PUBLIC PAPERS OF THE PRESIDENTS

OF THE UNITED STATES

PUBLIC PAPERS OF THE PRESIDENTS

OF THE UNITED STATES

Jimmy Carter

1977

(IN TWO BOOKS)

BOOK II—JUNE 25 TO DECEMBER 31, 1977

UNITED STATES GOVERNMENT PRINTING OFFICE

WASHINGTON : 1978

Published by the
Office of the Federal Register
National Archives and Records Service
General Services Administration

For sale by the Superintendent of Documents, U.S. Government Printing Office
Washington, D.C. 20402

Stock No. 022-003-00944-2

Foreword

The papers in this volume bring to a conclusion the official documentary record of my administration during 1977.

By the complexity of their subject matter they serve as a reminder of the difficult responsibilities that Americans are called upon to face in the last quarter of the Twentieth Century. Each generation must do its best with circumstances not of its own choosing, aware that in the eyes of history its character will be measured and its spirit tested by the response it gives to them.

The issues dealt with in these documents are the hardest and most intractable problems of our time. We have approached them in the knowledge that they must be resolved—but also in the knowledge that no government can hope to resolve them alone, without the patience and good will and active aid of the people we serve.

I am pleased by our accomplishments in this first year, but I also know the path ahead is not easy and much more remains to be done. Our challenge is to act while the times are opportune. As the Bible says, "Let us not be weary in well-doing; for in due season we shall reap, if we faint not."

Jimmy Carter

Preface

This book contains the papers of the 39th President of the United States which were issued by the White House Press Office during the period June 25–December 31, 1977. The material has been compiled and published by the Office of the Federal Register, National Archives and Records Service, General Services Administration.

The material is presented in chronological order within each week, and the dates shown in the headings are the dates of the documents or events. In instances when the release date differs from the date of the document itself, that fact is shown in the textnote. New to the Public Papers series this year are a digest containing the President's daily public schedule and other items of general interest, a list of nominations submitted to the Senate, a checklist of White House press releases not printed in the book, and a list of acts approved by the President. This information is compiled on a weekly basis and appears at the end of each week's coverage.

Every effort has been made to ensure accuracy. Tape recordings are used to protect against errors in transcription of Presidential remarks, and unless noted, signed documents are checked against the original to verify the correct printing. Textnotes, footnotes, and cross references have been provided by the editors for purposes of identification or clarity. Remarks were delivered in Washington, D.C., and other documents released there, unless indicated. All times noted are local times.

The index covers both Books I and II of the 1977 volume. In addition to the usual subject-matter entries in the index, the material has been classified in categories reflecting the type of Presidential activity. For example, a reader interested in the President's speeches will find them listed in the index under "Addresses and Remarks."

The Public Papers series was begun in 1957 in response to a recommendation of the National Historical Publications Commission. An extensive compilation of the messages and papers of the Presidents, covering the period 1789 to 1897, was assembled by James D. Richardson and published under congressional authority between 1896 and 1899. Since then, various private compilations were issued, but there was no uniform publication comparable to the Congressional Record or the United States Supreme Court Reports. Many Presidential papers could be found only in the form of mimeographed White House releases or as reported in the press. The Commission therefore recommended the establishment of an official series in which Presidential writings, addresses, and remarks of a public nature could be made available.

The Commission's recommendation was incorporated in regulations of the Administrative Committee of the Federal Register, issued under section 6 of the Federal Register Act (44 U.S.C. 1506), which may be found in Title 1, Part 10, of the Code of Federal Regulations.

The Weekly Compilation of Presidential Documents was begun in 1965 as a companion publication to the Public Papers to provide a record of Presidential materials on a more timely basis. Beginning with the administration of Jimmy Carter, the Public Papers series has expanded its coverage to include all material, as printed in the Weekly Compilation. This expanded coverage now provides the full text of proclamations and Executive orders, announcements of appointments and nominations, as well as selected statements or remarks of senior administration officials.

Volumes covering the administrations of Presidents Hoover, Truman, Eisenhower, Kennedy, Johnson, Nixon, and the first 2 years of President Ford are now available.

This series is under the direction of Fred J. Emery, Director, Ernest J. Galdi, Deputy Director, and Martha B. Girard, Director of the Presidential Documents Division, Office of the Federal Register. Editors of this volume were Margaret M. Donohoe, Richard L. Claypoole, Katherine A. Mellody, and Kenneth R. Payne.

White House liaison was provided by Walter W. Wurfel, Deputy Press Secretary. The frontispiece and photographs used in the portfolio were supplied by the White House Photo Office.

The typography and design of the volume were developed by the United States Government Printing Office under the direction of John J. Boyle, Public Printer.

JAMES B. RHOADS
Archivist of the United States

JOEL W. SOLOMON
Administrator of General Services
March 1978

Contents

Administration of Jimmy Carter

1977

Interview With the President

*Question-and-Answer Session With a
Group of Publishers, Editors, and
Broadcasters.   June 24, 1977*

THE PRESIDENT. Excuse me for interrupting you. I just wanted to come in and
spend a little time. I won't cheat you out
of the time. We had a half hour set up.
And I was having lunch with Congressman Jim Wright from Texas. He's been
very helpful to us, and we have a big
legislative agenda, as you know.

I'd like to spend a few minutes outlining
to you some of my own thoughts about
current circumstances in our administration's programs—domestic and foreign
affairs. And then we'll spend the balance
of the time answering your questions.

ADMINISTRATION PROGRAMS

We've got a heavy agenda, both in the
Congress and in our international negotiations. We've already had good success
in establishing a firm ethical standard,
initiated by the House and Senate. We've
got authority now to reorganize the structure of Government and to implement
some improvements in the management
capabilities of myself as President, others
who work with me. We approved six
major projects yesterday for reorganiza-

tion, and we'll have additional groups of
them approved from one week to another.

We are arriving at a point now of establishing a new Department of Energy. I
think the conference committees will meet
to resolve their remaining differences
probably before the Fourth of July. This
is extraordinarily rapid action on the part
of the Congress in bringing so many disparate agencies together in one major
department.

When President Johnson proposed the
Department of Transportation, when he
was supposed to have complete control of
the Congress, it took him 2 years, and the
final version of his proposal was hardly
recognizable as related to his original proposal. But we'll have that done.

We have also gotten a good package
together of economic stimulation, working on public works programs, training
and development, summer youth programs, and others. And now we are working on an energy policy which will have
far-reaching impacts and probably is the
most difficult, comprehensive congressional assignment undertaken that I've
ever known about. Maybe there have been
others. I can't recall them. We'll present
a comprehensive welfare reform package
to the Congress before they go home in
August, and before final adjournment of
the Congress, which I hope will be the

8th of October—that is our goal—we'll have a tax reform package to them as well.

In addition, we've proposed social security reform and other major issues that I need not outline to you now.

In foreign affairs, we've got an equally ambitious program underway. We are working very closely with some of our allies, Germany, France, England, Canada, in trying to resolve the Namibian question in formerly Southwest Africa, working with Mr. Vorster in South Africa. And I think we've made good progress on that recently. It's still a difficult thing.

We are working closely with the British on trying to resolve the Rhodesian question, leading there toward majority rule. We are in the process now of bringing the parties to agree to accept the broad outlines of a constitution under which free elections might be conducted.

In the Middle East, I've met with all the leaders there now except Mr. Begin. I met with Mr. Rabin when he was Prime Minister. And Mr. Begin will be coming over here on the 19th of next month to spend 2 or 3 days in our country, and I'm getting prepared for his visit.

We hope that this year we might make some progress in the Middle East. It's a very difficult question. It's one on which I've spent a great deal of time. At the same time, we are negotiating with the Soviets, trying to reach for the first time a comprehensive test ban on nuclear explosives.

We are prepared to accept the test ban with adequate safeguards that would apply both to military and peaceful explosive devices.

The British have asked to join this discussion, and both the Soviets and we have welcomed them in those talks, and they are being conducted in Moscow this minute.

We are also talking to them about reducing the military presence or restraining it in the future in the Indian Ocean,

prior notification of missile test firing, a prohibition against the capability of attacking observation satellites or others in space, and working as best we can to bring about a comprehensive, permanent agreement on SALT.

I feel at this point we've got a good framework for an agreement, but no specific agreement on the SALT negotiations. We are in a strong position on strategic weapons, and I think that strong position can be maintained for the foreseeable future, but we don't want a superiority there.

We'd like to reach an agreement with the Soviets where we can have a drastic reduction in total commitments with atomic weapons, but retaining an equivalent position with them so that either side will be strong enough to prevent—to permit a retaliatory attack, but not be subject to devastation that's overwhelming in an original attack—at least that we could still retaliate.

The other thing that we are trying to do is—and I'll just mention two more before I answer questions—is to prevent the spread of the capability for atomic explosions. I think it's accurate to say that 8 months ago there was a general feeling in the world that there was no way to restrain any more additional nations joining the nuclear explosive—I guess you would call it—fraternity. After India exploded a device, there was a general sense that with the spread of atomic power to produce electricity, that the development of explosives was inevitable.

I think that time has changed. And I believe there's a general hope now that with strict control over reprocessing plants and a long delay in shifting toward a plutonium society, that we might indeed prevent an expansion of the nuclear club.

The other thing that's been highly publicized is our commitment to human rights. We have addressed a subject that is very important to me and to the American people. It reestablishes our country, I think, as kind of a beacon light for a principle that's right and decent and compassionate.

I don't know if this would be liberal or conservative, but it prides—the concept of individuality, of the freedoms that our country has espoused.

And I don't think there's a national leader in the world right now who isn't constantly preoccupied with how well we measure up on the subject of human rights. Do our own people think that we abuse them too much through government, don't give them an equal opportunity, or what does the world think of us?

This has been brought about in part by our own attitude, but I think to a substantial degree because of the Helsinki agreement and the present Belgrade conference that is preparing to discuss this subject, among others, in October.

These are some of the things that are important. Of course, I'll make a decision this month about whether or not to go ahead with the production of the B–1 bomber and a few other incidental questions of that sort. [*Laughter*]

But perhaps it might be better than for me to go ahead with a dissertation, for me to answer your questions. And I would be glad to do so.

NUCLEAR POWERPLANTS

Q. Mr. President, with regard to energy, you have indicated that nuclear power was more or less a last resort as far as energy plans go. Last August, after you won the nomination, you came up to New Hampshire and indicated that nuclear plants shouldn't be placed where people don't want them, and you outlined your feelings on that.

A week ago today the Environmental Protection Agency gave the go-ahead to the Seabrook plant, which has been very controversial in New England—specifically New Hampshire—okayed the use of cooling tunnels, and this more or less gives them the green light to continue with their construction of the nuclear plant. What's your feeling on that decision last week?

THE PRESIDENT. Well, I think you probably know that the decision was a narrow and a technical one—whether or not the discharge of cooling water into the ocean would substantially affect the environment for marine life. And after a great deal of analysis, in which I did not participate, the director of our Environmental Protection Agency said there would be no substantial modification of marine life with the discharge of those warm waters.

This does not mean that final licensing has been approved. It does not mean that the plant will be constructed. I feel that our country and others in the world are going to have to rely quite heavily on atomic power as one of the energy sources in the future. I think that to the extent that we can conserve energy, quit wasting gas, oil, coal, that we can minimize the dependence upon nuclear power. The present severe constraint on the initiation of new atomic plant construction in our country now is economic.

And I think that as assessments are made by power companies, many of them have recently decided not to go with atomic powerplants but to shift toward coal. If we do have technical advantages demonstrated in the clean burning of coal, with liquid fuel beds and so forth, I think that trend will be enhanced.

But I think it would be a mistake for us to think that we can't have and won't need atomic powerplants. I'm very concerned about the control on an international basis of the waste products so that they can't be changed into explosives. But I have no aversion to the use of atomic powerplants as an energy source. Of course, the siting of those plants is something that basically has to be resolved by local power companies, State legislatures, which can prevent action by the power companies and the evaluation of land values.

In Georgia—we worked with North and South Carolina—we did a very early study of siting, and we have identified places where we would like to see atomic powerplants built, oil refineries built, and any oil that might be discovered in the Atlantic Ocean brought ashore.

And I would hope that all States would do that. Our State legislature participated along with power companies, but I think that the actual site is one that has to be determined by local people.

VIEWS ON THE PRESIDENCY

Q. Mr. President, you have now been in the Presidency about 6 months. What have you found to be more different, more complex, and more frustrating perhaps about being the President than you had ever anticipated before you took the office?

THE PRESIDENT. Well, that is hard to say. I might begin by stating clearly that I have enjoyed being President. It's been gratifying, challenging, and not unpleasant. I've had my family together most of the time. And the working conditions are good. The proximity of my office to my home is quite advantageous. [*Laughter*]

And I've chosen a Cabinet—most of whom I did not know ahead of time—who are superb. There's not a single member of my Cabinet that I consider to be weak or whom I would replace if I had a free option to do so. The same thing, obviously, applies to my White House staff. They've been very good. My working relationships with Congress have been good.

The complexity of some of the problems has been surprising. I can see why no previous President had been successful in evolving an energy policy or reforming the welfare system nor initiating zero-based budgeting or reorganizing the executive branch of Government or solving the depletion of the social security reserve funds or having basic tax reform. These things are enormously complicated, much more so when you get involved in actually making a final decision, than they are from a distance as viewed by a candidate.

I feel, also, that some of the international questions are going to take more time to resolve, if they are solved, than I had previously thought. Many of them, though, have been extant for decades or even generations.

There has been a surprising, adverse reaction in the Soviet Union to our stand on human rights. We've never singled them out. And I think I've been quite reticent in trying to publicly condemn the Soviets. I've never said anything except complimentary things about Mr. Brezhnev, for instance, but apparently that's provided a greater obstacle to other friendly pursuits of common goals, like in SALT, than I had anticipated.

We've had to do more traveling in foreign countries than we had thought—I haven't; I've only made one trip out of the country, to London. But the Secretary of State has found that because of past expectations built up, primarily under Secretary Kissinger, that foreign governments expect the American Secretary of State to come there, and his refraining from doing so and staying here in Washington is not well accepted by foreign nations. So, that's been one of the surprises, not particularly unpleasant.

COAL

Q. Mr. President, your energy program places heavy emphasis on coal.

THE PRESIDENT. Yes, it does.

Q. The United Mine Workers Union—the state of that union at present is at best unstable, no indication that it's going to change in the near future, particularly with contract talks coming up. How can the Nation place reliance on coal when it can't rely on the coal miners to get the coal out of the ground? Are you monitoring that situation?

THE PRESIDENT. Yes, to some degree. The coal labor contract will be negotiated this year. That's the schedule. And that's the last major labor contract that we face until the end of 1978. The recent election, of course, whose outcome will certainly be challenged, was an obstacle that had to be overcome before serious negotiations could commence. We are monitoring that situation very closely through Ray Marshall, the Secretary of Labor.

One of the exacerbating conditions about the coal mining relations are the wildcat strikes that take place outside the purview or without the approval of the elected leaders of the United Mine Workers and, of course, the rapid depletion of funds in the union treasury to pay legitimate claims. And all those things are going to create disharmonies.

We are projecting an ultimate coal production in 1985 of almost 1,300 million tons per year, which is about an 85-percent increase over the present production level. And I hope that increasing prices, increasing mechanization, opening up of new mine areas, and also I hope that after this year's negotiations that labor-management relationships might be improved—all those things are very important. But I don't have any way to control management-labor terms. And I think public concern about work stoppages, unless the reasons are very clear to the public, is a restraining factor, but that's the best I can answer your question.

TENNESSEE VALLEY AUTHORITY

Q. Mr. President, your support of nuclear power does not include the Clinch River breeder reactor.

THE PRESIDENT. That's correct.

Q. But you have stated that you would like to see the Tennessee Valley Authority use some sort of model in your energy program. Do you have any specific plans for what role you would like to see the TVA play?

THE PRESIDENT. Yes. If you don't mind, to save time, I would like to get you a copy of a letter that I have written to the Directors of the Tennessee Valley Authority that outline, I think, 14 or 15 different areas in which the Tennessee Valley Authority might play a leading role.

With roughly four million homes within the TVA system, they have an opportunity to test out the power suppliers' and homeowners' relationships on things such as peak-load pricing, insulation of homes, new price structures, and I think that these kinds of tests or pilot programs would be very helpful for the rest of the country.

TVA is also helping us with and helping themselves with research or pilot projects, for instance, concerning the fluid bed burning of coal and also, I believe, with the solvent, cleaned coal, along with, I think, the Georgia Power Company. So, these are a few of the things that come to mind.

But I've met with the Chairman of the TVA Authority. And he has contributed to this letter so that we could have a mutual exchange of ideas. The Directors have responded very well to this, and I think this would naturally tend to channel the large supply of research and development funds we have in the energy field toward TVA.

Obviously they'll be involved in additional matters concerning liquefaction, gasification of coal, solar energy, and heavily going into the atomic power field as well.

TVA has also become a very heavy coal producer, as you know. And the clean burning of coal is a very important aspect to them. Those are some kinds that come to mind offhand.

I'm not in favor of the shifting now toward the liquid metal fast breeder reactor in any sort of production model. My belief is that we won't need the breeder reactor, technology of that kind, to go into production for maybe 20 or 25 years. I think it is premature. It's extremely expensive and, in my opinion, completely unnecessary.

We have a budget authorization of roughly half a billion dollars for research and development in atomic energy. A major portion of that will go into testing different kinds of breeder reactors, which may or may not prove to be the best of all. But to make a heavy investment in one particular type of breeder reactor—that is, the liquid metal fast breeder reactor—I think is ill advised at this point.

I might add parenthetically that we do have a breeder reactor that will go critical either the last of August or the first of September at Shippingport which uses thorium as its base fuel.

But I don't have any doubt that in the future we'll need the breeder reactors. It's just too early to put so much of our financial and human resources into one particular model like the one at Clinch River.

Q. One little followup if I may while you are on the subject of TVA. Are you close to appointing a Director on the TVA?

THE PRESIDENT. Yes, sir.

Q. Could you give us any time frame on that?

THE PRESIDENT. I would guess within the next 2 or 3 weeks. That's my plan.

U.S. POSTAL SERVICE

Q. Mr. President, we've talked about the energy problem, which is certainly close to home. There's another one that's close to home to us all, I think, and that's the Postal Service. It took 5 days for the invitation to this festivity to come to me down in Arkansas, which is 800 miles away.

And it seems like the Postal Service is costing more and more and more and becoming more and more and more inefficient. What's going to happen?

THE PRESIDENT. I'd like to point out that one of the reasons is probably because it's not under my authority. [*Laughter*] No, I don't really know what to do about that. This is a matter that we are just getting started on.

As you know, the Postal Service is independent of the President and is ostensibly run as a business corporation with the corporate officers choosing the director. And I have met with him and have received voluminous recommendations from postal employees, postmasters, rural mail carriers, and others who cry out for some improvement in the service and the morale within the Post Office department.

I don't know what ought to be done as far as structure is concerned. I've not decided that it ought to be back as it was before with the President appointing the Postmaster General and being directly responsible for the Post Office. Now it's very difficult to decide who is responsible.

I think it's almost inevitable—although they did not take action in their June meeting—that there will be a call for increased postal rates, a call for an elimination of Saturday service, possibly combined with a realization of need for heavy subsidies, maybe not all three of those, but at least two of those.

I don't know how to answer your question, but as the time for the decision approaches, I'll be involved, because the appropriation of funds—and we face a deficit of about $200 million a month— will ultimately have to be approved by me and the Congress. I don't know how to answer your question any better. I'm concerned about it, too.

Q. Can you take a question from the peanut gallery?

THE PRESIDENT. I will get you next. Let me get this gentleman.

FEDERAL PROJECTS IN MICHIGAN

Q. Two local instances of a general problem: In the upper peninsula of Michigan, the Navy Department wants to install something called Project Seafarer, a method of communicating with submarines when submerged, and the Government is talking about nuclear disposal on a site around the city of Alpena.

In both cases citizens in the areas affected by one method or another have indicated they don't want those projects to go forward.

THE PRESIDENT. I understand.

Q. I'd appreciate both your response, if you may, to the specific questions, and also the general question of the interrelationship between what the Federal Government wants to do and the views of people in local communities who may be impacted by this.

THE PRESIDENT. I'm not familiar with any desire to bury nuclear wastes in that region. Most of our nuclear wastes now are retained within the control of the power companies who use the atomic fuel. But it's a matter that I could look into if you would like for me to do it. Alpena, you say?

As far as the Seafarer program is concerned, the plans for a massive burying of the transmission wires in broad areas of that region, I think, are ill advised.

We do need some way to communicate with our submerged submarines. We do have a way now, but we need some better ways.

The Defense Department is now assessing under the leadership of the Secretary of Defense, Harold Brown—who is a noted physicist—among other things,

some means by which, with two relatively small transmission line emplacements, we could get an adequate transmission to submarines submerged.

These would not be placed on private lands at all. And there is, I understand, absolutely no danger to people who would get anywhere near the transmission lines. This is just an exploratory thing.

But I am quite concerned about it, too. When I was campaigning there, the enormous placement of the transmission lines did concern me, and I spoke out against it. But as these alternative plans evolve, we'll be sure that the States would be thoroughly informed. But I think the essence of it is that it would likely be on public land, away from where anybody lives, and with a complete elimination of any possibility that any human being could be affected.

CONGRESSIONAL RELATIONS

Q. Mr. President, a few minutes ago you said working relationships with the Congress have been good. This is contrary to the analysis in some other quarters. And I just wondered what you based that conclusion on?

THE PRESIDENT. Well, the other quarters are the news media. [*Laughter*] And I really feel that this is a reporting job that hasn't been done well. It's inherent in the system, and I certainly recognize it and don't particularly deplore it, that altercations and debates and disharmonies and modifications in my proposals are the things that get the headlines.

But when I was at Blair House before I was inaugurated, I had meetings with almost all the Members of the Congress in groups of about 75 or so. And there were five goals that I had set for this year. One was the creation of the Department of Energy; one was reorganization authority; one was the establishment of ethics legislation in the House and Senate; one was the establishment of a comprehensive energy policy; and the other one was an economic stimulus package.

Well, I think any sort of an analysis by the news media as objective as possible would show that four of those things have already been carried out to almost complete fruition. The only remaining one is the energy policy, which is on schedule. So, I think the demonstration of this harmony is already there.

I might say one other thing. We've really loaded the Congress up with controversial matters, things that have been delayed for years or decades, sometimes generations, that hadn't been faced. They are controversial. They are very difficult. And I feel good about it.

The Congress does have still on the table some very important matters. One is how to deal with the social security reserve fund depletion. We've now got only a couple of years left in the disability fund, and whether the Congress will act permanently to resolve the problem as we have advocated or take action that would only provide temporary relief, I don't know yet. But either one, I think, would not be a sign of a schism between the White House and the Congress. And I think if you talk to any Members of the Congress, even Republican Members, you would see that they believe there's been more consultation, more exchange of ideas on domestic and international affairs than there has been in a long time.

But I feel good about it. My deep, visceral sense is that we have a good working relationship with Congress.

Q. Mr. President, a clarification, please.

THE PRESIDENT. Please.

Q. You mentioned five goals. I think I got energy twice.

THE PRESIDENT. One was energy policy; the other one was the construction of a new Department of Energy.

Q. I see.

NATURAL GAS PRICES

Q. Mr. President, will your energy program take any steps towards price equalization for the Northeast area?

THE PRESIDENT. Yes. We advocated, for instance, that there be a termination of the intrastate gas system and that interstate-intrastate would be treated the same. It would open up substantial amounts of gas we feel for the rest of the country.

Some of the gas-producing States don't like this, in particular. But I think we have a fairly good chance of succeeding.

Another thing that we implemented in our own plans—and none of these decisions have been made by Congress—is that there would be a guarantee to homeowners that any increase in fuel oil prices would be rebated to the homeowners who consumed that fuel for heating. This would provide some equalization. Any reduction in the amount of oil imported as a proportion of the total, I think, would benefit those regions like your own which are heavily dependent on imported oil. And more uniform prices around the country, which would result from a new energy policy, would certainly remove the discrimination that presently exists that has a slow but inexorable pressure on industry to decide to go to other parts of the country.

I think these aspects of the energy program would help to alleviate the present, I'd say, disadvantage, as far as energy goes, of the New England States.

Is the time up? I'll answer this one more question and then I'll have to go.

FOREIGN POLICY

Q. Mr. President, Henry Kissinger was in Denver on Wednesday and he was defending his old turf. And the message I got from listening to him was it's easy to criticize the State Department for lack of imagination when you are on the outside, but once you are in office many of these rosy-sounding dreams and ideas for change begin to wilt and the test for a huge, negative question that he saw is, what are the consequences of failure of a foreign policy move?

Do you gamble a little more on those kinds of questions than President Nixon, President Ford, and Mr. Kissinger did, do you think?

THE PRESIDENT. I don't disagree with what Kissinger says. We've had a very good series of conferences with Kissinger, either myself personally or more frequently the Secretary of State. And Dr. Brzezinski has participated in some of those as well. Obviously, it's easier to criticize any Government effort from outside than it is to solve a problem that's longstanding, once you have the responsibility yourself.

I think we've made some basic changes in the previous policies that might bear fruit, but we've not made any additional steps forward toward a SALT agreement. We hope we can. I think we are taking a much more bold approach to that question, not only seeking limitations on future construction, which is what was spelled out at Vladivostok, but actually asking the Soviets to join with us in a freeze of present deployment and development of nuclear weapons, and then a substantial reduction below what we have now. This has never been done before.

We are asking the Soviets to join with us in a comprehensive test ban that would prevent any nuclear explosives being tested. This has never been done before. Demilitarization of the Indian Ocean has never been attempted before, and so forth.

I don't say that in criticism of the previous administration. We have not achieved success yet in any of these efforts, and may not. I can't guarantee success.

I think that we have also taken a different approach in the Middle East. And it's a matter of judgment. Mr. Kissinger's position was to deal with the Middle East-

ern question in a step-by-step, incremental way. Our hope is that we can have an overall settlement by the participants in the Middle East discussion without delay, hopefully this year, and that once that settlement is reached, then the step-by-step implementation of the ultimate settlement is the best way to go about it. It's a completely different perspective.

I don't know that I can guarantee success. Again, we've tried to look on Latin America as a group of independent nations equal to us and to deal with them individually, not as a group or a homogeneous block.

We've been much more aggressive, I think, on the field of human rights. It means that to some degree our friendships and our allegiances in the different parts of the world, like Latin America, have changed.

We've tried to get away from blind support of totalitarian governments and tried to enhance and reward those countries that are shifting toward a more democratic process. And we've tried to compliment and encourage countries like Venezuela, countries like Ecuador that are shifting strongly toward more democratic processes. We've taken a very strong stand that has brought some adverse reaction on the control of nuclear weapons as far as new countries are concerned in the sales policies of our own nuclear-enriched fuels. And in addition to that, we've departed from Mr. Kissinger's past attitude, along with obviously the Presidents under whom he's served, in the sale of conventional weapons. We have some very strict standards now for the sale of conventional weapons.

And now it's the consumers' or the customers' responsibility to convince us that they need those weapons and that the sale of those weapons will be to the advantage of the United States rather than the other way around where arms manufacturers freely went to other countries, sold their products, and we were in effect quietly encouraging this escalation in nuclear arms—I mean in conventional arms sales around the world.

So, there are some differences in perspective, but I have to say that it's too early to assess tangible results.

Q. Mr. President, it's no more of a gamble as far as you see it?

THE PRESIDENT. I see no more of a gamble, no. I think our positions are much more clearly expressed in a public way. I think that all of you representing the news media and your readers and viewers and listeners have a much more accurate assessment of what we hope to achieve in SALT negotiations, what we hope to achieve with human rights and with non-proliferation of nuclear weapons, and what we hope to achieve in the Middle East, and what we hope to achieve in dealing with the People's Republic of China and Cuba, and so forth, very controversial matters, than they did in the past.

But I think the openness of it and the involvement of the public in the debates and discussions will prevent our making some of the mistakes that were so devastating to our country in the past. I don't think it's more risky to do this. I don't believe that open debate in itself is a risk. I think it possibly avoids the risk of a serious mistake when a decision is made in secret without the sound judgment and the experience and the common sense of the American people and the Congress being involved in making those crucial decisions.

Thank you very much. I enjoyed it. I hope you enjoyed your stay here. With whom have you met today?

Q. We met Mrs. Peterson.

Q. The Counsel.

Q. David Aaron.

Q. And a meeting with Geno Baroni.

THE PRESIDENT. Well, I hope you do enjoy it here. We are very honored to have you here.

This is a program that we think has been successful. I think if you have noticed the news in the last few weeks when the transcript of my answers are released, on, I think, Sunday, each time there has been a very heavy coverage of some of the points because you ask questions looking at your particular parochial viewpoint that bring out issues that quite often are not asked by the Washington correspondents who are here all the time at the center of government. And it also makes me think about questions that you raise that I would very rarely get in a Washington White House news conference. And I've been benefited greatly from it.

Thank you very much.

Q. Thank you, Mr. President.

NOTE: The interview began at 1:15 p.m. in the Cabinet Room at the White House. The transcript of the interview was released on June 25.

Prior to the interview, the group held meetings with Esther Peterson, Special Assistant to the President for Consumer Affairs, Robert J. Lipshutz, Counsel to the President, David L. Aaron, Deputy Assistant to the President for National Security Affairs, and Geno C. Baroni, Assistant Secretary of Housing and Urban Development for Neighborhood and Consumer Affairs.

Department of the Army

Nomination of Walter B. LaBerge To Be Under Secretary.   June 27, 1977

The President today announced that he will nominate Walter B. LaBerge, of Fairfax County, Va., to be Under Secretary of the Army. LaBerge is Assistant Secretary General for Defense Support at NATO.

He was born March 29, 1924, in Chicago, Ill. He received a B.S. in naval science (1944), a B.S. in physics (1947), and a Ph.D. in physics (1950) from the University of Notre Dame.

During World War II, LaBerge served as executive officer and then commander of the U.S. Navy Minesweeper YMS 165. He was program engineer (1950–1955) and then program manager (1955–1957) for the Sidewinder missile at the Naval Ordnance Test Station, China Lake, Calif.

From 1957 to 1963, LaBerge was the director of engineering at Western Development Laboratories, Philco-Ford Corp., in Palo Alto. From 1963 to 1965, he was director of the Philco-Ford Corporation's Houston operation, and in 1965 he became vice president for Philco-Ford's research and development corporate staff. From 1966 to 1971, he was first a division vice president, then vice president for the electronics group, at Western Development Laboratories.

In 1971 he became deputy technical director of the Naval Weapons Center in California, and in 1973 he became technical director. From 1973 to 1976, LaBerge was Assistant Secretary of the Air Force (Research and Development). Since 1976 he has been Assistant Secretary General for Defense Support at NATO.

LaBerge has served as a member of the U.S. Air Force Scientific Advisory Board and the Chief of Naval Operations Industry Advisory Committee. He has received the Navy Superior Civilian Service Award (1972) and the Air Force Exceptional Civilian Service Award (1975).

tional Commission on Employment and Unemployment Statistics. The President also indicated that if confirmed by the Senate, Levitan would be designated Chairman of the Commission. Levitan is director of the Center for Manpower Policy Studies at the George Washington University.

Levitan was born September 14, 1914, in Lithuania. He received a B.S. from City College of New York in 1937 and an M.A. (1939) and Ph. D. (1949) from Columbia University.

From 1946 to 1951, he was an associate professor of economics at the State University of New York in Plattsburgh, N.Y. He was a public member of the Wage Stabilization Board from 1951 to 1953, and from 1954 to 1960 he worked as a specialist in labor and economic development at the Legislative Reference Service of the Library of Congress.

In 1962–63 Levitan was a research professor of economics at George Washington University. He was senior economist at the W. E. Upjohn Institute in Washington from 1964 until 1967, when he became director of the Center for Manpower Policy Studies at George Washington.

Levitan has served as a consultant to various governmental agencies and has been on labor panels for the Federal Mediation and Conciliation Service and the American Arbitration Association. He is the author of numerous publications in the manpower area of labor economics.

National Commission on Employment and Unemployment Statistics

Nomination of Sar A. Levitan
To Be a Member.   June 27, 1977

The President today announced that he will nominate Sar A. Levitan, of Washington, D.C., to be a member of the Na-

Environmental Protection Agency

Nomination of William Drayton, Jr., To Be an
Assistant Administrator.   June 27, 1977

The President today announced that he will nominate William Drayton, Jr., of Cambridge, Mass., to be Assistant Administrator of the Environmental Protection Agency (Planning and Management). Drayton is a lecturer on public regulation and management reform at the Kennedy School of Government at Harvard University and a management consultant for McKinsey & Co. in New York City.

He was born June 15, 1943, in New York City. He received an A.B. from Harvard, an M.A. from Balliol College, Oxford University, and a J.D. from Yale Law School.

Drayton has been a management consultant with McKinsey & Co. since 1970. He has been on leave from McKinsey since 1975, serving as a visiting associate professor at Stanford Law School in 1975–76 and a lecturer at the Kennedy School of Government in 1976–77. In 1976 he worked on the Carter-Mondale campaign and transition staff on regulatory reform and reorganization.

U.N. Commission on the Status of Women

Appointment of Koryne Horbal as U.S. Representative. June 27, 1977

The President today announced the appointment of Koryne Horbal, of Minneapolis, Minn., as the Representative of the United States on the Commission on the Status of Women of the Economic and Social Council of the United Nations. Horbal is vice president and secretary of the American Contracting Corp. in Minneapolis.

She was born February 11, 1937, in Minneapolis. She worked for Batten, Barton, Durstine and Osborn advertising agency from 1955 to 1965, and has been with the American Contracting Corp. since 1958.

Horbal is a member of the Democratic National Committee, the DNC Charter Commission, and the National Organization of Women. She served on the Carter-Mondale National Steering Committee in 1976.

President's Commission on Military Compensation

Executive Order 11998. June 27, 1977

By virtue of the authority vested in me by the Constitution and statutes of the United States of America, and as President of the United States of America, in accordance with the Federal Advisory Committee Act (5 U.S.C. App. I), it is hereby ordered as follows:

SECTION 1. (a) There is established the President's Commission on Military Compensation, hereinafter referred to as the Commission, which shall be composed of not more than nine members who shall be appointed by the President.

(b) The President shall designate a Chairman from among the members.

SEC. 2. (a) The Commission shall review at least the analyses, findings, and recommendations related to military compensation which have been completed by the Quadrennial Reviews of Military Compensation, the Comptroller General, the Interagency Committee Study of Uniformed Services Retirement and Survivor Benefits, the Department of Defense Retirement Study Group, and the Defense Manpower Commission.

(b) The Commission shall identify, study, and make recommendations on critical military compensation issues, specifically addressing the following issues:

(1) What form of military compensation is the most effective for meeting the needs of the Nation in peace and war? Is the present pay and allowances system appropriate? If not, what changes (such

as some form of military salary) offer greater potential to serve the national purpose?

(2) Are specific standards appropriate and necessary for setting and adjusting military compensation? If so, what should the standards be? What elements of compensation should be based on such standards?

(3) What provisions are appropriate for differential compensations) such as special and incentive pays) and what are the appropriate criteria for using them?

(4) What are the purposes of the military retirement system? Is the present system effective in achieving these purposes? What changes are appropriate?

(5) Should the unique characteristics of military service be reflected in the compensation system, and, if so, how?

(c) The Commission shall submit a report to the President through the Secretary of Defense by March 15, 1978. The report shall recommend how the military compensation system can best be structured to serve the national interest. If changes are recommended, the Commission should estimate their cost and propose an implementation plan and timetable.

SEC. 3. In performing its functions the Commission shall conduct such studies, reviews, and inquiries as may be necessary. In addition to conducting open meetings in accordance with the Federal Advisory Committee Act, the Commission shall conduct public hearings to identify critical issues and possible solutions related to the structure of military compensation.

SEC. 4. The Commission is authorized to request from any Executive agency such information that may be deemed necessary to carry out its functions under this Order. Each Executive agency shall, to the extent permitted by law, furnish such information to the Commission in the performance of its functions under this Order.

SEC. 5. Each member of the Commission who is not otherwise employed in the Federal Government may receive, to the extent permitted by law, compensation for each day he or she is engaged in the work of the Commission at a rate not to exceed the maximum daily rate now or hereafter prescribed by law for GS–18 of the General Schedule, and may also receive transportation and travel expenses, including per diem in lieu of subsistence, as authorized by law (5 U.S.C. 5702 and 5703).

SEC. 6. The Chairman of the Commission is authorized to establish such additional advisory committees as may be deemed appropriate to carry out the purposes of this Order.

SEC. 7. All necessary administrative staff services, support, facilities, and expenses of the Commission shall, to the extent permitted by law, be furnished by the Department of Defense.

SEC. 8. Notwithstanding the provisions of any other Executive order, the functions of the President under the Federal Advisory Committee Act (5 U.S.C. App. I), except that of reporting annually to the Congress, which are applicable to the Commission, shall be performed by the Secretary of Defense in accordance with guidelines and procedures established by the Office of Management and Budget.

SEC. 9. The Commission shall terminate thirty days after submitting its report.

JIMMY CARTER

The White House,
June 27, 1977.

[Filed with the Office of the Federal Register, 4:42 p.m., June 27, 1977]

President's Commission on Military Compensation

Appointment of the Members of the Commission. June 27, 1977

President Carter today announced the appointment of a nine-member Commission to review previous studies of the military compensation system and to recommend changes to current pay and benefit programs.

The President's Commission on Military Compensation will be chaired by Charles J. Zwick, a former director of the Bureau of the Budget and now a Florida banker. It will submit a report to the President by March 15, 1978.

Studies to be reviewed include those of the Defense Manpower Commission and the Third Quadrennial Review of Military Compensation.

The President ordered the fresh review of pay, benefits, and the military retirement system since previous attempts to provide an equitable and efficient total military compensation system failed to achieve general agreement.

For example, in April 1976 the Defense Manpower Commission recommended that the members of the Armed Forces be paid in the form of a fully taxable salary, while the Third Quadrennial Review of Military Compensation concluded last winter that members should continue to be paid through a modified pay and allowances system. Similarly, the various reviews of military retired pay each came up with a different approach.

President Carter said he expects the Commission to resolve these differences and to propose one integrated, long-term solution to military compensation. He expects the solution to be fair to the taxpayers of the United States as well as members of the Armed Forces.

The members of the Commission are:

CHARLES J. ZWICK, Miami, Fla.—Chairman, director, Southeast Banking Corp.; former Director of the Bureau of the Budget

LT. GEN. BENJAMIN O. DAVIS, USAF, retired, Arlington, Va., former Commander, U.S. Forces Korea; and Chief of Staff, UN Command

GEN. WILLIAM E. DEPUY, Fort Monroe, Va., Commander, U.S. Army Training and Doctrine Command

THOMAS EHRLICH, Washington, D.C., President, Legal Services Corporation; former dean, Stanford Law School; Special Assistant to Under Secretary of State

JOHN H. FILER, Hartford, Conn., chief executive officer, Aetna Life and Casualty; former Connecticut State senator

PHILIP A. ODEEN, Lake Forest, Ill., vice president, Wilson Sporting Goods; former Deputy Assistant Secretary of Defense (Systems Analysis); and Director of Program Analysis, National Security Council

WALTER N. PAGE, Huntington, L.I., N.Y., president, Morgan Guaranty Trust Co.; director, Foreign Policy Association; and trustee of the Carnegie Institution

JANE P. PFEIFFER, Armonk, N.Y., Vice President, Communications, IBM Corp.; trustee, Rockefeller Foundation

HERBERT F. YORK, La Jolla, Calif., professor of physics, University of California at San Diego; former Director of Defense Research and Engineering

President's Commission on Military Compensation

Remarks to Members of the Commission. June 27, 1977

This afternoon we are establishing a Commission on Military Compensation, which I think will have great impact on the future of our country.

As a former military man myself, having spent 11 years in the Navy, I know how important it is to have both good pay and good morale within our military forces.

I also know how important it is to have the limited funds available spent in the most effective way to provide for our Nation's defense.

We now spend almost 60 percent of our total military budget on personnel. I'm not saying that this is too much, but I do say that when we spend this large a portion that it should be spent in the most effective way with the basic pay and the other compensations for those men and women who offer their very lives for the security of the United States.

I've asked this very fine Commission, headed by Chairman Charles Zwick, to do a complete analysis of the military compensation system in our country, to see if and how it should be improved, and I've asked them to make a report back to me within 9 months. Next March 1 [March 15], I believe, is the exact date.

This will not only be an assessment involving pay and retirement and other benefits of those who serve our country so well but in the process of the study there will be a renewed analysis of the effectiveness of our voluntary recruitment program.

This was put into effect to eliminate the gross discrimination that did occur during the Vietnam war and prior because poor people who couldn't go to college were the ones who were drafted and went to war.

And in the implementation of the voluntary recruitment program there was an accepted knowledge that compensation would be improved. So, we are not making any prior judgments. We want to be sure that when the study is completed, that our military personnel will be encouraged to enlist and to serve a long career, and that there's a proper balance among those who enjoy the benefits of offering their lives to our country in the military services.

I want to thank all the members of the group for being willing to serve. This is going to be a very time-consuming effort, very complicated and, as you can well imagine, very controversial.

The Chairman is Charles Zwick from Miami, who is an economist and who is now a banker. He is a former Director of the Office of Management and Budget.

Herbert York from La Jolla, California. He is a physicist. He is with the University of California in San Diego, and he is the former Director of Defense Research and Engineering and also a former Director of the Advanced Research Projects Agency.

Philip Odeen from Lake Forest, Illinois. He is a political scientist. He is vice president of the Wilson Sporting Goods Company. He is a former Deputy Assistant Secretary of Defense. He is a systems analyst, and he was a Director of Program Analysis for the National Security Council.

John Filer from Hartford, Connecticut. He is a lawyer, he is chairman and executive officer of the Aetna Life and Casualty Company. He is also a former State senator from Connecticut.

General William E. Depuy from Fort Monroe, Virginia. He is an economist. He is now at South Dakota University. He is Commander of the U.S. Army Training and Doctrine Command.

Jane Pfeiffer from Armonk, New York. She is vice president of communications of IBM. She was a participant in the White House Fellows Program in 1966, and she worked in the Council on Foreign Relations in 1967.

Lieutenant General Benjamin Davis, U.S. Air Force, retired. His credentials are superb. He is a U.S. Military Academy graduate. He was in the U.S. Armed Forces in Korea, Chief of Staff of the UN Command. He retired in January 1970, and he has extensive experience in transportation and also in the insurance field.

Walter Page, from Huntington, Long Island, New York. He is president of Morgan Guaranty Trust Company. He is associated with the Foreign Policy Association, a trustee of the Carnegie Institution.

And Thomas Ehrlich from Washington. He is a lawyer. He is president of the Legal Services Corporation; he is a former dean, Stanford Law School, and a Special Assistant to the Under Secretary of State.

These distinguished men and women have the background of analysis, of planning careers, of the legal profession, military profession, National Security Council, foreign affairs, and the trust of myself and the Secretary of Defense as well, and they and an adequate staff and detailed research and study, I think, will guide me and the other officials of our Government to make the right decision in giving the members of our Armed Forces in the future an attractive career opportunity with the most effective fighting force available to us.

I'd like to ask the Secretary of Defense to comment further.

NOTE: The President spoke at 2:08 p.m. in the Rose Garden at the White House.

Executive Schedule

Executive Order 11999.   June 27, 1977

RELATING TO CERTAIN POSITIONS IN LEVEL V OF THE EXECUTIVE SCHEDULE

By virtue of the authority vested in me by Section 5317 of Title 5 of the United States Code, and as President of the United States of America, Section 2 of Executive Order No. 11861, as amended, placing certain positions in level V of the Executive Schedule, is further amended by adding thereto "(14) Assistant to the Secretary and Land Utilization Adviser, Department of the Interior." and "(15) Executive Assistant and Counselor to the Secretary, Department of Labor.".

JIMMY CARTER

The White House,
    June 27, 1977.

[Filed with the Office of the Federal Register,
    12:38 p.m., June 28, 1977]

NOTE: The Executive order was not issued in the form of a White House press release.

Visit of President Carlos Andres Perez of Venezuela

Remarks of the President and President Perez at the Welcoming Ceremony.   June 28, 1977

PRESIDENT CARTER. This morning we have a great honor paid to our Nation by the visit of President Perez of Venezuela.

In our hemisphere, the nation of Venezuela has earned the great admiration of all those who believe in freedom and in the open, democratic processes of government.

President Perez represents a country which has set an example for many others in its firm and unswerving commitment to the proposition that the people of a nation should be the ones with universal suffrage and complete participation in an open and free electoral process to choose the leaders of that country.

But his influence has extended far beyond the borders of his beautiful and great nation. Because of his dynamism and his great leadership qualities, President Perez has become an active and effective spokesman for the Third World nations and one who can truly represent the highest aspirations of all the nations in Latin America.

His commitment to the basic principles of human rights, individual freedom, and liberty were vividly demonstrated recently at the Organization of American States conference at Grenada, when he and his people became leaders in pursuing these hopes for this hemisphere.

He has also espoused and has pursued his commitment to a reduction in expenditures for weapons and in trying to lay the groundwork for more peaceful relationships among the nations of the world.

He has also taken a strong stand against the proliferation of atomic explosives throughout the world and has joined with us and others in espousing the principles of the Tlatelolco Treaty, which prohibits the deployment of any nuclear explosives in the southern part of this hemisphere.

Venezuela has been a leader and was recently cochairman of the conference which tries to establish better relationships between the developed nations of the North and the developing nations of the South. He leads a country which has been blessed with great natural resources—oil among them—and they have been leading suppliers of that precious fuel to our country for many years.

During the 1973 embargo of our country by some members of OPEC, Venezuela maintained their staunch friendship to our country, and the interruption of oil to our shores was not part of their policy. And this past winter, when we faced a particular shortage because of the severity of our weather, Venezuela voluntarily increased their total export of oil and fuel from their country to meet our needs. At the same time, he's been strongly committed to the quality of the environment and to the careful conservation of his nation's precious oil and other fuel products.

We all know and admire the early and innovative commitment to freedom by the great liberator Simón Bolívar, and in more recent times, the great leadership of Don Rómulo Betancourt of Venezuela.

And I think I can say without any doubt that President Perez continues in this admirable mold of leadership which has come from the great nation and our close friend,the country of Venezuela.

Recently my wife, Rosalynn, was welcomed to your country, Mr. President, in the most hospitable way by you and your wife, Blanca. We deeply appreciate the personal friendships that have already been formed between your family and my own.

Señor Presidente, esta es su casa [Mr. President, this is your house.]

PRESIDENT PEREZ. Mr. President Carter, I must begin my words expressing to you my deep thanks and that of my wife for this cordial invitation that allows us to visit the great North American nation. I am a Latin American voice that, from Venezuela, comes to express an unreserved solidarity with your policy of great ethical substance addressed to affirm the essential values of the human being.

Many years have passed since nations, small and weak nations, have heard a voice rise from a great nation to tell the world that over the human values is the human being, the defense of his dignity, of the human rights. Those words have reconciliated us with other attitudes that we have not shared with this great nation, and they remind us of the voice of two other great Presidents, Franklin Delano Roosevelt and John Fitzgerald Kennedy, who are dear to the affection of all Latin Americans.

In my country—I mean all of Latin America, no matter what kind of governments our countries have, the people are feeling the warmth and the sincerity of these good words that constitute themselves in a commitment to make of America, of the New World, the true continent of freedom.

I have come, Mr. President, to exchange ideas with you and your officials with mutual respect, and as countries that do to each other the same treatment. Certainly, we will find points of coincidence very important within the global politics that are discussed today in the great forums of the world. Likewise, we are going to deal with matters that are essential for us, the relations between the United States and the Latin American community.

I already had the honor and the very pleasant opportunity to hear from the lips of your wife, in Caracas, many aspects of the talks that we are going to hold. Mrs. Carter brought the testimony of the friendship and admiration of the Venezuelan people and of all of the peoples of Latin America for the people of the United States and for the Government of President Carter.

For our hemispheric countries, the best perspectives are open. I sincerely believe that this is an historical moment without comparison, when the United States is going to assume a leadership role—which we do appreciate—not that of economic or military importance, but that of the great values of mankind.

Mr. President, Mrs. Carter, my wife and I in this first moment of our meeting give to you our thanks, and we express to you that beyond the formalities of protocol there exists a sincere friendship that will join in brotherhood the peoples of Latin America with the peoples of the United States.

NOTE: The President spoke at 10:39 a.m. on the South Lawn of the White House. President Perez spoke in Spanish, and his remarks were translated by an interpreter.

U.S. Special Representative for Non-Proliferation Matters

Nomination of Gerard C. Smith.
June 28, 1977

The President today announced that he will nominate Gerard C. Smith, of Washington, D.C., to be United States Special Representative for Non-Proliferation Matters, to be Ambassador at Large while serving in that capacity, and to be U.S. Representative to the International Atomic Energy Agency (IAEA).

As Special Representative for Non-Proliferation Matters, Smith will be responsible for coordinating preparation of executive branch studies, policies, and positions on the issues to be covered by this international effort and for carrying out negotiations and discussions here and abroad. The President has directed the heads of the U.S. departments and agencies concerned to give full support to this work.

Smith's responsibilities will also include coordinating and guiding, under the direction of the Secretary of State, overall U.S. efforts internationally to carry out non-proliferation policies, and he will be responsible for negotiations to that end. The President is nominating Smith as U.S. Representative to IAEA in view of the important role which that agency plays in non-proliferation matters.

In announcing Smith's nomination, the President stressed that international measures aimed at stopping the spread of nuclear explosives capabilities are of paramount importance to the security of this Nation and the world.

Smith was born May 14, 1914. He received a B.A. from Yale University in 1935 and LL.B from Yale Law School in 1938. He served in the U.S. Army from 1941 to 1946.

After practicing law in New York City from 1946 to 1950, Smith joined the Atomic Energy Commission as a Special Assistant. From 1954 to 1957, he was Special Assistant to the Secretary of State for Atomic Affairs. He served as Director of the State Department's Policy Planning Staff from 1957 to 1961.

From 1969 to 1972, Smith was Director of the Arms Control and Disarmament Agency and chief of the U.S. delegation to SALT. Smith has been a member of the Washington law firm of Wilmer, Cutler and Pickering since 1972.

Visit of President Perez of Venezuela

Toasts of the President and President Perez at a Dinner Honoring the Venezuelan President. June 28, 1977

PRESIDENT CARTER. First of all, I want to welcome all of you here tonight.

This is the first state visit we've had in quite a while. And one of the great things about having this kind of a banquet is to bring people to the White House from all over our country to meet distinguished visitors who mean so much to us.

During the morning sessions we have ceremonies on the lawn and then we have long, detailed, sometimes boring—but not this morning—discussions about matters of great world import. But in the evening we have a chance to get to know one another. And I've enjoyed it very much, talking to our good friend, President Perez, and his wife, Blanca.

We get to know about one another's government. We were discussing the problems of democracies all over the world, who are held back in quick decisions by the parliamentary process and congresses. [*Laughter*] We both agreed that these problems did not apply to Venezuela and the United States. [*Laughter*]

President Perez commented on the charm of the people at the table here with us, and particularly noticed that Jack Brooks—whenever he spoke I got very quiet and listened to what he said, sometimes even ignoring our guest. [*Laughter*] He pointed out how delightful and charming Jack was. I did not tell him that the conference committee on establishing a Department of Energy was going to meet very shortly, and Jack was the chairman of the Government Operations Committee. [*Laughter*]

But we have a chance to learn, and I was also very interested in his analysis of Rosalynn's visit. She was gone for a long time, and you may not be able to detect it from the atmosphere tonight, but this house was built when John Adams was President and it's gotten larger as time goes on. And I have never seen a lonelier place in my life than the White House when Rosalynn was in South and Central America and in the Caribbean. Chip and his wife were in England; later they went to California. Jeff was in Guatemala and Honduras and Mexico on an archeological expedition with George Washington University. Jack is building a grain and soybean elevator in Georgia. And I was here all alone.

He pointed out how brief her visit was to Venezuela. He wished she could have stayed longer. And I thought about the cartoon I saw, I think in the Milwaukee paper, which showed me talking to Jody Powell, my Press Secretary, Mr. President, and I was saying, "Jody, I don't give a damn about Idi Amin. Where is Rosalynn?" [*Laughter*]

So we have a chance to learn about one another. And there's an opportunity to draw ourselves together in the friendliest and most persuasive and personal way—not only between me and all of those of you who've come here to visit tonight from our country, but to get to know our distinguished visitors.

We share a great deal. But I think it's accurate to say that among all the visitors that we've had here at this great center of our Government's life, Venezuela is represented by a man who epitomizes the finest aspects of our own country's hopes and dreams and aspirations and ideals.

For 19 years now, there's been an absolute, total, and pure democracy in

Venezuela. Everyone is privileged to vote and is urged to vote and the decisions of the people on election day are binding without question. We also have seen a country evolve there, looking back on the superb leadership of the great liberator, Simón Bolívar, and President Perez' predecessor, President Betancourt, that is totally committed to the principle of basic human freedoms, the pride of people in their own individuality and the right to make their own decisions, and in the cherishing and nourishing enhancement of human rights.

At the recent Organization of American States meeting in Grenada, the leading country, above all others, even including our own, in insisting upon strong stands, unequivocal stands on the principle of human rights, was Venezuela. We felt a close partnership with them, and we felt a great gratitude toward them. They have been staunch and unswerving in this commitment in a part of the world, to be perfectly frank, where this has not always been a persuasive commitment. And I'm very proud of that.

When I think of any world leader and a strong, growing, and dynamic and fairly wealthy country with great material wealth and riches and oil and other products, who has looked on the weak and poor and deprived and small nations with understanding and compassion and mutual trust, the country again that comes to my mind, foremost, is Venezuela. And the leader who epitomizes that commitment is President Perez.

This is an interrelationship that's growing between our country and theirs on a relationship of complete mutual admiration and total equality. Our country may be larger in size; we may have a few more Spanish-speaking people than Venezuela—[*laughter*]—but we are equals in every way except in

those firm attributes where, I have to admit, they have achieved a superiority to us. But we are trying to emulate their example and move more and more toward a pure commitment to the principles on which our country was formed.

We have seen the great friendship demonstrated by President Perez and his wife toward our country. They will go to Philadelphia, and they will dedicate very shortly a statue to one of their liberators, Miranda, who, along with Simón Bolívar earlier, observed the American Revolution under George Washington. And this demonstration of mutual commitments to ideals by the establishment of this statue in Philadelphia very shortly is another symbol of our equality and mutual purpose.

He will also be dedicating a great sculpture by the great artist Otero, in Washington, D.C., another permanent indication of friendship between our countries.[1] And there is also a bust of a great writer, Vejo, in Austin, Texas. So, you can see that from one place to another, there are permanent indications being established of the friendships between Venezuela and the United States.

This is one kind of proliferation to which I have no objection, Mr. President. [*Laughter*]

The last point I'd like to make is this: Speaking of proliferation, our neighbors to the south at Mexico City, the suburbs of Mexico City called Tlatelolco, signed a treaty under the original auspices of the United Nations a few years ago, committing all the signatories permanently to prevent the deployment of nuclear explosives in the Southern Hemisphere.

There is no other part of the world that's done this. This was how long ago— 10 years ago? And we are now re-reviving

---

[1] The work by Venezuelan sculptor Alejandro Otero is located on the grounds of the National Air and Space Museum.

the impetus to get all countries in our hemisphere to sign this treaty.

Just before Rosalynn left for her trip, I signed the treaty. And as she visited the seven nations—some, early signatories like Venezuela—we tried to identify the problems. But one of the nations, again not coincidentally, who took the leadership in trying to spell out the principle that nuclear weapons should be kept at a zero level was Venezuela.

We in the United States sometimes think that we are the first in everything, that we take the first good action and that we are the strongest nation for commitment to the finest principles of life. But I just wanted, in my brief remarks tonight, in genuine admiration of our visitor and his great nation, to point out to you that there are many things in this hemisphere that we can learn from our neighbors, and there are many things that warrant genuine admiration on our part that they have already done. They have set standards that we are still trying to reach. So, we have great admiration for you and for your people and for your great nation.

And in a spirit of that admiration and expression of mutual friendship, I would like to propose a toast to President and Mrs. Perez and to the people of the great and free democratic nation, our friends, the people of Venezuela.

PRESIDENT PEREZ. *Mr. President of the United States and Mrs. Carter:*

You said at the University of Notre Dame that the United States can no longer separate the traditional issues of war and peace from the new global questions of justice, equity, and human rights. You also said a peaceful world cannot long exist one-third rich and two-thirds hungry.

The problem of world peace can no longer be defined within terms of strategic balance of power equilibrium, of areas of influence, of blocs, and of military alliances. Peace is not only the absence of war. The true problem of peace is that of the incorporation of the Third World to an international order in whose construction may participate all the nations that comprise it. The order imposed by the victors of the Second World War no longer exists.

Human rights cannot be spoken about, referred to only as respect for physical integrity and political liberties. The essential human right is the right to life, to well-being, to the integral dignity of each being, and this supreme right is flagrantly violated by those responsible for world economic order.

Venezuela looks with well-founded expectancy upon the orientation that the policies of the United States are taken in your hands and your forthright defense of human rights. We Venezuelans and all of the peoples of Latin America hope that this decorous, courageous, and firm position is going to help break the chains in the homelands that suffer oppression.

But we also believe that the Latin American dictatorships have as an essential cause and an efficient reason the economic instability generated by the unjust economic world order.

I may reiterate, Mr. President, that the validity of human rights in their noble and full meaning are summed up in the respect for the right of economic development for our peoples, giving them just value to our basic commodities and to the labor of our men and women and secure and proper access to the transference of technologies and capital.

The validity of democracy and human rights will be impossible with the social tensions that are experienced by a great number of nations and the dramatic economic differences that separate the nations today.

It is illusory to expect democratic development and implementation of human rights within an international order so deeply anti-democratic as the one in existence. The democratic transformation that your enlightened international policies search for cannot be reached without the disappearance of the economic structures and the privilege that characterize that international order.

The hopes that I place in the present direction of United States policies are conditioned in the first place by the establishment by the United States of the needed link between the ethical principles and aspirations and the policies, that there may be adequate understanding of world problems and their risks, political will to confront them, paying more attention to the reality that the people live with than to the formal and so often hypocritical relations between governments. This is the esteemable and beautiful worth that we give to the direct and sincere word with which you, Mr. President, are gaining the esteem and admiration of the people of Latin America, without genuflecting accents of the decayed diplomacy of half words and euphemisms. Confronting the biased criticism of actors and accomplices of the Latin American tragedy are raised the complacency of those who suffer torture, deprivation of liberty or persecution, and also of those like us who do not have enough influence to achieve alone the redemption of human dignity.

The efforts of the Third World in favor of dialog and cooperation for the establishment of the new international economic order have not found satisfactory answers on the part of the industrialized world, including the United States.

The less than encouraging results of the North-South conference indicate that the industrialized world resists in recognizing the need to transform the structures of privileges, and also show that they do not yet perceive with sufficient clarity the dangers inherent in this situation.

You, Mr. President, with true vision, have begun to speak another language. Without saying so expressly, you have understood that selfishness has presided until now over the lukewarm conduct of the great nations.

It is indispensable that the industrial world understand that the order of priorities no longer has in their first places the East-West conflict and the stabilization of the traditional power blocs, and that now the major efforts must be exerted in the resolution of the North-South conflict in order to create a new international order, just and equitable.

It is necessary that the industrial world understand that the creation of that new world order demands bold initiatives and global solutions, with major changes in the living standards of the rich nations insofar as they may be derived from the exploitation of the poorer nations.

The dissemination of conventional and nuclear arms in the world finds impulse in the vertical proliferation of all kinds of armaments in the hands of the industrial countries. Modern military technology creates specific problems of great complexity. But we believe that if the political will exists, those problems can be overcome. Détente and arms control are necessary conditions, but not enough to build world peace upon solid foundations. To assert otherwise would be to give military matters an autonomy that it does not have, to give it primacy over the political, and to disengage politics from social matters which would mean to repeat the mistakes that in the past have only driven to failure and tragedy.

The Third World wishes to dialog and to negotiate. The other alternative, deplorable as it may be, is confrontation—which nobody wants, but that, perhaps, many may be forced to resort to. From there stems the large responsibility of the developed countries if a confrontation situation is created with the Third World whose solidarity is already indivisible, and so that is the reason why its power is real.

A global reform is stated. No partial solution will overcome the problem. The new international order must be democratic and based not only on economic changes but on new economic and ethical premises, because another dramatic reality, which the great nations had not until now noticed, is that the world is neither an unlimited reservoir of resources nor that its exploitation could go on on the present terms impoverishing more and more the producing countries in order to maintain irritating levels of waste and consumption in the industrial ones.

Unfortunately, technological civilization could well be called the civilization of waste. It is founded upon an irresponsible arrogance of men who want to appropriate, without limit, the resources of nature and consume them as if they would never be depleted, in spite of the abuses which are inflicted upon it.

Fortunately, voices such as yours are beginning to be heard, which denounce this lack of suicidal prevention as well as these attacks against nature.

We must have as a starting point a deep criticism of the way of life of the industrial societies, greedy consumers of resources. The survival of human society is at stake.

The principles of classical liberalism and traditional capitalism have been revised in the national order. The policies of taxation, of social security, of social function of property, of the limitation of monopolies have originated in the requirements of the new society. In the international order the same must occur. We are beginning to realize that international controls must be devised to guarantee nations their economic rights. Likewise, it is imperative on the part of all countries in the international community, the acceptance of a code that regulates the actions of transnational companies, which have weakened and transgressed the national sovereignty of the developing countries and have deeply eroded their morals with the generalized practice of bribery.

Petroleum, a privileged one among the raw materials, confers upon the producing countries, members of OPEC, an historical responsibility vis-a-vis their countries and all of humanity.

OPEC has generated awareness with regard to interdependence in the world. It has shown the vulnerability of all countries, without exception, in a situation like the present, and it has made it much more difficult for the developed world to go on exploiting the developing world.

OPEC's actions have made clear the contradictions of the present world order as well as the possibilities that the third has at its disposal for dialog and understanding. The objectives of OPEC are not the price of oil; they go much further, to the achievement of that new international economic order. That is why I dare to affirm that it will be impossible to disrupt the unity of OPEC. No one has to fear it. It acts responsibly.

Mr. President, and Mrs. Carter, in our conversations we must talk about these and others of the many problems that deal with the bilateral relations between our two countries, with Latin America, with the Third World, and other aspects of world politics of common concern. We will have to talk about hidden conflicts in our hemisphere, of possible solutions, of the responsibilities of the United States and of our own.

With my words in this kind and friendly dinner expressive of the cordiality with which we have been received, I have wished to refer to fundamental aspects that commit the responsibility of nations and governments in the construction of the new world order, just and equitable.

We believe that a special responsibility falls on those nations that, like your great country, have a determining weight in the international context and in the definition of the political and economic rules of conduct. That is why I have tried to convey to you and to your great people a sincere and friendly message, with the irrevocable conviction that the true way for peace must be that of understanding between all countries with international justice.

As you have said with profound sense of justice, peace can only be affirmed on the basis of faithful observance of human rights, which give authentic and transcendental sense to man's life on Earth.

Venezuela joins the United States and will join you, Mr. President, so that you may achieve your noble purposes of universal justice, defense and promotion of human rights, and rigid action against proliferation of nuclear weapons. We identify in democracy and in the will, so that politics will serve high ethical purposes and humanistic principles.

With that trust, Mr. President, Mrs. Carter, I want to toast for the success of just and noble policy and for the great nation of the United States and for democracy in the Western Hemisphere.

NOTE. The President spoke at 9:40 p.m. in the State Dining Room at the White House. President Perez spoke in Spanish, and his remarks were translated by an interpreter.

Visit of President Perez of Venezuela

Remarks at the Entertainment Honoring President Perez. June 28, 1977

First of all, I'd like to welcome all the guests who've come here to be with us tonight with great faith in the weather, which I hope will be justified.

I would like to express my thanks at the beginning for the combined choirs of Wheaton College and Union College. They've just returned from a long tour in Venezuela, which they said did not seem long. They had made 11 performances in 11 days. They went there to honor a young choir group of 54 Venezuelans who were killed in the terrible airplane accident in the Azores. And this to us is a very good additional demonstration of the sharing of culture and beauty between our country and that of Venezuela.

The choir director has just informed me that they were received with open arms and deep appreciation and a mutual expression of the love for music which can cross national boundaries without detecting any impediment whatsoever. So, I do want to thank you both for being here and for this wonderful choir. And they will stay to see the ballet which will follow.

I would also like to introduce the two performers who will now entertain us, accompanied by the Marine Band, Cynthia Gregory and Ted Kivitt, who will begin by dancing "Giselle."

I've tried to think of some parallels between the performance tonight and our public servants, like myself and President Perez and the Members of Congress. The dance is obviously strong, forceful. People watch it with great interest, as is the case in politics. It's sometimes unpredictable, sometimes with a great deal of enthusiasm.

I think I'll abandon the parallel at this point—[laughter]—and talk about almost unanimous admiration of the observers. I think I'll talk about grace and beauty, and I think all of you will be inspired by the performance of these fine two internationally known dancers.

Following that, they will dance another selection, "Grand Pas Classique," and I think that you will be very pleased at this performance.

We are very grateful to have you here. And I think that this is the first time we've had a chance to have entertainment outside on the lawn. But it's a particularly beautiful setting, and I think that the beauty of the setting will be matched and even exceeded by the beauty of the performances.

Thank you very much.

NOTE: The President spoke at approximately 10:20 p.m. on the South Lawn of the White House.

United States Ambassador to Barbados and Grenada

Nomination of Frank V. Ortiz, Jr. June 29, 1977

The President today announced that he will nominate Frank V. Ortiz, Jr., of Santa Fe, N. Mex., to be Ambassador Extraordinary and Plenipotentiary of the United States to Barbados and to the State of Grenada. Ortiz is Deputy Executive Secretary at the State Department.

He was born March 14, 1926, in Santa Fe, N. Mex. He received a B.S. from Georgetown University in 1950 and an M.S. in 1967 from George Washington University. He served in the U.S. Army from 1944 to 1946.

From 1951 to 1953, Ortiz was an international relations officer at the State Department. He served as economic officer in Addis Ababa from 1953 to 1956, and as political officer in Mexico from 1956 to 1958. From 1958 to 1961, he was a foreign affairs officer.

From 1961 to 1963, Ortiz was special assistant to the Ambassador to Mexico. He was officer-in-charge for Spanish affairs from 1963 to 1966, and in 1966–67 attended the National War College.

Ortiz was supervisory political officer in Lima from 1967 to 1970, and Deputy

Chief of Mission in Montevideo from 1970 to 1973. He was Director for Argentina, Paraguay, and Uruguay from 1973 until 1975, when he became Deputy Executive Secretary at the Department.

Nuclear Regulatory Commission

Nomination of Joseph M. Hendrie To Be a Member. June 29, 1977

The President today announced that he will nominate Joseph M. Hendrie, of Bellport, N.Y., to be a member of the Nuclear Regulatory Commission. Hendrie is chairman of the department of applied science at Brookhaven National Laboratory in Upton, N.Y.

Hendrie was born March 18, 1925, in Janesville, Wis. He received a B.S. in physics from Case Institute of Technology in 1950 and a Ph.D. in physics from Columbia University in 1955. He served in the U.S. Army from 1943 to 1946.

Hendrie was a research assistant at Columbia University from 1950 to 1955. He worked at Brookhaven Laboratory from 1955 to 1972, beginning as an assistant physicist in the reactor physics division and ending as head of the engineering division in the department of applied science.

From 1972 to 1974, Hendrie was Deputy Director for Technical Review at the Directorate of Licensing of the U.S. Atomic Energy Commission. Since 1975 he has been chairman of the department of applied science at Brookhaven Laboratory.

Hendrie is a member of the board of directors of the American Nuclear Society and serves on the Risk-Impact Panel, Committee on Nuclear and Alternative Energy Systems, of the National Research Council. Since 1974 he has been the U.S. representative on the International

Atomic Energy Agency's Senior Advisory Group on Reactor Safety Codes and Guides. He was a member of the Advisory Committee on Reactor Safeguards of the U.S. Atomic Energy Commission from 1966 to 1972. He has had numerous articles published in professional journals.

Visit of President Perez of Venezuela

Remarks on the Departure of President Perez. June 29, 1977

This has been one of the most pleasant and productive meetings that we've ever had. The expressions of friendship between our countries are genuine, and we share deep commitments to common goals and common purposes.

A constant reminder in the center of our Capital City of the vision and hope of our two peoples is expressed by the Otero sculpture, and I'm very grateful for it. This is a photograph, and I think that we will have in the future a chance to enjoy this for many generations to come.

The discussions were compatible and harmonious, and the friendship that exists between our countries is absolutely unshakeable.

Thank you very much.

NOTE: The President spoke at 11:10 a.m. on the South Lawn at the White House following his final meeting with President Perez.

Exemption From Mandatory Retirement

Executive Order 12000. June 29, 1977

EXEMPTION OF ARTHUR S. FLEMMING FROM MANDATORY RETIREMENT

Arthur S. Flemming, Commissioner on Aging, Department of Health, Education, and Welfare, and Chairman, Commission on Civil Rights, became subject to mandatory retirement for age on June 30, 1975, under the provisions of Section 8335 of Title 5 of the United States Code unless exempted by Executive order. Arthur S. Flemming was exempted from mandatory retirement until June 30, 1976, by Executive Order No. 11869 of June 24, 1975. He was again exempted from mandatory retirement until June 30, 1977, by Executive Order No. 11924 of June 29, 1976.

In my judgment, the public interest requires that Arthur S. Flemming continue to be exempted from such mandatory retirement.

Now, THEREFORE, by virtue of the authority vested in me by subsection (c) of Section 8335 of Title 5 of the United States Code, I hereby exempt Arthur S. Flemming from mandatory retirement until June 30, 1978.

JIMMY CARTER

The White House,
   June 29, 1977.

[Filed with the Office of the Federal Register, 10:33 a.m., June 30, 1977]

Bicentennial Functions

Executive Order 12001. June 29, 1977

TRANSFERRING CERTAIN BICENTENNIAL FUNCTIONS TO THE SECRETARY OF THE INTERIOR

By virtue of the authority vested in me by Section 7(b) of the Act of December 11, 1973 (87 Stat. 701), hereinafter referred to as the Act, Section 202(b) of the Budget and Accounting Procedures Act of 1950 (64 Stat. 838, 31 U.S.C. 581c(b)), and Section 301 of Title 3 of the United States Code, and as President of the United States of America it is hereby ordered as follows:

SECTION 1. The Secretary of the Interior, hereinafter referred to as the Secretary, shall, through existing National Park Service programs, provide for the continuation of appropriate commemoration of events relating to the American Revolution until December 31, 1983.

SEC. 2. The Secretary shall administer existing contracts and grants of the American Revolution Bicentennial Administration, hereinafter referred to as ARBA.

SEC. 3. In performing the functions described in Section 1 and 2 of this Order, the Secretary may, in addition to any other available authority, exercise the following powers under the Act which are hereby transferred to him for such purposes until December 31, 1983, except as otherwise provided in subsection (b) of this Section:

(a) All powers described in Section 2(f) of the Act with respect to the expenditure of funds donated to ARBA prior to the effective date of this Order, and the expenditure of revenues received or which may be received pursuant to contracts described in Section 2 of this Order.

(b) Until December 31, 1977, all powers exercised by ARBA prior to the effective date of this Order which relate to enforcement of Section 2(i) of the Act.

(c) All powers described in Section 5(a) of the Act.

SEC. 4. All personnel, records, property and appropriations, including all funds and revenues described in Section 3(a) of this Order, as relate to the powers and functions assigned or transferred by this Order are hereby transferred to the Secretary.

SEC. 5. The Director of the Office of Management and Budget shall make such determinations and issue such orders as may be necessary or appropriate to carry out the transfers provided by this Order.

SEC. 6. Executive Order No. 11840 of February 18, 1975, is hereby revoked.

SEC. 7. This Order shall be effective June 30, 1977.

JIMMY CARTER

The White House,

June 29, 1977.

[Filed with the Office of the Federal Register, 10:34 a.m., June 30, 1977]

Executive Branch Reorganization Studies

Remarks to Reporters Announcing the Studies. June 29, 1977

I have a couple of very brief statements to make.

First of all, I'm particularly pleased with the action that was taken this afternoon by the Interstate and Foreign Commerce Committee when they accepted by, I think, a 22-to-21 vote the administration's proposal which retains ceilings for the time being on natural gas prices, but still provides adequate incentives for production of natural gas.

This fight, of course, is still not over. But I commend the members of the committee for their courage in the face of strong lobbying pressure. And I hope that their position will be maintained throughout the legislative process. I believe that their action is a major victory for American consumers.

The other item that I have is one that's very important to me, and I think to the American people. Over the last 2 years, there has been no theme that I have emphasized more often than a need to reorganize the Federal Government.

The American people overwhelmingly support this idea and that's one reason I was elected President. They know that reorganization is desperately needed, and neither they nor I underestimate the difficulty.

I've been encouraged by the progress that the administration and the Congress have already made together in the last 5 months, especially the legislation that I signed in April, which will now permit me to submit to the Congress reorganization plans during the next 3 years.

All of us know that the task will be a long one; it's taken these problems a long time to develop. And we must be patient in taking both small steps and large steps leading to a more effective and more efficient Government.

We've already begun many reorganization efforts, some of which have already been announced. But today I'm pleased to announce the beginning of four new reorganization studies which will bring order and simplicity and efficiency to major parts of our Government.

The four areas that we will study are, first of all, law enforcement; secondly, local and community economic development; third, human services; and fourth, administrative services, primarily under GSA. Together these areas account for $60 billion of Federal spending each year.

Our preliminary review indicates that there are at least 41 separate agencies involved in police and investigative activities. Twelve separate agencies are conducting personnel background investigations; 36 separate agencies have guard duties or security forces, for a total cost per year of about $2½ billion—I think about 164,000 employees in the District of Columbia area alone. There are 23 different Federal police forces.

A different study shows that a welfare mother with two children may now have to deal with 11 different agencies to get the services that she needs. And if there's an elderly person in the home, there are several additional agencies who are supposed to serve that same family.

In economic development, we now have more than a hundred different programs in 10 different agencies, all working to promote business in local areas, by doing so in a wasteful and uncoordinated way.

There are 46 different Federal sewer programs, for instance. And no one, either in or out of Government, benefits from this kind of confusion. All of us will profit from a more sensible and efficient organization.

These studies that I've announced will take from 5 to 9 months. These are very complicated agencies and programs, and we want to do a thorough and good job. The studies will depend upon how closely we can involve the Members of Congress, the officials of State and local governments, and private citizens from all parts of the country for their success.

I believe it's especially important for us to get continuing advice and counsel from the Members of the House and the Senate about the way our Federal programs are being administered, because they spend a good part of every day helping people cut through Government redtape, and they know first hand how the Government looks from the receiving end of the services.

On the day in 1974 when I announced my campaign for this office, I pledged to undertake this major task. At that time I said, and I quote: "This is no job for the faint-hearted. It will be met with violent opposition from those who enjoy a special privilege, those who prefer to work in the dark, or those whose private fiefdoms are threatened."

Well, it's still no job for the faint-hearted, but I intend to honor that pledge. I look forward to the cooperation of everyone involved—the Congress, the Federal employees, and the American people—to move toward that goal, which we all share, of having a Government that's efficient and effective but also sensitive to the needs of our people.

This afternoon Bert Lance and those who work with him on the reorganization studies will be available to answer your specific questions.

I have a full-scale press conference scheduled for tomorrow morning, at which time I'll answer your questions on any subject, including that one that interests you. [*Laughter*]

NOTE: The President spoke at 2 p.m. in the Briefing Room at the White House. Following his remarks, Bert Lance, Director of the Office of Management and Budget, and Harrison Wellford, Executive Associate Director for Reorganization and Management, held a news briefing for reporters on the studies.

Executive Branch Reorganization Studies

Memorandums for the Heads of Executive Departments and Agencies. **June 29, 1977**

Memorandum for the Heads of Executive Departments and Agencies

Subject: Comprehensive Review of Federal Law Enforcement

I have directed my Reorganization Project staff at the Office of Management and Budget to begin a comprehensive review of all Federal law enforcement missions, tasks, and priorities.

Today there is considerable jurisdictional ambiguity, overlap, and possible duplication among Federal organizations performing police or investigative activities. There are at least 75 different Federal agencies and 164,000 Federal employees involved in police or investigative work. Our goal is to make these functions more responsive to both individual rights and Federal law enforcement priorities. This effort will help us determine how best to structure these agencies to do so.

A major objective will be to re-examine the Federal role in law enforcement in light of the responsibilities and capabilities of State and local agencies. The Federal Government ought not to duplicate or overlap State and local law enforcement functions unnecessarily.

The Project will rely heavily on the advice and counsel of the Congress, Federal Departments and Agencies, State and local officials, interested private organizations, and the public.

You may be asked to contribute time, resources, and staff assistance to this effort. If so, I hope you will make your best effort to ensure its successful completion.

My Reorganization Project staff will contact you or an appropriate member of your staff shortly to discuss the appropriate role of your department or agency in the study.

I consider this to be a high priority matter. I know I can count on your cooperation and assistance.

In order to inform all affected parties that this review is underway, I have directed that this memorandum be published in the FEDERAL REGISTER.

JIMMY CARTER

Memorandum for the Heads of Executive Departments and Agencies

Subject: Comprehensive Review of Local Development Programs

I have directed my Reorganization Project staff at the Office of Management and Budget to begin a thorough review of the organization and structure of the major Federal local development programs, including the community economic development programs.

These programs have several problems, including jurisdictional uncertainty, duplication of effort, and lack of coordination.

This review will focus on the programs that comprise the core of the Federal local development assistance package:

• Business promotion, where over 100 different programs in more than ten different agencies provide financial and managerial assistance to businesses.

• Public facilities investment, where, for example, there are 46 sewage-related programs alone, dispensing about $6 billion through seven agencies in five departments, two independent agencies and eight regional commissions.

• Housing, where there are at least 77 different programs, administered by 15 different agencies and overseen by three separate government-chartered secondary mortgage agencies.

• Transportation, where 60 grant assistance programs are channelled through six semi-autonomous operating administrations of the Department of Transportation and an additional network of 25 agencies.

• Employment and training, where ten agencies administer 24 programs.

By examining how these various local development programs actually fit together at the local level, the project will identify ways to improve the Federal Government's contribution to community development, and help sort out the appropriate roles and responsibilities of Federal and non-Federal officials in this area.

The effort will need the active participation of State and local officials, the Congress, Federal Departments and Agencies, and the public.

You may be asked to contribute time, resources, and staff assistance to this effort. If so, I hope you will make your best effort to ensure its successful completion.

My Reorganization Project staff will contact you or an appropriate member of your staff shortly to discuss the appropriate role of your department or agency in the study.

I consider this to be a high priority matter. I know I can count on your support.

In order to inform all affected parties that this review is underway, I have directed that this memorandum be published in the FEDERAL REGISTER.

JIMMY CARTER

———

Memorandum for the Heads of Executive Departments and Agencies

Subject: Comprehensive Review of Human Services Program

I have directed my Reorganization Project staff to begin a study of the organization and delivery of human services. These services programs, ranging from day care to job training, are intended to help people whose special needs are not met by income assistance and health financing programs. This study will be coordinated closely with efforts underway to develop welfare and national health insurance proposals.

The Federal Government spends about $22 billion on more than 100 human services programs administered by ten departments and agencies. The numerous planning, administrative and eligibility requirements of these programs create fragmentation, waste, and confusion.

With your help, this study will lead to a more logical program structure at the Federal level and the delivery of services to families and individuals who need them in a simpler, more comprehensive and efficient way.

The success of this project will depend to a large extent on the cooperation and assistance of Federal departments and agencies, State and local officials, interested groups and individual citizens.

You may be asked to contribute time, resources, and staff assistance to this effort. If so, I hope you will make your best effort to ensure its successful completion.

My Reorganization Project staff will contact you or an appropriate member of your staff shortly to discuss the appropriate role of your department or agency in the study.

I consider this to be a high priority matter. I know I can count on your support.

In order to inform all affected parties that this review is underway, I have directed that this memorandum be published in the FEDERAL REGISTER.

JIMMY CARTER

Memorandum for the Heads of Executive Departments and Agencies

Subject: Comprehensive Review of Administrative Services Delivery

I have directed my Reorganization Project staff at the Office of Management and Budget to begin a comprehensive review of the management of administrative services within the Federal Government. The project will be administered jointly by OMB and the Administrator of the General Services Administration.

A preliminary staff review indicates significant problems with existing services. It has been 30 years since the first Hoover study led to the creation of the General Services Administration; it is time to reexamine the objectives and benefits of our present system in light of those years of operating experience.

A major objective of the study is to improve the delivery of administrative services to Federal agencies. It will assess the roles of the General Services Admin-

istration and others in the provision of services related to real and personal property, automated data processing, telecommunications, and records management.

The Project will rely heavily on the advice and counsel of the Congress, Federal Departments and Agencies, State and local officials, interested private organizations, and the public. Your agencies are the principal consumers of Federal administrative services. You have expressed your concerns about their quality. This is your opportunity to help improve them.

You may be asked to contribute time, resources, and staff assistance to this effort. If so, I hope you will make your best effort to ensure its successful completion.

My Reorganization Project staff will contact you or an appropriate member of your staff shortly to discuss the appropriate role of your department or agency in the study.

I consider this to be a high priority matter. I know I can count on your cooperation and assistance.

In order to inform all affected parties that this review is underway, I have directed that this memorandum be published in the FEDERAL REGISTER.

JIMMY CARTER

NOTE: Fact sheets on each of the studies were also included in the release.

Department of Health, Education, and Welfare

Nomination of Charles F. C. Ruff To Be Deputy Inspector General. June 30, 1977

The President today announced that he will nominate Charles F. C. Ruff, of Washington, D.C., to be Deputy Inspector General in the Department of Health, Education, and Welfare. Ruff is now an associate professor at Georgetown University Law Center and has been the Special Prosecutor on the Watergate Special Prosecution Force.

He was born March 1, 1939, in Cleveland, Ohio. He received an A.B. from Swarthmore College in 1960 and an LL.B. from Columbia Law School in 1963.

From 1963 to 1965, Ruff was an instructor at the Louis Arthur Grimes School of Law, University of Liberia, in Monrovia, Liberia. In 1966–67 he was an instructor in legal method at the University of Pennsylvania Law School.

From 1967 to 1970, Ruff was a trial attorney in the Organized Crime and Racketeering Section, Criminal Division, at the Justice Department. From 1970 to 1972, he was Chief of the Management and Labor Section in the Criminal Division at Justice.

Ruff was an attorney and professor at the Antioch School of Law in 1972–73. He has been an associate professor at Georgetown Law Center since 1973 and also served as Acting Chief Inspector of the Drug Enforcement Administration during 1975, as Assistant Special Prosecutor on the Watergate Force from 1973 to 1975, and Special Prosecutor from 1975 until that office was closed.

Harvard College in 1958 and a J.D. from Harvard Law School in 1962.

From 1962 to 1969, Frank worked in the Office of the Legal Adviser at the State Department, first as Assistant Legal Adviser, then as Acting Deputy Legal Adviser. He was a lecturer at George Washington University in 1967 on public international law and organizations and an adjunct professor at George Washington Law School in 1968–69, teaching "Negotiations—Concept and Technique."

In 1969 and 1970, Frank was a consultant and counsel to Investors Overseas Services. In 1970 and 1971, he was counsel to the law firm of Fisher and Gelband in Washington. Since 1971, Frank has been director of the International Project at the Center for Law and Social Policy, which has represented a wide range of public interest clients on international issues.

Frank serves on the Secretary of State's Advisory Committee on the Law of the Sea, and the State Department's Shipping Coordinating Committee. He has been adviser to several U.S. delegations in negotiations on vessel pollution and ocean dumping and is on the board of the Center for Oceans Law and Policy. He is the author of numerous articles.

National Oceanic and Atmospheric Administration

Nomination of Richard A. Frank To Be Administrator. June 30, 1977

The President today announced that he will nominate Richard A. Frank, of Washington, D.C., to be Administrator of the National Oceanic and Atmospheric Administration. Frank is director of the International Project at the Center for Law and Social Policy.

He was born November 4, 1936, in Omaha, Nebr. He received an A.B. from

United States Ambassador to Sri Lanka and the Maldives

Nomination of W. Howard Wriggins. June 30, 1977

The President today announced that he will nominate W. Howard Wriggins, of the Bronx, N.Y., to be Ambassador Extraordinary and Plenipotentiary of the United States to the Republic of Sri Lanka and to the Republic of Maldives. Wriggins is director of the Southern Asian Institute at Columbia University and professor of public law and government.

He was born February 14, 1918, in Philadelphia, Pa. He received a B.A. from Dartmouth College in 1940 and a Ph.D. from Yale University in 1951.

Wriggins was an instructor at Yale University in 1951–52 and an assistant, then associate, professor at Vassar College from 1952 to 1957. From 1958 to 1961, he was Chief of the Foreign Affairs Division of the Legislative Reference Service, Library of Congress, and also served as a part-time faculty member at George Washington University.

Wriggins was a member of the Policy Planning Council at the State Department from 1961 to 1966 and was a senior staff member on the National Security Council in 1966 and 1967. Since 1967 he has been director of the Southern Asian Institute at Columbia.

Wriggins has written several articles on Southern Asia and was co-editor of "Sri Lanka Journal of Social and Historical Studies" in the autumn of 1975. He serves on the board of trustees of the Asia Society and the Institute of Current World Affairs.

THE PRESIDENT'S NEWS CONFERENCE OF JUNE 30, 1977

THE PRESIDENT. I have a brief statement to make before we begin the questions.

B–1 BOMBER

This has been one of the most difficult decisions that I have made since I've been in office. During the last few months, I've done my best to assess all the factors involving production of the B–1 bomber. My decision is that we should not continue with deployment of the B–1, and I am directing that we discontinue plans for production of this weapons system.

The Secretary of Defense agrees that this is a preferable decision, and he will have a news conference tomorrow morning to discuss this issue in whatever detail you consider necessary.

The existing testing and development program now underway on the B–1 should continue to provide us with the needed technical base in the unlikely event that more cost-effective alternative systems should run into difficulty. Continued efforts at the research and development stage will give us better answers about the cost and effectiveness of the bomber and support systems, including electronic countermeasures techniques.

During the coming months, we will also be able to assess the progress toward agreements on strategic arms limitations in order to determine the need for any additional investments in nuclear weapons delivery systems. In the meantime, we should begin deployment of cruise missiles using air-launched platforms, such as our B–52's, modernized as necessary. Our triad concept of retaining three basic delivery systems will be continued with submarine-launched ballistic missiles, intercontinental ballistic missiles, and a bomber fleet, including cruise missiles as one of its armaments. We will continue thereby to have an effective and flexible strategic force whose capability is fully sufficient for our national defense.

Thank you.

QUESTIONS

B–1 BOMBER

Q. Mr. President, the House at least seems bent on providing the money for the B–1. Does this put you on a collision course with them on the whole subject?

THE PRESIDENT. No, I think not. The Congress took action last year to delay a final decision on the B–1 bomber pending my ability to analyze its needs.

When I came into office, I tried deliberately to have an open mind. And I've spent weeks studying all the aspects of our strategic defense forces. I've met with congressional leaders. I've spent a great deal of time with the Secretary of Defense and others in trying to understand all the ramifications of this very important decision.

The leaders in the House and Senate this morning have been informed of my decision, both by Frank Moore [1] and by the Secretary of Defense.

My belief is that the Congress will be supportive knowing that our previous requests for limited production funds were based on a previous decision. But my decision is that this production is not now necessary. And I believe that the House and the Senate will confirm my decision.

RELATIONS WITH THE SOVIET UNION

Q. Mr. President, in view of the growing difficulties between the United States and the Soviet Union, are there any early prospects in the coming months for a meeting with Brezhnev, between yourself and Brezhnev, and is August in Alaska—does that have any validity?

THE PRESIDENT. I don't agree that there are growing difficulties between ourselves and the Soviet Union. The technical discussions on SALT questions, comprehensive test ban, demilitarization of the Indian Ocean, a reduction in the sales of conventional weapons to developing nations of the world have been proceeding with very good attitudes on the part of the Soviets, and, of course, us. So, I don't believe that the relations between us are deteriorating.

I think that my own relationship with Mr. Brezhnev and other Soviet leaders

---

[1] Assistant to the President for Congressional Liaison.

should be one of continuing consultations, not just to ratify final agreements but to get to know one another. And I would welcome a chance this year to meet with President Brezhnev, to explore the ability of our countries to reach quicker decisions. But it would not be based on any deep concern about relations now, nor any frustration about what's gone on before.

The time or date or place would still have to be worked out, and it would be inappropriate, I think, to try to presume what those decisions might be on specifics until we determine accurately the attitude of the Soviet leaders.

Q. May I say that——

THE PRESIDENT. Please do.

Q. ——you yourself have expressed surprise at the reaction of the Soviets to your human rights drive, and Brezhnev has told Giscard that there are difficulties. So, I don't think it's exactly—I mean there is an atmosphere.

THE PRESIDENT. There are difficulties, obviously, in reaching final decisions on matters that are very controversial, very difficult, and which never have been successfully concluded. We've never tried as a nation to have a comprehensive test ban to eliminate all tests of all nuclear devices, both peaceful and military. We've never tried to open up the discussions of demilitarizing the Indian Ocean, first freezing the present circumstances, then reducing our military presence there. We've never tried for a sharp reduction in the deployment of nuclear weapons.

So, these new ideas obviously take more time to conclude. But I don't have any sense of fear or frustration or concern about our relationships with the Soviet Union. We have, I think, a good prospect of continuing our discussions, and I have every hope that those discussions will lead to success.

B-1 BOMBER

Q. Mr. President, what were the major factors that led to your decision against the B-1 bomber?

THE PRESIDENT. There are a number of factors. One is obviously the recent evolution of the cruise missile as an effective weapon itself. The tests of this system have been very successful so far.

Another one, of course, is the continued ability to use the B-52 bombers, particularly the G's and H's, up well into the 1980's, and the belief on my part that our defense capability using the submarine-launched missiles and intercontinental ballistic missiles combined with the B-52 cruise missile combination is adequate.

We will also explore the possibility of cruise missile carriers, perhaps using existing airplanes or others as a standoff launching base.

But I think in toto the B-1, a very expensive weapons system basically conceived in the absence of the cruise missile factor, is not necessary. Those are the major reasons.

Marilyn [Marilyn Berger, NBC News].

CRUISE MISSILE

Q. Mr. President, the Soviet Union has shown great concern about the cruise missile capability of the United States.

THE PRESIDENT. Yes.

Q. What limits are you ready to accept, if any, on air-launched cruise missiles so far as their range, and secondly, are you willing to accept the proposition that an airplane carrying cruise would be counted as a MIRV under the limits that you would set in a SALT agreement?

THE PRESIDENT. Those questions are being negotiated now. We have a fairly compatible position with the Soviets on maximum range of air-launched cruise missiles carried over from the Vladivostok discussions. I don't think there's any particular difference in that. It's an adequate

range in my opinion for the cruise missiles to be launched as a standoff weapon without the carrying airplane having to encroach into Soviet territory. This, though, is a matter that has not yet been finally resolved.

Also, the definition of what is a MIRVed weapon is one that is still in dispute. We don't believe that a bomber equipped with cruise missiles as a weapon ought to be classified as a MIRVed weapon. But depending upon the Soviets' attitude in reaching an overall comprehensive settlement, those matters are still open for discussion.

B-1 BOMBER

Q. Mr. President, in listening to factors involved in your decision, sir, you didn't mention or I didn't hear the fact that you had made a commitment or what many people took to be a commitment during the campaign against the bomber, I think particularly in the submission to the Democratic Platform Committee. Was that a factor, sir?

THE PRESIDENT. Well, when I went into office, as I think I said earlier, I tried to take the position of complete openmindedness, because obviously I've had available to me as President much of the classified analyses and information about weapons systems which I did not have before. And I tried to approach this question with an open mind.

I've spent many hours reading those detailed technical reports, the advice of specialists on both sides, an analysis of ultimate cost of weapons. And although, obviously, opinions are always hard to change, I deliberately tried not to let my campaign statements be the factor in this decision. I've made it, I think, recently with an original, very open mind, after carefully considering all aspects of the question and consulting very closely with the Secretary of Defense.

And I might say that with the advent of the cruise missile as a possible alternative, that the Secretary of Defense agrees with me that this is a preferable decision.

Q. Can I follow that up, sir? Mr. President, could I follow that up?

THE PRESIDENT. Yes, if you insist.

Q. This openmindedness that you describe, does that apply to other campaign commitments that you made in other areas outside of defense?

THE PRESIDENT. Well, I'll always try to keep an open mind and make my decision based on what I think is best for our country.

Q. Mr. President, is this decision on your part not to go ahead with the B–1 intended as any kind of a signal to the Soviets that you are willing to—that you want to do something quickly in the strategic arms talks?

THE PRESIDENT. I can't deny that that's a potential factor. But that has not been a reason for my decision. I think if I had looked upon the B–1 as simply a bargaining chip for the Soviets, then my decision would have been to go ahead with the weapon. But I made my decision on my analysis that, within a given budgetary limit for the defense of our country, which I am sure will always be adequate, that we should have the optimum capability to defend ourselves.

But this is a matter that's of very great importance, and if at the end of a few years the relations with the Soviets should deteriorate drastically, which I don't anticipate, then it may be necessary for me to change my mind. But I don't expect that to occur.

Mr. Sperling [Godfrey Sperling, Christian Science Monitor].

HUMAN RIGHTS POLICY

Q. Mr. President, is this emphasis on human rights now central to your foreign policy?

THE PRESIDENT. Yes. My emphasis on human rights is central to our foreign policy. As I've said since my first press conference, I see no relationship between the human rights decision, however, and matters affecting our defense or SALT negotiations. And I have doubts, based on analyses in our own country and from those who know the Soviet system very well in other countries, that there's any connection between the two in the minds of the Soviets.

Q. To follow there, has this emphasis helped or hurt those in the Soviet Union whose rights were being impaired?

THE PRESIDENT. It's hard for me to say. I think that in the long run our emphasis on human rights, the high publicity that has accrued to the human rights question because of the Helsinki agreement and the upcoming Belgrade conference in October—those two factors, combined, I think, dramatize every violation of human rights that is known.

And my guess is that the Soviets, like ourselves, want to put a good image forward for the world to observe, and I think in the long run that this emphasis on human rights will be beneficial to those who desire free speech and an enhancement of their own human freedoms.

THE MIDDLE EAST

Q. Mr. President, Senator Javits says you are pushing Israel too far. And other Americans sympathetic to the Israeli position say worse, that you are perhaps selling Israel down the river. My question is, first, do you think you are, and secondly, how difficult will it be for you to continue your policy if the American Jewish community sides with Mr. Begin instead of Mr. Carter?

THE PRESIDENT. I might say, first of all, that I look forward with great anticipation to the visit of Prime Minister Begin on the 19th of July. My determination is that the talks will be friendly and constructive and also instructive for both him and me.

He'll be received with the kind of friendship that's always been a characteristic of the American people's attitude toward Israel. An overwhelming consideration for us is the preservation of Israel as a free and independent and, hopefully, peaceful nation. That is preeminent. At the same time, I believe that it has been good during this year, when I hope we can reach a major step toward a peaceful resolution in the Middle East, to have the discussions much more open, to encourage the Arab nations and Israel to frankly understand some of the feelings that each of them has toward the other, and to address the basic questions of territories, the definition of peace, the Palestinian question.

I really think it is best for this next roughly 3 weeks before Mr. Begin comes that we refrain from additional comments on specifics because I think we've covered the specifics adequately. And if I or someone in the State Department or someone on my staff emphasizes territory and the definition of peace, the immediate response is: Why didn't you say something about the Palestinians, and so forth. So, I believe that we've discussed it adequately.

I believe all the issues are fairly clearly defined. It's accurate to say that our own Nation has no plan or solution that we intend to impose on anyone. We'll act to the degree that the two sides trust us in the role of an intermediary or mediator, and I still have high hopes that this year might lead toward peace.

But it will never be with any sort of abandonment of our deep and permanent commitment to Israel. And I have made this clear in specific terms to every Arab leader who has been to our country.

SUPPORT OF DEMOCRATIC PARTY
CANDIDATES

Q. Mr. President, as the leader of the Democratic Party, how important do you believe it is for Democratic leaders on the State and local level to support the nominees of their party even when their preferred candidates may happen to lose in a primary? And, second, sir, do you plan to support the Democratic nominee for mayor of New York City regardless of who it may be?

THE PRESIDENT. My general belief is that Democrats ought to support the Democratic nominees. I have not ever violated that premise in my own voting habits. I've never departed from voting for a Democratic nominee after they were chosen. My own inclination is to stay clear of Democratic primaries. Let the Democrats in a particular State or jurisdiction make their own choice.

But I think every Democrat, every American can reserve the right to participate with varying degrees of commitment or intensity or enthusiasm. And I would certainly not ever disavow a Democratic candidate unless he was completely abhorrent to me, which I think would be highly unlikely.

So, in general, I think Democrats ought to support their nominees. But I'm going to be fairly reluctant to inject myself directly and personally in very many elections around the country. We do have two important gubernatorial elections this year, and I think all Democrats will be looking with great interest on the outcome of the general election in Virginia and also New Jersey. And I hope personally that the Democratic candidates win. But that's a decision for the people in Virginia and New Jersey to make.

As far as New York is concerned, I

wouldn't want to make a prior commitment about the degree of my support for a candidate until I see who it is.

SALT NEGOTIATIONS

Q. Mr. President, given the numerous and obvious violations of the Helsinki accords by the Soviet Union, which they were pledged to uphold, could I ask why the United States should, on good faith, accept the Soviet word on a matter far more vital, say, for example, the SALT treaty, which you are in the process of negotiating?

THE PRESIDENT. We have never been willing simply to take the word of the Soviets on SALT agreements, and neither have they been willing to take our word alone. We have methods of confirming or verifying the carrying out of the agreement with various means, including aerial surveillance from space.

And I think that as we get down to the more technical agreements, that verification is becoming more and more a problem. For instance, if we should conclude a comprehensive test ban treaty with the Soviets of preventing any sort of nuclear tests, even including peaceful devices, then we would have to have some way to confirm that the Soviets indeed are carrying out their agreement, and vice versa.

There are sensing devices that might, for instance, be placed by us on Soviet territory or perhaps around the periphery of the Soviet Union. And we might conclude a similar agreement with them. Or if a factor in the agreement should be that certain kinds of uses of atomic weapons— not weapons, but explosives to divert the channel of a river, we might want to have actual observers there, and vice versa. My own hope is that we can conclude an agreement that there would be no testing. But verification is one of the aspects not just based on the word of us or the Soviets but on actual observations on site by sensing devices or by visual observations or others that I need not go into now.

PANAMA CANAL NEGOTIATIONS

Q. What is the status, Mr. President, of the Panama Canal treaty? Are you likely to sign such a treaty soon?

THE PRESIDENT. I don't know about the time schedule because it obviously takes two sides to agree to a treaty. We are putting in a lot of time on the Panama Canal treaty negotiations.

And I hope that we'll have a successful conclusion this summer. We've been encouraged so far. The major questions that were identified at the beginning have fairly well been concluded.

One of the disagreements at this point is on the payment of portions of the tolls from the Panama Canal to Panama and the exact financial arrangement.

But I hope still that we'll have one by summer. I think that General Torrijos feels the same way, and, of course, we have been aided by the good offices of President Perez from Venezuela and others who want to have a peaceful resolution here.

I can't give you an answer because I don't know yet. We are also trying to keep the Members of the Senate and others informed about progress as well as I'm being informed so that when we do reach a conclusion, it would be one that, with a major effort, we could have confirmed by the Congress.

OPEC OIL PRICES

Q. Mr. President, in view of the apparent moderation by the OPEC countries on oil prices lately, does that appear to be aimed at diffusing some of the stronger measures you'd like Congress to adopt, and what strategy can you have against that?

THE PRESIDENT. When Prince Fahd was over here, we discussed the prospects for OPEC prices, and he told me in confidence what he thought were the prospects. And I think that is going to come true, that the Saudi Arabians would raise their price to equal that of other OPEC nations and that the OPEC nations who had already raised their prices 10 percent would forgo their planned additional increases at least through this year.

I hope, and I believe the Saudis also hope, that that extension of a price freeze would go through 1978 at least. I think that our own strong country can accommodate additional increases in the price of oil.

I think the prices are too high. But there are obviously major adverse impacts on world inflation, and the poor countries that have to buy large quantities of oil and can't equal it by exports are very badly damaged.

But we can accommodate the change, but we are using our good offices when possible to hold down additional increases in the price of oil.

U.S.–CHINESE RELATIONS

Q. Mr. President, is it your intention to terminate either our defense commitment or diplomatic relations with Taiwan as a step towards normalizing relations with the People's Republic of China?

THE PRESIDENT. Our attitude on the Chinese question has been spelled out by my predecessors and confirmed by me as based on the Shanghai Communique which acknowledges the concept of one China. We also hope that Taiwan and the Mainland can work out the differences between them. We obviously hope that these differences can be resolved early, or perhaps in the future through peaceful means.

Other nations who have now full relationships with the People's Republic of China, on the Mainland have continued trade, cultural, social exchanges, sales of major equipment to Taiwan.

I can't give you a better answer than I've already described. The Secretary of State is planning to go to China, to Peking, in August. This was part of the Shanghai Communique agreement, that we would have consultations at the highest level, obviously at the Secretary of State level or the national leader level. But I can answer your question better after he returns in August.

Did you have one followup?

Q. Could I just follow that in a broader sense? Is it possible to have relations with the People's Republic of China and at the same time maintain a defense commitment to Taiwan?

THE PRESIDENT. This is a difficult question to answer now. My hope is that we can work out an agreement with the People's Republic of China having full diplomatic relations with them and still make sure that the peaceful lives of the Taiwanese, the Republic of China, is maintained. That's our hope, and that's our goal.

Q. Mr. President, in New York last night Secretary of State Vance spoke of a constructive dialog now on the way with Communist China. And I believe you have referred to this at least once publicly yourself. However, so far as I know, there have been only low-level talks with representatives of the Liaison Office here about property claims and also, there have been some other—an occasional meeting or two. What is involved in this dialog? Where and when are these exchanges taking place?

THE PRESIDENT. As you know, we don't have ambassadors exchanged. We have special representatives with the rank of ambassador. Ambassador Huang here in Washington meets with the Secretary of State. He's also been to the Oval Office to meet with me. We've had a very frank discussion about some of the relationships between our country and the People's Republic of China.

The first meetings at the foreign minister level or the head of state level will be in August in Peking. But the preparations for that visit will obviously be continuing through regular diplomatic channels. I think that's the limit of the discussions to this point.

PRESIDENT'S TAX RETURN

Q. Mr. President, you signed your income tax return on June 6 knowing then that you would owe no tax. Some days later you said you thought it had been filed. But it wasn't until about a week after that that you wrote the letter returning the $6,000. Was that an afterthought?

THE PRESIDENT. I had a substantial amount of income in 1976 from the sale of my book "Why Not The Best?" I think it was about $70,000. I'm not sure of the exact figure. That payment was made to me by the publisher on the first day of January, 1977. And the question arose whether or not we could count that as income in 1976 and therefore pay taxes on it.

We went to the Internal Revenue Service shortly before we published our statement and asked them for permission to include that income in 1976. They said that it would not be appropriate, that it would have to be included in 1977. So, because of that decision, I did not owe any income tax in 1976. Believing as I do that people in my income bracket ought to pay taxes, we took our adjusted tax income and paid the minimum tax on it, roughly 15 percent, and, of course, now I will pay the full income tax owed on the income from the book itself.

The difference in the total amount of tax that I would have had to pay either way was zero, so far as we could determine. But had we been able to include the book income in '76, I would have owed a substantial amount of tax and would not have had the problem.

I considered it to be a problem not because there was anything improper about it but I think that I, as President, ought to demonstrate that the present tax laws are not adequate and that someone who earns as much as I did in '76 ought to pay taxes. That was the reason for the delay.

U.S. POSTAL SERVICE

Q. Mr. President, we've talked today about sending a missile around the world. Could you talk——

THE PRESIDENT. Sending what?

Q. A missile halfway across the world. Could we talk about sending a letter halfway across town? [*Laughter*]

Have you made a decision yet on the future of the United States Postal Service? Will you ask Congress to bring it back into the executive branch?

THE PRESIDENT. I've not made a decision about that yet. I think in the July meeting of the board which governs the Post Office, which as you know is completely independent of the President—I have no responsibility for the Post Office—[*laughter*]—they will have to make a decision. I think, absent any decision on their part to forgo Saturday deliveries or to increase the price of postage, we will face about a $200-million-a-month deficit.

But after they make their decision—and I've not studied the problem—and make their recommendation to the Congress, then I think it would be an appropriate time for me to comment. I don't yet know what my preference would be, whether the Post Office should continue as an independent agency or whether it should be part of the Government itself.

STAFF MORALS

Q. Mr. President, Panax Newspapers has a tape-recorded statement by Dr. Peter Bourne that even though your own relationship is monogamous, you never held anything against people in your organization who were involved promiscuously with other women. My question is, is Dr. Bourne right or wrong in this recorded statement? [*Laughter*]

THE PRESIDENT. He certainly is right in part of it. My relationship—[*laughter*]—my relationship is monogamous.

Q. What about the rest of it? Can I follow up, Mr. President?

THE PRESIDENT. I am sorry?

Q. What about the second part of it? He has stated that you never held anything against people in your organization who were involved promiscuously with other women. Is he right or wrong?

THE PRESIDENT. My preference is that those who associate with me—in fact, all people—would honor the same standards that I honor. But I've never held it against people who had a different standard from myself. I've done everything I could properly and legitimately to encourage my staff members' families to be stable, and I have also encouraged the same sort of thing in my Cabinet.

If there are some who have slipped from grace, then I can only say that I'll do the best I can to forgive them and pray for them. [*Laughter*]

PRESIDENTIAL PAPERS

Q. Mr. President, can you give us your reaction to the Supreme Court decision on former President Nixon's tapes and documents, that they are the property of the Government, and the implications that this might have on the disposition of your own Presidential material?

THE PRESIDENT. My intentions are to make my own Presidential papers and documents the property of the people of the Nation after I leave office. And I have no objection, obviously, to the same thing being done in a mandatory way with the papers and documents of President Nixon.

I do have concern, however, about the enormous complexity of the requirement of making all those documents available for public scrutiny. I understand the cost of this process will be more than $55 million. There are literally millions of documents and hundreds and hundreds of tapes. And whether or not we should guarantee that any citizen of the country should have unimpeded access to any document and tape is one that does concern me. But, of course, I am constrained to abide by the 1974 law, and we are looking into how we can make sure that these documents and tapes are not concealed from the public, but still handle them in a rational way.

This is what I intend to do when I am no longer President, is to make my own papers available to the public.

HUMAN RIGHTS POLICY

Q. Mr. President, just one other aspect of human rights. Although you've expressed surprise, as Helen [Helen Thomas, United Press International] pointed out in the beginning, about some of the Soviet response, that reaction at the very beginning was predicted almost without exception by people who had long experience in dealing with the Soviet Union. My question is, did you consult any qualified, experienced people before undertaking your campaign? If you did, who were they? What did they tell you?

THE PRESIDENT. I would guess that the Secretary of State and my national security adviser, my staff, and others would be adequately qualified. I don't have any regrets at all about our enthusiastic endorsement of the principle of human rights, basic human freedoms, and the respect for individuality of persons.

I was asked by a group of local newspaper editors if there were any surprises to me. And I said that the degree of disturbance by the Soviets about what I considered to be a routine and normal commitment to human rights was a surprise. It has not caused me any deep concern, and I would certainly not do it otherwise in retrospect.

Q. Could I just follow up? Did any of them suggest that you not undertake this campaign?

THE PRESIDENT. No, never.

FRANK CORMIER [Associated Press]. Thank you, Mr. President.

THE PRESIDENT. Thank you very much.

NOTE: President Carter's tenth news conference began at 10:30 a.m. in Room 450 of the Old Executive Office Building. It was broadcast live on radio and television.

United States Ambassador to Norway

Nomination of Louis A. Lerner.   July 1, 1977

The President today announced that he will nominate Louis A. Lerner, of Chicago, Ill., to be Ambassador Extraordinary and Plenipotentiary of the United States to Norway. He would succeed William A. Anders. Lerner is publisher of Lerner Newspapers in Chicago.

He was born June 12, 1935, in Chicago. He received a B.A. in 1960 from Roosevelt University. In 1956–57, he studied Scandinavian affairs in Denmark.

From 1959 to 1962, Lerner was assistant to the publisher of Lerner Home Newspapers and an account executive for Times Home Newspapers. He was executive vice president of Lerner Home Newspapers from 1962 until 1969, when he became publisher.

United States Ambassador to Uruguay

Nomination of Lawrence A. Pezzullo. July 1, 1977

The President today announced that he will nominate Lawrence A. Pezzullo, of Bethesda, Md., to be Ambassador Extraordinary and Plenipotentiary of the United States to Uruguay. Pezzullo is Deputy Assistant Secretary of State for Congressional Relations. He would succeed Ernest V. Siracusa.

He was born May 3, 1926, in New York, N.Y. He received a B.A. in 1951 from Columbia University. He served in the U.S. Army from 1944 to 1946.

From 1951 to 1957, Pezzullo taught public school in Levittown, N.Y. He joined the Foreign Service in 1957, and from 1958 to 1960 served as consular officer in Ciudad Juarez. From 1960 to 1962, he was a foreign affairs officer at the State Department, and from 1962 to 1965 he was general services officer in Saigon.

Pezzullo was political officer in La Paz from 1965 to 1967, and political officer in Bogota from 1967 to 1969. From 1969 to 1971, he was political officer in Guatemala, and in 1971–72 he attended the National War College.

From 1972 to 1974, Pezzullo was international relations officer and the Deputy Director of the Office of Central American Affairs. He was Special Assistant to the Ambassador at Large from 1974 to 1975, and has been Deputy Assistant Secretary for Congressional Relations since 1975.

Visit of President Perez of Venezuela

Joint Communique Issued Following President Perez' Visit. July 1, 1977

The President of the Republic of Venezuela, Carlos Andres Perez, and Mrs. Perez made a State Visit to Washington June 28–29 in response to the invitation extended by the President of the United States of America, Jimmy Carter, and Mrs. Carter. Accompanying the President and Mrs. Perez were Minister of Foreign Relations Ramon Escovar Salon, Minister of Finance Hector Hurtado, Minister of Energy and Mines Valentin Hernandez, Minister of Information and Tourism Diego Arria, Minister of State for International Economic Affairs Manuel Perez Guerrero, the Ambassador of Venezuela and Mrs. Iribarren, Ambassador Simon Alberto Consalvi, and Ambassador Jose Maria Machin.

Participating in the talks on behalf of the United States were Vice President Mondale, Secretary of State Vance, Assistant to the President for National Security Affairs Brzezinski, Assistant to the President Schlesinger, and leaders of the Congress.

The Presidents of Venezuela and of the United States, accompanied by their respective parties, referred in their talks to the strong bonds existing between their two countries. They analyzed a wide range of political, economic and cultural affairs of mutual interest and they made special reference to the fact that international relations should be based on mutual respect and cooperation.

They confirmed their faith in the future and the importance of the ethical and political values of Western democratic society, and they reiterated their conviction that man should realize his full potential within a socially, politically, and economically just system which will foster the advantages of the democratic system and the importance which it attaches to the individual.

The two Presidents discussed fully the matters of human rights and agreed to issue a separate communique in this respect. They expressed their conviction that the scientific and technological application of nuclear energy for peaceful purposes and for economic development should be recognized and protected.

They recognized that dissemination of the capability to produce nuclear weapons has serious implications for peace and security, and they expressed their determination to continue their efforts on the international level to avoid those dangers.

Recognizing the contribution which could be made in this regard by adequate regional measures, they attached great importance to broad advocacy of the entry into force of the Treaty of Tlatelolco throughout Latin America. Therefore, States within and without the Latin American region whose decisions are required in order to bring the Treaty into effect are urged to take the necessary measures as soon as possible.

The two Presidents discussed the world energy situation, especially with respect to petroleum, and agreed to explore ways of cooperating and encouraging conservation and the development of alternative sources of energy.

They agreed on the need for intensifying and supporting the efforts of mankind to attain general and complete disarmament and on the desirability of perfecting international standards and instruments of control.

They made known their decision to combine their efforts to achieve a reduction in conventional arms transfers. They also expressed support for regional initiatives such as the Declaration of Ayacucho of 1974, the implementation of which would aid in reducing tensions and avoiding unnecessary expenditures on arms.

They recognized in terrorism a threat which endangers the lives of innocent persons and jeopardizes peace. They declared the intent of their governments to cooperate bilaterally and internationally to combat terrorism.

The two Presidents examined the work of the North-South Dialogue or Conference on International Economic Cooperation, they agreed on the need for continuing, within the framework of the United Nations, the constructive dialogue designed to establish an international system based on justice, equity, interdependence and cooperation among states.

President Carter and President Perez announced their intention to carry on direct consultation, as well as through their respective Ambassadors and other representatives, and to dedicate their best efforts to realizing moral values in terms of the goals and aspirations shared by the Presidents, Governments, and peoples of the United States and Venezuela.

President Perez expressed to President Carter his deep appreciation for the hospitality extended to him and the warm reception given him by the people and the Government of the United States of America, and his sincere satisfaction with the results of his talks with President Carter.

NOTE: The text of the joint communique was released simultaneously in Washington and Caracas.

Visit of President Perez of Venezuela

Joint Communique on Human Rights Issued Following President Perez' Visit.
July 1, 1977

The Presidents of the Republic of Venezuela and of the United States of America,

Recognize that the two countries share the same historic position regarding the protection of human rights as enshrined in their respective Constitutions;

Recognize that the Charter of the United Nations and of the Organization of American States obligate members to promote universal respect for human rights and fundamental freedom for all without distinction as to race, sex, language or religion;

Recognize that the Charter of the Organization of American States provides that member states should exhibit respect for the sovereignty of other nations, for peace, the rule of law, individual liberties, and social justice;

Recognize that the American Convention on Human Rights represents the reaffirmation of our commitment to promote the dignity of the individual in the Hemisphere;

Reaffirm their conviction that the protection and safeguarding of the rights and liberties of man should constitute an objective of all nations of the world;

Proclaim their dedication to those objectives and purposes and agree in their conviction that it is necessary to encourage efforts in support of the dignity of man and the universal protection of human rights as a major goal in the evolution of international law;

Affirm their common commitment to join with other nations in combatting abuses of human rights, including those caused by political, social, and economic injustice;

Affirm that the struggle for observance of human rights is an integral part of the political values of democratic societies;

Express the hope that the American Convention on Human Rights will be ratified and entered into force as soon as possible;

Affirm their continuing joint support for the excellent and effective work performed by the Inter-American Commission on Human Rights, underlining the indispensable need to provide increasingly efficacious means to promote effective respect for the rights of man;

Express interest in increasing the autonomy and resources of the Commission;

Express their interest in seeking ways to promote throughout the Hemisphere broadened programs in the care, protection and resettlement of political refugees; and

Strongly support the Costa Rican initiative to create the post of a United Nations High Commissioner on Human Rights.

NOTE: The text of the joint communique was released simultaneously in Washington and Caracas.

National Heart, Blood Vessel, Lung, and Blood Program

Message to the Congress Transmitting an Annual Report.   July 1, 1977

To the Congress of the United States:

I am transmitting herewith a copy of the Fourth Report of the Director of the National Heart, Lung, and Blood Institute, prepared in accordance with the requirements of Sec. 413(b)(2) of the Public Health Service Act, as amended by Public Law 94–278. The report contains two funding plans which have been generated by the National Heart, Lung, and Blood Institute. Both of these proposed levels are substantially in excess of my current budget request for 1978. While the research conducted by this Institute is of great importance, there are a large number of competing urgent national needs. Individual program activities and funding levels must be carefully considered not only on the basis of individual program merit, but also in light of overall resource availability and fiscal policy.

JIMMY CARTER

The White House,
  July 1, 1977.

NOTE: The report is entitled "National Heart, Blood Vessel, Lung, and Blood Program— Fourth Report of the Director of the National Heart, Lung, and Blood Institute" (Department of Health, Education, and Welfare, 173 pp.).

The message was not issued in the form of a White House press release.

Independence Day, 1977

Statement by the President.   July 1, 1977

The Fourth of July is Americans' traditional day of celebration, a chance to remind ourselves of the heritage we share with each other and with the men of great spirit and wise vision who brought our Nation into being 201 years ago today.

But July Fourth should also be a day of reflection. Freedom, the ideal which created our Nation and continues to give it meaning throughout the world, has flourished in human history far more seldom than we would like to believe.

The work of freedom can never be finished, for freedom is not a temple that is completed when the last stone is in place, but a living thing that each generation must create anew.

In 1977 we must face this task for ourselves and for the world—with a renewed sense of optimism, confident in the strength of our own beliefs and in the signs that other nations share them.

Digest of Other White House Announcements

The following listing includes the President's daily schedule and other items of general interest as announced by the White House Press Office during the period covered by this issue. Events and announcements printed elsewhere in the issue are not included.

June 25

The President met at the White House with:

—Vice President Walter F. Mondale, Secretary of State Cyrus Vance, and Zbigniew Brzezinski, Assistant to the President for National Security Affairs;

—Dr. Brzezinski.

June 27

The President met at the White House with:

—Dr. Brzezinski;

—senior White House staff members;

—the Cabinet;

—a group of administration officials, to discuss the reorganization of the executive branch;

—Vice President Mondale and Mrs. Carter, for lunch;

—Attorney General Griffin B. Bell and Secretary of Health, Education, and Welfare Joseph A. Califano, Jr., to discuss school busing;

—Secretary of Transportation Brock Adams, to discuss automobile safety issues;

—Representative Elliott H. Levitas, of Georgia.

June 28

The President met at the White House with:

—Dr. Brzezinski;

—Representative Dan Rostenkowski, of Illinois;

—Henry Howell, Democratic candidate for Governor of Virginia;

—Robert S. Strauss, Special Representative for Trade Negotiations, George Meany, president of the AFL-CIO, and labor and management representatives of the apparel industry.

June 29

The President met at the White House with:

—David L. Aaron, Deputy Assistant to the President for National Security Affairs;

—a group of Democratic Senators;

—Senator Wendell Ford and C. G. Morehead, an artist from Owensboro, Ky.;

—Secretary of Defense Harold Brown, to discuss the B–1 bomber;

—Dr. Brzezinski and Adm. Stansfield Turner, Director of Central Intelligence;

—Mrs. Carter, for lunch;

—Milan Marsh, president, and Warren J. Smith, secretary-treasurer, Ohio AFL–CIO executive board;

—Secretary of Agriculture Bob S. Bergland and a group of officials of the Agriculture Department;

—Attorney General Bell, Coretta Scott King, Horace Tate, and representatives of the Committee for the Appointment of Blacks to the Federal Judiciary in the Fifth Circuit, who were meeting in the Roosevelt Room.

The President has designated Earl H. Lubensky, American chargé d' affaires ad interim at San Salvador, as his representative to head the U.S. delegation at the inauguration of the new President of El Salvador, General Carlos Humberto Romero. Mr. Lubensky will hold the rank of Special Ambassador while heading the delegation. The inauguration is scheduled for July 1, 1977, in San Salvador.

The President today transmitted to the Congress the tenth annual reports on the administration of the Highway Safety and National Motor Vehicle and Traffic Safety Acts of 1966.

June 30

The President met at the White House with:

—Vice President Mondale, Secretary Vance, and Dr. Brzezinski;

—Dr. Brzezinski;

—Attorney General Bell;

—Judge Harlington A. Wood, Jr., who is under consideration for the position of FBI Director;

—Representative James M. Hanley, of New York;

—representatives of Xerox Education Publications which publishes "My Weekly Reader," a publication for elementary schoolchildren, and a group of children;

—Dr. Henry A. Kissinger, former Secretary of State;

—Neil J. Welch, who is under consideration for the position of FBI Director.

The White House announced that at the invitation of the President, Chancellor Helmut Schmidt of the Federal Republic of Germany will make an official visit to Washington from July 13 to July 15.

The President has transmitted to the Congress the 1976 annual report on the Privacy Act of 1974.

The White House announced that the President and the National Governors' Conference have jointly invited the Nation's Governors to the White House for a working session on energy on July 8–9.

July 1

The President met at the White House with:

—Dr. Brzezinski;

—Gerard C. Smith, the President's nominee to be Ambassador at Large and U.S. Special Representative for Non-Proliferation Matters and U.S. Representative to the International Atomic Energy Agency;

—Ray M. Zook, who is retiring as Chief of Telegraph and Transportation Services for the White House;

—Charles L. Schultze, Chairman of the Council of Economic Advisers;

—Representative Sidney R. Yates, of Illinois;

—Representative Mike McCormack, of Washington;

—Representative James F. Lloyd, of California.

The President left the White House for a weekend stay at Camp David, Md.

CHECKLIST OF WHITE HOUSE PRESS RELEASES

The following releases of the Office of the White House Press Secretary, distributed during the period covered by this issue, are not included in the issue.

Released June 27, 1977

Announcement: nomination of Kenneth J. Mighell to be United States Attorney for the Northern District of Texas

Released June 28, 1977

Announcement: on the meeting of the President with President Perez of Venezuela

Released June 29, 1977

Announcement: nomination of T. F. Gilroy Daly to be United States District Judge for the District of Connecticut; Peter E. Corning to be United States Attorney for the Northern District of New York; Joseph F. Dolan to be United States Attorney for the District of Colorado; James J. Gillespie to be United States Attorney for the Eastern District of Washington; Charles E. Graves to be United States Attorney for the District of Wyoming; D. Lee Rampey, Jr., to be United States Attorney for the Middle District of Georgia; Edward N. Keliikoa to be United States Marshal for the District of Hawaii; and Hubert T. Taylor to be United States Marshal for the Northern District of West Virginia

News briefing: on executive branch reorganization studies—by Bert Lance, Director, and Harrison Wellford, Executive Associate Director for Reorganization and Management, Office of Management and Budget

Announcement: appointment by USIA Director John Reinhardt of R. Peter Straus as Assistant Director of the United States Information Agency and Director of the Voice of America

Released June 30, 1977

Announcement: nomination of Harold M. Edwards to be United States Attorney for the Western District of North Carolina

CHECKLIST OF WHITE HOUSE PRESS RELEASES—Continued

Released July 1, 1977

Announcement: on the release of the comments made by Federal departments and agencies on the Federal Power Commission recommendations to the President on how best to transport Alaska natural gas to the Lower 48 States

News conference: on FPC recommendations concerning Alaska natural gas—by Leslie J. Goldman, Assistant Administrator for Energy Resource Development, Federal Energy Administration

NOMINATIONS SUBMITTED TO THE SENATE

The following list does not include promotions of members of the Uniformed Services, nominations to the Service Academies, or nominations of Foreign Service officers.

Submitted June 27, 1977

WALTER BARBER LaBERGE, of Virginia, to be Under Secretary of the Army, vice Norman R. Augustine, resigned.

KENNETH J. MIGHELL, of Texas, to be United States Attorney for the Northern District of Texas for the term of 4 years, vice Michael P. Carnes, resigned.

SAR A. LEVITAN, of the District of Columbia, to be a member of the National Commission on Employment and Unemployment Statistics (new position).

Submitted June 28, 1977

WILLIAM DRAYTON, JR., of Massachusetts, to be an Assistant Administrator of the Environmental Protection Agency, vice Alvin L. Alm, resigned.

Submitted June 29, 1977

GERARD C. SMITH, of the District of Columbia to be Ambassador at Large and United States Special Representative for Non-Proliferation Matters, and to be also the Representative of the United States of America to the International Atomic Energy Agency.

NOMINATIONS SUBMITTED TO THE SENATE—Continued

Submitted June 29, 1977—Continued

FRANK V. ORTIZ, JR., of New Mexico, a Foreign Service officer of Class one, to be Ambassador Extraordinary and Plenipotentiary of the United States of America to Barbados.

FRANK V. ORTIZ, JR., of New Mexico, a Foreign Service officer of Class one, to be Ambassador Extraordinary and Plenipotentiary of the United States of America to the State of Grenada.

T. F. GILROY DALY, of Connecticut, to be United States District Judge for the District of Connecticut, vice Robert C. Zampano, retired.

JOSEPH F. DOLAN, of Colorado, to be United States Attorney for the District of Colorado for the term of 4 years, vice James L. Treece, resigned.

D. LEE RAMPEY, JR., of Georgia, to be United States Attorney for the Middle District of Georgia for the term of 4 years, vice Ronald T. Knight, resigned.

PETER E. CORNING, of New York, to be United States Attorney for the Northern District of New York for the term of 4 years, vice James M. Sullivan, Jr., resigned.

JAMES J. GILLESPIE, of Washington, to be United States Attorney for the Eastern District of Washington for the term of 4 years, vice Dean C. Smith, resigned.

CHARLES E. GRAVES, of Wyoming, to be United States Attorney for the District of Wyoming for the term of 4 years, vice James P. Castberg, resigned.

EDWARD N. KELIIKOA, of Hawaii, to be United States Marshal for the District of Hawaii for the term of 4 years, vice Thomas K. Kaulukukui, resigning.

HUBERT T. TAYLOR, of West Virginia, to be United States Marshal for the Northern District of West Virginia for the term of 4 years, vice Walter M. Garrison, Jr.

Submitted June 30, 1977

W. HOWARD WRIGGINS, of New York, to be Ambassador Extraordinary and Plenipotentiary of the United States of America to the Republic of Sri Lanka.

W. HOWARD WRIGGINS, of New York, to be Ambassador Extraordinary and Plenipotentiary of the United States of America to the Republic of Maldives.

NOMINATIONS SUBMITTED TO THE SENATE—Continued

Submitted June 30, 1977—Continued

HAROLD M. EDWARDS, of North Carolina, to be United States Attorney for the Western District of North Carolina for the term of 4 years, vice Keith S. Snyder.

RICHARD ASHER FRANK, of the District of Columbia, to be Administrator of the National Oceanic and Atmospheric Administration, vice Robert M. White, resigned.

CHARLES F. C. RUFF, of the District of Columbia, to be Deputy Inspector General, Department of Health, Education, and Welfare (new position).

JOSEPH MALLAM HENDRIE, of New York, to be a member of the Nuclear Regulatory Commission for a term expiring June 30, 1981, vice William A. Anders.

Submitted July 1, 1977

LOUIS A. LERNER, of Illinois, to be Ambassador Extraordinary and Plenipotentiary of the United States of America to Norway.

LAWRENCE A. PEZZULLO, of Maryland, a Foreign Service officer of Class one, to be Ambassador Extraordinary and Plenipotentiary of the United States of America to Uruguay.

ACTS APPROVED BY THE PRESIDENT

Approved June 25, 1977

H.R. 3416_____Public Law 95–54
An act to amend section 316(c) of the Agricultural Adjustment Act of 1938 to provide that leasing of flue-cured tobacco acreage-poundage marketing quotas after June 15 of any year be permitted only between farms on which at least 80 per centum of the farm acreage allotment was planted for such year.

H.R. 7606_____Public Law 95–55
An act to authorize the Secretary of Agriculture to permit general recreational access

ACTS APPROVED BY THE PRESIDENT—Continued

Approved June 25, 1977—Continued

and geothermal explorations for six months within a portion of the Bull Run Reserve, Mount Hood National Forest, Oregon.

Approved June 27, 1977

H.R. 1440_____ Private Law 95–1
An act for the relief of Eun Kyung Park and Sang Hyuk Park.

H.R. 3314_____ Private Law 95–2
An act for the relief of Tri-State Motor Transit Company.

Approved June 29, 1977

H.R. 583_____ Public Law 95–57
An act to amend chapter 5 of title 37, United States Code, to extend the special pay provisions for reenlistment and enlistment bonuses, and for other purposes.

H.R. 4301_____ Public Law 95–58
An act to authorize appropriations for the National Sea Grant Program Act during fiscal year 1978, and for other purposes.

S.J. Res. 63_____ Public Law 95–56
A joint resolution to amend the Federal Home Loan Bank Act.

Approved June 30, 1977

H.J. Res. 525_____ Public Law 95–60
A joint resolution to provide for temporary extension of certain Federal Housing Administration mortgage insurance and related authorities and of the national flood insurance program, and for other purposes.

H.R. 1404_____ Public Law 95–59
An act for the relief of Smith College, Northampton, Massachusetts, and for other purposes.

Approved July 1, 1977

H.R. 6823_____ Public Law 95–61
An act to authorize appropriations for the United States Coast Guard for fiscal year 1978, and for other purposes.

PRESIDENTIAL DOCUMENTS

Presidential Medal of Freedom

Announcement of Award to the Rev. Martin Luther King, Jr., and Dr. Jonas E. Salk. July 4, 1977

The President today announced that he is awarding the Presidential Medal of Freedom to the Rev. Martin Luther King, Jr., and Dr. Jonas E. Salk.

The Presidential Medal of Freedom is the Government's highest civil award. It may be awarded only by the President to persons who have made especially meritorious contributions to the security or national interests of the United States, to world peace, or to cultural or other significant public or private endeavors.

The citations accompanying the medals follow:

"Martin Luther King, Jr. was the conscience of his generation. He gazed upon the great wall of segregation and saw that the power of love could bring it down. From the pain and exhaustion of his fight to fulfill the promises of our founding fathers for our humblest citizens, he wrung his eloquent statement of his dream for America. He made our nation stronger because he made it better. His dream sustains us yet."

———

"Because of Doctor Jonas E. Salk, our country is free from the cruel epidemics of poliomyelitis that once struck almost yearly. Because of his tireless work, untold hundreds of thousands who might have been crippled are sound in body today. These are Doctor Salk's true honors, and there is no way to add to them. This Medal of Freedom can only express our gratitude, and our deepest thanks."

President's Personal Representative to the Vatican

Designation of David Walters. July 6, 1977

The President has asked David Walters, of Miami, Fla., to act as his personal representative to the Vatican. Walters, a private attorney, succeeds Henry Cabot Lodge and will visit the Vatican from time to time to exchange views on international and humanitarian subjects of interest and concern to the Vatican and to the U.S. Government.

Walters was born April 4, 1917, in Cleveland, Ohio. He has a B.A. from Baldwin College and LL.B. and J.D. degrees from the University of Miami Law School. From 1940 to 1950, he worked for the Department of Justice, serving as an investigator, section head, then administrative hearing judge under the Administrative Procedures Act. From

1943 to 1946, he served in the U.S. Army Counter-Intelligence Corps.

Since 1950 Walters has practiced law with Walters and Costanzo in Miami, with an emphasis on international law. He is chairman of the National Leukemia Society and serves on the board of trustees of Variety Children's Hospital in Miami. He is a former member of the Governor's Advisory Council on Health.

Walters holds the title of Master Knight of the Order of Malta and is a member of Serra International, an organization to encourage young people to follow religious vocations.

Export Administration Act of 1969

Executive Order 12002.   July 7, 1977

ADMINISTRATION OF THE EXPORT ADMINISTRATION ACT OF 1969, AS AMENDED

By virtue of the authority vested in me by the Constitution and statutes of the United States of America, including the Export Administration Act of 1969, as amended (50 U.S.C. App. 2401, *et seq.*), and as President of the United States of America, it is hereby ordered as follows:

SECTION 1. Except as provided in Section 2, the power, authority, and discretion conferred upon the President by the provisions of the Export Administration Act of 1969, as amended (50 U.S.C. App. 2401, *et seq.*), hereinafter referred to as the Act, are delegated to the Secretary of Commerce, with the power of successive redelegation.

SEC. 2. (a) The power, authority and discretion conferred upon the President in Sections 4(h) and 4(1) of the Act are retained by the President.

(b) The power, authority and discretion conferred upon the President in Section 3(8) of the Act, which directs that every reasonable effort be made to secure the removal or reduction of assistance by foreign countries to international terrorists through cooperation and agreement, are delegated to the Secretary of State, with the power of successive redelegation.

SEC. 3. The Export Administration Review Board, hereinafter referred to as the Board, which was established by Executive Order No. 11533 of June 4, 1970, as amended, is hereby continued. The Board shall continue to have as members the Secretary of Commerce, who shall be Chairman of the Board, the Secretary of State, the Secretary of Defense, and the Chairman of the East-West Foreign Trade Board (Section 7 of Executive Order No. 11846, as amended). No alternate Board members shall be designated, but the acting head of any department may serve in lieu of the head of the concerned department. In the case of the East-West Foreign Trade Board, the Deputy Chairman or the Executive Secretary may serve in lieu of the Chairman. The Board may invite the heads of other United States Government departments or agencies, other than the agencies represented by Board members, to participate in the activities of the Board when matters of interest to such departments or agencies are under consideration.

SEC. 4. The Secretary of Commerce may from time to time refer to the Board such particular export license matters, involving questions of national security or other major policy issues, as the Secretary shall select. The Secretary of Commerce shall also refer to the Board any other such export license matter, upon the request of any other member of the Board or of the head of any other United States Government department or agency having any interest in such matter. The Board shall consider the matters so referred to it, giving due consideration to the foreign policy of the United States, the national security, and the domestic economy, and shall make recommendation thereon to the Secretary of Commerce.

SEC. 5. The President may at any time (a) prescribe rules and regulations applicable to the power, authority, and discretion referred to in this Order, and (b) communicate to the Secretary of Commerce such specific directives applicable thereto as the President shall determine. The Secretary of Commerce shall from time to time report to the President upon the administration of the Act and, as the Secretary deems necessary, may refer to the President recommendations made by the Board under Section 4 of this Order. Neither the provisions of this section nor those of Section 4 shall be construed as limiting the provisions of Section 1 of this Order.

SEC. 6. All delegations, rules, regulations, orders, licenses, and other forms of administrative action made, issued, or otherwise taken under, or continued in existence by, the Executive orders revoked in Section 7 of this Order, and not revoked administratively or legislatively, shall remain in full force and effect under this Order until amended, modified, or terminated by proper authority. The revocations in Section 7 of this Order shall not affect any violation of any rules, regulations, orders, licenses or other forms of administrative action under those Orders during the period those Orders were in effect.

SEC. 7. Executive Order No. 11533 of June 4, 1970, Executive Order No. 11683 of August 29, 1972, Executive Order No. 11798 of August 14, 1974, Executive Order No. 11818 of November 5, 1974, Executive Order No. 11907 of March 1,

1976, and Executive Order No. 11940 of September 30, 1976 are hereby revoked.

JIMMY CARTER

The White House,
July 7, 1977.

[Filed with the Office of the Federal Register, 4:13 p.m., July 7, 1977]

NOTE: The Executive order was not issued in the form of a White House press release.

Budget Rescission and Deferrals

Message to the Congress.   July 7, 1977

To the Congress of the United States:

In accordance with the Impoundment Control Act of 1974, I herewith propose rescission of $850,000 appropriated for the National Transportation Safety Board. In addition, I am reporting three new deferrals of budget authority totalling $170.1 million and revisions to two deferrals previously transmitted that contain increases totalling $22.2 million.

The details of the proposed rescission and the deferrals are contained in the attached reports.

JIMMY CARTER

The White House,
July 7, 1977.

NOTE: The attachments detailing the rescission and deferrals are printed in the FEDERAL REGISTER of July 13, 1977.

The message was not issued in the form of a White House press release.

Department of Justice

Nomination of John H. Shenefield To Be an Assistant Attorney General.   July 7, 1977

The President today announced that he will nominate John H. Shenefield, of Richmond, Va., to be an Assistant Attorney General. He would replace Donald I. Baker. Shenefield is Deputy Assistant Attorney General in the Antitrust Division of the Justice Department.

He was born January 23, 1939, in Toledo, Ohio. He received an A.B. (1960) and an LL.B. (1965) from Harvard University. He served in the U.S. Army in 1961 and 1962.

Shenefield was with the law firm of Hunton and Williams, in Richmond, from 1965 until April 1977, when he became Deputy Assistant Attorney General.

Civil Aeronautics Board

Nomination of Elizabeth E. Bailey To Be a Member. July 7, 1977

The President today announced that he will nominate Elizabeth E. Bailey, of Rumson, N.J., to be a member of the Civil Aeronautics Board for the remainder of the term expiring December 31, 1977, and for a term expiring December 31, 1983. She would replace John E. Robson.

Bailey was born November 26, 1938, in New York City. She received a B.A. in economics from Radcliffe College in 1960, an M.S. in mathematics from Stevens Institute of Technology in 1966, and a Ph. D. in economics from Princeton University in 1972.

She has been with Bell Laboratories since 1960, beginning as a computer programer and later working in the Traffic Studies Center, where she conducted mathematical studies of telecommunications traffic patterns and assisted in the development of a private communications network for the Department of Defense.

In 1968 she joined the Economic Modeling Group at Bell Labs to conduct research in regulatory theory, and in 1973 she became supervisor of the Economic

Analysis Group. Since 1975 she has been head of the Economics Research Department.

Since 1973 she has been an adjunct associate professor of economics at New York University, where her principal subject is pricing and industry regulation. She is on the editorial board of the American Economic Review and is a founder and former vice president of the School for Children with Learning Disability.

Bailey is the author of the book "Economic Theory of Regulatory Constraint" (1973) and of numerous articles on economics.

United States Ambassador to the German Democratic Republic

Nomination of David B. Bolen. July 8, 1977

The President today announced that he will nominate David B. Bolen, of Boulder, Colo., to be Ambassador Extraordinary and Plenipotentiary of the United States to the German Democratic Republic, which position has been vacant since the resignation of John Sherman Cooper. Bolen is Deputy Assistant Secretary of State for African Affairs.

Bolen was born December 23, 1923, in Heflin, La. He received a B.S. and M.S. from the University of Colorado in 1950, and an M.P.A. from Harvard University in 1960. He served in the U.S. Air Force from 1943 to 1946.

From 1950 to 1952, Bolen was administrative assistant and consular and reporting officer in Monrovia. He was an economic assistant in Karachi from 1952 to 1954 and was detailed to the Commerce Department from 1955 to 1957. In 1957 and 1958, he was an international economist at the State Department.

Bolen was Afghanistan desk officer in 1958 and 1959 and chief of the economic section in Accra from 1960 to 1962. From 1962 to 1964, he was staff assistant to the Assistant Secretary of State for African Affairs. From 1964 to 1966, he was officer in charge of Nigerian affairs, and in 1966–67 he attended the National War College.

From 1967 to 1972, Bolen was economic officer, then counselor of economic affairs, in Bonn. From 1972 to 1973, he was counselor of the Embassy for economic affairs in Belgrade. He served as Ambassador to Botswana, Lesotho, and Swaziland from 1973 until 1976, when he became Deputy Assistant Secretary of State for African Affairs.

United States Ambassador to Guyana

Nomination of John R. Burke. July 8, 1977

The President today announced that he will nominate John R. Burke, of Madison, Wis., to be Ambassador Extraordinary and Plenipotentiary of the United States to the Cooperative Republic of Guyana, which position has been vacant since the resignation of Max V. Krebs. Burke is Deputy Chief of Mission in Bangkok.

Burke was born December 7, 1924, in Madison, Wis. He received an A.B. (1947) and an M.A. (1950) from the University of Wisconsin. He served in the U.S. Navy from 1950 to 1953.

From 1953 to 1956, Burke was administrative assistant to the director of the Wisconsin State Historical Society. In 1954–55 he was also a teaching assistant at the University of Wisconsin.

He joined the Foreign Service in 1956, and in 1957 and 1958 served as Deputy Chief of the Southeast Asia Treaty Or-

ganization Division in Bangkok. From 1958 to 1961, he was consular officer in Paris, and from 1961 to 1963 he was an international relations officer at the State Department.

From 1963 to 1967, Burke was Deputy Chief of the political section in Saigon, and in 1967 he was special assistant to the Assistant Secretary of State. From 1967 to 1969, he was director of the Vietnam working group, and in 1969 he served as country director for Vietnam. In 1969–70 he was detailed to the National War College.

Burke was Deputy Chief of Mission in Port-au-Prince from 1970 to 1972, and Director of Caribbean countries in the Bureau of Inter-American Affairs from 1972 to 1975. In 1975–76 he was detailed to the Foreign Service Institute, and since 1976 he has been Deputy Chief of Mission in Bangkok.

United States Ambassador to Nicaragua

Nomination of Mauricio Solaun. July 8, 1977

The President today announced that he will nominate Mauricio Solaun, of Urbana, Ill., to be Ambassador Extraordinary and Plenipotentiary of the United States to Nicaragua. He would replace James D. Theberge. Solaun is an associate professor of sociology at the University of Illinois.

He was born September 22, 1935, in Cuba. He received a doctor of law degree in 1958 from the University of Villanova, in Cuba, an M.A. from Yale University in 1959, and a Ph. D. from the University of Chicago in 1971.

Since 1966 Solaun has been associate professor of sociology at the University of Illinois. He served as a consultant to the Colombian Planning Office in 1972 and 1973, and as a consultant to the United

Nations Development Program with the Chilean National Planning Office in 1975. He is the author and coauthor of several books and numerous articles on housing and urban policies, race relations, and politics.

United States Ambassador to Bulgaria

Nomination of Raymond L. Garthoff. July 8, 1977

The President today announced that he will nominate Raymond L. Garthoff, of Milford, Conn., to be Ambassador Extraordinary and Plenipotentiary of the United States to Bulgaria. He would replace Martin F. Herz. Garthoff is presently senior Foreign Service inspector at the State Department.

He was born March 26, 1929, in Cairo, Egypt. He received an A.B. from Princeton University in 1948, an M.A. from Yale University in 1949, and a Ph. D. from Yale in 1951.

From 1950 to 1957, Garthoff was a research specialist in Soviet affairs for the Rand Corporation. He served as a foreign affairs adviser to the Army from 1957 to 1961, and as Special Assistant for Soviet bloc politico-military affairs at the State Department from 1961 to 1968.

From 1968 to 1970, Garthoff was counselor for politico-military affairs at the U.S. Mission to NATO in Brussels. He was Deputy Director for politico-military affairs at the State Department from 1970 to 1973, and has been senior Foreign Service inspector since 1974.

Garthoff was also a professorial lecturer at George Washington University from 1962 to 1964, and a lecturer at Johns Hopkins University from 1964 to 1967.

Garthoff is the author of "Soviet Military Doctrine" (1953), "Soviet Strategy in the Nuclear Age" (1958), "The Soviet Image of Future War" (1959), and "Soviet Military Policy: A Historical Analysis" (1966).

Council on Wage and Price Stability

Nomination of Barry P. Bosworth To Be Director. July 8, 1977

The President today announced that he will nominate Barry P. Bosworth, of Silver Spring, Md., to be Director of the Council on Wage and Price Stability. He would replace Michael H. Moskow.

Bosworth was born August 14, 1942, in Kent County, Mich. He received a B.A. (1964) and Ph. D. (1969) in economics from the University of Michigan.

Bosworth was on the staff of the Council of Economic Advisers in 1968. He was an instructor at Harvard University in 1969, and an assistant professor from 1969 to 1971. He has been at the Brookings Institution since 1971, as a research associate from 1971 to 1976 and a senior fellow since 1976. He was a visiting lecturer at the University of California at Berkeley in 1974–75.

Bosworth is the author of several Brookings papers and other articles on economics.

International Conferences on Fish and Wildlife Matters

Nomination of John D. Negroponte for the Rank of Ambassador While Representing the United States. July 8, 1977

The President today announced that he will nominate John D. Negroponte, of New York, for the rank of Ambassador, which would pertain when he is representing the United States at international conferences and meetings on fish and wildlife matters. Negroponte is Deputy Assistant Secretary of State for Oceans and Fisheries Affairs.

Negroponte was born July 21, 1939, in England. He received a B.A. from Yale University in 1960. He joined the Foreign Service in 1960, serving as consular officer in Hong Kong in 1960 and 1961, and commercial officer in Hong Kong from 1961 to 1963.

In 1963 he was an administrative assistant in the Bureau of African Affairs, and in 1963–64 he took Vietnamese language training at the Foreign Service Institute. From 1964 to 1968, he was political officer in Saigon. In 1968 and 1969, he was a member of the U.S. delegation to the Paris peace talks.

Negroponte was detailed to Stanford University in 1969–70, and in 1970 he served as political officer at the Arms Control and Disarmament Agency. From 1970 to 1973, he was a staff officer on the National Security Council, and in 1973 he took Spanish language training at the Foreign Service Institute.

From 1973 to 1975, Negroponte was political officer in Quito, and from 1975 to 1977 he was Consul General in Thessaloniki, Greece. Since 1977 he has been Deputy Assistant Secretary of State for Oceans and Fisheries Affairs.

Digest of Other White House Announcements

The following listing includes the President's daily schedule and other items of general interest as announced by the White House Press Office during the period covered by this issue. Events and announcements printed elsewhere in the issue are not included.

July 4

The President returned to the White House from Camp David, Md.

July 5

The President met at the White House with:
—Zbigniew Brzezinski, Assistant to the President for National Security Affairs;
—James R. Schlesinger, Assistant to the President;
—Bert Lance, Director of the Office of Management and Budget.

July 6

The President met at the White House with:
—Dr. Brzezinski;
—senior White House staff members;
—Charles L. Schultze, Chairman of the Council of Economic Advisers;
—Secretary of the Interior Cecil D. Andrus and top-level officials of the Department;
—Dr. Robert E. Boyer, Family Doctor of the Year, and Dr. B. Leslie Huffman, Jr., president of the American Academy of Family Practice;
—Vice President Walter F. Mondale;
—leaders of the American Jewish community;
—Vice President Mondale, Secretary of Defense Harold Brown, Gen. George S. Brown, Chairman of the Joint Chiefs of Staff, and Dr. Brzezinski.

July 7

The President met at the White House with:
—Dr. Brzezinski;
—a group of administration officials, to discuss proposals for reorganization of the Executive Office of the President;

—Albert Shanker, president, Robert Porter, secretary-treasurer, and members of the executive committee of the American Federation of Teachers, AFL–CIO;

—Vice President Mondale, Adm. Stansfield Turner, Director of Central Intelligence, and Dr. Brzezinski;

—Mrs. Carter, for lunch;

—Marshall Shulman, Special Consultant to the Secretary of State for Soviet Affairs;

—Leonard Woodcock, Chief of the United States Liaison Office, People's Republic of China, Vice President Mondale, Secretary of State Cyrus Vance, Richard Holbrooke, Assistant Secretary of State for East Asian and Pacific Affairs, and Dr. Brzezinski, for a discussion prior to Ambassador Woodcock's departure for Peking.

July 8

The President met at the White House with:

—Vice President Mondale, Secretary Vance, and Dr. Brzezinski;

—Dr. Brzezinski;

—Secretary of the Treasury W. Michael Blumenthal, Mr. Lance, Dr. Schultze, Stuart E. Eizenstat, Assistant to the President for Domestic Affairs and Policy, Jack H. Watson, Jr., Assistant to the President for Intergovernmental Affairs, to discuss budgetary and economic projections for the period 1979–81;

—members of the Commission on Civil Rights, to discuss the Commission's recent report;

—Secretary of Labor Ray Marshall;

—Western and Plains States Governors who were meeting with Secretary of Agriculture Bob S. Bergland to discuss agricultural policy.

The President met with Soviet Ambassador A. F. Dobrynin, Academician V. A. Kirillin, Deputy Chairman of the Council of Ministers of the U.S.S.R., and Dr. Frank Press, Science Adviser to the President. Earlier in the day, in a ceremony at the Department of State, Academician Kirillin and Dr. Press had signed the renewal for another 5 years of the U.S.-Soviet Agreement on Cooperation in the Fields of Science and Technology of May 24, 1972.

CHECKLIST OF WHITE HOUSE PRESS RELEASES

The following releases of the Office of the White House Press Secretary, distributed during the period covered by this issue, are not included in the issue.

Released July 6, 1977

Announcement: nomination of Harold L. Murphy to be United States District Judge for the Northern District of Georgia

Released July 8, 1977

Announcement: nomination of Donald L. Beckner to be United States Attorney for the Middle District of Louisiana; Jose A. Canales to be United States Attorney for the Southern District of Texas; John H. Hannah, Jr., to be United States Attorney for the Eastern District of Texas; J. Albert Jones to be United States Attorney for the Western District of Kentucky; Theddis R. Coney to be United States Marshal for the Southern District of Texas; and Bennie A. Martinez to be United States Marshal for the District of New Mexico

NOMINATIONS SUBMITTED TO THE SENATE

The following list does not include promotions of members of the Uniformed Services, nominations to the Service Academies, or nominations of Foreign Service officers.

Submitted July 7, 1977

JOHN H. SHENEFIELD, of Virginia, to be an Assistant Attorney General, vice Donald I. Baker, resigned.

HAROLD L. MURPHY, of Georgia, to be United States District Judge for the Northern District of Georgia, vice James C. Hill, elevated.

NOMINATIONS SUBMITTED TO THE SENATE

Submitted July 8, 1977

DAVID B. BOLEN, of Colorado, a Foreign Service officer of Class one, to be Ambassador Extraordinary and Plenipotentiary of the United States of America to the German Democratic Republic.

RAYMOND L. GARTHOFF, of Connecticut, a Foreign Service officer of Class one, to be Ambassador Extraordinary and Plenipotentiary of the United States of America to Bulgaria.

MAURICIO SOLAUN, of Illinois, to be Ambassador Extraordinary and Plenipotentiary of the United States of America to Nicaragua.

JOHN RICHARD BURKE, of Wisconsin, a Foreign Service officer of Class one, to be Ambassador Extraordinary and Plenipotentiary of the United States of America to the Cooperative Republic of Guyana.

JOHN D. NEGROPONTE, of New York, Deputy Assistant Secretary of State for Oceans and Fisheries Affairs, for the rank of Ambassador.

ELIZABETH E. BAILEY, of New Jersey, to be a member of the Civil Aeronautics Board for the remainder of the term expiring December 31, 1977, vice John E. Robson, resigned.

NOMINATIONS SUBMITTED TO THE SENATE—Continued

Submitted July 8, 1977—Continued

ELIZABETH E. BAILEY, of New Jersey, to be a member of the Civil Aeronautics Board for the term of 6 years expiring December 31, 1983 (reappointment).

BARRY P. BOSWORTH, of Maryland, to be Director of the Council on Wage and Price Stability, vice Michael H. Moskow, resigned.

ACTS APPROVED BY THE PRESIDENT

Approved July 5, 1977

H.R. 3695_____Public Law 95–62
State Veterans' Home Assistance Improvement Act of 1977.

H.R. 3849_____Public Law 95–63
National Advisory Committee on Oceans and Atmosphere Act of 1977.

Approved July 6, 1977

H.R. 1437_____ Private Law 95–3
An act for the relief of Soo Jin Lee.

H.R. 3838_____ Private Law 95–4
An act for the relief of Tulsedei Zalim.

H.R. 4246_____ Private Law 95–5
An act for the relief of Hee Kyung Yoo.

Energy Conference With the Governors

Remarks of the President and Gov. Reubin Askew of Florida at a News Briefing Following the Conference. July 9, 1977

THE PRESIDENT. Good morning, everybody. I didn't know this many people worked on Saturday. [*Laughter*]

We've just completed a very important and helpful conference with, I think, 44 of the 50 Governors on the subject of energy, the interrelationship between the Federal and State governments, and the major responsibilities that fall on the shoulders of Governors. We got good advice, Dr. Schlesinger and I and other Cabinet officers, and the Vice President.

I'd like to introduce to you now for brief comments Governor Reubin Askew, who is chairman of the National Governors' Conference, and then I will respond briefly. And then he and Julian Carroll, who is the chairman of the Energy and Natural Resources Committee in the Governors' Conference, and Dr. Schlesinger will be available to answer your questions.

Governor Askew.

GOVERNOR ASKEW. Thank you, Mr. President.

On behalf of the Governors represented here today, I'd like to express our appreciation to you and to the Vice President, Dr. Schlesinger, Jack Watson, and the members of the Cabinet who participated in these meetings over the past day and a half.

There are three points, I think, that have been reflected in all of the discussions and the panel reports of this conference. First, there is a shared desire on the part of the States and the Federal Government to come to grips with the energy challenge. Secondly, the only way we are going to do the job effectively, whether in transportation, conservation, coal utilization, or other vital areas, is through cooperation between the Federal and the State Government. Third, the discussions have shown that there are many critical problems that affect individual States and regions more than others.

And that is why it is so important to have a Federal program that is responsive to State needs and concerns, and we feel this meeting marks such a good beginning. In fact, I believe that our meeting this weekend, particularly the meeting with the President this morning in which we spent close to 3 hours, is unparalleled and unprecedented, at least in my memory, where a President has given this much time on a single subject, as important as it is to the Governors.

We had an excellent exchange last night with Dr. Kissinger—[*laughter*]—excuse me, Dr. Schlesinger—welcome to Washington—and with the members of the Cabinet in what I thought was a very good give-and-take, and then this morning again discussing some vital areas. So, I think it's really been a very constructive and useful discussion.

I might add I was asked by one of the members of the press early on whether or not this was an attempt to use us to help lobby the President's program. That would be totally incorrect because there's been no attempt at any point on this. By and large it's been a very good exchange, not only in the areas that were structured by the staffs of the White House and the National Governors' Conference, but every Governor was given the latitude they would have otherwise asserted anyway to ask any questions on anything concerning energy.

And I truly believe that it marks a beginning, or I should say not the beginning, because we started at our last conference here, but a real dialog between the Federal Government that will be setting a lot of policies, and the States by and large will have to implement them. And I think it's been a very healthy situation.

I certainly am looking forward to some of the remaining discussions we will be having today on the question of welfare. Some of us will be meeting with Secretary Califano, some will be meeting with Secretary of Transportation Brock Adams, some of us met yesterday afternoon with Secretary Marshall. So, frankly, it's been a very constructive and productive day and a half for us.

And we thank you, Mr. President, not only for the continuing partnership that you truly have set up. It's really sort of a new thing, I guess, for Governors to find Cabinet members as easy to reach and to be as responsive as they have, and then also, the constant personal attention that the President has given them. So, we certainly thank you, Mr. President.

THE PRESIDENT. Thank you, Reubin. I'd like to respond briefly.

During the first 3 months that I was President we spent a great deal of time in evolving for the first time in our Nation's history a comprehensive approach to energy planning and policy, presented that proposal to the Congress. And we've been very pleased—the Vice President, Dr. Schlesinger, I, and others—at the good progress that's been made in Congress to date.

If we should not get 100 percent of our program this year, we'll be back next year. And I don't think there is any doubt that the Nation faces devastating consequences in the absence of a comprehensive and fair and understandable energy policy.

The implementation of such a policy—oil and natural gas exploration, production of those fuels plus coal, the proper use of atomic power, the increasing use of solar energy and other more exotic types of fuels, the reduction in environmental damage as new exploration is undertaken—these kinds of responsibilities fall to a major degree on the shoulders of Governors and also officials at the local level of government.

My own inclination, when a decision must be reached, would be to give those responsibilities to State and local officials. One of the obvious needs is to prepare for emergencies that might be very damaging to our country if not adequately anticipated.

We would have varying stages of this, from a total rationing plan to an allocation of fuel on the part of the Governors themselves, as was the case in the winter of 1973. But how to change from one responsibility to another between the Federal, State, and local levels of government and still maintain an efficient operation of the free enterprise system is something that we can't decide unilaterally here in Washington.

I think it's accurate to say that the Governors have been very frank in giving us their own advice, describing their experiences, and also have been very severe in their criticisms of aspects of the program with which they do disagree, and we've all learned in the process.

I and the Vice President have participated fully. Dr. Schlesinger, who will head up a new Department of Energy shortly, has been there throughout all the sessions, plus the Secretaries of Commerce, Labor, Interior, Transportation. And we've all learned in the process.

And I am deeply indebted to Governor Carroll and Governor Askew for having made it possible for this meeting to take place.

I might point out that there was decided this morning between Julian Carroll and Jim Schlesinger to have another meeting later on almost exclusively on the subject of enhanced production of energy, and this will also be of great benefit to us.

I think the country is well served when the different levels of government can cooperate and legitimately share responsibilities under our system of federalism.

Reubin, I thank you again for your support and for your helping to organize this meeting. And, Julian, you've brought together six study groups that have analyzed important facets of the energy program.

Now I'll turn the microphone over to you, Reubin. And I am sure the press will have some questions to propose to you, to Julian Carroll, and to Dr. Schlesinger.

Thank you very much.

NOTE: The President spoke at 12:25 p.m. in the Briefing Room at the White House. Fol-

lowing his remarks, Governor Askew, Gov. Julian Carroll of Kentucky, and Assistant to the President James R. Schlesinger held a news briefing for reporters on the conference.

United States Space Observance

Proclamation 4512.   July 11, 1977

By the President of the United States of America

A Proclamation

Our human race has always felt an urge to explore and understand the world around us. This drive lay behind the theories of Ptolemy and Copernicus, the discoveries of Aristotle and Newton, the journeys of Columbus and Magellan.

In our time, this spirit has led to the exploration of space. From single missions, designed to send satellites into orbit and land men on the Moon, the United States space program has grown into a much broader range of endeavors. Its purpose is not simply to study space, but to understand its relevance to life on earth. Satellites now orbiting the earth have helped us to forecast weather patterns accurately, discover mineral deposits, detect sources of pollution and establish a global communications network. International projects such as Apollo-Soyuz have helped bring the people of the world closer together through coordinated research and the cooperative use of land and sea resources.

To encourage the American people to reflect upon the purposes, goals and achievements of America's space program, the Senate (July 11, 1975) and the House of Representatives (September 30, 1976) have requested the President to issue a proclamation designating the period of July 16 through July 24 as "United States Space Observance" and calling for its appropriate observance (S. Con. Res. 47).

Now, THEREFORE, I, JIMMY CARTER, President of the United States of America, do hereby proclaim the period of July 16 through July 24, 1977, as United States Space Observance.

I urge the communications media, educators, the aerospace industry, scientific and public-service organizations and the American people to join with the Administrator of the National Aeronautics and Space Administration during this period in commemorating the achievements of the United States space program which demonstrate that advanced technology devoted to peaceful purposes can lead the way to a better life for people of all nations.

IN WITNESS WHEREOF, I have hereunto set my hand this eleventh day of July, in the year of our Lord nineteen hundred seventy-seven, and of the Independence of the United States of America the two hundred and second.

JIMMY CARTER

[Filed with the Office of the Federal Register, 4:07 p.m., July 11, 1977]

Commodity Credit Corporation

Nomination of Ray V. Fitzgerald To Be a Member of the Board of Directors. July 11, 1977

The President today announced that he will nominate Ray V. Fitzgerald, of Plankinton, S. Dak., to be a member of the Board of Directors of the Commodity Credit Corporation. He would replace Kenneth E. Frick. Fitzgerald was named Administrator-designate of the Agricultural Stabilization and Conservation Service (ASCS) by Secretary Bergland on May 4, 1977.

Fitzgerald was born May 19, 1923, in Plankinton, S. Dak., and received a degree in business from Xavier University in Cincinnati. He was secretary of agriculture for South Dakota in 1959 and 1960. He was Assistant Deputy Administrator of ASCS in 1961 and 1962 and Deputy Administrator for State and County Operations from 1962 to 1969.

From 1969 to 1971, Fitzgerald was a consultant to the U.S. Senate Select Committee on Nutrition and Human Needs. He was chief of the Agricultural Cooperative Development International (ACDI) technical team advising cooperatives, farmer associations, and the Agriculture Directorate in Vietnam from 1971 to 1974. He was president of ACDI from 1975 until he assumed his present position.

Presidential Medal of Freedom

Remarks on Presenting the Medal to Dr. Jonas E. Salk and to Martin Luther King, Jr. July 11, 1977

THE PRESIDENT. As you may know, the Medal of Freedom is the highest civilian award that's given in our country. It was begun when President Truman was in the White House, and the number of people who receive it is very small.

There are many Americans who do great things, who make us proud of them and their achievements, and who inspire us to do better ourselves. But there are some among those noble achievers who are exemplary in every way, who reach a higher plateau of achievement, and whose recognition almost demands being consummated by someone in my own position.

Today I have chosen to honor two great men, one who has alleviated suffering and despair in the field of health and one who has chosen to alleviate suffering and despair in the field of human freedom.

I'm very grateful today to have this opportunity on behalf of more than 200 million Americans to recognize these noble recipients of the award, one in life, one in death, but we know that they both live now and a thousand years from now, perhaps, will still live in the minds and hearts of Americans.

I'd like to first call Dr. Jonas Salk forward to present an award to him and to read a citation.

[*At this point, the President read the citation, the text of which follows:*]

THE PRESIDENT OF THE UNITED STATES OF AMERICA AWARDS THIS PRESIDENTIAL MEDAL OF FREEDOM TO DR. JONAS E. SALK

Because of Dr. Jonas E. Salk, our country is free from the cruel epidemics of poliomyelitis that once struck almost yearly. Because of his tireless work, untold hundreds of thousands who might have been crippled are sound in body today. These are Doctor Salk's true honors, and there is no way to add to them. This Medal of Freedom can only express our gratitude, and our deepest thanks.

I'd like to give this to Mrs. Salk to deliver to her husband later. Thank you.

DR. SALK. Mr. President, you have drawn special attention to me for the successful control of poliomyelitis. Our freedom from fear of this disease is the result of years of work by a great many who preceded me and who followed. This freedom was achieved to the mutual participation of the public as well as the scientific and medical communities.

I am deeply moved to receive the Presidential Medal of Freedom along with Martin Luther King, Jr., whose life and work contributed so richly to the ultimate freedoms we seek—freedom from human exploitation and oppression. Our Founding Fathers spoke about the right

to life, liberty, and the pursuit of happiness, but without freedom from oppression and from disease, the pursuit of happiness has little meaning.

I hope that all the world will see your own aspirations and commitments to life and to liberty, the world over, in the meaningful recognition that you have given to the importance of human rights and human health.

The achievements to which you have drawn attention serve as examples of more that might be accomplished through national and international commitments to improve the health and well-being of people everywhere.

Laurels are not to be rested upon. They crown what is valued and desired by society. They impose responsibility as well as offer encouragement.

In this spirit, I am pleased to accept the honor you bestow upon me and, in so doing, upon all those who work in the same vineyard toward improving the health and well-being of humankind. And I thank you, Mr. President.

THE PRESIDENT. When I was a child in Georgia, I, along with all other people, perhaps, in the world my age, were constantly fearful of the blight of a polio epidemic. In our own country alone in the years shortly before the Salk vaccine was developed, there were 52,000 people who were stricken with polio. And miraculously, because of the intelligence and commitment of Dr. Salk, this scourge was removed. And as he very generously described to us, many people before this achievement and since then have contributed as well to this alleviation of a constant threat.

When I was a child in Georgia, there was another threat as well which was even more all-encompassing and which afflicted us as did a physical disease, and that was racial discrimination, a deprivation of human freedom and a prohibition against the realization of the American dream for black people.

With unswerving dedication, superb courage, sensitivity, and humility and a dedication to peace, Dr. Martin Luther King, Jr., helped to remove this threat and this affliction. Although I never knew him personally, I've come to know the members of his family, and many thousands of people around the world now carry on his own deep commitments to which he gave his very life.

I'd like to ask Coretta King and Dr. Martin Luther King, Sr., to come and stand beside me as I read this citation.

[*At this point, the President read the citation, the text of which follows:*]

THE PRESIDENT OF THE UNITED STATES OF AMERICA AWARDS THIS PRESIDENTIAL MEDAL OF FREEDOM TO MARTIN LUTHER KING, JR.

Martin Luther King, Jr., was the conscience of his generation. He gazed upon the great wall of segregation and saw that the power of love could bring it down. From the pain and exhaustion of his fight to fulfill the promises of our founding fathers for our humblest citizens, he wrung his eloquent statement of his dream for America. He made our nation stronger because he made it better. His dream sustains us yet.

Signed, Jimmy Carter.

MRS. KING. *Thank you, Mr. President, Mr. Vice President, to our many friends who have gathered here today:*

This is indeed a very moving moment for me and, needless to say, a very fulfilling one for me and my family and our friends who have come here today to share this occasion with us.

It is highly significant that you, Mr. President, a white Southerner, would become the first American President to recognize the importance of Martin Luther King, Jr.'s contributions to the human rights movement in this country and bestow upon him the highest civilian award—the Presidential Medal of Freedom. For us as a family and the millions in our Nation who believed in Martin Luther King, Jr.'s teaching, we are greatly encouraged and feel this action is indicative of the new spirit of reconciliation which you and your administration are causing in this Nation.

Thank you, Mr. President, for renewing our hopes that our Nation can rise to true greatness and give due honor to one of its greatest national heroes.

This medal will be displayed with Martin's Nobel Peace Prize in the completed Martin Luther King, Jr., Center for Social Change, his official memorial in Atlanta, Georgia. It will serve as a continuous reminder and inspiration to young people and unborn generations that his dream of freedom, justice, and equality must be nurtured, protected, and fully realized, that they must be the keepers of the dream.

Let us all once again rededicate our lives to the fulfillment of Martin Luther King's dream, which was truly the American dream.

Thank you, Mr. President.

NOTE: The President spoke at 1:37 p.m. at the ceremony in Room 450 at the Old Executive Office Building.

United Nations Conference on Science and Technology for Development

Nomination of Jean M. Wilkowski for the Rank of Ambassador. July 12, 1977

The President today announced that he will nominate Jean M. Wilkowski for the rank of Ambassador while serving as coordinator of United States preparations for the United Nations Conference on Science and Technology for Development.

Wilkowski was born August 28, 1919, in Rhinelander, Wis. She received a B.A. from St. Mary of the Woods College in 1941 and an M.A. from the University of Wisconsin in 1944.

She was an instructor and publicity director at Barry College in Miami, Fla., from 1941 to 1943 and an agricultural reporter at Wisconsin College of Agriculture in 1944. She joined the Foreign Service in 1945 and served as consular and economic officer in Port of Spain in 1945 and 1946.

Wilkowski was economic and commercial officer in Bogotá in 1947 and 1948 and in Milan from 1949 to 1951. From 1951 to 1953, she was an economist on the Italian desk at the State Department and was detailed to the Office of International Trade at the Department of Commerce.

From 1953 to 1956, she was commercial intelligence officer in Paris. In 1956–57 she studied economics at the University of California at Berkeley, and from 1957 to 1959 she was financial officer in Santiago.

From 1960 to 1962, Wilkowski worked on the GATT negotiations, including preparatory work at the State Department and the conference in Geneva. In 1962–63 she attended the Senior Seminar in Foreign Policy at the Foreign Service Institute.

Wilkowski was assistant chief of the economic section in Rome from 1963 to 1966 and deputy chief of mission in Tegucigalpa, Honduras, from 1966 to 1970. In 1970 and 1971, she was counselor for commercial affairs in Rome, and in 1971 she was chief of the U.S. delegation to the Inter-American Commission of Wom-

en, Organization of American States, in Bogotá.

In 1971 and 1972, Wilkowski was minister-counselor for economic and commercial affairs in Rome. From 1972 to 1976, she was Ambassador to the Republic of Zambia. She was diplomat in residence at Occidental College in 1976-77 and in 1977 became coordinator of U.S. preparations for the United Nations Conference on Science and Technology for Development.

THE PRESIDENT'S NEWS CONFERENCE OF JULY 12, 1977

THE PRESIDENT. Good afternoon, everybody. Do you have any questions? [*Laughter*]

Ms. Thomas [Helen Thomas, United Press International].

ARMS AND WEAPONS

Q. Mr. President, how do you reconcile your decision to go ahead with the neutron bomb with your inaugural pledge to eliminate all nuclear weapons? Also, why didn't you know the money was in the bill? And three, doesn't this escalate the arms race? And I have a followup. [*Laughter*]

THE PRESIDENT. Well, it's a very serious question. In the first place, I did not know what was in the bill. The enhanced radiation of the neutron bomb has been discussed and also has been under development for 15 or 20 years. It's not a new concept at all, not a new weapon.

It does not affect our SALT or strategic weapons negotiations at all. It's strictly designed as a tactical weapon. I think that this would give us some flexibility.

I have not yet decided whether to advocate deployment of the neutron bomb. I think the essence of it is that for a given projectile size or for a given missile head size, that the destruction that would result from the explosion of a neutron bomb is much less than the destruction from an equivalent weapon of other types.

The essence of the question is that if the neutron weapon or atomic weapon ever should have to be used against enemy forces in occupied territory of our allies or ourselves, the destruction would be much less.

Before I make a final decision on the neutron bomb's deployment, I would do a complete impact statement analysis on it, submit this information to the Congress. But I have not yet decided whether to approve the neutron bomb. I do think it ought to be one of our options, however.

Q. Mr. President, if you decided to go ahead, would you renounce the first use of the bomb? For example, you would not use it unless there was an oppressive enemy action?

THE PRESIDENT. This is something that I have not yet decided. Of course, we hope that we can reach an agreement among all nations in the future to forgo the use of all atomic weapons and also to eliminate the possession of all nuclear weapons.

There are two distinct classes of weapons. One is the tactical weapons which have not been under the purview of discussions with the Soviets or others. The other one is the strategic nuclear weapons.

But the definition of under what circumstances we would use such atomic weapons has not yet been spelled out publicly. I obviously hope that our continuing inclination toward peace, shared, I'm sure, by the Soviets and others, will prevent any use of atomic weapons. They are there as a deterrent, however, and the option for their use has to be maintained as one of the viable options.

MINIMUM WAGE

Q. Mr. President, just today, I believe, you are reported on the brink of approving a compromise minimum wage proposal of $2.60 an hour. Now, if that's true, did you raise your sights because of political factors, economic factors, or a combination?

THE PRESIDENT. Well, the fact of the matter is that the minimum wage proposals are being handled by the congressional committees—Congressman Dent, Congressman Perkins. This afternoon, I think at 4 or 5 o'clock, Congressman Perkins will have a press conference to spell out the committee proposal.

We have no administration legislation to propose, and I do not intend to send the Congress any message on the minimum wage. I might say in advance that we have come to agree with the proposal that Congressman Perkins will propose, but it is not an administration bill.

ATOMIC WEAPONS

Q. Mr. President, may I go back to the neutron bomb?

THE PRESIDENT. Please.

Q. How much do you think there is to the argument that if you have a cleaner weapon, as you define it, it makes war more possible; that it might be used? And secondly, where do you stand on that age-old question of nuclear weapons in Europe, for instance, as to whether if you start using them it wouldn't automatically escalate to a full-scale nuclear war?

THE PRESIDENT. I think one of the concepts that must be avoided is an exact description ahead of time of what I as President would do under every conceivable circumstance.

The ownership of atomic weapons and their potential use is such a horrifying prospect—their use—that it is a deterrent to a major confrontation between nations who possess atomic weapons.

I believe that the nation that uses atomic weapons first would be under heavy condemnation from the other people of the world, unless the circumstances were extremely gross, such as an unwarranted invasion into another country.

But I'm eager to work with the Soviet Union, with China, with France, with England, on a continuing basis, so that there will never be a need for the use of those weapons.

To answer the other part of your question, my guess is—and no one would certainly know—that the first use of atomic weapons might very well quickly lead to a rapid and uncontrolled escalation in the use of even more powerful weapons with possibly a worldwide holocaust resulting.

This is a prospect that is sobering to us all, and that's why the Soviets and we and others have worked so hard to try to reach an agreement in the prohibition against atomic use.

Q. Sir, could I just follow it up with one question? Doesn't that give you a terrible paradox? Because if we are inferior on the ground in Europe with the Soviet and Warsaw Pact forces, if we don't use atomic weapons, can we and our NATO alliance stop a ground invasion?

THE PRESIDENT. My guess is and my belief is that without the use of atomic weapons, we have adequate force strength in NATO to stop an invasion from the Warsaw Pact forces.

There is some advantage in the commitment and effectiveness of the forces of a defending nation if they are fighting on their own invaded territory. And I think this would mean that in a rough balance

that the invading nations would have to have an overwhelming superior force.

We are now putting, as a much greater priority in our budget request for defense expenditures, moneys for improving our conventional forces in Europe. In years gone by, 15 or 20 years ago, we had an overwhelming superiority in nuclear weapons. Now I would say we have a roughly equivalent strength in atomic weapons. And so, we must ensure that within the bounds of measurement that our conventional forces are equivalent also. And I don't acknowledge at all the fact that an invasion of the Warsaw Pact nations would be successful without the use of atomic weapons.

FOREIGN EAVESDROPPING ON TELEPHONE CONVERSATIONS

Q. Mr. President, Senator Moynihan of New York says that the Government, both the Ford administration and yours, has avoided telling American citizens that they are the subject of massive eavesdropping on the part of the Soviet Union. If the Senator is correct, why has the Government not alerted American citizens to the situation?

Second, do you plan to demand that the Soviets withdraw their rooftop electronic equipment? And third, if they do not, will there be diplomatic reprisals?

THE PRESIDENT. Senator Moynihan, as you know, has been a member of the Nixon administration in the past in a very high official position, and he is well able to judge the knowledge that was possessed by that administration.

I think it's accurate to say that any detailed discussion of the electronics capabilities of different nations' intelligence forces is not a proper subject for complete discussion.

Within the last number of years, because of the radio transmission of telephone conversations, the intercept on a passive basis of these kinds of transmissions has become a common ability for nations to pursue. It's not an act of aggression or war; it's completely passive.

I don't know the full circumstances involved. When I became President, I asked to have a multidepartmental assessment of the threat to our own security. We have been embarked since I've been in office—and I think before—in an effort to make impervious to intercept those telephone lines that were involved directly in national security.

For instance, the lines going into and out of the Defense Department and my own office—we try to make sure that they are cables; they are buried underground; they are not subject to this electronics type of being overheard.

Some of the major commercial companies in our Nation who want to prevent any eavesdropping on their transactions, commercial transactions, not involving national security, also make an attempt to prevent intercepts by those who listen in on the free air waves.

But I would not interpret this use by the Soviet Union or by other embassies to be an act of aggression. And although it may be an intrusion into our security, I think we are taking adequate steps now to prevent its creating a threat to our country.

STOCK MARKET INVESTMENTS

Q. Mr. President?

THE PRESIDENT. Mr. Sperling [Godfrey Sperling, Jr., Christian Science Monitor].

Q. You obviously are doing well in the popularity polls, but how do you explain the uncertainty that investors in the stock market seem to have in you?

THE PRESIDENT. That was a very difficult thing for me to understand during the campaign. I thought that they should have given me their overwhelming support. [*Laughter*] The leading investors on Wall Street and others only gave me a 5-percent support compared to my opponent, President Ford.

I think that there's a general uncertainty in the world about future economic circumstances. We also, of course, are involved in a reassessment of some very controversial issues concerning energy, tax reform, welfare reform, that causes some governmental contribution to the uncertainty. We have an increasing dependence in the consuming nations on oil imports, which means that the OPEC nations have about a $40 billion trade surplus and the rest of the world has to absorb a $40 billion deficit.

So, I think there are many areas of uncertainty. I've been impressed with the long-range trend projections that have been given to me. We've had about a 1-percent reduction already in the unemployment rate since I became President, and the results last month on inflation were encouraging. But monthly figures fluctuate fairly widely. Since last November, we've had about a 3 million net increase in the number of jobs available in our country.

I feel very good about our economy. And I can't assess that feeling of mine as compared to investors in the stock market prices. But I think since the first of the year, the stock market prices, although they've fluctuated somewhat, have been relatively stable.

NATURAL GAS

Q. Mr. President, yesterday a congressional Republican group released a study showing that your natural gas plan, pricing plan, would cost American consumers about $48 billion more than deregulation of natural gas would by 1990. They mainly said that Americans would not be able to get as much gas under your plan and, therefore, would have to resort to other types of more expensive fuel. Could you respond to that?

THE PRESIDENT. Yes. I haven't heard of that report, but I can tell you that the Congressional Budget Office and the Library of Congress, independently of Dr. Schlesinger in his assessments, have confirmed our own figures. In fact, both those reports anticipate that deregulation of natural gas would be much more expensive than even the figures that we have put forward.

My estimate is that our own proposal, which I think gives an adequate incentive for production and exploration of new natural gas, would amount to about a $15 billion increase in income for the oil companies, natural gas producers, by 1985.

The Congressional Budget Office estimates that this would be, under deregulation, about $85 billion, which is $70 billion more with complete natural gas deregulation for new gas than what we proposed. The Library of Congress figures go up to about $150 billion. This means that the consumers of this country would have to pay to the oil and natural gas companies an enormous extra amount for a very slight increase in natural gas production, if it was completely deregulated.

I'm not in favor of complete deregulation. We estimate that if natural gas was completely deregulated, that the increased production would be about 1.1 trillion cubic feet of natural gas at an increased cost of more than $70 billion. This means that for every additional thousand cubic feet discovered, it would cost the American consumers about $60.

So, I think that our proposal is reasonable. I think that deregulation as proposed by some Members of the Congress would be a gross overburden on the American people and would not result in a substantial increase in production.

RELATIONS WITH THE SOVIET UNION

Q. Mr. President, what do you make of all the unfriendly rhetoric coming out of Moscow lately? And do your sources suggest that it may not just be because of your human rights campaign?

THE PRESIDENT. I don't know how to explain the unfriendly rhetoric. Our proposals have been fair and reasonable, and almost all of them have been made public. We have pursued our hopes for increased friendship with the Soviet Union, a reduction in nuclear weaponry, an easing of the tensions between ourselves and the Soviets through quiet diplomatic channels, with myself talking to the Soviet Ambassador, with Cy Vance, the Secretary of State, going to Moscow, and in continuing negotiations at Geneva and other places by Paul Warnke and other representatives of me. I believe that the Soviets, perhaps, have some political reasons for spelling out or exaggerating the disagreements. I don't know what those reasons are.

Our positions have been carefully contrived and constantly reassessed. I have no inclination to change the positions that we have taken; I think they are fair. And I believe that calm and persistent and fair negotiations with the Soviet Union will ultimately lead to increased relationships with them.

And the public statements that the Soviets make, attacking me personally or our own Nation's good faith, are both erroneous and ill-advised. But what their reasons for it might be, I do not know.

THE MIDDLE EAST

Q. Mr. President, with Mr. Begin coming to visit, I'd like to ask a question about the Middle East, a two-part question.

When you talk about the necessity for a Palestinian homeland, are you thinking of locating that homeland in territory that at one time was Palestine, or in your mind, could it be located anywhere?

The second part of the question is: Do you still believe, as you said a few weeks ago, that Israel eventually must withdraw with only minor changes to the pre-1967 borders?

THE PRESIDENT. I have not changed my opinion since the earlier statements that I made concerning the general outline of terms to be sought at a possible Geneva conference.

We have never tried to define geographical boundaries for a so-called Palestinian entity. My own preference, which I have expressed since I've been President and also as a candidate, was that the Palestinian entity, whatever form it might take and whatever area it might occupy, should be tied in with Jordan and not be independent. But I don't have the authority nor the inclination to try to impose that preference on the parties that will negotiate.

I think that in his coming over here to our country next week, on the 19th, that Prime Minister Begin is trying to bring with him an open mind and an ability to go to a possible peace conference with all items being negotiable. He said this publicly, and he's also sent me private messages to that effect.

I've seen an inclination in the Middle East in recent days toward an alleviation of tension. I got a private message from President Sadat, for instance, that he is going to make every effort again to comply with the Sinai agreement.

He had a few extra troops in the territory that had been identified. He's withdrawing those. He authorized me to announce that he's returning with full military honors 19 Israeli bodies that had been left in Egypt. He's expressed his willingness to go to Geneva without prior commitments. He's had negotiations or talks lately with the King of Jordan, and they have agreed that the Palestinian entity ought to be tied in with Jordan.

So, there's a general inclination on all parties for success, but I don't think it's advisable now for me to get any more specific than I have in the past.

And although I haven't changed my position, I want to reemphasize that we are not going to go to the different nations involved and say, "This is an American plan. You've got to accept it as a pre-condition to going to Geneva. It's what we think would be fair." It's been deliberately general in nature, and the ultimate results would have to be agreed to by the Arab and Israeli nations.

Judy [Judy Woodruff, NBC News].

ABORTION

Q. Mr. President, how comfortable are you with the recent Supreme Court decision that says the Federal Government is not obligated to provide money for abortions for women who cannot afford to pay for them themselves?

THE PRESIDENT. I do not think that the Federal Government should finance abortions except when the woman's life is threatened or when the pregnancy was a result of rape or incest. I think it ought to be interpreted very strictly.

In my opinion, the Federal Government being willing to finance abortions, as it has been in recent months, is an encouragement to abortion and its acceptance as a routine contraceptive means. And I think within that strict definition that I've given you, I would like to prevent the Federal Government financing abortions.

I think it's accurate to say that Secretary of HEW Califano agrees with me completely. And we are trying to make it possible for the people of this Nation to understand how to prevent unwanted pregnancies with education programs and with the availability of contraceptives and other devices, when they believe in their use, as an alternative to abortion. But I don't believe that either States or the Federal Government should be required to finance abortions.

Q. Mr. President, how fair do you believe it is then, that women who can afford to get an abortion can go ahead and have one, and women who cannot afford to are precluded?

THE PRESIDENT. Well, as you know, there are many things in life that are not fair, that wealthy people can afford and poor people can't. But I don't believe that the Federal Government should take action to try to make these opportunities exactly equal, particularly when there is a moral factor involved.

I know as well as anyone in the country, having faced this issue during the long campaign, about the intense feelings on both sides of the abortion issue. But my own personal feeling is that the Supreme Court rulings now are adequate, and they are reasonably fair, and that the Federal Government should not be required or encouraged to finance abortions other than I've spelled out.

RELATIONS WITH CONGRESS

Q. Mr. President, with the passage of time, your working relationships with Members of Congress seem to be improving. What accounts for the truce?

THE PRESIDENT. Well, I don't know that it's a truce, exactly. I think the Congress now understands much more clearly what I am, what I stand for, what proposals we put forward, and the priorities accruing to those proposals. I think we've had good success with the Congress already.

The passage of the economic stimulus package that we proposed was done expeditiously and is working well already. The authorization for me to reorganize the Government is doing well. The authorization for the new Department of Energy will be completed, I think, within the next few days.

The Congress has made good progress on strict ethics legislation. I think we have made good progress, also, in the effectuation of the energy policy which is very controversial, very difficult, and requires a great deal of courage on the part of Congress.

They've still got some hard questions to answer. One, of course, is how to finance the social security system, and then we will be proposing to them in the future a comprehensive welfare plan and a comprehensive tax reform proposal.

But I think in general it's just been a matter of getting to know one another, and we've been very forceful in our positions. There are some things on which the Congress and I still disagree. I thought the Senate made an improper decision yesterday on the Clinch River breeder reactor. I think there are excessive amounts of allocation of funds for water projects. I'm concerned about the Senate level of prospective expenditure on the farm bill. So we do have some differences. But I think in general there's been a good and mature working relationship between us.

FBI DIRECTOR

Q. Mr. President, are you going to go outside the list of FBI Director nominees supplied by your selection commission to choose the man to replace Clarence Kelley? And if so, isn't that an indictment of the manner in which that search was conducted?

THE PRESIDENT. I don't know yet. When I announced the five names that had been recommended to me, I pointed out that we would interview those five. If one of them is patently the best person to hold the job of FBI Director, in the judgment of the Attorney General and approved by me, then we would go with those five. But we reserve the right to interview others in addition to the first five recommended. If we do so, then we would use the information derived by the search committee as the basis for our own assessment of those additional candidates. I've only met so far with two of the five. I think, this week, I'm scheduled to meet with two others, and I'll meet with the fifth one. And then the Attorney General and I will decide together whether or not to interview others. It's not an indictment of them. I think they did a good job. We deliberately made public the names of those whom they did recommend to get information and so forth from those who knew the candidates that we would not have gotten otherwise.

We did not do an FBI, full-field background check on any of those five candidates or any of the other 225 who were assessed until they were recommended to us. And so we are now accumulating information about the nominees and then having an interview with them. The Attorney General meets with them 2 or 3 hours, gives me a report on what he thinks; I meet with them 15 or 20 minutes to get acquainted.

And my expectation is that the Attorney General will make a recommendation to me, and I will go along with his recommendation. But I will reserve the final judgment.

RELATIONS WITH THE SOVIET UNION

Q. Mr. President, could I get back to relations with the Soviet Union?

THE PRESIDENT. Yes.

Q. Despite the hopes that you expressed for better relations, there are several things that suggest that, in fact, relations have grown worse between the United States and the Soviet Union since you took office. Do you think that's the case, and if so, where are we headed in this? Are we seeing an end to the period of détente?

THE PRESIDENT. No. I don't think so. I believe that it's inherent that tough and public debates will accrue when controversial issues are addressed. It would be very easy for me and the Congress to get along completely harmoniously if I never made a proposal and if I agreed with everything the Congress did and we didn't address any of the controversial issues like welfare reform, tax reform, reorganization, or energy policy.

The same thing applies to the Soviet Union. We have never before made an attempt with the Soviet Union drastically to reduce the level of atomic weaponry. In the past, we've put limits on increasing production of atomic weaponry. We've never tried with the Soviet Union to get a complete prohibition against all testing of atomic devices. Now we are trying to work with the Soviet Union to get this very controversial and very difficult goal realized.

We've never tried before to work with the Soviet Union to demilitarize the Indian Ocean or to restrict any further militarization of that area. This is a controversial matter. It affects other nations as well—India, Australia, New Zealand, Iran, Somalia, and so forth.

So, we are now trying to address some questions that in the past have been avoided or delayed.

The question of human rights is one that obviously has caused some tough debate and difference of opinion, expressed publicly and privately. We could have sat quiescently and never raised the issue of human rights. I believe that our raising of the issue was compatible with the hopes and dreams and inclinations and commitments of the American people. And there have been varying kinds of responses to this pursuit.

We do not initiate all these controversies. As you know, the basket three aspect of the Helsinki agreement would have raised the human rights question to some degree, absent any commitment on my part.

But I don't think that this is an indication of deteriorated relationships between us and the Soviets because we are finally addressing, in a forceful way, from different perspectives, some extremely controversial but important issues.

So although I would like for us to agree on everything, I think the period of debate, disagreement, probing, and negotiation was inevitable. And I have no apologies to offer, and I have no regrets about the issues that have been raised that have proven to be controversial.

FRANK CORMIER [Associated Press]. Thank you, Mr. President.

THE PRESIDENT. Thank you, Frank, very much. Thank you, everybody.

NOTE: President Carter's eleventh news conference began at 2:32 p.m. in Room 450 of the Old Executive Office Building. It was broadcast live on radio and television.

Railroad Retirement Board

Nomination of Earl Oliver To Be a Member. July 12, 1977

The President today announced that he will nominate Earl Oliver, of Chicago, Ill., to be a member of the Railroad Retirement Board. He would replace Wythe D. Quarles. Oliver retired from Illinois Central Gulf Railroad in 1975, and since then has performed staff work for the National Railway Labor Conference and the Railroad Labor-Management Committee.

He was born February 25, 1917, in Monticello, Ky. He received a B.A. from Oklahoma A&M College.

From 1941 to 1947, Oliver worked for the Chicago and Northwestern Railway as a secretary, chief clerk, safety inspector, assistant trainmaster, and trainmaster. He was with Illinois Central Gulf Railroad from 1948 to 1975, working in various labor relations positions, then as manager of personnel, director of personnel, vice president for personnel, and finally senior vice president for personnel and administration.

Department of the Interior

Nomination of Forrest J. Gerard To Be an Assistant Secretary. July 12, 1977

The President today announced that he will nominate Forrest J. Gerard, of Bowie, Md., to be Assistant Secretary of the Interior for Indian Affairs. He would replace Albert C. Zapanta. Gerard is a lobbyist in Washington whose clients include several Indian tribes and the Association of American Indian Affairs.

Gerard was born January 15, 1925, in Browning, Mont. He received a B.A. from

Montana State University in 1949. He served in the U.S. Air Force from 1943 to 1945.

From 1949 to 1953, Gerard was a Federal field auditor for the Montana State Department of Public Instruction. From 1953 to 1955, he was a field consultant for the Montana Tuberculosis Association, and from 1955 to 1957 he was executive secretary of the Wyoming Tuberculosis and Health Association.

Gerard was a tribal relations officer for the Indian Health Service from 1957 to 1965. In 1966 and 1967, he was legislative liaison officer in the Bureau of Indian Affairs in Washington. He was Director of the Office for Indian Progress at the Department of Health, Education, and Welfare from 1967 to 1971.

From 1971 to 1976, Gerard was a professional staff member on the Committee on Interior and Insular Affairs. Since 1976 he has been self-employed as a lobbyist.

Gerard has served as Executive Secretary of the Surgeon General's Advisory Committee on Indian Health and has been on the advisory committee of the Capitol Conference on Indian Poverty and the National Indian Health Committee of the Association on American Indian Affairs. He is a member of the National Congress of American Indians and serves on its Advisory Committee on Indian Health. Gerard received the Indian Achievement Award from the Indian Council Fire in Chicago in 1966.

Nuclear Regulatory Commission
Designation of Joseph M. Hendrie as Chairman.   July 12, 1977

The President today announced his intention to designate Joseph M. Hendrie,

of Bellport, N.Y., as Chairman of the Nuclear Regulatory Commission upon his confirmation by the Senate.

Mr. Hendrie was nominated on June 30, 1977, to be a member of the Nuclear Regulatory Commission for a term expiring June 30, 1981.

Hendrie is a member of the board of directors of the American Nuclear Society and serves on the Risk-Impact Panel, Committee on Nuclear and Alternative Energy Systems of the National Research Council. Since 1974 he has been the U.S. Representative on the International Atomic Energy Agency's Senior Advisory Group on Reactor Safety Codes and Guides. He was a member of the Advisory Committee on Reactor Safeguards of the U.S. Atomic Energy Commission from 1966 to 1972. He has had numerous articles published in professional journals.

Nuclear Regulatory Commission
Nomination of Peter A. Bradford To Be a Member.   July 12, 1977

The President today announced that he will nominate Peter A. Bradford, of Augusta, Maine, to be a member of the Nuclear Regulatory Commission. He would replace Marcus A. Rowden. Bradford is commissioner of the Maine Public Utilities Commission.

He was born July 21, 1942, in New York City. He received a B.A. from Yale University in 1964 and an LL.B. from Yale Law School in 1968.

From 1968 to 1971, Bradford was assistant to then-Governor Kenneth Curtis for energy and the environment, in Augusta, Maine. Since 1971 he has been commissioner of the Maine Public Utilities Commission.

Visit of Chancellor Helmut Schmidt of the Federal Republic of Germany

Remarks of the President and the Chancellor at the Welcoming Ceremony. July 13, 1977

THE PRESIDENT. This morning we have the great honor and pleasure, in the United States, of welcoming to our country a great friend and one of the world's foremost leaders, Chancellor Helmut Schmidt, his wife, accompanied by Foreign Minister Genscher and distinguished leaders from industrial and labor and the cultural component parts of the society of the Federal Republic of Germany. We are very grateful that they've honored us by coming.

This friendship that exists between the United States and the Federal Republic has existed from the very day the Federal Republic was formed.

I've come to know Helmut Schmidt first of all at a distance, as a candidate and a new President, because of the admiration expressed by other leaders who've known him and worked with him over the years. Following my Inauguration, I had a chance to talk with him several times by phone and exchange diplomatic messages. And I've always welcomed his advice and his counsel and his friendship.

In London, recently, at the summit meeting with himself and me and five other leaders, we had a chance to exchange ideas and concepts and hopes and plans and aspirations for the future that vividly demonstrated to all of us that the ties that have been so strong between us and the people of Germany are still as strong as ever, and that our future is tied closely together.

I have a great admiration for him. The international questions determine our own attitudes toward other countries, and there are no differences between us. We have frank discussions, as is the nature of Helmut Schmidt. He's an accomplished economist, a very fine political leader, and an experienced and enlightened statesman.

The great progress that has been made in the Federal Republic of Germany has made it possible for him to demonstrate in many ways the restrained and enlightened and very effective leadership that is inherent in his own character and capabilities.

We're very proud that we share with the Federal Republic of Germany a complete commitment to democratic processes, a complete commitment for a hope of world peace, the alleviation of tensions, and the enhancement of the quality of life of those whose people are not so fortunate as those who live in our two countries.

We recognize that progress is only possible with joint efforts and that the private and public support between allies is always a crucial element of continued strength and beneficent influence.

And so this morning, my good friend, Helmut Schmidt, on behalf of more than 200 million Americans, we welcome you to our country with open arms and deep appreciation for what you and your leadership have meant to us and will mean to us and the world in the months ahead.

Thank you very much for coming. You are welcome, friend.

THE CHANCELLOR. *Mr. President, Mrs. Carter, ladies and gentlemen:*

Thank you, Mr. President, very much for this cordial reception and the friendly words of welcome which you have extended to me and the members of my party.

I have been visiting the White House several times in different capacities, but

1241

this is my first visit to the 39th President of the United States of America.

I've been looking forward to this meeting very much, because with it we are deepening an acquaintance and a mutual understanding which we were able to renew and to develop, as you mentioned, sir, in London. We shall be continuing discussions which got off to a favorable and constructive start at the summit conference.

Speaking from this spot about a year ago, I was able to pay tribute to the proud history of your great nation and to recall its achievements in the span of two centuries. Today my thoughts turn to that which lies ahead of us.

Let us together tackle our common problems with determination and with mutual understanding. Our two nations and two countries are joined in very strong bonds of friendship. And I would like to underline what you just said, Mr. President: This friendship has steadily been developed since the Federal Republic of Germany was constituted three decades ago, and it has never been closer than today.

As partners in the North Atlantic Alliance and among the industrialized nations, both our countries have a responsibility to carry in a world of growing interdependence. The security of our countries is indivisible, and you Americans can count on us to keep on making our full contribution towards maintaining it.

We shall continue our efforts to overcome existing tensions and to strive for peace and to strive for cooperation in all parts of the world, particularly in the European continent.

We do act on the basis of common beliefs which we have reaffirmed in the past few months. We can state with satisfaction that these meetings have emitted a message of confidence which has had a beneficial effect on the economic development of our two countries, in particular, and also on that of the international community.

We are at one in our determination to maintain peace, to enhance freedom and human dignity in a democratic order, to enhance free trade and economic cooperation, and to serve the well-being of our peoples. The identity of our ideals and of our interests gives strength to our alliance.

Mr. President, I'm looking forward to our talks and to our working together.

THE PRESIDENT. Thank you very much.

NOTE: The President spoke at 10:38 a.m. on the South Lawn of the White House.

United States Circuit Judge Nominating Panel for the Fourth Circuit

Announcement of the Membership of the Panel. July 13, 1977

The President today announced the members of the U.S. Circuit Judge Nominating Panel for the Fourth Circuit. The Panel will submit, within 60 days, a list of five names from which the President may select a nominee to fill the vacancy created by the death of the Honorable J. Braxton Craven, Jr. The President asked the panel to consider only persons from North Carolina for the vacancy.

The members of the panel are:

WESLEY M. WALKER, attorney, Greenville, S.C., chair;

JEAN GALLOWAY BISSELL, senior vice president, South Carolina National Bank, Columbia, S.C.;

KATHLEEN CARTER, president, Human Relations Concept, Inc., Baltimore Md.;

SANDY DUCKWORTH, DNC committeewoman, Alexandria, Va.;

PETER FISH, associate professor of political science, Duke University, Durham, N.C.;

J. CARLTON FLEMING, attorney, Charlotte, N.C.;

HENRY L. MARSH III, mayor, city of Richmond, Va.;

KATHY SEBO, North Carolina State senator, Greensboro, N.C.;

WILLIAM SPONG, dean, William and Mary School of Law, Williamsburg, Va.;

CHARLES B. STACY, attorney, Charleston, W. Va.;

EILEEN STEIN, attorney, Silver Spring, Md.

ACTION

Nomination of John R. Lewis To Be an Associate Director. July 13, 1977

The President today announced that he will nominate John R. Lewis, of Atlanta, Ga., to be an Associate Director (Domestic Operations) of the ACTION Agency.

Lewis was born February 21, 1940, in Troy, Ala. He holds degrees from the American Baptist Theological Seminary and from Fisk University.

From 1963 to 1966, Lewis was chairman of the Student Nonviolent Coordinating Committee. He served as associate director of the Field Foundation in 1966–67, and community organization project director for the Southern Regional Council from 1967 to 1970. Since 1970 he has been executive director of the Voter Education Project.

ACTION

Nomination of Irene Tinker To Be an Assistant Director. July 13, 1977

The President today announced that he will nominate Irene Tinker of Chevy Chase, Md., to be an Assistant Director (Office of Policy and Planning) of the ACTION Agency.

Tinker was born March 8, 1927, in Milwaukee, Wis. She received an A.B. in political science from Radcliffe College in 1949 and a Ph. D. from the London School of Economics and Political Science in 1954.

She has held a variety of academic positions at the University of California, Howard University, Federal City College, and American University. Since 1973 she has been head, Office of International Science, American Association for the Advancement of Science.

ACTION

Nomination of Mary F. Leyland To Be an Assistant Director. July 13, 1977

The President today announced that he will nominate Mary F. Leyland, of New York, to be an Assistant Director (Administration and Finance) of the ACTION Agency.

Leyland was born August 20, 1936, in Bennington, Vt. She received a B.A. in 1958 from Newton College of the Sacred Heart and an M.E. in 1967 from Boston State College.

From 1962 to 1966, Leyland worked at the Harvard Observatory and the Smithsonian Observatory, both in Cambridge, Mass. She later worked as a systems analyst for the IBM Corp. in New Haven, Conn., and for the Commonwealth of Massachusetts in Boston.

Since 1972 she has worked for the Environmental Protection Agency. She is currently Executive Officer in the Office of the Administrator.

Visit of Chancellor Schmidt of the Federal Republic of Germany

Toasts of the President and Chancellor Schmidt at a Dinner Honoring the Chancellor. July 13, 1977

THE PRESIDENT. First of all, I'd like to welcome all of you here to the White House on this very exciting and enjoyable evening for us.

In 1973, when I was still Governor of Georgia, my wife and I made our only trip to Europe. One of the obvious destinations that we chose was West Germany, the Federal Republic, and I wanted to see the leaders of the nations when I arrived there. In fact, long before I got there, they told me that it was not possible for a Governor to see the Chancellor, which——

THE CHANCELLOR. It was not me. [*Laughter*]

THE PRESIDENT. They said that the only one available was just a Finance Minister. [*Laughter*]

So, while we were in Bonn, I went by and was received by my friend, Helmut Schmidt. Although he was very busy, he spent about an hour and a half talking to me about Germany—its economic growth, the interrelationship between his nation and our own.

He asked me why I was making the trip, and I told him we were on a trade mission, trying to strengthen our ties with manufacturers of goods, with those who were experts in technology and those who might come to our own country with trade and investment opportunities.

One of the prospects that we had was Volkswagen, and I told him I had not been able to get an appointment with the Volkswagen people, and he said, "Well, why don't you let me give you some help." [*Laughter*]

So, when I arrived in Wolfsburg a couple of days later, having changed my itinerary, the entire board of directors was there waiting for me. We had a very productive visit.

I had left Rosalynn in Heidelberg. One of her favorite songs is "Student Prince" and we picked out Heidelberg because of that. And I had a chance to look at the nation of Germany, both on that trip and with my wife in other ways. We saw the tremendous rebirth of Germany, its hardworking farmers and factory workers. We talked to them and listened to them.

We had an opportunity to learn about their deep commitment to basic human freedom and the principles of democracy and the struggles that they had made successfully, since the Federal Republic was formed, to reconstitute their legitimate position as one of the leading nations of the world, admired and emulated by many, and having a special relationship that binds us together in many ways.

Those of us who have had some background in science have seen the preeminent scientific discoveries originate in Germany, in physics and mathematics, in space exploration. It's a very exciting realization of the origins of knowledge and innovation there.

There are very few families in our country who don't have a relative who has lived in Germany and served there in the combined armed forces that are dedicated to the mutual purpose of maintaining peace and the protection of homelands and the preservation of stability in one of the regions of the world which is still under a threat, the threat being assuaged and to some degree alleviated by the constant mutual commitment of many nations bound together in NATO.

And our young men, and some women, who have been there to serve with their families have formed ties of knowledge and friendship and even kinship in marriage with the people of the Federal Republic of Germany.

Those of us who love music are thrilled many times a week by the great artists who have made our own lives happy and spirited and moved with deep emotion. Some of my own favorite composers are from Germany and have set standards of excellence and achievement and inspiration that have been a pattern for world emulation.

We have seen the economic growth of Germany, a constant, sometimes plodding, but inexorable movement toward self-reliance and fairness and good relationships between entrepreneurs and members of unions who work with their hands. And there's been a very adequate and careful growth, with constant reticence and caution on the part of Germany not to be domineering but to be a trusted neighbor and a helpful neighbor.

And in spite of their strength and their growth and their influence, there is no fear, because they work in such good harmony and friendship with their allies and neighbors and friends in Western Europe and in other parts of our own hemisphere.

When other nations have deep needs for economic aid, Germany is there to help them. And we've shared these common purposes with Germany through the administrations of many Presidents. I've learned to appreciate this sense of strength and assurance that comes from having such an ally and such a friend. And I'm very proud of my own personal friendship with Helmut Schmidt, who took me in when I was not known.

He could have spent 10 minutes with me and had a photograph and said, "I'm glad you came by, Governor. I hope to see you some other time." But he didn't do that. He was busy, but he wanted me to learn about the achievements and aspirations of his people, and he wanted to learn about me and about Georgia and about the United States.

And I think this is typical of him. I had never met him again until we had the summit conference in London in May. And again he exhibited those qualities of leadership and personal commitment and friendship which increased my own admiration and friendship for him.

This is a time of challenge to the democracies of the world. And there are some who are weak, and there are some who are divided, some who are troubled, some who have very little sense of achievement, some who are doubtful about the future. But our country is not one of them, and the Federal Republic of Germany is not one of them. And that strength comes from the people who have a dedication and a willingness for self-sacrifice in times of challenge that make it possible to prevail.

We are eager to share our own problems and challenges and hopes and dreams and aspirations with others, and I think I am strengthened in my own resolve, knowing that I can consult with Helmut Schmidt when problems arise and questions come up about the growth of communism in some of the Western European countries. He's a statesman and he's wise and he's been there and he understands and he studies the present challenge and how to deal with it, and I listen to him and this is very helpful to me.

We have seen in the Federal Republic of Germany a great independence, and there are times when we don't agree on every item that comes before us for decision. But we are not reticent in our disagreements either, and we exchange views very firmly, without constraint, without subterfuge. And there again the communication between us, even in a disagreement, I think, is very constructive.

I learn from him, and perhaps he learns from me the attitudes and the concerns of the American people. This is a situation which is very helpful to us all. And I'm very proud of that.

We are honored tonight to have many of his key associates, particularly Foreign Minister Genscher, who works closely with Helmut Schmidt and who advises with him and who has helped to form the strength of their government, and the wives and others who have come here from industry, from labor, from the humanities, artists and musicians, news reporters who are leaders in that great country. We are honored by their visit. And I just want all of you to know and all those who listen and would read my words to know how much we appreciate this good relationship, which is staunch, unshakeable, sure, and also increasing in the future.

And I would like to propose a toast to the great people of the Federal Republic of Germany and to their great leader, Helmut Schmidt.

THE CHANCELLOR. *Mr. President, Mrs. Carter, ladies and gentlemen:*

Let me say first that I as a person am deeply moved by the generous words you just said. And I would like to express my personal gratitude, but express my thanks also on behalf of Minister Genscher and all our delegation. I would ask your permission to use a few notes which I have drafted this afternoon, being on a little handicap with your language.

And I would like to say that we today have carried on from where we left it off in London in May. Our meetings were preceded by Vice President Mondale's visit to my country. It's sad that he had to go back to the Senate tonight and didn't get a supper.

THE PRESIDENT. He's come back.

THE CHANCELLOR. Has he come back? You are wandering between the two places. [*Laughter*] But coming from a parliamentary democracy, and having been a Member of Parliament myself for 24 years, I know how it is. [*Laughter*]

This picture of close and sincere and trustful consultations between ourselves has been rounded off by various personal contacts between our foreign ministers and also by telephone and written communications between ourselves. The intensity of our dialog, to me, is a reflection of the unprecedented state of relations between the United States and the Federal Republic of Germany. It's a reflection also of the depth of our common, basic beliefs and basic convictions, a reflection also of our common interests and of the fact that the friendly nature of our meetings is very much a matter of course.

It's on this solid foundation of human and political links that this present meeting is based, like others in the past and more to come in the future.

I would like to emphasize already now that the talks and discussions of this first day of our stay in Washington, D.C., have been very fruitful and constructive.

I once again was deeply impressed by the profound sense of responsibility and understanding which you showed, Mr. President, when we were dealing with important aspects of international politics. And I once more have become aware of the tremendous burden which the President of the United States has to carry. His decisions very often have repercussions, consequences far beyond the borders of the United States. He needs great strength. His office requires confidence, and it does ask for an open mind with regards to the numerous problems which challenge the leading Western power.

Let me add that I have great admiration for the way in which President Carter is performing his tasks, and I would like to add for you personally, Jimmy, the way you have welcomed us today, to me, is just another proof of the common ground on which we stand, not only on general terms but also as friends working closely together.

We all know that the manifold problems facing the world today call more than ever for common effort and that they can be solved only if we proceed on the basis of common responsibility.

The Federal Republic of Germany will render its full contribution. And you, Mr. President, and your fellow Americans can rely on our firm will to pursue our common goals in close cooperation with you.

And I am quite sure that I can say this for all the citizens in my country, for all the German nation, as much as I can say this for all the members of my delegation, which as you already mentioned does not only consist of political leaders and civil servants but also eminent leaders from the trade unions, from industry, and from our cultural life and from our mass media.

We all know that the strength, quite a bit of the strength, and the confidence which you projected into our nation a couple of minutes ago—that they derive from the knowledge that my people can face up to great challenges of our times side by side with the United States.

I am convinced that our visit will help to even further increase, as you said, the determination and energy with which we on both sides of the Atlantic set about our great tasks.

We share with you, Mr. President, and with your country, and with your nation, the belief in the superiority of the spirit of freedom of the individual person. And like you, we are convinced that freedom can only prevail if the dignity of the individual and his or her civil rights, or as they are being called in our constitution, basic rights, are respected and exercised.

At the same time, we German people know from a bitter epoch in our history that freedom and basic rights can never be taken for granted, that they only thrive when they are protected and preserved by sincerity, by courageous involvement, and even by sacrifice.

You will always find the Federal Republic of Germany and its people at your side when it comes to safeguarding freedom for the individual and securing respect for his or her dignity and rights around the world.

I guess we need no special capacity of perception to recognize that without the Atlantic Alliance, which is the visible expression of our harmony in these objectives, freedom and basic rights in the western part of Europe might have been imperiled, perhaps even extinguished, in some parts over the past three decades.

We Germans never regarded the presence of the United States in Europe as part of a power political calculation, but we always regarded it as an involvement stemming from a deep commitment, for which we are grateful and which we reciprocate for the very same reason.

It becomes equally clear against this background how much importance is being attached to the patient continuance of the policy of détente, starting from the safe basis of our alliance and of its ability to defend ourselves.

Let me stress in this context that it is the most vital interest of my divided nation to continue and to further this policy of alleviating tensions, because there just is no other way to try and alleviate the human problems in millions of families in my nation stemming from the political and geographical division of my people.

There is, of course, a strong connection between elimination or alleviation of tensions in Europe and in other parts of the world and in the realization of all the three baskets of the Helsinki declaration, as was stressed by Secretary Vance just a couple of days ago.

One glance at the map or at the geopolitical and military facts shows ourselves the enormous differences between our two countries—at least some of the enormous differences between our two countries. In the United States people might not always realize that my country is no larger than the State of Oregon, with the one exception that there are living more than 60 million in that little state of the Federal Republic of Germany, 60 or 62 million.

Of course, no offense is being meant—no offense toward the good citizens of the State of Oregon—[*laughter*]—is being meant in using their fine State as a yardstick for the smallness in territory of my home country. I'm very well aware of the importance of Oregon, and of Portland especially. [*Laughter*]

But I like to point to the smallness of my country in order to make itself understood that neither are we a world power nor do we want to become one. We see ourselves as a European country integrating itself within the European community, with responsibilities determined by its membership of that community, responsibilities by its membership within the North Atlantic Alliance, responsibilities by our role in the economic system of the world. And we see our role as a country with very, very limited natural resources only.

To my view and to the view of most of my countrymen, intra-European coopération and the Atlantic Alliance comple-ment each other. And for us Germans, both of them are indispensable. Therefore, I welcome the practice of your administration to conduct particularly intensive consultations with European allies, with ourselves, and I have the feeling that our meeting today proves that this is not just theory but a very practical and successful reality.

My wife and I and the members of my delegation are grateful for your hospitality, Mr. President, which you have extended to us here in Washington. We are really glad of the opportunity to discuss questions and problems with close friends here in the United States in, as you correctly say, a frank and open-hearted manner, even if there may arise some points on which we might differ.

I do feel that if the world could show many more examples of talks conducted in such a spirit, the world would be quite a different and much better place.

I would now like to ask my fellow countrymen to raise their glasses and drink with me to the health of the President of the United States, Jimmy Carter, to continuing happiness of the American people, and to ever closer cooperation and friendship between our two nations.

THE PRESIDENT. Thank you very much.

NOTE: The President spoke at 9:30 p.m. in the State Dining Room at the White House.

Visit of Chancellor Schmidt of the Federal Republic of Germany

Remarks at the Entertainment Honoring Chancellor Schmidt. July 13, 1977

Again I want to welcome all of you here tonight. We are very thrilled and pleased to have Chancellor Helmut Schmidt, his wife, Foreign Minister Genscher and his wife, and other distinguished visitors from the Federal Republic of Germany.

As a special treat for them and for us, we have a performance tonight put on by five artists from the Metropolitan Opera Company, and I think you'll all recognize the beautiful music which exemplifies so well and so delightfully part of the American heritage.

When I was a young midshipman at Annapolis we had four weekends off per year—the second year we were at Annapolis; none the first year. One of my weekends I went to New York, and the first and only musical play that I ever heard was "Carousel." And tonight we have selections from "Carousel."

Following this performance, I'd like to make a special introduction to you of an extraordinary guest that we have. But I'll delay that until after the performance is completed.

I think you'll enjoy this, and I hope you will express your appreciation to these fine singers who have come here to put on this performance and to our fine Marine Band.

Thank you very much.

[*At this point, the entertainment began. At its conclusion, the President resumed speaking.*]

Did you like the music?

Fifty years ago a young man began to write perhaps the most beautiful music that our country has ever heard. His name is Richard Rodgers, and he's here tonight, and I'd like to ask him to come up on the stage with his wife, Dorothy.

Mr. Rodgers has a problem that I know many of you wish the politicians had. He can't speak very well, but we are so proud to have him and his wife here tonight. He and Lorenz Hart, better known as Rodgers and Hart, wrote 28 musical plays before Mr. Hart became unable to write. And then he formed another partnership with Oscar Hammerstein, and they produced some of the most brilliant and famous musical productions in our lifetime.

"Carousel" is just one of them—"Oklahoma," "South Pacific," "Sound of Music," "The King and I," and many others.

He's a man who is an inspiration to us all, one of the human treasures of the United States. He's received 10 honorary degrees. He's won the Pulitzer Prize twice. He's won two Oscars, he's won five Tony awards, and he's a man who exemplifies the finest in ensuring that other people of our Nation and the world have an enjoyable and inspired life.

And I'm very grateful and honored that Mr. Rodgers has come here tonight to be with us. This music, "Carousel," is just one of many tremendous examples of his noted work. And we are honored, Richard Rodgers, that you would come here to the White House with me and with Chancellor Schmidt and all these distinguished visitors from the United States and from the Federal Republic of Germany this evening.

Thank you very much, and God bless you, sir.

Typically of one who loves the way notes are put together, he wants us to recognize a brilliant performance of the Marine Band, and I wish you would stand, too. Mr. Rodgers said you did a superb job.

NOTE: The President spoke at 10:30 p.m. on the South Lawn of the White House.

Downing of U.S. Army Helicopter on Korean Peninsula

Statement by the White House Press Secretary. July 14, 1977

We have confirmation that a Chinook cargo helicopter with a crew of three is down north of the demarcation line in the Korean Peninsula. There are indications it was forced down by North Korean fire.

We are deeply concerned about this incident, and we are requesting a prompt explanation from North Korean authorities. Any penetration of North Korean air space that may have taken place would have been unintentional and regrettable. We do not know at this time the fate of the crew. We have requested that every consideration be given to them by North Korean authorities, and we have asked for their immediate return.

NOTE: Press Secretary Jody Powell read the statement at his news conference at the White House at 12:17 a.m. on July 14. At a news conference at 1:30 a.m., Mr. Powell stated: "We now have North Korean domestic radio reports monitored in South Korea which indicate that there were four people on board, three of whom are reported to be dead and one captured."

The statement was made available by the White House Press Office. It was not issued in the form of a White House press release.

Power Failure in the New York Metropolitan Area

Memorandum for Richard L. Dunham, Chairman, Federal Power Commission. July 14, 1977

Memorandum for Richard L. Dunham, Chairman, Federal Power Commission

Last night's power failure affecting 10 million people in New York City and parts of the metropolitan area is another dramatic reminder of the total dependence of this nation on reliable energy supplies. The Federal Power Commission is therefore directed immediately to investigate this power failure to ascertain the reasons why it occurred and to recommend specific actions to be taken to prevent a recurrence.

I am directing all agencies of the Executive Branch to support you in any way that their assistance may be useful. I hope that you will be able to report your findings at a very early date.

JIMMY CARTER

NOTE: The text of the memorandum was made available by the White House Press Office. It was not issued in the form of a White House press release.

Federal Energy Administration

Nomination of Hazel R. Rollins To Be an Assistant Administrator. July 14, 1977

The President today announced that he will nominate Hazel R. Rollins, of the District of Columbia, to be an Assistant Administrator (Conservation and Environment) of the Federal Energy Administration.

Ms. Rollins was born May 17, 1937, in Newport News, Va. She received a B.A. from Fisk University and an LL.B. from the Rutgers University Law School.

From 1974 to 1976, Ms. Rollins served as Director of the Office of Consumer Affairs for the Federal Energy Administration, leaving that post to become General Counsel of the Community Services Administration. She has also served as Director of the Public Sector Division of the Cost of Living Council.

An attorney and member of the New Jersey Bar, Ms. Rollins previously served as an assistant county prosecutor in Essex County, coordinator of the Community Action Workshop in Newark, and deputy attorney general for the State of New Jersey.

Visit of Chancellor Schmidt of the Federal Republic of Germany

White House Statement Issued at the Conclusion of the Chancellor's Visit. July 14, 1977

President Carter and the Chancellor of the Federal Republic of Germany, Helmut Schmidt, held three lengthy conversations during the Chancellor's official visit to Washington, July 13–15. The Chancellor came to Washington at the President's invitation, and the President hosted a White House dinner for the Chancellor and his party on July 13. The three meetings between the President and the Chancellor covered a wide range of economic, political, and security issues in which the two nations share an interest. Those discussions followed on the meetings the President and Chancellor had in May at the London Summit. In addition to the two scheduled meetings on Wednesday and Thursday mornings, the President met privately with the Chancellor for about 1 hour Wednesday night following the state dinner.

The President and the Chancellor emphasized the closeness of the consultation between their two governments and their basic agreement on major issues. They expressed the belief that the small differences between their governments in recent months have often become exaggerated in public accounts, and they committed themselves to be in direct touch with one another in the future to make sure that exaggeration does not recur.

In their first meeting, the President and the Chancellor discussed the spectrum of relations between East and West, focusing on SALT, other arms control negotiations, and the upcoming fall meeting in Belgrade of the Conference on Security and Cooperation in Europe. They also exchanged views on the situation in the Middle East and on how to move forward with international efforts to reduce the risk of nuclear proliferation, while still assuring all nations access to the nuclear energy they need. The President and the Chancellor also discussed the importance of basic human rights and its role in international affairs.

The second formal meeting between the two was devoted largely to MBFR and economic issues. The Germans presented some thoughts on MBFR, and the two sides exchanged views on how to move the negotiations forward. With regard to economic issues, there was broad agreement. The Chancellor met on July 13 with Secretary Blumenthal, and the President emphasized satisfaction, in his second formal meeting with the Chancellor, at the Federal Republic's efforts to assure domestic economic growth and deal with current accounts surpluses. The two men agreed on the importance of economic stability to the political cohesion of the developed countries and to the prospects for progress in the dialog between the North and South. The President and the Chancellor also agreed on the need to move forward this year with international trade negotiations—expressing pleasure at the results of recent meetings between the President's Special Trade Representative, Robert Strauss, and the European Communities—to assure adequate international financing and to implement the commitments their countries and others undertook at the London Summit in May.

The Chancellor, who last visited the United States in July 1976 to celebrate the American Bicentennial, was accompanied by Mrs. Schmidt. His party also included leaders from German business, labor, and cultural life. At the conclusion of their last meeting, the Chancellor invited the President to visit Germany, and the President accepted in principle, indicating that he looked forward to a visit.

Department of Agriculture

Nomination of Sarah Weddington To Be General Counsel. *July 15, 1977*

The President today announced his intention to nominate Sarah Weddington, of Austin, Tex., to be General Counsel of the Department of Agriculture.

Weddington was born February 2, 1945, in Alibene, Tex. She is a member of the Texas House of Representatives and a specialist in family law.

She was the first woman ever elected to the Texas Legislature from Travis County. As a State Representative since 1974, Ms. Weddington served as a delegate to the Texas Constitutional Convention of 1975, where she was a member of the Legislative Committee.

A graduate of the University of Texas Law School, she served for 3 years as assistant reporter to the American Bar Association Special Project to Reevaluate Ethical Standards. She practiced for a year as assistant city attorney for Fort Worth, resigning in 1971 to start her private practice in Austin.

United Nations

Nomination of Allard Kenneth Lowenstein To Be Alternate U.S. Representative for Special Political Affairs. *July 15, 1977*

The President today announced his intention to nominate Allard Kenneth Lowenstein, of Long Beach, N.Y., to be the Alternate Representative of the United States of America for Special Political Affairs in the United Nations, with the rank of Ambassador.

Mr. Lowenstein was born January 16, 1929, in Newark, N.J. He received his B.A. in 1949 from the University of North Carolina and LL.B. from Yale University Law School in 1954. He served in the United States Army from 1954–56.

He has taught at Stanford University, the City College of New York, Yale School of Urban Studies, University of Massachusetts, and the New School of Social Research. He served as a visiting fellow at John F. Kennedy School of Government, Harvard University. He has been a special assistant to United States Senator Frank P. Graham and a foreign policy assistant to Senator Hubert H. Humphrey. From 1969–71 he was United States Representative from the State of New York. He is currently a consultant with the Department of State.

United Nations

Appointment of Edward M. Mezvinsky as U.S. Representative on the Human Rights Commission of the Economic and Social Council. *July 15, 1977*

The President today announced the appointment of Edward M. Mezvinsky as the Representative of the United States of America on the Human Rights Commission of the Economic and Social Council of the United Nations.

Mr. Mezvinsky was born January 17, 1937 in Ames, Iowa. He received his B.A. in 1960 from the University of Iowa and his M.A. and J.D. in 1963 and 1965, respectively, from the University of California.

He was the legislative assistant to Congressman Neal Smith of Iowa from 1965–67. From 1967–72 Mr. Mezvinsky was an attorney in Iowa City, Iowa. From 1969–70 he served as a member of the Iowa State House of Representatives. In 1970–72 he was again an attorney in Iowa City. From 1973–77 he served as a United States Representative from the State of Iowa. Presently he is an attorney in Washington, D.C.

National Institute of Education

Nomination of Patricia A. Graham To Be Director. July 15, 1977

The President today announced that he will nominate Patricia A. Graham, of Cambridge, Mass., to be Director of the National Institute of Education, Department of Health, Education, and Welfare.

Dr. Graham was born February 9, 1935, in Lafayette, Ind. She holds bachelor's and master's degrees from Purdue University and a Ph.D. from Columbia University, as well as honorary degrees from Harvard University and Manhattanville College.

Dr. Graham is currently a professor in the Graduate School of Education at Harvard. She is also dean of Radcliffe Institute and Vice President of Radcliffe College. Her teaching career has included positions at Teachers College and Barnard College of Columbia University and Indiana University.

Executive Office of the President

Remarks to Reporters on Transmitting a Reorganization Plan to the Congress. July 15, 1977

Good afternoon, everybody.

Today we have submitted to the Congress the first in a series of recommendations for reorganizing the executive branch of Government. We are starting off with perhaps the most difficult one of all for me. That's the Executive Office of the President and the White House staff.

It's difficult because of the closeness of myself to the people involved. It's also difficult because, for many years, as the Congress and other elements in the Government have evolved special programs that cut across many departments' lines, they've put them in the Executive Office of the President. The closeness of the President is supposed to add stature to their influence and also permits them to deal with several departments simultaneously without any doubt about where the authority lies.

The basic thrust of the proposals today involving the Executive Office of the President is to strengthen Cabinet government. I'm very much opposed to having a concentration of large numbers of people and authority in the White House staff. I much prefer that Cabinet officers make their own decisions, manage their own departments, and that the coordinating effort rests in me.

We've initiated and maintained a weekly Cabinet meeting that further strengthens the Cabinet-level authority and responsibility. At the same time, these changes we are proposing today, which will be outlined by Bert Lance, the head of OMB, provide an unimpeded access of information, advice, counsel, criticism to me—a free flow of information from many diverse sources that eventually arrive on my desk, or with consultations with the President himself if they can't be resolved at a lower level of Government.

The historical authorized level of the White House staff has been about 485. I think the day of the election last November there were 489 people who were working in the White House, which is less than there had been some time in the past. We are proposing to cut that down to 351, a very drastic reduction amounting to about 28 percent.

In the Executive Office of the President we are reducing the overall staff size, including OMB and other entities that are very difficult to reduce, from 1,712 down to 1,459.

We have had, in the past, 19 separate units of Government within the Executive Office of the President. I have already eliminated two of those, and this proposal will eliminate seven others. This remaining 10 elements that work directly with me, we believe, are needed here, because there is no other logical place for them in Government and because I need their constant advice and counsel, almost on a daily basis, to make decisions that accrue to the President as a responsibility.

The 10 that are remaining will be simplified, and I think that this overall thrust will be a very successful effort to make the Executive Office of the Presi-

dent a model that can be emulated as we proceed aggressively now to reorganize other parts of the Federal Government.

Bert Lance will be here with his staff to answer your questions of a specific nature, but I am very pleased at the work they've done and believe that we have made the right decision that will stand us in good stead in the future.

I might point out that we've had additional responsibilities that have caused some increase in staffing. Under Jack Watson, we now have a superb interrelationship among Cabinet officers, since they are elevated to a much greater degree of importance than in the past. And this same additional group, which did not exist before, deals directly with Governors, mayors, county officials, local officials. And this is a very welcome addition to the Executive Office of the President.

We also have a few additional personnel here who work exclusively on the reorganization of the Government itself. But even including those additional people, this is very severe and, I think, adequate reduction.

I might say in closing that we think that every change we've made will lead to greater productivity of the right decisions and management of the Government and will also mean that each person has a much clearer definition of responsibility and authority than has been in the past.

I want to thank you for your attention and now turn the program over to Bert Lance.

NOTE: The President spoke at 1:38 p.m. in the Briefing Room at the White House. Following his remarks, Bert Lance, Director of the Office of Management and Budget, and A. D. Frazier, Jr., Project Manager of the Executive Office of the President Reorganization Study Group, held a news briefing for reporters on the reorganization plan.

Executive Office of the President

*Message to the Congress Transmitting
Reorganization Plan No. 1 of 1977.
July 15, 1977*

To the Congress of the United States:

I herewith transmit my plan for the Reorganization of the Executive Office of the President (EOP), Reorganization Plan No. 1 of 1977. This plan is the first of a series I intend to submit under the reorganization authority vested in me by the Reorganization Act of 1977 (P.L. 95–17). It adheres to the purposes set forth in Section 901(a) of the Act.

This plan in conjunction with the other steps I am taking will:

- eliminate seven of the seventeen units now within the EOP and modify the rest. There were 19 units when I took office; the President's Foreign Intelligence Advisory Board and the Economic Policy Board have already been abolished. Thus with this plan I will have eliminated nine of 19 EOP units.
- reduce EOP staffing by about 250 which includes the White House staff reduction of 134 or 28% which I have already ordered.
- improve efficiency by centralizing administrative functions; and
- improve the process by which information is provided for Presidential decisionmaking.

These recommendations arise from a careful, systematic study of the EOP. They are based on the premise that the EOP exists to serve the President and should be structured to meet his needs. They will reduce waste and cost while improving the service the President, and the nation, receive from the EOP.

The EOP now consists of the immediate White House Office, the Vice President's Office, the Office of Management and Budget, and fourteen other agencies. The EOP has a budget authority of about $80,000,000 and 1,712 full time employees.

The White House Office concentrates on close personal support including policy and political advice and administrative and operational services. The Office of the Vice President provides similar support to him. OMB's primary mission is to develop and implement the budget; it also carries out a number of management and reorganization activities.

Three EOP units have responsibility for policy development:

- National Security Council
- Domestic Council
- Council on International Economic Policy

The other 11 are more specialized offices that offer analysis and advice, help develop policy in certain areas, or carry out special projects. These are:

- Council of Economic Advisers
- Council on Wage and Price Stability
- Office of the Special Representative for Trade Negotiations
- Council on Environmental Quality
- Office of Science and Technology Policy
- Office of Drug Abuse Policy
- Office of Telecommunications Policy
- Intelligence Oversight Board
- Federal Property Council
- Energy Resources Council
- Economic Opportunity Council

To make the EOP more effective, four steps are necessary:

I. Strengthen management of policy issues.

II. Limit the EOP, wherever possible, to functions directly related to the President's work.

III. Centralize administrative services.

IV. Reduce size of White House and EOP staffs.

I. *Strengthen Process Management of Policy Issues.*

Perhaps the most important function of the President's staff is to make sure he has the wide variety of views and facts he needs to make decisions. By building a more orderly system for collecting information and advice, the President can make sure that he will hear all the views he should—and hear them in time. To better insure that this happens, I am taking the following actions to:

- Institute for domestic and economic issues, a system similar to the Presidential Review Memorandum process currently used for National Security issues.
- Create a committee of Presidential advisers, chaired by the Vice President, to set priorities among issues and oversee their staffing.
- Assure that Presidential decision memoranda on policy issues are coordinated with Cabinet and EOP advisers most involved with the issue.
- Consolidate under the Staff Secretary the two current White House paper circulation systems.
- Appoint a group of advisers to review the decisionmaking process periodically.
- Give the Assistant to the President for Domestic Affairs and Policy clear responsibility for managing the way in which domestic and most economic policy issues are prepared for Presidential decision.
- Assign follow-up responsibility for Presidential decisions as follows: immediate follow-up will be handled by the NSC or Domestic Policy Staff most directly involved in the issue; long term follow-up on selected issues will be handled by the Assistant to the President for Intergovernmental Relations.

These actions recognize that the White House and Executive Office staff must use their proximity to the President to insure that the full resources of the government and the public are brought to bear on Presidential decisions in a timely fashion. It is my purpose in instituting these changes to strengthen Cabinet participation in Presidential decisions.

II. *Rationalize EOP structure by limiting EOP, wherever possible, to functions which bear a close relationship to the work of the President.*

As the President's principal staff institution, there are several major things the EOP must do:

- Provide day-to-day operational support (e.g. scheduling, appointments) and help the President communicate with the public, the Congress, and the press.
- Manage the budget and coordinate Administration positions on matters before the Congress.
- Manage the Presidential decision-making processes efficiently and fairly, and bring the President the widest possible range of opinions.
- Help the President: plan and set priorities; monitor and evaluate progress toward achieving the President's objectives; understand and resolve major conflicts among line subordinates; manage crises, especially in national security matters.

In order to restructure the EOP around these basic functions, the functions of seven units should be discontinued or transferred, and ten units, including the White House Office, should be retained but modified.

Seven units should be discontinued or their functions transferred. These are:

1. Office of Drug Abuse Policy
2. Office of Telecommunications Policy

3. Council on International Economic Policy
4. Federal Property Council
5. Energy Resources Council
6. Economic Opportunity Council
7. Domestic Council

The functions of the *Office of Drug Abuse Policy* (ODAP) can be performed by a smaller staff reporting to a Presidential adviser in the EOP. The Office itself will be discontinued.

Much of the work done by the *Office of Telecommunications Policy* (OTP) can be more effectively performed outside the EOP. It is important that the EOP have the capacity to resolve differences and that the President have immediate advice on telecommunications and information policy, especially on national security, emergency preparedness and privacy issues. This only requires a small staff within EOP. The Office of Management and Budget would take responsibility for federal telecommunications procurement and management policy and arbitration of interagency disputes about frequency allocation. All other functions except developing Presidential policy options would be transferred to a new office within the Department of Commerce, headed by a new Assistant Secretary for Communications and Information, who will perform many of the functions previously performed by the head of the OTP.

I propose that the *Economic Opportunity Council* be discontinued; it is dormant and its only active function (preparation of the Catalogue of Federal Domestic Assistance) is being performed by OMB. Three other units are also inactive and should be discontinued: *Council on International Economic Policy, the Federal Property Council,* and the *Energy Resources Council.*

The *Domestic Council* should be abolished. It has rarely functioned as a Council, because it is too large and its membership too diverse to make decisions efficiently. Its functions have been performed entirely by its staff. This *Domestic Policy Staff* should report to the Assistant to the President for Domestic Affairs and Policy. Under the policy process system described earlier, they should manage the process which coordinates the making of domestic and most economic policy. They should work closely with the Cabinet departments and agencies to insure that the views of the Cabinet and agency heads are brought to the President before decisions are made.

The ten EOP units which will continue with some modification are:

1. White House Office
2. Office of the Vice President
3. Office of Management and Budget
4. Council on Environmental Quality
5. Council of Economic Advisers
6. Office of Science and Technology Policy
7. Office of the Special Representative for Trade Negotiations
8. National Security Council
9. Intelligence Oversight Board
10. Council on Wage and Price Stability

The operations of the *Office of the Vice President* reflect the combination of constitutional, statutory, and Presidentially assigned duties that make it unique among EOP units. Because his interests and assignments cover the same range as the President's, the Vice President requires a staff with expertise in diverse areas. Its basic functions should not be changed. However, I propose that certain support functions—involving accounting, personnel services, and supply—be transferred to a centralized EOP Administrative Unit.

The *Office of Management and Budget* would remain as a separate entity in the EOP, but some functional changes should be made. Four functions should be transferred from OMB to other parts of the government:

- Administration to the new EOP Central Administrative Unit;
- Executive Department/Labor Relations (except for Pay Agent, Executive Level Pools, and Legislative Analysis) to the Civil Service Commission;
- Advisory Committee Management Secretariat to the General Services Administration;
- Statistical Policy (except Forms Clearance) to the Department of Commerce.

I have asked the OMB to reorganize its management arm to emphasize major Presidential initiatives, such as reorganization, program evaluation, paperwork reduction, and regulatory reform.

The *Council on Environmental Quality* (CEQ) should remain in the EOP as an environmental adviser to the President. The CEQ's major purpose is to provide an independent assessment of our policies for improving the environment. Toward this end, it will analyze long term trends and conditions in the environment. It will advise OMB on the reorganization of natural resources functions within the Federal government. The Council will retain the functions it now has under NEPA and Executive Order No. 11514 with the exception of routine review of the adequacy of impact statements and the administrative aspects of their receipt and handling. The EPA will take over CEQ's evaluation responsibility under the Federal Nonnuclear Energy Research Development Act of 1974. The CEQ will continue to review and publish the Annual Report on Environmental Quality.

The strength of the *Council of Economic Advisers* (CEQ) lies in its economic analysis of current policy choices. It also presents objective economic data, makes macroeconomic forecasts, and analyzes economic trends and their impact on the national economy. It will continue with a small reduction in staff.

The *Office of Science and Technology Policy* (OSTP) should retain those science, engineering, and technology functions which can be so useful in helping the President and his advisers make decisions about policy and budget issues. Instead of the Intergovernmental Science, Engineering, and Technology Advisory Panels, the President should rely on an intergovernmental relations working group, chaired by the Science Adviser. The Federal Coordinating Council on Science and Technology should operate as a sub-Cabinet working group chaired by the Science Adviser. The reorganization work of the President's Committee on Science and Technology would be part of the overall reorganization effort. The responsibility for preparing certain reports should be transferred to the National Science Foundation.

The proposal places manageable limits on OSTP's broad mandate while emphasizing functions that support the President.

The *Office of the Special Representative for Trade Negotiations* (STR) is now operating effectively and will be retained essentially as is. With the difficult negotiations now underway in Geneva, the benefits of transferring the STR to another agency are outweighed by the potential reduction in its effectiveness as an international negotiator.

The *National Security Council* (NSC) will be retained in its present form and its staff slightly reduced.

Intelligence Oversight Board (IOB) should be retained to insure that abuses of the past are not repeated and to emphasize Presidential concerns regarding intelligence issues.

The *Council of Wage and Price Stability* (COWPS) is a necessary weapon in the continuing fight against inflation and will be retained. To be sure that its work is closely coordinated with the economic analyses performed by the Council of Economic Advisers (CEA), COWPS should be directed by the Chairman of CEA.

III. *Centralize Administrative Functions*

About 380 (22%) of the full-time, permanent EOP personnel perform administrative support services in EOP units. Most EOP units besides the White House and OMB are too small to provide a full complement of administrative services. They depend on the White House, OMB, GSA, other federal departments, or several of these sources for many of these services. This approach is inefficient; the quality is uneven and the coordination poor. Some services are duplicated, others inconsistently distributed (excess capacity in some units and deficiencies in others), and most too costly.

I propose to combine administrative support operations into a Central Administrative Unit in EOP to provide support in administrative services common to all EOP entities. It should be a separate EOP entity because of the need to assure equal access by all other units.

This consolidation will result in:
- saving of roughly 40 positions and about $1.1 million
- improved and more innovative services
- a focus for monitoring the efficiency and responsibility of administrative services
- a base for an effective EOP budget/ planning system through which the President can manage an integrated

EOP rather than a collection of disparate units.

The EOP has never before been organized as a single, unified entity serving the President. It is only by viewing it as a whole that we can improve efficiency through steps like the Central Administrative Unit.

IV. *Reduce the Size of White House and EOP Staffs*

I am reducing the White House staff by 28%, from the 485 I inherited from my predecessor to 351. This involves cuts in my policy and administrative staffs as well as transfers to the Central Administrative Unit.

I estimate that this plan and the other steps I am taking will reduce staff levels in the EOP by about 250, from 1,712 full-time permanent positions to about 1,460 and will save the taxpayers at least $6 million.

As in the rest of the government, I will be reluctant to add staff unless necessary to help me do my job better.

I ask that you support me in improving the operations of the Executive Office of the President by approving the attached reorganization plan.

In summary this plan would:
- Abolish the Domestic Council and establish a Domestic Policy Staff.
- Establish within the EOP a Central Administrative Unit.
- Transfer certain functions of the Council on Environmental Quality to the President for redelegation.
- Abolish the Office of Drug Abuse Policy and vest functions in the President for redelegation.
- Abolish the Office of Telecommunications Policy and transfer functions to the Department of Commerce and to the President for redelegation.

- Create an Assistant Secretary of Commerce for Communications and Information.
- Vest some Office of Science and Technology Policy functions in the President for redelegation.
- Abolish the Economic Opportunity Council and vest those functions in the President for redelegation.
- Transfer the Committee Management Secretariat function of the Office of Management and Budget to the President for redelegation.
- Make other incidental transfers attendant to those mentioned above.

Each of the changes set forth in the plan accompanying this message is necessary to accomplish one or more of the purposes set forth in Section 901(a) of Title 5 of the United States Code. I have taken care to determine that all functions abolished by the plan are done so only under statutory authority provided by Section 903(b) of Title 5 of the United States Code. The provisions in the plan for the appointment and pay of any head or officer of any agency have been found by me to be necessary.

As we continue our studies of other parts of the Executive Branch, we will find more ways to improve services in the EOP and elsewhere. This plan is only a beginning, but I am confident that it represents a major step toward a more efficient government that will serve the needs of the people and the President well.

JIMMY CARTER

The White House,
July 15, 1977.

REORGANIZATION PLAN No. 1 OF 1977

Prepared by the President and transmitted to the Senate and the House of Representatives in Congress assembled, July 15, 1977, pursuant to the provisions of Chapter 9 of Title 5 of the United States Code.

EXECUTIVE OFFICE OF THE PRESIDENT

SECTION 1. *Redesignation of Domestic Council Staff.*

The Domestic Council staff is hereby designated the Domestic Policy Staff and shall consist of such staff personnel as are determined by the President to be necessary to assure that the needs of the President for prompt and comprehensive advice are met with respect to matters of economic and domestic policy. The staff shall continue to be headed by an Executive Director who shall be an Assistant to the President, designated by the President, as provided in Section 203 of Reorganization Plan No. 2 of 1970. The Executive Director shall perform such functions as the President may from time to time direct.

SEC. 2. *Establishment of a Central Administrative Unit.*

There is hereby established in the Executive Office of the President the Central Administrative Unit which shall be headed by the President. There shall be a Director of the Central Administrative Unit. The Director shall be appointed by the President and shall serve as chief administrative officer of the Central Administrative Unit. The President is authorized to fix the compensation and duties of the Director.

The Central Administrative Unit shall provide components of the Executive Office of the President with such administrative services as the President shall from time to time direct.

SEC. 3. *Abolition of Components.*

The following components of the Executive Office of the President are hereby abolished:

A. The Domestic Council;

B. The Office of Drug Abuse Policy;

C. The Office of Telecommunications Policy; and

D. The Economic Opportunity Council.

SEC. 4. *Appointment of the Assistant Secretary of Commerce for Communications and Information.*

There shall be in the Department of Commerce an Assistant Secretary for Communications and Information who shall be appointed by the President, by and with the advice and consent of the Senate, and who shall be entitled to receive compensation at the rate now or hereafter prescribed by law for Level IV of the Executive Schedule.

SEC. 5. *Transfers of Functions.*

The following functions shall be transferred:

A. All functions vested in the Director of the Office of Science and Technology Policy and in the Office of Science and Technology Policy pursuant to sections 205(a)(2), 206 and 209 of the National Science and Technology Policy, Organization, and Priorities Act of 1976 (Public Law 94–282; 90 Stat. 459), are hereby transferred to the President. The Intergovernmental Science, Engineering, and Technology Advisory Panel, the President's Committee on Science and Technology, and the Federal Coordinating Council for Science, Engineering and Technology, established in accordance with the provisions of Titles II, III, and IV of the National Science and Technology Policy, Organization, and Priorities Act of 1976, are hereby abolished, and their functions transferred to the President.

B. Those functions of the Office of Telecommunications Policy and of its Director relating to:

(1) the preparation of national security, emergency, and other Presidential telecommunications policy options;

(2) disposition of appeals from assignments of radio frequencies to sta-

tions of the United States government; and

(3) procurement and management of Federal telecommunications systems, are hereby transferred to the President. All other functions of the Office of Telecommunications Policy and of its Director are hereby transferred to the Secretary of Commerce who shall provide for the performance of such functions.

C. The functions of the Office of Drug Abuse Policy and its Director are hereby transferred to the President.

D. The functions of the Domestic Council are hereby transferred to the President.

E. Those functions of the Council on Environmental Quality and the Office of Environmental Quality relating to the evaluation provided for by Section 11 of the Federal Nonnuclear Energy Research and Development Act of 1974 (Public Law 93–577, 88 Stat. 1878), are hereby transferred to the President.

F. Those functions of the Office of Management and Budget and its Director relating to the Committee Management Secretariat (Public Law 92–436, 86 Stat. 770, as amended Public Law 94–409, 90 Stat. 1247) are hereby transferred to the President.

G. The functions of the Economic Opportunity Council are hereby transferred to the President.

SEC. 6. *Incidental Transfers.*

So much of the personnel, property, records, and unexpended balances of appropriations, allocations and other funds employed, used, held, available, or to be made available in connection with the functions transferred under this Plan, as the Director of the Office of Management and Budget shall determine, shall be transferred to the appropriate department, agency, or component at such time or times as the Director of the Office of

Management and Budget shall provide, except that no such unexpended balances transferred shall be used for purposes other than those for which the appropriation was originally made. The Director of the Office of Management and Budget shall provide for terminating the affairs of all agencies abolished herein and for such further measures and dispositions as such Director deems necessary to effectuate the purposes of this Reorganization Plan.

SEC. 7. *Effective Date.*

This Reorganization Plan shall become effective at such time or times as the President shall specify, but not sooner than the earliest time allowable under Section 906 of Title 5 of the United States Code.

Community Services Administration

Nomination of Robert S. Landmann To Be an Assistant Director.   July 15, 1977

The President today announced that he will nominate Robert S. Landmann, of Santa Fe, N. Mex., to be an Assistant Director (Policy, Planning and Evaluation) of the Community Services Administration.

Landmann was born June 27, 1939, in New York City. He holds a B.A. from Mexico City College and an M.A. and Ph. D. from the University of New Mexico.

In 1965 Landmann was an administrative analyst for the State of New Mexico, leaving to serve as Peace Corps volunteer in Bolivia. He was a research consultant for the Joint Commission on Mental Health of Children, Washington, D.C., from 1967 to 1968. From 1969 to 1970, he was a consultant with the Hispanic American Development Corp., Austin, Tex., and Washington, D.C.

From 1971 to 1975, he held several posts at the University of New Mexico, serving last as associate director of the Institute for Social Research and Development and assistant professor of sociology. Since 1975 he has been deputy State planning officer for the State of New Mexico.

Community Services Administration

Nomination of John B. Gabusi To Be an Assistant Director.   July 15, 1977

The President today announced that he will nominate John B. Gabusi, of Tucson, Ariz., to be an Assistant Director (Management) of the Community Services Administration.

Mr. Gabusi was born February 3, 1941, in Florence, Ariz. He received his B.A. in history and political science from the University of Arizona in 1962, and an LL.B. from the University of Arizona in 1965.

From 1966 to 1968, he was director of Survey Research Associates, Tucson, Ariz. From 1969 to 1975, he was special assistant to Congressman Morris K. Udall, serving simultaneously during 1969–72 as staff director of the House Subcommittee on Postal Service.

He later was director of field operations for Energy Action, a public-interest organization, leaving in March 1976 to become national campaign director of the Udall '76 campaign. He resumed his position as special assistant to Congressman Udall in July 1976.

Community Services Administration

Nomination of Robert N. Smith To Be an Assistant Director.   July 15, 1977

The President today announced that he will nominate Robert N. Smith, of Bloomfield Hills, Mich., to be an Assistant Director (Office of Community Action) of the Community Services Administration.

Smith was born July 13, 1944, in Detroit, Mich. He received a B.A. in 1967 from the University of Michigan and a J.D. in 1970 from the University of Michigan Law School.

In 1970 he was the Midwestern field director for the Movement for a New Congress. From 1971 to 1974, Smith served as an attorney-advisor for the Federal Communications Commission. He was employed by the Democratic National Committee from 1974 to last January, holding several positions, the last as national coordinator for voter registration. Since January, he has served on the White House staff in the office of Joe Aragon, Special Assistant to the President.

Downing of U.S. Army Helicopter on Korean Peninsula

Statement by the White House Press Secretary.   July 16, 1977

I called the President that we were informed shortly after 7:30 a.m. that the bodies and survivor had been returned. I called the President immediately. The President welcomed the release of the survivor and return of the bodies; however, he deplored the loss of life and the excessive reaction to an unarmed and inadvertent intrusion.

He and Mrs. Carter again expressed their sympathy and condolences to the families of those who died.

NOTE: The statement was made available by the White House Press Office. It was not issued in the form of a White House press release.

Digest of Other White House Announcements

The following listing includes the President's daily schedule and other items of general interest as announced by the White House Press Office during the period covered by this issue. Events and announcements printed elsewhere in the issue are not included.

July 9

The President met at the White House with Zbigniew Brzezinski, Assistant to the President for National Security Affairs.

July 11

The President met at the White House with:
—Dr. Brzezinski;
—senior White House staff members;
—the Cabinet;
—Larry B. Sheafe, Special Agent of the Presidential Protective Division, U.S. Secret Service, who is being reassigned;
—Vice President Walter F. Mondale;
—Paul C. Warnke, Director of the United States Arms Control and Disarmament Agency, who reported on his recent trip to Moscow for discussions of the demilitarization of the Indian Ocean;

—a group of administration officials, to discuss proposals for reorganization of the Executive Office of the President;

—Senator and Mrs. Ernest F. Hollings, of South Carolina, and Senator and Mrs. Dale Bumpers, of Arkansas, for dinner.

The President transmitted to the Congress the Annual Report of the National Endowment for the Arts and the National Council on the Arts for the Fiscal Year ended June 30, 1976, and for the Transition Quarter ended September 30, 1976, and the Eleventh Annual Report on the Status of the National Wilderness Preservation System for calendar year 1974.

The White House announced that the President has invited President Julius Nyerere of the United Republic of Tanzania to make a state visit to the United States. President Nyerere will be in Washington August 4 and 5.

The President has appointed John G. Heimann, Comptroller of the Currency, as a member of the Board of Directors of the Federal National Mortgage Association.

July 12

The President met at the White House with:

—Dr. Brzezinski;

—the Democratic congressional leadership;

—members of the Privacy Protection Study Commission, who presented their report on a 2-year study of the impact of record-keeping relationships on individuals;

—a group of approximately 60 Republican Members of the House of Representatives from Eastern States;

—Dr. Brzezinski and Adm. Stansfield Turner, Director of Central Intelligence;

—Kenneth M. Curtis, chairman, and Paul Sullivan, executive director, Democratic National Committee;

—A. D. Frazier, Jr., Project Manager of the Executive Office of the President Reorganization Study Group.

The White House announced that at the invitation of the President, Prime Minister Giulio Andreotti of Italy will pay a 2-day official visit to Washington on July 26 and 27.

July 13

The President met at the White House with:

—Dr. Brzezinski;

—Representative Carroll Hubbard, Jr., of Kentucky;

—Gov. Brendan T. Byrne, of New Jersey, and his family;

—Senator and Mrs. Walter Huddleston and Mr. and Mrs. William E. Schmidt and their son, Larry, of Elizabethtown, Ky.;

—William Lucas, sheriff of Wayne County, Mich., who is under consideration for the position of FBI Director;

—Senator Mike Gravel, of Alaska, who presented a report on the Panama Canal which was written for the Senate Environment and Public Works Committee;

—Mr. and Mrs. Manuel Silva, of Reedley, Calif.

July 14

The President met at the White House with:

—Dr. Brzezinski;

—Vice President Mondale, Frank B. Moore, Assistant to the President for Congressional Liaison, and a group of seven Democratic Senators;

—Chancellor Helmut Schmidt of the Federal Republic of Germany;

—William Shannon, United States Ambassador to Ireland;

—W. Averell Harriman;

—Secretary of the Treasury W. Michael Blumenthal, Charles L. Schultze, Chairman of the Council of Economic Advisers, Bert Lance, Director of the Office of Management and Budget, and Stuart E. Eizenstat, Assistant to the President for Domestic Affairs and Policy;

—Secretary of Defense Harold Brown;

—Representative Shirley Chisholm, of New York;

—John Van de Kamp, who is under consideration for the position of FBI Director;

—a group of administration officials, to discuss Federal Regional Councils;

—Secretary of Agriculture Bob S. Bergland.

July 15

The President met at the White House with:

—Vice President Mondale, Secretary of State Cyrus Vance, and Dr. Brzezinski;

—Senator Mark O. Hatfield, of Oregon;

—members of the House Select Committee on Aging;

—Dr. Schultze;

—Judge William B. Gunter, the President's Special Representative to coordinate negotiations on the Indian claims matter in the State of Maine, who presented his recommendations on the issue, A. Stephens Clay, the judge's law partner, and Robert J. Lipshutz, Counsel to the President;

—Mrs. Carter, for lunch;

—a group of editors, publishers, and broadcasters;

—His Beatitude Elias IV, patriarch of the Antiochian Orthodox Church;

—Judge John Irwin, who is under consideration for the position of FBI Director;

—a group of administration officials, to discuss tax reform.

The White House made available the text of a letter sent to Senator Daniel K. Inouye, Chairman of the Select Committee on Intelligence, by Adm. Stansfield Turner, Director of the Central Intelligence Agency, at the President's direction. The letter reported on documents relating to drug experimentation activities of the CIA, which had been investigated by the committee in 1975.

The President left the White House for a weekend stay at Camp David, Md.

CHECKLIST OF WHITE HOUSE PRESS RELEASES

The following releases of the Office of the White House Press Secretary, distributed during the period covered by this issue, are not included in the issue.

Released July 8, 1977

Announcement: summary of issues for discussion at the energy conference with the Governors

Released July 9, 1977

News conference: on the energy conference with the Governors—by James R. Schlesinger, Assistant to the President, Gov. Reubin Askew, of Florida, and Gov. Julian Carroll, of Kentucky

Released July 15, 1977

Text: recommendations to the President concerning Indian land claims in the State of Maine

News conference: on his recommendations to the President concerning Indian land claims in the State of Maine—by William B. Gunter, the President's Special Representative for the negotiations

Fact sheet: on Reorganization Plan No. 1 of 1977 (Executive Office of the President)

News conference: on Reorganization Plan No. 1 of 1977 (Executive Office of the President)—by Bert Lance, Director, Harrison Wellford, Executive Associate Director for Reorganization and Management, Office of Management and Budget, and A. D. Frazier, Jr., Project Manager of the Executive

CHECKLIST OF WHITE HOUSE
PRESS RELEASES—Continued

Released July 15, 1977—Continued

Office of the President Reorganization Study Group

Announcement: nomination of William H. Shaheen to be United States Attorney for the District of New Hampshire, Edward F. Harrington to be United States Attorney for the District of Massachusetts, William G. Gray to be United States Attorney for the District of Vermont, Hubert H. Bryant to be United States Attorney for the Northern District of Oklahoma, Earle B. McLaughlin to be United States Marshal for the District of Vermont, William J. Evins, Jr., to be United States Marshal for the Middle District of Tennessee, and Wesley D. Lane to be United States Marshal for the District of Minnesota

---

NOMINATIONS SUBMITTED
TO THE SENATE

The following list does not include promotions of members of the Uniformed Services, nominations to the Service Academies, or nominations of Foreign Service officers.

Submitted July 11, 1977

RAY V. FITZGERALD, of South Dakota, to be a member of the Board of Directors of the Commodity Credit Corporation, vice Kenneth E. Frick, resigned.

J. ALBERT JONES, of Kentucky, to be United States Attorney for the Western District of Kentucky for the term of 4 years, vice George J. Long.

DONALD L. BECKNER, of Louisiana, to be United States Attorney for the Middle District of Louisiana for the term of 4 years, vice Douglas M. Gonzales, resigned.

JOHN H. HANNAH, JR., of Texas, to be United States Attorney for the Eastern District of Texas for the term of 4 years, vice A. Roby Hadden.

JOSE ANTONIO CANALES, of Texas, to be United States Attorney for the Southern District of Texas for the term of 4 years, vice Edward B. McDonough, Jr., resigning.

BENNIE A. MARTINEZ, of New Mexico, to be United States Marshal for the District of New Mexico for the term of 4 years, vice Doroteo R. Baca.

NOMINATIONS SUBMITTED
TO THE SENATE—Continued

Submitted July 11, 1977—Continued

THEDDIS R. CONEY, of Texas, to be United States Marshal for the Southern District of Texas for the term of 4 years, vice Marshall F. Rousseau, resigned.

Submitted July 12, 1977

JEAN M. WILKOWSKI, of Florida, a Foreign Service officer of Class one, for the rank of Ambassador while serving as Coordinator of United States Preparations for the United Nations Conference on Science and Technology for Development.

Submitted July 13, 1977

JOHN ROBERT LEWIS, of Georgia, to be an Associate Director of the ACTION Agency, vice Ronald E. Gerevas, resigned.

MARY FRANCIS CAHILL LEYLAND, of New York, to be an Assistant Director of the ACTION Agency, vice Willard H. Meinecke.

IRENE TINKER, of Maryland, to be an Assistant Director of the ACTION Agency, vice Harry J. Hogan, resigned.

FORREST J. GERARD, of Maryland, to be an Assistant Secretary of the Interior, vice Albert C. Zapanta, resigned.

EARL OLIVER, of Illinois, to be a member of the Railroad Retirement Board for the remainder of the term expiring August 28, 1978, vice Wythe D. Quarles, Jr., resigned.

PETER AMORY BRADFORD, of Maine, to be a member of the Nuclear Regulatory Commission for a term expiring June 30, 1982, vice Marcus A. Rowden, term expired.

Submitted July 14, 1977

HAZEL R. ROLLINS, of the District of Columbia, to be an Assistant Administrator of the Federal Energy Administration, vice Samuel J. Tuthill, resigned.

Submitted July 15, 1977

ALLARD KENNETH LOWENSTEIN, of New York, to be the Alternate Representative of the United States of America for Special Political Affairs in the United Nations, with the rank of Ambassador.

SARAH WEDDINGTON, of Texas, to be General Counsel of the Department of Agriculture, vice James D. Keast, resigned.

PATRICIA ALBJERG GRAHAM, of Massachusetts, to be Director of the National Institute of Education, vice Harold L. Hodgkinson, resigned.

NOMINATIONS SUBMITTED
TO THE SENATE—Continued

Submitted July 15, 1977—Continued

JOHN B. GABUSI, of Arizona, to be an Assistant Director of the Community Services Administration (new position).

ROBERT STERN LANDMANN, of New Mexico, to be an Assistant Director of the Community Services Administration (new position).

ROBERT NATHANIEL SMITH, of Michigan, to be an Assistant Director of the Community Services Administration (new position).

ACTS APPROVED BY
THE PRESIDENT

Approved July 11, 1977

H.J. Res. 539_____Public Law 95–64
A joint resolution to amend the statute of limitations provisions in section 2415 of title 28, United States Code, relating to claims by the United States on behalf of Indians.

H.R. 6668_____Public Law 95–65
An act to amend the Age Discrimination Act of 1975 to extend the date upon which the United States Commission on Civil Rights is required to file its report under such Act, and for other purposes.

S. 964_____Public Law 95–66
An act to provide that the salaries of certain positions and individuals which were increased as a result of the operation of the Federal Salary Act of 1967 shall not be increased by the first comparability pay adjustment occurring after the date of the enactment of this Act.

PRESIDENTIAL DOCUMENTS

Week Ending Friday, July 22, 1977

Interview With the President

Remarks and a Question-and-Answer Session With a Group of Editors and News Directors. July 15, 1977

THE PRESIDENT. I didn't get a chance to finish my lunch. I hope you have a chance to do it. [*Laughter*]

I don't know what Jody was talking to you about, but I'd like to maybe take about 3 or 4 minutes to outline some of the things that face us at this moment, on a topical basis, and then spend the time we have available answering your questions.

ADMINISTRATION POLICIES

We've just finished a superb meeting, I thought, with Chancellor Helmut Schmidt from Germany. Prior to that, we had a very good meeting with President Perez from Venezuela. On Tuesday, Prime Minister Begin will be here from Israel, and following that, we'll have Prime Minister Andreotti from Italy and, following that, President Nyerere from Tanzania.

This is a series of meetings that we've been conducting throughout the whole year, and I think it's given me a good chance to learn about foreign opinions, to re-cement our ties with nations who are naturally our allies and friends, as are those that I've mentioned to you this moment.

We also deeply are involved in the congressional appropriations legislation at this point. We have proposed to the Congress a comprehensive energy package, which was long overdue, and we've been very pleased so far with the action taken by both the Commerce Committee and the Ways and Means Committee. There's an ad hoc committee that's been set up to deal just with energy, and they will take over shortly that responsibility.

We hope that the House will finish with the entire energy package prior to the mandatory recess period that will begin on August 6. The Senate is now working on the energy package in a preliminary way, and they'll receive the legislation from the House before the summer work period.

We've done a lot of work on a comprehensive welfare reform proposal that we expect to go to the Congress, I'd say, well within the next month. And before they adjourn this year, we'll have a comprehensive tax reform proposal presented to them.

The Congress has moved very strongly on the major items that we put forward before the Inauguration—comprehensive ethics legislation, the authority for me to reorganize the Government, the evolution of a new Department of Energy, and so forth. We're very pleased with that relationship.

I have had some major disagreements with the Congress. One is to try to put at least a partial quietus on what I consider to be an unwarranted expenditure of moneys for water projects and the liquid metal fast breeder reactor production model at Clinch River, and so forth. We're trying to work that out to my satisfaction.

This year is one when we've addressed many problems that had been delayed for decades. I hope we can make progress in some of the international affairs that we face. We've got, I think, a very encouraging relationship with the Soviet Union in spite of the fact that some of the items are so controversial. But as I said at my last news conference, we are raising issues jointly with them which have not been addressed so substantively in the past.

We are working toward a comprehensive test ban treaty to prohibit the testing of all nuclear explosives, both military and peaceful. We now have no constraint on peaceful nuclear devices for underground explosions, and we have a 150-kiloton limit on military weapons. So this is quite a liberal restraint.

We've also put forward, as you know, the hope that we might begin demilitarizing the Indian Ocean, freezing our present level of deployment there, which is quite modest on both sides, and working on prior notification of missile test launchings, a prohibition against an attack of observation satellites by either country.

We've made two basic optional proposals to the Soviets on SALT talks. One is to ratify those items that were definitely agreed upon between Kissinger, Ford, and Brezhnev, and a much more deep series of cuts in nuclear weapon launchers and MIRV'd missiles, with a freeze on further deployment of the development of more advanced technology weapons.

We are trying to move, and we are working with the Soviet leaders. And al-

though we haven't been successful in these efforts yet, there are study groups working, and I think the tone of their own relationship is good within the study groups themselves. There have been some polemical discussions on their part, particularly about the absence of progress, but I think this is just a difference of interpretation.

I don't want to take up any more time. I would rather answer your questions about specific items, and I'll start——

QUESTIONS

MANDATORY RETIREMENT

Q. President Carter, I'm Linda Glazer from Saratoga Springs. How do you feel about efforts in Congress to abolish the mandatory 65 age requirement?

THE PRESIDENT. I think it's a good principle to evolve. There are still some details in the legislation that have to be worked out, with the rapidity with which the Federal laws have changed, the degree of interference of the Federal Government in private industrial, manufacturing, and professional agreements that involve long-standing terms between the employees and employers.

We have not yet done an adequate assessment of the impact on the Nation's economy. But, in general, I favor the relaxation of mandatory retirement laws. I think the first step would obviously relate to the Federal Government. But we've got superb people working in the Federal Government now on an exceptional extension—which I am authorized to pursue along with the Cabinet officers, themselves—which I think vividly demonstrates that when they reach 65, they still have a lot of production years ahead of them.

HOSPITAL COST CONTAINMENT BILL

Q. Mr. President, hospital costs containment bill—I'm aware of a proposal by the Community Hospital Association which would, in effect, self-regulate itself, limit capital expenditures and freeze employee ratios for a 2-year period to study the long-range aspects. And they approached Representative Rostenkowski and were told that his mind's made up, doesn't want to hear anything else about it.

Is your cost containment bill pretty much—are you very firm on this, or are we open to other suggestions for more long-range planning so that we can talk about freezing or controlling other costs to hospital suppliers; namely, doctors, others, other medical suppliers to the hospitals rather than just putting a freeze on the hospitals?

THE PRESIDENT. I think our mind is pretty well made up, except within the bounds of the congressional deliberations when I presume that adequate opportunity is given those who want to testify to do so. But I would not be willing to accept a 12-month or a 24-month or a 36-month study before we come back and make a recommendation to Congress.

We are faced now with an almost impossible proposition of having the cost of hospital care double every 5 years. And until we get some sort of constraint on hospital cost increases, I don't think there's any hope that we'll ever have a better health system for the money that is available. As you know, the cost of hospital care has gone up exorbitantly, in my opinion, compared to other inflationary costs.

So, to summarize, I would not be in favor of any delay other than that that would be part of the normal congressional process.

Q. Let me follow that up just a second. Has any thought been put to controlling other suppliers to the hospitals, such as doctors' fees, their regular, normal supplies that they have? As I understand it, under the cost containment bill, these costs are not frozen or limited to a 90-percent increase—or are they? Are they taken into account?

THE PRESIDENT. No. I think adjustments in wages have at least a partial exemption, and, of course, the fees that doctors charge to patients is not included in the hospital cost containment legislation. But we are pursuing independently of the cost containment bills some attempts to constrain the unnecessary purchase of very expensive machinery and equipment, where several hospitals in one area will spend an enormous amount of money on duplicative equipment which has got to be paid for.

I served 14 years on a hospital authority at home—and my mother is a registered nurse—and my uncle before me, my brother after me. And we've been able to see firsthand that many of the increases in hospital costs can be reduced without any deterioration, in my opinion, on the quality of the care given to the patients.

But I think this is just a first step in a move toward more preventive care, a heavier emphasis on outpatient care, without having to have the patient admitted to the hospital to receive treatment and insurance payments, and some constraint on expenditures for the very expensive equipment, and, also, increasing use of paramedical personnel. But this is a very complicated overall subject. This is the first of many steps.

UNEMPLOYMENT

Q. I am Chester Washington from Los Angeles. On the job picture, the National Urban League has just reported a dramatic increase in the unemployment of black citizens, and they say now it's down to the level during the recession period of the fourth quarter of 1975 and that the unemployment ratio among black youths is up to 58 percent.

I know money is being funneled into the city to help alleviate these problems, but is there anything else, any other areas where that problem may be helped?

THE PRESIDENT. I've never seen any statistics that equaled those. I wouldn't dispute them, because statistics can be used to prove a point. So far, since I've been in office, and I don't claim credit for it, the unemployment rate on a nationwide basis has decreased one full percent, which was the goal that we set for ourselves for the entire year—to get it down to a 7-percent level. It was 8.1 percent in December of 1976.

We've got, in addition to that, about a $21 billion stimulus package, a major portion of which is oriented toward employment with the Comprehensive Education and Training Act, public works jobs, and so forth. In addition, we've got 273,000 jobs for young people that would be included partially in those——

Q. What was that number again?

THE PRESIDENT. 273,000, I think; some of them in our National Park System, and so forth. Some of that is in the CETA programs.

In addition, we've got 1.1 million jobs approved for the summer work program. I think this is the highest level we've ever had. This last month's report on employment showed a slight increase, about 1½ points. But heads of families improve their percentage of employment. I think the increase in unemployment was primarily among housewives, women who were partial employees. And since last November, there've been 3 million new jobs provided in our country on a net basis. We've got 3 million more people working today than were working last November. In the last month alone, we increased 270,000 jobs in spite of a slight increase in unemployment percentage.

But we are deeply concerned about young persons' employment, particularly in minority groups. When we met in London at the summit conference, I would say the number one issue that we discussed among all seven heads of nations was youth unemployment. And we are trying to cooperate with our allies and friends who were there to deal with that particular subject. But I have never seen any sort of statistic as high as the one you've quoted. I wouldn't argue with it.

GOVERNMENT REORGANIZATION

Q. Mr. President, I understand that perhaps part of this program or meeting today, sir, is to get feedback, also. Of course, I don't think it's anything new to you, but I think one of the new—one of the prime concerns among the people in our area is that of the waste in Government, the seeming irresponsibility of Congress, and the unresponsiveness of the bureaucracy; a feeling of desperation that nothing can be done and feeling overwhelmed by it.

I put this in the context of requesting, sir, to know a little bit of what's going on in the area of reform, internally.

THE PRESIDENT. This afternoon, I'll present my first proposal to the public on reorganization. We started with the most difficult one of all, as far as I am concerned, and that is cutting down the Executive Office of the President. It's difficult because of the personalities involved; they're so close to me. It is also difficult because here is a repository of many special programs that Congress had established where closeness to the President himself would permit them to span across several departments as they made decisions. It's a very controversial subject.

We, I think, have done a good job in this respect. We have a series of reorganization studies that will proceed from this that have already been revealed. We have a 3-year authorization from the Congress to complete the reorganization effort before the bill, the legislation expires. This gives me almost unlimited authority to propose to the Congress modifications in existing structures. And when we want to form a new department—for instance, we're pulling together more than a dozen different departments into the Department of Energy—that has to be done with separate legislation because it requires an affirmative vote of both Houses of the Congress.

As you know, with the reorganization authority I can make modifications as I see fit, and they go into effect unless the Congress vetoes it, by a much easier process.

In addition, we're cutting down on paperwork. I was just notified Monday morning by the Secretary of Labor, Ray Marshall, that the number of forms that are used by OSHA, for instance, would be reduced 50 percent and that the remaining forms required would be greatly simplified. This touches 1½ million businesses in the United States. We are trying the same thing on all the other departments. We, in addition, are trying to simplify reports required and eliminate as many as we can.

And we have put a limit on the number of personnel who will be working in the Federal Government. My goal is that at the end of the following fiscal year, in October, on October 1 of 1978, that we would have no more employees in the Federal Government than we had in October of 1976. We are being very strict about that. This is in spite of the fact that many new programs are being as-sumed; that it is inevitable in any government.

So, we're doing the best we can in this early stage to bring about some restoration of confidence in the governmental process, and I enjoy it. It's a part of my experience and responsibilities as President that appeals to me. I think you will be pleased when you see the report this afternoon on the Executive Office of the President and the subsequent reports. But I don't think it's hopeless at all.

TOBACCO PRICE SUPPORTS

Q. Mr. President, the Surgeon General has ruled that cigarette smoking can kill you, and the Federal Government stepped in and told people they can't advertise—[*inaudible*]. I am from North Carolina. [*Laughter*] My question is this: How then can the Federal Government continue to give price supports to tobacco farmers? Is there any situation that you can envision where those supports will stop?

THE PRESIDENT. Well, only if the Congress votes that they would stop. I think that this is one of the most difficult philosophical questions to rationalize that I can think of.

We have, obviously, other conflicts; one that I addressed in my last press conference was on the abortion issue. Although I am strongly opposed to the concept of abortion on a morality basis, women insist on having the right to make their own decisions about their own body. The Supreme Court has ruled they can do this under limited circumstances. And then the next question is, should the Federal Government finance abortions? I don't think the Federal Government should.

The same thing applies to cigarette smoking. The Federal Government, long before I got here, decided it was a danger to one's health and put a warning notice on the cigarette packages and put constraints on advertising. The American people, in spite of that, still prefer to go ahead and smoke. I don't happen to smoke myself, but I don't condemn others who do.

But there's no way to rationalize inherent conflicts of that kind. I don't see any likelihood, though, that the Congress is going to eliminate the price supports on tobacco any time in the foreseeable future.

One of the things, as you know, is about sweeteners, artificial sweeteners now. It may be that the Congress will decide to put a warning on the diet soft drinks rather than completely prohibiting the use of saccharin. The present law, though, requires that saccharin be taken off the market altogether if it proves to be a danger to your health.

This is a difficult thing to rationalize. How much does the Government move in and constrain Americans' habits in that respect? This is not anything new, as you know. I'm reminding you of things that I'm sure you know.

I think the 18th amendment to the Constitution prohibited the sale of alcohol, which is obviously dangerous to one's health—if used in excess, at least—and after the trial period, that was repealed because the American people didn't accept that constraint on their lives. And now all the States and the Federal Government accept taxes from the sale of alcoholic beverages.

I would put the tobacco in the same category, roughly, with that where the American people demand the use of the product and the Federal Government tries to stabilize, tax, and modify, in the most beneficial way, the production and distribution of that product.

Q. Mr. President——

THE PRESIDENT. You go ahead. I'll get you next.

HUMAN RIGHTS

Q. If you had it to do all over again, would you find a different way to raise the human rights issue with the Soviet Union?

THE PRESIDENT. I can't think of any different way to do it. I've thought about that a lot, because it certainly was not done to aggravate any other government nor to single out any country.

Every time I've ever made a statement about human rights, I think without exception I have always included our country in as a people who are constantly searching for ways to alleviate or to reduce discrimination practices and to insure that our high standards for human rights would be realized.

So, I don't think I would do it any differently. To me, this is an integral part of the consciousness and commitment of America. It's another step forward in the realization of the goals and aspirations that we established 200 years ago.

We are not trying to send in troops to make other nations conform to us, we are not trying to punish anyone else. But I think there has to be some means in a democracy like ours, first of all, for a President to exemplify or to personify what the American people believe. And my opinion is that the American people believe very deeply in the concept of human rights.

I think it's important that this commitment be expressed publicly. We've been through some sordid and embarrassing years recently with Vietnam and Cambodia and Watergate and the CIA revelations, and I felt like it was time for our country to hold a beacon light of something that was pure and decent and right and proper that would rally our citizens to a cause. But I've been cautious not to single anyone out for condemnation.

And I might say that my own attitude on the human rights question has been fairly moderate. I'm proud of it. But I think it's accurate to say that some Members of Congress would go much further than I and even terminate all relationships with other countries who don't measure up to our standards of human rights. We can't do that.

So, I think a slow, careful, methodical but persistent expression of our concern about human rights violations has already been effective and will continue to be effective in the future. I don't believe there is a single leader of a nation in the world now who doesn't have at least in his or her consciousness the concept of human rights and how that country is measuring up to the expectations of one's own people or trying to avoid worldwide condemnation. So, I think our efforts have had an impact, and I would not do it otherwise.

Mr. POWELL. Mr. President, one more question.

Q. Mr. President?

THE PRESIDENT. I think I promised you.

ECONOMIC DEVELOPMENT AND GROWTH

Q. Thank you. This morning we had a presentation from Mr. Warren on the subject of environment and energy conservation, and the entire thrust of his presentation was conservation efforts.

There was no discussion and I'd like, if you could address yourself to this fundamental question, as to whether or not the administration is prepared to do or suggest anything to limit growth as a fundamental effort to deal with the environmental and energy questions confronting the country?

THE PRESIDENT. That's a concept that is partially my responsibility, yes. When we put forward the energy proposal to establish a policy for our country, one of

the presumptions was that we would continue to grow economically.

Our goal is to have, roughly, about a 5 percent per year growth in our own economy to sustain the needs of the rest of the world and also to keep our people employed.

We set as a goal for ourselves on energy consumption, however, an annual growth of about 2 percent.

We think the difference there might be achievable because of the efficiency and elimination of waste. For a given standard of living now, we use about twice as much energy as other peoples, like Germany, Sweden, Japan, who have an equivalent standard of living.

I think there's a historical trend that is almost inevitable that I detect and have to recognize; and that is, that we're shifting more and more toward having economic growth based on a higher quality of life, which means an increasing foundation of things like better health care, better education, more recreation, and not the long, tedious hours of labor that went into the production of goods.

So, I think that in general a shift towards service employment is a good part of the increase in the economic strength of our country.

This can be done with efficiency, compared to what we have been doing in the past, and without further deterioration in the quality of our environment. There again, without belaboring the point, just the expenditures on the protection of our environment, air pollution control, water pollution control, the handling of waste products, the protection of the purity of the oceans, for instance, those kind of things are expenditures which give us a better life, which don't waste our natural resources but preserve them and, at the same time, give us economic growth because of the expenditure that goes into production and effectuation of those efforts.

So, with proper understanding and constraints, I think that our economic growth can continue at a moderate and steady pace, give us at the same time an opportunity for full employment and a better quality of life and the elimination of waste of valuable raw materials and natural resources.

Compared to other countries, that growth is modest. I think the Germans are striving this year for 4½-percent growth. We'll probably have a good bit higher than that, maybe 5½-percent growth overall.

The Japanese are looking for about a 6½-percent growth rate this year. Other countries, a good bit lower.

But my goal is to maintain a rate of growth as I've just described.

Let me say in closing that I hope you've had a chance, while you're here, to get to know some of the members of the White House staff. We don't claim to know all the answers, you know. We're learning. I have never had a chance to serve in the Federal Government before, except when I was in the Navy. I have benefited from a sense of support and good will and, I'd say, counsel and constructive criticism since I've been in office.

We have done the best we could to stay in touch with people back home. We've made fairly frequent trips out through the country. I have made one trip overseas.

Later on, in just a few days, I will go down to Charleston, South Carolina, then over to Yazoo City, Mississippi, then on down to the coast of Louisiana.

We've instituted and maintained and will maintain an open press conference format every 2 weeks, which was predicted to be a failure, I think, by some, but which I think has proven to be good. And your coming here is an innovation that has meant an awful lot to us.

So, we would welcome your constant inquiries and your constant advice, and I know we'll get your criticisms when we deserve it in your opinion, whether I ask for it or not.

I've enjoyed being President so far and recognize that I still have a lot to learn.

Q. May I make one comment? I usually start with the taxicab driver. So I said, "How do you like President Carter?"

He said, "Well, he's brought back faith in the future to our people."

THE PRESIDENT. That's a good way to close.

I'll have to recognize you.

WATER PROJECTS

Q. May I ask one question about your water projects? My newspaper, the News Courier, in Charleston, where you'll be in a few days, has supported you on the water project issue with particular reference to the Russell dam and lake. Congress has given you a hard time, and some of the Congressmen have given me a hard time, too.

How do you feel about your success so far in this, and will you continue to press this issue with Congress?

THE PRESIDENT. Yes. I will continue to press this issue. We've made a tremendous amount of progress this first year. The Congress—the Senate, at least, has already agreed to eliminate about half the water projects. We've cut back severely on those that will be continued; they've eliminated all new starts for this year.

If we're not completely successful with this appropriation bill, then I will pursue this issue as long as I am in the White House.

I've really got to go. I appreciate it very much.

NOTE: The interview began at 1 p.m. in the Cabinet Room at the White House.

The transcript of the interview was released on July 16.

Labor Law Reform

*Message to the Congress Transmitting
Proposed Legislation. July 18, 1977*

To the Congress of the United States:

I am transmitting to Congress proposals to make the laws which govern labor-management relations work more efficiently, quickly and equitably.

I have pledged to make Federal regulatory agencies more responsive to the people they serve. Government regulation only works well if it is fair, prompt and predictable. Too often this has not been the case with the regulatory process that governs collective bargaining and labor-management relations. Our labor laws guarantee employees the right to choose freely their representatives, and to bargain collectively with employers over wages, fringe benefits and working conditions. But legal rights have limited value if many years are required to enforce them.

The National Labor Relations Board (NLRB) administers our labor laws. In recent years there has been growing agreement that those laws should be amended to ensure that the Board can function more effectively to protect employees rights. While the great majority of employers and unions have abided by the labor laws, a few have unfairly abused the procedures and practices under which the Board must operate.

As a result, the American Bar Association, many Federal courts, and the NLRB's own Task Force each recently suggested ways to improve the Board's procedures. The NLRB's internal report, which proposed a number of administrative changes, has already produced some beneficial changes. But it seems clear that legislation is actually needed to enable the Board to administer the labor laws properly.

Unnecessary delays are the most serious problem. In even the simpler cases, the NLRB typically takes almost two months to hold an election to determine whether workers want union representation. The enforcement of Board decisions is also subject to unnecessary delay: lengthy proceedings before the Board and extended litigation can sometimes delay final action for years.

The problem of delay has been compounded by the weakness of the Board's remedies. One of the reasons the regulatory process has worked so slowly is that a few employers have learned that, because of the problems the Board has in enforcing its decisions, delay can be less costly than initial compliance with the law. In one case, for instance, workers who were illegally fired for their union activities in 1962 are still awaiting payment for lost wages.

Because of these problems, workers are often denied a fair chance to decide, in an NLRB election, whether they want union representation. The same problems often deny employers the predictability they too need from the labor laws.

To help reduce the problems of delay, and to cure a number of related problems with our labor laws, I am today recommending to the Congress a set of reforms for the National Labor Relations Act. These reforms are designed to accomplish three important goals:

—To make the NLRB procedures fairer, prompter, and more predictable.

—To protect the rights of labor and management by strengthening NLRB sanctions against those who break the law.

—To preserve the integrity of the Federal contracting process by withholding federal contracts from firms that willfully violate orders from the NLRB and the courts.

I believe these goals can be met through the following changes in our labor laws:

• An election on union representation should be held within a fixed, brief period of time after a request for an election is filed with the Board. This period should be as short as is administratively feasible. The Board, however, should be allowed some additional time to deal with complex cases.

• The Board should be instructed to establish clear rules defining appropriate bargaining units. This change would not only help to streamline the time-consuming, case-by-case procedures now in effect, but would also allow labor and management to rely more fully on individual Board decisions.

• The Board should be expanded from five to seven members. This change would enable the NLRB to handle better its increasing caseload.

• The Board should establish procedures that would allow two members of the Board to affirm summarily the less complex decision of its administrative law judges. Similar procedures have already been adopted by the Federal courts of appeal.

• All appeals of Board decisions should be required to be filed within 30 days of the Board's decision. If no appeal is filed, the Board should refer its orders to the courts for enforcement without further delay. This procedure is similar to that used by such other Federal regulatory agencies as the Federal Trade Commission.

• When employers are found to have refused to bargain for a first contract, the Board should be able to order them to compensate workers for the wages that were lost during the period of unfair de-

lay. This compensation should be based on a fixed standard, such as the Quarterly Report of Major Collective Bargaining Settlements published by the Bureau of Labor Statistics (BLS). Workers would be entitled to the difference between the wages actually received during the delay and those which would have been received had their wages increased at the average rate for settlements reported during that period, as recorded in the BLS index.

• The Board should be authorized to award double back-pay without mitigation to workers who were illegally discharged before the initial contract. This flat-rate formula would simplify the present time-consuming back-pay process and would more fully compensate employees for the real cost of a lost job.

• The Board should be authorized to prohibit a firm from obtaining Federal contracts for a period of three years, if the firm is found to have willfully and repeatedly violated NLRB orders. Such a debarment should be limited to cases of serious violations and should not affect existing contracts. This restriction could be lifted under two conditions: if the Secretary of Labor determines that debarment is not in the national interest, or if the affected Federal agency determines that no other supplier is available.

• Under current law, the Board is only required to seek a preliminary injunction against a few types of serious union unfair labor practices, such as secondary boycotts or "hot cargo" agreements. The Board should also be required to seek preliminary injunctions against certain unfair labor practices which interfere seriously with employee rights, such as unlawful discharges.

There are related problems that should also be reviewed by the Congress in this effort to ensure that our labor laws fulfill the promise made to employees and employers when the Wagner Act was passed 42 years ago—that working men and women who wish to bargain collectively with their employers, in a way fair to both, shall have a reasonable and prompt chance to do so. In that way, the collective bargaining system, which has served this country well, can be strengthened for the benefit both of American workers and employers.

I have asked the Secretary of Labor to work closely with the Congress in the months ahead to explore these and other possible ways of improving our labor laws.

I ask the Congress to move promptly to pass legislation implementing the reforms I have recommended.

JIMMY CARTER

The White House,
July 18, 1977.

United States-Soviet Union Convention on Migratory Birds

Message to the Senate Transmitting the Convention. July 18, 1977

To the Senate of the United States:

I transmit herewith, for Senate advice and consent to ratification, the Convention between the United States of America and the Union of Soviet Socialist Republics Concerning the Conservation of Migratory Birds and Their Environment, signed at Moscow on November 19, 1976.

In the same manner as other Migratory Bird Conventions which the United States has with Canada, Japan and Mexico, this Convention provides for international cooperation in the protection and preservation of migratory birds. A fundamental function of this Convention is the identification of species of birds which migrate between the United States and the Soviet Union and species of birds which, while not actually migratory between the United States and the Soviet Union, have populations in both States and share common flyways or common breeding, wintering or feeding areas. With respect to these species of birds the Parties undertake certain strict management procedures as well as an ongoing interchange of information regarding the protection of these species.

In addition, as I mentioned in my May 23 Message to Congress on the Environment, this Convention and the legislation which will be submitted to implement it will establish new authority to conserve the habitats necessary to the survival of migratory birds. The Convention contains an undertaking by the Parties to list in an Appendix to the Convention, those Migratory Bird Habitats of special importance within the areas under their jurisdiction and, by mutual agreement, those which are outside the areas under their jurisdiction.

There are many species of birds which will benefit from the provisions of this Convention, which fills a major gap in the protection of the species of migratory birds which exists in the United States. I urge the Senate to act favorably on this Convention at an early date by giving its advice and consent to ratification.

JIMMY CARTER

The White House,
July 18, 1977.

Investigation of Korean CIA Involvement in Congress

Letter to Republican Congressional Leaders on Their Proposal for a Special Prosecutor.   July 18, 1977

To Senator Howard Baker: (To Congressman John Rhodes:)

I have reviewed your letter to me dated June 10, 1977, recommending on behalf of Republican Congressional leaders that a special prosecutor be appointed to investigate allegations of ". . . the Korean Central Intelligence Agency's involvement in domestic American politics." After discussions with Attorney General Bell and others, I have decided that appointment of a special prosecutor would be inappropriate and unwarranted, and would probably impede the investigation.

Your letter does not contain any specific information indicating that the Justice Department cannot conduct this investigation adequately. I assure you that any implication that the investigation has not been thorough and impartial is not well founded. I have been advised by Attorney General Bell that, in accordance with sound investigative procedures, the day-to-day conduct of the investigation is in the hands of experienced prosecutors, joined by career investigators of the F.B.I., the I.R.S. and other agencies. In addition, there continues to be active participation by a Federal Grand Jury, which has been meeting twice a week to hear testimony in this matter.

I am also advised by the Attorney General that the investigation is exceedingly thorough. To date, several hundred persons have been questioned, many repeatedly, and more than fifty witnesses have testified before the Grand Jury. Financial and other records, amounting to many thousands of individual documents, have been obtained, usually by grand jury subpoenas, from more than one hundred different sources. I am told that substantial progress is being made.

Your letter suggests that appointment of a special prosecutor is warranted because the controversy "is developing into a pattern of accusation by innuendo and trial by leak." You do not cite any facts to support the notion that media coverage of the matters under investigation has been based on leaks from the Justice Department.

In fact, I am advised by Judge Bell that many of the specific assertions in the press are entirely incorrect; some are unsupported by, and others are directly contrary to, the evidence and information obtained by the Justice Department.

I also believe there is a serious danger that appointment of a special prosecutor at this time would impede the investigation. The investigation has progressed to the point where potential prosecutions have been identified and, in several cases, the evidence-gathering process is nearly completed. The record thus far encompasses thousands of pages concerning hundreds of separate matters which occurred over a period of more than five years. Substitution of new personnel who would be entirely unfamiliar with this material would bring the investigation to a standstill for a number of months.

Finally, no suggestion has been made that members of the present Administration were in any way involved in the alleged illegal activities so as to raise a possible need for extraordinary measures in this investigation. As you know, the activities in question took place before this Administration took office. Furthermore, they involved individuals from both political parties. Attorney General Bell is advised continuously of the progress of the investigation, which is under the direct supervision of the Assistant Attorney General in charge of the Criminal Division.

I appreciate your concerns in this matter, and thank you for your letter. I am satisfied that the investigation is proceeding in a vigorous and impartial manner, and I therefore have determined that appointment of a special prosecutor is neither warranted nor advisable.

Sincerely,

Jimmy Carter

NOTE: This is the text of identical letters addressed to Representative John J. Rhodes, minority leader of the House of Representatives, and Senator Howard H. Baker, Jr., minority leader of the Senate.

Visit of Prime Minister Menahem Begin of Israel

Remarks of the President and the Prime Minister at the Welcoming Ceremony. July 19, 1977

THE PRESIDENT. This is a very important day in the history of our Nation and, I think, perhaps for the future of the Middle East and perhaps even for the future of the world.

We have with us a very distinguished visitor, Prime Minister Begin and his wife, Aliza. I'm particularly thrilled to have them come here. We've had many distinguished visitors this year, but he's the first one who comes as the head of a nation who is junior to me. All the others have been Presidents or Prime Ministers or Kings much longer. So, I welcome a chance to act as a senior statesman this morning, Prime Minister Begin.

We also have very important questions to discuss between us. We approach these conferences with deep common interests and with a sincerity of purpose that naturally binds us together.

Prime Minister Begin represents a nation which has just demonstrated again the importance of a true democracy where people in an absolutely unconstrained expression of individual preference in open elections can decide who their leader will be.

This has been a great test for Israel, and the orderly transition of authority and responsibility from one political party to another has been carried out not only with peace and cooperation but, I think, with an enhancement of the confidence in the people of Israel in the future.

I think, to me, having read the writings and biography of our distinguished visitor this morning, there's a great parallel between what Israel is, what it stands for, and what Prime Minister Begin is and what he stands for. He's a man who has demonstrated a willingness to suffer for principle, a man who has shown superlative personal courage in the face of trial, challenge, disappointment, but who has ultimately prevailed because of a depth of his commitment and his own personal characteristics. And this is a strong parallel with what his nation has been and is. He's a man of principle and a man of independence, and the nation of Israel is a people of principle and independence.

One of the important personal characteristics about Prime Minister Begin which I admire is his deep and unswerving religious commitments. This has always been a guiding factor in his consciousness and in his pursuit of unswerving goals. There's a quietness about him which goes with determination and a fiery spirit in his expressions of his beliefs to the public. And this is as it should be.

I was particularly impressed that the first official action of his government was to admit into Israel 66 homeless refugees from Vietnam who had been floating around in the oceans of the world, excluded by many nations who are their neighbors, who had been picked up by an Israeli ship and to whom he gave a home. It was an act of compassion, an act of sensitivity, and a recognition of him and his government about the importance of a home for people who are destitute and who would like to express their own individuality and freedom in a common way, again typifying the historic struggle of the people of Israel.

I've been encouraged by his statements that all the points of dispute with his Arab neighbors are negotiable; that this year might be a time of success in the so far frustrated efforts to bring permanent peace and security into the Middle East.

We share that common project. And although there might be differences of perspective and viewpoint between him and me, his nation and the United States, that common goal of finding a path to permanent peace will inevitably bind us together.

We are honored by his presence. We welcome him and his wife as our visitors.

And I would like to close my comments of welcome to him by quoting from Isaiah, from a Bible which he and I both read, given to us by God, whom we both worship. Isaiah said: "And the work of righteousness shall be peace, and the effects of righteousness, quietness and assurance forever."

Thank you very much, and welcome, sir.

[At this point, the Prime Minister responded. His opening remarks were in Hebrew, and the translation follows:]

THE PRIME MINISTER. Mr. President, I have come from the land of Zion and Jerusalem as the spokesman for an ancient people and a young nation. God's blessing on America, the hope of the human race. Peace to your great nation.

[The Prime Minister continued in English.]

Mr. President, I have come to you as the spokesman for an ancient people and a young renascent nation. In our own time these people were strewn into the abyss. It had to extricate itself from the depths of the pits with the last vestige of its strength through an unequaled fight for national self-liberation of the few against the many, of the weak against the strong, of right against might.

This is, Mr. President, the reason why we yearn for peace, pray for peace, and shall do everything humanly possible and make all the possible endeavors to bring about real peace between us and our neighbors. Peace is inseparable from national security.

May I assure you, Mr. President, that to us that concept is no excuse for anything; neither is it a cloak of anything. To us, with the experience of physical annihilation and spiritual redemption, national security may mean the lives of every man, woman, and child in Israel. The lives can be, under certain circumstances, directly threatened and put in jeopardy.

Mr. President, we in Israel see in you not only the fair citizen of your great, mighty country, but also the leader and the defender of the free world.

However, the free world has shrunk, indeed has been shrinking. It can be likened in our time to an island battered by bitter winds, by stormy seas, by high waves. Therefore, all free women and men should stand together to persevere in the struggle for human rights, to preserve human liberty, to make sure "that government of the people, by the people, for the people, shall not perish from the earth."

Mr. President, I am deeply grateful for the heartwarming words you said to me and about me today, which I do not deserve. But your appreciation is very dear to my wife and myself. We thank you.

You mentioned the decision by the Cabinet and myself in Israel to give refuge and haven to the Vietnamese refugees saved by an Israeli boat from the depths of the Pacific Ocean, threatened with drowning and exposure.

It was a natural act to us, Mr. President. We remembered, we have never forgotten that boat with 900 Jews, having left Germany in the last weeks before the Second World War for Cuba. When they reached the Cuban shores, their visas were declared nonvalid, and then they were 9 months at sea, traveling from harbor to harbor, from country to county, crying out for refuge. They were refused.

Eventually they went back to Europe. Some of them saved their lives. The majority of them went to the gas chambers. We have never forgotten the lot of our people, persecuted, humiliated, ultimately physically destroyed. And therefore, it was natural that my first act as Prime Minister was to give those people a haven in the land of Israel.

Mr. President, now we shall have Hebrews speaking Vietnamese in our country.

I share your view that we stand together for human liberty and dignity. And we may have difference of opinion, but we shall never disagree; we may only agree to differ.

Mr. President, my wife and I are deeply grateful to you and Mrs. Carter for the gracious hospitality you have bestowed upon us. We do hope that not in too distant a future we may reciprocate in Jerusalem. The people of Israel will re-

ceive you with an open and warm heart and with the traditional hospitality all of us inherited from old Abraham.

Thank you, Mr. President.

NOTE: The President spoke at 10:35 a.m. on the South Lawn of the White House.

Visit of Prime Minister Begin of Israel

White House Statement Issued Following the First Meeting Between the President and the Prime Minister. July 19, 1977

President Carter and Israeli Prime Minister Menahem Begin met in the Cabinet Room for 2 hours. The meeting was also attended by the Vice President, Secretary of State Cyrus Vance, Assistant to the President for National Security Affairs Zbigniew Brzezinski, Assistant Secretary of State Alfred L. Atherton, Jr., United States Ambassador to Israel Samuel Lewis, and William Quandt of the National Security Council staff on the American side; and Israeli Ambassador to the United States Simcha Dinitz, Advisor to the Prime Minister Shmuel Katz, Minister of the Embassy of Israel Hanan Bar-On, Director of the Prime Minister's Bureau Yechiel Kadishai, Political Advisor to the Prime Minister Eli Mizrachi, Military Secretary to the Prime Minister Brigadier General Ephraim Poran, and Advisor to the Prime Minister Yehuda Avner on the Israeli side.

The President began by repeating his personal pleasure at welcoming Prime Minister Begin to the White House so soon after his taking office last month. The President congratulated Mr. Begin once again on his accession to national leadership and expressed confidence that this first visit will inaugurate the close working relationship natural to the leaders of two democracies with such longstanding and deep ties of friendship. Their talks were conducted in the spirit of mutual respect common to that warm friendship between our two peoples. The President and Prime Minister agreed that their meeting and the others to follow here mark a good starting point for seeking ways toward a just and durable peace in the Middle East. They pledged their determination to achieve that peace, noting that imaginative and responsible statesmanship is essential to overcoming the challenges posed.

The meeting this morning was devoted to a thorough and searching discussion of how to move toward an overall settlement of the Arab-Israeli conflict. The President and Prime Minister each developed their ideas on the issues involved. They agreed that all the issues must be settled through negotiations between the parties based on United Nations Security Council Resolutions 242 and 338 which all the governments directly concerned have accepted. They also agreed that this goal would best be served by moving rapidly toward the reconvening of the Geneva conference this year, keeping in mind at the same time the importance of careful preparation. In this connection, they focused on the practical requirements for convening the conference, looking toward Secretary of State Vance's forthcoming trip to the area for more talks with all the leaders involved. They expressed a hope that the Prime Minister's visit will help lay the groundwork for rapid movement toward negotiations.

In the course of the talk this morning on the diplomacy of peace, the President reaffirmed the enduring American commitment to the security and well-being of Israel. He assured the Prime Minister that any differences that may occur from time to time should not be allowed to obscure America's and his personal dedication to this historic American commitment. He asked the Prime Minister to express to the people of Israel the determination of the people of the United States to help them find true peace. Discussions on how to get negotiations started between the parties will continue this afternoon in the Prime Minister's meeting with Secretary Vance. No bilateral issues were discussed at this first meeting. The President and Prime Minister will meet again tonight at the working dinner which the President is giving at the White House, and in the Cabinet Room again tomorrow morning at 10.

Tennessee Valley Authority

Nomination of S. David Freeman
To Be a Member of the Board of
Directors. July 19, 1977

The President today announced his intention to nominate S. David Freeman of Bethesda, Md., to be a member of the board of directors of the Tennessee Valley Authority.

Freeman was born in Chattanooga, Tenn., on January 14, 1926, and earned a civil engineering degree from Georgia Institute of Technology and a law degree from the University of Tennessee.

From 1949 to 1954, he worked for the Tennessee Valley Authority as an engineer designing steam electric powerplants and hydroelectric stations. After time out for law school, he rejoined TVA in 1956 as an attorney, serving in that capacity for 5 years.

From 1961 to 1965, he was assistant to the Chairman of the Federal Power Commission, and from 1967 to 1971 he served in the President's Office on a Government-wide basis. From 1971 to 1976, Freeman was a special energy and resources consultant to the Senate Commerce Committee, serving also, from 1971 to 1974, as director of the Ford Foundation's Energy Policy Project.

Last year, Freeman worked in the Carter campaign and later in the Carter-Mondale transition. Since January he has been an assistant to Dr. James Schlesinger in the Energy Policy and Planning Office of the Executive Office of the President.

Domestic Assistance Plans

Memorandum for the Heads of Executive Departments and Agencies.   July 19, 1977

Memorandum for the Heads of Executive Departments and Agencies
Subject: Review of Federal Plan Requirements for Domestic Assistance

Planning is a vital part of making any decision. State and local governments, however, have become plagued by too much of a good thing. The Federal requirements for State, regional, and local plans are unnecessarily numerous, and often overlap each other or conflict with local programs. The result is that everyone is overburdened by paperwork, and the original thrust of many of these plans is lost in the shuffle.

Accordingly, I am ordering a zero-based review of all Federal requirements that State and local governments submit plans when asking for assistance. All requirements, except for those established by Federal statute, should be abolished, combined with other plans or required only on a multi-year, rather than an annual basis. The requirement should remain in cases where 1) a compelling need is demonstrated, and 2) where the requirements reflect the wishes of top elected officials.

I have designated OMB to help each department carry out its review, with the goal of submitting final recommendations to me by November 30. I have also asked the White House intergovernmental staff to assist with the project.

As much as possible, each department should open its review to public participation. I also urge you to confer with Congress about eliminating any plan requirements established by statute which you do not believe are necessary.

I consider this an important part of our effort to make the government more efficient and productive. To ensure that it is successful, I request that you designate a high-level staff person to coordinate the review and to serve on an interdepartmental task force. This committee will examine any possible overlapping in the remaining plan requirements. OMB will be in charge.

I hope for prompt results from this effort. Specifically, I expect the number and complexity of planning requirements for Federal aid to be sharply reduced. Moreover, I want you to make a continuing effort to assure that no requirements are established unless they are essential to meet the responsibilities of government.

JIMMY CARTER

Budget Rescissions

Message to the Congress.   July 19, 1977

To the Congress of the United States:
In accordance with the Impoundment Control Act of 1974, I herewith propose

rescission of $462.0 million in procurement funds appropriated to the Department of Defense for the B–1 bomber. In addition, I am proposing rescission of $1.4 million provided to the Department of Defense for procurement of the short range attack missile (SRAM–B).

The details of the proposed rescissions are contained in the attached reports.

JIMMY CARTER

The White House,
   July 19, 1977.

NOTE: The attachments detailing the rescissions are printed in the FEDERAL REGISTER of July 22, 1977.

The message was not issued in the form of a White House press release.

Budget Rescissions and Deferral

Message to the Congress. July 19, 1977

To the Congress of the United States:

In accordance with the Impoundment Control Act of 1974, I herewith propose two new rescissions totalling $96.1 million in budget authority and report one new deferral of $12.5 million in budget authority.

The rescission proposals pertain to the foreign military credit sales program and the General Services Administration's Federal Buildings Fund. The new deferral relates to the Department of Defense, Uniform Services University of the Health Sciences.

I urge the Congress to act favorably on the rescission proposals.

JIMMY CARTER

The White House,
   July 19, 1977.

NOTE: The attachments detailing the rescissions and deferral are printed in the FEDERAL REGISTER of July 22, 1977.

The message was not issued in the form of a White House press release.

National Transportation Safety Board

Nomination of James B. King To Be a Member. July 19, 1977

The President today announced that he will nominate James B. King, of Boston, Mass., to be a member of the National Transportation Safety Board. He would replace William R. Haley. King is now Special Assistant to the President for Personnel.

He was born March 27, 1935, in Ludlow, Mass. He received a B.A. in 1960 from American International College in Springfield, Mass.

In 1960–61, King was national field secretary for Tau Kappa Epsilon fraternity, and in 1961–62 he taught seventh grade social studies at Ludlow Junior High School. In 1962 he also served as a full-time volunteer for Edward M. Kennedy's senatorial campaign.

King worked as a researcher for the Massachusetts State House library in 1963. From 1963 to 1965, he worked for the Massachusetts Department of Public Utilities Security Division, as an investigator of fraudulent securities, then supervisor of investigators.

In 1965 and 1966, King worked for the Commonwealth Service Corps as a community action technician, then as associate commissioner of the Commonwealth Service Corps, organizing community action groups. In 1966 and 1967, he was director of the Holyoke (Mass.) Program for the Aging.

From 1967 to 1975, King served as special assistant to Senator Edward M. Kennedy and was responsible for running his Boston office, setting up field hearings, and frequently traveling with him. From 1975 to 1977, King was director of community affairs and marketing for the

Massachusetts Bay Transportation Authority. He took leaves of absence from MBTA in July 1976 to work at the Democratic National Convention, and from August to November 1976 to serve as trip director for the Carter Presidential campaign. Since January 1977, he has been Special Assistant to the President for Personnel.

Visit of Prime Minister Begin of Israel

Toasts of the President and the Prime Minister at a Working Dinner for the Prime Minister. July 19, 1977

THE PRESIDENT. First of all, I want to welcome all of you here tonight—the Members of the Senate, the Cabinet, my own staff, the distinguished Members of the House, and also our very fine visitors from Israel, Ambassador Dinitz.

I was very much concerned a few weeks ago, when I discovered that this is a special night and I didn't know if we could induce anyone to come. The Speaker pointed out again tonight that this is the All-Star Game, the major baseball game of the year. [*Laughter*] And I was taken aback the day before yesterday, when my wife came and said, "Jimmy, we ordinarily have only 20 people come to your working suppers, and we are trying to cut the list down to 60."

I couldn't understand it. So, I talked to Cy and talked to Dr. Brzezinski, and they said that everyone wanted to come to meet the new Prime Minister of Israel. This is the largest group we have ever had, Mr. Prime Minister, and it's a great tribute to you and to the interest in your country and is demonstrative, I think, of the very close ties of friendship between the United States and the great nation of Israel. I'm pleased to be the host tonight to such a distinguished man.

As I said in my welcoming remarks this morning, this is very gratifying to me. He's the only foreign visitor I have had who is junior to me. I feel like a senior statesman tonight since he's very new in office. And he and I have a lot more in common.

Ambassador Dinitz was telling me that after the election somebody asked Prime Minister Begin how it felt to be unknown. And he said, well, he was known as Menahem who?—very similar to me, except the question was asked about him after he was elected Prime Minister, and it was asked about me when I first started running for President. [*Laughter*]

But he and I have a lot more in common than those ties that I've described to you, and we've explored some of them today. It's been one of the most gratifying and stimulating discussions that I have had since I have been President.

We've had a chance to get to know each other personally, and it's been obvious to me that our guest is a strong leader. He's a man of deep convictions and unshakeable principle. He's a man of truth and quiet dignity. He's a man who is polite and very modest. The only times today when I've seen him somewhat disconcerted is when he thinks that the praise and the compliments are excessive, and he's embarrassed then.

I think this is a tribute to him. And I know that the people in Israel and the many friends in our country who look with favor on him and his leadership are gratified to have him come to see us.

We've had far-reaching discussions today. We've explored differences of opinion in a very blunt and frank fashion. And I think we've resolved some of the differences; few still remain. But we've discovered and mutually recognized, in order to make them permanent, the agreements that are inherent in the attitudes of our people.

We both feel that this year is a propitious time to move toward real, permanent peace in the Middle East, a recognition by all nations that Israel has a right to exist, to exist as a proud and independent nation, to exist permanently, and to exist in peace. This is a basis on which we approach the coming crucial months.

We also recognize the sharp differences of opinion that exist between Israel and her Arab neighbors, the historical distrust that must be overcome. We also recognize the intense interest and legitimate concern and involvement of almost all the developed nations in the world and many of those who are still developing in a peaceful settlement of Middle Eastern differences.

We recognize that the basic security of Israel must not only be guaranteed in military terms and from the viewpoint of leaders who are involved, but the security of Israel must be guaranteed in the minds and hearts of people who live in that country and in the minds and hearts of people who would disturb that security if they thought there was hope for success. There must be a reassurance of the staunch friendship that binds our country to Israel.

I have met with the Arab leaders who've been here to see me and whom I've met in Europe, and we've always made clear to them in the early stages of discussion that the basic premise on which we approached a possible Middle East discussion leading toward progress and peace was our commitment to Israel.

We have also explored today some very sensitive questions, some that can prove to be embarrassing because of past statements made in the heat of anger or the heat of challenge or the heat of despair

or the heat or depths of insecurity. And with a new hope being generated, we see a need for a frank discussion of all the issues that in the past have appeared to be insuperable obstacles toward peace.

I've been very proud of the attitude taken by Prime Minister Begin, who has said that all issues are negotiable and who has already expressed publicly his hope that he and President Sadat and King Hussein and President Asad can meet with others in Geneva in October.

We don't know yet that we can resolve all the differences that might prevent such a meeting. But following this week, Secretary Vance will go to the Middle East to have private conversations with the leaders there and will also have a follow-up meeting with the Israeli leaders themselves.

The future, of course, is still in doubt. The historical differences still exist. But I am convinced, having spent hours and hours talking and listening to the leaders involved, that there is a unanimous hope that peace might come and a realization of the great benefits that can accrue to all the people in the Middle East with the coming of security and peace.

We are determined to do our share not to try to impose our will on anyone but to act as a trusted intermediary and, to deserve that trust, to give the same points of view to all the parties who will be negotiating—not to mislead anyone, not to avoid a controversial issue—and, wherever appropriate, to open those controversial issues up to public scrutiny, public analysis, public debate, even when at times it creates some hopefully transient dissension among people who have strongly held opposing views.

But there is no way to postpone any longer those issues that sometimes in the future will be divisive but which have historically been divisive either for 29 years or for 2,900 years.

Finally, I'd like to say this: Success this year is going to require a great deal of courage. As has often been pointed out, it's much more difficult to make peace than it is to make war, because in searching for peace there has to be an accommodation; in searching for war, there has to be an arousing of animosity and hatred and a using of innate dissension and distrust as a basis.

But the courage that exists in our fine visitor is one of the factors which encourages me to look toward great progress this year toward true peace in the Middle East.

We share a common religion. We share mutual economic trials, tribulations, successes, and hopes. We are bound together politically, culturally, ethically by blood relationships. And these common purposes and goals and characteristics provide a sure base which will withstand the trials and difficulties of a challenging year.

I look forward to it with a great deal of anticipation, and I'm very proud tonight to welcome to the White House the new Prime Minister of Israel and to offer a toast to this good and decent and courageous man in whom the hopes of many are focused, and on the brave and courageous people of the great and courageous nation of Israel.

To the people of Israel and to you, Mr. Prime Minister.

THE PRIME MINISTER. Mr. President, after having met you, I can say it was a great day in my life to be here, to speak to you, to listen to you. We have had very few good days in our lives in our generation. Most of the days were spent in struggle, in persecution; to time in being hunted, in dreams, in suffering. And the days of solace are not many.

This is one of the best days in my life, having met the President of the United States, having learned that this is a man, a great friend of humanity, a man of great understanding and feeling and, therefore, as I can say now wholeheartedly, a great friend of Israel.

Therefore, tonight, Mr. President, with your permission, I will say something about what I believed to be, perhaps since my childhood, the moral greatness of America.

In 60 years, America has saved mankind from three very grave dangers. The first was Prussian militarism, which during the First World War almost trampled under foot all of Europe and, ultimately, the world. 1917 was a crucial year. There were mutinies in the French Army. The great question was: "Whom? Who is going to break whom?" And then the outcry was heard throughout Europe: "The Yankees are coming." The army of General Pershing fought valiantly. Mainly, the spirit of the European armies, of the allies, rose. And then victory came.

The second time America saved mankind came during the period when, as Churchill said, all the embodiment of evil in mankind turned a great nation—a nation of poets and philosophers—into a bloodthirsty mob, thirsty first of all for Jewish blood. And in that hour, perhaps the darkest in our time, we lost a third of our people. That would mean 80 million Americans wiped out. Those are phantasmagoric figures which scientists make up in connection with the megatons. But megatons are produced never to be used. As we believe, all free men and all those who believe in divine providence, we have to live with those phantasmagoric figures to the last day on Earth.

A dark age started in Europe and throughout the world. We should always tell the truth. There was a time when England stood alone resisting that barbarous tyranny. And there was a time when the Soviet armies fought heroically against the onslaught by the Nazi hordes.

However, whoever studied history does know and should admit that were it not for America—for America's might and America's spirit and faith in justice and liberty—England would have succumbed, Russia would have fallen, and then a dark age would have started, perhaps for many, many years, perhaps for centuries, mankind never knew since the days of Nero and Caligula.

Ultimately, the United States won the day for all mankind, and so we were saved from the dark age under Nazi tyranny.

After the Second World War, Mr. President, there is no doubt whatsoever were it not for America, the Soviet armies long ago would have reached the shores of the Atlantic Ocean. There wasn't enough strength in Europe left to withstand such a possible onslaught. It was only because of America that part of mankind was saved from Soviet slavery, from Communist subjugation. This struggle still goes on, as we can see a tendency to take over country after country by proxy.

This is the moral greatness of America. It saved three times, in two generations, in 60 years, all the nations, all mankind. We free men bow to that greatness of America.

America knew crisis as well, economic and moral crisis. But as we follow those 200 years of American history, as we read Jefferson and the story of Lee and Hamilton and Citizen Tom Paine and the marvelous life story of Abraham Lincoln—who actually renewed all the great precepts taken from the Bible—when we follow this wonderful story, we see that after each crisis America becomes more democratic, more just, more free, and more devoted to our human tasks.

Now, with your permission, Mr. President, a few words about little Israel—and I do not say so for the sake of artificial modesty—we are a very little country. We shall always be. And in comparison with America's might, we are a very small, very small country and people in the Middle East. However, we rose in suffering and in heroism.

Sometimes, as I heard today as well, journalists have an undertone when they ask me about the Bible. I am not ashamed to say that I do believe with all my heart in divine providence. Were it not for divine providence, where would we be today or tonight? We were sentenced to death, all of us, and the life of every one of us is a present. We could have been there in the trains and in the camps, as the wife of my friend and secretary, a young lady, was, having spent 3 years in Auschwitz, having looked every day upon that smoke coming from the chimneys and knowing what happened.

So we suffered. And when people ask me about the Bible, then I can say our generation, my generation, is almost a Biblical generation.

Of course, we don't dare compare ourselves with our ancestors. But what was the Biblical generation? They achieved everything by suffering and with heroism. They suffered very much until they reached the Promised Land. And Moses, the great liberator, wasn't even allowed to come into the Promised Land.

In great heroism, Joshua was told, "Be strong spiritually, have courage and faith against overwhelming odds and forces."

That is our generation. Everything we achieved was through great suffering, almost inhuman suffering, having lost a mother, a father, a brother, a little nephew, everything dear and near to you being bereaved and orphaned; asking the question, "Wherefore will come my salvation?" And then saying to ourselves, "Rise for a just cause. Endanger your life; it is a present given to you. And create conditions in which never again will an enemy raise his hand on a Jewish child and escape with impunity."

So we did fight. And we suffered. And there was great heroism and singing of the Hatikvah with the last breath in one's lungs. But ultimately, with God's help—indeed, only with God's help—we won the day. We have a country, a parliament, a government, a land to till, cities to build, the field to make green, to take in our persecuted people from scores of countries, from the Arab lands. We took in 800,000 of our brethren from the Arab countries. The others came from Europe, what we call in Hebrew *Sharei Pleyta*—that term is absolutely unknown to other nations—the remnants of our people from generation to generation; we are the remnants of the remnants.

And now we want to have peace, more than anything in the world to have peace. We didn't have, in our time, one day of real peace there with all the tragic events, and in our own land, terror and bloodshed, always living on the hinge, always threatened with extinction and standing on guard for our people and for human liberty and for human dignity. This is the story of our generation.

Therefore, Mr. President, I have come to you, as the democratically elected Prime Minister of Israel, with a deep sense of responsibility. May I inform you, sir, that our spiritual leadership, the rabbinate, the day before yesterday asked the people to pray every day for the success of my mission. And they decided that there is a special song to say every day, a people praying for the success of one's mission.

This is some phenomenon, because they know we have a great friend, the United States of America. And we, Israel, are a faithful ally of the United States. We do whatever we can to serve the free world. We contribute to the national security—as tonight I will show you, Mr. President—to the national security of the United States.

We are a guardian of human liberty and democracy in the Middle East. We look around; I don't see any country in our neighborhood which can, through a free vote of proud citizens, say one leadership should take a vacation and there should be another leadership. And then the transfer of power is being carried out in so orderly a way—my predecessor waiting for me in his office; I coming in, shaking hands, expressing the best feelings for each other, and then the predecessor saying, "Now, take over," and I going into my office and then, indeed, giving the first order to bring in the Vietnamese refugees into our country.

Democracy is beautiful. When you look at what is happening under tyranny or whatever comes, and you compare democracy—as Churchill used to say, it also has its faults, but basically how beautiful is democracy.

We are proud that we are a democracy, as the United States carries the banner of democracy. This is our contribution to freedom, national security of the free world. We shall continue to do so to the best of our ability.

Our talks, Mr. President, I do hope, first of all, will result in the deepening of the friendship between our countries. One day, one day—I pray for it—perhaps I will be able to say that in pride I will call you my friend, in pride. And then our talks may result in progress towards that goal called peace.

We must have the sense of urgency, but we also must have some patience. May I respectfully submit that I prove to have patience. Some patience it was. [*Laughter*]

You, too, Mr. President, showed that you have patience. So some patience must be guarded, because it's an historical conflict; it is not a territorial problem. For 19 years there was no peace. For 19 years we didn't have the second part of Jerusalem or the Golan Heights, not one day of peace.

The question arises: Why not? Were it a territorial conflict, there was no reason not to make peace with Israel. It is an historical conflict. We came there. We have come there by right to the land of our ancestors. But it was not recognized, and time and again attempts were made to destroy us.

Sometimes you have a defeated aggressor claiming that he's the wronged victim. But we know what happened. We only defended ourselves against attempts, repeated, to destroy our people, our dream and our independence and, ultimately, our lives.

With a sense of urgency on one hand and some patience on the other, I think we can build a foundation of peace in the Middle East and the recognition of justice for all and fairness for all, as we believe.

We don't hate our neighbors. We don't want to humiliate them at all. We never wanted to defeat them. We never wanted to wrong them. But we had to defend ourselves. This is the whole story, as they used to say in those ancient days, on one foot. I can only speak very shortly standing on one foot, the whole story.

We are hopeful; we are optimistic. We have to be. Our people have always been optimistic.

So, Mr. President, the day after tomorrow I will be leaving Washington with a staunch heart, grateful for your gracious hospitality, for your friendship, for the encouragement you gave all of us, for your leadership.

At the time, ladies and gentlemen, the British used to say, because of their own reasons, thank God for the French Army. Now, paraphrasing that saying, I will raise my glass and say with all my heart, thank God for America.

To the President of the United States, the leader and defender of the free world: *Lechayim.*

NOTE: The President spoke at 9:02 p.m. in the State Dining Room at the White House.

Captive Nations Week, 1977
Proclamation 4513. July 20, 1977

By the President of the United States of America

A Proclamation

Since 1959 the Congress, by joint resolution (73 Stat. 212), has authorized and requested the President to designate the third week in July as Captive Nations Week.

Our own country was established on a profound belief in national self-determination. Throughout our history we have sought to give meaning to this principle and to our belief in liberty and human rights.

In recognition of this commitment, Now, THEREFORE, I, JIMMY CARTER, President of the United States of America, do hereby designate the week beginning July 17, 1977, as Captive Nations Week.

I call upon the people of the United States to observe this week with appropriate ceremonies and activities, demonstrating America's support for those who seek national independence, liberty, and human rights.

IN WITNESS WHEREOF, I have hereunto set my hand this twentieth day of July, in the year of our Lord nineteen hundred seventy-seven, and of the Independence of the United States of America the two hundred and second.

JIMMY CARTER

[Filed with the Office of the Federal Register, 11:38 a.m., July 20, 1977]

National Mediation Board
Nomination of Robert O. Harris To Be a Member. July 20, 1977

The President today announced that he will nominate Robert O. Harris, of Washington, D.C., to be a member of the National Mediation Board. He would replace Kay McMurray. Harris is staff director and counsel to the U.S. Senate Subcommittee on Governmental Efficiency and the District of Columbia.

He was born November 11, 1929, in New York, N.Y. He received an A.B. from Columbia College in 1951, an LL.B. from Yale Law School in 1954, an LL.M. from Georgetown Law School in 1961, and took the advanced management program at Harvard Business School in 1972–73.

Harris was an attorney in the Department of Health, Education, and Welfare from 1957 to 1959, and in the Department of Labor from 1959 to 1961. From 1961 to 1967, he was assistant to the Chairman of the National Labor Relations Board.

From 1967 to 1969, Harris was counsel to the U.S. Senate Labor Subcommittee, and from 1969 to 1971 he was staff director and counsel to the Senate Committee on Labor and Public Welfare.

From 1971 to 1977, he was staff director and counsel to the Senate Committee on the District of Columbia. Since 1977 he has been staff director and counsel to the Senate Subcommittee on Governmental Efficiency and the District of Columbia.

Harris is an alternate member of the National Capital Planning Commission and of the Temporary Commission on Financial Oversight of the District of Columbia.

Enforcement of Title VI of the Civil Rights Act
Memorandum for the Heads of Executive Departments and Agencies. July 20, 1977

Memorandum for the Heads of Executive Departments and Agencies

Title VI of the Civil Rights Act of 1964 writes into law a concept which is basic to our country—that the government of all the people should not support programs which discriminate on the grounds of race, color, or national origin. There are no exceptions to this rule; no matter how important a program, no matter how urgent the goals, they do not excuse violating any of our laws—including the laws against discrimination.

This Administration will enforce Title VI. This means, first, that each of you must exert firm leadership to ensure that your department or agency enforces this law.

Second, there must be central guidance and oversight of Title VI enforcement. Executive Order 11764 places with the Attorney General the responsibility for coordinating Title VI enforcement and for approving rules, regulations and orders which departments or agencies issue under Title VI. I want the Attorney General to work closely with each of you to help you make sure that your department or agency is doing an effective job, and I have asked him to give this matter a high priority. The Department of Justice will shortly be contacting each department and agency to determine what action has been taken to comply with the Attorney General's Title VI regulations. You should insist that your staff cooperate fully with the Department of Justice staff as they carry out this task and their other responsibilities under the Executive Order.

Finally, as you know, Title VI was intended to provide an administrative mechanism for insuring equal treatment in Federal programs. Consequently, administrative proceedings leading to fund terminations are the preferred method of enforcing Title VI, and this sanction must be utilized in appropriate cases. There may be some instances, however, where litigation is in order. You must make sure such cases are referred to the Department of Justice. The effective use of the sanctions provided by Title VI is an essential element of this Administration's effort to guarantee that Federal funds do not flow to discriminatory programs.

JIMMY CARTER

Post-Secondary Education in Micronesia

Letter Transmitting a Report to Congressional Committee Chairmen.   July 20, 1977

Dear Mr. Chairman:

Pursuant to P.L. 94–255, I am transmitting herewith a report concerning post-secondary education in the Trust Territory of the Pacific Islands.

The Congress of Micronesia originally requested the appropriation of $8 million in order to replace the facilities of the existing Community College of Microne-

sia located in Ponape. In authorizing the funds, Congress directed that no appropriation shall be made until a study is conducted to determine the educational need and most suitable educational concept for a Micronesian college and transmitted by the President to the appropriate committees of the Congress with his recommendation.

The Department of the Interior has conducted the study and has prepared the enclosed report. The report analyzes the educational system in Micronesia and recommends that several important steps be taken to revitalize and redirect Micronesian education before funds are appropriated to construct any new physical facilities for higher education in the Trust Territory.

The report does not deny the need for a quality institution of higher learning in Micronesia. It does recommend quite strongly, however, that a curriculum tailored to Micronesia's unique needs be developed before embarking on any new construction activities. I believe that this basic recommendation is sound, and I concur generally with the other recommendations contained in the report.

The Congress of Micronesia and the Micronesia Board of Education have written to me expressing their strong desire for immediate construction of physical facilities for the college. I appreciate their expression of interest and the symbolic value that a new college would have to the Micronesians.

Based on the findings of the enclosed report, however, I believe that constructing a new college before the Micronesian educational system is redesigned to be more responsive and more relevant to Micronesia's present and future needs would be of little benefit.

In response to the concerns of the Congress of Micronesia and the Micronesia Board of Education, as well as to the concerns expressed in the report, I have directed the Secretary of the Interior to work closely with the Micronesian people in the selection of a new president of the college and in the initiation of planning, research, and development efforts to prepare a program for the college which is relevant to Micronesia's special needs.

Further, I hope that the Micronesians themselves can provide some financial support for the college.

When these steps are accomplished, I believe it would be appropriate for the United States to consider financial assistance for the construction of college facilities in Micronesia.

Sincerely,

JIMMY CARTER

NOTE: This is the text of identical letters addressed to Senator Henry M. Jackson, chairman of the Senate Committee on Energy and Natural Resources, and Representative Morris K. Udall, chairman of the House Committee on Interior and Insular Affairs.

The 87-page report entitled "The College of Micronesia, the President's Report to Congress" was prepared by the Office of Territorial Affairs, Department of the Interior.

Visit of Prime Minister Begin of Israel

Remarks to Reporters Following the Prime Minister's Departure. July 20, 1977

REPORTER. Mr. President, how did this morning's talks go?

THE PRESIDENT. They went very well. The Prime Minister is going to have a press conference later on today, but I don't think the meetings with him could have been any better, and I believe that we've laid the groundwork now, barring some unforeseen difficulty, that will lead to the Geneva conferences in October.

Secretary Vance will be leaving the 1st of August to visit the Arab countries and also will visit Israel. And we believe that based on my past discussions with Arab leaders, and their desires, that the positions taken by Prime Minister Begin will lead to a convening of the Geneva conference.

Q. You once said there was no use to go to Geneva if it was not going to succeed. What are its chances of success?

THE PRESIDENT. Well, that's difficult to predict. Obviously there are still strong matters and differences that have to be resolved between the Arab and Israeli leaders. But we've not found any of them to be so adamant in their positions that they are not eager for accommodation. I think they all see that the transcendant goal is peace. They've all agreed that the basis for the negotiations themselves will be United Nations Resolutions 242 and 338.

They see that permanent peace is a requisite for accommodation, the definition of what will be done, and that territorial adjustments must be made.

There are obviously differences in how these territory questions should be resolved, and they all recognize the difficulty of the Palestinian question. But they're all eager to meet now. I believe I can say that accurately. And we see the convening of a Geneva conference as being very likely, the format of it, the participation there. And although there are strong differences between the Arab and Israeli leaders on territories and the Palestinian question, they want to work it out.

Q. [*Inaudible*]

THE PRESIDENT. I just cannot answer that question. I doubt it, though. I think that can be answered better by the Prime Minister.

Q. But they will negotiate on the West Bank?

THE PRESIDENT. I'll let the parties get down to the details of it.

Q. But you do think that.

THE PRESIDENT. That will certainly be one of the items on the agenda.

Q. [*Inaudible*]—on the territorial and Palestinian questions?

THE PRESIDENT. We didn't try to resolve those differences. I think it's inappropriate to try to draw lines or draw a map or decide on details at this point.

Those positions that will be put forward by the Arab and Israeli leaders at the Geneva conference are best left to them, because, obviously, strong differences of opinion—[*inaudible*]—any delineation of boundaries.

Q. Did you modify any of your well-known public views?

THE PRESIDENT. I'll stick to my public views, but I think now is the time to be quiet about specifics, and I think that this is a strong desire of Prime Minister Begin. And I think the recent comments and actions by the Arab leaders indicate that they feel the same way.

Q. Is there any significance to his leaving a little earlier than was planned?

THE PRESIDENT. We just had such an unexpectedly harmonious session this morning that we didn't find any reason for arguments.

Q. [*Inaudible*]

THE PRESIDENT. No.

Q. How did you find Mr. Begin as a personality to deal with?

THE PRESIDENT. I like him very much. As I said in my welcoming remarks, he's a man of courage and principle, and I have found in my discussions with him that my assessment was quite accurate.

Q. Is he easy to get along with?

THE PRESIDENT. Yes.

NOTE: The President spoke at 10:47 a.m. on the South Grounds of the White House.

The transcript of the remarks was made available by the White House Press Office. It was not issued in the form of a White House press release.

U.S. Shoe Industry

Announcement of Trade Adjustment Assistance Program. July 20, 1977

A program to revitalize segments of the American shoe industry injured by foreign competition was announced today at the White House. The plan includes formation of special teams of experts to assist affected companies in the design of "customized" strategies for recovery.

The 3-year, $56 million program was developed by the Department of Commerce, in consultation with other Government agencies, in response to President Carter's directive of April 1 to provide "an expanded and more effective program of assistance."

It was announced by Under Secretary of Commerce Sidney Harman and Stuart Eizenstat, Assistant to the President for Domestic Affairs and Policy.

Harman said the program reflects the President's observation that, "Over the long haul, the solution to difficulties in the shoe industry lies not in the restriction of imports but elsewhere—in innovation and modernization of our own production facilities and and the financing to make these possible."

The program will establish specialist teams of experts in the fields of management, production, marketing, and finance to provide consultative services to the estimated 150 trade-injured shoe manufacturers in 36 States. The firms employ approximately 80,000 employees—half of all U.S. nonrubber footwear workers. They produce 230 million pairs of shoes annually, which is approximately half the U.S. production total.

"The teams, each of which will consist of two to five experts drawn from the private sector, will work with the firms which indicate interest to develop custom analyses of their particular problems and to develop solutions. These solutions may involve new management initiatives, production, technology, or marketing improvements, worker-management innovations or a combination of these factors," Harman said.

The specialist teams will also assess the need for additional expertise and talent in each firm and help each company fill its needs. To aid in this effort, the Government will sponsor management development and technical training programs for industry members. The Commerce Department expects that teams will be in the field in October of this year.

Approximately $40 million will be made available to firms for investment in new plant and equipment, new technology, and, where they are integral parts of recovery programs, acquisitions, mergers, or other cooperative arrangements among industry members.

Harman explained that since the $40 million of Federal support for investment by the industry will take the form of loans or loan guarantees, a substantial portion of the Federal cost of the program should be recovered. Cost of the custom analyses of companies and training programs are expected to run to some $14 million over the 3-year period.

Another major aspect of the program is the voluntary cooperation of retailers in increasing orders to trade-injured shoe manufacturers as a spur to production.

"A number of major retailers have indicated their willingness to participate actively in such a program, and to facilitate increased orders," Harman said. "We will be providing them with information on the shoe firms' major product lines and size of orders that can be accommodated by those manufacturers who wish to participate in the program.

"As the consequence of increased volume created by increased orders, the affected companies should be able to cut production costs. This will permit them to reduce the selling price of shoes to be more competitive with foreign imports," Harman said.

"We think this program has advantages for manufacturers, labor, consumers, and the taxpaying public," Harman commented. "No new legislation is required to implement the recovery program. It should increase shoe industry employment. It should have no appreciable effect on the price consumers pay for shoes. The plan is a temporary mechanism designed to revitalize an industry and make it self-sufficient. It is a one-time experiment by the Federal Government operating in a new role—that of facilitator. The Government will do its job over the next 3 years and then get out. At that time a thorough assessment of the results and conclusions will be developed."

He said that the Economic Development Administration of the Commerce Department is "gearing up to contact all firms in the shoe industry about the program and to accelerate its certification process for companies eligible for assistance."

National Energy Plan

Letter to the Chairman of the House Ad Hoc Select Committee on Energy. July 20, 1977

To Lud Ashley

It is most gratifying to me to see the Ad

Hoc Committee begin its work of pulling together the various pieces of the energy plan this week. The cooperation which you, and each of the Committee Chairmen and members, have shown in keeping to a difficult and rigorous schedule for consideration of the plan has been strong and deserves commendation.

As your Committee proceeds with the work of integrating the various elements of the plan, however, I am concerned that we all be mindful of the critical need to keep the energy plan in fiscal balance.

The plan which I put forward to the Congress was consistent with achieving a balanced budget. Its receipts between 1978 and 1985 show a small surplus over its costs. While I do not view the energy plan as a means to balance the budget in and of itself, an internal balance within the plan is essential if we are to have the the resources to realize our goals in other areas such as tax reform, welfare reform and national health insurance, and to move toward a balanced budget. Any deficit created by excess expenditures on the energy plan will reduce our ability to attain these other goals.

It is also essential that, as we keep the energy ledger in balance, we retain the basic elements of equity and economic fairness which I believe we both agree are necessary ingredients of a workable energy program. Jim Schlesinger and I look forward to continuing to work closely with you and members of your Committee for the realization of these objectives.

Sincerely,

JIMMY CARTER

[Honorable Thomas L. Ashley, Chairman, Ad Hoc Select Committee on Energy, U.S. House of Representatives, Washington, D.C. 20515]

NOTE: The text of the letter was made available by the White House Press Office on July 21. It was not issued in the form of a White House press release.

Federal Employment of the Handicapped

Memorandum for the Heads of Executive Departments and Agencies. July 21, 1977

Memorandum for the Heads of Executive Departments and Agencies

When I addressed the White House Conference on Handicapped Individuals, I said that our nation can no longer tolerate discrimination against the handicapped. That means that we must enforce regulations to make sure that all facets of our national life—whether transportation, education, recreation, architecture, or others—are open to all our people.

Perhaps the most important of these areas is employment. I intend that the government should set an example for fair employment practices, by demonstrating what can be done to make the fullest possible use of the abilities of qualified handicapped people.

This is not a new effort. The government has already made progress toward removing barriers to federal employment. But I believe that we can do more. I ask that you actively review your annual affirmative action plans for hiring handicapped people and disabled veterans. As part of your review, I ask that you study the actions being taken to meet your goals, and that you take any extra steps that may be necessary to fulfill our commitment.

Our society has a duty to provide equal opportunities for our people, and an enlightened government has a duty to lead the way.

JIMMY CARTER

Energy Policy and Conservation

Executive Order 12003.　July 20, 1977

RELATING TO ENERGY POLICY AND
CONSERVATION

By virtue of the authority vested in me by the Constitution and the statutes of the United States of America, including the Energy Policy and Conservation Act (89 Stat. 871, 42 U.S.C. 6201 *et seq.*), the Motor Vehicle Information and Cost Savings Act, as amended (15 U.S.C. 1901 *et seq.*), Section 205(a) of the Federal Property and Administrative Services Act of 1949, as amended (40 U.S.C. 486 (a)), and Section 301 of Title 3 of the United States Code, and as President of the United States of America, it is hereby ordered as follows:

SECTION 1. Section 1 of Executive Order No. 11912 of April 13, 1976, is amended to read as follows:

"Section 1. (a) The Administrator of General Services is designated and empowered to perform, without approval, ratification or other action by the President, the function vested in the President by Section 510 of the Motor Vehicle Information and Cost Savings Act, as amended (89 Stat. 915, 15 U.S.C. 2010). In performing this function, the Administrator of General Services shall:

(1) Promulgate rules which will ensure that the minimum statutory requirement for fleet average fuel economy is exceeded (i) for fiscal year 1978 by 2 miles per gallon, (ii) for fiscal year 1979 by 3 miles per gallon, and (iii) for fiscal years 1980 and after by 4 miles per gallon.

(2) Promulgate rules which will ensure that Executive agencies do not acquire, subsequent to fiscal year 1977, any passenger automobile unless such automobile meets or exceeds the average fuel economy standard for the appropriate model year established by, or pursuant to, Section 502(a) of the Motor Vehicle Information and Cost Savings Act, as amended (15 U.S.C. 2002(a)); except that, such rules (i) shall not apply to automobiles designed to perform combat-related missions for the Armed Forces or designed to be used in law enforcement work or emergency rescue work, and (ii) may provide for granting exemptions for individual automobiles used for special purposes as determined to be appropriate by the Administrator of General Services with the concurrence of the Administrator of the Federal Energy Administration.

"(b) The Administrator of General Services shall promulgate rules which will ensure that each class of nonpassenger automobiles acquired by all Executive agencies in each fiscal year, beginning with fiscal year 1979, achieve for such fiscal year a fleet average fuel economy not less than the average fuel economy standard for such class, established pursuant to Section 502(b) of the Motor Vehicle Information and Cost Savings Act, as amended (89 Stat. 903, 15 U.S.C. 2002(b)), for the model year which includes January 1 of such fiscal year; except that, such rules (1) shall not apply to automobiles designed to perform combat-related missions for the Armed Forces or designed to be used in law enforcement work or emergency rescue work, and (2) may provide for granting exceptions for other categories of automobiles used for special purposes as determined to be appropriate by the Administrator of General Services with the concurrence of the Administrator of the Federal Energy Administration.".

SEC. 2. Executive Order No. 11912 of April 13, 1976, is further amended by adding the following new Section:

"Sec. 10. (a)(1) The Administrator of the Federal Energy Administration, hereinafter referred to as the Administrator, shall develop, with the concurrence of the Director of the Office of Management and Budget, and in consultation with the Secretary of Defense, the Secretary of Housing and Urban Development, the Administrator of Veterans' Affairs, the Administrator of the Energy Research and Development Administration, the Administrator of General Services, and the heads of such other Executive agencies as he deems appropriate, the ten-year plan for energy conservation with respect to Government buildings, as provided by section 381(a)(2) of the Energy Policy and Conservation Act (42 U.S.C. 6361(a)(2)).

(2) The goals established in subsection (b) shall apply to the following categories of Federally-owned buildings: (i) office buildings, (ii) hospitals, (iii) schools, (iv) prison facilities, (v) multifamily dwellings, (vi) storage facilities, and (vii) such other categories of buildings for which the Administrator determines the establishment of energy-efficiency performance goals is feasible.

"(b) The Administrator shall establish requirements and procedures, which shall be observed by each agency unless a waiver is granted by the Administrator, designed to ensure that each agency to the maximum extent practicable aims to achieve the following goals:

(1) For the total of all Federally-owned existing buildings the goal shall be a reduction of 20 percent in the average annual energy use per gross square foot of floor area in 1985 from the average energy use per gross square foot of floor area in 1975. This goal shall apply to all buildings for which construction was or design specifications were completed prior to the date of promulgation of the guidelines pursuant to subsection (d) of this Section.

(2) For the total of all Federally-owned new buildings the goal shall be a reduction of 45 percent in the average annual energy requirement per gross square foot of floor area in 1985 from the average annual energy use per gross square foot of floor area in 1975. This goal shall apply to all new buildings for which design specifications are completed after the date of promulgation of the guidelines pursuant to subsection (d) of this Section.

"(c) The Administrator, with the concurrence of the Director of the Office of Management and Budget, in consultation with the heads of the Executive agencies specified in subsection (a) and the Director of the National Bureau of Standards, shall establish, for purposes of developing the ten-year plan, a practical and effective method for estimating and comparing life cycle capital and operating costs for Federal buildings, including residential, commercial, and industrial type categories. Such method shall be consistent with the Office of Management and Budget Circular No. A–94, and shall be adopted and used by all agencies in developing their plans pursuant to subsection (e), annual reports pursuant to subsection (g), and budget estimates pursuant to subsection (h). For purposes of this paragraph, the term "life cycle cost" means the total costs of owning, operating, and maintaining a building over its economic life, including its fuel and energy costs, determined on the basis of a systematic evaluation and comparison of alternative building systems.

"(d) Not later than November 1, 1977, the Administrator, with the concurrence of the Director of the Office of Management and Budget, and after consultation with the Administrator of General Services and the heads of the Executive agencies specified in subsection (a) shall issue guidelines for the plans to be submitted pursuant to subsection (e).

"(e) (1) The head of each Executive agency that maintains any existing building or will maintain any new building shall submit no later than six months after the issuance of guidelines pursuant to subsection (d), to the Administrator a ten-year plan designed to the maximum extent practicable to meet the goals in subsection (b) for the total of existing or new Federal buildings. Such ten-year plans shall only consider improvements that are cost-effective consistent with the criteria established by the Director of the Office of Management and Budget (OMB Circular A–94) and the method established pursuant to subsection (c) of this Section. The plan submitted shall specify appropriate energy-saving initiatives and shall estimate the expected improvements by fiscal year in terms of specific accomplishments—energy savings and cost savings—together with the estimated costs of achieving the savings.

(2) The plans submitted shall, to the maximum extent practicable, include the results of preliminary energy audits of all existing buildings with over 30,000 gross square feet of space owned and maintained by Executive agencies. Further, the second annual report submitted under subsection (g)(2) of this Section shall, to the maximum extent practicable, include the results of preliminary energy audits of all existing buildings with more than 5,000 but not more than 30,000 gross square feet of space. The purpose of such preliminary energy audits shall be to identify the type, size, energy use level and major energy using systems of existing Federal buildings.

(3) The Administrator shall evaluate agency plans relative to the guidelines established pursuant to subsection (d) for such plans and relative to the cost estimating method established pursuant to subsection (c). Plans determined to be deficient by the Administrator will be re-turned to the submitting agency head for revision and resubmission within 60 days.

(4) The head of any Executive agency submitting a plan, should he disagree with the Administrator's determination with respect to that plan, may appeal to the Director of the Office of Management and Budget for resolution of the disagreement.

"(f) The head of each agency submitting a plan or revised plan determined not deficient by the Administrator or, on appeal, by the Director of the Office of Management and Budget, shall implement the plan in accord with approved budget estimates.

"(g) (1) Each Executive agency shall submit to the Administrator an overall plan for conserving fuel and energy in all operations of the agency. This overall plan shall be in addition to and include any ten-year plan for energy conservation in Government buildings submitted in accord with Subsection (e).

(2) By July 1 of each year, each Executive agency shall submit a report to the Administrator on progress made toward achieving the goals established in the overall plan required by paragraph (1) of this subsection. The annual report shall include quantitative measures and accomplishment with respect to energy saving actions taken, the cost of these actions, the energy saved, the costs saved, and other benefits realized.

(3) The Administrator shall prepare a consolidated annual report on Federal government progress toward achieving the goals, including aggregate quantitative measures of accomplishment as well as suggested revisions to the ten-year plan, and submit the report to the President by August 15 of each year.

"(h) Each agency required to submit a plan shall submit to the Director of the Office of Management and Budget with the agency's annual budget submission, and in accordance with procedures and requirements that the Director shall establish, estimates for implementation of the agency's plan. The Director of the Office of Management and Budget shall consult with the Administrator about the agency budget estimates.

"(i) Each agency shall program its proposed energy conservation improvements of buildings so as to give the highest priority to the most cost-effective projects.

"(j) No agency of the Federal government may enter into a lease or a commitment to lease a building the construction of which has not commenced by the effective date of this Order unless the building will likely meet or exceed the general goal set forth in subsection (b) (2).

"(k) The provisions of this section do not apply to housing units repossessed by the Federal Government.".

JIMMY CARTER

The White House,
July 20, 1977.

[Filed with the Office of the Federal Register, 12:11 p.m., July 21, 1977]

NOTE: The text of the Executive order was released on July 21.

Federal Pay Administration

Executive Order 12004. July 20, 1977

RELATING TO FEDERAL PAY ADMINISTRATION

By virtue of the authority vested in me by Sections 5304 and 5305 of Title 5 of the United States Code, and as President of the United States of America, in order to improve the process by which the President receives advice relating to the Federal pay systems, Executive Order No. 11721 of May 23, 1973, relating to

Federal pay administration, is hereby amended as follows:

SECTION 1. Section 201 is amended to read as follows:

"Section 201. The Secretary of Labor, the Director of the Office of Management and Budget, and the Chairman of the United States Civil Service Commission are hereby designated to serve jointly as the President's agent under section 5305 of title 5, United States Code, and shall be known in this capacity as the President's Pay Agent.".

SEC. 2. A new Section 204 is added as follows:

"Sec. 204. (a) The Advisory Committee on Federal Pay shall advise the President of its own opinion on any unresolved issues referred to it by the President's Pay Agent or the Federal Employees Pay Council. The Advisory Committee shall inform the President's Pay Agent and the Federal Employees Pay Council of its opinion on such issues as soon as practicable. To facilitate the exercise of this authority and the early resolution of such issues, the Advisory Committee shall attend, or be represented at, meetings between the President's Pay Agent and the Federal Employees Pay Council, and moderate and direct the discussion.

"(b) The President's Pay Agent, in its annual report to the President pursuant to section 5305 of title 5, United States Code, shall include a full discussion of each issue upon which the Advisory Committee has submitted, in accordance with subsection (a), an opinion.".

JIMMY CARTER

The White House,
July 20, 1977.

[Filed with the Office of the Federal Register, 12:12 p.m., July 21, 1977]

NOTE: The text of the Executive order was released on July 21.

Trust Territory of the Pacific Islands

Designation of Peter R. Rosenblatt as the President's Personal Representative to Negotiations on the Territory's Political Status. July 21, 1977

The President today announced that he is designating Peter R. Rosenblatt, of New York, as his Personal Representative to conduct negotiations on the future political status of the Trust Territory of the Pacific Islands. Rosenblatt will also be nominated for the rank of Ambassador. He would succeed Franklin Haydn Williams.

Rosenblatt was born September 4, 1933, in New York City. He received a B.A. from Yale College in 1954 and an LL.B. (J.D.) from Yale University Law School in 1957.

Rosenblatt was assistant district attorney of New York County from 1959 to 1962. From 1962 to 1966, he was an associate with the New York law firm of Stroock & Stroock & Lavan. He served as Deputy Assistant General Counsel for Near East and South Asia at AID in 1966, and from 1966 to 1968 was assistant to Special Assistant to the President Robert W. Komer.

In 1968 and 1969, Rosenblatt was Judicial Officer and Chairman of the Board of Contract Appeals at the U.S. Post Office Department. From 1969 to 1971, he was corporate vice president and director of Electronic Data Processing Technology, Inc., and chairman of International Development Services, Inc.

Rosenblatt was special consultant on political and foreign policy to Senator Edmund S. Muskie from 1970 to 1972, during his Presidential campaign. Since 1972 he has been in private law practice.

Future Farmers of America

Remarks to Representatives of the Organization. July 21, 1977

Almost every time when I come out to replace Midge Costanza, the audience is always disappointed. This is one group where I might have an advantage, though, because I'm part of you, not only now as President but also throughout my life. The first office I ever held was as secretary of the Plains High School FFA chapter.

I was an isolated and timid country boy, and I began to learn about organizational structure, and I began to learn about competition. I began to learn how to make a speech, and I began to learn how to work with other people. I also learned the value of agriculture, farm families, stability, commitment, idealism, hope, truth, hard work, patriotism, from the FFA.

Ours was a family that didn't have electricity on our farm then, and we lived and worked, as I said in a book I wrote, much more as farmers did 2,000 years ago than as farmers live today.

The Future Farmers of America have presented to farm adults, agricultural leaders, political leaders from cities and farms, new ideas and new concepts of innovation, experimentation, and growth. The FFA has always worked very closely in community problems, always worked very closely with experiment stations. And although my later training was in nuclear physics as a scientist and engineer, I recognize very clearly there is no single entity in our economic structure that's more innovative, much more eager to try new ideas and concepts than the farmers of this country. And it's paid rich dividends.

I learned about politics in the FFA in a good sense. I found even then that many of the battles that we fought during the thirties and forties, in which my father participated, were decided here in Washington. And although before the advent of the rural electrification program my father and our family had been very close to the farm geographically, without traveling much, my daddy, who was the first director of the Central Electric Membership Corporation, on occasion would have to come to Washington in a fight to protect the REA program when Roosevelt was President.

And it expanded the horizons of our family and taught me that there's a strong commitment and responsibility of agricultural leaders and workers to help shape the policies of our Nation not only for our own benefit and advantage, but for the benefit of the world.

My first building project—I had forgotten about it, but in your recent FFA magazine, I noticed my old "ag" teacher said it was a building of a little rough-hewn model of the White House. [*Laughter*] I have to admit that at that time I never thought I'd live here. I was hoping someday I might look at it through the cracks in the fence, but I've come further.

But I think, again, that illustrates that there is no limit on what we can do if we share experiences with one another and recognize the opportunities in the greatest nation on Earth, where background and a lack of experience is no obstacle to further achievement in politics or business or government or in the management of our own affairs.

When I came back home from the Navy in 1953, I continued a commitment that my father had made. And each year when the Plains FFA Chapter chooses its Outstanding Member of the Year, Carter's Warehouse, which is my business, always

sponsors the trip to the Kansas City Convention for that star FFA student. And I have to admit that I think because of that, I was made an honorary lifetime member of the FFA. But that kept me tied in with the FFA students at the junior and senior high school level.

I was able to come to Kansas City and speak to your convention, and I was excited and thrilled by the good response of almost 18,000 FFA delegates from around the country.

So, you have one of those precious possessions in your hands—the ancient history of future farmer organizations and the bright hope for the future. And I'm very proud to be part of one of the finest organizations on Earth, that's never lost its pride in what has been and its vision of what can be in the future.

I want to thank you for coming to the White House. You are leaders among tens of thousands of other leaders, and that puts not only a great pleasure and opportunity in your life but also a heavy responsibility on your shoulders. And it's a very reassuring thing for a President to be able to stand here in the Rose Garden, near the White House where every President has lived except George Washington—it was built while he was President—and to see the intelligence and the idealism mirrored in your faces, because I feel that in the future that our country will be even greater than it has been in the past.

I thank you for letting me be part of it.

NOTE: The President spoke at 10:05 a.m. in the Rose Garden at the White House. In his opening remarks, he referred to Midge Costanza, Assistant to the President for Public Liaison.

Deputy Special Representative for Trade Negotiations

Nomination of Alonzo L. McDonald, Jr.
July 21, 1977

The President today announced that he is nominating Alonzo L. McDonald, Jr., of Riverside, Conn., to be Deputy Special Representative for Trade Negotiations with the rank of Ambassador. McDonald is director of the New York office of McKinsey & Co., Inc.

McDonald was born August 5, 1928, in Atlanta, Ga. He received an A.B. from Emory University in 1948 and an M.B.A. from Harvard University in 1956. He served in the U.S. Marine Corps from 1950 to 1952.

He worked with the Air Conditioning Division of Westinghouse Electric Corp., from 1956 to 1960, rising from assistant to the sales manager to Western Zone manager, based in St. Louis. Since 1960 he has been with McKinsey & Co., Inc., in London, Zurich, Paris, and New York. He was principal in the London office, managing principal in the Zurich office, and managing director of the Paris office. McDonald became managing director of the firm in 1973 and assumed the additional function as director of the New York office in 1976.

From 1948 to 1950, McDonald was a reporter for the Atlanta Journal.

McDonald is: trustee, Committee for Economic Development; chairman, subcommittee on Role of Government Intervention in the Economy; member, Council on Foreign Relations; trustee and member of executive committee, U.S. Council of the International Chamber of Commerce; member, Advisory Council on Japan-U.S. Economic Relations; member, The Economic Club of New York; member, Center for Inter-American Relations; chairman, board of directors, Harvard Business School Club of Greater New York; member, Visiting Committee on Administration, Harvard University; director, The French-American Foundation; and warden at St. Joseph of Arimathea Episcopal Church (Elmsford, N.Y.).

Digest of Other White House Announcements

The following listing includes the President's daily schedule and other items of general interest as announced by the White House Press Office during the period covered by this issue. Events and announcements printed elsewhere in the issue are not included.

July 17

The President returned to the White House from Camp David, Md.

July 18

The President met at the White House with:

—Zbigniew Brzezinski, Assistant to the President for National Security Affairs;

—senior White House staff members;

—the Cabinet;

—Vice President Walter F. Mondale;

—Sam Brown, Jr., Director of ACTION;

—Bert Lance, Director of the Office of Management and Budget;

—Vice President Mondale and Attorney General Griffin B. Bell.

The President attended a briefing on foreign policy by Secretary of State Cyrus Vance for members of the Cabinet and senior White House staff and their spouses.

The White House released manifests listing passengers who have flown on White House authorized military aircraft from January 20 through June 23. The lists were sent to Representative Jack Brooks, chairman of the Legislation and National Security Subcommittee of the House Committee on Government Operations, and were also made available for inspection by the press.

July 19

The President met at the White House with:
—Dr. Brzezinski;
—a group of 12 Democratic Senators;
—Senator Daniel P. Moynihan of New York;
—Vice President Mondale, Adm. Stansfield Turner, Director of Central Intelligence, and Dr. Brzezinski;
—Secretary of Transportation Brock Adams, Secretary of the Treasury W. Michael Blumenthal, Charles L. Schultze, Chairman of the Council of Economic Advisers, and James R. Schlesinger, Assistant to the President, to discuss energy legislation.

The President transmitted to the Congress the annual report of the Saint Lawrence Seaway Development Corporation for 1976.

July 20

The President met at the White House with:
—Dr. Brzezinski;
—Prime Minister Menahem Begin of Israel;
—Mrs. Carter, for lunch;
—Dr. Schultze;
—Roy Wilkins, former executive director of the National Association for the Advancement of Colored People, and Mrs. Wilkins.

The President attended a portion of a briefing on foreign policy given by Secretary of Defense Harold Brown for a group of Congressmen and Senators.

The President today declared an emergency for the States of Georgia and Alabama because of the impact of a drought.

The President and Mrs. Carter hosted a picnic on the South Lawn for Members of Congress and their families.

July 21

The President met at the White House with:
—Vice President Mondale, Secretary Vance, and Dr. Brzezinski;
—Dr. Brzezinski;
—Representative Parren J. Mitchell of Maryland.

The President today declared a major disaster for the State of Pennsylvania as a result of severe storms and flooding beginning about July 19, which caused extensive public and private property damage.

In the afternoon, the President left the White House for a trip to South Carolina, Mississippi, and Louisiana.

CHECKLIST OF WHITE HOUSE PRESS RELEASES *

The following releases of the Office of the White House Press Secretary, distributed during the period covered by this issue, are not included in the issue.

Released July 18, 1977

News conference: on the President's message to the Congress on labor law reform—by Ray Marshall, Secretary, and Carin Ann Clauss, Solicitor, Department of Labor

CHECKLIST OF WHITE HOUSE PRESS RELEASES—Continued

Released July 19, 1977

Announcement: the President's memorandum to executive departments and agencies ordering a review of all Federal planning requirements that State and local governments and regional governmental organizations must follow when asking for Federal assistance

Announcement: nomination of Nicholas J. Bua to be United States District Judge for the Northern District of Illinois; Stanley J. Roszkowski to be United States District Judge for the Northern District of Illinois; Earl E. Veron to be United States District Judge for the Western District of Louisiana; and John C. Krsul to be United States Marshal for the District of Montana

Released July 20, 1977

News conference: on the trade adjustment assistance program for the U.S. shoe industry—by Stuart E. Eizenstat, Assistant to the President for Domestic Affairs and Policy, and Sidney Harman, Under Secretary of Commerce

Fact sheet: questions and answers on the trade adjustment assistance program for the U.S. shoe industry

Released July 21, 1977

Announcement: the President's signing of Executive Order 12003 on energy policy and conservation

Announcement: the President's signing of Executive Order 12004 on Federal pay administration

NOMINATIONS SUBMITTED TO THE SENATE

The following list does not include promotions of members of the Uniformed Services, nominations to the Service Academies, or nominations of Foreign Service officers.

Submitted July 18, 1977

WILLIAM H. SHAHEEN, of New Hampshire, to be United States Attorney for the District of New Hampshire for the term of 4 years, vice William J. Deachman III, term expired.

EDWARD F. HARRINGTON, of Massachusetts, to be United States Attorney for the District of Massachusetts for the term of 4 years, vice James N. Gabriel, term expired.

NOMINATIONS SUBMITTED TO THE SENATE—Continued

Submitted July 18, 1977—Continued

HUBERT H. BRYANT, of Oklahoma, to be United States Attorney for the Northern District of Oklahoma for the term of 4 years, vice Nathan G. Graham, resigned.

WILLIAM B. GRAY, of Vermont, to be United States Attorney for the District of Vermont for the term of 4 years, vice George W. F. Cook.

WESLEY DAVID LANE, of Minnesota, to be United States Marshal for the District of Minnesota for the term of 4 years, vice Harry D. Berglund.

WILLIAM J. EVINS, JR., of Tennessee, to be United States Marshal for the Middle District of Tennessee for the term of 4 years, vice Leon T. Campbell.

EARLE B. McLAUGHLIN, of Vermont, to be United States Marshal for the District of Vermont for the term of 4 years, vice Christian Hansen, Jr.

Submitted July 19, 1977

SIMON DAVID FREEMAN, of Maryland, to be a member of the Board of Directors of the Tennessee Valley Authority for the term expiring May 18, 1984, vice Donald Opie McBride, term expired.

NICHOLAS J. BUA, of Illinois, to be United States District Judge for the Northern District of Illinois, vice William J. Lynch, deceased.

EARL E. VERON, of Louisiana, to be United States District Judge for the Western District of Louisiana, vice Edwin F. Hunter, Jr., retired.

STANLEY J. ROSZKOWSKI, of Illinois, to be United States District Judge for the Northern District of Illinois, vice Richard W. McLaren, deceased.

JOHN C. KRSUL, of Montana, to be United States Marshal for the District of Montana for the term of 4 years, vice Louis O. Aleksich, term expired.

Submitted July 20, 1977

JAMES B. KING, of Massachusetts, to be a member of the National Transportation Safety Board for the term expiring December 31, 1981, vice William R. Haley, term expired.

ROBERT OBERNDOERFER HARRIS, of the District of Columbia, to be a member of the National Mediation Board for the term expiring July 1, 1980, vice Kay McMurray, term expired.

NOMINATIONS SUBMITTED
TO THE SENATE—Continued

Submitted July 21, 1977

PETER R. ROSENBLATT, of New York, for the rank of Ambassador during the tenure of his service as Personal Representative of the President to conduct negotiations on the future political status of the Trust Territory of the Pacific Islands.

ALONZO LOWRY McDONALD, JR., of Connecticut to be a Deputy Special Representative for Trade Negotiations, with the rank of Ambassador, vice William N. Walker.

ACTS APPROVED BY
THE PRESIDENT

Approved July 19, 1977

H.R. 6893_____ Public Law 95–67
An act to amend title 4 of the United States Code to make it clear that Members of Congress may not, for purposes of State income

ACTS APPROVED BY
THE PRESIDENT—Continued

Approved July 19, 1977—Continued

tax laws, be treated as residents of any State other than the State from which they were elected.

Approved July 20, 1977

H.R. 4585_____ Public Law 95–69
An act to authorize appropriations for the Indian Claims Commission for fiscal year 1978; to facilitate the transfer of cases from the Indian Claims Commission to the United States Court of Claims; and for other purposes.

H.R. 4992_____ Public Law 95–68
An act to amend the Indian Financing Act of 1974 by revising the appropriations for the Indian business development program.

Approved July 21, 1977

S. 1468_____ Public Law 95–70
Federal Energy Administration Authorization Act of 1977

Charleston, South Carolina

Remarks at the 31st Annual Meeting of the Southern Legislative Conference.
July 21, 1977

Senator Hollings and Senator Eastland, Senator Stennis, Governor Edwards, Chairman Bragg, distinguished Members of Congress, those representatives from State government, who share the leadership of America, and my friends in a personal way who come out to welcome me back to the South:

It's not often that a President comes as a substitute speaker. I realize that my brother, Billy, was the first choice. [*Laughter*] I understand that the Southern Legislative Conference—[*laughter*]—couldn't afford Billy here.

I was going to go by Plains on this trip, but I couldn't get a room there. [*Laughter*] I'm going to go to Yazoo City tonight and then to New Orleans later on.

I'm very grateful to be here as President of our country. I've learned a lot in this first 6 months. When I got to Washington and sought advice, someone said, "Just act like you're a President and treat Congress like the Georgia Legislature." It didn't work at first. [*Laughter*]

Very quickly I realized that the Congress was treating me like I was still Governor of Georgia, but now, with the help of a great number of friends in the Congress, we've formed a kind of relationship that ought to exist between the White House and our Nation's Capitol. I think there's a genuine sense of sharing of responsibility and the burden of government, and you are a part of that circle of leaders in the State legislature and the Governors' offices, who join in with the President, the Congress, and others in making sure that our government works.

I've become even more proud of being an American. And I have become even more proud of being a southerner, too. I'm also proud to be with you today where two great rivers come together, as they say in Charleston, to form the Atlantic Ocean. This is one of our Nation's most gracious cities.

And I want to talk to you today about the hopes and problems that we as southerners and as Americans share together. I feel a special kinship with your State legislators. For 4 years I was a member of the Georgia Senate, and I still prize State government not only for the talents of those who work in it but, as Fritz Hollings says, for the closeness to the people it represents.

Our Southern States have a proud tradition of local, independent government, and now you're the heirs of that tradition. But we in the South have also felt, perhaps more directly than many others, some of the rapid changes that have taken place in this modern age. More and more our own lives are shaped by events in other cities, decisions in other States, tensions in other parts of the world.

And as Americans we cannot overlook the way that our fate is bound to that of other nations. This interdependence stretches from the health of our economy, through war and peace, to the security of our own energy supplies. It's a new world in which we cannot afford to be narrow in our vision, limited in our foresight, or selfish in our purpose.

When I took office almost exactly 6 months ago, our Nation was faced with a series of problems around the world—in southern Africa, the Middle East, in our relationships with our NATO allies, and on such tough questions as nuclear proliferation, negotiations with our former adversaries, a Panama Canal treaty, human rights, world poverty.

We have openly and publicly addressed these and other many difficult and controversial issues—some of which had been either skirted or postponed in the past.

As I pointed out in a recent press conference, a period of debate, disagreement, probing was inevitable. Our goal has not been to reach easy or transient agreements, but to find solutions that are meaningful, balanced, and lasting.

Now, a President has a responsibility to present to the people of this Nation reports and summations of complex and important matters. I feel more secure as President making decisions if I know that either the most difficult, the most complex questions that face me have been understood and debated by you and understood and debated by the Congress.

In the past I think our Nation's leaders have been guilty of making decisions in secret. And even when the decision turns out to be the right one, it makes the President, the Secretary of State speak with a weak voice when they speak alone.

Today, I want to discuss a vitally important aspect of our foreign relations, the one that may most directly shape the chances for peace for us and for our children. I would like to spell out my view of what we have done and where we are going in our relations with the Soviet Union and to reaffirm the basic principles of our national policy.

I don't have any apology for talking about foreign affairs at a southern legislative conference, because foreign affairs and those difficult decisions ought never to be made with a concept that we can abandon common sense and the sound judgment and the constructive influence of the American people.

For decades, the central problems of our foreign policy revolved around antagonism between two coalitions, one headed by the United States and the other headed by the Soviet Union.

Our national security was often defined almost exclusively in terms of military competition with the Soviet Union. This competition is still critical, because it does involve issues which could lead to war. But however important this relationship of military balance, it cannot be our sole preoccupation to the exclusion of other world issues which also concern us both.

Even if we succeed in relaxing tensions with the U.S.S.R., we could still awake one day to find that nuclear weapons have been spread to dozens of other nations who may not be as responsible as are we. Or we could struggle to limit the conventional arsenals of our two nations, to reduce the danger of war, only to undo our efforts by continuing without constraint to export armaments around the world.

As two industrial giants, we face long-term, worldwide energy crises. Whatever our political differences, both of us are compelled to begin conserving world energy and developing alternatives to oil and gas.

Despite deep and continuing differences in world outlook, both of us should accept the new responsibilities imposed on us by the changing nature of international relations.

Europe and Japan rose from the rubble of war to become great economic powers. Communist parties and governments have become more widespread and more varied and, I might say, more independent from one another. Newly independent nations emerged into what has now become known as the Third World. Their role in world affairs is becoming increasingly significant.

Both the United States and the Soviet Union have learned that our countries and our people, in spite of great resources, are not all-powerful. We've learned that this world, no matter how technology has shrunk distances, is nevertheless too large and too varied to come under the sway of either one or two super powers. And what is perhaps more important of all, we have, for our part, learned, all of us, this fact, these facts in a spirit not of increasing resignation, but of increasing maturity.

I mention these familiar changes with which you are familiar because I think that to understand today's Soviet-American relationship, we must place it in perspective, both historically and in terms of the overall global scene.

The whole history of Sovet-American relations teaches us that we will be misled if we base our long-range policies on the mood of the moment, whether that mood be euphoric or grim. All of us can remember times when relations seemed especially dangerous and other times when they seemed especially bright.

We've crossed those peaks and valleys before. And we can see that, on balance, the trend in the last third of a century has been positive.

The profound differences in what our two governments believe about freedom and power and the inner lives of human beings, those differences are likely to remain; and so are other elements of competition between the United States and the Soviet Union. That competition is real and deeply rooted in the history and the values of our respective societies. But it's also true that our two countries share many important overlapping interests. Our job—my job, your job—is to explore those shared interests and use them to enlarge the areas of cooperation between us on a basis of equality and mutual respect.

As we negotiate with the Soviet Union, we will be guided by a vision of a gentler, freer, and more bountiful world. But we will have no illusions about the nature of the world as it really is. The basis for complete mutual trust between us does not yet exist. Therefore, the agreements that we reach must be anchored on each side in enlightened self-interest— what's best for us, what's best for the Soviet Union. That's why we search for areas of agreement where our real interests and those of the Soviets coincide.

We want to see the Soviets further engaged in the growing pattern of international activities designed to deal with human problems—not only because they can be of real help but because we both should be seeking for a greater stake in the creation of a constructive and peaceful world order.

When I took office, many Americans were growing disillusioned with détente— President Ford had even quit using the word, and by extension, people were concerned with the whole course of our relations with the Soviet Union. Also, and perhaps more seriously, world respect for the essential rightness of American foreign policy had been shaken by the events of a decade—Vietnam, Cambodia, CIA, Watergate. At the same time, we were beginning to regain our sense of confidence and our purpose and unity as a nation.

In this situation, I decided that it was time for honest discussions about international issues with the American people. I felt that it was urgent to restore the moral bearings of American foreign policy. And I felt that it was important to put the U.S. and Soviet relationship, in particular, on a more reciprocal, realistic, and, ultimately, more productive basis for both nations.

It's not a question of a "hard" policy or of a "soft" policy, but of a clear-eyed recognition of how most effectively to protect our own security and to create the kind of international order that I've just described. This is our goal.

We've looked at the problems in Soviet-American relations in a fresh way, and we've sought to deal with them boldly and constructively with proposals intended to produce concrete results. I'd like to point out just a few of them.

In the talks on strategic arms limitations, the SALT talks, we advanced a comprehensive proposal for genuine reductions, limitations, and a freeze on new technology which would maintain balanced strategic strength.

We have urged a complete end to all nuclear tests, and these negotiations are now underway. Agreement here could be a milestone in U.S.-Soviet relations.

We're working together toward a ban on chemical and biological warfare and the elimination of inventories of these destructive materials. We have proposed to curb the sales and transfers of conventional weapons to other countries, and we've asked France, Britain, and other countries to join with us in this effort.

We are attempting to halt the threatening proliferation of nuclear weapons among the nations of the world which don't yet have the ability to set off nuclear explosives.

We've undertaken serious negotiations on arms limitations in the Indian Ocean. We've encouraged the Soviets to sign, along with us, the Treaty of Tlatelolco, which would ban the introduction of nuclear weapons into the southern part of the Western Hemisphere.

We have begun regular consultations with the Soviet leaders as cochairmen of the prospective Geneva conference to promote peace in the Middle East.

We and our allies are negotiating together with the Soviet Union and their allies in the Warsaw Pact nations to reduce the level of military forces in Europe.

We've renewed the 1972 agreement for cooperation in science and technology, and a similar agreement for cooperation in outer space.

We're seeking ways to cooperate in improving world health and in relieving world hunger.

In the strategic arms limitation talks, confirming and then building on Vladivostok accords, we need to make steady progress toward our long-term goals of genuine reductions and strict limitations, while maintaining the basic strategic balance.

We've outlined proposals incorporating significant new elements of arms control, deep reductions in the arsenals of both sides, freezing of deployment and technology, and restraining certain elements in the strategic posture of both sides that threaten to destabilize the balance which now exists.

The Vladivostok negotiations of 1974 left some issues unresolved and subject to honest differences of interpretation. Meanwhile, new developments in technology have created new concerns—the cruise missile, the very large intercontinental ballistic missiles of the Soviets.

The Soviets are worried about our cruise missiles, and we are concerned about the security of our own deterrent capability. Our cruise missiles are aimed at compensating for the growing threat to our deterrent, represented by the build-up of strategic Soviet offensive weapons forces. If these threats can be controlled, and I believe they can, then we are prepared to limit our own strategic programs. But if an agreement cannot be reached, there should be no doubt that the United States can and will do what it must to protect our security and to ensure the adequacy of our strategic posture.

Our new proposals go beyond those that have been made before. In many areas we are in fact addressing for the first time the tough, complex core of long-standing problems. We are trying for the first time to reach agreements that will not be overturned by the next technological breakthrough. We are trying, in a word, for genuine accommodation.

But none of these proposals that I've outlined to you involves a sacrifice of security. All of them are meant to increase the security of both sides. Our view is that a SALT agreement which just reflects the lowest common denominator that can be agreed upon easily will only create an illusion of progress and, eventually, a backlash against the entire arms control process. Our view is that genuine progress in SALT will not merely stabilize competition in weapons but can also provide a basis for improvement in political relations as well.

When I say that these efforts are intended to relax tensions, I'm not speaking only of military security. I mean as well the concern among our own individual citizens, Soviet and American, that comes from the knowledge which all of you have that the leaders of our two countries have the capacity to destroy human society through misunderstandings or mistakes. If we can relax this tension by reducing the nuclear threat, not only will we make the world a safer place but we'll also free ourselves to concentrate on constructive action to give the world a better life.

We've made some progress toward our goals, but to be frank, we also hear some negative comments from the Soviet side about SALT and about our more general relations. If these comments are based on a misconception about our motives, then we will redouble our efforts to make our motives clear; but if the Soviets are merely making comments designed as propaganda to put pressure on us, let no one doubt that we will persevere.

What matters ultimately is whether we can create a relationship of cooperation that will be rooted in the national interests of both sides. We shape our own policies to accommodate a constantly changing world, and we hope the Soviets will do the same. Together we can give this change a positive direction.

Increased trade between the United States and the Soviet Union would help us both. The American-Soviet Joint Commercial Commission has resumed its meetings after a long interlude. I hope that conditions can be created that will make possible steps toward expanded trade.

In southern Africa we have pressed for Soviet and Cuban restraint. Throughout the nonaligned world, our goal is not to encourage dissension or to redivide the world into opposing ideological camps, but to expand the realm of independent, economically self-reliant nations, and to oppose attempts at new kinds of subjugation.

Part of the Soviet Union leaders' current attitude may be due to their apparent—and incorrect—belief that our concern for human rights is aimed specifically at them or is an attack on their vital interests.

There are no hidden meanings in our commitment to human rights.

We stand on what we have said on the subject of human rights. Our policy is exactly what it appears to be: the positive and sincere expression of our deepest beliefs as a people. It's addressed not to any particular people or area of the world, but to all countries equally, yes, including our own country.

And it's specifically not designed to heat up the arms race or bring back the cold war.

On the contrary, I believe that an atmosphere of peaceful cooperation is far more conducive to an increased respect for human rights than an atmosphere of belligerence or hatred or warlike confrontation. The experience of our own country this last century has proved this over and over again.

We have no illusions that the process will be quick or that change will come easily. But we are confident that if we do not abandon the struggle, the cause of personal freedom and human dignity will be enhanced in all nations of the world. We're going to do that.

In the past 6 months we've made clear our determination—both to give voice to Americans' fundamental beliefs and to obtain lasting solutions to East-West differences. If this chance to emphasize peace and cooperation instead of animosity and division is allowed to pass, it will not have been our choice.

We must always combine realism with principle. Our actions must be faithful to the essential values to which our own society is dedicated, because our faith in those values is the source of our confidence that this relationship will evolve in a more constructive direction.

I cannot forecast whether all our efforts will succeed. But there are things which give me hope, and in conclusion I would like to mention them very briefly.

This place where I now stand is one of the oldest cities in the United States. It's a beautiful town of whose culture and urban charm all Americans are proud—just as the people of the Soviet Union are justly proud of such ancient cities as Tbilisi or Novgorod, which there they lovingly preserve, as you do in Charleston, and into which they infuse a new life that makes these cities far more than just dead remnants of a glorious historical past.

Although there are deep differences in our values and ideas, we Americans and Russians belong to the same civilization whose origins stretch back hundreds of years.

Beyond all the disagreements between us—and beyond the cool calculations of mutual self-interest that our two countries bring to the negotiating table—is the invisible human reality that must bring us closer together. I mean the yearning for peace, real peace, that is in the very bones of us all.

I'm absolutely certain that the people of the Soviet Union, who have suffered so grievously in war, feel this yearning for peace. And in this they are at one with the people of the United States. It's up to all of us to help make that unspoken passion into something more than just a dream. And that responsibility falls most heavily on those like you, of course, but particularly like President Brezhnev and me, who hold in our hands the terrible power conferred on us by the modern engines of war.

Mr. Brezhnev said something very interesting recently, and I quote from his speech: "It is our belief, our firm belief," he said, "that realism in politics and the will for détente and progress will ultimately triumph, and mankind will be able to step into the 21st century in conditions of peace, stable as never before."

I see no hidden meaning in that. I credit its sincerity. And I express the same hope and belief that Mr. Brezhnev expressed. With all the difficulties, all the conflicts, I believe that our planet must finally obey the Biblical injunction to "follow after the things which make for peace."

Thank you very much.

NOTE: The President spoke at 3:08 p.m. in the Gaillard Municipal Auditorium. In his opening remarks, he referred to State Representative John T. Bragg of Tennessee, chairman of the conference.

Jackson, Mississippi

Remarks on Arrival at Allen C. Thompson Airport. July 21, 1977

Thank you very much, Governor Finch. Senator Stennis, Senator Eastland, Congressman Sonny Montgomery, and others who have come here to Mississippi from Washington with me, I want to express my thanks to you.

Just so nobody has any doubt that I know, and just so I don't have any doubt that you know, do you all remember what State put me over the top on election night? [*Applause*] Very good.

As a matter of fact, we were waiting to see who would be the next President. I was talking on a telephone with Governor Cliff Finch, and the television screens flashed, "Jimmy Carter wins," and I know that I busted Cliff Finch's eardrums when I shouted, "Mississippi did it! Mississippi did it!" And I thank you for it.

When I first came here, Mayor Russell Davis met me at the airport, and a group of business leaders and, later, a group of students, educators, both black and white, came to talk and to listen to me and to learn what I stood for.

I was a former Governor who was not well known. And over a period of time, the people of your State and the people of the country came to realize that I felt the same way that you do, that I tried to search in my own heart for those things that are conservative: basic decency and a pride in our past, a belief that those who are able to work ought to work, a belief that the best government is the government closest to the people, that budgets ought to be balanced, that there ought to be a careful attention paid to letting people's individuality be encouraged, that people should make their own decisions, that government officials ought to be accountable to the people back home.

These kinds of principles have bound us together, deep religious conviction, and combined with that in a changing world, as has been demonstrated in Mississippi, Georgia, Tennessee, Alabama, Louisiana, and other States, has been a willingness for us to change when we saw that the future could be better than the past. And we did not lack courage to reach our hands out to our black neighbors, those of us who were white, and say, "Join us in creating a better future for everybody." This was not an easy thing for us to do. But we have done it, and we are better off for it.

We also have seen in foreign affairs that some of our principles that are espoused throughout this country can be put into effect.

One of the most controversial issues so far has been that of human rights. But we say that government ought not to subjugate people, that people ought to have a right to speak their own voice, that they ought not be imprisoned because they believe in a certain political philosophy, and I have been criticized for this stand. But I'll never back down, as long as you stick with me.

We've also seen in our country a renewed faith, not because of me but because of you. Since last November, we've had 3 million additional people go to work. The unemployment rate since December has dropped one full percentage point. We've got a long way to go, but I think there's a general recognition now that the Congress—the Senate and the House—and the President in the White House are working closely with one another, not trying to blame each other for mistakes, but trying to share responsibility.

And we work very closely also with the Governors and mayors and county officials back home to be sure that when decisions are made about controversial questions, that your voice is heard by us and that our decisions are shaped by the sound judgment and the basic intelligence and the widely varying experience that you can bring to political decisions.

Another thing that I want to say before I close is I'm very glad that I was able to help bring the rain to Mississippi. I just hope it's raining in Plains, Georgia, as well as it is in Jackson.

We have a lot of characteristics as farmers in the agricultural region that I've described already. As I said a few minutes ago in Charleston, South Carolina, I'm proud to be an American, and I'm also proud to be a southerner.

For long weeks, long months, 2 years ago, people just didn't believe that a southerner could be elected President. But you and I together showed them they were wrong. And for the last 6 months, strangely enough, I haven't seen much in the newspapers or magazines about my being a southerner. Now I, like you, am an American.

And I think we have helped break down those barriers that used to separate us from the rest of the country. And now we see that, as is the case with our neighbors next door, we also share our hopes and our dreams with people throughout this great country. And I'm proud of that change that has taken place to a great measure because of your confidence in me.

In closing, let me say that I am very deeply grateful to you, and I pray God that, with your help, you'll never be disappointed that I am in the White House. I need your help, your encouragement, your advice, your sound judgment, and your prayers. And I hope you'll give me all those things as I fill the job which you have given to me.

Thank you very much. God bless you.

NOTE: The President spoke at 5:30 p.m.

Yazoo City, Mississippi

Remarks and a Question-and-Answer Session at a Public Meeting.   July 21, 1977

THE PRESIDENT. It's a great pleasure for me to come to the dedication ceremony of the Yazoo City new high school. I was told before I came that the new building was air-conditioned. [*Laughter*]

I think it's time for the rest of the country to see the southern self-propelled air-conditioner we have here tonight. It reminds me of going to church at home, and I appreciate you letting me come and the great welcome that I've received already.

I want to say just a word about the school itself, because I think it typifies the South, Mississippi, Yazoo City attitudes.

In a lot of places in our country you couldn't get a school bond issue passed, particularly if the school classrooms were going to be filled with roughly two-thirds black students and one-third white students, but the people of Yazoo City, believing in your young people, having confidence in one another, and looking forward to the future with great anticipation and courage and confidence, overwhelmingly voted to build this new school which will be occupied for the first time this fall, and I'm proud of you. It shows the good judgment of Mississippians.

And last November 3, I also witnessed the good political judgment of the State of Mississippi. If we could have just changed three votes, it would have shown the good political judgment of Yazoo County as well. [*Laughter*]

I've enjoyed this first, almost exactly 6 months of being your President. I've tried to open up the decisionmaking process of our country to you and the people like you all over the Nation.

I think Presidents, Members of Congress, Cabinet officers, Federal administrators can make better decisions to the extent that we receive the judgment, common sense, and the benefit of the experience of people around the country. So, I'm very grateful to have a chance to get out, away from Washington, to see and talk and listen to you and others like you.

Earlier this afternoon I went to Charleston, South Carolina, and I spoke to about 1,400 people there who represented the State legislatures of the Southern States. I didn't talk about highway funds, welfare programs, revenue sharing. I talked about foreign policy. I talked about the interrelationship between our country and the Soviet Union, a very important speech that spells out our Nation's policy which might affect the lives of you and your children and your grandchildren in years ahead, because I don't think that my visits to the South and other places ought to be limited to a discussion of just things that involve dollars and cents or even important things like inflation or welfare programs.

Our Nation's international policies ought also to be understood by you, debated by you, discussed by you, argued by you, and ultimately, decided by you. We've got a great country, and what we want, obviously, is to have the true character of the United States of America demonstrated in every action we take, not only in our own domestic affairs but also throughout the world.

And one of the great bursts of applause that came this afternoon was when I said that we are deeply committed to carrying out the purposes and the principles of the United States in our deep and permanent and unchanging commitments to human freedom and human rights, and you can count on that.

Tonight I want to take about an hour and a half to listen to your questions and try to give you the best answers I can. I don't claim to know all the answers. I have a lot to learn. I learn a lot from people like you and from the Members of your congressional delegation, from your State and local officials.

And I think it's also good for the citizens of our country, who are watching television tonight, to learn from your questions, to see what are the things that concern the people in Yazoo City, Mississippi.

So, we'll start on my right in just a moment with the first question, and I think we have four microphones in the audience and I'll try to keep my answers clear. I'll try to answer the questions that you actually ask me. If I don't know the answer, I'm going to tell you I don't know the answer.

But if there's a question now, we'll start with the first microphone.

Yes, sir? Would you tell me your name, first of all, and then your question?

FUTURE ECONOMIC GROWTH

Q. My name is Herman B. Desell of Yazoo City. My question, Mr. President, relates to your proposal to balance the budget by 1981. I think most of us agree with that proposition, but many of us are concerned about possible impairment of ongoing programs that are vital to our local people—revenue sharing, the youth work programs, our educational programs, and related programs that provide job opportunities.

My question is, how will you go about establishing priorities to determine which of these programs may be modified or altered, and in what way?

THE PRESIDENT. Fine. That's an excellent question. Our projections of the future economic growth of our country, based on normal circumstances, show that we can continue the programs that are doing a good job for our people, that are in effect now. And with proper management, reorganization of the Government itself, with the elimination of overlapping and duplicating Federal programs and bureaucracies, we can have enough growth in Federal revenues to give us both expanded programs and/or tax reductions which are very important to you, or a balanced budget.

I think that if we are fortunate, we can have both—not only continue the present programs but have some tax reduction and also balance the budget by fiscal year 1981.

We're going to have to be very strict about what the Congress and I approve in the way of increased spending. I'll have to use my best judgment, along with the Congress, to determine what is necessary to expand, what is necessary to cut back, what is necessary to eliminate. But everything I do, obviously, will be done in the open.

The Congress has a very close check on the President and vice versa. But I'm determined that in normal economic circumstances, to give you a balanced budget before this term is over.

CONGRESSIONAL ACTION ON PROPOSED LEGISLATION

Q. Hello, Mr. President, I'm Ted Webb, a student at Ole Miss. You have been in office for about 6 months now. At this point in time, are you personally satisfied with the progress made by the programs you sponsored, and if not, which program has been your biggest disappointment and why?

THE PRESIDENT. Okay. Does anybody mind if I take my coat off? I got wet at the airport in Jackson this afternoon when I landed, a rain that they needed very much. I've still got on the same clothes, so nobody can tell whether it's sweat or rain. [*Laughter*] I'll let you in on a secret: It's both.

I've been very pleased so far with the progress that the Congress has made in the programs that I've put forward in the campaign and also in my first meetings with the Members of Congress. We asked Congress to pass strict ethics legislation to remove the conflicts of interest that might exist between public officials in the executive and legislative branches, and they've done a good job with this. I asked them to give me the authority to reorganize the executive branch of Government, and the Congress gave me almost exactly what I wanted.

I asked the Congress, in addition, to help me create a new Department of Energy, to bring all the 40 or 45 or 50 different agencies that have been responsible for energy together in a coordinated, well-organized, bureaucratic entity so we could have a carrying out of an energy policy.

I think it's accurate to say this month I'll be able to sign that legislation.

I asked the Congress to help me stimulate the American economy, and they did so to the tune of about $21 billion to put our people back to work. Late in December, we had an unemployment rate of 8.1 percent. That's down now to about 7 percent. We have more than a million people at work now, more than we had when I came into office and, as you know, the inflation rate has now leveled off; still too high but it's leveled off.

We have summer programs for young people amounting to about 1.1 million jobs for them, and we have public works programs that will be putting our people back to work shortly, in addition, throughout the country. These basic programs have already been passed.

We've had a $4 billion permanent tax reduction already, which means that an average family that makes $10,000 a year will have a 30-percent permanent tax reduction.

So far we've had good progress. We're now dealing with some very difficult additional subjects. One is a comprehensive policy on energy. We've never had that in our country. We are one of the few developed nations in the world who hasn't. It's based primarily on conservation and an end of waste of energy and a shift toward increasing use of coal, solar energy and so forth, and a reduction of our consumption of oil and gas.

The Congress is now struggling with that. I think it's accurate to say they will complete this work before they adjourn for the year in October.

We have other things, like social security—to make sure that our social security reserve funds are sound. So far the Congress has not acted on that. There's no doubt in my mind that this year they will.

So, I would say that the major programs that we put forward already are well on the way to being passed with a lot of other programs—strip mining legislation, agriculture bills. Later, welfare reform, tax reform, are still to be presented.

So, to summarize, I'm very pleased. The things that have disappointed me, of course, are the things that disappoint you. We've still got too many people unemployed. Last month, we had 270,000 new jobs, but the work force has increased to such an extent that we still have about 7 percent of our people without work.

As we put the new welfare legislation to the Congress, one part of it will be to encompass an additional 1 million new jobs. I want to put people who are able to work, to work, and get them off of welfare. I also, of course, want to make sure that those who are on welfare who cannot work are treated with respect and decency and an ability to live with pride in themselves and not be ashamed. That's still got to come. The inflation rate is still too high. So, in domestic affairs, we still have not been completely satisfied.

We're working on a SALT talk with the Soviet Union to cut down on atomic weapons. We haven't made enough progress yet. We're still trying. We're trying to get a comprehensive test ban so we won't have any more tests of atomic weapons. We're trying to bring peace to the Middle East, peace to southern Africa, and these things still have to be done. But I think the progress is in the right direction. So, we've had kind of a mixed bag the first 6 months. I think we've done a lot of new things that had been avoided or ignored for a long time, and I have been, overall, pleased. I have enjoyed it. So far I like the job very much.

ENERGY PRICES

Q. Hello, Mr. President. My name is Sue Tatum, and I come to you tonight with a question on behalf of my friends who are low-income people and fixed-income people. As you can imagine, they are having increasing difficulty paying utility bills. On a day like today it doesn't make a lot of difference, unless you want a fan, I guess. But many times their utility bills approach, and sometimes exceed, their income. Is there anything on the horizon to help these people?

THE PRESIDENT. I wish I could give you good news, Miss Tatum. But I think no matter who's in the White House, no matter who's in the Congress, that the price of energy is going to go up. We are simply running out of oil and natural gas, and the production of coal, atomic power, solar energy is going to be more costly in the future.

The major effort that we are putting forward in the energy program is to cut down on waste and for a family that is poor, whose utility bills are very high, the insulation of homes, the stopping of the use of electricity during the time of day when the demand is very high, the change in the rate structure of electric power to make sure that big business doesn't get very cheap rates and the homeowners get very high rates, those are some of the things that we are doing.

But my guess is that in 5 years from now the price of electricity, the price of gasoline, the price of natural gas, the price of propane, the price of coal is going to be higher. So, the only solution, it seems to me, is a much fairer distribution of energy and also a great reduction in how much energy a family uses to meet its own needs. It's not a hopeless case.

I might close my answer by saying this: Germany, Sweden, Japan, other countries have the same standard of living as we do. Their families have just as good a life as we do, as far as the material things are concerned. They use only one-half as much energy as we do. So, I think we need to cut back on the consumption and waste of energy. That's the main thing to do.

The last point I want to make—another one is—we need to control inflation. The Government can't do it by itself. I've been very disturbed today to find out that one of the largest steel companies is increasing its price for steel products another 7 or 8 percent for tin plate materials.

This means that they've increased the price of that particular steel product 12½ percent this last September, less than a year. I don't think it's necessary. So, I would say that private homeowners, business leaders, industrial producers, and Government, all have to work together to hold down inflation, hold down the consumption of energy; but we can't depend on cheaper energy in the future. I'm sorry.

OIL COMPANIES

Q. Mr. President, my name is Roger McGrath, and I am employed by Southland Oil Company, a small independent oil company which built our first oil refinery here in Yazoo County almost 40 years ago. We compete in the marketplace against major oil companies, with abnormal advantages due to their control of crude oil supply, prices, and economy of scale.

In your energy address to the Nation on April 20—and we applaud you for facing the energy problem—you recognized the problems we independents face and called for improved antitrust enforcement based upon separate accounting for separate functional segments of the oil industry. But the proposed national energy legislation does not reach these issues and some administration spokesmen seem to express other views even to the effect that independent refiners are expendable in our Nation's overall energy program.

My question is, do you still intend to take these actions to protect competition and preserve the competitive viability of the small independent refiners; and pending long-term solutions, would you support the continuation of present Federal programs designed to provide temporary solutions?

THE PRESIDENT. Yes. The basic question is whether or not we will do what we can as an administration to treat the small and independent oil and gas companies on the same basis as the large ones; also, I understand your question is whether or not we're going to vigorously enforce the antitrust laws which do mean if they are enforced that the true competition in our country can be restored.

The answer to both those questions is yes.

HEALTH CARE COSTS

Q. Mr. President, I'm Dr. R. W. Harrison, a local dentist. I would like to ask what are your plans for increasing the availability of all phases of health care to rural, underserved areas, and do you believe that Public Law 93–641, dealing with health care delivery, can be implemented effectively?

THE PRESIDENT. You're going to have to tell me what Public Law 93–641 is. [*Laughter*]

Let me answer part of your question. I'll let you ask me that following up. The first step in the delivery of better health care to our people is to control runaway costs. In hospitals now, for instance, we have the cost of the same level of health care doubling every 5 years. So, no matter what kind of health program you have, if the hospital costs are twice as

high every 5 years, there's no way for the Federal Government or local and State governments or private citizens to pay for it.

We have introduced in the Congress this year a cost containment bill which will limit the increase in hospital charges to about 9 percent a year, with some flexibility in there to accommodate wage increases. That's the first step.

Another step is to cut down on the waste which goes into our health care system, when people are admitted into the hospital as inpatients, when they can just as well be treated either at home or in outpatient care, where the person comes to the hospital, gets treated, and goes back home. As you know, in many instances both doctors and hospitals benefit if the patient is admitted to the hospital. When you have a very simple operation, for instance, if you go into the hospital, stay 3 or 4 days, the costs are enormous. We need to do away with that as much as possible.

Another thing we need to do is that when people are treated in that fashion, that we have an increasing dependence upon nonphysicians—registered nurses, physicians' assistants, and others—who can give the same examinations, basic examinations and simple treatment, under the supervision of doctors so it won't cost as much.

We also need to have an emphasis on prevention of disease. When those of you who are my age were young, most of our contact either with private doctors or with the public health doctors and nurses was to prevent disease. We've gotten away from that now. We need to go back to the prevention of disease.

Another last thing I'd like to say on the cost of health care is this: There are increasingly wasteful, very expensive machines that are purchased by hospitals and health care centers, sometimes two or three in the same location and, of course, the patients who come there have to pay for those.

I think there needs to be an additional concern in reduction in this very high investment that has to be paid for by patients.

We also in some areas have too many hospital beds. When you have 40 percent of the hospital beds that are empty, then the patients that are in the other 60 percent are paying for their bed and also paying for those 40 empty beds that night. So, we need to have a much closer attention paid through local supervision, not the Federal Government, to make sure that we don't overbuild hospitals, hospital beds, machines, overadmit people to hospitals, and give them health care that they don't need.

But I think in all of these cases that the money that we do save can go back into giving people better preventive care and better and more complete care for those who actually need it.

Now, the particular bill that you refer to, if you'll tell me briefly what it says, maybe I can answer your other questions.

Q. It combines the functions of the old regional medical program, comprehensive health planning districts, and does some of the things that you just mentioned. You must establish a certificate of need for new beds, for new machines, any new facility.

THE PRESIDENT. Yes. I think that's very good legislation. And one of the best things about it, I understand, is that it lets the people who live in an area do the planning and make the decisions without having Federal Government supervisors or bureaucrats come in and do it for you. Is that correct?

Q. Correct.

THE PRESIDENT. I think that's a move in the right direction.

SMALL BUSINESS ADMINISTRATION

Q. Mr. President, my name is Tom Espy. In light of the recent developments in SBA's 8(a) set-aside programs, what is your posture or the posture of the President on the continuation and expansion of minority and disadvantaged economic development programs, especially those programs in the Department of Commerce?

THE PRESIDENT. I'm going to be frank with you. I think in the past that in many areas, the minority citizens have not been given an equal opportunity in the business world. When I came home from the Navy in 1953, I started a business and I needed, 3 or 4 years later, to get a loan. I went to the Small Business Administration and got a loan. I belonged to a prominent family in town and so I had every assistance that I needed from the local banks, from the Small Business Administration. They would send senior businessmen down to Plains to help me with my business, to make sure my accounts receivable were not too high, that I didn't overextend myself on loans, that my inventory was not too much, that I ran my business properly.

But quite often, minority new business people or sometimes women as well, when they get a loan from the Government or parts that are supported by the Government, have not been treated that way. Sometimes they've been given just enough of a loan to go into bankruptcy and have not been given a chance to work their way into the learning process.

This is what we're trying to address in the Small Business Administration—in the minority businesses part of it—and throughout the entire Department of Commerce.

As you know, there have been some scandals revealed recently where the Government had made loans to minority business people as a political payoff, I might add, before I came into the White House—and we're trying to stop that, also. I had a meeting today with Parren Mitchell, who is head of the Black Caucus, this morning, and as we put into effect changes in how to make these loans, we want to be sure that we don't have discrimination against minority entrepreneurs and also that when a loan is made, that it's not only sound but that that person who borrows the money has a constant attention given to him or her to make sure that the business is successful and that the loan is repaid.

I can't say to you that we have done enough in that respect in the past. But I can guarantee to you that we'll do much better in the future.

LIFE AS PRESIDENT

Q. Mr. Carter, my name is Mary Tucker and I would like to know how is it to be a President?

THE PRESIDENT. Thank you, Mary.

Well, Mary Tucker, nothing would please me better in about 30 years than to have you find out how it is to be President by living in the White House yourself as President. And if you're running, remind me and I'll vote for you if Amy doesn't run. Okay? [*Laughter*]

Let me say though, to answer your question additionally, it's a good life. I spent 2 years, Miss Tucker, campaigning around this country. I came into Mississippi a lot of times. So did my wife, all three of my sons, all three of my daughters-in-law, my mother and my sister and many Georgians. And we learned a lot about Mississippi and we learned a lot about the other States in the Nation. And I think a lot of people got to know me.

Now, I feel that people like you and your parents have put a lot of responsibility on my shoulders and a lot of faith in me. And I think that as long as I am able to come out like this and meet with you and others and learn, that I can do a good job.

We've brought our family back together. We had been separated for almost 2 years. Amy was only 2 years old when I was elected Governor and she was 3 years old when I moved into the Governor's Mansion. Now she's just 9, but she is enjoying living in the White House, too. She goes to the public school right down the street. She has a cat and a dog and a treehouse, and she has a lot of her friends come into the White House. So, we have a good family life.

I've had a good chance so far to work with the Members of the Congress. Your own Senator Stennis and Senator Eastland and Sonny Montgomery, your Congressman, have been a lot of help to me. I had Governor Finch up to the White House a week or so ago to help me with energy problems. So, I have a lot of help.

So, in general, it's been a very pleasant job. The working conditions are good. My office is near my home and the people have been very nice to me so far. And I just hope I don't ever betray the trust that all of you have placed in me. And I hope that you'll come up sometimes and visit me in the White House and also have a chance to play with Amy for a few minutes. Would you do that?

HUMAN RIGHTS

Q. Mr. President, my name is Everett Beers. I strongly support your position on human rights as manifested in your foreign policy statements. I'm very sorry that I missed your remarks on human rights this afternoon. But I would like to know, aside from the rhetoric that's been generated, can we really hope to influence the world community on human rights issues, and how can you conscientiously justify excluding our allies such as Korea and

Greece from human rights commitments and also, have you made an affirmative action plan to implement some long-range goals in this area?

THE PRESIDENT. That's a difficult question to answer, but I will do the best I can.

Obviously, throughout the world, I think in every country without exception in the heart and mind of every person, there's a desire to be free, to make one's own decision, to speak without fear, to have a chance to express one's political beliefs, to seek different kinds of employment without interference by government, not to be dominated by officials who have power, not to be imprisoned without adequate charge, and not to be tortured when one is arrested, whether or not a conviction has been carried out or not.

So, what we began to speak for 6 months ago is nothing new. It doesn't exist just in democracies or free countries like ours. It exists in the nations that are most dominated by totalitarian governments.

I think that my voice and others like mine all over the world, including, I hope, yours, when raised for liberty, for human dignity, for freedom, have a cumulative effect. We don't have any desire to go into a country with force and try to change their form of government. But I think it's accurate to say now that when an open spokesman for a minority group anywhere in the world is arrested, that it is a very newsworthy item.

We have seen recently in Argentina 342 political prisoners, who had been there for a long time, released. In Korea now, just this week, political prisoners who had been in prison for a long time are being released. And I think it's accurate to say that the trend is toward an enhancement of human rights.

In Belgrade, Yugoslavia, this October, there will be a very open and wide debate, I would say for at least a couple of months, part of which will be devoted to human rights, whether or not families can be joined together, whether people who want to leave a country can do so without being punished. And the Soviet Union signed the Helsinki treaty, and it will be debated—so did Poland, Yugoslavia, Czechoslovakia, the United States, the Western allies of ours. And all of us, including us, the United States, are trying to look good in the eyes of the world.

I think the progress is going to be quite slow. But I believe in the long run our efforts will be successful. But I am afraid if the United States does not take a strong position, that the cause of human rights is going to be damaged very severely. And I also believe we've ignored this question too long.

I think it was time this year, following our own 200th anniversary, to raise again a beacon light that will make our people proud and say we stand for something. We stand for the same thing that inspired Thomas Jefferson and George Washington, Benjamin Franklin, and others to offer their lives, if necessary, to found a country based on freedom. And I think this is a good move.

I've been criticized a good bit for being so outspoken about it, because it might make some leaders of other nations angry. I'm not trying to make anybody angry. I'm not trying to interfere in the internal affairs of other nations. I'm not trying to bring back the Cold War, but I'll say this: As long as the American people back me on the subject, we will never stay quiet on the subject of human rights.

ABORTION

Q. Mr. President, I am Dr. Will Thompson, a local family physician. I'm concerned about the issue of human rights also, but more particularly am interested in your opinion, your feelings on the abortion issue.

First of all, I'd like to commend you on your opposition to Federal funding for abortion on demand. And I would personally like to see you continue in your opposition to abortion on demand—this issue. My question is: Do you consider the issue of abortion on demand as a human rights issue since unborn children are human beings, created in God's image, and if you do not consider the abortion issue as a human rights issue, why not, and then if you do consider it, will you actively oppose abortion on demand in other areas during your administration?

Thank you.

THE PRESIDENT. Thank you, Doctor.

I think of all the questions that have faced me as a candidate, this was the one that was most widely discussed. The Supreme Court has ruled in several instances on the abortion question in recent years. One basic ruling has been that at the first stages of pregnancy that a woman has a right to have an abortion. Georgia had a law that prevented abortions except in the case of danger to the mother's life or when the pregnancy was caused by incest or rape.

As Governor, I personally supported that law. When the Supreme Court struck it down, we passed the most conservative abortion law possible under the Supreme Court ruling.

I do think that the abortion issue involves the question of human rights. There's an inherent conflict in the basic discussion: the right of a woman to have control over her own body, free from interference by government, and on the other hand, the right of the embryonic child to live.

The Supreme Court has drawn a line between the first 3 months of pregnancy, as you know, when abortions are permitted, and the other roughly 6 months of pregnancy when very tight constraints are placed on the right to have abortions. That's an arbitrary line that's drawn, and as President, I support the ruling and will enforce it to the best of my ability.

I don't favor the Federal Government financing abortions. The last year about 300,000 abortions were paid for by Federal funds. I was told that in the District of Columbia this past year there were more abortions than there were births. I'm afraid that to take a very permissive stand on abortions, paying for them, which puts them in the same category, roughly, as other contraceptive means, will be an encouragement to depend upon abortions to prevent pregnancy.

So, I would rather emphasize, as President—and I might say the Secretary of HEW agrees with me completely on this issue, Joe Califano—I would rather emphasize the prevention of the pregnancy at the time of sexual intercourse and not have the woman who might be very poor and very ignorant depend upon abortions as a way to terminate a pregnancy because of carelessness or sometimes a deliberate act.

It's very disturbing how many of the recipients of Federal payments for abortion in the past have been repeaters. They come back time after time for additional abortions which show that it's not entirely ignorance.

So, with a good education program, with a firm stand not to encourage abortions as a normal way of life, and with the provision to poor people of government-supported contraceptive devices if the person believes in their use, these are the alternatives that I personally favor in preference to abortions.

FEDERAL HOUSING SUBSIDY PROGRAM

Q. My name is Maurice King. I want to know if you are considering doing away with the Federal housing subsidy program, and, if so, why?

THE PRESIDENT. We are not considering doing away with the Federal housing subsidy program. There is no doubt in my mind that the program will be continued. We are constantly searching for a way to do a better job of providing good housing with the amount of money that we have available, and both Secretary Patricia Harris and Secretary Califano at HEW, Bert Lance at the Office of Management and Budget, myself, and others, are trying to see a proper balance on how limited Federal funds might be made available.

I believe in family homeownership and in many instances there's no way for a family to finance a home without Federal assistance in the acquisition of the loan, and sometimes interest subsidies. Among young people—I mean, older people, the 202 programs, to provide housing for them with a reasonable monthly payment, ought to be continued. We also, of course, need to continue the Section 8 program which provides decent housing for those with very low incomes.

The question that is being addressed is, with a limited amount of money for housing, how to make sure that we don't spend too much on very expensive homes for just a few people when many more hundreds of thousands of American citizens do without housing subsidies at all.

But the answer to your question in one word, about whether or not we are going to do away with the housing subsidy program—the answer is no.

PANAMA CANAL ZONE

Q. Hello, Mr. President. I am Jeff Davis, and my question is, with the Republic of Panama asking for complete control of the Panama Canal, do you feel it would be a mistake to grant their demand, and do you think that the Panama Canal Zone would be a vital base in case of a third world war, as Cuba is a threat to our Southern States?

THE PRESIDENT. Fine. In 1903 to 1907, our country worked out with Panama an arrangement to acquire control of the Panama Canal Zone and, of course, we built the Panama Canal. The treaty said that Panama retained sovereignty over the Panama Canal Zone; that we had control over the Panama Canal Zone as though we had sovereignty. So, even in the time of Theodore Roosevelt the agreement was that we and the Panamanians both, in effect, have sovereignty over the Panama Canal Zone—they have legal sovereignty, we control it—to operate after the building of the Panama Canal itself.

My hope is that we can sign a treaty with Panama to share with them, from now until the year 2000, the operation of the Panama Canal itself and to continue, after the year 2000, an adequate authority to protect the Panama Canal, to keep it open for international use, giving our own warships priority along with those of Panama in the use of the canal.

My guess is, that before many more years go by, we might very well need a new canal, one at sea level, that can handle very large ships. This was studied when Lyndon Johnson was President, and the cost of it was very high, several billions of dollars. Since then we have seen a much greater need for the canal.

We are now looking for a way to get Alaskan oil and gas to the central part and the Eastern seaboard of the United States. The large ships that bring the oil down from Panama [Alaska] can't go through the canal. If they bring oil, they come down to the Panama area, off-load the oil into small ships; the small ships go through the Panama Canal and bring the oil, in the future, up to the gulf coast or the eastern coast.

On natural gas, when it does come, it will be liquified at a very, very low temperature, put in large ships and brought down perhaps to the Panama Canal itself. There is no way to change it back into gas, send it across Panama, and reliquify it. It costs too much.

So, in the future, I would say that we will need a sea level Panama Canal that can handle our large warships and the large tankers and freighters that are part of international commerce now.

So, I think we ought to keep good relations with Panama. We can prevent an attack on the Panama Canal by a foreign government. It would be almost impossible to prevent the disruption or closing of the Panama Canal by sabotage if the Panamanians were determined to put it out of commission. So, it is important for us to work with Panama and not against Panama.

So, to summarize, between now and the year 2000, we will retain under the proposed treaty our control, partial sovereignty with Panama having sovereignty as well. This is derived from 1907. After the year 2000, we will give up the actual operation of the canal to Panama but retain the right to defend it with our armed forces and to keep it open, with first priority given to American warships and Panamanian warships to use it. I don't know what the treaty terms might be, but that's the best report that I can give you right now.

NATIONAL HEALTH INSURANCE

Q. Hello, President Carter. My name is Jeff Hogue, and I'm a student at the University of Tennessee. Last year, yourself and the Democratic Party proposed the creation of a national health insurance

program. I was wondering if you would briefly explain how such a program would work and how, at the same time, you could accomplish your goal of decreasing the budget and the national deficit with a program of such outrageous spending.

THE PRESIDENT. Okay. I have described in general already some of the principles that ought to be used to cut down on the cost, which is the first step under the bill we've already presented to Congress—to cut down on unnecessary health care, to have more emphasis on prevention, outpatient treatment, the use of paramedical personnel, and so forth. We presently spend in this country about $600 a year [per person] for health care; by far more than any other nation on Earth. And I believe that without any substantial increase in the total expenditures, we can have a good health care system.

If we put one in, and I would like to see it done, a comprehensive health care system, then the financing of it will still come, either from taxpayers, which it presently is now to some degree, private users of health care, and other organizations formed, like Blue Cross/Blue Shield, by the citizens ourselves. I personally prefer the health insurance program to be administered, to the extent that it can, on a competitive basis by private insurance firms, like Blue Cross/Blue Shield. When it's obvious to me and to the Congress and, ultimately, to the American people that the Government should play an additional role in managing the health care or insurance system, then I would not hestitate to do that.

No matter what we do, this program needs to be phased in over a fairly long period of time. By early next year, 1978, we will be prepared to present to the Congress a comprehensive, nationwide health insurance program, with emphasis on the things I've described to you—I think without substantial increase in the total cost and in a way emphasizing the private sector as much as possible, but without fear of having the Federal Government participate to the extent that I and the Congress think it's necessary.

HUMAN RIGHTS

Q. Mr. President, my name is Betty Rainey. I'm a housewife and mother of three. Welcome to Yazoo City.

THE PRESIDENT. Thank you.

Q. What aspects of what you consider to be your southern heritage have led to your concern with human rights in this Nation and abroad?

THE PRESIDENT. Okay. When I answer this, I don't want you to feel that all the characteristics that I'd ascribe to southerners are not also shared by people who live in other parts of the country. But I think that we have always been a deeply religious people in the South. When I was in a submarine, they used to tease me about being from the Bible Belt, and I am. And I think that our lives in this part of the country, perhaps more than most parts of our Nation, are built around the church. And, of course, our religious beliefs emphasize compassion, love, concern about downtrodden people, equality in the eyes of God, basic human freedoms, courage to stand up to one's convictions, and so forth.

The second thing that I believe that we admire, being basically a rural area, is not only the right but the duty of people to stand on their own feet, to make their own decisions, to manage their own affairs, to support themselves if they are able, kind of an independence of spirit which also, of course, persists in a lot of other parts of our Nation. Here again the value of individual human beings is very important.

We in the South, in the War Between the States, seceded from the Union as an expression of independence from the Federal Government. When the war was over, we came back into the Union. But I think there was engendered in our own hearts and minds an emphasis in the importance of local governments, ones close to us that we could see and control more directly, and somewhat of a distrust of the Federal Government.

I hope that that distrust is being lessened now as the days go by. But it's there. And I think the last thing is that, like all other people in this great country, we've been filled with the words of Thomas Paine and Thomas Jefferson, Benjamin Franklin and George Washington, and others—that all men are created equal, that we are endowed with certain inalienable rights, and that we have a government designed not to control us but to guarantee our rights.

So, human rights is a part of the American consciousness. These kinds of commitments that I share with all other Americans make it almost inevitable that our country will be a leader in the world in standing up for the same principles on which our Nation was founded.

The last thing I would like to say about it is this: In the South we were guilty for many years of the deprivation of human rights to a large portion of our citizens. Now, to look back 20 years, when black people didn't have a right to vote, didn't have a right to go to a decent school, quite often did not have equal opportunity to seek or acquire a job, or to get a decent home, is an indictment on us.

I think it was with a great deal of courage that the South was able to face up to that change. I personally believe it was the best thing that ever happened to the South in my lifetime. And we have seen the benefits from it. Now we white people and the black people who live near us can work together on common problems and share trials and difficulties and seek common solutions. I think it's strengthened the South.

I would not be here as President had it not been for the Civil Rights Act and for the courage of some leaders—and I don't claim to be one of them—who changed those bad aspects of the South to the present greatness of the South. So, from the good things and the bad things in our heritage, it made the human rights issue be very vivid to me. But I'd say the most important aspect of it is that it is part of the consciousness of the free people of the greatest nation on Earth, the United States.

U.S. CORPS OF ENGINEERS

Q. Mr. President, my name is Cindy Fuze, and I am also a local housewife. The United States Corps of Engineers presently has a project underway to strip large areas of hardwood forests from the banks of the Yazoo River, allegedly to aid navigation. Many landowners and conservationists oppose this project.

My question is, can you tell me an effective way that a concerned individual such as myself might have to oppose, to express opposition to this kind of wasteful project and proposition?

THE PRESIDENT. Yes, ma'am. I would say that one of the ways that you as a private citizen can help is to ask a question about the subject on nationwide television to the President of the United States.

I don't know about your specific project. I have to admit that I'm not familiar with it. But I think that the Corps of Engineers, at least since I've been in the White House, is beginning to change its concept about what is a good expenditure of taxpayers' money and what is not.

In my opinion, it's much more valuable to have a wild stream and swampland and hardwood forests the way God made it

than it is to have an open ditch that has been destroyed to some degree. But I think that the values that are attached to these questions are changing.

Obviously, a large part of the delta area of Mississippi that's so valuable to you and all others was former swampland that was drained. So, the balance needs to be struck and I am very eager to see wasteful water projects that are very, very costly, that were approved 25 years ago, or 15 years ago, be terminated, and that every project now be assessed on the basis of modern day concerns about environmental quality, open spaces as well as the value of dollars expended.

So, although I don't know about your specific project, it's one that ought to be looked at very closely. I'm very proud tonight that your Congressman and your two Senators are here. And I think that their hearing from you and others like you would be very important to them. I guarantee you that if Senator Eastland and Senator Stennis come to me and say, "Mr. President, we would like to see this project stopped," that I will stop it, if I can.

I might add very quickly that the House of Representatives passed over my objection almost all the water projects that I wanted to veto. But under the leadership of Senator Stennis, about half of those water projects were eliminated from the appropriations bill, and I'm very deeply grateful to him and others who supported my position.

TAX REFORM

Q. Mr. President, my name is Kenneth Helton, and I manage the local Sunflower grocery store. My question is, what is being done to ease the tax burden of the middle class working people, and how will the Federal Government go about this?

Also, Mr. President, as Jerry Clower might say, we need the Federal Government to shoot up here among us. We need some relief. [*Laughter*]

THE PRESIDENT. I think Jerry is here tonight. When I got off the plane in Jackson, Jerry Clower was there. When I was making my little, short talk, he held my raincoat for me. I have always been an admirer of his. He's one of the great products of Yazoo City. I want to congratulate you for giving him to the rest of the country.

A lot of the country philosophers and country comedians, even the country popular song composers, express concerns like yours very clearly to the rest of the world, and I'm thankful for it. So far, as I said a little earlier, we've had some tax reform. We have raised the standard deduction, which saves about $4 billion, most of which goes to the low-income and middle-income American families.

For a family, for instance, to repeat myself, that makes about $10,000 a year, their income taxes will be reduced because of this legislation already passed and signed into law, about 30 percent per year.

We are now working on a comprehensive tax reform package which has three basic goals, one of which is to be much simpler. The second one is to remove as many of the tax loopholes as possible and to be fairer. And the third is to be more progressive in nature, which means that those that have the higher income will pay a higher percentage of the taxes.

So, those three principles are the ones on which we are basing our tax reform study. I will be recommending to the Congress this comprehensive tax reform no later than the adjournment of Congress in October. They won't have time to vote on it this year, but when the Congress comes back into session next January, this tax reform package will be waiting for them, and you will have a chance and other Americans to know what is in it.

I'm very determined to remove the present tax law from the books which, as I said many times in the campaign, is a disgrace to the human race, and have a fair tax structure in this country, for a change.

FEDERAL REGULATORY AGENCIES

Q. Mr. President, my name is Sam Ray. The Occupational Safety and Health Administration has recently announced that they're screening their regulations to take out unrealistic ones.

Since 1970 small businessmen have been complaining to their Congressmen and others in Washington about OSHA's tactics. What will be done in your administration to safeguard against further abuses of power by Federal regulatory agencies?

THE PRESIDENT. I'm a small businessman, too, as you know. And in several of the magazine and newspaper articles recently there's been an analysis of the OSHA program by my brother, Billy, concerning his filling station and concerning Carter's peanut shelling plant. So, I know at first hand the problems with the program.

I think I want to make clear that the Occupational Safety and Health Act is a good piece of legislation. It's important that in the working places we protect the health and safety of employees, but the OSHA program is going to extremes.

The Director of OSHA this past week announced that 50 percent of all the report forms that had been used in this country are being eliminated altogether before the end of September, and that the other 50 percent of the reporting forms are being substantially simplified.

I believe, also, that we have had too much of an emphasis on detailed regulations on safety. For instance, if you had to go home and write for me every possible description of a safe chair or a safe stool or a safe ladder, it would take you a year to do it. And it would take a 200-page volume to describe every possible danger that could be related to a ladder or a chair.

I think the Federal Government ought to get out of those kinds of detailed safety precautions when the worker can observe with his or her own eyes that a danger exists, and then have the safety regulations covered perhaps by increases in the payment for workmen's compensation if an employer does have a dangerous place for the employees to work.

It's a little different in the case of health because, for instance, in my peanut shelling plant for years we treated peanut seed with what is called sericin, which is a mercury compound. I had no idea that it was poisonous, and neither did my other employees that worked with me in the shelling plant. But had we had OSHA back then in the fifties and early sixties they could have told us that a mercury compound was dangerous to our health because an employee can't tell what is dangerous.

For a long time nobody knew that breathing cotton lint would give you permanent lung disease or asbestos fibers would cause death. Nobody knew anything about radioactivity. So, I think in the field of health care that the regulations often are necessary.

In the safety area, I don't think many of them are necessary. But we are doing what we can now to simplify the whole system, to shift the program as I've described to you. I hope the Congress will help us with it and just a change in those regulation forms that I described to you will make a million and a half small businessmen happy before the end of September.

NEUTRON BOMB

Q. Good evening, Mr. President. My name is Michael Espy, and I'm presently a law student out of state. I understand the effect of the neutron bomb will serve to devastate human life through the spread of radiation, while leaving property, military structures, and other tangible objects relatively unaffected through the minimal blast and heat effect.

In light of this, what is the rationale behind your encouragement of a production of a weapon of this nature, which would seem to prioritize property over the preservation of human life?

THE PRESIDENT. Thank you very much. I have not yet decided whether to produce the neutron bomb or to deploy it among our own forces in Europe and other places. I will make that decision before this summer is over. I've not yet studied the subject.

But I might point out to you a few brief facts about it. Any nuclear weapon is horrible, and the first nation that uses nuclear weapons must be sure that the act is justifiable in the protection of invaded property or other very serious reasons for such use.

We now have the warheads of the Lance missile and our large gun projectiles, nuclear weapons. They destroy large areas of territory with both the bomb blast, fire from the explosion, and radiation. For the same projectile, you would have about the same radiation, much less blast or flames. This means in a way—and I think everybody agrees with it—that if you ever use a neutron bomb, it's much better than using a regular presently deployed projectile or Lance missile warhead. I hope never to use either one.

If we use them, for instance, on property that is invaded—our country or the countries of our allies—then you would need to move into that area as rapidly as possible with our own American forces. Under those circumstances, you would not want to have flames and long-lasting radiation. The neutron bomb radiation is quick-acting, and it's gone. The whole thing is very horrible to everybody who studies the subject.

I might point out to you, too, that an M–16 rifle destroys human life and not buildings and property. This is not a new concept in war when the destruction of enemy forces is the prime objective. So, I don't believe that the neutron bomb is more wicked or immoral than the present nuclear weapons we have and the Soviets have as well.

The argument against the neutron bomb is that because it is "clean," that there might be more temptation to use it. That would not be my own attitude as long as I am President, because I have a fear that once nuclear weapons are used, even the smallest ones are used, that there is a good likelihood that the nuclear war will escalate rapidly into the exchange of very heavy weapons between the warring countries.

So, there are arguments on both sides of the neutron bomb. If you have a projectile and use it, it's better. I would not let its characteristics cause me to use it quicker, and I don't look on it as a way to prevent war.

So, I'll make a decision later on this summer based on these principles that I've described to you. And I hope and pray that I'll make the right decision.

LABOR LAWS

Q. Mr. President, first off, I'd like to thank you for correctly pronouncing the name of this great city, Yazoo City. Secondly, I would like to ask you my question.

THE PRESIDENT. I might say some of my staff members, who speak with a heavy German accent, when they asked me where I was going, I said "Yazoo," and they said, *Gesundheit*. [*Laughter*]

But I've known about Yazoo City all my life, and I've known the good sides and the bad sides of Yazoo. As you know, one of the most horrible scandals that we had in Georgia was when Yazoo belonged to Georgia and we had the Yazoo frauds. But we didn't know then the value of your beautiful farmlands.

I also, of course, have seen the tremendous leaders that have come out of Yazoo City and all the people who live in the South. I think the rest of the Nation knows about Willie Morris and others who have written beautiful things about the South, and I'm very proud to be here. And I think after tonight maybe even more people will know how nice Yazoo City is.

I didn't mean to interrupt you. Go ahead.

Q. Fine. Recently you agreed to support major changes in the Nation's labor laws, which will have the effect of making it much easier for big labor to organize in the South. I wonder if you please could explain that for us.

THE PRESIDENT. Yes. I am not sure that the purpose of the legislation would lead to heavier organization by big labor in the South. What the legislation does is expedite and makes clearer the law under which factories can be organized.

If, under the existing National Labor Relations Board regulations and laws, workers in a plant vote to organize, then the new proposals would make sure that management has to comply with the law. There's no doubt about that. It also provides for a quicker determination of labor disputes. It also does protect workers who are injured in violation of the Federal law.

So, it would expedite the determination of a labor dispute. It would make sure that the present laws are enforced more quickly and fairly. But I don't think that the legislation would lead to more rapid establishment of union workers in the South.

There is a heavy emphasis now on unionizing some of our plants in the South. I don't think this legislation would affect it one way or the other in any material way. But it will be simpler, quicker, clearer, fairer legislation, and I think it will be beneficial to the country.

VIETNAM

Q. Mr. President, my name is Susan Griss. I, too, would like to welcome you to Yazoo City. I have seen on the news this week that the United States, under the support of your administration, has endorsed and supported the membership of Vietnam into the United Nations. The first thing that the Vietnamese asked for was financial aid from the United States to rebuild.

How do you feel about this? Do you expect the United States to, in fact, support the rebuilding effort and support the Vietnamese financially, and do you think the Congress will support you, too?

THE PRESIDENT. I want to answer—this is the last question I can answer I want to answer it in a little bit broader sense, but I won't ignore your question.

We have a basic decision to make in our country in our foreign policy about how to deal with nations who, in the past, have not been our friends and who, in some instances, have been our enemies on the warfield. Should we write them off permanently as enemies and force them to be completely under the control and influence of Communist powers, or should we start the process of giving them an option to be both our friends and the friends of others, hoping that they will come to a more democratic free society and join with us in making a better world?

I'm not in favor of writing those countries off. It's a controversial issue. I might point out that the Soviet Union, for instance, has a very strong effort being made to recruit as friends our own neighbors in Central America and South America. And I think that this peaceful competition with the Soviet Union for friendship of those nonaligned countries is good for our country, although it is controversial.

I have tried to open up relationships with Vietnam. The leader in the Congress in taking this initiative happens to be your own Congressman Sonny Montgomery. He went to Vietnam, I think, in a very courageous and effective way to try to get the Vietnamese to give us back the bodies of American servicemen lost in action.

When I got to be President, Congressman Montgomery came to the White House to give me a report on what he had done. Later, I sent another delegation back to them to ask them to find those bodies and to return them to us. They've done a great deal to try to find and return those bodies since that time. When Congressman Montgomery went to Vietnam, they brought back 11 American bodies and since then the Vietnamese have delivered others.

We have always for the last 25 years opposed Vietnam's entry into the United Nations. This year we did not oppose it. And now Vietnam will be a member of the world community in the United Nations. I don't have any apology to make about that action. I am not in favor of the United States paying any money or reparations to Vietnam, however.

Our time is up. The networks want to have about eight or ten minutes to close out after I go. It's now an hour and twenty minutes. And they tell me that I need to close.

Before I leave you, I would like to say this: I've enjoyed being here. The quality of your questions has been no surprise to me and, as you can see, they've covered a wide range of subjects—from the history of the South to the future of Vietnam. And this is typical of the intense interest in public affairs that exists among the American people.

As I said to begin with, I don't claim to know all the answers. I'm learning every day. I have a lot of people who believe in me. I have a lot of people who have doubts about me. I have a lot of people who voted for me; a lot who didn't. But I think it's accurate to say that almost every American wants to see me succeed in being a good President. Because to the extent that I do succeed, your own lives and those of your families will be better, freer, and fuller lives.

We are partners in shaping what our country will be. You are partners with me. And I hope that I can serve in such a way that would increase your own confidence in our government, increase your own confidence in the Federal Government, which in the South sometimes has not been a pleasant phrase, and that I can convince the American people that the Government in Washington is your government.

These hopes that I have are dependent on you for realization. If you withdraw and lash out and condemn and criticize your own Government as a general proposition because you don't like one or two things that happen, our whole country is weakened.

But to the extent that you participate in the debates and try to correct mistakes and let us know what you want done in Washington, and participate with us, to that extent we'll be a success.

I'll do the best I can not to disappoint you, and I ask for your support, your advice, your counsel, your criticisms when I

make mistakes, and your prayers every day.

Thank you very much.

NOTE: The President spoke at 8:02 p.m. in the gymnasium of the Yazoo City High School. The public meeting was broadcast live on the Public Broadcasting Service.

Prior to his remarks, the President took part in the dedication of the gymnasium.

Following the meeting, the President spent the night at the home of Mr. and Mrs. L. Owen Cooper, Sr., residents of Yazoo City.

New Orleans, Louisiana

Question-and-Answer Session With Reporters. July 22, 1977

THE PRESIDENT. This morning we're going to confine the press conference to the visit to the offshore drilling rig, or to the energy package that's before the Congress.

I have long wanted to visit one of these remarkable installations and I have been very pleased not only at the quality of the machinery, the technology, the electronics controls, but also with the training of the crew and the obvious dedication of those who are searching for oil or gas off our shores to prevent any recurrence of the environmental damage that occurred off the Santa Barbara coast, and recently in the North Sea.

There has been an enormous amount of time and effort and engineering skills in safety devices and controls for potential spills. And I think that we have made good progress in that area. I've also been convinced that American technology in the drilling exploration for oil is a very valuable national possession. Throughout the world, even in other countries there is a great need for this capability, and I think that we need to understand as best we can how the worldwide energy resources can be both husbanded, discovered and used, and distributed in the best way.

I hope that the progress of our energy policy legislation through the Congress will continue. I'm convinced that it's a well-balanced program, and I believe that an understanding of both the problems and potentials of offshore oil drilling can be understood by the rest of the Nation who haven't had a chance to observe it in person.

As Governor of Georgia, for instance, I joined with the Governors of North and South Carolina in laying plans for aggressive oil exploration and drilling and extraction off the coast of our Atlantic seaboard.

And we still have hopes that oil might be discovered there. And if so, working with environmental groups, university systems, State and local officials, we have already identified the places where we might bring the oil ashore or natural gas ashore, where the refineries might be located with a minimum adverse impact on the environmental quality, or recreation area or beauty of our shorelands.

I hope that the States north of us will take the same approach and make careful plans accordingly and that we can continue with an aggressive exploration policy on the Atlantic seaboard, as has been the case in the Gulf area.

The last point I'd like to make before I answer your questions is we need to have a good balanced Federal support program to the areas that are highly impacted by the consequences of oil production.

Senator Johnston and Senator Long have been leaders in this particular area and a bill has already been passed before the Senate and is now before the House.

We have made some progress in this already in the coal leases. We need to make the same type of progress in oil as well. And I believe that the distribution formulas that have already been established for coastal development and planning funds is the one the Governors prefer and one that's certainly suitable with me.

I don't have any way to know yet what the final action of the House will be on this legislation, but the Office of Management and Budget has worked, I think, a satisfactory understanding with the Senate leaders on this particular subject.

So, to summarize, I've been well educated this morning, have been pleased at what I have learned, and believe that the future of oil exploration in our country is assured to be both successful and compatible with the preservation of the quality of our life style.

I would be glad to answer any questions or refer the questions to these distinguished men and women behind me.

OIL AND NATURAL GAS PRODUCTION

Q. Mr. President, did you see anything this morning that would cause you to consider greater production incentives for the oil and natural gas industries than those you have already proposed, the $15 billion figure?

THE PRESIDENT. No, I didn't. I know that some of the leaders in the oil industry and certainly some political leaders from the oil-producing States think that higher production incentives are necessary. I do not. I believe that the incentives that we have put into the package devised by me, Dr. Schlesinger, and others, that those incentives are adequate.

Q. Mr. President, are you any more impressed with Governor Edwards' views on the energy situation than you were before?

THE PRESIDENT. I have always been strongly impressed by Governor Edwards' views. I think that the leaders from Texas, Louisiana, Mississippi, Oklahoma, Alabama, who represent States that are producing States, obviously have a different perspective from some of the parts of the Nation where we are primarily consuming States like Georgia. But I think all those views that are strongly held need to be understood, debated, and of course the Congress and myself together will make the final judgments from the Federal viewpoint. But I respect Governor Edwards' views. He's knowledgeable about the subject and I think he represents accurately the feeling of the Louisiana people.

But I have scheduled, along with Dr. Schlesinger and the Governors' conference, an additional meeting at the request of Governor Edwards and others just on the question of production, enhanced production of oil, gas, coal, nuclear, solar energy. And, I think, this is a very good suggestion that we received from him and it will be done within the next few weeks.

OFFSHORE DRILLING

Q. Mr. President, did you see anything on the rig that could be determined negative as far as persuading other areas of the United States for offshore drilling?

THE PRESIDENT. No. I didn't. I think it's accurate to say that this was one of the most advanced drilling rigs in existence in the world. It was obviously spotless and I asked them if it was always that clean, and they said that yes, every time they had a President visit—[laughter]— that it was. But it was superlative and the design of the rig, the control of the mechanisms for safety, the constant scanning of the bottom of the sea with television and other mechanisms, the obviously high-trained crew long experienced in this realm, the ability to drill at a depth of about 1,000 feet, the rapidity of drilling, which yesterday was 1,100 feet, drilled in one day, sometimes as high as 2,000 feet, I thought it was extraordinary.

And many of the advances that have taken place in the technology were a very pleasant surprise to me. I did not see anything there that caused me concern. I think at the present time because of a slowdown in exploration on the east coast, because of reluctance on the part of some political leaders in the northern part of the Eastern Coast and other reasons, that we have an excessive capacity now for drilling and I hope to do what I can, working with Dr. Schlesinger and the Congress and others, to expedite the drilling rate, particularly on the eastern seaboard. But I saw nothing that caused me concern this morning.

EXPLORATORY DRILLING

Q. Mr. President, there is a bill before Congress expanding the OCS act which will put the Federal Government into exploration and also put 3 to 5 years' delay into the timetable of finding and producing oil. This is going to affect and hurt the service companies and the contractors such as the people you visited today. What is your position on this bill as it stands now?

THE PRESIDENT. Well, there are two different bills that I know about. Now, I don't approve of either one of them. But I think that it's legitimate for the Federal Government to have the right, the authority for exploratory drilling in areas to be leased to the oil companies.

I think one of the bills, however, permits the Federal Government to drill on private property and State-owned property and also the Federal lands. And the other one makes it mandatory that the Federal Government drill in an area before it's leased. I don't like any one of those approaches.

But to give the Federal Government the authority when it's decided to be needed by the Secretary of the Interior and the

Secretary of Energy, I do favor that legislation.

GASOLINE TAX INCREASE

Q. Mr. President, I have a question on your energy package. What is your position on the recent proposal to increase the gasoline tax by 5 cents a gallon and use the revenue primarily for mass transit?

THE PRESIDENT. We have taken a position not to oppose the legislation. It is not part of the energy package that we put forward.

My understanding was that the proposal was 4 cents a gallon, 1½ cents of which would be used for a metropolitan rapid transit. One-half cent would go to the States. One-half cent would be used for research and development on energy, and the other 1½ cents could be used either for transportation or energy production.

I don't necessarily agree with the formula. I would rather see at least 1 cent returned to the States for maintenance on existing transportation systems. And I personally would prefer more flexibility in how the money should be paid.

This receipt of funds from gasoline taxes alone, if mandated to go into rapid transit, may not be fair. It also means that 1½ cents out of 4 cents would go to urban areas where rapid transit systems are needed, and the rural people who are paying part of the taxes would not benefit at all.

So, I have no objections to the allocation of additional tax on gasoline to be used on the highways, but I would like more flexibility in how the funds might be used.

TRANSPORTATION OF OIL AND NATURAL GAS

Q. Mr. President, I'd like to know if you saw the tanker that's on fire in the river this morning and if you considered that this is the latest in a series of accidents, involving long-distance transportation of oil, we've had tankers, the Alaskan pipeline, and if perhaps someone hasn't suggested that maybe it's better, rather than transporting fuels long distances, to use them closer to the area in which they are produced—to use the coal and such on the east coast, and use gas and oil down on the gulf coast?

THE PRESIDENT. Well, I did not see the tanker on fire. We left the airport nearby here and followed the route of the river to the sea. I did not see the tanker on fire.

Q. Were you aware of it, sir?

THE PRESIDENT. I was not. But I think it's obvious that whenever one can, it's better to use the fuel in the area where it's produced. That's obviously not possible in all respects. For instance, the northeastern part of our country, in its electrical requirements, might very well derive them from coal mine areas from West Virginia, Pennsylvania, Virginia, and other States, and then their electricity transmitted by powerlines.

But I don't think it is possible for us to use, for instance, Alaskan oil and natural gas in Alaska. It would be unreasonable to expect to burn those fuels in Alaska and transmit their electricity down to this country by power line.

But we have a great problem in how to distribute oil and gas. We had anticipated, as you know, the Alaskan oil and gas coming in, perhaps, in major quantities to California, as one place, and being distributed throughout the country in either existing pipelines or those where the flow might be reversed to new ones.

There is a great opposition among the public officials in California environmental groups and others against the offloading of large quantities of either liquefied natural gas or oil on the California coast.

This means there's more of a pressure to bring the oil down through the Panama Canal and up the gulf coast or eastern seaboard area.

So, I think we just have to keep an open mind as circumstances change and use the distribution systems that we have now and accommodate changing times. But I would be glad to have a followup question from you.

Q. If you would. Let me perhaps summarize. Does it make sense to build pipelines and such to bring slurry coal from West Virginia to Louisiana while at the same time we're sending gas from Louisiana to West Virginia? Wouldn't it make more sense to use the energy closer to where it is produced?

THE PRESIDENT. If there was a complete exchangeability among energy sources, I would agree with you instantly. I don't know how to answer your question definitively at this point. But there is a need in this country to use coal for stationary major powerplants and to use the much more valuable natural gas where it alone can be used.

Obviously, a balance has to be reached between transportation costs and the necessity to do as you originally suggest— use fuels where they are near their source. But we can't make, at this point, economically, nitrogen fertilizers out of coal. And many chemical processes require extremely clean-burning fuels. Natural gas fills the bill.

Coal can be used to produce electric power, and it might be advisable—I think it is necessary—to shift away from the use of natural gas for simple heat production and substitute coal. In Georgia, we produce about 85 percent of our electricity from coal-burning plants.

So, I would like to reserve the right now and in the future, whenever I think it advisable, as a President, to use any influence to transport coal even into areas which produce oil and natural gas in order to save the natural gas for more specific and a higher use.

PANAMA CANAL CONSTRUCTION

Q. Mr. President, last night you talked about the possible construction of the new Panama Canal primarily to transport oil. But you didn't go very far in telling us what your thinking, detailed thinking, of that might be.

THE PRESIDENT. I told you at least as much as I know. [*Laughter*]

Q. Let me ask you: Do you have any idea at this point how much it might cost, when you would start it, where it would be built, and just how far along your thinking on this subject is at this point?

THE PRESIDENT. No, I can't. I'll try to answer your questions briefly.

When President Johnson was in office, there was a very expensive analysis made—I think it cost about $22 million at that time—to determine the feasibility of a canal across the Isthmus of Central America. The outcome of that report was that the best location for a sea-level canal would be a little further north in Panama. I think the estimated cost at that time was about $7 billion.

We did not have the additional problem then of very serious disputes with Panama on continued management of the Canal under the 1907 treaty. We also did not have the additional problem of how to distribute Alaskan oil and natural gas to the eastern part of our country. I think at that time that price was considered to be shocking and unreasonable.

We have just spent $8 billion on the pipeline for oil in Alaska. We're now considering the construction of a natural gas pipeline that would cost maybe $12 billion. So, a new sea-level canal would not be unreasonable or exorbitant when compared with other alternative transmission capabilities.

The other part of the question is about its need. I have only mentioned the oil and natural gas transportation, but as you know, our major warships, large tankers and cargo ships cannot presently use the Panama Canal at all. And I would guess that before the year 2000 comes and the existing treaty with Panama and our control of the Panama Canal might expire, that the need for this larger, wider, deeper canal without the multiple locks might be in the interest of our national security, militarily as well as economically.

But all of these are conjectural points. I've not gone into the question in any depth and I'm not prepared to answer any further.

Go ahead.

Q. Are you planning to make any specific presentation to Congress or to start further study for expanding President Johnson's report?

THE PRESIDENT. Yes. We've begun to look now at the report that was prepared when President Johnson was in office to see its applicability now under the new circumstances that I've described. The two new factors that I've mentioned are the dispute with Panama with continued operation of the Canal under the existing treaty, and the other one is the need to transport Alaskan oil and natural gas. But those two new factors will be assessed, and I can't predict the outcome of it. I've not spent much time on it myself.

Q. [*Inaudible*]

THE PRESIDENT. I might see if the Senators or the Congress Members or the Governor have an additional comment to make, and then I'm going to have to leave. Senator? Senator Johnston.

SENATOR JOHNSTON. Mr. President, we are very pleased at the action you've taken lately that pertains to energy, and that is,

to give us what we think is a favorable statement on our offshore impact fund, and also the agreement to sign the bill that approves all of the Louisiana water projects, including the Boeuf, Black and Chene, which is the bayou that comes down from Morgan City, that through which the largest construction platform in the world just came this week. We think that is progress. We haven't gone all the way we want to go with you, but you're making progress.

THE PRESIDENT. I knew I made a mistake. [*Laughter*]

SENATOR LONG. I want to thank you for coming and seeing what our situation is here, Mr. President. You've been very kind to hear our views. I'm not one of those who complains about not being able to explain our position to you. I wish we could be sure you are going to agree with us after you heard it. But you're most kind to come and see what the situation is and decide this for yourself, and we very much appreciate it. Thanks for coming.

GOVERNOR EDWARDS. I want to personally express my appreciation to the President for coming to Louisiana, and for viewing firsthand the technology that exists in this area, and how we can produce oil and gas without doing any damage to the environment. And I think it shows a great willingness on his part to learn and to be involved and to be concerned, and I want to personally say how pleased and proud I am on behalf of the people of the State that he has chosen Louisiana this date to visit this facility.

So much of what's gone on in the world in the field of oil and gas, especially where water is concerned, came about as a result of the technology and the efforts and dedication of men and women in Louisiana. And we are very proud of that.

Mr. President, today you are where it's at. When you get to the East Coast you will be where it's going to be.

REPRESENTATIVE BOGGS. Mr. President, it was a joy and a privilege to have a President who was so well prepared, technically, to pose the right questions and then understand the answers on the rig. And I was especially pleased that you recognize the expertness with which the workers were performing their duties, because our onshore capabilities in Louisiana should help us in being able to acquire some of the research and development funds for the alternative sources of energy such as the o-tech (ocean technology) problems, and also geopressure (geopressurized brine). So that I hope you have been well impressed with the workmanship and with our capability.

NOTE: The question-and-answer session began at 11:30 a.m. at the Airport Hilton Hotel.

Earlier in the morning, the President had visited the Yorktown oil drilling rig off the coast of Louisiana.

Interview With the National Black Network

Question-and-Answer Session With Representatives of the Network. July 18, 1977

MR. SANDERS. We will begin our questions with Joe Brown.

MR. BROWN. Mr. President, welcome to "Black Issues and the Black Press."

THE PRESIDENT. Thank you. I am glad to be with you.

NEW YORK CITY POWER BLACKOUT

MR. BROWN. Some leaders say that the violence that erupted during New York City's blackout and the deprivation in New York City and other black communities is tied to what they call a powder keg with other cities around the country. And if that is true, do you prefer or do you favor a preferential treatment for blacks in order to work off this type of reaction around the country?

THE PRESIDENT. Well, obviously, it is of great concern to the whole Nation when violence occurs, when theft occurs or looting occurs or damage to property or persons occurs. There is no excuse for it. But it is also important that public officials like myself try to understand the reasons for it.

Obviously, the number one contributing factor to crime of all kinds, in my opinion, is high unemployment among young people, particularly those who are black or Spanish-speaking or in a minority age or group where they have such a difficult time getting jobs in times of economic problems.

We have begun to study the reasons for the entire incident in New York. I think had the power companies notified homeowners immediately to turn off air conditioners, TV sets, and cut down on power consumption, the crisis could have been avoided. If we had a comprehensive nationwide grid system where we could feed in power when a certain area has its source disrupted, that would have helped. If we had some closer working relationship between local, State, and Federal authorities with the power companies, that would have helped.

But the long-range problem is to restore confidence of citizens who live in a community in the structure of government, police officers, the housing opportunities, good jobs, and this obviously was not the case in New York. So, I think that this is an additional indication of the need to channel government programs for housing, health, education, job opportunities in the deteriorating urban areas that have been neglected too long.

ABORTION

MR. AGURS. Mr. President, in light of what you said about channeling resources and what-not, I would like to go back for a moment, if I might, to Tuesday's press conference during which a discussion of the abortion issue was taking place. And you were asked to reconcile your stand on abortion with your stand for—the statement I am getting at, sir, is there are certain things in this society—life is not fair, you said. Poor people cannot afford certain things that wealthy people can. How do you reconcile a statement like that with concern for deprivation and turning around the economic system?

THE PRESIDENT. Well, in any sort of societal structure or any degree of economic prosperity or need, and with any kind of Federal, State, or local budget, you have a limitation on money available for those who need help from government to give them an equal opportunity. Having that limited amount of money to spend in all, a President or Congress has to set priorities for expenditure; what is the greatest need? Is it a higher need to have preventive health care with physical examinations for children, immunization programs, the care for elderly, adequate housing, adequate food, adequate diet for a certain amount of money, or should you take a substantial portion of that money and pay for abortions from the Government?

I don't think that the Government ought to finance abortions except when the abortions are a danger to the potential mother's life or when they are caused by rape or incest. We have in this respect not a callous or unconcerned attitude toward the poor. But I personally find it very difficult to have a program which encourages abortion.

If the purpose of the Government—and I think its legitimate purpose—is to prevent the birth of unwanted children, I think the best way to spend limited Federal moneys, again, is in the education of sometimes ignorant young people, women and men, and making available to them family planning instruction plus contraceptive devices that would prevent a pregnancy to begin with.

I hate to see a government finance a very expensive program where young women get to depend upon abortion to correct a mistake that never should have occurred.

SOCIAL PROGRAMS

MR. SANDERS. You mentioned a long-range plan, and that has been your contention throughout your campaign. And you have also been described by a number of writers as being a man high on symbols. Do you feel if you had extended a few more symbols into specifically the New York area, the black community, that you probably would have contributed to heading off what did happen during the blackout?

THE PRESIDENT. This is hard to know. We have had a massive new effort made since I have been in office, for instance, concerning employment. We have passed legislation through the Congress that helps our economy, about $21 billion worth, which is a very major amount; about $4 billion for public works. We have provided for 1.1 million summer jobs for young people, plus about 435,000 new jobs in public service, working for local and State governments.

In addition to that, we have initiated now a health screening program for poor people. We have given a $4 billion tax reduction, where way over half of it goes to people who have less than $10,000 in income.

I have tried to make appointments in very major and sensitive positions to black people so that would be an obvious indication about my own concern about minority citizens.

Housing is a very important aspect, the rebuilding of downtown urban ghetto areas. That falls under the responsibility of the Housing and Urban Development Department. I put Pat Harris, who happens to be a black woman, in charge of that.

A lot of young people serve in the Army who are minority members of our communities. I appointed the first black Secretary of the Army. The head of all education programs in the Nation happens to be a black woman.

So, I have tried not only to give symbols but I have also tried to make sure we started programs that would be effective. Of course, the first budget that I have available to implement is the 1978 budget, which begins the first of October. And the brief period I have been in office, I think, has been a period that we have used to the utmost advantage so far. But the outcome of our efforts to give poor people a new lease on life and a new chance to improve themselves is one that can only be proven over the months ahead.

MR. SANDERS. President Jimmy Carter is our guest on this edition of the "Black Press." We will be back for more questions right after this word.

We continue our questions with Joe Brown.

HOUSING

MR. BROWN. You have said housing is important to particularly minorities and the poor. But it is reported that your administration wants to cut subsidized hous-

ing or the subsidized housing program, the program now, which is to provide about 400,000 homes per year, and it is reported that your administration wants to cut that back to 50,000 homes per year using additional moneys to go to welfare recipients.

If that is true, then, sir, how—it doesn't seem to add up that housing is important to minorities, but we are taking from one poor group and giving to another poor group.

THE PRESIDENT. The housing budget we put forward, which the Congress is going to approve without a doubt, is probably the greatest single step forward that has ever been taken in the country. We are now building at a rate of about 2 million new homes a year in this Nation, and this has been a standard rate of growth over the last number of months. Block grant programs for urban renewal are being approved by Congress, just as Pat Harris and I recommended.

The question that has been raised, not by me but by some of my heads of departments, is one that must be decided in the future, coming along as a part of a comprehensive welfare reform, and the basic question is, should you provide very nice homes for a few families in our country or should you give many poor people additional income so that the average quality of their housing should be improved for millions of people.

So far the basic philosophy of our Government has been to give very nice homes to just a few people and make many millions of people suffer. But this is a matter that will have to be addressed, I would say, in the next 12 months.

But overall, the amount of money that goes for better housing for poor people is going to increase, I guess, every year I am in the White House.

SOCIAL PROGRAMS

MR. AGURS. What you say, Mr. President, makes sense in one respect, but in terms of what you promised in the campaign, to reduce the military budget in favor of social programs, has not happened.

I would like to go to a statement by Representative Shirley Chisholm, with whom you met last week, who says, while your commitment to social programs and alleviating the social programs of the Nation is unquestionable, she finds she is concerned about a lack of that same commitment on the part of some of the individuals from whom you get advice.

Are you aware of that concern, and what do you plan to do to eliminate the fears and, I might add, which is shared by many in the black community?

THE PRESIDENT. Well, we have cut the military budget considerably. I recommended a reduction in the military budget of $3½ billion to begin with, which has been approved by Congress. They have reduced it a little more than I did, about an extra billion and a half dollars. And then in the last couple of weeks, I recommended the termination of the B–1 bomber program, which amounts to another reduction of $1.4 billion. At the same time, we have had about a $21 billion increase in making our economy grow more rapidly with job programs, public works programs, summer employment programs, better health programs, housing programs, and tax reductions. So, I think the essence of it so far is that we have done exactly what I promised during the campaign.

Representative Chisholm did come to see me and pointed out that in her opinion some of my employees or subordinates at the community level were not carrying out as enthusiastically as I was trying to do here at the White House, programs that would improve the lives of poor people. I think that this very well may be true. I have only been in office now about 6 months, and we have not been given the authority to change all the administrators that were left over from the Nixon and Ford administrations. But I think it is accurate to say Joe Califano and Pat Harris and others are trying to make changes now. And my guess is that the field workers who are at the community or city level working in the Federal Government agencies are making strides to carry out the programs that we initiate here in Washington.

I think that you probably know that the present budget under which we operate is a fiscal year '77 budget, which was passed by the Congress a year ago. And when our own new budget goes into effect in October, you will see another increase in the quality of services for poor people.

MR. SANDERS. Mr. President, can we shift that responsibility back here to the White House?

THE PRESIDENT. Sure.

MR. SANDERS. And find out really if these programs can be translated into the kind of language that would be at least acceptable and understandable to those people out there on the street? You are talking about reorganization——

THE PRESIDENT. That is right.

MR. SANDERS. ——and balancing the budget. Those are top priorities, but how does that translate to Joe Blow who needs a job?

THE PRESIDENT. Well, since last November when I was elected, we have had an increase in the number of people employed in this country of 3 million. In December the unemployment rate was 8.1 percent. We set as a goal for ourselves this year to cut it down to 7 percent. It has already been cut down to 7 percent

1343

in the first 6 months. We have had a $4 billion tax reduction. The average family that makes $10,000 a year, all the family members put together, have had their taxes cut already 30 percent. That is on a permanent basis. In addition to that, we have started many programs whose impact would not be felt for a year or two. But we are now beginning to see the benefits of the public works program, which is going to be building, say, in New York, Chicago, Indianapolis, and Los Angeles.

We also see the public service jobs, which will have 715,000 people employed plus over a million summer jobs for young people. These programs are just now beginning to be seen, because it took a while to get them started. But I think for the average family in this country there has been a change already in tone and attitude and confidence in the Government.

And the thing that I want to make sure of is that we deserve that confidence. We are not trying to rest on our laurels. We are not trying to brag on ourselves. There are other things that can be done and will be done.

We are trying to make sure the social security system is sound, and we are trying to make it sound not by cutting benefits to poor people, not by taxing the working family. If the Congress goes ahead with our recommendation, this can be done. We are trying to make sure people who have been kept from voting in the past have a chance to register to vote easily and to increase their participation in government. And I have directed all my Cabinet officers to get out in the field and in the streets of the cities to listen to suggestions and listen to complaints.

So, I cannot guarantee that everybody is living now a better life. That would be asking too much. But I think the trend

is in that direction, and I don't think there is a single member of my Cabinet or a single staff member who works in the White House who does not have as our major goal the improvement of the lives of the poor people in this country who have been ignored.

MR. SANDERS. We will have more questions right after this word.

We will resume our questions with Joe Brown.

WELFARE PROGRAM

MR. BROWN. Mr. Carter, your decision—it is reported you have made a decision to put an arbitrary ceiling on welfare—welfare and jobs programs when there has been no ceiling placed on such programs as tax reform, energy, defense, and the rest of it. We are wondering why has it been here that there has been a ceiling placed when the poor and the disadvantaged are at the very bottom of the special needs department?

THE PRESIDENT. We are trying to have a comprehensive welfare reform program. The defense budget has been cut, and as we change from a welfare program that is not fair to one that is simple and fair at the same time, we are trying to plow into it a combination work and welfare effort.

I want to be sure, for instance, that we add on to the new welfare program, in addition to the jobs I have described to you so far, about 1 million extra jobs. Our goal is to be sure that every family in the United States, that at least one member of that family will have a job, either in private life or a public job that pays a wage adequate to finance that family. So, as we shift away from welfare cost, not reducing it at all and make it more fair, more widely spread, with an emphasis on a job where there is no limit on income, that is a step in the right direction.

I might point out initial to that we have already advocated to the Congress or recommended to the Congress some additional improvements that I haven't mentioned yet. One, of course, is to remove from the food stamp program the requirement that cash money be put up to get food stamps.

We have removed that requirement, and I believe the Congress is going to go along with it. So, the overall approach for the welfare recipient is to make their income surer, higher, with better housing, better health care, and, at the same time, a constant opportunity for people within that family to get off dependence on welfare if they are able and willing and to have a productive job where there is no limit on that family's income.

ENFORCEMENT OF CIVIL RIGHTS LAWS

MR. AGURS. If I might shift the focus, the U.S. Civil Rights Commission in a recent report found a serious lack of administrative force behind the enforcement of civil rights laws and recommended that you appoint an individual whose sole responsibility would be a carrying out of legal mandates regarding individual rights. My question is: What is your reaction to their finding, and what do you plan to do with their recommendation?

THE PRESIDENT. I think their findings were very helpful to the whole Nation and certainly to me. As you probably know, the person that I have placed in charge of the equal opportunity commission, Eleanor Holmes Norton, is a very well experienced black woman, whose reputation is one of complete commitment to rooting out discrimination and making sure that corrective action is taken. The Solicitor General, who works within the Justice Department, Wade McCree, happens to be a black judge from Detroit.

His reputation as someone who will root out discrimination is superb. And at the same time in many other major departments of Government, in HEW, for instance, we have tried to do the same thing.

So, I don't think it would be better to have one person, for instance, working in the White House here, who would be responsible for civil rights, but the best thing to do is to have the prosecutor in the Justice Department, top officials in the equal opportunity commission, civil rights commission of HEW, working at this problem from a wide range of power bases.

One place, as I mentioned earlier, that has in the past been a root of discrimination is in the Armed Forces where many young men now volunteer to serve our country in danger to their lives. I thought the best approach to that would be to appoint, for instance, a black man to be the Secretary of the Army. This has been an unheard of thing in the past.

So, I believe that in general the Civil Rights Commission did point out areas of discrimination. They did recommend that the sensitive people be put in at the top of these agencies responsible for correction of discrimination, and I think the ones I have appointed will do a good job.

AFFIRMATIVE ACTION PROGRAMS

MR. SANDERS. Mr. President, the *University of California* v. *Bakke*—the Allen Bakke case is a formidable threat to most of the affirmative action programs that we have seen in the past. How far are you willing to go with your influence here at the White House to see that that case does not reverse some of the gains that have been made?

THE PRESIDENT. I have had a discussion with both the Secretary of HEW, Mr. Califano, and the Attorney General about this case. And I think that we will prevent a reversion to the previous discrimination that did exist; at the same time, we want to respect the need for an adequate level of education for minority groups in our country, and we also want to preserve the heritage and background and history that is part of the lives of minority families.

I think that it is accurate to say that I, the Vice President, the Secretary of HEW, and the Attorney General are all committed to making sure that these concerns that I have just outlined to you are met and that the discrimination that has been a part of our national life in the past is ended.

MR. SANDERS. Thank you, Mr. President.

THE PRESIDENT. I have enjoyed it very much.

NOTE: The radio interview began at 2:02 p.m. in the Oval Office at the White House. Participating in the interview were: Vince Sanders, vice president and national news director of the network, Joe Brown, editor, and Don Agurs, White House correspondent.

As printed above, this item follows the text of the White House press release which was issued on July 22.

The new agreement provides for continuing the basic principle of a fair and equal opportunity for the airlines of both countries to compete and dedicates both Governments to the provision of safe, adequate, and efficient international air transportation responsive to the present and future needs of the public and to the continued development of international air commerce. It emphasizes that both scheduled and charter air transportation are important to the consumer interest and are essential elements of a healthy international air transport system.

The United States seeks an international economic environment and air transportation structure founded on healthy economic competition among all air carriers. The new agreement is consistent with this objective. We shall continue to rely on competitive market forces as much as possible in our international air transportation agreements so that the public may receive the improved service at costs that reflect efficient operations.

The agreement is one that reflects well on our two great nations. Its quality, its fairness, and its benefits to the consumer and to airlines should make it last as long as the original 1946 Bermuda Agreement. It continues our long and historic relationship with the United Kingdom.

United States-United Kingdom Air Services Agreement

Statement on the Signing of the Agreement.   July 23, 1977

The agreement governing civil air services between the United States and the United Kingdom was negotiated over a period of several months and signed in Bermuda on July 23, 1977. It replaces and updates the predecessor agreement reached in 1946 and last amended in 1966.

Generalized System of Preferences for Developing Countries

Executive Order 12005.   July 23, 1977

AMENDING THE GENERALIZED SYSTEM OF PREFERENCES

By virtue of the authority vested in me by the Constitution and statutes of the United States of America, including Title V and Section 604 of the Trade Act of 1974 (88 Stat. 2066, 19 U.S.C. 2461 *et seq.;* 88 Stat. 2073, 19 U.S.C. 2483), and as President of the United States of America, it is hereby ordered as follows:

SECTION 1. In order to redefine an existing item for purposes of the Generalized System of Preferences (GSP), the Tariff Schedules of the United States (TSUS) are modified by deleting from item 791.74, TSUS, the description:

> "In part of textile materials the aggregate weight of which exceeds the weight of any individual non-textile material contained therein",

and substituting therefor the following description:

> "Containing 50% or more by weight of cotton, wool, or man-made fibers, or any combination thereof, or containing 50% or more by weight of textile materials with wool comprising 17% or more by weight of the article.".

SEC. 2. The amendment made by this order shall be effective with respect to articles that are both: (1) imported on or after January 1, 1976, and (2) entered, or withdrawn from warehouse, for consumption on or after March 1, 1977.

JIMMY CARTER

The White House,
July 23, 1977.

[Filed with the Office of the Federal Register, 5:02 p.m., July 25, 1977]

NOTE: The Executive order was not issued in the form of a White House press release.

National Urban League

Remarks at the League's National Convention.   July 25, 1977

Mr. McGannon and my good friend Vernon Jordan, distinguished members and guests of the Urban League:

The last annual convention I attended, I went as a guest. And I heard, as the main speaker of the final banquet evening, Eleanor Holmes Norton give a moving speech about the ties that bind families together and how the deprivations of poverty and the lack of an ability of primarily black males to be proud of themselves justifiably was a disruptive influence on the family structure. It was a moving speech.

And now, Eleanor Holmes Norton is in Washington, here with me, trying to bring together the thrust of the Federal Government to ensure equal opportunity in employment. And she'll be part of your program this year.

In Atlanta, as a joint friend of mine and Vernon Jordan's at the time when Vernon was thinking about running for Congress, the man who finally ran for that seat, Andy Young, has become throughout the world the exemplification of what this Nation stands for, what our Government stands for in the field of basic human rights. And Andy Young will be on your program this year as a member of our Cabinet, a man who has a voice of his own, but who works closely with me. And I might say other members of the United Nations have joined with him in letting the deprived people of the world know that the United States, with all its power and influence, is interested in them and is their friend.

We've been concerned about the deteriorating quality of urban centers, and we now have a Secretary of the Housing and Urban Development Department—a woman who understands because of her background and inclination, her experience and her heritage, the problem with struggling people who feel excluded from societal structures—Patricia Harris. And she'll be on your program later on as part of my own administration.

Griffin Bell will be here to explain the new thrust of the Department of Justice.

Joe Califano will spell out to you some of the programs that we have already instituted and are instituting to restore dignity to those who are and have been dependent upon government to give them a decent living. Ray Marshall is in charge of our program for bringing into being job opportunities, because we know that there is no end in itself to have a strong enough economy to balance budgets and control inflation, unless that is predicated upon employment—the provision of jobs for people to stimulate our economy and to make it viable and to benefit us all.

Friday night when I got home, my wife met me at the door. She said, "I just watched Vernon Jordan on television being interviewed"—[*laughter*]—"and he said your administration is not doing anything for people who need help." And I read the New York Times yesterday and this morning, and my wife called me again this morning about 7:30. She says, "Vernon doesn't think you are doing as well as I think you are doing, Jimmy." [*Laughter*] And I hope in the months ahead that I'll be able to work closer with Vernon Jordan at the White House—where I spend a great deal of time working and planning with Members of the Congress.

Parren Mitchell, the head of the Black Caucus, was in my office Thursday going over not only the accomplishments but the remaining needs that have been addressed and are being addressed by the Democratic Congress and the Democratic President. We haven't done everything we would like to do, nor have we done everything that we're going to do.

I've been in office now 6 months—have no apologies to make—and I was trying to think of a story to illustrate that sometimes an immediate transformation can't be accomplished when problems have been there for years or terms of Presidents or even generations. Griffin Bell, who will

speak to you later, has a favorite story about a man who was arrested for getting drunk and setting a bed on fire. When he got before the judge, he said, "Judge, I plead guilty to being drunk, but the bed was on fire when I got in it." [*Laughter*] Well, to some degree, the bed was on fire when I got in it. [*Laughter*]

The point I want to make is that we're trying as best we can to make progress. I think you'll judge before this convention is over that I don't speak with a lonely voice, that the members of my Cabinet are united with me, and that there is no division between the Urban League and my administration. But we do need to have a closer working relationship because it's obvious that we have a long way to go. And we can get to our destination of having a decent life for all Americans if we work close together in a constructive and cooperative fashion.

Among my first proposals as President was one to stimulate the overall economy and especially to provide jobs for teenagers in the inner cities. We've now established a program to provide 1.1 million jobs, summer jobs, for youth—more than ever in history. We proposed, in addition, a youth employment program with 1.5 million jobs for unemployed youth.

We've doubled the size of the Peace Corps, the Job Corps, and we've more than doubled the public service jobs for the unemployed—from 310,000 to 725,000, nearly half of these for the long-term unemployed.

Soon, before August 5, we'll be sending to the Congress our proposal for basic welfare reform. Jobs will be the thrust behind this reform program for those who are able to work and self-respect and adequate living conditions for those who are not able to work. Our goal is for all those who want to work to be able to find work so that they can be independent and so they can be proud and they can be self-sufficient.

And I'd like to point out that an emphasis on jobs and work for those who are able is not discriminatory, it's not moving backwards, and it's not a deprivation of basic rights. What we want is for people who are able not to be permanently dependent on government, but able to stand on their own feet, support their own family, and have a constructive attitude toward our society.

In this welfare proposal, there will be an additional 1 million job opportunities. Our goal is to make sure that every single family has a member of it with a guaranteed job, by government if necessary, and this is a goal that we intend to reach. But let me mention—[applause]—may I mention a few other items of major concern.

We're concerned about young people's health. We propose an $18.9 million program to immunize 5½ million poor children from preventable diseases over the next 30 months, and we'll raise the number of poor children screened for medical purposes from less than 2 million last year to 9.8 million before I go out of office.

I said during the campaign that the tax system was a disgrace, that it was most unfair to people with low and average incomes. We've been working now for 6 months on a tax proposal that will be simpler and fairer and will reduce the burden on the average American. But in the meantime, we have already gotten Congress to agree—the bill has been signed, it's been passed into law—to reduce taxes $4 billion with the primary emphasis on the low- and middle-income families, which means that a family that makes about $10,000 a year on a permanent basis would have a 30-percent reduction in their income tax payments. That's already been done.

Walter Mondale, my Vice President, worked for years unsuccessfully, 8 years, to try to get a $100-million increase in the Title I programs for a better education for poor people, poor children. We have already proposed, and the Congress has already agreed, to increase the Title I program more than $350 million.

We've made a major expansion in what is called countercyclical revenue sharing to focus into the most deprived urban ghetto, unemployed areas, to be administered by Patricia Harris. And I've already signed into law a $4 billion public works bill. Under a new urban program that we are proposing, the Secretary of HUD, Patricia Harris, will have the authority to target large amounts of this money, in her judgment, on areas that are the most needy.

For a long time in the past whenever a Federal program was approved by the Congress and the Republican Presidents, a large portion of that money went to areas where the need was least, in the suburban areas for housing and jobs went to areas with already low unemployment. We have reversed that now, and we're going to send the Federal money where it's needed most.

Another of my first tasks has been to reorganize the Federal Government and to handle discrimination complaints faster and more effectively than we have in the past. The Equal Employment Opportunity Commission now has a backlog of 130,000 cases. Many of these cases aren't considered for 3 years. There are seven different Federal agencies that are supposed to be taking care of these needs, these discriminatory practices. That's not been done yet.

Because these cases have dragged on so long, quite often the witnesses have disappeared and the victims have given up.

This is one of our top priorities—to reorganize the structure. It's not an easy or quick thing that can be done, and the person in charge of it is Eleanor Holmes Norton.

I'd like to outline very briefly for you, in the time I have available, some of the achievements already. But I want to emphasize again, I'm not bragging about it because we recognize, as does Vernon Jordan, my friend, that we have a long way to go. We've set as a goal for this year the reduction of the unemployment rate from 8.1 percent, which it was last December, to 7 percent by the end of this year. We've already reached that goal, and we expect it to go on down, perhaps as low as 6.5 percent before the end of the year, with a trend downward that will be maintained.

We have also created just a few of the jobs that I have described to you. Of the $4 billion public works bill—the benefits that have not mirrored in the reduction in unemployment that we've already seen; that's still to come because it takes a long time to get these programs going once the Congress approves the measure—of the $4 billion, we last week signed the first contracts for less than one percent of the money that's available. But beginning with this week, we will be approving 1,000 public works contracts per week, and we'll have all $4 billion allocated by September 30 and, for the first time, for the first time, 10 percent of every contract must go to a minority subcontractor or supplier. This can mean $400 million in additional, new income for minority business men and women.

Now, I mentioned an increase in the public service jobs from 310,000 to 600,000. That legislation is just now being passed, and it will be the end of September—September 30—before we have the 725,000 people involved.

Right now, we are adding 15,000 public service jobs per week. Our proposal for youth employment has now passed the Senate and House conference, and I expect to have it at the White House for signature next week. It will create over 200,000 jobs in a National Youth Conservation Corps, built on the old Civilian Conservation Corps that was put into effect by Franklin Roosevelt. And we are just doubling the Job Corps slots to 40,000. Now, this is a program that's been approved, but it hasn't yet been put into effect. But it will be put into effect rapidly now that we have it on the books.

Income security—a lot of people are concerned about the social security system. We have proposed to the Congress—I hope they'll act quickly—to make sure that we have a sound social security system. And we have made a proposal to put it back on a sound basis without increasing the tax rate of American workers above what's already been prescribed by law.

I want to mention food stamps—again, an income for poor people that's very valuable but, as you know, in the past they've had to have cash money to buy food stamps. We have proposed, and the Senate has already approved, and I hope the House will approve quickly, the elimination of any requirement to purchase food stamps. In the future they won't have to buy them.

We're taking the first step towards comprehensive health care by proposing to the Congress hospital cost containment. The price to sick people of hospital care has gone up too rapidly. It is now doubling. It's now doubling every 5 years, about twice the rate of growth of the normal, nationwide inflation rate.

By early next year, we'll have a comprehensive package of health care to put forward. And we're prepared to move more rapidly but, I have to tell you, frankly, that the Congress this year has almost all it can handle. But I've worked out with the congressional leaders that next year they'll start their full work on a comprehensive health care system for our country.

I want to add just a couple of more points. Then I'll be through.

We are concerned about the rebuilding of American urban centers. I won't cover what Patricia Harris is going to cover in her speech, but we've asked for $5 billion increase in budget authority and proposed new formulae to focus this attention where it's needed most. In housing we are increasing Title VIII sections of housing, reviving the 202 housing programs for elderly people. We've proposed an extension of $200 million in separate funding for private day care services, and action by both Houses of Congress is quite near. And we recently proposed major reforms in the foster care system to permit more easily approved adoptions and to hold families, again, together.

I could go on and on, because the list of programs is very long and the amount of money involved is very great, and the eagerness to implement these programs by me and the Democratic Congress is there and the Cabinet officers and administrators contains an attitude not of holding back what Congress has approved, as has been the case too often in the past, but an eagerness to put into effect these programs completely and without delay.

Now, I've mentioned a lot of figures to you. I've talked a lot about programs that we've already passed, about a lot of money that's already been appropriated. And then you might say, "Well, he's talking about a lot of money and a lot of help. But I haven't seen that money in my community yet." But the point I'm making to you is it takes time to change the trends of history and to reverse the bureaucratic mechanism to one of support and compassion and concern and enthusiasm from what was formerly reluctance or lack of enthusiasm.

We have, obviously, a long way to go. So, when I talk about these figures, it's not with a sense of final accomplishments. It's with a sense of dedication to the future to perform as President of our great country in such a way as to make you proud and to let you feel that there is in the White House and there is in the Democratic Congress and there is within the Cabinet members of my administration a partner with the Urban League, eager to work in the private and governmental sectors toward common goals. I'm talking about real money, real programs to help real people in real need of help.

And I'm not talking about just abstract figures—although a billion dollars is a lot of money—or meaningless statistics about percentages of reduction of unemployment. I'm talking about a flood of new programs that will be coming into your own community in the weeks and months ahead. I'm talking about my administration living up to its commitments to the poor and to the hungry and to the timid and to the weak and to the unemployed.

I need your partnership and you need my partnership. And I believe that that partnership is available to us and it can have a profound impact so that you and I and my Cabinet and the Congress together can make this a better place in which to live, particularly those who haven't yet realized the guarantees expressed 200 years ago by our Founding Fathers, of life and liberty and the pursuit of happiness.

We've made great strides in this country already. We still have a long way to go. And you've got my pledge to respond well to counsel, to advice, to caution, and to criticism. And I believe that this can be very constructive. And together we can put smiles on the faces instead of tears, and we can have a support of our system of government instead of a lashing out because deprived and unemployed people feel alienated from the structure of society that's been so good to all of us here.

Those are my hopes and my dreams and my prayers.

You're partners with me and Vernon and all of you. I'm proud of that partnership and what it can mean to us in this greatest of all nations on Earth.

Thank you very much.

NOTE: The President spoke at 9:05 a.m. in the International Ballroom at the Washington Hilton Hotel. Following his remarks, he met privately with Donald H. McGannon, president of the board of trustees, and Vernon E. Jordan, Jr., executive director, of the National Urban League.

Marine Pollution Protocol

Message to the Senate Transmitting the Protocol.   July 25, 1977

To the Senate of the United States:

I herewith transmit for your consideration the Protocol Relating to Intervention on the High Seas in Cases of Marine Pollution by Substances Other than Oil, 1973. I am also transmitting a report on this Protocol from the Department of State.

The Protocol complements the 1969 International Convention Relating to Intervention on the High Seas in Cases of Oil Pollution Casualties by providing that, under certain circumstances, governments may take action on the high seas to protect the interests of their coastal areas from marine pollution caused by substances other than oil. A list of such substances, compiled by the Inter-Governmental Maritime Consultative Organiza-

tion, accompanies the Protocol. Under the terms of the Protocol, the list can be amended to reflect future technological developments.

The Protocol is evidence of awareness by the international community that oil is not the only potential source of marine pollution, and that steps must be taken to prevent or reduce damage from other substances as well. I recommend that the Senate advise and consent to its ratification.

JIMMY CARTER

The White House,
    July 25, 1977.

Postal Rate Commission

Nomination of Simeon M. Bright To Be a Member.   July 25, 1977

The President today announced that he will nominate Simeon M. Bright, of Keyser, W. Va., to be a member of the Postal Rate Commission. He would replace Paul A. Miltich. Bright is owner of Sim Bright Real Estate & Investments and president of Bright Associates in West Virginia.

He was born September 11, 1925, in Keyser, W. Va. He received a B.A. (1949) and M.A. (1950) from West Virginia University.

From 1953 to 1962, he was an educational specialist for the Department of the Army. He worked for the Post Office Department from 1962 to 1969, serving as an employee development officer from 1962 to 1965 and as special assistant to the Assistant Postmaster General, Bureau of Personnel, from 1965 to 1969.

Bright was a lecturer at the University of Maryland in 1969–70, and from 1971 to 1974 he was manager of the J. Dorsey Real Estate Co. Since 1974 he has been owner of Sim Bright Real Estate & Investments. From 1973 to 1976, Bright was also coordinator of the cooperative education program at Potomac State College, West Virginia University.

Department of State

Nomination of Benjamin H. Read To Be Deputy Under Secretary.   July 25, 1977

The President today announced that he will nominate Benjamin H. Read, of Washington, D.C., to be Deputy Under Secretary of State for Management. He would replace Richard M. Moose. Read is president of the German Marshall Fund of the United States.

Read was born September 14, 1925, in Philadelphia, Pa. He received a B.A. from Williams College in 1949 and an LL.B. from the University of Pennsylvania in 1952.

From 1952 to 1955, Read practiced law in Philadelphia, and in 1955 and 1956 he was an associate defender with the Volunteer Defender Association there. In 1957 and 1958, he was an attorney adviser in the Legal Adviser's Office at the State Department.

From 1958 to 1963, Read was legislative assistant to U.S. Senator Joseph S. Clark of Pennsylvania. From 1963 to 1969, he was special assistant to the Secretary of State and Executive Secretary at the State Department.

Read was acting Director, then Director, of the Woodrow Wilson International Center for Scholars from 1969 to 1973. Since 1973 he has been president of the German Marshall Fund of the United States, a Washington-based foundation dedicated to assisting Americans and Europeans to understand and resolve the common problems of industrial societies.

Visit of Prime Minister Giulio Andreotti of Italy

Remarks of the President and the Prime Minister at the Welcoming Ceremony.   July 26, 1977

THE PRESIDENT. This morning it's a great honor for me, on behalf of the American people, to welcome to our country a personal friend of mine and a man who represents a nation which is a close partner and friend of the United States. Prime Minister Andreotti is one of the most experienced and accomplished leaders in the whole world. He's had a breadth of service in the Government of Italy, which is almost unbelievable in its complexity and in its diversity and accomplishments.

About 30 years ago, as a very young man of 27, he became the Under Secretary of State, and since then he's been the Minister of Interior, the Minister of Finance, the Minister of Defense, the Minister of the Treasury, of Commerce and Industry, the Minister of the Budget and Economic Planning. And before his present service, he has been Prime Minister of Italy on two different occasions. So, the great developments in Italy and its emergence as one of the world leaders is to a major degree a measure of the accomplishments of this fine man.

The last time he was in the United States was in December. He met then with Vice President-elect Walter Mondale. In January, when we made our first series of visits around the world to show how valuable those national friendships were, of course Italy was one of the places that the Vice President visited. He was well received by our good friend, Prime Minister Andreotti.

When I went to the London summit conference in May, I enjoyed working with Prime Minister Andreotti and five other world leaders in assessing the problems that we face together and the opportunities for improvement of the lot of those who live in our own countries and those who depend upon us to make decisions that can improve the lives of people in all nations.

The friendship between Italy and the United States is very dear to us and very important. The bilateral relationship is one of mutual significance and support. Obviously, Italy is one of the keystone nations in the European Community and is a valued partner of our own in the defense of the Atlantic region through NATO.

We have seen Italy's strong action and courageous action in recent years to overcome the tremendous burden of having to import 75 percent of their energy supplies at rapidly increasing prices. And the strict conservation measures and the sacrifice of the Italian people to restore the strength and integrity of their own economic system has been an inspiration to the rest of the world.

We work very closely with Italy. And now, we and they and a few other nations are analyzing the nuclear fuel cycle to determine how we can meet the needs of energy in the future from the atom without constraint on the economic well-being of the nations involved and at the same time prevent the proliferation of the ability of nations to develop nuclear weapons.

Our trade with Italy is of great mutual benefit, and there are large investments by American business in Italy and vice versa. We look on Italy as an avenue of advice and counsel and partnership in strengthening our own ties with the people of the developing nations of the world. And I think it is accurate to say that in world leadership the Government of Italy, under the leadership of Prime Minister Andreotti, is admired, respected, and also trusted.

So, we share with them a mutual responsibility for world security. We are interdependent. Their friendship means as much to us as does our friendship mean to the people of Italy.

We are also blessed in the United States with millions of Italian-Americans who have come here from their mother country and have enriched our own culture with the derivation of the historic achievements of ancient Italy.

For all these reasons it's a great honor to me this morning to welcome Prime Minister Andreotti who will now be sharing with me and others discussions about affairs that bind our nations together and challenges that address both our great countries. To use a phrase that Prime Minister Andreotti has made famous, "International solidarity among the democracies of the world is a very important foundation on which permanent peace can be found."

With great admiration, appreciation for his accomplishments, and an additional expression of the value of Italian friendship toward our country, Mr. Prime Minister, we welcome you to the United States.

Thank you very much.

THE PRIME MINISTER. Mr. President, I am particularly glad to find myself again on American soil in acceptance of the invitation that you addressed to me last December on the occasion of my visit to your predecessor and that you so kindly renewed last May in London when we met at the Downing Street summit and at the Atlantic Council.

There are two fundamental principles which guide the policies of democratic Italy, the frank and constructive friendship towards the United States of America and the passionate participation in the development of the European Community. And the latter in turn is tied to the American Continent by countless bonds, both historical and present.

This twofold aim is meant and lived by us not in a vision of hostility towards other regions of the world, but, on the contrary, as a stabilizing contribution to equilibrium and universal peace.

The Italian people, through hard sacrifices, certainly made less difficult by the breadth of the consensus in Parliament, were able to overcome last fall a critical moment which could have been dramatic for our economy and our finances.

The firm will to fight and tackle, with success, the present difficulty remains— first among them, unemployment and inflation. We know that only if our nation perseveres in fulfilling its duty, it can win the solidarity of its allies which at times is particularly vital to us—a solidarity which takes the form both of adequate credit from the international institutions and of the concrete availability of friendly countries to be ever more open and to accept the products of Italian labor.

But it is not only with the problems of the present moment that we must concern ourselves. There is an impelling need to discern the immediate and long-term possibilities and difficulties. First of all, that fundamental problem of energy to which you, Mr. President, have addressed yourself so vigorously and without delay in coordinated terms. We are eager for a close cooperation in this field, and this will figure in our discussions with you.

The country of Enrico Fermi and Guglielmo Marconi can, without committing a sin of pride, believe that it is a useful participant in the great research programs which will be all the more valid if formidable means, wills, and brains are concentrated on them.

Allow me, Mr. President, here from the White House to send a deep-felt message of fraternity and affection to the Italians of America, to their children, to their grandchildren. They represent in the number and quality a substantial component of the great American people and make up an indestructible basis for our friendship. The recent commemorations of the Bicentennial have drawn ample attention to their contribution, sometimes silent and humble, but always important, and of this we have been very proud.

Furthermore, our pride is in being able to show the old emigrants and their descendants that Italy is modernizing itself, it's strengthening itself in its spiritual heritage, and that it is capable of finding ways toward harmony and peace in the world.

Mr. President, on behalf of the Government, and interpreting the feelings of the Italian people, I address to you a warm and cordial greeting, which I wish to extend to Mrs. Carter, to the members of your family, and to all the American people.

NOTE: The President spoke at 10:40 a.m. on the South Lawn of the White House. Prime Minister Andreotti spoke in Italian, and his remarks were translated by an interpreter.

United States Ambassador to Qatar

Nomination of Andrew I. Killgore.
July 26, 1977

The President today announced that he will nominate Andrew I. Killgore, of Lakeland, Fla., to be Ambassador Extraordinary and Plenipotentiary of the United States to the State of Qatar. He would replace Robert P. Paganelli. Killgore is presently deputy chief of mission in Wellington, New Zealand.

Killgore was born November 7, 1919, in Greensboro, Ala. He received a B.S. from Livingstone University in 1943 and an LL.B. from the University of Alabama in 1949. He served in the U.S. Navy from 1943 to 1946.

Killgore served as a selector-analyst for the U.S. Displaced Persons Commission in 1949 and 1950 and as a displaced populations officer in Frankfort in 1950 and 1951. From 1951 to 1953, he was visa officer in London, and from 1953 to 1955 he was an evaluator at the State Department.

In 1955–56 Killgore took Arab language training at the Foreign Service Institute, and in 1956 and 1957 he served as political officer in Beirut. From 1957 to 1959, he was political officer in Jerusalem, and from 1959 to 1961, he was political officer in Amman.

In 1961 and 1962, Killgore was an international relations officer at the State Department. From 1962 to 1965, he was officer-in-charge of Iraq-Jordan affairs. From 1965 to 1967, he was detailed as a public affairs officer to USIA in Baghdad.

Killgore was political officer in Dacca from 1967 to 1970 and political-economic officer for the Arab North Directorate, Jordan Affairs, at the State Department from 1970 to 1972. From 1972 to 1974, he was counselor for political affairs in Tehran. In 1974 he was principal officer in Manama, and since 1974 he has been deputy chief of mission in Wellington.

replace David S. Smith. Kennedy-Minott is a professor of U.S. history at California State University at Hayward.

He was born June 1, 1928, in Portland, Oreg. He received an A.B. (1953), an M.A. (1956), and a Ph. D. (1960) from Stanford University. He served in the U.S. Army from 1946 to 1952.

Kennedy-Minott was at Stanford University from 1960 to 1965, serving as an instructor, then assistant professor of history, and as assistant director, then director of the summer sessions. In 1965–66 he was an associate professor at Portland State University.

In 1966–67 Kennedy-Minott was associate dean of instruction at California State University at Hayward, and from 1967 to 1969 he was head of the division of humanities there. Since 1969 he has been a full professor.

From 1971 to 1973, Kennedy-Minott was an adviser and researcher for Thames T.V. of London on European emigration to the United States and for "The World at War." He is the author of "Peerless Patriots: The Organized Veterans and the Spirit of Patriotism" (1962), "The Fortress That Never Was: The Myth of Hitler's Bavarian Stronghold" (1964), and "The Sinking of the Lollipop: Shirley Temple v. Pete McCloskey and the Politics of Suburbia" (1968).

United States Ambassador to Sweden

Nomination of Rodney O. Kennedy-Minott.
July 26, 1977

The President today announced that he will nominate Rodney O. Kennedy-Minott, of Atherton, Calif., to be Ambassador Extraordinary and Plenipotentiary of the United States to Sweden. He would

United States Ambassador to Haiti

Nomination of William B. Jones.
July 26, 1977

The President today announced that he will nominate William B. Jones, of Los Angeles, to be Ambassador Extraordinary and Plenipotentiary of the United States to Haiti. He would replace Heyward Isham. Jones is U.S. Permanent Representative to the United Nations Educational, Scientific and Cultural Organization (UNESCO) in Paris.

He was born May 2, 1928, in Los Angeles. He received an A.B. in 1949 from the University of California at Los Angeles and a J.D. in 1952 from the University of Southern California School of Law.

From 1953 to 1962, Jones practiced law in Los Angeles. In 1962 and 1963, he was supervisory educational and cultural exchange officer on the Plans and Development Staff at the State Department, and in 1963 and 1964 he was Chief of West Coast and Mali programs in the Bureau of Educational and Cultural Affairs.

Jones was Deputy Director of the Office of African Programs from 1964 to 1967, and Director of Programs Evaluation and Analysis staff from 1967 to 1969. From 1969 to 1973, he was Deputy Assistant Secretary in the Bureau of Educational and Cultural Affairs.

Since 1973 Jones has been U.S. Permanent Representative to UNESCO. He has also served as U.S. Representative to the 17th, 18th, and 19th sessions of the General Conference of UNESCO in 1972, 1974, and 1976. In 1973 he was designated U.S. delegate to the Third Extraordinary Session of the General Conference of UNESCO, and in 1976 he served as Chairman of the Legal Committee at the UNESCO General Conference in Nairobi.

Budget Rescission

Message to the Congress.   July 26, 1977

To the Congress of the United States:
In accordance with the Impoundment Control Act of 1974, I herewith propose rescission of $105.0 million in missile procurement funds appropriated to the Department of Defense.

The details of the proposed rescission are contained in the attached report.

JIMMY CARTER

The White House,
July 26, 1977.

NOTE: The attachment detailing the rescission is printed in the FEDERAL REGISTER of July 29, 1977.

The message was not issued in the form of a White House press release.

Budget Deferrals

Message to the Congress.   July 26, 1977

To the Congress of the United States:
In accordance with the Impoundment Control Act of 1974, I herewith report one new deferral of budget authority amounting to $11.0 million for the local public works program of the Department of Commerce. In addition, I am reporting a revision to a previously transmitted Energy Research and Development Administration deferral.

The details of each deferral are contained in the attached reports.

JIMMY CARTER

The White House,
July 26, 1977.

NOTE: The attachments detailing the deferrals are printed in the FEDERAL REGISTER of July 29, 1977.

The message was not issued in the form of a White House press release.

Customs Convention on International Transport of Goods

Message to the Senate Transmitting the Convention.   July 26, 1977

To the Senate of the United States:
With a view to receiving the advice

and consent of the Senate to ratification, I transmit herewith the revised Customs Convention on the International Transport of Goods under cover of Transport International Routier Carnets (TIR Convention), done at Geneva on November 14, 1975. I also transmit, for the information of the Senate, the report of the Department of State with respect to the Convention.

The revised TIR Convention is based on the TIR Convention of 1959 to which the United States is a party. The revised TIR Convention contains modernized technical provisions which will facilitate transportation of United States goods. The most important improvements are that the TIR Carnet is now to be printed in English as well as French, and United States goods transported to Europe which arrive late under the TIR Carnet will be protected against administrative delays.

I recommend that the Senate give early and favorable consideration to the Convention and give its advice and consent to ratification.

JIMMY CARTER

The White House,
July 26, 1977.

NOTE: The message was not issued in the form of a White House press release.

Federal Maritime Commission

Nomination of Richard J. Daschbach To Be a Commissioner. July 26, 1977

The President today announced that he will nominate Richard J. Daschbach, of Walpole, N.H., to be Commissioner of the Federal Maritime Commission. He would replace Ashton Barrett. Daschbach is maritime counsel to the Senate Commerce Committee.

He was born November 19, 1936, in Columbus, Ohio. He received a B.A. from Georgetown University in 1958 and grad-

uated from Georgetown University Law Center in 1962.

From 1963 to 1965, Daschbach was an area coordinator for the Area Redevelopment Administration in the Commerce Department. In 1965 and 1966, he was special assistant to the Assistant Administrator of the Economic Development Administration at Commerce.

Daschbach was Washington manager and counsel for Gulf South Research Institute from 1966 to 1968, and staff attorney for the Southern New Hampshire Legal Services Association in 1968 and 1969.

Daschbach was staff counsel to the Senate Commerce Committee from 1969 until 1973, when he became maritime counsel to the Committee.

Visit of Prime Minister Andreotti of Italy

Toasts of the President and Prime Minister Andreotti at a Dinner Honoring the Prime Minister. July 26, 1977

THE PRESIDENT. *Good evening, everybody.*

The first thing I'd like to say is that we're very proud to have you here with us tonight. It's been a delightful day for me, and I've thoroughly enjoyed the reunion with my good friend, Prime Minister Andreotti.

As you may or may not know, he doesn't speak English and I don't speak Italian. So we carry on a conversation in Spanish. [*Laughter*]

I got through with my first conversation with him today, and I discovered afterwards that we had promised to build 18 water projects in Italy. [*Laughter*] And he had promised to send the Communists over to help me run the Government. [*Laughter*] So we decided from then on to use an interpreter. [*Laughter*] We've made out much better since then.

There have been a lot of things that have made the Italian-Americans famous in our country. One of them was my acceptance speech at the Democratic Convention. [*Laughter*]

Afterwards, I went to an Italian-American appreciation banquet. And as a normal outgrowth of the fact that Rome was a republic 2,000 years ago and the fact that within the consciousness of Italians and their descendants there has been a strong commitment to orderly government, a deep sense of justice, truth, integrity, and a commitment to public service, I was there when the two most famous men in our Nation were recognized, along with some others, Judge John Sirica and Peter Rodino.

And I think it's accurate to say that it was not a coincidence that these Americans of Italian descent were the ones who—in a time of great challenge to our very system of government based on human freedom and the democratic process—that they stood tall and strong and reinspired our people to believe in our own system of government. And I particularly want to thank Peter Rodino, who's here, and my good friend, John Sirica, for that wonderful accomplishment.

That particular evening was during the general election contest. I had a chance to say a few words. I was very happy to introduce to several thousand Italian-Americans my runningmate, Fritz "Mondalli." [*Laughter*]

I think because of that and other reasons, we made out very well with Italian-Americans. But when we began to prepare the guest list for this evening, Rosalynn and I and all those who helped to make arrangements for this banquet were impressed at the overwhelming number of Italian-Americans who have been

an inspiration to us all, both those who are famous and those who are not very famous, and a re-awareness of the strong ties of heritage and kinship and friendship that has bound our countries together.

I'm very new at this job, as you know. But I've had a chance to learn from the experienced leaders who have, through long years of public service, learned themselves about the proper interrelationships between nations and the unchanging trends of history and the challenge that befalls democratic governments and how successfully to meet those challenges.

I was listening a few minutes ago to a very famous economist who is sitting at our table, Dr. Modigliani. And he has recently published an article in one of the famous Italian newspapers, pointing out that the government of Prime Minister Andreotti is, in his opinion, the first one in 20 years who's really moving that country and inspiring the people and correcting defects and carving out for the future a bright outlook on the prospects of the Italian people for maintaining their strength, economically and politically, and preserving their tremendous influence that's beneficial to the rest of the free world.

I've learned a lot from Prime Minister Andreotti, who's become a very close personal friend of mine. He's served, as I said in my welcoming remarks today, in many parts of government. I can't recall them all, but a little more than 30 years ago he began his service as Under Secretary of State. He served as Secretary of Finance and Treasury and Defense and Commerce and has managed the budget of Italy. And has been a solid and a very inspired leader for the people of Italy.

Several years ago, there was a great concern throughout the free world that the economic circumstances in Italy might deteriorate rapidly and be a stumbling block to further progress. But under the leadership of Prime Minister Andreotti, that crisis has been weathered. And now I think it's accurate to say, and almost everyone would agree, that the progress that has been made in that nation in recent months is inspirational indeed.

We value the friendship of leaders like him and the wisdom that he adds to international councils and, also, a sense of sharing of the responsibilities for leadership with the government and the people of Italy.

There is a great deal of common purpose, a common challenge, common problems, and a determination to solve them. I benefit personally from this friendship and this closeness. And I know that it is with a sense of reassurance that we recognize again the strength of the interrelationship between the people of Italy and the people of the United States of America.

As President of our people, representing about 215 million free men and women, I would like to propose a toast to the brave and courageous and fine friends of ours in Italy and to their inspired leader, Prime Minister Andreotti.

THE PRIME MINISTER. Mr. President, ladies and gentlemen, I am indeed very glad to be again in the United States for my third official visit as President of the Council of Ministers of the Italian Republic.

Your invitation, Mr. President, and tonight's wonderful reception in this historical house, which is deeply linked with so many memories of American greatness, had, first of all, evidence of the old, warm, and enduring friendship between our two countries.

I would like to thank particularly on this occasion our gracious hostess, Mrs. Carter, whose presence, whose courtesy

and, also, intelligence are so evident in so many activities of your great Nation.

Somebody suggested that I might address, in Latin, my host. [*Laughter*] By the way, I suppose that my Latin may be more understandable to many of you than my English. [*Laughter*]

But I would ask, Mr. President, your permission to use my language, which happens to be that, also, of so many Americans of Italian descent.

[*At this point, the Prime Minister continued in Italian, and the translation follows:*]

Mr. President, I wish to renew my warmest thanks for the welcome given to me and to Minister Forlani, for the cordiality shown to us, and for the appreciation toward our government at a time which is difficult but in which the Italian people are once again proving their great will for recovery and progress.

He who has the responsibility for political leadership always finds it hard to tackle programs of social reform. When the economic trends are favorable, one fears that an innovation may cause pauses and retrogressions. When, on the other hand, things do not go well, the requirements for first aid monopolize resources and energies.

Now, our Republican Constitution of 1948 provides for a general social progress and for the narrowing of excessive income gaps. It is not morally right that the contrast continues to exist between the few that possess very much and the many who have, if at all, the bare necessities.

In this period and within this framework, we are leading an energetic fiscal policy. This has proved so effective that in 24 months the taxation revenue has doubled, although the fiscal pressure on the less privileged has been appreciably lessened.

At the same time, we have had a prodigious expansion in the number of students up to the level of universities, which are open today to the children even of the humblest families.

Another item I would like to add—the proportion of Italians who now own their own homes has reached 50 percent. The road to be covered in the field of social justice is still long. We are conditioned by the grip of unemployment and of inflation. But the results of more than 30 years comfort us in our firm belief in the goodness of the democratic system. We consider freedom to be the fulcrum of any intention and design of our programs.

I am proud to speak these words in the presence of a chosen representation of Italian-Americans, almost all descendants of humble immigrants to whom for a long time our fatherland was not able to ensure bread and work.

On your soil the immigrants gave a strong contribution to the continuous growth of the American nation, sharing without exception joys and adversities.

Allow me today not to talk of those who have emerged socially in many fields. I would like instead to mention the contribution of blood given by the Italian-Americans when the United States has been engaged in war.

There is not a single military cemetery from Normandy to Nettuno in which the names of so many people of Italian origin do not bear witness to this participation in the greatest sacrifice of their new homeland.

When you, Mr. President, were serving in the Navy in Hawaii, you would certainly have paused in meditation in front of the historical memorial to the fallen of Pearl Harbor. Well, even on that stone are engraved significant names, such as those of machinist W. J. Bonfilio, of sailors E. I. Brigniole, E. Puzzio, M. I. Giovinazzo, F. J. Pidrotti, J. N. Ristivo, and R. D. Valenti, of yeoman M. Crisquolo, of shipfitter F. Riganti. Europe and Italy also owe those boys, twice in this century, their victorious liberation.

And it was the sacrifice of all this youth that inspired enlightened statesmen to give life in 1949 to the Atlantic Treaty, the prime purpose of which has been that of preserving peace. By associating themselves in time to effectively ward off the danger of a third world war, the United States, Canada, and 13 European countries have undertaken an affirmation of solidarity which had no historical precedent and which still remains an essential element of world stability.

We are pleased to say that this view is shared today in Italy by the widest majority of political forces, together with the other qualifying objective of the European Community.

Mr. President, on the occasion of every change here at the White House, we in Europe legitimately ask ourselves, what will be the policy of the United States towards our continent? It seems to us that a man from Georgia, the son, that is, of a State which counts among its cities a Rome and an Athens, must be by vocation more than others close to Europe. [*Laughter*]

You have given assurances of this many times during your electoral campaign, and you confirmed it without fear of doubt last May at the London summit. And on the same occasion, you also made it clear, without equivocation, that there is no contrast between the repeated raising of the issue of human rights and international policy of détente, to which we are also faithfully and earnestly committed.

I do not think I am far off the mark, because the statesman is first of all a man, if I connect your reaffirmations for human rights not so much to a high political strategy but rather to your youthful experiences as a son of the Deep South—sensitive, with foreseeing clearness to the appeal of civil unity and of the equality of man.

On the road of détente, the meeting in Belgrade offers us a proving ground to show that there is a convergence of ideas between America and Europe. And we must embark on it, both firmly and gradually, confident in the value of the principles in which we believe.

Mr. President, in the spirit of friendship and solidarity between our two countries and in view of the ever closer and more concrete cooperation which we intend to implement between our two Governments, I raise my glass in a toast to your personal happiness and to that of your family, to the prosperity of our two peoples, and to the well-being of all those present.

NOTE: The President spoke at 9:25 p.m. in the State Dining Room at the White House.

United States-Canada Maritime Boundaries and Related Resource Issues

Designation of Lloyd N. Cutler as the President's Special Representative for Negotiations. July 27, 1977

The President today announced the designation of Lloyd N. Cutler, of Chevy Chase, Md., as his special representative for maritime boundary and resource negotiations with Canada, with the personal rank of Ambassador. Ambassador Cutler, who is a Washington attorney, will conduct negotiations with Canada over the coming months in an effort to reach a comprehensive settlement of U.S.-Canadian maritime boundaries and related fishery and hydrocarbon issues.

The Government of Canada has named Ambassador Marcel Cadieux to conduct its negotiations. Ambassador Cadieux formerly served as Under-Secretary of the Department of External Affairs in Ottawa and as Ambassador of Canada to the United States. He is on temporary assignment from his position as Canadian Ambassador to the European Communities.

The two countries attempted to resolve their maritime boundary and fisheries issues in talks from late 1975 to early 1977. Failing agreement, earlier this year they entered into an interim Reciprocal Fisheries Agreement for 1977, to enable each country to continue fishing in the 200-mile zone of the other while negotiations for more permanent arrangements proceed. The new negotiations will resume under the direction of Ambassador Cutler and Ambassador Cadieux around August 1.

The two Governments have agreed that, with a view toward reaching a negotiated settlement between them, the special negotiators will be guided by the following terms of reference. The negotiators will report to Governments by October 15, 1977, on the principles of a comprehensive settlement encompassing:

—maritime boundaries delimitation;

—complementary fishery and hydrocarbon resource arrangements, as appropriate;

—such other related matters as the two Governments may decide.

The negotiators will develop the substance of an ad referendum comprehensive settlement for submission to Governments by December 1, 1977.

The negotiators will organize and conduct the negotiations in the manner and in the places which they judge will best facilitate a settlement.

Negotiations concerning West Coast salmon will be resumed separately on a priority basis. The special negotiators will determine the relationship, if any, between the courses and outcomes of the two sets of negotiations.

Cutler was born November 10, 1917, in New York City. He received an A.B. (1936) and an LL.B. (1939) from Yale University. He served in the U.S. Army from 1942 to 1945.

From 1946 to 1962, Cutler was a partner in the law firm of Cox, Langford, Stoddard & Cutler. He has been a partner with Wilmer, Cutler & Pickering since 1962.

Cutler was secretary of the Lawyers Committee on Civil Rights Under Law from 1963 to 1965, and cochairman from 1971 to 1973. He was vice chairman of the Business Leadership Advisory Council, Office of Economic Opportunity, in 1963. In 1968 and 1969, he was Executive Director of the National Commission on the Causes and Prevention of Violence.

Visit of Prime Minister Andreotti of Italy

White House Statement Issued Following the Conclusion of the Meetings Between the President and the Prime Minister. July 27, 1977

Italian Prime Minister Giulio Andreotti paid an official visit to Washington July 26–27 at the invitation of President Carter. He was accompanied by Foreign Minister Arnaldo Forlani. The President gave a White House dinner for the Prime Minister on July 26 and held two lengthy conversations with the Italian visitors. The talks between the President and the Prime Minister covered a wide range of political, economic, security, and cultural issues in which the two nations share an interest. These discussions were a follow-on to the meeting between the President and the Prime Minister in May at the London summit. The President and the Prime Minister expressed their intention to continue the process of close consultations between the two Governments and emphasized their basic agreement on major issues.

During their meetings, the President and the Prime Minister discussed East-West relations, focusing on SALT and other arms control negotiations; developments in Europe, with special reference to the European Community; the situation in the Mediterranean and the Middle East; and the upcoming fall meeting in Belgrade of the Conference on Security and Cooperation in Europe. The President and the Prime Minister also discussed human rights and their role in international affairs, agreeing on the desirability of continuing to stress implementation of these universally accepted values as an important element in the process of détente.

The Prime Minister described the Italian situation in its various aspects. The President expressed appreciation for Italy's continued contribution to Western cooperation and Allied solidarity, and its commitment to democratic institutions.

The President and the Prime Minister discussed the economic difficulties that beset many of the industrialized democracies and pledged to work for common solutions. The two leaders agreed that the Andreotti government's economic program has moved the Italian economy toward greater stability, less inflation, and a more favorable balance of payments. They agreed on the need to persevere along the lines agreed with the IMF, as well as on the necessity of implementing the consensus reached at the London summit to adjust payments imbalances in a context of expanding trade and economic development.

The President and the Prime Minister devoted a major part of their talks to world energy problems. They affirmed their intention to enhance and reinvigorate cooperation through the International Energy Agency and, bilaterally, through the U.S.-Italy Energy Working Group to coordinate policies and assist one another in this area of great significance. In this connection, the President agreed to explore ways of meeting Italy's needs for assured supplies of natural uranium as well as financing of its nuclear power program. The two leaders discussed the special energy requirements and objectives which Italy shares with other major industrialized countries heavily dependent on imported fossil fuels. They expressed their hope that the International Nuclear Fuel Cycle Evaluation would contribute to their common objectives in the field of nuclear nonproliferation and to a satisfactory solution of the participating countries' needs for assured fuel. They also agreed to expand cooperation in energy conservation, in safe and environmentally sound operation of nuclear reactors, and in the development of new sources of energy—solar, bioconversion, geothermal, and others.

Recognizing the importance of historical ties of friendship, a common cultural heritage, and the contribution of millions of Americans of Italian descent to the intellectual, spiritual, and economic life of the United States, the President and the Prime Minister agreed that every effort should be made to increase the already significant exchanges between the two countries in the fields of education and culture.

They agreed in particular on the desirability of a new effort of reciprocal assistance, in which Italy would assist in the strengthening of Italian language and study programs in the United States, and the United States would assist in the strengthening of English language teaching and American studies programs in Italy.

The two leaders also placed high priority on a two-way expansion of student and scholarly exchange and expressed their support for efforts now underway to finance additional exchanges, through loan funds made available by the private sector in the two countries.

The President and the Prime Minister discussed other areas where future cooperation between the two countries could lead to immediate results of mutual benefit, including an agreement on defense procurement, and follow-up visits by cabinet-level officials of the two Governments in the next few months. These visits will give impetus to U.S.-Italian cooperation in the areas of defense; economic, financial, and investment relations; scientific and technological cooperation; and exchanges of information on administrative matters.

During the course of the visit, the two Governments also agreed to announce that the Chicago Symphony will perform in Milan in September 1978, in return for the participation in our Bicentennial celebration of the La Scala Opera Company. In addition, a major exhibit called "Pompeii A.D. 79" will tour the United States soon.

Air Services Between the United States and United Kingdom

Letter to the Chairman of the Civil Aeronautics Board. July 21, 1977

To Chairman Alfred Kahn

On July 23, 1977, the United States intends to sign a new Air Services Agreement with the United Kingdom.

The Agreement authorizes new non-stop services to certain U.S. cities for U.S. and U.K. carriers. Also, the carrier authorizations and designations under the new Agreement at certain currently certificated cities must be revised pursuant to the Agreement's new provisions regarding multiple designation.

The United States is entitled to designate a U.S. carrier to provide immediate service in the Atlanta-London and Dallas/Fort Worth-London markets. Fairness to the public requires the authorization of immediate U.S.-flag service. And to promote our foreign commerce policy of increased competition worldwide we should act with the greatest possible speed. For these reasons, I am requesting that you submit a recommendation to me by early October designating a carrier to begin service to the Atlanta-London market and a carrier to begin service to the Dallas/Fort Worth-London market.

I hope to make designations by November 1, 1977, after considering your recommendation. Service could then begin shortly thereafter. The services you recommend should enhance the competitiveness of the U.S.-flag air system and be economically viable. I would also urge you to take into account in your recommendation the fact that a U.S. carrier may provide nonstop Houston-London service after July 23, 1980, and U.S. carriers may provide one-stop service in this market upon signing of the Agreement.

The United States must move promptly to issue the requisite foreign air carrier permits under § 402 of the Federal Aviation Act to those carriers designated by the United Kingdom for scheduled operations. Therefore, I request that you send me by early October, your recommendations for any necessary amendments of the § 402 permits of the designated U.K. carriers which have filed timely applications with the Board for such amendments.

With respect to those cities which are already gateways for service to the United Kingdom, the United States is required to submit new designations by November 1, 1977, and I also request your recommendation on these designations by early October, consistent with the provisions of the new Agreement regarding single and multiple designation.

Finally, I request that you move expeditiously to forward to me your recommendations concerning the other air services which were addressed by the Board in the Transatlantic Route Proceedings, but on which final action was postponed pending completion of the bilateral air negotiations with the United Kingdom.

I have directed the Secretaries of State and Transportation to provide any assistance that you may require in meeting these dates and implementing the new Agreement.

Sincerely,

JIMMY CARTER

[The Honorable Alfred Edward Kahn, Chairman, Civil Aeronautics Board, Washington, D.C. 20428]

NOTE: The text of the letter was made available by the White House Press Office on July 27. It was not issued in the form of a White House press release.

THE PRESIDENT'S NEWS CONFERENCE OF JULY 28, 1977

THE PRESIDENT. Good morning, everybody. I have two brief statements. One relates to foreign affairs and defense. The other one relates to domestic election processes.

NUCLEAR TEST BAN NEGOTIATIONS

I'm very glad to announce that our delegation in Geneva has just completed trilateral discussions with delegations from the United Kingdom and from the Soviet Union on the possible negotiation of a comprehensive ban against the testing of nuclear weapons or peaceful nuclear devices. Although there are still a number of problems that must be resolved, the results of these intense consultations have been sufficiently promising so that the three countries have decided to begin formal negotiations in Geneva on October 3. It's my hope that sufficient basis for agreement can be reached that all other nations of the world will join us in the ultimate prohibition against testing of nuclear devices.

SENATORIAL ELECTION CAMPAIGN FINANCING

The other point I'd like to mention is one that relates to the electoral process. Our greatest damage to the political process in our country comes when there is a perception among the public that the actions of their elected officials have been unduly influenced by special interest groups, and the major way that people get that feeling is in reviewing the large and single source campaign contributions received by those officials.

The Senate is now considering a bill which would help remove this obstacle to faith and confidence on the part of the people of this country. This bill, known as Senate Bill 926, would extend public financing to Senate campaigns. It would remove the appearance of obligation to special interests. It would give private citizens a larger role in choosing their Senators, and it would help enable deserving candidates to run for office even if they are not rich themselves. But, most importantly, it would help restore the public's confidence and trust in officials who have such a vital role to play in the future of the citizens of this country.

As you know, we now have public financing for Presidential campaigns. It worked very well last year—[*laughter*]—with not only the successful candidate but all of his challengers having gone through the entire campaign without being obligated to anyone because of political campaigns. I think this has been one of the major factors in restoring the confidence of our people in the system, and I hope that the Senate will approve their public financing bill. And I think that they, when it's tried, will find the same results to be applicable. The House will consider later on similar legislation for themselves.

Mr. Cormier [Frank Cormier, Associated Press].

QUESTIONS

ISRAELI SETTLEMENTS IN OCCUPIED TERRITORIES

Q. Mr. President, in your view, did the Israeli embrace of the three settlements on the West Bank diminish in any way the prospects for a negotiated settlement in that part of the world?

THE PRESIDENT. Yes. I think that any move toward making permanent the settlements in the occupied territories or the establishment of new settlements obviously increases the difficulty in ultimate peace.

It's not an insurmountable problem. The matter of legalizing existing settlements was a subject that was never discussed by me or Prime Minister Begin. My own concern was with the establishment of new settlements. And I let him know very strongly that this would be a matter that would cause our own Government deep concern.

This matter of settlements in the occupied territories has always been characterized by our Government, by me and my predecessors as an illegal action. But I think that the establishment of new territories [settlements] or the recognition of existing territories [settlements] to be legal, both provide obstacles to peace, obstacles which I think we can overcome, by the way.

FOREIGN ARMS SALES

Q. Mr. President, since you came into office, you have stressed so many times that your policy is to restrain arms sales, we should not be the arms merchant of the world. Now you are proposing arms to Egypt, Sudan, Somalia, Iran, and there are billions of dollars worth of arms in the pipeline for Israel—all areas of potential conflict. Why?

THE PRESIDENT. These proposals are compatible with my new arms sales policy, which is to reduce the level of arms sales in each succeeding year.

Many of these agreements are the result of longstanding commitments by our own Government to those nations which are our allies and friends. We have tried to keep a well-balanced approach to the whole question.

The most highly divisive issue recently has been the AWACS sale to Iran. They were contemplating a radar detection system using ground-based and air-

launched mechanisms that would have been about twice as expensive.

But we are determined to begin a downward trend in the sale of weapons throughout the world. But at the same time, of course, we have to have as a preeminent consideration the defense of our own country and an adequate defense capability for our allies.

And I would comply with my policy that after this fiscal year, 1977, that in '78 and subsequent years there would be an overall reduction in sales.

I am also trying to get our own allies, France, England, and others, and also the Soviet Union, to join us in this effort. And next year, under the auspices of the United Nations there will be a world disarmament conference in which we would not only participate but hope to play a leading role. But the policies that I have pursued will be a much greater constraint on arms sales than has been the policy in the past.

Q. Then you are not setting up a competition with the Soviet Union in Africa on the question of arms supplies?

THE PRESIDENT. No, ma'am, we aren't. I think it's accurate to say that in the case of Somalia, which has been almost completely under the friendly influence of the Soviet Union and to whom they've been completely obligated, there has been a change. We are trying to work not on a unilateral basis, but in conjunction with other nations like the Saudis, and France, Italy, and others, to deal with the Somalia-Ethiopian-Djibouti questions on a multinational basis to reduce the competition between ourselves and the Soviet Union.

I might say that in the Libyan-Ethiopian [Egyptian] conflict that's recently taken place, and which has now been changed into a peaceful relationship for the time being at least, both ourselves and the Soviets have deliberately shown complete constraint and restraint in our comments or actions in that area.

We want to confine those conflicts, when they unfortunately do occur, to as narrowly geographical an area as possible and prevent them being identified as a struggle between ourselves and the Soviet Union.

OIL IMPORTS

Q. Mr. President, in view of the projected $25 billion budget deficit this year, brought about largely by foreign oil increases, isn't this a far greater—imports rather—isn't this a far greater threat to the American economy than any energy crunch 8 years from now? Would you consider making the Government the sole importer of foreign oil, and at the very least, aren't you going to have to take far more serious energy conservation measures and proposals than what you've already got?

THE PRESIDENT. The early estimates this year on our trade deficit were about $25 billion. That's still our best estimate. There has not been a deterioration in that prospect. The fact is that by leaps and bounds the American people are importing and using too much oil. This has been the primary cause for our concern. We have a positive trade balance, excluding oil, of about $20 billion. But we are importing $45 billion worth of oil this year.

It's a vivid demonstration of the need for very tight conservation measures on the use of oil and natural gas. This is a reason for the long delayed proposal to establish a strict national energy policy.

Our hope is to cut down oil imports drastically by 1985—10 million barrels per day less than the present projected use by that time. But if the American people—business, industry, private persons, as well—will join in an effort to cut down on the waste of oil, then that

would be the major contributing factor toward balancing our trade with other countries.

I don't know what other actions we will take at this point. I think that we will continue to assess additional means by which we can constrain oil imports. But whether or not the Government would become the sole importer is a question that has not yet been considered.

THE MIDDLE EAST

Q. I'd like to go back to the Mideast, if I may. Some people believe that in your meetings with Mr. Begin, Mr. Begin came away with sort of the best of it. They think that you rather embraced him to the extent that our leverage with Israel has now been reduced. Would you comment on that, and would you also tell us what you think now the prospects for peace versus another war are in the Mideast?

THE PRESIDENT. After I met with President Sadat and King Hussein and President Asad, there were major outcries in Israel and among the American Jewish community that I had overly embraced the Arab cause. And I think now that Mr. Begin has visited me, there's a concern we have overly embraced the Israeli cause. Obviously, when these leaders come to see me or when I go to see them, there is an effort to understand one another, to have a base of comprehension and consultation that can provide hope for the future.

Our position on the Middle East has been very carefully spelled out to the degree of specificity that I choose. We've always made it clear that, ultimately, the agreement had to be approved and mutually beneficial to the Israelis and also their Arab neighbors as well.

I think that we have a good chance to go to Geneva. There are obstacles still to be resolved. I hope that every leader involved directly in the discussions, the four major countries there, will join with us and the cochairman of the prospective conference, the Soviet Union, in restraining their statements, not being so adamant on issues, and trying to cool down the situation until all can search out common ground, and then hope to minimize the differences.

Secretary Vance will leave this weekend to visit the three Arab nations plus Saudi Arabia, and then come back through Israel as well. When he returns to the United States after about a week or so, we'll have a clearer picture of the differences that still divide the countries.

I think the major stumbling block at this point is the participation in the negotiations by the Palestinian representatives. Our position has been that they ought to be represented and that we will discuss with them these elements that involve the Palestinians and other refugees at the time they forgo their commitment, presently publicly espoused, that Israel should be destroyed. But until the Palestinian leaders adopt the proposition that Israel is a nation, that it will be a nation permanently, that it has a right to live in peace—until that happens, I see no way that we would advocate participation by them in the peace negotiations.

But these matters are still very fluid. What gives me hope is that I believe that all national leaders with whom I've talked genuinely want to go to Geneva to try to work out permanent peace. That's the primary basis for my optimism. But it's difficult, and past statements by these leaders when they were at war, or in the status of prospective war, have been very rigid and very adamant and sometimes abusive and filled with hatred and distrust. We're trying to get them to change from those positions of distrust to one of genuine search for peace.

I think it's accurate to say, in closing my answer, that both sides now have at least a moderate amount of confidence in us, and I've tried to take a balanced position to enhance that trust in us. If I should ever take a biased position on the part of one of the parties, then the other parties would simply forgo any dependence upon us.

So, I'm very careful in my statements, privately and publicly, to be consistent, and also to be fair.

ISRAELI SETTLEMENTS

Q. Could I follow up on that, Mr. President? I believe you said just a moment ago that Mr. Begin gave you no advance hint of this action that he took this week on the settlements. You said that you discussed future settlements. Can you tell us what he said about that? Is he going to encourage new settlements there, and what did you tell him about that?

THE PRESIDENT. Mr. Begin did not give me any promise about his action on the settlement question. I did describe to him our longstanding position on the settlements, which I've already outlined, and told him that this was a major item of potential differences between Israel and the Arab countries and my strong hope that nothing would be done by the Israeli Government in establishing new settlements that might exacerbate an already difficult position.

He listened to me very carefully. He said this was a major political issue in Israel, that in many instances he and his opposition political parties in Israel, felt the same about it, but that he was certainly aware of our concern. But he did not give me any commitments about what he would do.

And to answer the other part of your question, he did not give me any prior notice that they were going to recognize the legality of the settlements involved.

PRIME MINISTER BEGIN

Q. Mr. President, isn't there a basic conflict between all the talk of progress we heard around here during the Begin visit and at the time he left, and the first action that he took upon returning to Israel and the rejection of the idea that we could have any influence over what moves he might make to the West Bank settlements?

THE PRESIDENT. Well, I think it's not fair to overly criticize Prime Minister Begin. The fact is that under the previous Mapai Coalition, the labor government, that settlements have been built there, a fairly large number. The number of people involved is quite small. And this is not a new thing. I think it would be a mistake to overemphasize it or to exaggerate the significance of it. We feel that any restraint that Prime Minister Begin might want to exert on this subject would certainly be contributory toward peace.

I think he's in a position now of great strength in Israel. I think that his voice would be honored by the Israeli people. But he, like myself, has run on campaign commitments, and I think he's trying to accommodate the interest of peace as best he can. That doesn't mean that the settlements are right, but I think it would not be proper to castigate him unnecessarily about it because he's continuing policies that have been extant in Israel for a long time. And the Israeli Government has never claimed that these settlements are permanent. What they have done is to say that they are legal at the present time.

I think that that's all I know about the subject, and that's certainly all that I'm going to say now.

Mr. Sperling [Godfrey Sperling, Jr., Christian Science Monitor].

VIEWS ON THE PRESIDENCY

Q. Mr. President, on your assessment of your first 6 months in office, I understand that you have said that you feel that, overall, your performance was good. But did you——

THE PRESIDENT. That's a biased expression. But go ahead. [*Laughter*]

Q. Anyway, did you do anything wrong, did you do anything that you would like to do differently, if you could do it over again?

THE PRESIDENT. Well, obviously, every day I make hundreds of decisions that in the light of subsequent events, in dealing with the Congress, in dealing with local and State governments, proposals that were rejected, slight amendments that could have been more acceptable, an inadvertent oversight in not calling a congressional committee chairman ahead of time before I made a public statement—those kinds of things always you would want to undo.

I think, though, that the final judgment would have to be the results of this year's work, at the time the Congress adjourns, hopefully, in October. In general, I think the Congress has responded well to my proposals. I think the results of their work have already been very good.

So, in minor things, obviously, I've made mistakes. But to be perfectly frank, I don't personally care to point them out. [*Laughter*]

Q. Have you learned anything in the first 6 months that in your opinion will make you a better President in the next 6 months?

THE PRESIDENT. I think so. I've learned——

Q. What?

THE PRESIDENT. I think the major issue that I'll point out that I've done before is I've learned how to work much more harmoniously with the Congress. I have been amazed at how hard the Congress works. Their results so far, I believe, are unprecedented: in having passed all of the major elements of the appropriations bills—this used to take place sometimes in November or December—they've already completed this major work; the establishment of a new Department of Energy, which is now on the verge of being concluded, and many other things.

I have learned to respect the Congress more in an individual basis. I've been favorably impressed at the high degree of concentrated experience and knowledge that individual Members of Congress can bring on a specific subject, where they've been the chairman of a subcommittee or committee for many years and have focused their attention on this particular aspect of government life which I will never be able to do.

And I think I've learned, too, the sensitivities of them, in trying to let them know ahead of time before my own positions were pronounced publicly.

I've now completed meeting at the White House with every Member of the House of Representatives, all the Democrats and then all the Republicans, to give them a chance in groups to ask me questions about parochial issues and to get to know them personally.

And I've now completed having a breakfast meeting with all the Democratic Members of the Senate. We'll now meet with the Republican Members of the Senate.

I think that's a major thing that I've learned, is the degree of respect that legitimately I ought to have for the Congress, and I have built up a great admiration for their individual competence and also for their dedication. That's the major thing——

WELFARE PROGRAMS

Q. Mr. President, how committed are you to keeping the pledge that you made earlier this year to hold welfare spending at its present level, in light of all the difficulties your advisers are having in coming up with a welfare plan that is within that limit?

THE PRESIDENT. Well, it's very difficult. I'm going to spend—I came over to my office this morning at 5:30 and I spent 3 hours working on the welfare question before my first appointments. And this afternoon I have 2 more hours of study and work with the Cabinet members on the welfare question.

I talked to Senator Long on the phone this morning when he called me to express his interest in it, and next week I'll be meeting with him and Chairman Ullman on the same subject. By the end of next week, we will have prepared for presentation to the public and the Congress my best assessment of what ought to be done.

There are obviously options that have to be exercised: the degree of fiscal relief for local and State governments, the amount of guarantees that even in a case where the benefits have been very liberal, that there will or will not be any reductions in those benefits for people who are well above the poverty level. Some families get welfare benefits that have an income twice as high as the poverty level, much greater than someone who works, say, full time at the minimum wage. But how to deal with these different questions, how to tie it in with a comprehensive tax reform is something that I'm spending a lot of time on.

I'm trying to hold down the cost of the overall program, and I think if you will look at the careful wording of my goals, it said the initial cost would not exceed present expenditures. We're trying now to estimate also the ultimate cost of these programs, what they will cost in 1980 and 1985.

But I can't respond any better to your question. It's a complicated and difficult subject. We're trying to make it fairer and simpler, and we're trying to have a heavy emphasis on a legitimate incentive to work for those that are able to work.

ISRAELI SETTLEMENTS

Q. Mr. President?

THE PRESIDENT. Mr. Schram [Martin J. Schram, Newsday].

Q. Mr. President, at the risk of going back over well-plowed ground, I'd like to ask you why it is that you did not ask Mr. Begin what his plans were concerning the existing settlements on the West Bank, and more specifically, were you led to believe from your own studies in advance of those talks that he was not going to take this action?

THE PRESIDENT. I hate to admit it to you, Mr. Schram, but I did not think about raising the subject of recognizing the legality of those settlements. The item that I wanted to discuss with him—and I did—both in the public meeting with Cabinet members and also privately upstairs in the White House, was the establishment of new settlements. And I pointed out to him, as I've said earlier, that I thought the establishment of new settlements would be a very difficult thing for public opinion to accept, both here and in the Arab countries, and that if— he pointed out to me that new settlers, as a result of his campaign statements and those of his opponents, were eager to go into the area—I don't think it's violating any confidence to tell you what I said, and that was that I thought it would be easier for us to accept an increase in the population of existing settlements than it would be to accept the establishment of new settlements. But I did not think about talking to him concerning the granting of legal status to those settlements. It was an oversight which never was discussed.

DISCRIMINATION

Q. Mr. President, there's a case coming up before the U.S. Supreme Court next term on the issue of whether institutions of higher learning can grant preferences in admission patterns to members of minority groups, and your administration has the opportunity to file an *amicus* brief in this case. What's your position on that?

THE PRESIDENT. I hate to endorse the proposition of quotas for minority groups, for women or for anyone else, that contravene the concept of merit selection. However, I think it is appropriate for both private employers, the public governments, and also institutions of education, health, and so forth, to try to compensate as well as possible for past discrimination, and also to take into consideration the fact that many tests that are used to screen applicants quite often are inadvertently biased against those whose environment and whose training might be different from white majority representatives of our society.

It's not an easy question for the courts to answer, or the Congress. It's not an easy question for me as President to answer, either. I just want to be sure that if we do make a mistake in this carefully balanced approach, that the mistake might be to end discrimination and not the other way around.

But, of course, I will have to comply with the Supreme Court ruling. And I might say that the Secretary of HEW and the Attorney General, who are lawyers— and I'm not—will prepare our position. I'll be involved in that preparation, but I've given you the best answer I can.

Yes?

SOCIAL PROGRAMS

Q. Mr. President, for some days now some of your constituencies have been publicly expressing concern that your interest in balancing the budget, your interest in working against inflation might cause you to ease up on your campaign commitments to the cities, to the poor, for employment programs, for national health insurance. One of those critics, Vernon Jordan, had a private meeting with you, and we were told that you told Mr. Jordan that you felt his public expression of these doubts would work against the interests of the poor and of black people.

I would like to know what you meant by that.

THE PRESIDENT. Okay. I think many of the expressions of concern are certainly legitimate. I want to be sure that the public and I and the Congress are always aware of deprivations, because quite often, those who are deprived most are not articulate enough or well-educated enough or influential enough to speak with a strong voice that can be heard. And I think it's completely legitimate for someone like the head of the Urban League or the head of the NAACP or other groups to speak out if they think that inadequate attention has been paid.

The second part of your question is, I think, that we've had a very good record so far, both my own administration and the Democratic Congress. We've initiated programs now, which are just beginning to be felt, that will greatly reduce the problems of those poor people in downtown urban areas, in particular, with public service jobs, public works jobs, CETA training programs, and the allocation of all Federal moneys on housing and so forth to the areas that in the past have not been treated fairly.

The third part of your question about my private conversation with Vernon Jordan: I did point out to him that when erroneous or demagogic statements were made—inaccurately reporting that neither I nor my own administration nor the Congress cared about those poor people— that since we are the last hope of those who are poor, that the Government would help them in some way, that this removed from them that prospect of a better life.

Accurate criticisms, fine. But I think to prey upon those who are poor or deprived or who are alienated from society and erroneously report that neither I nor my Cabinet members nor the Congress cares about them, does hurt the poor. That was the essence of the conversation.

Q. Mr. President, could I follow up on that question?

THE PRESIDENT. I was trying to recognize—yes, go ahead.

Q. I wanted to be sure I understood you correctly. Are you saying that Mr. Jordan's criticism of you was demagogic or that he was preying upon the fears of the poor people of this country?

THE PRESIDENT. No. As I said earlier, I think that Mr. Jordan's statements are certainly legitimate. He has a right to express his own opinion. But I will say this: To the extent that he alleged that neither I nor my administration nor the Congress was concerned about the poor, those statements were erroneous. But I think in his statements both before and after his speech, he presented to some degree both sides: that we had made progress that was not adequate, that our campaign promises had not been kept—they are being kept—and so forth.

But I have no quarrel with Vernon Jordan. I think he's a strong and able spokesman. I think, though, that my statement, my conversation with him, which was very friendly and mutually respectful, was an accurate assessment of what I've told you.

FEDERAL BUREAU OF INVESTIGATION

Q. Mr. President, sir, whom did you promise?

THE PRESIDENT. Go ahead. I'll be glad to answer your question.

Q. Will you take my question?

THE PRESIDENT. I will be glad to.

Q. Thank you, sir. [*Laughter*]

Sir, there's a very interesting question about the FBI. They were created, I believe, about 1908 by Teddy Roosevelt with an Executive order, and there's really no overall, comprehensive enabling law that applies to them. And they handle so many matters concerning criminal as well as civils—civilians.

I wondered if you don't think that we ought to patch up this piecemeal statute situation with the FBI and pass an overall, enabling law?

THE PRESIDENT. Yes, ma'am, I do think that we need to have a congressional charter evolved both for the FBI and also the CIA. And I think your concern is one that's well justified. I think it's accurate also to say that both my own administration, including the Attorney General and the Director of the Central Intelligence Agency, and the Congress leaders are working on this project, and I would hope that this would be one of the accomplishments of my administration.

Q. Mr. Carter, speaking of the FBI, can you bring us up to date on the search for a new Director, sir?

THE PRESIDENT. Well, we're proceeding very slowly and methodically and, I

think, with the prospect of good results. We have now interviewed six candidates for the job. We reserve the right to interview more in the future if we like. We've not made a final decision on who would be the Director. My own inclination is to defer to the recommendation of the Attorney General, unless we have an unanticipated difference of opinion. But we don't feel any time pressure to arrive at a final conclusion.

I might say that in the meantime, Director Kelley is doing a good job. He served on the selection committee, as you well know. But we'll have a good selection to make before the whole process is completed.

MR. CORMIER. Thank you, Mr. President.

THE PRESIDENT. Thank you, Mr. Cormier.

NOTE: President Carter's twelfth news conference began at 10:30 a.m. in Room 450 of the Old Executive Office Building. It was broadcast live on radio and television.

International Navigational Rules Act of 1977

Statement on Signing H.R. 186 Into Law. *July 28, 1977*

I have signed H.R. 186, a bill to implement the Convention on the International Regulations for Preventing Collisions at Sea, 1972. This convention brings International Rules of the Nautical Road in line with modern maritime practices and technology. The convention, which has been ratified by the Senate, became effective for its international signatories on July 15, 1977. This bill would implement the convention fully for United States vessels.

Although I have signed this bill, I want to make clear that I have serious constitutional reservations about section 3(d). That section permits Congress, by concurrent resolution, to disapprove a proposed amendment to the convention. The Congress concurrent resolution would not be presented to the President for approval or veto. This may violate Article I, Section 7 of the Constitution.

NOTE: As enacted, H.R. 186 is Public Law 95–75, approved July 28.

Mississippi River Commission

Nomination of Maj. Gen. Robert C. Marshall To Be a Member and President of the Commission. July 28, 1977

The President today announced that he will nominate Maj. Gen. Robert C. Marshall, Corps of Engineers, U.S. Army, to be a member and President of the Mississippi River Commission. He would replace Maj. Gen. Francis P. Koisch. Marshall is currently Deputy Chief of Engineers in the Office of the Chief of Engineers.

He was born November 10, 1921, in Washington, D.C. He received a B.S. in military science from the U.S. Military Academy and a B.C.E. in civil engineering from Cornell University.

Marshall has served in the U.S. Army since 1943. He served in Vietnam in 1968 and 1969. From 1969 to 1973, he was Commanding General of the SAFE GUARD Systems Command at Redstone Arsenal, Ala. In 1973 he was special assistant to the Chief of Staff, U.S. Continental Army Command, stationed at Fort McPherson, Ga.

In 1973 and 1974, Marshall was Deputy Chief of Staff for Logistics for the U.S. Army Forces Command at Fort Mc-Pherson. From 1974 to 1976, he was ballistic missile defense program manager in Arlington, Va. Since 1976 he has been Deputy Chief of Engineers.

Marshall holds the Distinguished Service Medal, the Silver Star, and the Legion of Merit with Oak Leaf Cluster.

National Credit Union Administration

Nomination of Eloise A. Woods To Be Chairman of the National Credit Union Board. July 28, 1977

The President today announced that he will nominate Eloise A. Woods, of Atlanta, Ga., to be Chairman of the National Credit Union Board. She would replace Richard H. Grant. Woods is secretary, treasurer, and general manager of the Georgia Telco Credit Union in Atlanta.

She was born January 19, 1927, in Okeechobee, Fla. She attended Florida Southern College.

Woods has been with the Georgia Telco Credit Union since 1947. She is also founder and former president, and currently director and secretary, of the International Telephone Credit Union Association. She has served as director and vice president of the Georgia Credit Union League and as chairperson of its legal and legislative committee.

Woods has also served as national director of the Credit Union National Association, as director of the Georgia Credit Union League Service Corp., as director and secretary of the National Share and Deposit Guaranty Corp., and as director and president of the Georgia Credit Union Deposit Insurance Corp.

Special Adviser to the Secretary of State for Soviet Affairs

Nomination of Marshall D. Shulman for the Rank of Ambassador. July 28, 1977

The President today announced that he will nominate Marshall D. Shulman, of Sherman, Conn., for the rank of Ambassador while serving as Special Adviser to the Secretary of State for Soviet Affairs.

Shulman was born April 8, 1916, in Jersey City, N.J. He received an A.B. from the University of Michigan in 1937 and a Ph. D. from Columbia University in 1949. He served in the U.S. Army Air Force from 1942 to 1946.

Shulman was a reporter for the Detroit News in 1937 and 1938, and a writer for the National Safety Council in 1938 and 1939.

From 1949 to 1950, Shulman was an information officer at the U.S. Mission to the United Nations. From 1950 to 1953, he was special assistant to the Secretary of State. He was associate director of the Russian Research Center at Harvard University from 1954 to 1960, and was a professor of international politics at the Fletcher School of Law and Diplomacy from 1961 to 1967.

Shulman was a professor of government and director of the Russian Institute at Columbia University from 1967 until 1977, when he became Special Adviser to the Secretary of State for Soviet Affairs.

Shulman is the author of "Stalin's Foreign Policy Reappraised" (1963) and "Beyond the Cold War" (1966), and of numerous articles in professional journals. He is a member of the Council on Foreign Relations and the International Institute for Strategic Studies.

Affirmative Action in the Executive Branch

Memorandum for the Heads of Departments and Agencies. July 26, 1977

Memorandum for the Heads of Departments and Agencies

Subject: Affirmative Action

Last March I wrote to each of you concerning my commitment to affirmative action in the Executive Branch. I indicated that at some future time I would expect progress reports on affirmative action from the executive departments and agencies.

I have directed the Presidential Personnel Office at the White House to assume responsibility for monitoring progress on affirmative action hiring for non-career positions throughout the Executive Branch.

The Presidential Personnel Office will be briefing each department or agency on the reporting procedures which have been established. If you have other ideas as to how affirmative action might be strengthened, please send them to me through the Presidential Personnel Office.

JIMMY CARTER

NOTE: The text of the memorandum was made available by the White House Press Office on July 28. It was not issued in the form of a White House press release.

National Credit Union Administration

Nomination of Lawrence Connell, Jr., To Be Administrator. July 28, 1977

The President today announced that he will nominate Lawrence Connell, Jr., of Connecticut, to be Administrator of the National Credit Union Administration. He would replace C. Austin Montgomery. Connell is bank commissioner for the State of Connecticut.

He was born September 30, 1936, in New York City. He received an A.B. in economics from Harvard College in 1958, a J.D. from Georgetown University in 1966, and an M.A. in economics from Trinity College in 1973.

Connell worked in the office of the U.S. Comptroller of the Currency from 1958 to 1968, beginning as a field examiner and ending as Deputy Regional Administrator of National Banks in New England. In 1962–63 he participated in the reorganization of the internal operations of the Washington office of the Comptroller of the Currency. He also participated in the first study of competition and branch banking by that office in 1963.

In 1968 he joined Hartford National Bank and Trust Co., as vice president and counsel, was promoted to cashier, and then became secretary of Hartford National Corp. He also served as an officer and director of a number of its subsidiaries.

Connell has been bank commissioner of the State of Connecticut since 1975. He served on the Governor's Commission to Study Uniform Consumer Credit Code.

International Bank for Reconstruction and Development

Nomination of William P. Dixon To Be U.S. Alternate Executive Director. July 28, 1977

The President today announced that he will nominate William P. Dixon, of Alexandria, Va., to be U.S. Alternate Executive Director of the International Bank for Reconstruction and Development. He would replace Hal F. Reynolds. Dixon is general counsel and deputy staff director of the House Committee on Banking, Finance and Urban Affairs.

Dixon was born December 12, 1943, in Buffalo, N.Y. He received a B.S. in 1965 and a J.D. in 1970 from the State University of New York at Buffalo.

From 1970 to 1972, Dixon was an associate attorney with the Milwaukee law firm of Foley and Lardner. In 1972 and 1973, he was chief counsel to Wisconsin Governor Patrick Lucey.

Dixon was counsel to the House Judiciary Committee from 1973 to 1975. Since 1975 he has been general counsel and deputy staff director of the House Banking, Finance and Urban Affairs Committee. In this position he has direct responsibility for all legal matters and legislation for the committee and shares administrative and policy matters with the staff director. Dixon has worked on legislation dealing with foreign banking, international multilateral development banks, supervision and reform of domestic financial institutions, and consumer protection.

Airborne Warning and Control Systems

White House Statement on Congressional Actions. July 28, 1977

In response to the suggestion of the Senate leadership and the Senate Foreign Assistance Subcommittee, the President will withdraw the notification of the sale for AWACS to Iran and resubmit it on the day the Congress returns, September 7, to be part of fiscal year 1977 arms sales.

Congress time is short because of other priority legislation. The President is anxious to give Members of the Senate and House sufficient time, as they have requested, to debate the complex technical issue of the proposed sale.

The President is confident that once Congress fully discusses the proposed sale and assesses the assurances we have provided regarding the security and management of the AWACS system in Iran, the sale will receive favorable congressional review.

National Cancer Institute

Appointment of Arthur C. Upton as Director. July 29, 1977

The President today announced the appointment of Arthur C. Upton, of Shoreham, N.Y., to be Director of the National Cancer Institute, Department of Health, Education, and Welfare. He would replace Frank Rauscher, Jr. Upton is a professor of pathology at the State University of New York at Stony Brook.

He was born February 27, 1923, in Ann Arbor, Mich. He received a B.A. in 1946 and an M.D. in 1949 from the University of Michigan.

Upton did his internship at University Hospital in Ann Arbor in 1947, and was a resident in pathology at the University of Michigan from 1948 to 1950. He was an instructor in pathology there in 1950–51.

From 1951 to 1954, Upton was a pathologist at Oak Ridge National Laboratory, and from 1954 to 1969 he was chief of the pathology-physiology section there. Since 1969 he has been a professor of pathology at the State University of New York at Stony Brook.

Upton has also served as attending pathologist for the medical department at Brookhaven National Laboratory since 1969, and was dean of the School of Basic Health Sciences at Stony Brook from 1970 to 1975.

He is a member of the American Association for Cancer Research and served as president of the association in 1963–64. He is representative of the association to the U.S. National Committee on the International Union against Cancer. He is also a member of the American Society for Experimental Pathology and the Radiation Research Society. He is a member of numerous medical advisory committees, including the National Cancer Institute Board of Scientific Counsellors and the International Commission on Radiological Protection.

Federal Government Reorganization

Announcement of Administration Survey of Congressional Members for Reorganization Purposes. July 29, 1977

The administration announced today that it is surveying Members of the House and Senate to identify which Federal programs result in the most day-to-day problems for their constituents. The results of the survey will be used in pinpointing targets for President Carter's Government reorganization program.

The survey is one of several administration efforts to develop information on Government performance. Other sources will include: meetings with affected groups, field interviews with State and local officials, Federal Information Centers, analysis of White House mail, and suggestions solicited from the general public.

The survey, which began earlier this week, asks Congressmen and Senators to list those Federal programs which, based upon their own constituent casework, cause the most public dissatisfaction, frustration, and confusion.

In a June 29 press briefing on reorganization, President Carter said that congressional casework offers a unique source of information on the Federal Government's performance.

"Members of the House and Senate spend a good part of every day helping people cut through Government redtape," he said. "They know firsthand how the Government looks from the receiving end of the services."

NOTE: The White House press release also included the text of a letter from Richard A. Pettigrew, Assistant to the President for Reorganization, which was sent to the Members of Congress to explain the purposes of the survey.

Voyager Spacecraft

Statement by the President. July 29, 1977

This Voyager spacecraft was constructed by the United States of America. We are a community of 240 million human beings among the more than 4 billion who inhabit the planet Earth. We human beings are still divided into nation states, but these states are rapidly becoming a single global civilization.

We cast this message into the cosmos. It is likely to survive a billion years into our future, when our civilization is profoundly altered and the surface of the Earth may be vastly changed. Of the 200 billion stars in the Milky Way galaxy, some—perhaps many—may have inhabited planets and spacefaring civiliza-

tions. If one such civilization intercepts Voyager and can understand these recorded contents, here is our message:

This is a present from a small distant world, a token of our sounds, our science, our images, our music, our thoughts, and our feelings. We are attempting to survive our time so we may live into yours. We hope someday, having solved the problems we face, to join a community of galactic civilizations. This record represents our hope and our determination, and our good will in a vast and awesome universe.

NOTE: The statement has been placed in a National Aeronautics and Space Administration Voyager spacecraft which is scheduled to be launched August 20. The statement is recorded in electronic impulses which can be converted into printed words.

Airline Industry Regulation

Letter to Members of the Senate Committee on Commerce, Science, and Transportation. July 28, 1977

To Members of the Senate Committee on Commerce, Science, and Transportation:

Reducing regulation of the airline industry is the first major opportunity to meet our shared goal of eliminating outdated and excessive government regulation. Sound regulatory reform is a top priority of my Administration. I commend you for the progress you and your colleagues have made in working toward that goal.

I urge you to speed the pace of your deliberations so that a bill can be acted upon by the Senate this year. You have already made significant decisions on many parts of the bill. But the most important decisions still lie ahead. I would like to elaborate upon the principles I set forth in my Message to Congress on March 4, 1977, and share with you my views on pricing and entry.

1. *Automatic Route Entry.* Pricing flexibility must be accompanied by strong entry provisions. It is entry, or the realistic threat of it, that prevents price flexibility from being abused. Automatic route entry is especially important in keeping prices low, and I consider it to be one of the most important elements of a reform bill. The current provision in the bill allows carriers to enter a very limited number of new markets each year without having to undergo the costly process of obtaining Board approval. The record developed by your Committee clearly supports even greater automatic entry than is provided by the current draft.

2. *Presumption in Favor of Entry.* Retention of the provision in the bill that would reverse the burden of proof in entry proceedings is essential. The presumption should be that competition is consistent with the public interest. Anyone who is against new competition should have to show that it would be harmful to the public—not the other way around. Indeed, I would prefer a provision reversing the burden of proof immediately upon enactment of the bill, rather than delaying its effectiveness of this provision for three years, as in the current draft.

3. *Unused Route Authority.* If a carrier has authority to serve a market but has chosen not to use it, a new carrier who would like to serve the public in that market should be given the opportunity to do so. There is simply no justification for preventing new carriers from serving markets which other carriers are not using. The draft bill makes entry against a carrier holding unused authority more difficult than entry into markets where no

such unexercised grants of authority are outstanding. I recommend that this provision of the current bill be strengthened.

4. *Pricing Flexibility.* One of the major aims of reform is to allow carriers to lower their prices wherever possible. The current regulatory scheme permits lower fares only by means of heavily regulated and highly restricted price discounts. I urge you to support the provisions in the bill which take meaningful steps to remove the artificial regulatory barriers to lower prices.

I believe that entry provisions and upward pricing flexibility are intimately related. To the extent that the automatic entry and dormant authority provisions are strengthened, and the burden of proof is reversed at an earlier date, some limited upward pricing flexibility may be warranted. But if these changes are not made, then I would support a move to limit carriers to price increases only where they are justified by rising costs. Alternatively, you might wish to consider explicitly tying entry to pricing; that is, providing for some easing of the bill's entry limitations in those instances where prices have been significantly increased.

There are many aspects of this complex reform legislation, but the value which the ordinary citizen ultimately gains from our efforts mainly depends on the Congress' resolution of these four basic issues.

Sincerely,

Jimmy Carter

[The Honorable Howard W. Cannon, United States Senate, Washington, D.C. 20510]

NOTE: The text of the letter was made available by the White House Press Office on July 29. It was not issued in the form of a White House press release.

Federal Power Commission

Nomination of Charles B. Curtis and Georgiana Sheldon To Be Members. July 29, 1977

The President today announced that he will nominate Charles B. Curtis, of Bethesda, Md., and Georgiana Sheldon, of Arlington, Va., to be members of the Federal Power Commission. Curtis would replace William L. Springer, and Sheldon would replace James G. Watt.

Curtis was born April 27, 1940, in Upper Darby, Pa. He received a B.S. from the University of Massachusetts in 1962 and an LL.B. from Boston University Law School in 1965.

From 1965 to 1967, Curtis was a staff attorney, then supervising staff attorney, in the Office of the Comptroller of the Currency. From 1967 to 1971, he served on the Securities and Exchange Commission, as special counsel to the Division of Trading and Markets; chief of the Branch of Regulation and Inspections; and attorney-advisor (finance).

Curtis was counsel to the House Committee on Interstate and Foreign Commerce from 1971 to 1976, with special emphasis on energy and securities regulation. From November 1976 to January 1977, he worked for the Carter-Mondale transition team as liaison to the Federal Energy Administration. Since January he has been with the Washington law firm of Van Ness, Curtis, Feldman & Sutcliffe.

Sheldon was born December 2, 1923, in Lawrenceville, Pa. She received a B.A. from Keuka College in 1945 and an M.S. from Cornell University in 1949.

From 1954 to 1956, Sheldon was registrar and director of admissions at Stetson University College of Law in Florida. From 1956 to 1961, she was assistant to the special assistant of the chairman of the Republican National Committee. In 1961 she was vice president of Sorin-Hall, Inc., a public relations firm, and in 1961 and 1962 she was executive secretary of the Foundation for Specialized Group Housing, an organization primarily for housing for the elderly.

From 1963 to 1969, Sheldon was executive secretary and personal assistant to then-Representative Rogers C. B. Morton. From 1969 to 1975, she was Deputy Director of the Defense Civil Preparedness Agency. In 1975 and 1976, she was Director of the Office of Foreign Disaster Relief and Deputy Coordinator for International Disaster Assistance at AID. Until June 1977 she was Acting Chairman and Vice Chairman of the U.S. Civil Service Commission.

Exemption From Mandatory Retirement

Executive Order 12006.   July 29, 1977

EXEMPTION OF G. JOSEPH MINETTI FROM MANDATORY RETIREMENT

G. Joseph Minetti, Member, Civil Aeronautics Board, will become subject to mandatory retirement for age on July 31, 1977, under the provisions of Section 8335 of Title 5 of the United States Code unless exempted by Executive order.

In my judgment, the public interest requires that G. Joseph Minetti be exempted from such mandatory retirement.

Now, THEREFORE, by virtue of the authority vested in me by subsection (c) of Section 8335 of Title 5 of the United States Code, I hereby exempt G. Joseph

Minetti from mandatory retirement until September 30, 1977.

JIMMY CARTER

The White House,
July 29, 1977.

[Filed with the Office of the Federal Register, 10:51 a.m., August 1, 1977]

NOTE: The Executive order was not issued in the form of a White House press release.

Digest of Other White House Announcements

The following listing includes the President's daily schedule and other items of general interest as announced by the White House Press Office during the period covered by this issue. Events and announcements printed elsewhere in the issue are not included.

July 22

The President returned to the White House following a trip to South Carolina, Mississippi, and Louisiana.

July 23

The President met at the White House with:

—Zbigniew Brzezinski, Assistant to the President for National Security Affairs;

—David Owen, British Foreign Secretary, Ewen Fergusson, Principal Private Secretary of State for Foreign and Commonwealth Affairs of Great Britain, Peter Jay, British Ambassador to the United States, Secretary of State Cyrus Vance, U.S. Representative to the United Nations Andrew J. Young, U.S. Ambassador to the United Kingdom Kingman Brewster,

Jr., and Dr. Brzezinski, to discuss developments and prospects for southern Africa and other international issues.

The President today declared an emergency for the State of Virginia because of the impact of a drought.

July 25

The President met at the White House with:

—Dr. Brzezinski;

—the Cabinet;

—Vice President Walter F. Mondale.

The President today transmitted to the Congress the 10th annual report of the U.S.-Japan Cooperative Medical Science Program.

July 26

The President met at the White House with:

—David L. Aaron, Deputy Assistant to the President for National Security Affairs;

—the Democratic congressional leadership;

—Secretary of the Treasury W. Michael Blumenthal;

—Vice President Mondale, Secretary Blumenthal, Arthur F. Burns, Chairman of the Board of Governors of the Federal Reserve System, Bert Lance, Director of the Office of Management and Budget, and Charles L. Schultze, Chairman of the Council of Economic Advisers;

—John A. Mintz, Assistant Director and Legal Counsel of the FBI;

—representative of the Theodore Roosevelt Association and members of the Roosevelt family, who presented him with a full set of the memorial edition of the Works of Theodore Roosevelt.

July 27

The President met at the White House with:
—Dr. Brzezinski;
—a group of 7 Democratic Senators;
—Prime Minister Giulio Andreotti of Italy;
—Secretary of Housing and Urban Development Patricia Roberts Harris;
—Representatives Joshua Eilberg and Peter W. Rodino, Jr., Attorney General Griffin B. Bell, and Secretary of Labor Ray Marshall, to discuss immigration;
—Secretary of Health, Education, and Welfare Joseph A. Califano, Jr.

The President and Mrs. Carter hosted a picnic on the South Lawn for Members of Congress and their families.

July 28

The President met at the White House with:
—Dr. Brzezinski;
—Members of the Executive Committee of the Senate and House Campaign Committees and representatives of the Democratic National Committee;
—Mrs. Carter, for lunch;
—Vice President Mondale, Adm. Stansfield Turner, Director of Central Intelligence, and Dr. Brzezinski;
—Secretary Califano, Secretary Marshall, Secretary Harris, and Dr. Schultze, to discuss welfare reform.

The President and Mrs. Carter hosted a picnic on the South Lawn for Members of Congress and their families.

July 29

The President met at the White House with:
—Vice President Mondale, Secretary Vance, and Dr. Brzezinski;
—Dr. Brzezinski;
—Vice President Mondale, Secretary Vance, Dr. Brzezinski, Ambassadors Ellsworth Bunker and Sol M. Linowitz, co-negotiators for the United States in the Panama Canal negotiations, Aristedes Royo, Minister of Education of Panama, Gabriel Lewis, Panamanian Ambassador to the United States, and Ambassador Ramon Escobar, chief negotiator for Panama in the canal negotiations;
—Dr. Schultze;
—George Parker, who recently retired as Chief of the Messenger Service for the White House;
—a group of editors, publishers, and broadcasters;
—Dr. Peter G. Bourne, Special Assistant to the President for Health Issues;
—Dr. Burns.

In a ceremony in the Oval Office, the President received diplomatic credentials from Ambassadors Abdul Wahid Karim of Afghanistan, Putteho Muketoi Ngonda of Zambia, Peter Milburn Towe of Canada, and Peter Jay of the United Kingdom.

The White House announced that Prime Minister Raymond Barre of France has accepted an invitation by the President to make an official visit to Washington September 15 and 16.

CHECKLIST OF WHITE HOUSE PRESS RELEASES

The following releases of the Office of the White House Press Secretary, distributed during the period covered by this issue, are not included in the issue.

Released July 21, 1977

Advance text: remarks at the annual meeting of the Southern Legislative Conference in Charleston, S.C.

Released July 23, 1977

Announcement: Federal assistance program for New York City following the power failure.

Released July 25, 1977

Advance text: excerpts from remarks at the national convention of the National Urban League

Announcement: nomination of George V. Grant to be United States Marshal for the Southern District of New York; Harvey N. Johnson, Jr., to be United States Marshal for the Northern District of Illinois; Robert E. Raiche to be United States Marshal for the District of New Hampshire; and Hugh Salter to be United States Marshal for the Eastern District of North Carolina

---

NOMINATIONS SUBMITTED TO THE SENATE

The following list does not include promotions of members of the Uniformed Services, nominations to the Service Academies, or nominations of Foreign Service officers.

Submitted July 25, 1977

BENJAMIN H. READ, of the District of Columbia, to be Deputy Under Secretary of State.

SIMEON MILLER BRIGHT, of West Virginia, to be a Commissioner of the Postal Rate Commission for the term expiring November 22, 1982, vice Paul A. Miltich.

HARVEY N. JOHNSON, JR., of Illinois, to be United States Marshal for the Northern District of Illinois for the term of 4 years, vice John J. Twomey, resigned.

ROBERT E. RAICHE, of New Hampshire, to be United States Marshal for the District of New Hampshire for the term of 4 years, vice Victor Cardosi.

GEORGE V. GRANT, of New York, to be United States Marshal for the Southern District of New York for the term of 4 years, vice Thomas E. Ferrandina, resigned.

NOMINATIONS—Continued
Submitted July 25—Continued

HUGH SALTER, of North Carolina, to be United States Marshal for the Eastern District of North Carolina for the term of 4 years, vice James R. Durham.

Submitted July 26, 1977

RODNEY O'GLIASAIN KENNEDY-MINOTT, of California, to be Ambassador Extraordinary and Plenipotentiary of the United States of America to Sweden.

ANDREW IVY KILLGORE, of Florida, a Foreign Service officer of Class two, to be Ambassador Extraordinary and Plenipotentiary of the United States of America to the State of Qatar.

WILLIAM BOWDOIN JONES, of California, a Foreign Service officer of Class one, to be Ambassador Extraordinary and Plenipotentiary of the United States of America to Haiti.

RICHARD J. DASCHBACH, of New Hampshire, to be a Federal Maritime Commissioner for the term expiring June 30, 1982, vice Ashton C. Barrett, term expired.

Submitted July 28, 1977

MARSHALL DARROW SHULMAN, of Connecticut, for the rank of Ambassador during the tenure of his service as Special Adviser to the Secretary of State for Soviet Affairs.

WILLIAM P. DIXON, of Virginia, to be United States Alternate Executive Director of the International Bank for Reconstruction and Development for a term of 2 years, vice Hal F. Reynolds, term expired.

LAWRENCE CONNELL, JR., of Connecticut, to be Administrator of the National Credit Union Administration, vice C. Austin Montgomery, resigned.

ELOISE A. WOODS, of Georgia, to be Chairman of the National Credit Union Board, vice Richard H. Grant, resigned.

MAJOR GENERAL ROBERT CREEL MARSHALL, 081-32-6336, United States Army, to be a member and President of the Mississippi River Commission, under the provisions of Section 2 of an act of Congress, approved 28 June 1879 (21 Stat. 37) (33 U.S.C. 642).

Submitted July 29, 1977

GEORGIANA H. SHELDON, of Virginia, to be a member of the Federal Power Commission for the remainder of the term expiring June 22, 1979, vice James G. Watt, resigned.

CHARLES BRENT CURTIS, of Maryland, to be a member of the Federal Power Commission for the term expiring June 22, 1982, vice William L. Springer, resigned.

**ACTS APPROVED BY
THE PRESIDENT**

Approved July 23, 1977

H.R. 1551_____Public Law 95–71
An act granting the consent of Congress to
an amendment to the Sabine River Compact
entered into by the States of Texas and
Louisiana

Approved July 25, 1977

H.J. Res. 24_____Public Law 95–72
A joint resolution to provide for the designation of a week as "National Lupus Week"

Approved July 26, 1977

H.R. 5638_____Public Law 95–73
An act to amend the Fishery Conservation
Zone Transition Act in order to give effect
during 1977 to the Reciprocal Fisheries
Agreement between the United States and
Canada

H.R. 7636_____Public Law 95–74
An act making appropriations for the Department of the Interior and related agencies for the fiscal year ending September 30,
1978, and for other purposes

Approved July 27, 1977

H.R. 186_____Public Law 95–75
International Navigational Rules Act of
1977

Interview With the President

*Question-and-Answer Session With a Group
of Editors and News Directors.
July 29, 1977*

THE PRESIDENT. I hope I didn't interrupt your meeting. [*Laughter*]

I think what we might do is just let me give you a quick report on the status of our administration as of the last couple of days and then spend the other 25 minutes answering your questions about any items that you want to raise.

ADMINISTRATION PROGRAMS

This last few days has been one of great activity around the White House, which is not different from most weeks. I'm putting the final touches on my own welfare reform proposal, which I will complete after meeting with Chairmen Russell Long and Al Ullman next week. I've spent a good bit of time on that recently, and we've been working on this with a great deal of enthusiasm and, I think, a good success ever since I've been in office.

We hope that the House and Senate, very quickly now, will take final action on the Department of Energy. They're making good progress on the overall energy policy. I think the House is very likely to finish that work before the mandatory summer recess.

I've been meeting frequently with foreign leaders. I think, so far, we've had

15 heads of state who have come here on official visits with me, and I've learned a lot from them. On my visit to Europe, I had about the same number with whom I met just a few minutes or extensively—a couple of hours, and I have a good relationship there.

This morning I had a meeting with the Panama Canal negotiating team, both our two Ambassadors and the two representing General Torrijos. And early this morning I met with Cy Vance, who will be leaving very quickly now to go to the Mideast. He'll go to Egypt and to Saudi Arabia, to Jordan and Syria, back through—Israel is the last stop this time, to try to put together some sort of framework on which we and the Soviet Union jointly can call for a Geneva conference this fall. We still have a lot of difficulties to overcome. My own belief is that they can be overcome.

Harold Brown is on the way back tonight from California, having finished a trip to Japan and to South Korea. Cy Vance is also preparing to go to China, and we'll spend all tomorrow morning, with me and him and Dr. Brzezinski and the Vice President and a few others, going over the component parts of his discussions with the Chinese Government.

We've embarked on a massive, 3-year reorganization program for the Federal Government, and I think this will be a slow, tedious, thorough improvement in the organizational structure of Government. It minimizes unnecessary intervention in the private lives and the business lives of our Nation and, at the same time, to be more efficient, more economical and simpler structured, with a clear delineation of authority and responsibility on the officers who will be responsible for certain functions.

We have, at the same time, tried to restore or improve our relationship with the developing nations of the world, with our own allies in Europe, with the African countries and, particularly, to deal with the long-standing problems in Rhodesia and Namibia. And at the same time, we've made strong and continuous overtures to our friends in the southern part of this hemisphere to make sure that we have as close as possible a relationship with them.

The last thing I'll mention, in passing, which is of crucial importance to us all, is the progress in our friendly relations with the Soviet Union. I put a lot of time on a speech that I made in Charleston last week to try to encapsulate, as best I could, the overall thrust of our policies.

We were successful yesterday in reaching an agreement with the Soviet Union and Great Britain to go to the detailed negotiations of an agreement on the comprehensive test ban. Our own desire is that we prohibit the testing of nuclear explosives completely, and we are making some progress in that direction. So far, the Soviets still would like to reserve the right to conduct some peaceful nuclear explosives.

But we've opened up new concepts of actual reductions in atomic weapons for the first time since they've been invented, to restrain military development in the Indian Ocean, to work with the Soviets on comprehensive SALT discussions, a prohibition against the destruction of observation satellites, prior notification of firing of test missiles, and so forth.

So we've a lot of things going on with the Soviet Union, which I think, potentially, are going to be very constructive. We have found them in their private atitudes toward us to be very forthcoming and cooperative. And these are difficult matters which have been ignored or postponed for decades, and we're trying to address them as forthrightly as possible.

I could go on with another long agenda, but I won't do that. I'd rather let you pick out the other items on the agenda that I have not mentioned, and I'll try to answer your questions as briefly and thoroughly as I can.

CUBA

Q. Mr. President, previous administrations and previous Presidents have made a strong commitment and promises to the Cuban people in behalf of their freedom. Example: President Kennedy at the Orange Bowl, Miami stadium: "I will return this flag"—he was referring to the 2506 Brigade flag—"in a free Havana." Now, we are approaching Communist Cuba. Are we abandoning our promise of support to the people of Cuba?

THE PRESIDENT. Well, I believe that, obviously, the Cuban-Americans here have complete freedom. We are not committed to the destruction by military force of the present Cuban Government; our hope and aspiration is that maximum freedom for people who live in Cuba can be achieved. But I think at the time of the Bay of Pigs, our country gave up the thought that we might do it by military attack.

We've proceeded very cautiously in our dealings with the Castro government. I've spelled out publicly on many occasions my own attitude toward this procedure.

We have signed now with the Soviets— I mean with the Cubans—a fishers agreement and a maritime agreement. And we are continuing in practical application the antihijacking agreement which has not been renewed.

We have also opened up the possibility, which will be realized very quickly, of diplomatic officials to be stationed in Washington and in Havana in the embassies of other nations. I don't see any possibility soon of normalizing relationships with Cuba. Castro's position has been that a prerequisite to this must be the removal of the trade embargo before negotiations can even commence.

As I've said on numerous occasions, my concerns about Cuba are that they still have large numbers of political prisoners incarcerated that ought to be released. They have large numbers of troops in Angola and other places in Africa which ought to be returned. And they still maintain an attitude of unwarranted intrusion into the internal affairs of some of the other nations or places in the Western Hemisphere.

So, I think all those factors tie together. But I assume from the tone of your question you were talking about a military overthrow of the Castro government. That is not part of our national purpose.

DEREGULATION OF NATURAL GAS AND OIL

Q. Mr. President, Governor Briscoe of Texas is circulating just today a document several hundred pages long which is called "The Texas Response to the National Energy Plan," and this bears heavily on what he sees as your failure to deregulate the price of natural gas as he says you promised in your preelection campaign. And this is perhaps the strongest way that the Governor has come out and said this, and I just wonder what—is the Governor correct when

he says that you went back on your promise?

THE PRESIDENT. No, he's not.

Dolph Briscoe is my friend, and I don't want to get into a personal interrelationship with him except on a basis of mutual understanding and friendship.

I think it's accurate to say that Congressman Krueger and several other Members of the Congress have adequately put forward the so-called Texas plan for energy development which, in my opinion, is primarily based on a complete deregulation of the price of oil and natural gas, which I think at this time would be inappropriate and a devastating load to the well-being of the consumers of this Nation. I also think it's unwarranted.

The degree of deregulation which we have advocated, a substantial improvement over what it is now, would result in the natural gas field alone in a $15–billion increase in the income of the natural gas companies between now and 1985.

There have been assessments made by the Library of Congress and by the GAO and other groups who advise Members of Congress, that the so-called Krueger Plan—I haven't seen the Briscoe Plan; I would guess they are similar and perhaps have a similar origin—would cost the consumers of our country maybe $70 billion more than what we advocate.

But I think that this is a crucial question in the overall energy concept— whether or not we should have extremely high prices to be established by the oil and natural gas companies without constraint and accept their proposition that exploration would build by leaps and bounds, that we would have unlimited supplies of oil and natural gas as a result, and that this is the best approach, or our own proposition on the other hand. I don't think that a crash program to extract oil and natural gas in a hasty fashion from American supplies is advisable under any circumstances.

I think that the emphasis on conservation and a shift toward coal, which we advocate, is the best approach. I also don't think there would be substantially increased exploration if oil was worth $20 a barrel and if natural gas was $3 or $4 a thousand cubic feet. I think the present rate of exploration would not be substantially enhanced, but it would be a great windfall to the oil and natural gas companies of our Nation.

As I said in the letter that Dolph Briscoe has, as I said in my speech on the energy proposal to the Congress back on April 20, our first move toward deregulation is one that will be followed later by others. It's a first move to carry out my commitment. But I can't bring myself to accept the proposition it ought to be done peremptorily. We've advocated, by the way, a $1.75 price for natural gas to be moved in interstate and intrastate supply lines, which is a substantial increase over interstate price now, and I think is adequate.

OIL LOCATION AND PRODUCTION

Q. Mr. President, last week in New Orleans when you visited the Zapata platform in the Gulf of Mexico, in your remarks after that, you indicated that you weren't disturbed by anything you had seen so far as a threat to the environment was concerned.

THE PRESIDENT. On that drill rig, that's correct.

Q. Does this mean you would step up encouraging drilling off the Atlantic seaboard?

THE PRESIDENT. Yes. But I think it's accurate to point out that the major impediment—one of the major impediments to increased drilling on the Atlantic sea-

board has been the oil companies themselves. They don't like the legitimate constraints that are placed on them by the Department of Interior and the Federal energy agency and others.

As Governor of Georgia, though, I worked with the Governors of our two neighboring States to the north—North and South Carolina—to provide, along with the oil companies, I might say, some assessment of what we ought to do. And we identified five places along the coast where we would like to see oil brought ashore, five places near this seacoast where we would like to see oil refineries built. And I would hope that all the States north of us on the eastern seaboard would do the same.

This new drill rig, one of the most modern in the world, I think, has greatly enhanced safety devices and oil spill control devices that were not extant when the Santa Barbara spills took place and were not applicable or installed in the North Sea spill. So, I don't think that we need fear, to the extent we did in the past, environmental consequences of offshore oil exploration and production.

So, to answer your question in a nutshell, I do favor a rapid increase in oil exploration and production on the eastern seaboard, and I hope that they find oil near the Georgia coast, first of all. [*Laughter*]

Q. Thank you, sir.

THE PRESIDENT. I think to do the oil companies justice and the drilling rig producers justice, it's a superb machine. And I was amazed at the quality of its construction, the electronics control devices, the safety devices, the training of the crew. I was really impressed with it. And as an engineer, it made me proud of what our country's technological ability could produce.

ENERGY CONSERVATION

Q. Mr. President, is there anything you can say to us about the state of voluntary public compliance with your energy use requests? My question is based on a story last week that gasoline usage in Michigan, for instance, was in excess of 455 million gallons, which was by 7.3 million gallons the highest in the State's history since those records have been kept. Is the public not paying attention?

THE PRESIDENT. The public is not paying attention. That's correct. And this has resulted in an enormous increase in the waste of fuel and also an increase in imports, which seriously unbalances our trade relationships with foreign countries.

I just spent some time right before lunch going over the reasons for it. There may be some indication that stockpiling is taking place in anticipation of the wellhead tax being imposed and because of the uncertainty of future price increases by the OPEC nations. But that's a relatively minor factor, although it is a factor.

I hope that the Congress will act expeditiously and not weaken the energy legislation, one of its primary purposes being to impose strict conservation measures. But I would say that at this point, the public has not responded well; that the absence of visibility to the impending oil shortage removes the incentive for the public to be concerned. And I'm afraid that a series of crises are going to be a prerequisite to a sincere desire on the part of the American people to quit wasting so much fuel.

We've seen this now on two or three occasions already, as a precursor. One, obviously, was the natural gas shortage this past winter; another one was the embargo in 1973, the rapid escalation in prices, and now the very severe trade imbalance. I think these are just predictions of what is to come.

I'm concerned that the public has not responded well. And I think voluntary compliance is probably not adequate at all. We will take what the Congress does this year and continue to build on it in subsequent years. I'm determined to have a complete and comprehensive energy package on the books before I go out of office. And what we don't get this year, we'll get in subsequent years.

GOVERNMENT REORGANIZATION

Q. Mr. President, aren't you finding it a lot harder as an insider than you thought it would be as an outsider to reform the bureaucracy? For example, I understand you probably no longer hope to cut the number of agencies from, say, 1,800 to 200. Are you having to sort of scale back your anticipation?

THE PRESIDENT. I haven't given up on that hope yet. Of course, a lot of those agencies, as we all know well, are minor commissions and boards and so forth that have been established by statute and you know can be eliminated when the need for them is no longer there. But I have not been unpleasantly surprised, Billy [Billy Watson, Macon Telegraph]. I had a good bit of experience, as you know, as Governor of Georgia and was familiar with at least a State bureaucracy. And I had heard such horrible stories about the Federal Government that I didn't expect to find a smooth-running, well-organized mechanism here in place. So, I wasn't very greatly surprised.

I have been pleasantly surprised at the quality of my Cabinet; that there is not a weak person on it, and not a single one

1391

that I would want to change if I had the whole choice to do over again. They've worked well together.

We have, for the first time in years—I don't know how long—we've got a weekly Cabinet meeting. And any defects that are carrying over in the governmental structure are partially overcome by the close-knit working relationship between the White House staff and the members of the Cabinet.

We have established now—almost completed the Department of Energy, which is to some degree a replacement for about 40 other Federal agencies. And our plan for reorganizing the entire structure of the Government is well in place. I've been through this before, for 4 years in Georgia, and I think there's a good parallel there to serve as a guide for me.

So to answer your question, I'm not disappointed nor unpleasantly surprised. And what defects are here, we are overcoming them by close relationship among the officials involved.

INNER CITIES

Q. Mr. President, you've been accused of, possibly unfairly, of not doing enough for the inner cities in this country. In view of the fact that many of the problems of the inner cities can be traced to the fact that crime and high taxes are chasing industry and jobs out of the cities, what exactly can the Federal Government do except to put all these people on welfare forever?

THE PRESIDENT. We obviously didn't cause the problem; it's an inherited problem that's been built up for long years. I think in the past there's been too much of an emphasis on major Federal programs when billions of dollars have been spent on helping people that didn't need the help very badly.

I'm from the Sun Belt States. I think there's been too much of a channeling of Federal moneys into Sun Belt areas. I think between the downtown ghetto areas on crime control, housing development, and so forth, the funds have quite often been channeled off into the suburbs because of more highly educated people, better organized people, more able to speak loudly and who understood the complexities of Federal programs. We're trying to change that and focus the attention of the Government, whatever it is, on the downtown, urban, deteriorating neighborhoods.

Another thing that we're trying to do is to concentrate on the rehabilitation of homes. I've seen this happen in Baltimore. I've seen it happen in Savannah, Georgia, and other places around the country, where with a small effort on the part of a chamber of commerce or the local officials, the banks, working with the Federal Government—that instead of seeing a neighborhood deteriorate, that existing structures can be rebuilt or renovated to make very attractive homes near the core area for executive and professional work without abandoning the central cities and moving out into the suburbs. We're trying to do that, too, with our general HUD programs.

And on crime, I think the major cause of crime in those downtown areas is unemployment, and we're trying to focus on this question. We've got now about 1.1 million jobs allotted during the summertime for young people, much more than ever has been before.

We are putting into realization at this moment 20,000 public service jobs per week, even a greater rate than Franklin Roosevelt put people in the CCC camps when you had the Army to do it and when the Nation was devastated by depression.

We are now approving 1,000 public works projects every week, with at least

10 percent of that allocation money being guaranteed to minority business people. And in addition to that, we have taken the CETA jobs, the comprehensive education and training jobs, and have multiplied them by more than a hundred percent, more than 200 percent.

We hope to increase those by 400,000 jobs between now and a year from now. None of these programs have yet been felt. Last week was the first week we ever were able to get a public works project approved.

This week the Congress has completed passing additional legislation on youth employment, above and beyond what I've just described to you. And I think by the time we feel the beneficial effect of all these programs, we'll be able to observe some improvements.

Obviously, we've got a long way to go in law enforcement. I think, to a substantial degree, the Law Enforcement Assistance Administration funds have been wasted in years gone by. We are trying to bring a more narrow focusing on them to prevent crime and to get out of the waste of buying very expensive and fancy machines and so forth and actually concentrate in the areas where the crime rate is highest.

I think I've seen statistics lately from the FBI and others that show that there's a general reduction in the crime rate. I think there's a better tone in the country, a little bit more trust in the Government. This was certainly subverted by the evidence in New York earlier this month. But I think, in general, throughout the country there's more of a respect being built up for public officials—not because of anything I've done, but just because we've recovered partially from the embarrassment of Watergate and the CIA and the Vietnam war and so forth.

But I think we ought not to give up on our urban cities and our downtown deteriorating neighborhoods. And my whole administration is focusing on this, and I feel hopeful about it.

ISRAELI SETTLEMENTS IN OCCUPIED LANDS

Q. Mr. President, do you have a commitment from Prime Minister Begin before he left here that he would not formalize or legalize the three settlements on the West Bank?

THE PRESIDENT. No, we did not discuss his legalizing those settlements. We did discuss my concern about the adverse impact of establishing new settlements. He did not promise me anything on the subject, and we did not even discuss the legalization question.

Q. So that you weren't upset by the fact that they did legalize these settlements?

THE PRESIDENT. Yes, I was upset. As I said I think it's an obstacle to peace. And I let Mr. Begin know very clearly that our Government policy, before I became President and now, is that these settlements are illegal and contravene the Geneva conference terms.

Mr. Begin disagrees with this. But we've spelled this out very clearly on several occasions in the United Nations and other places that these settlements are illegal.

I think that it's accurate to say that the Israeli Government has never maintained that they are permanent but, that on a temporary basis, maybe extending quite a while in the future in their view, that they are legalized, but not as a permanent settlement.

Israel has never claimed hegemony over the West Bank territory, as you know. And I think that it would be a mistake, as I said in my press conference yesterday, to condemn Mr. Begin about this action because this was a campaign commitment he made. I think what he did was in consonance with the desires of the Israeli people.

But I don't want anybody to misunderstand our feelings about it. We think it's wrong to establish these settlements, it's wrong to insinuate that they are legal, it's certainly wrong to ever claim that they are permanent. And to establish new settlements would be even more unsettling to their Arab neighbors, as we try to go to Geneva in a good spirit of compromise and cooperation, than the allocation of legality by the Government to those already in existence.

Q. Well, this hasn't passed your optimism for a resumption of a peace conference in Geneva?

THE PRESIDENT. No, I'm still optimistic about it. But it's an additional obstacle that we had not anticipated.

POWER FAILURE IN NEW YORK

Q. With that concern for the cities, how and why did you arrive at the decision not to declare New York a Federal disaster area after the blackout in the city?

THE PRESIDENT. We didn't consider it to fall in the legal definition of a disaster area. Those definitions are established very clearly in the Federal law. And the department leaders involved, Patricia Harris in HUD and others, analyzed the situation in New York as best we could, analyzed the definition of a disaster area in the law, and found out that it didn't match.

We did make a special allocation through Housing and Urban Development, Commerce, EDA, Labor, and other departments—including the Justice Department, to expedite the hearings on those that were accused of looting—I think a total package of about $11.4 million. I doubt that any more money would have been allocated to the city if it had received an official declaration. So we did all we could within the bounds of the law to recognize the problem in New York.

Q. Thank you, sir.

OPENNESS WITH AMERICAN PUBLIC

THE PRESIDENT. Thank you all. I'm sorry I have to go, but I've got another meeting in a few minutes. I've enjoyed it, and I hope that you had a chance to meet with some of our staff members.

I didn't make a speech at first, but I would like to say that it's important to us to have you come here. We learn, I'm sure, a lot more from listening to your questions and from my staff members talking to you about domestic and foreign affairs than you learn from us.

And I think it's important for your readers and listeners and viewers to know that this is their White House, and that we don't have anything to conceal here. We've made mistakes. We're obviously going to make them, like you do at home in your own business. But we don't try to cover up, conceal anything.

I've enjoyed the press conferences twice a week. Cy Vance has a press conference every month. It happens to be this afternoon.

And on many of the controversial issues that in the past have been decided in a very secret way between the Secretary of State and the President, for instance, are now discussed openly with the American people. I feel that's a good move. It exposes our doubts and uncertainties and controversies on occasion, but after that debate goes back and forth in the Congress and throughout the Nation, among American people, we monitor that opinion very closely. And I think that by the time I make a decision—which may or may not always agree with what the people are thinking at home—I have a much surer sense of what our country ought to do. And I think that foreign countries feel, for instance, that when I speak or Cy Vance speaks or the Vice President, that we speak for the country.

We also do the same thing with the Congress. I've met with every single Member of the Congress, Democrat and Republican, unless they just didn't come when they were invited. And if they missed one meeting, they've been invited to subsequent meetings. You know, very recently, I've had breakfast with all the Democratic Members of the Senate, and now we're starting to have breakfast with all the Republican Members. We've spent an hour and a half just sitting around a small table, and let them bring up any subject they want to me and I answer any question they ask me.

Q. [*Inaudible*].

THE PRESIDENT. So, it's kind of an open administration, sir.

RUSSELL DAM

Q. You going to veto Russell Dam?

THE PRESIDENT. I don't think Russell Dam ought ever to be built, and I'll do what I can to stop it. Whether I veto it this year, I can't tell you. But if I don't, I'll be trying to prevent it being built next year. I think it's a waste of money.

Thank you very much.

NOTE: The interview began at 1 p.m. in the Cabinet Room at the White House. The transcript of the interview was released on July 30.

Federal Oil and Gas Leases in Wyoming

Statement on Signing H. R. 2502 Into Law. August 1, 1977

I have signed H.R. 2502, which extends for 4 years, 17 Federal oil and gas leases in Wyoming. The purpose of the extension is to permit the lessees the additional time needed to drill an ultradeep well. Technological problems have prevented the lessees from drilling that well to date.

I want to make clear that my signing this bill is not part of an overall policy favoring the extension of such leases, nor is my signing intended to affect in any way pending litigation on drilling extensions for certain Federal oil and gas leases.

By signing H.R. 2502, I am only accepting Congress judgment that the special circumstances surrounding these leases require a 4-year extension.

NOTE: As enacted, H.R. 2502 is Public Law 95–77, approved July 30.

Securities and Exchange Commission

Nomination of Roberta S. Karmel To Be a Member. August 1, 1977

The President today announced that he will nominate Roberta S. Karmel, of New York, to be a member of the Securities and Exchange Commission. She would replace A. A. Sommer, Jr. Karmel is a partner in the New York law firm of Rogers & Wells and an adjunct professor at Brooklyn Law School.

She was born May 4, 1937, in Chicago, Ill. She received a B.A. from Radcliffe College in 1959 and an LL.B. from New York University School of Law in 1962.

From 1962 to 1969, Karmel worked for the Securities and Exchange Commission, as an attorney, then attorney branch chief, then Assistant Regional Administrator. From 1969 to 1972, she was an associate with Willkie, Farr & Gallagher in New York.

Karmel has been a partner with Rogers & Wells since 1972, and an adjunct professor at Brooklyn Law School since 1973. She has been a member of the American Bar Association Committee on Securities Regulation since 1973. She has also served on the New York City Bar Association's Committee on Securities Regulation and Committee on Administrative Law, and is presently on its Committee on Professional Responsibility.

She is the author of numerous articles in legal journals.

Consumer Agency Legislation

Announcement of a Proposal for Establishing the Agency. August 1, 1977

Today, a proposal for establishing the Agency for Consumer Protection entirely from existing resources was sent to Congress by Bert Lance, Director of the Office of Management and Budget. It will go into effect when the pending consumer bill becomes law.

The proposal would eliminate or merge 26 Government units that the President's Reorganization Project at OMB has identified as overlapping, duplicating, or conflicting with the functions of the new agency. These units currently spend $11.6 million annually and employ more than 200 people.

In anticipation of passage of the consumer agency legislation, President Carter also will direct all executive departments and agencies to rescind their so-called consumer representation plans. These plans, which cost $8.5 million to implement and maintain, were drawn up by the previous administration in an attempt to forestall creation of the consumer agency. The President has directed OMB to eliminate these funds in the next budget period.

In all, these actions will make more than $20 million available. The first year

budget of the proposed agency is only $15 million. In his letter, Lance said, "Prompt congressional action on the consumer agency legislation will result not only in more efficient conduct of consumer representation functions, but also in a savings to American taxpayers."

Esther Peterson, Special Assistant to the President for Consumer Affairs, said "today's release of the consumer reorganization proposal will answer charges of some opponents of the bill that the new agency will create more bureaucracy at increased cost."

The legislation currently provides that the President submit a consumer reorganization plan to the Congress within 180 days after passage of the bill. Release of the elements of the proposed plan now will "give a concerned Congress advance knowledge of the President's proposal and the information needed to make a positive decision on this bill," Peterson said.

NOTE: The White House press release also included the text of the letter which was sent to the Speaker of the House and the President of the Senate by Mr. Lance.

National Energy Plan

Statement on Pending Legislation. August 1, 1977

I deeply appreciate the efforts of the House leadership in moving the National Energy Plan forward for consideration by the full House in record time. I particularly want to commend Speaker O'Neill, Chairman Ashley of the Ad Hoc Energy Committee, Chairman Ullman of the Ways and Means Committee, Chairman Staggers of the Interstate and Foreign Commerce Committee, and Chairman Dingell of the Energy and Power Subcommittee, as well as many other committee chairmen and members. Each of these members themselves have shown, by putting their shoulders to the grindstone, that the Congress shares with me a commitment to taking decisive action on our energy problem.

As the House begins voting on the various energy proposals, there are five points which I consider to be critical.

First, I would urge the House to retain the natural gas pricing program which I proposed and which has been adopted by the Commerce Committee and by the Ad Hoc Committee. This program provides ample incentives for the production of natural gas from new reservoirs, it eliminates the artificial distinction between the interstate and intrastate gas markets, and assures that consumer costs for gas are kept within manageable bounds. If, as some Members of Congress have advocated, natural gas were deregulated, the consumers' bill would increase by billions of dollars and producers would reap extraordinary excess profits. Deregulation would only increase supplies by about 2 per cent above my program, and the price we would have to pay for that increase is exorbitant. A vote in favor of deregulation would undermine one of the basic tenets of my energy plan—fairness.

Second, I would urge the Members of the House to resist an amendment which would eliminate rebates to home heating oil users and to those taxpayers who most need assistance to meet higher fuel costs. I believe that the formula adopted by the Ad Hoc Committee for rebates of the crude oil equalization tax should not be changed.

Third, I do not believe that an amendment which would "plow back" some of the revenues collected under the crude oil equalization tax is necessary or fair. Drilling activity in the oil industry is at a 17-year high, and industry cash flows are so large that some major oil companies have made major acquisitions of non-energy companies. My plan provides for substantial incentive prices for new oil and gas exploration and production. In fact, the plan provides oil producers as high a rate of return as is available anywhere in the world. The Ways and Means Committee fully discussed and debated this issue and three times rejected a plowback proposal. I would urge that the House membership defeat this inequitable and unnecessary proposal.

Fourth, I understand that a 5-cents-per-gallon increase in the gasoline tax will be proposed by Congressman Howard. This tax would be earmarked for highway construction and maintenance and for mass transit. While I initially recommended a standby gasoline tax which would provide a specific disincentive on the wasteful use of gasoline, or a gasoline tax with greater flexibility for use of the revenues, I recommend positive action on this proposed tax which is supported by the House leadership.

Finally, I strongly support the Ad Hoc Committee's amendment to strengthen the tax on oil and gas use by large industrial consumers by striking the unnecessary exemption for certain new facilities.

I am convinced that the hard work that the Congress has undertaken over the last 3 months will result in a strong and effective bill. I commend the Congress for its work and am looking forward to seeing final passage of the National Energy Act this year.

United States Military Academy Board of Visitors

Letter to the Chairman of the Board on Receiving the Board's Annual Report for 1976. August 1, 1977

To General Wilcox

Thank you for the report on the United States Military Academy provided by you and your colleagues on the Board of Visitors. Please convey to each member of the Board my deep appreciation for his contribution to the report.

As you are aware, U.S. law requires the Board to examine academic and administrative procedures at the Academy, as well as physical and fiscal matters. In light of recent difficulties experienced at the Academy, I would hope the Board's report for April 1978 and subsequent years will focus more on academic and other training matters. I believe that your group offers a critical source of outside and expert evaluation, and I count on your judgment to help guide West Point in maintaining the high standards required to produce dedicated leadership for the United States Army.

Please accept my thanks for providing your distinguished and knowledgeable leadership as Chairman of the Board of Visitors.

Sincerely,

JIMMY CARTER

[Major General Howard S. Wilcox, USAR, 300 Board of Trade Building, Indianapolis, Indiana 46240]

NOTE: The text of the letter was made available by the White House Press Office on August 2.

United States Ambassador to Guinea-Bissau and Cape Verde

Nomination of Edward Marks.
August 2, 1977

The President today announced that he will nominate Edward Marks, of Los Angeles, Calif., to be Ambassador Extraordinary and Plenipotentiary of the United States to the Republic of Guinea-Bissau and to the Republic of Cape Verde. He would replace Melissa F. Wells. Marks is

Alternate Director of the Office of Central African Affairs at the State Department.

He was born April 22, 1934, in Chicago, Ill. He received a B.A. from the University of Michigan in 1956 and an M.A. from the University of Oklahoma in 1975. He served in the U.S. Army from 1956 to 1958.

In 1959 and 1960 Marks was an exchange program officer, and from 1960 to 1963 he was economic officer in Nairobi. He served as consular officer in Nuevo Laredo from 1963 to 1965 and as consular administrative officer in 1965 and 1966.

From 1966 to 1969, Marks was economic officer in Lusaka. In 1969 and 1970 he was an international relations officer, and in 1970 and 1971 he was an economic-commercial officer. From 1971 to 1974, he was economic-commercial officer in Brussels.

Marks was principal officer in Lubumbashi from 1974 to 1976. Since 1976 he has been Alternate Director of the Office of Central African Affairs.

National Endowment for the Humanities

Nomination of Joseph D. Duffey To Be Chairman.   August 2, 1977

The President today announced that he will nominate Joseph D. Duffey, of Washington, D.C., to be Chairman of the National Endowment for the Humanities. He would replace Ronald S. Berman. Duffey is Assistant Secretary of State for Educational and Cultural Affairs.

He was born July 1, 1932, in Huntington, W. Va. He received an A.B. from Marshall University in 1954, a B.D. from Andover Theological School in 1957, an S.T.M. from Yale University in 1963, and a Ph. D. from Hartford Seminary Foundation in 1969.

From 1960 to 1970, Duffey was an assistant professor, then acting dean and associate professor, at Hartford Seminary. He was also founder and director of the Center for Urban Studies there. In 1971 he was a fellow at the John F. Kennedy School of Government at Harvard University.

Duffey was an adjunct professor at Yale University and a fellow at Calhoon College from 1971 to 1973. From 1974 to 1976, he was chief administrative officer and spokesman for the American Association of University Professors. He worked on the Carter-Mondale transition team in 1976 and 1977 and has been Assistant Secretary of State for Educational and Cultural Affairs since early 1977.

Drug Abuse

Remarks on Transmitting a Message to the Congress. August 2, 1977

This afternoon I have a statement to make about the drug abuse problem following which, Dr. Peter Bourne will be available to answer specific questions.

Today I'm sending Congress a message which expresses my strong concern about the crime and sickness and death caused by the abuse of drugs, including barbiturates and alcohol.

The estimated cost of drug abuse in this country is more than $15 billion per year. I'm ordering the Attorney General to concentrate on breaking the links between organized crime and drug traffic, to enhance cooperation among all law enforcement agencies, and to ensure more certain conviction and quick punishment for those who traffic in drugs.

We will not have an effective and united Federal effort against drugs unless we reorganize the current Federal effort now divided among more than 20 different, often competing, noncooperative agencies, on occasion.

Therefore, I'm directing my staff to eliminate this duplication and overlap and also to end the long-standing fragmentation among our international drug enforcement programs and our treatment, rehabilitation, and prevention efforts.

We must also have international cooperation to control the production and transport of dangerous drugs into our country. We are making some progress on this already, in part because of the very good cooperation among the governments of foreign countries.

The influx of heroin from Mexico has been drastically reduced within this last 6-month period. In the Thailand-Burma area, cooperating with us, they have now mounted a very successful anti-drug campaign. I think last week, we had the largest confiscation of heroin on record, about 400 pounds of heroin. And recently, we formed a very good working relationship with the Government of Colombia.

Heroin sold in our streets is now in such short supply that it's only 4.9-percent pure, the lowest quality detected since records have been kept.

We will make further efforts to deal with the problem on an international level by cooperating with law enforcement officials abroad, by sharing treatment knowledge, by backing drug efforts of the United Nations, by helping to find alternate crops for drug-producing countries—particularly in the mountainous areas where heroin poppies are grown—and by supporting the ratification of the Convention on Psychotropic Substances.

In our own country, I'm ordering a study of how we can best control the abuse of barbiturates and other prescription drugs, which cause many deaths, while not interfering with their legitimate medical use.

I supported change in law to end Federal criminal penalties for possession of up to one ounce of marijuana, leaving the States free to adopt whatever laws they wish concerning marijuana. Decriminalization is not legalization. I do not condone any drug abuse, and we'll do everything possible to reduce the serious threat to our society. Federal civil penalties should be continued as a deterrent to the possession and use of marijuana.

Drug research and treatment programs will also be improved to lessen the adverse effect of drugs on the lives of our people. But it's ultimately the strength of the people of our country, of our values and of our society that will determine whether we can be successful in our fight against drug abuse.

The seriousness of this problem has caused us all in the Government, this first 6 months of my own administration, to try to come up with a coherent proposal to the Congress and with administrative action, both within our own country and in our relations with other nations.

The center of this effort, now and in the future, is and will be Dr. Peter Bourne, a man of international reputation, and has been an expert in the control of the production, transport, and treatment of the drug problem. Dr. Bourne is my personal adviser on this subject, and he will now be available to answer your questions about any aspects of the drug problem. Dr. Bourne.

NOTE: The President spoke at 2 p.m. to reporters assembled in the Briefing Room at the White House.

Drug Abuse

Message to the Congress.   August 2, 1977

To the Congress of the United States:

Drug abuse continues to be a serious social problem in America. The lives of hundreds of thousands of people are blighted by their dependence on drugs. Many communities remain unsafe because of drug-related street crime, and the immense profits made in the illicit drug traffic help support the power and influence of organized crime. Among young American men aged 18–24 years, drugs are the fourth most common cause of death: only automobile accidents, homicides, and suicides rank higher. The estimated cost of drug abuse in America exceeds 15 billion dollars each year. Among some minority groups, the incidence of addiction and the harm it inflicts are disproportionate.

Drug addiction, which in recent years was viewed as a problem peculiar to America, now affects people throughout the world. We can no longer concern ourselves merely with keeping illicit drugs out of the United States, but we must join with other nations to deal with this global problem by combating drug traffickers and sharing our knowledge and resources to help treat addiction wherever it occurs. We must set realistic objectives, giving our foremost attention domestically to those drugs that pose the greatest threat to health, and to our ability to reduce crime. Since heroin, barbiturates and other sedative/hypnotic drugs account for 90 percent of the deaths from drug abuse, they should receive our principal emphasis.

My goals are to discourage all drug abuse in America—and also discourage the excessive use of alcohol and tobacco—and to reduce to a minimum the harm drug abuse causes when it does occur. To achieve these goals with the resources available, effective management and direction are essential. Because the federal effort is currently divided among more than twenty different, and often competing, agencies, I have directed my staff to coordinate Federal action and to formulate a comprehensive national policy. This will end the long-standing fragmentation among our international programs, drug law enforcement, treatment and rehabilitation, prevention, and regulatory activities. I will also seek the counsel and active involvement of members of the Cabinet and heads of major independent agencies on all drug abuse policy questions, through a revitalized Strategy Council on Drug Abuse. My staff will examine the functions of the various agencies involved in this field and will recommend to me whatever organizational changes are appropriate.

INTERNATIONAL COOPERATION

For certain drugs originally derived from plant sources outside the United States, especially heroin and cocaine, diplomatic agreements against cultivation and trafficking are indispensable. Turkey—once virtually the sole source of heroin supply in this country—is now gone from the illicit market as the result of such an agreement. The enormous profits generated by the illicit drug traffic distort the economies of many smaller countries, aggravating inflation and draining tax revenues; they also engender corruption and corrode political stability. We must work closely with other governments to assist them in their efforts to eradicate the cultivation of drugs, and to develop legitimate alternative sources of income for the impoverished farmers who have for generations raised and sold crops such as opium.

We have made significant progress in the last few months. In February, I discussed with President Lopez-Portillo of Mexico my deep concern about the illegal cultivation of opium in his country. Under his strong leadership, the eradication program has been intensified and is producing dramatic results, significantly reducing the availability of heroin in many American cities. In addition, President Ne Win of Burma and Prime Minister Thanin of Thailand have shown a resolute determination to control drug cultivation and trafficking in their countries. Most recently I have received strong assurances from President Lopez-Michelsen of Colombia that he plans to give the problem of drug trafficking his highest priority. We are establishing a commission made up of government officials from our two countries to coordinate a stepped up effort to deal with the major international trafficking of cocaine and marihuana between our two countries, and the devastating economic impact of that traffic.

As a result of these efforts and those of the Drug Enforcement Administration, the purity of heroin in our country has dropped in the last six months to 4.9%, the lowest level in 4 years.

There is, however, more that we can do:

(1) I am directing the Secretary of State to give greater emphasis to the international narcotics control program and to reiterate to foreign governments our strong desire to curtail production of, and traffic in, illicit drugs.

(2) To this end, I am directing the Administrator of the Agency for International Development to include such measures as crop and income substitution in its development programs for those countries where drugs are grown illicitly. I expect the Secretary of State to continue to call on other agencies and departments, such as the Drug Enforcement Administration, the U.S. Customs Service, the U.S. Department of Agriculture, and the National Institute on Drug Abuse, to assist in the international narcotics control program according to the special expertise of each.

(3) I am directing the intelligence community to emphasize the collection and analysis of information relating to international drug trafficking.

(4) I strongly support the work of the United Nations Fund for Drug Abuse Control (UNFDAC), the United Nations Commission on Narcotic Drugs, the International Narcotics Control Board, the World Health Organization, and other organizations working within the framework of the United Nations in their efforts to help drug-producing countries find alternate crops, improve drug control measures, and make treatment resources available.

(5) I am instructing the United States representatives to the loan committees of the Regional Development Banks and other international financial institutions to use their votes and influence to encourage well designed rural development and income substitution projects in countries which now produce dangerous drugs, and to ensure that assistance is not used to foster the growth of crops like opium and coca.

(6) Because of the need to improve international controls over dangerous drugs which have legitimate medical uses, like barbiturates and amphetamines, I urge the Congress to adopt legislation implementing the Convention on Psychotropic Substances, and I urge the Senate to ratify this treaty promptly.

(7) In my communications with foreign leaders, I will emphasize international cooperation among drug law enforcement agencies, so that intelligence and technical expertise can be shared. I will encourage them to send law enforcement officials to work with us to stop the flow of drugs through other countries. This kind of cooperation has already begun in Bangkok among French, German, British, Dutch, American and Thai officials.

I will, in addition, promote the international sharing of knowledge and expertise in the treatment of drug abuse. We will make a special effort to share our experience, especially with those nations which have serious drug problems and which are working with us in the effort to control drug sources and prevent drug abuse. Our program will encompass training, research and technical assistance projects, including providing American experts as consultants.

LAW ENFORCEMENT

We must vigorously enforce our laws against those who traffic in drugs, so that the attraction of large profits is outweighed by the risk of detection and the likelihood of conviction. The Federal Government's job is to deter, and where possible prevent entirely, illegal importation and major trafficking of controlled substances. Often large-scale financiers of the illegal drug trade never come into direct contact with drugs. Through the cooperative efforts of the various agencies involved, we will attack the financial resources of these traffickers who provide the capital needed to support the smuggling of drugs into the country. Drug traffickers must understand that they face swift, certain, and severe punishment; and our law enforcement and judicial systems must have the resources to make this prospect a very real threat. We must allocate our resources intelligently, revise our penalty structure where necessary to concentrate on the actions (and the drugs) that are most dangerous, and improve the administration of justice.

Therefore:

• I am directing the Attorney General to intensify investigations of the link between organized crime and the drug traffic, and to recommend appropriate measures to be taken against these organizations.

• I am directing the Department of Justice in conjunction with the Departments of State and Treasury to study arrangements with other countries, consistent with Constitutional principles, to revoke the passports of known major traffickers, and to freeze assets accumulated in the illegal drug traffic.

• To ease the burden on the United States District Courts, which must hear major drug cases, I support legislation widening the jurisdiction of U.S. Magistrates under certain circumstances to include misdemeanor offenses which carry sentences of up to one year.

• In 18 United States Attorneys' Offices, special units devoted to the prosecution of major drug traffickers exist. The Department of Justice is now expanding this program to include additional units.

• I support legislation raising from $2,500 to $10,000 the value of property which can be seized and forfeited from drug violators by administrative action, including cash within the definition of seizable property. Amounts above this figure will continue to require court proceedings.

• I am directing my staff to recommend to me the appropriate Federal drug law enforcement role in the light of currently available resources—state, local and Federal. For nearly a decade, Federal support of state and local enforcement activity has steadily expanded. The time is ripe to evaluate the results of this effort, to determine whether federal participation should be altered, and to determine the proper division of responsibility between Federal and local officials. The Office of Drug Abuse Policy has already begun the first phase of this review, which includes consideration of border security and drug trafficking intelligence.

• I am directing the Attorney General to study the necessity for and constitutionality of proposals which would deny pre-trial release to certain persons charged with trafficking in drugs posing the greatest threat to health, and to give me his recommendations within 90 days. At the present time, some persons charged with major drug offenses can use their immense wealth to post bail and escape justice. If enactment of such proposals appears to be necessary and constitutional, their application should be tightly restricted and they should include a provision granting the accused an expedited trial.

• I am directing the Attorney General to review the adequacy of the penalties for major trafficking offenses and to give me his recommendations within 90 days.

• I also have considered requesting changes in the Tax Reform Act of 1976. Some of its provisions—such as those for disclosure and summonsing—were designed to protect the privacy of citizens but may also impede unnecessarily the investigation of narcotics trafficking cases. I am asking the appropriate Federal agencies to determine the difficulties these provisions present to effective law enforcement. If it appears they can be amended to improve law enforcement without infringing upon legitimate privacy interests, I will submit legislation to the Congress.

MARIHUANA

Marihuana continues to be an emotional and controversial issue. After four decades, efforts to discourage its use with stringent laws have still not been successful. More than 45 million Americans have tried marihuana and an estimated 11 million are regular users.

Penalties against possession of a drug should not be more damaging to an individual than the use of the drug itself; and where they are, they should be changed. Nowhere is this more clear than in the laws against possession of marihuana in private for personal use. We can, and should, continue to discourage the use of marihuana, but this can be done without defining the smoker as a criminal. States which have already removed criminal penalties for marihuana use, like Oregon and California, have not noted any significant increase in marihuana smoking. The National Commission on Marihuana and Drug Abuse concluded five years ago that marihuana use should be decriminalized, and I believe it is time to implement those basic recommendations.

Therefore, I support legislation amending Federal law to eliminate all Federal criminal penalties for the possession of up to one ounce of marihuana. This decriminalization is not legalization. It means only that the Federal penalty for possession would be reduced and a person would received a fine rather than a criminal penalty. Federal penalties for trafficking would remain in force and the states would remain free to adopt whatever laws they wish concerning the marihuana smoker.

I am especially concerned about the increasing levels of marihuana use, which may be particularly destructive to our youth. While there is certain evidence to date showing that the medical damage from marihuana use may be limited, we should be concerned that chronic intoxication with marihuana or any other drug may deplete productivity, causing people to lose interest in their social environment, their future, and other more constructive ways of filling their free time. In addition, driving while under the influence of marihuana can be very hazardous. I am, therefore, directing the Department of Transportation to expedite its study of the effects of marihuana use on the coordination and reflexes needed for safe driving.

DRUG TREATMENT

My immediate objective will be to widen the scope and improve the effectiveness of Federal drug treatment programs. In conception and in practice, they have been too narrow. Drug addiction can be cured; but we must not only treat the immediate effects of the drugs, we must also provide adequate rehabilitation, including job training, to help the addict regain a productive role in society. In the past, Federal programs have given disproportionate attention to the heroin addict while neglecting those who are dependent on other drugs.

To improve the quality of Federal drug treatment, I am recommending these steps:

• In recognition of the devastating effects that certain nonopiate drugs can have if abused, I am directing the Secretary of Health, Education, and Welfare to expand resources devoted to care for abusers of barbiturates, amphetamines, and multiple drugs used in combination, including alcohol.

• To help drug abusers return to productive lives, I am directing the Secretary of Labor to identify all Federal employment assistance programs which can help former drug abusers and to give me, within 120 days, his recommendations for increasing the access of drug abusers to them.

• A sustained effort must be made to identify the reasons that people turn to drugs, including alcohol and cigarettes. We should seek more effective ways to make people aware of the health problems associated with such substances (particularly cigarettes and alcohol) and to respond in more constructive ways to the human and psychological needs they satisfy.

DRUG RESEARCH

In the past, there has been no serious attempt to coordinate Federal research on opiates and alcohol despite the many similarities in the effects of these two drugs. A joint Federal research center might not only save money, but also lead to greater scientific understanding of addiction problems. Therefore I am directing the Secretary of Health, Education, and Welfare to study the feasibility of making the Addiction Research Center responsible for coordinated research on a variety of drugs, including opiates, alcohol, and tobacco.

ADMINISTRATIVE ACTION

Improved treatment and prevention programs should be accompanied by appropriate changes in Federal regulations, administrative practices, and enforcement, among which are these:

• *First,* I am recommending a conscious and deliberate increase in attention throughout the Federal Government to the problems related to the abuse of drugs that come originally from legitimate medical sources. Of particular concern are bar-

biturates, which despite their recognized medical use, are responsible for many deaths and are frequently used in suicide attempts. The withdrawal reaction of patients addicted to barbiturates can be more difficult and more dangerous than that associated with heroin withdrawal. They are frequently oversold, overprescribed, and overused.

Therefore, I will:

—Instruct the Secretary of Health, Education, and Welfare to undertake a study of barbiturates and other sedative/hypnotic drugs to determine the conditions under which they can be most safely used.

—Instruct the Secretary of Defense, the Secretary of Health, Education, and Welfare, and the Administrator of Veterans' Affairs to review the prescribing practices of physicians under their jurisdiction, and to discourage the medical use of barbiturates and sedative/hypnotics except in cases where it is unmistakably justified.

—Continue the program, already begun at my direction, by which the Drug Enforcement Administration has instructed its regional offices and regulatory task forces to give priority attention to barbiturate cases. DEA has also begun to investigate the "street" market in order to determine the source of illegal supplies so that suitable Federal action may be taken. In the near future, DEA will conduct a special accelerated audit of the 120 companies lawfully manufacturing barbiturates in this country and will also notify foreign governments of our desire to see them control their barbiturate exports strictly.

• *Second,* I am directing the Secretary of Health, Education, and Welfare to review those sedative/hypnotic drugs particularly subject to abuse to determine whether any should be removed from the market, taking into consideration not only their safety to the individual but also the dangers they pose to the public at large.

• *Third,* I support legislation giving the Food & Drug Administration the authority to apply standards of safety and efficacy to all drugs, by repealing those laws which exempt a variety of drugs because they were placed on the market before a certain date. A number of barbiturates fit into this category.

• *Fourth,* Some physicians still knowingly overprescribe a wide variety of drugs. Although, as a result of careful education, physicians have voluntarily reduced their prescriptions for barbiturates by 73 percent during the last five years, a few are continuing to misprescribe these and other drugs deliberately. I am directing the Attorney General, in full cooperation with State officials, to begin a concerted drive to identify and prosecute these violators.

No government can completely protect its citizens from all harm—not by legislation, or by regulation, or by medicine, or by advice. Drugs cannot be forced out of existence; they will be with us for as long as people find in them the relief or satisfaction they desire. But the harm caused by drug abuse can be reduced. We cannot talk in absolutes—that drug abuse will cease, that no more illegal drugs will cross our borders—because if we are honest with ourselves we know that is beyond our power. But we can bring together the resources of the Federal Government intelligently to protect our society and help those who suffer. The sufferers include the overwhelming majority of the public who never abuse drugs but for whom drug abuse poses the threat of broken families, a lost child or fear to walk the streets at night. Beyond that, we must understand why people seek the experience of drugs, and address ourselves to those reasons. For it is ultimately the strength of the American people, of our values and our society,

that will determine whether we can put an end to drug abuse.

JIMMY CARTER

The White House,
    August 2, 1977.

Review of Natural Resources and Environmental Programs

Memorandum for the Heads of Executive Departments and Agencies.   August 2, 1977

Memorandum for the Heads of Executive Departments and Agencies

Subject: Comprehensive Review of Natural Resources and Environmental Programs

I have directed my Reorganization Project staff at the Office of Management and Budget to review the organization of all Federal responsibilities for managing natural resources and protecting the environment.

These responsibilities are now dispersed among 8 Departments and numerous agencies, involving 160,000 employees and expenditures of more than $17 billion a year. Other Departments and agencies are involved less directly. There is no way to coordinate their policies and actions. This situation has led to difficulties in managing resources and safeguarding the environment; waste of time and money; confusion to the public; and ineffective coordination of geophysical and environmental research and technology.

This organizational review will seek better ways to set policy, make decisions about resource management and environmental quality, improve research and technical support, and assure consistency in programs.

Its success will depend on active participation by members of Congress, the Federal departments and agencies, State, local and regional officials, interested groups, and individual citizens.

JIMMY CARTER

International Boundary Commission, United States and Canada

Appointment of William M. Schreiber as a U.S. Commissioner.   August 2, 1977

The President today announced the appointment of William M. Schreiber, of Indianapolis, Ind., to be a Commissioner of the United States on the International Boundary Commission, United States and Canada. He replaces Richard L. Herman. Schreiber is administrator of the Marion County (Indiana) Board of Voter Registration.

He was born May 1, 1943, in Ottumwa, Iowa. He received a B.S. in secondary education in 1966 and an M.A. in political science in 1975 from Indiana University.

From 1969 to 1973, Schreiber was legislative assistant to Congressman Andy Jacobs of Indiana. Since 1973 he has been administrator of the Marion County Board of Voter Registration. In 1976 Schreiber was a visiting lecturer in State and local government at Indiana Central University.

Toxic and Hazardous Substances Regulation

Memorandum for the Heads of Four Agencies.   August 2, 1977

Memorandum for the Assistant Secretary of Labor, Occupational Safety and Health, the Administrator, Environmental Protection Agency, the Chairman, Consumer Product Safety Commission, the Commissioner, Food and Drug Administration

I was very pleased to receive your letter of July 27, describing the steps your four agencies are taking to develop a common, coordinated approach in regulating toxic and hazardous substances.

As you know, I am determined to protect the health of our people and the quality of our environment from damage done by toxic substances. We can better coordinate our efforts and make them both more effective and less burdensome.

I congratulate you on taking this step toward a better regulatory system. Your initiative will be a major contribution to the Administration's overall regulatory reform effort. It is especially useful that you are beginning the effort with a clear signal to your employees both in and outside of Washington of the seriousness of your aim to work together. Close cooperation among the regional and field offices of your agencies is essential if your efforts are to succeed.

Please keep me informed of your progress.

JIMMY CARTER

Surface Mining Control and Reclamation Act of 1977

Remarks on Signing H.R. 2 Into Law. August 3, 1977

THE PRESIDENT. I think it's obvious from the composition of the group here this morning, that the American people have an intense interest in preserving the quality of our lives and the beauty of the land that God gave us.

Many years ago, because of my help and the help of many others, Georgia passed a very strong strip mining law. And I know that many here have worked for 6 years, sometimes much longer, to get a Federal strip mining law which would be fair and reasonable, which would enhance the legitimate and much needed production of coal and, also, assuage the fears that the beautiful areas where coal is produced were being destroyed.

This has been in many ways a disappointing effort. The Congress has passed legislation that would meet these needs. Unfortunately, in the past, the bills have been vetoed. But I found, as I campaigned around our Nation for 2 years, that there's an overwhelming, favorable sentiment among the people of our country that this legislation be passed.

Because of the complexity of the subject, you can see the volume that is required to express the Government position in law. And I believe that the good work of Chairman Jackson, Henry Jackson, and Mo Udall, many others behind me, is a testimony of persistence and enlightened leadership.

I think all of you know that Louise Dunlap has, in the last 6 years, organized and worked and been persistent in the face of diversity and disappointment.

I'm not completely satisfied with the legislation. I would prefer to have a stricter strip mining bill. I'm concerned with some of the features that had to be watered down during this session to get it passed, but I think that this provides us a basis on which we can make improvements on the bill in years to come.

I have some deep concerns about the provision concerning surface rights for properties in the West. And I will be consulting with Senator Dale Bumpers and Cecil Andrus and others to see how we might pursue this question in the future.

But in general, I'm very proud of the good work that all of you have done, the fine and very courageous stands that the Members of the House and Senate have taken. And it's with a great deal of pleasure that I, as President of our beautiful country, sign into law the strip mining act, House Resolution 2, which will provide for protection of our country in the future.

And I want to express my thanks to all those who have done so much work long before I became President. It's a great pleasure for me to come in now and to take at least partial credit for the fine work that all of you around me have done for so long.

Perhaps the Senator would like to say a few words? Mo? Congratulations to you. Would you like to say a word?

REPRESENTATIVE UDALL. Well, thank you, Mr. President.

Someone once said that there's no limit to what can be done if it doesn't matter who gets the credit. And this is the work, as the President has said, of many people.

I see faces here from the coal fields in Kentucky and West Virginia, who were fighting a lonely battle in those company towns, 10 or 15 years ago, before I got interested, some of the Members of Congress got interested.

I see former Members of Congress, people like Patsy Mink, who cochaired the subcommittee, Members of the Senate and the House, all kinds of good people who love this Nation and love its land. And as I said so many times when I was fighting with this good man here around the country, the people who don't respect and love the land don't respect themselves. And by getting this bill passed today, we are showing that this Nation loves its land and respects it and is going to protect the land while at the same time we increase the production of coal.

Thank you, Mr. President.

THE PRESIDENT. I don't think Senator Jackson and Lee Metcalf are here, but Jennings Randolph is here.

SENATOR RANDOLPH. Thank you, Mr. President.

It's my purpose to thank Lee Metcalf. I expect no man in the Senate or House labored more diligently, Mr. President, to bring this well-balanced legislation to final passage than Lee Metcalf. My tribute is to him and to you and to all those who labored. I think what has been done is in the best interests of the country.

Thank you very much.

THE PRESIDENT. Well, I just want to shake hands with a few more people. We don't want the bill to get wet.

NOTE: The President spoke at 9:15 a.m. at the signing ceremony in the Rose Garden at the White House.

As enacted, H.R. 2 is Public Law 95–87, approved August 3.

Archbishop Makarios III

Statement on the Death of the President of Cyprus. August 3, 1977

I was greatly saddened to learn of the untimely death of President Makarios. His passing deprives the Republic of Cyprus and the world of a great statesman. We share the sorrow of the people of Cyprus over the loss of a man whose many years as leader of the Cypriot nation have left such a deep mark on history.

NOTE: Archbishop Makarios became President of the Republic of Cyprus in 1959.

Press Secretary Jody Powell read the statement at his August 3 news conference at the White House. It was not issued in the form of a White House press release.

Appropriations Bill

Statement on Signing H.R. 7556 Into Law. August 3, 1977

The President has signed H.R. 7556, which authorizes FY 1978 appropriations of $7,709,432,000 for the Departments of State, Justice, and Commerce, the Judiciary, the Small Business Administration, USIA, the Legal Services Corporation, and other related agencies and commissions. It also provides $211,515,000 in 1977 supplemental appropriations for the disaster loan fund of the Small Business Administration, for the Board for International Broadcasting, and for certain agencies to cover increased pay costs of the executive and judicial pay increases.

The bill also contains prohibitions against use of funds for the President's amnesty program, for making commitments of aid to Vietnam, Cambodia, or Laos, and for negotiating settlement of U.S. claims against private property confiscated by Cuba at less than principal value.

The President issued a statement on signing the bill, noting his constitutional objection to the section which interferes with the amnesty program. The statement follows:

"I am signing H.R. 7556, the Departments of State, Justice, and Commerce, the Judiciary, and Related Agencies Appropriation Act for fiscal year 1978. I wish, however, to express my strong disagreement with Section 706 of this act.

"On January 21, 1977, pursuant to my power under the Constitution, I issued a proclamation granting, with certain exceptions, an unconditional pardon for Vietnam era violators of the Selective Service laws. By Executive order, I directed the Attorney General to take certain actions to implement the pardon proclamation. Section 706 purports to prohibit the use of funds appropriated under this act to carry out the Executive order. The prohibition relates to the three types of action called for by the Executive order: dismissal of indictments for certain violations of the Selective Service laws, termination of investigations regarding those violations, and permitting entry into the United States of aliens who might be excludable because of possible violation of the Selective Service laws.

"The first two aspects of Section 706 will have no real practical effect because the matters in question—dismissal of indictments and termination of investigations— do not actually depend upon the expenditure of funds by the Department of Justice. The third aspect is intended to preclude entry of certain aliens who, as a result of the pardon and the Executive order, may be entitled to enter. I am advised by the Department of Justice that this aspect of Section 706 is unconstitutional. It amounts to interference with the pardon power which is invested in the President by the Constitution. Moreover, it would be a bill of attainder because it would impose punishment, without judicial trial, upon an easily ascertainable group. In addition, certain applications of

Section 706 would constitute a denial of due process."

NOTE: As enacted, the Departments of State, Justice, and Commerce, the Judiciary, and Related Agencies Appropriation Act, 1978, is Public Law 95–86, approved August 2.

Department of Energy Organization Act and Bill Amending the Small Business Administration Act

Remarks on Signing S. 826 and H.R. 692 Into Law. August 4, 1977

THE PRESIDENT. I have two legislative acts that have now been passed by the Congress, which I intend to sign this morning. One is a bill that has been very important to me. It's concerning changes in the Small Business Administration to make it more feasible for myself, as President, and for the executive branch of Government to deal with victims of catastrophe such as floods, tornadoes.

And this legislation has been sponsored by the Senators from West Virginia and others. It makes it possible for lower interest loans for people whose homes have been destroyed, whose businesses have been destroyed, and more direct and instant assistance.

I'm particularly grateful that the majority leader, Senator Byrd, and Senator Jennings Randolph and the congressional delegation from West Virginia took the leadership in this legislation.

This is House of Representatives act 692, and it is with a great deal of pleasure that I sign this bill.

[*At this point, the President signed H.R. 692 into law.*]

I might point out that because of the great influence of these two gentlemen that I've just recognized, in the Senate the bill passed with a voice vote; in the House the vote was unanimous, 392 to 0.

For the first time in 11 years, a Cabinet-level department is now being created. The impending crisis of energy shortages has brought about an unprecedented quick action by the Congress in establishing the new Department of Energy.

This in some ways has been controversial legislation because many agencies of Government are now being brought together under one roof, about 50 different agencies. And in the future, the head of this Department will be a person working directly under the President, who can be identified for those who want to work together in our Nation to at least alleviate the consequences of inevitable shortages of oil and gas and other energy supplies.

Senator Ribicoff in the Senate, Congressman Jack Brooks in the House, and others who have worked closely with them—Senator Jackson, Senator Percy, Congressman Horton, and others that I could name—have done extraordinarily good work in bringing this legislation to completion. In only about 5 months this extremely complicated effort has been realized.

I want to point out that the Department can now, I think, begin to deal in a much more aggressive and effective way not only with the needs of suppliers to increase the production of oil, gas, coal, solar, nuclear powers, but also to make sure that consumers of our country are treated fairly, that prices are adequate and not excessive.

It can also work with the State Department and others in relationships with foreign countries. I'm very proud of this accomplishment by the Congress, and I'd like now to sign into law the Senate bill 826, which establishes the new Department of Energy.

[*At this point, the President signed S. 826 into law.*]

Of course, the next problem that we face is the selection of a person to head up the new Department of Energy. This has been a matter that's been of great concern to me for the last few months. I've decided to establish a search committee— [*laughter*]—to choose a Secretary, and I have asked Dr. James Schlesinger to head up the search committee. And at his request, the membership of the committee will be limited to one person. [*Laughter*]

I think that everyone who serves in the executive or legislative branches of our Government knows that because of his preeminent knowledge and stature and his sound judgment and, I think, political awareness and the trust of the American people in him, that he is a natural leader for this tremendous undertaking. And without waiting for his recommendation, I would like to ask if he would serve as the Secretary of the Department of Energy, and I would like to sign now a nomination request to the Senate of the United States, nominating James R. Schlesinger of Virginia to be Secretary of Energy, which is a new position in our Government.

Jim, would you like to say a word?

MR. SCHLESINGER. I'd just say that I'm delighted to be here and want to congratulate you on the Department of Energy that the House and Senate worked together to achieve, with the help of your own administration. And I hope that it will light the way to a better energy solution for this Nation.

REPRESENTATIVE BROOKS. Mr. President, organization is really policy. You have a great energy program, but it is absolutely essential that you have in place an organization that can make it work.

Under your leadership and that of Dr. Schlesinger, I am confident that we will start on the solution of all our energy problems.

THE PRESIDENT. We've got a long way to go on the energy policy, but I want to express my thanks at this moment to the House and Senate for the superb work they are already doing in this difficult area.

I believe that before the Congress adjourns, hopefully in October, that we will have an energy policy to make our Nation proud. And I want to express my thanks to you, Senator Byrd, and to others.

NOTE: The President spoke at 9:24 a.m. at the signing ceremony in the Rose Garden at the White House. As enacted, H.R. 692 is Public Law 95–89, and S. 826 is Public Law 95–91, both approved August 4.

Secretary of Energy

Nomination of James R. Schlesinger.
August 4, 1977

The President today announced that he will nominate James R. Schlesinger, of Arlington, Va., to be Secretary of Energy. Schlesinger is Assistant to the President with primary responsibility for energy matters.

He was born February 15, 1929, in New York City. He received an A.B. (1950), an A.M. (1952), and a Ph.D. (1956) in economics from Harvard University.

From 1955 to 1963, he served as assistant and associate professor of economics at the University of Virginia. He was associated with the Rand Corporation as a senior staff member from 1963 to 1967 and as director of strategic studies from 1967 to 1969.

Schlesinger worked for the Bureau of the Budget from 1969 to 1971, serving as Assistant Director and as Acting Director. From 1971 to 1973, he was Chairman of the Atomic Energy Commission. From February to July 1973, he was Director of Central Intelligence.

From 1973 to 1975, Schlesinger was Secretary of Defense. He was a visiting scholar at Johns Hopkins University from 1975 until December 1976, when then President-elect Carter named him as Assistant to the President for energy matters.

Schlesinger is the author of "The Political Economy of National Security" (1960) and coauthor of "Issues in Defense Economics" (1967). He was associate editor of the Journal of Finance in 1964–65. He has been a member of the board of associates of the Foreign Policy Research Institute at the University of Pennsylvania (1962–63) and a Frederick Sheldon Prize Fellow at Harvard (1950–51).

Visit of President Julius K. Nyerere of Tanzania

Remarks of the President and President Nyerere at the Welcoming Ceremony.
August 4, 1977

PRESIDENT CARTER. Fourteen years ago, a young leader of our own Nation, John Kennedy, welcomed a young leader of a new nation, Julius Nyerere from Tanzania, to our country. There was a sharing of ideals and hopes and a mutual declaration of frustration about the hatred and racial discrimination and deprivation of the poor prevalent throughout the world. It was an honor for our country to have this new leader come to see us when his own country was only 2 years old.

He's a man who has come from a small village, with a father who shaped his concepts about caring for those who need help and public service, a mother who kept the family close together in times of trial and tribulation when it was dangerous to express one's views about political change; a man who has deep religious convictions and who's been successful in his own country in translating those convictions into demonstrable concern about freedom, justice, equality, the alleviation of hunger, poverty, and disease.

Now, this same man, President Nyerere from Tanzania, comes back to our Nation still a strong leader who in his own country is known as "Teacher." He epitomizes what his country is, what it stands for. But now he's much more than a national leader; he's a wise man, experienced, a superb politician who recognizes that the structure of government can be used for beneficial purposes. He is admired in every council of world leaders throughout this globe—a senior statesman whose integrity is unquestioned and which never has been questioned; a man who has forgone material wealth and ease in a sacrificial way for his own people.

In the troubled continent of Africa, he's recognized as preeminent in his commitment to the hopes and purposes of free people. He's a well-educated man, a scholar, a philosopher, a great writer, one who probes for new ideas and who expresses them succinctly and clearly to shape the minds of other people in a beneficent and constructive way.

Our own Nation is deeply concerned about and with Africa. As a new President myself, I need his advice and his counsel and his friendship and his guidance as we try to act in a responsible and constructive fashion to bring about peace with justice in the 30 or more nations in Africa in the years ahead.

He can help me and others take the right stand as we bring about proper change toward majority rule in Rhodesia or Zimbabwe, in Namibia, and in the alleviation of racial discrimination throughout the continent of Africa and the rest of the world. I value his friendship and look forward today and tomorrow in having a chance to learn from him.

It is with a great sense of appreciation of what he is and a clear recognition of the honor bestowed upon our country by the visit of President Nyerere, I would like to say, on behalf of the American people, Mr. President, welcome, or in your language, *Karibu*.

Thank you very much.

PRESIDENT NYERERE. Mr. President, you have been very kind and very generous in your remarks about myself. If I had not jotted down my remarks, I would have found it extremely difficult to say a few words, but I do thank you with great sincerity for the warmth of your welcome to me and to my colleagues. I can assure you that I have very great pleasure in coming to your country at your invitation.

We in Tanzania, Mr. President, and in Africa generally, follow American politics with close attention. There is the intrinsic interest of the affairs of the most powerful nation the world has ever known. But more to the point, your politics do affect us. Indeed, we in Tanzania sometimes think that the world should somehow join in the process of electing the American President—[*laughter*]—for though we realize that the American people do not elect an absolute monarch, the world power structure is such that other peoples in other nations have a vital interest in the person whom the American people choose as their executive head of state.

We appreciate your own recognition, Mr. President, of this fact in the message to audiences abroad which you issued on your inauguration.

Let me, therefore, once again offer you, Mr. President, our congratulations on the honor and the heavy responsibility which the American people have given you.

I'm very happy to be in the White House today as your guest, just as I was the guest of your distinguished predecessor and my friend, the late President Kennedy, in 1963.

Mr. President, I am glad of this opportunity to discuss with you the matters of common interest between our two countries, but in particular, the problems of southern Africa, for we in Tanzania have greatly welcomed your administration's new approach to matters related to the liberation of my continent from colonialism and racialism. I am, therefore, looking forward to my discussions with you and your colleagues and with Members of Congress.

I'm also very happy to have been invited to spend a few extra days in this country and to have been given the opportunity to visit different parts of the country. I do not expect to become an expert on America from my brief visits to the different States of your great country, but I'm sure that I shall learn a great deal of interest to me and to my countrymen.

Once again, Mr. President, I thank you very much.

NOTE: The President spoke at 10:37 a.m. on the South Lawn of the White House.

White House Conference on Balanced Growth and Economic Development

Statement Announcing the Conference. August 4, 1977

A White House Conference on Balanced Growth and Economic Development will be held in Washington in early 1978. I strongly endorse the action of Congress requesting and authorizing this Conference.

This country has been committed to the goal of economic growth and full employment with stable prices since the 1940's. We need to provide jobs for a growing work force—our labor force increased by 3 million people within the last year—so that all of our people who want to and are able can work to create a better life for all Americans. The economy is improving, and unemployment is down almost a full point since its peak last November, but much remains to be done if future recessions, high inflation, and high unemployment are to be prevented and if we are to make real progress in getting the remainder of our people back to work.

Balanced growth does not mean neglecting the environment or making our energy problems worse. We must make wise use of our Nation's land, water, and energy resources. We must also remain sensitive to the wide variations in local and regional resources, needs, and economic conditions, so that our national economic progress will not be at the expense of any one group or area.

This Conference is an important opportunity for citizens organizations, public interest groups, labor and business representatives, and State and local officials to recommend ways in which my administration can work toward balanced economic growth and development in the years ahead.

I am pleased to announce the appointment of Dr. Michael S. Koleda, former vice president of the National Planning Association, as Director of the Conference. Under his able leadership, the Conference will become a national forum through which our concern about these issues and our determination to seek solutions can be expressed.

I have asked Secretary of Commerce Juanita M. Kreps to coordinate the efforts of her Department with those of the Departments of Agriculture and Housing and Urban Development and other departments and agencies in preparing for this Conference.

NOTE: On the same day, the White House announced the appointment, by Secretary of Commerce Juanita M. Kreps, of Dr. Michael S. Koleda as Director of the Conference.

Undocumented Aliens

Remarks on Transmitting a Message to the Congress.   August 4, 1977

I have an announcement to make this afternoon, and then following my brief statement, the Attorney General and the Director of the Immigration and Naturalization Service and the Labor Secretary will answer your questions.

Within this last decade, the problem of undocumented aliens or illegal aliens or undocumented workers has become increasingly severe. It now comprises a total of literally millions of people who have come into our country against the law and who are still in the United States.

Last year alone, 875,000 undocumented workers were apprehended by the immigration officials, and the estimates are that only one out of three coming into our country are actually caught.

Last month alone, in San Diego County, 35,000 undocumented workers were apprehended, and this is a 25-percent increase over last year. So, the problem is not only severe but it's getting worse.

I'm today sending the Congress a message on this complex problem of undocumented aliens. As you may know, we've been studying this problem for the last several months, and the Congress has been working on it for the last several years.

I'm proposing actions that would meet four major needs: first of all, to regain greater control over our own borders; secondly, to limit employment opportunities of those who are illegally in our country and who are competing with American workers for scarce jobs; third, the registration and the regulation of the millions of undocumented workers who are already here; and, fourth, improving cooperation with countries from which these undocumented workers are coming into our own Nation.

The proposals that I'm making to Congress fulfill each of these needs. First of all, border controls would be improved by adding at least 2,000 additional enforcement officers at the borders and by concentrating their presence where the crossing of our borders is most likely. Also, we will target our efforts against smuggling rings which now provide entry of undocumented aliens into our country.

Secondly, the employment opportunities would be limited by prohibiting employers, with strong civil penalties, from hiring undocumented aliens. The Justice Department would be responsible for the enforcement of the laws against these employers who habitually hire undocumented aliens, and if they violated court orders, of course, they would also be subject to criminal penalties.

In the process, we must be fair to the Latin American, Chinese-American, and other citizens who are here legally, so that an employer might not discriminate against them simply because of their racial origin.

We want to get as many of the millions of undocumented aliens as possible registered. And the inducement for this and a step that would give us tangible benefits would be to give them status which they do not presently enjoy—legal status.

Those who have been in this country since before 1970 would be eligible for permanent resident status and might start their 5-year process ultimately to become United States citizens. Those who entered between 1970 and 1977 would be eligible for temporary status, permitting them to remain here and to work, but on a temporary basis only. Those entering since the beginning of 1977 would be subject to immediate deportation.

The last point—to increase employment opportunities in the home countries from which the undocumented aliens come. We will work with the Government of Mexico—already are—and with other nations involved, to develop economic and technical assistance programs so it might be more attractive for undocumented workers who are here to go back

to their home countries and others to refrain from coming here illegally.

I hope that the Congress will move quickly on these proposals so that the actions can take effect very soon. We've worked very closely with the congressional leaders, and in the House, Congressman Rodino and Congressman Eilberg will sponsor this legislation. In the Senate, Senator Jim Eastland from Mississippi and Senator Ted Kennedy will sponsor the legislation. They have already told me that they will do it enthusiastically, and prompt hearings will begin on this subject.

I'd like to turn the rostrum over now to the other Government officials who will answer your questions about this matter.

NOTE: The President spoke at 2:20 p.m. to reporters assembled in the Briefing Room at the White House. Following his remarks, Attorney General Griffin B. Bell, Secretary of Labor Ray Marshall, and Leonel Castillo, Commissioner of the Immigration and Naturalization Service, held a news conference for reporters on the President's message.

Undocumented Aliens
Message to the Congress.   August 4, 1977

To the Congress of the United States:

I am proposing to Congress today a set of actions to help markedly reduce the increasing flow of undocumented aliens in this country and to regulate the presence of the millions of undocumented aliens already here.

These proposed actions are based on the results of a thorough Cabinet-level study and on the groundwork which has been laid, since the beginning of the decade, by Congressmen Rodino and Eilberg and Senators Eastland and Kennedy. These actions will:

• Make unlawful the hiring of undocumented aliens, with enforcement by the Justice Department against those employers who engage in a "pattern or practice" of such hiring. Penalties would be civil—injunctions and fines of $1000 per undocumented alien hired. Criminal penalties could be imposed by the courts against employers violating injunctions. Moreover, employers, and others, receiving compensation for knowingly assisting an undocumented alien obtain or retain a job would also be subject to criminal penalties.

• Increase significantly the enforcement of the Fair Labor Standards Act and the Federal Farm Labor Contractor Registration Act, targeted to areas where heavy undocumented alien hiring occur.

• Adjust the immigration status of undocumented aliens who have resided in the U.S. continuously from before January 1, 1970 to the present and who apply with the Immigration and Naturalization Service (INS) for permanent resident alien status; create a new immigration category of temporary resident alien for undocumented aliens who have resided in the U.S. continuously prior to January 1, 1977; make no status change and enforce the immigration law against those undocumented aliens entering the U.S. after January 1, 1977.

• Substantially increase resources available to control the Southern border, and other entry points, in order to prevent illegal immigration.

• Promote continued cooperation with the governments which are major sources of undocumented aliens, in an effort to improve their economies and their controls over alien smuggling rings.

Each of these actions will play a distinct, but closely related, role in helping to solve one of our most complex domestic problems: In the last several years, millions of undocumented aliens have illegally immigrated to the United States. They have breached our nation's immigration laws, displaced many American citizens from jobs, and placed an increased financial burden on many states and local governments.

The set of actions I am proposing cannot solve this enormous problem overnight, but they will signal the beginning of an effective Federal response. My Administration is strongly committed to aggressive and comprehensive steps toward resolving this problem, and I am therefore proposing the following actions:

EMPLOYER SANCTIONS

The principal attraction of the United States for undocumented aliens is economic—the opportunity to obtain a job paying considerably more than any available in their own countries. If that opportunity is severely restricted, I am convinced that far fewer aliens will attempt illegal entry.

I am therefore proposing that Congress make unlawful the hiring by any employer of any undocumented alien. This employment bar would be implemented in the following way:

• Enforcement would be sought against those employers who engage in a "pattern or practice" of hiring undocumented aliens, with the Justice Department setting priorities for enforcement.

• Penalties for violation of the employment bar would be both injunctive relief and stiff civil fines—a maximum of $1,000 for each undocumented alien hired by an employer. A violation of a court injunction would subject an employer to a potential criminal contempt citation and imprisonment.

• An employer would be entitled to defend any charge of hiring an undocumented alien by proving that a prospective employee's documentation of legal residence, as designated by the Attorney General in regulations, was seen prior to employment.

• The Social Security card would be designated as one of the authorized identification documents; and we will accelerate the steps already being taken to make certain that such cards are issued, as the law now mandates, only to legal residents. Those steps include requiring personal interviews of card applicants and making the cards more difficult to forge. But no steps would be taken to make the Social Security card, or any other card, a national identification document.

• To further restrict job opportunities, criminal sanctions would be imposed on those persons who receive compensation for knowingly assisting an undocumented alien obtain or retain employment, or who knowingly contract with such persons for the employment of undocumented aliens. These sanctions are directed at the substantial number of individuals who broker jobs for undocumented aliens or act as agents for alien smugglers. It is *not* directed at those who inadvertently refer an undocumented alien to a job, such as an employment agency or a union hiring hall.

To make certain that all of these new sanctions are uniformly applied, they would pre-empt any existing state sanctions.

In addition to the creation of these new sanctions, efforts to increase enforcement of existing sanctions will be significantly increased. The Fair Labor Standards Act, which mandates payment of the minimum wage and provides other employee protections, would not only be strictly enforced, but its existing civil and criminal penalties would be sought much more frequently by the government. To date, the inability of the government to enforce fully this Act, due in part to a lack of

resources, has resulted in the hiring of undocumented aliens at sub-minimum wages, thereby often displacing American workers. Two hundred sixty new inspectors will be hired and targeted to areas of heavy undocumented alien employment. Similarly, the Federal Farm Labor Contractor Registration Act, which prohibits the recruiting and hiring of undocumented aliens for farm work, would be tightly enforced. The Departments of Justice and Labor will work closely in exchanging information developed in their separate enforcement activities.

While I believe that both the new and existing employer sanctions, and their strict enforcement, are required to control the employment of undocumented aliens, the possibility that these sanctions might lead employers to discriminate against Mexican-American citizens and legal residents, as well as other ethnic Americans, would be intolerable. The proposed employer sanctions have been designed, with their general reliance on civil penalties and "pattern or practice" enforcement, to minimize any cause for discrimination. However, to prevent any discriminatory hiring, the federal civil rights agencies will be charged with making much greater efforts to ensure that existing anti-discrimination laws are fully enforced.

BORDER ENFORCEMENT

The proposed employer sanctions will not, by themselves be enough to stop the entry of undocumented aliens. Measures must also be taken to significantly increase existing border enforcement efforts. While our borders cannot realistically be made impenetrable to illegal entry, greater enforcement efforts clearly are possible, consistent with preserving both the longest "open" borders in the world and our humanitarian traditions.

I am proposing to take the following increased enforcement measures, most of which will require Congressional approval for the necessary additional resources:

• Enforcement resources at the border will be increased substantially and will be reorganized to ensure greater effectiveness. The exact nature of the reorganization, as well as the amount of additional enforcement personnel, will be determined after the completion in September of our ongoing border enforcement studies. It is very likely, though, that a minimum of 2000 additional enforcement personnel will be placed on the Mexican border.

• INS will shift a significant number of enforcement personnel to border areas having the highest reported rates of undocumented alien entry.

• An anti-smuggling Task Force will be established in order to seek ways to reduce the number and effectiveness of the smuggling rings which, by obtaining forged documents and providing transportation, systematically smuggle a substantial percentage of the undocumented aliens entering the country. The U.S. Attorneys will be instructed to give high priority to prosecuting individuals involved in alien smuggling.

• The State Department will increase its visa issuance resources abroad to ensure that foreign citizens attempting to enter this country will be doing so within the requirements of the immigration laws.

• Passage will be sought of pending legislation to impose criminal sanctions on those who knowingly use false information to obtain identifiers issued by our Government, or who knowingly use fraudulent Government documents to obtain legitimate Government documents.

• The State Department will consult with countries which are the sources of significant numbers of undocumented aliens about cooperative border enforcement and anti-smuggling efforts.

COOPERATION WITH SOURCE COUNTRIES

The proposed employer sanctions and border enforcement will clearly discourage a significant percentage of those who would otherwise attempt to enter or remain in the U.S. illegally. However, as long as jobs are available here but not easily available in countries which have been the source of most undocumented aliens, many citizens of those countries will ignore whatever barriers to entry and employment we erect. An effective policy to control illegal immigration must include the development of a strong economy in each source country.

Unfortunately, this objective may be difficult to achieve within the near future. The economies of most of the source countries are still not sufficiently developed to produce, even with significant U.S. aid, enough jobs over the short-term to match their rapidly growing workforce.

Over the longer-term, however, I believe that marked improvements in source countries' economies are achieveable by their own efforts with support from the United States. I welcome the economic development efforts now being made by the dynamic and competent leaders of Mexico. To further efforts such as those, the United States is committed to helping source countries obtain assistance appropriate to their own economic needs. I will explore with source countries means of providing such assistance. In some cases this will mean bilateral or multilateral economic assistance. In others, it will involve technical assistance, encouragement of private financing and enhanced trade, or population programs.

ADJUSTMENT OF STATUS

The fact that there are millions of undocumented aliens already residing in this country presents one of the most difficult questions surrounding the aliens phe-

1419

nomenon. These aliens entered the U.S. illegally and have willfully remained here in violation of the immigration laws. On the other hand, many of them have been law-abiding residents who are looking for a new life and are productive members of their communities.

I have concluded that an adjustment of status is necessary to avoid having a permanent "underclass" of millions of persons who have not been and cannot practicably be deported, and who would continue living here in perpetual fear of immigration authorities, the local police, employers and neighbors. Their entire existence would continue to be predicated on staying outside the reach of government authorities and the law's protections.

I therefore recommend the following adjustments of status:

First, I propose that permanent resident alien status be granted to all undocumented aliens who have resided continuously in the U.S. from before January 1, 1970 to the present. These aliens would have to apply for this status and provide normal documentary proof of continuous residency. If residency is maintained, U.S. citizenship could be sought five years after the granting of permanent status, as provided in existing immigration laws.

The permanent resident alien status would be granted through an update of the registry provisions of the Immigration and Nationality Act. The registry statute has been updated three times since 1929, with the last update in 1965, when permanent resident alien status was granted to those who had resided here prior to 1948.

Second, all undocumented aliens, including those (other than exchange and student visitors) with expired visas, who were residing in the United States on or before January 1, 1977 will be eligible for a temporary resident alien status for five years.

Those eligible would be granted the temporary status only after registering with INS; registration would be permitted solely during a one-year period. Aliens granted temporary status would be entitled to reside legally in the United States for a five-year period.

The purpose of granting a temporary status is to preserve a decision on the final status of these undocumented aliens, until much more precise information about their number, location, family size and economic situation can be collected and reviewed. That information would be obtained through the registration process. A decision on their final status would be made sometime after the completion of the registration process and before the expiration of the five-year period.

Temporary resident aliens would not have the right to vote, to run for public office or to serve on juries; nor would they be entitled to bring members of their families into the U.S. But they could leave and re-enter this country, and they could seek employment, under the same rules as permanent resident aliens.

Unlike permanent resident aliens, temporary resident aliens would be ineligible to receive such Federal social services as Medicaid, Food Stamps, Aid to Families with Dependent Children, and Supplemental Security Income. However, the allocation formulas for Revenue Sharing, which are based on population, would be adjusted to reflect the presence of temporary resident aliens. The adjustment would compensate states and local communities for the fact that some of these residents—undocumented aliens— are currently not included in the Census Bureau's population counts. That undercount deprives certain states and communities of Revenue Sharing funds which, if Census figures were completely accurate, would be received and used to defray certain expenses caused by the presence of undocumented aliens. Those receiving adjustments of status through the actions I am proposing would be included in the 1980 Census, so that the allocation charges would have to be made only through 1980.

Third, for those undocumented aliens who entered the United States after January 1, 1977, there would be *no* adjustment of status. The immigration laws would still be enforced against these undocumented aliens. Similarly, those undocumented aliens, who are eligible for adjustment of status, but do not apply, would continue to have the immigration laws enforced against them.

In addition, the INS would expedite its handling of the substantial backlog of adjustment of status applications from those aliens entitled to an adjustment under existing law.

Finally, those persons who would be eligible for an adjustment of status under these proposals must not be ineligible under other provisions of the immigration laws.

TEMPORARY FOREIGN WORKERS

As part of these efforts to control the problem of undocumented aliens, I am asking the Secretary of Labor to conduct, in consultation with the Congress and other interested parties, a comprehensive review of the current temporary foreign worker (H–2) certification program. I believe it is possible to structure this program so that it responds to the legitimate needs of both employees, by protecting domestic employment opportunities, and of employers, by providing a needed workforce. However, I am not considering the reintroduction of a bracero-type program for the importation of temporary workers.

IMMIGRATION POLICY

Our present immigration statutes are in need of a comprehensive review. I am therefore directing the Secretary of State, the Attorney General, and the Secertary of Labor to begin a comprehensive interagency study of our existing immigration laws and policies.

In the interim, I am supporting pending legislation to increase the annual limitation on legal Mexican and Canadian immigration to a total of 50,000, allocated between them according to demand. This legislation will help provide an incentive to legal immigration.

I urge the Congress to consider promptly, and to pass, the legislation I will submit containing the proposals described in this Message.

JIMMY CARTER

The White House,
August 4, 1977.

Intelligence Community

Announcement of Decisions on the Organization and Functions of the Community. August 4, 1977

Following consultations with the Vice President, his principal national security advisers, and congressional leaders, the President has completed his review of the NSC studies on the organization and functions of the intelligence community.

The President's decisions provide for needed changes while retaining the basic structural continuity of the intelligence community. The purpose of these changes is to provide for strong direction by the President and the National Security Council and to centralize the most critical national intelligence management functions under the Director of Central

Intelligence (DCI)—tasking, resources, and national analytic production. Left unchanged are operational and support activities as they are performed adequately today.

This organizational arrangement builds on the experience of the past by strengthening the role of the NSC system and the DCI. At the same time, it assures responsiveness to both the intelligence requirements of major, national-level consumers of intelligence and the operational needs of the departments and military services.

—For the first time, the major consumers of intelligence will be charged with the formal responsibility for formulating their requirements for substantive intelligence. Thus, the real requirements of the policymaking level, rather than technology or ability to collect, will drive the entire intelligence process.

—The DCI will also have the ability to respond to these requirements through his full control of:

1. a new mechanism for setting specific tasks for all intelligence-collection organizations, the National Intelligence Tasking Center;
2. his mandate to manage the budgets for all predominantly national intelligence activities;
3. his sole responsibility for the production of national analytical products.

Placing full responsibility for the most critical management functions in one authority should result in more productive and cost-effective foreign intelligence activities.

—The National Security Council will continue to play the leading role in overall direction of the intelligence community. The NSC Special Coordination Committee will continue to assume responsibility for review of the most sensitive intelligence operations and collection activities. The new Policy Review Committee, when chaired by the DCI, will provide the direction to both the collection and analytical production effort that was missing in the past.

—The recently strengthened Intelligence Oversight Board will continue to assist the President in investigating possible illegal or otherwise improper activities within the intelligence community and assuring that appropriate corrective actions are taken.

Here are the specifics of the reorganization:

1. The National Security Council should continue to provide guidance and direction for the development and formulation of all national intelligence activities. The NSC Policy Review Committee, chaired by the Director of Central Intelligence, will define and assign priority for substantive intelligence requirements and will evaluate the production of analytical intelligence reporting. The PRC will submit semi-annual reports to the NSC on its activities. Its membership will include the Secretary of State, Secretary of Defense, Secretary of the Treasury, the Assistant to the President for National Security Affairs, and other attendees as deemed appropriate by the Chairman.

2. The Director of Central Intelligence will have peacetime responsibility and authority for translating PRC-validated national intelligence requirements developed by the PRC into specific intelligence collection objectives and targets and for assigning these to intelligence collection organizations. For these purposes a National Intelligence Tasking Center, jointly manned by civilian and military personnel, will be established under the direction of the DCI to assign tasks to all national intelligence collection systems. The Tasking Center will also be responsible for ensuring that the resulting flow

of intelligence is routed immediately to relevant components and commands. In periods of crisis or in wartime, the power to assign collection tasks may be delegated to the Secretary of Defense upon the express direction of the President.

3. The Director of Central Intelligence should have full and exclusive authority for approval of the National Foreign Intelligence Program (NFIP) budget prior to its presentation (through usual procedures) to the President, for its presentation to Congress, for reprogramming of NFIP funds, and monitoring the implementation of programs. In response to the DCI's guidance, the departments and agencies of the NFIP will submit their proposed national program budgets to the DCI and assure that the DCI has all information necessary to perform his budgetary responsibilities. The National Foreign Intelligence Board will advise the DCI on all of his budgetary responsibilities in the same manner as it does on national intelligence production and other activities of common concern. Department heads will retain the right to appeal the DCI's budget decisions to the President. The Director of Central Intelligence will be provided with adequate staff support to ensure his full access to relevant information and the capability to carry out audits and evaluations of intelligence programs.

4. The Director of Central Intelligence will continue to act as the primary adviser to the National Security Council and the President on substantive foreign intelligence and to have full responsibility for production of national intelligence in appropriate consultation with departmental analytical centers. He will retain all other powers provided to him under relevant statutes and Executive orders.

5. Apart from the foregoing, line authority will remain with the heads of the relevant departments and agencies. All other organizational and operational arrangements and responsibilities assigned under existing statutes and Executive orders shall remain in full effect. Personnel and administration, management and support activities, operational implementation of DCI tasking, and audit/inspector general functions will remain as presently assigned under departmental arrangements.

These decisions will be embodied in a new Executive order for the intelligence community as an interim measure until appropriate charter legislation can be introduced and enacted by Congress.

Visit of President Nyerere of Tanzania

Toasts of the President and President Nyerere at a Working Dinner for the Tanzanian President. August 4, 1977

PRESIDENT CARTER. Infrequently on the world scene, there arises a young leader at the beginning of the history of a nation who in a strange but all pervasive way represents what his people are and what his country hopes to be. And our guest tonight is that kind of leader.

Fourteen years ago, he came here when his nation was 2 years old. He had been searching for a role of leadership in a sacrificial way, came from a small town, and came to visit our young President, President John Kennedy. They exchanged ideas about the future, and he honored our country then by coming.

Now our guest, President Nyerere from Tanzania, has come here as a distinguished senior citizen—still young in body and in spirit, but experienced and respected and, a man who, when he speaks, has others listen; a man of modesty and great achievement who, in my opinion, holds the key to the future of peace and equality of treatment and opportunity and freedom in Africa as dearly and as closely as any person alive.

I'm very honored that he would come and meet with me today and tomorrow and to visit us in the White House tonight. I've been talking to him about ground nuts—[*laughter*]—and life in the rural area and his struggle for a good education and what his religious life means to him and the impact of his father on his social consciousness. And I've learned a lot about him in the process.

We have a need for advice and counsel and cooperation and mutual support, because the tremendous power of our country can be felt in the region of the world which is of great interest to President Nyerere.

The southern part of Africa, as you well know, is one that's troubled, where people are struggling to escape from the historical impact of colonialism and trying to do it peacefully.

We, like Tanzania, were formerly subjects of the British Crown, and we had a military victory to achieve independence. Tanzania had a victory in a peaceful fashion.

We now see other nations struggling for their own independence, where their own people might make a judgment as to who their leaders might be and the form of their government and the policies of their nation.

Rhodesia is one of those countries; Namibia is another. And the national leaders who hope to lead the new nation of Zimbabwe in the future look to our guest for counsel and for guidance and for support and for leadership and for inspiration.

He has joined with others for many years in struggling for a peaceful solution to the problems in Zimbabwe and Namibia. That has not yet been successful. And I think it's accurate to say that he and other front line Presidents and some of the leaders of the Western democracies in Europe and in our continent—if we are able to work in concert and to strive for justice and fairness—might very well bring a peaceful resolution to these questions in the southern part of Africa. That's my hope and my prayer. And I believe that this is the desire of the world.

Our Nation is blessed with great individual riches. The people in President Nyerere's country are relatively poor in material things, but they are blessed with a leader and officials of the government who are stable and respected and beloved, and justifiably so, by the people whom they lead.

We are honored at your presence, Mr. President, and I would like to propose a toast to the free and independent and lighthearted and hopeful people of your great country and to you, one of the leaders of the world.

PRESIDENT NYERERE. Mr. President, this is the second occasion I've listened to you talking about myself and my country. On both occasions, I feel a lump coming here, and then I feel, well, my notes are prepared, but I think the lump will go down. [*Laughter*]

I do want to thank you very much, Mr. President, for the encouraging words you've been saying about myself and my country, both this morning and now.

I have recently been reading some very good books about President Washington and his times. And I have come to the conclusion that the problems of young countries can be very similar. Although your Nation came into existence some 200 years ago, I suspect that if the first President of your country returned to Earth now, he might find it easier to understand the problems of Tanzania—[*laughter*]—better than he understands the problems which you face in the United States. I expect he might even be able to understand better my one-party system than your multi-party system. [*Laughter*]

For coming from Tanzania in 1977, I am very conscious of a few facts: Your country is now 201 years old; it is a firmly established political system, strong enough to withstand political crisis of great intensity and which cannot be upset by the intrigues or maneuvers of any other country. The United Republic of Tanzania became independent less than 16 years ago. Our union is just 13 years old, and we replaced our interim constitution only a few months ago. And not less relevant, in area, Tanzania is one-tenth the size of the United States; its population is less than one-thirteenth of your population. And the national income of Tanzania is a minute fraction of the national income of your country.

These facts, Mr. President, must affect the relationship between our two countries, and at least Tanzania's attitude towards your country. If you don't mind me saying it, where the law of the jungle still reigns, the pigmies are very wary of the giants. [*Laughter*]

For questions of world peace and justice do affect both of our countries, regardless of our differences in size. But your country is not only concerned about the problems of maintaining peace and building justice everywhere, as my country is; the great size and strength of your country and its economic power mean that the United States is also directly or indirectly involved in these matters everywhere in the world.

It is therefore not strange that in the United States and in our discussions, I should be concerned to learn more about your ideas and policies towards Africa. Nor is it surprising that I welcome the opportunity to explain to you and to your colleagues our commitment to the liberation of southern Africa from colonialism and racialism and our ideas about how this can be brought about.

Yet although the situation in southern Africa is simple in principle, it is not a simple one in practice. To achieve the liberation of Africa, we have to bring to an end the political, economic, and military structures in Rhodesia, in Namibia and South Africa, which are of longstanding and great, although varying, strength.

These structures will, sooner or later, be changed. The forces of nationalism cannot be defeated in the long run, and men will never willingly accept deliberate and organized humiliation as the price of existence. But how and how quickly these changes can be brought about is of vital concern to all the peoples of these areas, both black and white, to the rest of Africa, and also to the rest of the world.

It is unlikely that Tanzania and your country, Mr. President, will agree on all aspects of "how" and "how quickly" some of these changes will be able to be brought about in southern Africa. The problem of southern Africa has an urgency and a priority to Tanzania which this country may not share. But I believe that our two Governments will not, on this issue, again find themselves working for different objectives; I think we shall also find some points of agreement on how to assist the necessary changes.

For we in Tanzania have noticed with great pleasure the emphasis which you, Mr. President, and your colleagues give to support for human rights in the world. We welcome this emphasis. I am well aware that, as you yourself have said about America, no country warrants a clean report on this matter of human rights—certainly, Tanzania does not. No one in this country could be more aware of our faults than I am myself. But I do believe it to be important that this powerful country, whose Founding Fathers gave to the world that immortal liberation manifesto, the American Declaration of Independence, is now allowing this concern for human rights to influence its policies on major world issues and its relations with other countries in the world.

You have also said, Mr. President, that questions of human rights cannot be the only factor affecting America's relations with others, especially when the security of the United States is concerned. In saying that you were, it seems to me, just being honest and open with the people who elected you. For there is a realism in action forced upon practicing politicians, but which philosophers and others without responsibility can evade. This is also, unfortunately, the kind of realism which can lead to differences between statesmen who share the same broad political goals.

In the case of southern Africa, however, we believe that the long-term interests of the United States lie in the rapid end of racialism and colonialism in southern Africa.

In particular, the United States is now struggling to rectify the bitter effects of centuries of racial inequality and discrimination in your own country. I do not believe this struggle within your country would be made easier by the continued racial insult of apartheid in South Africa and the institutionalized racial domination in Rhodesia.

We have been greatly impressed and encouraged by what you, Mr. President, and your colleagues, the Vice President, the Secretary of State, and your Ambassador to the United Nations have been saying about these matters. And now I've had the chance to exchange views with you, and I'm greatly impressed and

greatly encouraged. For in the past, American power has been an impediment to Africa's liberation; now, we feel that your power can be an aid to our struggle.

Your coming to the White House, Mr. President, has not changed the international law of the jungle, but our apprehensions have been greatly reduced by your coming to the White House.

Mr. President, our two countries are also mutually involved in other issues, especially matters relating to the international economic system, the law of the sea, and the general relations between the rich and the poor nations of this world. On these and similar subjects, the differences in our power and wealth and our different approach to questions of production and distribution may continue to keep our representatives on different sides at relevant international conferences. I do not pretend that these matters are small matters. Malnutrition and preventable disease, ignorance, and the lack of any resources with which to fight these evils are very fundamental to those personally affected.

But even in this area, it may be that we can extend our points of agreement a little. And I do believe that greater mutual understanding can flow from our discussion on these topics also, and that this will be promoted by the good will which you and your colleagues have shown to me and my colleagues and which we in Tanzania feel towards you, Mr. President, and the people of your country.

And now, friends, I also ask you to stand up and join me in a toast to President Carter and to the people of the United States.

NOTE: The President spoke at 9 p.m. in the State Dining Room at the White House.

Youth Employment and Demonstration Projects Act of 1977

Remarks on Signing H.R. 6138 Into Law. August 5, 1977

THE PRESIDENT. I think this is a good week for my administration, for the Congress, and for the whole Nation.

This morning I will sign the final legislative act which implements the stimulus package that the Congress has approved to add to our economy crucial elements that it lacked 6 or 8 months ago.

We are now adding in public service jobs throughout our country 15,000 per week. In June, the taxpayers of our country began to receive permanent benefits in tax reductions amounting to $5.2 billion a year. Public service jobs that will improve the quality of neighborhoods and cities, towns, and provide additional jobs for our people are being contracted now at the rate of 1,000 per week. This is the first practical application of the beneficial legislation that Congress has passed.

This morning I want to express, first of all, my deep thanks to the congressional leaders who have been involved in the passage of a program to put our young people to work. Chairman Carl Perkins, Chairman Gus Hawkins, Senator Pete Williams, Senator Gaylord Nelson— all the chairmen of major committees have been very helpful; the Conservation Corps chairmen, Scoop Jackson and Lloyd Meeds, and I particularly want to recognize Senator Humphrey, who has been in favor of a Youth Conservation Corps for the last 20 or 25 years.

I think it's good to point out, too, that we have with us this morning Congressman Roybal and perhaps many others, including my own cousins—I was not quite old enough—who benefited from the

Civilian Conservation Corps back in the Depression years, implemented under President Franklin Roosevelt.

This House of Representatives act 6138 does four major things to correct a very serious deficiency. Although the unemployment rate has dropped in our country more than one percent already since last December, we still have enormous unemployment among young people. More than half the total number of unemployed in our country are under 24 years of age. And of course, this falls much more heavily on minority young people than it does those of us who are male and white.

This bill will take a great stride forward in trying to correct this serious affliction on our Nation's economy which is mirrored within the nations of all the Western democracies. I think all of us realize that if a young person reaches the age of 16, 17, 18, all the way up to 24 years of age and can't get a job in the formative years of a life, there is a feeling of despair, discouragement, a loss of self-esteem, an alienation from the structure of society, a lashing out against the authorities who are responsible, which can shape that life for years to come.

We are trying to address that now in the first major step forward. We will not only provide jobs under this program, but we will also learn about the best mechanisms for increasing jobs even more in the future.

The Young Adult Conservation Corps will permit young people from areas of high unemployment to go in the open spaces, in our farmlands, forest lands, parks, and work in constructive and enjoyable surroundings under the supervision of the Interior Department and the Agriculture Department.

During this summer, prior to the passage of this legislation, we have already run experimental programs so that the transition period will be very brief. In addition, the Youth Community Conservation and Improvement projects will provide similar job opportunities in the urban areas when, because of practical considerations, we can't and do not want to transfer young people away from their own homes.

We'll conduct pilot projects with the major part of the funds available, over a billion dollars in all, to provide innovative approaches to correcting this chronic unemployment among young people. In the process, we'll more than double the Job Corps, which is one of the programs that's already proven to be effective.

So the cumulative effect of this legislation will single out young people and give them a chance in life and is the last in a series of programs that have now been approved and funded by the Congress, whose beneficial impact is just beginning to be felt in our country.

I think there has been a restoration of trust among the people of our Nation. This has been indicated by an improvement in the economic circumstances throughout our country. These new programs will provide additional incentives for the people to believe that in our own country, that there is a chance to lead a productive life as part of a system; at the same time, to correct the deficiencies which we all deplore.

Saturday morning in Plains, I will reveal the proposal for changing in a beneficial way the confused welfare system. And we have worked on this at length.

But the cumulative total of all these efforts, which have been passed by the Congress and which will be addressed by the Congress, are extremely beneficial to our country. And I want to express my deep thanks to the Members of the Congress in the House and Senate, to the

mayors and Governors who are here, to representatives of business and labor, to young people who have already benefited from these programs and who look forward to doing it even more in the future, for their support in the passage of this fine legislation to cut down the blight of youth unemployment in the United States.

REPRESENTATIVE CARL D. PERKINS. Mr. President, to my way of thinking, your affixing your signature to this most important legislation is one of the greatest days in the history of our Government insofar as the employment of needy youth is concerned, which in that particular area in the forest is gradually becoming a lost art.

I certainly feel that the whole country wishes to compliment you for taking the lead in seeing that legislation of this type became law. You certainly deserve the compliments of all the youth in this country and all the taxpayers in this country in getting these youth off the streets.

Thank you.

SENATOR HARRISON A. WILLIAMS, JR. Thank you very much, Mr. President.

In your message, I think you addressed yourself to all of the thoughts that were on our minds as we fashioned this program to reach out to youth and to give them that start as productive citizens, believing in the system, believing in themselves.

I'm one here—and there aren't many that remember the Civilian Conservation Corps, CCC. We still hear, from people who were part of that, that that President Roosevelt measure, in that case, made men of poor boys that had a productive job. We have included that as part of this program.

I think that it's a message of great hope to the young people of our country, and I was glad to be part of it and applaud this administration and you, Mr. President, for passing it.

THE PRESIDENT. So many Members of Congress have helped, I think I will be safer if I don't call on other people to speak. [*Laughter*] But these were the two key chairmen, and there were at least six different congressional committees that played an instrumental role in this. And I want to express again my thanks to them all. Thank you and congratulations.

NOTE: The President spoke at 9:15 a.m. at the signing ceremony in the Rose Garden at the White House.

As enacted, H.R. 6138 is Public Law 95–93, approved August 5.

Task Force on Women Business Owners

Memorandum for the Heads of Certain Departments and Agencies. August 4, 1977

Memorandum for the Secretary of the Treasury, the Secretary of Defense, the Secretary of Labor, the Secretary of Commerce, the Secretary of Health, Education, and Welfare, the Administrator of General Services Administration, the Administrator of Small Business Administration

Subject: Task Force on Women Business Owners

As consumers, investors, and workers, women play a vital role in the nation's economy. But the number and size of women-owned businesses remain remarkably small. According to the 1972 Census statistics—the most recent available—the receipts generated by firms owned by women entrepreneurs represented only three-tenths of one percent of the total for all business firms.

In small business especially, women business owners face the traditional problems of lack of adequate capital, lack of marketing and procurement opportunities, and lack of management and technical assistance.

And in addition to these problems, they face the barriers created by negative attitudes toward women.

This Administration wants to encourage women to become business owners, to mitigate conditions and practices that place women at a competitive disadvantage, and to enhance Federal assistance to women entrepreneurs. However, there is a serious lack of current and accurate information on which to base actions in support of these commitments.

To provide this kind of information, I am establishing a Task Force on Women Business Owners. The Task Force shall:

1. Identify existing data on women entrepreneurs, assess its adequacy, identify needs for additional data and propose methods of collecting it;

2. Identify the primary practices or conditions
   a) which discourage women from becoming entrepreneurs; or
   b) which have the effect of discriminating against women entrepreneurs or placing them at a competitive disadvantage;

3. Assess current federal programs and practices
   a) which have the effect of discriminating against women entrepreneurs or placing them at a competitive disadvantage; or
   b) which are designed to mitigate the conditions and practices which place women entrepreneurs at a competitive disadvantage;

4. Based on these assessments, propose changes in federal law, regulation and practice for carrying out the commitment of the Administration, and advise as to the impact, if any, of such changes on the federal budget.

I request that the addressees of this memorandum designate a person to serve on this Task Force. Members from executive departments shall be of a rank of not less than Deputy Assistant Secretary, and members from other agencies should be of a comparable rank. The designee of the Commerce Department shall chair the Task Force. A member of the White House Domestic Policy staff shall serve as an ex officio member of the Task Force.

Executive departments and agencies not represented by membership on the Task Force may participate on committees established by the Task Force to carry out its work. In addition, I request that all heads of executive departments and agencies, upon request, furnish to the Task Force such information and assistance as is relevant to the purpose of the Task Force.

The Task Force is authorized to take such additional actions, not inconsistent with this Memorandum, as it determines to be necessary and appropriate in fulfilling its purpose. The Secretary of Commerce may appoint or designate staff to carry out the functions of the Task Force.

The Task Force shall report its findings and recommendations to me, conclude its work, and dissolve itself within 120 days of its first meeting.

JIMMY CARTER

cc: Heads of Executive Departments and Agencies

NOTE: The text of the memorandum was released on August 5.

Interagency Task Force on Occupational Safety and Health

Memorandum for the Heads of Executive Departments and Agencies.   August 5, 1977

Memorandum for the Heads of Executive Departments and Agencies

I have frequently expressed my commitment to review and reform the Federal role in combatting safety and health hazards in the workplace. My aim is to improve the effectiveness of our efforts to protect the health and safety of American workers.

The Secretary of Labor, Ray Marshall, and the Assistant Secretary for Occupational Safety and Health, Eula Bingham, have already moved vigorously to make our approach to occupational safety and health more sensible and effective. On May 19, 1977, the Labor Department announced a program to redirect the resources of the Occupational Safety and Health Administration (OSHA) away from trivial problems and toward more serious hazards to safety and health.

In another step towards common sense priorities, the Department of Labor announced on July 19 a program to reduce OSHA paperwork and streamline its recordkeeping requirements. The nation's 3.4 million small businesses will be exempt from filling out complicated job health and safety forms, and the paperwork for 1.5 million larger employers will be cut in half. Over the coming weeks, the Administration will take additional steps to reduce unnecessary burdens and allow OSHA to concentrate on the most serious hazards.

To complement these internal changes at OSHA, I have asked Ray Marshall and Bert Lance to head an interagency task force that will consider ways to strengthen the Federal role in protecting workplace safety and health. This task force will report to me with its first recommendations for action by April 30, 1978.

In addition to the Secretary of Labor and the Director of the Office of Management and Budget, this interagency group on worker safety and health protection will include the Departments of Commerce, Health, Education and Welfare and the Council of Economic Advisers, the Domestic Policy Staff, and the Small Business Administration. From time to time, I expect other departments and agencies to participate actively.

I want to be sure that federal programs actually do reduce threats to the health and safety of American workers, and that they help employers make the necessary adjustments. The inquiry will concentrate upon:

• Exploration of incentives that might supplement workplace safety regulations. These might include improved education and information services, economic aid and tax incentives to help employers improve workplace safety, changes in workers' compensation and liability laws and deterrent penalty structures.

• Evaluation of the government-wide administration of Federal workplace safety and health activities. This will include investigation of duplication, overlap and gaps in Federal agency jurisdiction.

• Review of other ways to improve the safety and health efforts of all Federal agencies, including those programs that affect Federal employees, and the resources devoted to them.

As you know, improvement of Federal health and safety protection measures is a matter of intense concern to the American people. This effort will be part of our larger program of looking at innovative approaches to many regulatory issues. It will help shape our reform program in other regulatory areas and will, I am confident, be one of this Administration's most valuable accomplishments.

You may be asked to contribute time, resources, and staff to this effort. I know I can count on your assistance.

In order to inform all affected parties that this review is underway, I have directed that this memorandum be published in the FEDERAL REGISTER.

JIMMY CARTER

International Security Assistance Act of 1977
Statement on Signing H.R. 6884 Into Law. August 5, 1977

I am signing into law H.R. 6884, the International Security Assistance Act of 1977. The programs made possible by this law include military assistance, international military education and training, and foreign military sales. The bill gives the United States an important tool with which to help meet reasonable and legitimate defense needs of our friends and allies. Such help contributes to our own security.

When I requested these authorizations from Congress in March, I emphasized my commitment to reducing conventional arms transfers throughout the world and to imposing greater discipline on our own arms transfers. Recently I announced a policy of restraint which is a major step toward my goal. And the military programs authorized by H.R. 6884 will help us make further progress by fostering the climate of security so important to lasting reductions in the world's arms trade.

I am pleased to note that some two-thirds of the funds authorized by the bill, as I had requested, will be for non-military programs. These will help bring economic and political stability to troubled regions of the world. The security supporting assistance programs in the bill differ somewhat from those which I proposed to Congress, but I believe that H.R. 6884 will nevertheless permit us to carry out an effective overall program in fiscal year 1978. I welcome, in particular, this bill's recognition of the special importance of security supporting assistance in the Middle East and in southern Africa.

However, I must note my serious concern over sections 16 and 20 of the bill. These provisions amend the Arms Export Control Act in such a way as to let Congress prevent Presidential action authorized under law simply by adopting a concurrent resolution of disapproval. Such provisions raise major constitutional questions, since Article I, section 7 of the Constitution requires that congressional action having the force and effect of law be presented to the President for approval. These provisions also have the potential of involving Congress in the execution of the laws, a responsibility reserved for the President under the Constitution. I am approving H.R. 6884 because of its importance to our foreign relations and national security, but I must express my deep reservations about these two provisions and my intention to preserve the constitutional authority of the President.

I intend to carry out the programs authorized by H.R. 6884—the first security assistance legislation of my administration—in such a way as to improve prospects for international peace and security.

NOTE: As enacted, H.R. 6884 is Public Law 95–92, approved August 4.

United States Naval Academy Board of Visitors

Letter to the Chairman of the Board on Receiving the Board's Annual Report for 1976.   August 5, 1977

To General Victor Krulak

I have just received from the Secretary of Defense the November 1976 Report of the Naval Academy Board of Visitors and wish to extend to you, as the elected Chairman of the Board, my sincere appreciation for the leadership so capably demonstrated in the preparation of this excellent report.

The comments and recommendations emphasize the Board's commitment to a Naval Academy whose growth will be equal to the challenge of the future. You have made a significant contribution to that vital undertaking and the security it provides our country.

Sincerely,

JIMMY CARTER

[Lt. General Victor H. Krulak, USMC (Ret.), President, Copley News Service, 350 Camino De La Reina, San Diego, California 92108]

NOTE: The text of the letter was made available by the White House Press Office. It was not issued in the form of a White House press release.

Visit of President Nyerere of Tanzania

Remarks to Reporters Following the President's Departure. August 5, 1977

REPORTER. Mr. President, has President Asad made it more difficult to arrange for a Geneva conference?

THE PRESIDENT. I don't know. I haven't gotten any reports lately. I'd rather not comment on it, not yet.

Q. What can you tell us, sir, about the outcome of the visit with President Nyerere?

THE PRESIDENT. Well, President Nyerere is a man who has the best insight into African problems of anyone I've ever met. I think he has the trust and confidence of almost all of the other nations in Africa and obviously is a natural scholar, student, historian, and political leader. He and I have reached, I think, almost complete agreement over the goals and purposes of diplomatic efforts relating to Rhodesia and Namibia. And we will try to carry out those purposes, working as closely as we can together, recognizing, of course, that many other nations and leaders will be involved.

But we have, I think, made a great deal of progress in our meetings these last 2 days, and I've developed an increasing respect for him.

Q. Did he say that he would let the American-British effort run to see if it could have a successful consequence?

THE PRESIDENT. Well, we hope and expect that the basic premises of a so-called British and American plan would be supported by President Nyerere. He can speak for himself. So far as I know, they are.

Secretary Vance will be consulting with the British officials in London, with perhaps the Foreign Minister of South Africa, and if the schedule can be arranged, subsequent to that meeting, with President Nyerere directly. And following that series of meetings, which will be completed, I think, on the 13th of this month, we'll have a much clearer picture of where we go from here on both Rhodesia and Namibia.

I think all parties have come a long way in the last few weeks. We don't know what the SWAPO leaders will decide. Sam Najoma is now in New York to give the viewpoint of the Namibian political leaders in exile, known as SWAPO, and I think they'll be consulting with our representative, Ambassador McHenry, within the next couple of days. We have not yet gotten from them their views.

If there is a general agreement between South Africa, the frontline presidents, ourselves, and SWAPO, then I think the United Nations would be prepared to move to implement free elections in Namibia without further delay.

Q. Mr. President, did President Nyerere agree to convene a conference of frontline states, or what was the—[*inaudible.*]

THE PRESIDENT. I think that would have to wait until after he met with Secretary Vance on the 13th. If things go according to our hopes, then I think that he would naturally bring together the other frontline presidents to see if their views were compatible with his own. I hope that will come about.

Q. Mr. President, President Nyerere also called for stricter enforcement of U.N. sanctions against the southern African minority—[*inaudible*]—as well as fewer American—[*inaudible*]—in South

Africa. Are you prepared to support those efforts?

THE PRESIDENT. Well, I think that that decision would have to depend on the degree of good faith which we detect among the South African leaders, in trying to bring about the purposes of the United Nations, and the citizens of Rhodesia and Namibia. We have lately been encouraged by constructive moves in South Africa concerning Namibia. There are still some difficult questions to be resolved. But I think at this point, the best thing to do is to encourage South Africa to continue their cooperative attitude and to join in under United Nations Resolution 385 in bringing about a free Namibia. If so, I think the threat of additional sanctions would be inappropriate.

Now, if the South Africans become an obstacle to further progress, then some sort of additional influence on our part against South Africa would probably be advisable.

Q. The reason we were asking about President Asad, we wonder if in turning down the working group concept, he wasn't, however, leaving the door open to some other way of making a preparation for Geneva?

THE PRESIDENT. I think it would be a mistake to attach too much importance to news reports and press conference statements at the conclusion of the meetings, because there are literally hundreds of options being discussed with each one of these leaders. Almost all of them are reluctant to make a unilateral statement until we know what the attitude of the other leaders might be.

And following the visit of Secretary Vance to Egypt, to Lebanon, to Syria and, now, to Jordan and Saudi Arabia, he'll go back to Israel and that will conclude his first interviews. If necessary, he will then consult with some of the Arab leaders about the reaction of Israel to their proposals.

Q. He might go back to Mr. Asad?

THE PRESIDENT. Either go back physically or communicate with him directly. But I think it's such a fluid thing, and there are so many conflicting options, that we are trying to find some formula by which those conflicting options might be harmonized, at least for a next step toward a peaceful resolution.

But it's an extremely difficult question, and I think to emphasize the few negative aspects of disagreements at this point possibly distorts the progress or minimizes progress that is being made.

I still believe that all the leaders in the Middle East genuinely want to have peace, obviously on their own terms. But I also believe that they are willing to negotiate and depart from their own previous terms if they feel that they can have their own security guaranteed and an end to the constant threat of war.

Q. Do you think Geneva is still a probability?

THE PRESIDENT. I think so, yes.

Q. With Palestinian representation?

THE PRESIDENT. I'll have to wait until later to answer that.

NOTE: The President spoke at 12:10 p.m. on the South Grounds of the White House.

Visit of President Nyerere of Tanzania

White House Statement Issued Following the Conclusion of the Meetings Between the President and President Nyerere.   August 5, 1977

President Julius K. Nyerere of the United Republic of Tanzania met yesterday and today with the President. They reviewed political and economic development in Africa and their relationship to global issues, as well as to subjects directly bearing on United States and Tanzanian relations.

President Nyerere outlined current political and development trends in Africa for the President, focusing in some detail on the problems of southern Africa. They discussed the prospects for negotiated settlements in southern Africa.

The President expressed his great pleasure at welcoming President Nyerere as not only the first African leader to pay a state visit to his administration, but equally as an African statesman. The President reaffirmed our deep and continuing interest in obtaining a peaceful solution to the problems of southern Africa, our interest in cooperating with Tanzania in solving its development problems, and discussed United States positions on matters of global interest to Tanzania. The President also declared his firm desire to make more intimate the warm and cooperative relations which exist between our two countries.

President Nyerere thanked the President for his cordial welcome to the United States. He reaffirmed Tanzania's commitment to just and, hopefully, peaceful, negotiated settlements in southern Africa. Further, President Nyerere expressed his pleasure at meeting President Carter and his keen desire to continue the close, personal relationship the two men achieved.

Government Steel Purchases

Memorandum for the Secretary of Defense and the Administrator of General Services. August 5, 1977

Memorandum for the Secretary of Defense, Administrator of General Services

In recent weeks several domestic steel producers have announced price increases for tin mill and structural steel products. If these price increases hold, they would bring the total price increases of steel mill products to 12½ percent over September a year ago. In contrast, the average price increases for all industrial commodities have been about 7 percent over the past year.

I am asking the Council on Wage and Price Stability to begin immediately a study of prices, costs, and the overall economic position of steel manufacturing. I have also asked the Council to monitor developments in tin mill and structural steel markets closely over the next few months. In addition, I am asking for your assistance.

Your agency is responsible for the procurement of a major portion of those goods and services purchased by the Federal Government. I would like your contracting and purchasing officers to be particularly alert to the comparative prices of steel supplies. Those regulations designed to insure the procurement of lowest cost goods should be carefully followed. Where existing procurement regulations provide an opportunity for judgments, or the exercise of your discretion, you should be aware of the importance to my anti-inflation program of purchasing steel at the lowest possible cost.

JIMMY CARTER

Study of Steel Industry Prices and Costs

Memorandum for the Chairman of the Council on Wage and Price Stability. August 5, 1977

Memorandum for Chairman of the Council on Wage and Price Stability

In the year since September, 1976, the price of steel products made in the United States will have risen 12.5 percent. This contrasts sharply with an annual rate of price increase for all industrial commodities of only 7 percent.

There is no doubt that the steel industry has experienced sharp increases in costs. Despite rapid price increases, profitability in the steel industry remains weak.

Nevertheless, the continuation of the kind of price and cost increases that we have been witnessing in one of our most basic industries clearly jeopardizes our efforts to achieve a deceleration in the overall rate of inflation. A steel industry able to produce steel at low cost, using the most modern techniques, is important to the overall well-being of the United States.

I am therefore directing the Council on Wage and Price Stability to begin immediately an updated study of prices, costs, and general economic conditions in the steel industry. I expect the Council to report to me by September 30, 1977. In its report the Council should pay particular attention to:

(1) identifying the sources and reasons for increasing costs in the steel industry.

(2) examining the impact of Federal policies on steel costs, prices, and economic conditions facing the industry.

(3) actions which the Federal Government might take to moderate cost and price pressures in this industry.

JIMMY CARTER

Digest of Other White House Announcements

The following listing includes the President's daily schedule and other items of general interest as announced by the White House Press Office during the period covered by this issue. Events and announcements printed elsewhere in the issue are not included.

July 30

The President met at the White House with:

—Zbigniew Brzezinski, Assistant to the President for National Security Affairs;

—Secretary of Defense Harold Brown, Secretary of State Cyrus Vance, Assistant Secretary of State Richard Holbrooke, and Dr. Brzezinski.

August 1

The President met at the White House with:

—William G. Hyland, senior staff member of the National Security Council;

—senior White House staff members;

—the Cabinet;

—Vice President Walter F. Mondale;

—Ben Brown, deputy chairman of the Democratic National Committee;

—Bert Lance, Director of the Office of Management and Budget.

August 2

The President met at the White House with:

—Dr. Brzezinski;

—Representative Al Ullman, Vice President Mondale, and Secretary of Health, Education, and Welfare Joseph A. Califano, Jr.;

—Vice President Mondale, Adm. Stansfield Turner, Director of Central Intelligence, and Dr. Brzezinski;

—Terence Cardinal Cooke, Archbishop of New York;

—Secretary Brown and Deputy Secretary of Defense Charles W. Duncan, Jr.

The President announced his intention to designate Charles B. Curtis, of Bethesda, Md., as Chairman of the Federal

Power Commission upon confirmation by the Senate. Mr. Curtis was nominated to be a member of the Commission on July 29.

August 3

The President met at the White House with:

—Dr. Brzezinski;

—Senator Russell B. Long, Vice President Mondale, and Secretary Califano;

—Mrs. Carter, for lunch;

—Charles L. Schultze, Chairman of the Council of Economic Advisers.

August 4

The President met at the White House with:

—Dr. Brzezinski;

—members of the Senate Select Committee on Intelligence;

—Secretary Brown and a group of leaders from private industry;

—Boy Scout Troop No. 139, from Calhoun, Ga.

The President designated Richard J. Daschbach as Chairman of the Federal Maritime Commission.

The President declared an emergency for the State of South Carolina because of the impact of a drought.

August 5

The President met at the White House with:

—Dr. Brzezinski;

—Aaron Henry, cochairman of the Mississippi Democratic Party;

—President Julius K. Nyerere of Tanzania;

—Vice President Mondale, Secretary Brown, Deputy Secretary of Defense Duncan, and the Joint Chiefs of Staff.

The White House announced that the President has signed an order designating Charles L. Schultze as Chairman of the Council on Wage and Price Stability, as part of the Executive Office reorganization.

The President attended the swearing-in ceremony for James R. Schlesinger as Secretary of Energy in the Rose Garden.

The President left the White House for a trip to Plains, Ga.

CHECKLIST OF WHITE HOUSE PRESS RELEASES

The following releases of the Office of the White House Press Secretary, distributed during the period covered by this issue, are not included in the issue.

Released August 1, 1977

Announcement: nomination of Juan G. Blas to be United States Marshal for the District of Guam; Wallace P. Bowen to be United States Marshal for the District of Oregon; Bernal D. Cantwell to be United States Marshal for the District of Kansas; Donald D. Forsht to be United States Marshal for the Southern District of Florida; Carl W. Gardner to be United States Marshal for the Northern District of Oklahoma; James I. Hartigan to be United States Marshal for the District of Massachusetts; and Louis J. Soscia to be United States Marshal for the Eastern District of New York

Released August 2, 1977

News conference: on the President's message to Congress on drug abuse—by Dr. Peter G. Bourne, Assistant to the President for Health Issues, and Lee Dogoloff, Deputy Director of the Office of Drug Abuse Policy

Fact sheet: the President's message to Congress on drug abuse

Announcement: reorganization review of natural resources and environmental programs

Released August 3, 1977

Announcement: national Women's Business Ownership Campaign by the Small Business Administration

CHECKLIST—Continued
Released August 3—Continued

News conference: on the national Women's Business Ownership Campaign by the Small Business Administration—by A. Vernon Weaver, Administrator, Pat Cloherty, Deputy Administrator-designate, Small Business Administration, and Midge Costanza, Assistant to the President for Public Liaison

Fact sheet: national Women's Business Ownership Campaign by the Small Business Administration

Released August 4, 1977

News conference: on the President's message to Congress on undocumented aliens—by Attorney General Griffin B. Bell, Secretary of Labor Ray Marshall, and the Commissioner of the Immigration and Naturalization Service, Leonel Castillo

Fact sheet: the President's message to Congress on undocumented aliens

Announcement: nomination Harry H. MacLaughlin to be United States District Judge for the District of Minnesota

Announcement: nominations of Frederick Weisberg and Carlisle Pratt to be Associate Judges of the Superior Court of the District of Columbia

Released August 5, 1977

Fact sheet: Youth Employment and Demonstration Projects Act of 1977

Announcement: nomination of Charles M. Adkins, Jr., to be United States Marshal for the Southern District of West Virginia, and Edward D. Schaeffer to be United States Marshal for the Eastern District of Pennsylvania

---

NOMINATIONS SUBMITTED TO THE SENATE

The following list does not include promotions of members of the Uniformed Services, nominations to the Service Academies, or nominations of Foreign Service officers.

Submitted August 1, 1977

JUAN G. BLAS, of Guam, to be United States Marshal for the District of Guam for the term of 4 years, vice John T. San Agustin.

NOMINATIONS—Continued
Submitted August 1—Continued

WALLACE P. BOWEN, of Oregon, to be United States Marshal for the District of Oregon for the term of 4 years, vice Everett R. Langford, term expired.

BERNAL D. CANTWELL, of Kansas, to be United States Marshal for the District of Kansas for the term of 4 years, vice Jack V. Richardson.

DONALD D. FORSHT, of Florida, to be United States Marshal for the Southern District of Florida for the term of 4 years (reappointment).

CARL W. GARDNER, of Oklahoma, to be United States Marshal for the Northern District of Oklahoma for the term of 4 years, vice Harry Connolly.

JAMES I. HARTIGAN, of Massachusetts, to be United States Marshal for the District of Massachusetts for the term of 4 years, vice John A. Birknes, Jr., resigned.

LOUIS J. SOSCIA, of New York, to be United States Marshal for the Eastern District of New York for the term of 4 years, vice Benjamin F. Butler, resigned.

ROBERTA S. KARMEL, of New York, to be a member of the Securities and Exchange Commission for the term expiring June 5, 1981, vice A. A. Sommer, Jr.

Submitted August 2, 1977

EDWARD MARKS, of California, a Foreign Service officer of Class three, to be Ambassador Extraordinary and Plenipotentiary of the United States of America to the Republic of Guinea-Bissau.

EDWARD MARKS, of California, a Foreign Service officer of Class three, to be Ambassador Extraordinary and Plenipotentiary of the United States of America to the Republic of Cape Verde.

JOSEPH D. DUFFEY, of the District of Columbia, to be Chairman of the National Endowment for the Humanities for a term of 4 years, vice Ronald S. Berman, term expired.

Submitted August 4, 1977

JAMES R. SCHLESINGER, of Virginia, to be Secretary of Energy (new position).

NOMINATIONS—Continued
Submitted August 4—Continued

CHARLES M. ADKINS, JR., of West Virginia, to be United States Marshal for the Southern District of West Virginia for the term of 4 years, vice Irvin W. Humphreys.

EDWARD D. SCHAEFFER, of Pennsylvania, to be United States Marshal for the Eastern District of Pennsylvania for the term of 4 years, vice Charles S. Guy.

FRANK JONES, of Virginia, to be an Assistant Director of the Community Services Administration (new position).

HARRY H. MACLAUGHLIN, of Minnesota, to be United States District Judge for the District of Minnesota, vice Earl R. Larson, retired.

CARLISLE EDWARD PRATT, of the District of Columbia, to be an Associate Judge of the Superior Court of the District of Columbia for a term of 15 years, vice Orman W. Ketcham, retired.

FREDERICK HOWARD WEISBERG, of the District of Columbia, to be an Associate Judge of the Superior Court of the District of Columbia for a term of 15 years, vice Charles W. Halleck, term expired.

ACTS APPROVED BY THE PRESIDENT

Approved July 30, 1977

H.R. 2502_____ Public Law 95–77
An act to extend certain oil and gas leases by a period sufficient to allow the drilling of an ultradeep well.

H.R. 4088_____ Public Law 95–76
National Aeronautics and Space Administration Authorization Act, 1978.

H.R. 5864_____ Public Law 95–78
An act to approve with modifications certain proposed amendments to the Federal Rules of Criminal Procedure, to disapprove other such proposed amendments, and for other related purposes.

H.R. 5970_____ Public Law 95–79
Department of Defense Appropriation Authorization Act, 1978.

ACTS APPROVED—Continued

Approved July 31, 1977

H.R. 7552_____ Public Law 95–81
Treasury, Postal Service, and General Government Appropriation Act, 1978.

S.J. Res. 77_____ Public Law 95–80
A joint resolution to provide for a temporary extension of certain Federal Housing Administration mortgage insurance and related authorities and of the national flood insurance program, and for other purposes.

Approved August 1, 1977

H.R. 4975_____ Public Law 95–83
An act to amend the Public Health Service Act to extend through the fiscal year ending September 30, 1978, the assistance programs for health services research; health statistics; comprehensive public health services; hypertension programs; migrant health; community health centers; medical libraries; cancer control programs; the National Cancer Institute; heart, blood vessel, lung, and blood disease prevention and control programs; the National Heart, Lung, and Blood Institute; National Research Service Awards; population research and voluntary family planning programs; sudden infant death syndrome; hemophilia; national health planning and development; and health resources development; to amend the Community Mental Health Centers Act to extend it through the fiscal year ending September 30, 1978; to extend the assistance programs for home health services; and for other purposes.

S. 1474_____ Public Law 95–82
Military Construction Authorization Act, 1978

Approved August 2, 1977

H.R. 4746_____ Public Law 95–84
An act to extend certain authorities of the Secretary of the Interior with respect to water resources research and saline water conversion programs, and for other purposes.

ACTS APPROVED—Continued

Approved August 2—Continued

H.R. 7556_____ Public Law 95–86
Departments of State, Justice, and Commerce, the Judiciary, and Related Agencies Appropriation Act, 1978.

H.R. 7557_____ Public Law 95–85
Department of Transportation and Related Agencies Appropriation Act, 1978.

Approved August 3, 1977

H.R. 2_____ Public Law 95–87
Surface Mining Control and Reclamation Act of 1977

H.R. 6714_____ Public Law 95–88
International Development and Food Assistance Act of 1977

Approved August 4, 1977

H.R. 692_____ Public Law 95–89
An act to amend the Small Business Act and the Small Business Investment Act of 1958 to increase loan authorization and surety bond guarantee authority; and to improve the disaster assistance, certificate of competency and Small Business set-aside programs, and for other purposes.

S.J. Res. 79_____ Public Law 95–90
A joint resolution to amend the Federal Home Loan Bank Act.

S. 826_____ Public Law 95–91
Department of Energy Organization Act.

H.R. 6884_____ Public Law 95–92
International Security Assistance Act of 1977

Approved August 5, 1977

H.R. 6138_____ Public Law 95–93
Youth Employment and Demonstration Projects Act of 1977

H.R. 7932_____ Public Law 95–94
Legislative Branch Appropriation Act, 1978.

PRESIDENTIAL DOCUMENTS

Secretary of Energy

Remarks at the Swearing In of
James R. Schlesinger. August 5, 1977

THE PRESIDENT. Good afternoon, everybody. I've come before you this afternoon to consummate an effort that began last fall in discussing with Dr. James Schlesinger the subject that's been on our mind perhaps more than any other throughout my own administration: the concept of energy shortages and the attitude of American people, how we might minimize the inevitable consequences that result from an overuse of scarce supplies.

I had known Dr. Schlesinger just a few months. He came down to Plains to talk to me late last summer, after returning to our country from a trip to the Far East, including China. And I think it's accurate to say that he and I liked each other immediately and began to confer on many subjects concerning defense, atomic energy, foreign affairs, budget matters, and then, finally, the most important subject of all—energy.

He has been the one that the Congress and I and the American people have trusted. He's put together, with the help of an extremely able staff, working sacrificially, a comprehensive energy proposal that the Congress is now addressing in a very effective way.

And I think it's accurate to say that here at the midpoint of the year's work, past the midpoint, that the success we've already witnessed has been in large measure due to the intelligence and capability and the esteem which is exhibited by Dr. Schlesinger and those who know him.

Yesterday, the Department of Energy was created. And in an absolutely unprecedented fashion, in just a couple of hours, he was confirmed by the Senate committee under Senator Scoop Jackson, and then on the same day was confirmed as the Secretary of the Department of Energy.

This is the 12th Cabinet-level department, the first one created in the last 11 years. And it comes at a time when it's greatly needed.

I think it's important that these new proposals be pursued through the Congress, authorized by law, and implemented in the most enlightened and effective way.

I also think that the new Department needs to be formed rapidly and efficiently and effectively. I think it's important that the head of this Department have the trust of other Cabinet members, of the President, of the Members of Congress, local and State officials, and the people of our country.

And I have chosen a person who fills all those very profound and very important requirements: Dr. James Schlesinger. He's had many important positions to play in his own life, privately and in Government. I think this is the most important of all. And it's with a great deal of appreciation to him and confidence in him that I have chosen him to be the Secretary of Energy.

And now I'd like to ask the Attorney General to administer the oath of office. And I'd like to congratulate ahead of time the American people for having this fine man to head up this important effort, which can rally our Nation in the future in a spirit of unity and common commitment and common trust.

Dr. James Schlesinger.

[At this point, Attorney General Griffin B. Bell administered the oath of office.]

SECRETARY SCHLESINGER. Mr. President, I am grateful to you for the confidence that you have reposed in me in assigning to me the responsibility of being the first Secretary of Energy.

Public service is our highest calling, and I am delighted to serve you and, through you, the American people.

Mr. President, yesterday you referred to a search committee. I am delighted that that committee acted so expeditiously. *[Laughter]* Senator Jackson was moving so fast that I was afraid that your nomination might be approved before it reached the Hill. *[Laughter]*

I see Admiral Rickover is here. I have had the honor, Mr. President, of serving Admiral Rickover now in three jobs. *[Laughter]* If you look at the organization charts, you might come to some other and erroneous conclusion.

I see my secretary, Evelyn, is here. Sometime ago when we were leaving the Atomic Energy Commission, she said to me, "Thank the Lord we will never hear about the liquid metal fast breeder reactor again." *[Laughter]* That, Mr. President, was not one of her better predictions.

I also see the entire staff of the Energy Policy and Planning Group. Mr. President, these men and women managed to produce, in 90 days time, a comprehensive energy plan. They achieved this by going without sleep. This has been maliciously charged by the critics of the plan, and some of our supporters fear that it may be true. I think I can confirm, indeed, that it is true.

On a more serious note, Mr. President, the Department of Energy provides you with a coordinated instrument for implementing whatever policies you and the Congress agree upon with regard to the long-run energy problems of this country.

I should emphasize, Mr. President, that our energy problems are serious, but they do constitute a challenge, a challenge to which you have just referred—an opportunity, once again, for all of us to pull together in a spirit of national cohesion and, once again, to have that sense of common purpose and common destiny by which to guide our efforts.

It will call on all of us to face the facts of our and the world's energy problem with total objectivity. But if we face those facts and we deal with them with determination, we shall be able to solve our energy problems. It will require us to act with speed and with prudence and, at the same time, to act out of a spirit of confidence and hope and, occasionally, charity. And in that spirit of charity, let me urge, Mr. President, that we will permit the assembled guests to escape from this excess of solar energy. *[Laughter]*

NOTE: The President spoke at 2 p.m. in the Rose Garden at the White House.

THE PRESIDENT'S NEWS CONFERENCE OF AUGUST 6, 1977

Held at Plains, Georgia

WELFARE REFORM

THE PRESIDENT. As I pledged during my campaign for the Presidency, I am today asking Congress to totally scrap our existing welfare system and to replace it with a Program for Better Jobs and Income, which will provide job opportunities for those able to work and a simplified, uniform cash assistance program for those who are unable to work due to disability, age, or family circumstances.

In May—I think May 1—after almost 4 months of intensive study, I said that the welfare system was worse than I had expected, and I stand by that conclusion.

Each of the individual programs has a high purpose and serves some needy people. But taken as a whole, the system is neither rational nor is it fair, and the welfare system is antiwork and antifamily. It's unfair to the poor and wasteful to taxpayers' dollars.

The defects of the current system are very clear. First of all, it treats people differently who have similar needs, and eligibility requirements vary for each separate program. Second, it creates exaggerated differences in benefits based on where people live. Third, it encourages the breakup of families. In most cases, two-parent families are not eligible for cash assistance, and a working father can most often increase his family's income by leaving home.

It also discourages work. In one Midwestern State, for example, a father who leaves part-time employment paying $2,400 a year and goes to a full-time job paying $4,800 a year, can actually lose more than $1,250. At the same time, well-intentioned efforts to find jobs for current recipients of welfare payments have floundered and been ineffective.

And finally, the complexity of current programs and regulations tends to waste, fraud, redtape, and errors. HEW has recently discovered even Government employees unlawfully receiving benefits and numbers of people receiving benefits in several different communities.

There is no perfect solution for these difficult problems, but it's time to begin. The welfare system is too hopeless to be cured by minor modifications; we must make a complete and clean break with the past.

The program that I propose today to the Congress does just that. It will provide for jobs for those who need work, a work bonus for those who do work but whose incomes are inadequate to support their family. It provides income support for those who are able to work part-time or who are unable to work due to age or physical disability or who need to care for little children 6 years of age or younger. It provides an earned income tax credit to strengthen work incentives and to provide tax relief for working families who have been hard hit by payroll tax increases.

If enacted by the Congress, this new program will have major benefits. It will significantly reduce the number of people who rely on welfare payments primarily by doubling the number of single-parent families who are supported primarily through work. Twice as many single-parent families will now be supported by work. It will insure that work will always be more profitable than welfare and that a private job or a public job not supported by the Federal Government will always bring in more income than a special job created with Federal funds. It will combine effective work requirements, strong work incentives, improved private sector placement services, and the creation of 1.4 million jobs. Those who can work will work. And every family with a full-time worker will have an income substantially above the poverty line for the first time.

This program will provide increased benefits and more sensitive treatment to those in need. It will provide simplicity by consolidating the current assistance programs, all of which have different eligibility requirements.

This new program will provide strong incentives to keep families together rather than tearing families apart and offering the dignity of useful work to the heads of families.

This program will reduce fraud and error and accelerate efforts to assure that deserting fathers meet their obligations to their families.

This program will also give substantial financial relief—$2 billion—to hard-pressed State and local taxpayers.

In my May 2, 1977, statement, I established as a goal that the new reform system involve no higher initial cost than the present system by making the new program more rational and efficient. Therefore, Secretary Califano, who is here on the stage with me, outlined a tentative, no-cost plan which embodied the major reforms we are seeking. It was a good plan.

After careful consultation with State and local leaders, Members of Congress, and many other interested persons throughout the country, we've now provided $2.8 billion in added benefits.

These additional funds will be used to make important improvements in our original plan—increased fiscal relief, as I've already outlined, for local and State governments, particularly those that have borne a heavy financial burden in the past.

Incentives which strengthen family ties have also been added. A deduction for child care will permit and encourage single parents to take work which will lift them out of poverty.

We've added up to 300,000 additional jobs, part-time jobs, for single-parent families with school age children. If adequate day care is available, such parents will be expected to take full-time jobs. And the earned income tax credit for working families, administered through the revenue system, has been expanded to provide tax relief for many who receive no income assistance, who work, and who have been hard hit by payroll tax increases.

So, with these improvements the program will help turn the low-income Americans away from welfare dependence with a system that is fair and fundamentally based on work for those who can and should work.

This Program for Better Jobs and Income stresses a fundamental American commitment to work, strengthens our family, respects the less advantaged in our society, and makes a far more efficient and effective use of our hard-earned tax dollars.

I'll now answer questions about this program. I have on the stage with me Joe Califano who heads up the Department of Health, Education, and Welfare, and Ray Marshall, who heads up the Department of Labor—two of the major Departments, along with Treasury, that will administer the new program.

And I'd like to also say that the House of Representatives yesterday—Speaker Tip O'Neill announced that a special welfare committee will be set up to implement the legislative work on this program for better jobs and income.

I'd now like to recognize Mr. Wes Pippert [Wesley G. Pippert, United Press International].

QUESTIONS

BERT LANCE

Q. I know that this is intended, Mr. President, to be a news conference on the all-important subject of welfare reform.

THE PRESIDENT. Yes, it is.

Q. But I do feel compelled to ask about something else that has just arisen that is also important. Budget Director Bert Lance has acknowledged that he received another big loan from a bank in which his own bank had an interest-free account.

Now, when did you become aware of these matters? Have you asked him for an explanation, and does he still have your full confidence?

THE PRESIDENT. Well, let me answer this question, and then I would like to have questions on the new system that I'm proposing, because some of the specialists on welfare programs have come down from Washington to both ask and answer questions. But I'll be glad to answer that question.

I became aware of the Comptroller's interest in the loan at the New York bank about, I guess, a week or 10 days ago. The Comptroller is conducting an inquiry with Mr. Lance. I've not talked to Mr. Lance about it. My understanding is that the inquiry is proceeding thoroughly and that all information concerning the loan will be made available to the public.

Mr. Lance, as you know, answered questions about this yesterday. He's much more familiar with it than I am, and I can only say that any information that is available that is known by Mr. Lance, by the Comptroller, will be made available to the public.

I know little about the details of the loan, but I have full confidence in both the Comptroller and Mr. Lance to handle it properly.

Now perhaps a question about the new program for better jobs and income.

WELFARE COSTS

Q. Mr. President, you said your program is designed to move people from welfare to work?

THE PRESIDENT. Yes.

Q. But you're projecting increased costs in the future. What will be the first year in which your program will actually reduce the total cost of welfare, and how low might it go?

THE PRESIDENT. Well, it's hard to say. Some estimates have shown that we might reduce the rolls for AFDC [Aid to Families with Dependent Children] as much as 50 percent when all of the part-time jobs that we envision are made available to families.

We will present this program to the Congress today in hopes that—by next spring, perhaps, is the target date that the Speaker has announced yesterday—that it might be passed into law. The full program will not possibly be implemented until fiscal year 1981, which is October of 1980.

However, in the meantime, the jobs part of the program will be initiated as rapidly as possible. And also, of course, the earned income tax credit, which will help working families, will be initiated along with tax reform much earlier, perhaps within the next 18 months or 2 years.

We obviously see that every time you provide a new job for a person with our present stimulus package—public works programs, public service jobs, the Youth Employment Jobs program that we initiated yesterday—a total package of $21 billion—that you put people to work and take them off welfare.

So, I think that this new program for both better jobs, more jobs and better income for those who do work will have an immediate impact, although it can't be fully effective until October of 1980.

Q. Could I follow up?

THE PRESIDENT. Please.

Q. Do you know what year though actual payout from the Treasury for welfare will go down, the actual money leaving the Treasury?

THE PRESIDENT. I don't believe that that question can be answered. I might say that immediately following this press conference, Joe Califano and Ray Marshall will be able to answer specific questions.

I doubt that even they, though, who are experts in this subject, can tell you exactly which year the welfare payments will be reduced and how much. But the primary impetus of this whole bill is to make sure that it's always profitable for a family to take a job.

We're trying to make sure that that job is available for every family to have—at least the head of that family—a job available, preferably in the private sector where the income would be highest; secondly, in the public sector without Federal supplement; and third, if necessary, public service jobs to be provided for and paid for by the Federal Government on a temporary basis—about a year—with a good strong training program involved.

Under the present system, quite often it is a serious sacrifice, quite often, financially, for a family to get off welfare and go to work.

Under this program, whenever a person goes to work, it's financially advantageous to them. And at the same time, there's a strong impetus in this program to hold a family together.

Miss Compton [Ann Compton, ABC News].

WELFARE FRAUD

Q. How much money and how much energy are you willing to expend to get fraud out of the system, considering that very often fraud is less expensive to go ahead and pay rather than to try to get rid of?

THE PRESIDENT. The benefits to be derived from eliminating fraud will be realized long before this entire program is implemented. Every time you simplify a system and remove the complexities you eliminate one chance of fraud.

Secretary Califano told me this morning that the estimated degree of fraud in the food stamp program, for instance— those who are not eligible to draw food stamps who do, those who get overpayments—amounts to about 17 percent.

So, in addition to the benefits that will be derived when this entire program goes into effect, we have an excellent chance to realize savings from the elimination of fraud of about $1.3 billion within the next 2 or 3 years just by simplifying, making more effective administration, a closer cooperation between the local, State, and Federal governments, and the computerization of the existing program, in preparation for the full implementation of this one.

So, how much the fraud savings would be after this full program goes into effect, I can't say. Before the full program goes into effect, though, the savings would be about $1.3 billion per year.

Q. But after the program gets going, how much money are you willing to invest at that point to make sure that fraud is done away with, after the program is under way?

THE PRESIDENT. Well, I can't answer that question, but I can say that whatever amount of money you put into the program to eliminate fraud, either in redesigning computer systems, simplifying the system, putting in more auditors, working closer with the State governments, you get a tenfold return on that expenditure, at least. Perhaps Secretary Califano has a better estimate.

Do you? Would you say——

SECRETARY CALIFANO. I think that's right, Mr. President. We'll actually both be saving money and eliminating fraud and error.

WELFARE COSTS

Q. Mr. President, you indicated initially that you were very concerned about keeping the cost of welfare reform at the current cost. But now it is going to cost $2.8 billion more. What changed your mind that it couldn't be done?

THE PRESIDENT. Well, in order to exercise tight discipline on the whole subject and to make sure that people just didn't add on new programs that were attractive, I required the Departments involved—Treasury, Labor, and HEW—to devise a complete program for me with absolutely no cost, which they did. And this was presented to the American public in outline form the first part of May.

Since May, for about 4 months, the Secretaries involved have been consulting with Governors, with mayors, with Members of Congress, and with private interest groups and analyzing in the computer programs how additional costs could be mirrored in improved benefits to the Nation.

As I said, we will now have about $2 billion in tax relief for local and State taxpayers. That is part of the advantages.

In addition, we have provided about 300,000 jobs that we did not anticipate at the beginning in May which would permit single-parent families, a mother or a father with small children, say 6 to 14 years old, to go to work part-time and to guarantee that they would have an opportunity to go work part-time or, if family day care centers are available, to work full-time. That obviously did cost more.

So, in the additional costs that we are putting forward, we are providing a much stronger incentive to work, providing more jobs for people and providing tax relief for local and State governments.

Q. What about your dream of balancing the budget, sir?

THE PRESIDENT. This program will not be incompatible with that dream to balance the budget.

CONSULTATION WITH CONGRESS

Q. Mr. President, you had considerable advice, strong advice from key Members of Congress to delay this package.

THE PRESIDENT. Yes.

Q. In your interests of working well with the Congress and establishing that good working relationship, why did you decide not to accept their advice?

THE PRESIDENT. Well, I might say that neither one of the Members of Congress with whom I consulted this past week urged me personally not to go ahead with the program. In their interviews with the press later, they said it might be better to wait.

There are obviously some differences that still exist between myself and Chairman Al Ullman in the House and Chairman Russell Long in the Senate. But I think that compared to the overall program those differences are quite minor in nature.

I think that what Chairman Ullman objected to was the supplementing of income for families who work being based on the number of children in a family. Obviously, this is already done, because when you file your income tax return, you get a credit for each child so that you can pay for that child's life.

The second thing is obviously the food stamp program that we presently have.

It's based on the number of people in a family. That's a difference of opinion between ourselves and Chairman Ullman. That has not been changed. Chairman Long has questions about how small a child should be in the family before the mother is encouraged—or the father, if it is a single-parent family—should be encouraged to go to work. And I think that the 6-year level is the proper level. I agree completely with that. I think maybe Senator Long would like a lower age. But I think that by the time the child is enrolled in school, that if a part-time job is available to the parent, or if a full-time job is available to the parent, with day care center services, that that parent ought to be in the expected-to-work category.

But those differences, which are sincere, compared to the overall breadth of the program, are relatively minor. And since we were quite ready, since all our plans had been made to reveal the programs to the other Members of the Congress, and since they did not request me personally to delay the program, we decided not to.

Q. Any idea as to why they would apply this indirect pressure, come out after talking with you when they had an opportunity to ask you to delay it personally.

THE PRESIDENT. No, I think they——

Q. And yet they left the impression that they did ask that?

THE PRESIDENT. No, I can't answer that question. I think that there are many Members of the Congress who would like to see this plan modified to mirror their exact desires. And of course, the Congress now will have a chance to go to work on it. I've been very pleased at the action that the Speaker announced yesterday in setting up a special committee, because in the past there have been several committees in the House directly responsible for welfare, in the Senate also three committees.

And I think in the case of energy legislation in the House, where the Ad Hoc Committee on Energy was set up, this expedited the process greatly. And the Speaker has set a target date for House completion on this very complex welfare program to be next spring. So, I think that the leadership in the House and Senate are ready for the legislation to be introduced. They'll have adequate time now to work their will, and I hope we'll be able to work compatibly.

FAMILIES ON WELFARE

Q. In your opening statement you mentioned the practice of welfare fathers leaving the family so that the family will indeed get more welfare benefits. How will your proposal counter that? What is there to keep the family together?

THE PRESIDENT. Well, now there will be no penalty on a family if the father lives in the household. If, say, a two-parent family with children exists and a job is available to that family through public service jobs or through the Employment Security Agency a private job is available, if the parent refuses to take the job, then those parents would lose their welfare benefits. We would then provide adequate payments for income maintenance to meet the needs of the children. But there would be a strong and very heavy financial incentive to that family, both to stay together and also for the mother or father who's the head of the household to work.

So, now, as you well know, if a father gets a job and moves out of the house or pretends to move out of the house, then the family's income is greatly increased. Under this proposed system, that would no longer be the case.

SUPPORT FOR WELFARE REFORM

Q. Mr. President, one of your predecessors, former President Nixon, proposed welfare reform. Senator Long essentially killed it. Senator Long has indeed been critical of your proposal so far, and conservative groups also criticized your proposals. My question is, without this conservative constituency, where is your constituency to reform, and who will support this?

THE PRESIDENT. My belief is that Senator Long will support the program. The chairman of the subcommittee in Senator Long's committee is Senator Pat Moynihan. He was extremely complimentary about the program as it was outlined to him. There's strong support for the program in the House. Every single State government has been consulted in depth about this program. And I would say it was overwhelmingly supported.

Families will be benefited. The ones who want to keep families together will be benefited. Almost all of the recipients of aid who are not able to work will be better off under this program. And I think this is part of the American way of life. To not only emphasize the desire for others to work but to provide jobs for them to be able to work is an integral part of this program that will make it politically attractive. I have very great confidence that this program, in its basic form, will be adopted by the Congress next year.

NEW YORK CITY WELFARE PROGRAM

Q. Mr. President, during your campaign you promised that you would lift the entire welfare load off New York City as soon as possible. This program contains substantial fiscal relief for New York, but still leaves them paying a great deal of welfare costs at the local level. How soon do you think it will be possible to lift the entire load off New York City, as you pledged in the campaign?

THE PRESIDENT. I can't answer that question. I think that the estimate here of financial relief for the States would amount to roughly $175 million for New York. The amount of reduction in cost to New York City under the present stimulus package far exceeds their welfare cost payments. This is brought about by housing and urban development programs, public works programs, and job programs for adults and youth.

But as far as the welfare system, which is being replaced by this new program, the direct benefit that we contemplate to New York would be $175 million.

Q. Could I follow that up? Would you envision in future years, after the program is put into effect, there would be additional dividends to the States and to the cities, such as the $2 billion that's estimated at the start of program? In other words, would they get more beyond the $175 million in the second, third, or fourth year of the program?

THE PRESIDENT. I don't know what my successor and the Congress might do after 1980, but I have to say this, that every time we reduce the unemployment roll, every time we put young people to work, that reduces greatly both unemployment compensation, it reduces welfare payments, and as we care for people with preventive health care programs and cut down hospital costs with the cost containment bill, it cuts down Medicaid and Medicare payments. So, I think the overall thrust of our programs has already far exceeded in benefits what we promised New York City on welfare cost reductions.

But as far as the welfare cost reductions themselves, I think that the most that they could hope for between now and the implementation of this program in the fall of 1980 would be what I've outlined to you.

What would happen after that, I have no idea.

PUBLIC OPINION OF WELFARE

Q. Mr. President, in your statement you obviously avoided using the word "welfare" except to say the system was a failure. Does this mean that you believe the word has become so stigmatized that under this approach you are advancing that you hope the word itself would become obsolete rather than rehabilitated?

THE PRESIDENT. Yes, I think there's a great deal of stigma attached to the word "welfare." And I can't shape the vocabulary of the Nation, obviously, but we've decided to call this program, during its work phase, a Program for Better Jobs and Income. And this is what we are trying to do.

I think the people of the country, according to my own interaction with them during the campaign and as President— and also my information derived from public opinion polls is that they don't like the word "welfare," but they do favor the programs that are provided for poor people, both those who work and those who cannot work.

But the abuses are being eliminated in this program, the abuses that people can make more money not working on welfare than they do if they get a job; the abuses that create confusion and complexity and fraud and cheating; the abuses that divide one member of the family from the rest of the family. Those are all being eliminated.

And I think that the elimination of those adverse parts of the present program will do a great deal to restore the beneficial image of the word "welfare" if it is used.

PUBLIC SERVICE JOBS

Q. In the interest of those who may have to go to work, can you spell out what the kind of jobs you are talking about, public service jobs, whether minimum wage—something like that?

THE PRESIDENT. Yes. The basic public service job will be at the minimum wage. If a local government or a State government supplements the basic payment for those who cannot work, then they are required to supplement the minimum wage salary.

The reason for that is that we don't want the welfare payment or the income payment for those who don't work to be above what a person could get if they worked. But now this can only amount to 10 percent, approximately 10 percent. So, these jobs will be at the minimum wage or slightly above the minimum wage.

Q. Is this like the WPA—or what kind of public service jobs? Like what occupation? Cleaning up roadsides?

THE PRESIDENT. I think there would be a wide range of jobs, working in centers for the elderly, teachers aides, perhaps, when desired, jobs providing for the beauty and cleanliness of municipalities or the countryside, almost any kind of jobs. I think the delineation of what particular job would be envisioned would depend upon the person's capabilities and the needs within the local community. But there will always be a heavy stimulus to move that person out of the public service job into a permanent job, either in the local or State government or preferably in the private sector.

REPORTER. Thank you, Mr. President.

THE PRESIDENT. Thank you very much. I might add that both Secretaries Califano and Marshall will be here now to answer additional questions and to correct any errors I may have made. [*Laughter*]

NOTE: President Carter's thirteenth news conference began at 10 a.m. at the Southwest Georgia Branch Experiment Station, in Plains, Ga. It was broadcast live on radio and television.

Welfare Reform

Message to the Congress.   August 6, 1977

To the Congress of the United States:

As I pledged during my campaign for the Presidency I am asking the Congress to abolish our existing welfare system, and replace it with a job-oriented program for those able to work and a simplified, uniform, equitable cash assistance program for those in need who are unable to work by virtue of disability, age or family circumstance. The Program for Better Jobs and Income I am proposing will transform the manner in which the Federal government deals with the income needs of the poor, and begin to break the welfare cycle.

The program I propose will provide:

—Job opportunities for those who need work.

—A Work Benefit for those who work but whose incomes are inadequate to support their families.

—Income Support for those able to work part-time or who are unable to work due to age, physical disability or the need to care for children six years of age or younger.

This new program will accomplish the following:

—Dramatically reduce reliance on welfare payments by doubling the number of single-parent family heads who support their families primarily through earnings from work.

—Ensure that work will always be more profitable than welfare, and that a private or non-subsidized public job will always be more profitable than a special federally-funded public service job.

—Combine effective work requirements and strong work incentives with improved private sector placement services, and create up to 1.4 million public service jobs. Forty-two percent of those jobs may be taken by current AFDC recipients. Those who can work will work, and every family with a full-time worker will have an income substantially above the poverty line.

—Provide increased benefits and more sensitive treatment to those most in need.

—Reduce complexity by consolidating the current AFDC, Supplemental Security Income (SSI), and Food Stamp programs, all of which have differing eligibility requirements, into a single cash assistance program, providing for the first time a uniform minimum Federal payment for the poor.

—Provide strong incentives to keep families together rather than tear them apart, by offering the dignity of useful work to family heads and by ending rules which prohibit assistance when the father of a family remains within the household.

—Reduce fraud and error and accelerate efforts to assure that deserting fathers meet their obligations to their families.

—Give significant financial relief to hard-pressed State and local governments.

THE NEED FOR REFORM

In May, after almost four months of study, I said that the welfare system was worse than I expected. I stand by that conclusion. Each program has a high purpose and serves many needy people; but taken as a whole the system is neither rational nor fair. The welfare system is anti-work, anti-family, inequitable in its treatment of the poor and wasteful of taxpayers' dollars. The defects of the current system are clear:

—It treats people with similar needs in different fashion with separate eligibility requirements for each program.

—It creates exaggerated differences in benefits based on state of residence. Current combined state and Federal AFDC benefits for a family of four with no income vary from $720 per year in Mississippi to $5,954 in Hawaii.

—It provides incentives for family breakup. In most cases two-parent families are not eligible for cash assistance and, therefore, a working father often can increase his family's income by leaving home. In Michigan a two-parent family with the father working at the minimum wage has a total income, including tax credits and food stamps, of $5,922. But if the father leaves, the family will be eligible for benefits totalling $7,076.

—It discourages work. In one Midwestern state, for example, a father who leaves part-time employment paying $2,400 for a full-time job paying $4,800 reduces his family's income by $1,250.

—Efforts to find jobs for current recipients have floundered.

—The complexity of current programs leads to waste, fraud, red tape, and errors. HEW has recently discovered even government workers unlawfully receiving benefits, and numbers of people receive benefits in more than one jurisdiction at the same time.

The solutions to these problems are not easy—and no solution can be perfect; but it is time to begin. The welfare system is too hopeless to be cured by minor modifications. We must make a complete and clean break with the past.

People in poverty want to work, and most of them do. This program is intended to give them the opportunity for self-support by providing jobs for those who need them, and by increasing the rewards from working for those who earn low wages.

Program Summary

The Program for Better Jobs and Income has the following major elements:

—Strengthened services through the employment and training system for placement in the private sector jobs.

—Creation of up to 1.4 million public service and training positions for principal earners in families with children, at or slightly above the minimum wage through state and local government and non-profit sponsors.

—An expansion of the Earned Income Tax Credit to provide an income supplement of up to a maximum of well over $600 for a family of four through the tax system, by a 10% credit for earnings up to $4,000, a 5% credit for earnings from $4,000 to the entry point of the positive tax system, and a declining 10% credit thereafter until phase-out. A major share of the benefit will accrue to hard-pressed workers with modest incomes struggling successfully to avoid welfare.

—Strong work requirements applying to single persons, childless couples and family heads, with work requirements of a more flexible nature for single-parent family heads with children aged 7 to 14. Single-parent family heads with preschool aged children are not required to work.

—A Work Benefit for two-parent families, single-parent families with older children, singles and childless couples. The Federal benefit for a family of four would be a maximum of $2,300 and, after $3,800 of earnings, would be reduced fifty cents for each dollar of earnings.

—Income Support for single-parent families with younger children and aged, blind or disabled persons. The Federal benefit would be a base of $4,200 for a family of four and would be reduced fifty cents for each dollar of earnings.

—New eligibility requirements for cash assistance which insure that benefits go to those most in need.

—Fiscal relief to States and localities of $2 billion in the first year, growing in subsequent years.

—Simple rules for state supplements to the basic program, in which the Federal government will bear a share of the cost.

Costs

In my May 2, 1977 statement I established as a goal that the new reformed system involve no higher initial cost than the present system. It was my belief that fundamental reform was possible within the confines of current expenditures if the system were made more rational and efficient. That belief has been borne out in our planning. Thereafter, Secretary Califano outlined a tentative no cost plan which embodied the major reform we have been seeking:

—Consolidation of programs.

—Incentives to work.

—Provision of jobs.

—Establishment of a national minimum payment.

—Streamlined administration.

—Incentives to keep families together.

—Some fiscal relief for State and local governments.

Subsequently, we have consulted with State and local officials and others who are knowledgeable in this area. As a result of those consultations we have gone beyond the no cost plan to one with modest additional cost in order to provide more jobs, particularly for current AFDC family heads, additional work incentives, broader coverage for needy families and greater fiscal relief for states and localities.

The Program For Better Jobs and Income will replace $26.3 billion in current programs which provide income assistance to low-income people. In addition, the program will produce savings in other programs amounting to $1.6 billion. The total amount available from replaced programs and savings is $27.9 billion.

Current Federal Expenditures and Savings

(1978 Dollars)

EXPENDITURES

	Billions
AFDC	$6.4
SSI	5.7
Food Stamps	5.0
Earned Income Tax Credit	1.3
Stimulus Portion of CETA Public Jobs	5.5
WIN Program	.4
Extended Unemployment Insurance Benefits (27–39 weeks)	.7
Rebates of per capita share of Wellhead Tax Revenues to Low-Income People if Passed by Congress [1]	1.3
Sub-Total	26.3

SAVINGS

Decreased Unemployment Insurance Expenditures	.4
HEW Program to Reduce Fraud and Abuse	.4
Decreases in Required Housing Subsidies Due to Increased Income [2]	.5
Increases in Social Security Contributions [3]	.3
Sub-total	1.6
Total	27.9

The new Program for Better Jobs and Income will have a total cost of $30.7 billion. The additional cost of the pro-

---

[1] The National Energy plan calls for rebate of the wellhead tax revenues to taxpayers through the income tax system and to "the poor who do not pay taxes" in effect through income maintenance programs.

[2] This does not decrease housing programs nor reduce the amount of cash assistance paid to residents of subsidized housing. It is merely an estimate of the savings to the Department of Housing and Urban Development's housing subsidy programs on account of higher incomes going to tenants under the new program.

[3] This does *not* increase anyone's Social Security Tax, nor does it take any money out of the Social Security Trust Funds. It merely recognizes that the millions of people taken off of dependence on welfare and given a job will become contributors to the Social Security System.

gram above existing costs is $2.8 billion in spending. In addition, $3.3 billion of tax relief is given to working low and moderate income taxpayers through an expanded income tax credit.

COST OF NEW PROGRAM

	Billions
Work Benefit and Income Support	$20. 4
Earned Income Tax Credit [4]	1. 5
Employment and Training	8. 8
TOTAL	30. 7

The additional cost above current expenditures has been used to make important improvements in our original plan:

—Increased fiscal relief has been provided for states and localities, particularly for those which have borne the greatest financial burdens.

—Incentives which strengthen family ties have been improved by adopting a broader definition of eligible applicants to permit more generous payment than in the earlier plan to older persons and young mothers with children who live in extended families.

—Work incentives for low wage workers have been increased by expanding the Earned Income Tax Credit for those in private and non-subsidized public work to cover and supplement approximately twice the income covered by the existing EITC.

—A deduction for child care will permit and encourage single parents to take work which will lift them out of poverty.

—Up to 300,000 additional part-time jobs have been added for single parent families with school age children (if adequate day care is available, such parents will be expected to accept full-time jobs).

------

[4] This is the cost of the portion of the expanded EITC which will be received by those who do not pay income taxes. Income taxpayers with families will receive benefits totalling $3.3 billion.

With these improvements the Program for Better Jobs and Income will help turn low income Americans away from welfare dependence with a system that is fair, and fundamentally based on work for those who can and should work.

PROGRAM DETAIL

EMPLOYMENT SERVICES AND JOB SEARCH

A central element of this proposal is a new effort to match low-income persons with available work in the private and public sector. It will be the responsibility of State and local officials to assure an unbroken sequence of employment and training services, including job search, training, and placement. Prime sponsors under the Comprehensive Employment and Training Act, state employment service agencies, and community-based organizations will play major roles in this effort.

JOBS FOR FAMILIES

A major component of the program is a national effort to secure jobs for the principal wage earners in low income families with children. The majority of poor families—including many who are on welfare for brief periods of time—depend upon earnings from work for most of their income. People want to support themselves and we should help them do so. I propose that the Federal government assist workers from low income families to find regular employment in the private and public sectors. When such employment cannot be found I propose to provide up to 1.4 million public service jobs (including part-time jobs and training) paying at the minimum wage, or slightly above where states supplement the basic Federal program.

This program represents a commitment by my Administration to ensure that families will have both the skills and the opportunity for self-support.

This new Public Service Employment Program is carefully designed to avoid disruptive effects to the regular economy:

—Applicants will be required to engage in an intensive 5-week search for regular employment before becoming eligible for a public service job. Those working in public service employment will be required to engage in a period of intensive job search every 12 months.

—In order to encourage participants to seek employment in the regular economy, the basic wage rate will be kept at, or where states supplement, slightly above, the minimum wage.

—Every effort will be made to emphasize job activities which lead to the acquisition of useful skills by participants, to help them obtain employment in the regular economy. Training activities will be a regular component of most job placements.

The development of this job program is clearly a substantial undertaking requiring close cooperation of all levels of government. I am confident it will succeed. Thousands of unmet needs for public goods and services exist in our country. Through an imaginative program of job creation we can insure that the goals of human development and community development are approached simultaneously. Public service jobs will be created in areas such as public safety, recreational facilities and programs, facilities for the handicapped, environmental monitoring, child care, waste treatment and recycling, clean-up, and pest and insect control, home services for the elderly and ill, weatherization of homes and buildings and other energy-saving activities, teachers' aides and other paraprofessionals in schools, school facilities improvements, and cultural arts activities.

EARNED INCOME TAX CREDIT

The current Earned Income Tax Credit (EITC) is an excellent mechanism to provide tax relief to the working poor. I propose to expand this concept to provide benefits to more families and provide relief to low and modest income working people hard hit by payroll tax increases, improve work incentives, and integrate the Program for Better Jobs and Income with the income tax system. The expanded EITC, which will apply to private and non-subsidized public employment, will have the following features:

—A 10% credit on earnings up to $4,000 per year as under current law.

—A 5% credit on earnings between $4,000 and approximately $9,000 for a family of four (the point at which the family will become liable for federal income taxes).

—A phase-out of the credit beyond roughly $9,000 of earnings at ten percent. The credit will provide benefits to a family of four up to $15,600 of income.

—The credit will be paid by the Treasury Department and the maximum credit for a family of four would be well over $600.

WORK BENEFIT AND INCOME SUPPORT

I propose to scrap and completely overhaul the current public assistance programs, combining them into a simplified, uniform, integrated system of cash assistance. AFDC, SSI and Food Stamps will be abolished. In their place will be a new program providing: (1) a Work Benefit for two-parent families, single people, childless couples and single parents with no child under 14, all of whom are expected to work full-time and required to accept available work; and (2) Income Support for those who are aged, blind or disabled, and for single parents of children under age 14. Single parents with children aged 7 to 14 will be required to accept part-time work which does not interfere with caring for the children, and will be expected to accept full-time work where appropriate day care is available.

These two levels of assistance are coordinated parts of a unified system which maintains incentives to work and simplifies administration.

—For those qualifying for income support the basic benefit for a family of four with no other income will be $4,200 in 1978 dollars. Benefits will be reduced fifty cents for each dollar of earnings, phasing out completely at $8,400 of earnings. Added benefits would accrue to those in regular private or public employment through the Earned Income Tax Credit.

—An aged, blind, or disabled individual would receive a Federal benefit of $2,500 and a couple would receive $3,750—more than they are now receiving. That is higher than the projected SSI benefit for either group—about $100 higher than for a couple and $120 higher for a single person.

—For those persons required to work who receive a Work Benefit, the basic benefit for a family of four with no other income will be $2,300. To encourage continued work, benefits will not be reduced at all for the first $3,800 of earnings and will thereafter be reduced by fifty cents for each dollar earned up to $8,400. Again, the Earned Income Tax Credit will provide added benefits to persons in regular private or public employment.

—We are committed to assure that inflation will not erode the value of the benefits, and that real benefits will be increased over time as federal resources grow. To preserve flexibility in the initial transition period, however, we do not at this time propose automatic indexing of benefits or automatic increases in their real value. (The figures contained in this message expressed in 1978 dollars will be adjusted to retain their real purchasing power at the time of implementation).

—Single parent family heads will be able to deduct up to 20% of earned income, up to an amount of $150 per month to pay for child care expenses required for the parent to go to work.

—No limits are placed on the right of states to supplement these basic benefits. However, only if states adopt supplements which complement the structure and incentives of the Federal program will the Federal government share in the cost.

Eligibility rules for the Work Benefit and Income Support will be tightened to insure that the assistance goes to those who are most in need.

—To reduce error and direct assistance to those most in need, benefits will be calculated based on a retrospective accounting period, rather than on the prospective accounting period used in existing programs. The income of the applicant over the previous six-month period will determine the amount of benefits.

—The value of assets will be reviewed to insure that those with substantial bank accounts or other resources do not receive benefits. The value of certain assets will be imputed as income to the family in determining the amount of benefits.

—Eligibility has been tightened in cases where related individuals share the same household, while preserving the ability of the aged, disabled and young mothers to file for benefits separately.

STATE ROLE AND FISCAL RELIEF FOR STATES AND LOCAL COMMUNITIES

Public assistance has been a shared Federal and State responsibility for forty years. The program I propose will significantly increase Federal participation but maintain an important role for the states.

—Every State will be assured that it will save at least ten percent of its current welfare expenses in the first year of the program, with substantially increased fiscal relief thereafter.

—Every State is required to pay ten percent of the basic Federal income benefits provided to its residents except where it will exceed 90 percent of its prior welfare expenditures.

—Every State is free to supplement the basic benefits, and is eligible for Federal matching payments for supplements structured to complement and maintain the incentives of the Federal program. The Federal government will pay 75% of the first $500 supplement and 25% of any additional supplement up to the poverty line. These State supplements will be required to follow Federal eligibility criteria to help achieve nation-wide uniformity.

—Where States supplement the income support they must also proportionally supplement the work benefit and the public service wage.

—There will be a three-year period during which states will be required to maintain a share of their current effort in order to ease the transition of those now receiving benefits. These resources must be directed to payment of the State's 10% share of the basic benefit, to supplements complementary to the basic program, and to grandfathering of existing SSI and partially grandfathering AFDC beneficiaries. The Federal government will guarantee a State that its total cost for these expenditures will not exceed 90% of current welfare costs. States can retain any amounts under the 90% requirement not actually needed for the mandated expenditures. In the second year of the program states will be *required* to maintain only 60% of current expenditures, in the third year, only 30%. In the

fourth year, they will only be required to spend enough to meet their 10% share of the basic benefit.

—States will have the option to assist in the administration of the program. They will be able to operate the crucial intake function serving applicants, making possible effective coordination with social service programs. The Federal government will operate the data processing system, calculate benefits, and issue payments.

—The Federal government will provide a $600 million block grant to the states to provide for emergency needs. These grants will assist the states in responding to sudden and drastic changes in family circumstances.

—The Federal government will provide 30% above the basic wage for fringe benefits and administrative costs of the jobs program, and will reimburse the states for costs of administration of the work benefit and income support program.

In the first year of this program, states and localities would receive $2 billion in fiscal relief, while at the same time ensuring that no current SSI beneficiary receives a reduced benefit and that over 90 percent of current AFDC beneficiaries receive similar protection.

In subsequent years as current recipients leave the rolls and as the maintenance of State effort requirement declines from 90 percent to zero within 3 years, the opportunities for increased fiscal relief will grow.

Under our program for fiscal relief, states will be required to pass through their fiscal relief to municipal and county governments in full proportion to their contributions. Thus, for example, in New York State, where New York City pays 33% of the State's share, New York City would receive 33% of the State's fiscal relief or $174 million.

REDUCTION OF FRAUD AND ABUSE

The few providers and recipients guilty of fraud and abuse in our welfare programs not only rob the taxpayers but cheat the vast majority of honest recipients. One of the most significant benefits of consolidation of existing cash assistance programs is the opportunity to apply sophisticated management techniques to improve their operation. The use of a central computer facility will permit more efficient processing of claims, reduce the incidence of error in calculating benefits, and facilitate the detection of fraud. No longer will people easily claim benefits in more than one jurisdiction.

We will strongly enforce current programs directed at assisting local officials in obtaining child support payments from run-away parents, as determined by judicial proceedings.

We will ensure that the Department of Health, Education, and Welfare will vigorously root out abuses and fraud in our social programs.

We will work for passage of current legislation designed to crack down on fraud and abuse in our Medicaid and Medicare Program. The administration of these programs will be a major challenge for federal and state officials. It provides a valuable opportunity to demonstrate that government can be made to work, particularly in its operation of programs which serve those in our society most in need.

IMPLEMENTATION

Because of the complexity of integrating the different welfare systems of the 50 states and the District of Columbia into a more unified national system, we estimate that this program will be effective in Fiscal Year 1981. Moreover, we recognize that the National Health Insurance plan which will be submitted next year must contain fundamental reform and rationalization of the Medicaid program, carefully coordinated with the structure of this proposal. However, we are anxious to achieve the swiftest implementation possible and will work with the Congress and State and local governments to accelerate this timetable if at all possible.

Given the present complex system, welfare reform inevitably involves difficult choices. Simplicity and uniformity and improved benefits for the great majority inevitably require reduction of special benefits for some who receive favored treatment now. Providing the dignity of a job to those who at present are denied work opportunities will require all the creativity and ingenuity that private business and government at all levels can bring to bear. But the effort will be worthwhile both for the individual and for the country. The Program for Better Jobs and Income stresses the fundamental American commitment to work, strengthens the family, respects the less advantaged in our society, and makes a far more efficient and effective use of our hard-earned tax dollars.

I hope the Congress will move expeditiously and pass this program early next year.

JIMMY CARTER

The White House,
   August 6, 1977.

Community Services Administration

Nomination of Frank Jones To Be an Assistant Director. August 6, 1977

The President has announced his intention to nominate Frank Jones of Arlington, Va., to be Assistant Director for Legal Affairs and General Counsel of the Community Services Administration. The position is a new one.

Jones is currently executive director of the National Legal Aid and Defender Association in Washington.

He was born in Clarksdale, Miss., on January 30, 1933, and holds degrees from Chicago State University, DePaul University, and the New York University Law Center.

He taught in the Chicago public schools from 1958 to 1964, then served with the NAACP Legal Defense and Educational Fund, Inc., in Jackson, Miss., and the Chicago Legal Aid Bureau. In 1969–70 he was Deputy Associate Director of Legal Services with the Office of Economic Opportunity in Washington.

He became executive director of the National Legal Aid and Defender Association in 1971 and served in that position until 1973, when he was named vice dean of the University of Pennsylvania Law School. He rejoined the NLADA in 1976.

Plains, Georgia

Exchange With Reporters at Carters Warehouse.   August 8, 1977

REPORTER. There's encouraging news out of the Middle East this morning. Any comment on the reports of the PLO?

THE PRESIDENT. No. We don't know yet what's going to happen until I get a complete report from Cy Vance—I get a message from him every night and then a briefing every morning. If the Palestinians will recognize the applicability of the United Nations Resolution 242, then it would open up a new opportunity for us to start discussions with them and also

open up an avenue that they might participate in the Geneva conference. But whether they'll do that, we don't know yet.

Q. If indeed they do recognize 242, wouldn't that more or less assure that the Geneva conference will indeed begin?

THE PRESIDENT. I can't answer that question because there might be other obstacles to it. But I think I can be able to answer that question when Secretary Vance gets back. He's now decided, I think, to double back and have a second conversation with some of the leaders in the Middle East. So, this might be an encouraging sign.

Q. He would go back to the other Arab countries again?

THE PRESIDENT. Either go back or have additional conversations with them before he leaves the Middle East. And he's going to stay over in London an extra day to talk to President Nyerere about Rhodesia and Namibia. So, I think things look better than they did. I hope we can work something out on the Palestinians. That is the biggest obstacle right now.

Q. We always ask you about the adverse developments. We give you a chance to talk about a positive development for a change. [*Laughter*]

THE PRESIDENT. Thank you very much.

Q. What about prospects for a Geneva conference in October? Still good?

THE PRESIDENT. Well, I'd say they are about the same as they were. The biggest obstacle that we've detected, of course, is whether or not the Palestinians would participate in the discussions. And our position has been that until the Palestinians and their leaders recognize Israel's right to exist that we would not have conversations with them ourselves.

So, if the Palestinians do adopt as a basis for the discussions the United Nations Resolutions 242 and 338, then that would certainly make it easier for them to go——

Q. Have we had any contact with the Palestinians formally—informally to indicate their position?

THE PRESIDENT. I think a better word would be "indirectly." We've not had any direct conversations with them. But, of course, they are sending us messages through the Syrians and the Saudi Arabians, the Jordanians and the Egyptians.

So, we have a means to contact them and to exchange ideas with them indirectly. But we are not going to meet with the Palestinian leaders as long as they are committed to the destruction of Israel.

Q. What were they saying, indirectly?

THE PRESIDENT. That they may adopt U.N. Resolution 242, which does recognize Israel's right to exist permanently and in peace with secure borders.

The thing that has made the Palestinians reluctant to do this is, at the time 242 was passed, it only referred to Palestinians as refugees. And if the Palestinians should say, "We recognize U.N. Resolution 242 in its entirety, but we think the Palestinians have additional status other than just refugees," that would suit us okay.

Q. Anything on your schedule today—softball again, maybe?

THE PRESIDENT. Maybe. I don't know yet.

Q. I don't know if we're up to it or not.

Q. How are you feeling?

THE PRESIDENT. I feel fine. Billy is in pretty bad shape this morning. [*Laughter*]

Q. You're not stiff?

THE PRESIDENT. No, I'm not stiff.

Q. We could tell you privately, perhaps, how he said he feels. [*Laughter*]

THE PRESIDENT. I'll probably go to the farm later on today.

REPORTER. Thank you, Mr. President.

NOTE: The exchange began at 9:10 a.m.

Clean Air Act Amendments of 1977

Statement on Signing H.R. 6161 Into Law. August 8, 1977

I am pleased to sign into law H.R. 6161, the Clean Air Act Amendments of 1977. This act is the culmination of a 3-year effort by the Congress to develop legislation which will continue our progress toward meeting our national clean air goals in all parts of the country. The issues involved in amending the Clean Air Act have been difficult and the debate lengthy. However, I believe that the Congress, under the leadership of Senator Muskie and Representative Rogers, has adopted a sound and comprehensive program for achieving and preserving healthy air in our Nation.

The automobile industry now has a firm timetable for meeting strict, but achievable emission reductions. That industry now knows with certainty what is required and can devote its full-time energies to designing cars which will further our clean air goals while continuing to improve fuel efficiency.

This timetable will be enforced.

With this legislation, we can continue to protect our national parks and our major national wilderness areas and national monuments from the degradation of air pollution. Other clean air areas of the country will also be protected, at the same time permitting economic growth in an environmentally sound manner.

The act provides us with a new tool to help abate industrial sources of pollution by authorizing use of economic incentives to reduce noncompliance. By directing the Environmental Protection Agency to establish monetary penalties equal to the cost of cleanup, those industries which delay installing abatement equipment will no longer be rewarded in the marketplace.

These three major provisions, coupled with the other authorities of H.R. 6161, provide the statutory framework for the Environmental Protection Agency to implement a firm, but responsible program for meeting and maintaining air quality standards which are necessary to protect the health of all of our citizens.

NOTE: As enacted, H.R. 6161 is Public Law 95–95, approved August 7.

The statement was released at Americus, Ga.

Public Works Appropriations Bill

*Statement on Signing H.R. 7553
Into Law. August 8, 1977*

I am signing H.R. 7553, the public works appropriations bill.

This bill is a precedent-setting first step in trimming spending on unnecessary, expensive, and environmentally damaging construction projects. In response to administration review of construction projects and recommendations to the Congress, nine unsound projects have been deleted and four modified. This is unprecedented progress. In addition to this action, the Congress has refrained from funding unbudgeted new construction starts.

I welcome this positive step. Action on this appropriations bill marks the beginning of a major effort on the part of this administration to cut back on waste in this area.

This effort will be continued.

I note that this bill contains funding for 10 projects for which I recommended deletion of funds. I remain very concerned about these projects.

Much remains to be done to accomplish lasting reform in water resources policy. My administration is developing water policy reform proposals and will continue to scrutinize carefully all ongoing and proposed water projects. In addition, with the exception of two projects which require further analysis by the Interior Department, the projects deleted by the Congress in this bill should be deauthorized immediately so that the first step is made permanent.

I am, therefore, signing this bill with the intention of accomplishing:

—deauthorization of deleted projects;

—continued close scrutiny of all projects; and

—institution of lasting reforms in water policy.

I would also note that H.R. 7553 appropriates over $500 million for research and development on breeder reactors and other advanced nuclear power technologies. The legislation does not, however, appropriate funds for the unnecessary Clinch River Breeder Reactor Project.

My FY 1978 budget proposal which H.R. 7553 will implement provides for a vigorous research and development program for breeder reactors. In FY 1978, we will complete the Fast Flux Test Facility at Hanford, Wash., which will tell us much more about how to design an advanced, environmentally sound, and economical breeder than Clinch River Breeder can. We will fund major research on alternative breeder technologies, improved safety systems, and other advanced atomic power sources.

Congress has yet to complete action on the legislation authorizing our nuclear breeder research and development program. I will urge Congress to reject proposals leading to an investment of over $2.2 billion of tax dollars in the Clinch River Breeder Reactor Project—a reactor which we do not now need, which is economically unsound, and which will be of little assistance in determining the commercial viability of breeder technology in the United States.

Without wasting the taxpayers' dollars on the Clinch River facility, we will be able to implement a breeder research program which will ultimately make this country better prepared to build, if and when we need to, a commercial breeder reactor which is technically, economically, and environmentally sound.

Finally, H.R. 7553 provides up to $14 million for such activities at the Barnwell Nuclear Fuel Plant as the Energy Research and Development Administration Administrator determines are consistent with the international nuclear fuel cycle evaluation. No funds appropriated in this act shall be used for the reprocessing of spent fuel.

NOTE: As enacted, the Public Works for Water and Power Development and Energy Research Appropriation Act, 1978, is Public Law 95–96, approved August 7.

The statement was released at Americus, Ga.

Red River Compact Commission

Appointment of Maj. Gen. Robert C. Marshall as Federal Representative and Non-Voting Chairman.   August 11, 1977

The President today announced the appointment of Maj. Gen. Robert C. Marshall, Corps of Engineers, U.S. Army, as the Federal Representative and non-voting Chairman of the Red River Compact Commission.

Marshall, 55, was nominated on July 28 to be a member and President of the Mississippi River Commission. He is Deputy Chief of Engineers in the Army Corps of Engineers. He has served in the Army since 1943.

Panama Canal Negotiations

Remarks on the Agreement in Principle Reached with Panama.   August 12, 1977

Good afternoon, everybody.

For 13 years, we have been engaged in negotiations for a Panama Canal treaty that would strengthen our security interests, be fair to ourselves and the people of Panama, and insure free international use of the Panama Canal in a spirit of cooperation and friendship among all nations in this hemisphere. In spite of difficulties and even bloodshed, each of my predecessors since President Lyndon Johnson has decided that this effort must be continued. And I'm pleased that it will now be completed during my own administration.

The Joint Chiefs of Staff and other principal advisers of mine have been involved in these talks at every stage. All of us believe that these agreements are good ones and that the implementation of the treaties incorporating these agreements are important to our long-term national interests.

Under the canal treaty that will now be prepared, we will have operating control and the right to protect and defend the Panama Canal with our own military forces until the end of this century. Under a separate neutrality treaty, we will have the right to assure the maintenance of the permanent neutrality of the canal as we may deem necessary. Our own warships are guaranteed the permanent right to expeditious passage, without regard to their type of propulsion or the cargo they carry. And the treaties will be a foundation for a new cooperative era in our relations with all of Latin America.

As provided by our United States Constitution, I will seek the advice and consent of the Senate for the ratification of these treaties. I know that each Senator and each Member of the House of Representatives will give the utmost and careful consideration to these agreements—not only to the treaties themselves but to the positive influence that their approval will have in our own country and in our position in the world as a strong and generous nation.

We will work with Panama to assess the need for a sea-level canal and will also cooperate on possible improvements to the existing canal.

I believe that these treaties will help to usher in a new day in hemispheric relations. All of the countries in Latin America are joined with us in a conviction that a new treaty which properly responds to the Panamanian aspirations and fully preserves our own security and other interests will give us an opportunity to work together more effectively toward our common objectives.

Our two leading negotiators have been Ambassador Ellsworth Bunker and Ambassador Sol Linowitz, and they are here this afternoon to answer specific questions that you might have on the treaties themselves and the negotiations and agreements that have been reached with Panama.

I'm glad now to introduce Ambassador Bunker and Ambassador Linowitz.

NOTE: The President spoke at 3:30 p.m. to reporters assembled in the Briefing Room at the White House.

Government Reorganization

Memorandum for the Heads of Executive Departments and Agencies.   August 11, 1977

Memorandum for the Heads of Executive Departments and Agencies

Government reorganization for better Government performance is one of my main goals, and I am encouraged by the progress made so far. How we handle the personnel aspects will be important to our ultimate success. I am committed to accomplishing the reorganization with a minimum of hardship to employees.

The reorganization will unquestionably require consolidation of functions and, in some cases, the closing of certain activities. In the event employees of your agency cannot be transferred with the same functions, you should do everything you can to place them in other suitable positions, including filling vacancies within your agency with qualified employees scheduled to be displaced, working through the Civil Service Commission's Displaced Employee Program to facilitate placements in other agencies, and providing opportunities for retraining.

This is a two-way responsibility. Just as I expect you to give all possible assistance to your own displaced employees, it is also your responsibility to give full consideration to hiring displaced workers of other agencies. This is the only way we can ensure that employees will not be adversely affected by the reorganization.

I have asked the Chairman of the Civil Service Commission to set up additional mechanisms to aid in the placement of employees affected, including mandatory priorities in hiring, and to provide you with other assistance as necessary. Chairman Campbell will follow through with these efforts and will report the results to me.

I am counting on your cooperation and resourcefulness to help us carry out the transition to greater governmental effectiveness as smoothly as we can.

JIMMY CARTER

NOTE: The text of the memorandum was released on August 12.

Combined Federal Campaign

Memorandum for the Heads of Departments and Agencies.   August 12, 1977

Memorandum for the Heads of Departments and Agencies

I am pleased to tell you that W. Michael Blumenthal, Secretary of the Treasury, has agreed to serve as Chairman of the Combined Federal Campaign for the National Capital Area this fall.

This campaign, which begins in September, combines the solicitation efforts of the United Way of the National Capital Area, the National Health Agencies, and the International Service Agencies. In this single drive we will seek to do our share to meet the needs of more than 150 local, national and international health, welfare and social service agencies.

The needs of the voluntary organizations supported by the Combined Federal Campaign are great. These organizations perform essential services in helping the disadvantaged, in serving youth and the aged, in healing the sick, and in helping those in need overseas. CFC gives all of us who are Federal employees, whether civilian or military, a unique opportunity to pledge our help to people in our community, our nation, and around the world—a pledge made more convenient by the availability of voluntary payroll deductions.

I request that you serve personally as Chairman of the campaign in your organization and that you appoint one of your top assistants as your Vice Chairman. Please advise Secretary Blumenthal of the person you designate as Vice Chairman. I am confident that Secretary Blumenthal will have your wholehearted support in this endeavor, and I urge you to commend the campaign to everyone in your organization.

JIMMY CARTER

Digest of Other White House Announcements

The following listing includes the President's daily schedule and other items of general interest as announced by the White House Press Office during the period covered by this issue. Events and announcements printed elsewhere in the issue are not included.

August 6

The President has declared an emergency for the State of Wisconsin because of the impact of high winds, hail, and rain.

August 10

In the evening, the President returned to the White House following a visit in Plains, Ga.

August 11

The President met at the White House with:

—William G. Hyland, senior staff member of the National Security Council;

—Secretary of the Treasury W. Michael Blumenthal;

—Arthur Goldberg;

—Ambassadors Ellsworth Bunker and Sol M. Linowitz, co-negotiators for the United States in the Panama Canal negotiations, Secretary of Defense Harold Brown, Acting Secretary of State Warren M. Christopher, and members of the Joint Chiefs of Staff.

The President declared an emergency for the State of North Carolina because of the impact of a drought.

August 12

The President met at the White House with:

—Mr. Hyland;
—Secretary Brown;
—Senator Frank Church of Idaho;
—Attorney General Griffin B. Bell.

The President transmitted to the Congress the 11th annual report of the National Endowment for the Humanities for fiscal year 1976 and the sixth annual report on the administration of the Railroad Safety Act of 1970.

ACTS APPROVED BY THE PRESIDENT

Approved August 7, 1977

H.R. 6161_____ Public Law 95–95 Clean Air Act Amendments of 1977.

H.R 7553_____ Public Law 95–96 Public Works for Water and Power Development and Energy Research Appropriation Act, 1978.

NOMINATIONS SUBMITTED TO THE SENATE

NOTE: No nominations were submitted to the Senate during the period covered by this issue.

CHECKLIST OF WHITE HOUSE PRESS RELEASES

The following releases of the Office of the White House Press Secretary, distributed during the period covered by this issue, are not included in the issue.

Released August 6, 1977

Statement: welfare reform (as read by the President at his news conference of August 6)

News conference: on welfare reform—by Secretary of Labor F. Ray Marshall and Secretary of Health, Education, and Welfare Joseph A. Califano, Jr.

Released August 8, 1977

Fact sheet: Clean Air Act Amendments of 1977

Released August 12, 1977

Statement: Panama Canal agreement in principle (as read by the President in the Briefing Room on August 12)

News conference: on the Panama Canal agreement in principle—by Ambassador at Large Ellsworth Bunker and Ambassador Sol Linowitz, co-negotiators for the United States in the Panama Canal negotiations

Fact sheet: summary of Panama Canal agreement in principle

ABC News Interview

*Interview With Correspondents
Harry Reasoner and Sam Donaldson
in Plains, Georgia.   August 10, 1977*

VIEWS ON THE PRESIDENCY

MR. REASONER. Mr. President, I suppose in 2 or 3 years before your election you were identified as a man who wanted the Presidency as much as any candidate in this century. Now that you've had it for 7 months or so, was it worth it? Are you having any fun?

THE PRESIDENT. Yes. So far, I've enjoyed it. It's been a pleasant life at the White House. I think it's brought our family back together after being divided all over the country for the last 2 or 3 years. I've been pleasantly surprised at the degree of cooperation and harmony that's evolved between me and the Congress after a shaky start. And we are now slowly but steadily putting into effect the campaign promises that I made on Government reorganization, welfare reform, energy policy, a new Energy Department, and so forth.

So, it's been a pleasant life the first 7 months, but I have to say that we've still got a long way to go. I'm learning. It's my first experience in serving in the Federal Government. But I think, in general, it's been pleasant.

MR. REASONER. As you know, Louis Harris' organization, for ABC, has taken a poll on the first 6 months of the administration and on how people feel about you. 1,515 people were talked to. Suppose you'd been one of the 1,515. What kind of marks would you give yourself as a leader and as a person for the first months?

THE PRESIDENT. Well, I think the major feeling that I have is that my own administration has fairly accurately represented what the American people both are and also want our country to be. I've tried to open up the White House and my own decisionmaking process to the public. I've learned from them. And I think that there has been a restoration of the confidence of people in the Government, not because of me but because there's such a deep desire on the part of our people to trust Washington, the Congress, the President, the White House for a change, after the war in Vietnam and the CIA and Watergate revelations.

So, I think to the extent that I've accurately represented what the people wanted our Government to do, it's been a good administration. Many people are impatient, perhaps overly so. We've made some good progress already in economic affairs, but everybody expected perhaps a much more rapid improvement.

When I took over, the unemployment rate was about 8 percent, and now it's, I think, 6.9 percent, which is some improvement. And the economic stimulus package, which is just now being approved by Congress and has been signed into law by me and is now being implemented, I think, will have an additional beneficial effect. I've been disappointed in the inflation rate, but it's this way all over the world almost.

So, I think as far as the tone of the Government and the attitude of our people toward the Government, the marks would be fairly high. As far as tangible results in this first 6 months on economy, they've been somewhat disappointing, but I think the slow progress is there. And we have not had any major breakthrough in foreign affairs, although we have a very coherent program that we are pursuing. We are tenacious and determined to improve the situation in southern Africa and in the Middle East, with the Soviets on SALT and test bans against atomic weapons. Our nonproliferation program has been a shock to some other nations but is making progress. And I think that in the organization of Government, our first budget is now being prepared using zero-base budgeting. So far, the progress has been good.

So, specific—too early to say. Tone, trust—pretty good.

MR. DONALDSON. You've retained a very high percentage of popularity. I think, except for the abnormal situation of Lyndon Johnson, at this point in your Presidency, you have more popularity than any recent President. And yet, that seems to be on a personal level; a lot of people don't like your programs and your initiatives.

My question really is: Down the road somewhere, does this line of Jimmy Carter—personally very popular—but President Carter's programs—not so popular—intersect? And what happens then?

THE PRESIDENT. I don't really believe there's that basic conflict between what I am, what I stand for, what I said during the campaign on the one hand, and our actual programs on the other. It's kind of a shock to certain elements in our society to come forward finally with an energy policy. The oil companies are mounting a massive advertising campaign saying that the Government ought to give them more money for additional exploration, which really translates into profits at the expense of consumers. This creates some confusion during the debate phase in Congress, for instance.

Nobody has attempted for a long time to completely revise the welfare system or to bring some renewed stability to the social security program. We've established a new Department of Energy. And we are addressing the basic question of tax reform and so forth. All these changes that will be coming forward with congressional action upset some very powerful and influential elements in our society.

But I think that after a period of 2 or 3 years, the difference between what I am and what the people perceived me to be during the campaign and what my programs actually are as they wind their way through the Congress—that difference will be narrowed and people will see that there's no difference.

ENERGY CONSERVATION

MR. DONALDSON. You mentioned energy, and you are quite correct—some interest groups, of course, are chewing away at the program. Perhaps Russell Long will in the Senate. But I had in mind the total American people. They don't want to pay a gasoline tax apparently, and they don't want to conserve in the tough ways. Did you miscalculate the mood of this country?

THE PRESIDENT. No. I think that the mood of the people is there—very supportive of a comprehensive and strict and profound energy policy designed, first of all, to conserve energy, to put the increased cost of energy equal to what it actually is worth, but to return those revenues back to the people directly in tax reductions or better programs, better insulated homes, more efficient automobiles, research and development in solar energy, and so forth. I think when the whole program is passed, they'll begin to see that although oil and gas is going to cost more—and by the way, the oil and gas companies will make more profits than they are now—the benefits to be derived from that will be long-range.

There's a growing awareness that our increasing imports of foreign oil is hurting our economy. It creates inflation. It means that we import more than we export. And this has got to be turned around. But there's no way to have a popular energy program. I think it's accurate to say that on generalities, the people are strongly in favor of a new, very tough energy conservation program. When you get down to specifics, where they have to cut a little themselves, perhaps they're not so much in favor of it.

But I think the shift toward coal, the savings in oil and gas consumption, the better insulation of homes, more efficient automobiles—these things are bound to come. And when they finally arrive, the people will, I think, favor them.

FOREIGN POLICY

MR. REASONER. Mr. President, at a news conference a couple of weeks ago you said, very understandably, that if you had made some mistakes, you didn't propose to list them. [*Laughter*] If we mentioned a couple of things some people think have been mistakes, maybe you'd have some comment.

THE PRESIDENT. I'll try.

MR. REASONER. In foreign affairs, the suggestion has been made that both in the SALT talks and in the Mideast that you have tended to perhaps be too open, that you have come out with what might seem to be an inflexible American program and just—it's sitting up there for everyone else to shoot at. Have you changed your attitude on how to do this kind of thing since you've taken office?

THE PRESIDENT. No. I think it's best for the American people to know the reason why we have not had a Middle Eastern settlement in 30 years or maybe 2,000 years and to understand not only our own Nation's positions in seeking a compromise or an agreement that might lead to permanent peace but also to understand, as best we can, the difference of opinion that exists between Israel and Egypt and Jordan and Syria and some of the other nations in the Mideast. I think the American people ought to understand and know the facts.

To the extent that there is an open debate in the Congress, in the news media, among the people themselves, I'll feel much more secure, when we take a strong position, that I have the backing of the Congress and the American people—that we ought not to evolve a complicated position in a sensitive area like the Middle East in secret and then spring it on people or negotiate privately.

No one can expect miracles. As I say, this is something that's been sought after for generations—this peace in the Middle East. We may or may not be successful, but we're going to continue to try in a very determined and tenacious way. And I'm going to continue to go public with the American position.

In the SALT talks, we've developed a comprehensive proposal to present to the Soviets. We are doing it both privately and, to some degree, publicly. We want a complete end of testing of nuclear explosives, both military and peaceful explosives.

We have put into effect a new policy on nonproliferation to try to prevent nations that don't presently have atomic explosives from developing them. This has upset some of our allies in Europe who want to sell factories and machines that can make explosive material. But I think we ought to be tenacious about it.

And I think it's good to let the American people know the facts behind the controversies and the debates. Obviously, when these kinds of debates are made public, it creates an image of confusion and a lack of a comprehensive policy, and it shows that our Nation is not a dictator for other countries.

We have to put forward ideas, and maybe over a period of time we'll have some progress. I think we will. But I've never had any doubt that the American people ought to be as thoroughly informed as possible and also involved in the decisionmaking process.

THE MIDDLE EAST

MR. REASONER. Keeping on the Middle East for just one minute, a number of Israeli leaders in private say that you have made drastic changes in America's attitude toward Israel and that they regard you with considerable trepidation. Are you aware of that feeling, and do you think there is justification for it?

THE PRESIDENT. Yes, I'm aware of that feeling and also many other feelings. There's no single attitude among all Jews in the world or all Israeli citizens. To the extent that Israeli leaders genuinely want a peace settlement, I think that they have to agree that there will be an acceptance of genuine peace on the part of the Arabs, an adjustment of boundaries in the Middle East which are secure for the Israelis and also satisfy the minimum requirements of the Arab neighbors and the United Nations resolutions, and some solution to the question of the enormous numbers of Palestinian refugees who have been forced out of their homes and who want to have some fair treatment.

These three basic elements are there. And we are trying not only to put forward our own ideas but to search among the different disputing nations for some common basis on which they can reach agreement. We can only act as an intermediary to the extent that the different countries trust us.

So, we've tried to be fair. We've tried to be open when possible. We've kept confidences when they have been given to us in confidence. And I don't know that we can reach a final solution. We are hopeful that we can, and I think world opinion is very powerful on disputing nations when there is a consensus about what ought to be done.

So, we'll continue to labor at it, taking slings and arrows from all directions, criticisms, publicly in nations when privately the leaders say we are willing to do this when we come out publicly for the same position. Quite often for domestic political consumption there's an adamant, very disputive, and antagonistic attitude taken on the part of some leaders. But we are willing to accept this consequence. I don't know how to guarantee an ultimate success, but I am willing to accept the criticism that comes from all parties as we struggle for success.

BERT LANCE

MR. DONALDSON. Mr. President, you talked a moment ago about one of your accomplishments. You said very proudly that the restoration of confidence in government was high.

THE PRESIDENT. Yes.

MR. DONALDSON. And all the polls show that people give you high marks for integrity. Against this background, what are you going to do about the problem of Bert Lance?

THE PRESIDENT. Well, the inquiry that's going on now by the Comptroller of the Currency concerning Bert Lance's banking practices before he came into the Government, I think, is a healthy circumstance.

When allegations are made in the news media or from private sources, it's incumbent on the Government to investigate those. Bert Lance is cooperating with the Comptroller. I have confidence in both the Government officials in the Treasury Department and also in Bert Lance. And as I've said before, I don't know the details and don't want to become involved in the details of what went on in 1975 or prior to that time. But I have confidence that both the Comptroller and Bert will make the facts known to the public and let the situation be judged accordingly.

MR. DONALDSON. But I think you have a higher problem than perhaps past Presidents because you had a higher standard. The question is not illegality. As I understand it, most of these investigations are not dealing on the question of illegality, but simply propriety of a man who might have been able to do something that is common practice in the banking field and yet personally benefit, whereas, the ordinary citizen—and you ran against people who didn't pay their fair share—wouldn't benefit. Don't you have to hold Mr. Lance to that higher standard?

THE PRESIDENT. Yes, I think so. And I believe that Bert would agree that a high standard has to be maintained. I'm not aware of any improprieties that have been proven against Bert Lance. Allegations or accusations have been made against me, Bert Lance, and many others. But I have complete confidence that when all the facts are known that the situation will be

judged by the American public to have been handled properly.

MR. DONALDSON. You know, one more question on this subject. Harry Truman, whom you admire greatly, had one failing that many people found as a failing. He stuck by his friends too long.

Now, at some point aren't you going to have to make a hard decision as to the good of your administration, maintaining the integrity that people have in your administration, versus a friend?

THE PRESIDENT. I don't have any qualms about that. I believe that if anything should be proven concerning Bert Lance that's either improper or illegal, that Bert would immediately take the initiative to either resign or step aside or offer to.

I don't have any concern about Bert Lance and his attitude toward me, my administration, his responsibility to the people. As I said before, though, it's something that ought to be decided between the Comptroller and Bert with a thorough investigation. All the facts ought to be and will be made public, and then a decision will be made accordingly. But——

MR. DONALDSON. But the buck stops there.

THE PRESIDENT. That's right. Well, I am ultimately responsible and don't hesitate to accept that responsibility. But I have enough confidence in Bert Lance to know that if any improprieties do exist, that he would take the initiative to step aside. So far, no improprieties have been proven.

ANDREW YOUNG

MR. REASONER. There are a lot of ways that friends can get you glory or get you in trouble besides improprieties. How do you feel these days about Andrew Young?

THE PRESIDENT. The same as I've always felt. I think that there is now and will be a growing realization of the value of Andrew Young to our country—both his work in the United Nations and also his work among the developing countries of the world, who in the past have been turned away from us almost unanimously.

There has been a time in years gone by when in the very crucial international organizations we couldn't get 20 percent of the other nations to support our positions even when we thought we had the right positions.

Now I think there's a growing feeling among those small and poor and weak countries that they can trust us for a change, that there's someone in our Government who can listen to them with an open mind, represent the best interests of the United States, and still represent their best interests as well.

Andrew Young is intelligent, courageous, articulate, accurately represents the position that I and the Secretary of State and others have evolved for our own country and is building up trust in our country among the nations who didn't trust us before.

He's a great national treasure, in my opinion, and he has my complete confidence and I think I have his complete confidence.

I might say that there has never been any difference of opinion on basic issues among Andrew Young, the Secretary of State and the National Security Council or myself.

RELATIONS WITH CONGRESS

MR. REASONER. Mr. President, you've been sleeping in the White House for nearly 7 months now. You campaigned sort of against the White House and Washington and the establishment and the bureaucracy.

Have you changed your attitude about that? There was a comic strip the other day that said that you were going

Washington, you are now an insider. [*Laughter*]

THE PRESIDENT. Well, I feel more and more like an insider. I think the thing that's made me naturally come to that sense of my position has been the increasingly good relationship between the White House and the Congress.

I've been deeply grateful at the spirit of cooperation and harmony that has evolved because of the leadership in the House and the Senate—I might say, on many occasions both Republican and Democratic leadership.

We face some tough decisions in the future that's going to require bipartisan support—Middle East questions; normalizing relations with China, if they want normal relations; how to deal with the Panama Canal treaty, which has been attempted for 13 years and which is now approaching a final conclusion; how to evolve our Nation's position on the matter of nuclear weapons or comprehensive test bans; the degree of commitment to different aspects of defense capability. All these matters involving defense and foreign affairs have got to be based on a bipartisan support.

But I feel part of the Washington Government now, not in an embarrassed way, but in a natural way. And I believe that there's been a restoration of harmony and cooperation and mutual purpose between the White House and Republicans and Democrats in the Congress, which is very healthy for our country.

THE PRESIDENT'S GOALS

MR. DONALDSON. Mr. President, the day before you took the oath of office I asked you if you thought you were just going to be an ordinary President or whether you had a chance for greatness, and you said you thought you had a chance for greatness.

THE PRESIDENT. A chance.

MR. DONALDSON. Now after 6 months of looking at the problems and finding that the bureaucracy doesn't move as rapidly as you might have thought and the Congress doesn't roll over as you might have suspected, what's your estimate?

THE PRESIDENT. Well, that's hard to say. I think it's primarily dependent on both the support that I can maintain among the people of the country and the Congress for the next 3½ years. A 6- or 7-month period is brief in the historical trends that relate to problems that have been there for generations. And if all of our programs are adopted, then I think this administration will be a great one.

But we're going to have a lot of failures and a lot of frustrations, and I think the American people have got to realize that the Government can't provide magic answers for difficult questions and problems. But I think history would have to decide that 20 years from now, looking backward, rather than for me to decide after just 6 months of experience in Washington.

We've got some great ideas and goals. I think the American people have seen a substantial rebuilding of pride in our country. I think that all the polls and my own relations with American people have indicated that there's a renewed sense that our country stands for something that's clean and decent and open, that the American people have more of a participation in the decisionmaking process.

I think there's a general feeling that when we make a mistake, that the mistake is not concealed but is instantly revealed. I think the frequent news conferences and the frankness with which we've discussed formerly secret issues has been constructive.

But as far as whether greatness or mediocrity will result from this administration, it's just too early to say.

MR. REASONER. Mr. President, one final question. We're sort of taking a poll, too. How would you rate Sam Donaldson as a White House correspondent? [*Laughter*]

THE PRESIDENT. I tell you, it's too early to say. [*Laughter*] Maybe history will reveal whether Sam has been adequate or below average or great. But after just 7 months, I've not been able to decide. I've put a lot of time in thinking about this question—[*laughter*]—but so far the answer has escaped me.

MR. DONALDSON. You've wasted your time, thank you. You owe about $10,000 back to the American people. [*Laughter*]

MR. REASONER. Thank you, Mr. President.

THE PRESIDENT. Thank you very much, Harry, Sam.

NOTE: The interview began at 11:30 a.m. on August 10 at the Pond House in Plains, Ga. The transcript was released on August 14 when portions of the interview were broadcast on an ABC News television program at 10:30 p.m.

Equal Employment Opportunity Commission

Designation of Daniel E. Leach as Vice Chairman.   August 15, 1977

The President today announced the designation of Daniel E. Leach, of Alexandria, Va., as Vice Chairman of the Equal Employment Opportunity Commission. He replaces Ethel B. Walsh.

Leach, 40, has been a member of the EEOC since March 1976. From 1966 to 1976, he was associate chief counsel of the Democratic Policy Committee in the U.S. Senate.

United States Ambassador to Burma

Nomination of Maurice D. Bean.
August 15, 1977

The President today announced that he will nominate Maurice D. Bean, of Los Angeles, Calif., to be Ambassador Extraordinary and Plenipotentiary of the United States to the Socialist Republic of the Union of Burma. He would replace David L. Osborn.

Bean was born September 9, 1928, in Gary, Ind. He received a B.A. from Howard University in 1950 and an M.A. from Haverford College in 1954.

He was with the Economic Cooperation Administration from 1951 to 1956, serving as a clerk in Djakarta, as assistant program officer, and as program analyst. He served as an international relations officer with the International Cooperation Administration from 1956 to 1959, and as assistant program officer in Bangkok from 1959 to 1961.

Bean served with the Peace Corps from 1961 to 1966 as Associate Director for Development and Operations, then Deputy Regional Director, then Peace Corps Representative in Manila.

He joined the Foreign Service in 1966, serving as country director for Malaysia-Singapore from 1966 to 1970. In 1970–71 he attended the senior seminar in foreign policy at the Foreign Service Institute. He was principal officer in Ibadan from 1971 to 1974, and Deputy Chief of Mission in Monrovia from 1974 to 1976. Since 1976 he has been a senior Foreign Service inspector.

United States Ambassador to Honduras

Nomination of Mari-Luci Jaramillo.
August 15, 1977

The President today announced that he will nominate Mari-Luci Jaramillo, of Albuquerque, N. Mex., to be Ambassador Extraordinary and Plenipotentiary of the United States to Honduras. She would replace Ralph E. Becker.

Jaramillo was born June 19, 1928, in Las Vegas, N. Mex. She received a B.A. in 1955 and an M.A. in 1959 from New Mexico Highlands University and a Ph.D. in 1970 from the University of New Mexico.

From 1962 to 1964, Jaramillo was a language arts consultant in the Las Vegas School System. From 1965 to 1969, she was assistant director of the Latin American education program at the University of New Mexico, and from 1969 to 1972 she was assistant director of instructional services of the Minority Group Center.

Jaramillo served as chairman and professor of the department of elementary education at the University of New Mexico from 1972 to 1975. In 1975–76 she was coordinator of Title VII teacher training. In 1976–77 she was an associate professor of education at the University of New Mexico, and since 1977 she has been a full professor.

Jaramillo is the author of numerous articles and chapters in professional journals and books and has taped several films used for educational instruction. She is a member of the National Association for Bilingual Education, the Latin Americanista Association, La Raza Films Coordinating Committee of McGraw Hill Broadcasting Co., and Bilingual Children's Television.

United States Ambassador to the Bahamas

Nomination of William B. Schwartz, Jr.
August 15, 1977

The President today announced that he will nominate William B. Schwartz, Jr., of Atlanta, Ga., to be Ambassador Extraordinary and Plenipotentiary of the United States to the Commonwealth of the Bahamas. Schwartz would replace Jack B. Olson.

Schwartz was born November 14, 1921, in Atlanta. He received a B.S. from the University of North Carolina in 1942. He served in the U.S. Navy from 1942 to 1945.

From 1945 to 1968, Schwartz was with National Service Industries, retiring as corporate vice president. Since 1969 he has been president of Weine Investment Corp., an Atlanta real estate investment firm.

Schwartz is a member of the president's council of Brandeis University and of the Chatham Valley Foundation. He has served on the board of the Metropolitan Atlanta Rapid Transit Authority.

National Science Foundation

Nomination of George C. Pimentel To Be
Deputy Director and F. James Rutherford
To Be an Assistant Director. August 15, 1977

The President today announced that he will nominate George C. Pimentel to be Deputy Director of the National Science Foundation. He would replace Richard C. Atkinson, who has been appointed Director of the Foundation.

Pimentel was born May 2, 1922, in Rolinda, Calif. He received an A.B. in 1943 and a Ph. D. in 1949 from the University of California.

Pimentel has been on the faculty of the chemistry department at the University of California at Berkeley since 1949 and has been a full professor since 1959. He was a Guggenheim Fellow in 1955.

The President also announced that he will nominate F. James Rutherford, of New York City, to be an Assistant Director of the National Science Foundation for Science Education. He would replace Harvey Averch.

Rutherford was born July 11, 1924, in Stockton, Calif. He received an A.B. from the University of California at Berkeley in 1947, an M.A. from Stanford University in 1949, and an Ed. D. in science education from Harvard University in 1962.

From 1962 to 1964, Rutherford was a science consultant and director of the science-humanities program for the San Mateo Union High School District. He was an assistant, then associate professor of science education and executive director of project physics at Harvard University from 1964 to 1971.

Since 1971 Rutherford has been chairman of the science education department at New York University.

National Science Foundation

Message to the Congress Transmitting the
Foundation's Annual Report.
August 15, 1977

To the Congress of the United States:

I am pleased to submit to the Congress the Twenty-Sixth Annual Report of the National Science Foundation, covering fiscal year 1976. This Report covers events prior to the beginning of my Administration.

The growth of scientific knowledge and its use in the service of mankind is an important concern of our times. The strength of our Nation depends in large part on the ideas and technologies that have emerged from our pursuit of questions at the frontiers of science. We must continue to invest in the development of fundamental knowledge to help meet the challenges and opportunities of the future. My 1978 Budget, now before the Congress, reflects the high order of importance this Administration gives to basic scientific research.

We are aware that the technological advances which result from scientific inquiry represent a mixed blessing, often creating strains upon the environment, our natural resources, and our ability to wisely manage progress. The remedy is not to retreat from new knowledge but to progress further in our understanding of the processes that underlie our universe, drawing upon the inventiveness of our people and keeping alive the political freedom that guarantees our scientists the right of free and open intellectual inquiry.

This annual Report of the National Science Foundation expresses in concrete terms the achievements of scientists and engineers supported by the Foundation's programs during the past fiscal year.

JIMMY CARTER

The White House,
    August 15, 1977.

NOTE: The report is entitled "National Science Foundation, Annual Report 1976" (Government Printing Office, 129 pp.).

The message was not issued in the form of a White House press release.

Jewish High Holy Days

Message of the President.   August 15, 1977

Rosalynn and I extend warmest greetings to our fellow Americans of the Jewish Faith on the occasion of your High Holy Days, in which symbolically "mankind passes in judgment before the heavenly throne".

As you solemnly review and judge your own conduct during the past year, we are all reminded that we serve God most faithfully by showing concern for our friends and neighbors.

In a world made small by modern technology, all peoples and nations have become closer together, and the concern for others has become more important than ever. This is the wellspring of our nation's commitment to human rights, and it is why we are determined that all of America's words and deeds will honor that commitment.

Among the Rosh Hashonah prayers recited in the synagogue is one which looks toward the day when mankind will be joined in universal brotherhood. This is a prayer to which all of us add our heartfelt *Amen* as we wish each of you a happy and prosperous New Year.

JIMMY CARTER

NOTE: The text of the message was made available by the White House Press Office. It was not issued in the form of a White House press release.

Advisory Commission on Intergovernmental Relations

Appointment of Six Members of the Commission.   August 15, 1977

The President has appointed the following persons to be members of the Advisory Commission on Intergovernmental Relations:

REUBIN ASKEW, Governor of Florida (replacing Philip W. Noel, term expired);

RICHARD KNEIP, Governor of South Dakota (reappointment);

RICHARD A. SNELLING, Governor of Vermont (replacing Daniel J. Evans, term as Governor expired);

LYNN CUTLER, chairperson of the Black Hawk County Board of Supervisors, Waterloo, Iowa (replacing Conrad Fowler, term expired);

MARTIN O. SABO, speaker of the Minnesota House of Representatives (replacing Robert Knowles, term expired);

RICHARD W. RILEY, attorney, Greenville, S.C. (replacing John Altorfer, term expired).

The Commission was created in 1959 to maintain a continuing review of the operation of the Federal system and to make recommendations for improvements. It consists of 26 members: 3 officers of the executive branch, 3 private citizens, 3 U.S. Senators, 3 Members of the House of Representatives, 4 Governors, 3 State legislators, 4 mayors, and 3 county officials.

National Advisory Council on Economic Opportunity

Appointment of Arthur I. Blaustein as a Member and Chairman. August 16, 1977

The President today announced the appointment of Arthur I. Blaustein, of Berkeley, Calif., as a member and Chairman of the National Advisory Council on Economic Opportunity. He replaces Winona Holmes, resigned.

Blaustein was born September 1, 1933. He received a B.A. from Bard College in 1957 and an M.A. from Columbia University in 1961. He is presently a Ph. D. candidate in public law and government at the University of California at Davis.

From 1961 to 1963, Blaustein was associate editor of WAR/PEACE Report, a journal on international relations. From 1963 to 1964, he was a program executive for the Foreign Policy Association. In

1965 and 1966, he was Director of Legislative and Public Affairs for the Northeast for the Office of Economic Opportunity (OEO).

In 1967 and 1968, Blaustein was Director of Interagency Coordination and Intergovernmental Affairs for OEO (Northeast). Since 1969 he has been codirector of the National Economic Development Law Project, a specialized support center for more than 150 community economic development corporations and 2,000 legal services attorneys throughout the country.

Blaustein is chairman of the board of directors of the Center for Rural Studies. He is on the board of the National Commission on Law, Social Action and Urban Affairs of the American Jewish Congress. He is on the editorial board of Social Policy and the advisory board of Advocates for Women.

Blaustein is the author of "The Star Spangled Hustle" (1972) and "World War III, Man Against Poverty" (1968), and of numerous articles.

Budget Deferrals

Message to the Congress. August 16, 1977

To the Congress of the United States:

In accordance with the Impoundment Control Act of 1974, I herewith report one new deferral of budget authority amounting to $11.3 million for the Energy Research and Development Administration's Intense Neutron Source Facility. In addition, I am reporting a revision to a previously transmitted deferral for the antirecession financial assistance fund in the Office of the Secretary of the Treasury.

The details of each deferral are contained in the attached reports.

JIMMY CARTER

The White House,
   August 16, 1977.

NOTE: The attachments detailing the deferrals are printed in the FEDERAL REGISTER of August 19, 1977.

The message was not issued in the form of a White House press release.

Death of Elvis Presley

Statement by the President.   August 17, 1977

Elvis Presley's death deprives our country of a part of itself. He was unique and irreplaceable. More than 20 years ago, he burst upon the scene with an impact that was unprecedented and will probably never be equaled. His music and his personality, fusing the styles of white country and black rhythm and blues, permanently changed the face of Amerian popular culture. His following was immense, and he was a symbol to people the world over of the vitality, rebelliousness, and good humor of his country.

Federal Bureau of Investigation

Nomination of Frank M. Johnson, Jr., To Be Director.   August 17, 1977

The President today announced his intention to nominate Frank M. Johnson, Jr., Chief Judge of the U.S. District Court for the Middle District of Alabama, to be Director of the Federal Bureau of Investigation.

Judge Johnson was appointed United States Attorney for the Northern District of Alabama in 1953, serving in that post until he was appointed to the Federal bench by President Eisenhower in 1955.

Judge Johnson became nationally known because of a series of decisions in civil rights cases, beginning with the famous Montgomery bus boycott case. He sat as a member of the three-judge court that abolished the Alabama poll tax; that handed down the first order requiring a State to reapportion its voting districts; that produced the first reapportionment plan designed by judges; that in 1967, ordered the desegregation of over 100 Alabama school districts—the first such statewide ruling in the Nation and one of the most important school orders since the Supreme Court decision of 1954.

In the field of women's rights, he was a member of the panel that gave women the right to serve on juries in the State courts of Alabama, and he was the first United States District Judge in the South to put women on Federal juries after the 1957 Civil Rights Act made it possible. He has ruled that an employer in considering employees for promotion may not discriminate against women on account of their sex, and that female salesclerks in department stores must be paid the same as male salesclerks. He was a member of the three-judge court called upon to decide a female Air Force officer's suit seeking benefits for dependents of female military personnel equal to those enjoyed by male personnel.

During the 22 years that Judge Johnson has been a Federal judge, in the trial of both criminal and civil cases, he has had the opportunity to appraise the performance of the FBI investigative techniques and procedures. He is familiar with the scope of the FBI's jurisdiction and the manner in which the members of that organization discharge their functions and responsibilities.

Judge Johnson has served as a member of the United States Judicial Conference Committee on the Federal Probation System and the Advisory Committee on Federal Criminal Rules. At present, he is a member of the committee which receives and reviews reports from other Federal judges on their extra-judicial income and activities. He is a member of the Joint Committee of Federal Judges that, in 1973, presented to the United States Judicial Conference a Code of Conduct and Ethics for Federal Judges. The Judicial Conference adopted that code in April 1973. He also serves as a member of the Emergency Court of Appeals, which reviews decisions of the various district courts in Economic Stabilization Act cases.

Judge Johnson was born October 30, 1918, in the northern part of Alabama, Winston County.

He attended grade schools in Winston County. He was graduated from Mississippi's Gulf Coast Military Academy, worked as a surveyor, spent a year in business college, and in 1938, married Ruth Jenkins, who is also from Winston County. Both worked their way through the University of Alabama.

When World War II separated them, Mrs. Johnson served as a WAVE lieutenant in Washington. Johnson, while a combat infantry officer in General Patton's Third Army, was awarded a commendation medal for outstanding action against the enemy during the Normandy invasion, was wounded, and in 1945 was sent back to England as a legal officer. He was discharged as a captain.

NOTE: Attorney General Griffin B. Bell announced the President's intention to nominate Judge Johnson at a news conference at the White House on August 17.

Federal Bureau of Investigation

Statement on the Nomination of Frank M. Johnson, Jr., To Be Director. August 17, 1977

I appreciate Judge Johnson's willingness to accept this important position. He brings a reputation as a tough, fairminded protector of justice and the law. My admiration for him is shared by those who have disagreed as well as agreed with his many difficult decisions from the bench. He will be a credit to the FBI, this administration, and the country.

I also commend the work of the selection commission and appreciate the large number of outstanding Americans who were willing to be considered for this position. My selection of Judge Johnson should in no way be considered a reflection on the commission's work.

NOTE: The statement was made available by the White House Press Office. It was not issued in the form of a White House press release.

U.S. International Trade Commission Appropriations Bill

Statement on Signing H.R. 6370 Into Law. August 18, 1977

H.R. 6370, which I am signing, authorizes FY 1978 appropriations of $11,522,000 for the International Trade Commission. The bill also provides the President with the power, starting in June 1978, to appoint a Chairman of the six-member Commission, but requires the appointment to be from among the four most senior Commissioners. In addition, the new Chairman must be of the opposite political party from the outgoing Chairman and from the new Vice Chairman.

I believe these restrictions on the selection of a Chairman may unduly limit the

President's ability to select the best available leadership for the Commission.

Accordingly, I hope that Congress will correct this defect prior to the appointment of the new Chairman by enacting legislation giving the President the flexibility to select any of the Commissioners as Chairman.

NOTE: As enacted, H.R. 6370 is Public Law 95–106, approved August 17.

Arms Control and Disarmament Act Amendments of 1977

Statement on Signing H.R. 6179 Into Law. August 18, 1977

I am signing H.R. 6179, the Arms Control and Disarmament Act Amendments of 1977. H.R. 6179 authorizes fiscal year 1978 appropriations of $16,600,000 for the Arms Control and Disarmament Agency.

The bill also adds a new section 37 to the Arms Control and Disarmament Act, declaring the sense of the Congress that adequate verification of compliance should be an indispensable part of any international arms control agreement. The section provides for the Director of the Arms Control and Disarmament Agency to furnish to the Congress information regarding verification, including the degree to which each element of any significant arms control proposal made to or by the United States can be verified by existing national technical means. The report of the Conference Committee points out that this provision is not intended to interfere with the President's ability to conduct arms control negotiations but is intended to emphasize the responsibility of the Arms Control and Disarmament Agency to keep Congress informed on these matters.

As Congress recognizes by the adoption of the Conference Report, the conduct of negotiations with other nations is the responsibility of the President under our Constitution. But I share Congress belief in the importance of consultation and close cooperation on these matters, and I am confident that we shall continue to work together in a manner that is consistent with our respective constitutional responsibilities in the conduct of the Nation's foreign policy. It is in this spirit that I am signing this legislation.

NOTE: As enacted, H.R. 6179 is Public Law 95–108, approved August 17.

Director of the Office of Management and Budget

Remarks of the President at a News Conference by Bert Lance Following an Investigation of His Finances. August 18, 1977

I have reviewed the report of the Comptroller of the United States, both personally and also with the White House Legal Counsel, Bob Lipshutz, and my faith in the character and competence of Bert Lance has been reconfirmed. I see no other conclusion that can be drawn from any objective analysis of these findings.

It's obvious that few individuals in Government or out of Government have ever undergone such an extensive and detailed investigation of their personal and business affairs by the Comptroller's Office, by the Justice Department, and twice by the Senate Committee. This process has not been an easy one for Bert, nor for those who are close to him. But I think I speak for him and his family, as well as for myself, when I say that we all recognize that intense scrutiny is a legitimate part of public life and public service.

I want to conclude by thanking Bert Lance for standing firm through difficult times, by answering every question put to him, and by going through this ordeal the last several weeks and, in all instances, conducted himself as a gentleman and as a man of complete integrity.

What is important is that Bert Lance is a man of competence, of honesty, trustworthy, and a man of integrity, and that his services to this country can and should continue. Bert Lance enjoys my complete confidence and support. I'm proud to have him as part of my administration.

As he has been throughout, Mr. Lance is now available to answer any questions that you might have. As far as I'm concerned, as President, the intense investigation and the Comptroller's report has answered questions that were raised against Bert Lance. And any questions that you might have now, in addition to those answered by the Comptroller or including those, Bert will be glad to provide those answers to you.

Bert, I'm proud of you.

NOTE: The President spoke at 3 p.m. to reporters assembled in Room 450 of the Old Executive Office Building.

United States Ambassador to Argentina

Nomination of Raul H. Castro.
August 19, 1977

The President today announced that he will nominate Raul H. Castro, of Scottsdale, Ariz., to be Ambassador Extraordinary and Plenipotentiary of the United States to Argentina. He would succeed Robert C. Hill, resigned.

Castro was born June 12, 1916, in Cananea, Sonora, Mexico, and became a naturalized U.S. citizen in 1939. He received a B.A. from Northern Arizona University in 1939 and a J.D. from the University of Arizona in 1949.

From 1941 to 1946, Castro was in charge of immigration and accounting at the American Consulate in Agua Prieta, Sonora, Mexico. From 1946 to 1949, he was a Spanish instructor at the University of Arizona.

From 1949 to 1955, Castro was senior partner in the law firm of Castro and Wolfe and an assistant Pima County attorney. From 1955 to 1959, he served as Pima County attorney. He was a judge of the Pima County Superior Court from 1959 to 1964.

Castro was U.S. Ambassador to El Salvador from 1964 to 1968 and U.S. Ambassador to Bolivia in 1968 and 1969. From 1969 to 1975, he practiced international and local law in Tucson. Since 1975 he has been Governor of Arizona.

World Law Day, 1977

Proclamation 4514. August 19, 1977

By the President of the United States of America

A Proclamation

The past twenty-five years have been marked by the unprecedented development of international law as nations have come to recognize that cooperation in international relations is the only alternative to chaos. This cooperation depends upon mutual respect, which in turn depends upon the development of legal norms upon which all parties can rely with confidence. These norms must be responsive to each nation's legitimate interests, must respect the feelings and beliefs of all peoples, and must foster a climate of justice and liberty in which each individual on this planet can achieve his or her full potential.

Representatives of the legal profession from every corner of the globe will gather in Manila during the week of August 21, 1977, under the auspices of the World Peace Through Law Center, to inaugurate the Eighth World Conference on World Peace Through Law. Together they will search for ways to further universal human liberty and security. Celebrations devoted to international legal protections for human rights will be held not only in Manila, but in more than one hundred countries. Accordingly, it is fitting that the United States join in this effort to focus the world's attention on the pressing need for continued vigilance in protecting fundamental rights and freedoms for all.

Now, THEREFORE, I, JIMMY CARTER, President of the United States of America, do hereby designate Sunday, August 21, 1977, as World Law Day in the United States. I call upon all public and private officials and organizations, members of the legal profession, the clergy, educators, the communications media, and all men and women of good will to join with the peoples of the world on this day in reflecting on the importance of the rule of law in achieving world peace as well as justice, freedom and dignity for all.

IN WITNESS WHEREOF, I have hereunto set my hand this nineteenth day of August, in the year of our Lord nineteen hundred seventy-seven, and of the Independence of the United States of America the two hundred and second.

JIMMY CARTER

[Filed with the Office of the Federal Register, 3:53 p.m., August 19, 1977]

Digest of Other White House Announcements

The following listing includes the President's daily schedule and other items of general interest as announced by the White House Press Office during the period covered by this issue. Events and announcements printed elsewhere in the issue are not included.

August 13

The President met at the White House with William G. Hyland, senior staff member of the National Security Council.

August 14

The President met at the White House with Secretary of State Cyrus Vance, who reported on his trip to Egypt, Lebanon, Syria, Jordan, Saudi Arabia, and Israel for discussions of the Middle East situation, and also his visit to London for talks concerning southern Africa.

August 15

The President met at the White House with:

—Zbigniew Brzezinski, Assistant to the President for National Security Affairs;

—Hobson R. Reynolds, Grand Exalted Ruler, and representatives of the Improved Benevolent Protective Order of Elks of the World, who presented the President with the Elijah Lovejoy Award and also named him the first recipient of the organization's Benjamin Franklin Howard Award;

—Alan S. Boyd, the President's Special Representative to negotiations for a United States-United Kingdom air services agreement;

—former Secretary of State Henry A. Kissinger;

—Bert Lance, Director, and James T. McIntyre, Jr., Deputy Director, Office of Management and Budget;

—Secretary of Labor F. Ray Marshall and G. William Miller, chairman of the board and chief executive officer of Textron and chairman of the President's Committee on HIRE;

—Matthew Brown, National Muscular Dystrophy Poster Child.

The President telephoned former President Gerald R. Ford in Vail, Colo., to discuss the Panama Canal agreement in principle. The President has asked Ambassador Sol M. Linowitz and Gen. George S. Brown, Chairman of the Joint Chiefs of Staff, to meet with the former President in Vail to brief him on the agreement.

The President transmitted to the Congress the 1976 annual report of the National Aeronautics and Space Administration.

The President left the White House for a stay at Camp David, Md.

August 17

The President met at Camp David with Secretary Vance and Dr. Brzezinski for a general foreign policy discussion with emphasis on the Secretary's forthcoming trip to the People's Republic of China.

August 18

The President transmitted to the Congress the seventh annual report on Hazardous Materials Control, prepared by the Department of Transportation.

The President returned to Washington to take part in a news conference by Bert Lance, Director of the Office of Management and Budget, and then returned to Camp David, Md.

CHECKLIST OF WHITE HOUSE PRESS RELEASES

The following releases of the Office of the White House Press Secretary, distributed during the period covered by this issue, are not included in the issue.

Released August 16, 1977

Announcement: nomination of Alvin B. Rubin to be United States Circuit Judge for the Fifth Circuit; Eugene H. Nickerson to be United States District Judge for the Eastern District of New York; Charles P. Sifton to be United States District Judge for the Eastern District of New York; Richard J. Dunn

CHECKLIST—Continued

to be United States Marshal for the District of Nevada; Franklin Payne to be United States Marshal for the Eastern District of Missouri; Paul J. Puckett to be United States Marshal for the Western District of Virginia; Howard J. Turner, Jr., to be United States Marshal for the Western District of Pennsylvania.

Released August 17, 1977

News conference: on the President's nomination of Frank M. Johnson, Jr., to be Director of the Federal Bureau of Investigation—by Attorney General Griffin B. Bell

Released August 18, 1977

News conference: following the conclusion of an investigation of his finances by the Comptroller of the Currency—by Bert Lance, Director of the Office of Management and Budget

NOMINATIONS SUBMITTED TO THE SENATE

The following list does not include promotions of members of the Uniformed Services, nominations to the Service Academies, or nominations of Foreign Service officers.

Submitted August 15, 1977

MAURICE DARROW BEAN, of California, a Foreign Service officer of Class one, to be Ambassador Extraordinary and Plenipotentiary of the United States of America to the Socialist Republic of the Union of Burma.

MARI-LUCI JARAMILLO, of New Mexico, to be Ambassador Extraordinary and Plenipotentiary of the United States of America to Honduras.

WILLIAM B. SCHWARTZ, JR., of Georgia, to be Ambassador Extraordinary and Plenipotentiary of the United States of America to The Commonwealth of The Bahamas.

GEORGE CLAUDE PIMENTEL, of California, to be Deputy Director of the National Science Foundation, vice Richard C. Atkinson, elevated.

FLOYD JAMES RUTHERFORD, of New York, to be an Assistant Director of the National Science Foundation, vice Harvey Allan Averch, resigned.

NOMINATIONS—Continued

Submitted August 16, 1977

ALVIN B. RUBIN, of Louisiana, to be United States Circuit Judge for the Fifth Circuit, vice John Minor Wisdom, retired.

EUGENE H. NICKERSON, of New York, to be United States District Judge for the Eastern District of New York, vice Orrin G. Judd, deceased.

CHARLES P. SIFTON, of New York, to be United States District Judge for the Eastern District of New York, vice John F. Dooling, Jr., retired.

RICHARD J. DUNN, of Nevada, to be United States Marshal for the District of Nevada for the term of 4 years, vice Denny L. Sampson.

FRANKLIN PAYNE, of Missouri, to be United States Marshal for the Eastern District of Missouri for the term of 4 years, vice Kenneth M. Link, Sr.

PAUL J. PUCKETT, of Virginia, to be United States Marshal for the Western District of Virginia for the term of 4 years, vice William A. Quick, Jr.

HOWARD J. TURNER, JR., of Pennsylvania, to be United States Marshal for the Western District of Pennsylvania for the term of 4 years, vice Charles W. Koval, deceased.

ACTS APPROVED BY THE PRESIDENT

Approved August 12, 1977

H.R. 7558_____ Public Law 95–97
An act making appropriations for Agriculture and Related Agencies programs for the fiscal year ending September 30, 1978, and for other purposes.

Approved August 15, 1977

H.J. Res. 372_____ Public Law 95–100
A joint resolution to authorize the President to issue a proclamation designating the week beginning on November 20, 1977, as "National Family Week".

H.R. 1952_____ Public Law 95–98
An act to amend the corporate name of AMVETS (American Veterans of World War II), and for other purposes.

ACTS APPROVED—Continued

Approved August 15—Continued

H.R. 2563_____ Private Law 95–7
An act for the relief of Velzora Carr.

H.R. 4991_____ Public Law 95–99
National Science Foundation Authorization Act, Fiscal Year 1978.

H.R. 7589_____ Public Law 95–101
Military Construction Appropriation Act, 1978.

S. 1235_____ Public Law 95–102
An act to authorize appropriations for the Peace Corps for fiscal year 1978.

S. 1377_____ Public Law 95–103
An act to amend the statute of limitations provisions in section 2415 of title 28, United States Code, relating to claims by the United States on behalf of Indians.

S. 1765_____ Private Law 95–6
An act for the relief of the Federal Life and Casualty Company of Battle Creek, Michigan.

S. 2001_____ Public Law 95–104
An act authorizing additional appropriations for prosecution of projects in certain comprehensive river basin plans for flood control, water conservation, recreation, hydroelectric power and other purposes.

Approved August 17, 1977

H.R. 6179_____ Public Law 95–108
Arms Control and Disarmament Act Amendments of 1977.

H.R. 6370_____ Public Law 95–106
An act to authorize appropriations to the United States International Trade Commission, to provide for greater efficiency in the administration of the Commission, and for other purposes.

H.R. 6689_____ Public Law 95–105
Foreign Relations Authorization Act, Fiscal Year 1978.

S. 1935_____ Public Law 95–107
An act to amend Public Law 95–18, providing for emergency drought relief measures.

Daniel "Chappie" James, Jr., Airmen and Industrial Museum

Message for the Groundbreaking in Tuskeegee, Alabama. August 19, 1977

A museum on the grounds of old Tuskeegee Airbase, where black airmen and support troops trained in World War II, is a useful and long overdue tribute to the sacrifice of these brave men. It is highly appropriate that the Air and Industrial Museum is being named for Gen. Daniel "Chappie" James Jr., who has served his country with such distinction. Despite segregation at the time, the black troops who trained here compiled an honorable record. Wallace and Wallace Chemical and Oil Corp. is to be commended for setting aside this museum area in their honor and for its plan to restore planes and equipment of the era so that future generations will better understand the contribution of black servicemen who fought and died for their country, and black industrialists and others who have contributed to the nation's economic well-being.

JIMMY CARTER

NOTE: The message was sent by telegram to Charles Wallace, president of Wallace and Wallace Enterprises, Inc., who read it at the ceremony in Tuskeegee on August 19.

The text of the message was made available by the White House Press Office. It was not issued in the form of a White House press release.

International Pacific Salmon Fisheries Commission

Appointment of Gordon Sandison as a Member. August 22, 1977

The President today announced the appointment of Gordon Sandison, of Olympia, Wash., as a member on the part of the United States of the International Pacific Salmon Fisheries Commission. He replaces Donald W. Moos, who has resigned. Sandison is director of the Washington Department of Fisheries.

He was born February 20, 1919, in Auburn, Wash. He received a B.S. from Seattle University and an LL.D. from St. Martins College.

Sandison served in the U.S. Marine Corps from 1942 to 1945. From 1947 to 1958, he was a member of the Washington State House of Representatives, and from 1958 to 1977 he was a Washington State senator.

Since 1977 Sandison has been director of the Washington Department of Fisheries.

Strategic Arms Limitation Talks

Nomination of Frank H. Perez for the Rank of Minister While Serving as State Department Representative. August 22, 1977

The President today announced that he will nominate Frank H. Perez, of Virginia, for the rank of Minister during the tenure of his assignment as the State Department SALT representative at Geneva.

Perez was born February 7, 1924, in Washington, D.C. He received an A.B. in 1949 and an M.A. in 1952 from George Washington University. He served in the U.S. Army from 1943 to 1946.

Perez was a military intelligence specialist in the Department of the Army from 1950 to 1951. From 1952 to 1967, he was senior air intelligence specialist in the Department of the Air Force and was detailed to the National War College in 1965–66.

From 1967 to 1968, Perez was an intelligence research specialist at the State Department, and in 1968 and 1969 he was a foreign affairs politico-military-scientific analyst, then Chief, at the Strategic Intelligence Division, Bureau of Intelligence-Research.

Between 1970 and 1974, Perez served as Deputy Director, then Director, of the Office of Strategic and General Research. He was a political officer at Brussels (NATO) from 1974 to 1977, and since 1977 has been the State Department representative to SALT.

Ohio River Valley Water Sanitation Commission

Appointment of Richard C. Armstrong as a U.S. Commissioner.   August 22, 1977

The President today announced the appointment of Richard C. Armstrong as a Commissioner representing the U.S. Government on the Ohio River Valley Water Sanitation Commission. He replaces Donald Williams, resigned.

Armstrong, 40, has been with the Army Corps of Engineers since 1960. Since 1976 he has been Chief of the Engineering Division, Ohio River Division, of the Corps.

UNESCO Executive Board

Approval of Henry E. Kerry, Jr., To Be the U.S. Member.   August 22, 1977

The President today announced his approval of the Secretary of State's selection of Henry E. Kerry, Jr., of Fort Worth, Tex., to fill the unexpired term of the present U.S. member of the executive board of UNESCO, Robert B. Kamm, who has resigned. Kamm's term expires in 1978. Kerry's name will be submitted to the board for approval.

Kerry was born November 5, 1932, in Longview, Tex. He received a B.A. in 1952 and an LL.B. in 1957 from the University of Texas.

From 1957 to 1977, Kerry was an attorney with the Fort Worth law firm of Hooper, Kerry, Chappell & Broiles. He was president of the State Junior Bar Association of Texas in 1963–64 and served on the Planning Commission of Judicial Selection, Administration and Tenure in 1964. He has contributed numerous articles to bar journals.

THE PRESIDENT'S NEWS CONFERENCE OF AUGUST 23, 1977

THE PRESIDENT. Good afternoon. I have three or four brief announcements to make before I answer your questions.

SOUTH AFRICA

First of all, in response to our own direct inquiry and that of other nations, South Africa has informed us that they do not have and do not intend to develop nuclear explosive devices for any purpose, either peaceful or as a weapon, that the Kalahari test site which has been in question is not designed for use to test nuclear explosives, and that no nuclear explosive test will be taken in South Africa now or in the future.

We appreciate this commitment from South Africa and this information. We will, of course, continue to monitor the situation there very closely. We'll also renew our efforts to encourage South Africa to place all their nuclear power production capabilities under international safeguards and inspections and encourage them along with other nations to sign the nuclear nonproliferation treaty.

PANAMA CANAL

Another item is that, as relates to the Panama Canal treaty, we have become interested, after the original discussions were concluded, in assuring that some definite commitment be made about a possible future development of a sea-level canal. As you know, the existing canal facilities cannot be used for large warships or cargo ships. And if it becomes necessary in the future for a sea-level canal to be constructed, we want to be sure that we have an opportunity to be involved directly in this construction and not have some possible hostile nation supplant us with our influence in the canal area.

We have asked Panama for this assurance, and this will be part of the treaties that we will sign—that if any sea-level canal or modification of the present canal is concluded, that we will be part of it if we choose and also, in return, that any sea-level canal to be built during the terms of the treaty will be built in Panama.

RHODESIA

A third item that I have to report to you is that in our effort to bring about a peaceful solution to the Rhodesian or Zimbabwe crisis, we have been trying to evolve, along with the British, a fair proposal that would be acceptable to the frontline nations, to the nationalist forces in Rhodesia, to the present Government of Rhodesia, to the South Africans, and others. And there will be a meeting of the frontline presidents in Lusaka, which is Zambia, beginning Friday.

And Ambassador Young, representing us, and Foreign Minister David Owen, representing the British, will be meeting with the frontline presidents in Lusaka on Saturday, the 27th of August. There they will go over our proposals on the Rhodesian question. And I believe this is a possible step toward a peaceful resolution of that question. We still have a lot of issues to resolve, but it is an encouraging thing.

PEOPLE'S REPUBLIC OF CHINA

The other I'd like to report is that Secretary Vance is continuing his discussions in China, primarily with Foreign Minister Huang Hua, and this evening he has been having a banquet sponsored by and hosted by Teng Hsiao-ping, who is the Vice Chairman of the Communist Party in China and who is also the Deputy Prime Minister.

We don't know what the results of these in-depth discussions might be yet. I won't be prepared to give you any detailed information until I hear from Secretary Vance at the conclusion of these talks.

I'd be glad to answer any questions.

Mr. Gerstenzang [James R. Gerstenzang, Associated Press].

QUESTIONS

PANAMA CANAL

Q. Mr. President, you have said that your foreign policy decisions should be made in consultation with the American people and that these decisions should reflect their thinking.

THE PRESIDENT. Yes.

Q. Yet there have been, so far, strong expressions of public disagreement with the Panama Canal treaty as we now see it.

How do you reconcile these differences, and what steps will be taken to convince the American people that you are right, that they are wrong, and that the canal treaty is in the best long-term interests of the United States?

THE PRESIDENT. We expect to conclude the drafting of the detailed language in the Pamana Canal treaties within the next few days, but they have to be compared to be sure that the Spanish text and the English text are compatible and that all the elements have been expressed in legal and proper language.

As soon as that is done, the text of the treaty will be released to the Members of the Congress and also to the American people and the news media. At this time we are going on a fairly detailed expression of principles which will be the basis for the treaty itself. And that set of principles in some minute detail has already been released.

I think there's been a great deal of misconception about what is being concluded in Panama, which may be one of the reasons that there is not popular support for the Panama Canal treaty at this point.

The negotiations were begun 13 years ago when President Johnson was President, as a result of an altercation, bloodshed, loss of life by both Panama and American troops there. And in my opinion, the terms of the canal protect American interests very well. We will retain control of the Panama Canal throughout this century. We will have an assurance in perpetuity following the year 2000 that the Panama Canal will be neutral, that our ships will have unlimited access to the canal, along with the ships of other nations. We have no constraints on the action that we can take as a nation to guarantee that neutrality. Our own ships and those of Panama will have priority for expeditious passage through the canal in a case—in a time of emergency.

And I think that this is an agreement that is very conducive to continued peace, to better relationships with nations and people in the Latin American area, and I think most of the objections that were raised earlier about a giveaway, a highly exorbitant payment to Panama, loss of control, takeover by some other government, a prohibition against the free use of the canal—all those concerns, which were legitimate in the past, have now been answered successfully for our Nation within the present negotiations.

But it will be a major responsibility of my own, through my own statements and through those of others who support the Panama Canal treaty to give the American people the facts. I think that to a substantial degree, those who do have the facts and have studied this situation closely concur that these two treaties are advantageous for us. This is a bipartisan support. It does involve, of course, myself and the members of my administration. The Joint Chiefs of Staff, with absolutely no pressure, encouragement from me, unanimously believe that this treaty is in the best interests of our own Nation's security. President Ford supports the treaty strongly, Secretary Kissinger supports it strongly, and so do many others.

But my belief is that as the American people become acquainted with the very good terms of the treaty, they will shift their support to the treaty itself.

Q. Would you say, then, that those who are criticizing it are not fully informed on it yet?

THE PRESIDENT. Obviously there are some who are fully informed who just don't want to make any change in the present terms concerning the operation of the treaty. I wouldn't want to say that anyone who disagrees with me is ignorant, but I believe that the way to arouse public support for the treaty is to let the American people know the advantages to our country of its terms.

I'm convinced that it's advantageous. I was not convinced of this fact, say, a year ago. But I think that the terms that we hope to achieve in our negotiations for the benefit of our country have all been achieved.

ISRAEL

Q. Mr. President, twice in recent weeks the United States has said that Israel is in violation of international law in terms of the West Bank settlements, which some view as an annexation plan. My question is: What does the United States plan to do to protect the rights of the people in the occupied lands?

THE PRESIDENT. Well, it's been the position of our own Government, long before I was elected President, that the West Bank territory, the Gaza Strip, areas of the Golan Heights, Sinai region, the occupied territories, in other words, were not a part of Israel. Our Government has expressed on several occasions—the President, our Ambassadors to the United Nations and otherwise—that the settlement of Israeli citizens in some of these areas was in violation of the Geneva Convention and that, therefore, the settlements were illegal.

We have private assurances and there have been public statements made by Mr. Begin that these settlements were not intended to show that Israel was to occupy these territories permanently, that the final boundaries to be established through mutual agreement between Israel and the Arab countries was to be decided without prior commitment, and negotiations would include these areas.

So, at this time, our pointing out to Israel that these three settlements that were just established are illegal because they were made on occupied territory, is the extent of our intention.

I concur with the statement that was made by Secretary Vance, the State Department, that this kind of action on the part of Israel, when we are trying to put together a Middle Eastern conference leading to a permanent peace, creates an unnecessary obstacle to peace. I believe that our opinion is shared by the overwhelming number of nations in the world, but we don't intend to go further than our caution to Israel, our open expression of our own concern, and the identification of these settlements as being illegal.

Q. But you don't feel that you have any leverage at all to move in any direction in terms of military aid to Israel to keep her from violating——

THE PRESIDENT. Obviously, we could exert pressure on Israel in other ways, but I have no intention to do so.

BERT LANCE

Q. Mr. President, 2 weeks ago you said in an interview that you had faith that Bert Lance would resign if the Comptroller's report showed any illegality or impropriety. And the report has confirmed that, indeed, he had lingering or was involved in lingering overdrafts, that there were large advances to bank officials, there were advances to his campaign for Governor.

Could you tell us what in the Comptroller's report—what words in that report convinced you that Bert Lance should not resign?

THE PRESIDENT. I don't know the details of Bert's relationship with the Calhoun National Bank where the overdrafts did occur. But my information, as derived from the Comptroller's report, is that in his own private accounts—that of himself and the other members of his family, plus a certificate of deposit which I think was in excess of $100,000—there was almost always a surplus amount of money on hand; in other words, that the overdraft in his campaign account was less than the amount of money he had on deposit at the bank; also that there was an agreement between not only Bert Lance but the customers of the bank, as a general policy, that if you had more than one bank account and you were overdrawn in one, but had more than enough money to cover that overdraft in other accounts, that this was accepted by the bank and the checks were honored. This is a common practice in a small or country bank. That's no excuse for an overdrawn account.

I think it is accurate to say that on one occasion, when this did not apply, that the money was paid back very quickly, that interest was paid on the overdraft, and it was handled in a completely normal way as it would have had I been the person who had the overdrawn account.

I've spent a great deal of time trying to become acquainted with the charges or allegations against Bert Lance. It means a lot to him. It means a lot to me personally as a friend of his. It means a lot to me as a President, responsible for the integrity and reputation not only of my Cabinet officers but myself. I don't know of any allegation that has been made or proven that Bert Lance did anything illegal or even unethical.

Now, I think that there are some possibilities that have been revealed in the practices of personal loans by bank officials from correspondent banks that might be changed in the future. But at the time these personal loans were made with correspondent banks—and I understand from one of the periodicals this is done with 93 percent of the correspondent banks and bank officials throughout the country—it may have been advisable for Bert and all others like him several years ago to make those loans public. That was not required. At the time that Mr. Lance ran for Governor in 1974, at the time Bert Lance submitted his name for approval by the Senate committee for OMB Director, he made a public statement of his debts owed and his net worth and how the debts were secured. I think it's obvious that he complied with not only the law and the ethics required but common loan practices among bank officers.

Now, it may be, as I say, that as a result of these investigations that stricter requirements should be implemented by law and also by the Comptroller in his standard operating procedures, but I don't know of anything either illegal or unethical even that Bert Lance has ever done.

Q. Mr. President, how can the Lance case be closed, as you seem to see it, as long as these investigations go on, the Comptroller's and the probes in the Senate?

THE PRESIDENT. I would not want to hasten their conclusion, using my own influence. I've never met the Comptroller, so far as I know. I've never had any conversation with him, have never tried to influence him, and wouldn't.

I think it's also been announced that the Senate committees, maybe two committees, will look further into the allegations against Mr. Lance. I think in the fairly voluminous report that the Comptroller filed, which I did read, that all of the allegations against him were listed, the investigative procedures were outlined, the findings were described and the facts revealed.

There may be some facts that have not yet been determined. But I think that it's part of our governmental process not to discourage, but to encourage the most detailed analysis and investigation when an allegation is made against a public official.

But I also think it's part of our process that if allegations are unfounded or if there is no illegal or unethical conduct revealed, that the accused public official should be exonerated. And this is the way I assess, after great study, the Bert Lance case. I have no objection to Senator Proxmire continuing with an investigation. And I think this is very good. I'd have no objection to Senator Ribicoff continuing with the investigation. But I think that that's part of our political process that ought to be encouraged.

Q. You don't see it, then, Mr. President, to be appropriate, as President, to keep an open mind until all these probes are completed?

THE PRESIDENT. I don't know how long the probes will be continued. So far as I know, the allegations with which I am familiar have been investigated and have been answered. And if any new information should be derived against Bert Lance or against the Secretary of State or the Secretary of the Treasury or anyone else in my administration, I would certainly have to assess new information as it arose.

But my judgment is that the investigation has been very complete. There's been a Comptroller's investigation in Atlanta. There's been, I think, two Department of Justice investigations, I think two Senate investigations, and now the U.S. Comptroller investigation. And as I say again, to repeat myself, there has been no evidence of either illegalities or unethical conduct and no conduct that was contrary to the normal practices that exist in the banking circles in our country.

Q. Mr. President, could I follow up? If the Comptroller's report had been made on, say, Mike Blumenthal or some assistant secretary in your administration, would you have found it acceptable for that person as you did for Lance?

THE PRESIDENT. Yes, sir.

Q. Mr. President, without belaboring this, during the transition, you and many of your top spokesmen said you wanted to avoid not only conflicts of interest in your top appointments but also the appearance of conflicts.

THE PRESIDENT. Yes.

Q. Mr. Lance has many loans out. And although they're held in a private trust, it is theoretically possible that someone who holds such a loan could come to him and ask a favor and without mentioning the loan, just ask the favor. Does that to you represent avoidance of the appearance of conflict? Isn't there the appearance of conflict here?

THE PRESIDENT. I don't know any alternative to that. As you know, Secretary Blumenthal was an official, for instance, in the Bendix Corporation. And he has put his holdings in a blind trust and instructed them over a period of time to dispose of those holdings or either to retain some of them.

I think that our Assistant Secretary of Defense has similar holdings in Coca-Cola Company. I have holdings in Carters

Warehouse and in my own farms. You can't expect a public official to dispose of all their net worth before they come to government.

And the legal framework of having those holdings put in a trust where the owner of that stock or property does not control the action concerning it, whether it's completely adequate or not, is the best that we can contrive.

There is also a complicating factor in the holding of bank stock. There's a U.S. law that prevents this resale of bank stock, I think within 6 months or 9 months after it's purchased. And this is designed to prevent the buying and trading and negotiations with bank stocks just for a profit motive in a transient way. And so there has been a time limit on when the Lance bank stock could be sold.

So, I do think that the appearance of impropriety or illegality or unethical conduct has been honored. But obviously, there could be those who say that because I still own several hundred acres of land in Georgia, that I have a conflict of interests relating to agricultural legislation. But I've done the best I could to isolate myself from it.

I think that's the best we can do, and I really believe that it's adequate.

Q. Mr. President, do you think the American taxpayer has reason to question the competence of a man in charge of the Federal budget who, after he has taken that job, wrote seven overdrafts on his own account?

THE PRESIDENT. I didn't know—you are referring to Mr. Lance?

Q. Yes. It's in the Comptroller's report.

THE PRESIDENT. I see. Well, obviously it's better not to write overdrafts. [*Laughter*]

I can't deny that I have written overdrafts on my own bank accounts on occasion and so has my wife, not deliberately, but because of an error or because of higher priorities that I assigned to other responsibilities that I had at the time. I think that there's no doubt that Bert Lance is one of the more competent and intelligent people that I have ever known in my life.

I realized 8 or 9 months ago, and I still realize, that the management of the Office of Management and Budget is one of the crucial assignments that will determine the success or failure of my own administration. And I cast about in my mind about who, among all those that I knew or knew about, would more competently fill that position.

My choice, without any competition, I might say, was Bert Lance. I still have that much faith in his honesty and his competence. And the fact that he has had overdrafts, I think—is obviously better had he not had them, but is no reflection on his basic judgment or competence.

He, like many other successful business leaders, has a multiplicity of bank accounts, stockholdings, business investments. And he has tried to sever himself from all those management responsibilities by placing his holdings into the hands of a trustee. And I can't answer the question about private bank account overdrafts. But my guess is that when an overdraft has occurred in a particular account, that his deposits in other accounts in that same bank were more than adequate to cover them.

PANAMA CANAL

Q. Mr. President, going back to the Panama Canal, do you favor a widening of the canal to make it usable for the largest modern warships and perhaps an American investment in a sea-level canal, as you mentioned earlier?

THE PRESIDENT. It's obvious to me that over a period of time the Panama

Canal in its original conformation has become inadequate. I think in the last 12 months, only four or five Navy warships have been through the canal at all. Any large ship, an aircraft carrier, for instance, would have to go around the southern area of South America.

Standard oil tankers that would bring oil, say, from Alaska to the gulf coast area, or the Atlantic area, could not possibly go through the Panama Canal. That oil, if transported through the canal, would have to be offloaded into small, lighter small ships and taken to the canal and then up to, say, New Orleans or some other gulf coast port.

Over a period of time, I think that the canal needs to be expanded. I think it's premature now, though, for me to decide whether or not a sea-level canal would be advocated or whether an expansion of the present canal facilities would be best. There has been a very elaborate study made of this, I think concluding only .a year or two ago, and, I think, initiated when President Johnson was in office, that showed that if a sea-level canal was needed, that it ought to be placed in Panama. That was before we had the additional opportunity to haul Alaskan oil and natural gas through the canal. So, that's an option for the future. I just want to be sure that we don't foreclose the option, if a sea-level canal is built, of our Nation playing a role in it, in harmony with and in partnership with Panama.

But whether we need it at this time, I doubt; in the future I think we will——

Q. Mr. President?

THE PRESIDENT. Yes, Judy [Judy Woodruff, NBC News].

Q. Mr. President, when you met with Secretary Kissinger last week, you told him in the presence of reporters that you had told President Ford that morning that you had what you called an absolute continuum of what you—referring to

Secretary Kissinger—and President Ford had started on southern Africa, the Middle East, Panama, and Chile.

THE PRESIDENT. No, I didn't mention those things, but go ahead with your question.

Q. This is according to a report that was written by reporters who were present.

At any rate, if you used the words "absolute continuum," what did you mean by that, and were you saying that the voters had no choice on those issues between you and President Ford?

THE PRESIDENT. I didn't mention any specific areas of the world where there was an absolute continuum. What Secretary Kissinger came to talk to me about was the Panama Canal. In some areas of foreign policy, there is a complete continuum as Presidents change. I have a different emphasis that I have placed on foreign affairs questions than did President Ford or President Nixon or their predecessors.

I think in the case of the Panama Canal negotiations, there was a complete continuum. We did appoint Sol Linowitz to help Ellsworth Bunker, and we added to the discussions a concept of guaranteed neutrality of the canal after the year 2000. That was an innovation. But the negotiations with the Panamanian officials continued without interruption.

Ambassador Ellsworth Bunker, who was the lead negotiator when President Ford was in office, continued as my lead negotiator. We added on Sol Linowitz. But I never mentioned anything about Chile or any specific nation in that comment.

BERT LANCE

Q. Mr. President, have you tried to ascertain, or have you ascertained that no one who worked during the transition for you was in contact with the U.S. Attorney's Office in Atlanta or the regional office of the Comptroller and discussing with them the inquiries into Mr. Lance that were extant at that point?

THE PRESIDENT. I have never heard of that before. And if there are any people who worked in the transition time who made an inquiry about Mr. Lance's affairs, they did it without my knowledge and without my authority, and it would have been contrary to my inclinations.

Q. May I follow that up? With all of your Cabinet appointments, before the nominations were made you had benefit of an FBI report, with the exception of Mr. Lance. Do you regret that now, that you made that nomination without the FBI report?

THE PRESIDENT. No, that has not been the case in every instance. For instance, my most recent appointment of Judge Frank Johnson to head up the FBI was made without an IRS and FBI check. There have been a few instances when this was not done because of the pressure of time and because we needed to move aggressively to make the decision or when I had absolute trust in them. But I don't have any regret about that.

MR. GERSTENZANG. Thank you, Mr. President.

NOTE: President Carter's fourteenth news conference began at 2:30 p.m. in Room 450 of the Old Executive Office Building. It was broadcast live on radio and television.

Presidential Advisory Committees
Executive Order 12007.   August 22, 1977

TERMINATION OF CERTAIN PRESIDENTIAL ADVISORY COMMITTEES

By virtue of the authority vested in me by the Constitution and statutes of the United States of America, and as President of the United States of America, in order to terminate certain advisory committees in accordance with the provisions of the Federal Advisory Committee Act (5 U.S.C. App. I), it is hereby ordered as follows:

SECTION 1. (a) The Citizens' Advisory Council on the Status of Women is terminated.

(b) Executive Order No. 11126 of November 1, 1963, as amended by Executive Order No. 11221 of May 6, 1965, is further amended as follows:

(1) Subsection (5) of Section 102 is revoked.

(2) Section 103, in order to delete a reference to the Council, is amended to read as follows:

"Annually the Committee shall transmit a report to the President concerning the status of women."

(3) Part II is revoked.

(4) The second sentence of Section 301, in order to delete references to the Council, is amended to read as follows:

"To the extent practical and to the extent permitted by law (1) all Executive agencies shall cooperate with the Committee and furnish it such information and assistance as may be necessary for the performance of its functions, and (2) the Secretary of Labor shall furnish staff, office space, office facilities and supplies, and other necessary assistance, facilities, and services for the Committee."

SEC. 2. (a) The Citizens' Advisory Committee on Environmental Quality is terminated.

(b) Part II of Executive Order No. 11472 of May 29, 1969, as amended by paragraphs (7) and (8) of Section 4 of Executive Order No. 11514 of March 5, 1970, is revoked.

SEC. 3. (a) The Advisory Council for Minority Enterprise is terminated.

(b) Section 2 of Executive Order No. 11625 of October 13, 1971, is revoked.

SEC. 4. (a) The Consumer Advisory Council is terminated.

(b) Executive Order No. 11583 of February 24, 1971, is amended as follows:

(1) The second sentence of subsection (b) (1) of Section 2 is amended by deleting "(including the Consumer Advisory Council established in section 5 of this order)".

(2) Section 5 is revoked.

SEC. 5. (a) The President's Advisory Board on International Investment is terminated.

(b) Executive Order No. 11962 of January 19, 1977, is revoked.

SEC. 6. Subsections (a), (g), (i), and (j) of Section 1 of Executive Order No. 11948 of December 20, 1976, which extended the above advisory committees until December 31, 1978, is superseded.

JIMMY CARTER

The White House,
    August 22, 1977.

[Filed with the Office of the Federal Register, 11:31 a.m., August 24, 1977]

NOTE: The Executive order was announced by the White House Press Office on August 24. It was not issued in the form of a White House press release.

Advisory Committee Review

Memorandum for the Heads of Executive Departments and Agencies. August 22, 1977

Memorandum for the Heads of Executive Departments and Agencies

Subject: Advisory Committee Review

We have completed the reviews of Federal Advisory committees directed by my memoranda of February 25 and May 24, 1977.

I am pleased that, as a result of the actions recommended, the 1,189 advisory committees reviewed will be reduced by 480 or forty percent of the total. I commend you for your part in this effort to make the government more effective and efficient.

The actions necessary to carry out the recommended terminations and consolidations should be completed as soon as possible. In addition, you should continue to give your personal attention to assuring that committees are terminated when no longer necessary, and that new committees are established only when absolutely necessary.

JIMMY CARTER

NOTE: The memorandum was announced by the White House Press Office on August 24. It was not issued in the form of a White House press release.

Executive Branch Reorganization Studies

Memorandums for the Heads of Executive Departments and Agencies. August 25, 1977

Memorandum for the Heads of Executive Departments and Agencies

Subject: Review of the Economic Analysis and Policy Machinery in the Federal Government

I have directed my Reorganization Project staff at the Office of Management and Budget to begin a review of the economic policy and analysis machinery of the Federal Government, to look for ways to improve the way economic policy decisions are made and carried out.

This review will focus primarily on the economic policymaking system outside the Executive Office of the President. It will involve 33 agencies employing approximately 5,000 economists.

The review will examine and develop recommendations about the best ways to:

- Eliminate overlapping functions among economic agencies;
- Repair weaknesses or gaps in the Federal Government's capacity to conduct economic analyses of particular industries or regions;
- Link foreign policy with economic decisions; and
- Ensure that economic decisions are carried out.

This effort will require the active participation of Federal departments and agencies. You may be asked to contribute time, resources, and staff assistance. I know that I can count on your support.

In order to inform all affected parties that this review is underway, I have directed that this memorandum be published in the FEDERAL REGISTER.

JIMMY CARTER

Memorandum for the Heads of Executive Departments and Agencies

Subject: Comprehensive Review of Federal Food and Nutrition Policy

I have directed my Reorganization Project staff at the Office of Management and Budget to begin a thorough review of the organization and structure of Federal food and nutrition programs.

The Federal Government is unable to respond as effectively as it should to the important changes taking place in the production, processing, marketing, and consumption of food. As a result, our capability to develop and implement a coherent food and nutrition policy is severely hampered.

This review will focus on seven major areas:

- Production and marketing of food;

- Regulatory activities affecting food which now involve 14 agencies and over 2000 regulations;
- Food research and education which is now conducted by 12 different organizations;
- International activities which involve 12 different organizations;
- Commodity procurement and distribution including the Federal feeding programs;
- Aquaculture activities which are dispersed among three major departments, and
- Conservation activities which affect the availability of good soil and water to grow crops.

The objective of this review is to improve the Government's capability to address the Nation's needs for adequate supplies of reasonably priced, safe, and nutritious foods.

As part of this overall project I have directed OMB's new Regulatory Policy and Reports Management staff to begin a specific review of Federal food inspection, labeling and grading as well as other related food regulatory practices. The comprehensive food and nutrition policy review and the food regulatory policy review will be closely coordinated within the Reorganization Project.

This important effort will need the active participation of the Congress, Federal Departments and Agencies, State and local officials, and the public.

You may be asked to contribute time, resources, and staff assistance to this effort. If so, I hope you will make your best effort to do so.

In order to inform all affected parties that this review is underway, I have directed that this memorandum be published in the FEDERAL REGISTER.

JIMMY CARTER

Memorandum for the Heads of Executive Departments and Agencies

Subject: Reorganization Study of Federal Preparedness and Response to Disasters

I have directed my Reorganization Project staff at the Office of Management and Budget to carry out a comprehensive study of the Federal Government's role in preparing for and responding to natural, accidental, and wartime civil disasters.

Three different departments have major responsibility for disaster and civil defense preparedness. Many other Federal organizations have some disaster planning, relief, or recovery responsibilities. In national emergencies the resources of the entire Federal Government are on call, but they must be deployed effectively. After local disasters Federal agencies should be effectively coordinated to be able to assist State and local authorities without delay.

A preliminary review indicates that there are opportunities for the Executive Branch to improve its performance in planning for and helping to cope with the effects of major disaster. But this is a shared responsibility. The cooperation of State and local government, Congress, private sector organizations, and individual citizens is essential. Successful completion of this important reorganization study will require their participation as well as the full cooperation of Federal departments and agencies. If you are asked to contribute staff support or other assistance to this effort, I encourage you to do so.

In order to inform all affected parties that the review is underway, I have directed that this memorandum be published in the FEDERAL REGISTER.

JIMMY CARTER

Memorandum for the Heads of Executive Departments and Agencies

Subject: Examination of the Federal Government's Legal Representation System

I have directed my Reorganization Project Staff at the Office of Management and Budget to review the Federal Government's system for providing legal advice and representation to its departments, agencies, and regulatory commissions.

This study is designed to improve the way governmental units use the legal resources at their disposal, which include their own legal offices and the services of the Department of Justice, including United States Attorneys. Better use of these resources should help prevent unnecessary litigation and administrative delay by enabling the Federal Government to do a better job of complying with its own rules and regulations.

A second objective will be to improve the way litigation is conducted in order to ensure better and more uniform application of the law.

This study will rely heavily on the advice and counsel of the Congress, Federal departments, agencies, and regulatory commissions, State and local officials, private organizations and the public.

I consider the effective use of legal resources to be a vital part of my Administration's effort to improve the performance of the Federal government; accordingly, I ask for your cooperation in providing staff assistance and other resources to assure the success of this review.

In order to inform all interested parties that this study is underway, I have directed that this memorandum be published in the FEDERAL REGISTER.

JIMMY CARTER

Memorandum for the Heads of Executive Departments and Agencies

Subject: Study of Federal Justice System Improvement Activities

The weaknesses of our present system of justice are painfully clear to many citizens. Lawyers are often available only to the wealthy or the very poor. There are substantial backlogs in the courts. While many people have proposed plans for resolving disputes outside of the courts, few of these plans are now operating. The Federal Government does not bear full responsibility for correcting these inequities, but it should make its own system a model and encourage State and local governments to improve the quality of their systems of justice.

I have therefore directed my Reorganization Project Staff at the Office of Management and Budget to review all Federal activities designed to improve the system of justice in this country. These include: (1) justice research programs; (2) justice information and statistical services; (3) justice policy and planning offices; (4) financial assistance for State and local systems; and (5) other reform activities such as juvenile justice and delinquency prevention programs.

This review will rely heavily on advice and counsel from Congress, Executive departments and agencies, the Judiciary, State and local officials, and the public.

You may be asked to contribute time, resources, and staff support to this effort. I consider this to be a high priority matter, and I know I can count on your cooperation and assistance.

In order to inform all affected parties that this review is underway, I have directed that this memorandum be published in the FEDERAL REGISTER.

JIMMY CARTER

NOTE: Fact sheets on each of the studies were also included in the release.

Presidential Management Intern Program

Remarks on Signing an Executive Order Establishing the Program. August 25, 1977

THE PRESIDENT. About a year ago at Syracuse University, I espoused a proposal that had been made earlier by others, including Elmer Staats, to begin a Presidential Management Intern Program, bringing into our Government graduates of the public management programs.

We now have about 20,000 graduate students in public management in about 150 universities and colleges. I'm sure we'll have intense competition for these jobs in Government.

Many of the people in the audience today in the educational institutions have been involved in the preparation of the program which I will initiate today by signing an Executive order. But equally important are the administrators of our Government agencies who are also in the audience, who will find very valuable, I'm sure, these interns who will come in to serve for 2 years.

There won't be a special allotment of funds for this program; the billets are there, and the normal budget processes will prevail. But we will have a chance to bring into our Government the finest graduates of our business management schools.

I think it's accurate to point out that those who serve in management positions in our Government now are also of superb quality—deeply dedicated, highly competent professionals in every way. Quite often, they are not adequately recognized, and I think it's accurate to say that these new interns—and the program will undoubtedly be highly publicized—will help to reassure the American public about the high quality of all those who serve professionally in our Government itself.

I'm very proud of this program. We will have about 250 men and women brought into the Government under it every year. They will serve for 2 years. We'll have a maximum of 500 at any one time, and they will be offered a job at a good salary. At the conclusion of the 2-year period, they can decide to stay permanently in the Government or not— we hope that many of them will—and they will have the advantage of knowing Government at its finest.

I think that in the future, it's likely that we will expand this program. Alan Campbell is already working on some possible improvements to it. One might be a cooperative program for graduate students who are still in college, whereby they might work part-time in Government and receive credit from the Government and from the university, both, for this experimental work.

We have high hopes that this will meet all of our objectives and that it will be successful in every way. I think one other ancillary benefit will be that we can more directly tap the tremendous reservoir of innovation, education, experiment, advice, and counsel that exist within our higher educational institutions that are not often used by Government. And I think the intern program itself, because it has to be a shared program, will help to tie together much more closely our educational institutions and the Government on a continuing basis.

I think at the same time, the benefits would flow to the universities, because as a common assessment of the experiences of these interns is examined by Government and the universities, I think the teaching institutions will then see some of the latest problems and achievements and challenges of the Government itself.

So for many reasons, I think this is one of the finest programs that I've had a part in, and I believe that all those assembled here today will insure the success of this effort.

I'd particularly like to express my thanks to Alan Campbell who heads our Civil Service Commission and who has been instrumental in bringing together these ideas. And it's with the greatest pleasure that I, as President of our country, sign an Executive order to implement the President's Management Intern Program for the first time in the United States Government. It will also be nice to have 250 other interns to join us newcomers to Government. [*Laughter*]

[*At this point, the President signed the Executive order.*]

MR. CAMPBELL. I believe the President has said it all. Those of us gathered here today are the ones who can make this program a success. I hope very much that all of us will make every effort to do that. I can assure you that you will have the full cooperation of the Civil Service Commission, both the Chairman and the other commissioners who are here with us today. It is, I believe, the first step—small, nonetheless significant—in our effort to totally revitalize the personnel system of the Federal Government.

Mr. President, you have the appreciation of all of us.

THE PRESIDENT. Thank you very much.

NOTE: The President spoke at 10 a.m. at the signing ceremony in the Rose Garden at the White House. In his opening remarks, he referred to Elmer B. Staats, Comptroller General of the United States.

Presidential Management Intern Program

Executive Order 12008. August 25, 1977

By virtue of the authority vested in me by Sections 3301 and 3302 of Title 5 of the United States Code, Section 301 of Title 3 of the United States Code, and as

President of the United States of America, it is hereby ordered as follows:

SECTION 1. There is hereby established the Presidential Management Intern Program, hereafter referred to as the Program, the purpose of which is to attract to Federal service men and women of exceptional management potential who have received special training in planning and managing public programs and policies.

SEC. 2. Outstanding individuals who have pursued a course of study oriented toward public management at a graduate-level educational institution and who, at the time of application, have recently received or will shortly receive an appropriate advanced degree, are eligible to apply for participation in the Program.

SEC. 3. The United States Civil Service Commission, hereafter referred to as the Commission, shall develop appropriate procedures for the recruitment, screening, and selection of applicants possessing the qualifications described in Section 2 of this order. In developing these procedures, the Commission shall be guided by the following principles and policies:

(a) The number of interns participating in the Program shall at no time exceed five hundred.

(b) Final selection of interns shall be made by the head of the department, agency, or component within the Executive Office of the President in which the intern is to be employed, or by the designee thereof.

(c) The procedures so developed shall provide for such affirmative action as the Commission deems appropriate to assure equal employment opportunity.

(d) To the extent permitted by law, the Commission is authorized to enter into appropriate cooperative arrangements with State and local officials and appropriate private institutions for recruitment and screening of candidates for the Program.

SEC. 4. Upon selection, candidates shall be appointed as interns to positions in Schedule A of the excepted service for a period not to exceed two years. Their tenure shall be governed by the following principles and policies:

(a) Interns shall be assigned responsibilities consistent with their public management backgrounds and the purposes of this Program.

(b) Continuation in the Program shall be contingent upon satisfactory performance by the interns throughout the internship period.

(c) Except as provided in subsection (d) of this Section, service as interns shall confer no rights to further Federal employment in either the competitive or excepted service upon expiration of the two-year internship period.

(d) Interns may be granted competitive civil service status if they satisfactorily complete their two-year internships and meet all other requirements prescribed by the Commission.

SEC. 5. The Commission shall prescribe such regulations as may be necessary to carry out the purposes of this order.

JIMMY CARTER

The White House,
    August 25, 1977.

[Filed with the Office of the Federal Register, 3:27 p.m., August 25, 1977]

The Cyprus Conflict

Message to the Congress Reporting on Progress Toward a Negotiated Settlement. August 25, 1977

To the Congress of the United States:

As required by Public Law 94–104, this report describes our efforts over the past sixty days to bring about a negotiated settlement of the Cyprus problem.

My last report, submitted to the Congress on June 22, noted that talks between the two Cypriot communities during the preceding sixty days had accomplished little. Regrettably, there has been no substantial change in the general situation.

The efforts of U.N. Secretary General Kurt Waldheim's Special Representative to Cyprus, Ambassador Perez de Cuellar, to persuade the two communities to hold a new round of talks in Nicosia in July and early August have proven unsuccessful.

Despite the failure of these efforts, however, the Administration has persisted in its efforts to bring the parties together in an effort to promote a settlement. In meetings in Washington with Ambassador de Cuellar and with House of Representatives President Kyprianou (now Acting President of Cyprus), Administration officials continually reiterated our view that the intercommunal forum should serve as the basis for substantive talks, and that they should be resumed as quickly as circumstances warranted. Moreover, we took the position that no time should be lost in pursuing a settlement once a new Turkish Government was formally installed.

The death of President Makarios on August 3 was an unfortunate development. The precise implications of his death for the future of the intercommunal negotiations are, as of this writing, difficult to assess.

Nonetheless, we see no reason to change course. As Clark Clifford stressed in his press conference in Nicosia on August 9, this Administration is as dedicated today to helping find a solution to the problems of Cyprus as it was last January, when he was appointed as my Special Repre-

sentative. We are prepared at any time to offer guidance and counsel to assist in the negotiating process, should the parties to the dispute so desire. It is my strong hope that constructive talks will be resumed and that the two Cypriot communities will again focus, with renewed energy, on the goal of achieving a just and lasting settlement which will enable everyone on the island to live in peace, harmony, and freedom.

JIMMY CARTER

The White House,
    August 25, 1977.

International Atomic Energy Agency

Nomination of U.S. Representative and Alternate Representatives to the 21st Session of the General Conference. August 25, 1977

The President today announced the persons whom he will nominate to be Representative and Alternate Representatives of the United States to the 21st session of the General Conference of the International Atomic Energy Agency (IAEA), which is scheduled to be held at Vienna, Austria, from September 26 to October 3, 1977.

As Representative, he will nominate Robert W. Fri, of Sumner, Md. Fri, 41, is Deputy Administrator of the Energy Research and Development Administration. From 1971 to 1973, he was Deputy Administrator of the Environmental Protection Agency.

The following persons will be nominated as Alternate Representatives:

RICHARD T. KENNEDY, Commissioner of the Nuclear Regulatory Commission;
LOUIS V. NOSENZO, Deputy Assistant Secretary of State for Nuclear Energy and

Energy Technology Affairs, in the Bureau of Oceans and International Environmental and Scientific Affairs;

Joseph S. Nye, Jr., Deputy to the Under Secretary of State for Security Assistance, Science and Technology;

Nelson F. Sievering, Jr., Assistant Administrator of ERDA for International Affairs;

Gerard C. Smith, Ambassador at Large and U.S. Special Representative for Non-proliferation Matters, and U.S. Representative to IAEA;

Galen L. Stone, Deputy U.S. Representative to IAEA, with the rank of Ambassador;

Robert D. Thorne, Acting Assistant Administrator of ERDA for Nuclear Energy.

Women's Equality Day, 1977

Remarks on Signing Proclamation 4515.
August 26, 1977

To Dean Virginia Allan and to others who are assembled here today, I'd like to say that I appreciate the chance to be part of this effort.

My wife is sorry that she cannot be here. She's at an international conference on mental health in Canada, making a speech there about the stigma of those who suffer from mental illness. She represents me there, as she does in so many other things.

My daughter-in-law, Judy Carter, is in California today working on the equal rights amendment in the Western States.

In an hour or two, I'll be having lunch with my daughter, Amy, and I'm sure she will bring up the subject as well. [*Laughter*]

During the modern day that we observe and in which we serve, it's not dangerous, politically or otherwise, to speak out for equality of opportunity. It's not a major sacrifice. We don't have to overcome fear of persecution or even incarceration.

Standing behind me is a woman, Ms. Hallinan, who in 1917 stood outside the gates of the White House when Woodrow Wilson was President, simply holding a sign in her hand that was photographed, saying, "How long will it be before women can have freedom?" She was convicted of a crime and jailed. Although we've come a long way since then, we still have a long way to go.

A recent survey by the Civil Rights Commission has shown that 3,000 governmental directives and laws have within them discriminatory concepts against women. Today, I've issued a directive prepared by the Justice Department to all heads of agencies and departments in the Federal Government, ordering them to take the personal responsibility to examine their own attitudes, policies, directives, laws, to root out those discriminatory practices that have so long been in existence.

We've not yet been successful in having the equal rights amendment ratified by enough States. I think we will succeed. In the process, however frustrating it has been, great achievements have already been realized. Inequities and discrimination against women have been revealed.

Many actions in local, State, and Federal governments have already been taken—I have to admit, in some cases, in order to block the passage of equal rights amendment—but those actions have been taken to lessen discrimination.

And we've also seen that there has been a great educational process taking place in this country. Although we've lost the ERA vote in several States this year, those losses have been much narrower than had been the losses in the same States before. So progress has been made, even in States where we have not yet been successful.

In dozens of cases when I or my wife, Rosalynn, have talked directly and personally with State legislators, they have said, "I believe the equal rights amendment is right, I think it ought to pass, but this year I can't vote for it because of pressure from the working women in my district." I think there is a growing realization that those who have suffered most have quite often been women who have taken the least action in encouraging the passage of equal rights amendment because they've been so hard at work in their homes and in their jobs that they've not been educated or inspired, nor have they had the time to become involved. This is changing very rapidly because of the leadership of many of you assembled here today.

So my commitment is the same as yours. I believe that if we work together, we can succeed. And I believe that we are going to work together and, therefore, I believe that we will succeed.

I would now like to read and to sign a proclamation entitled "Women's Equality Day, 1977."

[*At this point, the President read the text of the proclamation.*]

In witness whereof, I have today set my hand [*signing the proclamation*], and we are now mutually pledged to carry out the purposes of this resolution.

NOTE: The President spoke at 10:08 a.m. at the signing ceremony in the Rose Garden at the White House. In his remarks, he referred to Virginia R. Allan, special assistant to the

dean for women's studies of the Graduate School of Arts and Sciences of George Washington University, and Hazel Hunkins Hallinan.

Women's Equality Day, 1977
Proclamation 4515. August 26, 1977

By the President of the United States of America

A Proclamation

August 26, 1977, is the 57th anniversary of the adoption of the 19th Amendment to the Constitution guaranteeing that the right of United States citizens to vote shall not be denied or abridged by the Federal Government or any state on account of sex.

This was the successful culmination of the struggle of the American Women's Suffrage movement. The right to vote, to participate in the process of framing the laws under which we all live, is fundamental. But it was only the first step in achieving full equality for women. The late Dr. Alice Paul realized this, drafted the Equal Rights Amendment in 1923 and had it introduced in Congress over a period of 49 years, until it passed on March 22, 1972.

Dr. Paul and other early leaders of the movement who did not live to see their work completed were reviled and imprisoned, endured hunger strikes and force-feeding in order to further their cause. Their commitment is an inspiration to women and men today who seek to finally make their dreams a reality. Equal rights for women are an inseparable part of human rights for all.

Strong action is needed to guarantee women total equality in the areas of politics and government, education, employment and related benefits, health care, housing and justice. The needs, hopes and problems of a complex society demand the talents, imagination and dedication of all its citizens without regard to sex. As women achieve equality, men, too, are liberated from ancient prejudices and relieved of arbitrary barriers to personal fulfillment.

This is a crucial point in the struggle to achieve full equality for women under the law. Ratification of the Equal Rights Amendment must be completed by the required number of states by March 1979. The successes of the past were dearly bought, and this final effort will not be easy. Achievement of this goal is essential in order to secure meaningful equality for all our citizens.

Now, THEREFORE, I, JIMMY CARTER, President of the United States of America, do hereby proclaim August 26, 1977, as Women's Equality Day and do hereby call upon the people of the United States to observe this day with appropriate ceremonies and activity. I further urge all our people to dedicate themselves anew to the goal of achieving equal rights for women under the law.

IN WITNESS WHEREOF, I have hereunto set my hand this twenty-sixth day of August, in the year of our Lord nineteen hundred seventy-seven, and of the Independence of the United States of America the two hundred and second.

JIMMY CARTER

[Filed with the Office of the Federal Register, 3:24 p.m., August 26, 1977]

Sex Discrimination

Memorandum for the Heads of Executive Departments and Agencies.   August 26, 1977

Memorandum for the Heads of Executive Departments and Agencies

Today, on the anniversary of the ratification of the Women's Suffrage Amendment, I am requesting the Attorney General and all the Federal agencies to cooperate in eliminating sex discrimination from the laws and policies of the United States.

This country has a commitment to equality of opportunity for all citizens, yet a recent report from the Civil Rights Commission indicates that sex discrimination still exists in some Federal laws and policies. Last year the Department of Justice was directed to develop a plan for reviewing and revising Federal laws that discriminate on the basis of sex. At the request of this Administration, Congress has recently appropriated funds for the Task Force on Sex Discrimination in the Civil Rights Division of the Department of Justice to implement the plan.

I am now requesting the heads of all Federal agencies and departments to initiate a comprehensive review of all programs which they administer in order to identify any regulations, guidelines, programs or policies which result in unequal treatment based on sex. Some agencies have already begun such efforts.

I am requesting that the head of each department and agency cooperate with the Attorney General in collecting and furnishing existing information and developing additional information where necessary and that they develop proposals to change any laws, regulations and policies which discriminate on the basis of sex.

I am directing the Attorney General, as chief law officer of the Federal government, to coordinate all of the activities undertaken by the departments and agencies to eliminate sex discrimination. He has sent a letter to each agency today giving details of the proposed procedures.

Where statutory revision or repeal is necessary, I will recommend to the Congress that appropriate legislation be enacted. Where executive action will suffice, I will take appropriate steps to ensure that benefits and opportunities provided by the Federal government are made equally available to all, regardless of sex.

In taking this action, we intend to retain and possibly expand any existing protections and benefits provided for homemakers and families. We believe that offering opportunity to all should not threaten or diminish the protection provided those performing special functions in our society.

Federal law should be a model of nondiscrimination for every state and for the rest of the world. The Federal government, which is actively involved in eliminating sex discrimination in many areas, should not uphold it in others.

It is my hope that the project initiated today will result in such a model and the goal of equal rights and opportunity for all our citizens under the law will be realized.

JIMMY CARTER

United States Ambassador to Bolivia

Nomination of Paul H. Boeker.
August 26, 1977

The President today announced that he will nominate Paul H. Boeker, of Toledo, Ohio, to be Ambassador Extraordinary and Plenipotentiary of the United States to Bolivia. He would replace William P. Stedman, Jr., resigned.

Boeker was born May 2, 1938, in St. Louis, Mo. He received an A.B. from Dartmouth College in 1960 and an M.A. from the University of Michigan in 1967.

Boeker joined the Foreign Service in 1961, and served as a staff assistant in Bonn in 1961 and 1962. From 1962 to 1964, he was consular officer in Duesseldorf. He was economic officer in Bogota from 1964 to 1966, and a financial economist in the Office of Development and Finance at the State Department from 1967 to 1969.

Boeker was Chief of the Financial Operations Division in 1969 and 1970, and Director of the Office of Development and Finance in 1970 and 1971. In 1971 he also served as a member of the Policy Planning Staff.

From 1971 to 1974, Boeker was economic officer in Bonn. In 1974 he served as international relations officer at the State Department, and since 1974 he has been Deputy Assistant Secretary of State for Economic and Business Affairs.

Digest of Other White House Announcements

The following listing includes the President's daily schedule and other items of general interest as announced by the White House Press Office during the period covered by this issue. Events and announcements printed elsewhere in the issue are not included.

August 21

The President returned to the White House after a stay at Camp David, Md.

August 22

The President met at the White House with:

—Zbigniew Brzezinski, Assistant to the President for National Security Affairs;

—senior White House staff members;

—Vice President Walter F. Mondale;

—Dietrich Stobbe, governing mayor of West Berlin;

—Jesse Hill, Jr., president and chief executive officer of the Atlanta Life Insurance Co., and Herman J. Russell, president of H. J. Russell & Co., both of Atlanta, Ga.;

—Kenneth M. Curtis, chairman, and Paul D. Sullivan, executive director, Democratic National Committee.

The White House announced that the President has invited Prime Minister Leo Tindemans of Belgium to meet with him September 8.

The President declared an emergency for the State of Montana because of the impact of a drought.

August 23

The President met at the White House with:

—Dr. Brzezinski;

—Vice President Mondale, Adm. Stansfield Turner, Director of Central Intelligence, and Dr. Brzezinski;

—Mrs. Carter, for lunch;

—Secretary of Agriculture Bob Bergland and several officials of the Department;

—Senator and Mrs. Robert C. Byrd, of West Virginia, for dinner.

The President attended a briefing on the Panama Canal treaty, given for civic leaders from Kentucky and Mississippi in the State Dining Room.

August 24

The President met at the White House with:

—Dr. Brzezinski;

—W. Jack Davis, president, and other representatives of Rotary International;

—Vice President Mondale and Ambassador Robert S. Strauss, Special Representative for Trade Negotiations;

—Charles L. Schultze, Chairman of the Council of Economic Advisers;

—Vice President Mondale, Stuart E. Eizenstat, Assistant to the President for Domestic Affairs and Policy, and a group of people who had advised the President on economic matters during the campaign;

—Senator Ted Stevens of Alaska;

—Senator Spark M. Matsunaga of Hawaii.

August 25

The President met at the White House with:

—Dr. Brzezinski;

—Ambassador Gerard C. Smith, Special Representative for Non-proliferation Matters and U.S. Representative to the International Atomic Energy Agency;

—Bert Lance, Director of the Office of Management and Budget;

—Secretary of Defense Harold Brown;

—Cleve Ryan, who is retiring as lighting technician for the White House press corps, and members of his family.

The President has declared an emergency for the State of West Virginia because of the impact of severe storms, landslides, and flooding. The President's action will permit the use of Federal funds in the provision of temporary housing for those families who lost their homes as a result of the severe storms, landslides, and flooding.

The President has declared an emergency for the State of West Virginia because of the impact of a drought.

August 26

The President met at the White House with:

—Dr. Brzezinski;

—Senator Lloyd M. Bentsen of Texas;

—a group of editors, publishers, and broadcasters;

—Vice President Mondale and Senator Walter Huddleston of Kentucky;

—Representative Dawson Mathis of Georgia.

CHECKLIST OF WHITE HOUSE PRESS RELEASES

The following releases of the Office of the White House Press Secretary, distributed during the period covered by this issue, are not included in the issue.

Released August 23, 1977

News conference: following a briefing on the Panama Canal treaty—by Gov. Julian Carroll of Kentucky and Gov. Charles Finch of Mississippi

Released August 24, 1977

News conference: on the reduction of Federal advisory committees—by Harrison Wellford, Executive Director of the President's Reorganization Project in the Office of Management and Budget

Announcement: Federal advisory committee reduction and reorganization

Fact sheet: Federal advisory committee reduction and reorganization

Announcement: nomination of Gilbert S. Merritt to be United States Circuit Judge for the Sixth Circuit and Edward H. Johnstone to be United States District Judge for the Western District of Kentucky

Released August 25, 1977

Announcement: Executive order establishing the Presidential Management Intern Program

Released August 26, 1977

Announcement: nomination of Procter R. Hug, Jr., to be United States Circuit Judge for the Ninth Circuit; Thomas Tang to be United States Circuit Judge for the Ninth

CHECKLIST—Continued

Circuit; Ronald E. Angel to be United States Marshal for the Northern District of Georgia

NOMINATIONS SUBMITTED TO THE SENATE

The following list does not include promotions of members of the Uniformed Services, nominations to the Service Academies, or nominations of Foreign Service officers.

Submitted August 22, 1977

RAUL H. CASTRO, of Arizona, to be Ambassador Extraordinary and Plenipotentiary of the United States of America to Argentina.

FRANK H. PEREZ, of Virginia, for the rank of Minister during the tenure of his assignment as the State Department SALT Representative at Geneva, Switzerland.

Submitted August 25, 1977

The following-named persons to be the Representative and Alternate Representatives of the United States of America to the Twenty-first Session of the General Conference of the International Atomic Energy Agency:

Representative:
ROBERT W. FRI, of Maryland

Alternate Representatives:
RICHARD T. KENNEDY, of the District of Columbia
LOUIS V. NOSENZO, of Virginia
JOSEPH S. NYE, JR., of Massachusetts
NELSON F. SIEVERING, JR., of Maryland
GERARD C. SMITH, of the District of Columbia
GALEN L. STONE, of the District of Columbia
ROBERT D. THORNE, of California

GILBERT S. MERRITT, of Tennessee, to be United States Circuit Judge for the Sixth Circuit, vice William E. Miller, deceased.

EDWARD H. JOHNSTONE, of Kentucky, to be United States District Judge for the Western District of Kentucky, vice James F. Gordon, retired.

Submitted August 26, 1977

PAUL H. BOEKER, of Ohio, a Foreign Service officer of Class one, to be Ambassador Extraordinary and Plenipotentiary of the United States of America to Bolivia.

ACTS APPROVED BY THE PRESIDENT

NOTE: No acts approved by the President were received by the Office of the Federal Register during the period covered by this issue.

Interview With the President

Remarks and a Question-and-Answer Session With a Group of Editors and News Directors. August 26, 1977

THE PRESIDENT. I always hate to interrupt Jody when he's in the midst of answering a question, because I know that if he doesn't give an answer, that I might have to answer it later on.

These sessions have been very valuable to us because they've brought to me as President, I think to our whole White House staff, a different perspective about nationwide interests from what we ordinarily get at a Presidential news conference, or even a daily briefing by Jody Powell to the White House press corps.

There's a much more personal interest in specific issues that affect our country in domestic and foreign affairs, and some things that we take for granted here in Washington are quite often of intense interest to you or to the individuals that read your newspapers or listen to your broadcasts.

ADMINISTRATION POLICIES

We have now completed the first half year of our term, much more than a half year as far as relationships with Congress go, and I've been very pleased at the results. Most of the action so far has been

in the House of Representatives. But now the emphasis is going to shift very strongly to the Senate—one of the major reasons, of course, is because of the discussion on the comprehensive energy package.

Hearings will commence in the House and Senate on the comprehensive welfare reform package. And before the Congress adjourns, hopefully in October, we'll have available to them our proposal on tax reform.

Of the original priority items that we enumerated at the beginning of my administration, the Congress has taken care of all of them so far in a very expeditious way—the creation of a new Department of Energy, which will be put together and ready to go by the 1st of October, the economic stimulus package, which consists of about $21 billion, which is just beginning to be implemented. We figure that this quarter only about $3 billion of the $21 billion will be felt throughout the country. We are now letting public works contracts at the rate of about a thousand per week. We are putting public service jobs into effect at a rate even beyond what we had hoped to do.

We have also, of course, seen the Congress pass a very strong ethics legislation. We've been able to get authority for reorganization of the executive branch of Government. And we are embarked on a very determined effort, which will last all of 3 years, to reorganize the structure of our Government and to put into effect more efficient and economical ways to operate it.

In the field of foreign policy we have very carefully delineated a set of goals that will take us through a 4-year period, obviously recognizing that unforeseen challenges and opportunities can present themselves at any moment.

But some of those major goals that are obvious to all of you are the SALT talks. They will be recommenced next week when Cy Vance, after a short rest period, will go on over to Vienna. We are negotiating with the Soviets every day on that item.

The comprehensive test ban, for which we have good hopes at this moment, has been joined in by Great Britain. This may or may not materialize as we envision it.

We've been quite active in the Middle Eastern negotiations, and I think that it's completely accurate and a very cautious thing to say that Cy Vance's last trip to the Middle East was very successful, certainly compared to the news reports from it.

We've found a much more compatible relationship among the Arab leaders, a much more flexible attitude on their part. And I think we still have a chance for progress there. Obviously, the chances are directly determined by the attitudes of the parties involved, although we have a very major interest in the Middle East. We're not just idle bystanders. We don't play a narrowly defined negotiating or intermediary role. But we are not trying to impose an American or United States settlement upon the other nations involved. We will be aggressive. But I have to say that there's going to be a great deal of disillusionment on our part in the Middle East and around the world if some progress is not demonstrated within this year.

I doubt that our Government could continue to spend as much time and effort on my part, the State Department's, and all the other agencies involved, on a continuing basis, unless it's obvious to us that all the parties involved genuinely want a comprehensive peace settlement.

In southern Africa we have three major and simultaneous and interrelated goals. Again, we can't order people around. We can't impose a settlement on others. One is concerning Namibia, where we have taken the initiative and have recruited Germany, England, France, and Canada to join in with us to encourage South Africa to comply with the United Nations demands and international law concerning what was formerly Southwest Africa, now known as Namibia.

We have had encouragement from the South Africans. I think they want a settlement. We're now working with the so-called SWAPO group to get them to accept free and democratic elections. This is still conjectural, but we are encouraged now compared to what we were 3 months ago.

In Rhodesia, or Zimbabwe, we have the same problem. We and the British are working jointly on this project. The British have a tangible and a legal and historical responsibility in Rhodesia. Andy Young and David Owen, who is the Foreign Minister of Great Britain, will be meeting tomorrow with the five frontline presidents. We've evolved what I think is a rational and fair approach, which, if adopted, would be very beneficial.

And of course, the other problem is the continuing one with South Africa—their apartheid policy. We would like to encourage them to, at the most rapid possible rate, eliminate the grossly discriminatory practices that have been extant there for a number of years.

We're not trying to cause a revolution or to destroy their government. But this is a sensitive issue. There again, we have a limited role that we can play.

As you know, we've begun negotiations again with the People's Republic of China. Cy Vance will be returning now. He's just left Japan. He will be coming back home, and I'll be meeting with him Sunday afternoon to get a more detailed report from him.

This visit was exploratory in nature. No one in our Government had met Premier Hua before, certainly not since he's been in an ascendant position. Teng Hsiao-ping had been known by more of our people. But Cy had extensive talks with both those men, along with Huang Hua, who is their Foreign Minister. I think they understand our position better; we understand theirs.

I won't go into any detail on the Panama situation, except to point out that this treaty is one that I consider to be vital to our country. It's been negotiated now for 13 years.

I had serious concerns about it a couple of years ago, and I think that my concerns—to a very minor degree—but the concerns expressed by many Members of the Senate then have been taken into account.

I think that the present set of principles which are being drafted into treaty terms or language this week are completely compatible with our own Nation's best interests and our security needs.

We retain complete control over the operation of the Panama Canal for the rest of this century, with the right to defend it. There will be a nine-person board of directors, five of whom will always be from the United States. We will appoint all nine. Until 1990, the executive direc-

tor, who does not set policy, but carries out policy, will be an American citizen. Following 1990 that person will be a Panamanian citizen. Following the year 2000, the Panamanians will take operating control of the canal. We will retain the right, unilaterally, to decide what is necessary on our part to guarantee the neutrality of the canal, that it's open to all international shipping. In case of an emergency, we and the Panamanians have so-called rights of expeditious passage, which means that we get priority use of the canal for our warships and for strategic cargo to be passed through the canal.

I think in balance the treaty is fair to both sides, and for that purpose alone, I would favor it. But the additional major advantage is that it would enhance tremendously our own relationships with other countries in the Southern Hemisphere.

I think Mexico all the way down to the southern part of South America, our neighbors would know that we were trying to deal in good faith, that we were no longer attemping to act as a colonial power. And for that reason, again, there will be, I think, a great benefit to our business community, to our Nation's stature in the world, and I think in balance, the Panama Canal is much more likely now to be open, free, uninterrupted in its service to all nations of the world than it would be if we continued the constant altercations with Panama about the means by which it should be operated.

I could go on and on with other issues, but I think at this point I would prefer to let you ask questions, and I'll try to answer them as completely as I can.

QUESTIONS

U.S. POSTAL SERVICE

Q. Mr. President, I was wondering—I believe the postal bill or postal act appropriations will come up this fall. I believe you will present your—or Bert Lance will present the administration's views on it in about 2 weeks. Since newspapers are quite concerned with the Postal Service in several ways, both in rates and also in the lack of service that we are receiving, I was wondering what position the administration would take on that.

THE PRESIDENT. We have not yet decided on an administration position, and I have to say that I haven't put much time in on that yet. I have met with the director of the Postal Service. I've met with the representatives of both mail carriers and the postmasters. I've had some preliminary papers presented to me for study. But as far as our position on the actual organizational framework or the role to be played by the President in the future operation of the Postal Service, I haven't decided yet, but this will be done before our testimony is required on Capitol Hill.

It's not that we've ignored the subject, but I generally start becoming personally involved after all my department heads and other staff members have done their work, and then before the testimony is given, I do it myself.

Of course, what I want to see done is to have a maximum service to all people, and I would always put a heavy emphasis on the need for the Postal Service to provide to our readers of periodicals of all kinds that information without unnecessary financial burden. So, I favor the encouragement of a dissemination of news with beneficial postal rates, as we've always had as part of our Postal Service since I've known it.

Q. Are you familiar with H.R. 7700, the bill to provide appropriations for the Postal Service, for public service within the Postal Service?

THE PRESIDENT. Not in detail.

PANAMA CANAL

Q. Mr. President, to get back to Panama for a moment, would you hazard your assessment of what would be the immediate impact and the future impact of the rejection of the treaty, if it is rejected—the impact in Panama and Latin America generally?

THE PRESIDENT. I think if the treaty was rejected that our Nation would have the military capability to defend it in spite of a threat of sabotage or other similar threats. I believe that the cooperative arrangement that has been spelled out in the treaty between ourselves and Panama would greatly lessen the chance of violence and the need to defend the Panama Canal with force.

We have made an agreement with Panama that we would have access to the lands and waters, the military defense establishments in the Canal Zone as necessary to guarantee its safety and defense. The Joint Chiefs of Staff have been a party to the negotiations since I've been in office. They unanimously think that this is in the best interest of our country. And on their own initiative, without any orders or encouragement from me, they have said this publicly, even to the VFW and the American Legion.

We will have a signing ceremony in Washington the 7th of September. We have invited each of the Latin American countries who are supportive to send a high government official to represent their country. In some instances, the Presidents or the Prime Ministers themselves will come. In others, they might send the foreign minister, or some might choose not to support the treaty.

In all my travels in Latin America— and I've met with representatives, I think, of almost all the Latin American countries since I've been in office—I believe they're unanimously supportive of the treaty itself.

Had we never started the negotiations 13 years ago, the consequences of not having a treaty would be much more manageable. Now the expectation of Latin American people that we are going to have a resolution of this question has built up hopes of new friendship, new trade opportunities, and a new sense of commonality and equality of stature between their governments and our government that never existed before. I think if those hopes were dashed, if we signed the treaty, which we will do, if the other nations of Latin America signed the neutrality treaty which will take effect after the year 2000, and then our Senate rejects the treaty, I think that the consequences would be very severe. I hope to avoid that consequence.

I might add that several of the Senators who are strongly opposed to the treaty recognize this threat and this danger and this very difficult position in which we find ourselves.

I have received a report from the Joint Chiefs to corroborate the first statement I made that we can defend the treaty. Senator Goldwater has taken a very interesting position with which I do not agree—that if the American people are committed to fight in Panama against the Panamanians some time in the future, then, he says, he would favor our retention of present rights and the exclusion of Panama. If we are not willing to go to war with the Panamanians to retain the open canal, then the treaty is advisable. And this is basically the position that others have taken. Very conservative news columnists like Bill Buckley, to some

degree James Kilpatrick, agree with that position.

I don't want to have to go to war with Panama about the treaty, about the canal operation. The ownership of the canal is not nearly so important to me as the openness of the canal and its free access to all countries, as has been the case in the past with our having the right to defend it under any circumstances, to operate it to the end of this century, and to have our own warships, in case of an emergency, have priority.

Q. Mr. President, Governor Busbee made the statement that he did not believe you were receiving enough input from the American people on foreign policy. Before I left town, I asked the viewers of our newscast to call in on the questions of Panama and Cuba. And on the Panama treaty, in an hour's time, 822 said no to the treaty and 128 yes. Normalization of relations with Cuba: 589 said no and 357 said yes. So there's some input. But I'd like to know what you feel about Governor Busbee's statement.

THE PRESIDENT. I wish you'd ask Jody this if you see him again, but I think Governor Busbee called Jody to say that the text of the speech to which you refer, that was issued, was not the speech that he delivered, and I don't think he made those comments when he delivered the speech. But that was in the preliminary text that was prepared.

There are times in the life of any public official and in any news official when a position must be taken that's not completely compatible with the public view. There's been a great deal of legitimate concern about the Panama Canal expressed in the past, based on proposals that were put forward 5, 10, 13 years ago, that in the present treaty draft have been alleviated. The concerns are no longer there because the treaty terms are better than we had anticipated.

I have talked to 50 or 60 Members of the Senate myself since the treaty was completed, the terms of it. Many of the Senators who signed the so-called Thurmond resolution a year or so ago—I think there were 40 of them, urging that no treaty be signed—have now changed their minds, and they will vote for the treaty because they have been pleasantly surprised at the terms.

I have a responsibility to be sure that not only the Members of the Senate but the American people know the facts about the current terms of the treaty. My belief is that when those facts are known, the opinion of the American people will change.

I think it will have a beneficial effect when 8 or 10 or more leaders of foreign countries come here in September to ratify the treaty and express their support for it. I intend to go to the Nation with a fireside chat presentation some time in the not too distant future to explain the exact terms of the treaty.

We are also, at the request of individual Senators, inviting key opinion shapers from individual States to come here for a briefing by myself, the Joint Chiefs of Staff, the negotiators in the State Department. We've already had two States, Kentucky and Mississippi. And I think it's accurate to say that the people in Mississippi who came here were pleasantly surprised at the terms of the treaty.

So, I think a current assessment of the feeling of the American people about the Panama Canal, that can't yet be based on the actual terms, is not of overwhelming concern to me. It obviously is of some concern. But that's my responsibility, Dick [Dick McMichael, WRBL–TV, Columbus, Fla.], and if I can't sell the American people on the fact that the terms of the treaty are beneficial, then I'll have a very difficult time selling it to the Senate. But I'd predict that the treaty will be ratified.

OIL AND NATURAL GAS

Q. With most of the energy legislation still pending, I wonder what you foresee for this winter in terms of fuel shortages? Already in Louisiana they're talking about cutting off 300 to 400 businesses from natural gas as of November 1.

THE PRESIDENT. Well, as you know, we've made good progress already on shaping an energy policy backed up by strong legislation. And I hope the Senate will even strengthen what the House has done.

It is obvious to me, as one who has analyzed it as thoroughly as I can, that the energy shortages are going to be more and more severe each year. The shortage is not going to be alleviated. We now use about 60 million barrels of oil per day in the world. That is increasing at a rate of about 5 percent, most of the increase—a lot of the increase outside our own country. This means that the amount of oil that we will ever get out of Alaska would only meet about 9 months of that increase. In other words, we need a new Alaska North Slope every 9 months; we need a new Saudi Arabia every 3 years just to meet the increasing demands for oil. So, unless we cut back on the use of oil and natural gas we are going to have increasing demonstrations of crisis. We have had a few warnings already with which you're thoroughly familiar—one in 1973 with the embargo, and again, I think more recently, as you refer, this winter with the natural gas shortage.

We have increased our imports this year, I believe, 22 percent above last year so far. Part of that has been because of stockpiling. But we've now reached the point where about half the oil we use in this country is being imported. A lot of that is caused by waste. I think no matter how hard we try for new exploration, and there's a great incentive in the new energy bill for increased exploration, the production of oil in the continental United States is going to go down. It has been going down in spite of heavy exploratory efforts in the last 6 or 7 years about 6 percent a year.

We are heavily vulnerable to embargoes. We are trying to put a million barrels in the ground in salt dome storage to tide us over if there is such an embargo.

I think we have a need to recognize that we use about twice as much oil per person as other nations that have an equivalent standard of living, like Germany or Sweden or Japan. We've got an inclination on the part of the American people to do something about the energy problem until you get down to specifics. By an overwhelming majority, they want the Nation's Government to take a strong position on a new energy policy, but then when you ask specific questions—are you willing to sacrifice here or there—the answer quite often is no.

So, I think that the only approach to it is twofold: One is to have a department in the Federal Government, one entity, within which comprehensive decisions can be made and to which the American people can commit their questions or suggestions or criticisms. That's the Department of Energy that's already been done. The other one is to have a comprehensive policy on energy that will have to be improved year by year. It is weaker than I would have hoped for already, but I think it's going to take repetitive demonstrations of shortage that can be proven to the American people—and this is unfortunate—to arouse enough support to

give us a strong enough energy policy in the future.

So, conservation of oil and natural gas, a shift toward other sources, including obviously coal—these kinds of things must be encouraged by legislation.

Q. Things don't look too good for this winter, though, in your estimation?

THE PRESIDENT. It depends on the weather. I think if we have a winter as severe as we did this past winter, we are going to have another shortage as severe as this past winter.

THE MIDDLE EAST

Q. You said there'll be great disillusionment if progress toward the Middle East peace settlement isn't achieved by the end of the year. What will the United States do next——

THE PRESIDENT. Do next or ——

Q. ——if there isn't progress and if talks between Vance and the Middle East foreign ministers next month do not accomplish anything?

THE PRESIDENT. Let me say that our determination to bring about progress in the Middle East is as fervent as it has ever been. We're not going to slacken our effort. I'm convinced that the Congress and the American people can have their commitment to a peaceful settlement aroused even more than has been the case in the past.

We have found a growing impatience among the other nations of the world, in the European Community for instance, with a lack of progress. So, I think that any nation in the Middle East that proved to be intransigent or an obstacle to progress would suffer at least to some degree the condemnation of the rest of the world. That's a persuasive thing in itself.

The three basic problems have been obvious for decades. They are being addressed in detail now in a much more constructive way than 7 or 8 months ago when I came into office—territorial boundaries, defensible borders combined, the Palestinian refugee question, and a recognition by the Arab countries that Israel is there, that it has a right to exist, to exist in peace, and to be accepted as an equal.

I think we've made progress on all three of those basic areas. My hope is that we can bring the parties to Geneva for discussions under the aegis of ourselves and the Soviet Union and then let the world and the participating negotiators themselves realize that it's going to be a long, tedious process.

There is no instant solution. Disagreements that have existed in some cases 2,000 years can't be resolved overnight. But I think as long as each country proves that they are acting in good faith, which will require some flexibility, a moving away from adamant stands that have been expressed in the past, I think with that sort of demonstration on their part, then our commitment will continue to be very dedicated and very constant.

SMALL BUSINESS ADMINISTRATION

Q. Mr. President, with the temporary suspension of the 8(a) program that's havoc among the special minority businesses, what, if any—and what can you state to that minority businessman who still desires equitable treatment, which you espoused during your time seeking election, movement having occurred, but there is still dilemma there? What can we expect to occur?

THE PRESIDENT. The 8(a) program will be reinstituted very quickly. I think it will be put back into effect, eliminating the political prostitution of it that did oc-

cur during the last administration. We've seen, since my own early business experience with the Small Business Administration, a deterioration in its quality because it was injected into the political arena, as you know.

We got to the point where we were lending minority business men and women and others, as well, quite often enough money to go into bankruptcy. We'd make an original loan, there would be no followup, no constancy about it, no advice, no counsel, no support, and quite often the entrepreneur that was a newcomer—and that's the kind that the Small Business Administration quite often is designed to help—just couldn't stand alone.

I think all of those proven defects in the 8(a) portion of the Small Business Administration's effort will be corrected.

I think it's accurate to say that they will be corrected very quickly and the program in its reinvigorated form initiated very quickly. I can't give you a time schedule.

I've got to answer one more question, because I promised him.

PEOPLE'S REPUBLIC OF CHINA

Q. You characterized the Vance talks as exploratory.

THE PRESIDENT. Yes.

Q. Precisely what was being explored? Did we talk, for example, about the use of nuclear weapons, did we talk about Taiwan? What were the areas that you were exploring?

THE PRESIDENT. There was a long agenda prepared before Mr. Vance went to China that was of great interest to me for months. He covered a wide range of interests, different areas of the world—the Mideast, Africa, obviously, the Western Pacific, peace in Korea, the SALT talks, comprehensive test ban, the relationship between ourselves and the People's Republic of China if recognition is not initiated, the terms under which we could normalize relationships with the People's Republic of China on the mainland and also honor our longstanding commitment that the people on Taiwan could live in freedom—these kinds of questions were all explored at great length.

I had myself met with the Ambassador from the People's Republic of China—he's actually a trade representative, since we don't have an embassy here—and gone into these questions to some degree.

We've got at least 850 million people in China whose government we don't recognize diplomatically. We're one of the few governments who don't.

It's our hope that we can find some basis on which to have diplomatic exchange, an enhancement of trade, constructive cooperation—not against the Soviet Union or against anyone else, but for our mutual advantage to stabilize peaceful relationships in the far Pacific and also in the rest of the world—with Hua, Teng, and others—and at the same time honor our longstanding commitment to Taiwan—to continue trade with them, to make sure that any resolution of the China question is done peaceably.

I think that Secretary Vance spent an extended period of time talking to Premier Hua. He spent several hours talking to the Vice Premier and the Vice Chairman of the Party, Teng Hsiao-ping. And he spent a couple of days talking to Huang Hua, his equal as Foreign Minister or Secretary of State.

The only thing that I know about the discussion so far is what I received from dispatches that come in over the teletype. But I will meet with Cy Vance this weekend for an extended briefing. I don't feel under any constraint in this instance to

act precipitously just to get an agreement. Nor do I feel any constraint to act hastily to get a SALT agreement with the Soviets, or a comprehensive test ban with the Soviets, or to jump into something in Cuba or southern Africa that might get massive approval for me and my success in foreign policy that might in the long-run not be in the best interest of our country.

I feel like I've got time. I feel at this moment, at least, that I've got overwhelming support and trust from the American people, and I believe that we ought to act from a position of strength and soundness. But it is very important for us to understand the attitude of the Chinese leaders. It's very important for them to understand us. And because of the new leadership that has come there since either Nixon or Kissinger were there, I thought it was valuable to us to get acquainted with them, not just on a social basis but discussing the issues that are vital to world peace.

So, the agenda was very extensive and very long. But we try to be very frank with the Chinese and with others that we talk to or negotiate with. We don't violate confidences. We never tell one national leader one thing about a subject and tell a different country's leader a different thing about the same subject. Sometimes it takes longer to negotiate a settlement using that technique. But I think in the long run the trust in our negotiators, certainly Cy Vance, is enhanced.

Although I can't give you an accurate assessment of the progress made, Cy Vance's reports to me were very encouraging.

Q. They are encouraging, sir?

THE PRESIDENT. Yes, the reports are very encouraging. But we don't intend to act hastily. When we do make a decision about China which, if we make one of recognition, it's undoubtedly going to be well into the future and it'll be based on what I consider to be in the best interests of our country and one which I think the American people will support.

I want to say again how much I thank you for coming here. I'm sure that all of you on occasion watch the press conferences that I have with the national White House press corps. There's a different tone and a different kind of interest and a different kind of question. I personally favor strongly the attitude and the interests that are exhibited in these exchanges. Every one of these questions was substantive and of importance to your listeners and your viewers and your readers. And quite often in the national press conferences here, the major emphasis, almost exclusive interest, is on a transient question. But I want to express my thanks to you for coming to Washington. I hope you get a chance to be acquainted with not only Jody Powell and his staff but my other leaders.

I hope that you'll use this day's visit as a conviction that we need your constant input and that we are always eager to have you call us directly for the answer to a question that comes up about your own region of the country.

Yes. I don't want to see you.

BALANCING THE BUDGET

Q. Mr. President, I have a double-barreled question. The first part——

THE PRESIDENT. Well, I don't know if I have a chance for another question. I've got to go. [*Laughter*]

Q. The first part is: There is a restaurant right across the road from where the B–1's might have been built. It has a great big sign up that says, "Peanut butter sandwiches no longer for sale here." And down the street about two blocks is one which said, "We sell big peanut butter sand-wiches cut on the bias." Now, is this the way it is being done in Georgia, on the bias? [*Laughter*]

A serious question, please. I know you're intent on balancing the budget at the earliest possible date, with inflation and unemployment, and so forth, and I know what your target date is. How do you expect to do this, through a combination of reduced expenditures and income from revenues, and about when do you think you might actually get started toward some reductions on the deficit? How much importance do you place on that?

THE PRESIDENT. We spend a great deal of time on the concept of the balanced budget every day of my life. We'll prepare my first budget for fiscal year '79. I'll probably spend about 25 more actual hours in this room going over the budget figures in detail on all the Federal agencies with Bert Lance and others from the Office of Management and Budget. Any head of a department who disagrees with those decisions can appeal directly to me and I'll sit down and talk to him. But we hope the budget itself will be very tight, and the zero-base budgeting technique has been pleasantly a surprise to those who were not familiar with it before. I happened to have been familiar; so was Bert Lance.

The second thing is that we are trying through the reorganization effort to eliminate waste and inefficiency, unnecessary agencies. This will help in the long run.

Another thing is that we've put a lid on Federal employees. Our goal is that at the beginning of October, a year from now, that the total Federal employment will be at the same level, no higher than it was last October. In other words, for a 2-year period, because of efficiency and better assignment of responsibility, we won't have any further growth in personnel in the Federal Government.

We also are trying to eliminate various agencies and programs that have been in the past splintered and divided among administrators and consolidate them so that they can be administered better. The Department of Energy is the most obvious example.

Another thing that we hope to do is to have an economy with a reasonable rate of growth. As we put together the tax reform package, part of it will obviously be a substantial tax reduction, which will give more purchasing power to consumers, let them spend more, hopefully let employers hire more people, let the economy grow more, which will bring more money into the Federal Treasury to bring about a balanced budget.

So, in all those areas we are contributing to a balanced budget. Another one is to be very cautious about the future cost of new initiatives in programs. In other words, as you well know, quite often in the past the Congress has passed a law perhaps at the request of the President, with an estimated budget impact and 5 years later have found that the budget impact is 500 percent more than had been predicted.

But we're trying to make sure this doesn't happen in the future. So, through all those means and others that I don't have time to go into now—those are the major ones—but we are struggling every day to bring about a balanced budget, without reduction in services, through more efficiency, more economy, better organization and a much more careful husbanding of limited tax revenues and a stimulated economy with an average growth maintained at at least a 5-percent level.

We've had good success so far in reducing the unemployment rate. We hope to wind up this year with maybe 6.3 percent unemployment. It was about 8 per-cent when I came into office. But we're still quite concerned about the inflation rate which is on a worldwide basis, of growing concern to me and other leaders.

Again, let me thank you for the chance to meet with you.

Q. Thank you, Mr. President.

NOTE: The interview began at 1:03 p.m. in the Cabinet Room at the White House.

The transcript of the interview was released on August 27.

American Embassy Fire in Moscow

Message to Ambassador Malcolm Toon and Embassy Staff Members. August 27, 1977

To Ambassador Toon and the American Embassy Staff:

Your efforts and dedication to duty during the fire in the American Embassy in Moscow this week are in the highest tradition of our foreign service. My compliments to you for persevering under the most difficult conditions.

Secretary of State Vance's Trip to the People's Republic of China

Remarks on Secretary Vance's Return. August 27, 1977

THE PRESIDENT. It's with a great deal of both pleasure and pride that I welcome Cy Vance back to our country. He has had a very important mission to one of the most important nations on Earth, the People's Republic of China.

This is a country of central importance and also influence in the world, and we attach very high significance to this trip.

Although our objectives were deliberately limited—and as has been mentioned, I think, in the press, the discussions were exploratory in nature—they were highly successful.

Premier Hua has sent word back to me, along with Vice Premier Teng, that the discussions were very fruitful from their point of view. I believe that this is a major step forward in our ultimate goal of normalizing relationships with the People's Republic of China.

Discussions will be continued, and they could not have been in better hands, nor will they in the future be in better hands than those of our Secretary of State, Cy Vance.

Cy, we're proud to have you back. You are a great representative of our country, and of course, as always, our people have full faith in you.

SECRETARY VANCE. Thank you very much, Mr. President. I appreciate very much your coming out here to welcome us back.

Let me say it's very good to be home. We had a good and useful trip to China. I had the privilege of meeting not only with the Foreign Minister but also with Chairman Hua and with Vice Premier Teng. The conversations were described by them as earnest and significant. I felt them to be very useful.

As the President has said, this was an exploratory trip, and I think it was very important that we have this exchange of views for the first time with this powerful and great nation. We will be continuing our discussions in the future.

And let me close by saying again, it's very good to be back home.

NOTE: The President spoke at 2:48 p.m. at Andrews Air Force Base, Md.

Atlantic Treaty Association

Letter to a Meeting of the Association in Reykjavik, Iceland.   August 27, 1977

Dear Mr. Mommer:

I ask you to extend to the Association my warmest greetings as you assemble again to consider the current state of our Alliance. We look to you, opinion leaders in the North Atlantic Community, for insights on how we should move to strengthen even further the security on which the Atlantic Community vitally depends.

Your deliberations have never been more timely. We are faced with a renewed military challenge from the Warsaw Pact. In the last decade, the Warsaw Pact has steadily and impressively strengthened its forces deployed against Western Europe.

At last May's NATO Summit, I joined my Alliance colleagues in a thorough review of the challenge. We chose our response carefully—a major program of defense improvements, both short and long-term, as well as both conventional and nuclear. My government is solidly committed to these efforts, which we believe will maintain the credibility of existing NATO strategy into the 1980s and beyond. We are intensively engaged, in cooperation with our Allies, in charting concrete force improvements in pursuit of this objective.

I would also like to reiterate that the United States remains categorically committed to NATO's strategy of forward defense and flexible response. This is my own firm conviction, and it will remain the policy of the United States as long as I am President. Since this is also the firm conviction of the Congress and the American people, there is absolutely no doubt that my successors in office will continue this commitment.

We continue to be convinced that this strategy, kept credible through timely force improvements, can preserve the territorial integrity of all Alliance members.

My nation's commitment to the defense of Western Europe is at the center of our foreign and security policies. The security of the North Atlantic community continues to be vital to that of the United States itself.

JIMMY CARTER

[Mr. Karl Mommer, President, Atlantic Treaty Association]

National Hispanic Heritage Week, 1977

Proclamation 4516. August 29, 1977

By the President of the United States of America

A Proclamation

The Hispanic heritage of over sixteen million Americans, representing a broad diversity of cultures, has enriched our Nation by contributing to the advancement of art and science and by affirming the importance of family bonds and community spirit.

Today, Americans have come to recognize the important role of the Hispanic community both in the life and work of the United States and in our efforts to achieve understanding, mutual respect and common purpose with the Spanish-speaking nations of this hemisphere.

In recognition of our Hispanic heritage, the Congress, by joint resolution approved September 17, 1968 (36 U.S.C. 169f), has requested the President to issue annually a proclamation designating the week including September 15 and 16 as National Hispanic Heritage Week.

Now, THEREFORE, I, JIMMY CARTER, President of the United States of America, do hereby proclaim the week beginning September 11, 1977, as National Hispanic Heritage Week and call upon the people of the United States, especially the educational community, to observe it with appropriate ceremonies and activities; to reflect on the influence of Hispanic culture in our land; and to encourage the full participation of Hispanic Americans in every phase of American life.

In WITNESS WHEREOF, I have hereunto set my hand this twenty-ninth day of August, in the year of our Lord Nineteen hundred seventy-seven, and of the independence of the United States of America the two hundred and second.

JIMMY CARTER

[Filed with the Office of the Federal Register, 4:02 p.m., August 29, 1977]

Citizenship Day and Constitution Week, 1977

Proclamation 4517. August 29, 1977

By the President of the United States of America

A Proclamation

On July 4, 1976, we joyfully celebrated the 200th anniversary of our Nation's independence. Now, on September 17, 1977, we commemorate the 190th anniversary of a quieter but equally momentous event: the signing of the Constitution of the United States, at Independence Hall, Philadelphia.

The Constitution audaciously proposed a new plan of government—a government through which the new Nation's people could, in the words of the Preamble, "form a more perfect Union, establish Justice, insure domestic Tranquility, provide for the common defence, promote the general Welfare, and secure the Blessings of Liberty to ourselves and our Posterity . . ."

With amendments, notably the Bill of Rights, that Constitution has endured these 190 years as the supreme law of our land. We are its inheritors—the "posterity" whose liberty the Founding Fathers wished to secure—and it is fitting for us to mark the anniversary of what they did.

By a joint resolution of February 29, 1952 (36 U.S.C. 153), Congress designated September 17 as Citizenship Day, in commemoration of the formation and signing of the Constitution and in recognition of all who, by coming of age or by naturalization have attained the full status of citizenship, and authorized the President to issue annually a proclamation calling upon officials of the Government to display the flag on all Government buildings on that day. By a joint resolution of August 2, 1956 (36 U.S.C. 159), the Congress authorized the President to designate the period beginning September 17 and ending September 23 of each year as Constitution Week and to issue a proclamation calling for the observance of that week.

Now, THEREFORE, I, JIMMY CARTER, President of the United States of America, call upon appropriate Government officials to display the flag of the United States on all Government buildings on Citizenship Day, September 17, 1977, the 190th anniversary of the signing of the Constitution. I urge Federal, State and local officials, as well as leaders of civic, educational and religious organizations to conduct related ceremonies and programs on that day.

I also designate as Constitution Week the period beginning September 17 and ending September 23, 1977, and urge all Americans to observe that week with ceremonies and activities in their schools, churches and in other suitable places in order to foster a better understanding of the Constitution, and of the rights and duties of United States citizens.

IN WITNESS WHEREOF, I have hereunto set my hand this twenty-ninth day of August, in the year of our Lord nineteen hundred and seventy-seven, and of the Independence of the United States of America the two hundred and second.

JIMMY CARTER

[Filed with the Office of the Federal Register, 10:35 a.m., August 30, 1977]

National Endowment for the Arts

Letter to Chairman Nancy Hanks.
August 29, 1977

To Nancy Hanks

Although I fully understand and respect your desire to leave the chairmanship of the National Endowment for the

Arts at the conclusion of your second term, I also know that you will be greatly missed. The eight years of your leadership at the Endowment have been exemplary.

Under your thoughtful and creative stewardship, the Endowment has, among other things, firmly established in the country's consciousness the importance of broad-based public and private support for the arts. You and your colleagues have helped to foster a climate in which private resources and initiative play the leading role in shaping and nourishing the nation's artistic and cultural life. It is a source of pleasure and pride to us all that widely diverse arts activities of the highest quality are flourishing throughout the country on an unprecedented scale.

I am fully aware, as I know you are, of how much we all share in the inestimable benefits that spring from the creative visions of our artists. In carrying on the work you and others have so ably begun, I shall continue to seek the support and counsel of artists from every part of our great country.

Rosalynn joins me in wishing you well and in thanking you for your extraordinary efforts on behalf of us all.

Sincerely,

JIMMY CARTER

White House Fellows

Announcement of Opening of 14th Annual Program. August 29, 1977

The White House announced today that applications are now available for the White House Fellowship program for 1978–79. The program is seeking to increase the number of applicants from among women, minority groups, union and business careerists, and previously under-represented regions of the country, particularly the Southeast and Southwest.

The White House Fellowship program is beginning its 12th year. It was established by President Lyndon Johnson to give outstanding individuals, early in their careers, a unique, firsthand experience in his administration.

The program is open to all U.S. citizens at least 23 years old, except those in civilian Federal positions. Each Fellow is assigned to a Cabinet officer or senior member of the White House staff and participates in a program including seminars with top Government officials, leading scholars and journalists who deal with the National Government.

President Carter expanded the Commission which runs the program and appointed as its chairman John Gardner, who was among those instrumental in recommending the program to President Johnson. On June 22, President Carter told the 1976–77 and 1977–78 Fellows, "I think it is a rare occasion in our Nation's Government, history, when a man who has a brilliant idea that is innovative and constructive can come back several administrations later and help to keep the vigor and the quality of the program and to observe how it has continued beyond his own concept."

Application forms and additional information can be obtained by sending a post card to the President's Commission on White House Fellowships, Washington, D.C. 20415.

Northern Ireland

Statement on U.S. Policy.   August 30, 1977

Throughout our history, Americans have rightly recalled the contributions men and women from many countries have made to the development of the United States. Among the greatest contributions have been those of the British and Irish people, Protestant and Catholic alike. We have close ties of friendship with both parts of Ireland and with Great Britain.

It is natural that Americans are deeply concerned about the continuing conflict and violence in Northern Ireland. We know the overwhelming majority of the people there reject the bomb and the bullet. The United States wholeheartedly supports peaceful means for finding a just solution that involves both parts of the community of Northern Ireland and protects human rights and guarantees freedom from discrimination—a solution that the people in Northern Ireland, as well as the Governments of Great Britain and Ireland can support. Violence cannot resolve Northern Ireland's problems; it only increases them and solves nothing.

We hope that all those engaged in violence will renounce this course and commit themselves to peaceful pursuit of legitimate goals. The path of reconciliation, cooperation, and peace is the only course that can end the human suffering and lead to a better future for all the people of Northern Ireland. I ask all Americans to refrain from supporting with financial or other aid organizations whose involvement, direct or indirect, in this violence delays the day when the people of Northern Ireland can live and work together in harmony, free from fear. Federal law enforcement agencies will continue to apprehend and prosecute any who violate U.S. laws in this regard.

U.S. Government policy on the Northern Ireland issue has long been one of impartiality, and that is how it will remain. We support the establishment of a form of government in Northern Ireland which will command widespread acceptance throughout both parts of the community. However, we have no intention of telling the parties how this might be achieved. The only permanent solution will come from the people who live there. There are no solutions that outsiders can impose.

At the same time, the people of Northern Ireland should know that they have our complete support in their quest for a peaceful and just society. It is a tribute to Northern Ireland's hard-working people that the area has continued to attract investment, despite the violence committed by a small minority. This is to be welcomed, since investment and other programs to create jobs will assist in ensuring a healthy economy and combating unemployment.

It is still true that a peaceful settlement would contribute immeasurably to stability in Northern Ireland and so enhance the prospects for increased investment. In the event of such a settlement, the U.S. Government would be prepared to join with others to see how additional job-creating investment could be encouraged, to the benefit of all the people of Northern Ireland.

I admire the many true friends of Northern Ireland in this country who speak out for peace. Emotions run high on this subject, and the easiest course is not to stand up for conciliation. I place myself firmly on the side of those who seek peace and reject violence in Northern Ireland.

Federal Civilian and Military Pay

Announcement of Intention To Grant an Increase.   August 30, 1977

The President announced today that he intends to grant Federal white-collar employees and the military a pay increase so that their salaries will be comparable with salaries paid in the private sector for the same level of work, as required by the Federal Pay Comparability Act.

The President will make a decision on the size and distribution of the pay increase prior to October, when the increase becomes effective.

In making his decision on the size of the pay raise, the President is required by the Federal Pay Comparability Act to consider the recommendations of three separate advisory panels. The President has so far received two of the three necessary recommendations.

One recommendation came from the President's "Pay Agent," which consists of the Secretary of Labor, the Director of the Office of Management and Budget, and the Chairman of the Civil Service Commission, acting jointly. Their recommendation is for a 7.05 percent across-the-board pay increase.

A second recommendation came from the Federal Employees Pay Council, a five-member group of Federal employee union leaders. They argued that an 8.8 percent increase was justified this year.

The third recommendation is to be made by the President's Advisory Committee on Federal Pay, an impartial group of private sector experts established by law to advise the President on pay matters. The President has not yet received the recommendation of the Committee.

A total of about 1.4 million white-collar workers and approximately 2 million military personnel will be covered by the President's decision. Blue-collar workers and postal employees have their pay established by separate systems.

The 7.05 percent pay increase recommended by the Pay Agent would cost about $3.4 billion. There is an allowance currently provided in the budget to meet this increase. The 8.8 percent recommended by the Federal Employees Pay Council would cost about $850 million more than the Pay Agent's recommendation.

The Federal Pay Comparability Act provides that the President shall annually adjust the salaries of Federal white-collar workers so that they are comparable with salaries paid in the private sector for the same level of work as measured by a Bureau of Labor Statistics survey. The act also provides that the President may recommend an alternative plan to the Congress by August 31 if he decides that a "national emergency or economic conditions affecting the general welfare" would make the comparability increase inappropriate. The President has concluded that conditions warrant full comparability and he decided not to recommend an alternative plan this year.

Panama Canal Treaty

Remarks During a Briefing on the Treaty. August 30, 1977

I understand that Sol Linowitz was just in the process of giving you the points against the treaty. I'm not going to take that side. [*Laughter*]

I know that General Brown and the Joint Chiefs unanimously feel strong support for the Panama Canal treaty is a very important consideration from you, from Georgia and from Florida, and from me as President of our country.

Our Secretary of Defense, former Secretary of State, present Secretary of State, President Ford, Secretary Kissinger, and others who have studied this treaty in detail have concluded that many of the legitimate concerns faced about the treaty 2 years ago or 5 years ago, 10 years ago, 14 years ago, have been alleviated. And all those who in the past have been against the treaty and who would have preferred that no negotiations begin now say that since the negotiations have been initiated and concluded, that the adverse reaction throughout Latin America and throughout the world in rejecting the treaty would be profound.

I'd like to talk to you for a few minutes about the Panama Canal treaty from the perspective of a President and a political figure. This is one of those items that falls on the shoulders of leaders which is not a popular thing to assume. Because of longstanding misconceptions and because of rapidly changing circumstances that have not yet been explained, I think it is true that many American citizens, well-educated, very patriotic citizens, don't think the treaty at this point is a good idea.

To change their concept based on facts and explanations is my responsibility—not to mislead, not to pressure, not to cajole, but in a way to educate and to lead. And I would like for you to join with me, if you can in good conscience, in that effort.

It requires, as you know, a two-thirds vote in the Senate. There were 40 Senators within the past 12 months or so who signed a resolution deploring the concept of the Panama Canal treaty. I believe I've talked to every one of them, and I can tell you that their response has been very good because they see that their previous concerns have either been corrected or the circumstances are now different. There will obviously be strong opponents to the treaty. I think that our Nation's security interests are adequately protected.

Our original acquisition of the Panama Canal area is one that causes me some concern, speaking in historical terms. There was not a single Panamanian who ever saw the treaty before it was signed by Panama and by the United States, in the middle of the night, when the Panamanian leaders, including the President, were trying to get to Washington before the treaty was signed. Hastily, the treaty was signed, and that began the process of constructing the canal which has been beneficial to our country and to Panama and, I think, to the world.

We have never had sovereignty over the Panama Canal Zone, as you undoubtedly know by now. We had control of that zone, as though we had sovereignty, but we have recognized the sovereignty of Panama down through the years.

I believe that the most important consideration is that the canal be open to the shipping from all countries, that the canal be well operated, that there be harmony between us and the Panamanians, and that we, in case of emergency in this century and in perpetuity, have the right to protect the canal as we see fit and the preferential use of the canal by our own warships and by those cargo ships that have strategic purposes. And all those elements have been written into the treaty.

NOTE: The President spoke at 3:45 p.m. in the State Dining Room at the White House at a briefing for State officials and business and political leaders from Georgia and Florida. Reporters were present for this portion of the briefing.

55-Mile-per-Hour Speed Limit

Statement Urging Compliance With the Limit.   August 31, 1977

When I delivered my energy message last April, I hoped that the national 55-mile-per-hour speed limit—already in force—would help reduce gasoline consumption, which is essential if we are to extend the world's finite supply of oil. If we all drove within the speed limit, we could save more than 8 million gallons of gasoline a day. That's nearly a third of the reduction in total gasoline consumption I asked for in my energy program.

We *have* saved gasoline by driving slower. Tests by the Federal Highway Administration indicate that, depending on the type of car, drivers can get from 17 to nearly 50 percent better gas mileage at 55 miles per hour than at 70. And we have saved lives. Since the lower speed limit was adopted nationally 3 years ago, there have been approximately 9,000 fewer highway deaths each year than in 1973. The reduced speed limit has been the biggest single factor in this 17-percent drop in highway fatalities.

Unfortunately, highway speeds are again creeping up. Highway safety officials tell us that enforcement is difficult as average interstate speeds again approach 65. Worst of all, the numbers of people being killed or seriously injured in highway accidents are rising again with the increase in vehicle speeds. In July, 169 more Americans died on our highways than in July of last year; for June, the increase was 175.

This is a matter that deserves, and must have, greater Federal attention. General Davis, as special representative to Secretary Adams on 55-mile-per-hour speed limit education and enforcement, I hope you will redouble your efforts in communicating the importance of the 55-mile-per-hour speed limit to the safety leaders of our States and the people of America. Let it be clearly understood that by exceeding the speed limit, we are wasting fuel and, in too many instances, lives as well.

In your meetings with State law enforcement and safety officials, please convey my concern and assure those responsible for the safety of our highways that Federal support will be supplied and appropriate Federal actions taken to assist them in their programs. I will expect a report in 30 days on the status of speed limit compliance throughout the country, along with recommendations from the Secretary of Transportation on any additional measures considered advisable to save fuel and stem the tide of fatalities on the Nation's roads.

NOTE: The White House Press Office released the statement following the President's meeting with Secretary of Transportation Brock Adams, Joan B. Claybrook, Administrator of the National Highway Traffic Administration, and Lt. Gen. Benjamin O. Davis, USAF (ret.).

National Lupus Week, 1977
Proclamation 4518.   August 31, 1977

By the President of the United States of America

A Proclamation

The medical challenge which the disease lupus erythematosus presents is the subject of many research projects in hospitals and medical centers throughout the United States. The disease most often strikes during its victims' most active and productive years, and can affect many organs of the body with inflammation and changes in structure and function.

The cause of lupus still eludes investigators, but promising leads into its relationship to the immune system, as well as to other factors, may yield new understanding of the origin of this chronic inflammatory disease, which afflicts an estimated fifty thousand new victims annually.

The Federal Government is supporting an aggressive program of research into the cause and treatment of lupus, which, it is hoped, will ultimately lead to its prevention or control. Genetic studies suggesting the role of heredity in the occurrence of lupus have begun to provide important information. The study of immunity, the body's ability to resist disease, is now pointing the way to an understanding of the relationship to lupus of abnormal immune reactions of the body. Although a cure must await further knowledge of the basic cause, presently available forms of treatment can frequently delay the often grave consequences of the disease.

In recognition of the seriousness of lupus and America's commitment to its control, the Congress, by joint resolution approved July 25, 1977, has requested the President to issue a proclamation designating the week of September 18 through 24, 1977, as National Lupus Week and calling for its appropriate observance.

Now, Therefore, I, Jimmy Carter, President of the United States of America, do hereby designate the week of September 18 through 24, 1977, as National Lupus Week. I invite the Governors of the several States and the Commonwealth of Puerto Rico, the Mayor of the District of Columbia, the chief officials of local governments, the medical profession, and the people of the United States to observe that week with appropriate ceremonies and activities.

In Witness Whereof, I have hereunto set my hand this thirty-first day of August, in the year of our Lord nineteen hundred seventy-seven, and of the Independence of the United States of America the two hundred and second.

Jimmy Carter

[Filed with the Office of the Federal Register, 4:42 p.m., August 31, 1977]

United States Arms Control and Disarmament Agency

Nomination of Charles N. Van Doren To Be an Assistant Director. August 31, 1977

The President today announced that he will nominate Charles N. Van Doren, of Washington, D.C., to be Assistant Director of the Arms Control and Disarmament Agency (ACDA). He would replace Amrom Katz, resigned.

Van Doren was born April 7, 1924, in Orange, N.J. He received an LL.B. from Columbia Law School in 1949.

Van Doren practiced law in New York for 13 years with the firm of Simpson, Thacher and Bartlett. Since 1963 he has been at ACDA, serving as Assistant General Counsel (1963), Deputy General Counsel (1964–1973), Special Assistant for Treaty Implementation (1974), Deputy Assistant Director of the International Relations Bureau (1975), Deputy Assistant Director for Non-Proliferation (1976), and Acting Assistant Director for the Non-Proliferation Bureau (1977).

Committee on Selection of Federal Judicial Officers

Announcement of the Membership of the Committee. August 31, 1977

The President today announced the membership of the Committee on Selection of Federal Judicial Officers, which was established on May 24, 1977 to recommend candidates for vacancies on Federal courts other than Circuit Courts and District Courts.

The President asked the Committee to recommend candidates for two vacancies on the United States Court of Claims created by the retirements of Wilson Cowen and Byron Skelton. The Committee will report in confidence to the President, within 60 days, the names of no more than five suggested candidates for each vacancy.

The members of the Committee are:

HON. DAVID W. DYER, Senior Judge, U.S. Court of Appeals for the Fifth Circuit (retired), Miami, Fla. (Chairman);

LOLA DICKERMAN, attorney, Boston, Mass.;

H. STEWART DUNN, attorney, Washington, D.C.;

JAMES D. FELLERS, attorney, Oklahoma City, Okla.;

AMALYA L. KEARSE, attorney, New York, N.Y.;

J. LANE KIRKLAND, secretary-treasurer, AFL–CIO, Washington, D.C.;

RUDOLPH A. PETERSON, banker, Piedmont, Calif.

Occupational Safety and Health Review Commission

Designation of Timothy F. Cleary as Chairman. August 31, 1977

The President today announced the designation of Timothy F. Cleary, of Bethesda, Md., as Chairman of the Occupational Safety and Health Review Commission. Cleary has been a member of the Commission since 1973.

He was born September 30, 1925, in Cork, Ireland. He received a B.S. from Fordham University in 1955 and an LL.B. from Fordham University Law School in 1959. He served in U.S. naval aviation from 1943 to 1945.

From 1959 to 1967, Cleary was an attorney for the New York City Police Department Legal Bureau. From 1967 to 1969, he was a staff attorney at the Labor Department, and from 1969 to 1971 he was a trial attorney and Supervisory Assistant Counsel for Litigation in the Fair Labor Standards Division there.

Cleary was Chief Counsel to Commissioner Alan F. Burch of the Occupational Safety and Health Review Commission from 1971 until 1973, when he became a member of the Commission.

National Science Foundation

Nomination of John B. Slaughter To Be an Assistant Director. August 31, 1977

The President today announced that he will nominate John B. Slaughter, of Bellevue, Wash., to be Assistant Director of the National Science Foundation. He would replace Dr. Robert E. Hughes, resigned, and his area of responsibility would be astronomical, atmospheric, earth, and ocean sciences.

Slaughter was born March 16, 1934, in Topeka, Kans. He received a B.S. from Kansas State University in 1956, an M.S. from the University of California at Los Angeles in 1961, and a Ph.D. in engineering science from the University of California at San Diego in 1971.

Slaughter was an engineer at Convair Division of General Dynamics Corp., from 1956 to 1960, and was physical science administrator of information systems at the Naval Electronics Laboratory Center from 1961 to 1975. Since 1975 he has been director of the Applied Physics Laboratory at the University of Washington.

Since 1972 Slaughter has been editor of the Journal of Computer and Electrical Engineering. He received the Community Service Award of the Institute of Electric and Electronics Engineers in 1972.

Alaska Natural Gas Transportation System

Letter to the Speaker of the House and the President of the Senate. September 1, 1977

Dear Mr. Speaker: (Dear Mr. President:)

Section 7 of the Alaska Natural Gas Transportation Act of 1976 provides that my decision regarding an Alaska natural gas transportation system be transmitted to the House of Representatives and the Senate by September 1, 1977. The Act also provides that the decision may be delayed by as much as 90 days upon a determination that additional time is necessary to reach a sound decision. Although I intend to submit my decision to the Congress in the near future, it appears prudent to take some additional time prior to transmittal of that decision.

A decision on an Alaska natural gas transportation system is dependent upon a full and complete assessment of all options. Information and data concerning the proposal for building a pipeline across Alaska and then shipping Alaska gas to the lower-48 states via LNG tankers is complete and well understood.

Discussions with officials of the Canadian government to determine the route and conditions associated with any joint overland pipeline have been underway for some time. The general outline of the Canadian option is becoming increasingly clear, although several final details must still be resolved. While I expect these matters to be resolved in the course of the next several days, I have determined they will not be settled in time for a September 1, 1977, decision.

As soon as these discussions are completed, a final comparative assessment of all project options will be made and a decision regarding an Alaska natural gas transportation system reached.

I intend to transmit that decision to the Congress in the very near future so that action on this critical matter can be taken during this session of the Congress.

Sincerely,

JIMMY CARTER

NOTE: This is the text of identical letters addressed to the Honorable Thomas P. O'Neill, Jr., Speaker of the House of Representatives, and the Honorable Walter F. Mondale, President of the Senate.

The White House Press Office announced the letter on September 1. It was not issued in the form of a White House press release.

U.S. Special Representative to the States of Antigua, Dominica, St. Christopher-Nevis-Anguilla, St. Lucia, and St. Vincent

Appointment of Frank V. Ortiz, Jr. September 1, 1977

The President today announced that he has appointed Frank V. Ortiz, Jr., as U.S. Special Representative to the States of Antigua, Dominica, St. Christopher-Nevis-Anguilla, St. Lucia, and St. Vincent. Ortiz is Ambassador to Barbados and to the State of Grenada.

NOTE: The announcement of the President's intention to nominate Mr. Ortiz to be Ambassador to Barbados and the State of Grenada, which contains biographical information on Mr. Ortiz, is printed on page 1189 of this volume.

Labor Day, 1977

Message of the President. September 2, 1977

On Labor Day, our nation salutes the decency, grit and determination of the

American working man and woman.

The sweat and skill of American workers built this country and preserved it through wars and crises. Today, workers and their organizations are giving strong support to the national effort to restore our economy's health. This is in the finest tradition of organized labor, which has served not just its own members but all people through its century-long struggle for social and economic justice.

On this Labor Day, let us affirm our determination to build a future together in which all of us can enjoy the blessings of a more equitable and humane society.

JIMMY CARTER

Environmental Protection Agency

Nomination of Three Persons To Be Assistant Administrators. September 2, 1977

The President today announced three persons whom he will nominate for positions at the Environmental Protection Agency (EPA). They are:

Marvin B. Durning, of Seattle, Wash., to be an Assistant Administrator. He would replace Stanley W. Legro, resigned, and his primary area of responsibility would be enforcement.

Durning was born June 21, 1929, in New Orleans. He received an A.B. from Dartmouth College in 1949, a BA–MA from Oxford University on a Rhodes Scholarship in 1952, and an LL.B. from Yale Law School in 1959. He served in the U.S. Navy from 1952 to 1956.

Durning has practiced law in Seattle since 1959, and is currently a partner in the firm of Durning, Smith & Brucker. He is a founder and director of Mathematical Sciences Northwest, Inc., a research and development firm. He has taught law and economics at Yale University and the University of Washington. He served as chairman of the Washington State Interagency Committee for Outdoor Recreation from 1965 to 1967 and served on the Joint Committee on Urban Area Government of the Washington State Legislature in 1961 and 1962. He was the first chairman of the Seattle Design Commission, serving from 1968 to 1970.

David G. Hawkins, of Washington, D.C., to be an Assistant Administrator. He would replace Roger Strelow, resigned, and his primary area of responsibility would be air and waste management.

Hawkins was born July 8, 1943, in Hartford, Conn. He received a B.A. from Yale College in 1965 and a J.D. from Columbia University Law School in 1970. From 1970 to 1971, he was an environmental attorney at Stern Community Law Firm, and since 1971 he has been a staff attorney with the Natural Resources Defense Council.

Steven D. Jellinek, of Chevy Chase, Md., to be Assistant Administrator for Toxic Substances, a new position.

Jellinek was born May 22, 1940, in Brooklyn, N.Y. He received an A.B. from the University of Rochester in 1960 and an M.P.A. from the Maxwell School of Citizenship and Public Affairs at Syracuse University in 1961.

From 1961 to 1967, Jellinek worked for the Internal Revenue Service in various personnel management and administrative positions. From 1967 to 1969, he was staff assistant to the Assistant Commissioner of the IRS for Compliance, and from 1969 to 1971 he was special assistant to the Assistant Commissioner for Compliance.

In 1971 and 1972, Jellinek was a staff member at the Council on Environmental Quality, and in 1972 and 1973 he was a senior staff member there. Since 1973 he has been Staff Director of the Council.

International Whaling Commission

Appointment of Thomas Garrett as Deputy U.S. Commissioner. September 2, 1977

The President today announced the appointment of Thomas Garrett, of Laramie, Wyo., as Deputy U.S. Commissioner on the International Whaling Commission. He would replace Edwin J. Gould, resigned.

Garrett was born October 16, 1934, in Laramie, Wyo. He received a B.S. from the University of Wyoming in 1955. He served in the U.S. Army from 1957 to 1959.

In 1960 Garrett worked as a reporter for Reuters in Seoul and Tokyo. From 1960 to 1965 and from 1967 to 1971, he was a rancher on the Garrett Ranch in Garrett, Wyo. In 1966 he was chief engineer for the Knisely-Moore Construction Co.

Garrett served as director for conservation at Friends of the Earth from 1971 until earlier this year, when he became legislative director of Defenders of Wildlife.

Garrett has served on the U.S. delegation to five previous annual meetings of the International Whaling Commission, beginning in 1972. He also served as a member of the U.S. delegation to the conference which developed the Convention for Conservation of Antarctic Seals in 1972.

Digest of Other White House Announcements

The following listing includes the President's daily schedule and other items of general interest as announced by the White House Press Office during the period covered by this issue. Events and announcements printed elsewhere in the issue are not included.

August 27

The President met at the White House with Zbigniew Brzezinski, Assistant to the President for National Security Affairs.

August 28

The President met at the White House with Vice President Walter F. Mondale, Secretary of Defense Harold Brown, Dr. Brzezinski, and Secretary of State Cyrus R. Vance, who reported on his discussions in Peking with leaders of the People's Republic of China and his meetings in Japan with Japanese leaders.

August 29

The President met at the White House with:

—Dr. Brzezinski;

—the Cabinet;

—Secretary of Labor F. Ray Marshall, Alan K. Campbell, Chairman of the Civil Service Commission, and Bert Lance, Director of the Office of Management and Budget;

—Vice President Mondale;

—Secretary of Commerce Juanita M. Kreps to discuss minority employment;

—Secretary of Energy James R. Schlesinger.

The White House announced that in view of the consultations which will take place in Washington between the President and Western Hemisphere leaders in September, incident to the signing of the Panama Canal treaty, the President and

Prime Minister Leo Tindemans of Belgium have agreed to postpone the Prime Minister's official visit to Washington. The Prime Minister will now visit Washington October 18 and 19.

August 30

The President met at the White House with:

—Vice President Mondale, Secretary Vance, Dr. Brzezinski, and Adm. Stansfield Turner, Director of Central Intelligence;

—Vice President Mondale, Dr. Brzezinski, and Admiral Turner;

—Representative Clement J. Zablocki, of Wisconsin, and Dr. Brzezinski.

August 31

The President met at the White House with:

—Dr. Brzezinski;

—Vice President Mondale, Secretary of the Treasury W. Michael Blumenthal, and Representative Al Ullman, of Oregon, to discuss tax reform;

—Vice President Mondale and Representative Parren J. Mitchell, of Maryland, to discuss black issues;

—Representative Charles H. Wilson, of California, to discuss postal matters;

—Vice President Mondale, Mrs. Mondale, and Mrs. Carter, for lunch;

—Vice President Mondale, Secretary Blumenthal, Secretary Schlesinger, Stuart E. Eizenstat, Assistant to the President for Domestic Affairs and Policy, and representatives from the Departments of State and Treasury, to discuss the Alaska natural gas transportation system.

September 1

The President met at the White House with:

—Dr. Brzezinski;

—Mrs. Carter, for lunch;

—Attorney General Griffin B. Bell, Robert J. Lipshutz, Counsel to the President, and Mr. Eizenstat;

—Representative Lee H. Hamilton, of Indiana.

The President attended a briefing on the Panama Canal treaty, given for State officials and business and political leaders from Arkansas and West Virginia in the State Dining Room.

September 2

The President met at the White House with:

—Dr. Brzezinski;

—entertainers Willie Nelson and Emmylou Harris;

—Clara F. Hyatt, who is retiring as Chief of White House Correspondence;

—Charles L. Schultze, Chairman of the Council of Economic Advisers, to discuss minority employment;

—Representative David R. Bowen, of Mississippi, and Frank B. Moore, Assistant to the President for Congressional Liaison;

—Warren L. (Bill) Gulley, who is retiring as Director of the White House Military Office, and members of his family.

The President left the White House for a weekend visit at Camp David, Md.

CHECKLIST OF WHITE HOUSE PRESS RELEASES

The following releases of the Office of the White House Press Secretary, distributed during the period covered by this issue, are not included in the issue.

Released August 28, 1977

Announcement: Secretary of State Cyrus Vance's meeting with the President to report on his discussions with the leaders of the People's Republic of China during his visit to Peking on August 22–26, and also his meetings with Japanese leaders, in Japan, enroute home from Peking

CHECKLIST—Continued
Released August 29, 1977

News conference: on her decision to leave the Chairmanship of the National Endowment for the Arts at the expiration of her second term—by Nancy Hanks, Chairman of the National Endowment for the Arts

News conference: on the program concerning an international emergency food reserve, a set-aside for the 1978-crop wheat, and an increase in the loan rates for 1977-crop feed grains—by John C. White, Deputy Secretary, and Howard W. Hjort, Director of Agricultural Economics, Department of Agriculture

Fact sheet: the program concerning an international emergency food reserve, a set-aside for the 1978-crop wheat, and an increase in the loan rates for 1977-crop feed grains

Released August 30, 1977

News conference: following a briefing on the Panama Canal treaty—by Gov. Reubin Askew of Florida, Lt. Gov. Zell Miller of Georgia, and former Secretary of State Dean Rusk

---

NOMINATIONS SUBMITTED TO THE SENATE

The following list does not include promotions of members of the Uniformed Services, nominations to the Service Academies, or nominations of Foreign Service officers.

Submitted August 29, 1977

PROCTER R. HUG, JR., of Nevada, to be United States Circuit Judge for the Ninth Circuit, vice Ben Cushing Duniway, retired.

NOMINATIONS—Continued
Submitted August 29—Continued

THOMAS TANG, of Arizona, to be United States Circuit Judge for the Ninth Circuit, vice Richard H. Chambers, retired.

RONALD E. ANGEL, of Georgia, to be United States Marshal for the Northern District of Georgia for the term of 4 years, vice James H. Henson.

Submitted August 31, 1977

JOHN B. SLAUGHTER, of Washington, to be an Assistant Director of the National Science Foundation, vice Robert E. Hughes, resigned.

CHARLES N. VAN DOREN, of the District of Columbia, to be an Assistant Director of the United States Arms Control and Disarmament Agency, vice Amrom H. Katz, resigned.

Submitted September 2, 1977

MARVIN B. DURNING, of Washington, to be an Assistant Administrator of the Environmental Protection Agency, vice Stanley W. Legro, resigned.

DAVID G. HAWKINS, of the District of Columbia, to be an Assistant Administrator of the Environmental Protection Agency, vice Roger Strelow, resigned.

STEVEN D. JELLINEK, of Maryland, to be Assistant Administrator for Toxic Substances of the Environmental Protection Agency (new position).

ACTS APPROVED BY THE PRESIDENT

NOTE: No acts approved by the President were received by the Office of the Federal Register during the period covered by this issue.

Meeting With General Omar Torrijos Herrera of Panama

White House Statement Issued Following the Meeting. September 6, 1977

President Carter met with General Omar Torrijos Herrera, Chief of Government of Panama, for one hour this morning. The President was accompanied by Vice President Walter Mondale, Secretary of State Cyrus Vance, Assistant for National Security Affairs Zbigniew Brzezinski, Assistant Secretary of State Terence Todman, Ambassador to Panama William Jordan, and NSC Staff Member Robert Pastor. General Torrijos was accompanied by Foreign Minister Nicolas Gonzalez Revilla, Ambassador Gabriel Lewis, Minister of Planning and Economic Policy Nicolas Ardito Barletta, Advisor to the Head of Government Ambassador Rodrigo Gonzales, Aide-de-Camp of the Military Household Lieutenant Colonel Armando Beillido, and Aide-de-Camp of the Military Household Lieutenant Colonel Manuel A. Noriega.

President Carter and General Torrijos discussed the importance of the Panama Canal Treaty to the United States and Panama and efforts by both countries to gain widespread and popular acceptance of the treaty. The President noted that the treaty had been concluded without either side being under the pressure of the threat of violence and that the treaty would establish a new era of closer cooperation and friendship between the United States and Panama. The treaty, suggested the President, will be the first step in a series of improvements in the cooperation and friendship between the United States and Panama.

General Torrijos praised President Carter for pursuing the Panama Canal Treaty and said he too hoped the treaty would lead to a new type of relationship that will serve as an example for other Latin American countries.

President Carter said he hoped that the spirit of mutual respect and friendship which had guided the United States and Panama through the canal treaty negotiations will serve as an example to the other countries of the hemisphere as all our countries seek to resolve outstanding problems or disputes.

The two leaders agreed to consult closely on a continuing basis as the treaty moves toward ratification and implementation.

NOTE: The statement was made available by the White House Press Office. It was not issued in the form of a White House press release.

Meeting With President Francisco Morales Bermudez Cerruti of Peru

Remarks to Reporters Following the Meeting. September 6, 1977

THE PRESIDENT. Well, in every instance, I spent several hours studying about each country and am briefed as best I can be by the State Department and by the other leaders of our own Government concerning issues that are important between myself and the leaders of the visiting country.

I've already met with General Torrijos of Panama and this is Morales Bermudez, the President of Peru. We discussed a number of items with Peru. For instance, we are very grateful that they have signed the Treaty of Tlatelolco and also the non-proliferation treaty and the fact that they are moving strongly toward democratization of their government.

The President has announced that in 1980, if things go well, they'll have free elections, which is quite a step forward.

We also discussed matters that concern other countries, the possibility of Bolivia's having access to the Pacific Ocean, which they lost about a hundred years ago, and the possibility that Ecuador might have access to the Amazon River, which they desire very much.

We discussed the international copper prices and the possibility of an international sugar agreement, which is of great importance to almost all the countries to the south and also to us. But these are some of the items we discussed, in addition to the main question, which has brought all the countries here, and that is

their interest in a new era of cooperation and equality of treatment of the Latin American countries by our country as demonstrated so vividly in the signing of the Panama Canal Treaty.

So, in each individual instance, with 18 or 20 foreign leaders, there are general subjects that affect the whole hemisphere—the alleviation of tensions, the reduction of armaments, the nonproliferation commitment, human rights questions. Each country is quite different from one another. And I have tried to learn in every case what I can do to make our relationship with them better and also to alleviate any tensions that might exist with their neighbors.

Q. Realizing, Mr. President, that this is Panama week, if you will, you have the other matter pending, the matter of Bert Lance, the latest call for his resignation. What is your response to Chairman Ribicoff's and Senator Percy's call yesterday?

THE PRESIDENT. Well, I don't particularly want to talk about that now since I am engaged in other matters. But I have responded with appreciation to Senators Ribicoff and Percy for their early convening of the Senate committee for an expeditious presentation of all the allegations that have been made against Bert Lance and for giving him a chance to respond to them. And what I want is for it to be concluded quickly, for all the facts to be presented to the American people and to the Congress and to me.

REPORTER. Thank you.

NOTE: The President spoke at 2:45 p.m. on the South Grounds of the White House.

The transcript of the remarks was made available by the White House Press Office. It was not issued in the form of a White House press release.

Meeting With President Alfredo Stroessner of Paraguay

Remarks to Reporters Following the Meeting.
September 6, 1977

We have President Stroessner here with his Foreign Minister and other dignitaries to participate in the signing of a treaty between ourselves and Panama. We had an opportunity to discuss subjects of interest to our country and to Paraguay, to reemphasize the historic friendship that has bound our countries together, to discuss the present plans in Paraguay for the development of the country's economy, and also we made plans, I believe, to alleviate any differences of opinion that might exist between our country and Paraguay.

The President outlined the plans for elections in February and offered us an opportunity to come and observe the elections there. I told him that I might learn how to conduct a better campaign if I could see how the elections were conducted in Paraguay.

We had a discussion about the question of human rights and the fact that it has been a problem. And the President outlined to me the progress that is being made in this area.

We were pleased to learn about the cooperation between Paraguay and the neighbors in Brazil and Argentina in the development of water resources. And the President outlined to me the size of the fish which he quite often catches in the beautiful streams of Paraguay.

But we had a good discussion, and we are very grateful that he could come.

NOTE: The President spoke at 3:45 p.m. on the South Grounds of the White House. His concluding remarks in Spanish were not included in the transcript.

The transcript of the remarks was made available by the White House Press Office. It was not issued in the form of a White House press release.

Meeting With President Alfonso Lopez Michelsen of Colombia

Remarks to Reporters Following the Meeting.
September 6, 1977

THE PRESIDENT. This is Colombia?

REPORTER. Yes. We are from Colombia.

THE PRESIDENT. Fine. I am glad to see you.

Q. Can you tell me anything about your meeting?

THE PRESIDENT. Well, President Lopez and I had a very thorough discussion about many items. First of all, the preservation of Colombia's special rights in the use of the Panama Canal—they will be extended after the canal treaty goes into effect.

We also discussed the very important trade relationships that exist between ourselves and Colombia and the total commitment that Colombia has always made to democracy in its purest form and to the principle of human rights. And we discussed the importance of many nations being involved in pursuing the hope that all people might live in freedom and without oppression from government. And Colombia has set a very fine example for the rest of the world to follow.

We discussed the very serious problem of the traffic in drugs—marijuana, cocaine, and heroin—and the growing cooperation between our country and Colombia. President Lopez has been very helpful in this effort of ours, and we have been helpful, I hope, in his effort, as well.

We have no differences between our countries. There is great friendship and great cooperation, and this has existed historically. And I think that our own visit together was one of complete understanding and cooperation.

I also, of course, expressed my thanks to President Lopez and to his family for being so hospitable to my own wife when she was in Colombia recently and reminded him of my own visit to Colombia back in 1973 when I was Governor of Georgia.

So far as I know, the relationships between the United States and Colombia are excellent. It means a lot to us in this country to have the people of Colombia supporting the Panama Canal Treaty that has been evolved between the United States and Panama.

And I think it's accurate to say that President Lopez has been very helpful during the negotiations themselves.

NOTE: The President spoke at 6 p.m. on the South Grounds of the White House. His concluding remarks in Spanish were not included in the transcript.

The transcript of the remarks was made available by the White House Press Office. It was not issued in the form of a White House press release.

Meeting With President Augusto Pinochet Ugarte of Chile

Remarks to Reporters Following the Meeting. September 6, 1977

REPORTER. Mr. President?

THE PRESIDENT. Yes, ma'am.

Q. Do you mind telling us how it went this time?

THE PRESIDENT. Oh, very well. This was President Pinochet of Chile, and we

had a good discussion about matters that are important between us. We talked about the possibility of Bolivia having access to the ocean, the importance of Chile's ratifying the nonproliferation treaty and implementing the Treaty of Tlatelolco.

We also discussed the importance of holding down the armaments race in the Andean region. And I discussed with President Pinochet the problem that exists with the question of human rights in Chile, and he described to me some of the steps they are taking to improve the rights of the people there as they have recovered from the recent coup, and also we discussed the possibility of some observers who might go into Chile to observe what has been done there.

But these are matters that are, I think, important to Chile. They are certainly important to us and to the interrelationships that exist in our hemisphere.

Q. Did you ask him about missing Americans in Chile or anything about the problems concerning American citizens?

THE PRESIDENT. We talked about the release of prisoners and the right of those to be tried, the expedition of the judicial system, which has, he admitted, been delayed in some instances, and the elimination of their intelligence agency, I think a couple of weeks ago; also the new process by which a prisoner can be released from incarceration in exchange for extradition. In other words, if they want to be released, they leave the country.

We have had a very frank discussion about this serious problem. I think the Chilean leaders, including President Pinochet, recognize that the reputation of their country has been very poor in the field of human rights. He acknowledged that they have had problems in the past. He claimed that progress had been made in recent months and told me that their plans are for an increase in human freedoms in the future.

But I think that he can describe plans for the future better than can I. He knows that this is a very serious problem for Chile.

Q. Would you send observers?

THE PRESIDENT. No, we would not send observers. I think the observers that might—by the way, Assistant Secretary Todman was there recently—and the observers that we talked about would be from the United Nations.

Thank you very much.

Q. What do you say to people who say you shouldn't meet with these dictators? In other words, is there a problem meeting with people who have bad reputations?

THE PRESIDENT. Well, no, I don't feel that this should be an obstacle to my meeting with them, to describing to them the problems as I see them, to ask for their explanation in a very frank and forthcoming way and to request their plans for the alleviation of the problem or the explanation of the charges that have been made against their governments.

Obviously, the question of human rights has historically been a serious one in this hemisphere, Latin America in particular.

Most of the leaders have expressed to me great satisfaction at the progress that is now being made. Even when free elections do not exist, the commitments have been made among the leaders with whom I have met today that within a certain period of time and a date set by them that free elections would be held.

So, I think that my meeting with leaders of countries where human rights questions or others do exist—excessive armaments, border disputes, drug supply problems—I think it's healthy for them

and for us, for me to know their position better and for them to have the encouragement of our expressions of concern.

I think it's a good thing. Thank you.

NOTE: The exchange began at 7 p.m. on the South Grounds of the White House.

The transcript of the remarks was made available by the White House Press Office. It was not issued in the form of a White House press release.

United States Ambassador to El Salvador

Nomination of Frank J. Devine.
September 6, 1977

The President today announced that he will nominate Frank J. Devine, of Washington, D.C., to be Ambassador Extraordinary and Plenipotentiary of the United States to El Salvador. He would succeed Ignacio E. Lozano, Jr., who has resigned.

Devine was born June 30, 1922, in Albany, N.Y. He received a B.B.A. from Rensselaer Polytechnic Institute in 1942. He served in the U.S. Army from 1943 to 1946.

Devine joined the Foreign Service in 1946 and served in various posts in Central and South America and at the State Department. From 1962 to 1966, he was political officer in Lisbon, and from 1966 to 1970 he was deputy chief of mission in Santo Domingo.

He served as deputy chief of mission in Caracas from 1970 to 1973, and from 1973 to 1976 was Director of North Coast Affairs in the Bureau of Inter-American Affairs at the State Department. In 1976 and 1977, he was Director of the Office of Andean Affairs, and since earlier this year he has been Acting Deputy Assistant Secretary of State for Inter-American Affairs.

UNESCO

Nomination of Esteban E. Torres for the Rank of Ambassador While Serving as U.S. Permanent Representative.
September 7, 1977

The President today announced that he will nominate Esteban E. Torres, of Falls Church, Va., for the rank of Ambassador during his assignment as U.S. Permanent Representative to the United Nations Educational, Scientific and Cultural Organization (UNESCO) in Paris. He would replace William B. Jones, who is being transferred to another post.

Torres was born January 27, 1930, in Miami, Ariz. He has attended California State University at Los Angeles, American University, and the University of Maryland. He served in the U.S. Army from 1949 to 1953.

Since 1963 Torres has been with the United Automobile Workers of America, serving as international representative (1963), inter-American representative (1964–68), executive director of the Community Development Corporation of the East Los Angeles Community Union (on loan from 1968 to 1974), and assistant to the President (since 1974).

Torres has also served as a consultant to the U.S. Congress Office of Technology Assessment and as a member of the National Citizens Commission for Public Broadcasting. He has been a member of the National Center for Community Economic Development and the International Development Conference and is former president of the Plaza de la Raza Cultural Center of Los Angeles.

ACTION

Nomination of Carolyn R. Payton To Be an Associate Director. September 7, 1977

The President today announced that he will nominate Carolyn R. Payton, of Washington, D.C., to be Associate Director of ACTION. She would replace John R. Dellenback, resigned, and her area of responsibility would be international operations.

Payton was born May 13, 1925, in Norfolk, Va. She received a B.S. from Bennett College in 1945, an M.S. from the University of Wisconsin in 1948, and an Ed. D. from Columbia University in 1962.

From 1948 to 1953, Payton was an instructor in psychology and education at Livingstone College, and from 1953 to 1956 she was dean of women at Elizabeth City State Teachers College in North Carolina. From 1956 to 1959, she was associate professor of psychology and clinical counselor at Virginia State College.

Payton was an assistant professor of psychology at Howard University from 1959 to 1964. She worked for the Peace Corps from 1964 to 1970, serving as chief field selection officer for Latin America, deputy country director for the Eastern Caribbean, country director for the Eastern Caribbean, and special assistant to the Latin American regional director.

Since 1970 Payton has been director of the University Counseling Service at Howard University. She is chairperson of the American Psychological Association Committee on Scientific and Professional Ethics and Conduct, and a member of the APA's Task Force on Sex Bias and Sex Role Stereotyping in Psychotherapeutic Practice. She is a member of the National Association of Black Psychologists.

Advisory Committee for Trade Negotiations

Appointment of Douglas Fraser and Lloyd Mc-
Bride as Members.   September 7, 1977

The President today announced the appointments of Douglas Fraser and Lloyd McBride as members of the Advisory Committee for Trade Negotiations.

Fraser, 60, is president of the United Automobile, Aerospace and Agricultural Implement Workers of America (UAW). He replaces Leonard Woodcock, who has resigned from the Committee.

McBride, 61, is international president of the United Steelworkers of America and a vice president of the AFL-CIO. He replaces I. W. Abel, who has resigned from the Committee.

Occupational Health and Safety Review Commission

Nomination of Bertram R. Cottine To Be a
Member.   September 7, 1977

The President today announced that he will nominate Bertram R. Cottine, of Washington, D.C., to be a member of the Occupational Health and Safety Review Commission. He would replace Robert D. Moran, term expired.

Cottine was born April 2, 1947, in Kingston, N.Y. He received a J.D. from Boston University School of Law in 1972.

From 1972 to 1975, Cottine was a staff attorney and staff associate for the Occupational Health Research Group of Public Citizen. From 1975 to 1977, he was an adjunct professor at Georgetown University Law Center; deputy director of the D.C. Project: Community Legal Assistance and Street Law; and project coordinator and attorney on Law and the Developmentally Disabled.

Since April 1977, Cottine has been Special Assistant for Policy in the Office of the Assistant Secretary of Labor for Occupational Safety and Health.

Conference on Security and Cooperation in Europe

Nomination of Arthur J. Goldberg To Be Am-
bassador at Large and U.S. Representative
to the Conference.   September 7, 1977

The President today announced that he will nominate Arthur J. Goldberg, of Washington, D.C., to be Ambassador at Large and U.S. Representative to the Conference on Security and Cooperation in Europe (CSCE) and Chairman of the U.S. delegation to the CSCE.

Goldberg was born August 8, 1908, in Chicago. He received a B.S.L. in 1929 and a J.D. in 1930 from Northwestern University. He served in the U.S. Army from 1942 to 1944 as captain, then major.

Goldberg was senior partner of his own law firm in Chicago from 1933 to 1961. From 1948 to 1955, he was general counsel of the Congress of Industrial Organizations (CIO), and from 1948 to 1961 he was general counsel of the United Steelworkers of America. From 1952 to 1961, he was also senior partner in a Washington law firm.

In 1961 and 1962, Goldberg was Secretary of Labor. From 1962 to 1965, he was a Justice of the United States Supreme Court. From 1965 to 1968, he was U.S. Representative to the United Nations and U.S. Representative in the Security Council of the United Nations.

From 1968 to 1971, he was senior partner in a New York law firm.

Since 1971 Goldberg has practiced law in Washington. He has served on the President's Committee on Youth Employment, the President's Advisory Committee on Labor-Management Policy, and the President's Committee on Equal Employment Opportunity. He is former Chairman of the President's Committee on Migratory Labor.

Goldberg is the author of "AFL–CIO: Labor United" (1956), "Defenses of Freedom" (1966), "Equal Justice: The Warren Era of the Supreme Court" (1972), and numerous articles.

Mississippi River Commission

Nomination of William E. Read To Be a Member. September 7, 1977

The President today announced that he will nominate Brig. Gen. William E. Read, Corps of Engineers, to be a member of the Mississippi River Commission. He would succeed Maj. Gen. Charles I. McGinnis, who is being reassigned.

Read was born May 17, 1927, in Charlotte, N.C. He has served in the U.S. Army since 1950. He holds a B.S. in military engineering from the U.S. Military Academy and an M.S. in civil engineering from the University of Illinois.

Read served in Vietnam in 1970 and 1971. In 1971 and 1972, he was district engineer for the Tulsa District of the Army Engineer Division. From 1972 to 1974, he was Director of Procurement and Production for Army Aviation Systems Command in St. Louis, Mo., and from 1974 to 1976 he was Deputy Commanding General of that command.

Since 1976 Read has been division engineer for the Army Engineer Division,

Missouri River. He holds the Legion of Merit with Oak Leaf Cluster and the Bronze Star with two Oak Leaf Clusters.

Meeting With President Carlos Andrés Pérez of Venezuela

Remarks to Reporters Following the Meeting. September 7, 1977

President Pérez has developed into one of my best personal friends and is a great counselor and adviser for me on matters that concern the nations of the Caribbean and Central and South America.

Also, he was of great assistance in the negotiations between ourselves and Panama in developing the terms of the treaty.

The people of our country look upon President Pérez as a great leader in this hemisphere and also, of course, the leader of one of the great democracies of the world.

NOTE: The President spoke at 5:10 p.m. on the South Grounds of the White House. His concluding remarks in Spanish were not included in the transcript.

The transcript of the remarks was made available by the White House Press Office. It was not issued in the form of a White House press release.

Panama Canal Treaties

Remarks at the Signing Ceremony at the Pan American Union Building. September 7, 1977

Mr. Secretary General and distinguished leaders from throughout our own country and from throughout this hemisphere:

First of all, I want to express my deep thanks to the leaders who have come here from 27 nations in our own hemisphere, 20 heads of state, for this historic occasion.

I'm proud to be here as part of the largest group of heads of state ever assembled in the Hall of the Americas, Mr. Secretary General.

We are here to participate in the signing of treaties which will assure a peaceful and prosperous and secure future for an international waterway of great importance to us all.

But the treaties do more than that. They mark the commitment of the United States to the belief that fairness, and not force, should lie at the heart of our dealings with the nations of the world.

If any agreement between two nations is to last, it must serve the best interests of both nations. The new treaties do that. And by guaranteeing the neutrality of the Panama Canal, the treaties also serve the best interests of every nation that uses the canal.

This agreement thus forms a new partnership to insure that this vital waterway, so important to all of us, will continue to be well operated, safe, and open to shipping by all nations, now and in the future.

Under these accords, Panama will play an increasingly important role in the operation and defense of the canal during the next 23 years. And after that, the United States will still be able to counter any threat to the canal's neutrality and openness for use.

The members of the Organization of American States and all the members of the United Nations will have a chance to subscribe to the permanent neutrality of the canal.

The accords also give Panama an important economic stake in the continued, safe, and efficient operation of the canal and make Panama a strong and interested party in the future success of the waterway.

In the spirit of reciprocity suggested by the leaders at the Bogotá summit, the United States and Panama have agreed that any future sea-level canal will be built in Panama and with the cooperation of the United States. In this manner, the best interests of both our nations are linked and preserved into the future.

Many of you seated at this table have made known for years through the Organization of American States and through your own personal expressions of concern to my predecessors in the White House, your own strong feelings about the Panama Canal Treaty of 1903. That treaty, drafted in a world so different from ours today, has become an obstacle to better relations with Latin America.

I thank each of you for the support and help that you and your countries have given during the long process of negotiation, which is now drawing to a close.

This agreement has been negotiated over a period of 14 years under four Presidents of the United States.

I'm proud to see President Ford here with us tonight. And I'm also glad to see Mrs. Lyndon Johnson here with us tonight.

Many Secretaries of State have been involved in the negotiations. Dean Rusk can't be here. He has endorsed the treaty. But Secretary of State William Rogers is here. We are glad to have you, sir. And Secretary of State Henry Kissinger is here too.

This has been a bipartisan effort, and it is extremely important for our country to stay unified in our commitment to the fairness, the symbol of equality, the mutual respect, the preservation of the security and defense of our own Nation, and an exhibition of cooperation which sets a symbol that is important to us all before this assembly tonight and before the American people in the future.

This opens a new chapter in our relations with all nations of this hemisphere, and it testifies to the maturity and the good judgment and the decency of our people. This agreement is a symbol for the world of the mutual respect and cooperation among all our nations.

Thank you very much for your help.

NOTE: The President spoke at 7:35 p.m. in the Hall of the Americas at the headquarters of the Organization of American States. In his opening remarks, he referred to Alejandro Orfila, OAS Secretary General.

Following the President's remarks, General Torrijos of Panama spoke, and then the two leaders signed the Panama Canal Treaty and the Treaty Concerning the Permanent Neutrality and Operation of the Panama Canal.

Panama Canal Treaties

Remarks at a White House Dinner for Western Hemisphere Leaders Attending the Signing Ceremony. September 7, 1977

We are not going to have toasts tonight, but I would like to say a few words of welcome to all of you.

I would like to start with one of the best friends I have, and a great leader of our country, President Ford, and welcome him here this evening.

And someone else who has inspired our country, and who has set an example of leadership and beauty and gracious example for us, and who also recognized the Marine Strings from olden times—Lady Bird Johnson.

I know that most of you were at the ceremonies where the treaties were signed, so I won't try to introduce all our guests, but I would like to present to you again our special guest for this evening, General Torrijos from Panama and his wife, Mrs. Torrijos.

Some guests that General Torrijos cares much more about now than he does about me are the Members of the United States Senate. [*Laughter*] We are glad to have all of you here. It's a very fine thing for you to come.

I think that this was a very fine night, too, in the life of the Organization of American States. Secretary General Orfila, we are very proud to have you here.

Mr. Ellsworth Bunker and Sol Linowitz, would you stand just a moment? General Torrijos said he's going to be very lonesome in Panama in the future without Ambassador Bunker being there. [*Laughter*] He's been negotiating in Panama now for 14 years. And this is a great accomplishment for our country and also for Panama.

We invited a special guest from Brazil here tonight, Pele, but at the last minute he had to leave to go to Spain.

I was talking to General Torrijos. As you may know, the lightweight boxing champion of the world is Señor Durran from Panama, and he's very hard to match, but we tried to match him by the heavyweight champion of the world, Muhammad Ali, and we are very glad to have you here.

There's another man that I would like to introduce—he and his wife. I've been a very close reader of the sports page for the last several weeks, because we have a very distinguished Georgian who has, I think, come forward with a great deal of enthusiasm and skill, a great deal of understanding of the elements, the oceans in particular. He's exemplified, I think, the name of his boat. He's a very courageous man—Ted Turner. We are very proud to have you here tonight. And as you all know, he will represent us in the America's Cup races very shortly, having overwhelmed his opponents much better than has been the case with his baseball team, the Atlanta Braves. [*Laughter*]

This is an evening of historic importance, and I invited another special guest from Georgia, a woman whose husband inspired the world, Mrs. Martin Luther King, Jr.

I was talking to General Torrijos a few moments ago about how important the treaty was to Panama. It was shown throughout Latin America for a full hour live this evening—the ceremonies. And he said that because of the demands of his own people, that he used helicopters to carry to all the remote villages in Panama television sets; and since they didn't have electricity, that he also carried small electric generators so that he wouldn't have to carry all the people from the remote areas into Panama City this evening. And I think this demonstrates the importance of the treaty to Panama.

He said, "Mr. President, I can tell you without fear of being wrong that more than a million Panamanians wept this evening during the ceremonies."

And I could tell from his own private conversations with me the tremendous importance of this long search for an equitable treaty that has been consummated this evening.

There is another special difference between this treaty and the one that was signed in 1903. The Panamanians had a chance to read it before it was signed— [*laughter*]—which was not the case with the first treaty. And I believe that the American people are big enough and strong enough, courageous enough and understanding enough to be proud of what has been accomplished, initiated by President Johnson in 1963, following a temporary outbreak of violence in the Panama Canal Zone. And the demonstration that President Johnson gave of our good intentions caused an equal demonstration of patience and perseverance and good faith and good manners on the part of the Panamanians.

And the negotiations continued under President Nixon and under President Ford. And I am very glad that my predecessors, their Secretaries of State, their Vice Presidents and negotiators have led up to this successful conclusion of the effort this day.

We have an opportunity now in our own country to demonstrate again the respect and the appreciation which we feel toward our neighbors in the southern part of this hemisphere. This has not always been apparent to our neighbors, but I think the American people feel this deep within them, that the most precious friendships, the staunchest historical supporters, and those with whom we share a common history and a common future are those who live in Canada and in the nations to the south. And I believe that this treaty can open up a new era of understanding and comprehension, friendship and mutual respect, throughout not only this hemisphere but throughout the world.

It's not an easy thing to accept a change which has been so profoundly balanced in our favor and which can now be of equal benefit to both countries. But ours is a great country, and it's great enough to be fair.

I think it's accurate to say that never in the last 14 years has there been any semblance of a threat or an expression of displeasure on the part of the Panamanians toward our negotiators. Ambassador Bunker has told me this more than once.

And President Torrijos, I thank you for the good will that has been brought by you for the last 9 years as President and leader of your country to the negotiating table. And many other leaders who are represented here—27 countries in our hemisphere—have contributed a great deal of support and advice in times when the negotiations seemed to be on the verge of being broken off, when they gave quiet demonstrations of their interest in the treaty and what it might mean to all of us.

So, I am grateful to all of you leaders for coming here to give our people an expression of your interest and your support. And I think I can assure you that our Nation will rally itself to ratify the treaty, and also, General Torrijos feels sure that when the facts are presented to the Panamanians that in the plebiscite that will be held late in October, that his people will also give their approval to this great step forward toward peace and mutual respect.

We will have a chance during this 3 or 4 days—I will, and my Cabinet members—to meet with all of you leaders who have come from your own great countries. And I think that you are taking advantage of this opportunity to meet with one another to resolve longstanding disputes, to work out means of alleviating the threat of possible arms races that might lead to war or to conflict of some kind, and to restore friendships that perhaps in the past have been damaged and to join with one another in planning for the future, economically and politically, that will give us all a better life.

So, I believe that we'll always look back upon this event that has been made possible by General Torrijos and many of you as the first step toward even greater progress and greater friendship in what I think is the greatest hemisphere on Earth, the Western Hemisphere of our world.

Thank you very much.

I should have paused for the translations, but I didn't, and we will ask the translator to take his place now. And fol-

lowing that we will go and have a brief cup of coffee, and then I think you will hear some of the most delightful entertainment that you've ever heard.

NOTE: The President spoke at 11 p.m. in the State Dining Room at the White House.

United States-Canada Agreement on a Natural Gas Pipeline

Joint Statement by the President and Prime Minister Pierre Elliott Trudeau. September 8, 1977

Today, we have agreed in principle on the elements of a joint proposal to construct the Alcan-Foothills pipeline along the Alaska Highway to transport Alaskan natural gas through Canada to the lower 48 States and at a later time Canadian gas to Canadian markets.

This joint undertaking will be the largest single private energy project in history. The detailed agreement we hope to sign next week is an example of how both countries can work together to meet their energy needs.

After the agreement is signed, each of us intends to submit our decisions to our respective legislative bodies for the appropriate authorizations and assurances. We are both hopeful the project will be approved.

Major benefits from this project will accrue to both countries. When the pipeline is built, Canada will have a much greater ability to develop its own gas reserves, particularly in the frontier regions of the Mackenzie Delta.

The U.S., in turn, will have the enormous benefit of new natural gas supplies from the North Slope of Alaska at a significantly lower cost-of-service price than could have been achieved through an all-U.S. route.

This agreement serves the mutual interest of both countries and the national interest of each. Its underlying rationale is that both countries working together can move more energy more efficiently than either country working by itself. Under the expected cost estimates, this agreement improves the 20-year cost-of-service average price in 1975 dollars to the American consumer by at least $.08 per thousand cubic feet over the price that would have resulted from the route through Dawson and $.12 per thousand cubic feet for the Canadian consumer. At the expected volumes, the project will result in a $6 billion savings for American consumers over the life of the project when compared to the proposal to liquify and ship the gas from Alaska.

While providing Canada the opportunity to accelerate development of its gas reserves and providing for billions of dollars of additional investment in the Canadian economy, this pipeline will stimulate the gas industry in Canada, and together with the early prospect of connecting new sources of supply, will generally enhance the availability of gas to meet market needs.

The potential to secure increased Canadian, as well as Alaskan supplies, and the magnitude of consumer savings that can be achieved by an all-pipeline route guarantee the superiority of this proposal.

We have decided to embark together on this historic project which holds the promise of great benefits to both countries, and which confirms anew the strength of the ties that link us.

United States-Canada Agreement on a Natural Gas Pipeline

Remarks of the President and Prime Minister Trudeau Announcing the Agreement. September 8, 1977

THE PRESIDENT. *Good morning, everybody.*

I think a joint statement has already been issued to you just recently, concerning a very important agreement that President Trudeau and I have approved this morning in principle, that our countries will undertake the largest single privately financed energy project in history, an Alcan Highway pipeline to carry Alaskan natural gas through Canada to the lower 48 States.

This joint United States and Canadian system could deliver more than 3½ billion cubic feet per day of Alaskan and, later on, Canadian gas to both our countries.

The cost of this transportation system will be significantly lower than under the alternative pipeline, the El Paso line down due south through Alaska and then by ship into California.

The savings to the American consumers over the first 20 years of the project could total about $5 billion. The Alcan route is preferable to the El Paso route, which was the other one that we were considering, because it is more economical, it's safer, and has less damage to the environment, and because it will deliver gas more directly to the American markets where the gas is needed, in the northern midwestern part of our country, with perhaps a spur later on over to the California region.

The project will benefit Canada by facilitating development of its own gas reserves, particularly in the frontier region to the Mackenzie Delta area.

We have agreed in principle not to build the route diversion to Dawson originally required by the Canadian National Energy Board. But in exchange, the United States has agreed to share the cost of a Dempster Highway lateral from Dawson to Whitehorse if and when it is constructed. This lateral line would connect at Whitehorse with the main pipeline so that additional gas from the Mackenzie Delta could be brought to market.

The exact share of the U.S. cost for the extension will be determined by the percentage of cost overruns on construction of the main pipeline in Canada.

This formula will provide incentives for the most efficient construction of the pipeline. Both countries recognize the benefits from increased cooperation in developing our energy supplies. This agreement brings great benefits to both countries. We will continue to cooperate to our mutual benefit in many other matters of importance to our two nations as has always been the case between ourselves and Canada.

Once the agreement is signed, probably next week, Prime Minister Trudeau and I will then seek approval of the Alcan project from our respective legislative bodies. I hope the U.S. Congress will approve this critical energy project before the close of the session.

Once approved, I believe the project will be expeditiously built consistent with sound environmental practices.

Under the provisions of the Alaska Natural Gas Transportation Act passed by Congress last year, I will appoint a strong Federal construction coordinator and inspector to insure effective project design and management.

Again I want to express my deep appreciation to Prime Minister Pierre Trudeau and to the negotiators, and I look forward to another opportunity to demonstrate to the world and to our own people that our sharing of mutual projects and mutual purposes and a common philosophy about the future is a very valuable thing to our people and constantly demonstrates the good neighborship that exists across our borders.

Pierre, I do thank you very much for your cooperation. And I believe that when the details of the agreement are described within the next few days, that the Americans and Canadians will be pleased at the progress that we have made. It's a dramatic breakthrough, thanks to you and the cooperation of the Canadian Government.

THE PRIME MINISTER. Thank you, Jimmy.

I do want, Mr. President, to associate myself with these feelings. It's certain that what we have done and agreed upon in principle this morning is certainly in line with the spirit of good neighborliness that our countries have always attempted to practice.

We were successful in one other giant project a generation ago on the Seaway. This one is even bigger. In terms of energy, it's certainly more important.

And I am very happy to say that the spirit that you and I defined last February at our meeting of attempting to solve all these problems—not to one's greatest possible advantage at the disadvantage of the other, but so that both sides get the maximum amount of advantage—I am very glad that that spirit has underlined all the negotiations, and that I think in the process of them there was only one phone call that you and I had to make to insure that our people were negotiating in a spirit of complete openness, that both sides were endeavoring to make sure that the other side was operating on the same facts.

We weren't trying to hide things from each other in order to get maximum advantage from the other, but we were trying to make a project which would be to the advantage of the American people and to the Canadian people.

From our side, we are very happy with the cooperation that you, Mr. President, and your people have shown. It remains, as you say, to sign the fine print next week. But I am certain that with the agreed upon principles that there will be no difficulty there.

We will have to, apart from going to our legislature—we'll want to make sure that transmission of the energy itself is in keeping with the high principles as we have set for ourselves in terms of protecting the environment, making sure that the interests of the native peoples will be guarded in every way, and that, of course, our Provinces and our Yukon Council will be involved in the execution of this. But that is for us to follow up on. And so far as our bilateral negotiations are concerned, I am very happy with the spirit that pervaded them.

[*At this point, Prime Minister Trudeau summarized his remarks in French.*]

THE PRESIDENT. Thank you, Pierre.

I might say that I congratulated Prime Minister Trudeau on the tough negotiators that the Canadians have proven themselves to be. And I am now in the process of asking him to help us negotiate agreements with other nations; they've done so well in this particular project. [*Laughter*]

But we are proud of this. There has never been a larger project in the history of the world. And for two nations who have intense domestic political problems involving environment, involving cost to consumers, involving assured supplies of energy in the future, to look 20 or 40 years ahead and to undertake this project with

friendship and mutual trust is a major step forward.

And I think, again, it demonstrates vividly the longstanding friendship that exists between ourselves and the Canadians. We've had many other potential disagreements in recent months concerning the oceans, fisheries, and in every instance we've been able to work these potential problems out harmoniously.

And we still have some problems concerning United States and Canadian tax laws, extraterritorial questions concerning antitrust enforcements. But, again, we are trying—and I am sure with assured eventual success—to resolve these very important matters for our people in harmony and a spirit of cooperation.

But I want to reemphasize my thanks to you, Pierre, for your friendship and cooperation.

THE PRIME MINISTER. Well, Jimmy, I am very grateful for these final words. If I can help you with your elections at any point, I would like to—[*laughter*]——

NOTE: The President spoke at 10:30 a.m. to reporters assembled in the Briefing Room at the White House.

Meeting With Vice Admiral Alfredo Poveda Burbano of Ecuador

Remarks to Reporters Following the Meeting With the President of the Supreme Council of the Government of Ecuador. September 8, 1977

REPORTER. Mr. President, would you like to make any comment on your meeting with President Poveda?

THE PRESIDENT. I would be glad to. We had a very thorough discussion about matters that are of mutual importance to us, the common commitment that we have with the people and leaders of Ecuador for the enhancement of human rights, and our thanks to the leaders of Ecuador for supporting our strong position in improving human rights taken in the last Organization of American States meeting.

We also are very excited and pleased to see the move of the leaders of your country toward democratic elections that will commence perhaps next year. And we congratulated Admiral Poveda on this decision.

We discussed the statement by the Peruvian President that additional purchase of arms and weapons by Peru was not planned, the gratitude that we have for improved relationships between Ecuador and Peru. We discussed the future possibility of access by Ecuador to the Amazon River, although the prospects are not good at this point. The discussions, I think, will be accelerated in the future.

We discussed the delivery of landing craft from our country to Ecuador and the upcoming delivery of a new destroyer. And I also expressed my thanks that the desire of Ecuador for army and navy equipment was obviously predicated on defense of your country and not offense against any other nation.

We reemphasized our appreciation to the people of Ecuador for supplying oil to our country during the 1973 embargo and the gratitude that we feel for this expression of friendship to us.

We had long discussions about these items, and I think the meetings were very helpful to me in understanding the special problems and opportunities that exist in Ecuador.

We discussed other matters—oil exploration, enhancement of your port facilities, construction of new highways, the high percentage of your national budget that's spent for education, improvement of health care. These kind of things are very good for us to see.

REPORTER. Thank you very much, Mr. President.

THE PRESIDENT. Thank you again.

NOTE: The exchange began at 12:10 p.m. on the South Grounds of the White House.

The transcript of the remarks was made available by the White House Press Office. It was not issued in the form of a White House press release.

Meeting With President Hugo Banzer Suarez of Bolivia

Remarks to Reporters Following the Meeting. September 8, 1977

THE PRESIDENT. Well, we had a very thorough discussion with President Banzer of the good relationships between ourselves and your country. We examined the maps of the possible route to the sea for Bolivia, just north of Arica in Chile.

And our hope is that Bolivia, Chile, and Peru can agree on some corridor which will permit Bolivia to have direct access to the sea on Bolivian territory.

We have no authority over the nations involved, but we have expressed our hope to Presidents Pinochet and Morales Bermudez that this might be accomplished.

We also discussed the progress that Bolivia has made in reducing the traffic in drugs, particularly cocaine, that comes to North America.

And I expressed my sincere hope that the Americans who are in Bolivian prisons and who have not yet been tried might have their cases examined very soon. Three of these prisoners are very ill. And we hope that within the bounds of Bolivian law, that their cases might be resolved very early.

This is a serious problem in our country. The parents of these prisoners, and families, have aroused a great deal of interest among American citizens, and

President Banzer, I think, will take a personal interest, within the framework of Bolivian law, that attention will be given to their case.

We have good relations with Bolivia. And we appreciate the cooperation that has been evidenced between the Bolivian people and our people.

We expect good progress to be made in return of the political processes to civilian rule, hopefully by 1980 or before. President Banzer reemphasized his commitment to this process.

Q. Mr. President, what is the outlook for the sea corridor, as you see it——

THE PRESIDENT. No, I think there is a hope that President Banzer can meet with the Presidents of Peru and Chile, and what the prospects might be for success, I really don't know. But we have wished him well.

REPORTER. Thank you very much.

THE PRESIDENT. Thank you.

NOTE: The President spoke at 2 p.m. on the South Grounds of the White House.

The transcript of the remarks was made available by the White House Press Office. It was not issued in the form of a White House press release.

Meeting With President Joaquín Balaguer of the Dominican Republic

Remarks to Reporters Following the Meeting. September 8, 1977

REPORTER. Mr. President?

THE PRESIDENT. Yes, ma'am?

Q. Tell us all about it.

THE PRESIDENT. Well, we have an extremely good relationship with the Dominican Republic, as you know. President Balaguer has set an example for all leaders in this nation in changing his own country and his own people away from a former totalitarian government to one of increasingly pure democracy. And the commitment that he's shown in preserving human rights and leading the other nations in this effort have been an inspiration to me.

I doubt that any other two countries have worked more closely together in matters relating to our own hemisphere, in the United Nations than has the Dominican Republic and the United States of America. We cooperate on the sugar agreement. We cooperate in our debates in the General Assembly of the U.N. We cooperate in matters that relate to the Organization of American States.

We've been talking to President Balaguer about the upcoming elections next year, which will be open and free and, I think, which will be a model to everyone on the universality of the right to vote and the free expression of the people's will in choosing their own government.

So, in the last 7 years, there's been unbelievable progress made in the Dominican Republic. President Balaguer pointed out to me that there's a great need for us to realize that their major crop, their major export item is sugar, and what we do here in our own country has a profound impact on the well-being of his own people.

And of course, we hope that we'll have an international sugar agreement during 1977. We produce tremendous quantities of sugar in our own Nation from sugar beets and cane. And of course, we also import large quantities of sugar.

So, these discussions, particularly with him and with the other nations, are very important to me.

Q. When do you think the Senate is going to bring up these treaties, and are you confident of the result?

THE PRESIDENT. I'm going to do the best I can to have the treaties ratified. And I think that we will succeed. But the time schedule is something that I can't predict right now. It's going to be a matter of great importance to me and to our country and to this hemisphere, and I think a failure to ratify the treaty would have very serious consequences.

Q. The Hill leaders are saying it won't be 'til next year. Do you accept that that's probably what will happen?

THE PRESIDENT. Well, that is, I think, a guess at this point that would be good. But I've talked to the leaders on the Democratic and Republican sides, and if it seems apparent that we have enough votes to ratify the treaty during this session of Congress, they've all assured me that that would be their desire.

Q. Don't bring it up if you don't have the vote.

THE PRESIDENT. That's right.

Q. What do you mean by "serious consequences"? You've said that several times now. Do you mean war?

THE PRESIDENT. Well, no, I wouldn't want to predict war. But I think it would be a serious disappointment on behalf of all the nations of this hemisphere in the refusal to ratify the treaty by our country. I don't, obviously, predict war. But there would be a deterioration of the relationships between our country and almost every nation south of here.

Q. Do you see your own relationship to other foreign policy questions tied to your success or failure on this particular one?

THE PRESIDENT. Yes, to some degree, yes, because it tests the character and the will of the American people to do what's fair, what's right, what's decent, and to treat other nations with respect, and at the same time to enhance the security and well-being of our own people. And I

think it would be a reflection on our judgment and our fairness if the treaty was not ratified.

Q. And if it is ratified, do you then have a better hand in the Mideast, on SALT, on other questions?

THE PRESIDENT. I think my own position would be enhanced in that it would be a show of support for my administration by the Congress and the people, yes.

NOTE: The exchange began at 3:15 p.m. on the South Grounds of the White House.

The transcript of the remarks was made available by the White House Press Office. It was not issued in the form of a White House press release.

Meeting With President Carlos Humberto Romero of El Salvador

Remarks to Reporters Following the Meeting. September 8, 1977

THE PRESIDENT. Good afternoon.

President Romero from El Salvador was very gratifying to us.

In the past, there has been great concern in the United States about two questions: One, the question of human rights and the fact that charges have been made and allegations have been made that there were violations of these rights in El Salvador.

President Romero has informed me that he has requested that a commission on human rights from the United Nations or OAS go to El Salvador to see the great progress that has been made there in the last 2 months. And we are grateful to get this good news.

Another item that has been of great concern to us and all the nations of this hemisphere has been the absence of approval by the Congress of El Salvador of the mediation of the border disputes with Honduras, which has resulted in an interruption of free trade and transportation and exchange of people with Honduras to the north and the interruption of Pan-American Highway traffic.

But the President informed me that the Congress has today voted to accept the agreement that was signed here in Washington last year and that he anticipates a good chance now that the dispute with Honduras can be resolved without further delay.

So, these two problems that have existed between our countries have, I think, been substantially resolved, and we are very grateful that the new administration has been able to achieve these accomplishments in only 2 months in office.

I believe that we will have in the future a much closer relationship between our country and El Salvador, and I think the concern that has been expressed here in the Congress, among our people, and from the White House will be eliminated to a great degree in the future.

We believe that the President will carry out these statements with enthusiasm and with determination and with success. And this is very good news for all the nations and all the people of our hemisphere.

Q. Is there any indication, Mr. President, when the commission might be going to El Salvador?

THE PRESIDENT. No, but the President said that was one of his major purposes in coming to Washington. Since he has only been in office 2 months, this is really the first time for him to assess the needs in his country and to come to the OAS to specifically request that the commission go to El Salvador to witness, themselves, the progress that has been made.

But the time schedule for the sending of the commission, I guess, is now in the hands of the leaders of the international body.

Q. Did he see any progress for possible renewal of relations with Honduras, or did you just talk about mediation?

THE PRESIDENT. He just pointed out the fact that the Congress had today voted unanimously to take this action, which all of us have been hoping to see. But I think the President himself would have to answer the question about prospects for the renewal of relations. I don't know about that. We are very grateful for this good news.

Thank you.

NOTE: The President spoke at 4:30 p.m. on the South Grounds of the White House.

The transcript of the remarks was made available by the White House Press Office. It was not issued in the form of a White House press release.

California Debris Commission

Nomination of Col. Donald M. O'Shei To Be a Member.   September 8, 1977

The President today announced that he will nominate Col. Donald M. O'Shei, Corps of Engineers, to be a member of the California Debris Commission. He would replace Col. Fred Rockwell, retired.

O'Shei was born July 31, 1933, in Buffalo, N.Y. He graduated from the U.S. Military Academy in 1956 with a B.S. in engineering and has served in the Army since then. He also holds an M.S. in civil engineering from Princeton University (1961) and a J.D. from Georgetown University (1970). Since 1976 O'Shei has been district engineer for the U.S. Army Engineer District, Sacramento, Calif.

Meeting With Brigadier General Juan Alberto Melgar Castro of Honduras

Remarks to Reporters Following the Meeting With the Chief of State of Honduras. September 8, 1977

REPORTER. How did these talks go, Mr. President?

THE PRESIDENT. Well, they have all been very good. One of the most difficult threats to peace in our entire hemisphere has been the breakdown in relations between El Salvador and Honduras because of a border dispute that has been long-standing and which was aggravated by a conflict following a soccer game 7 or 8 years ago. And because of this, the Pan-American Highway has been severed for use and there have been no relations there and a constant threat of war.

Today, however, the El Salvadorian Congress voted unanimously to approve a pending agreement for mediation of the border disputes, and on the other hand, Honduras has reaffirmed its commitment to peace with El Salvador, and the two Presidents have been meeting at length while they have been in Washington.

We've also received good news from El Salvador, that they asked the Organization of American States to send their commission on human rights into El Salvador to witness the great progress that has been made in the last 2 months since the new administration took effect.

I've just met with President Melgar of Honduras, who has shown a great interest in multinational cooperation between Honduras and Guatemala and El Salvador and other countries in that region, like Nicaragua, in the development of energy resources. These are relatively poor countries as far as per capita income is concerned. And of course, this poverty has been aggravated by an absence of trade and commerce and cooperation with their neighbors.

And so, I think that many of these leaders have come here to Washington not only to participate in the ceremonies related to the Panama Canal Treaty but also to use the occasion as a chance to meet privately with one another and to try to resolve differences that have been in existence for decades, as an exhibition of their hope for peace and friendship which we showed, along with Panama, with our treaty.

So, I think the discussions have been good. It also gives me a chance to learn about their special needs.

There is a hydroelectric project, for instance, in Honduras, El Cajon, and of course, our attitude on the Board of Directors of the World Bank and the Inter-American Bank, the allocation of funds from some of the European countries and some of the Arab countries, Iran, for this project might very well make it possible now to be completed. It's been pending for years and years. And I think a common interest in this kind of project, whether or not this particular one is successful, is a constructive opportunity.

Q. I wonder if I could ask, Mr. President, if you've been told that your Harris approval rating has dropped from 69 to, today, 52 percent?

THE PRESIDENT. No.

Q. And to what extent you think that is related to the Lance affair?

THE PRESIDENT. It's hard to say, you know, what causes the ups and downs of a public official's approval rating. I think, though, that if I continue to make a judgment on each individual decision that confronts me on the basis of its merits, that ultimately I'll survive and will retain an adequate support from our people.

This, combined with the Panama Canal problem, the adverse report recently on unemployment, the chronic inflation rate, and also the controversial matters like welfare reform, energy problems, increased taxation on some kinds of energy sources—all of these matters contribute to the deterioration of the overwhelming approval rating that I did have, which I think was extraordinarily high.

But this is compatible with what has happened with other Presidents who were active, and although, of course, I would like to have a hundred percent approval, I'm perfectly willing to continue to be judged on what is the ultimate outcome of these affairs.

In my judgment, Bert Lance ought to have a chance for a hearing without delay, comprehensive in nature, with every allegation and fact produced for the American people to know and for the Congress to know and for me to understand. And I'm very eager to see the testimony presented by the Comptroller General's—by the Comptroller's report and the Senate investigating committees. And there has never been any doubt in my mind that the outcome of these investigations will be not only proper but also will be well accepted by the American people.

REPORTER. Thank you, Mr. President.

NOTE: The exchange began at 5:15 p.m. on the South Grounds of the White House.

The transcript of the remarks was made available by the White House Press Office. It was not issued in the form of a White House press release.

Meeting With President Jorge Rafael Videla of Argentina

Remarks to Reporters Following the Meeting. September 9, 1977

THE PRESIDENT. We discussed several items, but the two that we discussed at most length were, first, the question of nonproliferation of nuclear explosives. We are very hopeful that Argentina, which has been in the nuclear field for 25 years in the production of power, will join with other nations in this hemisphere in signing the Treaty of Tlatelolco to prevent any development of explosives. And I was very encouraged by what President Videla had to say.

The other item that we discussed at length was the question of human rights—the number of people who are incarcerated or imprisoned in Argentina, the need for rapid trial of these cases, and the need for Argentina to let the world know the status of the prisoners.

President Videla was very frank with me about pointing out the problems that have existed in Argentina and his commitment to make very rapid progress in the next few months. He wants Argentina to be judged not on his words alone, but on the demonstrable progress that he stated would be made.

We had a thorough discussion, and I think it was one of the most productive and most frank discussions that I've had with any leader.

I've had a chance to visit Argentina in the past and know the tremendous strength of your people and of your economy, the beauty of your nation, and the serious problem that presently exists in the opinion of the world about Argentina because of the repression of human rights and the terrorism that has existed there.

But we have great hopes that rapid progress might be made in alleviating this problem. And I was encouraged by what President Videla had to say.

REPORTER. Mr. President, it seems that Israel is intent on establishing yet more settlements on the West Bank. Does that make it even more difficult to find a peaceful settlement in that area?

THE PRESIDENT. Obviously, this creates additional problems. I will be meeting with Foreign Minister Dayan later on this month, and this will be one of the items on the agenda. Our country has taken a consistent stand for many years that the establishment of settlements in the occupied territories on the West Bank and otherwise by Israelis is illegal, and obviously, this creates a problem and we intend to pursue it.

Q. But despite our stand, in fact it seems to some in defiance of it, they persist in doing so.

THE PRESIDENT. You certainly analyzed it very well.

Q. Could you respond to Secretary Bergland's comments on Mr. Lance?

THE PRESIDENT. I haven't heard about it.

NOTE: The President spoke at 9:30 a.m. on the South Grounds of the White House. His concluding remarks in Spanish were not included in the transcript.

The transcript of the remarks was made available by the White House Press Office. It was not issued in the form of a White House press release.

Meeting With President Aparicio Méndez Manfredini of Uruguay

Remarks to Reporters Following the Meeting. September 9, 1977

THE PRESIDENT. President Méndez would like to make a statement to the press, and I think I'll make a brief statement and then leave him here with you for questions.

It's a grand pleasure for us to have in our country President Méndez, representing the people of Uruguay. We had a very thorough discussion about matters that are important to both our countries.

One of the major discussions was about the question of human rights, and President Méndez described to us the progress that is being made in Uruguay and invited any representative from our country, or group of representatives from our country to visit Uruguay to inspect personally the situations that do exist there.

I pointed out to him that there is a very grave concern in our Nation about allegations or charges that have been made. And it's important to Uruguay and also to us to have these questions answered.

In addition we discussed the question of the export of leather goods to our country, and we arranged for early additional negotiations to take place so that we can understand the law in Uruguay, the subsidies that exist, and so that Uruguay can understand the special American laws that restrict imports here when large subsidies are given in the exporting country.

But these negotiations and discussions will be expedited in the weeks ahead.

Again, thank you very much.

REPORTER. Mr. President, what is your feeling about the relations now between Uruguay and the United States?

THE PRESIDENT. I think I've described our position. We have very great concern about the status of human rights in Uruguay. But President Méndez has described to me the situation there, the reasons for the restraint, and his commitment to open up the country for observation by people from our country and to answer any questions. And my hope is that under his leadership the relationships can be improved very soon.

NOTE: The President spoke at 10:15 a.m. on the South Grounds of the White House. His concluding remarks in Spanish were not included in the transcript.

The transcript of the remarks was made available by the White House Press Office. It was not issued in the form of a White House press release.

Federal Grants-in-Aid

Remarks Announcing Reform of the System.
September 9, 1977

In the midst of the bilateral negotiations with leaders from the Latin American countries, we are continuing our effort to make the Federal Government more effective and more open and more efficient and to remove a burden that has existed on business and labor, agriculture, State and local governments.

As a former State and local official, I am keenly aware that the way that Federal grants are handled is increasingly irrational and inefficient and, also, insensitive to local needs.

Today, I'm proud to be able to announce a concentrated attack on redtape and confusion in the Federal grant-in-aid system. My own Presidential Assistant, Jack Watson, is making this same announcement today at the National Governors Association meeting in Detroit.

Making government work better is not the most dramatic or exciting subject, but there are a few things that we can do during this administration to assure the American people that this important subject is being resolved as successfully as possible.

In the case of Federal grants, reform will save tax dollars and will also enable the Federal, State, and local governments to give taxpayers maximum value for each dollar that is spent.

We will concentrate first on five areas where experience has shown the most serious problems exist:

First, paperwork requirements for the grants themselves. When I was Governor of Georgia, we estimated that 30 percent of the personnel hours in the State Department of Education was spent just in preparing grant requests.

Second, the Federal Government's financial management practices. This can result in enormous savings to make sure that funds that go to local and State governments and to private contractors in pursuit of work that they do are only expended when the money is actually needed. And there are tremendous savings in the tens of millions of dollars available here.

Third, Federal audit procedures. These are important, because there is a general feeling, which I share, that quite often there is waste, avoidable cost overruns, and then when later investigations are precipitated because of doubts about the efficacy of these programs, the data are not available to prove or disprove charges of mismanagement or outright fraud.

Fourth, the drafting of the regulations. This is a constant problem of mine, trying to change the sometimes confusing and unnecessary verbosity and also complexity of regulations. So, simplicity of regulations and minimizing the number of regulations is a very important issue.

The last one is the various requirements in the area of civil rights, of citizens' participation in the governmental process, the protection of environmental quality, and other associated elements of any decision involving these kinds of practices.

Most of these changes are straightforward, commonsense changes, and they are long overdue. There will be a group here after I leave to answer specific questions, but I'd like to outline them as quickly as I can.

Standard application and reporting forms will be used instead of a great variety of individual forms now in use. This has been underway for the last 3 or 4 months.

A limit on the number of copies that the Federal Government asks State and local governments to file, not more than the original and two copies. Sometimes, in the past, literally dozens of copies have been required to be submitted.

A halt to the practice of asking for duplicate information on a grant renewal which has already been supplied as part of the original application. There's just no reason, annually, to repeat large collections of data that have already been submitted to the Federal Government and which have not been changed since the original application was made and approved.

And consolidation and simplification of reports to reduce the amount of paperwork by at least 7 million hours per year, which will be implemented by the end of this month. I know from personal experience, that Federal grant regulations are often written in obscure, almost impenetrable language. Many were developed without adequate consultation with the State and local governments or with the public.

We will act to see to it that future regulations do take into account the public's interest and convenience from the beginning of the grant request procedure.

I have also directed that old regulations now on the books be reexamined, abbreviated, and canceled when their time has been served. All the executive departments and agencies will review their most unpopular regulations, those which are causing the greatest public outcry. We've run surveys, along with committees in the Congress, to determine which ones cause the most problems for the American people. Most of these will be either reformed or abolished altogether.

Making government work better is a long, tedious, and unglamorous process, but it must be done. It's been neglected too long, and if we do nothing, the situation, of course, will continue to become worse.

My own election, to a great degree, was an expression of the public's frustration at how government does its business and of their desire to see changes for the better. The measures that I am announcing today represent a substantial step in that direction, and there will be more steps taken as the months go by by me, by the members of the Cabinet and other agency heads, working with local and State government, in particular, and with business and labor leaders, to minimize paperwork, to make government more comprehensible, and to make sure that the expenditure of Federal moneys are made in the most advantageous way to our people.

Thank you very much.

NOTE: The President spoke at 11:45 a.m. to reporters assembled in the Briefing Room at the White House.

Federal Grants-in-Aid

Statement on Reform of the System.
September 9, 1977

The Federal grants-in-aid system has developed because of the importance, in a country as large as ours, of dealing decisively with national problems in a way that preserves and encourages innovative participation by State and local governments. In theory, the system is the basis of a balanced national partnership, an example of federalism at its best. Unfortunately, in practice, as grants have proliferated, it has grown increasingly irrational, inefficient, and insensitive to the various local needs and idiosyncracies it was originally designed to accommodate.

With Federal grants to State and local governments now amounting to $72 billion annually, the cost of administrative inefficiencies and the paperwork itself are staggering. Intelligent reform of this system will not only prevent the waste of tax dollars, it will ensure that the money which is spent produces superior results. Therefore, my administration is working to improve the management of Federal aid and improve the partnership with State and local governments, particularly in the following five areas of grant management where experience has shown the greatest problems exist:

• Application, reporting, and planning requirements
• Financial management practices
• Audit procedures
• Requirements to fulfill national goals
• Development of regulations

I. APPLICATION, REPORTING, AND PLANNING REQUIREMENTS

Many existing Federal requirements are confusing and unnecessarily difficult to comply with. They produce mounds of paper some grant applications arrive in Washington in crates rather than envelopes but the material they demand is too often duplicative, unhelpful, and sometimes even unread. To help relieve State and local government of this excessive burden, I am taking the following actions:

• *Simplification of application and reporting requirements.* By memorandum, I am today directing the heads of all executive departments and agencies to:

—ensure that no State or local official is required to provide, as part of a grant modification or renewal, information which was provided in the original application.

—use the standard application and financial reporting forms now available from the Office of Management and Budget.

—make reporting forms available no less than 2 months before aid recipients are required to use them or to

begin collecting data for inclusion in them.

—give the public an opportunity to comment on new application and reporting forms before the final version is decided upon.

—ensure that no State or local government is required to submit to the Federal Government more than one original and two copies of any grant application or reporting forms.

• *Reduction of the reporting burden on the public.* I have directed the heads of executive departments and agencies to combine reports where possible, eliminate unnecessary reports, require less frequent reporting, and share information among agencies themselves instead of asking grantees to provide such information repeatedly. By September 30, we will have reduced paperwork by at least 7 million hours a year, much of it in Federal grants. For example, the Department of Health, Education, and Welfare has revised the form which university administrators must complete to apply for student financial aid. The revision will save almost 100,000 hours of work for the school administrators. Similarly, the Department of Transportation has simplified its Federal highway program reporting system in a way which saves State employees and private contractors 67,000 hours a year.

• *Reduction in the number of plans required from State and local governments.* In a memorandum dated July 19, 1977, I directed the heads of all executive departments and agencies to perform a zero-based review of all federally imposed planning requirements with which State and local governments must comply as a condition for receiving grants. By November 30, I expect a substantial reduction in the number and duplication of plans from the 80 now required.

II. FINANCIAL MANAGEMENT PRACTICES

The Federal budget process inconveniences State and local governments because they never know from one year to the next how much money will be available to fund continuing programs. Federal payments are sometimes tardy and, when the check does arrive, it may fail to indicate which program it is for.

• *Advance appropriation.* State and local officials have pointed out that a lack of adequate advance information about Federal spending levels makes State and local planning and budgeting difficult. Since approximately 25 percent of State and local expenditures are from Federal sources, unexpected budget decisions in Washington have serious consequences around the country. As one way of dealing with this problem, the Office of Management and Budget is reviewing five major programs that the National Governors' Conference recommended be converted to an advance appropriation status, beginning in the FY 1979 budget. These programs are Basic Support for Vocational Rehabilitation, Maternal and Child Health Services, Special Programs for the Aging, Title XX Social Services, and Summer Youth Employment.

• *Letters of credit.* Delays in receipt of Federal grant payments have led many State and local officials (as well as the Federal Paperwork Commission) to recommend that letters of credit be used instead of checks. Letters of credit allow a grant recipient to draw funds from the Treasury for approved grants at the time the money is needed. At my request, the Department of the Treasury is expanding the use of letters of credit throughout the executive branch. This action will improve monitoring of Federal aid funds.

The next grant programs to be converted to letters of credit are Economic Adjustment Assistance, Rent Supplements for Lower Income Families, and Urban Mass Transit. The Federal Government is now saving about $180 million annually in interest which would be lost if cash advances were made to grant recipients before the money was actually needed. By introducing new payment techniques and increasing the use of letters of credit, Federal savings can double.

• *Electronic fund transfers.* Another method for speeding the payment of Federal grants is through the use of electronic fund transfers. Several experimental programs are now underway in, for example, the Department of Agriculture and the Department of Transportation. By memorandum today, I am directing the heads of executive departments and agencies to work with the Secretary of the Treasury to identify additional programs which can benefit from the use of electronic fund transfers. This is one way to reduce the occasions when grantees must spend their own money and wait for Federal reimbursement. State and local governments should not be put in the position of having to lend the Federal Government money, which is, in effect, what happens when they must borrow money to pay bills while awaiting Federal funds.

• *Labeling of checks.* When grantees receive checks from the Federal Government, the checks should indicate clearly what they are for. At present, they often do not. Consequently, State and local officials must spend time determining the correct account before they can deposit the check. As President, I encounter a great many problems that are complex and difficult, so it is refreshing occasionally to find one that is neither. By memorandum today, I am directing the heads of all executive departments and agencies to designate, on the face of all checks they send to grant-in-aid recipients, the specific program they are for.

III. AUDIT PROCEDURES

There is a substantial need for improved cooperation on audits. Since many grant recipients receive Federal funds from more than one program, many State and local governments often must submit to repeated audits of the same set of accounting books by several Federal auditors—each of whom represents a different funding source. Many grant recipients are audited by State and local auditors as well.

To make the audit process more orderly and predictable—and to help increase coordination among Federal, State, and local auditors—I am today ordering Federal executive departments and agencies to make their audit schedules systematically available to grant recipients and to State, local, and private auditors; to conduct single Federal audits wherever possible; and to increase their reliance on State and local audits.

IV. REQUIREMENTS TO FULFILL NATIONAL GOALS

In an effort to achieve certain worthy national goals, Federal agencies have sometimes required grant recipients to satisfy burdensome and overlapping requirements. There is room to simplify these requirements considerably without impeding progress toward the goals themselves.

The most chronic problems exist in three areas: environmental protection, citizen participation, and civil rights. Nearly every Federal department has produced its own Federal aid regulations, guidelines, and forms to assure that those who receive Federal money satisfy these national goals. The problem is that neither the departments, the Congress, the public, nor State and local governments know all the requirements governing the hundreds of Federal aid programs.

We need to determine whether the regulations are achieving their purpose, whether good-faith compliance with them involves unnecessary duplication of effort, and how the public can best use them to monitor the Government's performance.

In pursuit of those objectives, certain agencies are now gathering together for the first time the most important environmental, civil rights, and citizen participation requirements. During the next several months, they will be publishing (in plain English) explanations of:

- *Citizen participation grant requirements*—prepared by the Community Services Administration;
- *Federal legal requirements prohibiting discrimination in employment by State and local governments*—prepared by the Equal Employment Opportunity Commission;
- *The National Environmental Policy Act (NEPA) requirements and other environmental review statutes*—prepared by the Council on Environmental Quality.

The next step will be to identify redundancy and gaps in coverage so that we can develop simpler, uniform requirements.

Pursuant to my environmental message of May 23, 1977, CEQ is preparing a single set of binding regulations which will ensure a uniform approach for preparing all environmental impact statements.

V. DEVELOPMENT OF REGULATIONS

Whether they determine application or reporting procedures, set standards for the fulfillment of national goals, or establish financial management practices, Federal regulations are all too often written in obscure and confusing language. They can be, and frequently are, unnecessarily burdensome. Some of them have been changed so often that recipients find

1561

themselves engaged in a never-ending, losing battle merely to comprehend them, much less comply with them. Not surprisingly, many of these regulations have been developed without adequate consultation with State and local governments.

I have therefore taken the following actions:

• *Consultation with State and local officials.* Early in my administration, I directed the heads of all executive departments and agencies to consult with State and local officials when Federal regulations, budgets, and policy and reorganization proposals were first being formulated. This procedure, a sensible and long-overdue reform, is now becoming routine. I further directed each agency head to make a specific senior official responsible, fulltime, for consulting with State and local leaders and for insuring that their views are reflected in the development of departmental policy. These senior officials are now on the job.

In mid-October, I plan to issue an Executive order which will require agencies to take positive steps to improve the process by which regulations are developed and issued. This will include soliciting public advice, including that of affected State and local governments, early in the process of developing regulations. It will also call for the publication of a semi-annual schedule of significant regulations on which they plan to begin work.

• *Limitations on regulation changes during the program year.* From time to time, there is a legitimate need to change Federal regulations in the midst of a continuing program, but there is rarely any good reason to insist that grantees immediately follow the new rule instead of the old one. By memorandum to the heads of all executive departments and agencies, I am today directing that all new regulations be written to let grantees (at their own option) complete their program year by abiding by the regulations which existed at the beginning, except under extraordinary circumstances.

• *Simplification of existing regulations.* It is not enough to improve the process for drafting new regulations if existing ones remain complex and contradictory. There are several ways to improve existing regulations and thereby simplify Federal aid procedures. Among them are these:

—*Achieve uniformity of administrative requirements for all the grant programs administered by a single department.* For example, the Department of Health, Education, and Welfare is developing a single set of application, reporting, auditing, and payment procedures to replace the 300 separate regulations which now apply to grants administered there.

—*Make the concept of an integrated grant-in-aid work.* The Office of Management and Budget is now reviewing the Joint Funding Simplification Act, which act provides a way for grant recipients to combine several Federal grant programs in order to achieve a single objective. While jointly-funded projects ordinarily involve more than one Federal agency, the Department of Transportation is considering its own experiment in consolidated planning grants for State and regional organizations. The program will allow grantees to receive highway, mass transit, rail, and airport planning funds under one grant after meeting statutory requirements.

—*Consolidate grant programs.* In connection with both the government reorganization project and the budget, we are considering possible major grant consolidations.

—*Conduct sunset reviews.* Often regulations on the books become ineffective or outdated because they do not receive regular periodic review. For that reason, I will be instructing all departments and agencies to conduct sunset reviews of their regulations, beginning with one or more regulations or sets of regulations which have a significant impact on the public. Regulations which have been the target of public criticism or which conflict or overlap with the regulations of other agencies will be among initial targets.

PARTNERSHIPS FOR FUTURE ACTION

The actions I have outlined here represent my commitment to pursue and resolve the chronic management problems associated with Federal grants-in-aid. To ensure that we do not lose ground inadvertently, I have asked the Director of the Office of Management and Budget to develop a legislative checklist to alert Federal agencies and OMB analysts to provisions in pending legislation which might perpetuate or aggravate such problems in the future. I fully realize that executive actions alone are not enough. I am seeking to foster partnerships with:

- *State and local governments*—by establishing expeditious ways for State and local officials to help the Federal Government resolve major administrative problems;
- *the Congress*—by working with both Houses to make Federal aid programs and procedures more manageable;
- *the Advisory Commission on Intergovernmental Relations*—which I have asked to suggest, after one year, appropriate ways to further streamline Federal and administrative practices.

We shall continue to work together toward our mutual goal of improving the efficiency and effectiveness of government in the United States.

Federal Audit Plans

Memorandum for the Heads of Executive Departments and Agencies.   September 9, 1977

Memorandum for the Heads of Executive Departments and Agencies

Subject: Sharing Federal Audit Plans

The Administration is committed to forging new ties of cooperation among all levels of government. We want to eliminate the duplication and wasteful effort that too often has accompanied the management of Federal grants to State and local governments.

One area where improvements can be made is in coordinating the audit of these grants. All three levels of government have audit responsibilities, but it does not make sense for them all to audit the same transactions. Therefore, in order to improve coordination, I am ordering all Federal executive agencies to make public the State and local portion of the annual audit plans required by Federal Management Circular 73–2. The plans will be available to State and local governments, to the National and Regional Intergovernmental Audit Forums, and to other interested parties. The plans would also be available to the general public, and would be submitted to OMB prior to the beginning of the fiscal year in which they are to be implemented. They should be updated periodically throughout the year as significant changes are made.

I expect Federal agencies to use their audit plans as a basis for making greater efforts to improve interagency cooperation on audits, to increase Federal coordination with State and local auditors, and to increase reliance on audits made by others.

JIMMY CARTER

NOTE: The text of the memorandum was made available by the White House Press Office. It was not issued in the form of a White House press release.

Administration of Federal Aid System

Memorandum for the Heads of Executive Departments and Agencies.   September 9, 1977

Memorandum for the Heads of Executive Departments and Agencies

Subject: Cutting Federal Redtape for State and Local Grant Recipients

Both my own experience in State and local government and the advice and comments I have received from State and local officials over the past seven months have convinced me of the need to simplify and streamline the administration of the Federal aid system. Many departments have taken significant steps to reform their procedures. More should be done, however, to improve administrative practices, simplify application and reporting requirements, make consultation meaningful and timely, identify and eliminate inconsistent policies and programs, and modernize the way grant payments are made.

Accordingly, I am directing that all Federal agencies take steps to simplify and streamline their administrative procedures consistent with OMB directives. Particular attention should be given to the following areas:

* Application and Reporting Requirements
* Revision of Regulations

* Grant Payments

The specific steps which I am asking agencies to take with regard to grants made to State and local governments are outlined below:

I. *Application and Reporting Requirements*

* *Timely Distribution of Reporting Forms.* Reporting forms and requirements developed by program agencies for the use of State and local participants in Federal grant programs should be distributed as part of the application process or should be released no less than two months before aid recipients are required to begin collecting data. No agency may request information on grant activities from recipients for periods during which the reporting format was unavailable except when the Secretary personally determines otherwise within guidelines issued by the Director of the Office of Management and Budget (OMB).

* *Review and Comment.* Agencies should provide an opportunity for users and interested members of the public to comment on all proposed new application and reporting forms to be filled out by State and local grant recipients.

* *Duplicative Requests for Information.* In supporting grant modifications or renewals, State and local governments shall be required to submit only new and updating material, thereby eliminating the need to submit information provided with the original application.

* *Standard Forms.* All Federal agencies shall use the standard application and financial reporting forms developed by OMB pursuant to OMB Circular A–102. The standard forms shall be used to fulfill all agency financial reporting requirements except that additional data specifically required by statute or the Congress and not covered by the standard forms may also be requested. Agencies shall work

with OMB from time to time to revise the existing standard forms where experience indicates that a change is necessary.

• *Federal-State-Local Cooperation in Data Collection.* Agencies should establish cooperative data collection programs with State and local governments wherever practical to eliminate duplicative reporting of similar data by more than one level of government, so long as no legal prohibition against this exists.

• *Signatures.* Federal agencies should ensure that no State or local chief executive officer or other certifying official is required to sign a single reporting or application submission to Federal agencies more than one time, except as specifically required by law.

• *Copies.* Applicants and grantees shall be required to submit to Federal agencies no more than one original and two copies of any application, financial or performance report.

II. *Revision of Regulations*

• *Phase-In of Changed Regulations.* Whenever an agency revises a grant-in-aid regulation, grantees then participating in the program will normally not be required to comply with the revised regulation until the beginning of the first grant program year after the effective date of the new regulation. Exceptions would be when (1) immediate compliance is specifically required by law, or (2) the head of the promulgating agency demonstrates that deferral of the regulations would be detrimental to the public health or safety, or the rights of individuals. Grantees may choose to comply with the revised regulations immediately upon promulgation.

III. *Grant Payments*

• *Full Usage of Letters of Credit.* Agencies should work with the Department of the Treasury to convert all eligible grants to letters of credits. Grant payments should be made by letter of credit

if they are advanced for costs incurred and if they are made over a period of at least a year.

• *Timely Reimbursements.* Agencies should work with OMB and the Department of the Treasury to reduce to a minimum the time it takes to pay grantees under reimbursable programs.

• *Electronic Funds Transfer.* Agencies should work with the Department of the Treasury to identify grant programs for inclusion in an electronic fund transfer system as Treasury develops its EFTS capability for making payments to State and local governments.

• *Identification of Grant Payments.* Agencies should label all checks sent to grant-in-aid recipients, indicating the program to which each grant payment shall be credited. The Department of the Treasury will provide guidance on procedures.

I have asked that the Director of OMB take overall responsibility for implementing these directives except that those matters relating to grant payments shall be the responsibility of the Secretary of the Treasury.

JIMMY CARTER

NOTE: The text of the memorandum was made available by the White House Press Office. It was not issued in the form of a White House press release.

International Atomic Energy Agency

Nomination of Robert S. Rochlin To Be an Alternate Representative to the 21st Session of the General Conference. September 9, 1977

The President today announced that he will nominate Robert S. Rochlin, of Chevy Chase, Md., to be an Alternate Representative of the United States to the

21st session of the General Conference of the International Atomic Energy Agency (IAEA), which is scheduled to be held in Vienna, Austria, from September 26 to October 3.

Rochlin was born June 25, 1922, in New York. He received a B.E.E. in 1944 and a Ph. D. in 1952 from Cornell University. He served in the U.S. Navy from 1944 to 1949.

From 1951 to 1963, Rochlin was a physicist with General Electric Co. in Schenectady, N.Y. He has been with the U.S. Arms Control and Disarmament Agency since 1963, serving as a physical science officer (1963–66), Chief of the Office of Policy-Measures and Research (1966–68), Chief of Policy-Measures Division, Bureau of Science and Technology (1968–74), Chief of the Strategic Arms Division (1974–76), Chief of the Weapons Technology Division (1976–77), and since 1977 has been Deputy Assistant Director of the Bureau of Non-Proliferation.

Rochlin is coauthor of "Radioisotopes for Industry," "National Bureau of Standards Handbook 66," "The Technical Problems of Arms Control," and the author of numerous articles.

Meeting With Prime Minister Eric M. Gairy of Grenada

Exchange of Remarks With Reporter Following the Meeting. September 9, 1977

REPORTER. Mr. President——

THE PRESIDENT. Yes, Sam [Sam Donaldson, ABC News]. Do you have a question about Grenada?

Q. The former U.S. attorney in Atlanta, a man named Stokes, says that people in your administration withheld FBI reports from the committee on Bert Lance. Is that true?

THE PRESIDENT. Not as far as I know.

NOTE: The exchange of remarks began at 2:45 p.m. on the South Grounds of the White House.

The transcript of the remarks was made available by the White House Press Office. It was not issued in the form of a White House press release.

Meeting With President Daniel Oduber Quirós of Costa Rica

Remarks to Reporters Following the Meeting. September 9, 1977

REPORTER. Would you be so kind as to inform us about your discussions?

THE PRESIDENT. Well, it's very difficult to find any differences that exist between Costa Rica and the United States. If there is a pure democracy in the world which has been an example for all nations in preserving human freedoms, it would be Costa Rica.

This is a nation which has protected itself, not through military might, since you don't even have an army, but which has preserved its own freedom by making those freedoms so attractive.

We have followed in the footsteps of President Oduber and his predecessors in our own insistence on publicizing the deprivation of human rights in this hemisphere.

Our trade arrangements with Costa Rica are mutually advantageous. The friendship that has long existed between our countries is a very precious possession for us. I've been to Costa Rica to visit. My wife has been there twice; Ambassador Young has been there recently; Mr. Todman has been there recently. And we are very proud that President Oduber could come here for this meeting.

Another subject that's of great importance to all our people is the quality of the environment, and the first time I became acquainted with President Oduber was when he received an award as the outstanding environmentalist among all leaders in the world. He was here in Washington, and I called to congratulate him on that occasion.

The other thing I'd like to say—and then perhaps he would like to make a comment—is that 25 nations have come here to be represented and to sign the Declaration of Washington, which is a remarkable demonstration of mutuality of purpose and friendship that is perhaps unprecedented. And we have used the signing of the Panama treaty as an opportunity to bring these nations together. But I think in Central America, we have a much greater chance now to see the long-standing disputes—for instance, that have existed between El Salvador and Honduras—be resolved.

And there's been a major commitment to me and mutually among the leaders for the enhancement of basic human rights, which have long been a source of deprivation in some of the countries of our hemisphere.

So, Costa Rica represents the kind of nation that's worthy of admiration and emulation. And I'm very grateful that President Oduber has been here to represent these great people.

NOTE: The President spoke at 4:15 p.m. on the South Grounds of the White House.

The transcript of the remarks was made available by the White House Press Office. It was not issued in the form of a White House press release.

Digest of Other White House Announcements

The following listing includes the President's daily schedule and other items of general interest as announced by the White House Press Office during the period covered by this issue. Events and announcements printed elsewhere in the issue are not included.

September 5

The President returned to the White House after a weekend visit to Camp David, Md.

The President met at the White House with:

—Bert Lance, Director of the Office of Management and Budget, and Mrs. Lance;

—Senators Charles H. Percy of Illinois and Abraham A. Ribicoff of Connecticut, who briefed the President on the plans of the Senate Committee on Government Operations to open hearings on the financial situation of Bert Lance.

September 6

The President met at the White House with:

—Zbigniew Brzezinski, Assistant to the President for National Security Affairs;

—the National Security Council;

—Brig. Gen. Omar Torrijos Herrera, Chief of the Government of Panama;

—Vice President Walter F. Mondale;

—Gen. Francisco Morales Bermudez Cerruti, President of Peru;

—General of the Army Alfredo Stroessner, President of Paraguay;

—Adalberto Pereira dos Santos, Vice President of Brazil;

—Alfonso Lopez Michelsen, President of Colombia;

—Maj. Gen. Augusto Pinochet Ugarte, President of Chile.

The President declared an emergency for the State of Vermont because of the impact of a drought.

September 7

The President met at the White House with:

—Dr. Brzezinski;

—the Congressional Black Caucus;

—Senators John C. Stennis of Mississippi, Sam Nunn of Georgia, Henry M. Jackson of Washington, and Robert B. Morgan of North Carolina;

—Mrs. Carter, for lunch;

—Gen. Kjell Eugenio Laugerud Garcia, President of Guatemala;

—Carlos Andrés Pérez, President of Venezuela;

—former President Gerald R. Ford.

The President attended a briefing on the Panama Canal treaties, given for a group of about 70 institutional leaders and distinguished Americans in the State Dining Room.

The White House announced that the administration is resubmitting to Congress its proposed sale of seven AWACS (Airborne Warning and Control System) aircraft to Iran.

September 8

The President met at the White House with:

—Dr. Brzezinski;

—the leadership of the House of Representatives;

—Pierre Elliott Trudeau, Prime Minister of Canada;

—Vice Adm. Alfredo Poveda Burbano, President of the Supreme Council of Government of Ecuador;

—Gen. Hugo Banzer Suarez, President of Bolivia;

—Dr. Joaquín Balaguer, President of the Dominican Republic;

—Gen. Carlos Humberto Romero, President of El Salvador;

—Brig. Gen. Juan Alberto Melgar Castro, Chief of State of Honduras.

September 9

The President met at the White House with:

—Dr. Brzezinski;

—Lt. Gen. Jorge Rafael Videla, President of Argentina;

—Dr. Aparicio Méndez Manfredini, President of Uruguay;

—Vice President Mondale, Adm. Stansfield Turner, Director of Central Intelligence, and Dr. Brzezinski;

—Sir Eric M. Gairy, Prime Minister of Grenada;

—Lynden O. Pindling, Prime Minister of the Bahamas;

—Daniel Oduber Quirós, President of Costa Rica.

NOMINATIONS SUBMITTED TO THE SENATE

The following list does not include promotions of members of the Uniformed Services, nominations to the Service Academies, or nominations of Foreign Service officers.

Submitted September 7, 1977

FRANK J. DEVINE, of the District of Columbia, a Foreign Service officer of Class one, to be Ambassador Extraordinary and Plenipotentiary of the United States of America to El Salvador.

Submitted September 8, 1977

ARTHUR J. GOLDBERG, of the District of Columbia, to be Ambassador at Large and United States Representative to the Conference on Security and Cooperation in Europe (CSCE) and Chairman of the United States Delegation to the CSCE.

ESTEBAN EDWARD TORRES, of Virginia, for the rank of Ambassador during the tenure of his assignment as the United States Permanent Representative to the United Nations Educational, Scientific and Cultural Organization at Paris, France.

CAROLYN R. PAYTON, of the District of Columbia, to be an Associate Director of the ACTION Agency, vice John Dellenback, resigned.

NOMINATIONS—Continued
Submitted September 8—Continued

BERTRAM R. COTTINE, of the District of Columbia, to be a member of the Occupational Safety and Health Review Commission for a term expiring April 27, 1983, vice Robert D. Moran, term expired.

BRIG. GEN. WILLIAM EDGAR READ, 240–28–5658, United States Army, to be a member of the Mississippi River Commission, under the provisions of Section 2 of an Act of Congress, approved 28 June 1879 (21 Stat. 37) (33 U.S.C. 642).

Withdrawn September 8, 1977

PETER E. CORNING, of New York, to be United States Attorney for the Northern District of New York for the term of 4 years, vice James M. Sullivan, Jr., resigned, which was sent to the Senate on June 29, 1977.

Submitted September 9, 1977

RONALD L. RENCHER, of Utah, to be United States Attorney for the District of Utah for the term of 4 years, vice Ramon M. Child.

EDWARD L. SHAHEEN, of Louisiana, to be United States Attorney for the Western District of Louisiana for the term of 4 years, vice Donald E. Walter, resigned.

M. KARL SHURTLIFF, of Idaho, to be United States Attorney for the District of Idaho for the term of 4 years, vice Sidney E. Smith, resigned.

RALPH C. BISHOP, of Alabama, to be United States Marshal for the Northern District of Alabama for the term of 4 years, vice Johnny M. Towns.

WILLIAM L. BROWN, of Wisconsin, to be United States Marshal for the Eastern District of Wisconsin for the term of 4 years, vice Raymond J. Howard.

REX O. PRESLEY, of Oklahoma, to be United States Marshal for the Eastern District of Oklahoma for the term of 4 years, vice Laurence C. Beard.

ANTON T. SKORO, of Idaho, to be United States Marshal for the District of Idaho for the term of 4 years, vice Rex Walters, resigned.

ROY A. SMITH, of Ohio, to be United States Marshal for the Southern District of Ohio for the term of 4 years, vice Elmer J. Reis, resigned.

COL. DONALD MICHAEL O'SHEI, Corps of Engineers, to be a member of the California Debris Commission, under the provisions of Section 1 of the Act of Congress approved 1 March 1893 (27 Stat. 507) (33

NOMINATIONS—Continued

U.S.C. 661), vice Col. Frederick G. Rockwell, Jr., retired.

ROBERT S. ROCHLIN, of Maryland, to be an Alternate Representative of the United States of America to the Twenty-first Session of the General Conference of the International Atomic Energy Agency.

CHECKLIST OF WHITE HOUSE PRESS RELEASES

The following releases of the Office of the White House Press Secretary, distributed during the period covered by this issue, are not included in the issue.

Released September 7, 1977

Advance text: remarks at the signing ceremony for the Panama Canal treaties

Released September 8, 1977

Announcement: nomination of Ronald L. Rencher to be United States Attorney for the District of Utah; Edward L. Shaheen to be United States Attorney for the Western District of Louisiana; M. Karl Shurtliff to be United States Attorney for the District of Idaho; Ralph C. Bishop to be United States Marshal for the Northern District of Alabama; William L. Brown to be United States Marshal for the Eastern District of Wisconsin; Rex O. Presley to be United States Marshal for the Eastern District of Oklahoma; Anton T. Skoro to be United States Marshal for the District of Idaho; and Roy A. Smith to be United States Marshal for the Southern District of Ohio

Released September 9, 1977

New conference: on the United States–Canada agreement on a natural gas pipeline—by Secretary of Energy James R. Schlesinger

Announcement: reform of the Federal grants-in-aid system

List: actions taken by Federal departments and agencies in reforming the Federal grants-in-aid system

---

ACTS APPROVED BY THE PRESIDENT

NOTE: No acts approved by the President were received by the Office of the Federal Register during the period covered by this issue.

Newark, New Jersey

Remarks at a Fundraising Breakfast for
Governor Brendan Byrne.
September 10, 1977

Senator Pete Williams, and my good
friend, Brendan Byrne, Congressman Ro-
dino and Congressman Thompson, Con-
gressman Joe Minish, and to Mayor Gib-
son and to other friends who have formed
a relationship with me during the last 4
years which is very valuable to me:

I'm always interested in coming to New
Jersey to try to comprehend New Jersey
politics. [*Laughter*] In completely arriving
at a comprehension, I would guess that I
will be back in New Jersey again, even
after this meeting.

I tried to prepare myself this week with
a crash course on politics. I invited the
leaders of 27 Latin American nations to
come to Washington. [*Laughter*] I spent
about an hour with each one of them, and
I learned a great deal. But the thing that
I have learned most of all in New Jersey is
the value of leadership.

One of the news people yesterday said,
"You are probably going to New Jersey
because you're a Democratic President,
you're the titular head of the party, and
you feel an obligation to go." That's not
the case at all.

When I first heard about Brendan
Byrne in 1973, I had no obligations to

New Jersey. But I had heard about a man
who couldn't be bought. I heard about a
man who had never run in an election
campaign, a man whose quiet assurance
came from principles and beliefs that do
not change. I've come to know a man
with a quiet courage who didn't use his
office just to ingratiate himself with the
electorate, looking to the next election,
but who made one of the most difficult
decisions that I guess a Governor ever
makes, and that is to raise taxes when
they are needed, but to try to do it in such
a way that in the long run the people who
are affected will appreciate his courage.

The passage of the New Jersey income
tax was unpopular. As I campaigned
here last year, I could see that at first
hand. But in the process now, with property taxes going down, rebates, about a
quarter of a billion dollars to property tax
payers, lower property taxes, over $500
million extra money going into better
education for your children, and the
soundness of New Jersey's fiscal integrity
giving you a legitimate source of pride—
his courage and his good judgment and
that of many of you has begun to pay off.

I saw a public opinion poll in preparation for my visit here. As contrasted between the no-loophole income tax and an
increase in either sales tax or property
taxes, an overwhelming portion of the

New Jersey voters now prefer the judgment that Brendan Byrne made.

I have to tell you, quite frankly, that the first time I came to New Jersey, I was impressed with kind of a sense of discouragement. There was not much progress here; there was not much excitement here. But that time has changed. There's a new sense of honesty and commitment to principles of which all of you are proud.

A sunshine law has opened up government for your scrutiny. Public financing of the Governor's election has removed the inordinate influence of those who might tend to disrupt or corrupt government. Financial disclosure laws have been passed, a superb protection law for consumers. A corruption control effort under your good attorney general has been initiated.

And this sense of honesty and also achievement in New Jersey has been matched by dramatic programs that are symbolic in nature, yes, but which revivify the very determination that can insure the future greatness of your State.

There is no more successful sports complex in the entire United States than the new one that you have. Who would ever have thought that there would be a championship soccer team around here with 76,000 people coming to see a sport where 5 years ago, 2,000 people would not have come.

And Atlantic City, which in years gone by, generations gone by, was a place of enjoyment and growth and prosperity and brightness of life and which a few years ago had lost its hope for the future, now faces a prospect of thousands of new jobs and a strong center for the world to see of enjoyment because of Brendan Byrne.

I'm concerned about corruption. When gambling or horseracing or any other opportunity exists, there's always that possibility. But if there's one man in this Nation that I know can completely prevent the corruption that is always a potential, I think all of you would agree that it's Brendan Byrne.

I'd just like to mention a couple of other things that caused me to come here this morning, and to congratulate you on your good judgment 4 years ago and your coming good judgment this year as well. We've seen in the last 4 years, because of sound management in your State government, a better partnership evolve between New Jersey and Washington. Not just since I have been in office, but even under a Republican administration, New Jersey has now begun to benefit from the sound planning and the intense commitment to receive your fair share of Federal program assistance on a partnership basis.

When Brendan Byrne came into office, New Jersey was 49th among all the States in getting Federal program aid for housing, transportation, education, law enforcement. And now that situation has dramatically changed, and New Jersey has already moved up to 34th. Well, I don't want him to go much further. [*Laughter*] But I think this shows that with him in office, working with Pete Williams and the other congressional leaders that you've chosen, New Jersey can benefit by just getting back your fair share of the Federal tax dollars which you have been paying historically and which, too often, have been going to other States for their benefit and which are now coming to your State for your benefit.

I admire his quiet determination and tenacity. He exemplifies this in the most superb way. Once Brendan Byrne sets his mind on something, he'll never back down. And I'm just glad, along with you, that the things on which he is determined are the things that benefit the people of his own State.

Economic growth is good. Under Brendan Byrne's leadership, the Economic Development Authority has resulted in 24,000 new jobs; the sports complex itself, 900 permanent new jobs, plus thousands of jobs in its construction period.

Atlantic City will realize a permanent benefit of 3,900 new jobs permanently, plus all those that go into the revitalization of that city. This in itself is good. But at the same time, he has had the good judgment to also be one of the Nation's gubernatorial leaders on the protection of the quality of your lives. This is important for you, and it's important to me as President.

He's initiated an idea—which has been accepted by the Congress—called the Byrne amendment, giving Governors an input in the decisions made by the Environmental Protection Agency on water pollution, air pollution, and the protection of your beautiful beaches. This is an innovative idea which has caught on now around the world, around our Nation. And at the same time, we are eager to see exploration for new energy sources off the Atlantic freeboard to keep New Jersey's oil refineries operating at top capacity. Brendan Byrne has also had the sensitivity not to endanger the beauty of New Jersey's recreation areas on the coast.

Well, these kinds of achievements quite often are overlooked in a State like New Jersey where there is no major television station to serve your State and where the communications coming into your State, even from the newspaper medium, is mainly derived from Philadelphia and New York. So, quite often, these achievements are not apparent to people who watch this quiet and modest man in his good work.

I noticed that during the time of the New York City crisis a year or so ago, a little more than that, when it was almost impossible for New York City to sell its bonds and when the sports complex bonds were put up for sale, there was surprise in New Jersey because of a low interest rate and the ease of sale of your bonds. But it's because of the financial community's confidence in Brendan Byrne and the New Jersey government under his leadership that saved the taxpayers of this State tremendous quantities of money and gave you an opportunity for growth and improvement.

I'm opposed to runaway spending in government. And as Brendan mentioned in his introduction to me, this has been another notable achievement. Sometimes Democrats who are concerned about people, as Brendan Byrne is, are accused of wastefulness and of unnecessary government growth. Under his Republican predecessors, the annual increase in State expenditures went up twice as fast as it has under Brendan Byrne's leadership.

Well, obviously I could go on and on describing to you my reasons for pride in this good man. But I want to close by saying this: He's a man whose achievements are notable. He's a man whose past record is one that is a legitimate source of pride. He's a man who earns a continued and complete commitment of those intimate friends who know him best. He is a man who can't be bought. But the main thing I like about Brendan Byrne as the next Governor of New Jersey is that he loves his State. He loves his people. There's no way to shake his confidence in you.

And I know that he realizes that only if you honor that confidence and give him your complete support as he struggles courageously to overcome political odds, which he has done many times in the past—I don't believe he has ever lost an election so far, and I can't say that about myself—but only if you honor his trust and not just give him your quiet or quiescent or financial support, but let your neighbors and friends and all those who can hear your voice know how much you support him and actively struggle to see the reelection of this good man, will New Jersey reach its ultimate potential.

I'm proud of Brendan Byrne. I value his friendship. I know what he means to New Jersey. I know what he will mean to your State and to our Nation in the future.

You help him, I'll do my best, and we'll all benefit from his great leadership in the future.

Thank you.

NOTE: The President spoke at 10:13 a.m. at Airport Satellite A–2, Newark International Airport.

Newark, New Jersey

Remarks at the College of Medicine and Dentistry of New Jersey.   September 10, 1977

Governor Brendan Byrne, to Senator Pete Williams, to Congressman Pete Rodino, to Mayor Ken Gibson, and to my good friends from New Jersey:

I'd like to talk to you for a few minutes this morning about some of the things that are of great importance to you. The first thing I'd like to talk to you about is the New Jersey State income tax. There are people in this State who don't appreciate the great courage and good judgment of Brendan Byrne in putting into effect, along with your legislature, a State income tax which cuts your own property taxes in New Jersey by hundreds of millions of dollars.

This tax was designed to give you more than $500 million more for better education. This tax was designed to cut prop-

erty taxes. And your own mayor told me a few minutes ago that not only have property taxes been cut 7 percent in Newark but they will be kept cut next year as well.

This also prevents an increase in sales tax. And as you well know, the income tax is designed to be paid by rich people who can afford it best, rather than the working people and the older people of this country.

As a matter of fact, in New Jersey, 84 percent of all the senior citizens in this State pay zero New Jersey income tax. So this tax has given you a fair system which benefits poor people and working families and puts, for a change, some of the tax burden on the rich people that weren't paying taxes in the future—they will pay it in the future. They haven't been paying it in the past.

Another thing I'd like to mention is this: You've now got a Governor who looks to the future with great confidence in you and in this State.

This afternoon, Mayor Ken Gibson will take 2,000 of your children to see a football game between [Florida] College A&M and Howard University. If it hadn't been for the leadership of the mayor, they wouldn't be going. If it hadn't been for the leadership of the Governor, you would not have had the sport complex for them to play in. So, this is a sign of his looking to the future for your welfare and benefit.

As I look around me, in the distance I see new housing programs. In the last 4 years, New Jersey, in the area in which we are now located, Peter Rodino's district, Ken Gibson's city, has had more new housing come here than in all previous history put together. And we are just getting started together to give you a better place to live.

I'd like to talk to you for a minute about health care. Just behind us is a center to train medical doctors, nurses, physicians' assistants. In this center right here, under the leadership of Dr. Bergen and your mayor, your Governor, and others, there are more black students studying to be medical doctors than in any other integrated medical college in the United States.

And this program has been established and is now in operation without rigid quotas but based on the merit of the students who are studying, behind me, to hold down the disease that's always been so bad, and particularly among poor people.

There has not been another place in our country, so far as I know, where there's been such a dramatic reduction in deaths among the poor families and working families of your region. In the last 10 years alone, because of this kind of leadership, infant deaths have been cut 50 percent; deaths because of cancer have been cut 50 percent; deaths because of tuberculosis have been cut 60 percent. And there's no doubt in my mind that under the leadership of Ken Gibson, of Governor Brendan Byrne, of your congressional delegation working with Governor Byrne, that with the output of this great center behind me, new doctors will have an even greater reduction in the future.

We are now concentrating, also, on preventive health care. I know that Pete Williams, Pete Rodino, your Governor, and others are going to work to help congressional legislation get passed to cut down on the cost of hospital care. We now have a bill in the Congress to do this. If it doesn't pass, we'll have a doubling in the cost of hospital care every 5 years.

So, we must work together to give you better education, fairer tax programs, a good quality place to live, good housing, better health care, prevention of disease, and an opportunity for jobs. The worst

single domestic problem that I face—and it's also faced by your Governor and your mayor and the Congress—is unemployment, and particularly in urban areas.

A year ago the unemployment rate in your State was 10.3 percent. It's already been reduced by 2 percent. And with the kind of programs that have gone into effect, we have a good chance in the future to reduce it even further.

This is a State that now gets its fair share of Federal tax moneys. You've paid them, but in the past you've not been getting them back. When Brendan Byrne came into office, New Jersey ranked 49th among all the States in the Nation in getting your share of Federal money to pay for better housing, health care, law enforcement, transportation. Now New Jersey ranks 34th. And I believe it's fair to say that because of the cooperation that does exist between Governor Byrne and your Members of Congress, even when we had a Republican administration, that New Jersey began to cooperate and get programs that benefit you.

You've got a man in the Governor's office of great courage, of sound judgment, and one that's completely honest. And as you see Atlantic City in the future be a revived city, we don't want to see hoodlums come in and take it over. And if there's one man that's strong enough and honest enough to keep out corruption, it's Governor Brendan Byrne.

Well, I think all of you know how important it is for a candidate who takes courageous stands for people who don't have much influence to do so in the face of those like some of the demonstrators in this crowd that want special privileges for the ones that haven't paid their taxes in the future.

Brendan Byrne is a man who will fight for you if you don't have a job. Brendan Byrne is a man who will fight for you if you're a working-class family. Brendan Byrne is a man who will fight for you if you want better health care, better housing, better education.

He's also a man who has fought for you to let the rich pay their fair share of taxes and to let the working people benefit from lower property taxes. And if you want your property taxes to go up in the future, if you want your sales tax to go up in the future, if you want to put a burden on the poor and working-class and retired people, vote against Brendan Byrne.

But if you want fair taxes and better services, support Brendan Byrne in the election, which is what I'm doing and what those behind me are doing.

Thank you very much. I am proud to be back in New Jersey. God bless you all.

NOTE: The President spoke at 11:05 a.m. outside the college. Prior to his remarks, the President toured the college and was briefed on the facilities by Dr. Stanley S. Bergen, president of the college.

Trenton, New Jersey

Remarks at a Rally in the Chambersburg Neighborhood. September 10, 1977

Good afternoon, everybody. I'm glad to be here. The last time I was near the "burg," I was on a train and I was hungry and I had a great horseshoe made out of bread delivered to me at the train station from the "burg," and I do appreciate the good food and the expression of friendship.

I understand this is the home of some of the greatest pizzas in the world. Or as we say in Italian, tomato pies. [*Laughter*]

And also, of course, this great city of Trenton is the home of a President who was an inspiration to me and to many others. As you know, Woodrow Wilson lived for a while and practiced law in

Georgia, and he began his own political career at a rally and an endorsement back there at the old Taylor Opera House, which I understand is now a parking lot. And I hate to say that Plains, my hometown, is becoming a parking lot as well. But I think there's a lot that ties us together. My own family came to this country, my ancestor, as an indentured servant.

I was talking to Brendan Byrne on the way here from Newark this morning, and his parents arrived about 100 years ago. One of his grandfathers worked in the Stetson Hat Company. Another one was a caretaker and a gardener who worked for the wealthy people in the Orange area. And I know many of you and your families have come here from other European countries. This is a sign of two things: One, the strength of our Nation depends upon this diversification, the fact that we are different. We are proud of the differences that exist between us, but we all fit in together to comprise Americans. And that's what makes us have the greatest nation on Earth.

I've done a lot of campaigning in the last couple of years. And as I came down the street behind me and shook hands, I noticed a special thing. Quite often everybody rushes forward and reaches out to grab my hand. But down the street behind me, I noticed that almost every parent stepped back and pushed their little child forward to reach out and shake the President's hand, and I think that's a good sign.

The first time I heard of Brendan Byrne was a little more than 4 years ago. I was Governor of Georgia in 1973, and I began to hear radio programs and see on television about a man from New Jersey that couldn't be bought. And I became interested in him. And I came up to help him raise money and to help him plan his campaign for Governor of your State.

There is a characteristic about politicians that's important, and Brendan Byrne has these characteristics. One is courage. Now, I know that one of the most unpopular things that a Governor can do is to change the tax program of a State. This change was made because of the courage of Brendan Byrne.

I think this is becoming recognized, as the months go by, as an unpopular step at the beginning, but as people get more and more acquainted with the consequences and results of the income tax, they begin to like it more and more.

Mayor Holland just told me that it had been possible for him to lower property taxes in Trenton more than 40 percent. Another thing that I've learned is that retired families have an average property tax rebate of $240 a year.

This kind of tax change is good for both the poor people, the retired people, but primarily for the working people of New Jersey. Eighty-five percent of the retired citizens of New Jersey pay zero State taxes, and at the same time, you've been able to add to better schools for your children more than $500 million. So, what turned out at first to be an unpopular and a courageous decision is now beginning to be known as the proper thing to do.

I'd like to make one other comment about that. When you come down to a choice between high property taxes on the one hand, high sales taxes on the one hand, and the richer people in the State begin to pay their share of taxes, the choice for working families is very clear. And that choice is that Brendan Byrne, with the help of many of you, did the right thing last year.

I'm also glad to see this community restore—I believe last year—your celebration of the Festival of Lights. It's important for us to preserve not only our family heritage in countries in Europe and other places but, also, the commitment that we have to our own religions.

This is a festival that started more than 150 years ago. But I want to be sure that 100 years from now we still preserve these fine attributes that remind us of our backgrounds, our present and, also, our future. It ties us together, it's an enlightening thing, and also, I have understanding, at least in the "burg" it's a very enjoyable thing, because you have a festival every night for a week.

I'd like to comment on a couple of other things quite frankly with you. The first time I came to New Jersey to campaign, I have to tell you in complete frankness, that there was not a very good, hopeful spirit about the future. We have seen in the last 4 years some very quiet but very significant changes take place in your own life.

When Brendan Byrne became Governor of New Jersey, New Jersey ranked 49th in the amount of your Federal tax money that came back to your State for better education, better housing, better transportation, better law enforcement, and other programs that help your families—49th. Even when we had a Republican administration, there was great progress made with Frank Thompson, other members of the congressional delegation working with Brendan Byrne.

And now, New Jersey ranks 34th in getting back your tax money that you paid that formerly went to other States. Well, I don't want him to go too far with this, but I wanted to point out that he's gone a long way already in making sure that you are treated fairly.

I want to make another point, too. There have been some great new changes made that pay rich dividends and are going to pay more in the future. In many parts of the country, even including my own capital city in Georgia of Atlanta, we have not been very successful in bringing in professional sports. But there's not a better sports center in the whole Nation than the New Jersey sports complex that is now operating for your enjoyment and pleasure and pride, established by Brendan Byrne.

You've already shown, again, that New Jersey can be the State of champions. I just met Jersey Joe Walcott right behind me, who's a great champion and whom I admire.

I've observed very closely in recent months the decision that has been made to revitalize Atlantic City. There was a time, when I was a young man, when Atlantic City was looked upon as one of the finest, most beautiful, most progressive, most enjoyable places in the Nation to go. But it began to go downhill. But now, I think, with the new laws that have been passed, Atlantic City can be revived.

But there's a danger there, because we don't want to see the prospective recreation facilities, including gambling, being used to support illegal activities or leading to government corruption. And if there's one person in this country that I know can stand firm against the pressures of corruption and guarantee honesty and integrity in the future operations in Atlantic City, it's Brendan Byrne. And I know you agree with me about that, too.

Another thing that concerns me very much as President is the very high unemployment rate. In the last 4 years, in New Jersey, the unemployment rate has been reduced 25 percent. We've had more housing programs come into your State than we did in the 8 years gone by. And I just came from a medical center in Newark where, because of the good preventive health care that's now coming to New Jersey, the infant mortality rate has been reduced more than 50 percent, cancer deaths have been reduced more than 50 percent, and tuberculosis deaths have

been reduced more than 60 percent, just in the last 10 years.

So, in many ways, including environmental quality, health care, law enforcement, progress for education, pride, recreation, the Brendan Byrne administration has done you a good job.

One other point I'd like to make is this: It's very difficult for a politician to come from nowhere and to win an election.

This first time I heard about Brendan Byrne, he had never run for office before. He was given very little chance to win. But as you know, 4 years ago, he was elected Governor with your help. Earlier this year, because of the unpopularity of the income tax law, particularly, Brendan Byrne was given practically no chance to win the Democratic primary. Well, he's a fighter. He's slow in bragging about himself, but he believes in you and you have never betrayed his confidence.

And something that I cannot say about myself that I can say about Brendan Byrne is that he's never lost an election yet. [*Laughter*]

The last thing I want to say is this, about this good man: He's a personal friend of mine. I know him. I've visited him in his home. His wife, Jean, and my wife, Rosalynn, are good friends.

And I believe that it's important to you as a State that does have economic problems, a State that does have a new lease on life, a State that does now have strict controls over elections, openness in dealing with your own government, a good relationship between administrators and employees in State government, one that's struggling for better transportation, housing, health care, and education, to keep a good administrator in office.

As you well know, just a few months ago when New York City across the river couldn't sell its own bonds, there was a great outpouring of surprise when the bonds for the sports complex sold so easily at such a low rate of interest. And that's because of sound fiscal management.

Compared to the Republican administrations before him, the rate of increase in government spending has been cut in half. And although New Jersey has the highest population density of any State in this Nation, you have the lowest number of State employees per capita of any State in the country.

So, I think in almost every way you're getting a good bargain out of Brendan Byrne. And I want to be sure that when the election comes in November, that he gets a good bargain from you and your help and that New Jersey benefits all around with a partnership that's paid off so far and, I believe, is going to pay off even more in the future.

Thank you very much. I'm proud to be with you, and I'm proud of you.

NOTE: The President spoke at 2:06 p.m. at the corner of Butler and Hudson Streets in the Chambersburg area of Trenton. His visit coincided with the Feast of Lights, a week-long religious festival celebrated in Trenton.

Minority Business Enterprise

Statement by the President.
September 12, 1977

During the last decade, the Federal Government has played a crucial role in stimulating the development of minority businesses in this country. Working in partnership with private enterprise, the Government has sought to promote participation in our economy by entrepreneurs from socially and economically disadvantaged segments of society. There have been some successes and some failures in these minority business development efforts, but the important benefits to

society to be gained from these efforts have never been questioned. Building strong minority business enterprises is in the national interest because they contribute to our efforts to reduce unemployment and to stimulate community development.

It is the policy of this administration to promote the development of minority business enterprise. The experiences of the past decade show that the Government cannot solve all the problems in this area, but government at all levels has an important leadership role. This administration will actively support minority business development, and we strongly encourage the private sector to increase its involvement in this area. The overwhelming majority of existing minority businesses are in the retail and service fields. While I am confident that businesses in these areas will continue to prosper, it is my hope that we can promote the participation by minorities in industries with growth potential such as energy and telecommunications, where opportunities for development are greatest.

I have discussed this matter with the members of my Cabinet and found enthusiastic support among them for the Federal Government's promotion of minority business development. Some departments already have ongoing minority business development activities, but others do not. We must improve the performance of existing activities and create programs in other departments in recognition of the fact that all departments of Government have a role to play in minority business development.

I intend to rely on the Interagency Council, chaired by Sidney Harman, the Under Secretary of Commerce, to promote, coordinate, and monitor Federal programs relating to minority business enterprise. The Council should meet regularly to make certain that the issue of minority business development receives the attention of policymakers at the highest level of the Government.

In order to provide a focus for our efforts and to set achievable goals for this administration, I have taken the following actions:

First, I fully endorse the efforts underway to revamp and improve the SBA Section 8(a) program. Vernon Weaver has established an 8(a) Review Board. I have asked him to move expeditiously and to consult with interested Members of Congress and other concerned citizens to make certain that this key program operates in the most efficient, effective, and fair manner possible. We should not permit our disappointment at the manner in which this worthwhile program has been administered in the past to diminish our desire to make it work.

Second, I have instructed all executive departments to work with the Office of Minority Business Enterprise and the Small Business Administration to devise effective minority business assistance programs.

Third, I have asked the Office of Federal Procurement Policy to review and to revise procurement regulations to assure adequate involvement of minority and small business firms by requiring that recipients of major Federal contracts show how they will involve minority and small businesses before, rather than after a contract has been awarded.

Fourth, I have requested that the Treasury Department, as an Interagency Council member, lead a task force to prepare a report on sources of capital and mechanisms for financial assistance for minority business.

Finally, I have instructed all executive departments to double their purchases of services from minority firms through direct and indirect procurement activities during the next 2 fiscal years and to report to me on their progress in meeting this goal. This increase should raise the level of Federal Government purchases from minority firms to about $1 billion. We will closely monitor the effort of each department to see that this goal is achieved.

I believe that we should improve and strengthen existing programs rather than make wholesale changes at this time. However, we will assess the operation of these programs under their new leadership, and we will not hesitate to recommend changes where they seem warranted.

These steps provide a good beginning for our efforts in this area. We will show steady and sustained progress throughout my term of office in promoting the development of minority business enterprise.

Federal Communications Commission

Nomination of Charles D. Ferris To Be a Member. September 12, 1977

The President today announced that he will nominate Charles D. Ferris, of Boston, Mass., to be a member of the Federal Communications Commission. The President indicated that if confirmed, Ferris would be designated Chairman of the Commission. He would replace Richard Wiley, term expired.

Ferris was born April 9, 1933. He received an A.B. in physics from Boston College in 1954, and a J.D. from Boston College Law School in 1961.

In 1954 and 1955, Ferris was a research physicist for Sperry Gyroscope, and from 1958 to 1960 he was an assistant professor of naval science and marine engineering at Harvard University. From 1961 to 1963, he was a trial attorney in the Civil Division of the Department of Justice.

In 1963 and 1964, Ferris served as associate general counsel of the U.S. Senate Democratic Policy Committee, and from 1964 to 1977 he was chief of staff and general counsel of that committee. Since January 1977 he has been general counsel to Speaker of the House Thomas P. O'Neill, Jr.

Panama Canal Treaty Affairs

Accordance of Personal Rank of Ambassador to David H. Popper While Serving as Deputy to Ambassador Bunker. September 12, 1977

The President today announced that David H. Popper, of New York, has been accorded the personal rank of Ambassador while serving as deputy to Ambassador at Large Ellsworth Bunker for Panama Canal Treaty Affairs.

Popper was born October 3, 1912, in New York City, and received an A.B. in 1932 and an M.A. in 1934 from Harvard University. He served in the U.S. Army from 1942 to 1945.

Popper has worked for the State Department since 1945, when he began serving as a specialist and Assistant Chief of International Organization Affairs. From 1949 to 1951, he was officer in charge for General Assembly affairs, and from 1951 to 1954 he was Deputy Director of United Nations Political and Security Affairs.

In 1954 and 1955, Popper was Director of United Nations Political and Security Affairs, and in 1955–56 he attended the National War College. From 1956 to 1959, he served as Deputy U.S. Representative to international organizations in Geneva, and from 1959 to 1961 he

was Deputy U.S. Representative to the Nuclear Test Ban Conference in Geneva.

In 1961 and 1962, Popper was senior adviser to the U.S. Mission to the United Nations, and from 1962 to 1965 he was Director of the Office of Atlantic Political and Military Affairs.

Popper served as Deputy Assistant Secretary of State for International Organization Affairs from 1965 to 1969, and from 1969 to 1973 he was Ambassador to Cyprus. In 1973 and 1974, he was Assistant Secretary of State for International Organization Affairs. From 1974 until 1977, he was Ambassador to Chile.

Popper is the author of "The Puzzle of Palestine" (1938) and a contributor to professional publications.

Department of Energy

Executive Order 12009.   September 13, 1977

PROVIDING FOR THE EFFECTUATION OF THE DEPARTMENT OF ENERGY ORGANIZATION ACT

By virtue of the authority vested in me by the Constitution and statutes of the United States of America, including the Department of Energy Organization Act (Public Law 95–91; 91 Stat. 565), and as President of the United States of America, it is hereby ordered as follows:

SECTION 1. Pursuant to Section 901 of the Department of Energy Organization Act, I hereby prescribe October 1, 1977, as the effective date of that Act.

SEC. 2. The Director of the Office of Management and Budget, in consultation with the Secretary of Energy and the Federal Energy Regulatory Commission, as appropriate, shall take all steps necessary or appropriate to ensure or effectuate the transfer of functions provided for in the Department of Energy Organization Act, to the extent required or permitted by law, including transfers of funds, personnel and positions, assets, liabilities, contracts, property, records and other items related to the transfer of functions, programs, or authorities.

SEC. 3. As required by Section 901 of the Department of Energy Organization Act, this Order shall be published in the FEDERAL REGISTER.

JIMMY CARTER

The White House,
   September 13, 1977.

[Filed with the Office of the Federal Register, 10:01 a.m., September 14, 1977]

NOTE: The Executive order was not issued in the form of a White House press release.

Department of Energy

Remarks of the President and Secretary of Energy Schlesinger on the Activation of the Department. September 13, 1977

THE PRESIDENT. *Hi, everybody.*

I've just signed an Executive order that will activate the new Department of Energy on October 1. Creation of this new Department fulfills a campaign pledge that I made more than a year ago.

The Department of Energy will be in operation less than 2 months after I signed the enabling legislation, although the law does allow up to 4 months for the Department to be formed.

This new Department is the first major result of our efforts to reorganize the Federal bureaucracy to serve the American people more efficiently. As we move into another winter season, we need to be able to deal with the possible emergency shortages in a unified way. This was certainly not the case this past winter, and the Nation suffered because of it. Activation of this Department will do this by letting us combine many different individuals and agencies into a single unit.

Today, also I submitted my own nominations for key positions in the Department of Energy to the Senate, and I will be submitting additional nominations very shortly.

The creation of a Department of Energy is an important step toward dealing with our energy problems. It will give a clearer direction and focus to your energy future by providing the framework for carrying out a comprehensive and balanced national energy plan. This will help the public and the private sectors as they work together to bring energy supply and demand back into balance, both now and in the years ahead. But simply creating a department will not solve our energy problems. We will never do that without a clear will in Government and among our people to end waste, to use energy more efficiently, and to look for practical new sources of energy.

It's crucial that all of us understand the magnitude of the problem that we face. This summer, in spite of wide, maximum publicity that I and others gave to the problem of overconsumption, gasoline consumption has risen to an all-time high. We imported more oil during the first 6 months of this year than ever before in the history of our Nation. And these problems will grow worse every day until we act to solve them.

Whether we succeed or fail will largely depend on the choices we make as individuals and on our own ability to adapt and to share for our common long-term good as a nation.

We also need new legislation which, along with the Department of Energy, will be the backbone of our comprehensive energy plan. The rapid progress to date of national energy legislation through the Congress, having already passed the

House, reflects the determination on the part of both the Congress and this administration to end the years of delay in dealing with our energy problems. I hope that the Senate will complete its action as soon as possible on the balanced package of incentives and taxes in the national energy bill.

Cooperation between the administration and the congressional leadership has been essential to the progress of the bill so far. And I look forward to continued operation on this and other vital projects.

I met with the Senate leadership this morning for breakfast—Senator Byrd, Alan Cranston, Danny Inouye—plus Senator Long, who has responsibility for the tax aspects of the energy program, and Senator Jackson, who has responsibility for the conservation use elements of the energy plan.

I don't underestimate the difficulty, politically speaking, of evolving a comprehensive program. The one that we put forward to the Congress is the one we stand behind. We've had no reason to modify our basic proposals. The House has adopted a substantial portion of the package that we put forward. I know that the difficult decisions are multitudinous that yet need to be made and that pressures from special interests will continue to be an obstacle. But I remain optimistic that a sound, workable energy policy for the United States will be a reality before this Congress goes home this year.

I wish Jim Schlesinger and all those who will be working with him the best of luck in the difficult job they face. With the help and support of the American people, we can move together into a new era of energy security.

Dr. Schlesinger and his assistants are here to brief you on the organizational structure of the new Department. This is a rate of progress that has truly made me proud. The evolution of the energy plan, the expeditious passage through the House, the progress that it's made so far this week already in the Senate, and the evolution of major legislation to establish this Department has been at a rate that's almost unprecedented.

And I believe that it's because of his leadership and the urgent need of this legislation that's made our success possible so far.

Jim, I am very grateful that you have made these accomplishments, and we stand together as partners for the future.

SECRETARY SCHLESINGER. Thank you very much, sir.

THE PRESIDENT. Good luck to you.

SECRETARY SCHLESINGER. We have here, Mr. President, the seal of the Department of Energy. We know that you have many plans for reorganization. We don't know whether this will be the only department that you create during your tenure, sir, but we trust that it will be the first. The coloring indicates that we will strike the appropriate balance between energy and environment, and we will keep the sky blue and the grass green.

THE PRESIDENT. Thank you, Jim.

NOTE: The President spoke at 2:05 p.m. in Room 450 of the Old Executive Office Building.

Department of Energy

Announcement of Activation Date and Nominations for Positions in the Department. September 13, 1977

The President today submitted nominations to the Senate for key positions in the Department of Energy (DOE) and signed the Executive order setting October 1 as opening day for the new Cabinet Department.

Creation of the Department of Energy will give a clear direction and focus to America's energy future by providing the framework for carrying out a comprehensive, balanced national energy policy.

The new Department was proposed by President Carter on March 1 to provide the framework for carrying out national energy policy. On August 4, 1977, the Department of Energy Organization Act was signed into law, and the following day James R. Schlesinger was confirmed by the Senate as the first Secretary of Energy.

Among the major programs under the new Department are: conservation, resource development and production, research and development, data information management, and regulation.

With a first-year budget of almost $10.4 billion, the new Department will inherit almost 20,000 employees under this Government reorganization.

In addition to the Secretary, the act calls for the President to nominate, for confirmation by the Senate, candidates for the following positions: Deputy Secretary, Under Secretary, General Counsel, eight Assistant Secretaries, a Director of the Office of Energy Research, Administrators of the Economic Regulatory Administration and the Energy Information Administration, and an Inspector General and Deputy Inspector General.

A Federal Energy Regulatory Commission will be created within the Department, and the President will nominate, for confirmation by the Senate, five members, one of whom the President will designate as Chairman.

Nominations submitted today are:

JOHN F. O'LEARY—Deputy Secretary of Energy, currently Administrator, Federal Energy Administration. Mr. O'Leary will assist the Secretary in representing the Department before Congress and the public and will also

decide administrative matters of Department-wide scope. He will have special responsibility for overseeing and forming policy for the Department's energy regulatory functions (except those of the Federal Energy Regulatory Commission) and the energy data gathering, analysis, and reporting functions.

DALE D. MYERS—Under Secretary of Energy, currently corporate vice president of Rockwell International and president of North American Aircraft Operations in California. Mr. Myers will oversee those departmental programs requiring major budget outlays, such as energy research, development, and application, associated environmental programs, and the defense programs. In addition, he will have primary responsibility for the Department's energy conservation programs.

DAVID J. BARDIN—Administrator, Economic Regulatory Administration, currently Deputy Administrator of the Federal Energy Administration. Mr. Bardin will regulate the pricing and allocation of crude oil and natural gas liquids and products and assure the availability of these forms of energy. He will be responsible for developing and administering standby and emergency programs and administering the coal conversion and oil import programs. Mr. Bardin will also serve as the Department's chief spokesman before the Federal Energy Regulatory Commission and other Federal and State agencies on regulatory issues.

ALVIN L. ALM—Assistant Secretary of Energy (Policy and Evaluation), currently a senior member of the Energy Policy and Planning Staff, Executive Office of the President. Mr. Alm will be the Department's principal policy planner and coordinator of analysis and evaluation. He will also be responsible for assuring that DOE policies and programs promote competition in the energy industry.

HARRY E. BERGOLD, JR.—Assistant Secretary of Energy (International Affairs), currently a senior member of the Energy Policy and Planning Staff, Executive Office of the President, handling international energy matters. Mr. Bergold will be responsible for the international component in the Department's overall energy policy and will represent the Department in intragovernmental and international discussions on energy. He will assist the Secretary in providing independent advice to the President on international energy negotiations. In addition, he will handle cooperative international energy programs and will maintain relationships with foreign governments and international energy organizations.

ROBERT D. THORNE—Assistant Secretary of Energy (Energy Technology), currently Acting Assistant Administrator for Nuclear Energy at the Energy Research and Development Administration. Mr. Thorne will focus on making new energy technologies available for commercial application as early as possible. He will be responsible for research, development, and technology demonstration in all fields of energy. He also will administer the Department's nuclear waste management program. He will serve as the primary Department source of energy technology information.

JOHN M. DEUTCH—Director of the Office of Energy Research, currently chairman of the department of chemistry at the Massachusetts Institute of Technology. Dr. Deutch will advise the Secretary on the physical and energy research and development programs of the Department, the use of multipurpose laboratories, education and training for basic and applied research activities, and financial assistance for these activities. He will manage the basic sciences program and support certain research and development projects not performed elsewhere. He will advise on budget priorities for research and development projects. He will also chair the Department's R&D Coordination Council, which will ensure that the research and development activities of all program Assistant Secretaries are coordinated.

CHARLES B. CURTIS—member, Federal Energy Regulatory Commission, for a term of 2 years. Mr. Curtis is currently Chairman of the Federal Power Commission. Upon confirmation, the President will designate him as Chairman of the Federal Energy Regulatory Commission.

GEORGIANA SHELDON—member, Federal Energy Regulatory Commission, for a term of 3 years. Miss Sheldon is currently a Commissioner of the Federal Power Commission.

GEORGE R. HALL—member, Federal Energy Regulatory Commission, for a term of 3 years. Mr. Hall is currently a senior member of the Energy Policy and Planning Staff, Executive Office of the President.

The Federal Energy Regulatory Commission will be an independent organization within the DOE. It will retain many of the functions of the Federal Power Commission, such as the setting of rates and charges for the transportation and sale of natural gas and for the transmission and sale of electricity and the licensing of hydroelectric power projects. In addition, the authority of the Interstate Commerce Commission to establish rates for transporting oil by pipeline will be transferred to the FERC. While the initial terms of the members vary from 2 to 4 years, the standard term of office for each member is 4 years.

The Secretary of Energy announced appointments of additional officers who do not require Senate confirmation. They are:

JAMES BISHOP, JR.—Deputy Assistant Secretary for Public Affairs, currently serving as a senior member of the Energy Policy and Planning Staff, Executive Office of the President, and also serving as Director of Public Affairs, Federal Energy Administration. Mr. Bishop will serve as the adviser to the Secretary on media and public information matters and will direct the public affairs programs of DOE.

ROGER D. COLLOFF—the Special Assistant, currently serving as a senior member of the Energy Policy and Planning Staff, Executive Office of the President. Mr. Colloff will assist the Secretary, Deputy Secretary, and Under Secretary in providing White House liaison and in performing special projects as assigned.

MERWYN C. GREER—Controller, currently serving as Controller of the Energy Research and Development Administration. Mr. Greer will be the Department's principal budget and finance officer and the program review coordinator.

WILLIAM S. HEFFELFINGER—Director of Administration, currently serving as Associate Administrator for Management and Administration, Federal Energy Administration. Mr. Heffelfinger will be the principal officer for personnel, equal employment opportunity, organization and management studies, real property, and administrative services.

FREDERICK P. HITZ—Deputy Assistant Secretary for Congressional Affairs, currently serving as a senior member of the Energy Policy and Planning Staff, Executive Office of the President. Mr. Hitz will serve as the adviser to the Secretary on legislative matters and direct the congressional relations program of DOE.

WILLIAM E. PEACOCK—Deputy Assistant Secretary for Intergovernmental Relations, currently serving as a senior member of the DOE Activation Task Force, Energy Policy and Planning Staff, Executive Office of the President. Mr. Peacock will serve as the adviser to the Secretary on matters related to State and local affairs, provide a focal point for contact with Governors, mayors, and other government officials, and direct the Department's intergovernmental relations programs.

MICHAEL J. TASHJIAN—Director of Procurement and Contracts Management, currently serving as Director of Procurement, Energy Research and Development Administration. Mr. Tashjian will be the principal official and business adviser on all procurement contracts and other business agreement matters. He will also provide policy guidance on personal property matters, and he will support and provide policy on all source selection procedures.

RAYMOND L. WALTERS—Director, Executive Secretariat, currently serving as Special Assistant to the Chairman, DOE Activation Task Force, Energy Policy and Planning Staff, Executive Office of the President. Mr. Walters will be responsible for assuring proper coordination and follow up in the Secretarial decision process and for providing current, accurate, and complete information for the Secretary.

Announcements of additional Presidential nominees and other appointees will be made shortly.

The Department will be located in the James V. Forrestal Building, 1000 Independence Avenue, SW., but pending preparations, temporary headquarters for key officers will be at 730 Jackson Place, NW., Washington, D.C. Most Department personnel will remain in place until the Forrestal Building becomes available.

Veterans Day, 1977

Proclamation 4519. September 13, 1977

By the President of the United States of America

A Proclamation

The blessings of liberty which our ancestors secured for us are today, as they have always been, the birthright of every American. They have remained so because in each generation there have been men and women who have been willing to suffer the hardships and sacrifices necessary to preserve our rights for future generations.

No act of citizenship is more worthy of our respect than a willingness to serve in our armed forces and to protect and defend our ideals. There are nearly thirty million of our fellow citizens among us today who have earned that respect by their loyal and honorable service.

In recognition of the contributions our veterans have made to the cause of peace and freedom, the Congress has determined (5 U.S.C. 6103(a)) that one day each year should be set aside as a national holiday in order that all Americans may be able to take part in activities designed to show our respect for their dedication to their country.

Now, THEREFORE, I, JIMMY CARTER, President of the United States of America, ask all Americans to observe Monday, October 24, 1977, as Veterans Day in a manner that will let our Nation's veterans know that their sacrifices are and always will be recognized and appreciated.

I urge the conduct of public ceremonies, the visible tribute of members of the business community, and the personal participation of all Americans of all ages in honoring our Nation's veterans.

I especially encourage remembrance to those men and women who are sick and disabled and to those who are patients in our hospitals.

I call upon Federal, State and local government officials to mark Veterans Day by displaying the flag of the United States and by supporting and encouraging public involvement in appropriate exercises and programs.

IN WITNESS WHEREOF, I have hereunto set my hand this thirteenth day of September, in the year of our Lord nineteen hundred and seventy-seven, and of the Independence of the United States of America the two hundred and second.

JIMMY CARTER

[Filed with the Office of the Federal Register, 3:36 p.m., September 13, 1977]

President's Cancer Panel

Appointment of Elizabeth Miller as a Member. September 13, 1977

The President today announced the appointment of Elizabeth Miller, of Madison, Wis., as a member of the President's Cancer Panel. She replaces R. Lee Clark, term expired.

Miller was born May 2, 1920, in Minneapolis. She received a B.S. from the University of Minnesota in 1941 and an M.S. (1943) and Ph. D. (1945) in bio-

chemistry from the University of Wisconsin.

Miller was a Finney-Howell Fellow in Cancer Research at the University of Wisconsin from 1945 to 1947, and an instructor in oncology there from 1947 to 1949. She became an assistant professor in 1949, an associate professor in 1959, and since 1969 has been a full professor. She served as acting director of the McArdle Laboratory for Cancer Research at the University of Wisconsin in 1972 and 1973, and since 1973 has been associate director.

Miller is a member of the board of directors of the American Association for Cancer Research, and president for 1976–77. She is a member of the National Cancer Institute's Cancer Center Support Grant Review Committee and its Clearinghouse on Environmental Carcinogens. She has received numerous awards for cancer research.

United Nations Economic and Social Council

Appointment of James E. Baker and Ruth S. Morgenthau to Positions on the Council. September 14, 1977

The President today announced the appointment of James E. Baker as Deputy Representative of the United States on the Economic and Social Council of the United Nations, and Ruth S. Morgenthau as Representative of the United States on the Commission for Social Development of that Council.

Baker, of Santa Rosa, Calif., replaces Robert W. Kitchen, Jr., resigned. Baker was born January 21, 1935, in Suffolk, Va. He received a B.A. from Haverford College in 1956 and an M.A. (1957) and MALD (1960) from the Fletcher School of Law and Diplomacy. He served in the U.S. Army in 1956 and 1957.

Baker joined the Foreign Service in 1960. In 1960 and 1961, he was general services officer in Bamako, and in 1961 and 1962 he was economic officer in Niamey. From 1963 to 1967, he was economic officer in Tokyo. He served as an international economist at the State Department from 1967 to 1970, and as economic-commercial officer in Tokyo in 1971 and 1972. In 1972 and 1973, he took language training at the Foreign Service Institute, and in 1973–74 he was economic-commercial officer in Pretoria. Since 1974 he has been an adviser to the Economic and Social Council of the U.S. Mission to the United Nations.

Morgenthau, of Cambridge, Mass., replaces Jean Picker, resigned. Morgenthau was born January 26, 1931, in Vienna, Austria, and became a naturalized U.S. citizen in 1946. She received a B.A. from Barnard College in 1952 and a Ph. D. from Oxford University in 1958.

From 1960 to 1963, Morgenthau was assistant professor of government at Boston University, and from 1963 to 1968 she was an associate professor of politics at Brandeis University. Since 1969 she has been Adlai Stevenson Professor of International Politics at Brandeis University.

Morgenthau has also served as a lecturer at the Institute of African Studies, University of Ghana, in 1964, and as a research fellow at the Center for International Affairs, Harvard University, in 1965–66 and 1970–71.

Morgenthau served as a member of the African Advisory Council at the State Department from 1962 to 1969, and as a member of the board of directors of the African Studies Association from 1967 to

1970. She is the author of "Political Parties in French-speaking West Africa" (1964) and of numerous articles.

United States Ambassador to Chile

Nomination of George W. Landau. September 14, 1977

The President today announced that he will nominate George W. Landau, of Sumner, Md., to be Ambassador Extraordinary and Plenipotentiary of the United States to Chile. Landau would replace David H. Popper, resigned.

Landau was born March 4, 1920, in Vienna, Austria, and became an American citizen in 1943. He received an A.A. from George Washington University in 1969. He served in the U.S. Army from 1942 to 1947.

Landau was assistant vice president of International Foreign Freight Forwarders from 1942 to 1955, and general manager of an American automobile distributor in Colombia, South America, from 1955 to 1957.

He joined the Foreign Service in 1957 and served as commercial attaché and chief of the economic section in Montevideo from 1957 to 1962. From 1962 to 1965, Landau was political officer, then Deputy Chief of Mission in Madrid.

Landau attended the Canadian Defence College in 1965–66, and from 1966 to 1972 was country director for the Iberian Peninsula in the Bureau of European Affairs at the State Department. Since 1972 he has been Ambassador to Paraguay.

Presidential Domestic Policy Review System

**Memorandum for the Heads of Executive Departments and Agencies.
September 14, 1977**

Memorandum for the Heads of Executive Departments and Agencies

Subject: Establishment of the Presidential Domestic Policy Review System

The Presidential Domestic Policy Review System is hereby established to coordinate the work of the Departments and Agencies in developing the Administration's position on selected key domestic policy issues.

Objectives

This System was recommended in the Reorganization Project's report on the Executive Office of the President as a means to ensure greater Department and Agency participation in the domestic policy decision process. The System's principal objectives are to:

—Ensure that the full resources of government are brought to bear on particular domestic issues in a timely manner;

—Provide a full range of realistic and properly staffed options on an issue;

—Encourage advance planning and priority setting to promote coordination among issues;

—Establish procedures to ensure that Departments and Agencies have the opportunity to comment on issues relevant to their expertise and policy responsibilities; and,

—Provide for systematic follow-up on Presidential decisions.

Memoranda and Procedures

The System will make use of the following memoranda and procedures:

—Issue Definition Memorandum

Issues for inclusion in the Domestic Policy Review System will be selected through an Issue Definition Memorandum submitted for Presidential approval by the Assistant to the President for Domestic Affairs and Policy (at his initiative or the request of a Department or Agency) after full consultation with the Vice President, all affected Departments, Agencies, and senior Presidential advisers. The Issue Definition Memorandum will briefly state the questions to be covered and the Agencies to be involved, and shall designate a lead Agency and the membership of a coordinating committee at the Cabinet or sub-Cabinet level—including representatives of all participating Agencies. The memorandum shall include a date for submission of a Response to the memorandum. Upon Presidential approval, the Issue Definition Memorandum will serve as a directive for analysis to begin on the questions defined.

—Response Memorandum

The lead Agency will take responsibility, in coordination with the Domestic Policy Staff and with the full assistance and cooperation of participating Agencies, for development of a Response Memorandum providing background, analysis of decision options, and Agency recommendations on questions identified in the Issue Definition Memorandum. The Response Memorandum should analyze the issues set forth in the Issue Definition Memorandum and, in doing so, reflect the views of all Agencies represented on the review committee, as well as any other Agencies affected by the Memorandum.

—Decision Memorandum

Where appropriate, a Presidential Decision Memorandum summarizing decision options will be prepared by the Domestic Policy Staff with review by affected Departments and Agencies and Senior Presidential advisers.

—Domestic Presidential Directive

Where appropriate, Presidential decisions will be set forth through a Domestic Presidential Directive.

Organization

Because of the number of Departments and Agencies involved, there will be no permanent standing committees associated with the Domestic Policy Review System. There will, however, be a coordinating committee established for each issue and the composition of that committee will be defined in the Issue Definition Memorandum.

A member of the Domestic Policy Staff will be assigned responsibility for working with the appropriate lead Agency. In addition, these committees will normally include representatives from OMB and CEA.

Alternatives to Memoranda Process

Domestic issues which otherwise would be covered by the Domestic Policy Review System may have to be handled differently because of excessive time pressures or unusual policy sensitivity. And on some domestic policy issues, extensive and formal interagency coordination will simply not be required. However, in each of these circumstances, the intent of the System is to establish early and extensive involvement between the Domestic Policy Staff and the affected agencies, whether through the Memorandum process or more informal communication.

Confidentiality

Use of this process will result in increased circulation of domestic policy documents. Circulation of draft Memo-

randa must be closely supervised by all parties to maintain confidentiality and avoid premature disclosure.

Identification of current issues

As a first step in implementing the new System, I would like each of you to submit a brief list of domestic issues (indicating priorities among them) to Stu Eizenstat, for possible inclusion in the Domestic Policy Review System. The list should be limited to those issues which have substantial impact on domestic policy and which require significant interagency involvement. The list should be submitted by September 23.

JIMMY CARTER

Visit of Prime Minister Raymond Barre of France

Remarks of the President and the Prime Minister at the Welcoming Ceremony. September 15, 1977

THE PRESIDENT. *Prime Minister Barre and Mrs. Barre, other distinguished guests who have come here from France:*

On behalf of the more than 200 million people of our country, I would like to extend to you a hearty welcome to our country. This is the first time we've been honored by a visit of the French Prime Minister in more than 20 years. And we hope that in the years ahead, that we might be blessed with additional visits from you in order to further strengthen the understanding and mutual purpose and friendship that has always existed between our two great countries.

I think it's accurate to say that of all the nations in the world, our own country owes its greatest debt to France, because 200 years ago when we were struggling for our own independence, for the freedom of our people, for the formation of our country itself, our closest ally and friend and staunch partner in this difficult struggle were the people of France. Your military leaders supported and fought with George Washington and his troops, both on land and at sea. And we shared then an experience that became exemplified in the French Revolution, when the concepts of liberty, equality, fraternity became a worldwide slogan.

I think it's accurate to say, too, that in the last 65 years, we have shown more than once that when a challenge erupted against the concepts of freedom, that the French people and the people of the United States have stood shoulder-to-shoulder as brothers to meet those challenges successfully.

Yours is an ancient country, a nation of intense commitment to independence, to freedom, and to world leadership.

I have been blessed with an opportunity to meet with you previously, Prime Minister Barre, and with President Giscard. And I'm very proud of the fact that as we approach problems that are inevitably going to face us in the future that, as has been the case in the past, in the future we'll be bound with a spirit of mutual concern and mutual commitment. This is not an artificial partnership. It's one that comes because our people share common beliefs, common experiences, and a common future.

I read with great interest a recent speech made by President Giscard on the subject of human rights. I've seen with great admiration the fact that France, among all the developed nations of the world, allocates the greatest portion of your own riches to the developing nations of the world. And if there is a superb link between any of the democratic nations and the poor or struggling or new or weak countries of the world, it's France.

The advice and counsel that we receive from you and other French leaders in economic matters, as well as political and

military matters, is important to us. And there can be no greater purpose for me in pursuing the objectives of our own Government than to consult closely with and communicate constantly with and share the partnership with the people of France.

We do have problems of a mutual nature—a termination of the worldwide arms race, a prevention of the escalation of nuclear explosive capability, the problems of unemployment and inflation. And in this particular realm or subject, you bring to government leaders of the world a unique background, training, and sound judgment.

The economic efforts that have been initiated in France under your leadership are watched with great attention by us, and the success that you've already achieved so far has been one of great gratification to me personally and, I'm sure, to the people of France.

We will be meeting this morning, tonight, and tomorrow in private conversations that affect the future of our people. There is no restraint between us that would prevent mutual benefit being derived from exchanges of information, advice, and counsel in the most unrestricted and free and mutually beneficial fashion.

So, from our people, Mr. Prime Minister, we extend to you a welcome that's based on past history, on present mutual interests, and on the belief that in the future these superb achievements might even be enhanced.

Thank you for coming to visit us. It's a great honor for our country and our people.

Thank you very much.

THE PRIME MINISTER. *Mr. President, Mrs. Carter:*

I would like to thank you for the words of welcome you have just spoken for me, Mr. President, and for the warmth of your welcome.

A year and a half ago, I had the privilege to accompany President Giscard d'Estaing of the French Republic when he came to the United States to celebrate both the Bicentennial of American Independence and that of the unbroken friendship and alliance which binds our two countries.

Faced with the challenges of our time, this friendship, this alliance are necessary more than ever. My visit as your guest, Mr. President, displays the will of our two countries to seek, in concert with all the states sharing our ideals of democracy and freedom, the means to contribute to strengthening peace and prosperity throughout the world.

The conversations that you have been good enough to invite me to have with you will give me an opportunity to express, in the straightforward and candid manner that friendship requires, what is France's policy in her dignity and her continuity.

I do not doubt that profound concurrence of our basic objectives will come out of these meetings, even if, as is only natural, the different situations and the different interests are sometimes reflected in a different approach to the problems. What matters, above all, Mr. President, is the dialog in mutual good faith and friendship.

Mr. President, rest assured, you and the American people, that this is gratitude by the French Government, and I salute today the American people.

NOTE: The President spoke at 10:38 a.m. on the South Lawn of the White House. Prime Minister Barre spoke in French, and his remarks were translated by an interpreter.

Executive Office of the President

Message to the Congress Transmitting Amendments to Reorganization Plan No. 1 of of 1977. September 15, 1977

To the Congress of the United States:
I herewith transmit amendments to Reorganization Plan No. 1 of 1977, which I transmitted to you on July 15, 1977. Except as specifically amended hereby, Reorganization Plan No. 1 remains unmodified.

JIMMY CARTER

September 15, 1977.

AMENDMENTS TO REORGANIZATION PLAN No. 1 OF 1977

Prepared by the President and transmitted to the Senate and the House of Representatives in Congress assembled September 14, 1977, pursuant to the provisions of Chapter 9 of Title 5 of the United States Code.

Reorganization Plan No. 1 of 1977, which was transmitted to the Senate and the House of Representatives in Congress assembled on July 15, 1977, is hereby amended as follows:

A. Section 2. is amended to read:

"Section 2. *Establishment of an Office of Administration.*

"There is hereby established in the Executive Office of the President the Office of Administration which shall be headed by the President. There shall be a Director of the Office of Administration. The Director shall be appointed by the President and shall serve as chief administrative officer of the Office of Administration. The President is authorized to fix the compensation and duties of the Director.

"The Office of Administration shall provide components of the Executive Office of the President with such administrative services as the President shall from time to time direct."

B. Section 5. is amended to read:

"Section 5. *Transfers of functions.*

"The following functions shall be transferred:

"A. All functions vested in the Director of the Office of Science and Technology Policy and in the Office of Science and Technology Policy pursuant to sections 205(a)(2), 206 and 209 of the National Science and Technology Policy, Organization, and Priorities Act of 1976 (Public Law 94–282; 90 Stat. 459), are hereby transferred to the Director of the National Science Foundation. The Intergovernmental Science, Engineering, and Technology Advisory Panel, the President's Committee on Science and Technology, and the Federal Coordinating Council for Science, Engineering and Technology, established in accordance with the provisions of Titles II, III, IV of the National Science and Technology Policy, Organization, and Priorities Act of 1976, are hereby abolished, and their functions transferred to the President.

"B. Those functions of the Office of Telecommunications Policy and of its Director relating to:

(1) the preparation of Presidential telecommunications policy options including, but not limited to those related to the procurement and management of Federal telecommunications systems, national security, and emergency matters; and

(2) disposition of appeals from assignments of radio frequencies to stations of the United States Government; are hereby transferred to the President who may delegate such functions within the Executive Office of the President as the President may from time to time deem

desirable. All other functions of the Office of Telecommunications Policy and of its Director are hereby transferred to the Secretary of Commerce who shall provide for the performance of such functions.

"C. The functions of the Office of Drug Abuse Policy and its Director are hereby transferred to the President, who may delegate such functions within the Executive Office of the President as the President may from time to time deem desirable.

"D. The functions of the Domestic Council are hereby transferred to the President, who may delegate such functions within the Executive Office of the President as the President may from time to time deem desirable.

"E. Those functions of the Council on Environmental Quality and the Office of Environmental Quality relating to the evaluation provided for by Section 11 of the Federal Nonnuclear Energy Research and Development Act of 1974 (Public Law 93–577, 88 Stat. 1878), are hereby transferred to the Administrator of the Environmental Protection Agency.

"F. Those functions of the Office of Management and Budget and its Director relating to the Committee Management Secretariat (Public Law 92–463, 86 Stat. 770, as amended by Public Law 94–409, 90 Stat. 1247) are hereby transferred to the Administrator of General Services.

"G. The functions of the Economic Opportunity Council are hereby transferred to the President, who may delegate such functions within the Executive Office of the President as the President may from time to time deem desirable."

C. Section 7. is hereby amended to read:

"Section 7. *Effective date.*

This Reorganization Plan shall become effective at such time or times on or before April 1, 1978, as the President shall specify, but not sooner than the earliest time allowable under Section 906 of Title 5 of the United States Code."

NOTE: The White House Press Office announced the message on September 15. It was not issued in the form of a White House press release.

Radio-Television News Directors Association

Question-and-Answer Session by Telephone With Members Attending the Association's Annual Convention. September 15, 1977

MR. VRIESMAN. Good day, Mr. President. I am Wayne Vriesman, president of the Radio-Television News Directors Association and news director at WGN in Chicago.

Welcome to our RTNDA San Francisco convention. We thank you for taking time from your busy day to speak with us.

THE PRESIDENT. President Vriesman, it's a great honor for me to speak to the members of the Radio and Television News Directors Association. There have been so many developments recently that relate to the jobs of all of you that I'm very thankful for a chance to make a brief opening statement and then to answer your questions on matters that you consider to be important enough for emphasis.

ADMINISTRATION PROGRAMS

I've just finished the morning meeting with the Prime Minister of France, Mr. Barre. This is the first time a French Prime Minister has been to our country in more than 20 years. Then from now on in the coming months, I'll be meeting, be-

ginning next week, with Foreign Minister Dayan from Israel and then with all the foreign ministers of the Arabian countries around Israel, searching for a settlement in the Middle East.

I've spent last week, as you know, with the Panama Canal Treaty, which I consider to be crucial to our country's future, unimpeded use of the Panama Canal and a very important aspect in the mutual friendship and support that we can expect from Latin America.

We have constant negotiations going on with the Soviet Union on things concerning demilitarization of the Indian Ocean. The SALT negotiations are presently underway.

We have meetings with the Soviets and also with the British on the comprehensive test ban to do away with the testing of nuclear explosives.

I've met with several national leaders on reducing the opportunity for countries to go into the nuclear explosive field.

One of the recent concerns, of course, was South Africa's prospective test.

We are dealing with the United Nations and specific countries involved in trying to resolve the Namibian question down near South Africa and also the Rhodesian question.

We're working closely with the British, the French, the Germans, and the Canadians on these questions.

Of course, here in the Congress many of these matters spill over into joint decisions by me and the leaders in Congress.

In addition, the social security program is in danger of going bankrupt. We have guaranteed, of course, that this will not happen, but the Congress will have to take action on this matter this year. I've presented a comprehensive welfare reform proposal this week. We are dealing with the most important group of bills of all on energy this year, trying to come forward with a comprehensive energy package. We're proceeding now with the reorganization of the executive branch of Government, and I'll present tax reform proposals to the Congress before they go home this October.

So, I could go on and on listing important measures that come before me here in the Oval Office, where I'm sitting. But perhaps now it would be best to take your questions on these or any other items. I'll try to keep my answers brief so that we can get in as many questions as possible.

QUESTIONS

BERT LANCE

Q. Mr. President, I'm John Salisbury, news director for radio station KXL in Portland, Oregon. Last week, Senator Mark Hatfield—last weekend—defended Bert Lance as the best Director of the Office of Management and Budget in some time. And at the same time Hatfield blasted the media, particularly the Washington press, for overkill in the Lance case. Do you believe the press has been unfair and overzealous in this reporting of the Lance situation?

THE PRESIDENT. I had breakfast this morning with Senator Hatfield and a group of Republican Members of the Senate. I think, in general, the press has been fair. There have been some instances when, within the realm of my own specific knowledge, distortions have been put to the American people through the press, through the news media. Also, there have been overemphases placed on minor items.

And it's very difficult in the past to ensure that Mr. Lance has a chance to answer allegations, some of which had no foundation in fact. Today and tomorrow, as you know, Bert Lance is being given a chance to respond to the charges and allegations against him. And I think, as has been the case in the past, the press will go into as much detail as they can to give him an opportunity to present his views.

So, in general, I think the press has been fair. They've been very committed to digging up every possible fact about Bert Lance's past, also to publicize allegations. And now he's being given a chance to answer those allegations. So, I think Bert, at the end of this week, will have had a chance to pretty well balance the picture as far as his case is concerned.

WHITE HOUSE PRESS SECRETARY

Q. Mr. President, I am Curtis Beckman of WCCO-Radio in Minneapolis-St. Paul. Something very important to this crew happened in the last couple of days in the White House, and it involves Jody Powell, your Press Secretary, and his comment and tip to the Chicago Sun-Times.

The question is, were you aware of that comment before it was made? What is your response to what has happened since?

THE PRESIDENT. When Jody Powell found out about the revelation of his disclosure to the press, he came and told me it was inappropriate, inexcusable, and dumb. And I told him that I agreed with all three characterizations of his statement. He has not denied that he made that statement to the press.

I was certainly not informed about the fact that he was going to call the Sun-Times, the New York Times, or anyone else. I think it was a regrettable incident, and I believe that Jody has recognized the inadvisability of his action and has not only apologized publicly but has called Senator Percy and apologized to Senator Percy, as well.

This is one of those embarrassing things that, of course, has been difficult to explain once it was revealed. But I think that this has been an additional element or reason for caution on the part of Jody in the future. This was unfortunate. Jody has apologized, and I agree that there was grounds for his apology.

BERT LANCE

Q. Mr. President, Ernie Schultz, KTVY, Oklahoma City. Because Bert Lance was a personal friend, do you think the checks on his background before his appointment were as thorough as they should have been?

THE PRESIDENT. Yes, they were. I have not read the complete FBI file on Bert Lance. But members of my staff have reviewed it in the last few weeks, and I can state to you categorically that the assessment from 85 to 100 different people who were interviewed privately by the FBI, including three representatives from the Department of Justice and three additional people from the Comptroller's Office, all gave Bert Lance an overwhelming endorsement as the future Director of the Office of Management and Budget.

Of course, there were some elements of Bert Lance's past that we didn't have to investigate because I've known Bert for many years. He has built up a reputation in Georgia that is superb as a businessman and as a governmental leader. I worked with him intimately for 4 years when he was the Director of our Transportation Department in Georgia and knew at first-hand his competence and his general attitude toward public service.

So, I don't think that there is any indication that a more thorough scrutiny of Bert Lance's past record or his reputation among those who knew him would have changed my opinion that he was well qualified to be the OMB Director.

Q. Mr. President, Bill Wippel, news director of KIRO News Radio, Seattle. Chris Clark, at WTVF in Nashville, kind of put a question that is the same as mine.

You have set the moral standards for your administration. Even though Bert Lance may have done nothing illegal, does his ethical conduct measure up to the standards that you've set for your administration?

THE PRESIDENT. Well, of course, there's no way for me to excuse my own or anyone else's overdrafts. This is something that was obviously a mistake. I believe that rather than my trying to judge at this point the accuracy of the charges that have been made against Bert Lance, it would be better to wait for his completion of testimony under cross-examination before the Senate committee, which is being carried out right now.

If I believed all of the charges or allegations against Bert Lance that I have read or heard through the news media, I would have discharged him immediately. Some of those allegations I know to be incorrect, and the ones that prove to be correct, of course, I'll have to make a judgment on them.

But I have no reason to feel that Bert Lance is dishonest or incompetent nor that he has acted unethically. The propriety of Bert's loans, overdrafts, and so forth, obviously, will be assessed by me. And I think I can assess the entire series of charges made against Mr. Lance much more accurately and effectively at the conclusion of this week's hearings.

So, I'm keeping an open mind about the subject, eager to hear all the responses that are being made. I'm not familiar with them yet. I haven't had time nor the inclination to go into them in detail. But I'm sure that the decision that I make along with Bert Lance at the conclusion of the hearings will be satisfactory to the American people.

GEORGE WALLACE

Q. Mr. President, this is Bob Grip of WKRG–TV in Mobile, Alabama. Should

Federal Judge Frank Johnson be confirmed as the new FBI Director, would you, or have you given any consideration to nominating Governor George Wallace to that Federal judgeship?

THE PRESIDENT. No, I haven't given any consideration to who might fill that post. We are trying to select Federal judges on the basis of recommendations by merit screening committees.

My understanding is that Governor Wallace has other plans for his own future. And to repeat my answer, I have not given that appointment any consideration.

BERT LANCE

MR. VRIESMAN. Mr. President, this next question comes from Lewis Brooks of WSOC-Television in Charlotte, North Carolina. Are you satisfied with the testimony of Bert Lance thus far this morning?

THE PRESIDENT. I did not have a chance to watch Bert Lance as he testified this morning. I was in meetings throughout the morning with the Prime Minister of France. I'll have to depend upon the news media reports for my assessment. I have not even seen a copy of Bert Lance's testimony, which I do intend to read. So, I'm not prepared at this point to assess the effectiveness of his testimony.

PANAMA CANAL

MR. VRIESMAN. Mr. President, this question is from Michael Collins, WNOV in South Bend, Indiana. If the Panama Canal Treaty is not ratified in the Senate, what effect will this have on our relations with OAS countries?

THE PRESIDENT. Even before I was inaugurated, I had messages from eight different heads of state in Latin America urging me to put as our number one foreign policy matter the completion of a new Panama Canal treaty. For years, when the Organization of American States have met together, one of the prime items on the agenda has been to encourage our country and Panama to ratify a new treaty.

This past week we had a demonstration of support for the treaty terms from 27 different countries in this hemisphere. And as you probably have noticed in the news, last week we had 19 heads of state who took the time to leave their own jobs and to come to Washington to express publicly their support for the treaty terms. I met with all those heads of state and they considered this to be a crucial demonstration of our willingness to be fair.

I think there's a new sense of mutual purpose. There's also a new sense that we look upon our Latin American neighbors as equals. I think there's a new sense that there is a vista of improved friendship and common purpose between us and our Latin American friends in the years to come, not based on grants or loans or financial aid from us to them but based on the fact that this treaty corrects a longstanding defect in our relationship with countries to the south.

If the treaty should not be ratified, I think there would be very serious international consequences, not just with Panama but with all the nations in this hemisphere.

We have enjoyed the benefits of the presently existing treaty for a long time. No person from Panama ever saw that treaty before it was signed. No Panamanian, of course, was involved in the signing of that treaty.

In my opinion it's very beneficial to our Nation, to our security, and to our diplomatic relationships, to our business trade, and health to have this treaty ratified.

Every President since President Johnson has been involved in trying to get such a treaty ratified. Past Secretaries of State Kissinger, Rogers, Rusk have confirmed their support for the treaty. President Ford is strongly in favor of the treaty. And, of course, our Joint Chiefs of Staff unanimously, representing the Armed Forces, feel that this treaty is in our Nation's interests.

I think if we should fail to ratify the treaty that there would be a threat, at least, of disruption of the peaceful operation of the canal. I believe that we could defend the canal against such threatened disruptions. But it would be very difficult for us to do it.

It's not so important who actually owns the canal; Panama has always had sovereignty over the Panama Canal Zone. But what's important is whether or not the canal is open. And I believe that we can keep it open much more surely if we work in partnership with Panama rather than if we fail to ratify the canal and make an enemy, not only of Panama but betray the confidence that now exists in us by the other countries in our hemisphere.

So, you can tell from what I say that I consider it to be very important. And I'm very grateful that the American people's opinion is changing toward favoring the Panama Canal Treaty as they become familiar with the elements of it.

MR. VRIESMAN. Mr. President, what's your current assessment of the chances for the treaty in the Senate?

THE PRESIDENT. That's hard to say. As you know, a little more than a year ago, 40 Senators signed the resolution against the ratification of any treaty. Now many of those Senators have told me both privately and publicly that they favor the treaty itself. It's too early to say. Also, 6 months ago, according to some very responsible polls among the American people, only about 8 percent of our people favored the treaty. A more recent poll by Gallup, confirmed by some private polls that I have seen on a nationwide basis, show that about 40 percent now favor ratification of the treaty. There are about 45 to 50 percent still remaining who don't favor the ratification of the treaty. So, I would say that the trend is in the right direction, but we certainly don't have any assurance that we have a two-thirds majority yet.

PRESS COVERAGE OF INTERVIEW

MR. VRIESMAN. Mr. President, this next question is of special significance to us as news directors. It comes from Peter Herford of CBS News. He would like to know why, in view of your promise of an open administration, coverage of this news conference at the Washington end was limited to a single pool camera for only the first few moments of the news conference?

THE PRESIDENT. I don't have any idea. I walked into the Oval Office and found the office just about filled with electronics equipment and noticed that there was a television crew included. But the arrangements for who should come in is something that I was not involved in.

As you know, we've tried to have my administration as open as possible. I have had, and will have, two open press conferences every week (month) and frequent press exchanges in between. But I can't answer that question. I thought that we had accommodated your own association completely in this interview.

THE NATION'S ECONOMY

MR. VRIESMAN. Mr. President, the next question comes from Phil Mueller, KSL-AM, Salt Lake City. With interest rates going up and the Fed's discount rate moving up, are we on the brink of a recession?

THE PRESIDENT. No, I think not. As you know, I've met with probably 25 or 30 leaders of foreign nations. And the economic problems worldwide—France has a growth rate less than 3 percent per year, their inflation rate is about 9 or 10 percent, and their unemployment rate is, I think, the highest it has been in 25 or 30 years. They are a strong nation compared to many others in Europe.

We are not facing a recession. Our own growth rate this year has been extraordinarily high. There's no way that we can maintain the growth rate that we experienced the first 6 months. But I would say that, even in the last 6 months of this year, our growth rate would be averaging out for the entire year 5 or 6 percent, lowest in the last 6 months than in the first. This is in accordance with the projections that we made earlier. Our unemployment rate since last November, during the time I've been in office, has dropped about a full 1 percent. And, of course, the inflation rate is down as well.

We've got problems in the economy. There are some particular weak points among minority citizens and also, particularly, among young people, both white young people and otherwise. But every indication is that we'll have about the same rate of economic growth in 1978 as we will have the last half of 1977.

We anticipate that the unemployment rate will continue to decrease slowly, but steadily. And, of course, a big threat to us is to make sure that in the process we don't let inflation get out of hand. But I would say now the prospects are very good that we'll have a sustained growth in the economy that's adequate.

We've just got projections of business investment plans, and including inflation, they run about 13½ percent, which is very high. And even discounting maximum inflation rates, we think that business investments will be about 8½ percent higher than they were a year ago.

So, things look pretty good from my perspective.

ENERGY

MR. VRIESMAN. Mr. President, this will be your final question. The question, Mr. President, comes from Fred Blackman of WGHP-Television, High Point, North Carolina. Recent reports indicate there will be an oil surplus this winter, that the oil companies' estimates for consumer needs is too high. How can your administration justify calls for stringent conservation measures in the light of such reports?

THE PRESIDENT. I wouldn't vouch for the accuracy of that report. We've had in the first half of this year a rate of importing oil—it's higher than any we've ever experienced in the history of our country. We anticipate a trade imbalance, a negative trade balance this year of $25 to $30 billion primarily because of excessive oil imports.

Our consumption of gasoline this summer in automobile driving was up in a disturbing degree. We've just simply not conserved the consumption of energy in our own country. For the same standard of living, compared to countries like Sweden or Germany or Japan and so forth, we consume about twice as much energy per person as citizens in those other nations.

So, we have a very serious problem that's going to get worse in the future if we don't conserve energy. Of course, we're trying to the best of my own ability to induce the Congress to pass a comprehensive energy package which balances, on the one hand, adequate incentives for the increased production in our own country of oil and gas and coal and, on the other hand, a decrease in consumption just to eliminate waste.

We've done analyses that show if we could just eliminate the waste that can be prevented, then we can reduce our imports almost to zero. In other words, we are importing just about enough oil to meet our waste of oil.

So, it's a serious problem. It's going to get worse in the future. My guess is that we will not have as serious a natural gas shortage next winter as we had this past winter. I think those were extraordinary circumstances, particularly because of the prevailing low temperatures that lasted so long. But I think we'll go into this winter with a higher reserve supply of energy, just because we learned from sad experience last winter about the need for a kind of a buffer of supplies.

I'd like to say one other thing about this whole matter. It's difficult to convince the American people about the seriousness of the energy crisis. We've had two or three serious warning signs already, a quadrupling of the price of oil by the OPEC nations, extreme shortage of natural gas this past winter that disrupted schools and hospitals and private homes, and also rapidly escalating imports. These warning signs are not going to go away. And if we ignore them, they're going to get worse.

So, if we have made an error in the energy field, it's not because we have over-emphasized our problems. It's because we've not acted forcefully enough to prevent increasing problems in the future.

MR. VRIESMAN. Thank you, Mr. President.

THE PRESIDENT. I'd like to say in closing, Mr. President, that I've enjoyed this chance to answer your questions. The multiplicity of responsibilities that I have sometimes prevent my giving an adequate accounting to the American people.

I'm very grateful that you've given me this chance, through what I understand is a live broadcast, to cover some of the important issues. It's always a matter that I am concerned about—is how to communicate accurately with the American people. And I think even in the most controversial matters, I feel better about making the right decision to know that the subjects have been debated openly by the people of this country.

So, thank you again for letting me be with you in this means, and I hope that my answers have been adequate in the limited time available to me.

Thank you again very much.

MR. VRIESMAN. Thank you, Mr. President.

NOTE: The President spoke at 2 p.m. from the Oval Office by telephone hookup to members of the association meeting in San Francisco, Calif. The question-and-answer session was broadcast live on radio.

National Hispanic Heritage Week
Remarks at a Rose Garden Ceremony.
September 15, 1977

Last week I had a chance to practice my Spanish by meeting with 19 leaders of nations in Latin America—Central, South America, and the Caribbean. I think it's appropriate and also coincidental that this week is a week that we commemorate the Hispanic influence on American life.

There are only, I think, three other nations in the world that have more Spanish-speaking citizens than does the United States. And I think it's important that we're now beginning to recognize the tremendous contribution that was derived from Spanish-speaking people in our own country's history.

I come from a State which had its first settlements in the early 1500's by Spanish settlers. And, of course, had the history books been written in Spain instead of England, we would recognize this heritage much greater not only in Georgia and in Florida but in California and other parts of our own country.

I've tried to bring into our Government highly qualified leaders of Spanish-American communities. We haven't gone far enough, but we've made a good start at the top levels in the administrative branches of Government, to direct the Community Services Administration, the Immigration and Naturalization Service, as top officials, assistant secretaries of our major departments and above. No other President had ever appointed more than one Spanish-American citizen to that level. We've already appointed five. Also, we have superb people appointed to represent our own country at the ambassadorial level in international affairs.

So for these reasons, I'm very grateful that this week has been set aside to recognize our common heritage. I signed a proclamation on the 29th of August asking the American people to set aside this week to observe this special and important heritage.

I'd like to add just a word to this occasion, derived from my conversations last week. We had some very frank discussions, sometimes debates, with the leaders of nations which are highly democratic—Mexico, Costa Rica, Venezuela, Colombia, and others—and some leaders of nations that are not so democratic. There was a general sense that the importance of human rights was now being recognized in a more vivid way, and there was a general feeling that countries which had ignored the right of individuality and freedom and liberty were being damaged in their future trade relationships, acceptance in the world community, access in the future to atomic fuel for power production, and in other ways. And I think this is a good step in the right direction.

There was also a feeling of a new opportunity for friendship, the recognition of common purpose, cooperation, and mutual respect on an equal basis—not as a powerful nation looking down upon a weak nation; not as a father looking down on a son; not as a strong brother looking on a weak brother—but as equals, because I see very clearly we can derive as much or more benefit from good relations with our friends in Latin America even than they can derive from us.

With the signing of the Panama Canal Treaty we've demonstrated vividly that the American people can be fair, that the time for colonialism on our part is over, and that this can open up a new vista not only for better friendship with Panama but all the nations in the South and, also, that it can add to the enhancement of our trade, our international posture and reputation and, also, our Nation's security.

We are very eager to see the Panama Canal kept open for use by all countries. And to have 25 or 30 other nations now join in with us in a commitment that the canal will be kept neutral and open in perpetuity greatly strengthens our ability to guarantee its open use.

I might say that as we embark now on this new and improved relationship with Latin America, it's not on the basis of financial aid or grants or loans; it's on a nonfinancial basis of mutual benefit and equality and mutual respect.

So, for all these reasons I'm very grateful to have this chance to participate with you in the observance of this good week. I think we have 16 million Americans who speak Spanish, plus 3 Americans in the White House who are trying to learn Spanish—myself, my wife, and my daughter, Amy.

Es un gran placer para mi el estar con ustedes esta tarde. Muchas gracias a todos. [It is a great pleasure for me to be with you this afternoon. Thank you all.]

NOTE: The President spoke at 2:35 p.m. in the Rose Garden at the White House. Proclamation 4516, designating the week beginning September 11, 1977, as National Hispanic Heritage Week, is printed on page 1521 of this volume.

Meeting With Nobusuke Kishi of Japan

Remarks at a Meeting With the Former Prime Minister. September 15, 1977

Just for the benefit of the news media, this is one of the great leaders in the free world.

Prime Minister Kishi was courageous enough to support a friendship with our own country at a time when it was not popular for him to do so.

He's been instrumental in some of the finest international efforts that related to the well-being of humans throughout the world. And although he's had a lot of

years on Earth and a lot of experience, he's still young at heart.

It's a great honor for us to have him here in the United States.

NOTE: The President spoke at 3:15 p.m. in the Oval Office at the White House.

Designation of Federal Officials for Liaison With State and Local Leaders

Memorandum for the Heads of Executive Departments and Agencies. September 15, 1977

Memorandum for the Heads of Executive Departments and Agencies

Subject: Designation of Senior Intergovernmental Officials in Federal Agencies

To simplify the procedures of the Federal government and to make its programs more responsive to public needs, I have asked the head of each Federal agency having extensive contact with State and local leaders to designate a senior official for liaison with them in the development of policy. These intergovernmental officials are listed at the end of this notice.

I have also asked the agency heads to ensure that these officials respond to matters referred to them within two weeks. If a problem cannot be solved in this two week period, I have asked that the response indicate a definite plan of action and a timetable for reaching a resolution. State and local governments should, of course, direct their questions about pending applications to the appropriate grants offices and should take reasonable steps to resolve all questions at that level before enlisting the aid of the intergovernmental officials.

Where intergovernmental officials find that a problem raised by a grantee requires a decision by more than one Federal department, it is their responsibility to contact the other agencies to reach a decision. Matters that cannot be resolved at this level will be referred to Under Secretaries.

I invite comments and suggestions for improving this process; these should be sent to my Assistant for Intergovernmental Relations, Jack Watson, at the White House, Washington, D.C. 20500; telephone (202) 456–2335.

This document shall be published in the FEDERAL REGISTER.

JIMMY CARTER

NOTE: The list of intergovernmental officials is printed in the FEDERAL REGISTER of September 20.

The memorandum was not issued in the form of a White House press release.

Visit of Prime Minister Barre of France

Remarks of the President and the Prime Minister at a Working Dinner for the Prime Minister. September 15, 1977

THE PRESIDENT. Since I have been in office as President, we've had some very distinguished visitors come to our country, representing many of the great nations of the world. But as I said in my welcoming remarks this morning, to have Prime Minister Barre come here with other distinguished members of the French Government gives me an opportunity to say accurately that of all the nations in the world, our greatest debt is to France.

When we struggled 200 years ago for our independence and freedom, France was our staunch ally. We've never raised arms against France. I think during one

transient period we actually declared war, but the French ignored our little Nation. [*Laughter*] The President and the Congress eventually swallowed a couple of times and said, "France is our great friend, and we'll forget about our declaration, since they didn't even notice it in their newspapers." But with that one brief incident late in the 1700's, we've had the closest and most constant friendship with France.

We learned from them before our Nation was formed. Benjamin Franklin was our agent in Paris, representing the Colonies, and our own State of Georgia paid him an extra stipend every month—I think it was about $15 a month—to represent us and our farmers, our tobacco exporters in France. He never came to Georgia, but he always cashed the check that was sent to him—[*laughter*]—and I presume he did a good job.

When I walked in the front foyer of the Georgia's Governor's Mansion for 4 years, there was always a portrait hanging there of George Washington that was given to Count d'Estaing, who led naval forces, for helping our country in its struggle for freedom.

And, of course, we know that our Capital City itself was laid out by a Frenchman, and the first and earliest and most definitive assessment of the character of American people was written by a Frenchman. And although this was written more than 150 years ago, there's still an insight into our struggling Nation's character that's of great interest to those who are involved in politics in our country.

I reread some voluminous excerpts from de Tocqueville's analysis last year after the campaign was over, and I thought I was finally going to be here. I wanted to see what was thought about us then. I can't say that my own analysis of the American people was very much different from his.

I think it's also good to point out that Thomas Jefferson, as an Ambassador to France, absorbed the best elements of the French commitment to freedom and the worth of the individual human being, and this was part of his own contribution to our Nation's history, to our Nation's laws, to our Constitution. So, in those ancient days for us, recent days for an ancient nation like France, we derived our character from them and our freedom with their help.

And I've always felt an obligation to France, even as a schoolboy, because of this tremendous contribution in time of crisis and challenge.

As you well know, in this century we've stood side by side with France when freedom again was challenged and fought as brothers for liberty. And now I have learned more and more as a President the somewhat unique nature of France, to honor the friendship that ties them with us as an ally, which is crucial to us and to world peace and to the preservation of our democratic principles throughout the world, but also to retain a unique aloofness and independence which is, I think, admirable.

France has never been dominated by anyone else as long as they had control of their government. And they've retained even now a sense of autonomy and independence of action that can't be persuaded against their best judgment, even by the closest of allies. And that's an admirable trait in my opinion.

We have the closest relationship with France in matters that concern our own economy. We share common problems and common goals. And when we have a qualified economist who is both the Finance Minister and the Prime Minister come to our country, we were very eager to be students and to learn from him.

We've admired what they've done in the field of controlling energy consumption. I think we have a lot to learn from them, and I would like for the Prime Minister to repeat to you the comment that he made earlier to me today about our own efforts to conserve energy in this country.

When our White House was burned, Monroe—later President Monroe—was in France. And when he came back, he brought this particular gilded centerpiece, Mr. Prime Minister, from France back to our country. He delivered this here, I think, in 1818. And Rosalynn, in particular, wanted to put it on the table tonight to show that when the White House was rebuilt after being burned in 1812, that part of France's beauty was delivered here by our President.

So, those ties of history and those ties of the current day are very important to us. We seek France's advice and counsel as we deal with the problems of the world, in the Middle East, with their unique relationship with the European Community, as an adviser in Africa, as a generous nation. And we have a lot to admire there.

Of all the developed nations in the world, France devotes a larger portion of their gross national product to foreign aid than any other. And this sense of pride, independence, freedom, and also generosity is admirable, indeed.

We are honored to have the Prime Minister come here to be with us. We've not had a Prime Minister of France come here in the last 20 years. He did come here last year, but not as a Prime Minister. And we are very grateful that he would honor us in this way.

This is an opportunity for us to share our defense plans, to share military secrets with them, to nurture one another in times of trial, and to share common successes. And I believe that it's accurate to say that both nations are benefited by a relationship that is intimate, close, permanent, and valuable.

I'd like to express on behalf of the American people my thanks for these men who have come to visit us. And on behalf of our people, I'd like to offer a toast to Prime Minister Barre and to his distinguished colleagues, to the people of France, and to the spirit which has always made France such a great nation.

THE PRIME MINISTER. Mr. President, gentlemen, once again, here tonight, the United States and France are at a rendezvous of friendship, a friendship which over 200 years has never been denied.

As you have recalled yourself this morning, in warm terms which touched me deeply, our two countries have always stood side by side to fight for liberty and justice. It is true that France may sometimes appear to be a difficult ally and has sometimes appeared to be so. But how could it be otherwise when one has respect of oneself and respect of others?

France, who has existed for over 1,000 years and has withstood the vicissitudes of history, knows that strong friendship requires total vigilance. I have therefore appreciated, first of all, the frank, simple, and serious tone of the meetings that you have been kind enough to invite me to have with you. These meetings will have demonstrated to you, Mr. President, that where the great issues of the world of today are concerned, our preoccupations and our aspirations are fundamentally the same.

The United States is striving with patience, tenacity, and faith to contribute the best it has to contribute to peace and prosperity in the world. France is doing the same.

France believes, first of all, as she looks at the world as it has been shaped over the last 30 years, that a new economic order must be gradually defined, taking into account the legitimate aspirations of all nations. Whatever the framework within which this will, therefore, take place in the future, the constructive dialog between industrialized and developing nations is an obvious need. Those who would attempt to jeopardize it and who would substitute confrontation would assume a tragic responsibility in the face of history. It is also extremely important that the freedom of exchange of any and all kinds be preserved among nations.

Allow me to say to you, Mr. President, once again, that in a field which assumes particular significance in our bilateral relations, the field of aeronautical relations, we expect, confidently, the decisions of the United States Government and of United States justice. We are convinced that they could in no way contradict the traditions that your country declares itself to be so profoundly attached to.

France believes, in the second place, that in the East-West relations a policy of détente, understanding, and cooperation is necessary now more than ever. France knows from her own long experience that vigilant trust is far preferable to distrust, to a refusal to enter into a dialog, and to incomprehension. The American people, motivated by a blend of tolerance and conviction, which gives it its moral strength, and of which you, Mr. President, are the exemplification, cannot fail to be so persuaded.

France is also aware, as is the United States, of the dangers posed by nuclear proliferation. France fully assumes her responsibilities as a nuclear power. The measures France has taken in this connection attest to it. We are convinced that one can, one must, indeed, reconcile the means to stem proliferation of nuclear armaments with the indispensable development of nuclear energy production, for tomorrow all shall need that energy.

France, finally, is sensitive to the absurd, dangerous, overly wasteful, ruinous character of the unlimited accumulation of armaments. If it is justifiable and normal, so long as reason alone does not rule the world, for each country to seek to give itself the means to carry out its own defense, today we are witnessing an over-equipping in armaments, which is fraught with threats. And so the French Government shall endeavor, within the prospect of the next special session of the General Assembly of the United Nations, to bring her contribution to the common thinking in order to lead towards genuine disarmament.

Mr. President, I have dwelt upon four fundamental issues for the future of the world, but there are more immediate and more tragic threats bearing down upon peace in Africa, as in the Middle East. We have devoted a thorough exchange of views to these threats. I shall therefore simply express with fervor and anguish my wish that in these areas which could break out into flames at any moment, passions shall not rule out over reason.

We are aware of the efforts that you have undertaken to promote peace. You know that we shall not spare our own efforts.

A world at peace must not only be a world without war; it must also be a world without violence and without tyranny, where the furthering of the human being is the prime objective of society. Peace is not established only upon the silence of man.

Mr. President, may I propose a toast to yours and to Mrs. Carter's health, to the prosperity and the happiness of the American people, and the friendship between France and the United States.

NOTE: The President spoke at 8:45 p.m. in the State Dining Room at the White House. The Prime Minister spoke in French, and his remarks were translated by an interpreter.

General Pulaski's Memorial Day, 1977

Proclamation 4520. September 16, 1977

By the President of the United States of America

A Proclamation

Exactly two centuries ago, in 1777, the Polish patriot Casimir Pulaski arrived on our shores to help secure the liberty of the American colonies.

In exile from his native land, he fought courageously at Brandywine and in other battles. He formed and commanded the Pulaski Legion, the famous cavalry unit which contributed valiantly to the achievement of our independence.

In October, 1779, General Pulaski died of wounds received in the siege of Savannah. In commemoration of his heroic sacrifice on behalf of American independence, our Nation has for generations paid grateful tribute to him and to the millions of Americans of Polish descent who have played a role of enduring significance in the life of our country.

Now, THEREFORE, I, JIMMY CARTER, President of the United States of America, do hereby designate Tuesday, October 11, 1977, as General Pulaski's Memorial Day, and I direct the appropriate Government officials to display the flag of the United States on all Government buildings on that day.

I also invite the people of the United States to honor the memory of General Pulaski by holding appropriate exercises and ceremonies in suitable places throughout our land.

IN WITNESS WHEREOF, I have hereunto set my hand this sixteenth day of September, in the year of our Lord nineteen hundred seventy-seven, and of the

Independence of the United States of America the two hundred and second.

JIMMY CARTER

[Filed with the Office of the Federal Register, 2:56 p.m., September 16, 1977]

United States Arms Control and Disarmament Agency

Nomination of Ralph Earle II To Be Special Representative for Arms Control and Disarmament Negotiations. September 16, 1977

The President today announced that he will nominate Ralph Earle II, of Haverford, Pa., to be Special Representative for Arms Control and Disarmament Negotiations at the Arms Control and Disarmament Agency (ACDA). Earle is currently alternate Chairman of the U.S. Delegation to the Strategic Arms Limitation Talks.

Earle was born September 26, 1928, in Bryn Mawr, Pa. He received an A.B. from Harvard College in 1950 and an LL.B. from Harvard Law School in 1955. He served in the U.S. Army from 1950 to 1952.

Earle practiced law with the firm of Morgan, Lewis and Bockius in Philadelphia from 1956 to 1968, as an associate and then a partner. In 1968 and 1969, he served as Principal Deputy Assistant Secretary of Defense and Acting Assistant Secretary of Defense for International Security Affairs.

From 1969 to 1972, Earle was defense adviser to the U.S. Mission to NATO. In 1972 and 1973, he was a consultant for SALT in the Office of the Secretary of Defense. He was Representative of the U.S. Arms Control and Disarmament Agency to SALT from 1973 until earlier this year, when he became alternate

Chairman of the U.S. Delegation to SALT.

Visit of Prime Minister Barre of France

Remarks to Reporters Following the Prime Minister's Departure. September 16, 1977

REPORTER. Mr. President, are you planning to go to France this year?

THE PRESIDENT. I've been invited by President Giscard to come while I was in the summit meeting in Great Britain in May, and we're trying to work out a schedule where I might visit. But I can't tell yet. It will depend upon the prospects for Congress adjournment and some other uncertainties now. But I would like very much to visit France if I can.

Q. And what about the SST Concorde?

THE PRESIDENT. We'll make a decision on the Concorde, as far as our own Government can make the decision, on the 24th of this month, which is next week. And this will describe some of the noise limitations on the Concorde, the compliance with my own Government's position that the test period should be honored. And I think that we'll be making this report on time, as scheduled.

Q. Mr. President, was there electronic surveillance at the Panamanian negotiating delegation?

THE PRESIDENT. Well, I'd rather restrict my answers right now to the questions about France.

Q. Mr. President, tell us, please, about the professor, Mr. Raymond Barre; you spoke yesterday at the dinner about Mr. Barre was like a good professor.

THE PRESIDENT. Well, he is one of the more knowledgeable people in the world on international economics, and his unique position as Finance Minister and Prime Minister, with a long-standing history of experience in the European Community, makes him a very good source of information and advice for me in the field of international finance. And it's obvious that what his policies have done in his own country, France, has been very successful.

We've watched with great interest his economic policy being put into effect in the last 12 months. Obviously, we wish him good success with it. All of the countries of the world are faced with the problems of a sluggish growth, and we have a fairly rapid growth in our country compared to most others. The German and French and most European countries are not growing quite so rapidly as are we; the Japanese, a little bit more rapidly.

But Prime Minister Barre has made a study of this as his life's work and, as a student of international economics, I welcome him as one of my professors.

Q. Do you think it will be very difficult for you, the President of the United States, to go into France before the French election?

THE PRESIDENT. Well, I would not want to interfere at all in the French elections, which will be held next spring. And if I should find it possible to go to France, it would be with that complete commitment, because I think that the French people are so independent and so proud of their own right to make their own decisions that any sort of insinuation that I might interfere would be counterproductive. I have no intention of ever doing anything to try to influence the outcome of the French elections.

Q. Would it affect our relationship with France at all, however, if Commu-

nists should gain a participation in that government?

THE PRESIDENT. Well, of course, the ties between the French people and the American people are so strong historically that I doubt that anything could shake that friendship. Our own position is that we hope that democratic forces will always prevail in Europe; that we trust the Europeans to make their own decisions; and that the strength of the governments that are democratic now is the best factor in preventing the Communists from playing a more major role. So I think the French will make a good judgment.

Q. But you seem to be saying, sir, that if the Communists come to power through democratic methods, that we can have no objection.

THE PRESIDENT. Well, our preference is that the democratic parties prevail. There's no question about that. But we trust the judgment of the French people to make their choice in the election, and any interference from us, from the outside, I think, would be counterproductive.

Q. Are you aware that the CIA allegedly taped, bugged the Panama negotiators? And, if so, what do you think about it?

THE PRESIDENT. Well, as I say, I'd rather restrict my answers at this moment to the French——

Q. Did you discuss the nuclear facility that the French are planning to sell to Pakistan?

THE PRESIDENT. Yes, that was one of the items on the agenda.

Q. Did you and Mr. Barre discuss how Bert Lance was doing up on the Hill?

THE PRESIDENT. No.

REPORTER. Thank you very much.

NOTE: The President spoke at 11:30 a.m. on the South Grounds of the White House.

Visit of Prime Minister Barre of France

White House Statement Issued Following the Meetings Between the President and the Prime Minister.   September 16, 1977

French Prime Minister Raymond Barre paid an official visit to Washington September 15–16 at the invitation of President Carter. The President gave a working dinner for Prime Minister Barre on September 15 and held two meetings with the Prime Minister and his party. Their talks covered the range of political, economic, and other issues of importance to the two Governments.

These issues included the Middle East, developments in southern Africa, East-West relations, security and disarmament, nuclear nonproliferation, human rights, and economic policy. The two leaders agreed that close U.S.-French consultations are important on these and other issues.

Following discussions at the seven-nation summit in London last May in which they had taken part, the President and the Prime Minister reviewed economic conditions, both worldwide and in their own countries. Prime Minister Barre noted the significant improvement in France's foreign trade account and described the steps his government had taken to curb inflation, stimulate employment, and bring about conditions needed for sustained economic growth. President Carter reviewed the United States own economic prospects and expressed confidence that the U.S. economic recovery would continue into 1978.

President Carter emphasized the need to gain significant results in the multilateral trade negotiations in the near future. The Prime Minister stressed the impor-

tance of organized freedom of trade as a necessary condition for the orderly growth of that trade for the benefit of both developed and developing countries.

The President and the Prime Minister agreed on the importance of continued close consultation between the United States and France on international financial issues. The President said that the U.S. administration was seeking congressional authority for the United States to take part in the Supplementary Financing Facility (Witteveen facility), to assure that International Monetary Fund resources are sufficient to meet current needs for official financing.

President Carter praised France's leadership in proposing and helping to sustain the North-South dialog between industrialized and developing nations. The two leaders agreed that the Conference on International Economic Cooperation, concluded last June in Paris, had produced a number of positive benefits. They committed their two Governments to continue working for a more open and just international economic system.

The President and the Prime Minister reviewed major defense and disarmament issues. President Carter affirmed the unequivocal commitment of the United States to the defense of Western Europe. He reviewed U.S. steps, in line with the program he announced at last May's London meeting of the North Atlantic Council, to strengthen American forces committed to the defense of Europe. Prime Minister Barre described France's major program to modernize and upgrade its armed forces. The two leaders agreed that these efforts and similar efforts by other allies are essential to maintain the Alliance's security into the next decade.

President Carter and Prime Minister Barre discussed current and projected disarmament talks, including SALT and the U.N. General Assembly's Special Session on Disarmament scheduled for 1978. President Carter said he is convinced that France, as a major power, can make a positive contribution both to the maintenance of allied security and to the search for a more secure and stable international order. He was most interested in Prime Minister Barre's comment on these issues and the indications given on the views that France intends to put forward in the field of disarmament.

President Carter stated his appreciation for France's expressed willingness to participate in the International Fuel Cycle Evaluation, the opening conference of which is to occur next month, and noted that France's technological leadership in the field of nuclear energy makes its contribution particularly important. The President and the Prime Minister agreed that vigorous and imaginative measures are needed to develop nuclear energy while preventing any proliferation of nuclear weapons.

Prime Minister Barre explained the main features of the French energy conservation policy and stressed the vital importance of a rapid implementation of President Carter's energy program.

President Carter outlined U.S. policies on human rights. Prime Minister Barre emphasized that the concept of liberty and the rights of man will continue to inspire French foreign policy. The President and the Prime Minister discussed the Belgrade CSCE Review Conference. They agreed on the need for a thorough review of implementation of all aspects of the Helsinki Final Act, designed to promote further progress in each of these areas.

The President and the Prime Minister reviewed the situation in Africa. President Carter described U.S. steps to support the British effort to bring about a peaceful transition to majority rule in Rhodesia and expressed appreciation for French support. The two leaders agreed on the importance of progress toward social justice and majority rule in southern Africa. President Carter praised France's vital role in promoting economic development and political stability in Africa.

The two leaders also reviewed the situation in the Middle East and agreed on the importance of convening the Middle East Peace Conference.

Prime Minister Barre raised the subject of Concorde landing rights in the United States, emphasizing the importance of this issue to France. President Carter reiterated his support for a 16-month trial period for Concorde at Kennedy Airport and expressed the hope that this could be soon initiated. He also said that he would decide the future of landing rights at Dulles Airport in the very near future.

President Carter emphasized the vital importance of close cooperation between the United States and Europe. He expressed admiration for French leadership in resolving many international economic, social, political, and technological problems. Prime Minister Barre reiterated President Giscard d'Estaing's invitation to President Carter to visit France, and President Carter expressed the hope that he would soon be in a position to reply.

Part-time Federal Employment

Memorandum for the Heads of Executive Departments and Agencies.
September 16, 1977

Memorandum for the Heads of Executive Departments and Agencies

Subject: Part-time Employment

Part-time workers are an important, but relatively untapped national resource. Older people, those with family responsibilities, the handicapped, students and others who are unable to work full time can be valuable additions to an agency's permanent work force. To assure that we in the Federal Government take advantage of the many talents available, I am asking you to establish innovative programs to expand opportunities for men and women seeking part-time employment.

Such programs should include redesign of jobs and work schedules to open up permanent part-time opportunities, recruitment efforts to attract capable men and women to part-time work, review of rules, regulations, and procedures to eliminate artificial barriers to part-time employment, and pilot and research studies to determine where part-time employees can make the maximum contribution.

I believe that much can be done within existing employment ceilings. The Civil Service Commission will coordinate these efforts and will report to me periodically on the progress achieved and the need for any further actions.

JIMMY CARTER

Digest of Other White House Announcements

The following listing includes the President's daily schedule and other items of general interest as announced by the White House Press Office during the period covered by this issue. Events and announcements printed elsewhere in the issue are not included.

September 12

The President met at the White House with:

—Zbigniew Brzezinski, Assistant to the President for National Security Affairs;

—senior White House staff members;

—the Cabinet;

—Vice President Walter F. Mondale;

—Archbishop Joseph L. Bernardin, president of the National Conference of Catholic Bishops, and Bishop Thomas Kelly, general secretary of the U.S. Catholic Conference, to discuss the administration's human rights policies;

—members of the Interagency Council on Minority Business Enterprise, who were meeting in the Cabinet Room.

The White House announced that the President has recommended to the board of directors of the National Alliance of Businessmen that it consider the election of G. William Miller, chairman of the board and chief executive officer of Textron, Inc., and Chairman of the President's Committee on HIRE, to the post of chairman of the Alliance.

The White House announced that Lt. Gen. Olusegun Obasanjo, Head of State of the Federal Republic of Nigeria, has accepted the President's invitation to make a state visit to the United States, beginning in Washington on October 11.

September 13

The President met at the White House with:

—Dr. Brzezinski;

—the Democratic leadership of the Senate;

—Margaret Thatcher, British Conservative Party leader;

—Vice President Mondale, Dr. Brzezinski, and Robert R. Bowie, Deputy to the Director of Central Intelligence;

—Bert Lance, Director of the Office of Management and Budget;

—a group of national presidents of labor and postal management groups;

—Senator Ernest F. Hollings of South Carolina;

—Senator and Mrs. Russell B. Long of Louisiana, for dinner.

September 14

The President met at the White House with:

—Dr. Brzezinski;

—Senator Claiborne Pell of Rhode Island, honorary vice president, Coleman Burke, president, and Dr. Laton Holmgren, general secretary, of the American Bible Society;

—Senators Wendell R. Anderson of Minnesota and Dale Bumpers of Arkansas and Secretary of the Interior Cecil D. Andrus;

—Mrs. Carter, for lunch;

—Kenneth M. Curtis, chairman, Paul D. Sullivan, executive director, and Joel McCleary, treasurer, Democratic National Committee;

—Mr. Lance, James T. McIntyre, Jr., Deputy Director, Harrison Wellford, Executive Associate Director for Reorganization and Management, and F. Tread Davis, Jr., Deputy Associate Director for Reorganization, Office of Management and Budget, to discuss Government reorganization.

The President attended a briefing on the Panama Canal treaties given for Senator Lloyd M. Bentsen of Texas and a group of editors from Texas and South Carolina in the Cabinet Room.

The White House announced that Prime Minister Datuk Hussein bin Onn of Malaysia will be visiting the United States from September 23 to October 5. During his official stay in Washington, the Prime Minister will meet with the President on September 27.

The President declared a major disaster for the State of Missouri as a result of severe storms and flooding beginning about September 11, which caused extensive public and property damage.

September 15

The President met at the White House with:

—Dr. Brzezinski;

—a group of 12 Republican Senators;

—Mrs. Carter, Honorary Chairperson, and Dr. Thomas E. Bryant, Chairman, President's Commission on Mental Health, who presented the President with the preliminary report of the Commission;

—chief executives of the major recording studios represented in the Recording Industry Association of America, who were meeting in the Roosevelt Room.

September 16

The President met at the White House with:

—Vice President Mondale, Secretary of State Cyrus R. Vance, and Dr. Brzezinski;

—Prime Minister Raymond Barre of France;

—a group of editors, publishers, and broadcasters;

—members of the Advisory Committee on Federal Pay.

The President attended a briefing on the Panama Canal treaties, given for members of the U.S. Jaycees in the State Dining Room.

The President left the White House for a weekend visit at Camp David, Md.

NOMINATIONS SUBMITTED TO THE SENATE

The following list does not include promotions of members of the Uniformed Services, nominations to the Service Academies, or nominations of Foreign Service officers.

Submitted September 12, 1977

CHARLES D. FERRIS, of Massachusetts, to be a member of the Federal Communications Commission for a term of 7 years from July 1, 1977, vice Richard E. Wiley, term expired.

NOMINATIONS—Continued
Submitted September 13, 1977

The following-named persons to the positions indicated (new positions):

JOHN F. O'LEARY, of New Mexico, to be Deputy Secretary of Energy.

DALE D. MYERS, of California, to be Under Secretary of Energy.

ALVIN L. ALM, of the District of Columbia, to be an Assistant Secretary of Energy (Policy and Evaluation).

HARRY E. BERGOLD, JR., of Florida, to be an Assistant Secretary of Energy (International Affairs).

ROBERT D. THORNE, of California, to be an Assistant Secretary of Energy (Energy Technology).

JOHN M. DEUTCH, of Massachusetts, to be Director of the Office of Energy Research.

DAVID J. BARDIN, of New Jersey, to be Administrator of the Economic Regulatory Administration.

The following-named persons to be members of the Federal Energy Regulatory Commission for the terms indicated (new positions):

CHARLES B. CURTIS, of Maryland, for a term of 2 years.

GEORGE R. HALL, of Virginia, for a term of 3 years.

GEORGIANA H. SHELDON, of Virginia, for a term of 3 years.

Submitted September 14, 1977

GEORGE W. LANDAU, of Maryland, a Foreign Service officer of Class one, to be Ambassador Extraordinary and Plenipotentiary of the United States of America to Chile.

ROBERT J. DEL TUFO, of New Jersey, to be United States Attorney for the District of New Jersey for the term of 4 years, vice Jonathan L. Goldstein.

Submitted September 15, 1977

RAFAEL E. JUAREZ, of Colorado, to be United States Marshal for the District of Colorado for the term of 4 years, vice Doyle W. James.

Submitted September 16, 1977

RALPH EARLE II, of Pennsylvania, to be Special Representative for Arms Control and Disarmament Negotiations (new position).

LOUIS F. OBERDORFER, of Virginia, to be United States District Judge for the District of Columbia, vice William B. Jones, retired.

ROXANNE BARTON CONLIN, of Iowa, to be United States Attorney for the Southern District of Iowa for the term of 4 years, vice Allen L. Donielson, resigned.

NOMINATIONS—Continued
Submitted September 16—Continued

JACOB V. ESKENAZI, of Florida, to be United States Attorney for the Southern District of Florida for the term of 4 years, vice Robert W. Rust, resigned.

JULIAN K. FITE, of Oklahoma, to be United States Attorney for the Eastern District of Oklahoma for the term of 4 years, vice Richard A. Pyle.

ANDREA M. SHERIDAN ORDIN, of California, to be United States Attorney for the Central District of California for the term of 4 years, vice William D. Keller, resigned.

DAVID T. READY, of Indiana, to be United States Attorney for the Northern District of Indiana for the term of 4 years, vice John R. Wilks, resigned.

JAMES H. REYNOLDS, of Iowa, to be United States Attorney for the Northern District of Iowa for the term of 4 years, vice Evan L. Hultman.

BARRY E. TEAGUE, of Alabama, to be United States Attorney for the Middle District of Alabama for the term of 4 years, vice Ira De Ment, resigned.

ROBERT P. LAROCHE, of California, to be United States Marshal for the Eastern District of California for the term of 4 years, vice Arthur F. Van Court.

CHECKLIST OF WHITE HOUSE PRESS RELEASES

The following releases of the Office of the White House Press Secretary, distributed during the period covered by this issue, are not including in the issue.

Released September 12, 1977

Fact sheet: Interagency Council for Minority Business Enterprise

News conference: on the President's meeting with members of the Interagency Council for Minority Business Enterprise—by Sidney L. Harman, Under Secretary of Commerce and Chairman of the Council

Released September 13, 1977

News conference: on the organization of the Department of Energy—by Secretary of Energy James R. Schlesinger

Announcement: nomination of Robert J. Del Tufo to be United States Attorney for the District of New Jersey

Released September 15, 1977

Announcement: nomination of Rafael E. Juarez to be United States Marshal for the District of Colorado

CHECKLIST—Continued
Released September 15—Continued

News conference: on the President's meeting with Prime Minister Raymond Barre of France—by Jerrold L. Schecter, Associate Press Secretary

Released September 16, 1977

Announcement: nomination of Louis F. Oberdorfer to be United States District Judge for the District of Columbia; Roxanne B. Conlin be United States Attorney for the Southern District of Iowa; Jacob V. Eskenazi to be United States Attorney for the Southern District of Florida; Julian K. Fite to be United States Attorney for the Eastern District of Oklahoma; Andrea M. Ordin to be United States Attorney for the Central District of California; David T. Ready to be United States Attorney for the Northern

CHECKLIST—Continued

District of Indiana; James H. Reynolds to be United States Attorney for the Northern District of Iowa; Barry E. Teague to be United States Attorney for the Middle District of Alabama; Robert P. LaRoche to be United States Marshal for the Eastern District of California

News conference: on the President's meeting with Prime Minister Raymond Barre of France—by Jerrold L. Schecter, Associate Press Secretary

ACTS APPROVED BY THE PRESIDENT

NOTE: No acts approved by the President were received by the Office of the Federal Register during the period covered by this issue.

Interview With the President

Remarks and a Question-and-Answer Session With a Group of Editors and News Directors. September 16, 1977

THE PRESIDENT. I want to welcome all of you to the White House. Some of you have been here before. I think you've had a chance to meet with some of our staff this morning. And I hope that the day will be fruitful for you.

One of the most important things to me as President is to have a means by which I can understand the problems and the questions that arise throughout the country—sometimes removed from Washington itself—to get a different perspective and also, of course, during my news conferences, that have been held and will always be held, I hope, twice a month, to receive questions from the Washington press corps.

The number of issues that confront me are very voluminous. I'd just like to outline a few of them for you in preparation for your questions.

ADMINISTRATION POLICIES

This morning I concluded my own talks with the Prime Minister of France, and this is a final meeting with him. He'll now, this afternoon, meet with economic advisers, the Secretary of State, Secretary of Defense, Secretary of Energy, and others so that we, in shaping our own policies for the future, will know the special problems of France, and vice versa. These discussions which I have had with many foreign leaders have been very helpful to me.

As you know, I've never served in Washington before January. I've got a lot to learn about the processes, and I've gone out of my way this year to expand my own circle of knowledge outside just domestic issues.

Last week, I met with, I think, 19 heads of state of the Latin American countries. And I think we have a new relationship with them, brought about primarily by the prospect of the ratification of the Panama Canal Treaty.

We are continuing our negotiations with the Soviets on the SALT question; also, on a comprehensive test ban of nuclear weapons. And as you know, the Soviet Union in addition is a cochairman, along with us, of the Mideast talks that we hope will take place before the end of this year.

This coming week, I'll have the first of a series of foreign ministers who will come and meet with me from the Middle Eastern region—Foreign Minister Dayan from Israel. And during the following weeks, I'll meet with all the others. These meetings that come to me directly are preceded, of course, by long discussions with the Secretary of State and others.

We have, in addition, many other defense matters that have come to my desk. Quite often, we have foreign matters that don't relate to the prospect of war or the issue of peace. A recent one, concluded last week, was with the Canadians, on a means by which we might bring natural gas down to our country. And this is the biggest construction project ever undertaken in the history of the world, and I think we arrived at a common purpose there.

We have already implemented the construction of a new Department of Energy. I approved it this week. Dr. Schlesinger has been working on this ever since I've been in office.

We have finished in the House, I think, substantial legislation to set up an energy policy that might guide the new Department in its functions. We are running into additional problems in the Senate. The political pressures are enormous from the oil companies and others on the subject of energy. I think the House took very courageous action in this respect, and my hope and expectation is that the Senate will do the same.

Welfare reform has been presented to the House and to the Senate this week in its final, legally drafted version of legislation. And before the Congress adjourns this year, hopefully in October, I will present to them my tax reform package as well. This will take a great deal of debate and study, along with welfare. And that, obviously, can't be concluded during this calendar year.

We have, I think, been fairly successful so far. We've been learning, and I think that we put together a good organization here.

I've obviously been concerned recently about the Bert Lance case, and I've not let it interfere with my own functions. I don't think Bert has let it interfere with his

functions as the Director of the Office of Management and Budget.

This is an agency with which I'm most intimately involved, personally, on a multiple basis every day. And because of my own engineering background and my habits acquired while I was Governor, I set very specific and rigid time schedules for the accomplishment of each component part of a major undertaking. And I can assure you that there has been absolutely zero slippage in the Office of Management and Budget because of this series of allegations that are now being answered by Bert Lance to the Senate—I hope, successfully.

We've initiated this year—and this is the last point I'll make—a brand new budgeting system that I used in Georgia, called zero-based budgeting. It's a massive undertaking for a bureaucracy of our size to completely change its mechanism by which next year's budget will be prepared. But the fiscal year '79 budget will be prepared in its entirety using the zero-based budgeting technique, where you don't make any assumptions that present programs or expenditures are sacred. You don't just deal with the new additions next year for the budget considerations, but you start from zero and analyze the entire appropriation of funds.

The reorganization effort is on schedule, and I think by the end of the 3-year period that's been given me by the Congress, we will complete it to the satisfaction of the people of our country.

I'll be glad now to answer any questions that you might have.

John [John McCormally, Hawk Eye, Burlington, Iowa].

QUESTIONS

BERT LANCE

Q. Mr. President, you say you read the editorials, so I might as well get what's coming to me. [*Laughter*] We are very well aware of your concern for the need for fairness to Mr. Lance, and you're respected for that by the people who support you the most; those same people are the most concerned about the success of your Presidency. And on another issue, recently you remarked that life isn't always fair. I wondered if you are confronted with the problem of whether a resolution may be necessary which is not altogether fair to Mr. Lance, but which is necessary for the larger concerns of the Presidency?

THE PRESIDENT. Yes, that's something I'll have to balance. And as I said yesterday in a telephone talk to the news programers of television and radio stations, I don't know of anything illegal that Bert Lance has done. I don't know of any unethical conduct on his behalf. And I'm keeping an open mind about this entire subject until the Senate goes through its present procedure of analyzing in detail all of the new charges and allegations and claims and statements that have been made about Bert Lance.

He's now being given a fair chance to say these are all of the charges, this is my answer to them. And of course, I will certainly have an eagerness to learn of any reason for me to change the assessment that I've just made. But I want to be fair about it, and I have a sure sense of the basic fairness of the American people.

The facts, if divulged, will be conclusive, I think, in the shaping of public opinion. And one problem about the whole incident that I can't comprehend, perhaps, adequately, is—let's leave Bert Lance out of it for just a moment; just take any of you, or myself. If a series of, say, incorrect allegations are made day after day after day with the highest possible publicity, the lead story on every television network every night and the headlines in the Washington Post and

other newspapers every day, and then all those allegations are proved to be false, how much of those allegations remain to damage the character of the person who might be totally innocent?

And then you say, well, this person is damaged so that he can't perform his functions adequately, when the damage has been caused either erroneously or falsely. Well, if that was the only factor, then my decision would be easy. But if I also have confidence that as the American people learn—and it might take a while—that the allegations were basically false and have successfully been answered, that the character of the person, say, yourself, would be restored, then my decision would be a different one. And I really have been concerned about this matter, as you know.

I don't know an easy answer. But at this point, I have no evidence to indicate that Bert's done anything illegal or unethical. I wish that every one of you could read the FBI report which has been the subject of many references. Bert has an ability, under the law, to get the FBI report under the Freedom of Information Act and make it public.

They interviewed, I guess, a hundred people—three of those people were in the Comptroller's Office; three additional ones were in the Department of Justice. And the FBI questioned them about these same allegations, and the response of those, I think, all men, six men, were unanimously almost effusive in their recommendation of Bert. But now their testimony under the pressure of Senate interrogation is a little bit different. But at the time that the Senate investigated first, I think the information was offered to them. Obviously, a lot of new questions have been raised. But in general, I'm still keeping an open mind about it.

Q. Mr. President, I am from New England, and we don't engage in overdrafts, as Mr. Lance calls some of his actions. When you were a businessman in Georgia, did you ever become involved in overdrafts? He gives the impression that it's a common practice in the State of Georgia.

THE PRESIDENT. There are several people here, I think, from Georgia. I don't think that this is——

Q. But did you, in your business——

THE PRESIDENT. Well, I can't say that I depended on overdrafts to run my business, but as I have said in one of my regular news conferences that was televised nationwide, yes, I've had overdrafts. Let me add one other thing.

There is a fairly common practice—and I am not trying to criticize banks, because I don't know how wide the practice is—but there's a general sense at home, not because it's in the South, but because I live in a small town, that if you have several accounts and a substantial balance in all those accounts, but then you become overdrawn in one of those accounts, then that's not considered to be an illegal or an unethical act.

I run, I would say in my business, six or seven individual accounts, different aspects of my farm or my warehouse business. Also, I have a personal account. I never write any checks. I haven't written three checks in the last 5 years. My wife does all the check writing. But if we should have $50,000 or $100,000 in my warehouse account, and in my own personal account my wife should buy a dress and give a $25 check to pay for it and the check bounced because we were overdrawn, they would not send for the sheriff or call me on the phone to say, "You've disgraced yourself by having an overdraft." They would say, in effect, "We'll honor this check. We'll put a notice in your mailbox, and then you can shift some money from your warehouse account over into the personal account."

But I don't excuse overdrafts. You know, it's obvious that I would rather my own life have been completely free of any overdraft. But I can't say that it's an acceptable thing. But I still don't believe that it's an unethical or illegal thing in the banking circles in which I've had to operate.

ENERGY

Q. Mr. President, people in the Northeast are as concerned about energy as anything. I know that Secretary Schlesinger yesterday told the Senate Finance Committee that he wasn't sure how you were going to react to the idea of diverting the wellhead tax to energy production rather than tax rebates. I wonder, can you tell us today how you feel about it?

THE PRESIDENT. My preference is to have the wellhead tax receipts go to tax rebates. There are some alternatives that obviously will be considered by the Congress with or without my approval, and I can't say that my own position will prevail ultimately. But there are different ways to use wellhead taxes. My preference is, as we presented it to the Congress, the rebates. One reason for that preference is that it's fair. Another one is that it doesn't create a tremendous withdrawal from the national economy of substantial amounts of money. If you have increased wellhead taxes and immediately return that money to people in better paychecks on a 2-week basis, then there's not a shock to the country. If you withdraw that money and wait 3 months, 6 months, or a year before it gets back into the economy, you have a tremendous dampening effect on our national economy, which is bad.

Now, if some of the wellhead tax should be shifted to enhance the effectiveness of the energy goals, then I can't see anything very bad about that. If you had better rapid transit systems, better insulation of homes, more research and development, for instance, for new energy sources, that would be one thing. But the constant threat is that because of political pressures, that money is going to be returned to the oil companies under the guise of enhancing production.

I think the oil companies have enough cash flow right now—certainly the majors do—to have an adequate degree of exploration. In fact, that exploration, in my opinion, is adequate at this point. And I'm just as afraid that there is a threat that the wellhead tax is going to be given to the oil companies to reward them financially.

I think that our package has a gracious plenty of incentives for enhanced exploration and enhanced production of oil in this country. We have by far the highest price for newly discovered oil in this energy package of anywhere on Earth, and I don't think the oil companies deserve to get this money taken out of the consumers' pockets and put in the pockets of the oil companies.

TAX CREDIT FOR HOMEOWNERS

Q. Sir, in light of the fact that many people are having a hard time affording a home these days and some are depending, apparently, on the mortgage tax deduction which you have proposed to eliminate or reduce, do you have any idea what the impact is going to be? Have you done any studies on whether this is going to be preventing many people from buying homes?

THE PRESIDENT. In the first place, I have not decided on any specifics of a tax reform package at all. I've certainly not decided on eliminating credits for interest paid on homes or property taxes paid for homes.

During the political campaign, I promised that there would not be a reduction in the stimulus for American families to own their own homes, and if there should be any change it would be compatible with that commitment of mine.

Now, I have some doubt about whether this same level of interest rate deduction should be applicable to a $500,000 home or a second or third or fourth home for very wealthy families, as contrasted with the average American working family who's trying to pay for one home in which they live.

Also, you have to remember that if the credit is on a percentage basis, then a family that has a $15,000 income, if given a certain amount of credit for interest, only gets, say, 20 percent of that interest payment credited on their tax. But if you're in the 70-percent bracket, you get 70 percent of any interest that you pay on your home.

So, equalizing those homeownership credit incentives is part of the package. But it will not hurt the average family in trying to purchase or pay for their own dwelling place.

Q. What limit do you propose, sir?

THE PRESIDENT. I don't know the specifics yet.

BERT LANCE

Q. Mr. President, do you think Bert Lance has strengthened or weakened his position since yesterday morning?

THE PRESIDENT. I've not had a chance to watch the television programs, except that my staff puts together an 18- or 20-minute recap on some of the highlights. And I see those on occasion. I spent all yesterday and today in my regular business and meeting with Prime Minister Barre.

But my assessment from the brief time I've watched it, and also from my own staff, is that he has enhanced his position, because he was in a situation where, literally, for weeks, all kinds of allegations or charges were made, including criminal violation of the writing of checks to avoid paying of taxes, which is fraudulent and illegal. He was alleged to be an embezzler by a convicted felon. And on that basis, the chairman and the minority leader of the Senate [committee] had called for his immediate resignation, and he had not had a chance to answer those charges.

Now that he has answered the charges—I hope and believe successfully—I think he's certainly enhanced his position.

PUERTO RICO

Q. Mr. President, I'm from San Juan, Puerto Rico. *Buenas tardes.*

THE PRESIDENT. *Muchas gracias.*

Q. Would you object to a U.N. fact-finding team going to Puerto Rico to look into the idea, the charges that have been raised, that we are a colony of the United States?

THE PRESIDENT. Yes, I would object to that. I don't have any objection to any analysis of the question, but I think my own statement and the statement of all the leaders of our country that whatever Puerto Rico's people want to do is acceptable to me. If the Puerto Rican people want to be a commonwealth, I will support it. If the Puerto Rican people want to be a State, I will support it. If the Puerto Rican people want to be an independent nation, I would support it.

Q. But the U.N. has no jurisdiction?

THE PRESIDENT. I don't think the U.N. has any jurisdiction. And particularly when this question is raised by Cuba, a government that has no respect for individual freedom or individual liberty and permits no vote of any kind in their own country, to accuse us of trying to sub-

jugate the people of Puerto Rico, to me, is absolutely and patently ridiculous.

TRAVEL TO LATIN AMERICA

Q. Are you planning a trip down that way or the Caribbean way in the Latin American trip?

THE PRESIDENT. I would like to come down there as soon as I can. An important goal of my administration is to build up a renewed understanding and trust and communication with the nations and the people who live south of here in our hemisphere. My wife's already visited seven nations, as you know.

Q. She is coming to San Juan in 2 weeks?

THE PRESIDENT. Yes, she's coming there in 2 weeks to make a speech to a news group. In addition to that, Andy Young has been down to visit several of the countries in the South. Assistant Secretary Todman has been down. Very shortly, I think next month, the Secretary of State will come down to Latin America. And I hope to come, too. I don't have any specific date yet.

NATURAL GAS PIPELINE

Q. Mr. President, you mentioned the pipeline from the North Slope. The Governor of our State, California, Governor Brown, has been running around saying that you have given California a finger instead of a leg regarding the western leg that goes into California. Would you comment on that?

THE PRESIDENT. Well, I would like to say one thing to start with, that the people of California are my constituents just as much as they are the Governor's constituents, and I have just as deep a concern about the future prosperity and good life of the people of California as the Governor or anyone else.

I've never had any disagreements with Governor Brown. So far as I know, he's never mentioned the western leg of the pipeline to me. If he corresponded with some of my staff members and I'm not familiar with it, then, of course, that would be understandable.

I've been with him several times this year, both in California, and he spent a night with me at the mansion. We've had long discussions, but I did not know he was dissatisfied with the arrangement at all.

One of the problems, however, with the El Paso route, which was the alternative, was the reluctance of California to provide some means by which oil or natural gas could come into the State to be used there and also to be transported to other parts of the country. I don't say that in a spirit of criticism, because I'm concerned about environmental questions and possible oil spills and, also, the deterioration in the quality of air, because of heavy shipping transport, as well.

But I would expect that Governor Brown and I and other State and Federal officials would eagerly search for a basis on which we could assure California adequate energy supplies in the future.

My decision to go with the Alcan route was one of great importance to our country. But certainly none of the factors involved was to damage California people whom I care about very much.

BUSINESS TAXES

Q. Mr. President, I appreciate the honor of being here and meeting you. I've been an admirer of yours. The one thing that concerns me and, I think, concerns you and the country, is the tax reforms that are getting into the magazines, et cetera.

You see what's happening to the stock market. I, like you, was a poor boy in Washington that became affluent. Now, I don't like to see small business—which, I believe I read in Fortune, contributes 90 percent of the gross national product—now, where you make statements that capital gains might go to 50 percent, more social security taxes to a small businessman, it's killing the American incentive. And I do hope that you will give it serious thought to keep venture capital going, not for the big corporations. We support the big corporation.

THE PRESIDENT. Well, one of the major considerations in evolving the tax reform package is obviously to provide adequate incentive for business expansion. And I believe that when the tax reform package is made public, that there will be a sigh of relief and also a removal of the inevitable uncertainty about what the terms of the tax proposal might encompass.

Also, of course, through long weeks of House and Senate hearings, any possible improvements on the tax reform package would be explored.

We have met with many leaders—I have personally—representing small businesses, large businesses, the professions, labor, consumers, tax experts, in trying to evolve a good package. And I think it will be good. We hope that there will be equity. We hope that there will be a reduction in tax rates. We hope that there will be simplicity, and we hope that we can provide an adequate assurance of improved venture capital in the future. And we hope that there will be substantial tax reductions.

Those are about five factors that I hope will be in the tax reform package and which I can predict to you with great assurance will be in the tax package.

Q. With the 15-percent tax investment credit, you cut the unemployment rate to 4 percent.

THE PRESIDENT. That sounds very good.

DON TUCKER

Q. Mr. President, do you plan to withdraw your nomination of Don Tucker to the CAB, and do you think the Lance matter has hurt that?

THE PRESIDENT. I haven't any intentions to withdraw the nomination. I understand that there has been some concern raised within the committee. I have not received that report; I've just read about it in the news. But I will look into it, and if there are some provable allegations there that I didn't know about when the recommendation was made, then I would certainly reconsider. But I don't have any intention now, knowing what I know, to withdraw the recommendation. Don Tucker is speaker of the house in Florida. He's been recommended strongly by the two Senators in Florida. He's been recommended strongly by Governor Reubin Askew from Florida. And I don't even know what the reason for the hesitancy in the Senate staff is at this point.

SUGAR PRICE SUPPORTS

Q. Mr. President, during the House-Senate conference committee on this year's agriculture act, an administration spokesman said he felt that tariffs should be used—or tariffs would be used to maintain the price of sugar, rather than a price support program of Government subsidies.

Yesterday, Secretary of Agriculture Bergland announced that a payments program, very similar to the one declared illegal by the Comptroller General, was going to be proposed. Why are you insisting on Government subsidies rather than tariffs or import restrictions to support the price of sugar? And, secondly, do you think that sugar prices should be supported at all?

THE PRESIDENT. Yes, I think that sugar prices ought to be supported. I

think that a 13½-cent sugar price is about the minimum that would be advisable, both for domestic producers and also for imported sugar. We have supported the new farm bill which provides price supports until the international sugar agreement can be implemented.

I did this reluctantly, as you may know. We did not support the de la Garza amendment in its original form and accepted it only if the conferees would agree that the price support mechanism would be terminated at the time an international sugar agreement was reached, if the international sugar agreement encompassed a price of about 13½ cents.

Tariffs are a terrible thing to impose, because many of our friends in Latin America depend heavily upon sugar. One of the most democratic nations in the world derives almost its entire income from the export of sugar. And for us to put an obstacle to their shipment of sugar to our country would, I think, almost destroy their economy, their government, probably shift it toward a complete dependence on totalitarian assistance and would not be fair, as well.

We've tried to avoid a protectionist policy since I've been in office. And I think the best way to do it is through international agreements that, in effect, set minimum and maximum prices for commodities whose prices, without constraint, fluctuate so wildly.

We've seen this happen in the case of coffee. We've seen it happen in the case of sugar, where it went almost up to a dollar and then dropped down to about 8 cents. Well, we can accommodate that. It's devastating to a sugar farmer or to the sugar producers, but our national economy is so varied that we can accommodate it. But for a country where 85 percent of all their exports is sugar, this is devastating.

So, I don't like tariffs as such. They would particularly be damaging to our closest friends and allies in this hemisphere. They also, I think, would cost the American taxpayer a great deal more. And I think that an international agreement on sugar of about 13 cents would be the preferable approach, and until that can be put into effect, I have reluctantly agreed to support the price support aspects of the new farm bill.

THE MIDDLE EAST

Q. Mr. President, Jim Wisch, with the Texas Jewish Post, Dallas and Fort Worth.

First of all, on behalf of the American Jewish Publishers Association, I want to thank you for the profound message you sent from your wife, Rosalynn, and yourself to the American Jewish community. It was indeed very sincere. And with regard to your sincerity, which was recognized by all editors across the country, regardless of their background, I want to point up to you your profound statement on the Mideast which we published right before the election, which was highly informative and set out many things that you had proposed to do.

I just returned from the Mideast, where I had a long, long conversation with Ambassador Lewis. And it seems to me there's a great deal of apprehension going on amongst American Jews and Jews of the world, and somehow it rests upon what some of your decisions are going to be.

I think this apprehension could be cleared, because I think there may be a disagreement, perhaps, in semantics rather than in objectives. And I wonder if you had been concerned about your popularity or your interpretation vis-a-vis your embracement of the PLO, and that your regard for them has given them a prop-

aganda ploy where they have become recalcitrant—they still employ Chapter 16, the complete destruction of Israel. Now, people think that you are pushing Israel to sit down and recognize the PLO, regardless of that point in the PLO's platform. 242, your resolution, which you so eloquently described last July, says that nobody can sit down unless it's a face-to-face discussion and they recognize the entity of each nation as being a sovereign nation like we are doing with Panama.

And in view of this regard, I wonder if you plan to clear this up or elucidate or however you plan to handle this.

THE PRESIDENT. With all due respect, that's one of the most distorted assessments of my own policy that I've ever heard.

Q. It is not my assessment—[*laughter*]——

THE PRESIDENT. I understand.

Q. But it's incumbent upon me to bring it to you.

THE PRESIDENT. I've never endorsed the PLO. Our Government has had no communication, at all, directly with the PLO. The only communication has been when representatives of the PLO have been to Arab leaders immediately prior to a Cy Vance visit with them or their visit to our country and have delivered messages to us indirectly.

Our agreement with the Israeli Government several years ago, before I became President, was that we would not communicate with the PLO as long as they did not refute their commitment to destroy the nation of Israel and did not accept the right of Israel to exist. Our public position is the same as our private position. There is no difference between them.

We have said that if the PLO would accept publicly the right of Israel to exist and exist in peace, as described under

United Nations Resolution 242, that we would meet with them and discuss the future of the Palestinians in the Middle East. We have never called on the PLO to be part of the future negotiations. We have said that the Palestinian people should be represented in the future negotiations. That is one of the three major elements of any agreement that might lead to lasting peace—one is the territorial boundaries; the other one is the Arab countries accepting Israel, to live in peace as neighbors; and the third one is some resolution of the Palestinian question.

I've never called for an independent Palestinian country. We have used the word "entity." And my own preference as expressed in that talk that I made in New Jersey, I think, and now, is that we think that if there is a Palestinian entity established on the West Bank, that it ought to be associated with Jordan, for instance. I think this was the case among many Israeli leaders as their preference in the past.

So, we have been very cautious, very careful, very consistent in spelling out our posture on the Middle Eastern settlements. When we have gone around, for instance—I haven't, but Cy Vance has gone around to Israel, to Jordan, to Syria, to Egypt, to Saudi Arabia—to talk about a future Middle Eastern conference and, hopefully, a settlement, we have taken the same exact written set of principles so there would be no difference among them, and discussed it with Sadat and Hussein and Asad and Fahd and with Mr. Begin, so that there would never be any allegation on any part of theirs that we took one position with the Israelis and a different position with the Arabs.

Sometimes the Israelis would say, "We

don't accept this principle number 4." Sometimes the Arabs would say, "We don't accept principle number 1." But we've tried to negotiate in good faith.

I might say one other thing. We are not just an idle bystander. We are not just an uninterested intermediary or mediator. Our country has a direct, substantial interest in a permanent peace in the Middle East. And I sincerely hope and I believe that the nations who live there also want to have a permanent settlement and a permanent peace in the Middle East. And the principles that I described in that speech, the principles that the Vice President described in a speech he made in California earlier this year, and the principles that we espouse in our public and private conversations with Arabs and Israelis and with Prime Minister Barre, yesterday, from France, and others who are interested, are exactly the same. We've never deviated.

We have learned a lot. And as we've learned, we've added additional new items onto our basic proposal. But ultimately, the Middle Eastern settlement has got to be an agreement among the parties involved.

Now, I hope that all the countries are eager to negotiate in good faith. I hope that none of them are putting up deliberate obstacles to prevent a Geneva conference from being convened. That's my hope and that's my present expectation.

Q. Thank you, sir.

THE PRESIDENT. I'm sorry that I have to leave. I've enjoyed it. You asked superb questions, and I always appreciate your coming.

NOTE: The interview began at 1 p.m. in the Cabinet Room at the White House.

The transcript of the interview was released on September 17.

Panama Canal Treaties

Message to the Senate Transmitting the Treaties. September 16, 1977

To the Senate of the United States:

I transmit herewith, for the purpose of receiving the advice and consent of the Senate to ratification, the Panama Canal Treaty and the Treaty Concerning the Permanent Neutrality and Operation of the Panama Canal, which I signed on behalf of the United States at the headquarters of the Organization of American States on September 7, 1977. I also transmit, for the information of the Senate, the report of the Department of State with respect to those Treaties.

When ratified, the Treaties will establish new arrangements for operating and defending the Panama Canal, and for ensuring its continuing neutrality and accessibility to all shipping. These objectives will be achieved through a new, cooperative relationship between the United States and Panama under which the United States will continue to operate the Canal until December 31, 1999. After this period of preparation, Panama will assume control of Canal operations, with the United States sharing permanent responsibility for maintaining the Canal's neutrality.

The Treaties serve the essential interest of the United States in an efficient and safe Canal. They permit a new relationship with Panama based on friendship and mutual respect. Moreover, they remove a major obstacle to the betterment of our relations with the countries of Latin America and the Caribbean area, and will substantially improve our standing with other nations, particularly those of the developing world.

I believe that these Treaties are fair to both countries, consistent with our heritage, and right for our times. They protect United States interests in the Panama Canal for the future better than the 1903 Convention which they will replace. Undue delay in ratification could cause serious problems for our foreign relations and jeopardize our long-term interests in the Canal and in the Hemisphere. Accordingly, I urge the Senate to give these Treaties early and favorable consideration.

JIMMY CARTER

The White House,
September 16, 1977.

NOTE: The text of the message was released on September 17.

United Nations

Nomination of U.S. Representatives and Alternate Representatives to the 32d Session of the General Assembly. September 19, 1977

The President today announced the persons he will nominate as Representatives and Alternate Representatives of the United States to the Thirty-second Session of the United Nations General Assembly, which will be held in New York from September 20 to December 17. They are:

Representatives:

ANDREW J. YOUNG, U.S. Representative to the United Nations;

JAMES F. LEONARD, JR., Deputy Representative of the United States to the United Nations;

LESTER L. WOLFF, U.S. Representative from New York, member of the House International Relations Committee;

CHARLES W. WHALEN, JR., U.S. Representative from Ohio, member of the House International Relations Committee;

CORETTA SCOTT KING, lecturer and writer, president of the Martin Luther King, Jr., Foundation and the Martin Luther King, Jr., Center for Social Change.

Alternate Representatives:

DONALD F. MCHENRY, Deputy Representative of the United States in the Security Council of the United Nations;

MELISSA F. WELLS, Representative of the United States on the Economic and Social Council of the United Nations;

ALLARD K. LOWENSTEIN, Alternate Representative of the United States for Special Political Affairs in the United Nations;

MARJORIE C. BENTON, employed by Films, Inc., of Wilmette, Ill., president of the Better Government Association (Chicago), chairperson, Illinois 51.3% Committee;

JOHN C. KENNEDY, partner and general manager of an Oklahoma real estate and insurance firm, chairman of the Oklahoma Department of Transportation.

Fire Prevention Week, 1977

Proclamation 4521. September 19, 1977

By the President of the United States of America

A Proclamation

The United States of America and its people continue to be victims of destructive fires at a rate unmatched in the industrialized world. For this reason, it is essential that we all be aware of the potential for tragedy from fire and that we do all within our power to eradicate the threat of unwanted fire.

The most recent figures available indicate that about 7,500 Americans die, over 300,000 are injured, and more than $4 billion in property is lost annually because of fire. These fires occur in all areas of America, in homes, factories, offices, schools, nightclubs, prisons, and homes for elderly, and affect all Americans. Professional fire fighters bear a disproportionate burden of the human costs of fire; theirs is still one of the most hazardous professions in America. In addition, thousands of individuals face the dangers of fire without pay, as volunteer fire fighters.

Through the efforts of the fire services, concerned citizens, the private sector, and government, Americans are becoming increasingly aware of the problem, and some of its solutions.

NOW, THEREFORE, I, JIMMY CARTER, President of the United States of America, do hereby designate the week beginning October 9, 1977, as Fire Prevention Week.

I call upon all Americans to learn basic fire prevention and personal fire safety practices and to apply these safeguards to reduce the toll of death, burn injuries and property loss due to fire.

I urge all Federal, State and local agencies concerned with such national problems as energy conservation, environmental protection, and economic well-being to consider fully how their programs can help assure that all Americans live and work in an environment that is as safe as possible from the danger of fire.

I urge the continued cooperation of Government and the private sector in encouraging the use of smoke detection and fire suppression systems.

I call upon the members of the Joint Council of National Fire Service Organizations, the National Fire Protection Association, all other organizations concerned with fire safety, and the National Fire Prevention and Control Administration to provide the leadership, planning, and innovation necessary for an effective national fire prevention and control effort.

Finally, let us all recognize the valiant and determined efforts of the fire services, code enforcement officers, Federal officials, and State and local government officials in fire prevention and control.

IN WITNESS WHEREOF, I have hereunto set my hand this nineteenth day of September, in the year of our Lord nineteen hundred seventy-seven, and of the Independence of the United States of America the two hundred and second.

JIMMY CARTER

[Filed with the Office of the Federal Register, 12:49 p.m., September 19, 1977]

Meeting With Foreign Minister Moshe Dayan of Israel

White House Statement Issued Following the Meeting Between the President and the Foreign Minister. September 19, 1977

President Carter and Israeli Foreign Minister Moshe Dayan met in the Cabinet Room for 1 hour, 35 minutes. The meeting was also attended by Vice President Walter Mondale; Secretary of State Cyrus Vance; Zbigniew Brzezinski, Assistant to the President for National Security Affairs; Hamilton Jordan, Assistant to the President; Robert J. Lipshutz, Counsel to the President; David Aaron, Deputy Assistant for National Security Affairs; Alfred L. Atherton, Jr., Assistant Secretary of State for Near Eastern and South Asian Affairs; Samuel Lewis, U.S. Ambassador to Israel; and William Quandt, National Security Council staff member, on the American side; and His Excellency Simcha Dinitz, Ambassador of Israel to the United States; The Honorable Ephraim Evron, Director General, Ministry of Foreign Affairs; The Honorable Hanan Baron, Minister, Embassy of Israel; Mr. Meir Rosenne, Legal Advisor to the Foreign Minister; Mr. Naphtali Lavie, Foreign

Ministry Spokesman and Advisor to the Foreign Minister; and Mr. Elyakim Rubinstein, Director, Foreign Minister's Bureau, and Advisor to the Foreign Minister, on the Israeli side.

The President began by expressing personal pleasure at his first opportunity to welcome Foreign Minister Dayan to the White House. He noted that his talks today inaugurate a series of detailed and concrete discussions with foreign ministers from the Middle East in the intensive search for a comprehensive peace settlement. The President repeated his determination to help the parties reach that settlement. He underlined his conviction that a just and lasting peace in this vital area of the world requires compromise and courageous leadership from all the parties to the negotiations.

The President and Foreign Minister emphasized the importance of instituting negotiations between the parties through resuming the Geneva conference. The President and the Foreign Minister reviewed the substantive issues of a settlement and discussed questions related to organizing the conference. There was an exchange of views on the question of the Palestinian representation and the question of Israeli settlements. The Foreign Minister elaborated on the draft treaty of peace the Government of Israel had submitted to us for a comprehensive settlement. As a follow-on to this meeting, Secretary Vance will discuss the Israeli plan in depth with the Foreign Minister and will also discuss with him some specific American suggestions for reconciling the differences between the parties.

The talk between the President and the Foreign Minister will be useful in proceeding with the discussions the President, and later the Secretary of State, are having with the other foreign ministers. Their talk was conducted in the open and friendly spirit of relations between our two countries which permits differences to be discussed candidly and in the knowledge that both the United States and Israel have a heavy stake in achieving their shared goal of peace in the Middle East. In this connection, the President reaffirmed the commitment of the United States to the security of Israel.

Consumer Protection Act Amendments

Remarks on Signing H.R. 5294 Into Law.
September 20, 1977

I'm glad to see there's a lot of interest in this legislation. It's a great pleasure for me to meet with all of you this morning to sign H.R. 5294, which is a fair debt collection bill.

And before I sign this legislation, I would particularly like to thank Senator Proxmire and Senator Riegle, who did so much hard work on this, and Congressmen Reuss, Annunzio, Wylie, and others behind me, who fought a very difficult fight—very close in the House, very overwhelming in the Senate—to get this legislation into law.

This is the first consumer bill that I've had the opportunity to sign, and it's one of the first times, I think, in the history of our country when a consumer bill has been signed here at the White House. [*Laughter*] But I believe it's important for me as President to indicate my strong interest in this legislation.

It's not a minor matter to treat consumers fairly in this country. And if there's one major gap in what has been accomplished by my predecessors in the White House and by previous Congresses, it is in the protection of consumers. I hope that this is the first of a series of bills

that I'll be able to sign here on the White House lawn.

I believe that we need to pursue the opportunity for consumers to be represented before the agencies of the Federal Government which determine their right to a fair opportunity in our economic structure. I hope that we'll have a chance to enhance the use of responsible class action suits. And above all, I hope that I'll have a chance to sign into law an act creating the consumer protection agency, which I believe is of very great importance to our country.

The deliberate misinformation that's been promulgated about this legislation is disheartening to me. And I hope that the Members of Congress who have already shown their courage in protecting consumers against what is often very strong pressure will again renew their effort to pass this law which will create the agency that I've described.

We now have consumer protection scattered so diversely throughout the Federal Government that it's impossible to make it effective. And it would be a great saving in taxpayers' money; it would be a great saving in the wasted efforts of public employees; and it would also be a great step forward in letting American people know that our free enterprise system can be fair—to implement this agency in the future.

This bill assures that collection procedures are fair. Testimony that was given during the hearings on this bill showed that quite often innocent consumers— some of whom had even been misidentified as debtors—were harassed by profane language, by false statements made to them directly or by telephone, by calls after midnight to disturb a family, by threats which were contrary to the law, by alleging that consumers were violating the law when in fact they weren't. And these practices will now be made illegal among about 5,000 collection agencies, most of which are honest and law-abiding and do a proper job; some of which, though, need to be corrected. About $5 billion a year are collected by these agencies. And this is a great step forward in indicating to the American people that the Congress believes that consumers need to be treated fairly.

So, because of these reasons and many others, I congratulate the Members of the House and Senate behind me, who represent many others, and express my congratulations to the consumers of America and my own pride in being able to sign this legislation, which is a great step forward.

NOTE: The President spoke at 10 a.m. at the signing ceremony in the Rose Garden at the White House.

As enacted, H.R. 5294 is Public Law 95–109, approved September 20.

Federal Farm Credit Board

Nomination of Owen Cooper and Edgar C. Rutherford To Be Members. September 20, 1977

The President today announced that he has nominated Owen Cooper and Edgar C. Rutherford to be members of the Federal Farm Credit Board, Farm Credit Administration, for terms expiring March 31, 1983.

Cooper, of Yazoo City, Miss., would replace Ernest G. Spivey, term expired. Cooper was born April 19, 1908, in Warren County, Miss. He received a B.S. in agriculture from Mississippi State University in 1929, an M.A. in political science and economics from the University of Mississippi in 1936, and graduated from Jackson School of Law in 1938.

Cooper was a teacher of vocational agriculture from 1930 to 1935 and served as assistant director of the Mississippi State Planning Commission from 1936 to 1938. From 1938 to 1949, he was executive director of the Mississippi Farm Bureau Federation. He was chief executive officer of Mississippi Chemical Corp., from 1949 until his retirement in 1973.

Cooper is a member and former director of the Mississippi Council of Farm Cooperatives and the National Council of Farm Cooperatives. He is former chairman of the board of Mississippi Action for Progress. He is a member of the executive committee of the Southern Baptist Convention and the board of directors of the Mississippi Religious Leadership Council.

Rutherford, of Brawley, Calif., would replace Earl S. Smittcamp, term expired. Rutherford was born February 9, 1916, in Brawley, Calif. Since 1937 he has been a farmer and farmland owner in the Imperial Valley of California. He has also raised cattle since 1937. Rutherford was director of the Federal Land Bank Association of El Centro, Calif., for 10 years.

20th Anniversary of the Commission on Civil Rights

Message of the President. September 20, 1977

With the creation of the Civil Rights Commission by Title I of the Civil Rights Act of 1957, a new era emerged in the protection of the equal rights guaranteed to every citizen by the Constitution of our nation. For the first time in history, our country had an official advocate to press for the full realization of these rights in the daily lives of our people.

As we mark the twentieth anniversary of this great institution, I welcome the opportunity to express my strong personal commitment to expanding equality of opportunity for our citizens, to ending all remaining discrimination in every sphere of American life and to maintaining rigid enforcement of all Federal laws in this area.

Mindful of the oath of office I took, I am determined that my Administration will remain committed, in both spirit and action, to the enforcement of the civil rights acts that defend the individual freedoms of all our citizens.

JIMMY CARTER

NOTE: The text of the message was made available by the White House Press Office. It was not issued in the form of a White House press release.

Federal Civilian and Military Pay

Announcement of Adjustment of Certain Rates of Pay and Allowances. September 20, 1977

The President announced today that he intends to grant a 7.05 percent across-the-board pay increase for the 1.4 million Federal white-collar employees and a matching increase for the 2 million military personnel. The pay adjustments will be effective on the first day of the first applicable pay period beginning on or after October 1, 1977.

Under the Federal Pay Comparability Act of 1970, the President has responsibility for determining annually the increase needed to maintain comparability between Federal white-collar and private sector salaries for the same level of work. In making his decision on the size of the pay raise, the President is required by the Federal Pay Comparability Act to consider the recommendations of three separate advisory panels.

One recommendation was made by the President's "Pay Agent," which consists of the Secretary of Labor, the Director of the Office of Management and Budget, and the Chairman of the Civil Service Commission, acting jointly. The Pay Agent recommended a 7.05 percent across-the-board increase.

A second recommendation was made by the Federal Employees Pay Council, a five-member group of Federal employee union leaders. The Council argued that an 8.8 percent increase was justified this year.

The third recommendation was made by the President's Advisory Committee on Federal Pay, an impartial group of private sector experts established by law to advise the President on pay matters. The Committee endorsed the Pay Agent's recommendation for a 7.05 percent increase.

The 7.05 percent pay increase will cost about $3.4 billion. There is an allowance currently provided in the budget for this increase. The 8.8 percent recommended by the Federal Employees Pay Council would have cost about $850 million more than the 7.05 percent increase.

Affected by this increase are the salary schedules for Federal civilian employees of the General Schedule, the Foreign Service, and the Department of Medicine and Surgery, Veterans Administration. Federal blue-collar workers and postal employees have their pay adjusted by separate systems.

Additionally affected are the basic pay, quarters, and subsistence allowance schedules of the Uniformed Services. The law gives the President some flexibility in distributing the 7.05 percent increase among these schedules. A final decision on the precise distribution has not yet been made.

Child Health Day, 1977

Proclamation 4522. September 20, 1977

By the President of the United States of America

A Proclamation

This Nation was established to provide its people with the chance for better lives. Our early settlers and those who expanded the Nation westward bore their sacrifices and hardships with the assurance that in this free land future generations would enjoy opportunities still undreamed of.

The health of America's children today often determines what their future can be tomorrow. Over the years the number of deaths among babies has been drastically cut and we have made great strides toward eliminating the diseases and handicaps of childhood. We still have much to learn and accomplish, especially in the areas of birth abnormalities, child abuse, teenage alcoholism and drug addiction, lack of availability of medical care, and damage brought on by environmental factors.

But it is tragic for a child to die or endure lifelong handicaps from conditions we can prevent. Although such diseases as polio, measles, rubella, diphtheria and whooping cough have been subdued for the time being, they are not beaten. It is in our power to protect all our children, but nearly 40 per cent of those under the age of 15 are inadequately immunized. Some of these children will die or have serious disabilities and unborn babies will be permanently damaged from these preventable diseases and their complications.

No American child should die or suffer needless handicaps from diseases for which safe and effective vaccines are readily available. Neither should any child be deprived of adequate nutrition or a safe environment. While pushing back the walls of our knowledge and improving medical techniques may be restricted to scientists and medical experts, this is an area where every citizen can have an impact on giving our children the opportunity for better health, both now and in the years to come.

To encourage awareness of the fundamental necessity of a year-round program for the protection and the development of the Nation's health, the Congress, by joint resolution of May 18, 1928, as amended (36 U.S.C. 143) has requested the President to issue annually a proclamation designating the first Monday in October as Child Health Day and calling for its appropriate observance.

NOW, THEREFORE, I, JIMMY CARTER, President of the United States of America, do hereby proclaim Monday, October 3, 1977, as Child Health Day. I invite all Americans, as well as all agencies and organizations dedicated to the well-being of children, to unite on that day in support of activities that will alert each of us to our separate and collective responsibilities to protect and enhance the health of America's children and to provide them with the opportunity to live in safety and to grow up strong and knowledgeable about their own and their families' health needs.

IN WITNESS WHEREOF, I have hereunto set my hand this twentieth day of September, in the year of our Lord nineteen hundred seventy-seven, and of the Independence of the United States of America the two hundred and second.

JIMMY CARTER

[Filed with the Office of the Federal Register, 5:03 p.m., September 20, 1977]

Presidential Task Force on the District of Columbia

Remarks of the Vice President on the President's Decisions on Task Force Recommendations. September 21, 1977

For the past several months a congressional, District government, and executive branch task force has been meeting at the request of the President to review the major issues in Federal relations with the District of Columbia. On behalf of the President, I would particularly like to express our appreciation for the advice, help, and cooperation of the members of that task force. They include the Chairman, Charles Diggs, Senator Thomas Eagleton, Mayor Walter Washington, Chairman William Natcher, District Delegate Walter Fauntroy, Congressman Stewart McKinney, Senator Patrick Leahy, Senator Charles Mathias, and Council Chairman Sterling Tucker.

The President has now reviewed the major issues identified by the task force and reached his conclusions based on the facts and views presented, and we are outlining his decisions here this morning.

Three overriding commitments are reflected in the President's judgments on the individual issues that have been reviewed.

First, the President is dedicated to upholding the principle of full voting representation for the citizens of the District. He believes that there is no justification for denying citizens equal representation at the Federal level simply because they happen to reside in the District of Columbia.

Second, we are determined to reduce and eliminate, where possible, Federal intrusion in decisions that are of purely local concern. The people of this city should not be subjected to burdensome and wasteful executive review procedures in matters that involve no significant Federal interest whatsoever. Where substantial Federal interest may be involved, we propose to streamline and simplify review procedures wherever possible.

Third, while the financial relationship between the Federal Government and the District are extremely complex, we have tried to identify several specific areas in which progress can be made now toward greater equity, predictability, and comparability with other cities and to pinpoint other areas and issues which require longer and more detailed analysis.

Following are some of the highlights of some of the specific decisions reached by the President, and attached to my statement is a more detailed analysis of many of the other issues.

First, to promote equal representation the administration supports approval of a constitutional amendment proposed by District Delegate Fauntroy, which would provide full voting representation in both Houses of the Congress, as well as in the selection of the President and the Vice President and in the ratification of constitutional amendments.

Secondly, to expand home rule for the District, the President supports congressional action to eliminate Presidential review of mayoral vetoes that are overridden by the City Council and to repeal the so-called Federal enclave and to streamline the procedures for congressional review of locally enacted legislation.

Third, to provide greater equity and predictability in the financial relationship between the Federal Government and the District, the administration is committed to an increase in the fiscal '79 Federal payment authorization from $300 to $317 million, with a simultaneous effort by the District to improve use of existing resources through reductions in any excessive employee authorization levels; to share financial responsibility for the RFK Stadium and pension plan funding; and to extend the city's authority to borrow from the Federal Treasury.

Creation of the D.C. task force last spring by the President reflects the high priority that he attaches to the key issues affecting our Nation's Capital and the people who live here. I'm proud of the decisions that have been made as the result of this process. I believe they represent the most progressive steps taken toward resolving problems of our Capital City by any administration in recent years.

As I indicated, fact sheets indicating more detail on these decisions are attached. And I'm asking Bunny Mitchell, who served as the convener of these meetings and of the task force and who serves as a special assistant to the President on these matters, and Jim Dyke, of my staff, to answer any questions that you might have.

NOTE: The Vice President spoke at 10:05 a.m. to reporters assembled in the Briefing Room at the White House. On the same day, the Vice President's Press Office released a fact sheet on the President's decisions.

Meeting With Foreign Minister Ismail Fahmy of Egypt

White House Statement Issued Following the Meeting Between the President and the Foreign Minister. September 21, 1977

President Carter and Egyptian Foreign Minister Ismail Fahmy met in the Cabinet Room for 1 hour, 5 minutes. The meeting was also attended by Vice President Walter Mondale; Secretary of State Cyrus Vance; Zbigniew Brzezinski, Assistant to the President for National Security Affairs; Hamilton Jordan, Assistant to the President; Robert Lipshutz, Counsel to the President; David Aaron, Deputy Assistant to the President for National Security Affairs; Alfred L. Atherton, Jr., Assistant Secretary of State for Near Eastern and South Asian Affairs; Herman Eilts, U.S. Ambassador to Egypt; and William Quandt, National Security Council staff member, on the American side; and Ashraf Ghorbal, Egyptian Ambassador to the United States; Minister of Foreign Affairs, Under Secretary Osama al-Baz; First Secretary Dr. Mohammed Baradai, Executive Secretary of Foreign Minister's Cabinet; and Minister Counselor Mohammed Shaker, Egyptian Embassy, on the Egyptian side.

The President began by expressing his pleasure at welcoming Foreign Minister Fahmy to the White House in this latest round of his meetings with Middle Eastern foreign ministers. The President was gratified to receive a personal letter from President Sadat conveyed by the Foreign Minister. He repeated to the Foreign Minister his support for the key role Egypt continues to play in efforts to reach a negotiated peace settlement of the Middle East conflict. The President underlined his own conviction that a just and lasting peace in this vital area of the world requires compromise and courageous leadership from all the parties to the negotiations.

The President and Foreign Minister agreed on the importance of reconvening the Geneva conference by the end of this year, thus beginning the process of negotiations between the parties. To that end, they discussed the substantive issues of a settlement. Secretary Vance will pursue the discussion of these issues with the Foreign Minister, both to hear Egypt's concrete ideas on these issues and to explain some specific American suggestions on the elements of a peace treaty designed to help reconcile the differences between the parties. The President and the Foreign Minister also addressed the problem of Palestinian representation at Geneva, with a view to finding a solution during the course of these current talks the President and Secretary Vance are holding with Middle East foreign ministers.

The President reaffirmed the importance he attaches to U.S. relations with Egypt and continued American support for Egyptian economic development efforts. Finally, the President asked the Foreign Minister to convey to President Sadat assurances that the United States remains committed to the search for a comprehensive peace settlement in the Middle East.

International Labor Organization

Letter to the President from Prime Minister Leo Tindemans of Belgium, President of the Council of the European Communities. September 21, 1977

The President received yesterday the following letter from Prime Minister Leo Tindemans of Belgium, acting in his capacity as President of the Council of the European Community—Nine. President Carter announced that he will study with care all the points raised in the letter.

———

Brussels, September 9, 1977

Mr. President,

I am writing to you on behalf of the Nine member Governments of the European Communities to convey to you our views on the present situation in the International Labour Organisation.

The member Governments of the European Communities have been following recent events in the ILO with keen concern. We share the preoccupations of the United States Government. Like the US Government, we consider that certain developments at the annual Conference of the ILO, held in June 1977, were damaging to the Organisation. One of the results of that Conference, the failure to adopt the report of the Committee on the Application of Conventions, seems to us particularly regrettable. It is our firm view that the successful operation of the ILO requires that the annual reports of this Committee should be adopted and should be acted upon. It is our intention, which we believe is shared by many member Governments, to ensure that the main points in this years report, and in particular its endorsement of the need for a single standard in judging performance, are actively pursued within the organisation.

The 1977 Conference was the more disappointing in that we consider the ILO to be an element of major and indeed growing importance in the UN system. As the World Employment Conference showed, the ILO has a significant role to play in the attempts of the United Nations to tackle the crucial problems of north/south relations and of global economic development. It has a substantial contribution to make to the success of the basic needs strategy. Similarly it has a major contribution to make in the field of human rights where the ILO machinery is the longest established and, so far, the most effective of that deployed by any international organisation. Finally the regular work of the ILO, the only world-wide tripartite organisation, in standard setting and in improving conditions of work throughout the world seems to us of undiminished importance.

For these reasons we consider the ILO remains an organisation fully worthy of our support. It would be a major blow both to the Organisation itself and to the

UN system as a whole if the US were to withdraw. Nor do we believe that the resulting situation would be readily rectified. The task of reform and of achieving the objectives we share in the ILO might well be impossible in the absence of the United States even though the Governments of the Nine would continue their efforts to preserve and enhance the value of the ILO's services to the international community.

On the other hand, working together with the United States in the organisation and seeking the support and goodwill of the many member states who share our objectives, we consider that there would be a reasonable prospect of making progress in the right direction and of preserving the integrity of the Organisation. This would of course require flexibility on the part of all involved in the negotiations which lie ahead. We believe it will be possible to secure a strenghthening of the defence of due process through amendment of Article 17 of the Standing Orders. The necessary restructuring of the Organisation, including, for instance, changes in voting procedures, will require the most careful consideration. But if the discussions are approached in a spirit of mutual understanding the essential requirements of the membership of the Organisation, including the preservation both of the principles of tripartism and of the partnership between the industrial and developing countries can be satisfied.

There is of course no prospect of resolving these complicated issues in the next two months. But a recent opinion by the Legal Adviser to the ILO in response to our inquiry concludes that notice of intent to withdraw from membership can be extended for a defined period of time. We greatly hope that the United States will withdraw its notice of intent. If however there are factors which make that impossible, we urge that you take appropriate steps to extend the formal notice for a new period so as to allow time to work out lasting solutions to the problems which confront the ILO. Such an extension would cover next year's Conference, to which any results of our work in the months ahead will need to be submitted.

In this way all of us, together, will be able to work effectively in support of an organisation whose historical commitment to social justice is so consonant with the purpose of your Government.

Respectfully yours,

LEO TINDEMANS

THE PRESIDENT'S NEWS CONFERENCE OF SEPTEMBER 21, 1977

RESIGNATION OF BERT LANCE

THE PRESIDENT. I would like to read first a letter that I have just received from Bert Lance.

"My Dear Mr. President: There is no need for me to go into the events of the last few weeks. You know them well as do the American people.

"You also know that previously I had said three things to you about the importance of the so-called 'Lance affair.' I will recall those for you:

"First, it was and is important that my name and reputation be cleared for me, my wife, my children, my grandchildren, and those who have trust and faith in me; and, I believe that this has been done. As I said at the Senate hearings, my conscience is clear.

"Second, it was and is important for me to be able to say that people should be willing to make the necessary sacrifices and be willing to serve their government and country. This I can still say, and say proudly.

"Third, I believe in the absolute need for government to be able to attract good people from the private sector. We must find ways to encourage these people.

"As to my position as Director of the Office of Management and Budget: I hope the American people feel that during my eight months in office I have met well my responsibilities and performed well my tasks. This has been an important aspect of the entire matter.

"However, I have to ask the question at what price do I remain? My only intention in coming to Washington in the first place was to make a contribution to this country and to you.

"I am convinced that I can continue to be an effective Director of the Office of Management and Budget. However, because of the amount of controversy and the continuing nature of it, I have decided to submit my resignation as Director of OMB. I desire to return to my native State of Georgia.

"It has been a high privilege and honor to be a part of your administration. Hopefully, I have made a contribution which will be of lasting value. Respectfully yours."

Signed, Bert Lance.

Bert Lance is my friend. I know him personally, as well as if he was my own brother. I know him without any doubt in my mind or heart to be a good and an honorable man.

He was given, this past weekend, a chance to answer thousands of questions that have been raised about him, unproven allegations that have been raised against him, and he did it well. He told the truth. And I think he proved that our system of government works, because when he was given a chance to testify on his own behalf, he was able to clear his name.

My responsibility, along with Bert's, has been and is to make sure that the American people can have justified confidence in our own Government. And we also have an additional responsibility which is just as difficult, and that is to protect the reputation of decent men and women. Nothing that I have heard or read has shaken my belief in Bert's ability or his integrity.

There have been numerous allegations which, I admit, are true, that a lot of the problem has been brought on Bert Lance by me, because of the extraordinary standards that we have tried to set in Government and the expectations of the American people that were engendered during my own campaign and my Inauguration statement and as has been so strongly supported by Bert in his voluntary sacrifice, financially and otherwise, to come to Washington.

It was I who insisted that Bert agree to sell his substantial holdings in bank stock. Had he stayed there, in a selfish fashion, and enriched himself and his own family financially, I'm sure he would have been spared any allegations of impropriety. But he wanted to come to Washington and serve his Government because I asked him to, and he did.

I accept Bert's resignation with the greatest sense of regret and sorrow. He's a good man. Even those who have made other statements about Bert have never alleged, on any occasion, that he did not do a good job as the Director of the Office of Management and Budget. He's close to me and always will be, and I think he's made the right decision, because it would be difficult for him to devote full time to his responsibilities in the future.

And although I regret his resignation, I do accept it.

I would be glad to answer any questions you might have about this or other matters.

Ms. Thomas [Helen Thomas, United Press International].

QUESTIONS

Q. Mr. President, there have been reports that you knew early on what the charges were, that Mr. Lance had told you some of the allegations last January. Is that so, and can you tell us what you knew? And also, did you ask for his resignation or encourage it, and what made you accept it?

THE PRESIDENT. I did not ask for Bert's resignation. Bert Lance and I communicate without embarrassment, without constraint, and without evasion of issues. I thought Bert did a superb job Thursday, Friday, and Saturday in answering all the questions that had been leveled about him and against him.

Monday morning about 6 o'clock, Bert came to my office, and we spent about 45 minutes going over all the present questions that still remained, the prospects for the future. I told Bert I thought he had exonerated himself completely, proven our system worked, and asked him to make his own decision about what his choice would be.

He told me yesterday afternoon that he had decided that it would be best to resign. He wanted to talk to his wife again. He wanted to discuss the question with his attorney, Clark Clifford, before he made a final judgment. Mr. Clifford was in Detroit, came back this afternoon, and that was why the press conference was delayed.

This was a decision that Bert made. I did not disagree with it, and I think he's made a very unselfish and wise judgment.

The other question that you asked was whether and when I knew about charges that were made against Bert. The only thing that I ever heard about before Bert became OMB Director was last fall I knew that there had been questions about the Calhoun National Bank and overdrafts. My understanding at that time was that the overdraft question referred to his 1974 campaign debt.

The first time I heard about it was when Bert mentioned it to me in Plains about 2 weeks later. I think the date is now determined to be the 1st of December. I was called from Atlanta and told that the matter had been resolved by the Comptroller's Office and by the Justice Department.

On that date was the first time that either Bert or I knew that the Justice Department had been involved at all. And my understanding then was that it was an oversight and, had the oversight not occurred, that the Justice Department would have resolved the issue long before.

So, I would hope that in the future the complete FBI report might be made available. That's a decision for Bert Lance to make. But I think if any of you would read it, you would see that approximately a hundred people were interviewed—three of them from the Justice Department, three of them from the Comptroller's department. All of the analyses of Bert Lance's character and ability were good and favorable.

And I don't think that any mistake was made. I think he was qualified then; I think he's qualified now. And there was no attempt to conceal anything from me nor my staff.

Q. Mr. President, you've spoken so highly of Mr. Lance again this afternoon. I wonder if you feel that he was unfairly drummed out of the Government?

THE PRESIDENT. That's a difficult question for me to answer. I have had personal knowledge of many of the statements and happenings that have been widely publicized. Some of them were greatly exaggerated; some of them were actually untrue. On some occasions, the report of an incident was not unbiased, but unfair. In general, I think the media have been fair. There are some exceptions. In general, I think that the Senate committee has been fair.

Bert has now had a chance to let his own positions be known, and I think that at this point, his resignation is voluntary. He needs to go home and take care of his own business. I think it's obvious that if he stayed here he couldn't serve completely and with full commitment to his job. And I think his honor and his integrity have been proven.

Q. Mr. President, Mr. Lance was in charge of some very important subjects: the Federal budget, of course, and Government reorganization. What are your plans for short-term continuity in those areas, and in the long term, do you have a successor in mind?

THE PRESIDENT. I've not thought about a successor because the vacancy has just become apparent to me recently. I haven't given any thought to that yet.

If there's one agency of the Government in which the President is daily involved, not only with the director but also with immediate subordinates, it's the Office of Management and Budget. This is, in effect, an extension of the Oval Office.

And I happen to know Bert Lance's immediate subordinates much better than I do the subordinates of any other department in Government. They are highly competent. They've been chosen by him and me or are long-time professionals there, and there has been in the past few weeks absolutely no slippage in the schedules that Bert and I and others had evolved earlier this year.

There has been no instance where a major question has been ignored nor where responsibility has been delayed. And for the time being, I and those assistants that Bert and I have chosen together will continue.

I have not yet had a chance to talk to Bert about how quickly he can leave, how long he can stay. I would guess that he'll be wanting to leave fairly shortly. But there will be an orderly transition, and I will decide beginning after today on who a successor might be.

Q. Mr. President, you said, sir, that you did not ask for the resignation. But you said it was, you felt, the right decision. Does that mean, sir, that you really came down to feel that he could no longer be an effective advocate for the administration on Capitol Hill?

THE PRESIDENT. No, I think it would be a mistake to attribute Bert's decision to the fact that he could not be an effective advocate of the administration's positions. There are so many advocates that even if one were completely incapacitated, other advocates could put forward the arguments for the administration's position.

I think that it would be better to let Bert answer this question, because some of it involves his own personal affairs back home. But he has suffered greatly in a financial way. The value of his stock, if purchased, in his major holdings in the National Bank of Georgia is quite greatly above the market value, because it involves a substantial controlling interest in the bank itself. Several would-be purchasers, I understand, in the last few days, have come forward wanting to buy the stock but are reluctant to do so because of the high focus of publicity on the sale.

They would be scrutinized thoroughly. And I think, perhaps, that's expectable; I don't deplore that. So, they've been reluctant to do it.

I think ·Bert can very quickly get his own financial affairs back in order if he takes care of them himself. He has complied stringently in removing himself from his own affairs in the blind trust arrangement. He could have cheated on that arrangement; he did not. So, part of his reasons for resigning, with which I have an understanding, is to help himself, to get his own family affairs and financial affairs back in good shape. I don't know what the future might hold if he couldn't do that. I'm afraid it might get even worse than it is now. This is no fault of his. If there's any fault there, it's mine because of the strict requirements we placed on him.

Obviously, it takes a great deal of Bert's time to look up ancient data that goes back to '72, '73, '74. Did you have a power of attorney? How many overdrafts did your in-laws have? How many trips did you take on the plane to your home in Sea Island, and so forth. This has required an enormous amount of Bert's time.

And my expectation, along with Bert's, is that this kind of investigation and demand on his time might continue. Bert is the kind of person who comes to work at 5 o'clock in the morning. He puts in, even in these past few weeks, I'd say, 12 hours a day or more on his OMB job.

But it obviously is disconcerting to him. And I think, to be perfectly frank, the constant high publicity that has accrued to this case, even if completely fair and unbiased, creates doubt among the news media, among the people of this country, about the integrity of me and our Government, even though I think there is no doubt about Bert's being a man of complete integrity.

So, there are multiple reasons for his decision. And I don't think any of them should be interpreted as being a reflection on him.

Q. I suppose there's an obvious follow-up, Mr. President, and that is, if he had not offered to resign, would you have wanted him to stay on?

THE PRESIDENT. That's hard to say. As I have said several times in brief, impromptu news encounters in the last few weeks, the decision that Bert Lance and I make together will be acceptable to the American people. And I have had large numbers of people who have asked me not to let Bert Lance resign. A group from Tennessee and North Carolina were in the White House this afternoon for a briefing on the Panama Canal Treaty. They rose, and the Governor of Tennessee said, "We all hope that Bert Lance will not resign." I had twelve speakers of the house of State legislatures here last Friday. They unanimously voted and importuned me not to let Bert resign. I felt, and still feel, that it's basically a decision for him.

I don't know the details of Bert's financial dealings back home. I don't have the time nor the inclination to learn them. All I know about it is what I have had a chance to read in the news media. So the decision was Bert's. And when he discussed it with me, it was not from a posture of a subordinate talking to a superior; it was in the posture of friends who understood one another, discussing mutually what ought to be done about a difficult situation.

I think it was a courageous and also a patriotic gesture on Bert's part to resign.

Q. Mr. President, how much has your credibility been damaged by this incident and by Mr. Lance's resignation?

THE PRESIDENT. I don't know. I think that as best I could from one hour to another, one day to another, and as best Bert could from one hour and one day to another, we've done what was right, as judged by what we knew at that time.

We've been partners in every sense of the word since he's been here, and you, having covered the government of Georgia, know that we were equally close partners in Georgia.

I have never known the head of a State or Federal agency who is more competent and has better judgment and who understands me better and can work in closer harmony with me. But whether my own credibility has been damaged, I can't say. I would guess to some degree an unpleasant situation like this would be damaging somewhat, but I just have to accept that if it comes.

Q. How will you replace the kind of close relationship that you've had with him, and how much does that concern you?

THE PRESIDENT. I don't think there's any way that I could find anyone to replace Bert Lance that would be, in my judgment, as competent, as strong, as decent, and as close to me as a friend and adviser as he has been. And obviously, the Government will continue, and I hope to do a good job as President, and I'm sure a successor will be adequate.

But there has been a special relationship between me and Bert Lance that transcended official responsibilities or duties or even governmental service over the last 6 or 7 years. So, he has occupied a special place in my governmental career, in my political career, and in my personal life, and I don't think there's any way anyone could replace him now.

Q. Mr. President, apart from Mr. Lance's reasons for resigning, can you share more of your thoughts for accepting his resignation? You said that your belief in his integrity has not been shaken.

THE PRESIDENT. That is correct.

Q. Just recently, House Speaker O'Neill said he can be an effective Budget Director in the future. Why do you feel, sir, that Mr. Lance did have to go?

THE PRESIDENT. I've described to you my assessment of Bert Lance's reasons, and I have read his letter, which I'm sure was very carefully prepared by Bert to emphasize the most important reasons for his resignation. I don't have any way to know anything further beyond that answer.

Q. Mr. President, you referred to the high standards you set for your people during the campaign. You said often that you would not tolerate impropriety or even the appearance of impropriety.

Sir, I think now a lot of people are looking at your standards against the Bert Lance case. You now know what the charges and allegations were. I'd like to ask you whether you, today, still feel that Mr. Lance has avoided the appearance of impropriety or whether a new standard is now in operation?

THE PRESIDENT. The standards were high at the beginning, the standards are still high, and the standards have been high in the service of Bert Lance. There has been not even one allegation that I have ever heard of that Bert Lance did not perform his duties as Director of OMB in a superlative way.

There's not been one allegation that he violated his responsibility or his oath when he was sworn in, that he's done anything improper at all, that he's violated any law. And even those allegations that were made about his life several years ago, in my opinion, have been proven false and without foundation.

I think there has been an adequate opportunity for Bert, after some unfortunate delay, in presenting his answers in the Senate hearings this past week. So, I don't think that any blame should accrue to Bert Lance for having acted improperly or having lowered the standards of our Government.

Q. Mr. President, I would like to follow that up with a little more specific question. During the campaign, you not only campaigned on the promise that your appointees would avoid the appearance of impropriety but you also campaigned against the privileged few who had too much influence and against expense account padders and that sort of thing.

Mr. Lance, by his own admission—I think this isn't in doubt—overdrew his checking accounts by thousands of dollars on a regular basis. He flew on corporate planes for what appear to be political and, perhaps, personal reasons. What I think many of us are interested in, sir, is your justification for reaffirming your belief in his integrity, given the positions you took as a candidate.

THE PRESIDENT. My impression is that I've answered that question already, but I would be glad to reaffirm what I've said. I have seen the statements about him. I've read the charges against him. I've heard the allegations about him of even criminal acts. I've seen some of his accusers apologize publicly for having made a serious mistake, for having made a peremptory and a preliminary judgment without hearing his explanation which, when it came, was adequate.

I just don't feel that I can preserve just the appearance of the White House to the exclusion of everything else. I also have a responsibility as President to be interested in justice and fairness and in giving someone who is accused erroneously a chance to answer the questions.

There has always been a possibility that in the last week's Senate hearings that Bert could not answer the allegations adequately, that he would prove to have violated a law. That was not the case. And I think my judgment that Bert had a right to officially answer every question, in 3 hard days of interrogation by highly competent Senators and well-qualified staffs after they've had months to prepare, was justified.

He's answered them adequately. So, it would not be possible for me, just because one of my leaders or employees was accused of something, to discharge them or demand their resignation on the basis of an accusation about which I had doubt and which later proved to be false.

Q. Mr. President, sir, I'd like to ask you about your statement, repeated statement that Mr. Lance never did anything illegal. The Comptroller of the Currency reported that Mr. Lance's overdraft loans of more than $5,000 violated the banking law, and Mr. Lance, I think, conceded that his failure to report loans to board of directors of the two banks he ran also was an infraction of the banking statutes.

It's true there are no civil—they are civil statutes and there are no criminal penalties. But how do you justify this with your statement that he never broke any law?

THE PRESIDENT. Well, my assessment is that you are trying to succeed where the Senate committee failed. There was no judgment made that Bert Lance did anything illegal. The only Comptroller's report that I saw specifically said that he had done nothing illegal, and I think that he's adequately explained his position. He had 3 days to do it in. I think he did it well. And I have no information to add to what Bert has already revealed to the Senators and to the public.

Q. Mr. President, I'd like to follow up on Judy's [Judy Woodruff, NBC News] question, not directly, on how this may have damaged you. At the first meeting of your Cabinet appointees, Cabinet designees at St. Simons Island—there was a meeting which Mr. Lance attended, and you were there—it was pointed out to every member of this Cabinet a feeling on your part and those of some of the staff closest to you, that because of the recent past political history in the country and partly because of the expectations that had been raised by your campaign, that this was sort of a last chance; that if the public became disappointed and disillusioned in your administration, that the result would be very, very damaging.

Early in this press conference, you said Bert Lance is my friend, I have known him personally as well as my own brother and without any doubt in my mind or heart that he could be, that he was a good and honorable man.

THE PRESIDENT. That's correct.

Q. Do you think that you may have been, if only slightly, less than fully prudent and diligent because of your feeling towards Mr. Lance in the way you read some of these things, when he talked to you on November 15, when he talked to you on December 1, when the FBI report, which I understand has also an appendix with some of these judgmental matters about the propriety of some of Mr. Lance's banking practices—in retrospect, do you feel that in effect two standards were applied: one, a very firm, strong standard which you set, and one for Mr. Lance, who you knew so well that you felt you didn't have to examine it that closely?

THE PRESIDENT. No. I don't think I've been remiss in that incident at all, even looking at it from this retrospective point of view.

Obviously, you can make a much better judgment on someone who comes in as a member of a Cabinet if you yourself have known that person for years, if you know

that person's general reputation, if you've worked intimately with that person in times of stress and matters of challenge and have seen the basic competence, courage, honesty, unselfishness there. This existed in Bert Lance.

And I don't think there's any doubt that the FBI check of Bert Lance was just as thorough as was the FBI investigation of any other member of the Cabinet. I think that if you examine the entire FBI report now, that you would confirm that if that was all you knew about him and had never seen Bert Lance before, you would agree that he was superlatively qualified to be a Cabinet-level officer.

So, I don't think there's any feeling on my part that my friendship with him distorted my point of view in assessing his competence. My friendship for Bert Lance, my long knowledge of him just confirmed a very favorable assessment of his qualifications by those who did not know him.

Q. Has the Lance case diverted your attention at all away from important matters at home and abroad? Has there been a price that you've had to pay there and the American public has had to pay because of the Lance case and the heavy attention being placed upon it?

THE PRESIDENT. Well, I have to admit that there has been some diversion of my attention. I've been deeply concerned about the case. I've been concerned about Bert Lance personally. I've been concerned about the impact on my administration if some of those serious allegations proved to be true. And it hasn't taken nearly so much of my own time as it has that of, say, Jody Powell, who's had to face this questioning every day, which I think was a good thing.

Bob Lipshutz on my staff has had to confirm the accuracy of the answers to questions that were raised by the Comptroller's report and by other testimony that has come forward. Some of my staff have put a lot of time on it. I don't think their effort was misplaced. I think it was good for us to be informed. I think it was good for Jody, in his daily briefings to you, to be accurate. And I think had we, through error or through neglect, given you a false statement, even though it might have been completely unintentional, that would have been a very serious matter.

But as far as my own time and effort was concerned, it's had a slight but detectable effect of diverting me from some things. I don't think the country has suffered, and I think that's one of the reasons that Bert decided to resign—not for his own benefit, but to make sure that I didn't have this potential problem in the future.

Q. If Mr. Lance had not decided to resign, were you prepared to have him stay on or would you have tried to persuade him to resign?

THE PRESIDENT. I can't answer that question because it's, first of all, hypothetical. As I said before, it wasn't a matter of Bert Lance operating in isolation from me. We had thorough discussions about the matter. I left it completely up to him. He and I talked about the advantages of his staying, the disadvantages of his staying to him, to my administration, to the Government, to his family. And Bert consulted with his own attorney, he consulted with several Members of the Congress, he consulted with the people back home.

He talked it over with members of his family, and he came to me and said he had decided it was best for him and for me if he resigned. And as has always been the case between me and Bert, I was honest with him. I didn't artificially try to talk him out of it, because as we discussed

the same facts and the same issues and the same prospects for the future, I think that our minds were working in the same direction.

But I have always trusted Bert Lance to do the proper and the unselfish thing. And my guess is that he was much more concerned about me and my administration and the reputation of the Government and the diversion of our attention to his case away from things that were important for the people. I think that was by far the most important factor in his decision.

Thank you very much.

NOTE: President Carter's fifteenth news conference began at 5 p.m. in Room 450 of the Old Executive Office Building. It was broadcast live on radio and television.

National School Lunch Week, 1977

Proclamation 4523. September 22, 1977

By the President of the United States of America

A Proclamation

Since 1946, the National School Lunch Program has been serving nutritious lunches to the school children of America. In its first year, the program served lunch to 6 million children daily; today nearly 25 million children in 92,600 schools and residential child care institutions take advantage of this program every day. Lunches under this program are available to 94 percent of all children attending public schools in America.

As the program begins its fourth decade, its dedicated workers are making a significant effort to improve the nutritional quality and appeal of the food while developing menus in keeping with the changing tastes of our children. Those involved in the program maintain their commitment to recognize the children's needs in order to serve them better.

In recognition of the program's contribution to America's youth, the Congress, by a joint resolution of October 9, 1962 (76 Stat. 779; 36 U.S.C. 168), has designated the week beginning the second Sunday of October of each year as National School Lunch Week, and has requested the President to issue annually a proclamation calling for its appropriate observance.

Now, THEREFORE, I, JIMMY CARTER, President of the United States of America, do hereby urge the people of the United States to observe the week of October 9, 1977, as National School Lunch Week and to give special recognition to the role of good nutrition in building a stronger America through its youth.

IN WITNESS WHEREOF, I have hereunto set my hand this twenty-second day of September, in the year of our Lord nineteen hundred seventy-seven, and of the Independence of the United States of America the two hundred and second.

JIMMY CARTER

[Filed with the Office of the Federal Register, 3:39 p.m., September 22, 1977]

United States Parole Commission

Nomination of Three Persons To Be Commissioners.   September 22, 1977

The President today announced three persons whom he will nominate as Commissioners of the United States Parole Commission. They are:

Benjamin J. Malcolm, of St. Albans, N.Y., who would replace Curtis C. Crawford, term expired. Malcolm was born August 24, 1919, in Philadelphia, Pa. He received a B.A. from Morehouse College in 1940 and an M.P.A. from New York University in 1970. He served in the U.S. Army from 1942 to 1946.

Malcolm worked for the New York City Parole Commission from 1948 to 1967, serving as a parole officer, then deputy chief parole officer. From 1967 to 1970, he was assistant director of labor relations for the city of New York. He has been with the New York City Department of Correction since 1970, serving as deputy commissioner from 1970 to 1972 and commissioner since 1972.

Cecil M. McCall, of Roswell, Ga., who would replace Maurice H. Sigler, resigned. McCall was born June 22, 1936, in Pickens, S.C. He received an A.B. from the University of South Carolina in 1961. He served in the U.S. Air Force from 1954 to 1958.

McCall worked for the March of Dimes Foundation from 1961 to 1969, rising from representative to regional director. From 1970 to 1972, he was director of the Georgia Probation Department. Since 1972 he has been a member of the Georgia State Board of Pardons and Paroles, and from 1972 to 1976 he served as chairman.

Robert D. Vincent, of Oklahoma City, Okla., who would replace Lawrence A. Carpenter, resigned. Vincent was born November 15, 1942, in Tucson, Ariz. He received a B.A., M.S., and Ph. D. from Oklahoma University.

In 1968 and 1969, Vincent was a research psychologist at Battelle Memorial

Institute in Columbus, Ohio. From 1969 to 1972, he was president of Action-Analysis in Washington. He served as president of Antec, Inc., in Oklahoma City from 1970 until 1972. Since 1972 he has been a member of the Oklahoma State Regents for Higher Education.

Rehabilitation Services Administration

Nomination of Robert R. Humphreys To Be Commissioner. September 22, 1977

The President today announced that he will nominate Robert R. Humphreys, of Alexandria, Va., to be Commissioner of the Rehabilitation Services Administration. He would replace Andrew S. Adams, resigned.

Humphreys was born May 7, 1938, in Eugene, Oreg. He received a B.A. from the University of Washington in 1959 and an LL.B. from George Washington University Law School in 1965. He served in the U.S. Army from 1959 to 1962.

Humphreys worked as a law clerk in 1963 and 1964, and from 1965 to 1971 he was with the Air Transport Association of America, serving as manager of public affairs services, then assistant to the vice president for Federal affairs.

Since 1971 Humphreys has been special counsel to the U.S. Senate Committee on Human Resources, where he is chief legislative adviser on the committee to Senator Jennings Randolph, the ranking majority member.

Humphreys is a director of the National Center for a Barrier Free Environment, a nonprofit corporation promoting access of handicapped individuals to manmade environment. He has spoken at the conventions of the American Coalition of Citizens with Disabilities and the National Council of State Agencies for the Blind.

Alaska Natural Gas Transportation System

Message to the Congress. September 22, 1977

To the Congress of the United States:

Natural gas has become the Nation's scarcest and most desired fuel. It is in our interest to bring the reserves in Alaska to market at the lowest possible price. Consequently, I am today sending the Congress my decision and report on an Alaska Natural Gas Transportation System.

The selection of the Alcan project was made after an exhaustive review required by the Alaska Natural Gas Transportation Act of 1976 determined that the Alcan Pipeline System will deliver more natural gas at less cost to a greater number of Americans than any other proposed transportation system.

The Alcan proposal, taken together with the recently signed Agreement on Principles with Canada, demonstrates that our two countries working together can transport more energy more efficiently than either of us could transport alone.

Unnecessary delay would greatly increase the total cost of the pipeline system. I urge the Congress to act expeditiously to approve this important project.

JIMMY CARTER

The White House,
September 22, 1977.

United States Ambassador to Colombia

Nomination of Diego C. Asencio.
September 23, 1977

The President today announced that he will nominate Diego C. Asencio, of Waldwick, N.J., to be Ambassador Extraordinary and Plenipotentiary of the United States to Colombia. He would replace Phillip V. Sanchez, resigned.

Asencio was born July 15, 1931, in Nijar, Spain. He received a B.S.F.S. from Georgetown University in 1952. He served in the U.S. Army from 1955 to 1957.

Asencio joined the Foreign Service in 1957 and served as an intelligence research analyst at the State Department until 1959. From 1959 to 1962, he was consular officer in Mexico City, and from 1962 to 1964 he was political officer in Panama.

From 1964 to 1965, Asencio was an international relations officer at the State Department, and from 1965 to 1967 he was special assistant to the Assistant Secretary of State for Inter-American Affairs. From 1967 to 1972, he was political officer, then Deputy Chief of Mission, in Lisbon.

Asencio was counselor for political affairs in Brasilia from 1972 to 1975, and since 1975 has been Deputy Chief of Mission in Caracas.

Department of Energy

Nomination of Lynn R. Coleman To Be General Counsel. September 23, 1977

The President today announced that he will nominate Lynn R. Coleman, of Washington, D.C., to be General Counsel of the Department of Energy.

Coleman was born August 17, 1939. He received a B.A. from Abilene Christian College in 1961 and graduated with honors from the University of Texas School of Law in 1964.

Since 1965 Coleman has practiced law with the Houston-based firm of Vinson & Elkins. In 1973 he established the firm's Washington office, and he has been in Washington since then, engaging principally in an energy-related practice. His experience includes litigation, both civil and criminal, oil and gas law, legislation, and practice before the Federal Power Commission and the Federal Energy Administration.

Department of Energy

Nomination of Phillip S. Hughes To Be an Assistant Secretary. September 23, 1977

The President today announced that he will nominate Phillip S. Hughes, of Maryland, to be Assistant Secretary of Energy. His area of responsibility would be intergovernmental and institutional relations.

Hughes was born February 26, 1917. He received a B.A. from the University of Washington in 1938.

Hughes worked for the U.S. Bureau of the Budget from 1949 to 1969, serving as a budget examiner, Head of Congressional Affairs, and retiring as Deputy Director.

In 1969 and 1970, he served as acting president of the National Institute of Public Affairs. In 1971 and 1972, he was a senior fellow at the Brookings Institution, in charge of the public management studies project.

Hughes worked for the General Accounting Office from 1972 to 1977, serving as Director of the Office of Federal

Elections from 1972 to 1973, and as Assistant Comptroller General after 1973. Since January 1977, he has been a consultant to the Development and Resources Corp. and the Smithsonian Institution.

Federal Energy Regulatory Commission

Nomination of Matthew Holden, Jr., To Be a Member. September 23, 1977

The President today announced that he will nominate Matthew Holden, Jr., of Wisconsin, to be a member of the Federal Energy Regulatory Commission for a term of 4 years.

Holden was born September 12, 1931, in Mound Bayou, Miss. He received a B.A. from Roosevelt University in 1952, and an M.A. (1955) and Ph. D. (1961) from Northwestern University in political science. He served in the U.S. Army from 1955 to 1957.

From 1959 to 1961, Holden was a research associate at the Institute of Government and Public Affairs at the University of Illinois. He was a lecturer in political science at Northwestern University in 1961, and was on the faculty at Wayne State University from 1961 to 1963 and from 1966 to 1969, rising from instructor to professor. From 1963 to 1966, he was an assistant professor at the University of Pittsburgh.

Holden has been a professor at the University of Wisconsin since 1969. Since 1975 he has been on leave, serving on the Public Service Commission.

Holden is a member of the National Urban League's Education Advisory Committee, and was a member of the Urban League's Delegate Assembly in 1971, 1972, and 1973. He was a charter member of the Pennsylvania Negro Democratic Committee in 1965 and 1966 and served on the U.S. Air Quality Advisory Board from 1971 to 1974. He was appointed by the Governor to the Wisconsin Citizens' Study Committee on Metropolitan Problems from 1971 to 1973.

Budget Rescission

Message to the Congress. September 23, 1977

To the Congress of the United States:

In accordance with the Impoundment Control Act of 1974, I herewith propose rescission of $2.7 million in general criminal justice and corrections grant funds appropriated to the Department of Justice.

The details of the proposed rescission are contained in the attached report.

JIMMY CARTER

The White House,
    September 23, 1977.

NOTE: The attachment detailing the rescission is printed in the FEDERAL REGISTER of September 29, 1977.

The message was announced by the White House Press Office. It was not issued in the form of a White House press release.

Leif Erikson Day, 1977

Proclamation 4524. September 23, 1977

By the President of the United States of America

A Proclamation

Once again it is appropriate for Americans to honor the intrepid Norse explorers who overcame hardship and adversity to reach our shores so long ago.

The United States is a young Nation, but our debt to that courageous Norseperson, Leif Erikson, predates 1776 and recalls a distant age when brave adventurers sailed forth into the unknown. As a people we continue to embody this spirit of bold discovery, and we take pride in his historical exploits.

As a mark of respect for Leif Erikson and the Norse explorers, the Congress of the United States, by joint resolution approved September 2, 1964 (78 Stat. 849, 36 U.S.C. 169c), authorized the President to proclaim October 9 in each year as Leif Erikson Day.

NOW, THEREFORE, I, JIMMY CARTER, President of the United States of America, do hereby designate Sunday, October 9, 1977, as Leif Erikson Day and I direct the appropriate Government officials to display the flag of the United States on all Government buildings that day.

I also invite the people of the United States to honor the memory of Leif Erikson on that day by holding appropriate exercises and ceremonies in suitable places throughout our land.

IN WITNESS WHEREOF, I have hereunto set my hand this twenty-third day of September, in the year of our Lord nineteen hundred seventy-seven, and of the Independence of the United States of America the two hundred and second.

JIMMY CARTER

[Filed with the Office of the Federal Register, 10:27 a.m., September 26, 1977]

Digest of Other White House Announcements

The following listing includes the President's daily schedule and other items of general interest as announced by the White House Press Office during the period covered by this issue. Events and announcements printed elsewhere in the issue are not included.

September 18

The President returned to the White House after a weekend stay at Camp David, Md.

September 19

The President met at the White House with:

—Bert Lance, Director of the Office of Management and Budget;

—Zbigniew Brzezinski, Assistant to the President for National Security Affairs;

—Secretary of Energy James R. Schlesinger and Senators Pete V. Domenici of New Mexico and Henry L. Bellmon of Oklahoma, to discuss energy legislation;

—the Cabinet;

—Secretary of Labor Ray Marshall, Secretary of the Treasury W. Michael Blumenthal, Secretary of Commerce Juanita M. Kreps, and a group of administration officials to discuss mandatory retirement policy;

—Vice President Walter F. Mondale.

The President attended a briefing on the Panama Canal treaties, given for a group of State legislators from Southern States in the State Dining Room.

The White House announced that Dr. Brzezinski will travel to Paris, London, and Bonn on September 25–28, to review international developments with his French, British, and West German counterparts.

September 20

The President met at the White House with:

—Dr. Brzezinski;

—the Democratic congressional leadership;

—Secretary of Transportation Brock Adams and several Members of Congress to discuss the SST Concorde;

—Attorney General Griffin B. Bell, Robert J. Lipshutz, Counsel to the President, Stuart E. Eizenstat, Assistant to the President for Domestic Affairs and Policy, and John M. Harmon, Assistant Attorney General;

—Vice President Mondale, Dr. Brzezinski, and Adm. Stansfield Turner, Director of Central Intelligence;

—Secretary of Defense Harold Brown and Dr. Brzezinski.

The President declared a major disaster for the State of Kansas as a result of severe storms and flooding beginning about September 11, which caused extensive public and private property damage.

September 21

The President met at the White House with:

—Dr. Brzezinski;

—a group of 12 Republican Senators;

—Secretary Adams and several Members of Congress to discuss the SST Concorde;

—Senator Edward M. Kennedy of Massachusetts.

The President attended a briefing on the Panama Canal treaties, given for State officials and business and political leaders from North Carolina and Tennessee in the State Dining Room.

September 22

The President met at the White House with:

—Dr. Brzezinski;

—Senator Jennings Randolph of West Virginia;

—Attorney General Bell;

—Secretary Blumenthal;

—Stanley E. Schneider, international president of Kiwanis International.

September 23

The President met at the White House with:

—Vice President Mondale, Secretary of State Cyrus R. Vance, Secretary Brown, Paul C. Warnke, Director of the U.S. Arms Control and Disarmament Agency, and Dr. Brzezinski;

—A. A. Gromyko, Minister of Foreign Affairs of the Union of Soviet Socialist Republics;

—Mrs. Carter, for lunch;

—Meno Vardas Gilford, of Tulsa, Okla., the sickle cell anemia poster child;

—Vice President Mondale, Secretary Kreps, Secretary Blumenthal, Charles L. Schultze, Chairman of the Council of Economic Advisers, James T. McIntyre, Jr., Acting Director of the Office of Management and Budget, Sidney L. Harman, Under Secretary, and Jerry J. Jasinowski, Assistant Secretary for Policy, Department of Commerce, and a group of business leaders;

—members of the Inaugural Committee for a reception in the State Dining Room.

The President attended a briefing on the Panama Canal treaties, given for State leaders from New Hampshire and Indiana in the State Dining Room.

The White House announced that the President will visit Venezuela, Brazil, Nigeria, India, Iran, France, Poland, and Belgium on November 22–December 2.

The White House announced that at the invitation of the United States Government, Edvard Kardelj, Member of the Presidency of the Socialist Federal Republic of Yugoslavia, will pay an official visit to Washington, D.C., from September 28 to October 5, and will meet with the President.

The White House announced that the President and Prime Minister Robert Muldoon of New Zealand have agreed that in view of the President's trip abroad in late November, the Prime Minister's official visit to Washington, originally scheduled for November 22 and 23, will now take place on November 9 and 10.

NOMINATIONS SUBMITTED TO THE SENATE

The following list does not include promotions of members of the Uniformed Services, nominations to the Service Academies, or nominations of Foreign Service officers.

Submitted September 19, 1977

The following-named persons to be Representatives of the United States of America to the Thirty-second Session of the General Assembly of the United Nations:

ANDREW J. YOUNG, of Georgia

JAMES F. LEONARD, JR., of New York

LESTER L. WOLFF, United States Representative from the State of New York

CHARLES W. WHALEN, JR., United States Representative from the State of Ohio

CORETTA SCOTT KING, of Georgia

The following-named persons to be Alternate Representatives of the United States of America to the Thirty-second Session of the General Assembly of the United Nations:

DONALD F. McHENRY, of Illinois

MELISSA F. WELLS, of New York

ALLARD KENNETH LOWENSTEIN, of New York

MARJORIE CRAIG BENTON, of Illinois

JOHN CLIFFORD KENNEDY, of Oklahoma

HUGH H. BOWNES, of New Hampshire, to be United States Circuit Judge for the First Circuit, vice Edward M. McEntee, retired.

A. LEON HIGGINBOTHAM, JR., of Pennsylvania, to be United States Circuit Judge for the Third Circuit, vice Francis L. Van Dusen, retired.

The following-named persons to be members of the Federal Farm Credit Board, Farm Credit Administration, for terms expiring March 31, 1983:

LAWRENCE OWEN COOPER, SR., of Mississippi, vice Ernest G. Spivey, term expired.

EDGAR C. RUTHERFORD, of California, vice Earl S. Smittcamp, term expired.

Submitted September 22, 1977

BENJAMIN J. MALCOLM, of New York, to be a Commissioner of the United States Parole Commission for the term of 6 years, vice Curtis C. Crawford, term expired.

NOMINATIONS—Continued

Submitted September 22—Continued

CECIL M. McCALL, of Georgia, to be a Commissioner of the United States Parole Commission for the term of 6 years, vice Maurice H. Sigler.

ROBERT D. VINCENT, of Oklahoma, to be a Commissioner of the United States Parole Commission for the term of 6 years, vice Lawrence A. Carpenter, resigned.

Submitted September 23, 1977

DIEGO C. ASENCIO, of New Jersey, a Foreign Service officer of Class one, to be Ambassador Extraordinary and Plenipotentiary of the United States of America to Colombia.

ROBERT D. KINGSLAND, of Missouri, to be United States Attorney for the Eastern District of Missouri for the term of 4 years, vice Donald J. Stohr, resigned.

EDWARD G. WARIN, of Nebraska, to be United States Attorney for the District of Nebraska for the term of 4 years, vice Daniel E. Wherry.

WILLIE D. DURHAM, SR., of Tennessee, to be United States Marshal for the Western District of Tennessee for the term of 4 years, vice Richard N. Moore.

RICHARD D. DUTREMBLE, of Maine, to be United States Marshal for the District of Maine for the term of 4 years, vice Charles J. Pooler.

ROBERT R. HUMPHREYS, of Virginia, to be Commissioner of the Rehabilitation Services Administration (new position).

PHILLIP SAMUEL HUGHES, of Maryland, to be an Assistant Secretary of Energy (Intergovernmental and Institutional Relations) (new position).

LYNN R. COLEMAN, of the District of Columbia, to be General Counsel of the Department of Energy (new position).

MATTHEW HOLDEN, JR., of Wisconsin, to be a member of the Federal Energy Regulatory Commission for a term of 4 years (new position).

CHARLES J. CHAMBERLAIN, of Illinois, to be a member of the Railroad Retirement Board for the remainder of the term expiring August 28, 1979, vice Neil P. Speirs, resigned.

CHECKLIST OF WHITE HOUSE PRESS RELEASES

The following releases of the Office of the White House Press Secretary, distributed during the period covered by this issue, are not included in the issue.

CHECKLIST—Continued

Released September 19, 1977

Announcement: nomination of Hugh H. Bownes to be United States Circuit Judge for the First Circuit, and A. Leon Higginbotham, Jr., to be United States Circuit Judge for the Third Circuit, U.S. Court of Appeals

Released September 20, 1977

Announcement: Lt. Gen. George M. Seignious II, USA (ret.), to fill the position of the "at large" chair on the U.S. delegation to the strategic arms limitation talks in Geneva

Released September 21, 1977

News conference: on the President's decisions on recommendations of the Presidential Task Force on the District of Columbia—by Martha M. Mitchell, Special Assistant to the President for Special Projects, and James Dyke, Assistant to the Vice President

News conference: on the meeting of the President and Ismail Fahmy, Deputy Prime Minister and Minister of Foreign Affairs of Egypt—by Jerrold L. Schecter, Associate Press Secretary

Released September 22, 1977

Announcement: nomination of Robert D. Kingsland to be United States Attorney for the Eastern District of Missouri; Edward G. Warin to be United States Attorney for the District of Nebraska; Willie D. Durham, Sr., to be United States Marshal for the Western District of Tennessee; and Richard D. Du-

CHECKLIST—Continued

tremble to be United States Marshal for the District of Maine

Released September 23, 1977

News conference: on the President's forthcoming trip to eight nations on November 22-December 2—by Zbigniew Brzezinski, Assistant to the President for National Security Affairs

News conference: on the President's meeting with Cabinet members and business leaders to discuss the Nation's economy—by Juanita M. Kreps, Secretary of Commerce, W. Michael Blumenthal, Secretary of the Treasury, Reginald H. Jones, chairman of the board, General Electric, and Irving Shapiro, chairman of the board, Dupont Corp.

ACTS APPROVED BY THE PRESIDENT

Approved September 20, 1977

H.R. 5294_____ Public Law 95–109 Consumer Credit Protection Act, amendments.

S. 1153_____ Public Law 95–110 An act to abolish the Joint Committee on Atomic Energy and to reassign certain functions and authorities thereof, and for other purposes.

Approved September 21, 1977

H.R. 7933_____ Public Law 95–111 Department of Defense Appropriation Act, 1978.

Roanoke, Virginia

Remarks at a Campaign Rally for Democratic Candidates for State Office.
September 24, 1977

Thank you, everybody. Right on. Thank you very much.

It's a great pleasure to me to be back in Virginia with men who will be important in your lives in the future, as they have been in the past—Attorney General Ed Lane, Lieutenant Governor Chuck Robb, Governor Henry Howell.

I thought I knew Henry Howell well. I've always heard he was a man of the people. He's the first person I ever saw that came to the White House and ate a cheeseburger with a knife and fork. [*Laughter*]

I've always been proud of the fact that when I first came to Virginia to begin my campaign a couple of years ago and didn't have very many friends, I went to Henry Howell's home, and he and Betty were nice enough to let me sleep there. I think Henry may have mentioned that on occasion. [*Laughter*] And I need for you to help me in the next few weeks, because 15 or 20 years from now, I would like very much to be able to tell my grandchildren that I slept in the same bed that was used by the Governor of Virginia. [*Laughter*]

You have a beautiful State. Of course, I come from a beautiful State, but when I do come to Virginia, I feel an extra degree of humility, because your State has produced eight Presidents and mine has only produced one. [*Laughter*] It's not an accident that Virginia has produced men and women who have laid the cornerstone of our country, because in historic times and in modern times alike, the characteristics that fill your heart are the ones that have made our Nation great.

In 1973 I was Governor of Georgia. I didn't have much time to be away from my own duties. I did not have any responsibilities for the national Democratic Party. But I heard about a man who was running for Governor. I was a small businessman, and I wanted to be sure that I could come to give my own help in a very small way to a man who believes in sound management, balanced budgets, no tax increases. As a farmer, I wanted someone who understood agriculture and the proper interrelationship that must exist between State government and the Federal Government. And I wanted someone as my friend who truly represents the best interests of those who are not rich, not influential, and don't want to dominate government for themselves, but want to see government controlled by consumers and housewives and the working people of this country.

So, I took a Saturday off, and I came to Virginia to campaign for Henry

Howell in 1973. And then a couple of weeks later, I took another Wednesday afternoon off, and I came to Virginia and got in Henry Howell's bus—he was not with me then; he was campaigning in another place—and I campaigned through the small towns and livestock sale barns and tractor dealerships of Virginia on behalf of Henry Howell. And he lost that Governor's race by less than 1 percent. It was a great disappointment to me, because a lot of those who believed in him so deeply and knew he would do a good job and knew he cared about him didn't get out and work hard enough in the last few days. And the distorted news reports about him, in my opinion, cost him the Governorship. But now is the year to correct that mistake and put him in the office.

He's a man who believes in home rule. And if he were to live in Roanoke, people who live in Boones Mill, and those others of you who believe in local government and who believe that a citizen ought to have as many decisions as possible made in the city hall and the county courthouse and not in the State capitol and not in Washington, ought to support Henry Howell, because he is fighting for a home rule provision that'll let every decision possible be made as close as possible to you. That's my kind of government. I believe it's your kind of government.

There was one other reason that I wanted to come to Virginia. I had seen some little pins that were even circulating through Georgia with five or six initials on them. And the secret of that slogan was "Keep the big boys honest."

I believe in the free enterprise system. I'm part of it. And I know there's a very important place for telephone companies and power companies to fill in our lives. But most other States have had a tight control over the step-by-step increase in charges that are levied against consumers and a very tight control over waste that sometimes exists when there is no regulation of increased prices.

And I understand—it's hard to believe, but I understand in Virginia that every time energy costs go up that the utility companies automatically raise your rates, and the regulatory agencies don't have a thing in the world to say about it. That ought to be changed. It's just a matter of fairness. It's just a matter of justice. And I would guess that in the long run, even the utility companies themselves would not be hurt if they knew that any increase in their costs would be carefully examined by public representatives and a reasonable profit allowed. But in your neighboring States they cannot raise rates 15 percent in 1 year without a utility regulatory body saying this is fair to the consumers. That ought to be changed. I understand Henry Howell is the one that can change it.

I tried to look at some poll results before I came to Virginia to see what advice I could give Henry Howell. You know how easy it is to give Henry Howell advice. He's so close to the people himself that he doesn't get his counsel and his advice from other politicians. And I'm not going to go in a posture of getting between you and him, because he listens to you, and that's the way it ought to be.

But one of the main concerns about Henry Howell is that he's sometimes indiscreet. He brings up subjects that, when examined by the news media, create controversy. But as far as I can see as a politician, that's not anything to be ashamed of; that's something to be proud of. Issues need to be discussed openly and controversial issues ought especially to be discussed openly.

The last time that I was in Virginia, before the general election, I was in Williamsburg, where I'll be tonight. Does anybody remember why I came there, to Williamsburg? What was it? That's right, to debate the President of the United States. And I believe that if I had not been willing to enter in those open, frank, free debates with my opponent, that the American people would not have known me and my stand on issues that are important to every one of you. They would not have had a chance to examine Mr. Ford and his stand on issues that are important to you. And I possibly would not have been elected President. Nobody knows. But I do know one thing: I didn't have anything to hide, and I was willing to debate. My understanding is that Henry Howell is not hiding, and he's willing to debate.

Some people may think that it's just a political tactic and kind of a trick when a candidate wants to have open debates. I think it's important. And if there are factors in Henry Howell's philosophy or in his background, in his private life, in his finances, of which he's ashamed, I think they ought to be brought out.

So, I believe that it's part of the American system, that began right here in Virginia, to have two candidates, seeking the highest office in your State, meet each other, debate, let you understand how they stand on issues.

There's another question that I think is much newer than debates. As you well know, your first President, from Virginia, and others after him believed in debate. But that was a time when it was not ordinarily expected that a public servant or Governor or President would reveal financial holdings. These days, it's different.

I believe for the last 11 years, I have disclosed my income tax returns. And I've made a habit every year since I've been a candidate for Governor of Georgia to give a net worth statement to the American people now and to the Georgia people before. I think it's important that this be done, because it lets the people know what is the origin of a person's income, what obligations do they have, what stocks do they hold, what possible conflicts might arise. And even for the most honest man or the most honest woman seeking office, it's a constraint on us to be sure we're not tempted to vote a certain way because we've got stock in a certain company.

So, I'm very proud that Henry Howell has been willing to make his net worth a matter of information for you. And he told me on the way here from the airport that Wednesday he's going to reveal his income tax returns. This is good. I hope everybody involved in the Governor's race will do the same.

Now, I just want to make one other statement, and then I would like to close. I like to see someone who seeks a major office have courage. I don't know of any issue that's come along in the Southland in my life or in the last 100 years that's been more important nor more controversial than the question of equality, freedom, voting rights, good education for the black people who live among us.

In 1959 I was not in politics. I was just a farmer. But Georgia was looking at Virginia, because Virginia politicians—maybe some of you in the audience—had decided, "We will not integrate our schools. We'd rather close them down and let our children do without any public education than to take that difficult step." It was a common thing all over the South. But there was at least one man that I know about in Virginia that ran for the State Legislature, and he said, "Let's take the padlocks off the schoolhouse doors." Do you know who that was? It was Henry Howell.

That's kind of ancient history, I know, but the reason I brought it up was because in the next 4 years there are going to be other decisions that will confront the Governor of Virginia that will provide a serious test of that person's courage. And I hope that in the Statehouse, representing you, is a man who cares about you personally, who is eager to openly debate the issues that are important to you, that has a long record of service, that believes in home rule, that understands business, balanced budgets, no tax increases, that can work closely with local and Federal officials, who casts his lot not with powerful and influential people, but directly with the voters of his State, and a man of courage, and coincidentally, a man who is my personal friend and whom I know well. And that's the man I hope that you'll help elect Governor this year—Henry Howell.

NOTE: The President spoke at 2:40 p.m. at the Roanoke Civic Center.

Norfolk, Virginia

Remarks at a Campaign Rally for Democratic Candidates for State Office. September 24, 1977

THE PRESIDENT. *Thank you, Henry Howell. Thank you very much, everybody.*

BYSTANDER. That's northern Virginia over there.

THE PRESIDENT. Hi, northern Virginia. [*Laughter*] Thank you, everybody. Let me get started.

After I got the nomination for the highest office in the world, my first day I came to this spot from Warm Springs, and a brief stop in between and then right here. And the friendship that you showed to me here in Henry Howell country, is something that I'll never forget.

And of course, I watched with a great deal of interest your recent primary campaign, and I'm very proud of the choices that you did make for attorney general, Lieutenant Governor, and for Governor. You formed a rainbow team that can't be beat, a rainbow team that will not let you down, and I'm here to speak for them.

One of my staff members asked me if I knew what a rainbow team meant. I told him that when I ran for Governor of Georgia and was elected, my Lieutenant Governor was Lester Maddox. [*Laughter*] And I had to say that at the end of the campaign, it was not any way that the Georgia people could tell which end of the rainbow I was on. I ran as an individual and, as has always been the case with Democrats, provided they are close to the people, any sort of definition about conservative, liberal, moderate, liberal-moderate, moderate-liberal, moderate-conservative has very little meaning.

When I ran for President, one of the first questions I would always get from the newcomers to the news ranks was, "Are you a liberal or a conservative?" My answer has always been, "I vote on each issue as it arises. I make my judgments on the basis of merit. I remember who put me in office. And I try to represent you."

You've got a team on my right that can represent you well. Ed Lane, as a very young man, went to the House of Delegates. He's a man who has the backing and the trust of Virginians of all kinds. His record is a good one—sound conservative management, active in the appropriations committee, understands zero-based budgeting, committed to fairness and equality for all people—a man who is eager to see the office of the attorney general be made more open to serve you. You couldn't find a better platform. And my judgment is that he's strong enough, courageous enough, knowledgeable enough, experienced enough, close enough to you, so when he is elected, he'll carry out his platform. You can't ask for any more, and I believe you can depend on that.

Quite different is Chuck Robb, a relative newcomer to politics running for Lieutenant Governor; ran an extraordinary campaign, nobody thought he had a chance; married into a great family; wanting to represent a great State; eager to see the office of Lieutenant Governor become directly responsible for bringing in new industry, new jobs; being a spokesman for Virginia throughout the world; and at the same time, looking at county and city officials and problems with a special eye to how the State government can be more responsive to local needs.

And you've already seen welded together Chuck Robb and Henry Howell, so you won't ever have to worry about the Governor and the Lieutenant Governor disagreeing on major issues that affect you. An integral part of the team, and a proven vote-getter, who has great political prospects for the future—even greater, perhaps, than Lieutenant Governor of Virginia—I have great confidence in him, and I'm very proud that Chuck Robb is my friend and I can be here to speak for him.

And before I forget, I'd like to say a word about Henry Howell.

It's always good in politics to have longtime friends whom you know, whom you understand, in whose house you've visited, whose family you know, whom you observed over several years in trying times—in office and during a campaign, his campaign and my campaign.

In 1973 I was the Governor of Georgia; I had no responsibility to Virginia. But I heard about a man who stands on his own feet. I heard about a man who wanted

to "keep the big boys honest" and has proven he knows how to do it. I heard about a man who puts his complete faith not in powerful bigshot financiers, bankers, utility company magnates, or even powerful political people, but puts his faith in the average Virginia voter, the working family, the elderly, the struggling, and the proud, who know that our own system of government is best when the people's voice is a voice of a Governor. And when Henry Howell is Governor, your voice will be his voice. That's why I'm proud to be his friend and proud that I came in 1973 to help him in his campaign then.

Unfortunately, he lost by just a few votes, because the rest of Virginia didn't have as good judgment as the Tidewater area. But I think the rest of Virginia has now learned. But if just a few more people here in his home area had gone to vote, he'd have been elected then.

And it would be a serious mistake, when the election comes along this year, for you to take anything for granted. It's very important that his home people who know him best and whom he knows best works hard throughout the State with your kinfolks and relatives and friends, to say, "I know Henry Howell; he'll fight for us. Give him your time and your support and your vote."

I came in on a Wednesday afternoon and campaigned for him in '73. I came back later on, because I liked him so well, and campaigned for him on a Saturday afternoon in farmers' markets, tractor dealerships, up and down the street. And I was disappointed that he lost.

But I've seen him grow even since then, and I believe he has a much sounder judgment now of your needs and the challenges of the Governorship even than he did have then. It won't hurt that he's got a friend in the White House when he becomes Governor of Virginia.

There's no doubt that I'll treat Virginia fair no matter how the campaign comes out. But there won't be any problem in constant communication between Henry Howell and me in the years ahead because he's promised me that if there's ever a need for Virginia people to have the services of a President, that he will not keep me waiting outside the door of the Governor's office in Virginia.

There are some basic changes that need to be made in your State. I started my married life here in Norfolk—1009 Buckingham—as a young Navy ensign. And the greatness of our military forces, the greatness of your shipyard capabilities, the constant expansion of job opportunities, the closeness between your unique community and our Central Government in Washington are all a very precious possession that you have. It would be hard to hope to see a major improvement.

But I think that if Virginia has one failing, it's that the interests of consumers have not been given adequate attention in the years gone by. Now, I believe that every family has got to have the services of a good telephone system and a good power distribution system. But in your State and mine, too, I don't want to see an uncontrolled monopoly.

Henry Howell understands this. And when the price of energy goes up, in most States increases in your power rates have to be approved by a regulatory agency answering to you. But in Virginia the charges are passed on to you automatically. That ought to be changed. And I believe Henry Howell can change it.

I understand that one year the rates went up 15 percent—decided only by the power company. I think that if there was a constraint on them that reasonable cost increases could be passed along. But they'd be a lot more careful not to waste

money, and they would begin to realize that it's their money they were wasting instead of your money that they were wasting. This is important to you and to all of us.

We have the same problem in Washington about powerful companies having too much influence. I put forward to the Congress a comprehensive energy package. Part of it calls for deregulation, over a period of time, of natural gas. And it has, in the proposal, enough incentive to encourage increased exploration and a shifting of natural gas into the interstate pipelines so it comes to States like your own and to Georgia, away from the States where the gas is produced. I'm in favor of that.

But the gas companies—very powerful in Washington, as you well know—want to deregulate immediately and add tremendous cost to the American public, not only for new gas to be discovered in the future but for gas that already has been discovered and that will be coming to you in any case.

This latest proposal in the Senate would add about $20 billion to the price of natural gas already discovered in Alaska alone and scheduled to be brought down here. I hate to veto a bill that a Democratic Congress passes, but you can depend upon it; I'll protect your interests when the bill comes to my desk.

So, I've come here in a spirit of friendship, appreciation to you for your confidence in me as President, to ask you for your help now and in the future on behalf of a longtime personal friend in whom I have complete confidence, and to ask your strong, active, dedicated, sacrificial support in these next few weeks for a Democratic ticket that will serve you well.

And it'll make a lot of difference to you who is elected attorney general, who is elected Lieutenant Governor, and who is elected Governor—Ed Lane, Chuck Robb, Henry Howell are a good team. And I believe you and our country will be served well if they are elected. I trust the judgment of Virginia people. And that's why I predict that you and they are going to be very happy when the election night comes.

Thank you very much. I'm glad to be with you.

NOTE: The President spoke at 5:07 p.m. at the Azalea Gardens.

Williamsburg, Virginia

Remarks at a Democratic Fundraising Dinner. September 24, 1977

In every State, there are a few people who are willing to sacrifice their time and their financial wealth and their own personal investment for the benefit of their fellow men and women. And I want to let you know how much I appreciate the generous contribution that you are making tonight by being here.

I'm touched to be present, not touched quite as much as some of you have been, perhaps—*[laughter]*—but it's an enjoyable and a voluntary thing on my part, and I know an enjoyable and a voluntary thing on your part.

Virginia is a great State with a history that makes us all proud who know it.

Three hundred and almost forty years ago, my own Carter family settled not too far from here, just across the James River from Jamestown in what was then the Isle of Wight County and later became Surry County; later moved to North Carolina, and later, then moved on down to Georgia. And when I was first married,

I lived in Norfolk with my new bride, and that's where my first son was born.

As President, I feel an even deeper sense of kinship with Virginia. Georgia has now produced one President; Virginia has produced eight. *[Laughter]* I have to say that the quality of some of your Presidents has been very, very good, and I hope to measure up to that standard.

But our country is a partnership for us, and State government is also a partnership. Our Nation is, in a way, a child of the States. And of course, county government, city government are children of the State. But the interrelationship has got to be a strong one for our basic system of government, federalism, to continue to exist.

The number of democracies in the world is not as great as it should be. I spent 3 hours yesterday in detailed discussions with Foreign Minister Gromyko about matters that are transcendent in their importance to our own people and our future—to world peace and world progress, to a lessening of tension, a reduction in armaments, an enhancement of human freedom, the protection of human rights. And it was a very real responsibility on me to prepare carefully for that exchange of ideas.

I believe some progress was made in establishing terms for a comprehensive test ban that would prohibit all testing of nuclear explosions in the future by our countries. And I believe that progress was made in limiting strategic nuclear weapons with unbelievable destructive power. We don't yet know what our success might be, but at least we made progress forward.

Virginia is a State that's always prided itself on strength and unchanging principle and a search for candidates for public office who represent the finest aspects of your heritage—an old State, but always vigorous and young in your attitude. You are confident about the future, confident in yourselves, eager to search out common ground on which we can approach problems jointly, as partners.

I'm grateful to come back to Virginia. I was here in this room, as some of you may remember, the night after the third debate that I had with President Ford. And I thanked you then and thank you now for a chance to participate in your lives now and in the future.

Tonight I'm here not to speak on my own behalf but to speak on behalf of you and the citizens of Virginia who have an opportunity, in my opinion, to elect fine men to represent you as Governor in Henry Howell, Lieutenant Governor in Chuck Robb, and Ed Lane as your attorney general.

These men have formed a team. They're different from one another—newcomers to politics, those with long years of experience, those who've served in the legislative branch of Government, those who've served in the executive branch of Government, one who's not served yet but has a bright future ahead of him. And I know that as history evolves in the future, you'll all be proud that you've had a part tonight and, hopefully, with an even greater fervor in the next few weeks to participate in the election of these good men, good men to lead your State.

Virginia also has a commitment and almost a unique heritage, particularly in the South, to nonpartisan approach to the election of public officials. It's been difficult for me in the past to know who was an Independent and who was a Democrat and who was a Republican, and particularly in Virginia. [*Laughter*] Tonight I hope, and in the next few weeks

I hope, that we'll all be Democrats because we have such a fine ticket here.

But this, I think, again, is a symbol of your own independence. I've examined, in preparing for this visit, the campaign platforms of Ed and Chuck and Henry, and I can certainly endorse them without equivocation or doubt. They are eager to be examined. They are eager to debate the issues publicly, whether those issues might be safe ones or controversial. And I think in particular my longtime friend, Henry Howell, has what some people describe as a problem but which I describe as a very fine political attribute, and that is a willingness to express himself openly and publicly and without fear or trepidation and with a maximum of courage on issues that are not safe because those are quite often the issues that are most important to people like yourselves and those who look to you for leadership.

I know that attendance here tonight in a way is a mark of esteem, and I was proud to get what was a very hurried picture with each one of you because I know that you are leaders in your own, in business or the professions, in education, in labor, in protecting the interest of people who depend upon you.

Most of you are not in public office, but you are in public life, and you are public servants whether you are attorneys or teachers or in the business community or operate a railroad—those kinds of things don't separate you from Henry and Ed and Chuck and me in our responsibilities now and in the future.

This is an opportunity for our country this year, I think, to overcome some of the problems of the past, the embarrassing things that have afflicted our people in Vietnam and Watergate and CIA. But there's a burgeoning hope, changing into a quiet confidence, that our country is so strong and our system of government is so well-planned and our leaders are so directly subject to the constant scrutiny and mandatory approval of the people that we can withstand challenge, that we can overcome mistakes that might very well destroy a lesser government or a lesser people.

I've learned a lot about politics in the last 2 years, a lot about my country and your country. And I've learned a lot about economics and a lot about the interrelationship that ought to exist between the different levels of government. Our economic system is strong. And although the monthly figures go up and down slightly, there's a basic stability there that I want to maintain working with strong State leaders like these here with me.

So, I'd like to summarize my own comments by saying that Virginia epitomizes an attitude and a character that is typical of our country. Your heritage is a basis for a finer future for you and our Nation.

You have nominated candidates who represent you well and who are worthy of your support and of my support. And I believe that if they are elected, Virginia will be well-blessed and there will be an enhanced relationship between the State-house in Virginia and the White House in Washington that will be of benefit to us all.

As I mentioned this afternoon in Norfolk, a close communication and friendship between a Governor and a President can be a very healthy thing for the people who look to us for leadership. And I'm very grateful that when Henry is in the Governor's office and I'm in the White House, that he has promised that when a problem comes up that affects Virginia, especially in which he and I have a direct personal interest, that he will not keep me waiting long outside the Gov-

ernor's office if I want to see him. [*Laughter*]

I'd like to close by saying this: I have to go to another banquet tonight; I'll be meeting with about 3,000 of the black leaders of our country, the annual Black Caucus banquet. And I'll be talking to them about the future of our minority citizens who are represented so well.

But I want to point out to you that this is just a brief visit for me into Virginia. I'm not trying to tell the Virginia people how to vote. I trust your good judgment, and I respect your independence and your eagerness not to be influenced or dominated in an unwarranted way from the White House or from anywhere else.

But in trusting that judgment, I know that you will make the right decision and that the rainbow team will be successful on election night, and then you and I can celebrate together.

Thank you very much.

NOTE: The President spoke at 7:35 p.m. in the Virginia Room at the Colonial Williamsburg Convention Center.

Congressional Black Caucus

Remarks at the Caucus' Annual Dinner. September 24, 1977

I appreciate the chance to come. You've probably noticed that I was a little late in arriving. I met Alex Haley outside, and I made the mistake of saying, "Alex, how's your family?" [*Laughter*] Unfortunately, he told me. And it took a while to get in. [*Laughter*]

Alex and I have a lot in common. I just came up a few minutes ago from an afternoon of campaigning in Virginia, and was in Williamsburg right across from where my own folks came to this country, I think 340 years ago, across the river from Jamestown. He and I were both in the Navy. We both were famous enough last year to be interviewed by Playboy magazine. [*Laughter*]

We both wrote a book. Mine was called "Why Not The Best?"; his was. [*Laughter*]

Of course, all of you know how much I depend on Andy Young. Andy is valuable in more ways than one. Of course, he's a great diplomat. But there was a time, whenever things were going bad with me and my administration and I didn't want my name to be in the headlines— [*laughter*]—Andy would always take over, and he saved me from a lot of embarrassing attention. [*Laughter*] Unfortunately, he taught Bert Lance the same thing the last few weeks. [*Laughter*] I guess Andy and I are back on our own, beginning this week.

As a diplomat, however, Andrew Young is always in there fighting and pitching for our country, giving the world and me new ideas. He's just told me tonight about a brilliant political and diplomatic achievement that we now have in progress; I haven't announced it before. As you know, we have a problem in the Mideast. We have a difficult fight on our hands with the Panama Canal Treaty. I'd say we're lucky that 50 percent of the people favor the treaty. And his proposal is that we give the East Bank to Panama— [*laughter*]—that we keep the West Bank and make it a Palestinian homeland. [*Laughter*]

Andy and I have not yet decided who would be the ruler of this new entity, but Andy tells me that before long, Ian Smith's going to be looking for a new job. [*Laughter*]

One thing that I want to talk about tonight is that we share, the Black Caucus, all of its supporters, and I, a common, ultimate dream for America. It's going to be a long time coming because this dream is so great.

We want a time to come when all Americans will be well off enough to afford the same tailor that Ron Dellums [1] has. [*Laughter*]

Now, to be serious for a few minutes, I'd like to say that I've had a very interesting relationship with the Black Caucus in this first part of my administration. Sometimes we've been in complete harmony. Sometimes I haven't exactly satisfied Parren Mitchell and the other members of the Black Caucus.

I can tell the difference when I get my mail. [*Laughter*] In the low times, the mail that comes from Parren Mitchell to the White House is just addressed to "Occupant." [*Laughter*] But I have to say that in many ways the partnership that I have formed with the Black Caucus has been good for me, good for my administration, good for the entire Government, and good for our country.

We've got a long way to go. And expectations are high, and they ought to be high. But because of that, quite often achievements that a year ago or 5 years ago would have been greeted with a great sense of jubilation and a sigh of relief— that an enormous achievement had been accepted by the American people with only a response, "It should have been more."

The Congress and your President has done a great deal already. The programs that are in place now to improve the economic conditions of our people who need it most are beginning to bear fruit. We are now completing a thousand public works contracts every week, and because of the good work of the Black Caucus members, of course joined by other

---

[1] Representative Ronald V. Dellums of California.

Members of the Congress, the law requires that 10 percent of all those contracts for the first time in the country have to be given to minority businesses, and that's the way it ought to be.

And the rate of new jobs that are going into our urban centers now are at 35,000 per week, which exceeds even what was done during the depths of the Depression with the New Deal, the WPA, the CCC—35,000 a week. It's still not enough, but it's a great step forward, and we're now channeling those jobs deliberately and with a great commitment as they have not been channeled in the past to the young people of our country and, particularly, to young people who happen to be black. And that's the way it ought to be, and it's going to be more in the future. We've had a billion dollars put in the youth employment programs. I asked for a billion and a half. We are now going back to the Congress for the other half billion dollars.

We are evolving an urban policy. Within the next week or 10 days, there will be a final decision made on the form of the Humphrey-Hawkins bill, so that for the first time in the history of our country—[*applause*]—we'll have, as a national policy, full employment.

When we presented our welfare reform package to the Congress, which will be passed next year, an integral part of it, which can be phased in early, would be an additional 1.4 million jobs, and, of course, these jobs will be channeled to families that have in the past been supported by welfare.

So, we are making some progress. And one of the things that we've done, too, is to direct by executive order that the rate of purchases of Government supplies from black enterprises must be doubled in the next year.

Parren Mitchell and the Black Caucus members were gracious enough to help us prepare a recent brief in the Department of Justice. [*Laughter*] We confirmed strongly the principle of affirmative action, and we made it clear that race can be and ought to be an integral part in alleviating discrimination that has existed far too long.

Where do we go from here? The progress has in the past been a source of pride to all of you assembled in this room, long before I became involved in our own Federal Government.

But the extrapolation of what you have already accomplished to the future is a goal of yours and also a commitment of mine. Many of you suffered anguish of heart, and sometimes physically, in the years gone by, to achieve civil rights in our own country. And now, we're involved together on a concept of enhancing human rights, here and around the world. And the example you've set is now an inspiration to many throughout the globe.

Just this past week, I publicly endorsed a concept, for the first time, of human rights for the District of Columbia. [*Applause*] Thank you; you're welcome.

The endorsement by the President, of course, is not the final step. The Congress must act, and the people have to ratify a change in the United States Constitution. As I say, we still have a long way to go.

We join together in matters that affect all human beings—a search for peace in the world, a reduction in armaments, a channeling of scarce financial and human resources to give people a better life, a life with education possible, better health care, more human freedom, the rule by the black majorities in the African nations.

And there has been a change among the developing nations of the world in their attitude toward us. And I would say that the crucial factors that have been involved are represented very well by the three men who stand behind me—Parren Mitchell, Alex Haley, and Andrew Young—and many others in this audience who have come before them and who have marched with them and will join with us in the future in a spirit of brotherhood to make sure that the great achievements that we've seen in our own country can be enhanced and that they can be made available to the needy and downtrodden people throughout the world.

Thank you very much. I love you all. Thank you.

NOTE: The President spoke at 10:40 p.m. in the International Ballroom at the Washington Hilton Hotel. In his remarks, he referred to Alex Haley, author of "Roots," and Representative Parren J. Mitchell of Maryland, chairman of the Congressional Black Caucus.

United Nations Day, 1977
Proclamation 4525.   September 26, 1977

By the President of the United States of America

A Proclamation

Each year on October 24, Americans join with the people of other countries in celebrating the anniversary of the United Nations—an institution created to maintain international peace and security, to promote the self-determination of peoples, to encourage respect for human rights, and to foster economic and social welfare.

Americans have been instrumental in creating the United Nations, in advancing cooperation through its forums, and in providing, over the years, the largest share of its financial support.

Since its establishment at San Francisco in 1945, the United Nations has undergone profound change. Its membership has nearly trebled from the original 51 members, as most of the former colonial areas of Asia and Africa received their independence. New problems brought on by developments in science and technology and by global interdependence have tested the ability of governments to cooperate harmoniously. Problems like the arms race, the spread of nuclear weapons, the international economic order, the disposition of the world's oceanic resources, energy, and environmental pollution transcend national boundaries, making the United Nations and its specialized and technical agencies of continuing importance to the international community.

Now, THEREFORE, I, JIMMY CARTER, President of the United States of America, do hereby designate Monday, October 24, 1977, as United Nations Day. I have appointed Henry Ford II to be United States National Chairman for United Nations Day and I urge appropriate observances to inform citizens of the aims and achievements of the United Nations and its affiliated agencies.

IN WITNESS WHEREOF, I have hereunto set my hand this 26th day of September, in the year of our Lord nineteen hundred seventy-seven, and of the Independence of the United States of America the two hundred and second.

JIMMY CARTER

[Filed with the Office of the Federal Register, 11:32 a.m., September 26, 1977]

Railroad Retirement Board
Nomination of Charles J. Chamberlain To Be a Member.   September 26, 1977

The President today announced that he will nominate Charles J. Chamberlain, of Illinois, to be a member of the Railroad Retirement Board. He would replace Neil P. Speirs, resigned.

Chamberlain was born August 7, 1921. From 1938 to 1956, he worked for the Chicago and North Western Railroad as a signalman and signal maintainer. Since 1941 he has held various posts in the Brotherhood of Railroad Signalmen, beginning as recording secretary for Local 108. Since 1970 he has been president of the union.

Since 1970 Chamberlain has been chairman of the Railway Labor Executives' Association. He is a member of the Railroad Safety Research Board and the Railroad Industry Labor-Management Committee.

American National Red Cross

Appointment of Six Persons to the Board of Governors. September 26, 1977

The President today announced that he will appoint the following persons to the American National Red Cross Board of Governors:

SECRETARY OF STATE CYRUS VANCE
SECRETARY OF DEFENSE HAROLD BROWN
SECRETARY OF HEALTH, EDUCATION, AND WELFARE JOSEPH CALIFANO
SECRETARY OF HOUSING AND URBAN DEVELOPMENT PATRICIA HARRIS
ASSISTANT SECRETARY OF DEFENSE FOR MANPOWER AND RESERVE AFFAIRS JOHN P. WHITE
ASSISTANT SECRETARY OF HEALTH, EDUCATION, AND WELFARE FOR HEALTH JULIUS B. RICHMOND.

Department of Labor

*Nomination of Julius Shiskin
To Be Commissioner of Labor
Statistics. September 26, 1977*

The President today announced that he will nominate Julius Shiskin, of Maryland, for reappointment as Commissioner of Labor Statistics at the Department of Labor. Shiskin has held the position since 1973.

He was born October 13, 1912, in New York City. He received a B.S. and an M.A. from Rutgers University.

Shiskin was an instructor of economics and statistics at Rutgers University from 1934 to 1938, and a staff assistant at the National Bureau of Economics Research from 1938 to 1942. From 1942 to 1945, he was head economist for the Planning Division of the War Production Board.

From 1945 to 1969, Shiskin was Chief Economic Statistician and Assistant Director of the Bureau of the Census. From 1969 to 1973, he was Chief Statistician at the Office of Management and Budget and U.S. Representative to the United Nations Statistical Commission. Since 1973 he has been Commissioner of Labor Statistics at the Labor Department.

Shiskin has served as a consultant to the Council of Economic Advisers, the Organization for Economic Cooperation and Development, the United Nations, and the International Monetary Fund. He is the author of numerous articles and several books on economics and statistics.

Federal Election Commission

Nomination of John W. McGarry To Be a Commissioner. September 26, 1977

The President today announced that he will nominate John W. McGarry, of Massachusetts, to be a Commissioner of the Federal Election Commission. He would replace Neil Staebler, term expired.

McGarry was born June 11, 1922, in Boston, Mass. He served in the U.S. Navy during World War II, and after the war graduated from Holy Cross College and earned a law degree at Georgetown University Law Center.

From 1959 to 1963, McGarry served as assistant attorney general of Massachusetts. He then combined private law practice with service as chief counsel for the Special Committee to Investigate Campaign Expenditures, which was created as a temporary unit every 2 years until 1972 to oversee House elections.

Since 1973 McGarry has been special counsel on elections to the Committee on House Administration of the U.S. House of Representatives.

National Labor Relations Board

Nomination of John C. Truesdale To Be a Member. September 26, 1977

The President today announced that he will nominate John C. Truesdale, of Westgate, Md., to be a member of the National Labor Relations Board (NLRB) for a term expiring August 27, 1980. He would replace Peter D. Walther, resigned.

Truesdale was born July 17, 1921, in Grand Rapids, Mich. He received an A.B. from Grinnell College in 1942, an M.S. in industrial and labor relations from Cornell University in 1948, and a J.D. from Georgetown University Law Center in 1972.

Truesdale worked for the NLRB from 1948 to 1957, serving as a field examiner, then administrative analyst. From 1957 to 1963, he was at the National Academy of Sciences, serving as Deputy Director, then Director of Information for the International Geophysical Year.

In 1963 Truesdale returned to NLRB, where he served as Associate Executive Secretary until 1968, Deputy Executive Secretary from 1968 to 1972, and Executive Secretary since 1972.

United States International Trade Commission

Nomination of William R. Alberger To Be a Member. September 26, 1977

The President today announced that he will nominate William R. Alberger, of Portland, Oreg., to be a member of the United States International Trade Commission for a term of 9 years. He would replace Will E. Leonard, Jr., resigned.

Alberger was born October 11, 1945. He received a B.A. from Willamette University, Oregon, in 1967, an M.B.A. from the University of Iowa in 1971, and a J.D. from Georgetown University Law Center in 1973.

Alberger served as legislative assistant to Representative Al Ullman from 1972 to 1975, and as his administrative assistant from 1975 to 1977. Since March 1977, he has been administrative assistant to the House Ways and Means Committee.

Copyright Royalty Tribunal

Nomination of Five Commissioners of the Tribunal. September 26, 1977

The President today announced the persons he will nominate as Commissioners of the Copyright Royalty Tribunal. They are:

Thomas C. Brennan, of New Jersey, for a term of 7 years. Brennan was born January 16, 1935, and received a J.D. (1959) and LL.M. (1962) from Georgetown University. He has been a professional staff member of the Senate Judiciary Committee since 1959, and served as counsel to both the Majority and Minority in the Senate throughout the decade of proceedings on the general revision of the copyright law.

Douglas Coulter, of New Hampshire, for a term of 7 years. Coulter was born January 26, 1941, and holds M.B.A. degrees from Harvard Business School and the European Institute of Business Administration. Coulter is self-employed as a freelance writer. He worked as a campaign director on the Carter Presidential campaign in Indiana and also worked as an organizer on the 1972 McGovern Presidential campaign, and as a field director on the 1973 Henry Howell gubernatorial campaign in Virginia.

Mary Lou Burg, of Wisconsin, for a term of 7 years. Burg was born February 10, 1930. She received a B.S. from the University of Wisconsin in 1952. She served as Vice Chairman and Deputy Chairman of the Democratic National Committee between 1970 and 1977. She was a Democratic National Committeewoman from Wisconsin from 1968 to 1976.

Clarence L. James, Jr., of Ohio, for a term of 5 years. James was born October 13, 1933, and received a J.D. from Cleveland Marshall College of Law, Cleveland State University, in 1962. From 1968 to 1971, he was director of law for the city of Cleveland. Since 1971 he has practiced law in Cleveland, and since 1972 he has been special counsel to the attorney general of Ohio.

Frances Garcia, of Texas, for a term of 5 years. Garcia was born July 21, 1941. She received a B.B.A. from Midwestern University in Texas in 1968 and became a certified public accountant in 1972. Since 1968 she has been an audit manager for Arthur Andersen & Co.

Copyright Royalty Tribunal

Order Designating Order of Seniority of the Commissioners. September 26, 1977

Pursuant to the provisions of Public Law 94–553 of October 19, 1976, I hereby designate the order of seniority of the Commissioners of the Copyright Royalty Tribunal as follows:

> Thomas C. Brennan
> Douglas Coulter
> Mary Lou Burg
> Clarence L. James, Jr.
> Frances Garcia

This Order shall be published in the FEDERAL REGISTER.

JIMMY CARTER

The White House,
September 26, 1977.

[Filed with the Office of the Federal Register, 11:58 a.m., September 26, 1977]

NOTE: The order was not issued in the form of a White House press release.

Law of the Sea Conference

Appointment of George H. Aldrich as Deputy Special Representative of the President and Deputy Chief of the U.S. Delegation. September 26, 1977

The President today announced that he will appoint George H. Aldrich, of Alexandria, Va., to be Deputy Special Representative of the President for the Law of the Sea Conference and Deputy Chief of the Delegation. Aldrich replaces John N. Moore, resigned.

Aldrich was born February 25, 1932, in St. Louis, Mo. He received a B.A. from De Pauw University in 1954 and an LL.B. from Harvard Law School in 1957.

In 1959 and 1960, he was an attorney in the Office of the General Counsel, Department of the Navy, and from 1960 to

1963 he was an attorney in the Office of the Assistant General Counsel for International Affairs at the Defense Department.

From 1963 to 1965, Aldrich was legal adviser to the U.S. Delegation to the North Atlantic Council in Paris. From 1965 to 1969, he was assistant legal adviser for East Asian and Pacific Affairs at the State Department. Since 1969 he has been deputy legal adviser of the Department of State.

Aldrich was head of the U.S. Delegation to the Fourth Session of the Diplomatic Conference on the Reaffirmation and Development of International Humanitarian Law Applicable in Armed Conflicts, held at Geneva in 1977, and of the U.S. Delegation to the Conference of Government Experts on Possible Prohibitions or Restrictions on the Use of Certain Conventional Weapons, held in Lugano, Switzerland, in 1976.

Aldrich was legal adviser to Dr. Henry Kissinger for the Vietnam negotiations in Paris in 1972 and 1973, and principal drafter of the Protocols to the Agreement on Ending the War and Restoring the Peace in Viet Nam. He was Chairman of the U.S. Delegation to the 1971 and 1972 Geneva Conferences of Government Experts on International Humanitarian Law Applicable in Armed Conflicts, and to the 1974, 1975, and 1976 Diplomatic Conferences on the same subject.

Transatlantic Air Fares

Announcement of Approval of New Low-Cost Fares. September 26, 1977

President Carter today overruled the Civil Aeronautics Board and approved new low-cost transatlantic air service. The specific fares approved by the President are a $256 budget fare, roundtrip between New York and London, and a $290 advanced purchase excursion ("super-APEX") fare, roundtrip between London and New York. Similar super-APEX fares will be offered from Boston, Philadelphia, Chicago, Detroit, Los Angeles, Washington, and Miami.

The CAB has recently allowed a $256 standby fare and a $280 budget fare, but on September 16 it ruled against the $256 budget fare and the $290 super-APEX fare.

In his letter to the Board, the President stated that "I have decided to reject the Board's order as inconsistent with this Administration's foreign economic policy. I must emphasize that my international aviation policy carries with it a commitment to low fare, competitive international air service for the benefit of American consumers."

In its decision, the Civil Aeronautics Board expressed concern that low fare service by scheduled airlines might adversely affect the charter industry.

To make sure that consumers have the widest variety of low fares available to them, the President urged the Board to move as rapidly as possible to remove Federal regulations that impede low cost charter service. The Departments of State and Transportation will also be undertaking discussions with European government aviation authorities to remove restrictions on both charters and other low fare services.

The fares approved today are experimental and will be available to the public through March 31, 1978. Transportation Secretary Adams will study these winter fares to determine how responsive they are to the public need and how these fares and charter services might be made more widely available as the basis for long-term, low-cost transatlantic service.

Transatlantic Air Fares

Letter to the Chairman of the Civil
Aeronautics Board.   September 26, 1977

Dear Mr. Chairman:

I have reviewed your proposed order
(Docket 31363) dated September 16,
1977, which suspends passenger fares filed
by Pan American World Airways, Inc.,
Trans World Airlines, Inc., British Airways, Air-India, Iran National Airlines
Corporation, and Aerlinte Eireann Teo-
ranta for foreign air transportation.

Under my authority pursuant to section
801(b) of the Federal Aviation Act of
1958, as amended, I have decided to reject the Board's order as inconsistent with
this Administration's foreign economic
policy. I must emphasize that my international aviation policy carries with it a
commitment to low fare, competitive international air service for the benefit of
American consumers. I am not convinced
that these innovative, carrier-initiated,
low fares would damage the international
aviation system. If the Board obtains new
evidence after these fares are in effect that
they are indeed predatory, I will consider
a suspension of the rates at that time
under the terms of the *ad hoc* agreement
negotiated on September 19, 1977, with
the United Kingdom.

I would also take this opportunity to
suggest that the Board give serious attention to reforming present rules covering
charter flights to permit those services to
be more competitive with the new low
fare scheduled flights and more responsive to the foreign economic policy reasons
for encouraging low fare passenger service. Liberalizing charter rules will assist in
the expansion of air travel markets and
should provide real benefits to consumers
and carriers alike.

Sincerely,

JIMMY CARTER

[Honorable Alfred E. Kahn, Chairman, Civil
Aeronautics Board, Washington, D.C. 20428]

World Bank Group and International Monetary Fund

Remarks at the Opening Session of the Annual
Meetings of the Boards of Governors.
September 26, 1977

Mr. Colley, Mr. Witteveen, Mr. Bob
McNamara, and my own Secretary of
Treasury, Mike Blumenthal, distin-
guished visitors to our country from all
over the world:

I'm very glad to welcome you to Washington, as you begin your annual meeting.

After being President for a few months,
after dealing with the Congress, after
facing many difficult questions, it's a great
pleasure to meet with a group where
there's an absence of disagreement, where
complete harmony prevails—*[laughter]*—
and where you have discovered the answers to all the difficult questions.

This meeting is important to all of us
because the partnership that exists among
nations and among people is so evident
in this room. These meetings provide an
opportunity for the leaders of the world's
financial institutions, both public and
private, to consider the economic problems and also the economic opportunities
that our nations share. And through the
Bank and the Fund, we are able to meet
the challenges to our shared well-being.

The two greatest challenges we face are
to restore and to maintain steady, noninflationary expansion of the world econ-

omy and to increase the pace of growth in the developing nations of the world, with the benefits of the growth among us all more widely and equitably shared.

The health of the international economic system depends upon the health of our individual domestic economies. Just as none of us can prosper without a stable system, so the system will not be sound unless we act responsibly at home.

I am pleased that the United States economy is healthy and growing. Our rate of inflation, while still too high for our liking—about 6 percent—is moderating and is below that, of course, in most other countries.

We will meet our economic growth targets for this year—about 6 percent in real terms. And we will also maintain a vigorous and noninflationary growth next year.

And I am committed to take such actions as are necessary as President to insure that this optimistic prediction comes true. We will do so principally because it is good for our own country, but also because it contributes to the economic health of the rest of the world.

Our unemployment rate is steadily going down. We have very little doubt about this. And there's a sense of commitment in our country and a strength of our economic system. They bode us good for the future. Strong economic growth in the United States and a slowing pace of growth in other countries, combined with an excessive United States import of oil, have all led to a rise this year in the United States trade deficit, which has continued even through last month.

With respect to oil imports, I have proposed to the Congress—really for the first time in the history of our country—a comprehensive energy program, which in the years ahead, is designed to reduce our oil

imports substantially below what they are now and to less than one-half the previous projections for the next 8 years.

We know that it is critical that the Congress enact strong and effective energy measures. The U.S. must have a credible program to limit the growth of oil consumption and, therefore, to reduce oil imports.

I urge all nations, and especially the major industrial countries, to reduce energy waste along with us and to pursue economic growth and stabilization policies along with us, leading to an expanding, noninflationary world economy, growing international trade, and an improved pattern of world trade balances.

The International Monetary Fund has played already a vital role in keeping the international monetary system both flexible and effective. I'm particularly grateful for the enlightened fiscal discipline which the Fund and the Bank encourage throughout the world with their loans. The present system is working well.

The United States has ratified the amendments to the Articles of Agreement of the IMF, and we hope that other nations, other members will do the same so as to increase the Fund's resources and strengthen its capacity for surveillance of exchange rate policies and the oversight of monetary agreements.

The new IMF supplementary credit facility adds an important element to the IMF capabilities. It has my country's full support. The United States will also join with others in working toward adequate increases in IMF quotas during the Seventh Special Review of these quotas.

The United States remains firmly committed to policies that will promote freer and wider trade without the deleterious consequences of protectionism. My country joins others in pledging to seek substantive progress in the ongoing multinational trade negotiations by the end of this year.

Restoring health to the world economy will help us toward what we all recognize is a vital, human obligation—assisting poor countries in the task of human development. If the roughly 1 billion people who now live in extreme poverty are to have their chance, every nation must take more effective action. And the United States is ready to join such an international campaign.

The study of world development issues now being undertaken by the Bank and the Fund should provide a framework in which all nations can expand our efforts toward common development efforts.

Of course, the developing countries are ultimately responsible for their own growth. Only they can mobilize the skills and the resources necessary for development. Only they can be sure that the benefits of growth, when and if it does come, extends throughout the country involved, to those who need it most. But the industrialized countries like our own must provide more outside capital.

I'm glad to report that the United States Congress has authorized more than twice as much money for the World Bank and the regional development banks this year as we did last year.

I hope that the negotiations for a major, general capital increase will permit the World Bank to increase the level of its lending in real terms.

All this will take time. Our goals will not be achieved overnight. Perseverance will be the key to success. There will be many difficulties to overcome, many complicated questions to answer, many national interests that might separate countries, to be overwhelmed by a common commitment to mutual responsibility.

The United States wants to cooperate with all of you. We are prepared to stay the course, and you can depend upon us.

Thank you very much.

NOTE: The President spoke at 3:02 p.m. in the Ballroom at the Sheraton-Park Hotel to representatives of the International Monetary Fund, the International Bank for Reconstruction and Development (World Bank), the International Development Association, and the International Finance Corporation.

In his opening remarks, the President referred to George Colley, Chairman of the Boards of Governors of the IBRD and IMF, H. Johannes Witteveen, Managing Director of the IMF, and Robert S. McNamara, President of the IBRD.

Natural Gas Prices

Remarks on Senate Consideration of Price Deregulation.   September 26, 1977

Good afternoon, everybody.

Sam asked did I have a statement to make this afternoon, and I thought I'd accommodate him.

This week the Senate is voting on natural gas pricing, an issue which directly affects almost 50 million American families who depend on natural gas to heat their homes.

The Congress has been lobbied continuously by the oil and gas industry to deregulate the price of new natural gas. The House has faced this lobbying pressure and has acted both wisely and courageously to protect the integrity of the basic energy policy that I presented to the Congress at the beginning of this year. The Senate is now facing the same challenge. By 1985, the industry proposal will cost the average American family that heats with natural gas an additional $150 per year. It will cost consumers almost $10 billion every year and will produce little, if any, new supplies. Natural gas already discovered in Alaska will cost about $20 billion more if natural gas is completely deregulated, as proposed by the industry.

There comes a time when we must ask how much is enough. Fair treatment and equal sacrifice by every member and segment of our society are fundamental principles of the National Energy Plan submitted by my administration and already passed by the House.

Our proposed price under this plan would give producers strong incentives to explore and to develop new supplies of natural gas through a price which will be six times higher than the price was 5 years ago. That is enough. It's time for the public interest to prevail over special interest lobbyists.

I appreciate very much the leadership which the Senate majority leader, Senator Byrd, is providing on this particular and very important question. And I call on the Senate to act responsibly in the interest of the great majority of Americans to reject narrow, special interest attacks on all segments of the National Energy Plan.

This Nation faces a serious and a growing energy problem. Our balance of trade is very disturbing; it's so high, primarily, because of excessive oil imports. We need to discourage the waste of energy. But the lobbying efforts of oil and gas industries on deregulation itself show how the special interests are trying to block the enactment of the entire energy program.

As we depend more and more on energy imports, the special interests must not be allowed to jeopardize our energy future. We need adequate supplies. We need reasonable prices.

I realize that there have been some preliminary votes in the Senate which cause concern. But I have confidence in the judgment of the Senate and the entire Congress. And I believe that because of the great interest of the American people in this broad question of energy policy and because this is a major domestic issue that we're faced with this year, that I and the American people can continue to have confidence that the outcome of these proposals will be acceptable to me as President and will be a source of gratitude to the House and Senate by the American people when adjournment day comes.

Thank you very much.

NOTE: The President spoke at 4:40 p.m. to reporters assembled in the Briefing Room at the White House. In his remarks, he referred to Sam Donaldson of ABC News.

National Employ the Handicapped Week, 1977

Proclamation 4526.   September 27, 1977

By the President of the United States of America

A Proclamation

America needs the talents and energies of all her citizens, including the physically and mentally handicapped. But many handicapped people have been kept from full participation in our society. To the handicaps they must overcome have been added the barriers of an environment constructed without them in mind, a lack of equal education, and exclusion from rewarding and useful employment.

In recent months, however, progress has been dramatic. New laws are promoting equality for handicapped people. The recent White House Conference on Handicapped Individuals stimulated plans for the future. New ideas in education, housing, jobs, and transportation are adding to the opportunities for handicapped people to be independent, to lead fuller lives and to contribute to society. In support of these goals, I have asked the heads of Executive departments and agencies to set an example for fair employment practices by demonstrating what can be done to make the fullest possible use of the abilities of qualified handicapped people.

To affirm our commitment to the handicapped, the Congress, by joint resolution of August 11, 1945, as amended (36 U.S.C. 155), has called for the designation of the first week in October of each year as National Employ the Handicapped Week.

Now, THEREFORE, I, JIMMY CARTER, President of the United States of America, do hereby designate the week beginning October 2, 1977, as National Employ the Handicapped Week. I urge all Governors, Mayors, and other public officials, leaders in business and labor, and private citizens to take affirmative action to ensure equal employment opportunities for handicapped people and to join during this week and afterwards to work toward full equality in all aspects of American life.

IN WITNESS WHEREOF, I have hereunto set my hand this 27th day of September, in the year of our Lord nineteen hundred seventy-seven, and of the Independence of the United States of America the two hundred and second.

JIMMY CARTER

[Filed with the Office of the Federal Register, 3:20 p.m., September 27, 1977]

would replace William H. Sullivan, transferred.

Newsom was born January 6, 1918, in Richmond, Calif. He received an A.B. from the University of California in 1938 and an M.S. from Columbia University in 1940. He served in the U.S. Navy from 1942 to 1946.

Newsom was a newspaper reporter from 1938 to 1941 and publisher of the Walnut Creek (California) Courier-Journal from 1946 to 1947. He joined the Foreign Service in 1947 and from 1948 to 1950 served as information officer in Karachi.

From 1950 to 1951, Newsom was visa officer in Oslo, and from 1951 to 1955 he was public affairs officer in Baghdad. From 1956 to 1959, he was officer in charge for Arabian Peninsula affairs at the State Department.

Newsom attended the National War College in 1959, and from 1960 to 1962 he was political officer in London. In 1962 and 1963, he was Deputy Director of the Office of Northern African Affairs at the State Department, and from 1963 to 1965 he was Director of that office.

Newsom served as Ambassador to Libya from 1965 to 1969 and as Assistant Secretary of State for African Affairs from 1969 to 1974. Since 1974 he has been Ambassador to Indonesia.

United States Ambassador to the Philippines

Nomination of David D. Newsom.
September 27, 1977

The President today announced that he will nominate David D. Newsom, of Berkeley, Calif., to be Ambassador Extraordinary and Plenipotentiary of the United States to the Philippines. He

United States Ambassador to Romania

Nomination of O. Rudolph Aggrey.
September 27, 1977

The President today announced that he will nominate O. Rudolph Aggrey, of Washington, D.C., to be Ambassador Extraordinary and Plenipotentiary of the

United States to Romania. He would replace Harry G. Barnes, Jr., resigned.

Aggrey was born July 24, 1926, in Salisbury, N.C. He received a B.S. from Hampton Institute in 1946 and an M.S. from Syracuse University in 1948.

Aggrey was a publicity assistant for the United Negro College Fund of New York in 1947 and 1950. In 1948 and 1949, he was a newspaper reporter and correspondent, and in 1950 he was publicity director of Bennett College.

Aggrey joined the Foreign Service in 1951 and served as information assistant and vice consul in Lagos until 1953. In 1953 and 1954, he was assistant public affairs officer in Lille, and from 1954 to 1957 he was youth activities officer in Paris. From 1957 to 1961, he was director of the American Cultural Center in Paris.

From 1961 to 1964, Aggrey was Deputy Public Affairs Adviser in the Bureau of African Affairs at the State Department. In 1964–65 he was a fellow at the Center for International Affairs at Harvard University. From 1966 to 1968, he was deputy public affairs officer and first secretary in Kinshasa.

From 1968 to 1970, Aggrey was program manager for the Motion Picture-TV Service. From 1970 to 1973, he was Director of the Office of West African Affairs at the State Department. From 1973 until earlier this year, he was Ambassador to Senegal and the Gambia.

Columbus Day, 1977

Remarks on Signing Proclamation 4527.
September 28, 1977

This is a happy day for us. I notice the expressions on everyone's face are pleasant.

I think it's important for us, at least once a year, to recognize the significance with which Americans look upon Columbus Day. There are only two official holidays of our Nation that recognize people, men. One is Washington's Birthday, the founder of our country, and the other one is Columbus, who discovered our continent.

This is a significant occasion because it represents two basic purposes of our country. One is the spirit of discovery. Recently, we've been proud of the fact that Americans were first to the Moon, and we've admired the courage of those men who went into space. But I think an equal degree of courage was aboard the *Niña* and the *Pinta* and the *Santa María,* who embarked on an unknown path with very little support, no contact with a home base, and with very little acknowledgment at the time of their tremendous accomplishment.

And of course, the reason that they came to our country was for opportunity. Not only material wealth and a better life for people resulted from this trip but also it was the first step in a new degree of human freedom.

We have only 15 more years to go before we celebrate the 500th anniversary of Columbus' discovery. And I hope I'm around to join with you in the celebration, which I would guess would be one of the most sustained and enjoyable occurrences that ever took place in our country. I think it's not too early for us to start planning that occasion. [*Laughter*]

Five hundred years is a long time, but I think when you go back into the history of Italians, more than 2,000 years, and if you would inventory all the great achievements of humankind, those of the ancestors of Italian Americans would stand out very clearly in science, art, music, medicine, and the concepts of government and politics. And it's a heritage of which I know all of you are very deeply proud.

That heritage has not been wasted. There are great moments of pride with highly publicized, international achievements—the ones I've just mentioned—but there's another characteristic that to me is important, and that is the emphasis on family values, the tightness of the home, and the fact that the development of human beings begins with a close-knit environment of love. This has made you and other Italian Americans instrumental in the strength of neighborhoods and the preservation of values which are unchanging.

Father Geno Baroni is now a special person in my own administration, an Assistant Secretary in the Housing and Urban Development Department, but especially responsible for neighborhoods and the development of a better quality of life, again, in our urban centers.

And, of course, we all know the tremendous contributions made by many of these men and women assembled around me. I find it hard not to mention specifically Judge John Sirica and Congressman Peter Rodino who, in a moment of greatest challenge to our very system of government, extracted from their background and heritage and their love for this country, wisdom and courage that preserved our system of life.

And for all these reasons, I'm proud to be a part of this ceremony as President of our country, and I'd like to read and to sign a brief proclamation that was first signed by a President in 1934.

[*At this point, the President read the text of the proclamation.*]

In witness whereof, I have hereunto set my hand this day, and I urge all of you to be careful not to forget the celebration of this notable occasion.

NOTE: The President spoke at 9:17 a.m. at the signing ceremony in the Rose Garden at the White House.

Columbus Day, 1977
Proclamation 4527. September 28, 1977

By the President of the United States of America

A Proclamation

On October 10 we once again pay tribute to the great Italian mariner and explorer whose historic voyage of discovery led to the permanent settlement of the New World by the Old.

With the support of the Spanish Crown, Columbus journeyed across uncharted waters to open the way for future generations of immigrants who would found the new nations of the Americas.

As his heirs, we take pride in commemorating the spirit of Christopher Columbus as part of our national heritage.

In tribute to the achievement of Columbus, the Congress of the United States, by joint resolution approved April 30, 1934 (48 Stat. 657), as modified by the Act of June 28, 1968 (82 Stat. 250), requested the President to proclaim the second Monday in October of each year as Columbus Day.

Now, THEREFORE, I, JIMMY CARTER, President of the United States of America, do hereby designate Monday, October 10, 1977, as Columbus Day and invite the people of this Nation to observe that day in schools, churches, and other suitable places with appropriate ceremonies in honor of the great explorer.

I also direct that the flag of the United States be displayed on all public buildings

1675

on the appointed day in memory of Christopher Columbus.

IN WITNESS WHEREOF, I have hereunto set my hand this twenty-eighth day of September, in the year of our Lord nineteen hundred seventy-seven, and of the Independence of the United States of America the two hundred and second.

JIMMY CARTER

[Filed with the Office of the Federal Register, 4:31 p.m., September 28, 1977]

United States Arms Control and Disarmament Agency

Nomination of Barry M. Blechman To Be Assistant Director. September 28, 1977

The President today announced that he will nominate Barry M. Blechman, of Reston, Va., to be Assistant Director of the U.S. Arms Control and Disarmament Agency. His area of responsibility would be weapons evaluation and control, and he would replace Robert M. Behr, resigned.

Blechman was born April 7, 1943, in New York City. He received a B.A. from Queens College in 1963, an M.A. from New York University in 1964, and a Ph.D. from Georgetown University in 1971.

From 1965 to 1966, Blechman was an operations research analyst for the Army's Strategy and Tactics Analysis Group. From 1966 to 1971, he was on the professional staff at the Center for Naval Analyses, where he participated in several major studies of force structure issues and directed two studies on political-military questions.

Since 1971 Blechman has been a senior fellow at the Brookings Institution. He is head of Brookings' Defense Analyses Staff.

Blechman is a consultant to the Defense Department and a member of the Council on Foreign Relations. He is the author of numerous articles.

Government Printing Office

Nomination of John J. Boyle To Be Public Printer. September 28, 1977

The President today announced that he will nominate John J. Boyle, of Silver Spring, Md., to be Public Printer. He would replace T. F. McCormick, resigned.

Boyle was born January 25, 1919, in Honesdale, Pa. Following his apprenticeship and several years in the private printing industry, he joined the Government Printing Office as a proofreader in 1952.

In 1960 he became principal technical assistant in the Office of the Production Manager and the Production Manager's representative on the Scheduling Committee. In 1964 he was appointed special assistant to the Production Manager for electronic printing.

In 1971 Boyle became Deputy Production Manager (electronics). He was detailed as Production Manager in 1972. Since 1973 he has been Deputy Public Printer.

Federal Energy Regulatory Commission

Nomination of Don S. Smith To Be a Commissioner. September 28, 1977

The President today announced that he will nominate Don S. Smith, of Arkansas, to be a Commissioner of the Federal Energy Regulatory Commission for a term of 2 years.

1676

Smith was born October 9, 1937, in Ouachita County, Ark. He received a B.A. from the University of Arkansas in 1960 and an LL.B. from the University of Arkansas School of Law in 1962.

From 1963 to 1967, Smith was an assistant professor, then associate professor of law at Emory University School of Law. He was the Arkansas securities commissioner from 1967 until 1969, when he became a member of the Arkansas Public Service Commission. Since 1973 he has been a Commissioner of the Federal Power Commission. He served as Vice Chairman of the Commission for 1975 and was reelected Vice Chairman for the latter half of 1977.

Smith has served as Arkansas member and chairman of the Southern Interstate Nuclear Board, chairman of the Laws and Regulations Committee of the Southern Governors' Conference Task Force on Nuclear Power Policy, and Arkansas member of the Steering Committee of the Southern Regional Environmental Conservation Council. He is a member of the Executive Committee of the National Association of Regulatory Utility Commissioners and designated official FPC observer on the Interstate Oil Compact Commission.

Meeting With Foreign Minister Abd al Halim Khaddam of Syria

White House Statement Issued Following the Meeting Between the President and the Foreign Minister.   September 28, 1977

The President and Syrian Deputy Prime Minister and Foreign Minister Abd al Halim Khaddam met in the Cabinet Room for 1 hour and 5 minutes. The meeting was also attended by Vice President Mondale; Secretary of State Cyrus Vance; Hamilton Jordan, Assistant to the President; David Aaron, Deputy Assistant to the President for National Security Affairs; Alfred L. Atherton, Jr., Assistant Secretary of State for Near Eastern and South Asian Affairs; Richard Murphy, U.S. Ambassador to Syria; and William Quandt, National Security Council staff member, on the American side; and His Excellency Dr. Sabah Kabbani, Ambassador of the Syrian Arab Republic to the United States; and Mr. Abd al-Salam Aqil, private secretary to the Deputy Prime Minister, on the Syrian side.

The President began by expressing his pleasure at this opportunity to meet again with Minister Khaddam, recalling their friendly talks at the White House last April and at the time of President Carter's meeting with President Asad in Geneva in May. The President underlined the importance he attributes to Syrian participation in the peace efforts underway in the Middle East and reaffirmed his determination to continue those efforts to reach a comprehensive settlement of the Arab-Israeli conflict. In this connection, the President repeated his own conviction that a just and lasting peace in this vital area of the world requires compromise and courageous leadership from all the parties to the negotiations.

The President and the Minister agreed on the importance of working to reconvene the Geneva conference by the end of this year. They discussed the substantive issues of a settlement and, while noting that differences exist between our respective views on some points, they agreed that these efforts at finding concrete solutions to the core issues of the conflict should continue. Secretary Vance will pursue the discussion with the Minister, listening to his ideas and explaining in detail American suggestions for reconciling differences between the parties on the key elements of a settlement. The President and the Minister also discussed the problem of Palestinian representation at Geneva, agreeing that this question must be resolved if the Geneva conference is to be reconvened.

The President concluded by expressing his gratification with the steady improvement in relations between Syria and the United States. He emphasized that these good relations aid the cause of reaching a just and lasting peace in the Middle East. The President asked the Minister to assure President Asad that he intends to carry on American efforts to that end.

Meeting With Jordanian Representatives

White House Statement Issued Following the Meeting Between the President and Chief of the Royal Court Sharif Abdul Hamid Sharaf and Foreign Minister Hassan Ibrahim. September 28, 1977

The President and Chief of the Royal Court Sharif Abdul Hamid Sharaf and Jordanian Minister of State for Foreign Affairs Hassan Ibrahim met in the Cabinet Room for 1 hour and 20 minutes. The meeting was also attended by Vice President Mondale; Secretary of State Cyrus Vance; David Aaron, Deputy Assistant to the President for National Security Affairs; Alfred L. Atherton, Jr., Assistant Secretary of State for Near Eastern and South Asian Affairs; Thomas Pickering, U.S. Ambassador to Jordan; and William Quandt, National Security Council staff member, on the American side; and by Jordanian Ambassador to the United States Abdullah Salah.

The President welcomed the two Jordanian representatives to the White House by reaffirming the longstanding friendship and support of the Government and people of the United States for His Majesty King Hussein and the people of the Hashemite Kingdom of Jordan. The President noted that these strong ties are a firm basis for our mutual search for a just and lasting peace in the Middle East. As he had in his earlier meetings here with foreign ministers from the area, the President underlined his own conviction that peace requires compromise and courageous leadership from all the parties to the negotiations.

The President and Jordanian representatives agreed on the importance of finding a formula to begin negotiations through reconvening the Geneva conference by the end of the year. They discussed procedural issues involved in resuming the conference and the substantive issues to be resolved in an overall settlement. The Jordanian representatives presented Jordan's ideas for a just settlement. The President responded that the Jordanian ideas will be useful in the continuing talks with Middle East foreign ministers. Secretary Vance, who had begun talks with the Jordanians here at an earlier meeting, will be pursuing the discussion both of their ideas and American suggestions for reconciling differences between the parties. The meeting today devoted some time to the specific problem of how the Palestinians should be represented at the Geneva conference. The President and Jordanian representatives agreed that this current round of talks should seek a solution to this question, so as to achieve the common goal of reconvening Geneva as soon as possible.

The President concluded by asking the Jordanian representatives to convey to King Hussein his assurances that he remains committed to doing all possible in continuing efforts toward a comprehensive settlement in the Middle East.

Country Music Month, October 1977

Message of the President.
September 28, 1977

As a native of rural America, I grew up with country music and join with great enthusiasm with all those who celebrate Country Music Month.

Anyone who has spent time living and working on a farm or touring the rural areas and small towns of our nation has learned to appreciate the musical legacy of this part of our country. It embraces the joys, sorrows, experiences and hopes of daily life. It echoes the greatness, goodness and diligence of hard working men and women.

Along with millions of fans, I salute the creative genius of those to whom country music owes its ever-growing popularity.

JIMMY CARTER

NOTE: For the President's proclamation on Country Music Month, see page 1697 of this volume.

Food and Agriculture Act of 1977

Remarks on Signing S. 275 Into Law.
September 29, 1977

THE PRESIDENT. I think all of you can see before me the results of a tremendous amount of work and cooperation among all those in our Government who are interested in the present and future strength of our Nation's number one economic resource, and that's agriculture.

I think it's also accurate to point out that more than has ever been the case in the past, that professional nutritionists and their representatives, private citizens, consumer groups, have been involved in the preparation of this legislation.

Another fact that I think would be undisputed is that in the last 40 years, there has never been such a far-reaching and important piece of legislation passed relating to American agriculture. There's been a heavy emphasis in this bill on the strength of the American farm family. This is an important concept for us all.

We are very eager to continue our preeminent position in international agricultural trade circles. Public Law 480, which permits us to dispose of American food products in a beneficial way, is enhanced. Foreign trade with the sale of our own agricultural commodities is enhanced.

We have in this bill, too, a new approach to the food stamp question. This has sometimes been considered as an anomaly or an anachronism in a modern day Department of Agriculture. But I think this legislation that has been included in the Food and Agriculture Act of 1977 is a great step forward in providing a simple food stamp system and one that would be easy to administer, one that is more equitable, which eliminates the pervasive threat of fraud.

I'd also like to point out that this bill includes many other features—a renewed emphasis and an enhancement of our research program in agriculture that's so important to every family.

It, for the first time, makes a major step toward tying target prices to actual production costs. This has been one of the most controversial issues that the Congress has had to face. Obviously, because production costs vary so widely from one community to another, and a bill of this kind has to deal with average prices or cost of production throughout the country, there still remain and will inevitably remain some inequities.

But this bill makes a giant step toward tying target prices with production costs, and it also narrows its focus on individual commodities so that there can be more equity insured.

This bill also sets up a means for maintaining adequate food reserves. Although we have been blessed recently with bountiful crops, we don't have an excessive reserve supply of crucial food and feed items on hand. This bill permits us to maintain adequate reserves, and it also encompasses a provision that's very dear to me, and that is that most of the reserves will be under the control of farmers and that there's a very careful safeguard against the dumping of agricultural products on the market, artificially, to force prices down and, therefore, to damage the economy of farm families.

We have moved in this bill to correct a very serious economic problem that exists among the farm communities of our Nation by increasing target and loan prices for the 1977 crop. And I believe that this will certainly be a good investment both this year and in the future.

Another aspect of this bill that particularly appeals to me is the reduction of Government interference in the agricultural economy. This is always devoutly to be sought, and I think the Congress has very wisely achieved this goal in this current legislation.

We've eliminated acreage allotments. Quite often in the past, acreage allotments historically have evolved into a financial measure of the benefit of Government programs, and they are bought and traded like actual property. This bill moves to eliminate those acreage allotments.

We've also maintained an important element in the set-aside authority for the Agriculture Secretary. And very shortly now, set-aside regulations will be promulgated by this Department.

I have to admit that the bill is about $300 million more costly than I had personally preferred to see. But I think the investment is a good one. And I think the cost of this bill, because of its wise drafting, will be less and less as the future years go by.

We have an exceptional case at the present time in agriculture, where additional expenditures are required. One of the elements of agricultural legislation and appropriations which is often overlooked is that at least half the costs that are normally attributed to an agricultural bill are actually in the form of redeemable loans. And this is not an expenditure from the Federal Government; it's an investment in a very good and sound commodity. The loan is secured and the loans are repaid, but under our present accounting system, this is identified as an expenditure, and it tends to distort in the public mind the degree of Federal investment in agriculture.

I'd like to close by saying that I'm very proud of the good work that has been done this year, and in years gone by, by Senator Talmadge, the chairman of the Senate committee and, of course, by Tom Foley and Bob Poage and all those Democrats and Republicans who've worked with them, both within the committee and on the floor of Congress.

These have been tedious studies and negotiations. Bob Bergland and his staff in the Department of Agriculture have worked very harmoniously with the congressional leaders. And as the President of our country, as a farmer myself, as someone who feels a direct responsibility to the consumers of this country, I'm very proud now to affix my signature onto the Food and Agriculture Act of 1977 and ratify into law one of the most progressive and far-reaching pieces of legislation that has come before me.

Thank you very much, all of you.

Unaccustomed as he is to public speaking, I would still like to ask Senator Talmadge to say just a word, if he would. [*Laughter*]

SENATOR HERMAN E. TALMADGE. Thank you very much, Mr. President. I think you've correctly summarized the purpose of the Agriculture Act of 1977 and properly paid respect to Bob Bergland, Tom Foley, all the members of the committee, your staff in the White House who worked so very cooperatively and so diligently in formulating this legislation. It's a big asset to the American people, and to the world, for that matter.

THE PRESIDENT. I certainly agree with that, Senator.

Chairman Tom Foley.

REPRESENTATIVE THOMAS S. FOLEY. Mr. President, I can only echo those remarks of Senator Talmadge and express our deep appreciation to you and to the Secretary and to all of those in your administration who have worked so cooperatively with all of those members of the committee, Republicans and Democrats, House and Senate, to bring this bill about. And I want to also say that I join with you in expressing appreciation to Bob Poage, the vice chairman of our committee and a man who I think on our side represents the most skilled and knowledgeable single Member of the House of Representatives in agriculture. He's leaving us next year when he retires, but he takes with him all of our good wishes and thanks for all he has done on this bill and every other bill in agriculture.

THE PRESIDENT. Well, I know that all of you in the audience and in the press are very eager to read this legislation in detail. [*Laughter*] And I would like very much to have your comments about it after you've read it word by word. It's an exciting document and one that I think is going to be a great boon not only to American family farmers but to everyone who consumes our products.

Thank you very much.

NOTE: The President spoke at 10:30 a.m. at the signing ceremony in the Rose Garden at the White House.

As enacted, S. 275 is Public Law 95–113, approved September 29.

Federal Civilian and Military Pay Increases

Executive Order 12010.   September 28, 1977

ADJUSTMENTS OF CERTAIN RATES OF PAY AND ALLOWANCES

By virtue of the authority vested in me by the Constitution and the laws of the United States of America, and as President of the United States of America, it is hereby ordered as follows:

SECTION 1. *Statutory Pay Systems.* Pursuant to the provisions of subchapter I of Chapter 53 of Title 5 of the United States Code, the rates of basic pay and salaries are adjusted, as set forth at the schedules attached hereto and made a part hereof, for the following statutory pay systems:

(a) The General Schedule (5 U.S.C. 5332(a)) at Schedule 1;

(b) the schedules for the Foreign Service (22 U.S.C. 867 and 870(a)) at Schedule 2; and

(c) the schedules for the Department of Medicine and Surgery, Veterans Administration (38 U.S.C. 4107) at Schedule 3.

SEC. 2. *Pay and Allowances for Members of the Uniformed Services.* Pursuant to the provisions of Section 1009 of Title 37 of the United States Code, the rates of monthly basic pay (37 U.S.C. 203 (a) and (c)), the rates of basic allowances for subsistence (37 U.S.C. 402), and the rates of basic allowances for quarters (37 U.S.C. 403(a)) are adjusted, as set forth at Schedule 4 attached hereto and made a part hereof, for members of the uniformed services.

SEC. 3. *Effective Date.* The adjustments in rates of monthly basic pay and basic allowances for subsistence and quarters for members of the uniformed services shall be effective on October 1, 1977. All other adjustments of salary or pay shall be effective on the first day of the first applicable pay period beginning on or after October 1, 1977.

SEC. 4. *Superseded Orders.* Executive Order No. 11941 of October 1, 1976, is superseded.

JIMMY CARTER

The White House,
    September 28, 1977.

[Filed with the Office of the Federal Register, 2:30 p.m., September 29, 1977]

NOTE: The pay schedules attached to the Executive order are printed in the FEDERAL REGISTER of September 30.

The text of the Executive order was released on September 29.

Federal Civilian and Military Pay Increases

Message to the Congress.   September 29, 1977

To the Congress of the United States:

In accordance with the provisions of section 5305 of title 5 of the United States Code, I hereby report on the comparability adjustment I am ordering for the Federal statutory pay systems in October 1977.

The Secretary of Labor, the Director of the Office of Management and Budget and the Chairman of the United States Civil Service Commission, who serve jointly as my agent for Federal pay, have proposed a 7.05 percent across-the-board increase in pay rates for the Federal statutory pay systems. The Advisory Committee on Federal Pay has concurred with this recommendation.

While the Federal Employees Pay Council recommended a larger increase, I have decided that the 7.05 percent increase fully satisfies the principles set forth in the Federal Pay Comparability Act of 1970 that Federal salaries be comparable with those in private enterprise for the same levels of work.

I am transmitting herewith the reports of my Pay Agent and the Advisory Committee, as well as a copy of the Executive order I have promulgated to put this pay adjustment into effect.

JIMMY CARTER

The White House,
    September 29, 1977.

Military Pay Increase

Message to the Congress.   September 29, 1977

To the Congress of the United States:

In accord with 37 U.S.C. 1009(c), I am hereby advising the Congress that I plan to exercise the discretionary authority provided by 37 U.S.C. 1009(c), as added by section 303 of the Department of Defense Appropriation Authorization Act, 1977 (Public Law 94–361), with respect to adjustments in the levels of compensation for the members of the uniformed services.

The amendments to 37 U.S.C. 1009 made by that act provide discretionary authority to apply the adjustments (based on the overall average percentage increase in General Schedule rates of basic pay, in accord with 37 U.S.C. 1009(a)) to the basic pay, quarters allowances and subsistence allowances of the uniformed services on a percentage basis other than an equal percentage basis. Those amendments also provide discretionary authority to pay a partial quarters allowance to bachelors in government quarters, on field duty and on sea duty.

The current levels of the military allowances for quarters and for subsistence are less than the costs of the services they are intended to procure. Because of this deficiency in the current level of these allowances, it is my considered judgment that a reallocation of the October 1, 1977 military basic pay increase is appropriate. However, in consideration of the negative impact of reallocation on some military members, I am not going to reallocate the full 25 percent which I am authorized by law to do. I plan to reallocate 12 percent of the basic pay increase, by grade, all to the basic allowance for quarters, and to increase the partial quarters allowance to bachelors in government quarters, and to those on sea duty or on field duty, by an amount equal to that reallocated from the basic pay increase. This action takes a positive step toward improving the current relationship of the quarters allowance to the costs of off-post housing and, at the same time, recognizes the adverse impact of reallocation on some military members by limiting it to a moderate amount.

Specifically, the amount allocated to the element of monthly basic pay for each grade shall be 88 percent of the amount that would have been allocated to that element under 37 U.S.C. 1009 (b) (3); the elements of monthly basic allowance for subsistence and monthly basic allowance for quarters for each grade shall be increased by an amount which is of the same percentage as the overall average percentage increase in the General Schedule rates, except that the element of monthly basic allowance for quarters shall be increased by an additional amount by grade equal to 12 percent of the amount that would have been allocated to the element of monthly basic pay under 37 U.S.C. 1009(b) (3). Members without dependents, who, under 37 U.S.C. 403 (b) or (c), are not entitled to

receive a basic allowance for quarters, shall be paid an increase in the monthly partial basic allowance for quarters in an amount equal to the additional amount allocated by grade to the element of monthly basic allowance for quarters under 37 U.S.C. 1009(c).

JIMMY CARTER

The White House,
    September 29, 1977.

Federal Maritime Commission

Nomination of Thomas F. Moakley To Be a Commissioner. September 29, 1977

The President today announced that he will nominate Thomas F. Moakley, of Whitman, Mass., to be a Commissioner of the Federal Maritime Commission for the remainder of the term expiring June 30, 1978. He would replace Bob Casey, resigned.

Moakley was born November 3, 1921, in Boston, Mass. He graduated from Bentley College in 1940.

Moakley worked in steamship operations and administration for the United Fruit Co. for 12 years and in 1960 was cofounder of Dataman Associates, a consulting company specializing in electronic data processing and personnel. He was treasurer of Dataman Associates until 1966.

From 1966 to 1968, Moakley was a personnel consultant, and from 1968 to 1970 he was postmaster of Whitman, Mass.

Since 1970 he has worked for the Massachusetts Port Authority, serving as port auditor, then comptroller and assistant treasurer, and currently as port director of the Port of Boston.

White Cane Safety Day, 1977

Proclamation 4528. September 29, 1977

By the President of the United States of America

A Proclamation

The white cane, an ingeniously simple device in an age of complex technology, helps assure that those with impaired or lost vision can lead rich and useful lives.

Remarkable progress in public attitudes toward blindness has been made in recent years. It is now widely understood that blindness need not be a barrier to full participation in social and economic life, and the white cane is responsible for some of this progress.

Nevertheless, in certain situations—on a busy street, near construction sites, or wherever there are unusual obstacles or hazards—a white cane user may still need help. Yet some people may be reluctant to offer it, for fear of saying or doing the wrong thing. Most blind people understand this hesitancy and are glad to explain their needs if they are asked.

The white cane also signals to motorists and cyclists that the user is blind—but it cannot signal the user that a vehicle is approaching. Thus it is the driver's responsibility to exercise extra caution.

To heighten public awareness of the importance of the white cane to the independence and safety of thousands of blind and visually handicapped Americans, the Congress, by a joint resolution approved October 6, 1964 (78 Stat. 1003· 36 U.S.C. 169d), has authorized the President to proclaim October 15 of each year as White Cane Safety Day.

Now, THEREFORE, I, JIMMY CARTER, President of the United States of America, do hereby proclaim October 15, 1977, as White Cane Safety Day.

IN WITNESS WHEREOF, I have hereunto set my hand this twenty-ninth day of September, in the year of our Lord nineteen hundred seventy-seven, and of the Independence of the United States of America the two hundred and second.

JIMMY CARTER

[Filed with the Office of the Federal Register, 11:32 a.m., September 30, 1977]

THE PRESIDENT'S NEWS CONFERENCE OF SEPTEMBER 29, 1977

THE PRESIDENT. Good afternoon, everybody.

After the last press conference, I had an uneasy feeling that I had not adequately covered the question about energy and some foreign affairs, so I thought we would have another press conference fairly soon after that one.

NATIONAL ENERGY PLAN

About 5 months ago, in April, I spoke with the American people and with the Congress about one of the most pressing national needs—to develop a comprehensive energy policy. The reason that we have to act is not because we have crises or emergencies at this present time, but because they are imminent, and we need to begin preparing now to protect our own economic and our national security well-being for the future.

With every passing day, our energy problems become more severe. We have, almost unbelievably, spent $23 billion so far this year on imported oil, and we are likely to spend almost $45 billion before the year is over. This is by far more than we have ever bought before. Gasoline consumption was higher this summer than it has ever been before, and now half of the oil that we use, much of it wastefully, came from foreign countries.

No matter how hard we try to ignore it, our energy problem is not going away. There is no easy way to establish a comprehensive energy policy. No interest group or organization can be totally satisfied with every part of our plan. But the House of Representatives has met this very difficult and controversial issue courageously and has adopted almost all of the program that was proposed to them last April.

This proposal is balanced, fair, and comprehensive, and it contains incentives for adequate production and also protects the interest of consumers.

By relying on incentives rather than prohibitions and regulations, it keeps to a minimum the direct Government involvement that would otherwise be necessary to control our energy problems and which exist at the present time.

Oil producers will receive the equivalent of the world price for newly discovered oil, and between now and 1990 oil and gas profits from domestic exploration and production, under my own program, will exceed $430 billion.

We accept these incentives, knowing that they are necessary to guarantee future supplies of oil and natural gas. What we do not accept is the argument that we hear from the oil and gas companies that we need to provide incentives for wells that were drilled in 1970 or 1972, or even earlier, when oil prices were about one-fourth what they are now. We do not accept windfall profits for efforts that the producers have already made and for oil and gas already discovered.

I do not support complete deregulation of natural gas prices, which would provide windfall profits without significantly increasing supply. Deregulation would cost consumers an extra $70 billion by 1985 but would increase supplies very little, if any. Gas prices have already risen by 500 percent over the last 6 years, but we are producing less natural gas than we did in 1972, 6 years ago.

Along with production incentives, the National Energy Plan also contains vital measures to conserve energy and to replace our precious oil and gas with more abundant fuels, such as coal. Let me mention quickly in closing three of the most important of these conservation measures.

Unless we pass the oil equalization tax, we will in effect continue to subsidize, with an extremely complicated Government program, imports of oil. The gas-guzzler tax is crucial because it provides a continuous economic incentive for consumers to buy and automobile makers to produce more efficient automobiles.

The large industrial users of oil and gas must be persuaded to convert to coal and to other fuels. This effort alone could account for about 40 percent of the total oil savings that we project in the energy program.

And, finally, the rate structure for electric power must be modified to discourage waste.

We are now at a turning point in establishing a comprehensive energy program. The House of Representatives has acted. The Senate is still in the process. I'd like to take this opportunity to thank the majority leader and many of the Senate leaders for their work toward resolving the difficult questions that now face the

Senate. It's a difficult job, I know, and at times an unpleasant one, but the price of failing to enact a comprehensive energy program is just too high for our Nation.

I think the American people are expecting their Government—the Congress and the President—to establish an energy program. And I sincerely hope that the Senate will not let the American people be disappointed.

Thank you very much.

Mr. Cormier [Frank Cormier, Associated Press].

QUESTIONS

SENATE ACTION ON ENERGY

Q. Mr. President, the Senate hasn't obviously completed action, but on the basis of their votes in committee and elsewhere so far, the difference between them and the House is so marked, how do you account for it? Are they less representative? Are they more susceptible to lobby pressures? How do you figure it?

THE PRESIDENT. Well, first of all, I'd like to point out that no final action has been taken by the Senate. And there were times several weeks ago when we were quite disappointed at the progress that had been made in the House. As the Members of the House of Representatives began to realize the enormity of the consequences of their timid action and as the Speaker and other leaders moved forward to assert their influence, the House acted responsibly after giving us a disappointing time for a few weeks.

I think the Senate is now in that posture. I think the Senate realizes that this is the major domestic legislative product that we expect this year. And for us to devote a full year of work and come out with an inconsequential or inadequate energy program is something that I don't

believe the Senate will face. They have their own reputations to protect.

I think they want to act responsibly. And I think that it is obvious, in my own experience in the legislative branch in Georgia, that the focusing of the powerful lobby pressure is always on the second legislative body that has to act, the final body that has to act. So, there is a tremendous pressure on the Members of the Senate now from the lobbyists, many of whom are well-meaning people—I am not criticizing them necessarily—but I think as they hear the voice of the American people, as they realize the consequences of an absence of courageous action, then I think they will move to adopt the major parts of the program.

The last thing I'd like to say is that when the Senate acts, we still have what is in effect a third branch of government to consider and to exert its will, and that's the conference committees. And I think the House is going to be very adamant in maintaining their position. And the likelihood now is that I would be much more inclined to support the House position, which is compatible with my own.

So, we still have a long way to go. I'm not discouraged, but I think my own voice is helpful in encouraging the American people to let the Senators know what their duties are and to encourage them to act objectively. And I'm sure they will.

GENEVA CONFERENCE

Q. Mr. President, there have been a lot of confusing statements from the White House and from leaders who have seen you recently on where exactly the United States stands in terms of Palestinian—PLO participation in a Geneva peace conference, if one comes about. Can you really clarify this point?

THE PRESIDENT. I doubt it— [*laughter*]—but I would be glad to try. What we are trying to do now is—as a first and immediate goal—is to bring all the parties in the Mideast dispute to Geneva for a conference. We are dealing with Israel directly. We are dealing directly with Lebanon, Syria, Jordan, and Egypt. We are trying to act as an intermediary between Israel and each one of those Arab countries that border their own country.

There are some differences among the Arab nations, which we are trying to resolve, concerning a unified Arab delegation or individual Arab delegations and the format which might be used to let the Palestinian views be represented.

At the same time, we have a further complicating factor in that we are joint chairmen of the Geneva conference along with the Soviet Union. So, in the call for the conference, in the negotiations preceding the format of the conference, we have to deal with the Soviet Union as well. So, on top of all that, and perhaps preeminent in my own mind, is that we are not an idle observer or bystander, we are not just an intermediary or mediator. We have a vital national interest in the ultimate peace in the Middle East.

It's obvious to me that there can be no Middle Eastern peace settlement without adequate Palestinian representation. The Arab countries maintain that the PLO is the only legitimate representative of the Palestinian interests. The Israelis say that they won't deal with the Palestinians, or certainly not the well-known PLO members, because they have been identified in the past as committed to the destruction of the nation of Israel.

So, we are trying to get an agreement between the Israelis and the Arab countries, with widely divergent views, about the format of the meeting and, also, who would be welcomed to the conference to represent the Palestinians.

This is something that is still in the negotiating stage, and I cannot predict a final outcome. We have no national position on exactly who would represent the Palestinians or exactly what form the Arab group would take in which the Palestinians would be represented. I just can't answer that question yet because the question has not been answered in my mind.

PALESTINE LIBERATION ORGANIZATION

Q. Does the United States recognize—"recognize" is the wrong word—but accept the PLO as a representative of the Palestinians?

THE PRESIDENT. We have pledged to the Israelis in the past, and I have confirmed the pledge, that we will not negotiate with, nor deal directly with the PLO until they adopt United Nations Resolution 242 as a basis for their involvement, which includes a recognition of the right of Israel to exist. We have let this be known to the PLO leaders through various intermediaries, through intermediaries through the United Nations, leaders in Saudi Arabia, Syria, Egypt, Jordan, and so forth. They know our position.

If the PLO should go ahead and say, "We endorse U.N. Resolution 242; we don't think it adequately addresses the Palestinian issue because it only refers to refugees and we think we have a further interest in that," that would suit us okay.

We would then begin to meet with and to work with the PLO. Obviously, they don't represent a nation. It is a group that represents, certainly, a substantial part of the Palestinians. I certainly don't think they are the exclusive representatives of the Palestinians. Obviously, there are mayors, for instance, and local officials in the West Bank area who represent Palestinians. They may or may not be members of the PLO. So, we are not trying to define an exact formula that we would prescribe for others. We are trying to find some common ground on which the Israelis and Arabs might get together to meet in Geneva.

I think, by the way, that both the groups, the Arabs and the Israelis, have come a long way. They are genuinely searching for a formula by which they can meet. They want peace. And I think they are to be congratulated already, because in the past number of years they have made very strong and provocative statements against one another, and now, to move toward an accommodation is a difficult thing for them. And we are trying not to make it any more difficult.

Q. Mr. President, what are the assurances given to the PLO in the event of accepting 242?

THE PRESIDENT. If they accept U.N. 242 and the right of Israel to exist, then we will begin discussions with the leaders of the PLO. We are not giving them any further assurance of that because we are not trying to prescribe, as I said, the status of the PLO itself in any Geneva conference. But it would give us a means to understand the special problems of the Palestinians. And as you know, many of the Israeli—some of the Israeli leaders have said that they recognize that the Palestinian question is one of the three major elements. But I can't and have no inclination to give the PLO any assurances other than we will begin to meet with them and to search for some accommodation and some reasonable approach to the Palestinian question if they adopt 242 and recognize publicly the right of Israel to exist.

RELATIONS WITH CONGRESS

Q. Mr. President, this morning a group of Republicans who came over here to meet with you reported that you told them that on certain matters you perhaps worked even more closely with them than the Democratic majority. I wonder if, noting what has been happening to some of your programs in the Congress, that you feel more comfortable with the Republicans now, and what effect do you think those words this morning will have on the eventual outcome of certain energy matters in the Senate which must, of course, receive support from the Democrats?

THE PRESIDENT. Energy was not one of the examples I used. I did point out the almost unanimous approval of the Republicans, for instance, for the AWACS sale to Iran, which I think is important and advisable, and I pointed that one out.

I also pointed out the extreme inadvisability of the Congress trying to put tight controls over our international financial institutions allotments. For instance, the Congress has said, in a very serious mistake, that we could not contribute to the World Bank or to the international regional banks if any of the money was to be used in a country that produced citrus fruits or palm oil or sugar, or if it was to be used for loans to, I think, eight different nations.

This is an unprecedented encroachment on the independence of the World Bank, and it would mean that our contribution to the World Bank could not be made. This is another item where the Republicans see the matter much more clearly, in my opinion, than do some of the Democrats.

But in general, of course, I am a very loyal Democrat. I appreciate what the Democrats have done, but in some areas the Republicans have helped me more.

I would say another example would be the reorganization effort. I think as a matter of philosophy, the moderate-to-conservative Members of the Congress and I see compatibly a need for strict Government reorganization. But this means, certainly, that many Democrats have cooperated just as well.

VICE PRESIDENT'S ROLE

Q. Mr. President, you have been underscoring of late how very important the Vice President—very important role he is playing in your administration. And I was just wondering whether the Vice President has become in actuality as well as in effect your deputy, the deputy President or assistant President?

THE PRESIDENT. I probably meet with the Vice President on a daily basis more than all the other staff members that I have combined. He brings to my own inner circle of advisers an experience in the Congress and in Washington. He, obviously, has a stature, political stature inherent in his office itself. And his wide-ranging interests, that I have welcomed and encouraged, include domestic politics, our relationships with the Congress, domestic matters like tax reform, sensitive civil matters like the Bakke case, international matters like southern Africa or the Middle East. He has a detailed knowledge of the SALT negotiations now and the history of SALT negotiations in the past.

So, there is no aspect of my own daily responsibilities as President that are not shared by the Vice President. He has a unique background in the Congress of having been both a member, simultaneously, of the Senate Finance Committee and also the Senate Budget Committee. So, here again, he's had a broad range of experience.

I would say, without derogating the other members of my staff, that there is no one who would approach him in his importance to me, his closeness to me and, also, his ability to carry out a singular assignment with my complete trust.

SALT NEGOTIATIONS

Q. Mr. President, it is said that we have modified our SALT position somewhat and, on the basis of that, we may be very near an agreement, and, on the basis of that, you may be meeting with Mr. Brezhnev in a few weeks or months. Is any or all of that true? [*Laughter*]

THE PRESIDENT. I will resist the temptation to comment on the accuracy or veracity of past comments made in the news media—and by you—[*laughing*]—I understand.

I think some of those statements are fairly accurate. We have been encouraged recently by the cooperative attitude of the Soviets. I have met several hours, on two occasions, with Foreign Minister Gromyko. And they have been fairly flexible in their attitude, and we have tried to match their cooperative stance.

There has been no decision made about a time or place for a meeting between me and Mr. Brezhnev. In fact, the meeting itself is certainly not a sure thing at all. It is, as a matter of record, his time to come to the United States, if and when a meeting does take place, and he has that permanent standing invitation which he can accept as he sees fit.

Our purpose in the SALT negotiations this year has been generally twofold: One is to reduce the overall level of nuclear armaments; and secondly, to have an assurance that there is an equivalent capability in the future to give a reasonable sense of security to both nations. And I think, at the same time, integrally with this is to let the Soviets know that we are negotiating in good faith, that we are not trying to pull a trick, or to take unfair advantage over them.

At the same time, I recognize that progress on SALT leads to further progress on comprehensive test ban, on the matter of nonproliferation, on general reductions in armament sales around the world. And I think it would lessen tensions between us and the Soviets that have existed historically.

So, we are making some progress. An immediate agreement is not in prospect. We have narrowed down the differences to a relatively small number which could take quite a long time to resolve. Our negotiators are now going back to Geneva to try to eliminate as many of the differences as possible. So, reasonable progress has been made.

I wouldn't be too optimistic about an early settlement. And there is no plan at this time for a meeting with Mr. Brezhnev.

STEEL AND TELEVISION INDUSTRIES

Q. Mr. President, important segments of the steel and television manufacturing industries have been laying off thousands of workers recently because of foreign competition, some of which they allege is unfair. What, if anything, do you plan to do about that?

THE PRESIDENT. Well, we have already negotiated in the television industry a voluntary constraint on the Japanese, who are the major exporters to us. This was worked out this year by Robert Strauss, working even directly with Prime Minister Fukuda. I think this will alleviate the increasing imports of color televisions which were causing a problem.

The steel question is one that is obviously a highly complex question. I would not be willing to lay all the blame on imports. We have obviously some elements in the steel industry, where the plants themselves are older—they are not quite as efficient as some of the more modern plants overseas. We have a problem that the steel industry points out frequently in the compliance with fairly strict environmental quality standards, which I certainly would not change.

But I think it's fair to point out the Japanese and the West Germans have the same degree of quality constraints now on air pollution and water pollution. So, this is not an unnecessary advantage for them.

I might add quickly that we are addressing the steel industry with a multidepartmental approach. This is under the control of an Assistant Secretary [Under Secretary] in the Treasury Department, Mr. Solomon, who is an expert on the steel industry. He is working with Robert Strauss, our Special Trade Representative, and with Charles Schultze, my Council of Economic Advisers Chairman, with the Secretaries of Commerce and Labor.

Where large unemployment has been a factor with the closing of at least one steel mill, we have already moved to provide retraining and economic assistance for those workers involved. And within the next few weeks, I plan to receive the report of this group whose work was begun several weeks ago and then to meet with labor and industry leaders in the steel industry and also with Congress Members who have large steel interests in their own areas.

But we believe that the problems are chronic. I don't think any basic changes need to be made in our import laws or in the national statutes. And I think that perhaps my own involvement in it can cause some alleviation of the problem. But some of the problems are chronic.

The worldwide economic structure is not growing as rapidly as it has in the past. Ours is better off than most of the other nations'. And when the growth rate in our country drops down to 6 percent this year and many other major nations' drop to 4 percent or less, there is just not as many orders for steel. It's complicated. We are moving on it. And when I receive this report and decide what to do, I will make it public.

Charlie [Charles Mohr, New York Times].

RICHARD HELMS

Q. Mr. President, Admiral Turner of the CIA did a speech this week at Annapolis in which he said that the Attorney General would have to make a decision as to whether it would further the national interests to prosecute the case of Mr. Richard Helms, or whether it would be better to waive the case in order to save the secrets. But the Attorney General said that he was going to consult you on this.

I wonder if you can tell us your views on how you are reaching this decision as to whether certain material should be declassified for a possible trial in this case?

THE PRESIDENT. He has not consulted with me, nor given me any advice on the Helms question. I am familiar with it through reading in the press. I have no way to know yet the strength of the possible indictment or charges. I have no way to know yet the seriousness of the offense with which he will be charged (instead of "he will be charged.", the President meant "he may be charged.")[1] And I have no way to know yet the seriousness of possible damage to our own

---

[1] Printed in the White House Press Office transcript.

national security if massive revelations of intelligence techniques and documents are made either to ourselves or to our friends and allies.

When I get all this information, then I would certainly consult with the Attorney General as to what action should be taken. I think it's a very serious thing for anyone to commit perjury (instead of "commit perjury" the President meant "commit alleged perjury")[1] before a congressional committee or anywhere else. And the matter would not in any case be treated lightly.

My understanding is that the Attorney General is now going over the data that have been presented to him. I think he will make a report to me and possibly a recommendation fairly soon. But until this moment, he has not yet done so.

I promised Marty [Martin J. Schram, Newsday].

BERT LANCE

Q. Mr. President, pardon me, I would like to go back to the subject of last week's press conference. You told us twice that you'd learned on December 1, which was just 2 days before you appointed Mr. Lance—nominated him——

THE PRESIDENT. Yes.

Q. ——that aspects of the Lance case had been referred to the Justice Department. Jody Powell has told us that you didn't know at that time, you didn't learn until much later. Who is right? Is Jody right, or are you?

THE PRESIDENT. I don't recall—I did say that in the last press conference. And when Jody asked me about it afterwards, I told him I was mistaken. I don't recall at all ever knowing that the Justice Department itself was involved in the Bert Lance overdraft or other problems last year. Bert Lance told me that he did not know that the Justice Department was involved in it until December 1. The information that I got from Bert Lance—I now know that it was November 15—was derived from Lance himself. And he states to me—and my memory confirms it—that he only referred to me the problem with the Comptroller's Office.

My guess is that on December 1 they did not specifically point out to me that the Justice Department was also involved. My memory of it is that they said that the problem that had been described to me had been resolved and that a press statement would be made then.

So, I would believe—certainly my memory confirms—that I did not know anything about the Justice Department itself anytime in 1976 and that Bert Lance did not know anything about the Justice Department being involved until the 1st of December.

If you have a followup, you can ask it.

Q. Just to follow up on that——

THE PRESIDENT. Please.

Q. ——would it have made a difference to you if you had known at that time that there had been a Justice Department investigation?

THE PRESIDENT. No.

Q. Would you have delayed your appointment perhaps to see what the investigation had been about?

THE PRESIDENT. No, I doubt it because on the 1st of December when Lance himself found that the Justice Department was involved, it was also to learn that same day or the day after that the Justice Department had determined that there were no grounds for a further pursuit of the case.

WEAPONS PROGRAMS

Q. Mr. President, on the strategic arms situation.

THE PRESIDENT. Thank you.

Q. In the absence of an agreement as of next Monday, could you tell us what your attitude will be toward major American weapons systems that have been under research? For example, where do we stand now after this 5-year agreement expires on the MX missile; what is your attitude toward it? And how about on the cruise missile? During the period after the agreement expires, will you be observing any constraints, or do you think constraints ought to be reserved, for example, on the range of the cruise missile, the air-launched cruise missile?

THE PRESIDENT. We are proceeding with our research and development program on the items that you described. As you know, under the present agreement with the Soviets, there is no restraint on the mobile missiles nor on air-launched or ground- or sea-launched cruise missiles. Pending an agreement with the Soviets, we are free to proceed with those matters.

We are continuing to conduct active tests with the cruise missile. And I might say, the tests have been very successful so far. We have not proceeded that far along with the MX. We are negotiating with the Soviets on those two items for the so-called SALT II agreement. We have not completely resolved those two questions yet.

ENERGY TAXATION

Q. Mr. President, may I ask you something about your energy program? When you started talking about a wellhead tax, as I understood it, virtually all the money collected on that tax would be rebated back to consumers.

THE PRESIDENT. That's correct.

Q. Do you think, given Senator Long's attitude, that that kind of a wellhead tax is possible if you still give that tax? Or are you going to have to put part of that revenue into Government programs to spur energy exploration and development?

THE PRESIDENT. This was a matter that was debated very thoroughly among my own advisers and myself before we presented our proposal to the Congress on April 20. Our judgment was that the tax ought to be rebated directly to the American consumer. It's a fair and equitable way to dispose of that money. It would lessen greatly the American Government involvement in the oil industry. It would remove the very complicated entitlements program. And also it would not withhold large sums of money from an already kind of dormant economy.

If you gave the money immediately back in reduced payroll taxes, then the money would be circulated and you would not hold it in the reserve fund. I would have to retain some flexibility on that subject.

The thing that I don't want to do is to take the money from the American consumers in the increased price of gasoline and other products and give it as a reward to the oil companies. Now, matters that might relate to better transportation system or mass transit or better insulation of homes, combined with a tax rebate to consumers—I would consider all those as options.

Q. So, in other words, it won't all be coming back to the consumers now?

THE PRESIDENT. My preference is that it would all come back to the consumers. And as you know, that's the version that was passed by the House of Representatives. If I had my preference and could write the bill without congressional involvement, that would be my choice.

But I can't say that I would veto or fail to support any alternative. There are some alternatives that I could accept without too much reluctance.

MR. CORMIER. Thank you, Mr. President.

THE PRESIDENT. Thank you very much.

NOTE: President Carter's sixteenth news conference began at 2:30 p.m. in Room 450 of the Old Executive Office Building. It was broadcast live on radio and television.

Defense Appropriations

Letters to the Speaker of the House and the Senate Majority Leader.   September 29, 1977

Dear Mr. Speaker:

Unless the Congress acts soon, over one-half billion dollars will be wasted on unneeded defense purchases.

In acting on 1978 appropriations for Defense, the Congress agreed with my proposals for no additional B–1 bombers or Minuteman III missiles. Despite that agreement, the House Appropriations Committee recommended that no Congressional action be taken to rescind funds previously appropriated for the same purposes. This means that the Congress will force the Defense Department to produce weapons systems that the Congress has agreed are no longer needed.

Mr. Speaker, my opinion is that this matter has not yet been fully considered and I hope that you will personally help me to prevent a serious mistake.

Additional B–1 bombers and Minuteman III missiles are simply not needed to defend our country. The enclosed summary sheet outlines the reasons for my concern. The Secretary of Defense and members of the Joint Chiefs of Staff will be glad to provide further information and the reasons for our urgent request that you and the House give this matter further consideration.

Sincerely,

JIMMY CARTER

[The Honorable Thomas P. O'Neill, Jr., Speaker of the House of Representatives, Washington, D.C. 20515]

Dear Senator Byrd:

I have sent the enclosed letter to Speaker O'Neill about my concern that over one-half billion dollars may be wasted on unneeded B–1 bombers and Minuteman III missiles.

I hope that you and the Senate will assist me in this effort to avoid unneeded spending.

Sincerely,

JIMMY CARTER

[The Honorable Robert Byrd, Majority Leader, United States Senate, Washington, D.C. 20510]

NOTE: The texts of the letters were made available by the White House Press Office. They were not issued in the form of a White House press release.

American Education Week, 1977

Proclamation 4529. September 30, 1977

By the President of the United States of America

A Proclamation

At the base of any democracy must lie a commitment to education for all.

Americans, accordingly, have an enormous stake in the vitality of our schools.

Parents, instead of being strangers to the classrooms in which their children spend so much of their lives, must become partners with teachers.

But parents and teachers cannot do the job alone. In our attitudes and our actions, in a hundred different ways, each of us influences young people toward education or away from it. This is the significance of this year's theme for American Education Week: "Working Together for Education".

By sharing our expertise and interests with the schools, we can all enrich educational programs and help determine the course along which our young people will lead America in the years to come.

Now, THEREFORE, I, JIMMY CARTER, President of the United States of America, do hereby designate the week beginning November 13, 1977, as American Education Week.

I ask every American to consider how he or she can work with our Nation's educational community to help America prepare its youngsters to meet the responsibilities they will some day assume.

IN WITNESS WHEREOF, I have hereunto set my hand this thirtieth day of September, in the year of our Lord nineteen hundred seventy-seven, and of the Independence of the United States of America the two hundred and second.

JIMMY CARTER

[Filed with the Office of the Federal Register, 1:02 p.m., September 30, 1977]

National Guard and Reserve

Statement by the President.
September 30, 1977

I have today signed a statement pledging that all Federal agencies will support their employees' participation in the programs of the National Guard and Reserve. Our Nation continues to depend for its defense upon our Reserve forces. Under the total force concept, Reserve forces would perform critical missions in any future conflict. My administration is committed to ensuring that these vital forces are fully manned, well trained, well equipped, and capable of rapid mobilization and integration into the active force in time of national emergency.

The programs available in the Reserve offer an excellent opportunity for many young men and women to learn valuable skills while also serving their Nation.

I call upon employers throughout the Nation, both public and private, to join me in continued support of these programs which are so necessary to our national defense.

Working Group on Food and Agricultural Policy

Memorandum for the Heads of Executive Departments and Agencies.
September 30, 1977

Memorandum for the Heads of Executive Departments and Agencies

This Administration is determined to develop food and agricultural policies which help the people who need help most, both in the United States and abroad. By encouraging efficient agricultural production, especially on the family farm, we can ensure reasonable incomes for producers and fair prices for consumers. An efficient productive system will also help us meet the demands of foreign markets. Our policy should give our producers the greatest possible access to foreign markets, while helping poor nations

improve their own ability to produce and distribute food.

The Secretary of Agriculture has primary responsibility in the Executive Branch for developing policies and actions in food and agriculture. In order to exercise this responsibility, the Secretary of Agriculture must weigh and balance interests represented in other parts of the Executive Branch. Accordingly, I am directing the Secretary of Agriculture to form a Working Group on Food and Agricultural Policy. This Working Group will be chaired by the Secretary's designee and will be composed of representatives at the level of assistant secretary from these organizations:

Department of State
Department of the Treasury
Department of Agriculture
Office of the Special Representative for Trade Negotiations
Agency for International Development
Council of Economic Advisors
Office of Management and Budget
National Security Council

The Secretary of Agriculture may invite representatives of other organizations in the Executive Branch to serve in the Working Group.

In consultation with the Secretary of Agriculture and the White House Domestic Policy Staff, the Working Group will develop an agenda for policy considerations on domestic and international food and agriculture. The Secretary of Agriculture, in consultation with the Domestic Policy Staff, will inform me of policies adopted and actions taken and will refer to me policy options on issues requiring Presidential decision.

A subcommittee of this Working Group will serve as the vehicle for developing an

Administration policy on world hunger. This Subcommittee will report its findings and recommendations directly to me and to the Secretary of Agriculture.

To insure coordination, I am asking the Domestic Policy Staff to inform other organizations in the Executive Branch of policy issues to be addressed and decisions made on domestic and international food and agriculture.

The Department of Agriculture and the Domestic Policy Staff will provide staff for the Working Group on Food and Agricultural Policy.

JIMMY CARTER

World Hunger Working Group

Memorandum for the Heads of Executive Departments and Agencies.
September 30, 1977

Memorandum for the Heads of Executive Departments and Agencies

As you know, I have repeatedly emphasized as a major goal of U.S. foreign policy the importance of meeting basic human needs—in particular, the alleviation of world hunger and malnutrition. In order to develop a major initiative in this area, I have formed a World Hunger Working Group headed by my Special Assistant, Peter Bourne, to coordinate a White House study of world hunger with other U.S. domestic and international food and agricultural policies. Peter Bourne, representing the Working Group, will participate on the soon to be formed Cabinet Level Committee on Food and Agricultural Policy, chaired by the Secretary of Agriculture.

The Working Group consists of Executive Office Organizations—National Security Council (NSC), Domestic Council

(DC), White House Intergovernmental Relations Office (WHIGA), Office of Science and Technology Policy (OSTP), Council of Economic Advisors (CEA), Office of Management and Budget (OMB), Office of the Special Assistant for Consumer Affairs (OSACA), Council of Environmental Quality (CEQ), and Office of the Special Representative for Trade Negotiations (STR)—as well as representation from the U.S. Department of Agriculture (USDA), State, Agency for International Development (AID), Treasury, and Commerce.

The purpose of the Working Group is to prepare a list of options to combat world hunger and malnutrition with the full participation of several departments and agencies. This anaylsis will be the basis for a Presidential statement outlining the following goals:

—to provide more equitable access to available food and to improve nutritional well-being;

—to increase the supply of food relative to need;

—to offer food assistance to those unable to purchase enough food for adequate nutrition;

—to assure a decision-making process, management, and resources adequate to implement these policies.

Departments and agencies affected by this memorandum should submit to the chairman of the Working Group their recommendations by close of business on October 21st.

The Working Group will review the recommendations and develop a set of U.S. government policy options designed to make a significant impact on world hunger. Departments and agencies will have an opportunity to comment on the Working Group's list of options before it is submitted to me.

PHOTOGRAPHIC PORTFOLIO

President Jimmy Carter

Overleaf: Addressing a public meetin[g] at Yazoo City High School, Yazo[o] City, Mississippi, July 21. *Above:* We[l]coming Chancellor Helmut Schmid[t] of the Federal Republic of German[y] to the White House, July 13. *Lef[t]:* Presenting the Presidential Medal [of] Freedom for Martin Luther King, Jr[.,] to Mrs. King and Martin Luthe[r] King, Sr., at a White House cere[]mony, July 11. *Right:* Visiting th[e] Headquarters of the Strategic A[ir] Command at Offutt Air Force Bas[e,] Nebraska, October 22.

Above left: Breakfast meeting with Senate Democratic leaders in the Family Dining Room, September 13. *Below left:* The President and Brig. Gen. Omar Torrijos Herrera of Panama signing the Panama Canal Treaties in a ceremony at the Pan American Union Building, September 7. *Right:* Campaigning in Trenton, New Jersey, on behalf of Gov. Brendan Byrne, September 10. *Below:* Veterans Day address in the Amphitheater at Arlington National Cemetery, October 24.

Above: Boarding Air Force One with Senator and Mrs. Hubert H. Humphrey at the Minneapolis/St. Paul International Airport, October 23. *Left:* Talking with participants in a public policy forum in Detroit, Michigan, October 21. *Right:* Walking to the Oval Office with Prime Minister Pierre Elliott Trudeau of Canada, September 8.

Above: Meeting with Secretary o
State Vance and Soviet Ambassado
A. F. Dobrynin in the Oval Office
November 18. *Left:* At a ceremony i
the Oval Office with Adm. Hyman G
Rickover as the Shippingport, Penn
sylvania, light water breeder reacto
was increased to full power produc
tion, December 2.

I would appreciate your cooperation to enable the Working Group to complete its task on or about November 11th.

JIMMY CARTER

National Forest Products Week, 1977

Proclamation 4530.   September 30, 1977

By the President of the United States of America

A Proclamation

From the time the first explorers and settlers set foot on this land, the abundant products of America's forests have been regarded as a major resource. Today they still provide a significant portion of our materials for construction, furniture and other important industries and create millions of jobs.

Unlike many of our precious natural resources, our forest products can be replenished. The need to make optimum use of these important resources must be balanced with vital environmental concerns, so that we make the best possible use of our forest lands, preserving the irreplaceable, conserving the beauty and ecological balance while providing important raw materials for our Nation's economic well-being. Small, private non-industrial interests own 59 per cent of our commercial forest land. We encourage them to make wise use of this land. As a Nation we must all work together to prevent and control pollution, fires, insects and diseases that damage our forests, while striving to maintain and improve fish and wildlife habitats.

In recognition of the importance of America's forest resources and in the contributions of the forest products industry to our Nation's growth, the Congress has, by joint resolution of September 13, 1960 (74 Stat. 898), designated the week beginning the third Sunday of October in each year as National Forest Products Week and has requested the President to issue an annual proclamation calling for its observance.

NOW, THEREFORE, I, JIMMY CARTER, President of the United States of America, do hereby call upon the people of the United States to observe the week beginning October 16, 1977, as National Forest Products Week, with activities and ceremonies designed to direct public attention to, and demonstrate our gratitude for, the forest resources with which we are blessed.

IN WITNESS WHEREOF, I have hereunto set my hand this thirtieth day of September, in the year of our Lord nineteen hundred and seventy-seven, and of the Independence of the United States of America the two hundred and second.

JIMMY CARTER

[Filed with the Office of the Federal Register, 4:14 p.m., September 30, 1977]

Country Music Month, 1977

Proclamation 4531.   September 30, 1977

By the President of the United States of America

A Proclamation

Country music, once the simple expression of America's isolated hill country and farms, has spread to our most sophisticated cities. It has always told of the basic human emotions and experiences—of childhood heroes and lost places, forgotten dreams and everyday goodness and disappointments as well as great sadness, love and loneliness, honor and humor. It vibrates with the passions and scenes that make up our common heritage. Country music is as universal as a sunset and as personal as a baby's smile. It is fitting that we acknowledge the importance of a form that reflects so much the lives and hopes of the people who make up our nation and pay tribute to the talented people who have contributed to its growing popularity.

Now, THEREFORE, I, JIMMY CARTER, President of the United States of America, ask the people of this Nation to mark the month of October 1977, with suitable observances as Country Music Month.

IN WITNESS WHEREOF, I have hereunto set my hand this thirtieth day of September, in the year of our Lord nineteen hundred seventy-seven, and of the Independence of the United States of America the two hundred and second.

JIMMY CARTER

[Filed with the Office of the Federal Register, 5:04 p.m., September 30, 1977]

NOTE: For the President's message on Country Music Month, see page 1433 of this issue.

Exemption From Mandatory Retirement

Executive Order 12011.   September 30, 1977

EXEMPTION OF G. JOSEPH MINETTI FROM MANDATORY RETIREMENT

G. Joseph Minetti, Member, Civil Aeronautics Board, became subject to mandatory retirement for age on July 31, 1977, under the provisions of Section 8335 of Title 5 of the United States Code unless exempted by Executive Order. Mr. Minetti was exempted from mandatory retirement until September 30, 1977, by Executive Order No. 12006 of July 29, 1977.

In my judgment, the public interest requires that G. Joseph Minetti continue to be exempted from such mandatory retirement.

Now, THEREFORE, by virtue of the authority vested in me by subsection (c) of Section 8335 of Title 5 of the United States Code, I hereby exempt G. Joseph Minetti from mandatory retirement until October 31, 1977.

JIMMY CARTER

The White House,
    September 30, 1977.

[Filed with the Office of the Federal Register, 5:09 p.m., September 30, 1977]

NOTE: The White House Press Office announced the Executive order on September 30. It was not issued in the form of a White House press release.

Digest of Other White House Announcements

The following listing includes the President's daily schedule and other items of general interest as announced by the White House Press Office during the period covered by this issue. Events and announcements printed elsewhere in the issue are not included.

September 24

The President sent a letter, dated today, to Bert Lance, accepting his resignation as Director of the Office of Management and Budget. In a letter to James T. McIntyre, Jr., also dated today, the President officially designated Mr. McIntyre as Acting Director of the Office.

September 26

The President met at the White House with:

—David L. Aaron, Deputy Assistant to the President for National Security Affairs;

—senior White House staff members;

—the Cabinet;

—Vice President Walter F. Mondale;

—Senator Robert P. Griffin of Michigan;

—Robert A. Frosch, Administrator of the National Aeronautics and Space Administration.

The President briefly attended a party for Mr. Lance in Mr. Lance's office in the Old Executive Office Building.

The President transmitted to the Congress the ninth annual report on the administration of the Natural Gas Pipeline Safety Act of 1968.

The White House announced that Prime Minister Lee Kuan Yew of Singapore will visit the United States from October 4 until mid-October. During his official stay in Washington, the Prime Minister will meet with the President on October 7.

September 27

The President met at the White House with:

—Mr. Aaron;

—the Democratic congressional leaders;

—Representative Robert N. C. Nix of Pennsylvania;

—Vice President Mondale, Mr. Aaron, and Adm. Stansfield Turner, Director of Central Intelligence;

—Prime Minister Datuk Hussein bin Onn of Malaysia;

—Representative Henry S. Reuss of Wisconsin;

—Benjamin L. Hooks, executive director, and members of the executive committee of the National Associa-

tion for the Advancement of Colored People;

—Representative Edward I. Koch of New York and Bess Myerson, consumer consultant, Bristol-Myers Co., New York, N.Y.;

—Barry Jagoda, Special Assistant to the President for Media and Public Affairs, and White House staff members, to discuss public broadcasting legislation;

—A. A. Gromyko, Minister of Foreign Affairs of the Union of Soviet Socialist Republics.

September 28

The President met at the White House with:

—Mr. Aaron;

—Mrs. Carter, for lunch;

—members of the Commission on Federal Paperwork, who presented the Commission's final report.

The President attended a briefing on the Panama Canal treaties, given for State officials and business and political leaders from Arizona, Colorado, and Delaware in the State Dining Room.

The President announced that he will nominate Carolyn R. Payton to be Director of the Peace Corps. Ms. Payton was nominated to be Associate Director of ACTION on September 7.

September 29

The President met at the White House with:

—Zbigniew Brzezinski, Assistant to the President for National Security Affairs;

—a group of Republican Members of the House of Representatives from Midwest and Western States;

—Vice President Mondale, Secretary of the Treasury W. Michael Blumenthal, Arthur F. Burns, Chairman of the Board of Governors of the Federal Reserve System, Charles L. Schultze, Chairman of the Council of Economic Advisers, and Mr. McIntyre;

—representatives of the Motion Picture Association of America who were meeting with administration officials in the Roosevelt Room.

September 30

The President met at the White House with:

—Dr. Brzezinski;

—Senators Robert C. Byrd, Henry M. Jackson, John C. Stennis, and Howard H. Baker, Jr., to discuss the progress of the SALT negotiations;

—a group of eight Republican Senators;

—a group of approximately 100 Members of Congress to discuss appropriations for international financial institutions;

—Edvard Kardelj, Member of the Presidency of Yugoslavia;

—Representative George H. Mahon of Texas;

—members of the Newspaper Farm Editors of America (transcript will be printed next week);

—Lloyd Klabunde and family, of Emmet, N. Dak., the Farm Family of the Year;

—Chief Justice of the United States Warren E. Burger;

—the Justices of the Supreme Court of the United States for their traditional White House visit, marking the opening of the Court's new term.

The President left the White House for a weekend stay at Camp David, Md.

NOMINATIONS SUBMITTED TO THE SENATE

The following list does not include promotions of members of the Uniformed Services,

1700

NOMINATIONS—Continued

nominations to the Service Academies, or nominations of Foreign Service officers.

Submitted September 26, 1977

JULIUS SHISKIN, of Maryland, to be Commissioner of Labor Statistics, United States Department of Labor, for a term of 4 years (reappointment).

Submitted September 27, 1977

DAVID D. NEWSOM, of California, a Foreign Service officer of the Class of Career Minister, to be Ambassador Extraordinary and Plenipotentiary of the United States of America to the Philippines.

O. RUDOLPH AGGREY, of the District of Columbia, a Foreign Service Information officer of Class one, to be Ambassador Extraordinary and Plenipotentiary of the United States of America to Romania.

THOMAS A. BALLANTINE, JR., of Kentucky, to be United States District Judge for the Western District of Kentucky, vice C. Rhodes Bratcher, deceased.

The following-named persons to be Commissioners of the Copyright Royalty Tribunal for the terms indicated (new positions):

For a term of 7 years from September 27, 1977:

THOMAS C. BRENNAN, of New Jersey
DOUGLAS COULTER, of Virginia
MARY LOU BURG, of Wisconsin

For a term of 5 years from September 27, 1977:

CLARENCE L. JAMES, JR., of Ohio
FRANCES GARCIA, of Texas

JOHN WARREN MCGARRY, of Massachusetts, to be a member of the Federal Election Commission for a term expiring April 30, 1983, vice Neil Staebler, term expired.

JOHN C. TRUESDALE, of Maryland, to be a member of the National Labor Relations Board for the remainder of the term expiring August 27, 1980, vice Peter D. Walther, resigned.

WILLIAM R. ALBERGER, of Oregon, to be a member of the United States International Trade Commission for the term expiring December 16, 1985, vice Will E. Leonard, Jr., term expired.

Submitted September 28, 1977

BARRY M. BLECHMAN, of Virginia, to be an Assistant Director of the United States Arms Control and Disarmament Agency, vice Robert M. Behr, resigned.

NOMINATIONS—Continued
Submitted September 28—Continued

DAMON J. KEITH, of Michigan, to be United States Circuit Judge for the Sixth Circuit, vice Wade H. McCree, Jr., resigned.

DON SANDERS SMITH, of Arkansas, to be a member of the Federal Energy Regulatory Commission for a term of 2 years (new position).

CAROLYN R. PAYTON, of the District of Columbia, to be Director of the Peace Corps.

JOHN J. BOYLE, of Maryland, to be Public Printer, vice Thomas F. McCormick, resigned.

Submitted September 30, 1977

THOMAS F. MOAKLEY, of Massachusetts, to be a Federal Maritime Commissioner for the remainder of the term expiring June 30, 1978, vice Bob Casey, resigned.

FRANK M. JOHNSON, JR., of Alabama, to be Director of the Federal Bureau of Investigation for the term of 10 years, vice Clarence Marion Kelley, resigning.

ROBERT T. O'LEARY, of Montana, to be United States Attorney for the District of Montana for the term of 4 years, vice Thomas A. Olson.

ARCHIE P. SHERAR, of Washington, to be United States Marshal for the Eastern District of Washington for the term of 4 years, vice George A. Locke.

CHECKLIST OF WHITE HOUSE PRESS RELEASES

The following releases of the Office of the White House Press Secretary, distributed during the period covered by this issue, are not included in the issue.

Released September 26, 1977

Announcement: nomination of Thomas A. Ballantine, Jr., to be United States District Judge for the Western District of Kentucky

CHECKLIST—Continued
Released September 28, 1977

Announcement: nomination of Damon J. Keith to be United States Circuit Judge for the Sixth Circuit

News conference: on the President's meeting with Chief of the Royal Court Sharif Abdul Hamid Sharaf and Foreign Minister Hassan Ibrahim of Jordan—by Jerrold L. Schecter, Associate Press Secretary

Released September 30, 1977

Announcement: nomination of Robert T. O'Leary to be United States Attorney for the District of Montana and Archie P. Sherar to be United States Marshal for the Eastern District of Washington

News conference: on the President's meeting with Edvard Kardelj, Member of the Presidency of Yugoslavia—by Zbigniew Brzezinski, Assistant to the President for National Security Affairs, and Jerrold L. Schecter, Associate Press Secretary

ACTS APPROVED BY THE PRESIDENT

Approved September 24, 1977

S. 1752_____ Public Law 95–112 Education Amendments of 1977.

Approved September 29, 1977

S. 275_____ Public Law 95–113 Food and Agriculture Act of 1977.

Approved September 30, 1977

S. 1731_____ Public Law 95–114 Armed Forces, physicians and dentists, etc., special pay provisions, extension.

PRESIDENTIAL DOCUMENTS

Week Ending Friday, October 7, 1977

Newspaper Farm Editors of America

Interview With Members of the Organization.   September 30, 1977

THE PRESIDENT. First of all, let me apologize for interrupting your meeting. [*Laughter*]

It's a great pleasure to be with you. I think that all of you noticed with great attention yesterday the signing of the 1977 agriculture bill, which is probably the most far-reaching and innovative farm legislation in the history of our country, certainly in the last 35 or 40 years.

I just had lunch with Chairman George Mahon from Lubbock, Texas, and he agrees with that assessment. So, it's not just a newcomer's assessment. He told me that in his district this year they will produce 3.2 million bales of cotton, which is an unbelievable quantity.

ADMINISTRATION POLICIES

I would like to say that I know that your interests are broad-ranging because you represent literally millions of families in this country who look to you for leadership and guidance and whom you serve. I believe that so far this year we've had a good beginning of our administration. We've approached some questions that your readers, listeners, and viewers are deeply concerned about.

I've gotten authority from the Congress to reorganize the executive branch of Government, which we're doing now, and we have a 3-year period in which that can be accomplished. We've formed a new Department of Energy. We now see the Senate engaged in dealing with the energy questions which the House has already successfully accomplished, in my opinion, in a very courageous way.

We've proposed to the Congress a far-reaching reform of our welfare system to give our people a better chance for both jobs and income, and this will primarily be decided by the Congress early next year. And before the Congress adjourns, I'll present to them a comprehensive tax reform package.

In addition to that, we are trying to work on the international field and resolve some of the longstanding questions that confront us. The Middle East is difficult, southern Africa is difficult, the SALT negotiations are difficult, the strengthening of NATO is quite difficult.

We also are trying to enhance international trade, the export of our agricultural and industrial products. We have had, so far, good success.

The only very serious cloud is that we are importing too much oil. This is going to give us an adverse trade balance this year of about $30 billion. If we didn't have the excessive oil imports, we would have a positive trade balance of about $15 to $20 billion.

Agricultural products exports in the last 12-month period was about $24 billion, which is as high or higher than it's ever been before.

I've met this week with a series of foreign leaders, which has been my custom and, I guess, my predecessors'. I spent this morning meeting with the heir apparent to President Tito of Yugoslavia, Mr. Kardelj. Earlier this week, I met twice with Foreign Minister Gromyko, with the head of the Government of Malaysia, Prime Minister Hussein, and with leaders from Jordan and Syria, and another group last week.

So, this is a continuing obligation of mine, which I welcome. I think we are making good progress, and I've been pleased so far with my own life here in the White House. This is my first experience in serving in the Federal Government, except for the Navy, and I think the Congress has been very cooperative and I've got a good Cabinet.

I think since we have a limited amount of time, I would rather spend the next few minutes answering questions that you might have, if I can.

QUESTIONS

COLOGNE FOOD FAIR

Q. Mr. President, you mentioned international trade, expansion of international trade. Recently, Governor Thompson of Illinois sent a two-man agriculture team over to Europe on a trade mission. They reported that when they were at the Cologne Food Fair, the United States was about the only country that did not have a national food display, a national agricultural display, and they thought that was in the eyes of many of these nations a loss of face in some way. There were

about five or six states exhibiting there, but not the United States. Do you think we ought to have a unified effort like that?

THE PRESIDENT. Yes, I do, and I would just about guarantee you that the next time such an occasion arises we'll have a display there. I didn't know about it, and I'll contact Bob Bergland about that this afternoon and find out why we didn't. That would be Agriculture and Commerce combined.

We do have a fairly substantial budget allocation which we expend with enthusiasm for displays in international fairs and other opportunities of this kind. But why we missed the Cologne Food Fair, I don't know. But I'll find out.

FOOD AND AGRICULTURE ACT OF 1977

Q. Mr. President, were there any sections of the farm bill that you were dissatisfied with?

THE PRESIDENT. Well, as you know, a bill of that complexity is a result of innumerable conferences and compromises. And my own presentation to the Congress was about $300 to $600 million lower in cost than the final bill was, not counting food stamps. We don't know if it's $300 or $600 million, depending upon how the question of oats will be handled. But I think in its final form, I didn't have any reluctance about signing it.

I think there's a great improvement in allocation of funds for research and development. It eliminates the concept of acreage allotments, which have, I think, been abused in the past. It fairly well equates production costs with target prices, at least on an average. There are some places which have very high production costs which can't be accommodated exactly.

I think the loan levels are reasonable enough to give us a competitive place in the international market. It establishes the concept of increased food reserves, the control of which is primarily in the hands of farmers, which was an important consideration to me as a farmer. It has adequate safeguards on that concept to prevent Government dumping of farm products on the market to artificially lower prices. It changes the food stamp program to one that's much simpler, much more free of fraud, and much more equitable in its concept. And I think, in general, the agriculture bill, for all those reasons, is good.

We did have a difference of opinion of about 10 cents here and 10 cents there on some of the farm prices. I think, for instance, the price of rice is too high. But that's not a serious objection. But that was a result of negotiations.

We still have a problem with sugar. The de la Garza amendment on sugar did cause me some concern. I would like for the Congress to have placed a greater emphasis on encouraging the international sugar amendment. We do have in the bill a provision that we were successful in implementing, that at the time an international sugar agreement is confirmed by the Senate, that the present support price structure would be replaced.

But I'm afraid that if the international sugar agreement price is even slightly below the 13½ cents, roughly, that's in this bill, that the Senate might lose its incentive to ratify the agreement.

There were just a few technical negotiating points like that, but in a 150-page bill, those are relatively minor.

ROBERT H. MEYER

Q. Mr. President, there have been some questions raised lately about Mr. Robert Meyer, Assistant Secretary of Agriculture. Have you looked into this

matter, and do you have any thoughts on it at this point?

THE PRESIDENT. I've not talked to either Robert Meyer nor Bob Bergland about this. I read about it in the news and understand from my staff reports that there has been nothing illegal done. But I have written Bob Bergland a note and told him that I wanted the practice stopped, whether or not there was an illegality.

I really don't feel that anyone in Government, including myself, should use the official position to pursue a goal that would result in financial advantage or other advantage for the public official. I'm not alleging that Bob Meyer has done anything improper or illegal; I don't know that much about it. But I just don't want to have the accusation of impropriety there.

Q. You plan no action against Mr. Meyer?

THE PRESIDENT. I certainly have no information about Bob Meyer's actions at this point that would indicate any action needing to be taken, except that I have asked Bob Bergland to stop the effort of Bob Meyer to determine land policy in the Imperial Valley.

As all of you know, this is an ancient problem. The law that the Congress passed, I think back in 1902, limited the ownership of land in some irrigated areas of the West to 160 acres. And in some instances, a husband and a wife can own 320 acres. In the Imperial Valley and in other places, the acreage owned by single families is much greater. The law was just not enforced.

The altercation has been not between Washington and farmers, honest farmers in the West; it's been between farmers in the West and their neighbors—their neighbors wanting to have an easier ability to acquire land; the farmers wanting to hold the land that they possessed. This ultimately went to the Federal courts. The Federal courts have ruled that the U.S. law has to be enforced. And Cecil Andrus, who is the Secretary of Interior, has no alternative except to enforce the law.

So, we're not trying to intrude ourselves gratuitously or on an initial basis into this controversy; we inherited it. And under the present law, I'm sworn on my word of honor to enforce the law and will have to enforce it.

But I recognize, as do many of you, that 75 years ago, 320 acres for a husband and wife of irrigated land was all they could handle. And now, with massive investments in large machinery, a larger acreage is sometimes necessary for an economically viable farm operation.

So, the law needs to be changed. But we don't have any alternative except to enforce the law. And I think Bob Meyer was not doing anything except expressing, basically, what I've just said. I don't think he was trying to do anything surreptitiously or improperly. But I think that there are other people that can be adequate spokesmen, even including myself. I don't think Bob needs to do that.

DIRECTOR OF THE OFFICE OF MANAGEMENT AND BUDGET

Q. Is Charles Zwick of Connecticut a serious candidate for Director of the Budget—being considered?

THE PRESIDENT. I'm not looking at this point for any Director of Office of Management and Budget. I'm completely satisfied with James McIntyre, who was my OMB director in Georgia and who was Bert Lance's deputy, and I think that it would be an improper time for me to change the directors of that department while we are well involved in the preparation of the fiscal year '79 budget preparation.

So, I'll wait until the end of this year before I start considering a permanent OMB Director, and when I do, James McIntyre would be one of those I would consider. But I don't have any intention to pursue that at this time.

NUCLEAR REPROCESSING

Q. I understand that you are against any more plutonium recycling. We have a nuclear plant to the east of us, with three reactors, and we have another one going up to the west of us with two more reactors. And we're wondering, with all these reactors in the area, the huge quantities of nuclear waste material that will be generated there, well, what are we going to do about the disposal of these materials without any recycling? Do you not think that it might increase our Nation's energy independence to extend this nuclear fuel supply through the recycle?

THE PRESIDENT. Well, you know, recycling or reprocessing, as it's most often called, is not an answer to the question that you raised. We've been involved in nuclear power production now for 35 years, and also weapons production for 35 years. The nuclear wastes, even if they were reprocessed, would still have to be stored somewhere. And, as you know, there have been two major plants of the most modern possible design already completed to reprocess spent nuclear fuel. Both of them have been abandoned because they simply didn't work economically, they were not feasible, and also they created environmental questions of contamination that just were never resolved.

The thing that we are trying to do is to provide some long-range and comprehensive spent fuel storage capability, maybe injecting the Federal Government into it more deeply than it has been in the past, to handle spent fuel from commercial powerplants.

At the same time, we are trying to prevent countries that don't have a nuclear explosive capability from getting into the reprocessing field. This reprocessing capability also means that a nation could very well acquire the atomic bomb.

I have no objection to the plutonium age coming. I have no objection to breeder reactors. I don't think that the time has yet come. We are now about to waste, in my opinion, about $2 billion if the congressional action on the Clinch River breeder reactor is carried out where we don't need the particular breeder reactor that's in question.

I think 25 or 30 years from now—maybe not quite that long—we will need to go into the breeder reactor field. By that time there's no doubt in my mind that major advances will be made in the technology. We have a massive research and development program that would include pilot plant operation in the plutonium field. So, this is a problem, again, that I've inherited.

My background and graduate work is in nuclear physics. I think I understand most of the principles involved. So, we are reprocessing spent fuel now under the Government programs. There has not yet been resolved the problem of whether to reprocess and how to store spent nuclear fuel from commercial plants. In most instances, they are storing that spent fuel on their own premises and sometimes, perhaps, carelessly—I can't prove that. Past efforts to reprocess commercially have been a complete failure, and I just think that the emphasis ought to be in the prevention of the proliferation of explosives around the world. And we will be ready to move into the plutonium or breeder field when the time comes and when we need it.

We do have a breeder reactor operating today. It began operation about a month ago. It's at Shippingport, Pennsylvania. It was developed under the auspices of Admiral Rickover, and it uses a thorium base for the breeding capability. It'll be up to a hundred percent operating level within the next few days. So, the breeder reactor concept is with us.

PRESIDENT'S SUPPORT IN FARM AREAS

Q. Sir, the New York Times recently carried a story that indicates you're losing support among farm people. I was wondering if you're aware of this, and if so, do you plan anything to counteract this possible loss of support as indicated in this newspaper article?

THE PRESIDENT. Well, as you know from looking at the maps the day after the election, my political support was about equally divided between urban and rural people. There were geographical delineations. I didn't carry many of the States in the Midwest or in the Far West. I carried the rural areas in the South and in New England and in States like Wisconsin and Minnesota, Ohio, very well.

I don't think any of our polling results indicate that I've lost support in the Farm Belt. The farmers are disturbed, and I'm a farmer and I'm disturbed as well. We've had a complete, total failure of our corn crop. We won't make any cotton at home. Our soybean crop is very badly damaged. Our peanut crop is probably going to be off 25 or 30 percent—because of weather, not because I became President. [*Laughter*] But I know from experience that farmers tend to blame the President when they have a short crop or when the prices are low.

I think this new farm bill, when it's analyzed by farm groups, and also the set-aside program for wheat and some feed grains next year will be, I think, an indication of my understanding of the farm needs. And I think the increase in support price and target prices for the '77 crops will also help.

But I would guess that political popularity with the President will always go up and down, depending upon the general attitude of farmers.

When I wasn't in office, I used to cuss the President and cuss the Secretary of Agriculture when my crop was poor. And when it was good, of course, I didn't give the President and the Secretary of Agriculture any credit for it. I figured it was because of me.

And so, my answer in a nutshell is, I don't think that I've varied much in my political support among farm families. I do think that the new legislation that I've helped to provide will be an indication that the farm families can trust me not only to understand their problems but to carry out my campaign commitments.

TRADE WITH THE PEOPLE'S REPUBLIC OF CHINA

Q. Mr. President, several times this morning in our conversations with people on your staff, the question was raised about penetrating the Chinese market with American exports. And thus far, we've been effectively shut out. And I'm wondering if this is a concern of yours?

THE PRESIDENT. It is. Nothing would please me more than to see our trade with all the nations in the world build up.

There's some question now about the result of the Russians' crop year. There's a possibility they might buy 5 million more tons of food grains, for instance. We don't know that yet. I would hope that we could provide the major part of that to the Soviet Union. As you know, we have a permanent contract now with them, a multiyear contract, for the sale of specified quantities of wheat.

Since Nixon went to China, there has been, first of all, a brief flurry of trade with China—nothing earthshaking, but at least some—and there's been a steady decrease since then.

I think the Chinese have, this past 8 or 9 months, bought large quantities of wheat from some of the other countries—Canada, Argentina, and perhaps, Australia. I would like to see us get our share of those Chinese purchases, and we are doing everything we can to meet that goal. This was one of the items on the agenda when Secretary Vance met with the new Chinese leaders.

Q. What are some of the roadblocks immediately to trading with China, as you said?

THE PRESIDENT. It's a very complicated question. Let me give you one example. We have an old claims question with China that has never yet been resolved. When the Communist Chinese took over from Chiang Kai-shek 35 years ago or so, they confiscated some property that was owned by Americans. In retaliation for that, we impounded Chinese bank deposits and other financial resources in this country. The amount of money involved is in the neighborhood of $200 million. We've never yet been able to work out with the Chinese an agreement of how to settle those counterclaims.

There are lawsuits involved on our part. For instance, if a Chinese ship should come into, say, New Orleans or to Los Angeles to load a cargo of wheat, that ship would be subject to impoundment by some American citizen who still claims they've got property in China and the Chinese owe it for them. I would guess that the American courts would uphold that American citizen's claim. That's one of the complicated obstacles to it.

Another one, of course, is the Chinese relationship with us. They refuse to send any of their major officials into the city of Washington because we have an ambassador here who represents the Republic of China in Taiwan. And I would guess that if the situation existed a hundred years that they would never deviate in that policy.

They will send top officials into New York to attend the United Nations, but as a matter of principle, they won't send their top persons like the foreign minister or one of their premiers into the city of Washington because they claim that we erroneously have relationships with Taipei. That's another question that arises.

And another one is that the Chinese insist upon being very independent. They're cautious about how they buy goods from any other country.

I think that my own judgment is that under the new government with Premier Hua and Deputy Premier Teng, that the Chinese are going to expand their interrelationship with other countries on a foreign trade basis, and perhaps we can benefit from that.

We are eager to meet them more than half way in order to enhance American sales and, I think, through trade, to improve our relationships with the Mainland Chinese.

It's so complicated; it's hard to explain briefly.

AGRICULTURAL LOANS

Q. Probably the most severe problem right now seems to be this financing, refinancing, keeping the loan levels in certain areas. Do you think that there might either through cooperative credit agencies or through the Farmers Home Administration, might be some bridge that will allow farmers—see, the thing, like banks just run out of loan—and they're really getting pressed on this, and the drought, last year's bills are coming due, and 1974's early freeze coming due, and all these things putting hundreds of millions of dollars in Wisconsin alone coming due to the Government, and by golly, they can't have the comeback quite to make it. And I just wondered if this type of immediate problem might be addressed through an existing agency or some special program, just a loan, not——

THE PRESIDENT. I know. We've had an extraordinary demand this year for agricultural disaster loans because of floods, droughts and so forth, and we've met those requirements. I think that about at least two-thirds of the counties in the United States are now eligible for disaster loans, and still we've had one of the most bountiful crops on a nationwide basis we've ever had.

As you know, we did increase the price support of milk, which certainly helped Wisconsin. Also, we've increased the loan and price support levels of 1977 crop commodities, which does mean that the banks would have a more secure loan at a higher level of the loan itself. If you increase the loan level of wheat that the farmer has in storage, then he can go back to the bank and on a secured basis get a higher loan or extend his loan more carefully as far as the bank is concerned.

We also have tried to encourage, through decisions made from the Agriculture Department, more easy loans, both in the paperwork involved and also a higher level of loans for the installation of storage equipment for wheat, soybeans, feed grains, and so forth.

So, within the present structure, the extension of credit is enhanced. We've also had Bob Bergland, who's an excellent man, working very closely with Arthur Burns and with the Secretary of Treasury, Mike Blumenthal, to analyze from one region of the country to another if the banks were truly overextended in loans or if they did have lending reserves that they were withholding for some other reason.

I think those are some of the things that come to mind just offhand that have already been done and obviously can be continued in the future.

Maybe one more question, then I have to——

AGRICULTURAL RESEARCH

Q. Mr. President, probably our peanut farmers in Texas have benefited as much as anyone on agricultural research, basic research. The gap is closing faster all the time on what research has to offer to the better farmers to stay in business. I understand that the Congress is contemplating—or making a move to increase the amount of funds for basic agricultural research.

THE PRESIDENT. That's correct.

Q. How would the administration go along with that, sir?

THE PRESIDENT. We favor that. In fact, in the new agriculture bill that I signed yesterday, there is a substantial increase in commitment of the Federal Government for the basic research program. I, myself—and you use peanuts as an example—have seen production rates of peanuts, I'd say, either tripled or quadrupled because of the results of basic research.

In the case of peanuts, the basic finding was that the less you cultivate peanuts, the more they made. We used to cultivate peanuts so much that we destroyed the vines, injured them, and created problems for the growing nuts.

But I think that some of the money that pays the richest dividend is in the field of basic research, because one or two scientists who are adequately financed can change the basic production rates of crops.

We've got a lot of needs because of changing times. We're going to have to learn how to produce crops with less fuel being used. And the environmental standards that are being enforced—passed by the Congress and obviously enforced by us—are making it necessary to produce crops with fewer herbicides and insecticides which we used as a substitute for the massive cultivation in the past.

We also have insects that are growing immune to the standard pesticides that have been used on the farms for literally decades.

We are now seeing one of our basic insecticides challenged as far as toxicity to human beings is concerned, and that's toxaphene. I can close my eyes now and smell toxaphene. I've lived with it 25 or 30 years.

But all these changing demands on farmers require that we stay up with the basic research.

I'd like to say one other thing. I happen to be a nuclear-trained person, but there's no group in the world that's more eager to take advantage of basic research in practical and immediate application than farmers. Farmers are not conservative at all in the way they produce food and feed and fiber. What has always been a concern to us in Georgia is trying to encourage farmers to wait 2 years or wait 3 years to let the experiment stations complete their testing program before the farmers adopt it on a massive scale. And some of the more successful farmers have, in effect, turned their farms automatically over into an experiment station which they themselves have been willing to finance.

I've been part of that. As a small warehouseman that had 200 or 300 farm customers, my farmers, if you came out with any sort of a new planting technique or cultivating technique or herbicide or pesticide or curing technique, they were eager to try it out and take all the risks themselves. And you quite often would say, "Now please, don't do this yet. It hasn't been proven." "I don't care if it's been proven or not. I'm willing to try it on my own farm."

And the competitive nature in the agricultural community has been eager to take basic research and, rather than wait for a long period of delay in the applied research field, they'd just skip over that completely and implement basic research techniques right on their farm, in the production, which I think is a tremendous contribution to the country, voluntarily carried out by farmers. And so, that makes in agriculture, especially, basic research pay immediate dividends which it wouldn't pay in many other areas of life where basic research is followed by applied research and years later by prototype models and then years later by a small production model and then later on by the final consumer product. Agriculture shortcircuits all that almost immediately and jumps directly from basic research into full production application.

I'd like to stay with you longer, but I have got to go. I want to say this in closing: I don't claim to know all the answers about agriculture. It's my life, and I always feel at home when I'm meeting with or talking to farm groups like yourselves.

I have learned, as Bob Bergland is learning very well, that we have a highly diverse agricultural economy in this country. It's our most important industry by far. And when I assess in my own mind—sometimes in the quietness of my office, late at night, looking at a globe—the advantages that our country has over, perhaps, competing nations, our agricultural production is one of the greatest, constant, unshakable advantages, and I'm very thankful for what the American farm family and ranch family have done to give

us this advantage. It's one also that contributes not to competition leading to bloodshed, but it contributes to competition leading to peace.

And I am very grateful that you would come here and take a day of your time getting to know some of my own fellow workers in the White House, and hope that the day is productive for you.

I hope you'll extend my personal best wishes to all of your readers and all of your friends when you go back home, because they've got a friend and a farmer in the White House.

Thank you again very much.

NOTE: The interview began at 1 p.m. in the Cabinet Room at the White House.

The transcript of the interview was released on October 1.

Juvenile Justice Amendments of 1977

Remarks on Signing H.R. 6111 Into Law.
October 3, 1977

THE PRESIDENT. Good morning, everybody. We've assembled here this morning to discuss House of Representatives act 6111, the Juvenile Delinquency Act of 1977.

One of the most serious problems that faces our country, of course, is that of rampant crime. And we know from experience and from examining the statistics that almost half of the crimes are committed by juveniles. We also realize that, unfortunately, in our country there has been an absence of adequate distinction between those juveniles who commit serious crimes, such as murder, rape, robbery, on the one hand, and those who commit crimes that are no threat to their neighbors, like being a runaway child.

In many communities of our country, these two kinds of crimes—one serious and one not very serious—are treated the same, and young people have been incarcerated for long periods of time, who have committed offenses that would not even be a crime at all if they were adult. It costs about $12,000 a year to keep a young person in prison. This act very wisely draws a sharp distinction between these two kinds of crimes. It also encourages local administrators, States, and local governments to deinstitutionalize those young people who have not committed serious crimes.

We are extending here the Runaway Youth Act for 3 years, which I think is a good step forward, and in this bill is adequate financing for this act itself. There's also an allocation in fiscal year 1978 of $150 million for juvenile justice under the Law Enforcement Assistance Administration.

I'm very proud of the work that has been done. As you may or may not have heard, some of the Senators are not able to show up this morning because of other business before their body. I'm particularly sorry that Senator Bayh can't be here. He's been very instrumental in the passage of this act. But we have some of the Members of the House behind me who have been very effective in dealing with this very serious problem of juvenile crime—Congressman Pepper and others.

It's with a great deal of pleasure that I now sign into law act 6111, the Juvenile Delinquency Act of 1977.

[At this point, the President signed H.R. 6111 into law.]

I want to congratulate you gentlemen behind me for the good work you've done.

REPRESENTATIVE PEPPER. Mr. President, we are so grateful for your recognition of the importance of trying to preserve from the area of criminality the younger people of the country. We realize that any approach to the problem of crime is a very difficult one. We've tried the orthodox approach. I wish we could, in the future, put more emphasis upon the preventive aspects of crime. And I believe we can do that best by trying to stop school dropouts, trying to provide jobs for the younger people, perhaps after school, in the summers, give them incentives to do creative and constructive work and to live useful lives.

I'm convinced that if we could put into effect an effective, adequate preventive program, we could reduce crime in this country at least 25 percent. I hope this is a good beginning in that direction.

THE PRESIDENT. Thank you very much. It's not an accident that the foremost spokesman for the elderly in this country is also Claude Pepper, who's also—*[laughter]*—who's the foremost spokesman for young people.

I want to again thank all of you for coming. I think it's a good step forward today. And I believe that if this program can be administered effectively through LEAA and through the Department of HEW, that we'll have a good program that will take our Nation forward on fighting crime, and particularly among the young people of our Nation.

Thank you very much.

NOTE: The President spoke at 11:34 a.m. at the signing ceremony in the Rose Garden at the White House.

As enacted, H.R. 6111 is Public Law 95–115, approved October 3.

Veterans Disability Compensation and Survivor Benefits Act of 1977

Statement on Signing H.R. 1862 Into Law. October 3, 1977

I am pleased to sign into law H.R. 1862, a bill which will provide a 6.6 percent increase in compensation payments for over 2 million disabled veterans and their survivors. These increases will become effective Saturday, October 1, 1977.

The enactment of H.R. 1862 carries out my recommendation that compensation payments be adjusted this year to keep pace with the cost of living.

NOTE: As enacted, H.R. 1862 is Public Law 95–117, approved October 3.

Corporation for Public Broadcasting

Nomination of Sharon Percy Rockefeller and Gillian M. Sorensen To Be Members of the Board of Directors. October 3, 1977

The President today announced that he will nominate Sharon Percy Rockefeller and Gillian M. Sorensen to be members of the Board of Directors of the Corporation for Public Broadcasting for terms of 6 years.

Rockefeller, 32, of West Virginia, would replace Thomas W. Moore, term expired. She is an active board member of WETA–TV in Washington and served on the Advisory Board of Education during the Johnson administration.

Sorensen, 36, is associate producer at Talent Associates and assistant producer of New York Television Theater. She has produced a charity telethon and commercial television programs and has been involved in broadcasting and communications since 1964.

National Advisory Committee for Juvenile Justice and Delinquency Prevention

Appointment of Seven Members to the Committee. October 3, 1977

The President today announced that he has appointed the following persons as members of the National Advisory Committee for Juvenile Justice and Delinquency Prevention for 4-year terms:

GEORGE P. BELITSOS, of Ames, Iowa. Belitsos, 30, has been director since 1973 of Youth and Shelter Services Inc., a community-based corrections and diversion program. He is a commissioner of the Iowa Crime Commission. He previously served as director of the Story County Youth Service Bureau, a consultant to the Iowa Drug Abuse Authority, and community program director for the Ames YMCA.

TIMOTHY S. DAVIS, of Tulsa, Okla. Davis, 23, is presently at the Democratic National Committee. He worked for Unified Delinquency Intervention Service in 1975 as a case manager, researcher, and evaluator. In 1974 he worked as administrative assistant to the warden at the Atlanta Correctional Center. Davis has done academic research on alternatives to child institutionalization, urban planning on police relations, and zoning and segregation patterns.

MARGARET C. DRISCOLL, of Bridgeport, Conn. Driscoll, 65, is chief judge of the Connecticut Juvenile Court. Before becoming a judge, she served as counsel, then legislative counsel to the Connecticut State Labor Council and practiced law in Bridgeport. She is president of the National Council of Juvenile Court Judges.

STEVEN D. STARK, of Atlanta, Ga. Stark, 25, is a student at Yale University Law School. He was issues coordinator for the Carter campaign in 1975 and early 1976 and before that was a reporter for several newspapers. In 1970 he was a researcher and counselor at the Narcotics Treatment Agency in Washington.

BARBARA T. SYLVESTER, of Florence, S.C. Sylvester, 48, is active in civic and community affairs in South Carolina. She is a member and former chairman of the South Carolina Board of Youth Services and a former chairman of the State Board of Juvenile Corrections. She worked on the creation of the South Carolina Department of Mental Retardation and is chairman of the Mumford G. Fuller Developmental Center Board, a community school for retarded children.

DIANA M. TAMEZ, of San Antonio, Tex. Tamez, 22, is completing a B.S. in psychology at the University of Texas. She works on a child abuse project at the Mexican American Neighborhood Civic Organization.

GENEVIEVE H. WILSON, of Baltimore, Md. Wilson, 59 has been a housewife since 1958. Before that she was an advertising sales representative for the Johnson Publishing Company in Chicago. She is a director of the Children's Guild in Baltimore, the National Conference of Christians and Jews, and the Family and Children's Society.

Civil Aeronautics Board

Letter to Donald L. Tucker on the Withdrawal of His Nomination To Be a Member of the Board.   October 3, 1977

To Don Tucker

I wish to express to you my sincere and deep felt appreciation for your willingness to serve in my Administration as a member and Vice Chairman of the Civil Aeronautics Board.

Nevertheless, I understand the reasons which you have given for your request that I now withdraw your nomination for this position. I will honor your request.

I have complete confidence in your competence and integrity, and regret that our nation will be deprived of your good services.

Sincerely,

JIMMY CARTER

[The Honorable Don Tucker, State Capitol, Tallahassee, Florida]

NOTE: The text of the letter was made available by the White House Press Office. It was not issued in the form of a White House press release.

Budget Deferrals

Message to the Congress.   October 3, 1977

To the Congress of the United States:

In accordance with the Impoundment Control Act of 1974, I herewith report 42 deferrals of fiscal year 1978 funds totalling

$1,480.6 million. The deferrals are primarily routine in nature and do not, in most cases, affect program levels.

The details of each deferral are contained in the attached reports.

JIMMY CARTER

The White House,
   October 3, 1977.

NOTE: The attachments detailing the deferrals are printed in the FEDERAL REGISTER of October 7, 1977.

The message was announced by the White House Press Office. It was not issued in the form of a White House press release.

White House Fellowships

Executive Order 12012.   October 3, 1977

By virtue of the authority vested in me by the Constitution and statutes of the United States of America, and as President of the United States of America, Executive Order No. 11183, as amended, is further amended as follows:

SECTION 1. The word "young" is deleted wherever it appears in the preamble and in Section 2(a).

SEC. 2. Section 2(b)(2) is amended to read:

"(2) Are presently early in their chosen careers and show exceptional promise of future development;".

SEC. 3. Section 2(b)(4) is deleted, the word "and" is added at the end of Section 2(b)(3), and Section 2(b)(5) is redesignated as Section 2(b)(4).

SEC. 4. Section 2(c) is amended by adding "age" after "national origin,".

JIMMY CARTER

The White House,
   October 3, 1977.

[Filed with the Office of the Federal Register, 11:15 a.m., October 4, 1977]

NOTE: The Executive order was not issued in the form of a White House press release.

UNITED NATIONS

Address Before the General Assembly.   October 4, 1977

Mr. President, Mr. Secretary General, assembled delegates, and distinguished guests:

Mr. President, I wish to offer first my congratulations on your election as President of the 32d General Assembly. It gives my own Government particular satisfaction to work under the leadership of a representative from Yugoslavia, a nation with which the United States enjoys close and valued relations. We pledge our cooperation and will depend heavily on your experience and skill in guiding these discussions which we are beginning.

Mr. President, I would also like to express again the high esteem in which we hold Secretary General Waldheim. We continue to benefit greatly from our close consultations with him, and we place great trust in his leadership of this organization.

Thirty-two years ago, in the cold dawn of the Atomic Age, this organization came into being. Its first and its most urgent purpose has been to secure peace for an exhausted and ravaged world.

Present conditions in some respects appear quite hopeful, yet the assurance of peace continues to elude us. Before the end of this century, a score of nations could possess nuclear weapons. If this should happen, the world that we leave our children will mock our own hopes for peace.

The level of nuclear armaments could grow by tens of thousands, and the same situation could well occur with advanced conventional weapons. The temptation to use these weapons, for fear that someone else might do it first, would be almost irresistible.

The ever-growing trade in conventional arms subverts international commerce from a force for peace to a caterer for war.

Violence, terrorism, assassination, undeclared wars all threaten to destroy the restraint and the moderation that must become the dominant characteristic of our age.

Unless we establish a code of international behavior in which the resort to violence becomes increasingly irrelevant to the pursuit of national interests, we will crush the world's dreams for human development and the full flowering of human freedom.

We have already become a global community, but only in the sense that we face common problems and we share for good or evil a common future. In this community, power to solve the world's problems, particularly economic and political power, no longer lies solely in the hands of a few nations.

Power is now widely shared among many nations with different cultures and different histories and different aspirations. The question is whether we will allow our differences to defeat us or whether we will work together to realize our common hopes for peace.

Today I want to address the major dimensions of peace and the role the United States intends to play in limiting and reducing all armaments, controlling nuclear technology, restricting the arms trade, and settling disputes by peaceful means.

When atomic weapons were used for the first time, Winston Churchill described the power of the atom as a revelation long, mercifully withheld from man. Since then we have learned in Dürrenmatt's chilling words that "what has once been thought can never be un-thought."

If we are to have any assurance that our children are to live out their lives in a world which satisfies our hope—or that they will have a chance to live at all—we must finally come to terms with this enormous nuclear force and turn it exclusively to beneficial ends.

Peace will not be assured until the weapons of war are finally put away. While we work toward that goal, nations will want sufficient arms to preserve their security.

The United States purpose is to ensure peace. It is for that reason that our military posture and our alliances will remain as strong as necessary to deter attack. However, the security of the global community cannot forever rest on a balance of terror.

In the past, war has been accepted as the ultimate arbiter of disputes among nations. But in the nuclear era we can no longer think of war as merely a continuation of diplomacy by other means. Nuclear war cannot be measured by the archaic standards of victory or defeat.

This stark reality imposes on the United States and the Soviet Union an awesome and special responsibility. The United States is engaged, along with other nations, in a broad range of negotiations. In strategic arms limitation talks, we and the Soviets are within sight of a significant agreement in limiting the total numbers of weapons and in restricting certain categories of weapons of special concern to each of us. We can also start the crucial process of curbing the relentless march of technological development which makes nuclear weapons ever more difficult to control.

We must look beyond the present and work to prevent the critical threats and instabilities of the future. In the principles of self-restraint, reciprocity, and mutual accommodation of interests, if these are observed, then the United States and the Soviet Union will not only succeed in limiting weapons but will also create a foundation of better relations in other spheres of interest.

The United States is willing to go as far as possible, consistent with our security interest, in limiting and reducing our nuclear weapons. On a reciprocal basis we are willing now to reduce them by 10 percent or 20 percent, even 50 percent. Then we will work for further reductions to a world truly free of nuclear weapons.

The United States also recognizes a threat of continued testing of nuclear explosives.

Negotiations for a comprehensive ban on nuclear explosions are now being conducted by the United States, the United Kingdom, and the Soviet Union. As in other areas where vital national security interests are engaged, agreements must be verifiable and fair. They must be seen by all the parties as serving a longer term interest that justifies the restraints of the moment.

The longer term interest in this instance is to close one more avenue of nuclear competition and thereby demonstrate to all the world that the major nuclear powers take seriously our obligations to reduce the threat of nuclear catastrophe.

My country believes that the time has come to end all explosions of nuclear devices, no matter what their claimed justification, peaceful or military, and we appreciate the efforts of other nations to reach this same goal.

During the past 9 months, I have expressed the special importance that we attach to controlling nuclear proliferation. But I fear that many do not understand why the United States feels as it does.

Why is it so important to avoid the chance that 1 or 2 or 10 other nations might acquire 1 or 2 or 10 nuclear weapons of their own?

Let me try to explain why I deeply believe that this is one of the greatest challenges that we face in the next quarter of a century.

It's a truism that nuclear weapons are a powerful deterrent. They are a deterrent because they threaten. They could be used for terrorism or blackmail as well as for war. But they threaten not just the intended enemy, they threaten every nation, combatant or noncombatant alike. That is why all of us must be concerned.

Let me be frank. The existence of nuclear weapons in the United States and the Soviet Union, in Great Britain, France, and China, is

something that we cannot undo except by the painstaking process of negotiation. But the existence of these weapons does not mean that other
nations need to develop their own weapons any more than it provides a
reason for those of us who have them to share them with others.

Rather, it imposes two solemn obligations on the nations which have
the capacity to export nuclear fuel and nuclear technology—the obligations to meet legitimate energy needs and, in doing so, to ensure that
nothing that we export contributes directly or indirectly to the production
of nuclear explosives. That is why the supplier nations are seeking a
common policy, and that is why the United States and the Soviet Union,
even as we struggle to find common ground in the SALT talks, have
already moved closer toward agreement and cooperation in our efforts to
limit nuclear proliferation.

I believe that the London Suppliers Group must conclude its work
as it's presently constituted so that the world security will be safeguarded
from the pressures of commercial competition. We have learned it is not
enough to safeguard just some facilities or some materials. Full-scope,
comprehensive safeguards are necessary.

Two weeks from now in our own country, more than 30 supplier and
consuming nations will convene for the International Fuel Cycle Evaluation, which we proposed last spring. For the next several years experts
will work together on every facet of the nuclear fuel cycle.

The scientists and the policymakers of these nations will face a tremendous challenge. We know that by the year 2000, nuclear power reactors could be producing enough plutonium to make tens of thousands of
bombs every year.

I believe from my own personal knowledge of this issue that there are
ways to solve the problems that we face. I believe that there are alternative
fuel cycles that can be managed safely on a global basis. I hope, therefore,
that the International Fuel Cycle Evaluation will have the support and
the encouragement of every nation.

I've heard it said that efforts to control nuclear proliferation are
futile, that the genie is already out of the bottle. I do not believe this to
be true. It should not be forgotten that for 25 years the nuclear club did
not expand its membership. By genuine cooperation, we can make certain
that this terrible club expands no further.

Now, I've talked about the special problems of nuclear arms control
and nuclear proliferation at length. Let me turn to the problem of conventional arms control, which affects potentially or directly every nation

represented in this great hall. This is not a matter for the future, even the near future, but of the immediate present. Worldwide military expenditures are now in the neighborhood of $300 billion a year.

Last year the nations of the world spent more than 60 times as much—60 times as much—equipping each soldier as we spent educating each child. The industrial nations spent the most money, but the rate of growth in military spending is faster in the developing world.

While only a handful of states produce sophisticated weapons, the number of nations which seek to purchase these weapons is expanding rapidly.

The conventional arms race both causes and feeds on the threat of larger and more deadly wars. It levies an enormous burden on an already troubled world economy.

For our part, the United States has now begun to reduce its arms exports. Our aim is to reduce both the quantity and the deadliness of the weapons that we sell. We have already taken the first few steps, but we cannot go very far alone. Nations whose neighbors are purchasing large quantities of arms feel constrained to do the same. Supplier nations who practice restraint in arms sales sometimes find that they simply lose valuable commercial markets to other suppliers.

We hope to work with other supplier nations to cut back on the flow of arms and to reduce the rate at which the most advanced and sophisticated weapon technologies spread around the world. We do not expect this task to be easy or to produce instant results. But we are committed to stop the spiral of increasing sale of weapons.

Equally important, we hope that purchaser nations, individually and through regional organizations, will limit their arms imports. We are ready to provide to some nations the necessary means for legitimate self-defense, but we are also eager to work with any nation or region in order to decrease the need for more numerous, more deadly, and ever more expensive weapons.

Fourteen years ago one of my predecessors spoke in this very room under circumstances that in certain ways resembled these. It was a time, he said, of comparative calm, and there was an atmosphere of rising hope about the prospect of controlling nuclear energy.

The first specific step had been taken to limit the nuclear arms race—a test ban treaty signed by nearly a hundred nations.

But the succeeding years did not live up to the optimistic prospect John F. Kennedy placed before this assembly, because as a community of nations, we failed to address the deepest sources of potential conflict among us.

As we seek to establish the principles of détente among the major nuclear powers, we believe that these principles must also apply in regional conflicts.

The United States is committed to the peaceful settlement of differences. We are committed to the strengthening of the peacemaking capabilities of the United Nations and regional organizations, such as the Organization of African Unity and the Organization of American States.

The United States supports Great Britain's efforts to bring about a peaceful, rapid transition to majority rule and independence in Zimbabwe. We have joined other members of the Security Council last week and also the Secretary General in efforts to bring about independence and democratic rule in Namibia. We are pleased with the level of cooperation that we have achieved with the leaders of the nations in the area, as well as those people who are struggling for independence.

We urge South Africa and other nations to support the proposed solution to the problems in Zimbabwe and to cooperate still more closely in providing for a smooth and prompt transition in Namibia. But it is essential that all outside nations exercise restraint in their actions in Zimbabwe and Namibia so that we can bring about this majority rule and avoid a widening war that could engulf the southern half of the African Continent.

Of all the regional conflicts in the world, none holds more menace than the Middle East. War there has already carried the world to the edge of nuclear confrontation. It has already disrupted the world economy and imposed severe hardships on the people in the developed and the developing nations alike.

So, true peace—peace embodied in binding treaties—is essential. It will be in the interest of the Israelis and the Arabs. It is in the interest of the American people. It is in the interest of the entire world.

The United Nations Security Council has provided the basis for peace in Resolutions 242 and 338, but negotiations in good faith by all parties is needed to give substance to peace.

Such good faith negotiations must be inspired by a recognition that all nations in the area—Israel and the Arab countries—have a right to exist in peace, with early establishment of economic and cultural exchange and of normal diplomatic relations. Peace must include a process in which the bitter divisions of generations, even centuries, hatreds and suspicions can be overcome. Negotiations cannot be successful if any of the parties harbor the deceitful view that peace is simply an interlude in which to prepare for war.

Good faith negotiations will also require acceptance by all sides of the fundamental rights and interests of everyone involved.

For Israel this means borders that are recognized and secure. Security arrangements are crucial to a nation that has fought for its survival in each of the last four decades. The commitment of the United States to Israel's security is unquestionable.

For the Arabs, the legitimate rights of the Palestinian people must be recognized. One of the things that binds the American people to Israel is our shared respect for human rights and the courage with which Israel has defended such rights. It is clear that a true and lasting peace in the Middle East must also respect the rights of all peoples of the area. How these rights are to be defined and implemented is, of course, for the interested parties to decide in detailed negotiations and not for us to dictate.

We do not intend to impose, from the outside, a settlement on the nations of the Middle East.

The United States has been meeting with the foreign ministers of Israel and the Arab nations involved in the search for peace. We are staying in close contact with the Soviet Union, with whom we share responsibility for reconvening the Geneva conference.

As a result of these consultations, the Soviet Union and the United States have agreed to call for the resumption of the Geneva conference before the end of this year.

While a number of procedural questions remain, if the parties continue to act in good faith, I believe that these questions can be answered.

The major powers have a special responsibility to act with restraint in areas of the world where they have competing interests, because the association of these interests with local rivalries and conflicts can lead to serious confrontation.

In the Indian Ocean area, neither we nor the Soviet Union has a large military presence, nor is there a rapidly mounting competition between us.

Restraint in the area may well begin with a mutual effort to stabilize our presence and to avoid an escalation in military competition. Then both sides can consider how our military activities in the Indian Ocean, this whole area, might be even further reduced.

The peaceful settlement of differences is, of course, essential. The United States is willing to abide by that principle, as in the case of the recently signed Panama Canal treaties. Once ratified, these treaties can transform the U.S.-Panama relationship into one that permanently protects the interests and respects the sovereignty of both our countries.

We have all survived and surmounted major challenges since the United Nations was founded. But we can accelerate progress even in a world of ever-increasing diversity.

A commitment to strengthen international institutions is vital. But progress lies also in our own national policies. We can work together to form a community of peace if we accept the kind of obligations that I have suggested today.

To summarize: first, an obligation to remove the threat of nuclear weaponry, to reverse the buildup of armaments and their trade, and to conclude bilateral and multilateral arms control agreements that can bring security to all of us. In order to reduce the reliance of nations on nuclear weaponry, I hereby solemnly declare on behalf of the United States that we will not use nuclear weapons except in self-defense; that is, in circumstances of an actual nuclear or conventional attack on the United States, our territories, or Armed Forces, or such an attack on our allies.

In addition, we hope that initiatives by the Western nations to secure mutual and balanced force reductions in Europe will be met by equal response from the Warsaw Pact countries.

Second, an obligation to show restraint in areas of tension, to negotiate disputes and settle them peacefully, and to strengthen peacemaking capabilities of the United Nations and regional organizations.

And finally, an effort by all nations, East as well as West, North as well as South, to fulfill mankind's aspirations for human development and human freedom. It is to meet these basic demands that we build governments and seek peace.

We must share these obligations for our own mutual survival and our own mutual prosperity.

We can see a world at peace. We can work for a world without want. We can build a global community dedicated to these purposes and to human dignity.

The view that I have sketched for you today is that of only one leader in only one nation. However wealthy and powerful the United

States may be, however capable of leadership, this power is increasingly only relative. The leadership increasingly is in need of being shared.

No nation has a monopoly of vision, of creativity, or of ideas. Bringing these together from many nations is our common responsibility and our common challenge. For only in these ways can the idea of a peaceful global community grow and prosper.

Thank you very much.

NOTE: The President spoke at 10:20 a.m. in the General Assembly Hall.

Prior to his remarks, the President met briefly with United Nations Secretary General Kurt Waldheim and General Assembly President Lazar Mojsov.

United Nations

Remarks at a Working Luncheon for Officials of African Nations. October 4, 1977

That's the briefest speech I've ever heard Andy Young make. [*Laughter*]

It is an honor for me to meet with the distinguished representatives of so many countries in Africa. President Machel and I were just noticing that we have 50 States in our Nation and about 220 million people. In Africa, there are also about 220 million people—49 states now; Zimbabwe will be 50 and Namibia will be 51.

In the past, we have not always enjoyed as close a spirit of friendship and cooperation with the nations of Africa as we would have liked. I think it's accurate to say, however, within the last 9 months, because of the good services of our Secretary of State, Cy Vance, and our Ambassador to the United Nations, Andrew Young, that those relations have improved greatly, and we are very thankful for this progress.

Our purpose is the same as yours—to see a strong, vigorous, free, and prosperous Africa with as much of the control of government as possible in the hands of the residents of your countries. We believe in majority rule. We believe in human rights. We believe in peace. And we, of course, also believe in strong harmony among neighbors and also between ourselves and you across the Atlantic Ocean.

This luncheon is a chance for me to get acquainted with all of you, and we are very eager for this chance to grow into closer and more constant consultations between myself, all of you, and the leaders of your great countries.

We have benefited greatly in the evolution of our own national policy from close consultation with many of you. I believe that our purposes are the same as yours.

We face together the problem of how to resolve the Rhodesian, Zimbabwe question. Our own cooperation with the British, with the Organization of African Unity, with the strong leaders of nations who are neighbors of Zimbabwe have been very helpful in forming a common purpose. And now this question, as you know, has been presented to the United Nations. As the months ahead give us an opportunity for increasing realization of our hopes for majority rule and peace in Zimbabwe, we would welcome your constant advice and counsel about how we can use the influence of the United States in the most constructive way.

Of course, we are also dedicated to carrying out the resolutions which already exist concerning Namibia, and we hope for early and complete peace in the Horn of Africa. And we are eager to cooperate with you in these noble efforts.

I might add, also, that we want to have very close and friendly bilateral relationships between the United States and every one of your countries. We now have about 2,000 Peace Corps volunteers in 23 nations in Africa. In the past, I know that this has been an effort about which there has been some doubt. But if you have a special need for technical help or help with agriculture, education, health, if you would let me know or Secretary of State Vance or Ambassador Andrew Young, we would be glad to participate with you on this basis, with your having control, of course, over how these volunteers might strengthen the ties between our country and yours.

We do this and offer this in a spirit of partnership and equality. And, of course, we also welcome delegations of your own citizens or individual students or others, who would like to come to our country and to learn about us and to form closer ties of friendship between our people.

I might close by saying that we are very eager to have a reduction in expenditures for weapons and arms, as I mentioned in my speech this morning. We have a substantial aid program. Our hopes would be that this could be in the form of humanitarian aid and not military aid.

We need to understand your special problems and your special hopes and dreams and aspirations for the future so that the opportunities in your own country might be realized. And I would personally appreciate direct communication from the leaders of your nations if a special occasion should arise where the United States might be of help in some matter that is important to your people.

Again, let me say how deeply grateful I am for the honor of meeting all of you.

We share a common purpose. Friendship can bind us together, and I'm very eager to meet you more than halfway.

I hope that those of you who represent your countries here will extend my heartiest and personal best wishes to the leaders of your country. And I know that many of them have been here already; some will come next year. And I look forward to a chance in the future, perhaps, of visiting your nation, to extend a stronger expression of friendship from the United States to the people whom you represent.

Thank you very much.

NOTE: The President spoke at 2:03 p.m. at the headquarters of the U.S. Mission to the United Nations in New York City. He was introduced by Andrew J. Young, U.S. Representative to the United Nations.

The President hosted the luncheon for foreign ministers and heads of delegations to the United Nations.

Natural Gas Deregulation

Statement on Senate Action.   October 4, 1977

This legislation is unacceptable. It is an injustice to the working people of this country.

The bill passed by the House is a fair one and one that I and the American people can support. I hope and expect that a reasonable bill will emerge from the conference committee and be approved by both Houses.

I look forward to signing legislation that provides adequate production incentives while protecting the interests of American consumers. I will not sign an unfair bill.

NOTE: Earlier in the day, the Senate had passed H.R. 5289, a bill to establish a comprehensive natural gas pricing policy.

The statement was made available by the White House Press Office. It was not issued in the form of a White House press release.

United Nations

Remarks to Members of the U.S. Delegation and U.S. Officials of the United Nations Secretariat. October 4, 1977

In case you're wondering, additionally, who I am, I'm the one who works for Andy Young. [*Laughter*]

I know it's not appropriate for me to charge you with a special responsibility just to our own great Nation alone, because in a special way you represent the United States in an expanded role. You work in the international community which we were very grateful to have come, with its headquarters, to our free country.

In the past years there has been, I think, a constant growth in the influence of the United Nations. And more and more, there has been a realization that without the U.N. there could be no resolution of any regional disputes and problems and the realization of hopes that, if thwarted, could possibly even embroil our own country in warfare quite unnecessarily.

I, myself, have a deep commitment to the United Nations and want to see its role expanded in the future. The world is too complex to be dealt with even as well as in the past by one powerful country or three or four powerful countries. The other nations of the world resent it, and it's much better to have a forum where each nation's voice can be heard.

I want to say, also, that there's a special reason for the U.N. to be in our country. This kind of a kinship sometimes goes unrecognized because our Nation for the last 200 years has, in effect, done what the United Nations has done in the last 32 years.

There's hardly a country represented in this body now or its predecessors that doesn't have citizens who come to our country to learn how to get along with one another, to share religious compatibilities and differences, to compare social compatibilities and differences, to share past political compatibilities and differences.

Those who have been mortal enemies in the heart of Europe or in Africa or other parts of the world, when they come here to our country to be citizens, they've had to learn to live in harmony. And at the same time, they've also preserved their own precious heritage in a unique and very proud and effective way.

The foundation of the United Nations, as you know, is similar to our own. The Charter of the United Nations, signed in 1945, I believe, has as its basic premise individual freedom, the reaching for a higher capacity for human life, existence with the worth of each human protected, a search for equality of opportunity. These kinds of bases, not coincidentally, exist in both our own Constitution and Declaration of Independence and in the United Nations Charter.

I think it's accurate to say that there is a growing realization that the United Nations is accepted better by the American people. It hasn't always been a fact that the U.N. could take the major responsibility in a potential trouble spot like Namibia and retain that role, deal with South Africa, deal with SWAPO, deal with the other nations in southern Africa, deal with the other parts of the world who are interested.

I know that as far as our own role is concerned in Zimbabwe, we and the British are very eager to see the United Nations come in and play a larger and larger role.

Just the prevention of war is certainly not enough. But the enhancement of education opportunities, better health care for the people of the world, a searching out of commerce, dealing with the laws

1725

of the seas and elimination of racism and many other of the most complicated and challenging confrontations with human beings are now being channeled more and more into the United Nations.

I know that you're searching, along with others who administer the U.N. for a better way to spend the limited amount of money that's available to you, and the organization of the structure of the United Nations is being reexamined. And this is compatible with governments throughout the world.

I'd like to say in closing that I, personally, am deeply indebted to you. We have a fine delegation at the United Nations. Without any derrogation at all to past ambassadors here, I want to say that I'm extremely proud of what Andrew Young is, what he means, what he says, what he does, what he stands for. In my opinion, he epitomizes in many ways the greatness of our own country. And the new harmonious relationship that now exists between our own country and some of the developing nations of the world can be credited directly to the influence of Andrew Young and the trust that those deprived people have in him.

He's one of those Americans whose ancestors came here, perhaps involuntarily—[*laughter and applause*]—but you can see how well he's done. [*Laughter*] And I'm very glad politically to have him on my side. But I think this does illustrate very clearly what our country is and what it's made of itself, and what the United Nations is and what it is making of itself, because some of the finest expressions of hope and commitment in the international community have not yet been realized.

Many of our realizations were slow in coming. As you well know, when our country was founded there was a premise that slavery was accepted, although we were founded on a basis of equality and freedom. And it's been in recent years that women had a right to vote and young people had a right to vote and we could elect our United States Senators directly, and so forth. Our country has grown with the last two centuries' experience. And we still have a long way to go before we can assure that the future of the international community will be based on peace and that people with diverse interests can indeed live with mutual respect and in harmony.

I came here as a candidate to speak about the proliferation of nuclear weapons. And I came back last spring as a new President to speak about human rights. And I came here again this morning to speak about the elimination of a threat of war. So, I think I've already demonstrated my deep commitment to the institution which you serve so well.

So, I'm proud of you, and I hope that my own administration, our United Nations delegation, our State Department, and other aspects of it will make you proud.

I think as we deal with the North-South question, which is one of the most difficult of all, it's accurate to say that we've had similar struggle within the United States, too. And perhaps I've proven that if you struggle long enough, the Southerners don't have to worry about eventually coming out on top. So, we've got a long way to go. We'll go there together.

I hope that we can learn as a nation from the harmony in the United Nations, and I hope that your organization, the United Nations, can also learn from the great experience of what I still consider to be the greatest country on Earth, the United States.

Thank you very much.

NOTE: The President spoke at 5:49 p.m. at the United Nations Building in New York City.

United Nations

Remarks at a Working Dinner for Officials of Western and Eastern European Nations. October 4, 1977

It's very nice for a President to have an Ambassador who when he's unpopular takes the blame and when he's popular gives the President the credit for it. [*Laughter*]

There were a few months ago when I had doubts about Andrew Young—[*laughter*]—and his popularity with the American people. But I think all of you have seen very clearly that he's now one of the greatest international assets that we have, and the American people now recognize that. And, Andy, I want to thank you for it.

I've had a delightful day here as President of our country, visiting the distinguished representatives of so many nations around the world. And this evening during the meal I had a chance to come around and meet all of you. And to think for just a moment about the remarkable harmony that exists here between or among diplomats and foreign ministers, prime ministers, presidents, whose people share even as deep or even deeper a feeling of friendship to one another and a yearning of peace and harmony and mutual commitment to solving problems. And at the same time we go ahead mounting armaments races, and we have difficulty communicating with one another at the top level. And there's often an inability to bridge a gap which separates our people.

I think that in a remarkable way we have an opportunity to correct that defect in our societal arrangement. The United Nations has been an entity now for 32 years, I believe. We're very proud of the fact that its basic home is here. But many of you share in a commitment that it's your home, too. And I think there's a growing awareness among ourselves and the Soviets and the Israelis and the Arab countries, the African nations and those in the Far East, that this is a place to bring our challenges and our problems and our differences and our opportunities and our dreams, and hopefully, to get other nations to join in a common understanding of the realization of those hopes and the resolution of differences.

As President of one of the great nations, I'm very eager to do everything I can to show the world that we have confidence in the community-of-nations approach. We realize that power and might and influence and strength and economic well-being can't provide leadership unless there is a community of effort. And as a newcomer to the international scene, as a newcomer even to the National Government in our own country, I've already benefited greatly from my contact with many of you and the leaders from your own countries. You've been very helpful to me in giving me advice and counsel privately, sometimes publicly, which I also appreciate. And we hope to learn in the process, and I think we have learned some things.

We have a great opportunity to move forward in the next few years. There are some crises that must be addressed between ourselves and the Soviet Union in the SALT talks and the elimination of testing of nuclear weapons and the elimination of explosives from countries that don't have them, as I mentioned today in my talk, and the questions in the Middle East, in southern Africa, in the recognition of newborn nations, and the alleviation of disharmonies that still exist from past wars.

Those things are challenges to us all. And this is a challenge that's so great that it's just imperative that we work together—not in a quiescent or quiet or reticent way, but in a constructive, forceful, and courageous fashion, because there's no doubt in my mind that among our people there is an intense desire for harmony and friendship. The leaders sometimes are the obstacle to the realization of those hopes that exist among those who have put us in powerful offices.

I would like to say in closing that we are very grateful to have you here with us tonight. It's an honor for us to welcome you. Those of you who are not heads of state, I've had a chance either to meet with your own chosen leaders or will soon be taking advantage of that opportunity. And this again is a way for the American people to learn about the common problems that we face and the need for closer attention to those at all levels of government.

And this is a time, also, to break down barriers that exist to trade, to tourism, to share the battle against hunger and disease and poverty, and to share the battle against disease.

These are challenges I hope we can face, once we eliminate the threat of war and remove our deep and debilitating commitment to the purchase of weapons and threat of nuclear destruction. The challenge is there for us. I think we have a great and exciting prospect in the years to come.

You know these things better than I. And I'm very proud of a chance to make friends here tonight and to let you know that the commitment of our Nation is to join with you in these high and exciting and challenging and difficult common purposes for a brighter future.

Thank you very much.

NOTE: The President spoke at 9:40 p.m. at the headquarters of the U.S. Mission to the United Nations in New York City. The President hosted the dinner for foreign ministers and heads of delegations to the United Nations.

Geneva Peace Conference on the Middle East

United States-Israel Joint Statement Issued Following a Meeting Between the President and Israeli Foreign Minister Moshe Dayan. October 5, 1977

The U.S. and Israel agree that Security Council Resolutions 242 and 338 remain the agreed basis for the resumption of the Geneva Peace Conference and that all the understandings and agreements between them on this subject remain in force.

Proposals for removing remaining obstacles to reconvening the Geneva Conference were developed. Foreign Minister Dayan will consult his Government on the results of these discussions. Secretary Vance will discuss these proposals with the other parties to the Geneva Conference.

Acceptance of the Joint U.S.-U.S.S.R. Statement of October 1, 1977, by the parties is not a prerequisite for the reconvening and conduct of the Geneva Conference.

NOTE: The text of the joint statement was released at New York, N.Y.

The text of the U.S.-U.S.S.R. statement is printed in the Department of State Bulletin of November 7, 1977, page 639.

New York City

Exchange With Reporters Following a Tour of the South Bronx.   October 5, 1977

THE PRESIDENT. [*Inaudible*]—but I was encouraged in some way, because there is obviously—[*inaudible*]—to rebuild this. And the Public Housing Authority in New York, which is well known as probably the best in the Nation, has done a superb job.

I have asked the Department of Housing and Urban Development, Secretary Pat Harris, who was with me this morning, to work closely with the Interior Department in putting down some plans along with the city and State for recreation areas and park areas in regions where buildings need to be destroyed.

And our CETA funds, training programs can provide employment for people to rebuild their own neighborhoods and, of course, with the public works programs that we put through the Congress now, we have a good chance to renovate that area.

We'll put together a comprehensive plan, working with Mayor Beame both while he's mayor and, I hope, after he's no longer mayor—and the new mayor of New York. I think we will have a good prospect——

REPORTER. You once said you thought New York City has changed for the better in the last few years under Mayor Beame. Have——

THE PRESIDENT. It has.

Q. Did you change your mind after your tour—[*inaudible*].

THE PRESIDENT. No, I haven't changed my mind. I think even among the people who live in the South Bronx and who are very disturbed about their own neighborhoods, that there's a spirit of hope, and I think that there's a spirit of determination to take what they still have—there is a friendly attitude toward me, toward Mayor Beame—[*inaudible*].

I believe that in the last 2 years there has been a substantial transformation for the better in the general attitude of New Yorkers, and I think they are confident—[*inaudible*].

Q. Sir, could you tell us what job you might consider Mayor Beame for in Washington?

THE PRESIDENT. Well, I particularly need him in government, tying together in a more forceful way the different levels of government, because the Federal Government can't deal with these problems alone.

Of course, almost all of the South Bronx property, outside of government housing—[*inaudible*]—are owned by private citizens. So, that's a resource that we haven't adequately tapped. And with his superb experience and background and knowledge, that's one area that I see a possibility of—[*inaudible*]—but I won't expect him to make a decision all alone. If he is willing to help me I'd like to work closely with him on a nationwide basis, for making sure that the different levels of government can work in harmony.

Q. Would there be an official appointment for Mr. Beame, or would this be in an unofficial capacity?

THE PRESIDENT. Well, I would prefer an official capacity, but that would be—[*inaudible*].

Q. Can you make a suggestion about what type of office?

THE PRESIDENT. No, I think that's something that ought to be announced later on.

Q. Mr. President, were you upset at all by Mr. Koch's giving you that letter yesterday, objecting to your position?

THE PRESIDENT. No, not at all. No, I was glad to see Mr. Koch. I think it's a completely logical thing for him to express his concern to me, and I was not disturbed at all.

Q. Will the letter, sir, in any way jeopardize your relationship with New York City through Mr. Koch?

THE PRESIDENT. Of course not. Ed Koch expressed some of the concerns in his letter that I feel myself. We've obviously got a very difficult job as a negotiator, a mediator, and an interested party in the Middle East. We have ties with Israel that are absolutely unshakable. The security of Israel is vital to the security of our own country.

We had meetings last night for 4, 5, 6 hours—I don't know exactly how long—with Foreign Minister Dayan. I met with the Foreign Minister of Egypt, Mr. Fahmy, yesterday. Cy Vance is meeting this morning with the Foreign Minister of Syria. And we're continuing our discussions with all the interested parties.

I'll be meeting today with the Foreign Minister of Lebanon. So, I think that a public expression of concern is completely legitimate, and I don't feel badly about it at all.

Q. Won't you come back and campaign for Mr. Koch in New York?

THE PRESIDENT. I don't know about that. I really don't think I need to. And I doubt that I'll be able to come back before the election.

Q. [*Inaudible*]—microphones, set up at the heliport, prepared for you to make a statement in behalf of the Koch candidacy for mayor. You apparently at the last minute——

THE PRESIDENT. I didn't know about that.

Q.——changed your mind. You did not know about that at all?

THE PRESIDENT. No, I didn't. I didn't know it.

Q. Your advance people didn't discuss this with you at all?

THE PRESIDENT. No, I never heard about that.

NOTE: The President spoke at 10:15 a.m. outside the U.N. Plaza Hotel.

Earlier in the day, the President and Mayor Abraham Beame of New York City met at the U.N. Plaza Hotel and then proceeded to the South Bronx area of the city for the tour.

New York City

Statement by the President.   *October 5, 1977*

When I addressed the United States Conference of Mayors last year, I committed this administration to develop a long-term, comprehensive urban policy. I pledged an overall strategy to improve the quality of life and strengthen the economic base of this Nation's cities.

In the first 8 months of my administration, I believe that we have taken sig-

nificant steps to begin to fulfill that commitment, while at the same time preserving sound budget policy. The brief list below of the new fiscal and economic assistance provided to New York this year indicates the importance that I attach to helping our distressed urban areas.

The steps this administration has taken over the past 8 months represent a strong beginning, but they will not substitute for a comprehensive urban policy.

The Cabinet-level Urban and Regional Policy Group is formulating a long-term program that will address the critical problems facing residents of urban areas. The initiatives this group will recommend will provide particular benefits for cities such as New York.

Summarized below are significant administration actions which will provide fiscal or economic relief for New York City:

1. *New Social Services Authorization*

I am announcing today my approval of a settlement of $543 million against $2.4 billion in claims under the Title XX Social Services program, subject to congressional concurrence. New York State is expected to receive at least $214 million of this settlement. A substantial portion of this amount is expected to be passed through to New York City to provide significant new fiscal relief. The administration will send the necessary legislation reflecting the agreement to Congress in the next 2 weeks.

This agreement settles the largest outstanding financial dispute between the Federal Government and the States. I believe that this settlement, which involved close consultations with State officials, reflects a new atmosphere of cooperation between this administration and State and local officials. (Attached is a detailed description of the background and terms of this settlement.)

2. *Seasonal Financing Loans*

The Federal Government is continuing to provide loans to New York City under the New York City Seasonal Financing Act. A total of $1.5 billion has been loaned the city since July 1, including a $325 million loan on October 4. An additional $575 million is expected to be loaned during the remainder of the year.

The Treasury Department is working closely with State and city officials to facilitate the city's return to the public market.

The administration is also reviewing the city's borrowing needs for the post-FY 1978 period, and remains committed to working with the city to assure that those needs are met.

3. *Countercyclical Revenue Sharing*

The administration's extension of countercyclical assistance, which provided $121 million for the city in its fiscal year 1977, is expected to increase to over $130 million in fiscal year 1978. These funds are used by the city to maintain vital services, to prevent municipal employee layoffs, and to relieve the burden of local taxation.

4. *Employment Training*

The administration is increasing the city's funding under the Comprehensive Employment Training Act from $180 million in the city's fiscal year 1977 to $411 million in 1978. These funds have significantly helped the city to provide important services during its fiscal crisis and to create jobs for the unemployed.

5. *Local Public Works*

Under the administration's $4 billion public works program, assistance in the city will nearly double from $102 million in the city's fiscal year 1977 to $192 million in 1978. This assistance will provide a particularly critical boost to the city's depressed construction industry.

6. *Community Development Block Grant*

This special revenue sharing program supports a wide range of community and economic development activities. The administration proposed and the Congress has now enacted a dual distribution formula which increases aid for older distressed cities. This will add some $64 million more to the city's grant in the next fiscal year, for a total of $229 million.

The city will also be eligible for assistance under the newly enacted $400 million Urban Development Action Grant program, which permits the Secretary of HUD to make discretionary grants to stimulate private sector investment in distressed cities.

This proposal should be effective in leveraging significant private investment in cities such as New York.

7. *Urban Mass Transit*

On Monday, Secretary Adams announced discretionary mass transit grants totalling $280 million to the city's transit system and the commuter rail network surrounding the city. Most of the assistance is for the modernization of existing facilities, with the balance going to further progress on major additions to their system which began in previous years.

8. *Westway Highway*

The administration has approved an $800 million grant for this highway project, which State and city public officials believe will stimulate economic development on Manhattan's West Side.

In addition, the Federal Department of Transportation has approved the sale of the right-of-way of the Westway Interstate Highway to New York State. This sale is expected to result in approximately $80 million in revenues to the city, 90 percent of which is financed by the Department of Transportation and 10 percent by New York State. These funds will provide significant budget relief to the city.

9. *Mitchell-Lama Housing*

The Federal Government is in the process of insuring Mitchell-Lama housing projects, which will enable the city to raise $280 million in 1978 either through the sale of the projects or issuance of bonds.

10. *Child Health Assessment*

The administration's proposed Child Health Assessment Program, if enacted by Congress, in Federal fiscal year 1978, will provide $8.8 million in increased health services for children in New York City. This program is a major reform of Medicaid's periodic diagnostic program for children.

11. *Welfare Reform*

The administration's welfare reform package will result in an estimated $525 million in fiscal relief to New York *State* with approximately $175 million of that going to New York *City*. This added relief would be effective in 1981 under the proposal.

12. *Fuel Bill Payments*

A new program under the Community Services Administration assists people who had difficulty meeting last winter's large fuel bills. Of the $200 million available, $21.1 million went to New York *State,* including $1.1 million to New York *City,* to supplement other funds also available to help city residents.

13. *Trends in Federal Grants*

New York City's Financial Plan Statements show the following trends in total Federal grants:

City fiscal year	Federal grants [1] (in millions)	Federal grants [2] as a percent of city revenues
1976	$2,750	19.9
1977	3,188	22.2
1978	3,670	24.5

[1] Including capital grants.
[2] Excluding capital grants.

In 2 years, from FY 1976 through 1978, total Federal grants are projected to increase by 33 percent. In the same period, Federal non-capital grants will provide over 4.5 percent more of current city revenues.

Detailed Description of the Retroactive Social Services Claims Settlement

President Carter has approved an agreement, negotiated by the Department of Health, Education, and Welfare with State representatives, to settle the largest outstanding financial dispute between the Federal Government and the States. The agreement involves payments to 28 States for the cost of social services provided to low-income families and individuals from 1969 to 1975.

Under the agreement, 19 States will receive Federal payments totaling $532 million, and 22 States (13 of them also members of the group of 19) will have Federal Government claims against them dropped. The States, in turn, will drop all further actions against the Federal Government.

The Congress will be asked to authorize $543 million for the settlement. Eleven million dollars will be held as a contingency figure to be allotted as a part of the final agreement.

The action, contingent upon the approval of Congress, is part of a settlement between HEW and a total of 28 States of some $2.4 billion in disputed payments. Of this $2.4 billion, $1.56 billion represented State claims that were never paid by HEW, and the balance represented payments that had been made by HEW but whose validity the Department disputed.

The dispute over these claims goes back into prior administrations. It has resulted in years of expensive and inconclusive litigation between the States and the Federal Government. It has been a nagging irritant in the relations between HEW and the States.

The dispute began in the early 1970's when HEW took two actions: (1) it refused to pay 19 of the States some $1.56 billion in social services claims; and (2) it sought reimbursement from 13 of these 19 States, plus 9 other States, of Federal funds already paid to the States for social services.

The focus of the dispute has chiefly been over the types of social services for which the Federal Government should reimburse the States and whether certain State procedures were proper.

These services were covered under the old Titles I, IV, VI, X, XIV, and XVI of the Social Security Act, which became obsolete on

October 1, 1975, when Title XX became effective. Title XX of the Social Security Act is the new consolidated Title authorizing Federal payments for social services provided by the States.

The social services covered such areas as day care for children, protective services for neglected or abused children, drug and alcohol abuse services, counseling on family planning, and a variety of services for aged, blind, or disabled persons.

The agreement now reached would pay, on a formula worked out between the Department and the States, a portion of the pending unpaid claims. In addition, 22 affected States will not be asked for reimbursement of funds already given them. (See attached table.)

The amounts to be paid to the States may be adjusted slightly if existing claims by the States are adjusted, or if additional claims are filed.

Proposed settlements by State

[In millions]

State	Claimed payment due from HEW (1969–75)	Proposed payment	U.S. claims against States dropped
Alabama	....	....	$1. 0
Alaska	....	....	. 7
Arizona	....	....	5. 2
Arkansas	$3. 8	$2. 2	.....
California	....	....	1. 5
Connecticut	38	22	6. 0
Florida	28. 7	11	29. 1
Georgia	. 7	. 3	6. 0
Idaho	1. 1	. 6	.....
Illinois	87. 3	32. 1	188. 4
Kentucky	....	....	2. 4
Louisiana	....	....	16. 7
Maine	2. 2	1. 3	.....
Maryland	24. 7	14. 3	.....
Massachusetts	142	75	.....
Michigan	57. 1	32. 6	8. 4
Minnesota	49. 4	28. 6	4. 0
Missouri	....	....	. 2
New Jersey	1. 3	. 7	.....
New York	914	214. 4	490. 0
Ohio	15. 1	5. 7	5. 0
Oklahoma	....	....	13. 8
Pennsylvania	4. 2	1. 6	2. 8
Rhode Island	....	....	1. 2
Tennessee	. 004	. 0015	. 5
Texas	92. 7	34	34. 7
Washington	32. 8	19	5. 6
Wisconsin	65	36. 5	6. 3
Total	1, 560	532	830. 0

NOTE: The statement was released at New York, N.Y.

United Nations

Remarks on Signing International Covenants on Human Rights.   October 5, 1977

Mr. Secretary Waldheim, I'm beginning to feel at home here at the United Nations.

I am honored to sign on behalf of the United States of America these two international covenants on human rights.

Of the many affinities between the United States and the United Nations, perhaps the most important is that both had their origins in a vision of the greatness of the human possibility.

The American Declaration of Independence speaks of the idea that, and I quote, "all men are created equal . . . endowed by their Creator with certain inalienable rights . . . Life, Liberty, and the pursuit of Happiness."

The Charter of the United Nations speaks of "faith in fundamental human rights, in the dignity and worth of the human person, in the equal rights of men and women and of nations large and small."

Though separated by a century and a half in time, these visions are identical in spirit. The covenants that I signed today are unusual in the world of international politics and diplomacy. They say absolutely nothing about powerful governments or military alliances or the privileges and immunities of statesmen and high officials. Instead, they are concerned about the rights of individual human beings and the duties of governments to the people they are created to serve—the rights of human beings and the duties of government.

The Covenant on Civil and Political Rights concerns what governments must not do to their people, and the Covenant on Economic, Social and Cultural Rights concerns what governments must do for their people.

By ratifying the Covenant on Civil and Political Rights, a government pledges, as a matter of law, to refrain from subjecting its own people to arbitrary imprisonment or execution or to cruel or degrading treatment. It recognizes the right of every person to freedom of thought, freedom of conscience, freedom of religion, freedom of opinion, freedom of expression, freedom of association, and the rights of peaceful assembly, and the right to emigrate from that country.

A government entering this covenant states explicitly that there are sharp limits on its own powers over the lives of its people. But as Thomas Jefferson once wrote about the Bill of Rights, which became part of our own American Republic, and I quote again from Thomas Jefferson: "These are fetters against doing evil which no honest government should decline."

By ratifying the other Covenant on Economic, Social and Cultural Rights, a government commits itself to its best efforts to secure its citizens a basic standard of material existence, social justice, and cultural opportunity.

This covenant recognizes that governments are the instruments and the servants of their people. Both of these covenants express values in which the people of my country have believed for a long time.

I will seek ratification of these covenants by the Congress of the United States at the earliest possible date.

It would be idle to pretend that these two covenants themselves reflect the world as it is. But to those who believe that instruments of this kind are futile, I would suggest that there are powerful lessons to be learned in the history of my own country.

Our Declaration of Independence and the Bill of Rights expressed a lofty standard of liberty and equality. But in practice, these rights were enjoyed only by a very small segment of our people.

In the years and decades that followed, those who struggled for universal suffrage, those who struggled for the abolition of slavery, those who struggled for women's rights, those who struggled for racial equality, in spite of discouragement and personal danger, drew their own inspiration from these two great documents—the Declaration of Independence, the Bill of Rights and our own Constitution. Because the beliefs expressed in these documents were at the heart of what we Americans most valued about ourselves, they created a momentum toward the realization of the hopes that they offered.

Some of these hopes were 200 years in being realized. But ultimately, because the basis was there and the documents signed at the origins of our country, people's discouragements and disappointments were overcome, and ultimately these dreams have prevailed.

My hope and my belief is that the international covenants that I sign today can play a similar role in the advancement and the ultimate realization of human rights in the world at large.

The last time I was here at the United Nations, shortly after I became President, I made an entire speech on the subject of human rights. Yesterday I made a speech on peace. And today I've taken tangible steps toward the realization both of peace among nations and the preservation of human rights for individual men and women throughout the world.

My hope and my prayer is that the high and noble expressions in these documents will be realized throughout all nations as the high and noble expressions of hope in our own Bill of Rights, 200 years ago, is being realized in our great country.

Thank you very much.

NOTE: The President spoke at 11:35 a.m. in the Economic and Social Council Chamber at the United Nations Building in New York City.

Following his remarks, the President attended a reception and then met with United Nations Secretary General Kurt Waldheim.

United Nations

Remarks at a Working Luncheon for Officials of Asian Nations. October 5, 1977

I've been trying to define the geographical area represented here. I've noticed that Cyprus is present, and Mongolia is present, and the Philippines is present, and Korea is present, Vietnam is present. I've not quite yet gotten oriented about which particular part of the world this luncheon is supposed to encompass.

But I do see one or two things in common. One is that the ancient civilizations of the world are represented here—the fountainhead for knowledge and science and education, mathematics, medicine, culture, music, art, drama. And it's a very stimulating and exciting thing for me to meet representatives of those historic peoples who have meant so much to the formation of human society.

I've also noticed that many of you represent countries that are quite new, having been formed only in recent years. But you've been able to bridge the gap between an ancient civilization of your peoples' heritage and also a new form of government.

I notice also that many of you have moved strongly toward a concept of preservation of human freedoms and the right of people to be treated well. I've noticed expansion of the definition of human rights in my own consciousness to encompass the right of someone to have a place to work and a place to live and an education and an absence of disease, and, perhaps, an alleviation of hunger. And I know that in many countries of the world represented here, those are ever-present problems for you as they are even for a wealthy and powerful nation like the United States.

I've also observed that it's important for us to have good relations with you, not just politically and in a military way but also for commercial advantages. We have about $75 billion in trade with your countries every year. And this encompasses the most rudimentary raw materials as well as the most advanced electronics and automotive technology. And it's crucial to us to have your friendship and your understanding and a constant means of communication and consultation with your nations.

I know that in the brief time that I've been President, I have personally asked you or your own national leaders to help with bilateral and multilateral and regional problems. And the constructive attitude that you have taken in forming either transient or permanent partnerships with us is very important indeed.

We also have changing relationships with many of your nations. In Southeast Asia we are trying to repair the damages of recent war and stretch out a hand of friendship to those countries with whom in the past we have had animosity.

A few of you are nations where we don't yet enjoy full diplomatic relations. We would like to establish those diplomatic exchanges with you without delay so that we might probe to alleviate the differences that divide us and also assess and take advantage of the common problems that we can address together. So, we are eager to proceed to repair the damages of the past and to approach the future in a spirit of friendship and cooperation.

In parts of your world, economic development is the most important part of your national purposes, and we want to be a part of that, because when your people's progress is enhanced, it helps the life of everyone who lives in my own country.

In the Middle East, I've spent a great deal of time in the last 9 months working with many of you represented here and have been encouraged so far with the prospects for ultimate success. What seemed to be despair and an absence of communication and consultation a year ago is now, I think, improved. And it will require flexible attitudes on the part of countries that in the past have been inflexible and confidence in one's neighbors where in the past confidence has been completely absent.

And I hope and expect a growing trust in our own good offices to help bring the parties together to arrive at mutual peace, because a war in the Middle East could be a devastating blow to the entire world.

These opportunities that we have together are very important to me, and I'm honored and pleased to be part of this luncheon. I have a lot to learn. I'm new in national political affairs. I'm an eager student, and I would always welcome a chance to learn from you.

We value the friendship that has been exhibited here in this room. And my dream is that this kind of relationship that exists in the United Nations environment might, ultimately, spread to the national capitals and, I think, mirror accurately the natural friendship which the peoples of the world have toward one another. It's leaders like myself and, perhaps, some of your own leaders that might be an obstacle to the realization of peace which exists in the hearts of those whom we represent. And it's incumbent upon us always to search for those openings and opportunities when they present themselves.

I am also grateful, as the President of our host country here, of your presence in the United Nations. I'm determined, during my own term in the White House, to do everything I can to strengthen the role that the United Nations plays in helping the lives of our people. And I will depend in a more deeply committed way, each year that I am in office, in using the good services of the United Nations and letting the people of our country realize what already occurs here.

I think very few Americans know the broad scope of good services that is a daily contribution of the special committees of the United Nations in civil aeronautical safety and in the protection of our people against nuclear proliferation and expanding the health care around the world—better chance for children, the alleviation of hunger.

These kinds of projects, which are a constant responsibility of mine in the United States, are carried on around the world in a routine fashion by the special agencies of the United Nations. But quite often the nations that support the U.N. with financial contributions don't realize the tremendous return that we get on our investment in the United Nations itself.

So, in the establishment of peace, in the alleviation of regional problems, in the sharing of contributions, which we all are eager to make, I know that you realize along with me that the United Nations plays an integral role.

Again, let me thank you for coming to this luncheon. I hope that you'll give Andy Young your constant friendship and advice and counsel, criticism when he deserves it. [*Laughter*]

I meet with Ambassador Young every Monday morning. He's a part of our Cabinet structure. We use his influence among you, and you can use his influence with me to make sure that this transient luncheon is transformed into a permanent intercommunication and strong relationship.

Thank you again for being here.

NOTE: The President spoke at 2:10 p.m. at the headquarters of the U.S. Mission to the United Nations in New York City. The President hosted the luncheon for foreign ministers and heads of delegations to the United Nations.

Public Broadcasting System

Message to the Congress.   October 6, 1977

To the Congress of the United States:

I am transmitting to the Congress today proposals to strengthen our public broadcasting system and to insulate it from political manipulation.

The impact of television and radio on our lives can scarcely be overestimated. Television now bulks larger than all its rivals for our leisure time. In the daily routine of many individuals, it consumes more hours than family, school, church, or job. Radio is just as important; with some 400 million receivers in American homes, cars, and workplaces, radio listening is nearly as pervasive as the air that carries it.

In these circumstances, a strong and varied public broadcast system has a crucial role to play. Because it is free of the scramble for ratings, public broadcasting has room for experimentation and risk-taking. Public broadcasting is for all Americans. It can meet the needs of audiences that number in the millions but are seldom served anywhere else. That is why, during my campaign for the Presidency, I pledged my best efforts to strengthen it.

The bill I am submitting with this message continues and increases long-term Federal funding for public television and radio. Financial stability is needed if public broadcasting is to provide better programs for more citizens and protect those programs from political pressures.

The bill also makes statutory changes to increase cooperation, reduce overlap, and clarify the missions of the three primary national organizations in the field—the Corporation for Public Broadcasting (CPB), the Public Broadcasting Service (PBS), and National Public Radio (NPR).

These changes will also increase public broadcasting's insulation from inappropriate political influence. Other amendments will give it greater journalistic independence. I want to encourage public broadcasters at all levels to engage in active news reporting and public affairs programming. This Administration will not try to stifle controversy on public television and radio. No President should try to dictate what issues public broadcasting should cover or how it should cover them. And this legislation will make such an attempt more unlikely.

This bill also proposes amendments that require public broadcasting to:

—Devote more resources to high-quality national programming.

—Set long-range goals by which its progress can be judged.

—Plan how public television and radio signals can be brought within reach of all citizens.

—Provide greater accountability to the public.

—Stimulate greater participation by minorities and women.

Without these statutory changes, not even a long-term authorization bill would insure diverse and high-quality programming.

Public broadcasting's organizational problems and its need for better planning and greater diversity should not blind us to its accomplishments. In the ten years since the Public Broadcasting Act first provided Federal funds for programming, public broadcasting has set new standards in children's programs, drama, music, science, history, and educational services. Its coverage of local, state, and national hearings, its documentaries, and its in-depth news analyses have helped make government more understandable.

Public broadcasting has done more than simply entertain us. It has encouraged us and our children to think and to act. It has also pioneered in such technical innovations as captioning for the deaf and satellite broadcasting.

This bill will renew Federal funding while improving the ways the money is spent. The money will be used, among other purposes, to:

—Strengthen the PBS national television service to provide a first-rate schedule of cultural and public affairs programs.

—Support and expand National Public Radio, which provides a lively alternative schedule that includes music, public hearings and events, news analysis, and original radio drama.

—Plan the best use of the public broadcasting satellite system and other new communications technologies. These advances make possible new television and radio networks devoted entirely to adult instruction, children's programming, or the special needs of Hispanics, Blacks, women, the elderly, or other distinct audiences.

—Extend the reach of public television and radio signals. All taxpayers contribute to public broadcasting, but only about half receive a good public television signal, and fewer than two-thirds can receive public radio.

—Increase public broadcasting's contribution to in-school and adult instruction. Public television's most popular prime-time series have been widely used for college extension courses. Lifelong learning should remain one of its principal goals.

—Increase employment, training, and ownership opportunities for minorities and women.

—Support local, state, and regional programming. Programming of local interest is an important resource.

Except for the key area of national programming, this legislation does not mandate specific allocations of Federal funds for each of these purposes. It is desirable to allow CPB the flexibility to choose among competing priorities. But the bill does set a direction that allows all these efforts to be pursued.

My specific proposals are as follows:

Assure Long-range Funding

Enactment of this legislation will allow continuation of the present system of five-year authorization and two-year advance appropriations, which was designed to assist planning and enhance insulation.

Congress is currently considering an appropriation of $152 million for fiscal 1980, the last year of the current authorization. New legislation is needed early next year for public broadcasting to be included in next year's appropriations process.

The funds authorized in the enclosed bill total $1.041 billion. This includes a five-year authorization for CPB at $180 million for fiscal year 1981 and $200 million in each of the four succeeding years. It also includes a separate grant program of $30 million annually for technical facilities in fiscal 1979 and 1980, and $1 million for telecommunications demonstrations by HEW in fiscal 1979. These figures represent recommended authorization levels. Appropriations requests must come from the annual budget review process.

This bill maintains an authorized level of Federal funding at $200 million after the second year. Such leveled funding will ensure that both we and the public broadcasting system will reexamine appropriate funding levels based on its needs and potential in 1979, after the new Carnegie Commission on the Future of Public Broadcasting delivers its report. This Commission has taken on the difficult job of looking at the public system's creative process in light of new technology. It is also examining both the existing sources of Federal and non-Federal funding and potential new ones. The Task Force that established the Commission has urged us and Congress to move forward with a long-term authorization and related structural issues so that it can concentrate on funding methods, technology, and programming.

Leveling the authorization also insures that in two years we and Congress will evaluate the success of the organizational and other changes proposed in this bill.

Clarify Functions of National Entities

Since 1967, most Federal funds for public broadcasting have gone to the Corporation for Public Broadcasting (CPB). CPB is an independent unit run by a 15-member Board appointed by the President and confirmed by the Senate. One of CPB's key missions is to distribute Federal funds for programming in ways that shield program content from political pressure. Another is to provide system-wide leadership in planning, budgeting, resource allocation, research, evaluation, fund-raising from private sources and government agencies, and development of new communications services.

The public radio and television networks are run by two other units that represent the local stations: National Public Radio (NPR) and the Public Broadcasting Service (PBS). The stations decide what programs get on the air. There are also five regional television networks and several special program exchanges like the Latino Consortium. National production centers exist at larger stations and at independent entities like Children's Television Workshop. All these units have their own programming staffs.

At present, CPB itself often chooses which individual programs or series to fund. This:

—Reduces CPB's effectiveness as a political insulator.

—Reduces its ability to focus on long-range planning and new educational services.

—Duplicates staff, wastes money, and causes unproductive feuds between CPB and PBS, NPR, and other public broadcasting organizations.

The public cannot afford to pay duplicate organizations to do the same job.

The greater the bureaucratic overhead, the smaller the sums that can be used for programming. It is time to define organizational roles clearly so that the public and program producers can understand how the system operates and there can be a rational, efficient basis for future planning.

I propose three steps to resolve this issue:

—CPB's role would be clarified to be that of a system overseer operating much like an endowment or foundation. Based on its planning process, it would make broad allocations among radio, TV, and other distribution systems and among children's, public affairs, minority, and other program types. It would implement these decisions by giving annual or multi-year bloc grants to PBS, NPR, regional and other specialized networks, and production centers. The grantees would select the specific programs to be produced.

—Two members chosen by PBS and two by NPR would be added to the CPB Board to increase both cooperation and insulation. (Four Presidentially appointed slots would be phased out to keep the total at 15.)

—CPB would be required to prepare a five-year development plan for public broadcasting in concert with PBS and NPR to guide the allocation of Federal resources and update it annually in its report to Congress.

This will decentralize creative decisions, place them further from any potential political control, and refocus CPB on the important job of overall system development. But, under this mode of operation, CPB should require only a limited full-time staff to assist its Board in its priority setting and oversight tasks. It can draw upon distinguished experts in the arts, science, journalism, and education to help it evaluate current and future needs. This does not eliminate, but makes more appropriate, CPB's critical role in programming.

CPB would not need a substantial staff for program decision-making and program-related legal, public information, audience research, and similar functions. These operational tasks can be done by PBS, NPR, and other grantees without adding persons to their staffs.

CPB would need substantially fewer than its current staff of 130 to carry out its missions. The savings from these cuts and greater efficiency in CPB's retained functions should go into programming.

Increase Funds Allocated for National Programming

There are now 271 public television stations and 203 public radio stations. They provide a vital service to their states and communities. But each of these stations cannot separately produce the high quality cultural, public affairs, and instructional programming their communities need.

Federal support for strong national program services was a principal recommendation of the first Carnegie Commission. It was a primary aim of the 1967 Act that created CPB. But CPB now devotes only $17 million of its current $103 million appropriation directly to national programming. In addition, about $19 million of the $58 million CPB gives to local stations is pooled for that purpose.

More Federal funds should be concentrated on national programming. By devoting more funds to national needs, public broadcasting can give producers adequate lead time and budget to create high quality domestic productions. It can and should support more first-rate production centers, like Children's Television Workshop and similar centers for independent producers, minorities, educators, and

women. It can provide the complete coverage of news events, such as important Congressional hearings, that commercial broadcasting rarely offers.

This bill provides that at least 25% of funds appropriated to CPB in future years shall be used for a National Programming Fund for bloc grants for such productions. This will insure that by FY 1982 up to $50 million, depending on the appropriation level, would be ear-marked for national programming. These programs will continue to be produced on a decentralized basis, by producers throughout the country, but intended for national distribution.

In addition, I call on the public broadcasting system to devote another 25% of the Federal money to national programming. The stations can do this by pooling money, as the TV stations do now through the Station Program Cooperative, or it can be done by any other mechanism. This would provide a total of up to $100 million for national programming in FY 1982. Minorities, women, and independent as well as station producers should have access to these funds as well as those in CPB's National Programming Fund.

Local, state, and regional services also need substantial support. A significant aspect of that support has been the funds CPB passes through to local stations for their discretionary use for local or national purposes. Unlike the current law, my bill does not place either a ceiling or floor on those funds. Allocations for this purpose should be made from year to year, as determined through CPB's cooperative planning process with PBS, NPR, and the licensees.

I also call on the other funding sources—particularly the states—to hold up their end of this funding partnership. Currently, non-Federal sources such as state and local governments, individuals, foundations, and corporations still supply the vast bulk of funds for local public stations. But, while Federal funds and individual contributions have increased during the past few years, state funds have levelled off.

As a former governor, I know the pressures on state budgets. But state support of public broadcasting, which brings state legislative proceedings and other vital services to citizens, should be maintained. I urge states that have contributed to do more, and those that have not, to begin.

Reduce the Percentage Public Broadcasting Must Raise to Match CPB Funds

The current law requires the system to raise $2.50 for every $1.00 the Federal Government gives CPB. CPB has indicated that such levels of non-Federal support cannot be achieved to match the proposed increased authorizations.

Even if states increase their share, there are realistic limits to the amounts that public broadcasting can hope to raise by on-air appeals to its audience and by corporate and foundation support. I am therefore proposing a reduction in the match to $2.25-to-$1.00. This figure assures a continued incentive for fund-raising without asking the system to achieve the impossible. The minimum dollar amount of matching funds that could be required to meet the upper limit of appropriations under this bill would rise gradually until the authorization is levelled off.

CPB itself can also increase incentives for non-Federal funds. It might revise its formula for allocation of local community service grants to encourage such support. Individual citizens should recognize that their funds help maintain the diversity and independence of their local stations.

I intend to review the matching concept and formula in 1979 after assessing its impact on fund raising and the Carnegie Commission's report as to future funding sources and needs.

Transfer Public Communications Facilities Program From HEW to CPB

A key part of my plan is the effort to bring public broadcasting to as many people as possible. Much of the Federal funding for station facilities comes from the Educational Broadcast Facilities Program now run by HEW. That effort should be fully coordinated with the system's own long-range planning. I am therefore recommending that this program be transferred to CPB.

As part of the planning required by this bill, CPB will estimate the cost of reaching as close to the total American population as would be feasible using the most efficient technologies. For the next two years, pending submission of such a plan, I propose to continue the Facilities Program's present $30 million annual authorization.

I also propose changes in the Facilities Program to:

—Make assistance to minority public television and radio stations a funding priority. No public television station in the continental United States is operated by a minority-controlled institution, although Howard University and others have applied for licenses. There are only a handful of minority-controlled public radio stations.

—Allow planning grants to be made to groups wishing to start stations. These grants would enable them to do the legal, engineering, and other studies needed to apply for actual communications facilities.

—Make regional networks and other groups of stations eligible for facilities funds.

—Make facilities grants open to any broadcast or nonbroadcast communications technology chosen by an eligible applicant. Federal funds should support the most efficient technical means to make publicly funded programming available to the widest audiences.

CPB will be able to use a portion of the facilities funds being transferred for demonstrations of new public service delivery systems, such as two-way communication via satellite.

Encourage Journalistic Independence

Unlike commercial broadcasters, public broadcasters are forbidden by current law to editorialize on issues of public importance. This ban makes sense for stations licensed to a state or local government instrumentality. But Congress has recently amended the tax code to allow private non-profit organizations to advocate positions on public issues. The Public Broadcasting Act should be similarly amended to allow non-governmental licensees to exercise their First Amendment rights.

This change would not require editorials, but it would permit them. Public broadcasters should have an equal opportunity with commercial broadcasters to participate in the free marketplace of ideas.

States hold about half of the U.S. public television station licenses. Another step toward journalistic independence would be for state and local governments to better insulate these stations. The danger of undue political control is as real here as at the Federal level. This bill does not compel any particular form, but I want to encourage states to establish independent boards to assure insulation.

Require Public Accountability

Independence from government control does not mean a public station has no obligation to account for its stewardship.

But such accountability is best exercised directly to the local citizens who contribute to the station's support. I therefore propose sunshine for public stations that receive Federal funds; they should be required to open their board meetings and financial records to the public.

This legislation is not intended to restrict a public station board's privacy on personnel matters, or otherwise sanction unwarranted invasions of personal privacy. But local citizens should have access to the basic decisions public stations make in allocating tax funds and private donations. This is already standard practice at CPB, PBS, NPR, and many public stations.

Increase Participation of Minorities and Women

This bill makes it clear that the employment discrimination laws apply to stations and other producers that receive CPB funds. It conditions such grants on nondiscrimination, just like receipt of a grant from a Federal agency. Since CPB is not a Federal agency, enforcement of this requirement will be delegated to a Federal agency with expertise in this field.

This change, combined with making minority ownership a goal of the facilities program, will help bring greater diversity to the decision-making levels of public broadcasting. But statutory amendments alone are not enough. Public broadcasting should make its own effort to become an entry-level training ground and model for the other media in meeting the needs of women, Blacks, Hispanics, and other minorities.

Study of Federal Agency Program Funding

Last year approximately $25 million was contributed to public broadcasting directly by four agencies—HEW, the National Endowment for the Arts, the National Endowment for the Humanities, and the National Science Foundation.

This is an important source of Federal funds that is outside of the CPB appropriation. It accounts for one-fourth of the national public TV schedule, as well as many local and State productions. And it is not covered by CPB's insulation from political pressure.

This funding should be coordinated with the work of CPB, PBS, and NPR to assure that it is used efficiently for programs that get on the air. I propose that CPB inventory all such grants in its annual report to Congress and that it act as a consultant to the agencies and a clearinghouse for grant information. In addition, we are drafting administrative rules for the agencies to assure there is no improper manipulation of program content.

Public Station Frequency Allocations and Reception

Most public television stations are on UHF channels, and most public radio stations are on the FM band. I urge the Federal Communications Commission to seriously consider pending proposals that would bring public television and radio closer to parity with commercial stations. These include proposals for better standards for TV set reception of UHF channels and better allocation of FM channels for public radio. I am hopeful that the new leadership at the FCC will give UHF and FM improvements priority attention.

Better spectrum management and reception standards may do more to make public broadcasting more widely available than substantial Federal grants for transmitters and increased power. The costs and benefits of each approach should be carefully weighed.

I urge Congress to consider promptly, and to pass, the legislation I am submitting containing the proposals described in this message. This will provide a firm foundation for planning the next decade of public communications in this country.

JIMMY CARTER

The White House,
   October 6, 1977.

Indochina Refugees

Letter to Six Senate and House Committee Chairmen.   October 4, 1977

Dear Mr. Chairman:

In accordance with the provisions of the Indochina Migration and Refugee Assistance Act of 1975, I am reporting to you on the status of refugees from Cambodia, Laos, and South Vietnam.

Though we continue to make progress in helping the Indochina refugees to become self-sufficient members of their communities, problems remain. I therefore have asked the Congress to extend the Indochina Migration and Refugee Assistance Act for three years with a gradual phasedown in program assistance. I am also concerned over the plight of Indochinese stranded on the shores of the South China Sea and in temporary Thai refugee camps. Therefore, at my request, the Attorney General has announced that he is using his parole authority to admit an additional 15,000 refugees into the U.S. I have also directed that an interagency task force be established to develop a longer term solution to the Indochina refugee problem.

As my report to you shows, a large portion of the Indochina refugees are independent and productive members of their communities. With the continued assistance of the private and public agencies that have contributed so generously to this program, I am confident that the adjustment to life in the United States will be made by the refugees from Indochina.

Sincerely,

JIMMY CARTER

NOTE: This is the text of identical letters addressed to the Honorable James O. Eastland, chairman, Senate Committee on the Judiciary; the Honorable Peter W. Rodino, chairman, House Committee on the Judiciary; the Honorable John J. Sparkman, chairman, Senate Committee on Foreign Relations; the Honorable Clement J. Zablocki, chairman, House Committee on International Relations; the Honorable John L. McClellan, chairman, Senate Committee on Appropriations; and the Honorable George H. Mahon, chairman, House Committee on Appropriations.

The report is entitled "Task Force for Indochina Refugees, Report to the Congress, September 21, 1977."

The letter was announced by the White House Press Office on October 6. It was not issued in the form of a White House press release.

Andres Figueroa Cordero

Announcement of the Commutation of Mr. Figueroa Cordero's Prison Sentence. October 6, 1977

The President today granted clemency to Andres Figueroa Cordero, convicted in 1954 along with three other Puerto Ricans in connection with the shooting and wounding of several Congressmen.

The President commuted his sentence to the time served.

Mr. Cordero has terminal cancer. The President commuted Mr. Cordero's sentence on humanitarian grounds because of his physical condition.

Mr. Cordero was convicted of assault and conspiracy to overthrow the Government and was serving a 25- to 75-year sentence. He would not have been eligible for parole until 1981.

The commutation order, which is not a pardon, was an act of clemency on the part of the President.

Mr. Cordero was expected to be released from the Federal Medical Center for Prisoners at Springfield, Mo., within 24 hours.

Democratic National Committee

Remarks at the Committee's Quarterly Meeting. October 7, 1977

After spending 2 days in New York this week, meeting with representatives of almost every nation in the world, and staying up to well after midnight talking about controversial issues, after spending the last 2 days dealing with the Congress—particularly the Senate—it's a great pleasure to come over where absolute harmony and peace prevail—[*laughter*]—where there are no differences, and complete support for everything that is suggested by leadership is accepted without question.

This is a time that I have welcomed, meeting with my friends and my fellow workers, my partners, who represent the greatest political organization in the entire world, the Democratic Party.

I know you've been considering the 1978 conference, among other things. This is important to us all. I know that all of you want to meet there, to have tough debates without delay, to move expeditiously, to make quick decisions. And in order to ensure this, I've asked Vice President Mondale to preside over the sessions. [*Laughter*] I'm sure he'll show his strong leadership characteristics as he has recently in other trying times.

As you know, there has never been, I believe, as close a relationship between a President and a Vice President as exists in our country today, and I'm very proud of him, what he means to me personally and politically and in the governance of this country. He's a great ally and friend to have.

What you decide as far as the mechanism of the Democratic Party, what you decide as an equitable way to ensure representation in all our conferences, what you decide about the site, the format, the choosing of delegates, the size of the delegations is very crucial to me.

I want to be sure that the 1978 conference, for instance, can consider in some depth the controversial issues that face me and our country and you, and so that I can deal with the conference in a personal way, so that members of my own administration can come to the convention site and receive from you and from other delegates accurate assessments of the needs and desires and hopes and dreams and aspirations and concerns and advice of Democrats throughout the country.

I personally hope that you will maintain a manageable size, and I'm sure you've already agreed to do that. That will be very helpful.

I'm involved, along with many on this stage and many of you, in raising money for the Democratic Party. I hope the costs can be held within reasonable bounds and, at the same time, without interfering with an open, frank, thorough discussion of all the issues that face us.

I've enjoyed my own administration so far. I have welcomed the controversy that has swirled around the White House since I've been in office. It's not been a sign of weakness. It's not been a sign of failure. It's been a sign that we as Democrats intend to carry out the commitments that we made to the people of the United States in the 1976 campaign, and that's what I intend to do.

Many of the issues that we are now approaching strongly and boldly and for the best interests of the American people have been avoided for years, for decades, for generations, because of a fear of arousing controversy and open debate. But they can't be avoided any longer, and I have no inclination to do so.

When I campaigned throughout this country in every one of your States, for the 2 years preceding my own election, I listened, I considered very carefully, I made my own position known, which accurately, I believe, represents the inclinations of the American people. And now we're trying to carry out those commitments.

We have proposed, as you know, an energy policy for our country, for the first time to avoid an almost inevitable crisis that might afflict every person in our Nation. It's not easy. The shadow of the oil lobby hovers over Capitol Hill. This has got to be addressed frankly, and we have to make sure that when the energy package comes out this year, it doesn't work contrary to the best interests of the consumers and the homeowners and the people of this country.

The House of Representatives, under the leadership of Tip O'Neill, has acted strongly and courageously and well, and Bob Byrd in the Senate is doing the best he can to bring forth the crucial elements of our energy package, but it is difficult. It is difficult. What we don't get this year, I'll be back next year again. I don't intend to fail, because the people need it.

We've also proposed to the Congress a comprehensive revision of the welfare programs to give our people a better job and income possibility. It's an integral part of what we are trying to do as an administration. It treats with respect and dignity and compassion those who are unable to work, but it gives those members of families who are able to work a chance to work.

The cost of the program is completely compatible with present expenditures, slightly increased, but primarily because of the provision of job opportunities. This is an excellent investment in the present and future of our country. And next year I believe that the Congress will accept at least the major provisions of our welfare package, hopefully all.

But I know how difficult it is, how controversial it is. But this question has to be openly debated so that the American people can understand the challenges that have been presented and the solutions that have been proposed.

It's a well-balanced program. It ties in very well with the tax reform package that will be presented to the Congress before they adjourn this fall. And I'll be spending all this weekend putting my own final judgment on the options that have been presented to me. Then early next week, I'll meet with my key advisers to discuss my choice of options, and the package will then be put into a proposal that will go to the Congress.

Nothing could be more controversial than tax reform. But, as I've said many times last year and before, our present income tax structure is a disgrace. It needs to be simple, equitable, and progressive; and that those who are able to pay the taxes ought to pay their fair share for a change. And the working families of this country, the middle-income families of this country, ought to be helped by removing the unnecessary and unfair burdens that have rested on their shoulders.

And along with the reform that I've described I predict will come a substantial

reduction in the overall tax burden on the American people.

We've begun now a 3-year program to reorganize the executive branch of Government. Our first reform package, reorganization package is before the Congress this coming week. This is going to be a long, tedious, sometimes unpleasant process, but it's necessary. We committed ourselves to do it as a party, and I believe that our success will bring credit to all of you.

We are dealing with international matters that have escaped a solution again, for hundreds of years in some instances.

I think we're making good progress in the Middle East. We're treating fairly all parties. There's no way that I can act as a trusted negotiator—not just an idle bystander, but the leader of a nation that has crucial interest in the Middle East—unless I have the complete confidence of the leaders of the nations involved in the upcoming Geneva conference.

I've got to be fair and I will be fair. I'll never tell one leader one thing and a different leader something else. And so far we've made substantial progress. There's now evolving with a growing trust in our character and good will and fairness and truthfulness a much more flexible and accommodating attitude on the part of all nations.

The key element in American policy in the Middle East, in the negotiations that are going on literally day and night now, and which will be a crucial element when we go to Geneva, is a strength, independence, freedom, and peace of the people of Israel.

This is not a simple issue. It's probably the most complex international question that's ever been addressed in a comprehensive way. There's a crucial interest among many hundreds of thousands of Americans in the outcome of the negotiations.

The Soviet Union, since 1973, has been a cochairman with us in Geneva. In the past their attitude has been one of disruption and the creation of unnecessary obstacles.

Recently, they've become much more moderate in their positions. It's an achievement of unprecedented significance that we were able recently to sign a statement with the Soviet Union where they recognized Israel's right to exist, although they still do not have diplomatic relations. They did not insist upon an independent Palestinian state. They did not insist upon naming the PLO. They did not insist upon complete withdrawal of Israel from the territories acquired in 1967. It took a moderate attitude.

This statement is a simple declaration to the world that we are sincere in bringing about a successful conclusion of the Geneva conference. It broke down immediately in October of 1973. We don't want that to happen again. This statement between us and the Soviet Union is not a prerequisite for the Arab or Israeli Governments to adopt in its entirety before they go to Geneva. Neither the Arabs nor the Israelis like every part of it, but it's a good step forward. And I can tell you that the leaders of all the nations involved with whom I have held long, tedious, complete discussions now have a constructive attitude toward Middle Eastern peace, and I believe that we will ultimately be successful.

We're dealing with another very crucial threat to world peace in southern Africa. For too long our country ignored Africa. Soon I will be making the first state visit in our Nation's history to a leading African nation, Nigeria. Cy Vance and Andrew Young and others have already let the people in those developing nations in Africa and throughout the world know that we care about them, we want to treat them as equals, we want to treat them with respect.

And there's a new attitude of friendship to the United States in the United Nations which has been absent for decades. This is a constructive step forward, because those nations are crucial to us. And they know that we ourselves are crucial to them.

In worldwide disarmament, nonproliferation, our SALT negotiations with the Soviet Union, an end to the testing of atomic weapons, in many other areas of international diplomacy involving our national security, we are moving without timidity, openly, which does quite often create controversy. These challenges are not easy, but the prospect of success is exciting to me. And I know that all of you share the ultimate goals. And I need your active, constant help in your own community, because you are all leaders in supporting these difficult challenges that I have accepted with pleasure. This is important.

We're trying to deal with a controversial question of unemployment. We got statistics this morning that showed that the unemployment rate has dropped somewhat, dropped substantially for black citizens.

We need to do more. We'll have a comprehensive urban policy shortly to present to the Congress and to the Nation. We're trying to make sure that the economic stimulus package, which is just now being felt, is challenged in the right areas of our country to alleviate the most serious suffering that causes me and you such grief and pain.

I wish that everyone here could go to the South Bronx area of New York where I visited earlier this week and see the devastation there. It's absolutely heartbreaking, and I realize after campaigning throughout this country that this is not a unique area. There are other urban areas like this where crime is rampant, where living conditions that we all take for granted are completely absent, where deterioration diminishes hope, and where there's an ingrained distrust of the concern and the ability of government to meet legitimate needs.

But I believe that the people there exhibited a sense of confidence and appreciation and hope, and I'm determined not to disappoint them. And I need your help in this effort.

There are just a couple of other points I want to make.

On a worldwide basis we have restored our own Nation's commitment to basic human rights. There's not a single leader in the world among almost 150 nations who doesn't have before him or her a constant concern about this question: "How am I and my government treating the people who look to me for leadership? What does the outside world think about my nation as I deal with the needs of human beings and the question of human freedom?" It's a new development.

And in the conference that's going on now in Belgrade to assess the progress from the Helsinki signing of the treaties, there's a deep and penetrating and nonconfrontational assessment of how well we are all doing.

We don't claim to be perfect or holy. We've got our own problems in this country. The first time I met Ambassador Dobrynin, that was a major subject of the discussion. And he said to me, "At least in the Soviet Union our women have equal rights."

We are moving to assess our own problems, to correct our own defects and, at the same time, in a constructive way holding open for complete debate the deprivation of rights in other countries. This is not an easy subject to raise. It's sensitive. It creates controversy. But it could not any longer be ignored.

I want our Nation to be one where there is an intense internal pride in what we stand for and a reaffirmation of our commitment to the principles on which our Nation was formed. And I believe that we've restored that spirit, because now the United States of America is again identified with the question of human freedom and human rights, and I want to keep that image before the world as long as I'm in office.

Just one other thing: I know that in many of these issues—and I could go on for another 10 minutes itemizing them for you—there will be specific portions and sometimes misinterpretations presented to you that cause you to doubt and also to refrain from giving me your full support. I need your support, your open, aggressive, and courageous support.

In a few minutes, you'll be receiving an analysis of the Panama Canal Treaty from Ambassador Bunker. There is no doubt in my mind that our country's best interest will be served by the ratification of this treaty, these treaties—two of them.

Eisenhower, Kennedy, Johnson, Nixon, Ford have all seen a need to modify the present treaty arrangements with Panama. And now we've been successful in bringing forth two treaties that serve our Nation well, our Nation's defense.

Jim Schlesinger, Melvin Laird, the five Joint Chiefs of Staff, our present Secretary of Defense, Paul Nitze, many others agree that our defense needs are well served by these treaties. President Ford, Secretary Kissinger, Secretary Rogers, Secretary Dean Rusk have all committed themselves to help passing these treaties through the Senate.

Obviously, our own administration is completely unanimous in believing that we have made a major step forward. We retain the right to defend, to choose the lands and waters, to operate and manage the canal throughout this century, 23 more years, and after the year 2000, to insure that the canal will be open for all commerce, and neutrality guaranteed, our ships granted the right of expeditious passage, our interests have been met.

But, in addition, the signing of these treaties alone prior to ratification has been a vivid proof to the people of the nations of our hemisphere that there's a new era of friendship and cooperation and an affirmation of mutual purpose, an end to colonialism that's profound.

Every business leader that I know of has come out in favor of the Panama Canal treaties who have expressed themselves at all. Trade, commerce, mutual defense will all be enhanced with this new interrelationship.

A few weeks ago, I met with 19 heads of state from nations in South and Central America and the Caribbean. Every one of them pointed out to me the new interrelationship. Not a single one predicated future progress on grants or aids or financial contributions. This is a tremendous bonus that our Nation will derive from the ratification of these treaties.

I need your help on this most controversial of subjects this year. The matter is in doubt. It's not going to be easy. But the Democratic Party has never asked for ease.

I want to be a good President. With your help, I can be a good President. But I also want to be a good Democratic President.

Thank you very much.

NOTE: The President spoke at 9:30 a.m. in the International Ballroom at the Washington Hilton Hotel. In his remarks, he referred to former Secretary of Defense Melvin R. Laird, former Secretary of the Navy Paul H. Nitze, and former Secretaries of State Henry A. Kissinger, William P. Rogers, and Dean Rusk.

Judge John J. Sirica

Exchange of Letters on the Retirement of the U.S. District Court Judge.   October 6, 1977

To Judge John Sirica

On behalf of the American people, I congratulate you for your distinguished career in the Federal judiciary since 1957.

You have been given an opportunity afforded to few of us who enter upon public service: to exhibit, at a time of the greatest challenge to our system of government, the personal courage and wisdom needed to sustain it, and by these actions to become a lasting symbol of unflinching devotion to duty.

As you retire now from regular active service, you have my warmest wishes for good health, happiness, and more years of fruitful contributions as a Senior Judge.

Sincerely,

JIMMY CARTER

[The Honorable John J. Sirica, United States District Court for the District of Columbia, Washington, D.C.]

October 4, 1977

My dear Mr. President:

This is to formally advise you that I have decided under the provisions of Section 371(b) of Title 28, United States Code to retire from regular active service as a Judge of the United States District Court for the District of Columbia and to assume the role and status of a Senior Judge of that Court effective at the close of business Monday, October 31, 1977.

For over twenty years now I have been privileged to serve as a Judge of this great tribunal, and can only hope I have contributed to and measured up in some slight degree to the high responsibilities thus imposed.

With every good wish for your health and happiness, I am

Respectfully yours,

JOHN J. SIRICA

[The President, The White House, Washington, D.C. 20500]

NOTE: The texts of the letters were released on October 7.

United Nations Conference on Science and Technology for Development

Nomination of Theodore M. Hesburgh for the Rank of Ambassador While Serving as Chairman of the U.S. Delegation.
October 7, 1977

The President today announced that he will nominate Theodore M. Hesburgh, of South Bend, Ind., for the rank of Ambassador while serving as Chairman of the U.S. Delegation to the United Nations Conference on Science and Technology for Development, to be held in Geneva in 1979.

Hesburgh was born May 25, 1917, in Syracuse, N.Y. He received a Ph. B. from Gregorian University in Rome, Italy, in 1940, and a doctorate in sacred theology from Catholic University in 1945. He was ordained to the priesthood in 1943.

In 1943 and 1944, Hesburgh was chaplain for the National Training School for Boys in Washington. From 1945 to 1977, he was at the University of Notre Dame,

serving as chaplain to veterans from 1945 to 1947, assistant professor of religion, then head of the religion department in 1948–49, executive vice president from 1949 to 1952, and president of the university from 1952 until earlier this year. Since then he has been serving as Chairman of the U.S. Delegation to the U.N. Conference on Science and Technology for Development.

Hesburgh was a member of the U.S. Commission on Civil Rights from 1957 to 1970 and served as Chairman of the Commission from 1967 to 1970. He is the author of numerous books.

Export-Import Bank of the United States

Nomination of Donald E. Stingel To Be a Member of the Board of Directors.
October 7, 1977

The President today announced that he will nominate Donald E. Stingel, of Pittsburgh, Pa., to be a member of the Board of Directors of the Export-Import Bank. He would replace John C. Clark, resigned.

Stingel was born January 31, 1920, in Pittsburgh. He graduated from Carnegie-Mellon University in 1941 with a degree in metallurgical engineering. He served in the U.S. Army from 1941 to 1946.

Stingel worked for Union Carbide metals division from 1946 to 1965, serving as division works manager from 1960 to 1965. From 1965 to 1969, he was with Airco Corp., serving as president of the national carbide division from 1965 to 1968, and president of Airco alloys division in 1968 and 1969.

Stingel joined Swindell-Dressler (now Pullman Swindell) in 1969 as senior vice president, became executive vice president in 1971 and president in 1973. As president, he had complete responsibility for sales, administration, and operation of the division's activities in over 30 countries and the United States. He resigned in June 1977.

Stingel is Vice Chairman of the commerce Department's Committee on East-West Trade and a member of the Commerce Department Advisory Committee on Multilateral Trade Negotiations.

National Labor Relations Board

Nomination of John H. Fanning To Be a Member.   October 7, 1977

The President today announced that he will nominate John H. Fanning, of Rhode Island, for reappointment as a member of the National Labor Relations Board for a 5-year term. He indicated that, on confirmation, Fanning would be redesignated Chairman of the NLRB.

Fanning, 61, has been a member of the NLRB since 1957, when he was appointed to the Board by President Eisenhower. His current term would have expired in December 1977. He was designated Chairman by President Carter on April 14, 1977.

Department of Transportation

Nomination of Mortimer L. Downey III To Be an Assistant Secretary.   October 7, 1977

The President today announced that he will nominate Mortimer L. Downey III, of Reston, Va., to be an Assistant Secretary of Transportation. His area of responsibility would be budget and programs,

and he would replace Hamilton Herman, resigned.

Downey was born August 9, 1936, in Springfield, Mass. He received a B.A. from Yale University in 1958 and an M.P.A. from New York University in 1966.

From 1958 to 1962, Downey was a management trainee and staff assistant in various departments of the Port Authority of New York and New Jersey. From 1962 to 1968, he was assistant to the chief of the central research division in the planning and development department of the Port Authority, and from 1968 to 1973 he was principal transportation planner for that department.

Downey was supervisor of rail public services for the Port Authority from 1973 to 1975. He was a budget priority analyst for the House Budget Committee in Washington from 1975 until January 1977, when be became Deputy Under Secretary of Transportation.

United States-Mexico International Fishery Agreement

Message to the Congress Transmitting the Agreement.   October 7, 1977

To the Congress of the United States:

In accordance with The Fishery Conservation and Management Act of 1976 (P.L. 94–265; 16 USC 1801), I transmit herewith a governing international fishery agreement between the United States and Mexico, signed at Washington on August 26, 1977.

This Agreement is significant because it is one of a series to be negotiated in accordance with that legislation. It is also significant in the context of the warm and close relationship which the United States has had with Mexico for many years. I, therefore, urge that the Congress give favorable consideration to this Agreement at an early date.

JIMMY CARTER

The White House,
October 7, 1977.

NOTE: The message was announced by the White House Press Office on October 7. It was not issued in the form of a White House press release.

United States-United Kingdom Reciprocal Fisheries Agreement

Message to the Senate Transmitting the Agreement. October 7, 1977

To the Senate of the United States:

I am pleased to transmit for the advice and consent of the Senate to ratification the Reciprocal Fisheries Agreement between the Government of the United States of America and the Government of the United Kingdom of Great Britain and Northern Ireland. The Agreement was signed, and an accompanying Agreed Minute initialed, in Washington, D.C. on June 24, 1977.

The Agreement provides United States commercial fishermen access to the new 200 mile fishery zone of the British Virgin Islands and commercial fishermen of the British Virgin Islands access to the 200 mile United States fishery conservation zone. It secures the United States objective of providing for U.S. commercial fishermen the opportunity to continue fishing at traditional levels in areas which have recently become subject to the fishery jurisdiction of the British Virgin Islands. The Agreement reflects the close ties which exist in the Caribbean area between the United States and the British Virgin Islands.

I also transmit for the information of the Senate the report of the Department of State with respect to the Agreement.

I urge the Senate to consider the Agreement at an early date and to give its advice and consent to ratification.

JIMMY CARTER

The White House,
October 7, 1977.

NOTE: The message was announced by the White House Press Office on October 7. It was not issued in the form of a White House press release.

Digest of Other White House Announcements

The following listing includes the President's daily schedule and other items of general interest as announced by the White House Press Office during the period covered by this issue. Events and announcements printed elsewhere in the issue are not included.

October 2

The President returned to the White House after a weekend stay at Camp David, Md.

October 3

The President met at the White House with:

—Zbigniew Brzezinski, Assistant to the President for National Security Affairs;
—senior White House staff members;
—the Cabinet;
—Senator Wendell H. Ford of Kentucky to discuss the energy program;
—Senator John H. Chafee of Rhode Island to discuss the energy program;
—Senator Quentin N. Burdick of North Dakota to discuss the energy program;

—Senator Dennis DeConcini of Arizona to discuss the energy program;

—James T. McIntyre, Jr., Acting Director of the Office of Management and Budget.

October 4

While in New York City, the President met at the U.N. Plaza Hotel with:

—Ismail Fahmy, Foreign Minister of Egypt;

—Gaston Thorn, Prime Minister of Luxembourg;

—Samora Moises Machel, President of Mozambique;

—Moshe Dayan, Foreign Minister of Israel.

October 5

While in New York City, the President met at the U.N. Plaza Hotel with:

—Fuad Boutros, Foreign Minister of Lebanon;

—Emil Wojtaszek, Foreign Minister of Poland;

—Spyros Kyprianou, President of Cyprus;

—Carlos P. Romulo, Foreign Minister, and Imelda Marcos, First Lady, of the Philippines;

—Governor Hugh Carey of New York.

The President attended a reception at the headquarters of the U.S. Mission to the United Nations, hosted by Secretary of State Cyrus R. Vance for Latin American and Caribbean Foreign Ministers and heads of delegations to the United Nations.

In the evening, the President returned to the White House.

October 6

The President met at the White House with:

—Dr. Brzezinski;

—a group of Senators from Western States;

—a group of 27 Members of Congress to discuss the Middle East situation;

—Secretary of Labor F. Ray Marshall.

The White House announced that a White House conference on steel will be held on October 13 to discuss issues concerning the steel industry in this country. The meeting is to be chaired by Ambassador Robert S. Strauss, Special Representative for Trade Negotiations, and the invitees include representatives from steel industry, organized labor, manufacturers, economists, environmentalists, consumer groups, and Members of Congress from steel-producing States.

October 7

The President met at the White House with:

—Dr. Brzezinski;

—Vice President Mondale, Dr. Brzezinski, and Adm. Stansfield Turner, Director of Central Intelligence;

—Lee Kuan Yew, Prime Minister of Singapore;

—Mrs. Carter, for lunch;

—Charles L. Schultze, Chairman of the Council of Economic Advisers.

In a ceremony in the Oval Office, the President received diplomatic credentials from Ambassadors Olujimi Jolaoso of Nigeria, Kasongo Mutuale of Zaire, Farid Mubarak Ali al-Hinai of Oman, Ibrahima Camara of Guinea, and N. A. Palkhivala of India.

The President left the White House for a weekend stay at Camp David, Md.

NOMINATIONS SUBMITTED TO THE SENATE

The following list does not include promotions of members of the Uniformed Services, nominations to the Service Academies, or nominations of Foreign Service officers.

NOMINATIONS—Continued
Submitted October 4, 1977

The following-named persons to be members of the Board of Directors of the Corporation for Public Broadcasting for terms expiring March 26, 1982:

GILLIAN MARTIN SORENSEN, of New York, vice Robert S. Benjamin, term expired.

SHARON P. ROCKEFELLER, of West Virginia, vice Thomas W. Moore, term expired.

Withdrawn October 4, 1977

DONALD L. TUCKER, of Florida, to be a member of the Civil Aeronautics Board for the remainder of the term expiring December 31, 1979, vice G. Joseph Minetti, which was sent to the Senate on June 16, 1977.

Submitted October 7, 1977

THEODORE M. HESBURGH, of Indiana, for the rank of Ambassador during the tenure of his service as Chairman of the United States Delegation to the United Nations Conference on Science and Technology for Development.

JAMES S. BRADY, of Michigan, to be United States Attorney for the Western District of Michigan for the term of 4 years, vice Frank S. Spies.

G. WILLIAM HUNTER, of California, to be United States Attorney for the Northern District of California for the term of 4 years, vice James L. Browning, Jr.

ISAAC GEORGE HYLTON, of Virginia, to be United States Marshal for the Eastern District of Virginia for the term of 4 years (reappointment).

RUFUS A. LEWIS, of Alabama, to be United States Marshal for the Middle District of Alabama for the term of 4 years, vice James T. Lunsford.

HARRY H. MARSHALL, of Illinois, to be United States Marshal for the Southern District of Illinois for the term of 4 years, vice Carl H. Slayback, resigned.

MORTIMER L. DOWNEY III, of Virginia, to be an Assistant Secretary of Transportation, vice Hamilton Herman, resigned.

DONALD EUGENE STINGEL, of Pennsylvania, to be a member of the Board of Directors of the Export-Import Bank of the United States, vice John Conrad Clark, resigned.

JOHN HAROLD FANNING, of Rhode Island, to be a member of the National Labor Relations Board for the term of 5 years expiring December 16, 1982 (reappointment).

NOMINATIONS—Continued
Submitted October 7—Continued

DOUGLAS COULTER, of New Hampshire, to be a Commissioner of the Copyright Royalty Tribunal for a term of 7 years from September 27, 1977 (new position).

Withdrawn October 7, 1977

DOUGLAS COULTER, of Virginia, to be a Commissioner of the Copyright Royalty Tribunal for a term of 7 years from September 27, 1977 (new position), which was sent to the Senate on September 27, 1977.

CHECKLIST OF WHITE HOUSE PRESS RELEASES

The following releases of the Office of the White House Press Secretary, distributed during the period covered by this issue, are not included in the issue.

Released October 4, 1977

Advance text: address before the United Nations General Assembly

Remarks: following the first session of his meeting with the President at the U.N. Plaza Hotel—by Moshe Dayan, Foreign Minister of Israel

News conference: on the President's meeting with President Samora Moises Machel of Mozambique—by Jerrold L. Schecter, Associate Press Secretary

Released October 5, 1977

News conference: following his meeting with the President at the U.N. Plaza Hotel—by Moshe Dayan, Foreign Minister of Israel

News conference: following their tour of the South Bronx area of New York City with the President—by Mayor Abraham Beame of New York and Secretary of Housing and Urban Development Patricia Roberts Harris

Released October 6, 1977

Announcement: nomination of James S. Brady to be United States Attorney for the Western District of Michigan; G. William Hunter to be United States Attorney for the Northern District of California; Isaac G. Hylton to be United States Marshal for the Eastern District of Virginia; Rufus A. Lewis to be United States Marshal for the Middle District of Alabama; and Harry H. Marshall to be United States Marshal for the Southern District of Illinois

CHECKLIST—Continued
Released October 6—Continued

News conference: on the President's message to Congress proposing public broadcasting legislation—by Barry Jagoda, Special Assistant to the President for Media and Public Affairs, Richard M. Neustadt, Deputy Special Assistant for Media and Public Affairs, and Frank Lloyd, consultant to the Office of Telecommunications Policy

Released October 7, 1977

News conference: on the President's meeting with Prime Minister Lee Kuan Yew of Singapore—by Jerrold L. Schecter, Associate Press Secretary

ACTS APPROVED BY
THE PRESIDENT

Approved October 3, 1977

H.R. 1862_____ Public Law 95–117
Veterans Disability Compensation and Survivor Benefits Act of 1977.

H.R. 5262_____ Public Law 95–118
An act to provide for increased participation by the United States in the International Bank for Reconstruction and Development, the International Development Association, the International Finance Corporation, the Asian Development Bank and the Asian Development Fund, and for other purposes.

ACTS APPROVED—Continued
Approved October 3—Continued

H.R. 6111_____ Public Law 95–115
Juvenile Justice Amendments of 1977.

H.R. 6502_____ Public Law 95–116
An act to amend title 38 of the United States Code to provide an automobile assistance allowance and to provide automotive adaptive equipment to veterans of World War I.

Approved October 4, 1977

H.R. 7554_____ Public Law 95–119
Department of Housing and Urban Development—Independent Agencies Appropriation Act, 1978.

H.R. 9290_____ Public Law 95–120
An act to increase the temporary debt limit, and for other purposes.

Approved October 6, 1977

H.R. 6951_____ Public Law 95–121
An act to amend the Council on Wage and Price Stability Act to extend its termination date, and for other purposes.

S. 1322_____ Public Law 95–122
An act to revise the basis for estimating the annual Federal payment to the District of Columbia for water and water services and sanitary sewer services furnished to the United States.

Approved October 7, 1977

S. 126_____ Public Law 95–124
Earthquake Hazards Reduction Act of 1977.

S. 602_____ Public Law 95–123
Library Services and Construction Act Amendments of 1977.

Veterans Benefits

Statement on Signing S. 1307 Into Law.
October 8, 1977

I am today signing S. 1307, a bill which provides standards for discharge review and benefit eligibility for those persons whose discharge is upgraded by the Department of Defense under the Special Discharge Review Program and for certain other veterans.

While I believe several of the bill's provisions can be improved—and I will propose legislation next year to do so—S. 1307 properly recognizes the need for an equitable and compassionate attitude toward the many veterans who received less than honorable discharges.

One of my first official acts as President was the pardon of those persons who violated selective service laws during the era of the Vietnam war, a war which divided the American people. By this action, thousands of persons were relieved of possible prosecution for violations of the Military Selective Service Act.

In addition, I directed the Secretary of Defense to develop an administrative program to deal with those persons who received less than honorable discharges during the Vietnam war era. Under the Special Discharge Review Program developed by the Department of Defense, with the advice of the Joint Chiefs of Staff, 28,000 applicants have been reviewed to date, and 16,000 persons have had their discharges upgraded. The Review Program has freed many young persons from the social and employment hardships that resulted from their less than honorable discharges.

This Special Discharge Review Program gave Congress the opportunity, by passing S. 1307, to evaluate the treatment given to all veterans with less than honorable discharges, regardless of the era in which they served. Through S. 1307, the Congress has provided all veterans with less than honorable discharges the opportunity to apply for an upgraded status.

Nothing in this bill detracts from the impact of the Presidential pardon or the Special Discharge Review Program in helping to wipe the records of these veterans clean.

S. 1307 accomplishes many positive benefits for veterans:

—For the first time, all veterans, regardless of the time of their service, will have their applications for discharge upgrading and for benefit eligibility determined by uniform nationwide standards. Thus, pre-Vietnam era, post-Vietnam era, and Vietnam era veterans will all be judged by the same nationwide standards.

—Veterans with less than honorable discharges, as well as those upgraded under the Special Discharge Review Program, will automatically be eligible for

VA health care benefits for their service-incurred injuries.

—The bill provides an opportunity for veterans upgraded under the Special Discharge Review Program to receive veterans benefits.

My hope is that the Department of Defense and the Veterans Administration will be forthcoming and compassionate in upgrading veterans and extending benefit eligibility to them. Each of these is a clear step forward in the Nation's treatment of many of those who served in the Armed Forces.

This act establishes procedures for granting relief from administrative discharges in the future. Nothing we are doing, however, should create an impression of weakness in the resolve of the Government to ensure that discipline is maintained in our Armed Forces.

While the Special Discharge Review Program would have automatically provided benefit eligibility to those whose discharges have been upgraded, without the cumbersome procedures provided in S. 1307, I am pleased that Congress has deleted the amendment by Congressman Beard to the Department of Housing and Urban Development appropriations bill. That amendment would have totally denied veterans benefits to those whose status was upgraded under the Special Discharge Review Program.

Despite the benefits of the act, there are some provisions of S. 1307 which are troubling and which I will attempt to alleviate by submitting legislation next year.

While the primary purpose of the Special Discharge Review Program was to eliminate the stigma attached to persons with less than honorable discharges, another tangential result was to provide VA benefit eligibility to those upgraded under the program. Under S. 1307, however, those upgraded under the program will be required to have their benefit eligibility reevaluated by the Discharge Review Board, whether or not they have sought or plan to seek VA benefits.

In addition, I am also concerned that the bill completely bars benefit eligibility to those upgraded under the program whose records indicate they were absent without official leave for more than 180 consecutive days. This adverse impact of this provision is tempered by the fact that the upgraded status of such veterans would not be affected by this provision, the VA Administrator would be permitted to waive the bar if there were mitigating circumstances for the veteran's absence from service, and Defense Department records indicate that there are very few upgraded veterans actually in this category.

But the fact that this 180-day bar applies only to those whose upgrade discharges resulted from the Special Discharge Review Program raises serious equal protection problems. The Justice Department believes this denial of equal treatment to certain upgraded veterans is probably unconstitutional. I am asking the Attorney General's advice on the way in which this provision should be administered in light of the Justice Department's opinion.

On balance, I believe this bill will help veterans, because it expands the number of veterans who are eligible for benefits, while preserving the opportunity for those whose status has been upgraded under the Special Discharge Review Program to qualify for benefits.

NOTE: As enacted, S. 1307 is Public Law 95–126, approved October 8.

Maine Indian Land Claims Dispute

Appointment of Three-Member Working Group.   *October 8, 1977*

The White House announced today the appointment of a three-member working group to discuss with the parties certain aspects of Judge William Gunter's proposal for resolving the Maine Indian land dispute. The group will consist of A. Stephens Clay, Judge Gunter's law partner; Eliot Cutler, Associate Director for Natural Resources, Energy and Science at the Office of Management and Budget; and Leo M. Krulitz, Solicitor of Interior.

The purpose of the working group is to attempt to reach a consensual agreement for resolution of this dispute within the framework recommended by Judge Gunter.

The President wishes to express his personal gratitude to all parties for the good faith they have demonstrated in approaching this difficult problem.

Statistical Policy Functions

Announcement of Signing of Executive Order 12013.   *October 11, 1977*

The President has signed an Executive order transferring certain statistical policy functions previously centered in the Office of Management and Budget to the Commerce Department. The order implements a section of the Reorganization Plan for the Executive Office of the President.

Functions transferred as a result of the Executive order include:

—authority to develop programs and issue regulations for the gathering of statistics by Government agencies;

—authority to determine, with the approval of the Secretary of State, what statistical information to provide in response to requests from international organizations;

—functions relating to study of international investment statistics and access to information collected under the Investment Survey Act of 1976.

The Executive order also establishes the Statistical Policy Coordination Committee, headed by the Secretary of Commerce. It will advise the President on development and coordination of statistical services.

OMB will retain a general oversight role in statistical collection through its responsibilities for reviewing collection and use of statistical information under the Federal Reports Act. In other words, the Executive order assigns to the Commerce Department primary responsibility for interagency coordination of statistical policy programs but retains in OMB sufficient authority to resolve any differences between agencies which cannot be handled by Commerce.

Statistical Policy Functions

Executive Order 12013.   *October 7, 1977*

Relating to the Transfer of Certain Statistical Policy Functions

By virtue of the authority vested in me by the Constitution and statutes of the United States of America, including Reorganization Plan No. 2 of 1970 (5 U.S.C. App. II), Section 202 of the Budget and Accounting Procedures Act of 1950 (31

U.S.C. 581c), and Section 301 of Title 3 of the United States Code, and as President of the United States of America, in order to transfer certain functions from the Director of the Office of Management and Budget to the Secretary of Commerce and for other purposes, it is hereby ordered as follows:

SECTION 1. Section 1 of Executive Order No. 11541 of July 1, 1970, is amended by adding thereto the following new subsection:

"(c) The delegation to the Director of the Office of Management and Budget, pursuant to subsection (a) of this Section, of the functions vested in the Director of the Bureau of the Budget by Section 103 of the Budget and Accounting Procedures Act of 1950 (31 U.S.C. 18b) and subsequently transferred to the President by Part I of Reorganization Plan No. 2 of 1970 (5 U.S.C. App. II) is terminated on October 9, 1977.".

SEC. 2. Executive Order No. 10253 of June 11, 1951, is amended as follows:

(a) "Director of the Bureau of the Budget" is deleted in Section 1 and "Secretary of Commerce" is substituted.

(b) "Director" is deleted wherever it appears in Sections 1, 2, 4, 5, and 6 and "Secretary" is substituted therefor.

(c) "Bureau of the Budget" is deleted in Section 6 and "Department of Commerce" is substituted.

(d) a new Section 8 is added as follows:

"Sec. 8. The performance of the functions vested in the Secretary by this Order shall be subject to any authority or responsibility vested in the Director of the Office of Management and Budget, including Chapter 35 of Title 44 of the United States Code (the Federal Reports Act).".

SEC. 3. Executive Order No. 10033, as amended, is further amended as follows:

(a) "Director of the Bureau of the Budget" is deleted in Section 1 and "Secretary of Commerce" is substituted.

(b) "Director" is deleted wherever it appears in Sections 1, 2(a), 2(b), 2(c), 3, 4, and 5 and "Secretary" is substituted therefor.

(c) A new Section 7 is added as follows:

"Sec. 7. The performance of the functions vested in the Secretary by this Order shall be subject to any authority or responsibility vested in the Director of the Office of Management and Budget, including Chapter 35 of Title 44 of the United States Code (the Federal Reports Act).".

SEC. 4. Section 4 of Executive Order No. 11961 of January 19, 1977, is amended by deleting—

"the Council on International Economic Policy shall perform the function of making periodic reports to the Committees of the Congress as set forth in Section 4(a)(3) of the Act"

and substituting therefor—

"the Secretary of Commerce shall perform the functions set forth in Sections 4(a)(3) and (5)(c) of the Act".

SEC. 5. The records, property, personnel, and unexpended balances of appropriations, available or to be made available, which relate to the functions transferred or reassigned from the Director of the Office of Management and Budget to the Secretary of Commerce by the delegations made in this Order, are hereby transferred to the Secretary of Commerce.

SEC. 6. The Director of the Office of Management and Budget shall make such determinations, issue such orders, and take all steps necessary or appropriate to ensure or effectuate the transfers or reassignments provided by this Order, including the transfer of funds, records, property, and personnel.

SEC. 7. The Secretary of Commerce shall provide advice to the Director of the Office of Management and Budget with respect to the review and preparation of that portion of the annual Budget of the U.S. Government dealing with the gathering, interpreting, and disseminating of statistics and statistical information.

SEC. 8. (a) There is hereby established the Statistical Policy Coordination Committee, hereinafter referred to as the Committee, which shall be composed of the following members, and such other heads of Executive agencies as the President may designate:

(1) The Secretary of Commerce, who shall be the Chairman.

(2) The Secretary of State.

(3) The Secretary of the Treasury.

(4) The Secretary of Defense.

(5) The Attorney General.

(6) The Secretary of the Interior.

(7) The Secretary of Agriculture.

(8) The Secretary of Labor.

(9) The Secretary of Health, Education, and Welfare.

(10) The Secretary of Housing and Urban Development.

(11) The Secretary of Transportation.

(12) The Secretary of Energy.

(13) The Chairman, Council of Economic Advisers.

(14) The Director of the Office of Management and Budget.

(15) The Chairman, Board of Governors of the Federal Reserve System is invited to be a member.

(b) The Chairman may designate any other member to act as Chairman during the absence of the Chairman. Each member of the Committee may designate an alternate to serve whenever the regular member is unable to attend any meeting. The Chairman may invite the heads of other Executive agencies or their alternates to participate in Committee deliberations whenever matters which affect the interests of such agencies are to be considered.

(c) The Committee shall advise and assist the President with respect to the improvement, development, and coordination of Federal and other statistical services, and shall perform such other related duties as the President may prescribe.

(d) The Secretary of Commerce, to the extent permitted by law, shall provide such administrative support and such funds as may be necessary to support the functions of the Committee.

(e) Executive agencies shall, to the extent permitted by law, provide such information and assistance as the Committee or the Chairman may request to assist in carrying out the functions of the Committee.

SEC. 9. Any rules, regulations, orders, directives, circulars, or other actions taken pursuant to the functions transferred or reassigned from the Director of the Office of Management and Budget to the Secretary of Commerce by the delegations made in this Order, shall remain in effect until amended, modified, or revoked pursuant to the delegations made in this Order.

SEC. 10. This Order shall be effective October 9, 1977.

JIMMY CARTER

The White House,
    October 7, 1977.

[Filed with the Office of the Federal Register, 11:59 a.m., October 11, 1977]

NOTE: The White House Press Office announced the Executive order on October 11. It was not issued in the form of a White House press release.

Visit of Lieutenant General Olusegun Obasanjo of Nigeria

Remarks of the President and the Nigerian Head of State at the Welcoming Ceremony. October 11, 1977

THE PRESIDENT. This morning we're greatly pleased and honored to have as our guest General Obasanjo, the head of state of one of the great nations of Africa, indeed, one of the great nations of the world.

Historically, Nigeria has been a friend of our country. This is a nation with about 80 million people—a federation, like ours, of 19 states, a country fairly new in its own present government.

And our distinguished guest this morning was not only a courageous fighter for liberty and independence but, in his first visit to our own Nation, he came here as one seeking to reconstruct the economy and the people's lives of Nigeria. He's a distinguished military man in war and also has proven himself to be a distinguished military leader in peace.

Nigeria is a country of great importance to us. There is no doubt that this is a most important nation economically in Africa. We have great trade already between our country and Nigeria, a total of about $6 billion per year. Nigeria is a nation making great social and political progress. A new constitution has already been drafted for this great country, substantially similar to our own, providing for a president, a bicameral legislature, and the continuation of a completely independent judiciary, which has always been a part of the political life of Nigeria.

Nigeria has also moved to establish universal primary education and to use the wealth that has come from their natural resources, as has our own country in the past and at present, to enrich the lives of the people who live there.

Nigeria is a nation of great pride and also a growing leadership, not only among the nations of Africa but throughout the developing world and, indeed, throughout all nations on Earth.

We are very proud of the presence of this great leader. Seventeen years ago President Eisenhower met with the Prime Minister of Nigeria. A year later President Kennedy met with the Prime Minister of Nigeria. And now we have the head of state of a new and independent Nigeria. It's a great honor for us to have General Obasanjo here with us, with his leading fellow executives and diplomats, to consult with me and my own Cabinet members.

We will be probing ways of increased mutual partnership in dealing with the troubled region of the world and seeking for ways to tie our countries even closer together in a mutual partnership involving politics and economics.

I'm very proud that General Obasanjo has been able to come to our country. And I will be visiting his country in about 6 weeks. This will be the first state visit of a President to the black nations of Africa, and it's no coincidence that my point of visit will be Lagos, the capital of Nigeria.

Let me say in closing that in addition to forming mutual positions and compatible positions on matters of great moment to us and to the rest of the world, I will be seeking General Obasanjo's advice in how best we can orient our own foreign policy to accommodate the special needs, the special problems, and the special hopes of the great continent of Africa.

So, in many ways this will be a fruitful meeting for us, for Nigeria, I believe, for the continent of Africa, and for the entire world.

General Obasanjo, we are very proud to have you here. And on behalf of 215 million Americans, I extend to you our heartiest welcome and our gratitude for your superb leadership and the greatness of your country.

LIEUTENANT GENERAL OBASANJO. *President Carter, your Excellencies, distinguished guests, ladies and gentlemen:*

I am delighted to be here in this great country and to have the opportunity of personally conveying to you, Mr. President, the Government and the people of the United States, greetings and good wishes of the Government and people of Nigeria.

My present visit to the United States marks a new and favorable tone in the efforts to foster cooperation and amity between our two countries.

Mr. President, Nigeria and the United States share many common experiences. Our two countries have behind them a history of colonial rule and political struggles for independence. Both have progressive, dynamic, and resourceful peoples deeply committed to freedom, equality, social justice, and the pursuit of international peace and security. Of equal importance is the element of ethnic affinity between our two countries. I have no doubt that this visit will afford both our Governments the opportunity to build upon these and the many other bonds that unite us.

We also look forward to elaborating upon the initiatives and dialog we have started regarding the many matters of crucial importance to Africa and the world. Indeed, it is only recently that the Western Powers as a whole have come to realize that the quest for global peace and security also involves ensuring the stability and rapid development of Africa.

We in Nigeria, particularly, welcome such a realization on the part of the United States Government and people. We hope that our discussions will contribute towards the progress of the Afri-

can Continent, a process in which your Government and people can make significant and welcome contributions. In this respect, Mr. President, I am sure that we shall pay appropriate attention to the specific issues of the highly volatile and potentially dangerous situation in southern Africa, a situation which threatens international peace and security.

Human degradation, oppression and deprivation, as rationalized and perpetuated in southern Africa by the racist regimes there, is a crime against which not only Africa but all mankind as a whole must fight.

Needless to say, we also attach great importance to other elements of our bilateral relations, particularly in the economic and technical spheres. We in Nigeria have embarked upon a program of economic and industrial development for the period 1975 through 1980. We are happy to note that the major industrialized countries are already actually participating in this program. It is our hope that the United States, with its enormous economic and technological capabilities, will find ample opportunities in the program for fuller participation.

Mr. President, may I express the immense appreciation of myself and my delegation to you and the Government and people of the United States for inviting us to visit you. We look forward to a happy stay in your country.

Thank you.

NOTE: The President spoke at 10:37 a.m. on the South Lawn of the White House.

United States Ambassador to Paraguay

Nomination of Robert E. White.
October 11, 1977

The President today announced that he will nominate Robert E. White, of Melrose Heights, Mass., to be Ambassador Extraordinary and Plenipotentiary of the United States to Paraguay. He would replace George W. Landau, transferred.

White was born September 21, 1926, in Stoneham, Mass. He received an A.B. from St. Michael's College in 1952 and an M.A. from the Fletcher School of Law and Diplomacy in 1954. He served in the U.S. Navy from 1944 to 1946.

White joined the Foreign Service in 1955 and served as an international economist, foreign affairs officer, and then information specialist at the State Department. In 1958 and 1959, he was vice consul in Hong Kong, and from 1959 to 1961 he was economic officer in Ottawa.

From 1961 to 1963, White was a foreign affairs officer at the State Department, and from 1963 to 1965 he was deputy principal officer in Guayaquil, Ecuador. From 1965 to 1968, he was chief of the political section in Tegucigalpa.

From 1968 to 1970, White was detailed to the Peace Corps and served as Deputy Regional Director, then Regional Director, for Latin America. From 1970 to 1972, he was deputy chief of mission in Managua.

From 1972 to 1975, White was deputy chief of mission in Bogotá. Since 1975 he has been Deputy U.S. Permanent Representative to the Organization of American States.

Inter-American Tropical Tuna Commission

Appointment of Gerald V. Howard and Wymberley DeR. Coerr as Commissioners. October 11, 1977

The President today announced the appointment of Gerald V. Howard and Wymberly DeR. Coerr as Commissioners on the Inter-American Tropical Tuna Commission.

Howard, of Rancho Palos Verdes, Calif., replaces Wilvan G. Van Campen, resigned. Howard was born September 18, 1918, in Nottingham, England, and became an American citizen in 1956. He received a B.A. (1941) and M.A. (1947) in biology from the University of British Columbia.

Howard was with the International Pacific Salmon Fisheries Commission in British Columbia from 1942 to 1948 and served as a fishery biologist for the Food and Agriculture Organization of the United Nations from 1948 to 1951. From 1951 to 1959, he was senior scientist for the Inter-American Tropical Tuna Commission.

From 1959 to 1966, Howard was laboratory director for the Bureau of Commercial Fisheries Biological Laboratory in California. Since 1966 he has been Regional Director of the National Marine Fisheries Service Southwest Region.

Coerr, of Carmel, Calif., replaces Glenn H. Copeland, resigned. Coerr was born October 2, 1913, in New York City. He received a B.S. from Yale University in 1936.

From 1939 to 1944, Coerr was a Foreign Service officer serving in Canada, Honduras, and Mexico. From 1944 to 1947, he was manager and education director of the Consumer Cooperative Corps in New York. He returned to the Foreign Service in 1947 and served in Fiji, Indonesia, Guatemala, Bolivia, at the State Department as Deputy Assistant Secretary for Inter-American Affairs, as Ambassador to Uruguay (1962 to 1965), and as Ambassador to Ecuador (1965 to 1968). He retired from the Foreign Service in 1973.

From 1973 to 1975, Coerr was Director of the Office of International Environmental Programs of the Smithsonian Institution. Since 1976 he has been West Coast Representative for Defenders of Wildlife and for Monitor, Inc.

Agency for International Communication

Message to the Congress Transmitting Reorganization Plan No. 2 of 1977. October 11, 1977

To the Congress of the United States:

I transmit herewith Reorganization Plan No. 2 of 1977 to consolidate certain international communication, educational and cultural, and broadcasting activities of the United States Government. I am acting under the authority vested in me by the Reorganization Act, chapter 9 of title 5 of the United States Code. I am also acting pursuant to section 501 of the Foreign Relations Authorization Act, Fiscal Year 1978 (Public Law 95–105), which provides that my recommendations for reorganizing these activities be transmitted by October 31, 1977.

This reorganization will consolidate into a new agency, to be known as the Agency for International Communication, the functions now exercised by the State Department's Bureau of Educational and Cultural Affairs and the United States Information Agency.

The principal aspects of this proposal are:

—The new agency will take over USIA's international communications programs (including the Voice of America) and the international educational and cultural exchange activities now conducted by the Bureau of Educational and Cultural Affairs.

—The agency's Director will be the principal advisor on international information and exchange activities to the President, the National Security Council, and the Secretary of State. Under the direction of the Secretary of State, the Director will have primary responsibility within the Government for the conduct of such activities. The Director, the Deputy Director and the Associate Directors of the new agency will be confirmed by the Senate.

—The two commissions that now advise USIA and the Bureau of Educational and Cultural Affairs will be combined into a single seven-member commission. Members of this nonpartisan commission will be chosen from fields related to the agency's mission. The commissioners will be appointed by the President and confirmed by the Senate.

The purpose of this reorganization is to broaden our informational, educational and cultural intercourse with the world, since this is the major means by which our government can inform others about our country, and inform ourselves about the rest of the world.

The new Agency for International Communication will play a central role in building these two-way bridges of understanding between our people and the other peoples of the world. Only by knowing and understanding each other's experiences can we find common ground on which we can examine and resolve our differences.

The new agency will have two distinct but related goals:

• To tell the world about our society and policies—in particular our commitment to cultural diversity and individual liberty.

• To tell ourselves about the world, so as to enrich our own culture as well as to give us the understanding to deal effectively with problems among nations.

As the world becomes more and more interdependent, such mutual understanding becomes increasingly vital. The aim of this reorganization, therefore, is a more effective dialogue among peoples of the earth. Americans—mostly immigrants or the descendants of immigrants—are particularly well suited to enter into such an undertaking. We have already learned much from those who have brought differing values, perspectives and experiences to our shores. And we must continue to learn.

Thus the new agency will lay heavy emphasis on listening to others, so as to learn something of their motivations and aspirations, their histories and cultures.

Several principles guided me in shaping this reorganization plan. Among the most important were:

—Maintaining the integrity of the educational and cultural exchange programs is imperative. To this end, the plan retains the Board of Foreign Scholarships, whose strong leadership has done so much to insure the high quality of the educational exchange program. In addition, I intend to nominate an Associate Director who will be responsible for the administration and supervision of educational and cultural functions consolidated in the new Agency. The responsibilities presently exercised by the Department of State in relation to the Center for Technical and Cultural Interchange Between East and West, Inc., will be transferred to the new agency without alteration.

—Keeping the Voice of America's news gathering and reporting functions independent and objective. The Voice's charter, enacted into law in 1976, provides that "VOA news will be accurate, objective, and comprehensive"; that VOA will "present a balanced and comprehensive projection of significant American thought and institutions"; and that VOA will present U.S. policies "clearly and effectively, and will also present responsible discussion and opinion on these policies." Under this Administration, VOA will be solely responsible for the content of news broadcasts—for there is no more valued coin than candor in the international marketplace of ideas. I also plan to nominate an Associate Director who will be responsible for the administration and supervision of the Voice of America.

—The new agency's activities must be straightforward, open, candid, balanced, and representative. They will not be given over to the advancement of the views of any one group, any one party or any one Administration. The agency must not operate in a covert, manipulative, or propagandistic way.

—Rights of U.S. Information Agency and State Department employees must be respected. In the new agency, their career achievements will be recognized and the best possible use made of their professional skills and abilities.

The Director of the new agency will assess and advise on the impact on worldwide public opinion of American foreign policy decisions. The Agency will coordinate the international information, educational, cultural and exchange programs conducted by the U.S. Government and will be a governmental focal point for private U.S. international exchange programs. It will also play a leading role within the U.S. Government in our efforts to remove barriers to the international exchange of ideas and information.

It is not practicable to specify all of the expenditure reductions and other economies that will result from the proposed reorganization, and therefore I do not do so. The reorganization will result in greater efficiency by unifying in Washington the management of programs which are already administered in a consolidated manner in the field. For example, field officers will no longer report to two separate sets of supervisors and headquarters at home.

This plan abolishes the functions of the Advisory Committee on the Arts authorized by section 106(c) of the Mutual Educational and Cultural Exchange Act of 1961, as amended (22 U.S.C. 2456(c)). Also abolished, as a result of the consolidation of certain functions of the United States Advisory Commission on Information and the United States Advisory Commission on International Educational and Cultural Affairs in the United States Advisory Commission on International Communication, Cultural and Educational Affairs, are the functions authorized by section 603 of the United States Information and Educational Exchange Act of 1948, as amended (22 U.S.C. 1468) (requiring submission by the United States Advisory Commission on Information of a quarterly report to the Director of USIA and a semiannual report to the Congress). The new commission will report annually and at such other times as it deems appropriate (as does the existing Advisory Commission on International Educational and Cultural Affairs). Since appointments of all members of the new commission will be on a nonpartisan basis, as has been the case with the Advisory Commission on International Educational and Cultural Affairs, the requirement of section 602(a) of the U.S. Information and Educational Exchange Act (22 U.S.C. 1467(a)) that not more than three members of the Advisory Commission on Information shall be of the same political party is abolished.

Various obsolete or superseded functions under Reorganization Plan No. 8 of 1953 (22 U.S.C. 1461 note), which created the USIA, are superseded by this plan. Finally, the Plan abolishes a provision authorizing the Secretary of State to pay the expenses of transporting the bodies of participants in exchange programs who die away from home, since State no longer will conduct such programs (22 U.S.C. 2670(e)). All functions abolished by the reorganization are done so in compliance with section 903(b) of title 5 of the United States Code.

After investigation, I have ·found that this reorganization is necessary to carry out the policy set forth in section 901(a) of title 5 of the United States Code. The provisions in this Plan for the appointment and pay of the Director, Deputy Director, and Associate Directors of the Agency have been found by me to be necessary by reason of the reorganization made by the plan and are at a rate applicable to comparable officers in the executive branch.

In presenting this plan, I ask the support of Congress to strengthen and simplify the machinery by which we carry out these important functions of the United States Government.

Such action will make us better able to project the great variety and vitality of American life to those abroad, and to enrich our own lives with a fuller knowledge of the vitality and variety of other societies.

The new Agency for International Communication will help us demonstrate "a decent respect for the opinions of mankind," and to deal intelligently with a world awakening to a new spirit of freedom.

JIMMY CARTER

The White House,
　October 11, 1977.

REORGANIZATION PLAN No. 2 OF 1977

Prepared by the President and transmitted to the Senate and the House of Representatives in Congress assembled, October 11, 1977, pursuant to the provisions of chapter 9 of title 5 of the United States Code.

AGENCY FOR INTERNATIONAL
COMMUNICATION

SECTION 1. *Establishment of the Agency for International Communication.*

There is hereby established in the executive branch an agency to be known as the Agency for International Communication (the "Agency").

SEC. 2. *Director*

The Agency shall be headed by a Director (the "Director"), who shall serve as the principal advisor to the President, the National Security Council, and the Secretary of State on the functions vested in the Director. The Director shall report to the President and the Secretary of State. Under the direction of the Secretary of State, the Director shall have primary responsibility within the Government for the exercise of the functions vested in the Director. The Director shall be appointed by the President, by and with the advice and consent of the Senate, and shall be entitled to receive compensation at the rate now or hereafter prescribed by law for Level II of the Executive Schedule.

SEC. 3. *Deputy Director*

A Deputy Director shall be appointed by the President, by and with the advice and consent of the Senate. The Deputy Director shall act for, and exercise the powers of, the Director during the Director's absence or disability or during a vacancy in said office and, in addition, shall perform such duties and exercise such powers as the Director may from time to time prescribe. The Deputy Director shall be entitled to receive compensation at the rate now or hereafter prescribed by law for Level III of the Executive Schedule.

SEC. 4. *Associate Directors*

The President, by and with the advice and consent of the Senate, may appoint four Associate Directors, who shall perform such duties and exercise such powers as the Director may from time to time prescribe and who shall be entitled to receive compensation at the rate now or hereafter prescribed by law for Level IV of the Executive Schedule.

SEC. 5. *Performance of Functions*

The Director may establish within the Agency bureaus, offices, divisions and other units. The Director may from time to time make provision for the performance of any function of the Director by any officer, employee or unit of the Agency.

SEC. 6. *Negotiations*

(a) Under the direction of the Secretary of State, the Director shall prepare for, manage and conduct negotiations with representatives of foreign states or international organizations on matters for which responsibility is vested in the Director or in the Agency.

(b) For the purpose of conducting such negotiations, or for the purpose of exercising any other authority vested in the Director or in the Agency, the Director may

(1) consult and communicate with or direct the consultation and communication with representatives of other nations or of international organizations; and

(2) communicate in the name of the Secretary of State with diplomatic representatives of the United States in this country and abroad.

SEC. 7. *Transfer of Functions*

(a) There are hereby transferred to the Director all functions vested in the President, the Secretary of State, the Department of State, the Director of the United States Information Agency, and the United States Information Agency pursuant to the following:

(1) the United States Information and Educational Exchange Act of 1948, as amended (22 U.S.C. 1431–1479), except

to the extent that any function in sections 302, 401, or 602 is vested in the President;

(2) the Mutual Educational and Cultural Exchange Act of 1961, as amended (22 U.S.C. 2451–2458a), except for: (A) such functions as are vested by sections 102(b)(6), 102(b)(10), 104(a), 104(e)(1), 104(e)(2), 104(f), 104(g), 105(a), 105(b), 105(c), 106(a), 108; (B) to the extent that such functions were assigned to the Secretary of Health, Education and Welfare immediately prior to the effective date of this Reorganization Plan, sections 104(b), 105(d)(2), 105(f), 106(d), and 106(f); and (C) to the extent that any function therein is vested in the President or the Secretary of State, sections 106(b) and 106(c).

(3) Public Law 90–494 (22 U.S.C. 929–932, 1221–1234), to the extent that such functions are vested in the Director of the United States Information Agency;

(4) Sections 522(3), 692(1), and 803 (a)(4) of the Foreign Service Act of 1946, as amended (22 U.S.C. 922(3), 1037a(1), and 1063(a)(4)), to the extent such functions are vested in the Director of the United States Information Agency or in the United States Information Agency.

(5) Section 4 of the United States Information Agency Appropriations Authorization Act of 1973, Public Law 93–168;

(6)(A) Sections 107(b), 204 and 205 of the Foreign Relations Authorization Act, Fiscal Year 1978, Public Law 95–105, 91 Stat. 844; and (B) to the extent such functions are vested in the Director of the United States Information Agency, section 203 of the Act;

(7) the Center for Cultural and Technical Interchange Between East and West Act of 1960 (22 U.S.C. 2054–2057);

(8) Sections 101(a)(15)(J) and 212 (e) of the Immigration and Nationality Act (8 U.S.C. 1101(a)(15)(J),1182 (e));

(9) Section 2(a)(1) of Reorganization Plan No. 8 of 1953 (22 U.S.C. 1461 note);

(10) Section 3(a) of the Arts and Artifacts Indemnity Act (20 U.S.C. 972(a));

(11) Section 7 of the Act of June 15, 1951, c. 138, 65 Stat. 71 (50 U.S.C. App. 2316);

(12) Section 9(b) of the National Foundation on the Arts and Humanities Act of 1965 (20 U.S.C. 958(b));

(13) Section 112(a) of the Higher Education Act of 1965 (20 U.S.C. 1009 (a)), to the extent such functions are vested in the Department of State;

(14) Section 3(b)(1) of the Woodrow Wilson Memorial Act of 1968 (20 U.S.C. 80f(b)(1));

(15) Section 201 of Public Law 89–665, as amended by section 201(5) of Public Law 94–422 (16 U.S.C. 470i(a)(9));

(16) The third proviso in the twenty-third unnumbered paragraph of title V of Public Law 95–86 (headed "UNITED STATES INFORMATION AGENCY, SALARIES AND EXPENSES"), 91 Stat. 440–41;

(17) The twentieth unnumbered paragraph of title I of Public Law 95–86 (headed "CENTER FOR CULTURAL AND TECHNICAL INTERCHANGE BETWEEN EAST AND WEST"), 91 Stat. 424;

(18) Sections 4(d)(1)(F), 4(f)(1) (F), 4(g)(1)(F), and 4(h)(1)(F) of the Foreign Service Buildings Act, 1926, as amended (22 U.S.C. 295(d)(1)(F), 295(f)(1)(F), 295(g)(1)(F), and 295 (h)(1)(F)); and

(19) Sections 1, 2, and 3 of the Act of July 9, 1949, c. 301, 63 Stat. 408 (22 U.S.C. 2681–2683).

(b) There are hereby transferred to the Director all functions vested in the Assistant Secretary of State for Public Affairs pursuant to Section 2(a) of the John F. Kennedy Center Act (20 U.S.C. 76h(a)).

SEC. 8. *Establishment of the United States Advisory Commission on International Communication, Cultural and Educational Affairs*

(a) There is hereby established an advisory commission, to be known as the United States Advisory Commission on International Communication, Cultural and Educational Affairs (the "Commission"). The Commission shall consist of seven members who shall be appointed by the President by and with the advice and consent of the Senate. The members of the Commission shall represent the public interest and shall be selected from a cross section of educational, communications, cultural, scientific, technical, public service, and business and professional backgrounds. The members shall be appointed on a nonpartisan basis. The term of each member shall be three years except that of the original seven appointments, two shall be for a term of one year and two shall be for a term of two years. Any member appointed to fill a vacancy occurring prior to the expiration of the term for which a predecessor was appointed shall be appointed for the remainder of such term. Upon the expiration of a member's term of office, such member may continue to serve until a successor is appointed and has qualified. The President shall designate a member to chair the Commission.

(b) The functions now vested in the United States Advisory Commission on Information and in the United States Advisory Commission on International Educational and Cultural Affairs under sections 601 through 603 and 801(6) of the United States Information and Educational Exchange Act of 1948, as amended (22 U.S.C. 1466–1468, 1471 (6)), and under sections 106(b) and 107 of the Mutual Educational and Cultural Exchange Act of 1961, as amended (22 U.S.C. 2456(b), 2457), respectively, are hereby consolidated and vested in the Commission, as follows:

The Commission shall formulate and recommend to the Director, the Secretary of State, and the President policies and programs to carry out the functions vested in the Director or the Agency, and shall appraise the effectiveness of policies and programs of the Agency. The Commission shall submit to the Congress, the President, the Secretary of State and the Director annual reports on programs and activities carried on by the Agency, including appraisals, where feasible, as to the effectiveness of the several programs. The Commission shall also include in such reports such recommendations as shall have been made by the Commission to the Director for effectuating the purposes of the Agency, and the action taken to carry out such recommendations. The Commission may also submit such other reports to the Congress as it deems appropriate, and shall make reports to the public in the United States and abroad to develop a better understanding of and support for the programs conducted by the Agency.

(c) The Commission shall have no authority with respect to the Board of Foreign Scholarships or the United States National Commission for UNESCO.

SEC. 9. *Abolitions and Supersessions*

(a) The following are hereby abolished:

(1) The United States Information Agency, including the offices of Director, Deputy Director, Deputy Director (Policy and Plans) (5 U.S.C. 5316(67)), Associate Director (Policy and Plans) (5 U.S.C. 5316(103)), and additional offices created by section 1(d) of Reorganization Plan No. 8 of 1953 (22 U.S.C. 1461 note), of the United States Information Agency, provided that, pending the initial appointment of the Director, Deputy Director and Associate Directors of the Agency

their functions shall be performed temporarily, but not for a period in excess of sixty (60) days, by such officers of the Department of State or of the United States Information Agency as the President shall designate;

(2) One of the offices of Assistant Secretary of State provided for in section 1 of the Act of May 26, 1949, c. 143, 63 Stat. 111, as amended (22 U.S.C. 2652), and in section 5315(22) of title 5 of the United States Code;

(3) The United States Advisory Commission on International Educational and Cultural Affairs (22 U.S.C. 2456(b));

(4) The United States Advisory Commission on Information (22 U.S.C. 1466–1468);

(5) All functions vested in or related to the United States Advisory Commission on International Educational and Cultural Affairs and the United States Advisory Commission on Information that are not transferred to the Director by section 7 or consolidated in the Commission by section 8 of this Reorganization Plan;

(6) The Advisory Committee on the Arts, all functions thereof, and all functions relating thereto (22 U.S.C. 2456 (c)); and

(7) The functions vested in the Secretary of State by section 3(e) of the Act of August 1, 1956, c. 841, 70 Stat. 890 (22 U.S.C. 2670(e)).

(b) Sections 1, 2(a)(2), 2(b), 2(c) (3), 3, 4, and 5 of Reorganization Plan No. 8 of 1953 (22 U.S.C. 1461 note) are hereby superseded.

SEC. 10. *Other Transfers*

So much of the personnel, property, records, and unexpended balances of appropriations, allocations and other funds employed, used, held, available, or to be made available in connection with the functions transferred or consolidated by this Reorganization Plan, as the Director of the Office of Management and Budget shall determine, shall be transferred to the appropriate department, agency, or commission at such time or times as the Director of the Office of Management and Budget shall provide, except that no such unexpended balances transferred shall be used for purposes other than those for which the appropriation was originally made. The Director of the Office of Management and Budget shall provide for terminating the affairs of all agencies, commissions, and offices abolished herein and for such further measures and dispositions as such Director deems necessary to effectuate the purposes of this Reorganization Plan.

SEC. 11. *Effective Date*

This Reorganization Plan shall become effective at such time or times, on or before July 1, 1978, as the President shall specify, but not sooner than the earliest time allowable under section 906 of title 5 of the United States Code.

Council on Wage and Price Stability

Message Transmitting a Quarterly Report.
October 11, 1977

To the Congress of the United States:

In accordance with section 5 of the Council on Wage and Price Stability Act, as amended, I hereby transmit to the Congress the tenth quarterly report of the Council on Wage and Price Stability. This report contains a description of the Council activities during the first quarter of 1977 in monitoring both prices and wages in the private sector and various Federal Government activities that lead to higher costs and prices without creating commensurate benefits. It discusses in some detail the Council's studies of the outlook for collective bargaining negotiations for 1977, health care costs, automobiles, cement and the trends in industrial plant construction, as well as its filings before various Federal regulatory agencies.

During the remainder of 1977, the Council on Wage and Price Stability will continue to play an important role in supplementing fiscal and monetary policies by calling public attention to wage and price developments or actions by the Government that could be of concern to American consumers.

JIMMY CARTER

The White House,
    October 11, 1977.

NOTE: The 38-page report is entitled "Council on Wage and Price Stability—Quarterly Report, April 1977."

The message was not issued in the form of a White House press release.

Visit of Lieutenant General Obasanjo of Nigeria

Toasts of the President and Lieutenant General Obasanjo at a Dinner Honoring the Nigerian Head of State. October 11, 1977

THE PRESIDENT. First of all, let me welcome all of you here. This is one of those great occasions in our country's history when a new relationship between two great nations is beginning to take form and the advantages of that relationship are becoming obvious to all those involved.

This weekend I went to Camp David, and I spent probably 18 or 20 hours studying tax reform options, and I spent 2 or 3 hours reading a very interesting book called "Things Fall Apart," written by a great modern novelist called Achebe from Nigeria. This was an intriguing book about the life of a small community in Nigeria and how it was changed with the

advent of the intrusion of white missionaries and the British Government officials and how there was a struggle to retain both the freedom and independence and heritage that was precious to the Nigerians in the face of inexorable changing social and economic times. It was a very fine book, and I would recommend it to any of you here who haven't read it.

This is a time of great admiration in my own life for General Obasanjo and the people who come with him, and also the great country that General Obasanjo represents.

There is a common theme that runs through the advice to me of leaders of African nations: "We want to manage our own affairs. We want to be friends with both of the great super powers and also with the nations of Europe. We don't want to choose up sides. We don't want you or the Soviet Union to inject yourselves into the internal affairs of the nations of our continent. We believe that we are able and we are certainly willing to resolve challenging and very difficult disputes."

And if there's one nation that has come into the forefront because of great population, 80 million, because of economic advances, the wealthiest nation in Africa, probably, because of enlightened leadership, it's Nigeria.

This is a country that went through a very terrible civil war. And those of us who live in either the North or South in our own country know that it took us a hundred years to overcome the consequences of a divisive civil war in our own country. But under the leadership of General Obasanjo and the Military Council, Nigeria has healed its wounds and has carved out for its own citizens a very fine and rapidly improving quality of life and at the same time, in an almost unprecedented fashion has earned the confidence and trust of the other leaders of Africa and perhaps of the world as far as integrity is concerned and sound judgment and fairness.

I don't know, in my own limited experience as a statesman, a public official, but as a long student of history, that I've seen this happen before so quickly. It's also an almost unprecedented thing to know that a group of military leaders love their nation so much and love the principles of human freedom so much that without fanfare or turmoil or bloodshed they've laid a firm basis for rapid transfer of authority to the people themselves through free elections and through civilian rule.

And a democratically chosen constitutional convention comprised of about 230, 240 people are already completing the first draft of the constitution which will have a president and a bicameral congress, legislature, and they have maintained an absolutely free judicial system.

And the anticipation is that the first elections might take place in 1979, perhaps no later. They've extracted the finest aspects of British jurisprudence, in my opinion, and retained it. They have a unique system, Cy,[1] of choosing judges. The Chief Justice of the Supreme Court of the nation and the chief justices of the supreme courts of the states choose the new appointees to be judges, and they are submitted to the Military Council and, as a pro forma thing they're approved. This is something that I would welcome here in the United States. It would take off me the responsibility of appointing judges. [*Laughter*]

But the point I'm making is that there is a remarkable trend of change with pride and determination of preservation of human rights and absolute human freedom, a deep commitment to democracy in an extremely rapid way, and an acquisition,

---

[1] Secretary of State Cyrus R. Vance.

because of fulfillment, of the trust of the other nations of Africa and, indeed, of the whole world.

And I'm very proud to see our own relationship with Nigeria improving rapidly.

As we've discussed today, the problems with Chad and Libya, the advice that I've had is, "Let us handle it. We're already working with the Chadeans and the Libyans, and I believe that we can resolve it." And as we are deeply concerned about the Horn of Africa, I've learned today that the OAU has a standing committee and that Nigeria will be the lead nation in bringing Somalia and Ethiopia together if things go well. And through negotiation, perhaps the differences can be resolved with an alleviation of the bloodshed that's being demonstrated there now.

Well, I'm very proud to have this friendship, because our hopes are the same for Africa as those that exist in the hearts of our visitors here tonight—that there might be peace, that there might be an honoring of national borders, that there might be a complete absence of military intrusion or unwarranted influence from the European nations or the super powers, ourselves or the Soviets, or any other outside force, that there might be the establishment of majority rule, an end to racism and discrimination, that there might be maximum autonomy for the nations that exist there, enhancement of human freedom, and an improvement in the quality of life of people who live in Africa.

These are exactly the same things we hope for. And because of my own limited knowledge of Africa, but a burgeoning interest in Africa on the part of our own Nation, it helps me to have a friend, adviser, and counselor like our guest here tonight to make sure that our own decisions are made on the basis of sound advice and accurate analysis of things as they exist.

I'd like to close by saying that we have very strong ties with Nigeria at the people level, even though there have been differences of opinion in the last few years which are now being rapidly alleviated. There are more than 15,000 Nigerian students in the United States, and this in the future will help to tie our countries together.

And I'm determined, as a fellow Baptist—[*laughter*]—and as a fellow engineer and as a fellow leader of my Nation, to join in with General Obasanjo to assure that these demonstrations of progress are continued at an accelerating rate in the future.

On behalf of the people of this country, I would like to offer a toast to the great leader and leaders of Nigeria and to the people of that great country who have served so well, our friends.

LIEUTENANT GENERAL OBASANJO. *President Carter, distinguished guests:*

I wish to thank you most sincerely for the excellent dinner we have just had and for the warm and friendly reception which you and your government have so graciously accorded me and members of my delegation.

I also thank you for the kind and generous terms in which you spoke about my country and myself. We have seen demonstrated in this short period of our visit a new awareness of the need to establish a bridge of communication between our two countries and our two peoples. But I believe that a close affinity already exists between our two countries. History and shared ancestry bind us to a large section of your population. This affinity for that derives from our common attachment to freedom and independence and all their ramifications.

You attained your independence 200 years ago. We have been independent for only 17 years. For us in Nigeria, independence is indivisible and total, and we regard our independence as incomplete so long as parts of the African Continent remain under the yoke of colonialism.

Our perception of the policies of successive United States administrations was that concern for Africa and its problems played an insignificant role in the formulation of these policies. It appeared to us that Africa had become a mere pawn in a global chess game which had no serious relevance to our concerns and interests. Even if such a policy served the interests of the United States at that time, the effect of its implementation was to alienate the vast majority of the people of Africa whose history and even aspirations cut them out to be staunch friends and allies of the American people.

At our independence all the indications to us were that it was almost natural that the United States and Nigeria would enjoy a cordial and close relationship. Events subsequently showed that the genuine desire of Nigeria to walk in close collaboration with the United States to promote freedom and understanding could not be reciprocated.

There are those who hold the view that such setbacks are natural in the history of relations between nation states. Some maintain that both the United States and Nigeria did not utilize the opportunity which their common belief and historical ties offered them. Even at that time, while relations between our two Governments were at their lowest ebb, there were individuals in both countries who, because of their determination and foresight, resisted the temptation to give up all attempts at fostering friendly relationships and kept open the lines of communication and dialog between our two peoples until the atmosphere improved.

Hence, we are again in a position to indicate our readiness to work together for the cause of freedom and understanding and to foster cooperation in areas of mutual benefit. While we seek to forge closer relations between our two countries, let us, Mr. President, remember that the commitment of our peoples to freedom is total and that we can only carry our people along with us if we continue to uphold and nurture those principles which motivate their action.

As far as we are concerned, we are happy to note that for the first time a United States administration is showing signs of recognizing the necessity of placing Africa in its proper position as a major focal point in the quest for international peace and stability. Nowhere in the world is there a greater assault on human rights than in Africa. Nowhere is the continued exportation of weapons of war and the technology of destruction likely to have graver consequences than in Africa. And so long as Africa remains unstable, for whatever due political reasons, so long will developments there continue to pose a threat to world peace.

This is why we welcome with pride the place which you and your administration have given to human rights. This has kindled a new awareness of freedom and its overall importance in the overall context of relations between nation states.

If this policy is consistently pursued, the peoples of Africa will have no difficulty in accepting that your stand and commitment to freedom and justice is more than mere rhetoric. The basic rights of all human beings, which your administration upholds, remind us all that one of the primary responsibilities of all governments is to jealously protect and assure the fundamental rights of their peoples. We in Nigeria share this belief with you, Mr. President.

There is hardly any need for me to recount here the steps we are taking in Nigeria to restore the government of our country to a democratically elected body by 1979. While our own traditions of government and historical experience will inevitably influence the form and content of our constitution and the style of government in our country, we cannot ignore the lessons and experiences of older republics.

Mr. President, since our arrival here, you and I have discussed at length the situation in southern Africa. If we have devoted so much time to the subject, it is largely because we share the view that nowhere else in the world are the ideas of freedom, justice, and human rights so wantonly and systematically trampled upon than in that unhappy part of our continent.

While I do not wish to go over the issues again here, I would like to stress that they are of paramount importance in the relations between our two countries and peoples. I am sure, therefore, that we shall continue to monitor events in the three problem areas of southern Africa.

Here again, Nigeria, for her part, is prepared to support all efforts aimed at finding just and peaceful solutions to the problems of southern Africa. Those of us who are skeptical about the current well-intentioned international efforts directed at bringing about desirable change in southern Africa through peaceful means are led to that conclusion by our understanding of racism and colonialism. Peaceful negotiations can only be carried out in an atmosphere of mutual respect and confidence. Neither Vorster nor Smith inspire any confidence, trust, or respect. Indeed, given the very systems they are committed to maintain, it is idle and unrealistic to expect them to miraculously abandon their chosen course on their own.

Apartheid and the belief in the superiority of one race over another is the fundamental belief among the white groups in South Africa and Rhodesia. This belief has been systematized and sustained by a whole range of state operators of violence. We therefore believe that only the eventual bankruptcy of the system will bring about acceptable change in southern Africa. But this will be a long process, which we cannot expect the principal victims to patiently endure. This is why we believe that an armed liberation struggle by the oppressed is justifiable and bound to succeed. This is a commitment which we in Africa have a duty to support.

While we acknowledge that some countries outside Africa may not feel able to subscribe to this position, we think they can assist in this effort by discontinuing their current involvement with the racist system in terms of their massive investment and their deliveries of arms and, in particular, the technology of armaments.

If, as almost the whole world seems to be agreed, apartheid is a uniquely evil system, then no one should hesitate to feel we have a moral duty to humanity to take these minimum steps.

Mr. President, other aspects which touch directly on the bilateral relations between our two countries flow from the premise of our mutual commitment to common ideals. In spite of the undue and often misleading publicity given to Nigeria's petroleum resources, ours is a developing country. Eighty percent of Nigeria's working population is in the agricultural sector. Our per capita income is less than $350 per annum. Thus we cannot be considered as a rich nation. It is our hope, therefore, that we will continue to enjoy the cooperation of the United States in the execution of programs designed to improve the quality of life for our people.

Our resources and available technology cannot yet support self-sustained improvement in the standard of living of the bulk of our population. As with other technologically and industrially advanced countries, we shall seek to consult more closely with the United States in exploring further ways of strengthening cooperation in our endeavor to develop a strong technological base for the mechanization of production and the resultant improvement to the material well-being of our people.

Mr. President, as you are aware, the dialog between the industrialized countries and the developing nations on the structure of a new world economic order ended inconclusively, and there was no agreement as to what system should replace the existing one.

We are encouraged to know that the United States is committed to work towards the creation of a more just world economic system, because we also desire the elimination of a situation in which nations of the world are prominently categorized as industrialized and developing states, haves and have-nots. I am happy that we are both committed to the creation of a new world order which will take due cognizance of the interdependence between states, a world in which nation states will relate to one another on the basis of equality, understanding, and mutual respect.

May I once again express my sincere gratitude and that of my delegation for your generous hospitality. I also seize this opportunity to assure you that we welcome your impending visit to Nigeria. It certainly will add a new dimension and impetus to the efforts of all who desire to forge meaningful and mutually beneficial relations between the peoples and governments of our two countries.

Honorable Members of Congress, distinguished ladies and gentlemen, may I invite you to rise and drink with me a hearty toast to the continued good health and happiness of President Carter and to the well-being of the people of the United States of America.

NOTE: The President spoke at 8:47 p.m. in the State Dining Room at the White House.

Housing and Community Development Act of 1977

Remarks on Signing H.R. 6655 Into Law.
October 12, 1977

Good morning, everybody. I'm glad to be here on this occasion, which I think is a very happy one for our country.

There's been a great deal of work that's gone into the production of the Housing and Community Development Act of 1977. One of the first recommendations that I made to Congress was to stimulate improvements in the housing field, which had come in a sad state, I think, in the last number of years.

During the campaign, I spent a couple of years moving around the country, trying to learn about our people's needs. And there are some devastated areas where American citizens live that are a disgrace to our great country.

There's no immediate solution that can be offered. I visited the South Bronx last week, which is enough to shake our confidence in the structure that we've evolved. And I know that in many other places in the country there are similar areas which need to be addressed by all of the leaders in this country in the private and public sector. We have made some progress in the last 9 months under Pat Harris' leadership.

We've already more than doubled the number of assisted houses being constructed. Now, as a matter of fact, about a fourth of the total multifamily houses in the Nation are assisted housing.

But this bill takes a giant step forward and gives me and the administration, the lending institutions, private developers, local and State officials, a framework within which we can make great improvements in the housing of our people. Because of the good work of the Members of the House and the Senators behind me, there's been a focusing of attention to the more devastated and needy communities of our country, in large and small cities and in rural areas.

The formulae that have been evolved will permit this to be done. There will be $12.4 billion over the next 3 years that will go into the community development block grant program, again concentrated in older and more distressed communities of our country.

In the urban development action grant, which is designed primarily to stimulate private investment, there will be $400 million a year. Rent subsidies will permit a substantial increase. 317,000 more families can be housed under the Section 8 program, again stimulating primarily private investment into renovation and building of adequate housing for our people.

The Congress has added a restraint on unwarranted redlining of depressed areas. Although this will require some additional effort in administration, I think it spells out the Congress attitude that this is not a proper way to deal with areas that are on the decline, that we need to work together to restimulate them.

In general, this is a very excellent piece of legislation. There's one portion of it that does cause me some concern and that's Title VII, which removes the constraints on the building of homes in flood plain areas.

We will be considering how we can salvage the flood damage insurance program and also restrict the building of homes in areas that are very likely to be flooded in the future. With this provision it's been estimated that we might have $4½ billion of flood damage to homes that are built in areas where the rivers and streams are going to flood. And whether or not to come back with corrective legislation next year or whether to try to deal with this administratively is something we haven't decided.

But I would like to congratulate the distinguished Members of the House and Senate for the very fine work they've done with this legislation—it's a controversial piece of legislation—in devising the formulae to channel funds into areas that are most in need. But I think they have done a superb job. And with a great deal of appreciation to the Congress and, I think, congratulations to the people who seek better housing in the United States, I'm very glad to sign this House of Representatives bill 6655, which is the Housing and Community Development Act of 1977.

Thank you very much.

NOTE: The President spoke at 9:18 a.m. in the Rose Garden at the White House.

As enacted, H.R. 6655 is Public Law 95–128, approved October 12.

Hospital Cost Containment Legislation

Letter to the Chairmen of Three Congressional Subcommittees. October 12, 1977

One of my most important priorities is to secure strong legislation to restrain the skyrocketing increase in health care costs.

As subcommittees in both the House and Senate prepare to resume their work in this area, I wish to reaffirm my strong personal commitment to the Administration's Hospital Cost Containment legislation.

Last month, HEW announced that it was required to increase the deductible for hospital coverage under Medicare from $124 to $144, reflecting rising hospital costs. These rising costs affect not only the elderly, but all Americans. Today, 95,000 Americans will enter community hospitals. By the time they leave the hospital, their care will have cost $124 million. Our people already spend more for health care than the people of any other nation—yet the cost of that care doubles every five years. The American people simply cannot afford yearly increases in their hospital bills of 15% and more.

The Administration's Hospital Cost Containment bill will restrain this escalation in hospital costs. It will save billions of dollars—not only in Federal and State budgets, but in the budgets of American families as well. This legislation is important in our twin efforts to restrain inflation and improve the quality of health care for all Americans.

I deeply appreciate your leadership to this date.

Sincerely,

JIMMY CARTER

NOTE: This is the text of identical letters addressed to the Honorable Herman E. Talmadge, chairman of the Subcommittee on Health of the Senate Finance Committee, the Honorable Paul G. Rogers, chairman of the Subcommittee on Health and the Environment of the House Committee on Interstate and Foreign Commerce, and the Honorable Dan Rostenkowski, chairman of the Subcommittee on Health of the House Ways and Means Committee.

Alcohol, Drug Abuse, and Mental Health Administration

Nomination of Gerald L. Klerman To Be Administrator.   October 12, 1977

The President today announced that he will nominate Gerald L. Klerman, of Chestnut Hill, Mass., to be Administrator of the Alcohol, Drug Abuse, and Mental Health Administration. He would replace James Isbister, resigned.

Klerman was born December 29, 1928. He received an A.B. from Cornell University in 1950 and an M.D. from New York University College of Medicine in 1954.

From 1954 to 1956, Klerman was an intern and resident in medicine at Bellevue Hospital in New York. From 1956 to 1959, he was a resident in psychiatry at the Massachusetts Mental Health Center.

Klerman was a research associate at the National Institute of Mental Health from 1959 to 1961. From 1961 to 1965, he was at the Massachusetts Mental Health Center as a psychiatrist, then assistant director of psychiatry. He was at the Connecticut Mental Health Center from 1965 to 1969, serving as director of clinical services, then general director.

From 1970 to 1976, Klerman was superintendent at the Erich Lindemann Mental Health Center in Boston. Since 1976 he has been professor of psychiatry at Harvard Medical School and director of the Stanley Cobb Laboratories in Research Psychiatry at Massachusetts General Hospital.

Klerman is a consultant to the American Medical Association Council on Drugs, the National Institute of Mental Health Clinical Research Branch, the Medical Letter, Drug and Therapeutic Information, and the Veterans Administration Cooperative Studies Evaluation Committee. He has been a principal investigator on a number of research studies.

Council of the International Civil Aviation Organization

Appointment of John E. Downs as U.S. Representative.   October 12, 1977

The President today announced the appointment of John E. Downs, of St. Joseph, Mo., as Representative of the United States on the Council of the International Civil Aviation Organization. He replaces Betty C. Dillon, resigned. The President also announced that he will nominate Downs for the rank of Minister while serving in this position.

Downs was born May 12, 1917, in St. Joseph, Mo. He received an LL.B. (J.D.) from the University of Missouri in 1941. He served in the U.S. Marine Corps from 1941 to 1945.

From 1947 to 1949, Downs was a group attorney with the Securities and Exchange Commission, and from 1950 to 1954 he was a prosecuting attorney for Buchanan County, Mo. Since 1954 he has been a trial lawyer. He has also served as a member of the Missouri State Legislature in 1956 and 1957, and a Missouri State senator from 1960 to 1970. He is licensed as a commercial pilot for single- and twin-engine airplanes.

Department of the Navy

Nomination of George A. Peapples To Be an Assistant Secretary.   October 12, 1977

The President today announced that he will nominate George A. Peapples, of

Dexter, Mich., to be an Assistant Secretary of the Navy. He would replace Gary D. Penisten, resigned, and his area of responsibility would be financial management.

Peapples was born November 6, 1940, in Benton Harbor, Mich. He received a bachelor's degree in economics (1962) and an M.B.A. in finance (1963) from the University of Michigan.

After graduation Peapples joined the General Motors Corp. financial staff in Detroit. In 1968 he was transferred to General Motors treasurer's office in New York as a staff assistant.

In 1971 Peapples was appointed director of the capital analysis and investments section of the General Motors New York treasurer's office. In 1973 he became assistant divisional comptroller of the Delco Moraine Division of General Motors, and since 1975 he has been assistant treasurer, bank relations, of GMC.

Peapples is a member of the board of directors and executive committee of the American Freedom Train Foundation.

National Institute of Education

Appointment of P. Michael Timpane as Deputy Director. October 12, 1977

The President today announced that he has appointed P. Michael Timpane, of Arlington, Va., to be Deputy Director of the National Institute of Education. He would succeed Emerson Elliott, resigned.

Timpane was born November 27, 1934, in Troy, N.Y. He received a B.A. (1956) and an M.A. (1964) from Catholic University and an M.P.A. in education policy, government, and economics from Harvard University in 1970.

Timpane served as special assistant to the deputy for civil rights in the office of

the Assistant Secretary of Defense for Manpower from 1964 to 1968. From 1968 to 1972, he worked in the office of the Assistant Secretary of HEW for Planning and Evaluation, serving as Deputy Assistant Secretary and Director of Education Planning in 1971 and 1972.

Timpane then served as a senior fellow at the Brookings Institution in the economic studies program. Since 1974 he has been on the staff of the Rand Corp. in Washington, serving as director of studies for the Aspen Institute of Humanistic Studies Program for Education in a Changing Society, principal investigator of "Youth Policy in Transition," and, currently, director of the Center for Educational Finance and Governance.

Timpane has served as a consultant to the National Institute of Education and an editorial consultant to "Evaluation" magazine. He is the author of numerous articles.

National Museum Services Board

Nomination of 15 Members of the Board. October 12, 1977

The President today announced that he will nominate the following persons as members of the National Museum Services Board:

For 5-year terms:

LLOYD HEZEKIAH, director of the Brooklyn (New York) Children's Museum;

PETER H. RAVEN, director of the Missouri Botanical Garden in St. Louis;

GEORGE C. SEYBOLT (to be designated Chairman of the Board on confirmation), of Westwood, Mass., chairman of the American Association of Museums' trustees committee;

For 4-year terms:

LEWIS DAVIS, a New York architect who has done extensive work in museum design;

RAUL A. LOPEZ, curator of New World Collections and Communication Publication Program at UCLA's Museum of Cultural History;

E. LELAND WEBBER, director of the Field Museum of Natural History in Chicago;

For 3-year terms:

GARY K. CLARKE, director of the Topeka, Kans., Zoological Park;

GEORGE HORSE CAPTURE, an Indian curriculum researcher and instructor at the College of Great Falls in Montana;

CHARLOTTE FERST, member of the executive committee and chairman of the endowment committee of the High Museum of Art in Atlanta;

For 2-year terms:

MAMIE P. CLARK, executive director of the Northside Center for Child Development in New York;

BENJAMIN W. HAZARD, curator of special exhibits in education at the Oakland (California) Museum;

NANCY NEGLEY, president of the San Antonio Conservation Society;

For 1-year terms:

DOUGLAS DILLON, president of the Metropolitan Museum of Art in New York;

NEIL HARRIS, professor of history at the University of Chicago;

JOAN MONDALE, former director of the Associated Council of the Arts and author of "Politics in Art."

Visit of Lieutenant General Obasanjo of Nigeria

Remarks to Reporters Following the Nigerian Head of State's Departure. October 12, 1977

REPORTER. Mr. President, did you solve all the problems with them or only half?

THE PRESIDENT. Well, we made a great stride forward. I think the recognition of Nigeria as an enlightened and very influential nation has been a long time coming in our own country.

The respect with which the Nigerian Government and people are held in Africa is obvious to us now. A year ago, we had nothing but animosity between our own country and the Nigerian Government. Now we have nothing but friendship. And I'm very grateful that this exchange has taken place and the change in our relationships have taken place.

In almost every trouble spot in Africa, the Nigerians are looked upon as a major factor for peace and for the resolution of differences. They comprise about a third of the population of Africa, about half of the gross national product of all the black African nations.

The key to success in resolving the problems in Rhodesia, Namibia, between Somalia and Ethiopia, between Chad and Libya—I think that this is because of their complete commitment to democracy. The fact that the military leaders have healed the wounds of the civil war, the fact that they have an absolute commitment to a democratic means of writing a new constitution with complete civilian rule, these things are admirable, as measured by American standards.

The compatibility between us is very profound. And I think this new development in the relationships between our countries will be very helpful to us, to Africa, and, I think, to the entire world.

Q. Are you pleased with the Israeli Cabinet action?

THE PRESIDENT. I'm sorry?

Q. On the peace plan, so-called, the procedures for going to Geneva, are you pleased with that?

THE PRESIDENT. Yes, I'm pleased with that. And it's not a final decision, obviously, because we don't yet know the private concerns on the part of the Israelis—I don't.

1781

Of course, we are consulting constantly with the Arab nations as well. But I think every week now is bringing about some progress toward a Geneva conference. And I think there's been a substantial alleviation among the leaders of the Middle Eastern nations of their concern about the results of a Geneva conference.

I think they all are beginning to see now that it's not something that they need to fear, that it's a first step toward a possible final peace settlement. But it's extremely sensitive, extremely complicated.

The national leaders, even those presently in office, have made very abusive statements in the past. It's hard for them to correct or to modify those statements in a constructive fashion, but they're doing their best. And I don't think there's any nation now that I couldn't say is genuinely striving for the convening of the conference and also ultimate settlement that brings about peace.

Q. Are the stories about the breakthrough in SALT correct?

THE PRESIDENT. Well, there has been substantial progress, as I've already said, on the SALT negotiations. We don't know yet what the Soviet attitude is on the very important remaining differences. We are negotiating at Geneva. These negotiations have just recommenced. And we have nothing to indicate that there's been an irresolvable difference. So, I can't really comment specifically on SALT, except to say that the results so far have been encouraging. We don't know how much progress will be made in the future.

Q. Mr. President, we understand you are going to step up your public role in behalf of the energy program to a large extent in the next few weeks. What kinds of things do you have in mind?

THE PRESIDENT. Well, back in April and May, when we described very accurately the threat to our country of the energy crisis, there was a rapid growth in public awareness. The oil companies, through their advertising program and so forth, on an almost hourly basis, present their point of view about the energy problem. That's completely legitimate. I don't criticize them because of it.

But I don't think that anything has happened since April that's caused an alleviation of the problem. I think that it's patently obvious that the problem is much more severe now than it was 6 months ago and that the inevitability of an energy crisis that can be devastating to us and to the rest of the world is becoming more and more obvious.

The major effort of the entire Government this year, the Congress and myself together, has been the energy legislation. A very large investment of time and effort has gone into it. And it's predictably controversial. What the Congress decides will touch the lives of every person in this country, not only in the immediate future but even more severely in years to come.

The basic struggle is whether or not the average family in this Nation is going to be treated fairly, whether energy supplies are going to be adequate, whether there can be international stability where the security of our country can be maintained on the one hand, or whether special interest groups can derive an unwarranted advantage at the expense of most American people, and the conservation efforts that we have proposed would be negated.

I consider it to be of crucial importance. And as we approach the end of the congressional session, I think it's important for me again to go back to the country and reaffirm the reasons, which have not changed, for a comprehensive energy policy to be adopted.

Q. Are you now going over the heads of Congress?

THE PRESIDENT. No, I think I'll be working with most of the Members of Congress.

Q. Mr. President, do you think the creation of a Palestinian state would lead to the destruction of Israel—or entity——

THE PRESIDENT. I've never advocated an independent Palestinian state.

NOTE: The President spoke at 12 noon on the South Grounds of the White House.

THE PRESIDENT'S NEWS CONFERENCE OF OCTOBER 13, 1977

ENERGY LEGISLATION

THE PRESIDENT. Good morning, everybody.

Back in April when a national energy policy was presented to the Congress and to the people, I said that because of the importance of it that this was a moral equivalent of war. I haven't changed my mind. In fact, the seriousness of the energy crisis is even more acute than it was then.

But as is the case in time of war, there is potential war profiteering in the impending energy crisis. This could develop, with the passing months, as the biggest ripoff in history. And the issues involved here are extremely important. We live in a nation and we believe in the free enterprise system where market forces determine prices. But the oil and gas industry is not part of that system because prices are not free. They are heavily influenced by decisions made outside our country by the OPEC nations, and they are heavily influenced by some control over the rate of production by American companies. And there's an inevitable increasing short-

age of oil and gas, which we all recognize, I believe, without dispute.

Prices have gone up drastically in the last few years. They are going to go up some more. That also is inevitable. But the question is: Who will profit from these prices and to what degree?

The package that was presented to the Congress in April is fair. It's well-balanced. It assures that the American people are not robbed. It also ensures that the oil companies get enough incentive to ensure adequate exploration and production. But the oil companies apparently want it all.

And we are talking about enormous amounts of money. Never before in our history has this much money been involved in a decision controlled by Government policy and by legislation.

The struggle is intense. It's going to go on for a long time. But the basic question is going to be resolved within the next few weeks in the Congress.

Now, the oil companies deserve incentive, and our proposals have been both fair and they have been adequately generous. In 1973, for instance, just before the OPEC price rise and the oil embargo, the oil and gas industries had an income of $18 billion. Under our proposal, by 1985 their annual income would be about $100 billion, an enormous increase. What the oil companies and gas companies are now demanding—and making some progress—is $150 billion. The difference will not encourage increased production of oil. But that difference will come out of the pockets of the American consumers and go into the pockets of the oil companies themselves.

Our proposal, if adopted, would give the oil companies, the producers themselves, the highest prices for oil in all the world. But still they want more.

If we deregulate natural gas prices, then the price will go to 15 times more than natural gas prices were before the oil embargo. These billions and billions of dollars are at stake; whether that money should be given partially to the oil companies to encourage production and partially to the American people in a fair way or whether it should all be grabbed by the oil companies at the expense of the American consumer.

There is one other point I want to make very briefly. The international circumstances of the energy crisis are now being recognized as being very, very serious. Dr. Schlesinger just returned from a meeting with the nations who comprise the International Energy Agency, almost all the developed nations in the world, the industrialized nations in the world. We now consume about 23 million barrels of oil a day. The prospect is that we might go to 36 million by 1985, a demand that simply cannot be met.

So, all the countries, including us, have resolved to cut down our consumption, not below what it is now, but below the anticipated amount, to about 26 million barrels a day.

We believe that production can meet those demands. But the biggest single question in international councils is the will of the American people. Do we have the will as a nation to cut down our enormous oil imports?

I have confidence in the American people, looking to the future, but past performance has been very disappointing. We were shocked in 1973 when the oil embargo was imposed on us and prices went up. We began to move to cut back on imports. Imports this year will be about $45 billion in oil, 87 percent more than just 4 years ago. We import more oil than all the European countries combined, in spite of the fact that we have enormous produc-

tion in our own country, which they don't have.

So, I cannot overemphasize the importance of this question to the present and future security of our country, our independence, our economic structure, and also the fairness of a distribution of increased prices, which are inevitable.

It is absolutely important that the legislation be passed. The House has done a good job. They have come forward with legislation that I can accept.

It's up to the Senate. I have confidence in the Senate. And I believe that we'll come out of this legislative session with a reasonable policy established for our country.

It's the most important domestic issue that we will face while I am in office. And I attribute the highest possible importance to it in my own administration.

I'm going to devote most of my time the next few weeks while the Congress is in session trying to make sure we have a fair and adequate energy package. And I hope that the American people will join in with me to encourage the Congress to act accordingly.

QUESTIONS

SENATE ACTION ON ENERGY
LEGISLATION

Q. Mr. President, you have struck out against the oil lobbies, but not against the Senators in your own party who may be listening to them and who have decimated your energy program. You say you have confidence in them. Also, your administration undercut a filibuster against the natural gas deregulation, and one Senator called your credibility into question. Who is to blame?

THE PRESIDENT. I think at this point no one is to blame. With the encouragement and cooperation between the White House and the Congress, the House of

Representatives has passed an energy bill which is not completely adequate as we proposed it, but is a major step forward. The Senate has not yet decided.

There are five major component parts of the energy legislation. The Senate has acted on four of them. The other one involves pricing and tax. Those questions have not yet been resolved.

The present proposal by the Senate leaders—and I have no alternative except to go along with it, of course—is that there will hopefully be a bill passed by the Senate. I don't think it's accurate to say that it will be in final form. And then that bill will be transmitted to the conference committee, the members of which have already been appointed. Then the negotiations between the House and the Senate will take place and the agreed-upon compromise, hopefully compatible with what we recommended, would go back to both Houses for rejection or acceptance.

The filibuster was not initiated by me. It was not terminated by me. And I believe that that was a step in getting the House and Senate to a conference. But I still believe that if the American people can recognize the importance of this issue, as the House Members have already done, that we will have acceptable legislation this year.

TAX REFORM

Q. Mr. President, are you or your people giving even tentative thought now to the possibility of an economy-stimulating tax cut next year, quite apart from tax revision?

THE PRESIDENT. Yes, but the tax revision, tax reform, tax cut will all be one package. Tax reform is long overdue. It is, as I have discovered recently, an extremely complicated matter. Scars are left over from previous tax reform efforts, some of which have been successful.

But I would say that the tax reductions, which may come next year or perhaps later—I think next year—will be tied integrally with an overall tax reform package.

Q. Would they be motivated by the state of the economy, Mr. President?

THE PRESIDENT. Yes, the rapidity with which tax cuts would be instituted would certainly be motivated by the state of the economy, whether or not it does need stimulation early or whether that stimulation would come late. The major unresolved question is how much impact this year's stimulus package is going to have in a beneficial way to keep our economy moving. I have good hopes about it. But we won't really know until about January or February.

REDUCTION OF OIL CONSUMPTION

Q. Mr. President, I take it from the strength of your opening statement that if Congress doesn't come up with an energy bill that you like, you would move administratively to do what you could to cut down on oil consumption.

Secretary Schlesinger has already talked about an import tax on foreign oil. And I would like to ask you if that is your view and also if you would then move to gasoline rationing administratively or some other measure?

THE PRESIDENT. We are considering all those options. And without knowing the form of the congressional action, it's hard for us to say now. If the bill in my opinion is not a substantial step forward, then I would not accept it after it's passed. And I say that very reluctantly, because it would mean that a substantial part of an entire year's work by the executive and the legislative branches of Government would have been wasted in the energy field.

I hope and believe that I can sign the bill as introduced to me. In the absence of new legislation, there are many options that will be considered within the present authority of the President and the new Department of Energy. Those that you mentioned are among the options, but we certainly have not decided on which option to choose.

Q. Mr. President, gasoline rationing is one of the options that you would seriously consider?

THE PRESIDENT. That's one of the options, yes.

RELATIONS WITH THE SENATE ON ENERGY

Q. Mr. President, Speaker O'Neill said yesterday that if you had made a mistake with your energy package in the Senate, it's perhaps that you didn't follow it along with your lobbyists on the Hill step by step as you did in the House. I'm wondering if you feel that your inexperience in Washington and the inexperience with the so-called outsiders you brought with you to Washington has caused your programs to suffer?

THE PRESIDENT. Well, to tell you the truth, I had more experience when the bill got to the Senate than I did when it got to the House first. We did put in an enormous of time with the House Members. I did myself with breakfast meetings two or three times a week and bringing the different subcommittee members and full committee members over.

The reason that I did that, more than I did with the Senate, was because this was when the bill was first introduced, not only to the Congress but to the people of our country. And there were many questions about the ultimate impact of the legislative proposals that we put forward. In the process, though, of the House meetings with me, with Dr. Schlesinger, and others, and the House debates and news coverage, of course, the Senate Members naturally became better acquainted with what our proposals were.

I think that in retrospect it would have helped had I had more meetings with the Members of the Senate. But the fact that I did not meet with them personally doesn't mean that they didn't have an adequate awareness of what our own proposals were and what their impact might be, because Dr. Schlesinger and all of his people have spent full time there, and I have met several times with the key leaders of the Senate about energy.

So, I don't deny the fact that that may have been a factor, but there are reasons for my having spent more time with the House in the initial stages of energy debate than I did with the Senate after the debate had been carried on in the House.

OIL COMPANY DIVESTITURE

Q. Mr. President, if you are serious about the oil industry and the oil lobbies working contrary to what you perceive the public interest to be, you've got a club in the closet, and that's divestiture. Why don't you move to break them up?

THE PRESIDENT. Well, there's a matter of raising too many issues at once. And I'm not trying to threaten anybody or use a club. It's obvious that the influence of the oil companies, both in the legislative process, in the executive branch of Government as well, in the economic structure of our country is enormous.

Part of that is inevitable, and part of it is not to be deplored—it's appropriate. There is a concern to me. For instance, in the uranium industry, which is another major and future alternative for large portions of our energy supplies, the oil companies already own about 50 percent of the uranium deposits. They have substantial holdings in coal.

But whether or not divestiture is needed is a matter on which I have not yet decided, and I don't think that now is the time to go into that detailed study or analysis.

URBAN POLICY

Q. Mr. President, last week you visited the South Bronx and took a tour of that area. Right now you have a task force under Mrs. Harris developing an urban policy. Sir, did your visit to the South Bronx and what you saw there—the vacant buildings and the unemployed people—have any impact on your thoughts on what kind of urban policy we should have and what you are going to present to the Congress?

THE PRESIDENT. Yes, it certainly did have an impact on me and my own conscience. It was not the first time I had been to the South Bronx. I went there as a candidate.

And I think it's important in two ways—three ways. One is to let me understand, personally, the devastation in the South Bronx, and similar places like it throughout the country—that's not unique. It's good for me to consult with my Cabinet officers. And they are now visiting the South Bronx and other similar areas. I think when I am in Detroit later on this month I'll also talk to families who live in this kind of devastated area.

It's important for me to demonstrate accurately my deep concern about this urban deterioration. And it's also important, through the news media—the radio and newspaper reports, the television pictures—to let the American people know that such places exist in our country.

I think the bill that I signed this week, the Housing and Urban Development Act of 1977,[1] will provide us with a base or a framework on which we can make substantial improvements in the urban areas.

---

[1] For the President's remarks on signing H.R. 6655 into law, see page 1777 of this volume.

The formulae that are being put forward now—and the Congress is accepting them—will orient more and more of the rehabilitation money of all kinds to the more blighted areas of our country, both rural and urban.

So, it's an educational process for me, an assurance to people who live in those areas that we do indeed care, and also an educational process for the people of the country who don't know about these instances.

BRIGADIER GENERAL TORRIJOS OF PANAMA

Q. Mr. President, Panama's General Torrijos will come to this country late this week in an atmosphere in which a lot of confusion has been generated over the language of the treaty and how that will be used.

How are you going to use his visit? What is he going to do here? And will you perhaps get into the language of the treaty itself in terms of trying to clarify what he thinks?

THE PRESIDENT. I think the language of the treaty is adequate. I've had a chance to meet with General Torrijos at length on his other visit here and also to meet on one occasion with both the negotiators from Panama and our own country when the negotiations were at a crucial stage. Both General Torrijos and I are faced with a difficult political problem—as he described it accurately, to sell the same product in two different markets.

We are determined that the canal will be open, neutral, and free for use as long as it is there beyond the end of this century.

We do not have any inclination to intervene in the internal affairs of Panama. And when we say in this country, "We reserve the right to take action to keep the canal open," when they say in their country, "We do not intend to permit the United States to intervene in the internal affairs of Panama," we are both right. But the language didn't go into that much detail.

We agreed for expeditious passage of American and Panamanian ships through the Panama Canal when necessary. That language to me is adequate. But that particular phrase, "expeditious passage," has been interpreted differently here than it has in Panama.

I want to be sure that the American people, when the Senate votes ratification, and the Panamanian people, when they have a plebiscite or referendum on the same treaty the 23d day of this month, both understand the terms of the treaty very clearly.

So, General Torrijos and I will be meeting tomorrow to make sure that we have a common agreement on what the treaty means, and we may or may not issue some clarifying statement. But it's a constructive proposal, because both of us want to be sure that our people don't labor under any misapprehensions about the intentions or interpretation of the other country.

HUMPHREY-HAWKINS BILL

Q. Sir, obviously you have made statements regarding your energy proposal and it being the most important issue you will face during your term. But full employment, national full employment, is a topic you discussed with the Congressional Black Caucus numerous times. Have you made a final decision regarding the Humphrey-Hawkins bill?

THE PRESIDENT. During the campaign I promised to support the Humphrey-Hawkins bill, but expressed some concern about the detailed factors included in the Humphrey-Hawkins bill at that time and did not approve the version as it then existed. It's been constantly amended over the last 2 or 3 years since introduction.

My staff have recently been working with Congressman Hawkins, with Senator Humphrey on the telephone, with their staffs, and others, to evolve a full employment bill that we could indeed support without equivocation or hesitancy. We are making good progress about that. And I would guess that within the next few days we would be prepared, if things go well, to announce our support of the Humphrey-Hawkins bill.

PANAMA CANAL TREATIES

Q. Mr. President, back on the canal issue, if you cannot come to some mutually agreeable statement with General Torrijos tomorrow, aren't the canal treaties doomed?

THE PRESIDENT. Well, I think it would be very difficult to get ratification of the treaties if there is any doubt that General Torrijos and I, the Panamanian people and the United States citizens, agree on what the canal treaties mean.

I don't believe there's any need to amend the treaty language. To me it's clear because I've been involved in the discussions with the negotiators and also with General Torrijos. But it may be necessary, after he and I discuss the situation, to issue some clarifying statement. I've not talked to him personally the last few days. I did extend an invitation by letter. He has been in the Middle East, the Scandinavian countries, Europe, and he's coming back here tonight, I think.

But I did extend a written letter to him asking him to meet with me. He was eager to do so. And we will be meeting tomorrow. But I think the clarification is crucial. A written agreement or modification to the treaty may or may not be necessary. I don't think we need to modify the treaty itself.

ENERGY LEGISLATION

Q. Mr. President, what was the moral equivalent of war last spring has now become the object of most of the attention of your administration until Congress is out—a last-ditch effort perhaps to salvage what you can in the Senate.

Certainly that's not entirely the fault of the oil lobbies. Shouldn't the administration and people in the Senate, like Russell Long, take some of the blame?

THE PRESIDENT. Yes. I take my share of the blame. I don't know how to define it. I think that Senator Russell Long is working long and hard to come up with an acceptable energy package. And my own hope is that before this year is over, legislation at least equivalent to what the House passed will be in its final version.

But I'm not trying to blame all the problem on the oil companies. The grabbing for the financial rewards is what I deplore in the oil companies. And that is a major issue on gas deregulation and also in the price structure for oil.

Part of the blame falls on me, my predecessors, and the American people. We are simply wasting too much energy. For the same standard of living, we use twice as much energy as is used in Japan, West Germany, Sweden, and other countries of that kind. So, we've got to cut down on our waste through conservation measures, voluntary action, and also a realization of the seriousness of this question.

And I am also concerned as Commander in Chief of our country about the serious security implications of becoming increasingly dependent upon foreign oil supplies which may for some reason be interrupted. So, I consider this to be a crucial issue, not just economically, not just who gets the gross profits, but also for our own Nation's security.

U.S. STEEL INDUSTRY

Q. Mr. President, you have a special meeting here today on the steel industry, and also you have a special task force working on the domestic steel problem.

But what do you see, offering on a more immediate basis, to stop the loss of jobs in the U.S. steel industry—perhaps through some sort of voluntary quotas with other steel-exporting countries?

THE PRESIDENT. Well, steel imports are just one part of a fairly large number of problems that affect the United States steel industry and which, I might say, affect the steel industry all over the world.

I met with the Prime Minister of Luxembourg the other day, and he said, "The biggest single problem that I have is the low quantity of orders for my steel products and the relatively low price." The Luxembourg steel industry is in just as bad a shape. The rest of them are, too.

One of the things that have taken place already is a voluntary reduction in exports to our country by some of the other steel producers in West Germany and Japan. But that's an exceptionally artificial and simplistic approach to the problem of the steel industry.

Our analysis has shown that reduction in imports would not materially increase the supplies or the demand for steel among our own American suppliers, that any benefit to them financially would probably come from greatly increased prices, which would have to be paid for by the American consumers. It's an extremely complicated question.

The general, overall world recession or slow growth means that you are just not building as many things all over the world that require steel.

But my hope and expectation is to learn as much as I can, personally, about the steel industry, all of its problems, and then to propose to the Congress and to the steel industry itself and to negotiate perhaps with other countries that export steel to us a resolution of these problems.

It's longstanding. It's historic. The trends have been there, of course, long before I came in office. But this afternoon will be the first time I will meet with steel producers, steel laborers or workers, and the interested congressional Members.

I have a task force headed by Mr. Solomon in the Treasury Department. And he's working on a multidepartmental basis to give me specific recommendations for Government action. This will be coming to me later on this month. So, we are acting very rapidly on it to try to deal with the longstanding, chronic problem that exists not only in our own country but also in other countries around the world.

ENERGY SHORTAGE

Q. Mr. President, you touched on this just a moment ago, but I wonder if you would elaborate. You talk about energy being a crucial issue yet it does not seem to have caught on in the country——

THE PRESIDENT. I know.

Q. ——as an issue. Do you have any views on why that is?

THE PRESIDENT. Well, you know, it caught on in the country in 1973 when our oil imports were reduced substantially and there were waiting lines at the gaspumps and the price rose quite rapidly. That was just the first warning sign of an inevitable shortage of oil and natural gas. It aroused the American consciousness this past winter when natural gas supplies were scarce, and we had schools close down, factories shut; transportation was interrupted. These are just the first warning signs. It's going to get worse instead of better. And I don't think there's any responsible international economist or analyst who doesn't agree with this fact.

Now, there are several ways that it can be dealt with. One is to increase production, which we are trying to do on a worldwide basis. Another one is to cut down on consumption. Another one is to develop alternative or new kinds of energy supplies. But there's no doubt that the American people at this point simply do not recognize the seriousness of the present problem and the future problems, because it doesn't touch them individually yet.

But I don't want to see the American consciousness raised because of a devastating crisis that they have to experience. We are trying to prevent the crisis, not just react to one.

DOMESTIC POLICY PROPOSALS

Q. Mr. President, you are now focusing on energy, but some of your critics have been saying that you are doing too many things and all at the same time. What is your response to that?

THE PRESIDENT. Well, I think if anyone analyzes already what the Congress has done in response to my request and on their own initiative, and the major legislation that they have presently before them, they would see that we have made substantial progress.

I doubt that anyone would want to eliminate a particular proposal that we have put forward—the establishment of the Department of Energy, reorganization of the executive branch of Government, or reform to our very complicated and wasteful welfare system, and so forth.

I don't think we are dealing with too many issues. The fact is that these issues are difficult, they are controversial, they are complicated. And I think we are making fairly good progress. But in my mind, on domestic affairs, there is no doubt that the energy question is the most important.

ROBERT H. MENDELSOHN

Q. Mr. President, if I could have a clarification here. I wonder if you could clarify the ethical standards of the administration. Is it now and has it been——

THE PRESIDENT. Did you say "ethical standards?"

Q. The question was asked about this two press conferences ago. Is it now and has it been the position of the Carter administration in the past or present that illegal, unethical, and/or improper conduct as well as actual, potential conflicts of interest and the appearance of impropriety would not be tolerated?

THE PRESIDENT. That's correct.

Q. That being the case, in light of the fact that the California Fair Political Practices Committee decided to charge a campaign committee of Robert H. Mendelsohn, the Assistant Secretary of the Interior for Policy, Budget, and Administration-designate, with illegal conduct, which you said you would not tolerate, in connection with accepting a total of $16,500 in watered campaign contributions—by the way, the reports were signed by Mr. Mendelsohn and sort of a pro forma campaign treasurer who said that he really didn't know anything about the details and Mr. Mendelsohn knew all about the finances, or indicated that— why are you continuing to support the Mendelsohn nomination, especially in the wake of the trauma we have just been through on Watergate?

THE PRESIDENT. I have to say I am not familiar with that case. And I don't know if what you've described are just allegations or whether improprieties have been proven.

Q. It is the report of the committee——

THE PRESIDENT. But I'm sure that if any of those allegations are proven, that neither I nor the Secretary of Interior nor the congressional committee who will confirm his nomination will approve of it.

FRANK CORMIER [Associated Press]. Thank you, Mr. President.

THE PRESIDENT. Thank you very much.

NOTE: President Carter's seventeenth news conference began at 10:30 a.m. in Room 450 of the Old Executive Office Building. It was broadcast live on radio and television.

United States Ambassador to Guinea

Nomination of Oliver S. Crosby.
October 13, 1977

The President today announced that he will nominate Oliver S. Crosby, of Tacoma, Wash., to be Ambassador Extraordinary and Plenipotentiary of the United States to the Republic of Guinea. He would replace William C. Harrop, resigned.

Crosby was born April 27, 1920, in Philadelphia, Pa. He received a B.A. from the University of Pennsylvania in 1946 and an M.A. from Johns Hopkins School of Advanced International Studies in 1947. He served in the U.S. Navy from 1942 to 1946.

Crosby joined the Foreign Service in 1947 and served as consular-political officer in Athens until 1950. From 1950 to 1952, he was political officer in Tabriz, and in 1952–53 he took German language and area training at Harvard University.

From 1953 to 1958, Crosby was transportation officer, then economic officer in Berlin. He was at the State Department from 1958 to 1962 as an intelligence research specialist, then a foreign affairs officer. He was political officer in Nicosia from 1962 to 1964 and attended the National War College in 1964–65.

From 1965 to 1968, Crosby was deputy chief of mission in Bamako. He was country director for southern African affairs at the State Department from 1968 to 1972, and since 1972 has been deputy chief of mission in Lagos.

United States Ambassador to Mauritania

Nomination of E. Gregory Kryza.
October 13, 1977

The President today announced that he will nominate E. Gregory Kryza, of Falls Church, Va., to be Ambassador Extraordinary and Plenipotentiary of the United States to the Islamic Republic of Mauritania. He would replace Holsey G. Handyside, resigned.

Kryza was born March 12, 1922, in Detroit, Mich. He served in the U.S. Navy from 1943 to 1947 and from 1950 to 1952.

From 1947 to 1950, Kryza was a fiscal accountant for the Department of the Navy in Tangier and Ciudad Trujillo. From 1952 to 1954, he was disbursing officer in Curaçao for the State Department, and from 1954 to 1957 he was budget and fiscal officer in Brussels.

Kryza was budget and fiscal officer in Belgrade from 1957 to 1959. From 1959 to 1963, he was at the State Department as a supervisory audit officer, then supervisory budget analyst. He was administrative officer in Nairobi from 1963 to 1967.

Kryza attended the Air War College in 1967–68, and from 1968 to 1970 he was administrative counselor in Kinshasa. He served as administrative counselor in Rio de Janeiro from 1970 to 1971 and in Brasília in 1971.

From 1971 to 1974, Kryza was a Foreign Service inspector at the State Department. Since 1974 he has been Executive Director of the Bureau of African Affairs.

National Day of Prayer, 1977

Proclamation 4532.   October 13, 1977

By the President of the United States of America

A Proclamation

Throughout our Nation's history Americans of all faiths have turned to Divine Providence for the strength and wisdom to meet whatever challenges were put before them with honor and dignity.

The tasks we face today are as great as those faced by any generation of Americans. Our actions and choices will, for many years to come, affect not only ourselves but all the peoples with whom we share this tiny planet.

It is therefore fitting that we set aside a day of prayer and meditation to ask the Almighty for the vision to see our duty as individuals and as a Nation and for the courage to pursue it, even at the cost of personal or collective sacrifice.

Recognizing this, the Congress by joint resolution approved April 17, 1952 (36 U.S.C. 185; 66 Stat. 64) has called upon the President to set aside a suitable day each year as a National Day of Prayer.

Now, THEREFORE, I, JIMMY CARTER, President of the United States of America, do hereby proclaim Thursday, December 15, 1977, as National Day of Prayer. I ask all Americans to join with me on that day in asking God's help that we may see and understand our responsibilities and discharge them in a manner that befits a just and good people.

IN WITNESS WHEREOF, I have hereunto set my hand this thirteenth day of October, in the year of our Lord nineteen hundred seventy-seven, and of the Independence of the United States of America the two hundred and second.

JIMMY CARTER

[Filed with the Office of the Federal Register, 11:02 a.m., October 14, 1977]

NOTE: The text of the proclamation was released on October 14.

Federal Communications Commission

Nomination of Tyrone Brown To Be a Member. October 14, 1977

The President today announced that he will nominate Tyrone Brown, of Washington, D.C., to be a member of the Federal Communications Commission for the unexpired term of 7 years from July 1, 1972. He would succeed Benjamin L. Hooks, resigned.

Brown was born November 5, 1942, in Norfolk, Va. He received an A.B. from Hamilton College in 1964 and an LL.B. from Cornell Law School in 1967.

Brown was law clerk to Chief Justice Earl Warren in 1967, and an associate with a Washington law firm from 1968 to 1970. He was a special investigator for the President's Commission on Campus Unrest in 1970. From 1970 to 1971, he served as assistant to Senator Edmund S. Muskie, then staff director of the Intergovernmental Relations Subcommittee of the Senate Government Operations Committee.

From 1971 to 1974, Brown was director and vice president for legal affairs of Post-Newsweek Stations, Inc., and its subsidiary companies. Since 1974 he has been with the Washington law firm of Caplin & Drysdale.

Treaty Concerning the Permanent Neutrality and Operation of the Panama Canal

Joint Statement of Understanding Issued Following a Meeting Between the President and Brigadier General Omar Torrijos Herrera of Panama. October 14, 1977

Under the Treaty Concerning the Permanent Neutrality and Operation of the Panama Canal (the Neutrality Treaty), Panama and the United States have the responsibility to assure that the Panama Canal will remain open and secure to ships of all nations. The correct interpretation of this principle is that each of the two countries shall, in accordance with their respective constitutional processes, defend the Canal against any threat to the regime of neutrality, and consequently shall have the right to act against any aggression or threat directed against the Canal or against the peaceful transit of vessels through the Canal.

This does not mean, nor shall it be interpreted as a right of intervention of the United States in the internal affairs of Panama. Any United States action will be directed at insuring that the Canal will remain open, secure and accessible, and it shall never be directed against the territorial integrity or political independence of Panama.

The Neutrality Treaty provides that the vessels of war and auxiliary vessels of the United States and Panama will be entitled to transit the Canal expeditiously. This is intended, and it shall so be interpreted, to assure the transit of such vessels through the Canal as quickly as possible, without any impediment, with expedited treatment, and in case of need or emergency, to go to the head of the line of vessels in order to transit the Canal rapidly.

1793

Death of Bing Crosby

Statement by the President.   October 14, 1977

For all the roads he traveled in his memorable career, Bing Crosby remained a gentleman, proof that a great talent can be a good man despite the pressures of show business. He lived a life his fans around the world felt was typically American: successful yet modest, casual but elegant. He revolutionized popular music, sang the biggest hit of all time, yet was a man who would be at ease in any American home.

Digest of Other White House Announcements

The following listing includes the President's daily schedule and other items of general interest as announced by the White House Press Office during the period covered by this issue. Events and announcements printed elsewhere in the issue are not included.

October 10

The President returned to the White House after a weekend stay at Camp David, Md.

The President met at the White House with Secretary of the Treasury W. Michael Blumenthal, James T. McIntyre, Jr., Acting Director of the Office of Management and Budget, Charles L. Schultze, Chairman of the Council of Economic Advisers, Laurence N. Woodworth, Assistant Secretary of the Treasury for Tax Policy, and Stuart E. Eizenstat, Assistant to the President for Domestic Affairs and Policy, to discuss tax reform.

October 11

The President met at the White House with:

—Zbigniew Brzezinski, Assistant to the President for National Security Affairs;
—Senate Majority Leader Robert C. Byrd, Senate Minority Leader Howard H. Baker, Jr., and Senators Clifford P. Case, Frank Church, Alan Cranston, James O. Eastland, Barry Goldwater, Daniel K. Inouye, Henry M. Jackson, Sam Nunn, John J. Sparkman, John C. Stennis, and Ted Stevens, to discuss the Panama Canal treaties;
—Members of Congress from Pennsylvania to discuss economic conditions in the Delaware Valley;
—officers of the National Association of Counties;
—Secretary of Housing and Urban Development Patricia Roberts Harris.

October 12

The President met at the White House with:

—Dr. Brzezinski;
—the Democratic congressional leadership;
—Vice President Walter F. Mondale, Adm. Stansfield Turner, Director of Central Intelligence, and Dr. Brzezinski;
—Vice President Mondale;
—Mr. McIntyre.

The President attended a briefing on the Panama Canal treaties, given for State officials and business and political leaders from Pennsylvania, Vermont, and Minnesota in the State Dining Room.

October 13

The President met at the White House with:

—Dr. Brzezinski;

—Mrs. Carter, for lunch;

—Kenneth M. Curtis, Chairman of the Democratic National Committee.

The President met with representatives of the Young Presidents' Organization, Inc., who were meeting with administration officials in the Old Executive Office Building.

The President attended the White House Conference on Steel, which was chaired by Ambassador Robert S. Strauss, Special Representative for Trade Negotiations, in the Roosevelt Room. Participants included representatives from the steel industry, organized labor, manufacturers, economists, environmentalists, consumer groups, Members of Congress from steel-producing States, and White House and other administration officials.

The President and Mrs. Carter hosted a barbecue supper on the South Lawn for 500 members of the "Peanut Brigade," a group of Georgians who campaigned for Mr. Carter beginning with the early 1976 primary campaigns for the Democratic Presidential nomination.

October 14

The President met at the White House with:

—Dr. Brzezinski;

—Secretary of State Cyrus R. Vance and Dr. Brzezinski;

—a group of Congressmen from Western States to discuss water policy;

—Dr. Schultze;

—a group of editors, publishers, and broadcasters (transcript will be printed next week);

—Ambassador Strauss.

The President attended a reception for members of the Finance Council of the Democratic National Committee in the State Dining Room.

The President announced that he has accorded Patricia Derian the personal rank of Ambassador while serving as Chairman of the U.S. Delegation to the International Conference of the Red Cross, to be held at Bucharest, Romania, from October 15 to October 21.

The President announced that he will nominate George H. Aldrich for the rank of Ambassador while serving as the Deputy Special Representative for the Law of the Sea Conference and Deputy Chief of Delegation.

The White House issued a correction concerning the October 7 press release on the nomination of Theodore M. Hesburgh for the rank of Ambassador while serving as Chairman of the U.S. Delegation to the United Nations Conference on Science and Technology Development (see page 1751). The release stated that the conference will be held in Geneva in 1979. In fact, no decision has been made on where the conference will be held.

NOMINATIONS SUBMITTED TO THE SENATE

The following list does not include promotions of members of the Uniformed Services, nominations to the Service Academies, or nominations of Foreign Service officers.

Submitted October 11, 1977

ROBERT E. WHITE, of Massachusetts, a Foreign Service officer of Class one, to be Ambassador Extraordinary and Plenipotentiary of the United States of America to Paraguay.

Submitted October 12, 1977

JOHN E. DOWNS, of Missouri, for the rank of Minister during the tenure of his service as the Representative of the United States of America on the Council of the International Civil Aviation Organization.

GEORGE A. PEAPPLES, of Michigan, to be an Assistant Secretary of the Navy, vice Gary Dean Penisten.

NOMINATIONS—Continued
Submitted October 12—Continued

GERALD L. KLERMAN, of Massachusetts, to be Administrator of the Alcohol, Drug Abuse, and Mental Health Administration, vice James D. Isbister, resigning.

The following-named persons to be members of the National Museum Services Board for the terms indicated:

For a term of 1 year:

DOUGLAS DILLON, of New York
NEIL HARRIS, of Illinois
JOAN MONDALE, of Minnesota

For a term of 2 years:

MAMIE P. CLARK, of New York
BENJAMIN W. HAZARD, of California
NANCY NEGLEY, of Texas

For a term of 3 years:

GARY K. CLARKE, of Kansas
GEORGE HORSE CAPTURE, of Montana
CHARLOTTE FERST, of Georgia

For a term of 4 years:

LEWIS DAVIS, of New York
RAUL A. LOPEZ, of California
E. LELAND WEBBER, of Illinois

For a term of 5 years:

LLOYD HEZEKIAH, of New York
PETER H. RAVEN, of Missouri
GEORGE C. SEYBOLT, of Massachusetts

Submitted October 13, 1977

OLIVER S. CROSBY, of Washington, a Foreign Service officer of Class one, to be Ambassador Extraordinary and Plenipotentiary of the United States of America to the Republic of Guinea.

E. GREGORY KRYZA, of Virginia, a Foreign Service officer of Class one, to be Ambassador Extraordinary and Plenipotentiary of the United States of America to the Islamic Republic of Mauritania.

HERMAN SILLAS, JR., of California, to be United States Attorney for the Eastern District of California for the term of 4 years, vice D. Dwayne Keyes.

GEORGE L. MILLER, of North Carolina, to be United States Marshal for the Middle District of North Carolina for the term of 4 years, vice P. Ellis Almond.

NOMINATIONS—Continued
Submitted October 13—Continued

JOHN A. ROE, of Iowa, to be United States Marshal for the Northern District of Iowa for the term of 4 years, vice Melvin A. Hove, term expired.

CHECKLIST OF WHITE HOUSE
PRESS RELEASES

The following releases of the Office of the White House Press Secretary, distributed during the period covered by this issue, are not included in the issue.

Released October 11, 1977

Fact sheet: Reorganization Plan No. 2 of 1977—Agency for International Communication

Released October 12, 1977

Fact sheet: Housing and Community Development Act of 1977

News conference: on the President's meeting with Lt. Gen. Olusegun Obasanjo of Nigeria—by Jerrold L. Schecter, Associate Press Secretary

Announcement: the President's meeting with Brig. Gen. Omar Torrijos Herrera of Panama at the White House on October 14

Released October 13, 1977

Announcement: nomination of Herman Sillas, Jr., to be United States Attorney for the Eastern District of California, George L. Miller to be United States Marshal for the Middle District of North Carolina, and John A. Roe to be United States Marshal for the Northern District of Iowa

News conference: on the White House Conference on Steel—by Ambassador Robert S. Strauss, Special Representative for Trade Negotiations, Secretary of the Treasury W. Michael Blumenthal, Edgar Speer, chairman of the board of U.S. Steel, and Lloyd McBride, president of the United Steel Workers

Released October 14, 1977

News conference: on the statement of understanding issued by the United States and Panama on the Treaty Concerning the Permanent Neutrality and Operation of the Panama Canal—by Ambassador Sol M. Linowitz, conegotiator for the United States in the Panama Canal negotiations

ACTS APPROVED BY THE PRESIDENT

Approved October 7, 1977

S. 213_____ Public Law 95–125
An act to amend the Accounting and Auditing Act of 1950 to provide for the audit, by the Comptroller General, of the Internal Revenue Service and of the Bureau of Alcohol, Tobacco, and Firearms.

Approved October 8, 1977

S. 1307_____ Public Law 95–126
An act to deny entitlement to veterans' benefits to certain persons who would otherwise become so entitled solely by virtue of the administrative upgrading under temporarily revised standards of other than honorable discharges from service during the Vietnam era: to require case-by-case review under uniform, historically consistent, generally applicable standards and procedures prior to the award of veterans' benefits to persons administratively discharged under other than honorable conditions from active military, naval, or air service; and for other purposes.

ACTS APPROVED—Continued

Approved October 12, 1977

H.R. 6655_____ Public Law 95–128
Housing and Community Development Act of 1977.

S. 1435_____ Public Law 95–127
An act to amend the Federal Election Campaign Act of 1971 to extend the authorization of appropriations contained in such Act.

Approved October 13, 1977

H.J. Res. 626_____ Public Law 95–130
A joint resolution making continuing appropriations for the fiscal year 1978, and for other purposes.

H.R. 5645_____ Public Law 95–132
Civil Rights Commission Authorization Act of 1977.

H.R. 6530_____ Public Law 95–131
An act to amend the District of Columbia Self-Government and Governmental Reorganization Act with respect to the borrowing authority of the District of Columbia, and for other purposes.

S. 1331_____ Public Law 95–129
An act to provide for the establishment of a Center for the Book in the Library of Congress, and for other purposes.

Interview With the President

*Remarks and a Question-and-Answer Session
With a Group of Editors and News
Directors.   October 14, 1977*

THE PRESIDENT. I apologize for interrupting your meeting. This has been kind of a busy day for us. We had an extra hour and a half or 2 hours this morning with General Torrijos from Panama. And we had not put it on our long-range schedule. But it was very productive, and it's put me a little bit behind.

I think it might be good for me to make just an opening statement to you about some of the things on which we are working during these last few weeks of the congressional session.

ADMINISTRATION POLICIES

The number one issue for us on the domestic scene, by far, is energy. We've got a very acceptable energy package from the House. So far we've gotten practically nothing from the Senate. But they'll be considering what to do within the next few days. We hope to have a productive conference committee, as is well understood by many of the Senators, and then the joint package will go back to the House and Senate for an up or down vote.

I think the Members of Congress recognize the seriousness of our problem. We've got a terrible adverse trade balance because of oil imports. We'll probably import about $45 billion worth of oil this year, which puts us about $30 billion in the hole on trade balance.

As you can well see, we'd have a $15 billion or so surplus if it wasn't for oil imports, which are very excessive. This is one of the problems. It makes us much more susceptible to severe damage in the future if those oil imports should be interrupted for any reason. And, of course, the inevitability of increased shortages means that we've got to start conserving oil and natural gas.

We are working on several foreign matters. I just mentioned the Torrijos visit this morning. I think that his and my statement, which has already been prepared—it's not been released yet, I don't believe—will successfully resolve the major difference of interpretation that has been raised about our right to defend the canal and also about the right of our ships to have expeditious passage through the canal.

And, of course, we are also very interested to point out that we have no intention to intervene in the internal affairs of Panama in order to challenge their sovereignty. But the questions have arisen both in Panama and in our country, and we want to get those differences explained. There are no differences between me and Torrijos or among our negotiators, and there never have been since the text was approved.

Another thing that we're working on that's been highly publicized is the SALT agreement. I think we are approaching a settlement with the Soviets, if they continue to act in as constructive a fashion as they've exhibited the last few weeks.

We are working on a comprehensive test ban treaty. Now we are both permitted to test nuclear weapons up to 150,000 tons, which, as you know, is seven or eight times larger than the Hiroshima explosion. But we would like to eliminate those tests altogether. We personally would prefer to eliminate all peaceful nuclear devices being tested. So far, the Soviets have not been willing to agree to that.

But we've already got good, substantial progress, I believe, assured. We are trying to agree with the Soviets to prevent any arms buildup in the Indian Ocean, to prevent attacks on one another's satellites in space, and to prohibit chemical, biological, radiological warfare.

Lately, I've been encouraged. We've been able to get the Soviets, for the first time, to take a moderate position on the Middle East. We think the recent American-Soviet statement has been very constructive there, and we're making slow, tedious progress toward a Geneva conference.

This is one of the most complicated international questions which has ever been addressed, I guess, in the history of human beings. We have to negotiate with the Soviets, who are our cochairmen and have been since 1973. We're negotiating with the Lebanese, with the Syrians, with the Jordanians, with the Egyptians, individually. We're negotiating between each one of those countries and the Israelis.

We are also negotiating among the Arab countries, who have differences, and we're trying to keep a good and successful presentation to the American public about what we are doing, without betraying the confidences of the heads of state who deal directly with me.

I've enjoyed being President so far. It's a job with obviously great challenge and an adequate diversity so that we don't ever suffer from boredom. [*Laughter*]

As you probably have noticed, many of the items that I've described—and I could go down the list with welfare reform and tax reform and social security, and so forth, and our new farm bill, dealing with the problems of the urban areas—are all highly controversial, inevitably, predictably, and almost all of them have been delayed too long.

Some should have been addressed many years ago. Some of them have been in existence as problems for decades, even generations. But I feel encouraged about them.

We have a good working relationship with Congress. We've all learned a lot since we've been up here. And one of the best things about my own administration, from a personal point of view, is when I am able to communicate directly with the people back home.

This is an unprecedented effort that Jody has initiated to bring you into the White House. And I don't think we've ever had a session with television, radio, and newspaper people like you that we didn't have innovative questions that brought a fairly substantial news story. I don't know exactly how Jody handles the embargo, but I think they have been productive; I know for me.

I would be glad now to answer any questions that you might have for awhile.

QUESTIONS

STEEL STRIKE

Q. Mr. President, northern Minnesota and northern Michigan are both suffering from the steel strike. Now, about 20,000 people are off in a 3-month-old steel strike. The Governor of Minnesota has been attempting and has met, I understand, with some members of the White House staff trying to end the strike. Is there any indication, sir, that you may get involved personally to try to end the strike? And, if so, how has the strike up to this point affected the current steel situation?

THE PRESIDENT. No, I don't have any inclination to get involved in the strike. I believe that it's better for us not to do this, because if both parties feel that the White House or the Labor Department is going to get precipitously involved in the negotiations, they're not nearly so eager to negotiate themselves.

Obviously, when I reach a point of thinking that the national security might be endangered, that either the ore stocks or the steel stocks are being reduced too much, then I would not hesitate to get involved. But as is the case in the longshoremen's strike, as has been the case in the past with coal and other very important industries, my inclination is not to get involved in those. And I might say that Ray Marshall, the Secretary of Labor, shares my belief very deeply.

We did have a meeting, as you know, yesterday on the basic steel industry. It was surprisingly productive and suprisingly successful and surprisingly harmonious. I dreaded going into the meeting— [*laughter*]—but it turned out very well.

The steel leaders said that they did not want to see import quotas established, they did not want to see import tariffs raised, they did not want to build a wall around our country in order to prevent competition; they wanted open trade and fair trade.

We will go into depth in an analysis of the entire steel industry between now and, I'd say, 4 weeks from now, at which time

the recommendations will come to me from Mr. Tony Solomon,[1] who is a very highly qualified person in this area. And at that time, I will release it to the public after very close consultation with steel executives, consumers, and labor leaders representing the steel workers, Members of Congress that were there yesterday. I think it's going to be a very constructive thing.

As you know, our American steel industry is crucial to us. It's now operating at about a 70-percent capacity. There are large steel imports which are legitimate and needed, in my opinion, to ensure competition. But we certainly do not want to have illegal sales of foreign steel in our country below the cost of production and transportation. That kind of sale is illegal. It has been occurring for the last number of years. We're determined to stamp it out.

Q. If I may follow up on that for just a second, was there any indication, Mr. President, in yesterday's meeting, that the strike has had any effect on the steel industry now?

THE PRESIDENT. Well, to answer your question specifically about the meeting yesterday, no, that did not come up while I was there. The threat of continued strike is always present. That's the leverage that a strike presents. Sometimes when inventories are very low, the strike has an immediate adverse impact. Sometimes when inventories are fairly substantial, as is the case in this instance, the threat of a continued strike is always serious. But that did not come up in the meeting yesterday.

UNDOCUMENTED ALIENS

Q. Mr. President, we have some serious troubles in El Paso right now with illegal

---

[1] Anthony M. Solomon, Under Secretary of the Treasury for Monetary Affairs.

aliens. And I would like to know what you're going to do to help control the illegal aliens, particularly in El Paso, when our border patrol agents have been cut down. When you were running for office, you were going to help us increase the size of our border patrol. We only have 325 border patrol agents guarding both the Canadian and Mexican border, and that's not enough; they're eating us alive.

THE PRESIDENT. Well, we have completed now the drafting of illegal alien legislation. We call them undocumented workers or undocumented aliens.

Again, this is a very complicated subject, as you know—to protect the basic civil rights of people who might be from a Chinese family or from a Mexican family and who are here legally, to be sure that employers don't discriminate against them just because of the color of their skin. That's a problem.

Another one is the demand among employers of adequate labor supply, particularly in areas where it's seasonal and also in areas where the available domestic labor doesn't fill the need. We have as many as 7 or 8 million illegal aliens. They're coming in now at a rate that's hard to estimate, maybe approaching a million a year. They obviously contribute to our unemployment rate. And we're determined to both reduce the flow of illegal aliens, to register those that are here, let them stay here temporarily, and then give them the freedom to move back and forth across the border without any establishment of citizenship rights and, as has been the case in the past, historically, to maybe give permanent residency rights to those that have been in our country as long as 7 or 8 years.

I don't know what the Congress will do about that part of it, but it's a very comprehensive bill; it's been worked out after hard debate and close study. Along with

that will be an increase in the number of personnel assigned to patrol the borders and also a much closer correlation among the different Federal agencies that have that responsibility.

Q. What are you going to do about the people, particularly in our part of the country—the Mexican-Americans are the ones that are fighting the amnesty program. And if amnesty is not accepted among our people and can be pursued by the Government, then what alternative do you have to suggest?

THE PRESIDENT. Well, amnesty is a gross oversimplification. The only thing that we are doing is for those that have been in this country since 1970, 7 years, to give them the legal right to stay here. They won't be citizens, but they do have a right to apply for citizenship.

The ones that have come in since, if they register, they would have a temporary right to work. But they could only— I think that—I've forgotten the exact details of the bill—but I think they could only do that for a year, then they would have to leave our country. And they would have the right to apply for work permits.

But to distinguish between those who have become legal citizens, that we don't want to hurt, to distinguish between those who have been here for a long time and have performed well, established homes, and who don't yet have citizenship rights but who want it in the future is another question. To try to find out who and how many illegal aliens we presently have and to have an ability to send them back home is a third level of the question. And the fourth question is to keep the illegal aliens from crossing the border. But just to say that the entire complicated program consists of amnesty is a ridiculous oversimplification.

The only amnesty involved is one that has historically been the case when about every 7 years, in retroactivity, you say that those that came in before 1970 or before 1962, you know, do have the right to stay here and ultimately apply for citizenship.

SELECTION OF FEDERAL JUDICIAL OFFICERS

Q. Mr. President, two U.S. attorneys, Philip Van Dam of Detroit and Jonathan Goldstein of New Jersey, criticized you for not fulfilling your campaign pledge to select Federal prosecutors on a merit basis. Mr. Goldstein has a nationwide reputation as a tough and honest prosecutor and, in fact, was cited by Federal authorities as having done an outstanding job.

You had said before your election that topflight prosecutors would be retained. And Mr. Goldstein now says that he is a victim of the political spoils system which you have decried.

Can you tell me if there were other than political reasons for Mr. Goldstein's reluctant departure, or would you otherwise comment on that question?

THE PRESIDENT. Quite often, I've observed in a case like this that the incumbent officeholder considers himself or herself to be superior to the one who replaces that person. [*Laughter*] And I'm sure that Mr. Goldstein's predecessor felt that he was better qualified than Mr. Goldstein when he came in. In both these instances, the case was decided on the basis of merit. I don't think anyone has alleged, other than Mr. Goldstein or Van Dam and their own close friends, that they are decidedly better qualified than their replacements. And all of our appointments have been made on the basis of merit.

We have turned down literally hundreds of recommendations from many sources because we did not consider them at least as well qualified or better qualified than the incumbents. I cannot say that we have never made a mistake.

These two have been highly publicized, primarily because Mr. Goldstein feels very strongly that he is better qualified than anyone we could choose as his replacement.

But historically this has been the case, and I don't think anyone has ever gone as far as we have, myself and the Attorney General, to make these appointments on the basis of merit. In all circuit judgeships, we have selection panels—first time in the history of our country—where a group of distinguished people, both legal and nonlawyers, meet and give me a recommendation, through the Attorney General, of the five best qualified people in that area to fill vacancies, and then we choose from those five who ought to be appointed.

As you know, the Senate plays a major role in the selection of district judges and also U.S. attorneys. A number of the Senators have already set up similar selection committees in an individual State, I think 14 to 16—I have forgotten exactly the latest figure. But we've tried to do it on the basis of merit. And I don't know of any case where there's been a demonstrable lowering of standards.

I don't deny that Mr. Goldstein and Van Dam are well qualified. In my judgment, as assessed by people on the scene, those who know them both, by the Attorney General, their replacements are at least as well qualified as their predecessors.

THE MIDDLE EAST

Q. How do you deal, Mr. President, with Israel's fears that if they come to some sort of settlement on the West Bank, any kind of settlement on the West Bank, first they'll be subjected to ongoing terrorism from irreconcilable Arabs over a long period of time or the new government, having gained a new position, declares itself to be hostile towards the State of Israel? How do you deal with those kinds of fears and are these fears legitimate?

THE PRESIDENT. Well, in the first place, any agreement reached in the Middle East would have to be accepted voluntarily by the Israelis and by their Arab neighbors. There won't be any imposition of a settlement by us or the Soviet Union or anyone else. So, you have that much of a safety factor to start with, that no settlement would be reached unless the Israelis wanted that settlement. Secondly, I do not favor and have never favored an independent Palestinian state in the West Bank area or in the Mideast area in presently occupied territory.

We have always, since the first few minutes of the foundation of Israel, had a national policy supporting the integrity, the independence, the freedom, the permanence of Israel, and hoping for peace. All of those factors, I think, have been met—sometimes challenged, but always met—except peace.

Now the Israelis and their neighbors, Arab countries, see the prospect of peace. The Arab leaders are making statements now that they could and would never have made a year ago, recognizing Israel's right to exist, being willing to negotiate with Israel directly if we get to Geneva.

There is a serious question about Palestinian representation. My belief is that when we consider the future status of the West Bank, Gaza Strip, and the Palestinians, that it ought to be negotiated with some participation by Palestinians. I personally think that Israel has agreed—I think this has been announced—that they would accept those Palestinians from the West Bank and the Gaza Strip and that that area would be negotiated by those Palestinians, Jordan, Egypt, and Israel on a multinational basis, because it's all wrapped up in one.

We have also got the prospect of considering as a separate item, but certainly a directly related item, the future of the refugees as such—some Jewish, some, of course, Palestinian. This would be on a multinational basis. But I think every possible right and prospect of Israel's existence, freedom, security in the future will be honored, certainly, by Israelis, backed by us.

MAYOR MICHAEL BILANDIC OF CHICAGO

Q. Mr. President, Mayor Bilandic's political organization in Chicago is feeling that you are ignoring us since Mayor Daley died, and some have said that they wanted you to come out and do some fundraising and you haven't. Do you have any problem with the Bilandic organization in Chicago?

THE PRESIDENT. No, of course not.

Q. The Vice President was out there just the other day.

THE PRESIDENT. I understand. I haven't raised money for anybody. I didn't even know he was running for election this year.

Q. He's not. The organization constantly raises money.

THE PRESIDENT. I have been to one fundraiser in New York for the Democratic National Committee, and I'm going to another one at the end of this month in Los Angeles for the Democratic National Committee. I've campaigned a half day for Brendan Byrne as Governor of New Jersey and a half day for Henry Howell as Governor of Virginia. Those are the only political involvements that I have had.

But, no, I get along well with the Bilandic administration. He's been here to visit with me. I've talked to him on the phone several times. There's no difference between us at all.

Q. So there's no problem with the political organization?

THE PRESIDENT. No. The only question that's been raised is concerning some of the management of the CETA funds. But that's all been public, and that's been between the Labor Department and the city administration.

But, no, between me and Bilandic or the Chicago Democratic organization, there is no difference.

REPRESENTATIVE EDWARD I. KOCH

Q. Mr. President, as a followup on that, there are some people concerned back in New York, especially at the lower end of the economic and political spectrum—as you know, there are now no city-wide black elected officials and Puerto Rican elected officials in New York. Some people were concerned, very seriously, that when you came to New York and Mr. Koch handed you the letter and there seemed to be a snubbing—well, he claims that he was not available to go with you to the South Bronx that day. But actually there seems to be some concern among people that, in fact, since Mr. Koch is going to be or presumed to be the next mayor of New York, that in fact, that he'll have a positive relationship with you that people at the local level could count on to get aid and assistance.

THE PRESIDENT. Well, there's no doubt that if he is elected mayor that he will have a close relationship with me. He has a close relationship with me now, and nothing has been done to shake that. I was amazed at any news attention being given at all to his handing me the letter. This was not something that I anticipated ahead of time. I didn't ever expect to make a public statement with Mr. Koch.

When I got off the helicopter, there were five or six people standing there, and I met Mayor Beame first, who is the senior person, talked to Ed, congratulated him again on his primary victory. He said, "Mr. President, I have a letter to give you about the Middle East question." I said,

"I appreciate it." And I took it and handed it to Jody Powell to keep for me. I went on down and met with Carol Bellamy and the rest of them, and then I got in the car and went to the United Nations.

A couple of hours later, my wife came, after I had been through a couple of U.N. meetings, and said, "What's the problem between you and Ed Koch? I just heard something about it on the radio." [*Laughter*] I said, "I don't have the slightest idea. I just got off the helicopter, shook hands with Ed, patted him on the shoulder, he handed me a letter, and I got in the car and drove off."

It was apparently a local media concentration or expectation—I don't know what the origin was—that I was going to endorse him there or make some public statement and so forth. But as far as I was concerned, it was a very harmonious exchange.

Shortly after that, Ed came here to meet with me in this room. We sat together and discussed, I think, the Mideast question, and completely harmonious.

Yesterday, the Vice President went up to New York to campaign with him. I mean, the whole thing has just been blown out of nothing.

Q. He made statements, though, to the effect that he had given you the business on the Middle East.

THE PRESIDENT. Well, you know, I can't speak for him. I was not aware of that.

NATIONAL ENERGY PLAN

Q. Mr. President, I'd just like to ask you, after you've handled the man in Chicago and the illegal aliens and Koch in New York, I would like to ask a parochial question. You may consider this an easy one.

After what happened yesterday here in Washington and with the oil companies all over the country and especially down in my part of the country, which is Louisiana—big gas producers, oil companies—I'm sure they feel that some kind of an all-out war has now been declared between the White House and the oil companies. Could you comment on that?

THE PRESIDENT. I'd be glad to. There is no all-out war. I deeply and genuinely believe that the proposal that we put to the Congress back in April is not only fair but very generous to the oil and gas industry in ensuring adequate profits, prices, accumulation of capital, to continue an effective exploration program and, also, a production program for oil and gas. I think the price structure also is very generous and much superior to what we have now. There would be a commensurate reduction in the involvement of the Federal Government in the oil and gas industry. And over a fairly short period of time, the circumstances that I've just described to you would be improved year by year.

The major thrust of our own program is to cut down on consumption. The price of oil and gas in this country at the present time, I think, is abnormally low, compared to the value of the oil and gas and the cost of replacement. So, what we'd like to do is to increase the price of those products gradually toward a free and uncontrolled price, certainly based all the time on factors such as the international oil market, the equivalent heat value in natural gas, and the distinction between oil and gas that has been discovered and is being produced now and new gas and oil to be discovered.

I think that the rejection by some, not all, of the members of the oil and gas industry of this proposal is unwarranted. And they are faced with a possibility of failure this year to come out with any legislation concerning oil and gas production and pricing. If that should occur, then the present laws and administrative rulings would stay in effect, a much less attractive prospect than what we have proposed.

I have spent literally weeks working on this question and many others related to it—the building up of adequate reserves, the bringing of oil and gas down from Alaska, the adverse impact of rapidly increasing imports, the definition of what is new gas, what is new oil, the future construction of pipelines, the use of the Panama Canal to bring about oil and gas from Alaska to our eastern freeboard, and so forth.

I'm convinced that the oil and gas companies, through their efforts on Capitol Hill to get more profit, to define what is actually old gas as new gas under the subterfuge of exploration, to also cover tax benefits and price benefits for production of gas which has already been discovered and so forth, that they are trying to get an unwarranted advantage at the expense of the American consumers. And I'm just not going to stand for it.

Now, nothing would please me better than to see the House version of our package, which is not completely what I want, go ahead and pass. But I think that I've been fair about it. And there's no way that I can deal with the question by being quiet or timid or quiescent. We've gone as far as we can.

I made a statement to the public last April with a fireside chat, my only speech to the Congress since I was inaugurated, and since then, of course, there's been a tremendous volume of constant and legitimate advertising by the oil companies and the natural gas companies over a period of days and weeks and months. There's a cloudy impression built up among the American people that we do have adequate supplies of oil and gas if the Government would just let the oil and gas companies set whatever price they choose and take the profits, which they claim to earn, and invest it back into additional production, which I think is a very gross distortion of the facts. Other than that, I agree with them completely. [*Laughter*]

MISSILE SYSTEMS

Q. Mr. President, when Safeguard went down the tube a few years ago when we negotiated the SALT agreement, since then the technology has become pretty well obsolete. Is anything at all being done in the area of ABM's, other than some studies going on back in Huntsville? I believe there's no hardware in production. Are we putting all our eggs in the basket of negotiation? How long would it take us to gear up, for instance, if we should discover that the other side is putting an ABM system into place?

THE PRESIDENT. Well, as you know, we have the right to build ABM's, if we choose. In the original negotiation, both sides agreed that they could build two. Later, the Soviets decided to build one. We almost finished one out in the Dakotas.

About a year ago, before I went into office, a decision was made to decommission the one in the Dakotas. The Soviets still have an ABM system, antiballistic missile system, around Moscow. I think they feel that if they hadn't already built it, that it would not be a warranted expenditure.

I believe that because of the advent of many technological improvements—the MIRV'd weapon is the most obvious— that an antiballistic missile system, compared to its cost, is simply not effective. So, we have an adequate means for verifying compliance with nuclear agreements—not perfect. We can accurately assess the location of missile silos. We can accurately maintain an inventory of submarines that are used for ballistic missile firing. We can count the number of missiles that are on each submarine. We can

monitor their testing program and determine when missiles are improved. We have fairly accurate estimates of their range.

It's very difficult to discern when a missile has one warhead or multiple warheads on the same missile. But we've reached an agreement with the Soviets that, if they ever MIRV one missile of a type, that all missiles in that type are assumed to already have been MIRV'd, so that we don't have to say, "You have got 300 missiles of this kind—100 have been MIRV'd and 200 have not." If they MIRV the first group of those missiles, we just assume that all of them have been MIRV'd.

So, there are some things that you can't confirm. But I would say that the balance between those is of equal concern to us and the Soviets.

The new era of cruise missiles is one that opens up an additional difficulty of verification. It's hard to look at a cruise missile from a satellite and determine how far it can go. And it's hard to look at a cruise missile from a satellite to determine whether it's got a nuclear warhead on it or a conventional warhead.

This is a new technological era that we're just approaching, and this is one of the difficulties of the present SALT negotiations. But I would say that our verification capability is adequate, that we do not have a handicap in the inadequacies that exceed the handicap of the Soviets.

Q. But there is no research and development in any kind of a system based upon these theories?

THE PRESIDENT. Yes, there is a constant research and development on better means of verification. And, of course, if we do get a comprehensive test ban in effect that would prohibit any level of explosion of a military weapon, then that would be much more difficult to discern because it's easier to detect. I think you would have a hundred percent capability of a 150,000-ton weapon. But if you tested, say, a 20-ton weapon, it would be very difficult to detect if you wanted to conceal it.

I think you also ought to remember, though—I don't want to overemphasize this—both we and the Soviets recognize that if we ever cheat and get caught, that the consequences are very severe. And there's a mutual trust that has to be maintained, based on maximum verification—not just word, but confirmation.

But if we ever detected specifically that the Soviets had deliberately violated a written agreement, it would destroy the tenuous, mutual confidence that's so imperative. And the Soviets recognize this, and so do we.

When I met with Secretary Kissinger about a year ago, after I was elected and before I was inaugurated, I asked him if he knew of any instance where the specific agreement between us and the Soviets had ever been violated. He said no, that he had never known of an instance of that kind, that in some cases the SALT negotiations had not been as specifically worded as they should have been and new technologies had come along later that were not covered in the original agreements, but both sides had taken advantage of those so-called loopholes. But it was so important that we not cheat and get caught because of the catastrophic consequences of that, that he thought except when you actually were going to attack, that that would be highly unlikely.

Q. Thank you, Mr. President.

THE PRESIDENT. I'll take one other question. Then I'll go, Walt,[2] thank you. This will be the last one.

---

[2] Walter W. Wurfel, Deputy Press Secretary.

ADMINISTRATION'S PRIORITY PROGRAMS

Q. Mr. President, you referred again to a very ambitious program, a lot of which you say is urgent. There is, as you know, some criticisms—too much too soon. Do you have, in light of your congressional experience since inauguration, developed a priority program? Is there anything you want to get out of the way first and, particularly, before next November's elections?

THE PRESIDENT. Well, I've had a priority program already, and some of it has been put into effect. When I first came into office, I wanted to see ethics legislation passed; that has been done. I wanted to get authority to reorganize the Government; that has been done. I wanted to get an economic stimulus package in effect; that's been done. I wanted to enhance employment opportunities among young people and others through public works project and so forth; that's been done. I wanted to get a bill on the books that would permit me to deal with urban blight. The housing and urban development bill was signed last week. And I wanted to get an energy package through this year; that has not yet been done.

Over a longer period of time—and I announced this at the time—we want to have welfare reform, and that bill has now been introduced, as you know, after a great deal of work. And then next year, we intend to address the tax reform question.

That's on the domestic scene, and that encompasses the major items that I've described. We don't expect the welfare program to be completely implemented until 1981. We may or may not try to implement some portions of the tax reform package next year, or they may be delayed until 1979. That will depend on the need for additional stimulus. But so far, the scorecard, I think, is very good. We don't get every item of what we put into the Congress, and we can't expect to. There are some other items that I have not tried to name.

On the international scene, I've named the major ones. There is nothing on the international scene in which we are deeply involved that I would undo. Now, we are trying to resolve the problem in Rhodesia, Namibia, and we are trying to add our good offices to the Middle Eastern question, deal with the Soviets on these questions that I've already described to you. We wanted to strengthen NATO and to revive the spirit of support for NATO among our European allies. I think we've done that successfully. And we also wanted to restore a sense of compatibility and friendship with nations that in the past have looked on us almost as enemies.

The visit that I had this week from the Nigerian leader, Obasanjo, was a point in fact. I wish that when all of you get home that you would get an atlas and read about Nigeria, what the country is. They've got 80 million people in Nigeria. This is more than a third of all the population of Africa. It's by far the greatest country economically in Africa. It's been torn by civil war. General Obasanjo was the leader of the armed forces in the civil war. He's an engineer and helped to rebuild the country.

They have got a military government now of 23 people. They have already had elected, through completely democratic means, a 236-person constitutional convention. They've just about completed the first draft of a constitution. They will have a freely, democratically elected president, a bicameral legislature. They have kept intact already a completely independent judiciary. And a year ago Secretary Kissinger, for the third time, tried to get permission to go into Nigeria, unsuccessfully.

Because of Andy Young's good work and so forth, we've kind of turned that around.

It's just a typical example of one of the most difficult political questions that I have to face—is the one I mentioned first this afternoon, and that's the Panama Canal treaties. If they can be ratified, our country will be greatly benefited through this process.

So, the multiplicity of these questions is almost overwhelming, and I know that politically speaking, it's not very good. If we've got 10 different major things on the fire at one time, and we win and finally finish, say, a reorganization package or an urban program or a stimulus package, and we still have 9 or 10 more that we're working on, it looks like everything is all confused, we're not making any progress.

But I recognize the legitimacy of having too many things going at once. I am trying to carry out my promises that I made during the campaign. It would be much easier for me to deal in foreign affairs just with SALT and let the Middle East and Africa and everything else drift. But that is not my nature, and I don't think it's in the best interest of the American people.

We can't succeed in every international effort. I don't expect to. And I recognize the natural inclination of the news media and the American people to concentrate on the exciting stories, the defeats and the combat and the debates and the disagreements and arguments. That's okay. But I think as far as the best interests of the country is concerned, there's nothing that I've mentioned in this kind of a rambling and fairly brief analysis that I would withdraw from just to create an increased sense of harmony or achievement.

I have enjoyed being with you. I wish I had more time. And I thank you again for being here.

NOTE: The interview began at 1 p.m. in the Cabinet Room at the White House.

The transcript of the interview was released on October 15.

Department of the Interior

Nomination of Walter N. Heine To Be Director of the Office of Surface Mining Reclamation and Enforcement.   October 17, 1977

The President today announced that he will nominate Walter N. Heine, of Newville, Pa., to be Director of the Office of Surface Mining Reclamation and Enforcement.

Heine was born February 21, 1934, in New York City. He received a B.S. in civil engineering from Drexel Institute of Technology in 1959 and an M.S. in sanitary engineering from the University of Michigan in 1964.

From 1955 to 1970, Heine worked for the Pennsylvania Department of Health, serving as a staff engineer, operations engineer, regional sanitary engineer, and chief of the Division of Mine Drainage Control. In 1970 and 1971, he was director of environmental engineering for a Harrisburg consulting firm.

Since 1971 Heine has been associate deputy secretary for mines and land protection in the Pennsylvania Department of Environmental Resources. He has been responsible for developing the organizational structure of the Office of Mines and Land Protection and for implementation of State-wide programs for surface mine reclamation, mine safety, solid waste management, occupational health, mine subsidence control, and oil and gas well-drilling regulation.

Heine assisted in drafting Federal coal surface mine regulation bills. He is the author of several technical articles on mining.

West German Rescue of Hostages in Somalia

White House Statement.   October 17, 1977

At 7:49 p.m., President Carter received a telephone message on behalf of Chancellor Helmut Schmidt informing him of the successful operation conducted by a special unit of West German border guards who freed the Lufthansa hostages at Mogadishu, Somalia. The President asked that the Chancellor be congratulated on the courage of his decision. The President feels that the West Germans have struck a blow for all of us who are vulnerable to this kind of terrorism. He wishes that the participants in the operation be commended and the Somalian Government thanked for its cooperation. The President sends his warmest greetings and his deepest feelings of relief to the hostages and their families.

NOTE: The Lufthansa Boeing 737 was hijacked by terrorists on October 13 during a flight from Palma de Mallorca, Spain, to Frankfurt, Germany.

The statement was made available by the White House Press Office. It was not issued in the form of a White House press release.

National Railroad Passenger Corporation

Nomination of Six Members of the Board of Directors.   October 18, 1977

The President today announced that he will nominate the following persons to be members of the Board of Directors of the

National Railroad Passenger Corporation (Amtrak):

ANTHONY HASWELL, of Chicago, Ill., for the term expiring July 18, 1981. He would replace Donald Jacobs, term expired. Haswell, 46, is an attorney who worked for the law department of the Illinois Central Railroad from 1958 to 1960. He organized the National Association of Railroad Passengers in 1967 and served as executive director, then chairman. From 1975 to 1977, he was managing director for passenger services for Rock Island Lines.

RONALD G. NATHAN, of Washington, D.C., for the term expiring July 18, 1981. He would replace Frank Besson, term expired. Nathan, 32, is a Washington attorney. From 1974 to 1977, he was a consulting attorney for the Interstate Commerce Commission's Office of Public Counsel, providing legal representation to communities facing discontinuance of rail service.

HARRY T. EDWARDS, of Ann Arbor, Mich., for the term expiring July 18, 1980. He would replace Joseph MacDonald, term expired. Edwards, 36, is a professor of law at the University of Michigan and has also taught law at Harvard University Law School. His areas of specialization are labor law and collective bargaining and labor arbitration. He has served on numerous arbitration panels and is the author of books and articles in legal journals.

CHARLES LUNA, of Dallas, Tex., for reappointment for the term expiring July 18, 1980. Luna, 70, served as president of the Brotherhood of Railroad Trainmen from 1963 to 1969 and as president of the United Transportation Union from 1969 to 1972. Since 1970 he has been on the Board of Directors of the National Railroad Passenger Corporation (Amtrak).

JAMES R. MILLS, of San Diego, Calif., for the remainder of the term expiring July 18, 1978. He would replace Gerald Morgan, deceased. Mills, 50, is a California State senator and has also served as a California State assemblyman. He serves as Acting Governor of California in the absence of the Governor and Lieutenant Governor. Mills received the Gold Spike Award from Citizens for Rail California for his efforts to improve intercity passenger rail service in California.

FRANK NEEL, of Thomasville, Ga., for the remainder of the term expiring July 18, 1978. He would replace Edward Ullman, deceased. Neel, 61, is president of Neel Air Conditioning and Heating Co., a firm operating in several southeastern States and handling electrical, mechanical, and solar energy planning, research, and installation in construction work.

United States Ambassador to Indonesia

Nomination of Edward E. Masters.
October 18, 1977

The President today announced that he will nominate Edward E. Masters, of Savannah, Ohio, to be Ambassador Extraordinary and Plenipotentiary of the United States to the Republic of Indonesia. He would replace David D. Newsom, transferred.

Masters was born June 21, 1924, in Columbus, Ohio. He received a B.A. from George Washington University in 1948 and an M.A. from Fletcher School of Law and Diplomacy in 1949. He served in the U.S. Army from 1943 to 1946.

In 1949 and 1950, Masters was an intelligence research analyst at the State Department, and from 1950 to 1952 he was resident officer, then military liaison officer in Frankfurt. He was political officer in Karachi in 1953 and 1954 and took Hindustani language and area training in 1954–55.

From 1955 to 1958, Masters was political officer in Madras. He was an intelligence research specialist at the State Department from 1958 to 1960. From 1960 to 1962, he was Chief of the Indonesia-Malaya Branch of the Office of Intelligence Research-Analysis for Asia, then international economist. In 1962 and 1963, he was officer in charge of Thailand affairs at the State Department.

Masters attended the National War College in 1963–64. He served as counselor for political affairs in Djakarta from 1964 to 1968, and as country director for Indonesian affairs at the State Department from 1968 to 1970. In 1970 and 1971, he was Director of the Office of Regional Affairs at the Bureau of East Asian and Pacific Affairs.

From 1971 to 1976, Masters was Deputy Chief of Mission in Bangkok. Since 1976 he has been Ambassador to the People's Republic of Bangladesh.

International Nuclear Fuel Cycle Evaluation

Remarks at the First Plenary Session of the Organizing Conference. October 19, 1977

About 25 years ago, I was a student doing graduate work in nuclear physics and reactor technology, not too many years after the first atomic weapons had been used to destroy human beings. My study was the peaceful use of this tremendous force, working under Admiral Rickover in the development of atomic submarine powerplants.

And now we've come to a time when we can look back with a clear historic perspective at what has transpired during this quarter century. It's a great honor for us to have you leaders come from, I believe, 36 nations and 3 international organizations, to think back to 1945, to remember our own President Eisenhower's proposal called Atoms for Peace, part of which was adopted, the later establishment of the International Atomic Energy Agency, which has provided for us, so far, a very effective mechanism by which explosions could be reduced and power could be produced.

We then went into a time of at least embryonic discussions of nuclear test bans, and now we have one that still permits the testing of weapons which have the equivalent of 150,000 tons of TNT. Even this has been recognized as an achievement. And, of course, we are discussing with the Soviet Union means by which we can eliminate, sometime in the future, our dependence upon atomic weapons altogether. We've lived under a threat which so far has not yet been realized, and I pray that it never shall.

In the last 32 years, there have been no people killed by the use of atomic weapons. But with the rapidly increasing price of oil and the scarcity of fuel which we have taken for granted in years gone by, there's an increasing pressure for expanding atomic power use. And commensurate with that use is also the threat of the proliferation of nuclear explosives among nations that have forgone voluntarily that opportunity up until now.

We have seen regional actions taken in the southern part of this hemisphere. The Treaty of Tlatelolco is now being ratified by the last nations, we hope, to prevent the deployment of any atomic explosions—or explosives in that part of the world. We hope that this will prevail in many other parts of the world.

We've also seen progress made recently between ourselves and the Soviet Union. We are eager to see drastic reductions in the deployment of nuclear weapons. And we are now negotiating with the Soviet Union and with Great Britain for a complete elimination of the testing of atomic explosions.

At the same time, the challenge presents itself to this group and to me, as one of the world leaders, to find a means by which the consuming nations who need atomic power to produce electricity and to serve peaceful purposes—to draw a distinction between that need, which is legitimate, and the threat of the development of atomic explosions themselves.

I have a feeling that the need for atomic power itself for peaceful uses has perhaps been greatly exaggerated. And I hope that all the nations represented here and others will assess alternatives to turning to this source of power, if for no other reasons than because of economic considerations.

Recent studies that I have read show that we can gain the equivalent of a barrel of oil per day by conservation measures at very little or any cost, often zero cost or up to $3,500. North Sea oil costs capital investment about $10,000 for every barrel of oil per day derived from that source. Our own Alaskan oil will cost $20,000 in capital investment for every barrel of oil per day, or its equivalent derived at the ultimate site of use. And for the equivalent of a barrel of oil per day at the end-use site for atomic power, the capital investment is between $200,000 and $300,000.

So, there's a tremendous cost even for the potential peaceful use of atomic power. Even so, we recognize that there will be a need, and we are eager to cooperate.

It's important that we understand your problems, that those nations that supply enriched uranium—ourselves, the Canadians, others—those who have major deposits of uranium ore that have presently not been exploited, like Australia, understand the need of nations that are not well blessed with uranium fuel supplies. It's important that you understand from those of us who unfortunately are nuclear weapon nations, our special commitment to reducing this threat.

I believe that in this brief session that you will have this week, followed by weeks and months of tedious, I'm sure, argumentative but productive discussions and debates, that common knowledge will benefit us all.

It's important that we combine our ingenuity, our foresight, our own experience, our research and development efforts, so that we don't duplicate the very expensive efforts to use atomic power in a useful way. And this exchange of ideas among us will be very helpful.

It's important that we know what potential nuclear fuel cycles are available to us, the quantity and the location of uranium and thorium and other nuclear fuels, the methods used for extraction, the methods used and the costs for enrichment, possible distribution systems, the proper design and use, standardization of powerplants, safety of people who live near them, proper siting considerations, the political objections to atomic powerplants themselves, the possible need for breeder reactors, the handling of spent fuel, the need or absence of a need for reprocessing the spent fuel, and international safeguards that will prevent the development of explosives.

We are eager to cooperate as a nation which is a consumer and also a supplier. We want to be sure that where there is a legitimate need and where there's a mutually agreed upon nonproliferation restraint, that there be an adequate supply of nuclear fuel.

I think an international fuel bank should be established, so that if there is a temporary breakdown in the bilateral supply of nuclear fuel, that there might be a reservoir of fuel to be supplied under those circumstances. And we'll certainly contribute our own technical ability and our own portion of the enriched uranium supplies for that purpose.

We are very eager, also, to help solve the problem of the disposal of spent nuclear fuel itself. We can't provide storage for the major portion of the world's spent fuel, but we are willing to cooperate. And when a nation demonstrates to us your need for spent nuclear fuel storage, we hope to be prepared to accept that responsibility, working closely with you.

All the costs of the nuclear fuel cycle should be accurately known as well as possible. And there should be an open-minded approach to this very controversial and very difficult subject.

I hope, as the President of our country, to learn from you, and I will welcome your advice and your counsel. I welcome your caution and, on occasion, your criticism about American policies. And I believe that we'll find a common ground on which we can work together in harmony to make sure that our people do have a better quality of life, that alternate fuel supplies are evolved in an effective and adequate way, that energy is conserved to an optimum degree, and that the threat of nuclear destruction is minimized.

I want to congratulate all of you on being willing to come here to meet together, because there has been an inclination to avoid controversy. This question is inherently controversial. The interests on occasion are highly divergent, and many of these matters have not been discussed adequately in the past.

I'm very grateful that the International Atomic Energy Agency is here because there is no conflict between this effort and the tremendous contribution that that Agency has been making and will make in the future.

We want to do everything we can to strengthen the safeguard system already established. And if there is a recommendation from this group that the functions of the International Atomic Energy Agency should be expanded, we will certainly

be willing to contribute our own financial and other support to make that possible.

In closing, let me thank you for being willing to participate in this international discussion. I am very eager to study your own debates and derive information from you. We will cooperate in every possible way that we can to give our people of the world adequate power sources and, at the same time, to keep their lives from being endangered.

Thank you very much.

NOTE: The President spoke at 10:15 a.m. in the Loy Henderson Conference Room at the State Department. The organizing conference of the International Nuclear Fuel Cycle Evaluation was hosted by the State Department.

Visit of Prime Minister Leo Tindemans of Belgium

Remarks of the President and the Prime Minister at the Welcoming Ceremony. October 19, 1977

THE PRESIDENT. On this beautiful day, it's a great pleasure for me to welcome to our country one of the great world leaders who has shown, through the influence of his own nation and his own strength of character and reputation, what can be done to enhance the principles of democratic government, a better way of life for our people, and the basic human freedoms throughout Europe and, indeed, throughout the world.

When I was first inaugurated President, the first official visit of my administration was by Vice President Mondale to Brussels. And Prime Minister Tindemans and the people of Belgium welcomed this early visit as a true indication of the strong friendship that has always prevailed between our countries and, also, the importance that we attach to this nation whose influence spreads far beyond its own national borders.

Belgium has been one of our strongest democratic allies, and the reputation that Prime Minister Tindemans has, has not only been exemplified in an enormous electoral victory recently in his own country, which shows the faith of his own people in him, but the fact that he has been chosen the President of the Council of the European Community.

We are very interested in a stronger and an even more united European Community. And the leaders and people of our own country have observed with great admiration and appreciation the unique role that Prime Minister Tindemans has played in spelling out the future evolution of this strong and united Europe.

We see the European Community as being an integral part of our own Nation's future well-being. And, of course, NATO is also a crucial matter for our own Nation's security.

We have problems that we share as well as friendship and achievements. We're concerned about economics. We're concerned about security. We're concerned about employment among our young people. We're concerned about energy. We're concerned about friendship that must exist between ourselves and the Soviet Union, between the democratic nations and the nations of Eastern Europe and further east. We're concerned about the prevention of proliferation of atomic explosives. And we are concerned about a curtailment in the sale of the weapons of war.

Prime Minister Tindemans and I will be discussing these and other matters later on today. But I especially want to emphasize again how much we value his friendship, his leadership, his counsel and advice, and how proud I am on behalf of 215 million Americans to welcome the leader of the great people of Belgium.

Welcome, Mr. Prime Minister, to our country.

THE PRIME MINISTER. Mr. President, first of all, I wish to thank you for the kind words which you have just expressed for my country and for myself, as well as for the warm welcome which has been given us in the United States. Based on a common heritage and common ideals, our two countries have developed a very strong and close relationship.

In the multilateral field, I would just mention our common membership in many multilateral and international organizations as NATO, OECD, the United Nations, and all the organizations of the U.N. family.

In each of these we work closely together, and Belgium has always attached the greatest importance to the invaluable contribution that the United States has made to help these international organizations and specialized agencies to achieve their goals.

On the bilateral front, Mr. President, our friendship has been enshrined in blood on the battlefield and, in time of peace, in a community of ideals in defense of peace, justice, democracy, and the dignity of the human being.

Last year, the United States celebrated their 200th anniversary of its birth as a nation. No doubt, the path has been difficult. Perhaps there have been setbacks, difficulties, and controversies. But nevertheless, the United States has, during those 200 years, never wavered from its main purpose of creating a society where men and women stand free. For this magnificent achievement, I must express my admiration to the United States of America.

We Belgians are an ancient people, but not such an old state. Indeed, we are now eagerly looking forward to celebrating, in 1980, the 150th anniversary of our independence as a nation. Appropriate ceremonies will mark this occasion in our own country and throughout the world, including, of course, the United States. I hope I shall not be misunderstood if, in the present context, I say that we look upon the United States as a big brother. Both our countries, Mr. President, are today faced with tremendous challenges, both in the field of politics and that of economics.

I do believe that while, of course, varying in degree, our responsibilities are identical in nature and our search for the proper solutions. We both believe in the dignity of man. We both stand for an economic system which is at the same time free and equitable. We both share preoccupation for the progress of the developing countries.

Rest assured, Mr. President, that in its quest for answers to our present day problems, Belgium will not lose sight of those guiding principles in the firm belief that we shall join company with the United States on this common ground.

By nature, by temperament, and by necessity, we Belgians are internationalists. We learned long ago that we cannot live in isolation. And since the signing of the Belgo-Luxembourg Economic Union in 1921, my country has not ceased to enlarge its cooperation with our neighbors and other countries of the world in a series of concentric circles—Belgium-Luxembourg Economic Union, Benelux, European Economic Community, OECD, the world organizations. More than ever, as the interdependence of nations increases, we are convinced that progress for mankind is dependent on international consultation and cooperation.

In this respect, we have been especially happy to maintain a close relationship with the United States. At the beginning of this year, immediately after your in-

auguration, we had the pleasure of receiving in Brussels the visit of Vice President Mondale. And in May, it was my privilege to meet you, Mr. President, in London.

Following my present visit to the United States, we shall be anticipating with the greatest interest and pleasure the visit that you plan to pay to Belgium on the first day of December next. These meetings at the highest level are proof enough of our common desire to work closely together.

May I finally add, Mr. President, how eagerly we are looking forward to your visit to Brussels, because it will give us the opportunity to repay all the warmth and kindness that you show us today.

Thank you very much.

NOTE: The President spoke at 11:08 a.m. on the South Lawn of the White House.

Federal Regional Councils

Designation of Chairpersons for the 10 Federal Regions. October 19, 1977

The President has designated 10 persons for 1-year terms as Federal Regional Council Chairpersons for the 10 Federal regions.

In letters to the 10 persons chosen, the President stated that the Federal Regional Council should help implement his initiative in streamlining and simplifying the Federal grant-in-aid system. "I am relying on you to identify problems and potential solutions for management improvement in concert with State and local officials in your region," the letters state.

The 10 persons are:

Region I (Boston)—Ivan Ashley, Regional Director, Community Services Administration

Region II (New York)—Eckardt Beck, Regional Administrator, Environmental Protection Agency

Region III (Philadelphia)—Thomas Maloney, Regional Administrator, Housing and Urban Development

Region IV (Atlanta)—Sara Craig, principal regional official, Health, Education, and Welfare

Region V (Chicago)—Loran Wittner, regional representative of the Secretary, Department of Commerce

Region VI (Dallas)—William Harris, Regional Administrator, Employment and Training Administration, Department of Labor

Region VII (Kansas City)—John Kemp, Regional Director, Department of Transportation

Region VIII (Denver)—Betty J. Miller, Regional Administrator, Housing and Urban Development

Region IX (San Francisco)—Bill Arntz, Regional Administrator, Department of Energy

Region X (Seattle)—Bernard Kelly, principal regional official, Health, Education, and Welfare

Corporation for Public Broadcasting

Nomination of Irby Turner, Jr., To Be a Member of the Board of Directors. October 19, 1977

The President today announced that he will nominate Irby Turner, Jr., of Belzoni, Miss., to be a member of the Board of Directors of the Corporation for Public Broadcasting for a term expiring March 26, 1982. He would replace Virginia B. Duncan, term expired.

Turner was born May 7, 1932. He holds a B.A. from Millsaps College and an LL.B. from the University of Mississippi Law School. He served in the U.S. Army from 1955 to 1957.

Turner has practiced law since 1957 and has been city attorney for Belzoni, Miss., since 1959. He served in the Missis-

sippi House of Representatives from 1960 to 1968.

Turner was a director of the Mississippi Authority for Educational Television from 1970 to 1976 and chairman of the board from 1972 to 1976. He was a member of the Board of Governors of the Public Broadcasting Service from 1973 to 1976.

Outstanding Contributions by Federal Employees

Memorandum for the Heads of Departments and Agencies.   October 19, 1977

Memorandum for the Heads of Departments and Agencies

If we are to improve the quality and performance of our government, we must involve all government employees in that task. We need their determination, their energy, and their ideas to set high standards and see that we meet them. One way to give public employees a greater stake in the government's performance is to recognize those who have made exceptional contributions—especially, these days, in the crucial area of energy conservation.

I intend to recognize these major contributions myself, to illustrate the importance I attach to them. Therefore, I want you to bring to my attention contributions by civilian and military personnel, recognized through awards made under the Federal Government's Incentive Awards Program since January 1, 1977, which produce first-year benefits of $5,000 or more. I also intend to recognize energy-saving actions, when you are satisfied that they are especially significant and deserve additional recognition. The best of these contributions will be considered for

Presidential Management Improvement Awards, to be presented at a White House ceremony early next year.

I urge you to give your full support to this special effort. I ask that you review the structure and processes within your agency to ensure that they encourage your employees to develop and propose innovative ideas. In order that this effort, and my interest in its success, be made clear, I want you to convey this message to all civilian and military personnel along with your own expression of the need for their personal involvement.

JIMMY CARTER

Visit of Prime Minister Tindemans of Belgium

White House Statement Issued Following the Meeting Between the President and the Prime Minister. October 19, 1977

The President met today at the White House with Prime Minister Leo Tindemans of Belgium. The Prime Minister, who is also the current President of the European Council, is visiting Washington at the invitation of the President. The President hosted the Prime Minister, Foreign Minister Simonet, and the Belgian party at a White House working lunch. The discussions covered a wide range of political and economic topics in both our bilateral relations and U.S. relations with the Community.

The President and the Prime Minister reviewed economic conditions in their two countries, the European Community, and the world, and agreed on the need for continued close cooperation among the industrial democracies in sustaining economic growth and addressing global economic problems. The President reaffirmed U.S. support for the European Community, noting that he will be visiting E.C. headquarters, as well as that of NATO, during his upcoming visit to Belgium. The two leaders both stressed the importance of significant results in the multilateral trade negotiations currently underway, agreeing on the importance of resisting protectionist measures and recognizing that freer trade would promote the orderly economic growth of both the developed and developing countries.

The President reiterated the U.S. commitment to the defense of Western Europe and to the strengthening of the NATO Alliance. He expressed satisfaction that positive steps were being taken in the Alliance to implement initiatives he had suggested and that had been adopted at the NATO summit meeting in May. The Prime Minister indicated that Belgium fully concurred in the need for a strong Europe and pointed to his country's good record in sharing the defense burden, noting that the United States and Belgium were cooperating in joint production of MAG-58 machineguns and the F-16 aircraft.

The President and the Prime Minister discussed a wide range of arms control and disarmament issues. The President welcomed Belgium's participation in the International Nuclear Fuel Cycle Evaluation. Both leaders agreed on the need to reduce both the quality and quantity of arms sold by all weapons-producing countries. The Prime Minister noted that his country had been using considerable restraint over the export of arms to sensitive areas and that Belgium had taken important initiatives in the U.N., proposing that controls on arms sales be considered in the context of regional disarmament measures.

The President and the Prime Minister expressed their satisfaction with the agreement reached by the United States and Belgium on October 18, under which Belgium acquires a route to Atlanta in addition to the one already enjoyed to New York. The two leaders also endorsed the emphasis given by the new agreement to promoting low-fare scheduled service and liberalized charter arrangements over the Atlantic.

Prime Minister Tindemans offered the President his analysis of the state of the movement towards European unification. Specifically he mentioned the progress represented by direct election of the European Parliament, which is scheduled for 1978. The Prime Minister also underlined that Greece, Portugal, and Spain had all applied for membership in the Community. President Carter repeated that the United States remained unequivocally committed to European unity and a strong Community.

Prime Minister Tindemans expressed his view that the Community should be represented at Western summit meetings and involved in any followup. The President said that we fully support the principle of E.C. participation but believe the nature of that participation must be determined by the Community itself.

The Prime Minister and the President agreed on the importance of cooperative efforts to assist developing countries with sustaining economic growth and meeting the basic needs of their poor. In that context, Prime Minister Tindemans raised the issue of a major economic development program for Zaire to be implemented in the framework of a joint international effort, an issue which had been raised with the Belgian Government by President Mobutu in June. The President indicated that he supported the principle of such an aid program for Zaire, and he expressed the hope that Belgium would continue to promote a joint program within a multilateral framework, in harmony with the important economic and reform measures now underway in Zaire.

The Prime Minister and the President noted the close harmony in the approaches of their two Governments to the CSCE review conference in Belgrade, and expressed their intent to consult closely on developments at the conference. They emphasized the need for a full, frank review of the entire Final Act, without polemics, and stressed the importance of human rights aspects. The Prime Minister and the President reiterated their support for participation at the conference by the Community.

President's Award for Distinguished Federal Civilian Service

Executive Order 12014.   October 19, 1977

RELATING TO THE PRESIDENT'S AWARD
FOR DISTINGUISHED FEDERAL CIVILIAN
SERVICE

By virtue of the authority vested in me by the Constitution and statutes of the United States of America, and as President of the United States of America, the Distinguished Civilian Service Awards Board is hereby abolished and Executive Order No. 10717, as amended, is further amended by deleting Sections 3, 4, 5, 6, 7, 8 and 9 and by adding the following new Sections:

"Sec. 3. The Chairman of the United States Civil Service Commission shall advise and assist the President in selecting persons to receive this award. In performing this function, the Chairman shall carefully review nominations submitted pursuant to the provisions of Section 4 of this Order and decide which of them, if any, warrant presentation to the President. The Chairman shall thereupon transmit to the President the names of those persons who, in the opinion of the Chairman, merit the award, together with a statement of the reasons therefor. Recipients for the award shall be selected by the President.

"Sec. 4. The form and procedures for making nominations for this award shall be prescribed by the Chairman of the United States Civil Service Commission, in accord with the following principles:

"(a) The Chairman shall be guided in the performance of this function by the provisions of Section 4504 and 4505 of Title 5 of the United States Code, and by additional criteria which the Chairman may prescribe.

"(b) The Chairman shall not recommend any person for the award without the concurrence of the head of the agency in which that person was employed at the time of the achievement for which the award is recommended.

"(c) Persons appointed by the President are not eligible for this award unless, in the opinion of the Commission, they are currently serving in a career position.".

JIMMY CARTER

The White House,
    October 19, 1977.

[Filed with the Office of the Federal Register,
    5:13 p.m., October 19, 1977]

NOTE: The Executive order was announced by the White House Press Office on October 19. It was not issued in the form of a White House press release.

United States Sinai Support Mission

Message to the Congress Transmitting a Report. October 19, 1977

To the Congress of the United States:

I am pleased to transmit herewith the Fourth Report of the United States Sinai Support Mission. It highlights the Mission's operation of the United States early warning system in the Sinai and the relationship of the system to the overall disengagement arrangements of the Agreement signed by Egypt and Israel on September 4, 1975—the Sinai II Agreement. This report is provided to the Congress in conformity with Section 4 of Public Law 94–110 of October 13, 1975.

Since the beginning of operations on February 22, 1976, there have been no serious intrusions into the area of the early warning system by either party. Some 40 minor or accidental intrusions have been detected and reported to both sides and to the United Nations, but none of them appears to have had any hostile purpose.

The Director of the Sinai Support Mission raised with senior Egyptian and Israeli officials the Congressional interest in the feasibility of substituting nationals of other countries for some of the Americans working in the Sinai. They expressed strong opposition to this proposal as, in their view, such a change would create difficult problems for their governments and risk upsetting arrangements which are now working to their complete satisfaction. Both parties continue to make clear their full support for the role of the United States in maintaining the disengagement arrangements in the Sinai.

At a time when we are engaged in intensive discussions to help Israel and the

Arab states make further progress in the search for a lasting peace, it is essential that the United States meet fully its commitments under the Sinai II Agreement. The Sinai Support Mission is an important element in meeting these responsibilities, and I urge the Congress to continue its support for this peacekeeping mission.

JIMMY CARTER

The White House,
    October 19, 1977.

NOTE: The 18-page report is entitled "Report to the Congress, SSM, United States Sinai Support Mission, October 13, 1977."

Department of Justice

Announcement of Signing of S. 2089, Establishing the Position of Associate Attorney General, and Nomination of Michael J. Egan for the Position.   October 20, 1977

The President has signed S. 2089, which establishes the position of Associate Attorney General, by statute, as the third-ranking position in the Justice Department, with appointment by the President and Senate confirmation.

The President has also nominated Michael J. Egan for the position. Egan has been serving as Associate Attorney General under appointment by the Attorney General since February.

Egan was born August 8, 1926, in Savannah, Ga. He received a B.A. from Yale University in 1950 and an LL.B. from Harvard Law School in 1955.

Egan practiced law in Atlanta from 1955 to 1977. He was a member of the Georgia House of Representatives from 1966 to 1977 and served as minority leader from 1970 to 1977.

NOTE: As enacted, S. 2089 is Public Law 95–139, approved October 19.

National Farm-City Week, 1977

Proclamation 4533.   October 20, 1977

By the President of the United States of America

A Proclamation

One of our most important national objectives is the establishment of a national food policy. This is vital to our own welfare and security as well as to our search for world peace. It requires the mutual respect and intelligent cooperation of all our people.

Once each family's farm supplied almost all of the raw materials and finished products to feed, clothe and warm the family. As our means of production have progressed and farmers as well as factories and businesses have increasingly specialized, each family has come to depend on many others for the tools and equipment and materials to keep our complex system running and meet our individual daily needs.

Our production of food is the marvel of the world. It depends on not only our farmers, but also researchers, the makers and sellers of equipment and supplies and the providers of services to farms and farmers, and those who transport, process and sell our harvests. All are vital links in maintaining the wholesomeness, abundance and availability at reasonable cost of our varied food supply. Many of the links in this food chain are in distant cities. All of us, on farms, in cities and suburbs, are consumers of these vital products.

Now, THEREFORE, I, JIMMY CARTER, President of the United States of America, do hereby proclaim the period of November 18 through November 24,

1977, as National Farm-City Week and ask all Americans to observe that period with suitable activities.

IN WITNESS WHEREOF, I have hereunto set my hand this twentieth day of October, in the year of our Lord nineteen hundred seventy-seven, and of the Independence of the United States of America the two hundred and second.

JIMMY CARTER

[Filed with the Office of the Federal Register, 5:03 p.m., October 20, 1977]

Transfer of Defense Articles to the Republic of Korea

Letter to the Speaker of the House, the President of the Senate, and the Senate Majority Leader Transmitting Proposed Legislation. October 21, 1977

I am transmitting today for the consideration of the Congress legislation which will authorize the transfer of certain United States-owned defense articles to the Republic of Korea. A draft bill and a section by section analysis of its provisions are enclosed.

In the Korean War the independence and security of the Republic of Korea were preserved at a cost of 34,000 American lives and many billions of dollars. Since then, a major objective of United States foreign policy has been the avoidance of renewed hostilities and the maintenance of peace on the Korean peninsula. Our security relationship with the Republic of Korea, which has been the cornerstone of this policy, has consisted of three principal elements—our 1954 Mutual Defense Treaty, a program of military and economic assistance, and the presence of United States Armed Forces in Korea.

Peace and stability in Northeast Asia are vital to our national interests, and

stability on the Korean peninsula is essential to that goal. I am determined, therefore, to maintain our commitment to the security of the Republic of Korea. However, our security relationship is not a static one, and the specific ways in which we seek to accomplish our basic policy objectives must be evaluated in light of present circumstances.

Within this context, I have concluded that the withdrawal of U.S. ground combat forces from Korea over a four- to five-year period can be accomplished in a manner which will not endanger the security of the Republic of Korea. So long as it is conducted in a way which will assure continued peace and stability in Northeast Asia, the ground force withdrawal is a natural evolution of our ongoing security relationship. Both governments have understood that the presence of U.S. ground forces was not permanent and is related directly to the maintenance of the military balance. With appropriate assistance, such as that included in the legislation I am proposing, the Republic of Korea will be able to assume a larger share of its defense burden and assume the tasks of U.S. units being withdrawn.

I have established a tentative schedule for the withdrawal of ground combat forces: 6,000 men, including one brigade of the Second Division, will be withdrawn by the end of 1978. The remainder of the ground forces will be withdrawn incrementally with the final withdrawal taking place in 1981 or 1982. U.S. air forces will remain in Korea with a small U.S. Army element to provide communications, intelligence and logistic support to our forces and those of the ROK.

My decision to withdraw U.S. ground combat forces from Korea rests on certain basic considerations:

—Korea's impressive economic growth over the past decade and the corresponding increase in Korea's ability to defend itself;

—our continued firm determination to maintain our basic security commitment to Korea, and to retain a significant military presence there, composed mainly of air and key support units, together with the continuing presence of U.S. naval units in the area; we believe that these forces, as well as the major U.S. forces remaining in the Western Pacific, provide a clear and visible U.S. deterrent to North Korean miscalculation;

—our assessment of the broader international context of the Korea question, particularly the pattern of interrelationships between the great powers in the area;

—our readiness, subject to Congressional consultations and approval, to take appropriate actions to assure that the ground force withdrawal does not weaken Republic of Korea defense capabilities.

The decision to withdraw ground combat forces from Korea has involved full consultations with the Korean Government. The Governments of Japan and other friendly nations in Asia have been kept fully informed, both of our withdrawal intentions and of our continuing firm commitment to Korean security. We have made it clear to both the People's Republic of China and the Soviet Union that the withdrawal decision signals no weakening of our commitment. The North Korean Government should be in no doubt about our position.

The legislation I am proposing is designed to help make certain that Korean defense capabilities are not weakened by our ground force withdrawal. It provides for the transfer of certain U.S.-owned military equipment (primarily in the custody of U.S. forces in Korea) and related services to the Korean Government, without reimbursement. We envisage at most the transfer of equipment with a depreciated value of about $800 million.

Even with this no-cost transfer, the withdrawal will require the Korean Government to devote a larger share of its financial resources, both foreign exchange and local currency, to defense. In my judgment, the transfer provided for in the draft legislation will ease the incremental fiscal burden of withdrawal on the Korean Government to an amount which can be borne without diverting excessive resources from the high priority task of economic development.

The bill provides that the President shall transmit an annual report to the Congress, through the five-year period during which the anticipated equipment transfer will take place, detailing the types, quantities and value of defense articles furnished to Korea under this Act.

The transfer of equipment to the Korean Government to be authorized by the bill will ensure that the withdrawal of U.S. ground forces is accomplished in a way that will not disturb the stability that must be maintained in the region. Since the initial phase of that withdrawal will take place in 1978, I urge the Congress to enact promptly the proposed legislation.

Sincerely,

JIMMY CARTER

NOTE: This is the text of identical letters addressed to the Honorable Walter F. Mondale, President of the Senate, the Honorable Thomas P. O'Neill, Jr., Speaker of the House of Representatives, and the Honorable Robert C. Byrd, Majority Leader of the Senate.

Department of Defense

Nomination of Harold W. Chase To Be Deputy Assistant Secretary for Reserve Affairs.   October 21, 1977

The President today announced that he will nominate Harold W. Chase, of

Minneapolis, Minn., to be Deputy Assistant Secretary of Defense for Reserve Affairs. He would replace Will H. Tankersley, resigned.

Chase was born February 6, 1922, in Worcester, Mass. He received an A.B. (1939), M.A. (1948), and Ph.D. (1954) from Princeton University. He served in the U.S. Marine Corps from 1950 to 1952.

Chase was an associate professor at Princeton University from 1952 to 1957. Since 1957 he has been a professor at the University of Minnesota.

Chase holds the rank of major general in the Marine Corps Reserve, and since 1976 has been a member of the Reserve Forces Policy Board.

Federal Election Commission

Nomination of Samuel D. Zagoria To Be a Member. October 21, 1977

The President today announced his intention to nominate Samuel D. Zagoria of Maryland to be a member of the Federal Election Commission for a term expiring April 30, 1983.

Mr. Zagoria, formerly a member of the National Labor Relations Board, is director of the Labor-Management Relations Service, which is sponsored by the U.S. Conference of Mayors to provide leaders of local government with information and education on municipal labor-management relations.

A 1954 Nieman Fellow at Harvard University, Mr. Zagoria served for 10 years as administrative assistant to Senator Clifford Case of New Jersey. Previously, he was a reporter and an editor for the Washington Post for 10 years.

United States Parole Commission

Nomination of Audrey A. Kaslow To Be a Commissioner. October 21, 1977

The President today announced his intention to nominate Audrey A. Kaslow of California to be a Commissioner of the U.S. Parole Commission for the term of 6 years.

Ms. Kaslow has been employed by the Los Angeles County Probation Department since 1950 and is now a probation director.

A native of Miami, Ariz., Ms. Kaslow holds a bachelor's degree from the University of California and a master's degree from the University of Southern California.

She has served as a special representative on the California Fair Employment Practices Commission.

Department of Defense

Announcement of Signing of S. 1372, Creating the Post of Under Secretary of Defense for Research and Engineering, and Nomination of William J. Perry for the Post. October 21, 1977

The President today announced his intention to nominate William J. Perry of Virginia to fill the newly created post of Under Secretary of Defense for Research and Engineering.

Simultaneously, the President signed S. 1372 which creates the post.

On March 11, the President has nominated Mr. Perry to be Director of Defense Research and Engineering in the Department of Defense.

S. 1372 redesignates the Director of Defense Research and Engineering as Under Secretary of Defense for Research and Engineering.

NOTE: As enacted, S. 1372 is Public Law 95–140, approved October 21.

Digest of Other White House Announcements

The following listing includes the President's daily schedule and other items of general interest as announced by the White House Press Office during the period covered by this issue. Events and announcements printed elsewhere in the issue are not included.

October 15

The President met at the White House with Zbigniew Brzezinski, Assistant to the President for National Security Affairs.

October 17

The President met at the White House with:

—Dr. Brzezinski;
—senior White House staff members;
—the Cabinet;
—Vice President Walter F. Mondale and members of the Committee of Americans for the Canal Treaties, Inc.;
—Vice President Mondale;
—El Hadj Omar Bongo, President of Gabon and Chairman of the Organization of African Unity, and William Eteki of Cameroon, Secretary General of the Organization;
—Senator Russell B. Long of Louisiana.

The President transmitted to the Congress the 1976 annual report of the Administration on Aging.

The White House announced that during the President's trip abroad from November 22 to December 2, he will stop in Saudi Arabia following his visit to Lagos, Nigeria. The President will meet with King Khalid and Crown Prince Fahd.

October 18

The President met at the White House with:

—Dr. Brzezinski;

—the Democratic congressional leaders;
—Representative Thomas L. Ashley of Ohio to discuss energy;
—Vice President Mondale, Adm. Stansfield Turner, Director of Central Intelligence, and Dr. Brzezinski;
—Mrs. Carter, for lunch;
—James T. McIntyre, Jr., Acting Director of the Office of Management and Budget;
—Amory Lovins, physicist and British representative of Friends of the Earth, to discuss energy;
—Senator Abraham A. Ribicoff of Connecticut to discuss energy;
—Senator Lloyd M. Bentsen of Texas to discuss energy.

October 19

The President met at the White House with:

—Dr. Brzezinski;
—Representatives Al Ullman of Oregon, Harley O. Staggers of West Virginia, Dan Rostenkowski of Illinois, and Thomas L. Ashley of Ohio, to discuss energy;
—Secretary of Defense Harold Brown;
—J. Lane Kirkland, secretary-treasurer of the AFL–CIO;
—Senator Edmund S. Muskie of Maine.

The White House announced that at the invitation of the President, the Shah of Iran will pay a state visit to Washington on November 15–16.

The President has designated Joseph Duffey as Chairman of the Federal Council on the Arts and the Humanities. Mr. Duffey is Chairman of the National Endowment for the Humanities.

October 20

The President met at the White House with:

—Dr. Brzezinski;

1825

—Representatives Edward I. Koch and Herman Badillo of New York;

—Senator Edward M. Kennedy of Massachusetts;

—Senators James Abourezk of South Dakota, Dale Bumpers of Arkansas, and Howard M. Metzenbaum of Ohio;

—Charles L. Schultze, Chairman of the Council of Economic Advisers;

—Secretary of the Treasury W. Michael Blumenthal;

—John C. West, United States Ambassador to Saudi Arabia;

—representatives of several consumer groups to discuss energy.

October 21

The President met at the White House with:

Vice President Mondale, Secretary of State Cyrus R. Vance, and Dr. Brzezinski;

—Dr. Brzezinski;

—Senator John A. Durkin of New Hampshire.

The President left the White House for a weekend trip to Michigan, Iowa, Nebraska, Colorado, California, and Minnesota.

The White House announced that the President will meet with Saudi Arabian Foreign Minister Prince Saud on October 25 to discuss the Middle East situation and matters involved in bilateral relations.

NOMINATIONS SUBMITTED TO THE SENATE

The following list does not include promotions of members of the Uniformed Services, nominations to the Service Academies, or nominations of Foreign Service officers.

Submitted October 17, 1977

GEORGE H. ALDRICH, of Virginia, for the rank of Ambassador during the tenure of his

NOMINATIONS—Continued
Submitted October 17—Continued

service as Deputy Special Representative of the President of the United States for the Law of the Sea Conference, and Deputy Chief of Delegation.

TYRONE BROWN, of the District of Columbia, to be a member of the Federal Communications Commission for the unexpired term of 7 years from July 1, 1972, vice Benjamin L. Hooks, resigned.

PIERRE N. LEVAL, of New York, to be United States District Judge for the Southern District of New York, vice Donald B. Bonsal, retired.

Submitted October 19, 1977

WALTER N. HEINE, of Pennsylvania, to be Director of the Office of Surface Mining Reclamation and Enforcement (new position).

The following-named persons to be members of the Board of Directors of the National Railroad Passenger Corporation for the terms indicated:

For the remainder of the term expiring July 18, 1978:

FRANK H. NEEL, of Georgia, vice Edward L. Ullman, deceased.

JAMES R. MILLS, of California, vice Gerald D. Morgan, deceased.

For a term expiring July 18, 1980:

HARRY T. EDWARDS, of Michigan, vice Joseph V. MacDonald, term expired.

CHARLES LUNA, of Texas (reappointment).

For a term expiring July 18, 1981:

ANTHONY HASWELL, of Illinois, vice Donald P. Jacobs, term expired.

RONALD G. NATHAN, of the District of Columbia, vice Frank S. Besson, Jr., term expired.

EDWARD E. MASTERS, of Ohio, a Foreign Service officer of Class one, to be Ambassador Extraordinary and Plenipotentiary of the United States of America to the Republic of Indonesia.

MICHAEL J. EGAN, of Georgia, to be Associate Attorney General (new position).

IRBY TURNER, JR., of Mississippi, to be a member of the Board of Directors of the Corporation for Public Broadcasting for a term expiring March 26, 1982, vice Virginia Bauer Duncan, term expired.

CHECKLIST OF WHITE HOUSE PRESS RELEASES

The following releases of the Office of the White House Press Secretary, distributed during the period covered by this issue, are not included in the issue.

Released October 17, 1977

Announcement: nomination of Pierre N. Leval to be United States District Judge for the Southern District of New York

News conference: on the President's meeting with El Hadj Omar Bongo, President of Gabon and Chairman of the Organization of African Unity, and William Eteki of the Cameroons, Secretary General of the OAU— by Jerrold L. Schecter, Associate Press Secretary

Released October 19, 1977

News conference: on the President's meeting with Prime Minister Leo Tindemans of Belgium—by Jerrold L. Schecter, Associate Press Secretary

Released October 20, 1977

Announcement: nomination of David T. Wood to be United States Attorney for the District of Guam

Released October 21, 1977

Announcement: nomination of Elsijane Trimble Roy to be United States District Judge for the Eastern and Western Districts of Arkansas

Announcement: nomination of Gerald D. Fines to be United States Attorney for the Southern District of Illinois

---

ACTS APPROVED BY THE PRESIDENT

Approved October 15, 1977

H.R. 6550_____ Public Law 95–134
An act to authorize certain appropriations for the territories of the United States, to amend certain Acts relating thereto, and for other purposes.

S. 667_____ Public Law 95–133
An act to declare certain federally owned land held in trust by the United States for the Te-Moak Bands of Western Shoshone Indians.

ACTS APPROVED—Continued
Approved October 15—Continued

S.J. Res. 89_____ Public Law 95–135
A joint resolution to amend an act entitled "To authorize certain appropriations for the territories of the United States, to amend certain Acts relating thereto, and for other purposes" (enrolled bill H.R. 6550, Ninety-fifth Congress, first session).

Approved October 18, 1977

H.R. 5742_____ Public Law 95–137
An act to amend the Controlled Substances Act to extend for three fiscal years the authorization of appropriations under that Act for the expenses of the Department of Justice in carrying out that Act.

H.R. 9354_____ Public Law 95–138
An act to amend the Act of August 25, 1958, with respect to staff allowances for former Presidents.

S. 1060_____ Private Law 95–8
The George Washington University Charter Restatement Act.

S. 1522_____ Public Law 136
An act to authorize appropriations for fiscal year 1978 to carry out the Marine Mammal Protection Act of 1972.

Approved October 19, 1977

S. 2089_____ Public Law 95–139
An act to establish within the Department of Justice the position of Associate Attorney General.

Approved October 20, 177

H.R. 1934_____ Private Law 95–9
An act for the relief of Doctor Lawrence C. B. Chan.

Approved October 21, 1977

S. 1372_____ Public Law 95–140
An act to amend title 10, United States Code, to abolish one of the two positions of Deputy Secretary of Defense and establish the position of Under Secretary of Defense for Policy and to change the title of the Director of Defense Research and Engineering to the Under Secretary of Defense for Research and Engineering.

Detroit, Michigan

Remarks in a Panel Discussion and Question-and-Answer Session at a Public Policy Forum Sponsored by the Community Services Administration. October 21, 1977

THE PRESIDENT. First of all, let me say that I'm very grateful for a chance to come back to Detroit. I was here the first time as Governor in 1973 and then came back again as Governor in 1974. Then in 1975 I came back several times during the campaign and not—well, more than once in 1976.

This is a regional meeting, extending in many directions from Detroit—suburbs and urban areas—with representatives here who bring to this panel table a wide range of interests and also experience and also advice for me. The purpose of the meeting is to make sure that I, as President of our great country, am able to learn in a human way about the special needs of people who have quite often been most deprived, most alienated from the sometimes distant Government in Washington, and to see from a personal perspective how well-meaning programs that are poorly administered don't serve the needs of those who need the services most and sometimes how Presidents and Members of Congress, Governors and even mayors overlook opportunities for providing a better life for our people.

I'm very proud of Detroit. This city has come a long way. Two years ago the unemployment rate here when I came was about 25 percent—23.4 percent. This past month it was down about 8 or 9 percent, which is still too high. But to have that drastic a reduction in unemployment is a very great credit to those who serve you so well.

I was living in Atlanta as Governor, and Detroit was known as the murder capital of the Nation. In the last 2 years alone, with the good work of your mayor and with close cooperation from officials in the suburban areas, the State government, and particularly the police, the murder rate has been reduced 64 percent. And the crime rate in Detroit in the last year has dropped 21 percent—the greatest reduction in crime of any major city in the whole country.

So, these achievements are notable, but we're here today not to brag on one another but to point out how we can make our people have an even better life.

The format for this meeting has already been described to you, I'm sure, but I will call on each member of the panel just to comment briefly on your own background and then bring up an issue that you'd like to discuss with me. I don't claim to know all the answers. But I think in this general discussion that we'll have, I think all of us are quite relaxed at this point. This will probably take about an hour. I think many of the issues that have been on the minds of the audience who will later participate will have been answered. But then we'll turn to the audience members, who are not around the table, for additional questions.

I want you to know that, again, I'm here as a student, first of all, to learn how I can be a better President and, secondly, to let you understand what the present and future services might be, coming from your Federal Government.

I'd like to call now on Mr. Lawrence Hall to make a brief comment and perhaps ask a question, and then we'll go around the table.

Lawrence, it's good to have you here.

PANEL DISCUSSION

UNEMPLOYMENT

MR. HALL. Thank you, Mr. President. My name is Lawrence Hall. I'm from Gary, Indiana. I'm 56 years old, and I'm an unemployed steelworker. My views about the problem—it's a personal problem, and I'm only speaking for the other 1 million unemployed.

I'm in a desperate situation now. I need a job. I'm at the age now where I can't seek other employment. The type of work that I have—I was unable to prepare myself to do something on the side. I'm not a homeowner; I'm a home buyer. I have four children. I have one daughter at home; she's just 10.

I have 37 years' service in the steel mill. I work at Youngstown. This is one of the places that has been completely—5,000 people put out of a job, just overnight. What are they going to do? We're in the same situation in Gary, Indiana. We finished up working last week. There's not a piece of material to be worked in. They welded up our operation. "Go home; we'll call you; don't call us."

This money that we're able to get through subpay and et cetera—it's only 85 percent of our earnings. To those of you who don't know, 85 percent sounds pretty nice. But when you lose 15 percent of your earnings, one week you can make it, but when it goes over a period of 3 years, this means a house note every month, your food every month, your utilities every month that you're losing. You can't make any plans. You don't know how you're going to work.

My situation is that I feel that—the terminology is I'm being ripped off by the company I've dedicated my life to, trying to give them a fair day's work for a fair day's pay. And they say now, "The only way I can give you a job is the Government has got to subsidize you."

I feel frustrated because my union has not been able to help me to prepare myself or to tell me these things are going to happen. And then the leaders that I talked to—there are so many problems in the world—I don't say they're not concerned, but they don't realize how desperate I am, that I don't feel much like talking about energy and foreign policy. I'm concerned about how am I going to live. And I don't want to take up as much time as I'm allowed, but these are my personal feelings. I can't be too concerned about other things when I have a daughter to raise and I don't have a job and I'm 56 years old.

THE PRESIDENT. Very good statement. Many of us in Government, when we see a 6- or 7-percent unemployment rate, are quite pleased if a year ago it was 8 or 9 percent. And we tend to forget the human suffering and the challenge and the loss of self-respect and a deep fear about the future that comes with someone who is, as you say, 56 years old, who has worked all your life in one industry, and now is unemployed.

I also have a 10-year-old daughter, as you know. She was 10 this week. So, I feel a kinship with you. I can point this out to you to begin with: You are one of the fortunate unemployed, in that the steel industry is a special impacted industry and there are special assistance programs for you. But that's not the way you want to live. You want to earn your own living by working and not get even the assistance that comes from the impacted area.

I had a meeting this past week with executives, your own labor leaders, the Members of Congress who represent the steel industry, who came to the Oval Office, to the White House, to meet about what we are going to do concerning the steel industry itself.

One of the problems, obviously, is a worldwide semirecession. The growth rate in our economy, the construction of buildings, the construction of homes, the construction of machinery is not growing as rapidly as it has been sometimes in the past, and the order for steel from European, Japanese, and American sources is just down. I think that we will see in our own Nation an increasing demand for steel. Our housing construction now is the highest it's been in many years. Over 2 million housing units per year is the present rate. I think, with passage of a new energy bill—although you're not concerned with energy right now; you're concerned with a job—will provide increasing demands for steel.

One of the first things that the steel executives and labor leaders told me when I came into the room to meet with them was that they don't want to build a wall around our country. They don't want import quotas. They don't want high tariffs, because that hurts the trade on which our Nation relies so heavily. But they want to stop the dumping procedures that have been in place for steel this year and in years past where producers of steel in other

nations, in Europe and Japan, for instance, sell on our market—against the law, I might say—steel at a price below what it costs them to produce it.

And we can stay competitive with other nations if they comply with our law. So, that's one thing that I can promise that we will do, is enforce the antidumping laws, cut down on the illegal competition from overseas, continue the impacted area or industry programs that will keep you at least on your feet until we can get you another job, and with our public works programs, which I'll discuss later after some other questions, with our housing programs that we're keeping going, and also with our new tax reform measures that will be forthcoming next year that will stimulate the economy, I believe we have a good chance, Mr. Hall, to put you back to work. I'll do my best on this subject. And every time I consider a measure that might relieve the unemployment question, you're one of those people that I'll be thinking about.

Mrs. Emma Molina.

MIGRANT WORKERS

MRS. MOLINA. My name is Emma Molina, and I'm the mother of 10 children, and I'm an ex-migrant. Presently, I'm minority affairs director with the Community Action Agency in Findlay, Ohio.

Mr. President, my hopes today are to make you aware of the problems of the poor people that I have come to represent from my area. They could not be here personally, but I will try to speak for them.

First of all, their needs in the housing area. Now, in our area housing is so poor, poor people are forced to live in substandard homes because they have no choice. And they're asking why, if there are so many projects that are designed to help the low-incomed, why can't it be for everybody. In our county we have not been able to get our people interested in forming a metropolitan housing commission, and so we cannot bring projects for the low-income. So, they are forced to live in very poor housing.

And another area that we're lacking is in minority employment. Minorities, blacks, Mexican Americans—when they come to the employment agencies, they're not given the opportunities for the good jobs. If you're black, you're offered jobs to clean. If you're Mexican American, you're offered the farm work. And I believe we have the potential also to hold good jobs if we're given the opportunity.

And also the elderly people, poor people, and minority people, they're left out of the good programs that are offered to them. I have contact with different senior centers, and participants come from backgrounds—like they're professionals, maybe teachers or people of this kind. But low-income people are not really taking advantage of the programs that are designed to help them.

And also the migrants in my area, they have many problems. When I was a migrant 20 years ago, Mr. President, the conditions were bad. And I have worked with migrants as a volunteer and as a staff person, and I see the same problems. There is no change in wages, in housing. Housing codes are not being enforced, and the wages—20 years ago I used to pick tomatoes—14 cents a basket. And today, migrants are still being paid 17 cents, which means there's only 4 cents difference. And all these things I have brought to you because you are the hope of the poor people, and you know in your own capacity what you could do for poor people in this country.

So, I'm speaking for the poor people all over the country, and we appeal to you for your help.

Thank you very much.

THE PRESIDENT. I don't think anybody could make a better speech, if they prepared it for a long time, than you and Mr. Hall have made. And what makes you so able to express yourself is because you've been there as a migrant worker and you see at first hand what a job means—first of all, what a low-paid job means, secondly, what an absence of housing means. And even not having a home community aggravates all those other problems.

For someone who is poor, who is a minority member of our society, but who has a stable home, there are services available to them, like public health and so forth, that are not there if you are a migrant. One of the things that we are doing, for instance, is to make sure and to require that Medicaid and Medicare provisions be made available to all migrants, which has not been the case in the past.

I've picked tomatoes by the hamper myself, and I've picked cotton, and I've shaken peanuts. And my first home when I got out of the Navy was in a public housing project. And I understand, at least to some degree, the environment that you have described.

We've made some good progress already in this first 9 months or so that I've been in office. The Congress has cooperated, and I think the Nation will begin to feel the benefits of what we've done in the next few months in an increasing degree.

For instance, I just signed this month a housing and community development act, which in 3 years will provide about $12½ billion to improve the quality of housing, both low-rent housing for poor people and better loans, community development projects, and funds that will be made available to mayors and others to provide housing.

We also have put money into programs, which are just now being felt, to put our poor people back to work. In the Comprehensive Education and Training Act, for instance, and in the public works projects, many of these programs are designed specifically for minority groups.

Detroit, just to take an example, has received approval already for, I think, $67 million under the public works projects—money—and for the first time in the history of our Nation, 10 percent of that money has to be spent with minority contractors or builders. This means that the Spanish-speaking, the black, and other minority groups can participate not only in the benefits of projects once they get finished but also can provide the workers to build those projects, which is a step in the right direction.

One of the things that's concerned me very much is that among poor people we have a very inadequate health care system. Quite often a medical doctor will not be available to serve transient workers or others. And I was talking to Senator Herman Talmadge yesterday about a bill that will, for the first time, permit the service of what's called physician extenders, who are men and women who have training a little bit above and beyond a registered nurse, who can act as a medical doctor when doctors themselves are not available. I would predict to you that the Congress will finish their action on this legislation this month, and I'll sign it into effect, obviously, as soon as it's completed.

We have put into effect, to close out my answer, under Ray Marshall, who is the Labor Secretary, I think a much better way to place both local workers who are unemployed and also migrant workers in contact with the jobs that are available. I think he's the kind of person who

will get out with his workclothes and get to know people who really are suffering because of the lack of services and jobs. Pat Harris, the Secretary of Housing and Urban Development, is the same way. She's been here and been many other places to try to see how we could improve the housing area.

So, we have made some first major steps toward meeting the needs of the people that you represent, Mrs. Molina. And I believe that in the future, after assessing what you've said, we can make even greater steps for those people.

I might say, before the next panelist starts, that I try to take notes, as you've mentioned the housing and minority employment and migrant workers problems. And if any of you ask me a question that I fail to answer, then don't hesitate to follow up, because I'll try to keep notes and answer all the questions.

Father Hernady came here from Hungary in 1950, and I'm very glad to be with you today, Father. And it's time for you to comment.

NEIGHBORHOOD REVITALIZATION

FATHER MARTIN HERNADY. Thank you, Mr. President. I'm Father Hernady from Toledo, Ohio. We had the privilege of having President Carter in our place, in Americas' nicest ethnic neighborhood— [*inaudible*].

THE PRESIDENT. I will never forget.

FATHER HERNADY. We'd like to have you back again. I come from a typical ethnic workingclass neighborhood in the Midwest. I speak for the people of the neighborhoods who decided to stay in the cities instead of fleeing to the suburbs. They decided to stay in the city because they loved the city and the place of their heritage, the place of their roots. And they joined the precious heritage of their forefathers, which is still strong in our neighborhoods. They are determined that their city will not become black, brown, and broke, as Monsignor Baroni [1] says. It could happen if the practices of financial institutions, the real estate industry, big business, and the local and State and even the Federal Government are not stopped.

During your campaign, Mr. President, you encouraged us to revitalize our neighborhoods, and we were encouraged to do so. But at the present time we wonder about the depth and the extent of the commitment of your administration to the cities. As we hear of your proposed urban development policies, we are afraid that your administration perceives the urban problem as only a black problem, as a problem of totally devastated areas, such as the Bronx in New York. We are also concerned that the revitalization of the downtown areas of our cities, often with massive new programs, sounds suspiciously like the urban renewal programs in the sixties. We wonder how the new action grants will affect our cities, and are they going to reach people or only their industry or business?

We believe that young people should stay in our neighborhoods. At the present time the enticements of the banking industry are sucking our young people to suburbia.

I would like to demonstrate it with an example. I am in this parish 23 years. And when our boys returned from the war, from Korea and Vietnam, they wanted to buy a home in our neighborhood, let us say, for $12,000. In order to buy a home in a good ethnic neighborhood they had to have 50 percent down, $6,000. In the meantime, if they had only $500, they could go to suburbia and buy a home for $25,000.

And they were always told, "How can you invest your money in an old neighborhood?" They couldn't understand that those people love the roots of their ancestors.

We are dreaming of a community where people can walk to church. We are dreaming of a community where our children are walking to school, when the child can go down three, five blocks, and he knows everybody, Mr. Naggie or Mr. Kovach, and the parents don't have to be afraid that somebody might pick him up. We are dreaming of a neighborhood where people know each other on a first-name basis.

This is a beautiful life, what our people enjoy. And this is a beautiful way of life that we would like to keep. And we resented in the past when some people tried to antagonize various ethnic neighbors, like the blacks and the Hungarians and the Polish people. We are not enemies; we are friends. And we want to combine our efforts to revitalize our neighborhood, our cities. We have to realize there are no cities in America if you don't have neighborhoods. And if you don't have nice, sound neighborhoods, you are not going to have nice family life in our Nation.

We wonder again how your banking policy is going to affect our neighborhood, whether the banking industry is going to be people oriented or only for business or for industry? We would like to see that they would invest money in people whom we love very much.

THE PRESIDENT. Very good. Thank you Father.

As Father Hernady said, I have visited his neighborhood, and, as some of you may remember, I got in trouble during the campaign talking about ethnic purity

---

[1] Geno Baroni, Assistant Secretary of Housing and Urban Development for Neighborhoods, Voluntary Associations, and Consumer Protection.

or ethnic heritage. I think it's very important for us Americans who are black or Spanish-speaking or Hungarian or Polish or Irish to have a continuing pride in our background, in our history, in our characteristics as human beings, and also in the preservation of the quality of our neighborhoods. I'm proud of where I live, the little town of Plains, Georgia. And I know that all of you, to the extent that one is proud of a family or community or a home, the quality of that family or community or home will be maintained. When pride leaves, then the neighborhood deteriorates.

And I think one of the greatest contributions to our country, in my lifetime at least, has been the pride of black people in their own heritage and a refusal to accept the proposition that was put forward by many that there was an inferiority in being a minority. There's just as much pride and strength in a minority group of any kind as there can be in a majority group.

We have a very deep concern about the destruction of the neighborhood fiber and strength. You mentioned banking. In this bill that I signed last week, which is now being put into effect by Housing and Urban Development, there is a tight constraint that will prevent the red-lining practices that have been implemented before. This was an amendment placed on the bill by Senator Proxmire. And I believe that that, combined with a voluntary effort to bring in the State and local governments, the Federal Government, and the private business leaders in a community, is the best way to stop a neighborhood deterioration.

Here in Detroit, for instance, there's a superb example of that, where the downtown area is being rebuilt with local, State, and Federal funds, yes, but also with the support of neighborhood groups and also the support of the local banking and other leaders.

One of the major contributing factors to the dramatic reduction in crime that does permit the children to walk to school and does permit people to go out on the front porch at night without being fearful is the close relationship between people who live in a neighborhood and the police officers who serve there.

I rode in from the airport today with the mayor of Detroit, Coleman Young, and I asked him, "How in the world have you and the police officers had such an unprecedented reduction in the crime rate?" And he said that one of the major reasons is that the police officers now are closely related to the community in which they serve. And they become friends of the people who live there, and eventually that friendship is reciprocated.

Quite often in a community that is very poor, that is going downhill, the people distrust the police officers and look on them almost as enemies instead of friends. I think that that permanent, friendly, mutually supportive relationship with the police officials among the neighbors who live in that community is a very vital part that can prevent a deterioration. Obviously, our public works programs, the community development programs, the housing programs, the red-lining programs, the crime control programs will be of help.

Another couple of things that I'd like to mention briefly is that we're trying to hold down the exorbitant costs of, for instance, medical care for people that you care about. We have a hospital cost containment bill that's already passed the two major committees in the House and the Senate. And this will stop the rapid increase in the cost of families, like in your neighborhood, where the income is fairly fixed.

A very high portion of people whom you serve are older. I think about 60 percent in your neighborhood, I understand, are maybe 65 or older—an extraordinary percentage. And they live on a fixed income. So, we're trying to do something to hold down inflation of all costs. We got some statistics this morning that show that the inflation rate, at least for last month, is less than 4 percent. I would like to maintain this permanently. I don't think we can, but at least we're making a step in the right direction.

The last point I want to make is that under the Housing and Urban Development Department, for the first time, we have a special Assistant Secretary for neighborhoods. His name is Father Baroni. And I know you're familiar with him.

During the campaign, two things that I emphasized almost everywhere I went was, one, the importance of the neighborhood, and the second was the importance of the family. I think if we can keep those family structures intact, that will make a great step forward.

And now, to get to someone who has always been very reluctant to express herself openly—[*laughter*]—Gladys Woodard.

SENIOR CITIZENS

Ms. WOODARD. Thank you, Mr. President. I'm going to make this very short because we have some more panelists here, and they're going to have to talk to you, too. I've talked to you a lot, and I'm going to talk to you again. I'll be in Washington next weekend. [*Laughter*]

The Older Americans Act is concerned with the quality of life for the elderly. In Michigan and particularly in Detroit, many senior citizens are living on limited, frozen incomes, in many instances as low as $3,000 per year or less.

Many of the persons here, and especially elderly people, they always face gas heat shutoffs or threats to shut it off because they have no money to pay the gas bills. It's too high. This is caused by delinquency as a result of last winter's severe cold wave. Now, I know you talk about energy, Mr. President, but these people must keep warm. Otherwise, they'll have pneumonia—anything. Even though the application for utilities relief was filed with the Department of Social Services, the threats and actual shutoffs has been taking place in a ruthless fashion here in the city of Detroit.

We are deeply concerned that, in addition to last winter's severe cold, we may face another severe, cold winter this winter. And we urge you, Mr. President, to use your power in your office to intervene on the behalf of the lives of thousands of senior citizens, not only of Detroit but across this country. We also urge a moratorium on heat shutoff from now until the winter is over, especially for senior citizens and for ADC mothers that have a house full of children.

There's a need to address the problems of the ethnic poor, especially senior citizens, who cannot receive services because of inability to communicate. There's a need to urge Social Security, the Department of Social Services, and other service agencies to develop a sensitivity to the needs of those who are isolated by language and cultural barriers. Those people are suffering, too. We don't have enough people to teach these people to take steps to recruit bilingual personnel and to avail themselves of community resources persons who can help and advocate and temper their language, and they suffer.

Also, in low-income areas we are also suffering in housing. And I agree with Father here: Everybody doesn't want to leave their rightful neighborhood. I also am the director—you know what I am—and I have all ethnic groups—Hungarians, Latinos, Poles, Appalachian whites, Mexicans—and all of those people are 65 percent, and the black is about 40 percent in my area, and I also head those organizations.

And there's about 14,000 people in my little neighborhood, and we need housing, Mr. President. I will be coming to Washington next week to see about that again. We need housing, and we need housing in that neighborhood, not because people said, "Oh, you live out there." Everybody can't live on the boulevard. Everybody can't live on Woodward. You have got to live in your respective neighborhoods. And we urge you to talk to HUD. And HUD is the people that will make some old broke-down houses; they don't care where you live. So, we want you to use your power to try to help us to get some houses for low-income families.

THE PRESIDENT. In order to get around the panel, I am going to make my answers very brief.

First of all, on the energy special funds for those that have their power cut off or their heat cut off, as you know, last year, quite late in the freezing winter, we came forward with $200 million under Graciela Olivarez, who runs the Community Services Agency [Administration]. This money was distributed to the local and State governments very efficiently, very effectively, in a hurry, too late. I've already had Senator Muskie and Senator Kennedy come to see me this week saying, "What about this coming winter?" And I can promise you that we're not going to be too late this coming winter.

On the bilingual approach to many problems, not just in education—of course, this is something we are pursuing. I promised this during the campaign and will continue with it.

And you mentioned that HUD hasn't cared where people lived or what kind of houses they lived in. This may have been the case in the past, that there have been housing funds frozen and impounded in the past. That won't ever happen as long as I'm in the White House because I know you'll be watching me too closely. I don't think we could have a better Secretary of Housing and Urban Development than Pat Harris, that we've got now. She's there with you, she cares about you, and you can depend on her and me not to let this happen again.

Thank you very much, Gladys.

Now, Courtney Matthews.

YOUTH UNEMPLOYMENT

MR. MATTHEWS. Good afternoon, Mr. President. My name is Courtney Matthews, and I'm 20 years old. I came to Detroit in 1966 from Chicago, Illinois. After I graduated from high school, I found it necessary that I work in order to attend college. I worked as a cook and a custodian and an unskilled laborer at Chrysler. And then, together with funds and savings I saved up and my mother's financial help and a basic opportunity grant, I was able to attend Tuskeegee Institute for 1 year, before financial forces forced me to return back to Detroit to seek employment. Now I live with my brother and his family. And my sister-in-law and I were the only ones supporting the family this summer because my brother was on disability. Now our program is over with, and there's no income coming into the house at all.

So now, my question is to you: What is a 20-year-old man to do when he wants to work and he wants to help his family and he wants to get a job in a city where there's no jobs for minority youth at all? Youth programs like that are our only jobs we have to look for, where private employers can give us the attention we need to become a productive citizen in today's job world. Thank you.

THE PRESIDENT. That's a good and a tough question to answer. And, Courtney, I can't tell you that I've got the answer. We have, in the whole country, now brought the unemployment rate down, I'd say, about 1 percent below what it was a year ago. And as you've already heard, in Detroit itself in the last 2 or 3 years, the unemployment rate has dropped about 75 percent. But that still means that when you have a 6 or 7 percent unemployment rate nationwide among young men like you, who are black, who have a fairly good education even, the unemployment rate runs 35 or 40 percent, which is entirely too high.

What we have tried to do already—and I would say the Congress has cooperated—is to concentrate our efforts on the Comprehensive Education and Training Act among young people themselves. We are now building up those jobs to 725,000. It will take a while to get up to that level. We are adding about, I'd say, in that particular program about 15,000 new jobs per week, which is a fairly big increase. About half those jobs will go to minority young people.

In addition, we've got a $1½ billion youth employment bill that the Congress passed, I signed into law. This has been within the last month or so. And it's just beginning to be put into effect.

Another thing that will help you is that in the public works projects that will be built in your area—and we're concentrating them more and more not in the wealthy suburban areas, but in the downtown areas where the need is greatest—at least 10 percent of those contracts in the future must go to minority business enterprises, and we're trying to make sure that the business is actually owned by a mi-

nority and not owned by the majority with just a figurehead black person whose name is used to qualify for the funds themselves.

Another thing that I'd like to point out to you is this: We've got a better economy than most of the nations of the world, but we've still got a long way to go. My goal, already established, is that before this term of mine is over that we'll bring that unemployment rate down from 8 percent, which it was last December, to well under 5 percent by the time 1981 rolls around.

There are not any automatic or easy answers. It's a very tough proposition. But the only thing we can do is make sure the jobs are made available in private industry, first of all, in government, second of all, and to make sure that the discrimination that has existed in the past against minority young people like you is wiped away and that we give a first priority in all our programs to the areas of the Nation, the areas of cities that have been hurt the worst. All those things are of substantial change or improvement over what we've seen in the past. But it's going to be a hard, long, tough proposition, and I wish you well.

Are you unemployed right now?

MR. MATTHEWS. Right now, yes, sir.

THE PRESIDENT. Well, we'll try to help you in those ways.

Joan Shaw.

COMMUNITY ACTION PROGRAMS

MS. SHAW. Afternoon, Mr. President. My name is Joan Shaw, and I'm from St. Cloud, Minnesota, and I work for a CAP agency. I guess I worked on your Crisis Intervention Program, and I'd like to say that our State of Minnesota spent its $8.5 million in 5 weeks' time about. And there's lots of people out there, thousands, that our agency had alone that we couldn't help because the funds ran out. So, we're asking you to consider giving us some more money.

THE PRESIDENT. We will do that.

Ms. SHAW. Thank you. CAP's need, I guess—more money to run to really help the people. It seems like we have one program at a time. Like right now we have a food shelf and a little bit of money to buy food stamps for people who we're trying to help get on assistance. Well, we'll have it for awhile, and then all the money runs out, and we can't help any more. We're kind of in-between all the time. So, you know, it's really a great need.

As for myself, I guess I'd like to also talk on health problems. Like I said, I'm a mother of five, and I don't qualify to get medical assistance, and yet I don't make enough money to pay the dental care of my own children who need it badly.

So, I'm asking you to really be concerned about the low-income, who feel that the poor get poorer and the rich get richer, and help us, too. Thank you.

THE PRESIDENT. Thank you very much.

Well, you have been very active, I understand, in representing consumers in a strong and very effective fashion, and I want to congratulate you on it. We are now facing a major decision by the Congress and by the Nation on energy legislation. And one of the toughest battles that I have to fight is to protect the consumers and to make sure that the Congress doesn't give the oil companies all the financial breaks as we put into effect an energy package. I might say that I have had superb support from the Vice President, from the Members of Congress from your own State in the House and Senate, and I'm going to go by Sunday afternoon and pick up the finest American that I have ever known—Senator Hubert Humphrey—and he's going to go back to Washington with me.

The Michigan delegation came with me. They are helping me, too, with this very difficult energy legislation. But it could mean, if we make a serious mistake, a devastating blow to the people who are not sometimes adequately represented by the lobbyists in Washington. And I hope that you all will look on me as your prime lobbyist in Washington for those who don't have strong representation at times.

We have done a few things, just to answer your specific questions, on food. This year already the Congress has very wisely removed the purchase requirement for food stamps, which, I think, will make the program much easier to administer in the future, and it will prevent poor people from having to put cash money into food stamps. They'll get the food stamp themselves now in the future without having to put money into it.

We also have done the best we could to provide some help for fuel costs during the rough winter we had last year. We'll have the same program, I don't have any doubt, this winter to take care of families who might have their energy cut off.

We have put forward, in addition, some programs that will be of great help to the poorer-built homes, with direct aid for those who want to insulate their homes. Quite often the poorer a family is, the more inefficient their home is in preserving heat and energy, and we want to be sure that that's corrected in this bill so that it will be a protection for you in the future.

We want to make sure that the money collected on oil price increases goes back to the consumers directly. And as you know, there's a great deal of pressure to give a large part of this money to the oil companies.

We are trying to have electricity rate reform. At this time the electric power companies charge the highest electric rates to those homeowners who use the least amount of electricity. If you have a big building like this or a big office building or a big factory, the more electricity you use, the less you pay per kilowatt-hour. And we want to be sure that that's turned around.

We also want to make sure that there's an end to the construction of unnecessary electric powerplants, because when there is a waste of electricity and the power companies have to build new plants to meet that need—increased demand that's not necessary—then the present consumers of electricity have to pay for the construction costs. This has not been addressed adequately in the past.

The other point I'd like to say is we are very concerned about health. We have put into effect a new immunization program. Now only about 45 percent of our young people are immunized against diseases.

When I was a child, or when some of you were children, almost a hundred percent of us had had immunization shots. We hope to increase that very quickly. And, you know, our CHAPS program, where we give full physical examinations for young people at a very early age—we now have only about 1½ million children who get that program. We intend, before I go out of office, to increase this 500 percent and have about 8 million more young people get these physical examinations and when things are found wrong with them at an early age, to give them health care that they need. Because if they go into the teenage years and later years, if they've had an early disease or problem that could have been corrected, it becomes very expensive for the public and also, of course, destroys their lives.

So, we have many programs that are now being put into effect very quickly under me and the Democratic Congress that I think are going to meet the needs of some of the people that you represent so well in Minnesota.

Ms. SHAW. Thank you.

THE PRESIDENT. Thank you very much, Joan.

Mike Maloney.

APPALACHIAN MIGRANTS

MR. MALONEY. Mr. President, I'm Mike Maloney. I'm the son of an Appalachian coal miner. I'm now an Appalachian migrant and director of the Urban Appalachian Council in Cincinnati, which is an advocacy organization for Appalachian migrants.

We now know who the urban poor are. The urban poor are black Southerners, even though they may be third generation from the South. They are white Southerners from the Appalachian South and from the flatland South. They're internal migrants from Puerto Rico. They're Chicanos or Mexican Americans. And they are the elderly that you and Father Hernady were talking about, of the national ethnic minorities. The bulk of the urban poor are in those groups. Our concerns as Appalachians are the same as has already been expressed.

I do need to mention that there are 6 million first- and second-generation mountain people now living outside the Appalachian region and that we're one of the largest ethnic minorities in the urban North. And it doesn't seem that the Federal Government knows that we exist. In many cases, the local governments don't know that we exist.

But if the Government has programs that help with unemployment, that help with the education of low-income children and housing, and if Government programs give some emphasis on the development of the neighborhoods, which are where people live, and consult with the people who live in neighborhoods, and if, perhaps, you could appoint a Presidential commission on urban neighborhoods to make sure you're not just dealing with city hall, but to make sure that programs are relating to neighborhoods, that would help all of us.

Thank you.

THE PRESIDENT. Thank you.

When I was Governor, I was chairman of the Appalachian Regional Commission. There are 13 States that belong to it, as you know. And this is an area that has been devastated in the past, was perhaps the poorest region of our Nation, may still be the poorest region of our Nation, geographically speaking. This poverty, as you point out so well, has forced many, several million people, from that mountain region into the urban centers. Quite often, they don't have the technical skills or the educational background or experience to survive and help themselves once they get in an urban environment. I think that this is likely to improve.

I would like to suggest that you make a point of coming to Washington and meeting with Father Baroni on the neighborhood question. He's a very sensitive man. This is a new office that has been established just to deal with neighborhoods themselves, because I'm afraid that he might overlook the special problems of the Appalachian migrants because he's not acquainted with your and my region of the country. So, if you would do that, Mike, I'm sure he'd be glad to see you. It might be possible, if you call him, that he could come and meet with you in a group who represent these 6 million migrant persons.

MR. MALONEY. He's a man that I trust.

THE PRESIDENT. He's a good man, and I think if he knew you better that the two of you might help to alleviate some of these problems that you describe. There is no program specifically for migrant Ap-

palachians who now have settled in the downtown areas of the cities. But I think that the programs that we have outlined already, which I won't repeat, would be applicable, but we need to know the special problems of the folks that you have in mind.

Would you do that for me? And I'll tell Father Baroni to expect you.

MR. MALONEY. I'll be glad to.

THE PRESIDENT. Thank you, Mike.

Mr. Doss.

URBAN PROGRAMS IN DETROIT

MR. DOSS. I'm Larry Doss, Mr. President. I'm president of New Detroit, Incorporated, the urban coalition in Detroit which works on improving the quality of life for people in the entire metropolitan area, but with special emphasis on the problems of the poor and minorities.

And you mentioned earlier that some positive things were happening in Detroit, and we're very conscious that Detroit is moving upward. Much of this is because of the kind of partnership and coalition that's been forged here in Detroit between government leaders, between labor and business and people in the community—the partnership that is turning many things around. But one particular important component has been generally absent from that partnership in the degree that we would like to have it present, and that has been the Federal Government. There are many, many programs and many needs that we have in Detroit that we would like to see the Federal Government be very much more involved in in terms of that partnership.

We brought to Washington a delegation led by Mayor Young—I think a very dramatic 5-year plan for moving Detroit forward—back in June. And there has been some limited response to that plan.

But we haven't yet seen the full Federal partnership response to that plan.

Some of the specific things in that plan and other crucial problems that we're trying to deal with in Detroit now, which really relate to moving ahead on our poverty problems and our economic development problems, are first of all jobs. Even though we've made that progress you talked about, from 24 percent to 8.8 percent, we're still something like 70,000 jobs short in Detroit, 70,000 people unemployed.

Secondly, we have still very pressing educational problems. Even though we are making some progress in education here, we still have 40,000 young people in Detroit between the ages of 16 and 20 that are dropouts from the school system. And our regular programs don't take care of them. No State programs are dealing with these young dropouts. So, we need new alternative education programs that give us a chance to recapture these young people and provide a new quality of life for them, because they will have the educational base they need.

Another crucial thing in Detroit is to strengthen our economic base so that we can become self-sufficient over the long run. In the short run it's going to take a great partnership of input from the Federal Government to accomplish this, and the kinds of things that we need on that are things like an urban development bank and other kinds of Federal incentives that will help to encourage business and jobs to locate in urban areas. We're getting an outflow rather than an inflow of businesses and the jobs they bring, and that's one of the things that creates our 70,000-job shortage.

So, those are some of the crucial kinds of things that we need in Detroit. And, most of all, we need to expand this partnership that we've developed here, that's

helping to move us forward, by having the Federal Government help us on these kinds of things, move us closer to full employment, and be a full partner in our efforts to restore Detroit.

The President. Thank you, Mr. Doss.

In order to save time, I'm going to ask three of the panelists to speak at a time, and then I'm going to ask my good friend Grace Olivarez to comment. I think we've covered most of the basic questions on the left about new health programs, job programs, public works programs, and so forth. Then I'll reserve a right after Grace comments to add my own, if necessary.

Mrs. Prieto.

ROLE OF WOMEN IN URBAN PROGRAMS

Mrs. Prieto. Mr. President, I am Luz Maria Prieto of Chicago, Illinois. I work for a group called Mujeres Latinas en Accion, or Latin Women in Action. We're a group of Latino women in Chicago. And knowing that—we know the problems of the barrios and the problems of the women. We have to struggle just to survive. And the woman has the greatest burden to survive for her family. We have to struggle through a disastrous educational system, a health system that we don't understand and sometimes does us a great deal of harm, and a great deal of underemployment because we are working women and have to work just to keep our families afloat. We're away from all the debates of things that affect us—domestic violence, abortion, drug abuse.

The sad part is not that we not only have no voice in these debates, but these are all debates about reactions to the problems. The women in the neighborhoods don't want just to react. We want to control our own destinies. And we need very simple answers, it seems to us, if we could say something about it. We need quality education, all the way down from child care, all around the clock, that's bilingual and bicultural, education for our children, education for the women who have to go back so we'd have real skills, skills that would benefit us and our families and would build up our communities, not just being dumped from one public sector job to another.

So, we're asking people to really work on the causes. It seems very simple. And if you talked to poor women and the Latino women of the barrios, we would tell you that that's what we need. We need programs that would just help us be self-sufficient.

THE PRESIDENT. Thank you very much.

Mr. Oscar Webb.

JOB PROGRAMS

MR. WEBB. Yes. Mr. President, my name is Oscar Webb and I represent Target Area I, which is part of the poverty program. And I imagine everything that I want to say has been hit on slightly, because it would take a multitude of things for me to explain to you some of the things that we need.

I would like to give you a good example. One of the things is that a father look at his child and say, "I'm on a fixed income. I can't work, can't find work, don't know where to go." You know, it's agony in a child's face, the father's face, the mother's face for this person to have to look and say that my family looks at me as a failure. There's no way for me to go. What am I going to do, you know? But now we are asking, you know, that maybe we can put someone up there in Washington who understands what's going on down here in these areas. And the only way that you can really find an answer is to ask the hungry man what it feels like. You know? We cannot ask a person that

doesn't understand what he's going through.

Other than that, education, you know—we have dropouts. It's many a reasons for these dropouts. We never had a committee to go out and find out why these dropouts are out of high school. We need people that's in the community to get into these programs.

We ask that when these guidelines are written, is it possible that maybe 40 percent or 60 percent of these jobs, paying jobs, go to the people who are in poverty, since it's poverty money? We would like to see these people's response. And that money that we're getting for welfare, that money can be used for other people who are on the waiting list. Do you understand?

I want to thank you for coming to Detroit to hear our complaints, and we hope that you will have this session again. I'm sorry that I didn't have enough time to give you all of the information on subjects that was on my mind.

Thank you.

THE PRESIDENT. I'd like to introduce Grace or Graciela Olivarez, who heads up our program in the Government—Community Services Agency—that deals directly and specifically and quickly with programs that have been outlined in this panel already.

I might point out that Mr. Webb is not only unemployed but he's disabled because of an accident. And this adds a special problem to a father who wants to be proud before his children. And when you talk about the problems of hungry people, I think that makes a great impression on me and on Ms. Olivarez and on the news media and on the rest of the people of the country who have heard or will hear tonight on the evening news what you've had to say, Mr. Webb.

I'd like to ask Ms. Olivarez to comment on the points that you three people have raised.

Ms. OLIVAREZ. I'd like to point out to Mr. Doss, I heard the Boston plan being introduced yesterday in the White House. And listening to Mr. Maloney, to the Detroit plan, and the Boston plan, I think that there's an ingredient missing, and that is that we can't talk about urban development without talking about rural development simultaneously. Because as you start improving the cities, they continue to be the magnet that create the situation that Mr. Maloney explains. But no provision was made for that type of magnet that is being created in the revitalization of cities.

So, I guess my recommendation, or my plea, would be for all who are developing urban redevelopment or regeneration plans not to forget that we've got to do the same thing in the rural areas simultaneously, or we're not going to be solving the problem.

I would like to mention, Mr. President, that Mrs. Prieto's father is an M.D. in Chicago who has done more work, probably more free-of-charge work, among the poor than any other M.D. who I know in the country. He has dedicated his life as a doctor and his services to people who don't have access to doctors. So, I'm very pleased to get to know her because I've known her dad for a while.

Let me just say, Luz, that I'm not trying to polish the President's apple. There's one great thing in Washington right now. There are a lot of women in key positions who are making policy. So, the problems of the women that you were describing can be addressed right now if you're willing to go in a joint partnership—Federal, State, city. And I would recommend that you get in touch with people like Blandina Cardenas, Arabella Martinez. Both of

them are in the Office of Human Development at HEW. By the same token, you might want to talk to some of the women on our staff or at the regional office in Chicago, because the type of program that you're doing—if we could do more of the preventive rather than the remedial, through training, I think that would help.

For Mr. Webb, I know what you're talking about when you say that the people who need the jobs didn't get them. I think you have to understand that during the last 8 years, the poverty agency has been victimized, brutalized, gutted, defunded, maligned. But under this administration we're trying to slowly bring it back together again, not necessarily to make it a larger agency, but to be a more effective spokesperson for the poor. And because of the last 8 years—there was no supervision, there was no monitoring— I'm sure that in some instances, the people who didn't deserve the jobs got them. I can assure you that under some of our regulations that we've issued recently and for which I'm getting a lot of flak, that is not going to continue, because we are constantly monitoring to be sure that the people who understand the problems are working at the solution as paid employees and not perpetual volunteers.

THE PRESIDENT. Let me add a brief comment. I noticed all three of you have talked about some problems that didn't arise before. One thing that hasn't been mentioned yet is the welfare reform proposal that we've put to the Congress. This program is designed to give our people better jobs and income. That's the name of it—Better Jobs and Income Program. And we have in there a heavy allotment of funds and programs for day care, for child care, that would specifically relate to women who want to work. And we also have included in the program 1.4 million jobs, Mr. Webb, for the heads of families.

That is above and beyond anything that I've described here to you so far.

We recognize that almost every person who is on welfare that's able to work would rather work if they are given an opportunity. And that will be the thrust of the welfare reform proposal that Congress will be working on and, hopefully, will pass next year. They already have the legislation on their desk. They have already started hearings on the subject.

So, to put people back to work that are able and want to work will be a major new thrust of the welfare proposals that Congress has now.

I'd like to call on Ms. Franckowiak first.

UTILITY ASSISTANCE PROGRAM

LORETTA FRANCKOWIAK. Most of what I was going to speak of about the utilities and the fuel shortage and so on has been very well put, but I would like to add to that. I think we need to continue the utility assistance program for poor people and the aged on a low-income basis with as much money as possible that can reach them.

In addition, we need programs to educate our youth. In the energy conservation our youth must get involved in the energy crisis, and I think employing low-income youth in helping out with energy problems is possibly a way to do it. It's very brief, but I want to thank you for your time.

THE PRESIDENT. Very good, too.

Mr. Carl Fox.

SENIOR CITIZENS

MR. FOX. Mr. President, this is my sixth year working for the senior citizens. I'm a volunteer man, from the area agencies. The area agencies on aging and other States and Federal organizations who serve the elderly need to coordinate their programs of the Community Service Ad-

ministration and local community action agency.

I'll skip along, Mr. President. The time lags between increases in social security benefits and increases in the Community Services Administration—poverty guidelines makes many needy clients ineligible for important service. If these increases took place at the same time, this would resolve the problem. The difference between the State and the Federal poverty guidelines should be eliminated to remove the roadblocks to service to the poor.

Now, Mr. President, I will go on. I know your time is limited. More lead time is needed between requests for our proposals and the due dates of our applications to allow seniors input and proper planning. More elderly low-income housing—well, I will skip that. Laws must be designated to remove certain zoning restrictions which have been used as a tool to prevent senior citizens low-income housing in many communities. More government grants should be geared to establish employment opportunity for low-income.

Okay, Mr. President, for a long time it has been recognized that it is less expensive for the taxpayer to provide support service for the elderly than it is to place the elderly in a nursing home. Certainly, almost all older persons are happier in their own home than they are in nursing homes. Therefore, it is important for this country to spend more of its resources on providing support service for the elderly. The existing support service programs, such as chore service, visiting nurses, home-bound meals, and so forth, have waiting lists of people who need the service but cannot get it because the programs are not sufficiently funded to handle the needs in their communities. Some of our elderly are lucky enough to get into elderly housing projects. These lucky persons receive housing subsidies to cover rent, utilities, taxes, insurance, and maintenance. The unlucky ones remain in their own home and try somehow to pay taxes, utilities, insurance, and maintenance. If they cannot cover their costs, they often find themselves in nursing homes.

For community development, Mr. President, it would be better for the older person and cheaper for the taxpayer to provide a subsidy to the older persons who own their own home to assist them with taxes, insurance, utilities, and maintenance. What I am suggesting, Mr. President, is that the Federal Government put more of the resources into full-range support service to assist the elderly to remain independent in their own home with dignity. This will also help maintain the stability of our Presidential community.

Thank you.

THE PRESIDENT. Ms. Evelyn Chappell.

INCREASING COST OF ENERGY

Ms. CHAPPELL. Mr. President, my name is Evelyn Chappell. I am a Head Start parent coordinator from Oak Park, Michigan.

My concerns mostly have been answered as you went around the table—about low-income housing, the lack of low-income housing, adequate low-income housing, high utility bills for ADC and low-income families.

Also, there seems to be a conflict between Housing and Urban Development and the Department of Social Services regarding utilities. For instance, utility allowances: Department of Social Services has one, and HUD has one. The difference in those allowances are subtracted and added onto ADC recipients' rents. I am an ADC recipient. I live in public housing. I know. Your rent goes up, and they add these charges onto your rent. They only allow you "x" amount of dollars for gas, "x" amount of dollars

for lights, when your one bill—your light bill—is higher than both that they allow you.

The winterization program is very, very good for the senior citizens. Okay, but what about the ADC and the low-income mothers who own their own home, who cannot afford to get roof leaks fixed, basements repaired, and windows repaired? What do we do?

Thank you, Mr. President.

THE PRESIDENT. Very good.

Ms. OLIVAREZ. I would just like to point out to you, Loretta, that the President has already indicated that we're going to make every effort to be sure that we do have a supplemental amount of money to help people with their high utility bills, so they don't go into the winter without that kind of assistance. Secondly, I would also advise that you continue to work on weatherization. And then, the third phase, which we must get involved in—that is looking at alternative sources of energy. I think we've been dragging our feet too long on this.

I come from a State—New Mexico—where we've already experimented with solar energy units that cost us $300, that were very effective in reducing heating costs by 30 percent—and then discovered that we could grow vegetables and flowers in them. So, we have an added dimension to it.

I guess what I'm saying is that there are hopes and plans and even some successes on alternative energy sources, particularly for people on fixed income, because I'm sure we're not going to be able to get supplemental appropriations every year for this type of problem. So, we must work on the alternative sources and on education, on the real issues surrounding energy.

As far as Mr. Fox is concerned—Mr. Fox, you know our agency gets a total of $10 million a year to work with senior citizens, simply because we're not the lead agency in serving senior citizens.

You pointed out the guidelines and the time involved in getting your application in. May I point out to you that Mr. Glenwood Johnson, the Regional Director in our Chicago office—would you stand, Glenwood?—I'd like you to get together with him after this, and would you repeat to him your concerns on the guidelines and when the application goes in and all that, to be sure that if there's a major problem that we take care of it immediately.

Like I said, we don't have the responsibility for senior citizens. We get $10 million. And our job is to be sure that we identify as many of those who are eligible for the existing programs. But that amount has been static for the last 4 or 5 years. We're hoping that we'll get a little bit more. But I'm not sure that it's only money that's going to solve the problem. I think we need to coordinate a little bit better.

And then, lastly, I should tell you that we do have an interagency group looking at the whole issue of who is in poverty and who isn't in poverty, and what do they mean by poverty guidelines, and how do you measure poverty in this era where people, even the middle class, can't afford to pay utility bills and buy houses.

THE PRESIDENT. We're going to go to the audience now. I would like to say, though, one thing about, particularly, Mr. Fox's comments, since he represents the elderly. The Senate, as you know, passed this week a change in the mandatory retirement age from 65 to 70. I have always felt that it was better for a person that age who wants to work to be allowed to do so, rather than to force them into retirement or onto the unemployed rolls.

Also, we are moving strongly to take advantage of what you've just described, that it's always cheaper for someone to receive services in their own home than

it is to go into a nursing home or go into a public institution. Almost invariably, too, the elderly person or retired person is much happier if they can live in one's own home. And that involves public meals. It also involves health care. It also involves recreation. And we know that there are many who need help with housing. We are continuing and restrengthening the 202 housing program that provides public housing for the elderly, and of course, the Section 8 rent supplements will help all those around this table and those whom you do represent.

I thought that Ms. Chappell—I'm sorry I pronounced your name wrong—made some very good points on the special problems of people who are not elderly, who are not disabled, but who do qualify and genuinely need the services of the welfare program under HEW.

There's too much of an overlap and a lack of communication among the different Federal agencies. We're trying to bring some order out of chaos in making sure that these agencies do have a special responsibility, that they have to cooperate, communicate, and work with one another, because if it's hard for me in the White House, with all my authority, to understand which Federal agency does what, it's impossible for you to understand which Federal agency does what.

We do have an outstanding group of women at the top levels in our Federal Government. Graciela Olivarez is only one of them. At the head of the Housing and Urban Development Department, we have a strong, competent woman; at the head of the Commerce Department, responsible for all public works programs and EDA programs, we have a strong and competent woman; at the head of the Equal Employment Opportunity Agency [Commission], as you know, we have a strong and competent woman, and many others in Cabinet and sub-Cabinet levels.

This is a fairly new development in our Government. But, I think, quite often women who have been activists in fighting for poor people, deprived people, minority groups, the elderly, and women are now helping to make policy for our own administration.

Before we take the first question from the audience, I'd like to say that although I've tried to provide some answer or explanation to you when you've had a criticism or a question, we've got a long way to go. We've made some progress, and I don't want you to think that I believe that all the questions have been answered. When we leave here today, Courtney Matthews will still be unemployed. And when we leave here today, there will still be problems for Mrs. Prieto and the women, and particularly minority group women, in having equal rights in our country. There will still be urban areas that are left blighted. There will still be a lack of communication between you and Federal, State, and local officials who are trying to work with you.

We are not solving all the problems here today, but as the head of our Government, I have learned a lot. And I hope that all of you will keep your direct connections with me, with Ms. Olivarez, and others. This is a first step.

Is Father Baroni here? Where? Come up here a minute. Stand up again. I want all of you to see Father Baroni.

Almost every question that has been raised this afternoon relates directly to the family and the life structure of a neighborhood. And, of course, my neighborhood responsibility is to 215 million Americans. But the only way that I can do that job well is to make sure that each family, each home, each street, each small community is addressed as a unit and that people there join in with me in making their own lives better.

When the members of a neighborhood rebel against government or look on the policemen as an enemy or provide hatred or misunderstanding against a neighbor who might be different from you, to that extent it makes it impossible for me or the Federal Government or your local or State governments to do anything. And Father Baroni's only responsibility is to work with people like you, who represent neighborhoods, to make sure that all of our programs strengthen that basic foundation on which our country rests.

Father Baroni, I'm very glad you came here today. This is a new job in the Federal Government, and I think as time goes by, you'll see the advantages of having a man like him who has that responsibility to you.

Now, I don't know what the exact arrangement is, but I understand we have microphones on each side. We'll start with this gentleman on my right.

QUESTIONS

PROGRAMS FOR SPANISH-SPEAKING

Q. *Buenos tardes* [good afternoon], President Carter.

THE PRESIDENT. *Buenos tardes, Señor.*

Q. My name is Rafael Acalá. Some of my qualifications: I was an ex-migrant, President Carter, I'm a student. Some of the problems that I represent here—I think I've been kind of contemplating on what the question I could ask you, kind of put everything in a nutshell, and it possibly could fit in with Ms. Olivarez to help you—that as the second largest minority in the United States, representing not only the city of Detroit but the whole United States.

The question I want to ask you, President, is that, what is the reason why, when programs are funded for Latinos, Chicanos, or Hispanic communities—and they are just getting off the ground—they seem to be taken away from us, including the city of Detroit? What I want to ask you, President Carter, is, for example—at the present time there is a need for this type of education, of programs, not only in the black community but in the Latino communities. For example, at the present time, President Carter and Ms. Olivarez, LULAC National Education Service Centers has only a chance to be funded until December. This is the one and only top educational center mechanism that the Latino community has all over the United States. They only have fundings up to December. I am concerned, because it deals with all the issues that Mrs. Prieto and Mrs. Molina have addressed in the Latino community. I am concerned, just like all my brothers here in southwest Detroit. I am also a product of Michigan. I am concerned with what will you, President Carter, do in alleviating our problem when our funding for our Latinos programs, for Hispanic communities, are detailed, are not funded to the capacity that is needed. We need an answer on that, Mr. President.

THE PRESIDENT. Thank you, Mr. Acalá. Ms. Olivarez is familiar with the specific question that you asked. I'm going to ask her to give you the answer.

Ms. OLIVAREZ. Mr. President, that particular project is an educational project that isn't designed exclusively for poor people. They have been funded by our agency for—it will be 4½ years in January. And we have asked them to go to the Office of Education for that kind of money, because we don't have enough money to fund educational centers. Sometimes I think we wind up subsidizing the other agencies that have larger budgets.

THE PRESIDENT. What are the prospects for success in getting it continued?

Ms. OLIVAREZ. The prospects for their getting funding from the Office of Education are good, except that there's going to be a lull of about 5 months simply because of the bureaucratic situation. But I am working with the leaders of the organization to see if we can help them in the interim while they get their funding from the Office of Education.

THE PRESIDENT. Do you think I can help?

Ms. OLIVAREZ. Yes, sir.

THE PRESIDENT. I'll help. Thank you.

COMMUNITY ACTION PROGRAMS

Q. President Carter, my name is Audrey Francis, and I'm the mother of nine, and four are at home. I'm here for the CAP program. They've insulated my home and fixed the roof. I need their help badly, and they are working with the same funds that they started with 7 years ago. And every year it's still the same amount, and they are running out. The ones that are doing the work are the young people that are unemployed and out of work. And it's a case where the poor is helping the poor, and they're helping me help myself.

THE PRESIDENT. I understand. Grace also knows the answer to this. [*Laughter*]. Since she has a specific responsibility, I'll let her answer, and I'll follow up.

Ms. OLIVAREZ. Okay. Thank you. I just wanted to point out that seated behind you is part of the Michigan congressional delegation, who have been very good friends of the Community Action Agency. And through the help of them and others, we understand that our funding this year, particularly for the type of programs that you're talking about that are administered at the local levels through the CAP agency—that we'll get a little bit more money than we had been getting in the past. So, we expect to be weatherizing a lot more homes of poor people.

Q. Thank you very much.

THE PRESIDENT. Before we go further, I'd like to ask the members of the Michigan congressional delegation to stand. I don't believe there's any other group in the country that has been more eager to help work with me and others in alleviating these problems than this group has. And I would like for them to stand and let you recognize them.

SPECIAL EDUCATION PROGRAMS

Q. Hello, Mr. Carter. Thank you for inviting me here this afternoon. My question deals with health care, and it's something that has touched my life and lives of other children.

What is your administration doing today for the children with learning disabilities, in terms of education, specialized training, and especially financial support for the children in low-income houses? People with low income can't afford the training their children need and have to send them to school where the teachers and the programs are not geared for the children with learning disabilities. These children suffer, and it's an emotional problem. It is a physical problem, and it scars them for the rest of their lives. And most of society neglects it and ignores it. The problems surface later, sometime in dropouts, in crime, and in many other areas. Thank you.

THE PRESIDENT. Thank you very much.

One of the first things I did when I was elected was to appoint a special commission on those Americans who have mental problems and those who have disability problems. My wife is the Honorary Chairman, and as you may know, she has had hearings all around the country and has just recently given me her report. In the meantime, though, we've been learning from this special study.

One of the things that we are doing is, as we set up the day care centers and child care centers and expand that program, we're giving first priority to chil-

dren who have learning disabilities and other problems of that kind. In the past they have been the last priority. We have now moved them up and will move them up to the first priority.

The second thing we are doing is to make sure in all our programs that deal with disabilities that we are emphasizing not institutional care, but community-oriented small units, where the children can be close to their families, close to their own homes, where the cost is much less and the benefit of training programs and education programs are greatly magnified.

Another thing that we've done is to increase greatly the Head Start programs, which give the children in low-income communities an early start in the learning experience. The first Head Start program that ever existed in Georgia—I happened to have been the head of it. And I learned at that time the tremendous benefit that can be derived for children who come from deprived homes, not only handicapped because of emotional or mental or physical problems but also because of social problems and environmental problems, where the families are so poverty-stricken that the kids have never seen a book, they've never heard a bedtime story, they don't have any base on which to compete with the other children.

And the last thing I'll mention very briefly is the so-called CHAPS program, which I think is very crucial in the future. This will provide early, complete physical examinations which will include not only teeth and eyes and their bodily functions but also will include any disabilities that are at least apparent at that time. We now have about 1½ million children a year who are given this kind of early, thorough examination. We expect to expand this very rapidly to about 9½ million, which is an additional 8 million or about a fivefold increase. This will be done as rapidly as the bureaucratic structure can be established. Again, we want this to be done as nearly as possible to the children's natural living environment, either in the Head Start program, the first days when they attend the first grade, or in the home or community structure.

So, we are moving very quickly to correct some of the defects that have existed in the past and also to give special emphasis to those children who have special learning disabilities. Thank you very much.

SOCIAL SERVICE AGENCIES

Q. Mr. President, my name is Cleophus Young. I am president of the Community Action Agency in south Cook County. They have over 60,000 recipients.

My problem is that—we commend you on your redesigning or reorganizing human services as they relate to Washington and the fiscal control—our concern is that if a community action agency is supposed to be its clients' advocates, how can we deal effectively when human service agencies are compartmentalizing our clients? We have a big problem with one has their arms, one's got their legs, and there's never a case conference. We, at this point in time, demand some kind of vehicle that we can determine and monitor and be a part of the services that are given to our clients. One social worker might tell him to stand on his right foot, and a juvenile officer will tell him to stand on his left leg.

And please, in the winterization money we have one big problem—the way the paying agencies are taking their time to pay the utility companies, which should be sensitive to the problem, which they are not. We help a low-income person by paying the bill, but next week after the bill is paid, they get a request for deposits. So, you haven't helped them anyway. This program has only helped, this year,

the utility companies. It has not really helped us. Please take this into consideration. Thank you.

THE PRESIDENT. The reason that the agencies compartmentalize your clients is because the agencies are compartmentalized in Washington. And there's no way to make it possible at the community level to have a client-family deal with one key person who can take care of the needs, without running all over the community, unless we have some coordination coming out of Washington. This is what we are trying to do with our reorganization proposal.

When I became Governor of Georgia, we had this same problem. We did an analysis and found that in some poor families we had seven different State agencies going to that one family. Every one of those agencies had a separate file on that family. And there was no way for the poor, sometimes ignorant people in the family that didn't have a telephone and didn't have an automobile to find the right agency when they had a problem.

But we had what we called a one-door policy that we established. We brought all those agencies together in a human resources department, and we arranged it so that in every community there was one place where a family could go for advice or counsel or even services, themselves, and for financial assistance. And we tried to make sure that one lead agency person—it might be a mental health worker, it might be a social worker, or others—would go into that family and get to be friends of theirs. And that family had that person's telephone number. And if an aged person had a problem, and the social worker that worked with that family happened to be a specialist in mental health, they could call that person in the middle of the night, and that person would know who the aged counselor might be.

But we now still have a grossly disorganized Federal Government. At the regional office you have the same thing. But we're working on that. And the Congress gave me early this year authority to reorganize the structure of the Government. I'm going to do it, and I need for you to help me reach this great goal. I believe we can do it together.

We only have time for one more question, I understand from my staff.

CITIZEN PARTICIPATION IN COMMUNITY PROGRAMS

Q. Mr. President, my name is Romelia M. Carter, Youngstown, Ohio. As you probably already know, with the closing of the steel mills in Youngstown, we have a terrific problem.

THE PRESIDENT. Yes, I know.

Q. I'm representing the Youngstown Community Action Council. We would like to know, President Carter—now that it seems as if you are fully aware that the services that are to be given to the poor and money for jobs are being used up now in political patronage—if you have a way to or if you can explain to us what your plans are to alleviate this so that the old meaning of meaningful citizens participation once more comes back into stress. We used to know about citizens participation, and it was meaningful at one point. But now it's no longer meaningful. Can you give us some idea as to what you're going to do or what method you're going to use to make us meaningful again?

THE PRESIDENT. Thank you. I might say that it's always nice to meet my cousins, and I'm glad you are here. [*Laughter*] During the campaign I was able to visit Youngstown, as you may remember, several times, and you and Mr. Hall make a very good representation from that community today.

I believe that you would agree that when John Kennedy was President and when Lyndon Johnson was President, that the community action agencies had a life of their own and helped to make decisions about government programs. In the last 8 years—and I won't call the names of the Presidents who were in the White House—[*laughter*]—those community action agencies were put into a very secondary position and lost the influence and the decisionmaking authority that they formerly had under the leadership of people like Joe Califano in HEW, who helped to put into effect many of the Johnson programs 10 years ago. And under the leadership of Pat Harris and Juanita Kreps and Grace Olivarez and others, we're trying to bring back the life of those community action groups.

I think that it's impossible, no matter how intelligent or how dedicated a Washington official might be—it's impossible for them to know what the needs are in your community as well as you know them. That's the reason that I brought Grace Olivarez with me today, because that's her responsibility, working with the people that I've just named, to make sure that in the future we have a reviving of the community group influence and authority, whether it's a Hungarian American community or a Spanish-speaking community or a predominantly black community in Youngstown where a steel mill has shut down or a community of older people in Florida who have moved down there on a very low income; that doesn't matter. I want that particular community to let me know, through the Government agencies, how we can best address your problems.

I want to thank you for that good question. I think Grace would agree that we're making a move in the right direction. And I think meeting with you today will help to expedite what we want to do.

I think that everybody in the audience would agree that we've had a superb panel. They've asked very good questions, brought forward very good ideas for us. And I and all my staff members who are here, the different Federal agencies represented—and almost all of them are represented—the national news media that will repeat what you have said to the world at large tonight will benefit greatly from the sound, good judgment that you have provided and the personal experience that make your words carry even more authority than the words of a President. You know what you're talking about. I'm trying to learn what you're talking about.

Thank you very much.

NOTE: The President spoke at 1:30 p.m. in the Ballroom at the Veterans Memorial Building.

Des Moines, Iowa

Remarks on Arrival at Des Moines International Airport. October 21, 1977

Did any of you see the plane that just took off? During the campaign, I traveled through Iowa seven different times. I visited 110 of your cities and towns. And all those times put together, I never saw this many people. The small plane that took off just before the airline plane, the single engine, was much larger and much more modern than the one that I used to fly around over your beautiful fields.

I was reading the other day about the great American poet Robert Frost who, the first time he came to Iowa and saw your rich black earth, said he saw no reason to process that earth through vegetables, for it was good enough to eat.

And I feel almost that good, coming from Washington back here.

As I told your own congressional delegation a few minutes ago, as is the case with all of you, with Iowa Congressmen and Senators, I feel like I'm coming home. And I do feel like I've come home to you.

When I was lonely, you took me in. When I needed support, you gave it to me. The first time I came to Iowa there was a Gallup poll. There were 36 names on the Gallup poll. Mine was not even on the list.

But still, many of these folks that are standing in the front row here let me come in your homes. You introduced me to your friends. I got to know you. You got to know me. And it was the beginning of a successful campaign.

I think one of the things that tied me closer to the Iowa people than anything else, at least in those early days, was the fact that I was a farmer; I understood the soil and the earth. I knew then and I know now that in all the economy of our great Nation, the single most important factor is farming and agriculture. And that made me feel at home when I came to Iowa.

Ours is the nation that's the greatest food producer on Earth. Iowa is number one in corn production, number one in hog production. You produce 10 percent of all our Nation's food. And this gives us a tremendous strategic weapon to be used in a peaceful way to tie the nation to the world together.

During this past 12 months, we have exported $24 billion worth of food and feed products, and Iowa is an integral part of all that. We've got great needs in our country. But I think you represent the solutions to many of those problems, because you are an agricultural State and, at the same time, are moving forward in technology, in industry, and business.

Because the Iowa people believe in hard work, you have the lowest unemployment rate of any of the 50 States in the Nation, and I want to congratulate you on that as well.

You've always represented what makes our country strong. I think of all the States I know, there's a closer sense of family and a closer sense of community and a closer sense of brotherhood and sisterhood in Iowa, because you know that many of the problems of the future cannot be resolved by individuals alone; there must be cooperation.

And there's a deep sense here, too, of what this Nation has meant to our forefathers who came to our country, staked out a small claim of land, and began to carve out for ourselves a great future and a great country.

I'm glad to come back as a Democrat, and I know that you share with me a great pride in your own congressional delegation. We've just signed, a few days ago, a new comprehensive farm bill which will help to bring order out of chaos, to let us have strengthening prices, to let food reserves be kept within the control of farmers, that will expand greatly agricultural export potential, that will give us greater research and development programs for agriculture.

They see and I see, together, that as we face other problems like the energy package, that this decision to be made will affect every life here, whether you live in the city or live on a farm. And of all the delegations that I know in the Congress, I've not had stronger friendship nor stronger support than I have from your own congressional delegation. And I'd like for them to hold up their hands and for you to express your appreciation to them, as I do from the bottom of my heart.

They not only take care of your own personal needs but they are leaders. We had a very crucial vote last night to decide whether to go on building the unnecessary B-1 bomber or not. They voted with me, and I believe that that bomber will not be built anymore, and I thank them for it.

We're trying to bring peace to the world by eliminating the threat of nuclear weapons and the proliferation of nuclear explosives, and this is a great group of allies for me to bring about peace for which we all search. And I believe we're going to find it with the help of the Congress, particularly your delegation from Iowa.

I've had a chance to learn about—a lot about your State. I don't claim to know all the answers. But I believe that my campaigning around Iowa, my knowledge of you, your friendship for me will stand me in good stead in the future.

We've got some problems in our country; no one could deny that. But we're making progress. The unemployment rate in the last 8 or 9 months has dropped 1 full percent. I just came here from Detroit. Two years ago, the unemployment rate in the downtown urban area was 24 percent; now, it's down to about 8 percent.

We got figures this morning that showed that the inflation rate is coming under control, an annual rate of only 3.6 percent. We've still got a long way to go, but we're going in the right direction.

If you'll stand with me, give me your support, give me your confidence, give me your friendship as you did before, I'll try to do you a good job as President, to continue to learn from you, to derive my strength from you, and to work with you to make sure that we keep our Nation as it always has been—the greatest country on Earth.

Thank you very much for coming out to meet me. God bless every one of you.

NOTE: The President spoke at 5:15 p.m. at the Air National Guard Facility. During the flight from Detroit to Des Moines, the President met on Air Force One with members of the Iowa Democratic congressional delegation—Senators Dick Clark and John C. Culver and Representatives Berkley W. Bedell, Michael T. Blouin, Tom Harkin, and Neal Smith.

Des Moines, Iowa

Remarks at the Democratic Party Jefferson-Jackson Day Dinner. October 21, 1977

When I think of Iowa, I think of people, mostly. I think about Marie Jahn, Soapy Owens, Harry Baxter, Floyd Gillotti, and literally dozens of other people who had confidence in me months and months before I was able to convince the rest of the world that I was a political figure who needed watching.

Two years ago, I came to speak to the annual Jefferson-Jackson Day Dinner in Iowa at Ames. I was not the only main speaker on the program. [*Laughter*] But when the evening was over, we had won what proved to be a great national victory. I have to admit that most of my votes came from people who were sitting in the balcony in the $5 seats. And even now a lot of them are wondering whether or not they got their money's worth. [*Laughter*] But it formed a tie or a cement between myself and your State and your people that will last until the last day I live. I'm grateful to you, and since then I've had a chance to learn more about this country, more about its people.

My family have become the centers of attention—there has been 2 or 3 weeks of publicity about whether Amy was playing "Three Blind Mice" or "Twinkle, Twinkle, Little Star" on her violin. We've had a chance to learn about the rest of the world. We'll be making a long overseas trip beginning the last of November. We'll be going down to Brazil to pick up the sweater that Rosalynn left there last spring. We'll be making several stops on the way—in Venezuela, Nigeria, Iran, Saudi Arabia to refuel our plane and to get special dealer's rates from the oil-producing countries. [*Laughter*]

It's really kind of a pleasure trip for me as President. You get to do things that everyone wants to do but very seldom has a chance to accomplish. How many of you have ever had Thanksgiving Day in Lagos? [*Laughter*] See what I mean? But I hope to take to those countries an accurate image of our Nation, representing you.

My family has been affected in other ways. My brother, Billy, has found another way to make a living other than growing peanuts. He can go to Canada and do a bellybuster in the swimming pool and make more money than he made all year on the farm. [*Laughter*] When I mentioned that to Billy, he said, "Well you forgot, Jimmy, that I don't know how to swim." [*Laughter*] But anyway, he is doing his share for the Nation's economy. He's put the beer industry back on its feet—almost alone. [*Laughter*]

A lot of people criticize Billy, but his standing in the public opinion polls is substantially above my own. [*Laughter*] As a matter of fact, lately—you couldn't tell it by tonight—but the polls have been down a little. But I remind myself that even in the worst of polls, I've only dropped 3 percent since election night. So, I'm pretty good there. And in the more responsible and reliable polls, we're still up pretty high, as you know, and I have enjoyed it.

Tonight, I went to the hotel room for a couple of hours before coming over here, and I wanted to write some notes for my speech. I thought back to a little more than 3 years ago when I first came to Iowa. I traveled across your State. I think I stopped in seven towns and cities. And I began to talk about issues that were important to you and important to me and important to our country. Quite often very few people came. Harry Baxter and his wife arranged for two or three hundred to come to a reception here in Des Moines. I think three people came, including Harry Baxter's wife and Jody Powell and one other. And I was invited over to the courthouse and went through and shook hands.

But way back in those days we were already talking about human rights. We were talking about stopping the construction of the B–1 bomber. We were talking about bringing lasting peace to the Middle East. We were talking about holding down weapons sales, not only from our country, which is the worst violator of all, but among arms producers throughout the world. We were talking about a better relationship with the Soviet Union, a comprehensive SALT agreement that would put a limit on atomic weapons of all kinds. And we are making great progress on this effort. And I can tell you that in a few weeks, my prediction is that we will have a SALT agreement that will be a pride of our country, and following that, we will proceed toward my ultimate goal of reducing nuclear weapons in this world to zero.

Back in those early days, even a year ago, there was a general feeling that nothing could be done to stop the proliferation of nuclear explosives among countries that presently don't have them. But in the last 9 months we have formed a commitment among the nations of the world to permit some use of atomic power to produce electricity, but to prevent the production of

weapons. And I believe that we'll never see another nation again added to that horrible club that we started of countries that have nuclear destructive weapons in our repertoire.

This week 36 nations came together in Washington to talk about the international nuclear fuel cycle and how we might bring into being this dream of all people in the world.

We talked about the reorganization of the Federal branch of Government, the executive branch, to bring some order out of bureaucratic chaos. And the Congress has given me authority now, for 3 years, to carry out this effort. And I am as determined now as I was 3, 2, or 1 year ago, to do it successfully.

We talked about inflation. A year ago the inflation rate was very high—last December, 10 percent. We've brought it down slowly and steadily. The information that was given out this morning on a 1-month-only basis was that the inflation rate is below 4 percent for the first time in quite a while. I think the prevailing inflation rate is about 6 or 6½ percent. It's going to be almost impossible to hold it down. But we are making some progress.

We're doing the same thing on the unemployment rate. Last December it was 8 percent. Now it's down to 7 percent, a little bit lower. It's still a great challenge to us all, but we are making some progress.

I was in Detroit earlier today. Two years ago, the unemployment rate in that urban city was 24.4 percent; now, it's 8.8 percent. But we still have an unemployment rate among minority groups, particularly young people, 35 or 40 percent.

It's not going to be an easy thing to do, but I'm just as determined as I was before to carry out my commitment to you to bring some order out of chaos in our economy. We're working orderly and persistently with other nations of the world to address these matters on a multi-national basis, and I believe that we are making some progress.

I know that our country's persuasive effort around the world to bring about peace in Africa, in the Middle East, better relationships with our former enemies, depends upon a strong economy.

Tonight, I'd like to mention two subjects that are important among all those others. One is the economy as it relates to agriculture.

Yours is a great agricultural State. It provides one of the ties between me and you. The economy of our country is based upon agricultural production. We're the greatest nation on Earth in the production of food and feed and fiber. Your State is preeminent. But we have some problems in agriculture that we're also trying to address.

Agriculture and the people who participate in this effort are not well understood. It would be a serious mistake to think that we have no inherent problems. We can't take for granted bountiful crops. We can't take for granted economic health. We can't take for granted food supplies.

We are now forming efforts to bring about our hopes. We have an Agriculture Secretary, Bob Bergland, who's a dirt farmer. He's the kind of man who understands the special problems of farm families. He's been there. He went to Florida as a migrant worker. He came back home and borrowed money to start a small rent farm operation. He now has about 600 acres of farmland, as you know, in the northernmost part of Minnesota. And he's working on the extremely complicated subjects that deal with the farmers' lives in a very enlightened, down-to-earth, practical, and effective way.

We've come out this year with a comprehensive farm bill that will help in many ways to carry out the promises that I made to you when I was campaigning in your State. We've established target prices which on an average will meet production cost, and it's done in a conservative way which will help to hold down the rapidly escalating prices for farmland.

We've also set price supports that will keep our products competitive. We've increased exports. In this last 12 months our farm exports were $24 billion, the highest they've ever been in the history of our country. This year, on a worldwide basis, we have fairly good crop weather. Exports may not be as good in fiscal year 1978 as they have been last year, but we'll try to hold them up.

One of the promises that I made to the farmers of this State and others during my campaign was there would be no more grain embargoes, and you can depend on that. There won't be as long as I'm in the White House.

We're trying to establish, for instance, a noncommercial insurance program to make sure that farm product exporters are protected from losses that they can't anticipate. We're trying to expand Public Law 480 to increase the export of our farm products, food and fiber and feed, to nations that are destitute and hungry. We're trying to cut down artificial trade barriers in the multinational trade negotiations now going on in Europe. We're opening agricultural trade offices in places around the world where they haven't existed before.

We're trying to make it possible for farmer-owned cooperatives to negotiate directly in the sale of feed grains and food grains. We're making sure that we bring together the different departments of our Federal Government in the common effort to sell agricultural products—the Labor Department, our Special Trade Representative, the Commerce Department, the State Department, as well as the Department of Agriculture.

We're trying to establish a comprehensive world food policy to match the tremendous production that we have with the tremendous need among the hungry people of the world. And we're trying to explore new markets, not only in Western Europe and Japan but in Eastern Europe and other countries as well.

So, in the export of food we're trying to increase the quality of service that the great farm areas of our Nation provide for the rest of the world. We've got a long way to go. We have to work out the problem with food reserves, and my promise to the farmers of this area was that when we did have high-yielding crops—and this is the greatest crop we have ever had in corn; it's the greatest crop we've ever had in soybeans—that we would have reserves that would be not under the control of the Government, but supported and controlled by farmers so there can be no dumping on the market, artificially, to lower prices. And I promised you that we'd do the best I could to get the Government out of interference in the production, storage, and marketing of crops. These kinds of challenges are constantly on my mind.

We have a long way to go in soil and water conservation efforts, and we've got a long way to go in providing a comprehensive disaster assistance program.

There's another item I'd like to mention tonight, and that's the subject of energy. I presented to the Congress and to the American people last April, for the first time in the history of our Nation, a comprehensive energy policy.

We had a severe blow in 1973 when the prices of oil were quadrupled almost overnight. And when an oil embargo was slapped on our country, that economically almost brought us to our knees.

Other nations suffered the same challenge. They have reacted well. The consumption of oil in Germany, compared to 1973, is down. The consumption of oil in Sweden is down, France down, Italy down, Japan down. The consumption of oil in the United States since 1973 is up 87 percent. This year we are importing $45 billion worth of oil from overseas, half of the oil we use. And that's almost exactly the amount that we waste, that we don't have to waste. Notice that this is twice as much oil imported as all the agricultural products that we export. Something must be done.

It's not easy to remove the hold on our government processes that have been in existence for a long time by the oil and gas companies, but I'm determined to do it with your help. In many ways, the acceptance by the American people and the acceptance by the American Congress of a comprehensive energy policy is a test of our strength and a test of our national will. The rest of the nations of the world watch us very closely to see if we can sacrifice in a time of international need.

The proposal that we've put forward is bitter medicine, but it's not nearly so bitter as the catastrophe that might befall us if we don't take rapid action. We have put forward a well-balanced program that will induce our own selves to conserve energy of all kinds. It will induce us, without hurting us deeply, to shift to other forms of energy, away from oil and natural gas. I'm determined that the consumers of our Nation will not be hurt and that the oil suppliers, the companies that produce oil and gas, will not be enriched in an unwarranted fashion. We have built into our proposal adequate incentives to encourage oil and gas exploration and production.

Under our own program new oil discovered by American companies in the future will have the highest price on Earth. But still the oil companies want more. And unless we stand firm, they may get it. And if they do, it will come out of the pockets of those who need it, who need the money and who need adequate energy supplies most.

As a farmer, I know that we, just a small part of the American population, use $6 billion worth of oil and gas every year. About 75 percent of all the energy we use is oil and natural gas. This means that we have got to have a supply in the future, because it takes natural gas and propane to dry our crops.

It takes oil to drive our tractors and our trucks and our other machinery. We can't very easily shift to coal. So, as we conserve and shift to other supplies of energy, in the production of electric power, for instance, it makes that much more available to farmers in the future when energy supplies become even more scarce.

There are some myths that are exploited on your television set several times a day, sometimes several times an hour.

The first myth is that the oil and gas industry is controlled by free market forces. All of us believe in the free enterprise system, but there is no free enterprise system in the oil and gas market. The prices are not established by competition. The prices are established arbitrarily when the OPEC nation leaders meet in secret and say, next year this is what we will charge for oil. And, as you well know, immediately that oil price prevails in new oil discoveries in our country.

We have a need, at least for our Government, to play a stronger role, as is played in other countries. But we ought to get away from the proposition or the thought that free market forces control oil or natural gas prices.

Another myth is that there's an inherent conflict between conservation and production. This is not true. We are making good progress in exploration for oil. There's about an 8-month waiting period right now for new oil drilling rigs. If we triple the price of oil and natural gas, there could be no substantial increase in the rate of exploration. It would be just an enormous windfall of profits. The cheapest oil is what we save, and the cheapest natural gas is what we save. Quite often it costs nothing to save the equivalent of one barrel of oil per day.

When we add expensive conservation measures, it costs maybe from zero to $3,500 to provide the saving of one barrel of oil per day. The oil that we are now going to bring down from Alaska costs about $20,000 in capital investment for one barrel of oil per day, used at its final place to heat a home. For the production of electricity, the capital investment required is much greater, maybe $50,000 to $100,000 for the equivalent of one barrel of oil used in your home in electricity. For nuclear powerplants, the investment is $200,000 to $300,000 per barrel of oil per day, when it's actually delivered to your home for use.

So, to conserve a barrel of oil is much better than producing that barrel of oil in investment alone. And at the same time it reserves for future use these extremely scarce supplies.

I wanted to mention tonight especially those two among many subjects that fall on my shoulders—agriculture and energy. The tests of political strength are severe; the responsibilities are great; the complexities are very difficult; the questions are hard to answer. But what gives me a sense of assurance and confidence is the degree with which I am close to you. When I base my opinion and my decision and my efforts on what I know you feel and what I know that you want, to that degree I feel that I represent you and our Nation well.

I have a feeling that we are making good progress in correcting some of the deep concerns that we felt a year, 2 years, 3 years ago. The spirit of our country had been damaged severely by the Vietnam war. It had been damaged severely by the Watergate revelations, by the CIA investigations. There was a sense of concern about what our Nation stood for.

I think now there's a new spirit in our Nation. I believe with our stand on human rights, our efforts to bring peace, to reduce the nuclear threat, to alleviate the hatreds in the Middle East, to bring majority rule and peace to southern Africa, that there is a sense of purpose again.

And in my own way as a human being with limits that you and I both recognize, but occupying the most important office perhaps in the whole world, I want to be sure that the American flag is once more lifted high and when anyone on Earth sees it, they think about freedom, they think about the worth of an individual human being, they think about hope, they think about a sense of compassion and love, they think about high ideals, they think about openness of government, they think about democratic principles, they think about compassion and concern, and they think about the worth of our people who live in harmony from so many different places on Earth.

These are the hopes that I have as President. I thank you for your involvement in the democratic processes, your support of our party, your friendship toward me. I thank you for the fine congressional delegation that you've sent to Washington who represent you and our Nation so well. And I know that I can speak for them as I repeat a phrase that

I used thousands of times in my long campaign: All I want and all they want is a government as good as the people of our country.

Thank you very much.

NOTE: The President spoke at 9:02 p.m. in the Ballroom at the Veterans Auditorium. In his remarks, he referred to Marie Jahn, honorary chairperson, and Edris "Soapy" Owens, Harry Baxter, and Floyd Gillotti, members of the Iowa steering committee for Mr. Carter during the 1976 Presidential primary campaign.

Offutt Air Force Base, Nebraska

Remarks to Strategic Air Command Personnel. October 22, 1977

This is the President at the Command Base. I have been here several hours studying the readiness of the forces that are under my command, and I've spent the last 9 months learning about the superb qualities of all you men and women who are prepared to defend our country in a time of extreme emergency.

What I've learned has made me very proud of you. I think that you know that the freedom of human beings throughout the world depends upon the qualities that you exhibit, the high standards of training and readiness that you always are supposed to maintain. And my own observations as the President of our country has reconfirmed my confidence in you.

The two things that I'd like to say is that I want to congratulate you on the fine standards that are maintained and express my appreciation to you on behalf of the people of our country, and secondly, to let you know that my position in the White House and your position throughout the world is one of partnership. The closeness with which we communicate in preparing for an emergency will prevent, as nothing else could possibly do, the possible destruction of our Nation. And the closeness with which we cooperate in a time of extreme emergency, when an attack is imminent, will mean the defense of our country and, perhaps, of the free world itself.

I have a great feeling of assurance that you will perform your jobs well, and I'm determined, as your commanding officer, as President of our country, to work closely with you to prevent any possible successful attack on our country that's not met instantly and competently and adequately from our own forces.

So, I'm thankful for what you are and reaffirm my own partnership and commitment to join with you, on a daily basis, to prevent our great Nation from being attacked successfully and also provide for a successful response if such an attack should be launched.

Thank you, again, very much for giving me this sense of assurance in your superb qualities of leadership and performance of duty.

NOTE: The President spoke at 11:40 a.m. from the Headquarters of the Strategic Air Command via the Red Telephone System to SAC facilities around the world.

During his visit to the base, the President toured the SAC Headquarters and was briefed by U.S. Air Force personnel.

Denver, Colorado

Remarks in a Panel Discussion and a Question-and-Answer Session on Western Water Policy. October 22, 1977

THE PRESIDENT. Let me say first of all that I am very glad to be back in Colorado, in Denver. This is one of the more important meetings that I will have a chance to attend this year.

WESTERN WATER POLICY

I realize that in the Rocky Mountain States, indeed throughout the West, that water is the lifeblood of the people who live here. And I am especially grateful that the members of the Colorado congressional delegation came in with me on Air Force One today. And we have, I think, 10 Western Governors who joined this group to listen to the discussion with the panelists and with the audience, and later they'll be meeting with me privately to pursue additional items that concern water and other matters that relate directly to Governors and their responsibilities.

We have times that are changing, that require, in my opinion as President of our country, the evolution of a national water policy. Up until about a month in the future, we will be accumulating advice and questions, proposals, criticisms from public officials and from private water users that will come to the Secretary of Interior, Cecil Andrus, on my right.

In February this analysis will be presented to me, and I will make a decision then as to what portions of the national water policy are ready for final form and which elements of that policy proposal option will be needing additional study by me and others. I will not make a decision on any of the controversial items without first discussing these matters thoroughly with the Members of Congress, with the Governors involved, and with the local and private users of water, not only in the West but throughout the country.

I want to make clear from the very beginning that there absolutely will be no Federal preemption of State or private prerogatives in the use or management of water. This is not the purpose of the policy at all.

But as you well know, I have a responsibility as President, working with the Congress, to make sure that we have an effective program in carrying out the responsibilities, the legal responsibilities, of the Federal Government. We must make sure that Federal water programs are effective, that they meet the needs of the American people. We have got to be sure also that we don't waste money in some Federal programs and projects that are not needed or are of a very low priority and at the same time rob projects that are needed in other parts of the country.

It's a very important concept to me to have the direct input of people like those on the panel today—Governors, mayors, farmers, those who develop energy sources, those who are interested in environmental quality and the preservation of wildlife—to work together. It's also very important for people in Colorado to understand the problems of people in California and Utah as well as Arizona and Oregon and the northeastern part of our country. And as we evolve a national energy policy, a national water policy, we'll be sure that the two are tied together, because this is an encroaching demand for water that wasn't present in your region in years gone by.

We've seen a rapidly rising demand on the part of urban areas, as contrasted with longstanding use of water in the rural areas. We've seen increasing conflicts develop between States as water supplies that were formerly adequate now become inadequate.

We've got an increasing problem in international matters, particularly between the United States and Mexico. And we've got an increasing demand for water supplies by energy producers, coal, shale, also electric power producers, on the one hand, compared to longstanding users in agriculture and other needs of water.

We have not adequately addressed conservation matters. And in the past when water has been assumed to be of unlimited quantity, conservation was not an ever-present consideration in our minds. Now conservation has got to be addressed, not only by me as President and others in Washington but by the average family here in Denver and other parts where it hasn't been an ever-present consideration in the past.

Just a couple of other points very quickly and we'll start around the panel, after Governor Lamm makes a brief statement. There are some questions that have not yet been assessed.

The question of Indian rights to water—no one knows what future years might bring in court decisions interpreting longstanding ancient treaty rights between the Indians and the white population. And no one has adequately explored yet the responsibilities of the Federal Government in lands under Federal Government control. So, I believe that this year's work with an open, free, unbiased, and, hopefully, complete discussion of the water problem will make sure that in the future our needs are met.

But I can assure you again that I'm here as a student to learn as best I can from you the facts about your special needs, to answer your questions when I know the answer, to get help from Cecil Andrus and others when I don't know the answers. And then I'll go back to Washington with a much clearer concept of how to carry out my responsibilities to you.

Again, let me thank you for letting me be here. I'd like to ask Governor Dick Lamm now to make a few remarks and then we'll call on the panel to discuss the different questions that must be addressed today about this crucial question of water in the West.

Governor Lamm.

PANEL DISCUSSION

COLORADO'S WATER SYSTEM

GOVERNOR LAMM. Mr. President, we want you to know first and foremost that we're pleased by your visit. We're honored by your visit. We are not unaware of the political and personal courage that it comes in the West to come here to talk about water, which is truly our most sensitive subject.

We further appreciate the whole forum which you have given us, the idea of coming and listening rather than making a speech—of listening to our citizens. That is very much appreciated, and we very much honor you and respect you as our President.

There are four brief points that I have been asked to make, and I will make them briefly, but they are in my mind and the minds of a great many other people in this State, sort of the heart of Colorado's water system. First of all, it's important to understand that Colorado and the West is a semiarid State. For the first 50 years, when mapping in this area was called the Great American Desert, that water in fact revolves—everything revolves around water. I remember a very poignant scene that I know is poignant to you, too, from "Gone With the Wind," where Scarlett O'Hara's father is standing there and says land—that land is everything worth fighting for, land is worth dying for, land is the only thing. And you remember it well. I think that basically that same picture is a great part of our heritage here in the West, except—except that it isn't land, it's water, because we literally have hundreds and millions of acres of land that,

in fact, only can bloom and grow and produce and be made productive if it has water. So, water in fact, as John Gunther said, "Touch water in the West and you touch everything."

Point number two is the way we get our water, and it's extremely important to understand that because our water doesn't come evenly over the year, but in fact it comes—about 80 to 90 percent of it comes, of our usable water, comes through snow. It accumulates in our mountains, and in one fast 60-day period it runs off. And what we don't store we don't use. And that is extremely central to remembering the problems of the West, that basically no great rivers, major rivers, flow into Colorado. Only one flows in at all, and all the rest flow out. We are the mother of rivers. Some 16 States get their water in whole or in part from Colorado. But we have to store our water if we're going to use it. Without it, cities and crops both die.

In Colorado, for instance, of our 20 major cities, every one of them relies on water storage—every one of them. Not that some of them might not have some direct stream flow rights, but without that water storage, those cities would dry up and people would have to leave.

A great part of our agricultural commodities, two-thirds of our agricultural production related to irrigated agriculture, water that is stored at some point in that 60-day period and then is allowed to be used in the other part. So, our ability to produce crops and allow our civilization to continue in this area is directly related to this storage and irrigation of water.

Point number three, Mr. President, is we've historically had a good Federal-State partnership, that the Federal Government has been very helpful to the West and for which we are appreciative.

In the Reclamation Act, in grazing and a number of other of these areas, it is very important to understand that the West, however, hasn't necessarily been just an endless beneficiary. In Colorado, for instance, during the last 70 years, we have built—70 reclamation projects have been completed, costing $248 million.

In 1975 alone, in one year alone, those reclamation projects were related to $331 million worth of crops. So, in one short year there was gross production from those crops far exceeding the investment made from the very beginning and all of those reclamation projects. Eighty-four percent of the total Federal investment is reimbursable to the Federal Treasury in these reclamation projects, and again it is not only part of our lifeblood but it is also something that has been part of a longstanding Federal-State partnership.

The last point, Mr. President, is how vulnerable we are to Federal policy. Our water—there is 94 percent of all of the lands that you are the landlord of, the Federal Government—94 percent of all Federal lands are in the 16 Western States. So, a mistake in a Federal policy in some other doesn't have near the ramifications in much of the country as it does here because of how closely we're tied.

Thirty-six percent of our State is owned by the Federal Government. The water policy, the Federal policy, grazing policy—all of these things again go right to the very heart of Colorado and our economy. Our social and economic planning is done on into the future relating to projections and policies as set down in the past, and much of them—most of them revolve around water.

In summary, Mr. President, again, the overriding thing is we're honored to have you here, and we're pleased that you've come to listen. We've disagreed with some of your water policies in the past, but we

want to work with you in a partnership, and we're happy you're here.

THE PRESIDENT. We're going to move our discussion along as rapidly as possible, and I'd like to call on any panel members now who want to discuss the first item on the agenda, which is the competition that is evolving—already exists between States for water or between regions for water.

Mr. el-Ashry.

COLORADO RIVER BASIN

MOHAMED EL-ASHRY. To me, Mr. President, talking about water in an important region of the West is talking about the Colorado River Basin, one example of the tremendous competition that's taking place between the States.

It started in 1922 when the Basin was divided artificially into an Upper Basin and a Lower Basin, and using a very high flow assumption at that time for the river—it happened to be a wet year at the time—the water of the river was apportioned among the seven States or among at least the Upper Basin and the Lower Basin.

From that point on, water planning in the Colorado River Basin became focused upon competition on which State develops its water first.

As a result, those who were in a position to develop—southern California in particular—not only developed on their apportioned water but developed also on borrowed water, water that does not belong to them. And without learning from past history, central Arizona right now is developing on borrowed water, water that does not belong to Arizona. And in the very near future, both States will be asked to relinquish the water that they have used that does not belong to them. This resulted in the fact that the Upper Basin States became very nervous about what's going to happen when they are ready to develop their water. Are they, in fact, going to lose what they were guaranteed in the compact that they will have and legitimately so?

However, it does not justify really the push that's being made by the Upper Basin States to develop every drop of water in the Upper Basin at any cost, by building all the storage projects that they can get their hands on, so that they can have the water that they are entitled to although the need for the use for this water does not exist at the present time.

One major aspect of the water planning in that basin has been based on full development of the available supply without any concern for the water quality implications of developing these supplies. As a result, salinity has reached dangerous proportions, threatening productive agriculture in the Lower Basin, costing over $50 million per year in damages to water users in the Lower Basin and requiring hundreds of millions of dollars in Federal expenditures to control it. Instead of considering efficiency and conservation of water use, it has been often assumed that additional water supply is the only means to further local and regional development, and it is the lack of consideration of alternatives in considering water management in this basin where the available supply is not adequate to meet all the demands that are placed upon it.

As a matter of fact, if all demands that are being projected at the present time go on line—water-related development plans go on line as projected by 1990, it is expected that the demands will exceed the available supply. So, something is needed to be done. And the major reason for the problem is that there was tremendous lack of basinwide planning; the planning became focused on local, regional, or State level—not on a basinwide planning.

An inescapable fact, also, Mr. President, is that there is not enough water in the basin to meet all the demands that are placed upon it, and the solution has got to be in the form of reordering these demands that are placed on the water supply, but again the reordering has to be done on a basinwide basis. The Upper Basin should not really suffer just because they have not developed in time and somebody else locked up all the water in some other things.

So, it has got to be a fair and equitable means of reordering the future needs for water use in the basin. And I'll stop at this moment. Thank you.

THE PRESIDENT. I might point out that Mr. el-Ashry is a geologist and a hydrologist. He's also the staff scientist for the Environmental Defense Fund. In the future there's no doubt in my mind that the competition among the States and between the United States and Mexico is going to be even much more intense than it has been in the past or present. And this is going to require that Congress look with a great deal of attention at the relative priority of new construction projects and that everyone concentrate on a self-imposed conservation effort so that we use every drop of water to a maximum degree and don't waste it as has been the case in the past.

Perhaps one other panelist would like to comment on the competition aspect. Mr. Carlos Lucero.

INTERSTATE COMPACTS

MR. LUCERO. Mr. President, water rights in Colorado are popular. It seems to me the discussion of interstate rights to water really has to be based at a recognition that the water rights of Coloradans have been hardly fought for and have been settled either through litigation at the Supreme Court level through equitable apportionment or by interstate compact.

Now, it seems to me that we have—and it's Colorado's position that we do—that these interstate compacts finally and forever settle the question of what the relative right of the States are to the water, that where Colorado can benefit from the Federal Government's assistance is in developing programs either for salvaging water or for managing water so that we can have the maximum ability to meet our compact obligations.

In the San Luis Valley where I'm from, for example, we have a valley the size of Connecticut. The series of rivers run into the valley. The Conejos River, the Trinchera, the La Jara all join to form the Rio Grande, which flows into New Mexico and Texas, and, as you wisely recognized, creates obligations to the Republic of Mexico as well.

In that area we have had shortfalls close to a million acre-feet of water in our delivery obligations under the compact. At the present time, we have an obligation of in excess of 700,000 acre-feet. How can the Federal Government help Colorado to meet its obligations in a manner consistent with your policies of environmental soundness, economic feasibility, nonstructural approaches?

It seems to me that the Closed Basin Project there is a logical place to look. That project would take water from parts of the valley that are in the Closed Basin, so-called, and pump those waters into the Rio Grande River. That water would then permit Colorado to receive credit on its interstate compact obligation to the two lower States, Texas and New Mexico, and, of course, make water available to the Republic of Mexico as well.

One last point on that, Mr. President, is that when we start talking about further competition between States, that's very disturbing to us, because we feel that we've already settled some of those matters. But when we start talking about coal slurry pipelines, for example, what we are talking about there is we have already had equitable division of the waters. When we take fresh water from Colorado, mix it with coal, and send it to the Gulf of Mexico—to Houston, for example—it seems to me like it's a little bit more of a division. And it's Colorado's position that any water that's going to be taken from the State, Colorado would have to receive credit on its interstate compacts for that water.

THE PRESIDENT. I might point out that Mr. Lucero is the president of the Colorado Bar Association and a recognized legal expert on the water question. We are not only going to have competition, as you know, between States but within States as well.

I've seen some projections that have been evolved for Denver that show a doubling in population between now and the year 2000. We have a lot of water in Georgia, an average rainfall of anywhere from 45 to 70 inches. But all of our homes, so far as I know, have water meters on them. [*Laughter*]

MR. LUCERO. We're starting that, Mr. President.

THE PRESIDENT. I think in the future that the competition between farmers and urban dwellers and—between farmers and urban dwellers and the energy—either coal miners or energy producers, is going to be just as intense or perhaps more so than between States. But this applies all over the Nation. It doesn't only apply to the West.

I think we might have some comment now on an extension of what Mr. Lucero has said, and that is what elements do you panelists see as being important to be included in a national water policy to make sure that these kinds of problems can be addressed in a fair way with a minimum of intrusion by the Federal Government, but a recognition of the rights of different people.

I think Mr. Fischer had his hand up first, and then I'll get Mr. Wright.

NATIONAL WATER POLICY

MR. FISCHER. Thank you, Mr. President. First of all, thank you for coming. We appreciate it.

I'd like to, by way of preliminary comment, state that we very much appreciate the opportunity for improved communication with the White House. The communication, we hope, will not stop today. With your concurrence, I would like to continue dialog, especially on the Colorado River, with Jack Watson's office on your staff. We would like to comment—and appreciate very much your comment on not preempting by the Federal Government's actions the Colorado water priority system, the appropriations system or that of all the West. And by way of competition and certainly by way of improved relationships with each other, we would like to assume that your policy will permeate the departments both directly and indirectly. We would like to comment that in the problem area, one of our problems is that the Federal Government, and especially the agencies of Interior—with respect, Mr. Secretary—have been very reluctant to quantify and adjudicate their claims in the Western States courts and particularly in Colorado where we believe we have three precedent-setting United States Supreme Court decisions, Mr. President, that require that. We hope that we will not continue to find the aggressive

reluctance on the part of Federal agencies for quantification and adjudication.

As you know, the Colorado River is the most controversial, one of the most controlled, and certainly the most litigated river in the world. It is the subject of two compacts, one international treaty. It's presently very tenuously balanced.

The people of the State of Colorado look forward to the opportunity to use that water. We are in the process of addressing the water quality and salinity issues. We believe that salinity is from several sources: loading, by man-made activities, natural, and the out-basin diversion of increasing amounts of very high quality water to the detriment of the basin itself. We would hope that these things could be addressed.

In the areas of competition certainly we are going to have competition between energy and agriculture. But there is no requirement, we don't believe, to assume that agriculture, Mr. President, has to take the shortage. It does not.

There is under Colorado's compact apportion share of the river, the Colorado River where I am from, enough water for present and future agriculture projects, irrigation, reasonable energy use, but Mr. President, it will take storage. That storage can be economically and environmentally sound. We believe it can be. I would like to talk to the staff about that. But we believe, Mr. President, that the energy industry should supply and pay for its own storage. Thank you.

THE PRESIDENT. I might point out that Rolly Fischer is the secretary of engineering of the Colorado Water Conservation District and an acknowledged expert on Western Slope water.

The Federal Government has some very clear responsibilities that we hope to outline. One is, of course, as I've already mentioned, the congressional responsibility to set priorities on which major construction projects are financed first. Secondly, to make sure that the environmental laws of our Nation are carried out. That not only applies to water quality but also to air quality, the life of marine animals and fish, and also, of course, to guarantee the safety of dam projects and so forth. So, the Federal Government has a very clear responsibility in some ways.

I'd like to call now on Mr. Ken Wright.

INTERSTATE COMPACTS

MR. WRIGHT. Thank you, Mr. President.

I would like to comment further on the point made by Carlos Lucero regarding the Rio Grande compact and the competition for water between regions as it affects the policy. The valley that he referred to, the San Luis Valley, sits on roughly perhaps one billion acre-feet of water in ground water storage. And in our administration of the Rio Grande compact within Colorado, there are water shortages, in spite of this huge underground water reservoir. And within the basin you could say there are two regions—the Conejos River Basin and the Rio Grande River Basin. There is tremendous competition between those two basins within the San Luis Basin. And there just isn't enough water. And we see, in effect, the water chaos in the San Luis Valley. The people with the earliest water rights on the Conejos, we see as being the shortest in water supply.

THE PRESIDENT. Shortest on water supply?

MR. WRIGHT. Shortage—yes, because of the interstate commitment to New Mexico and Texas. And what it's gotten down to is that we don't know how to resolve this particular dispute within the State courts for a number of reasons. But we felt that one of the solutions would be a nonstructural, integrated water management investigation and plan to show us the way to solve this problem.

We feel there are good opportunities for economic benefits from this water, for fair distribution of the benefits to the people in the southern part of the valley, and also for environmental enhancement. We think it's a good opportunity for the Geological Survey and the Bureau of Reclamation to help us here in Colorado on a nonstructural, integrated water management plan.

THE PRESIDENT. What about agricultural water problems? Does anybody want to comment on that? Mary, did you want to say something else? Ms. Taylor.

CONSERVATION

MS. TAYLOR. I did want to say something on water policy—Mary Taylor, president of the Colorado Open Space Council, which is a statewide environmental coordinating council composed of conservation, recreational, and service organizations.

There are two or three points I would like to make regarding Federal water policy. The first thing we would like for you to know is that you have very broad grassroots support for your efforts to reform, to reevaluate Federal water policy. There are a great many citizens in Colorado who support you in that. Not everyone believes that water storage—large Federal water storage projects are the way to go.

There is a very vocal and a very well-funded water development lobby that would like you to think so, but this is simply not so. We feel that there is a great need for a Federal water policy with conservation as its cornerstone, as you have proposed. We feel that conservation—the primary reason for conservation should be to protect in-stream environmental uses which now seem to be ignored or they certainly are not the primary concern.

We feel that the Federal water policy should be very comprehensive, including water supply and water quality. They are interrelated, and they should be integrated. The water policy we feel there should be overall coordination with other Federal policies.

In Colorado, for instance, there is the Bureau of Land Management, the Bureau of Reclamation, Forest Service, five districts of the Corps of Engineers, the Environmental Protection Agency, the HUD flood insurance program, and others—all dealing with water resources.

THE PRESIDENT. Department of Energy now.

MS. TAYLOR. Yes.

A Federal water policy should also have a sunset provision, we feel, or continued review and evaluation of all water programs according to objective criteria.

And lastly, the role of the Federal Government, we feel, should be to provide strong incentives to the States to do a comprehensive water quality, water resource planning. And we do feel that the Federal Government has an important role to play. We in the West know a great deal about our water. We know what our water problems are. We understand them.

But we really, up until now, have done very little about them. And we feel that there is a role for the Federal Government to provide the incentives for us to get on the right track.

THE PRESIDENT. As a farmer, I've gone as far as I can without getting into agriculture. [*Laughter*] I would like to call on Mr. John Fetcher, who is a rancher, who is a member of the Colorado Water Conservation Board, a former county commissioner, a member of the Farm Bureau and the Cattlemens Association, and he's been involved in a ski area development as well. So, he has a broad range of background, just to comment if he will. He didn't know

I was going to call on him on how the discussions so far relate to agriculture.

COLORADO AGRICULTURE

JOHN FETCHER. I'm ready, Mr. President.

THE PRESIDENT. I figured you might be. [*Laughter*]

MR. FETCHER. But I didn't realize I was a county commissioner. So, your information there isn't quite correct.

But I am a cattleman. And we have an irrigated ranch in northwest Colorado where we run about 300 cows and we have to raise about 600 tons of hay to keep those cows fed during the wintertime. So, obviously we depend on water for our hay crop.

By the way, here is a picture. I'd like to say a little bit about what has been probably put to you that agriculture tends to waste water and over-irrigate. Perhaps you have read this report which was written by the Comptroller of the United States. And I am not exactly sure what the Comptroller knows about irrigated agriculture. [*Laughter*]

THE PRESIDENT. I see you were ready, Mr. Fetcher. [*Laughter*]

MR. FETCHER. Well, there are statements in this report that say that if you don't use the water, you're going to lose it. This statement made in this report is to the effect that this tends to make us irrigators waste it—you know, we're afraid of losing it. Well, this isn't quite the way the law says. The law says you are to use the water beneficially and as efficiently as possible. But it doesn't say you are going to lose it. And I don't know of any cases of my fellow ranchers who have lost any water because they didn't use their full quota of water.

Now, on the subject of waste, we know that when we over-irrigate—and I am talking primarily about flood irrigation,

1869

not sprinkler irrigation—that the grasses that grow as a result of over-irrigation are the bad grasses, the grasses the cattle don't eat. Heck, we know that. And there's implications in this report that we don't know it.

So, I think the question of waste is truthfully exaggerated. Furthermore, every bit of water that we put on the land that isn't used by the plants goes back to the stream in return flow and is used by the next fellow.

Now, I'll say one more thing, because I know everybody wants a crack. I'll admit that this year on our ranch we tended to over-irrigate during May and June because we were really fearful that we wouldn't have any water because of the drought. And this is actually what happened: We ran out of water on our ranch on some of the tributaries of the main river in July, and we had a hard time making our hay crop. In fact, our hay crop was down about 150 tons.

Now, the reason that we tended to over-irrigate during that period is because we didn't have any storage. And if we had had storage, we would have apportioned the water that Governor Dick spoke about over the growing season rather than trying to get it all at the beginning.

THE PRESIDENT. Very good.

I would like to call now on Mr. Elton Miller, who is an irrigated farmer on the South Platte River, and he's a member of the Farmers Union and also a member of the Colorado State Agricultural Commission.

Mr. Miller.

MR. MILLER. Thank you, Mr. President.

I would like to relate the importance of water to Colorado agriculture. It's very important. Colorado's base has been built around agriculture over the last hundred years. Agriculture has either been first or second in production and industry in Colorado. So, it's important. We want to keep the agriculture base in Colorado.

Only 4 percent of Colorado's land is irrigated, yet it produces two-thirds of the value of the crops that we sell each year. So, that gives you some idea.

With our short rainfall we can't produce the crops that we are producing with this water. And we think that our valleys that are irrigated are as fertile as any place in the United States. I would just like to remind you, Mr. President, in 1974 Colorado ranked 15th in the country in agriculture sales, just ahead of 16th place Georgia. [*Laughter*] I'm sure you knew that.

But the water is vital to us, and I think some of our concerns in agriculture—and I would like to thank you for the statement you made. I think it eases a lot of our minds on the opening about our water rights. My own water right dates back to 1864, a direct flow water right. And when you talk about changing this, it really worries us farmers.

THE PRESIDENT. I understand.

MR. MILLER. So, we do appreciate your opening remarks on that. I think it's important—we are going to have some energy development. We're going to have some growth in from the energy development, also probably some growth here in the front range. It's important that we develop some more sources of water. If we don't, that water is going to come from agriculture, because we cannot compete in the free marketplace for water with the energy companies and urban development.

So, as that is inevitably coming, we need some water storage. We have years when we have water running out of Colorado and we need some storage for that, because otherwise our irrigated agriculture, I am afraid, is going to have to pay the price. Thank you.

THE PRESIDENT. Thank you, Mr. Miller. One thing that I know will relieve your mind—and I hope that's one of the results of my visit out here—is that this water policy will not be developed in secret. It's going to be thoroughly and openly debated, and you and others will have a complete knowledge of what we are doing. We are not going to spring anything on anyone. I have already met with every Member of Congress from the Rocky Mountain and Western States, both in the House in one meeting and also in the Senate. And this is just a series of discussions we will have. The Governors will all be in Washington for their annual meeting in February. I am not going to firm up any aspects of the water policy without consulting with the Governors, during your winter meeting, Governors.

I would like to call on Mr. Alvey and then shift and let one part of our energy industry respond right after Mr. Alvey. Mr. Bill Alvey.

MR. ALVEY. Thank you, Mr. President. I would like to touch on farm prices. I know that's a touchy subject right now.

I want to thank you for signing the farm bill. It wasn't exactly what the farmers wanted. And they still want more, and you can't blame them. But it is a step up the hill.

THE PRESIDENT. Yes, sir.

MR. ALVEY. As I say, I am not going to criticize you about that. However, when you were campaigning in Wisconsin, you said the farmer should have cost of production plus a reasonable profit. Now, we are getting close to the cost of production. But I'm still looking for that reasonable profit. [*Laughter*]

THE PRESIDENT. Mr. Alvey, let me say I know you are my friend, but I very specifically said in Wisconsin that I thought we ought to have a farm bill that would guarantee the cost of production, but not guarantee the farmers necessarily a profit.

MR. ALVEY. The news media misquoted you, then.

THE PRESIDENT. Well, that's the first time the news media have ever done that, then. [*Laughter*]

MR. ALVEY. Anyway, I was your delegate from Colorado and probably the only farmer outside of Georgia that was a delegate to the national convention.

THE PRESIDENT. Yes, sir. [*Laughter*]

MR. ALVEY. But anyway, we are going to leave that. But I did want to bring that out.

THE PRESIDENT. I think we have a good farm bill, by the way, and as you say, it's a step in the right direction.

MR. ALVEY. Yes, but I think with the help of our western Congressmen, Senators and Representatives alike, that maybe in the next few months we can get over that hill so the farmers can—because they are getting in a bind, and we just can't go on with the farm economy slipping. Its impact on even the city of Denver will be felt sooner or later. But what I wanted to bring out as, of course, a farmer in eastern Colorado, which is mostly pump irrigation where there is any irrigation—and, believe me, there is a lot of acres under irrigation there—but we have had some squabbles along the State line about whether Colorado should take all the water before it slips across the line, because it does flow southeast into Kansas.

But what I am wanting to mention more specifically, and I want to thank Governor Lamm for his wonderful effort on this, is weather modification. Now, Governor Lamm has instigated $960,000 for weather modification in Colorado. As I say, you can have all the dams in the world, but if you don't have any rain or snow, you're not going to have any irrigation water. And I am not criticizing you on that point. [*Laughter*]

I know that some of the dams were dropped off. I believe that you should go ahead and in light of the fact, in order to keep peace in the family, all over the country, go ahead, when these dams or reservoirs or flood protection dams that are in the process of being formulated—you should go ahead and put them on and finish them up, because the cost is getting higher all the time.

But in the future, I think we should look deeper into this and all the aspects of safety as well as economic feasibility for any more projects. So, in other words, we should declare a moratorium of a few years on any new projects.

This weather modification point I am trying to bring out, you say—I know you have 40 to 70 inches of rainfall in Georgia. You lose a lot of it. But we get moisture here. And if we could just figure out some way to wring it out of the clouds and increase our moisture content by 3 or 4 inches in the West, it would really make a great deal of difference.

THE PRESIDENT. I understand.

MR. ALVEY. Another thing: They are worried about the neutron bomb. But I believe that a nation that controls the weather in the future won't need any neutron bombs.

THE PRESIDENT. Thank you, Mr. Alvey. That's a great statement.

I think we have had the question of energy production and commercial use of water raised several times. And I would like to call on Ralph Atkins to comment on this. He's raised his hand earlier. He is the director of the water operations of Colorado Fuel & Iron, which is a steel company, as you know, and he also is the

president of the Colorado Water Congress.

Ralph Atkins.

POLLUTION CONTROL

MR. ATKINS. Thank you, Mr. President.

I would like to start with a comment in regard to the matter of water use versus waste that has been referred to earlier and move now to the Arkansas River, which is in the southeastern part of the State of Colorado, with which I am most familiar.

The Arkansas River, many years in the spring and in the fall, goes dry at Pueblo. The only water that is in that river east of Pueblo is the return flow from the CF&I Steel Corporation and from the city of Pueblo. At the present time, we return from the steel plant 85 percent of the water which we divert originally from the river. That water meets the 1977 best practical technology standards and also meets the drinking water supply standard.

As that water flows east from Pueblo, it is used and reused, and what may be thought by some to be waste is the next downstream irrigator's sole supply that he has for his crops. Salinity has been mentioned here, but let me say to you on the Arkansas River we have a viable agricultural economy which is irrigating with water that is four to five times in salinity what we are supposed to deliver to the Republic of New Mexico at the border.

Now, in connection with this matter of use and return flow, we have some serious concerns dealing with the Water Pollution Control Act Amendments of 1972, better known as Public Law 92–500, which calls for best practical technology level July of this year. It calls for the best available technology in 1983, and then, in Section 1, of course, it calls for zero in 1985.

We support the 1977 best practicable technology level. But at that point then I think we need to bring into play the Section 208 of that law, which is the area-wide waste management planning section, which will cover a major part area-wide of the State of Colorado, because the greater part of it is rural, and go in that direction first before we push too hard for the 1983 best available technology.

And I say that for this reason: I said earlier that we return 85 percent of the water that we use in that plant to the river for use east of Pueblo. If we at this point in time, while we are meeting the standards now—if we have to go to the best available technology level, we are going to have to destroy a volume of water equal to 10 percent of what will be brought into the Arkansas River Basin by means of the Franklin Arkansas Project.

We think that that destruction and what it will do to the economy east of Pueblo, plus what it's going to require in energy use to get that destruction, puts us into an economically unsound area. And we believe that we should move into the 208 area at this point and bring it to fruition with the planning which is one of the best things in that bill, because it allows local participation to set the needs.

And in that connection, I would like to mention, I understand the conference committee on 3199 has made a recommendation, whether it will clear or not, that the funding for that section should be extended at least 2 years in order to allow orderly and continuing planning under that 208 section, because, as you recall, that's a 2-year program, and what many areas are doing in order to get the funding and get in, they are rushing it. We are getting hurried planning, and I'm afraid we are not going to get good

enough planning for what we want in the future.

THE PRESIDENT. Thank you very much, Mr. Atkins.

I mentioned earlier the special concern about Indian rights. We have with us today Leonard Burch, who is the tribal chairman of the Southern Utes, and I would like to call on him. And I would like to ask him and the other panelists, since most of the items have been covered, to be as brief as you can, because at about 2:30 I would like to go to the audience for questions. So, please keep your statements as brief as you can, the other panelists.

Mr. Burch.

INDIAN TRIBAL RIGHTS

MR. BURCH. Thank you, Mr. President.

As representative of the Indians that call Colorado their home, we would like to welcome you to our State. I hope this is not your last visit. We would like for you to come back and see us.

On the national Indian water policy, there was a meeting in Washington on October 12, and the two national organizations—the National Tribal Chairmen's Association and the National Congress of American Indians—are working together with Assistant Secretary Forrest Gerard in coming up with a national Indian water policy.

So, I am certainly glad that you brought this up in your opening remarks, Mr. President, about the concern that is the concern of all the Indians across the country, of the water issues that face them. Each one of these issues that do face the Indian tribes across the country is very unique in certain ways. So, I am glad that you have mentioned it and that Secretary Andrus, in working with the national organization and the consultation with the Indian leaders that you mentioned is most encouraging to me and I am glad to hear that from from you, Mr. President.

We hope that during this time that we can come up with a very good, meaningful water policy that will be endorsed by all the tribes across the country in working hand in hand with your administration and your staff, Mr. President.

I would like to mention about the Indian water rights. It is also a very important and different concern to us as Indians. We love our land. It is our mother earth. And we want to keep it as the Great Spirit has put us there, because we talk about environmental issues—we have talked about a lot of these other concerns that we have got—but the Indian loves his land. His water means quite a bit to him. So, therefore, he, the Indian, will follow steps to be taken to protect his water rights. And this is what the two Ute tribes in the State of Colorado have gone that route. Some of the court decisions that have been made was not too interesting, but it concerns us.

Now moving on, we like to work with your administration in perhaps coming up with a national policy, how this can be worked out rather than going to the courts, because we feel that Indian rights belong to the Indian people. It's not a national right, but it belongs to the Indian, and that he should be given the right to use that water in some way.

Mr. President, I would like to thank you on behalf of this Ute Mountain Tribe for the Dolores Project that is now under construction.

That has gone into construction. This has taken us quite a long time in working with the non-Indian neighbors that we have in southwest Colorado, on the congressional delegation, the former Governors and our present Governor Lamm in working together—this is what

we have come up with. And we certainly appreciate your help and your concern that the Dolores Project will be a benefit to the tribe.

Lastly, Mr. President, I would like to comment on another project that we are working on and have been working on for many years.

I have, as a spokesman and leader for my tribe, been the last 11 years going back to Washington and testifying before the committees of Congress in support of this particular project. It will mean quite a bit to my people, the Southern Utes and the Ute mountain people in the Four Corners area. We are very interested in this project. We have worked with our non-Indian neighbors, planned with them, and that's the Animus LaPlata Project. I hope, Mr. President, that you could give that a priority so that this project, meaningful to the Indian tribes in the State of Colorado—we would appreciate it very much. Again, Mr. President, thank you for this time in listening to me.

THE PRESIDENT. Thank you, Mr. Burch. On that last project, as you know, we did support that project.

I would like to go now to Mr. Ray Wells, who is from one of the major suburban areas and ask him to comment specifically on the need of growing communities in the use of water. Ray.

Again let me remind everybody to be as brief as you can, because I do want to go to the audience.

Ray.

WATER TREATMENT FACILITIES

MR. WELLS. Yes, sir. Thank you, Mr. President. As I am sure you are aware, the Denver metro area is rapidly becoming the transportation and energy center for Western United States.

Mr. President, if we are to meet that destiny, we must have a supply of water, because that involves people, and people need the water. Whether it's a matter of the foothills treatment facility, a matter of high-mountain storage, the water must be made available to meet that, as I see it, a charge.

As you are probably aware, this summer the drought has severely limited the growth of housing and other important industries to accommodate those people.

I am also interested, Mr. President—I can't help but comment when in over 20 years of trying to deal with urban problems, I become a little pessimistic when the Federal Government says, "We'd like to help."

THE PRESIDENT. You could turn all your Federal funds back in. We could distribute them somewhere else. [*Laughter*]

MR. WELLS. Well, that sort of is the answer today, when we encounter the States rights question, that withdrawal of funds always seems to be the way around it.

THE PRESIDENT. Well, we want to be helpful.

MR. WELLS. Yes, sir. [*Laughter*] That's like when the auditor walks in to the manager and he says, "I am glad to see you," and the auditor says, "I am just here to help." [*Laughter*] As a member of the State Water Quality Commission, Mr. President, I am also interested particularly in the Clean Water Act, which is the other end of the water cycle, as I see it.

I am particularly interested in increased funding for that act. I have some agreement with my peers across the table. However, I believe in the accomplishment of those goals as set forth and, in particular, the recycling and reuse of water, Mr. President.

If somehow we could reach some type of funding which would encourage re-

cycling, reuse, and, especially, land treatment of our waste water, I think it would be of particular benefit to the urban areas of this country.

THE PRESIDENT. Thank you very much, Mr. Wells.

I would like to call now on Ms. Beverly Haddon, who is the vice president for marketing operations of United Banks, Incorporated.

WATER POLICY PRIORITIES

Ms. HADDON. Thank you, Mr. President.

Actually, I won't take up too much time, because most of the points have been made. And as you know, in the banking industry we are a service industry, and we attempt to support all of the people that you have been talking to today. So, we are very interested in all of the industries, in two of the key industries, agriculture; we think it has been very important to this State, and we hope to protect that in the future.

We also think that an orderly approach to the development of energy can take place, and I guess our most important concern would be what the final priorities are and how you do approach those. We need the input back from you so that we, too, can plan. I might be interested, if you have a moment, what your sense of those priorities are today, in terms of those industries.

You've referred to the most important projects first. In terms of the tradeoffs which are tough decisions on energy and agriculture, do you have a sense of those priorities?

THE PRESIDENT. Well, I think it's obvious that the priorities have already been established basically for our country. Obviously, drinking water for human beings would come first, then agricultural production for food. I think obviously after that, quality of life, the beautification of our lands, the production of energy.

I don't think that we need to establish exclusive priorities for any of those needs. I think we do have adequate water supplies throughout our country to meet our needs if they are husbanded well, not wasted, and if we can work in harmony.

But one thing that happens—and I have already noticed in the brief time I have been in the White House—is that when people see the threat of a future shortage, they tend to increase their wastefulness to be sure they get their share of water that might be even scarcer in the future that's not scarce today. And I know that this is the case not only in water but in many other areas.

I think a thorough and open debate and the expression of a multifaceted approach to the single question of water as we have had here today will make sure that we can kind of relax to some degree, at least as we learn about one another and grow to trust one another and see the special needs that each of us has.

And I don't think there's any doubt that I and the Congress and my successors in the White House in years to come will have to establish priorities in the allocation of scarce financing for major water projects. But I don't think that we need to be concerned at this point that we don't have adequate water to meet our needs.

We don't know what the energy situation might be in the future. I think that here is the greatest unknown quantity that has recently come on the scene that bothers me and everyone else. But when I say priorities, that doesn't mean that we are going to deprive urban dwellers in order to keep farms in operation or deprive farm operations in order to control floods. I think they all can be harmonized within a common effort.

Let me call on Joe Sullivan now, who is a dry land farmer producing both wheat and grains. He is a past president of the Colorado Association of Wheat Growers. He serves on the State Mine Land Reclamation Board. And he is particularly familiar with the energy impacts on agricultural land.

So, Joe Sullivan, for a brief remark, please, Joe.

POPULATION GROWTH

MR. SULLIVAN. Thank you, Mr. President.

Many of the remarks that I wish to address have already been addressed, so I will bypass them. But I think that it is important that we consider the population expansion that western Colorado is seeing and will probably see accelerate in the next few years.

And I live in Rio Blanco County in western Colorado where much of the oil shale and the coal development is taking place. I believe that there is water available, that this can be done without detriment to agriculture, but I think that we need to plan now for storage facilities in order to do this.

I would like to point out also that in western Colorado, that as far as agriculture is concerned, that much of the land that is used for agriculture is used for livestock production. And the livestock production is dependent upon our irrigated valleys for hay to maintain them.

So, rather than just the loss that we may have in a valley, we affect several thousands of acres if we are not able to produce the hay that is necessary to maintain our livestock herds.

Thank you.

THE PRESIDENT. Very good. I think that you have put your finger on one of the impending conflicts between energy production and agricultural production that we need to address. And I think to the degree that we can analyze it together, it will remove the fear of the future that does exist in some parts of our country.

I would like to call on Betty Salazar now. She is the director of the United Way Agency in Denver and head of the Latin American Research Center.

UTILIZATION OF MINORITIES

Ms. SALAZAR. Thank you, Mr. President.

I guess my primary concern would be as these Federal permits are issued and so forth, that there be a real consideration and an assertive effort in terms of utilizing inner or core city persons to work in those projects and also a concerted effort in terms of utilization of minority contractors.

And as a social service representative, certainly these are the people we work with. And we would hope that as the policies develop, there would be consideration for utilizing those persons.

THE PRESIDENT. Thank you very much, Betty.

In the local public works bill that the Congress passed, which encompasses about $4 billion of improvements for communities like you represent, 10 percent of the contracting must be to minority enterprises. This is the first time the Congress has done this. I think it's a good move. But you made a very excellent point.

I believe that as we see the evolution in the future of both agriculture and energy production and other things, that we can have a very heavy improvement in employment opportunities that don't exist at this time.

Bob Botel has a very interesting experience in making sure that we do use water efficiently. He's a member of the International Brotherhood of Electrical Workers and a foreman at the Honeywell plant.

And I would like to ask him to make a brief comment.

WATER STORAGE

MR. BOTEL. Thank you, Mr. President.

I think it needs to be pointed out that labor is interested in storage, because storage of our water is the only way we can grow economically in the State.

And I think also that another point that we should bring out—you have been talking about water reuse in harmony. I think the city of Northglen has a program where water sharing is a feasible thing, and it's something that the urban dweller and the agricultural farmer have agreed on. I think it's a program that will work, and I think it adds to the soil vital minerals and nutrients that the soil needs from an organic basis.

THE PRESIDENT. This project is one that's of great interest to me. Northglen does use their supply of water, but they have worked out an arrangement with surrounding farmers to supply the waste waters to enrich the soil to produce more crops. I think this might be a vista of what we will see on a broad basis in the future.

The last panelist is Jonni Jones, and I would like to call on her now. She is an associate professor of urban planning at the University of Colorado, and she is in the Graduate School of Design.

URBAN PLANNING

Ms. JONES. Thank you, Mr. President.

I don't know how you can talk about growth in a short period of time; there are so many issues involved. But I will try to make two quick points.

I think people who live in the cities are concerned about growth—where it happens, how it happens, and at whose expense.

One of the things Denverites are concerned about is that as development occurs around the city, the inner city, that they not be asked to subsidize it.

The other point I would like to make is that people are concerned about growth. They want it managed. They want to be involved with the planning of it. And I think our Governor has made a very good step in developing the Planning and Coordinating Council. We have not been planning and managing growth well so far.

Many of us are in fear of the problems of cities in the East being repeated here and the sprawl of Los Angeles happening here. And I think that we can avoid those mistakes with the kinds of talent and energy and commitment here in Denver. And I hope that we do and not repeat the past.

The third point I would like to make is that though we want managed growth, controlled growth, it doesn't mean that many of us are antigrowth. Growth is very important for minorities particularly. With economic development and growth, minorities can participate as entrepreneurs as well as workmen. The economy in its expansion hopefully will take those on the bottom rung of the economy along with them.

One of the things that concerns the minority community, however, is that there are not enough minorities on policymaking level commissions or boards so that the minority input is made on energy planning.

The other concern is that most of the energy development will occur on the Western Slope. It is expected that about 14,000 new jobs will be created in production and construction. But most of the minorities live here in Denver on the Eastern Slope.

The other point is that if these minorities are going to participate in the economy and going to benefit from those jobs,

some sort of program will have to be developed to get them over on the Western Slope. Many of them perceive that, perhaps, it is an unknown territory and even hostile. A lot of the companies there are not familiar with affirmative action programs. We don't know whether or not they will take the initiative. So, a program has to be developed along those lines.

I guess people in the cities are concerned about a whole range of issues. But I think not only minorities but everyone here in Colorado wants to maintain our lifestyle, see our economy grow and keep Denver the way it is. Thank you.

THE PRESIDENT. Thank you very much.

I think the audience would agree with me that the panel has done an extraordinarily good job in bringing a multifaceted approach. It shows how many different voices there are, when you start talking about energy, that want to be heard. I would like to call now on any member of the audience who would like to ask a question. We have about 15 minutes left for that, and then I have a meeting with the Governors to pursue some of these matters.

Can you just identify yourself before you ask a question?

QUESTIONS

FARM PRICES

Q. Mr. President, my name is John Stulb, and I farm and ranch in Lamar, Colorado. Today we have talked about the relationship between water and agriculture. And of prime concern to agriculture, not only here in Colorado but across this Nation, is our present price situation. The agriculture producers of this country at this time are receiving a comparative value for their product at an alltime low, never before exceeded except in the Great Depression.

The farm bill that you have just signed into law provides some aid, but it is not enough. It limits the family farmer to less than 70 percent on his products, as compared to those products that he is having to buy to produce and to live in this country. We cannot go on working for 70 cents or less on the dollar when the products and services we have to purchase are costing us a dollar on the dollar.

I ask you, surely you do not feel that the American family farmer is a subparity citizen?

THE PRESIDENT. The answer to your question is no. [*Laughter*] As you may or may not know, I am a farmer myself. And I believe that the Congress has placed on my desk and I have signed a farm bill that's very far-reaching in its benefits to agriculture.

In spite of the fact that two-thirds of all the counties in this Nation are designated officially as disaster areas, we have had the highest production of corn in history. We have had the highest production of soybeans in history. And throughout the world there is a fairly good growing season, which means that the demand for our exports is not as great as it has been in the past.

In spite of that, in this last year which ended the end of September, we had the greatest exports also in the history of our country—$24 billion. We expect to pay out to farmers in this new fiscal year that began the 1st of October three times as much as we did during this past fiscal year just completed.

This farm bill will cost the taxpayers about $6½ billion, and I think it's money well spent.

Of course, much of that which is charged against the Federal Treasury because of longstanding bookkeeping principles are not payments, but they are loans. But I believe that within the framework of the Federal budget restrictions that the agriculture bill that has just been signed is the best that we can expect. And I believe that it is adequate.

The farmers in many areas have made a bumper crop. The price is presently low. But based on information that has been received from the land grant colleges and other sources, with the exception of land depreciation, we have tried to meet the average cost of production in our target price base. And as you well know, there are some areas that have much higher cost of production than does the average, and those areas do suffer. I certainly realize that. We hope to continue our increase in agricultural exports in the years ahead.

The last point I would like to say is that in addition to the President having a background in agriculture, we have a dirt farmer who is Secretary of Agriculture. And the new bill does give the Secretary a great deal of flexibility. And I believe that his own background, a man who went to Florida as a migrant worker in his young age, came back to the northernmost parts of Minnesota, borrowed some money, started a small operation, now farms about 600 acres—his background, I think, is close enough to your own so that as he administers this bill, he can take full advantages of all the potential that exists in it to make you and the other American farmers have a prosperous and an enjoyable life. So, it's not everything you would have wanted. There are budget constraints that keep us from having a perfect bill, but I believe that as Mr. Alvey said, it's a great step in the right direction.

Thank you very much, sir.

FOREIGN AID

Q. Mr. President, my name is Dave Sanders. I am from Boulder, and I have a question about the direction of foreign aid. Given the example of South Africa, your administration has moved away from backing the developed group there, which is the whites, to moving behind the underdeveloped group, which is the blacks.

What I would like to know is if this is some kind of an across-the-board policy change, that we are going to start giving foreign aid more directly to those people who are in need of it?

THE PRESIDENT. Yes. As you know, the Congress has just completed its action on the foreign aid bill, and I believe the emphasis has been more and more toward getting the foreign aid directly into the hands of those who need it and not into the hands of those in poor countries who don't need it.

As I said several times in the campaign, I don't think it's right to tax the poor people in our rich country and give the money to the rich people in the poor countries. And this is something that we have tried to do this year.

We also have the prospect—since I just had a question on agriculture—to increase substantially the benefits from Public Law 480, which will take our great food and feed grain reserves of which we are very proud and use them as an integral part and a growing part of our foreign aid program. But I hope that we can measure up to what you have just described, that we are now trying to make sure that the aid programs of all kinds are more efficiently administered and do get the money and the aid and the food in the hands of those who need them most.

Thank you very much, Mr. Sanders.

OIL AND GAS PRICES

Q. Mr. President, my name is Max Ellison, and I am from Salt Lake City. I am just completing a 2-year term as the president of the Rocky Mountain Oil and Gas Association, which covers an eight-State area. Now, I am also a farm boy, as you are, and as a farm boy I realize the importance of having adequate supplies of oil and natural gas.

All of this discussion about water and so on will be moot unless we have the energy to run our farms and our factories. My question is this, and it relates to a campaign letter which you wrote last year to Governor Boren. And in that letter you pointed out that it was necessary and important for us to have adequate supplies of oil and gas in order to have full employment and so on in this country and to have a growing economy.

And in there you outlined three steps which you said were necessary for us to increase domestic supplies, and the first one that I would like to read is this. You said, "I will work with the Congress, as the Ford administration has been unable to do, to deregulate new natural gas. The decontrol of producers' prices for new natural gas would provide an incentive for new exploration and would help our Nation's oil and gas operators attract needed capital."

Now, we agree 100 percent with that justification, and we believe that it's critical that oil and natural gas prices be decontrolled.

Now, I have two related questions for you. The first is, why did you change your position on deregulation of natural gas prices and also proposed that regulation be extended to the intrastate market? And related to that is, where is the fairness in an energy program which includes price controls by which the value of a product, oil or natural gas, is taken from the owner of that product and distributed to other people through taxation?

THE PRESIDENT. I will be glad to answer your question. As I also said in my speech to the Congress in April—it's the only speech that I have made to the Congress since I was President—our goal is to deregulate new natural gas. We proposed to the Congress an adequate step, in my opinion, a first step, toward that ultimate goal. And that is to increase the value of natural gas, the market price, to $1.75.

Of course, the oil and gas industry want immediate deregulation, and they want to define new natural gas to include gas that already has been discovered, that has not yet been produced. There is a limit to how much we can take out of the pockets of consumers and give to the oil and gas companies.

I want to be sure, as President, that there are adequate incentives to explore for and to discover new sources of natural gas. And I believe that the proposal that we made to the Congress is very liberal and provides adequate incentives and would ensure that the capital required would be there.

As you know, we have had a rapid increase in exploration in the natural gas field and the oil field in recent years. There is an 8-month waiting list now for new drilling rigs. And I think if we quadruple again the price of oil and natural gas, there would be no substantial increase in the rate of exploration or production.

So, I believe that the package that we put together is adequate. It does take a major step toward deregulation. But I think that the oil and gas companies have shown that they are not only satisfied with this, but they want to define old gas as new gas, and in the acquisition of immediate complete deregulation, it would just be too expensive for the rest of the country and I think would result in very little increase in production itself.

I know that the oil and gas companies disagree substantially with the rate of moving toward deregulation, but I think the proposal we made is compatible with my statement during the campaign and is certainly adequate.

Q. May I give you this copy of a talk which I presented here in Denver about a month ago?

THE PRESIDENT. I would very much like to have it.

Q. May I just make one other comment, Mr. President?

THE PRESIDENT. Certainly.

Q. I also own a mineral interest in two oil wells out in Duchesne County, Utah. That oil is being sold for $10 a barrel because of price controls. Some of our neighbors are selling their oil, or being forced to sell their oil, for $5 a barrel.

Now, the value of oil is about $15 per barrel in this country. Now, that means that under price control, every month about one-third of the value of my oil is being taken from me and given to someone else. I am a landowner. Now, I just cannot understand how in this country that type of thing can continue. I consider that confiscation of my property.

In other words, I get about $500 a month income from those two wells. If the true value was given to me as a landowner, I would be getting $750 a month. In other words, I feel like someone is stealing $250 a month from me, and I speak not just for myself but for the owners of oil and gas production throughout this country. And that's part of the problem with this energy program and part of the reason why unless adequate profits are given to the oil and gas industry, any energy program which is developed will be a failure.

THE PRESIDENT. Mr. Ellison, can I ask you a question?

Q. Certainly.

THE PRESIDENT. What was the price of that oil when it was first discovered on your place?

Q. That oil was discovered in about 1973, so it started out at about $9 a barrel. It's now about $10.

THE PRESIDENT. That was a very good price in 1973. [*Laughter*]

I am not trying to put you on the spot, Mr. Ellison, because I understand your point of view. The thing is, I believe and I think everybody here believes very strongly in the free enterprise system. But the oil and gas industry don't function within a free enterprise system.

The price that you say is the proper or fair price for oil is a price that has arbitrarily been set in a secret meeting of OPEC nations and not set in a free and open market condition in our country.

We have provided, proposed to the Congress that newly discovered oil would be at the full world market price, which means that oil discovered in our country, under the proposal we made to the Congress, would be the highest price for oil in the entire world.

But I don't think that we can afford to go back to oil that has been under production for several or many years that was originally profitable at a $2- or $3-a-barrel price, raise the price to $14 or $15 just because the OPEC nations have imposed that price on the rest of the world arbitrarily, and let the consumers pay that exorbitant profit to the oil companies in the process. It just doesn't seem fair to me.

I want to say that I don't want to use my position as President to win an argument with Mr. Ellison. This is one of the most difficult and controversial issues and the most important that has ever come before our country's Government, and that is to evolve an energy policy that's fair to the consumers, that's fair to the producers, and also provides adequate incentive for future discovery of new oil and gas.

There are not any easy solutions to it, and I am very grateful that these different points of view do come out freely, and I particularly appreciate Mr. Ellison being so forceful in his expounding of the viewpoint of those who do produce oil and gas.

I have another meeting with the Governors and this will be the last question that I can take.

I understand that you are president of the Chamber of Commerce in Denver.

FEDERAL BUDGET

Q. Yes, Mr. President. My name is Rex Jennings. I live in Denver, I am president and general manager of the Denver Chamber of Commerce. More importantly, perhaps, I am a former peanut farmer——

THE PRESIDENT. I can see why you changed jobs.

Q.——and a Southern Baptist. And the way I figure it, that almost makes you and me kinfolks. [*Laughter*]

I want to make two quick points and one quick question. Number one, I have great admiration for your commitment to reduce unemployment in this country. I have great admiration for your commitment to balance the Federal budget during your first term in office. I think you and I would agree that in order to reduce unemployment, we must create new jobs. And that's particularly important to the low-income, the minorities, and the youth of this Nation.

In order to create new jobs in the private sector, American business and industry must have access to capital. As long as the Federal Government is incurring an increasing deficit, going to the money market itself for 50, 60, 70 billion dollars a year, it reduces the amount of money available for private industry to borrow for plant and equipment to create new jobs to, in essence, provide full employment and reduce unemployment.

My question to you is, after having been in office now for 9 months, do you still feel strongly that you will be able to balance the budget before the end of your first term?

THE PRESIDENT. If we can have a reasonable level of economic prosperity in our country, the answer is yes. Of course, I can't control, as you know, and no one else can control, the worldwide trends and shortages, inflation, and absence of export. But with reasonable growth, 5, 6 percent GNP growth per year, the answer is yes.

Q. Thanks for being here, sir.

THE PRESIDENT. I want to close this out now very quickly. I would like to ask Dick Lamm to give a very brief closing statement. He said he only needs one minute. I would like to ask Cecil Andrus, the Secretary of Interior, to make a brief statement. And then I would like to ask the Governors, if they will, to meet with me privately after this meeting adjourns. Dick Lamm.

SUMMARY

GOVERNOR LAMM. Mr. President, very briefly, in your office I noticed a plaque that says, very appropriately, "O Lord, Thy sea is so vast and my boat is so small." I think when you think of that occasionally, if you could think that in the West we look at that and we say, "O Lord, our land is so vast, but our water is so little." It really is.

Second, Mr. President, Colorado, as you can see, does speak with many voices, as does every area. I think it's important for you to know a couple of things, however. Number one is that with regards to the water projects that our State legislature, which is a representative body— sometimes I argue with them, but never-

theless, it is our elective representatives— they voted 97 to 3 in favor of actually going ahead with those water projects that were on your "hit list."

But thirdly, most important, I think it is important that you do understand that not only in terms of the reclamation projects that we do need, that we do recognize the wisdom of much of what you say.

The West is running out of the amount of water that we can supply, that we are going to have to start learning better water conservation, we are going to have to better manage what we have, and that we definitely have a common cause.

We are very honored that you came here so we can listen and learn together. Thank you.

THE PRESIDENT. Almost all of the responsibilities that have been brought out here today fall directly under the Secretary of Interior, Cecil Andrus. As you know, he is a former Governor of Idaho. He's a westerner. He understands, I think, many of the problems that you have described. But he, like myself, is eager to learn more. He has been out here several times since we have been in office, works closely with many of those who have already spoken today. And I would like to call on Cecil to make a brief statement as we close out our meeting.

SECRETARY ANDRUS. Thank you very much, Mr. President.

Ladies and gentlemen, I think it was much more beneficial to all of us that any time that I might have spent at the microphone was used by the panel members that you see here and members of the audience to have the opportunity to express their opinion to the President of the United States.

Now, we might disagree with one another, but where else in the world other than in America, and in Denver, Colorado, do you have this opportunity? I think we are very fortunate and we have to understand that. That is probably the strength from which we will speak on all things, even when we differ. So, I would— yes, I recognize the water situation that has been pointed out here. I remind you that I was Governor of the State of Idaho.

But let me also say that when the President gave us some of the charges that he has given us, he took the tough road. It had been a lot more politically beneficial to him to have ignored the future problems of water, because the people that Mary was describing and that other people are describing, some of them haven't even been born yet. They don't have a very strong constituency in the Congress yet, and the President could have ignored it. But the beneficiaries will be all America if we'll work together in this regard.

There is nothing secret about water policy. It affects all of our lives. The President said it's the lifeblood of America, and it particularly is in the West. So, we'll continue to work with you in the Department of Interior. We'll come forth with our proposals the best we can, submit them to the President in February. Then he'll make the difficult call as to what we have to do to see that all people have the balance that you touched upon.

Every person at this table indicated that we need this, and we can, if we'll balance it. But we must work together to balance it.

The closing footnote I would like to make is to the question the president of your Chamber of Commerce asked. He said, can you balance the budget? Well, if the President treats all members of the Cabinet as he treats me, when I submit my budget, I'm telling you that he'll balance that budget. [*Laughter*]

So, I thank you very much for being here, and we are going to listen. And the decision will be his, as all the difficult ones are. But it will be made before the American public, and I think that is the important thing.

THE PRESIDENT. Thank you again, everybody. I appreciate it.

NOTE: The President spoke at 1:30 p.m. in the Ballroom at the Denver Hilton Hotel.

Following the panel discussion, the President met in the Cedar Room at the hotel with a group of Western States Governors to discuss water policy.

Denver, Colorado

Remarks and a Question-and-Answer Session at a Briefing on the Panama Canal Treaties.   October 22, 1977

THE PRESIDENT. I know that you've already had an excellent briefing from Ambassador Sol Linowitz and from my own national security adviser, from the Secretary of Defense and from our representative, the Chairman of the Joint Chiefs of Staff, about one of the most controversial and, perhaps, one of the most important issues that our country has to face, and that is the Panama Canal Treaty—or treaties.

I'd like to take a few minutes to talk to you from the perspective of the Presidency of our great country and from the perspective of the Commander in Chief of our Armed Forces.

President Eisenhower, President Kennedy, President Johnson, President Nixon, President Ford, and myself have all seen a need to modify or amend the present treaty with Panama concerning the Panama Canal. The negotiations have been taking place for 14 years, and the treaty that we have evolved, after tough, now completely publicized negotiations, are very good for our country, for our defense, our Nation's security, our Nation's prosperity brought about by trade, the political alliance or friendship that must exist between ourselves and our neighbors in this hemisphere, and from the spirit, I believe, of the rest of the world that our country is large and strong and fair.

It would be a serious mistake for anyone to assume that the Panama Canal Treaty is not important. It would also be a very serious mistake for anyone to assume that the Panama Canal is not important. It is important. It has been important to our country for the last 75 years; it will be important to our country for the next 75 years.

It would be a mistake for anyone to say that our country couldn't defend it if it were attacked by insurgents, by terrorists, or by well-meaning patriots of Panama in opposition to the stance of the Panama Government.

We could defend the Panama Canal, and if it is attacked by any means, I will defend it, and our country will be able to defend the canal.

The Joint Chiefs of Staff have said, in a concerted effort even by nongovernmental forces against the wishes of the Panama Government, it might take 100,-000 or 200,000 troops to defend the canal. But it can be done, and it will be done.

I believe that it's best not to face this prospect, not to take an action that would bring about an attack on the Panama Canal. We can do this with these treaties by forming a continuing partnership with Panama to help us keep the canal well operated, well maintained, open for our use, at the same time guaranteeing it to our country, which the treaties do, the absolute right to defend the canal as we see fit for the rest of this century.

The Joint Chiefs of Staff, the Secretary of Defense, the Secretary of State, and the President of our country has a right to choose, within the zone itself, the lands and waters necessary to be occupied by our own forces to keep the canal open.

We also have the right under the treaties, confirmed by a recent joint statement between myself and General Torrijos, after the year 2000, to take what action we see fit as a nation to defend the canal, to keep it open, and to keep it available for our ships.

During the rest of this century and after the year 2000, we have the right of what is called expeditious passage. In time of emergency or in time of need, as judged by us, our ships have a right to go through the canal as quickly as possible and also, when needed, to move to the head of the line if our Nation's security is at stake or if I or my successors in the White House think there is a need.

This is a common agreement between us and Panama. There is no doubt about it. And these two basic questions—do we have a right to defend the canal; do we have a right for our ships to have priority in using the canal—have been seriously distorted in the past, now clarified by precise English and Spanish language between myself and the leader of Panama.

I might say also that the Panamanian negotiators and General Torrijos have acted in good faith. Throughout the last 14 years there have been no threats, no implied statements that if you don't approve the treaty, the Panama Canal might be damaged. They have never done this. Although Panama does not have a democratic government like our own, General Torrijos has gone a second mile in making sure that not only he as a leader approve the treaties, along with his own chosen Cabinet, but the Panamanian people had a right, in an unprecedented expression of democratic principles, to vote in an open and free referendum or plebiscite that will take place, as a matter of fact, tomorrow.

He's invited the United Nations to come in and witness the procedures that are being used.

So, not only does General Torrijos and I—do we approve the canal treaties but the Panamanian people will vote in a referendum, and as you well know, the United States Senate, under our own Constitution, must approve the treaties themselves.

I'd like to add one other thing. We are not taking any taxpayers' money to pay the Panamanians. There will be a sharing of income from the canal use fees. The second thing is we have never owned the Panama Canal Zone. We've never had title to it. We've never had sovereignty over it. There's always been recognized by Theodore Roosevelt originally, the Supreme Court has confirmed since then that this is Panamanian territory. People born in the Panama Canal Zone are not American citizens. We've always paid them an annual fee, since the first year of the Panama Canal Treaty that presently exists, for the use of their property.

This canal will also be operated jointly by us. There will be the rest of this century a nine-person board that will set the policy for and manage the canal itself. Five of those members will be American citizens. Four of them will be Panamanians. All nine of them will be appointed by the United States.

So, you can clearly see that in economic matters, defense matters, priority of use, fair action on the part of the Panamanians, that our country comes out very well in this Panama Canal treaty arrangement.

Now, the original treaty that presently exists—I don't condemn my predecessors for having signed it. The fact is that no Panamanian has ever signed it. Before it was signed in 1903, no Panamanian ever saw it. But I'm proud of the fact that our Nation was strong enough and able enough, no matter what the circumstances were about the arrangements with Panama—I'm proud that we had the will and the technical ability to build a canal, because it's been better for our country and it's also been better for Panama. It's been better for all the other maritime nations of the world. So, in balance, in every aspect of measuring the treaty terms, our Nation comes out very well in the negotiations.

The Panamanians wanted very high monetary payments; they did not get them. Panama wanted immediate transfer to them of operating rights of the canal; they did not get them. Panama wanted an immediate withdrawal of our Armed Forces; they did not get them. But I think they've negotiated in good faith, and our country has come out very well.

Assuming, which I think is completely accurate, that we have a good equal deal in the Panama Canal treaties, we also have tremendous advantages with other countries. Under Franklin Roosevelt, under John Kennedy, under Lyndon Johnson, there were massive efforts made by the President and the Congress to strengthen the ties of friendship and trade and common purpose between ourselves and our neighbors to the south.

To some degree, to some variable degree, these efforts were successful. But almost invariably their success depended upon financial payments or financial loans or monetary aid. It was kind of like a big brother giving handouts to smaller nations to the south to buy their friendship.

During the week that we signed the Panama Canal treaties in the ceremonies in Washington, I met with 19 leaders of countries to the south of us. There was a new spirit of friendship and cooperation and equality and partnership. There was no mention of this new feeling being based on economics. So, symbolically, the fair treatment of Panama, the end of what they look upon as colonialism by the United States will be a tremendous boon to us.

Almost without exception, the business leaders of our country approve the Panama Canal treaties. They are outspoken in their support because they know that trade and jobs and exchange and exports of our agricultural products and so forth are heavily dependent upon this good will that ought to exist between ourselves and other nations of the hemisphere.

President Ford has endorsed the treaties. Secretary Kissinger has endorsed the treaties. Secretary William Rogers has endorsed the treaties. Secretary Dean Rusk has endorsed the treaties. Former Secretary of Defense Melvin Laird has endorsed the treaties. All five members of the Joint Chiefs of Staff have endorsed and support strongly the treaties as being in the best interest of our Nation's defense.

There is almost unanimity among those who are responsible for our foreign affairs, our trade, and the Nation's defense to support the treaties. With all these advantages for it—and these statements are absolutely accurate—what is the political problem?

There's an emotional feeling about the Panama Canal. And there is a lot of distortion about the significance of the Panama Canal. People say we bought it; it's ours; we ought not to give it away. We've never bought it. It's not been ours. We are not giving it away. There is no semblance between the status of, say, the Panama Canal Zone and Texas or Alaska that were bought and paid for and over

which we've always had sovereignty. There's no similarity at all.

What we're doing is continuing a partnership that has existed for a long time between ourselves and Panama. They will continue to have sovereignty over the canal. But we will continue to guarantee that the canal is open. And we have the absolute right, in this century and later, to defend the canal against any attack from Panamanian terrorists or from other countries. We have the right for our ships to use it.

So, I believe that when the American people know the facts about these treaties, that you will give us your support. It's very important that this be done.

I think, had the canal negotiations not begun 14 years ago, we might very well withstand, for a time being, no action. But there's been a tremendous expectation built up in Panama because of the negotiations that have taken place now under four Presidents. And the treaties have been signed with a great deal of ceremony. And they feel that we are treating them fairly. They feel that in the past we have not treated them fairly. And now to have the treaties rejected, I think, might very well arouse in them a feeling of resentment and deep animosity.

The last point I want to make is this: One reason that there is such a feeling about Panama is that we withdrew from Vietnam after we had committed major efforts of our country in that war, and that our country was almost universally condemned by the rest of the world for our investment of military effort in Vietnam. Most of the people of our country felt at the initial stages, and maybe even later on, that we should have been in Vietnam as we were in South Korea to defend democracy and freedom and let people have the right to choose their own government.

But I think you'll remember there was a slight difference. When we went into South Korea, we did not have the condemnation of the rest of the world because we went in with a legitimate position. The United Nations voted, the Security Council, that South Korea should be defended. And we went in as part of the United Nations forces—the strongest force of all, of course, legally.

We went into Vietnam with the same good intentions and with the same commitment of forces, but we were looked on as being an illegal entity in South Vietnam.

With the passing of these two treaties, if we later have to go into Panama—and I don't believe we will—but if we should later have to go into Panama, it will be with the endorsement of the Panamanian Government, the Panamanian people. It will be with the endorsement of 30 or 40 or 50 other nations who will sign the neutrality treaty going into effect after the year 2000, saying, we think that the treaty with Panama and the United States is a good one. We support it and we endorse the principle of either the United States or Panama having the right—not just the right but the duty—to defend the canal against any attack and to keep it open.

So, it gives us a legitimacy and an endorsement of the rest of the world to do what we want in the first place to keep the canal open, well managed, and to meet the security needs, the trade needs of our own country.

So, in every aspect of controversy, there's a good and responsible and truthful answer. But the distortions and the incorrect information that has been put out about these treaties is very, very damaging to the truth.

I'm very proud to have a chance to come here, and I think for the few minutes we have remaining I'd like to answer any questions that you might have on the treaties themselves. I've tried to cover as quickly as I could some of the questions that I thought you might ask in the future.

QUESTIONS

Q. Mr. President, Roger McDaniel from Wyoming. I'd like to ask that with the reasonable assumption that tomorrow's plebiscite in Panama will show the anticipated overwhelming support for the enactment of the treaty, what kind of a timetable do you see as necessary for the ratification by the United States Senate?

THE PRESIDENT. I think there's a general feeling in Washington, I think, the rest of the Nation, that the most important single thing that the Congress can address this year is a comprehensive energy policy. And following that, I think the Congress will be ready to turn its attention to the ratification of the Panama Canal Treaty. I was hoping we could do it this year. But the obstacles that have been placed in the way of rapid Senate consideration of the energy package, I think, has delayed it.

I have talked privately with Senator Robert Byrd, the majority leader, and his response is, "Whenever you get an assured vote of 67 votes in the Senate, why, I'll be willing to call it up." [*Laughter*] And that's why I need your help. I'm not asking you in particular to call your U.S. Senator and say please support the treaty. But I do hope that when you go back home, if you are convinced that the treaties are in the best interest of our country that you will let your own voice be heard.

It takes a great deal of courage on the part of a U.S. Senator to vote for the canal treaties if he has any doubts whatsoever if the people in his home State are overwhelmingly opposed to the treaties based upon incorrect information.

I think you've had a very good opportunity this afternoon to learn the facts about the treaties. And I hope that you will exhibit not only a knowledge of the treaties themselves when you go back home but some political courage and make speeches to the Lions Clubs or Rotary Clubs or Jaycees or be interviewed by your own local television or radio stations or your local editorial board and let your own voice be heard and say this is a difficult and unpopular political question, but our country will be well-served by these treaties.

So, I think that the vote in the Senate might very well come early next year. I think there's been a great deal of alleviation of previous concern about the treaties with the recent exchange of clarifying language between myself and the Panamanian leaders.

Q. Mr. President, I was in favor of the treaty before I came, so, you know, I haven't changed my mind.

THE PRESIDENT. Very good.

Q. But most people in Utah aren't in favor of the treaty, I believe. What specifically—somehow, if I could say respectfully without walking around this question—would be your position in case the Senate doesn't ratify the treaty?

THE PRESIDENT. I would be reluctant to bring the treaties to the Senate for action unless I was reasonably sure the Senate would vote affirmatively, because I am afraid that even with the best-meaning intentions among the Panamanian governmental leaders, that a rejection of the treaty might have very serious consequences in our relationship with Panama—the ability to keep the canal open without armed conflict—and also would damage severely our relationship with countries in the southern part of this hemisphere.

So, my expectation is to try to secure enough votes in the Senate before I actually ask the Senate to vote on the subject. Yes, would you have a followup question?

Q. I don't know how to ask the President of the United States, but——

THE PRESIDENT. You're welcome.

Q. ——what if you don't get the votes?

THE PRESIDENT. I think we've got a good chance to get them. But if I don't see that we're going to get the votes, then my own inclination would be to delay submission of the treaties for a vote.

Q. And would that create havoc for Panama?

THE PRESIDENT. It would create a very difficult condition which we might very well use as time for me to let the Senators know how serious the question is. When the Senate does adjourn this year, a group of them, the leaders, many of whom oppose the treaties at this point, will go to Panama on their own initiative to see what the circumstances are there and to see the advantages of ratification and the very serious disadvantages that might come with rejection.

So, I believe that time and education and knowledge about the treaties will lead to increasing support in the Senate. So, I have confidence that the Senate will ratify when the vote does come.

Q. Mr. President, as another supporter of the Panama treaties, I want to ask you a question that's asked of me often. Isn't the ratification—the potential ratification of the Panama Canal treaties a symbolic step in what people perceive as the continuing process of withdrawal of the United States from the world, such as we've seen in Vietnam, Korea, and in other places in the world? People talk about withdrawing troops involved in NATO. It's more of a symbolic question than it is a pragmatic question.

THE PRESIDENT. Yes, I think that's part of the emotional commitment to the canal, because we were, as a nation, embarrassed in Vietnam. I think there's a sense that we've got to show our strength and show our ability to stand firm no matter what the challenges to us might be.

I look on the ratification of the Panama Canal treaties as a show of strength and as a show of national will and as a show of fairness and as a show of confidence in ourselves now and in the future to act if necessary, but not to have to show that we are strong just because we can run over a little country.

It's much better for us to show our strength and our ability by not being a bully and by saying to Panama, let's work in harmony, let's form a partnership. If the canal is challenged either by insurgents or terrorists from your own country or by outside forces we'll be there to work with you to defend the canal, but not to throw down a gauntlet and tell Panama, we dare you to do anything about the canal because we're strong enough to defeat any forces that you might put forward.

We don't have to show our strength as a nation by running over a small nation because we're stronger than they are. So, I don't see the treaties as a withdrawal. We are retaining permanent rights to defend the Panama Canal. We will operate it with a dominant position the rest of this century, and after the year 2000, and this century, of course, we'll have a complete right for our ships to use the Panama Canal on a priority basis in time of either need or emergency.

So, I don't believe we're giving up anything by showing that we can work in harmony with a small nation. We can suffer tremendously in our reputation among the small nations of the world not just in Latin America but throughout the world if we continue to try to run over Panama just because we're strong militarily.

I don't think anybody thinks that Panama is stronger than we are militarily, and I don't think we have to prove it by trying to push them around. I think they've been very fair in the negotiation period, which has lasted 14 years. They've been very patient. And their original, very extreme demands, which they thought were legitimate, have not been accepted by us, and I think General Torrijos has acted fairly with me. He's very concerned about the Senate action. He's gone out of his way to make it possible for the Senate to vote for the treaties.

And, of course, we've tried to help him as well. I think there'll be a new sense of partnership and commitment based on the strength of our country, not weakness, in the Panama Canal Treaty effort.

Q. Thank you. Mr. President, I'm Betty Orten from Colorado. I support the Panama treaty, and I thank you for the briefing. And I ask you, sir, please to consider the opinions of Colorado and the West regarding water. [*Laughter*]

THE PRESIDENT. I might say that that's been ever present on my mind ever since I got off the plane here. [*Laughter*] And for the benefit of Coloradans and also Georgians, I'm determined to keep the Panama Canal full of water and to keep our ships moving through it. [*Laughter*]

Q. Mr. President, firstly, I'd like to be able to tell my children that I chatted with the President. [*Laughter*] Norm Johnson from Salt Lake City. I understand that the board which governs the Panama Canal will change makeup after a period of time, and at some point——

THE PRESIDENT. No.

Q. That is not true?

THE PRESIDENT. No. Let me explain it to you.

The board will always consist of nine people for the rest of this century—five Americans, four Panamanians. The four

Panamanians will come from a list submitted to us by Panama that the United States chooses and approves. The chairman of the board will be an American for the first part of the treaty. The administrator, the executive officer, who can only carry out the board's policy, will be an American up through 1990 and for the last 10 years of this century will be a Panamanian. But that person will not set policy. He'll only carry out the policy of the board itself dominated by Americans.

And, of course, one of the things that that board will do, which is very important, is to set fees for the use of the canal to decide which projects will take priority in repair or expansion of the canal. So, we'll keep complete control of that board for the rest of the century.

Q. At some point are we in jeopardy of coming under economic duress? In other words, we talked about 30 cents, at the time, I believe, in terms of tonnage price. Is there some point in history under the terms of the treaties wherein—or whoever is running the canal could raise that to $10, $20, whatever would make it fiscally impossible, or——

THE PRESIDENT. Yes. That's always a possibility, that the board of directors would go wild and set a transit fee that would be extraordinarily high. If so, the ships just wouldn't use the canal. Some might even go around the southern coast of South America. Others might choose to offload on the east or west coast or the gulf coast and let rail shipment replace transit shipment. But I think that even if the use of the canal doesn't increase in the future, that the fees will be much less, for instance, than they are with the Suez Canal, and with any increase in the use of the canal, it's almost inevitable, in my opinion, as we start shipping more and more oil and natural gas from Alaska, down around the coast, through the canal

up to the gulf coast, that as you increase the volume of shipment through the canal, then the fees per ton will go down.

Q. Mr. President, my name is Greg Olin, and I'm from Salt Lake City. I was wondering if I could have a comment on the current furor over disregard of the constitutional provision—and I'll have to read this——

THE PRESIDENT. All right.

Q. ——found in Article IV, Section 3, Clause 2, which says, "The Congress shall have power to dispose of and make all needful rules and regulations respecting the territory or other property belonging to the United States," my question being, I think you're being accused by some people of having circumvented the House.

THE PRESIDENT. I understand.

Q. The second question that I had for you is, you'd mentioned that you'd like to keep the canal full. I guess the rumor that you were going to adhere to EPA standards, drain it, put your dirt back into it—[inaudible]—[laughter].

THE PRESIDENT. That's all right. We'll keep the canal open and work it. We've got legal rulings on the constitutionality of my signing the treaties and the Senate advising and consenting toward the ratification of the treaties. I might say that the House of Representatives will be involved in the process. For instance, a very crucial element of the treaties themselves will be the establishment of the nine-person board to which I just referred. Now the Panama Canal Corporation is a private nongovernmental entity. After the canal treaties are ratified, then that will be replaced by a government agency which will consist of this nine-person board, and the House and Senate will have to approve the establishment of that board. So, that's one of the necessary parts of the completion of the treaty process. So, the House will have an adequate chance to participate in that. Historically in our country, the President and the Senate, ratifying a treaty, has been able to take action as we are taking now.

Q. Mr. President, I am Sue Joshel from Denver. You told us that a number of Congressmen who are now against the treaty will eventually go over to Panama. And you are pretty sure that they will come back and have their minds changed. What will it be—what will they hear and see which will change their minds?

THE PRESIDENT. Well, you know, I can't really predict the details, and it may be presumptuous of me to think that the Senators who go down there will all come back convinced that the treaties will be advantageous. I can't say that for sure. But my own experience so far has been that as people in a position of responsibility, like you all and the other public leaders, have studied the treaties and understand the provisions and the advantages to our country in carrying out the treaties, they've become convinced that it was good.

I've seen a shift among Senators who give me their private commitments toward approval for the treaties themselves. One thing that has always been a consideration is how do the American citizens who live in the zone have their rights guaranteed.

Whenever we've discussed that point with the negotiators, we have had representatives of the citizens there in the meetings themselves and also labor leaders who in the past have opposed the treaties. But we have guaranteed the right in the treaties themselves for American citizens to have their jobs protected, to have promotion rights, to have all their retirement benefits protected.

So, that was one of the major obstacles in the past that did exist to the treaties

being ratified. And now the UAW, the AFL–CIO, and others who represent those American workers in the canal for the first time have endorsed the treaties.

Maybe one more question. We've just about run out of time.

Q. My name is Abbott Sekaquaptewa, Mr. President. I'm the chairman of the Hopi Indian Tribal Council from Arizona.

THE PRESIDENT. Yes, sir.

Q. This afternoon we have heard many things, and as I understand it, one of the goals of the treaty is to channel our relations to a more positive atmosphere, not only in the Western Hemisphere but in the larger world community, in the process to give a better status and self-respect and better opportunities to the Panamanians in the process.

THE PRESIDENT. Yes.

Q. Now, based on your support for these treaties I would like to know, my people would like to know, I'm sure, does this then set a policy for your administration and the administration of internal decisions made for the Indian people of this country with the same high goals as these two treaties seem to aspire to?

THE PRESIDENT. The answer is yes, it does. Thank you, sir.

I see you represent the American Legion?

Q. Yes, sir.

THE PRESIDENT. I'm a Legionnaire myself. I want to have your question.

Q. Mr. President, I'd just like to make a few comments here. I'm Harry Taylor, State commander of the Republic of New Mexico American Legion. I have the pleasure, of course, to address you now, Mr. President, and explain the position of the American Legion in regard to the Panama Canal, the Canal Zone.

As you are aware, the American Legion held our national convention here in Denver on August 19 to the 26th.

THE PRESIDENT. Yes, I heard about that. [*Laughter*]

Q. And the delegates at that time unanimously endorsed Resolution 445 concerning the rejection of the treaty to turn the Canal Zone back to the Panamanians.

We have been warned of this over a long time and by many of the former high military naval personnel of our Government that if this would happen and it would result in the greatest economic, geographical, and sovereignty loss that our country as a republic has endured in the last 200 years.

The American Legion will not stand still or wait for this to happen. We intend and we will use our influence to inform the United States Senate and the American people to reject this treaty, and with the help of God and the wisdom of the American people, we will succeed, because we dare to care about the future of America and the American people.

Thank you.

THE PRESIDENT. Thank you very much, sir. I understand how the American Legion felt back in those days, and perhaps you haven't changed your mind. Certainly, you haven't.

I think there has been some clarification, as I said a little earlier, about the two most important questions that were raised at your convention. One was a claim that our country did not have the right to defend the canal the rest of this century and into the next century. I believe that to the best of my ability that particular question has been answered.

And the other major question that was raised then and since by the American Legionnaires has been that we didn't have the right to use the canal in a time of emergency ahead of other ships in order to defend our country. I think that to the best of my ability that has also now been answered.

Very great military leaders, including our own Joint Chiefs of Staff, have endorsed the canal. In the last week, for instance, Admiral Zumwalt, who was a very forceful and very strong naval leader, has endorsed the canal itself. The Chief of Naval Operations of the Navy now strongly endorses the canal. Former commanding officer of our forces in South Korea, Matthew Ridgway, this past week came out, endorsed the canal. Melvin Laird, former Secretary of Defense under the Republican administration, has endorsed the canal, and others who are deeply concerned about the defense of our Nation.

As a fellow Legionnaire, though, I know that there is a very strong and forceful desire on the part of Legionnaires to express your opinion openly and aggressively, and I'm very glad to have you do that this afternoon, sir.

Thank you very much, everybody.

NOTE: The President spoke at 3:55 p.m. in the Silver Room at the Denver Hilton Hotel. The briefing was attended by approximately 150 citizens from the States of Arizona, Colorado, Idaho, Montana, Nevada, New Mexico, Utah, and Wyoming.

Los Angeles, California

Remarks at a Democratic National Committee Fundraising Dinner.
October 22, 1977

Thank you very much, everybody. I see all the Imperial Valley farmers are not outside—[*laughter*]—and I want to thank you for it.

It's really a great pleasure for me to be back in Los Angeles with you and with the California Democrats. I've been looking forward to coming. This has been something that is obviously the result of a lot of work.

I got a personal handwritten letter from your Governor, Jerry Brown. I decided to come on out here anyway. [*Laughter*] And as you know, we formed a partnership way back in the campaign, and we've been moving toward the same goal for a long time. [*Laughter*] I'm very thankful I finally made it.

I see how successful the evening is, and I want to thank personally all the cochairmen and, particularly, Lew Wasserman, one of the greatest people I know. It's obvious that he met his goal and that the supper is a very fine financial success.

I was hoping that you would meet my goal to raise enough money to have my brother, Billy, come out and speak next year. Billy brings me a lot of good publicity, as you well know. I wish we could have gone along with my plans to involve him in the Government. I had it all arranged. I was going to reorganize and put the CIA and the FBI together, but Billy said he wouldn't head up any agency that he couldn't spell, so that fell through. [*Laughter*]

As you know, my family is very close to California. My mother has been following the Los Angeles Dodgers around the country for the last couple of weeks. She's really angry at the Yankees. She was supposed to spend a night or two with us at the White House, but after the World Series game, she refused to come. She said I live too close to the Mason-Dixon line. She wasn't going to have anything to do with me anymore. As you know, we've had trouble with the Yankees around Atlanta, too. At least they didn't burn Los Angeles. [*Laughter*]

Tonight I want to talk to you about a few things that are important to me as the head of the Democratic Party and also as the leader of our great country. I spent 2 years campaigning and learned a lot about our Nation and got to know many of you and formed some close and fast friendships and learned from you.

On this very brief trip, since I left Washington, I've had a chance to go into Iowa, where I won my first primary victory, and to meet with farmers. And I got up early this morning to talk to them about the new farm legislation. Before that, I was in Detroit, in a city that 2 years ago had a 24 percent unemployment rate, and they're very proud now to be down to 8 percent. They've cut the murder rate 64 percent in the last couple of years and are making great progress. I talked about the poverty-stricken areas of our Nation. Later this morning I went to Omaha, Nebraska, to visit, as Commander in Chief, the Command Center for our Strategic Air Forces, on which the defense of our country and the free world rests. And then I went from there to Denver, Colorado, to spend all afternoon meeting with a broad representation from the central Rocky Mountain West on all aspects of the water problem, and then had an encounter or a debate or meeting with leaders from eight States on the Panama Canal treaties. And there was a live television coverage of it. And now I've come here.

And after spending 9 or 10 months in the White House, I've begun to value very deeply my own knowledge of the interests and concerns and yearnings and hopes of you and other people who gave me your friendship and your support when I was running for President.

We've begun to make progress on the strategic arms limitation talks. For the first time there seems to be a desire on the part of the Soviet Union to put a lower limit on strategic launches and MIRV'd warheads and a limit on the production of new weapons. And I believe that in a few weeks we'll be able to announce some success in our negotiations with the Soviets that will make you proud. That's my hope and my belief.

A little more than a year ago in San Diego, I made a speech about nonproliferation, and I think it's accurate to say that then and even at the time I went into office, there was a general feeling throughout the world that it was too late to recapture a commitment against the spread of atomic explosives, to put the nuclear genie back in the bottle. But now we've built up a hope and a belief among the nations of the world that we can have at least a limited use of atomic power to produce electricity and to meet our legitimate need and to stop once and for all the spread of atomic explosives. I believe that this is a realization that will soon be appreciated by the world.

We've had this past week 36 countries come together in Washington to talk about this subject. And I hope that we'll never again see another nation added to the club of those who can destroy human beings with nuclear explosives. This is my belief, and this is my hope.

I want to say just a word about our efforts to reorganize the Government of our country. The Congress has courageously given me the authority to carry out this effort over a 3-year period, and I believe that you will be pleased with what is being done in that respect. It's a project that will make the Democratic Party proud. And I know that a great responsibility lies on my shoulders not to disappoint the people who have given me this effort that has been so long overdue.

The Congress has also passed a very strong economic stimulation package, and we are beginning to see the results of it. Our economy is in danger of causing us

grave concern. Among the nations of the world, ours is one of the strongest, and we have an inherent advantage in our Nation with our great productivity and the commitment of our people to hard work and our free enterprise system.

The latest estimates of the inflation rate from September were less than 4 percent, but there is still an underlying inflation rate of 6 or 6½ percent that we hope to bring down in the future. Last December, shortly before I became President, we had an unemployment rate of 8.1 percent. Now it's down below 7 percent, and I believe it will continue to go down the rest of this year and next year, but very, very slowly. So, we are making some progress.

I believe that our country needs to get the spirit of what we have been given, and I believe there's too much whining and complaining about some of the temporary setbacks that do cause us legitimate concern. But I believe, if all of us Democrats speak out about the greatness and the strength and the bright future that lies ahead of us and the tremendous blessings that have fallen upon us, that our country can benefit even more by a concerted effort to make that future even greater.

I want to say just a word about three basic subjects that I haven't talked about to you in a good while. One is the question of human rights. As you well know, our Nation has been deeply wounded in the last few years. The war in Vietnam— our withdrawal from that country caused our people to be embarrassed and brought the condemnation of most of the rest of the world on our Nation. We have been embarrassed by the Watergate revelations and by the CIA investigations. There was a sense of malaise and a sense of discouragement and a sense of distrust of our own Government, a sense of betrayal of the fine ideals on which our country was founded.

But I think it's accurate to say that a strong emphasis on human rights and every aspect of them has restored to our people a pride again. And we now have raised the banner of commitment to the principles that were filling the hearts of Americans 200 years ago, of a pride in the individuality of human beings and a pride in the basic freedoms and a pride in what our Nation stands for.

I think now there's a sense among every national leader in the world that how we treat the people in our countries is of crucial importance for a change. And the condemnation of the rest of the world is a powerful force on those who in the past have been the most guilty of depriving our people and other people around the world of these rights.

We are not perfect yet, but I think there is a general sense now that the United States does stand for the principles that have made us a great nation.

We've had some serious problems in Czechoslovakia recently when four dissidents were tried and convicted just because they were dissidents. And South Africa recently has made a major retrogressive step in depriving people of the right of free speech and free press. We have just announced the withdrawal of our Ambassador from South Africa for consultations, and we hope to use all the pressure we can to bring this course of action.

I think that our Democratic Party, my own leadership, the accomplishments of the Congress are going to be measured by what we do about the comprehensive energy policy. As you know, this effort is long overdue, and I don't have time tonight to go into the domestic implications of it. But I would like to point out to you in just a few sentences the international implications of what we have failed to do in the last few years.

In 1973 the world was shocked when the price of oil quadrupled almost overnight. And we realized that we were in trouble with excessive waste of the increasingly scarce fossil fuels. Great Britain has reduced their consumption of oil since 1973; Germany has reduced their imports of oil since 1973; France has reduced their imports of oil since 1973; Italy has done the same; so has Japan. But our country since 1973 has almost doubled our imports of oil. We now import more oil. In spite of the fact that we can produce a great deal ourselves, we now import more oil than all the European Community nations combined. We are the OPEC countries' greatest customer. We purchase 25 percent of all the oil exported from the OPEC nations.

This year we will purchase overseas $45 billion worth of oil—approximately half of all the oil we use and just about exactly the amount that we waste that we could be saving. This is making us increasingly vulnerable and actually can endanger our own Nation's security as we come much more heavily on foreign oil, the supply of which can be interrupted without our being able to prevent it. It removes the freedom of action that we ought to have in dealing with other countries and causes a constraint on us economically that is very devastating.

This past year we had the greatest year for exports of farm products in history—$24 billion—but we imported twice as much oil as we exported all our farm products combined. This year we'll have a trade imbalance of $30 billion, and if we could just hold down oil imports, we would have a trade surplus of $15 billion. This robs our economy of very scarce moneys. It dampens the prospect for jobs and growth. And unless we act courageously, our reputation as a nation with will and strength will be severely damaged, and we will be in serious trouble, even more than we are now.

I hope and believe that the Congress will act with courage to meet this very serious need and that we can do this in such a way—shifting toward conservation, toward alternate sources of energy—that we'll provide an adequate incentive for the oil and gas producers and not rob the consumers in the process.

This also makes it very important for us to reexamine one of the most important foreign policy responsibilities that falls on our shoulders, and that's in the Middle East. As you well know, we have made progress this year in trying to bring peace, and permanent peace, to the Middle East. My overwhelming commitment and the commitment of the Nation is to guarantee a strong, independent, secure, and peaceful Israel.

A few days ago in a conversation with about 30 Members of the House of Representatives, I said that I would rather commit suicide than to hurt the nation of Israel. I think many of them realize that the two concepts are not incompatible. [*Laughter*] If I should ever hurt Israel, which I won't, I think a political suicide would almost automatically result, because it's not only our Jewish citizens who have this deep commitment to Israel but there's an overwhelming support throughout the Nation, because there's a common bond of commitment to the same principles of openness and freedom and democracy and strength and courage that ties us together in an irrevocable way.

I think it's important, though, for the people of our Nation to remember that now that we are moving toward a comprehensive settlement of the Middle East disputes, that we have two roles to play. One role is the one that I've just described: an unshakable partnership with Israel, an unshakable support of Israel—

the only staunch and dependable major ally on which Israel can depend. That's one of the two roles. The other one is as a mediator, a trusted political entity that cannot afford to betray the trust of all those that we hope to bring together in Geneva before this year is over to talk about the terms of a genuine peace.

I've had long, detailed, private conversations with the leaders of Israel and her neighbors. And I'm convinced that the Egyptians want permanent peace, and I'm convinced that the Jordanians want permanent peace, and I'm convinced that the Syrians want permanent peace, and I'm convinced that the Lebanese want permanent peace, and I know also, of course, that Israel wants permanent peace. But if I ever betray any of those leaders as they look to me and to our country to bring them together to discuss the extremely sensitive and divisive issues that have caused hatreds and animosities to exist, closed borders and barbed wire to exist, a lack of communication and common purpose to exist for generations, even centuries, then the hopes for peace will be dashed for many years to come.

My own belief is that we do have a chance for success. There is a very delicate balance, because there have been strong statements made in the past that now must be forgotten. And there must be an inexorable movement toward an open discussion on a bilateral basis, where Israel can sit down with Syria on an equal basis and discuss the Golan Heights and sit down with the Egyptians and discuss the Sinai and on a multinational basis discuss the problems of the Gaza Strip and also the West Bank and the Palestinian refugee question. These must be addressed, and I believe that all the leaders agree that this is a prospect for the future.

It's very difficult for me at times to explain to the public the private negotiation terms that have convinced me that we are making good progress. This is a year when hopes are growing, and I believe that we have a good chance to see a vision realized that fills my heart and my mind— a vision of borders that are not closed, a vision of trade, an exchange of students, an exchange of tourists, of commerce, a sense of political commitment to common purpose, diplomatic recognition between nations, an alleviation of the arms race, and a repair of the economic chaos that exists in many of the nations that I have described. We want to be sure that there is economic growth there so that private contributions and Government aid programs that go into that region can be used not just for weapons, overwhelmingly, but to repair the lives of those who have lived there in torment for so long.

I don't know that we will be successful. But I am committed to this hope with my uttermost commitment as a human being who loves Israel, as a President of a country that feels a sense of partnership. And I hope that everything that you do as Democrats and as leaders of one of our great States will be contributing to a realization of these hopes that we share so deeply.

I've enjoyed being President this year. There have been many responsibilities that have not been so enjoyable. But I see the prospects for progress. But I can do really very little without a sense of partnership with you, because my judgment must be based on a realization of the hopes and dreams of the American people. And your demonstration tonight of support for our party is very encouraging to me. I appreciate your confidence in our government in spite of the fact that it has had problems in the past, and I appreciate your confidence in me as President.

I want to continue to have an open government where even controversial subjects can be discussed without fear, because sometimes the longstanding problems of unemployment and inflation, of nuclear weaponry and nuclear proliferation, an absence of an energy policy and a comprehensive farm legislation, rebuilding our cities, bringing peace with the Soviet Union and peace to southern Africa, an emphasis on human rights and peace in the Middle East—none of these questions are easy. It would be much easier to ignore them or delay the resolution of them. But with your strength and support and the commitment or the principles of a Democratic Party, I believe that we can be successful.

Tomorrow morning, I and those traveling with me will get up early, about 5 o'clock, and we'll get on a plane, and we'll fly to Minnesota. And as I get off that plane, I would like to be able to extend the love of the California Democrats to the greatest Democrat of all—Hubert Humphrey. Senator Humphrey and Muriel will fly back to Washington with me on Air Force One. And as I travel that short distance with him, I will be expressing my thanks to him for what he means and has meant to our country, and I'll extend to him your love and a recommitment from you to the principles for which he stands, for which our party stands, and for which stands also the greatest nation on Earth—our country.

Thank you very much.

NOTE: The President spoke at 8:40 p.m. in the Los Angeles Room at the Century Plaza Hotel.

Minneapolis, Minnesota

Remarks of the President and Senator Hubert H. Humphrey at Minneapolis/ St. Paul International Airport. October 23, 1977

THE PRESIDENT. This is one of the great days of my life, to be able to come back to

Minnesota to join with the greatest American that I know, the number one Democrat in our country, and a man who has been admired and is admired throughout the world.

I was in Los Angeles last night, Senator Humphrey, and hundreds of Democrats who came to help finance our party all send you their personal love.

But I came to express my thanks to Senator Humphrey. I've missed him in Washington, and I'm looking forward to getting him back to the U.S. Senate where he's been needed so badly.

He's got renewed strength. He's feeling very well, and he's eager to get back to Washington and join his fellow Senators and bringing this congressional session to a successful close.

On the plane, after we take off, I'm going to sign a bill that will name the newest building of the Health, Education, and Welfare Department after Senator Humphrey.

As a mayor of Minneapolis, as a Senator from Minnesota, and a Vice President, as a Presidential nominee, and a great candidate and, now, as a U.S. Senator, I know no one who exemplifies what our Nation stands for better than he.

If there's a retarded child in our country who hasn't been helped by Senator Humphrey, I don't know about it. Every elderly person in our Nation, every poor person in our Nation, every black person in our Nation, everyone who has come here from overseas who doesn't speak English well, everyone who lives in something of despair knows that they have one staunch and undying friend in Senator Hubert Humphrey.

This naming of the building for him would be just a small gesture on the part of the House and the Senate to make sure that everyone in our country, for this year and for many years to come, will connect this building and the great work that he's done with the humanitarian efforts that have been typical of him.

He's a friend of mine. He has been down to Georgia to help me. He's given me advice when I was Governor. I met him when I was a Georgia senator. He's been a man who has been an idol of farmers throughout the country, and I'm really looking forward to having him back in his workclothes, back in Washington as a staunch ally for me as President and as a leader of our Congress. It's going to mean a great deal to our country to have him back where he belongs, again serving the American people.

Senator Humphrey, I'm glad you're going back to work, and I'm glad you've let me provide the taxi service to get you back where you belong. Congratulations to you, and congratulations to the Minnesota football team yesterday. That was great.

SENATOR HUMPHREY. Mr. President, I know I speak on behalf of the almost 4 million people in this State when I say thank you for stopping by on this Sunday to pay us a visit, to share with us your optimism, your confidence, your friendly smile, and above all, your love of people and country. It's these things that I find so much of meaning to me. And it's in these ideals and these attitudes that I share so much with the President—a great faith in the Nation, in our people, a faith in our institutions of government, and a knowing that we've got to work at it and never give in and never give up.

I am happy to report to you that I do feel so much better. Everything, of course, is relative. I'm not quite as good as I was when I was 50, but I'm doing mighty good, considering what we've gone through. Getting back to Washington is going to be good therapy. That's what my doctors told me.

They've done about as much for me here as they think they can. It's been remarkable. With a strong faith in the Lord, with the best doctors, with the loving care of a family, with the friendship and the— indeed, the devoted friendship of people all over this country, I really have felt the healing strength that comes from all of this.

I want to thank you for coming out. Mrs. Humphrey is here with me. My grandchildren are here, my three sons and daughter, my sister, nephew; all the family are here.

I'm sure my doctor is over there, Dr. Najarian, and Dr. Levitt, possibly Dr. Kennedy. I hope they are. They have been helping me so much.

Yesterday, I was a little tired because I gave a good deal of my strength to the Gophers. [*Laughter*] I'm going to let you in now on a high state secret. On Friday night, the former President of the United States, Mr. Ford, called me. And he said, "Hubert, I understand that the University of Michigan is coming to Minnesota." I said, "Yes." I said, "Please, just don't mention it," because Michigan, up to that time, was unbeaten. He said, "Well, now, Hubert, don't you think we ought to have a little wager?" I said, "I think that's proper." He said, "I'll give you 14 points." I said, "That's Republican conservatism." [*Laughter*] I said, "I demand three touchdowns—21." He said, "Well, how about 20?" I said, "That's a deal." He said, "What's the amount?" I said, "Five dollars." Now, I hope that's legal. I'm not sure. If it isn't, I ask for forgiveness.

THE PRESIDENT. I pardon you on that one. [*Laughter*]

SENATOR HUMPHREY. You pardon me on that, would you, Mr. President? Thank you.

So yesterday, after the game, as soon as I could get the White House switchboard to help me, which they did readily, I got

ahold of my old friend, President Ford. I said, "Mr. President, send the check." [*Laughter*] And I gave him two or three addresses so that he couldn't possibly miss. So if the IRS is here, we'll include it.

I just wanted you to know that great developments have taken place within the last 24 hours. Thank you, and God bless you today. Thank you very much.

NOTE: The President spoke at 12:30 p.m. at the Hubert H. Humphrey Charter Terminal.

Following their remarks, Senator Humphrey returned to Washington with the President. Upon arrival at Andrews Air Force Base, they were joined on Air Force One by Vice President Walter F. Mondale, and the President signed S. 2169, designating the South Portal Federal Office Building of the Department of Health, Education, and Welfare as the Hubert H. Humphrey Building.

As enacted, S. 2169 is Public Law 95–141, approved October 23.

Veterans Day

Remarks at Ceremonies at Arlington National Cemetery. October 24, 1977

As I stand here this morning representing the greatest nation on Earth, and as I've heard the prayer of Captain James Carter and joined in the Pledge of Allegiance with General Rogers, and then introduced by my own close, personal friend, Max Cleland, I've been overwhelmed, as I have many times in the past in my life, with a sense of love and gratitude for those who have offered, and sometimes who have offered and given their lives in service to our country. Our hearts are filled with love and appreciation and gratitude and closeness and brotherhood. And at the same time, we think about the horrors of war, when those attributes are missing from the hearts and lives of people who have to fight.

I come from the South, as you know. We are one of the parts of the Nation who have suffered severely, along with those who fought in the War Between the States. And I think Robert E. Lee gave a good analysis of this duality of feeling when he said to his wife in a personal letter, "What a cruel thing is war, to separate and destroy families and friends and mar the purest joys and happiness that God has granted us in this world, to fill our hearts with hatred, instead of love, and to devastate the fair face of this beautiful world."

We are here to commemorate the dead. The Tomb of the Unknown Soldier was dedicated in 1921, and the body of an unknown soldier from the First World War was buried here. Later, we had the bodies of unknown soldiers from the Korean war and the Second World War. We don't have the body of a Vietnam veteran, because every body so far discovered has been identified. But they share in the commemoration of their heroism perhaps in a special way.

Since the Revolutionary War in 1776, 45 million Americans have been part of the Armed Forces during conflict. About 140 years after my own family came to this country, the first James Carter in our family who lived in Georgia fought in the Revolutionary War. My great-grandparents participated in the War Between the States. My own father was a first lieutenant in the First World War. I wore the uniform of our country during the second war and the Korean war.

I represent the kind of family that's close to all your hearts. And the prospect in the service in war has touched almost every life in our country. Francis Bacon said that peace is much better than war, because in peace, sons bury fathers and in war, fathers bury sons.

My son Jack served in Vietnam. And although I came back from the wars as something of a hero—although I was not a hero—my son came back unappreciated, sometimes scorned by his peer group who did not join in the conflict. And I think there's a special debt of gratitude on the part of American people to those young men and women who served in Vietnam, because they've not been appreciated enough.

It's difficult enough to fight in a war that's popular with our people because of a sense of patriotism and dedication and gratitude that is a sustaining force when one's life is threatened to the danger of combat. But to fight in a self-sacrificial way in Vietnam, when there was not this depth of gratitude and commitment on the part of the people back home, is an extremely difficult thing, even above and beyond the difficulty of previous wars.

I have a deep sense of this responsibility on me as President. And we've tried, since Max Cleland has been in office and since I've been in office, to recommend— and the Congress has responded well—to increase Veterans Administration compensation, to increase Veterans Administration pensions, to increase GI bill coverage, and to reverse the effort that had been made to reduce the time during which Vietnam veterans would qualify for the GI bill.

When we initiated our jobs program this year, we put veterans at the top place in the responsibility to give them gainful employment.

We have with us today a special person, Chairman George Mahon, who will be retiring after this term after long service in Congress. In a speech the other night, he pointed out that he had fought in the Congress to allocate more than $2 trillion for the defense of our country. And I know that all our people feel very deeply that we must have peace.

Those who love peace most are those who serve in the Armed Forces and whose lives would first be lost if conflict occurs. But we know that peace can best be preserved by maintaining the strength of our Nation. We must be strong enough militarily, we must have a strong commitment of the American people, and there must be a demonstrable will to defend freedom in order to prevent war. Those are the commitments that I make to you.

Those are the commitments that I make to you, and I ask you today and millions of Americans to join me in assuring that the future will hold peace for all of us, because our will for freedom and our commitment to the principles of our Nation will always be strong in gratitude to those in the past who have given their lives and those today who are willing to give their lives for the preservation of the greatest nation on Earth.

Thank you very much.

NOTE: The President spoke at 11:28 a.m. at the Amphitheater after laying a wreath at the Tomb of the Unknowns.

In his remarks, the President referred to Rev. James Paul Carter, chaplain, Audie Murphy Veterans Administration Hospital, San Antonio, Tex., and Maj. Gen. Charles C. Rogers, USA, winner of the Medal of Honor.

Medicare-Medicaid Anti-Fraud and Abuse Amendments

Remarks on Signing H.R. 3 Into Law.
October 25, 1977

We seem to have some happy people here today.

As most of you know, I was Governor for 4 years and later spent 2 years campaigning around the country to be elected President. I think one of the greatest problems that we have in this Nation is a distrust of government and its ability to administer programs of great benefit to our people in an honest and efficient way.

Perhaps one of the most sensitive issues is in health care. We have seen the cost of a day's stay in the hospital increase since 1950 more than 1,000 percent. The cost of hospital care is going up a hundred percent, doubling every 5 years.

At the same time, we see highly publicized instances when the Medicaid and Medicare programs in recent years have been shot through with fraud. This was one of my frequent campaign comments. And I'm very proud today to sign into law a bill that has been evolved with close cooperation between the executive branch of Government, particularly HEW, and the House and Senate.

This bill will go a long way to eliminating fraud in the administration of the health care programs of our country. It will shift to heavier penalties for those who are convicted of false claims, kickbacks—changing these from misdemeanors to felonies—and also prohibiting those who are convicted of this crime from delivering any services in the future.

This legislation also permits—in fact, requires—the Department of HEW to set up both simplified and also standardized forms for reporting the delivery of services in the health care field and also the charging for those services.

In the past it's been quite difficult, as you know who have watched the evening news, to determine exactly who owns the health provider entities that deliver health care and quite often conceal who is responsible when a violation of the law does exist. This legislation requires that anyone who owns as much as 5 percent in a health provider company or hospital or health care center must reveal their identity to the public.

We have included also in this bill an allocation of aid funds to establish among the States, or within each individual

State, a fraud unit to detect and to root out and to prevent fraud from continuing. And this bill also provides more effective use of the PSRO's, or the professional standards review organizations, that are designed to let health care providers themselves monitor their own activities and their own efficiency of operation.

The overwhelming majority of doctors and hospital and nursing home administrators are honest, patriotic, and deeply dedicated to giving good health care according to the law and in the best interests of their patients. And we want to make sure that they who are honest can have a more efficient means by which they can patrol or monitor their own professions.

I'm very thankful today to sign into law the House of Representatives bill number 3. And I want to congratulate Danny Rostenkowski and Paul Rogers and Senator Talmadge and their fellow workers in the Congress behind me for having been so successful in passing this bill.

We hope, without too much delay, to have a hospital cost containment legislation passed as well. All these men and their committees are working on this. And I hope, certainly early next year, we might get this additional law on the books.

But this is a major step forward. And as I sign this legislation, it's with a great deal of gratitude to them for their fine leadership in moving our Nation one step forward toward better health care, more efficient for the taxpayers, and with a restoration of the confidence in our government that is so well deserved.

[*At this point, the President signed H.R. 3 into law.*]

Thank you very much. I made it.

NOTE: The President spoke at 1:31 p.m. at the signing ceremony in the Rose Garden at the White House.

As enacted, H.R. 3 is Public Law 95–142, approved October 25.

Meeting With Prince Saud of Saudi Arabia

White House Statement Issued Following the Meeting Between the President and the Foreign Minister. October 25, 1977

The President and Saudi Arabian Foreign Minister, His Royal Highness Prince Saud, met in the Cabinet Room this morning for 1 hour and 30 minutes. The President was accompanied by Vice President Walter Mondale, Secretary of State Cyrus Vance, Deputy Assistant for National Security Affairs David L. Aaron, Counsel to the President Robert J. Lipshutz, Assistant to the President Hamilton Jordan, Assistant Secretary of State for Near Eastern and South Asian Affairs Alfred L. Atherton, U.S. Ambassador to Saudi Arabia John West, and National Security Staff member William Quandt; and Prince Saud by Ambassador Ali Alireza, Deputy Prime Minister for Foreign Affairs Sheikh Abdullah Alireza, Ambassador Ahmed Siraj of the Ministry of Foreign Affairs, and First Secretary of the Saudi Arabia Embassy Dr. Nazar Madani.

The President began by expressing his pleasure at this opportunity to discuss with Prince Saud the wide range of ties which unite Saudi Arabia and the United States in friendship. The President asked the Foreign Minister to convey his personal best wishes to His Majesty King Khalid in anticipation of the meeting he will be having with His Majesty and His Royal Highness Prince Fahd next month in Saudi Arabia.

The President and Prince Saud spent a good deal of their time today reviewing the current efforts to resume negotiations on a settlement of the Middle East conflict. The President informed the Foreign Minister of the results of previous meetings he has had over the past few weeks with foreign ministers of the governments involved. The President reaffirmed his determination to help these parties to the conflict work out procedures for reconvening the Geneva conference by the end of the year. The President expressed his conviction that differences over procedure should not be permitted to prevent negotiations on the substance of the conflict which all the parties have said they desire. As he has in his other meetings, the President repeated his own conviction that a just and lasting peace in this vital area of the world requires compromise and courageous leadership from all concerned. He thanked Prince Saud for the understanding and support Saudi Arabia has shown for the efforts to advance the prospects for an early resumption of peace negotiations. Secretary Vance will pursue the discussion with the Minister, listening to his ideas and explaining in detail suggestions for reconciling differences between the parties.

The President and Prince Saud also discussed a number of matters of mutual interest pertaining both to our bilateral relations and to the challenges facing the international community. In particular, the President emphasized to the Foreign Minister his determination to obtain the comprehensive energy conservation program which is currently before Congress. He expressed again his appreciation of the policy which Saudi Arabia, the world's largest oil exporter, has pursued in petroleum production and pricing.

The President emphasized the importance to the international community of maintaining world oil price stability over the coming year. The President and Prince Saud noted with satisfaction that the economic ties between the United States and Saudi Arabia continue to expand, and that the close cooperation and

consultation between the two Governments in international finance and development lending remain a major contribution to world economic growth.

The President assured the Foreign Minister that the United States intends to continue its role in helping Saudi Arabia meet legitimate defense needs.

Constitution of the Northern Mariana Islands
Proclamation 4534.   October 24, 1977

By the President of the United States of America

A Proclamation

On February 15, 1975, the Marianas Political Status Commission, the duly appointed representative of the people of the Northern Mariana Islands, and the Personal Representative of the President of the United States signed a Covenant, the purpose of which is to provide for the eventual establishment of a Commonwealth of the Northern Mariana Islands in political union with the United States of America. This Covenant was subsequently approved by the Mariana Islands District Legislature and by the people of the Northern Mariana Islands voting in a plebiscite. The Covenant was approved by the Congress of the United States by joint resolution approved March 24, 1976 (Public Law 94–241; 90 Stat. 263).

In accordance with the provisions of Article II of the Covenant, the people of the Northern Mariana Islands have formulated and approved a Constitution which was submitted to me on behalf of the Government of the United States on April 21, 1977, for approval on the basis of its consistency with the Covenant and those provisions of the Constitution, treaties and laws of the United States to be applicable to the Northern Mariana Islands. Pursuant to the provisions of Section 202 of the Covenant, the Constitution of the Northern Mariana Islands will be deemed to have been approved by the Government of the United States six months after the date of submission to the President unless sooner approved or disapproved.

The six-month period of Section 202 of the Covenant having expired on October 22, 1977, I am pleased to announce that the Constitution of the Northern Mariana Islands is hereby deemed approved.

I am satisfied that the Constitution of the Northern Mariana Islands complies with the requirements of Article II of the Covenant. I have also received advice from the Senate Committee on Energy and Natural Resources and the Subcommittee on National Parks and Insular Affairs of the House Committee on Interior and Insular Affairs that the Constitution complies with those requirements.

Sections 1003(b) and 1004(b) of the Covenant provide that the Constitution of the Northern Mariana Islands and the provisions specified in Section 1003(b) of the Covenant shall become effective on a date proclaimed by the President which will be not more than 180 days after the Covenant and the Constitution of the Northern Mariana Islands have both been approved.

Now, THEREFORE, I, JIMMY CARTER, President of the United States of America, do hereby proclaim as follows:

SECTION 1. The Constitution of the Northern Mariana Islands shall come into full force and effect at eleven o'clock on the morning of January 9, 1978, Northern Mariana Islands local time.

SEC. 2. Sections 102, 103, 204, 304, Article IV, Sections 501, 502, 505, 601–605, 607, Article VII, Sections 802–805, 901 and 902 of the Covenant shall come into full force and effect on the date and at the time specified in Section 1 of this Proclamation.

SEC. 3. The authority of the President under Section 1004 of the Covenant to suspend the application of any provision of law to or in the Northern Mariana Islands until the termination of the Trusteeship Agreement is hereby reserved.

IN WITNESS WHEREOF, I have hereunto set my hand this twenty-fourth day of October, in the year of our Lord nineteen hundred seventy-seven, and of the Independence of the United States of America the two hundred and second.

JIMMY CARTER

[Filed with the Office of the Federal Register, 5:06 p.m., October 25, 1977]

NOTE: The text of the proclamation was released on October 25.

National Commission on Neighborhoods

Nomination of Joseph F. Timilty To Be Chairman. October 25, 1977

The President today announced that he will nominate Joseph F. Timilty, of Boston, Mass., to be Chairman of the National Commission on Neighborhoods.

Timilty was born October 3, 1938, in Boston. He attended Providence College and served in the U.S. Marine Corps.

Timilty worked on Edward M. Kennedy's campaign for the U.S. Senate in 1962. He was elected to the Boston City Council in 1967 and served until 1971, when he ran for mayor of Boston. Since 1972 Timilty has been a Massachusetts State senator.

Timilty is chairman of the Massachusetts Legislature's Joint Committee on

Urban Affairs, which handles legislative activity in such areas as public housing, private government-assisted housing, urban redevelopment, tenant-landlord relations, and zoning. He is on the faculty of the Boston University urban affairs department and has been a teaching fellow at the Kennedy Institute for Politics at Harvard University.

Department of Agriculture

Exchange of Letters on the Resignation of Robert H. Meyer as Assistant Secretary. October 25, 1977

To: Robert H. Meyer

I received your letter of October 20 and accept with regret your resignation as Assistant Secretary of Agriculture.

However, I fully understand your feelings as expressed in this letter.

I also wish to express my sincere gratitude to you for all of the assistance which you have rendered to me and to the country over such a long period of time and I look forward to seeing you frequently in the future.

Sincerely,

JIMMY CARTER

[Mr. Robert H. Meyer, Assistant Secretary of Agriculture, U.S. Department of Agriculture, Washington, D.C. 25250]

October 20, 1977

Dear Mr. President:

The issue of individual water rights raised by the Interior Department bears heavily on questions of national water, and food and agriculture policies, which I know firsthand to be of a high priority to you and your Administration. As the Interior position applies to the Imperial Valley of California, I feel strongly that it goes beyond reliability of water and food supplies. At the heart of the matter is the commitment of our government to its people. For over 75 years, generations of family farmers have invested their lives and resources in the Imperial Valley. For slightly more than 40 years, they have been farming and relying on the word of their government that the 1902 Reclamation Act did *NOT* apply to them. Going back over three generations, these family farmers originally developed this Valley in 1901 and delivered water to themselves and their ground without any government help. The fact that the courts, so far, have ruled against them does not remove the moral obligation that our government has to these people.

I never anticipated any higher honor than that you have given me nor higher privilege than the opportunities of service entrusted to me.

Because I feel so deeply that I must be free to voice my personal convictions, I regretfully offer my resignation as Assistant Secretary of Agriculture.

I will continue to do all that I can to serve my country and you as a private citizen. You have my abiding gratitude and loyalty.

Sincerely,

ROBERT H. MEYER

[The President, The White House, Washington, D.C. 20500]

NOTE: The texts of the letters were made available by the White House Press Office on October 26. They were not issued in the form of a White House press release.

President's Executive Interchange Program

Memorandum for the Heads of Executive Departments and Agencies.   October 26, 1977

Memorandum for the Heads of Executive Departments and Agencies

To improve understanding between the Federal government and the private sector, I ask for your support of the President's Executive Interchange Program. It is designed to give executives from the Federal government and the private sector the opportunity of working in responsible positions in the opposite sector for a one-year period. Only those with a record of significant managerial accomplishments and potential for advancement to senior positions are chosen to participate.

This exchange of talent and expertise can help us use our human resources in the most effective way. This Program has my complete endorsement, and I urge all Federal Departments and Agencies to support it in two ways: by seeking out nominees from the career employees of your department for assignment in the private sector, and by accepting on assignment an appropriate executive from outside government.

The Executive Director of the President's Commission on Personnel Interchange, which administers the Program, will contact your office to follow up on this request.

JIMMY CARTER

Department of the Treasury
Nomination of Stella B. Hackel To Be Director of the Mint. October 26, 1977

The President today announced that he will nominate Stella B. Hackel, of Rutland, Vt., to be Director of the Mint. She would replace Mary T. Brooks, resigned.

Hackel was born December 27, 1926, in Burlington, Vt. She received a J.D. from Boston University School of Law in 1948.

She was elected city grand juror (city prosecutor) of Rutland in 1956, and was reelected annually until 1963. From 1963 to 1973, she was commissioner of the Vermont Department of Employment Se-

curity and chairman of the Employment Security Board.

Hackel practiced law in Rutland from 1973 to 1975. From 1975 to 1977, she was treasurer of the State of Vermont. She was the Democratic candidate for Governor of Vermont in 1976. Since earlier this year she has been city attorney of Rutland.

Work-Study Program Students
Executive Order 12015. October 26, 1977

PERMITTING STUDENTS COMPLETING APPROVED CAREER-RELATED WORK-STUDY PROGRAMS TO BE APPOINTED TO CAREER OR CAREER-CONDITIONAL POSITIONS IN THE COMPETITIVE SERVICE

By virtue of the authority vested in me by Sections 3301 and 3302 of Title 5 of the United States Code, and as President of the United States of America, it is hereby ordered as follows:

SECTION 1. As used in this order "career-related work-study programs" are those programs established by the United States Civil Service Commission which provide for a formally-arranged schedule of periods of attendance at an accredited school combined with periods of career-related work in a Federal agency under a Schedule B appointment.

SEC. 2. The appointment of a student to a position in a career-related work-study program may be converted noncompetitively to a career or career-conditional appointment if the student:

(a) has completed within the preceding 120 days an educational program that meets the provisions established by the Civil Service Commission;

(b) has satisfied all course requirements leading to completion of the related curriculum at an accredited school;

(c) is recommended for such an appointment by the employing agency in which the career-related work was performed; and,

(d) satisfies such other requirements and conditions as the Civil Service Commission may prescribe for career or career-conditional appointment of an individual in career-related work-study programs.

SEC. 3. The Civil Service Commission shall prescribe such regulations as it deems necessary to carry out the provisions of this order and to provide for the continuation of planning, implementation and evaluation of employment programs for students throughout the Government. These regulations shall provide for the periodic evaluation of the work of each student and require that each student's continuation in the program shall be dependent upon a finding of satisfactory performance.

SEC. 4. Executive Order No. 11813 of October 7, 1974, is hereby revoked.

JIMMY CARTER

The White House,
   October 26, 1977.

[Filed with the Office of the Federal Register,
   3:25 p.m., October 27, 1977]

NOTE: The Executive order was announced by the White House Press Office on October 26. It was not issued in the form of a White House press release.

THE PRESIDENT'S NEWS CONFERENCE OF OCTOBER 27, 1977

THE PRESIDENT. Good afternoon. I have a brief statement to make before I take questions.

ENERGY AND TAX REFORM LEGISLATION

Action on a national energy policy is a test of the ability of our democratic system to respond to a recognized threat before it seriously damages our Nation and our economy, and we will all be measured by the courage which we are able to muster to face up to this energy problem.

The debate that's now going on concerning the National Energy Plan is not a contest between the executive branch and the Congress nor between the House of Representatives and the Senate. It's a test of our national will.

We must protect the American people and also avoid unfair windfall profits. We must also meet our stated objectives on conservation, on production, and on the shift of consumption to other sources of energy other than gas and oil. And we must not let the formation of a national energy policy break our budget.

Nothing less is at stake than the ability of our own Nation to act independently as a country. We cannot allow uncertain foreign oil supplies to obtain a stranglehold over the United States. We cannot continue to import $45 billion worth of oil annually, almost half the total amount that we consume and about how much we waste that we don't need to waste.

And we cannot let this excessive dependence on foreign oil continue to increase our trade deficit, to drain off purchasing power of our economy, and also to affect our economic stability.

Both the Congress and I know that enactment of comprehensive energy legislation must be our top priority.

Now, as you know, I had planned to send by now to the Congress a major tax reform package. Although most of the work has already been done, I've decided to submit that program after Congress completes its work on both social security and also energy legislation.

The Congress right now needs an opportunity to concentrate its attention more fully on the entire energy package, including the tax proposals.

I will have more time working with my staff and with the Congress and with labor and business leaders to evolve the difficult answers to complicated tax proposals. We have an early need to simplify the tax system, to provide more equity to modify the tax rates and to improve capital formation.

The tax reform proposals will be a major element in a comprehensive economic program designed to promote a strong economy and to deal further with reducing inflation, which has recently been on the way down, to reduce unemployment, which is also going down quite slowly, and to do this both immediately and in the years ahead.

The principal component parts of this program have to be carefully integrated also in our budgetary proposals for fiscal year 1979. I prefer to make these final decisions on the tax reform program after the Congress has completed action on the energy program, particularly its tax components, and social security, which has heavy tax connotations.

Both of these proposals can be assessed, obviously, after the Congress adjourns. By the end of the year we will have more information also on the state of the economy, to know how much of our tax reform proposal should be devoted to stimulating the economy.

We have a full agenda this year, and I have discussed this delay in the tax reform proposal until after the Congress adjourns with the leaders of Congress. And I might say they unanimously agree with this delay.

Mr. Cormier [Frank Cormier, Associated Press].

QUESTIONS
TAX REFORM

Q. On taxes, Mr. President, depending on economic conditions, might you in the end give higher priority to a stimulative tax cut and seek action on that first before the broad overall reform program?

THE PRESIDENT. No. I think the tax reform package has got to fulfill three basic elements. One is improved equity, which means more progressivity and an end to many of the unnecessary tax incentives and loopholes; secondly, to create investment capital; and third, greatly to simplify the entire tax structure. The degree to which we will have tax cuts to stimulate the economy can only be assessed after we see how much of a drag on the economy the increased social security taxes might be and the rate of growth in the economy.

We've just gotten returns this morning, for instance, from overseas balance of trade. We had the highest rate of exports last month in the Nation's history. And imports were reduced somewhat. Obviously, the trade imbalance comes from energy imports.

We also have had a substantial decrease in the last couple of months in the inflation rate, but a very slow decrease in unemployment.

So, I would say that the rate of tax reduction and stimulation from the tax reform measures could only be assessed at the end of this year.

ARTHUR BURNS

Q. Mr. President, what is your reaction to Arthur Burns' criticism of your economic policy, and do you plan to reappoint him as the Fed Chairman?

THE PRESIDENT. I haven't decided about reappointment, but as you well know, Mr. Burns is a very able and outspoken and independent man. And the Federal Reserve System is legally an independent agency.

I, as President, the Congress, and the Federal Reserve System all have independent roles to play in the evolution of tax law, budget proposals, and of course, the supply of money primarily from the Federal Reserve Board.

I think Mr. Burns' primary concern is that we have created uncertainty in the business community by our major proposals, and this is a concern which I share. But when I'm faced with the problem of whether to ignore a depleting reserve, for instance, on social security and letting the integrity of the social security system be threatened on the one hand, or proposing bold measures to correct the social security problems—and I, of course, propose those corrections to the Congress.

I think we had delayed too long the addressing of the energy crisis, and these weeks, when there is a time of uncertainty, creates a dampening effect on the economy and on the attitude of businessmen toward future investment. But the alternative was to ignore the energy problem additionally for months and perhaps years.

The same thing applies to welfare reform; the same thing applies to tax reform. I believe that these kinds of criticisms that might have come from Mr. Burns, that the volume of proposals might have created uncertainty, are just honest differences of opinion. And I think I've made the right decision. I agree with Mr. Burns that the profitability of our free enterprise system—the business profits ought to be up, and one of the things that I hope to do with the tax reform proposals and others is to improve capital retention so that new investments can be made to provide new jobs.

I might say in closing that I welcome his public criticisms, and I think that I can understand his point of view. I have a luncheon meeting monthly with Mr. Burns, which is an innovation since I've been in office, and we exchange our views very frankly with each other. Sometimes there's a sharper disagreement at our private luncheons even than there is in public. But we're working toward the same goal, and I respect him very much and the right of him to make his independent judgments of what I do.

SOUTH AFRICA

Q. Mr. President, on the subject of sanctions against South Africa, could you share your thinking on the course the United States should follow in this situation?

THE PRESIDENT. Yes. Our hope has been and our goal has been to work harmoniously with South Africa in dealing with the threats to peace in Namibia and in Zimbabwe in particular and to encourage South Africa to move toward the elimination of some of those racial problems which they've had historically, to do away with apartheid, to give an equal opportunity for employment, job promotion, education, and the participation in the political and economic affairs of South Africa for all its citizens.

The crisis was engendered last week when South Africa took away the rights of the free press and eliminated many of the organizations themselves who had been working toward improved equality for the citizens of South Africa. I think it's important that we express in no uncertain terms our deep and legitimate concern about those actions of South Africa.

We are working in harmony with our Western Alliance friends. We are working in harmony with leaders in Africa and throughout the rest of the world. My decision has been to support strong sanctions against the sale of weapons to South Africa. This will be carried out immediately by us.

My prediction is that the United Nations will adopt such a resolution and it will be overwhelmingly supported by the nations of the world. This will be joined with a direction from me that this be carried out. It would include prohibition against the sale of spare parts to weapons. And we will also, of course, assess other actions that might be taken in the future.

We don't know yet what the negotiations might bring between us and the nations that I described to you. But this is an appropriate action, in my opinion, and we still hope that South Africa will not sever themselves from the rest of the world community, that they will cooperate with us in bringing peace, that they will move in a rapid but evolutionary way toward restoring—or granting for the first time those human rights that we hold so dear.

ENERGY LEGISLATION

Q. Mr. President, there's talk on Capitol Hill that the administration would accept a bill that sets the pricing of natural gas at $1.85 per mcf. And you've said that you would only sign a bill that's fair to consumers. If the Congress were to pass a bill setting the price at $1.85, would you sign it? And I have a followup.

THE PRESIDENT. Judy [Judy Woodruff, NBC News], I don't want to get into the role of saying I will or will not sign a bill that has this or that in it. As you know, the negotiations on the House and Senate side both are very sensitive at this point. And we had prospects several months ago, in June and July, of having a complete failure in the House. They debated and worked and very courageously came out with an acceptable package fairly close to what we proposed.

I still stand behind the proposals that we made to Congress in April. I believe that's the best approach. The price for natural gas that we put forward was $1.75. It involves a slow but predictable increase in the price of natural gas that would be compatible with world prices,

and it had an accurate, I think an adequate description of the definition of new gas.

We also proposed to include both intrastate and interstate gas in this new program. That's still my position, and that's what I'm going to fight for and work hard for in the conference committee, and then when the conference committee comes back to the House and Senate.

I've not had any secret or private agreements with anyone to modify our own original proposal. We stuck with that proposal throughout the House deliberations, and because of that tenacity that we demonstrated, I think it kept our whole program together. And that's my present stance, and that's my future stance.

I have told Members of the House and Senate who come to see me, I've told labor leaders, business groups, and also consumer groups that before I modify at all our own official position on these very controversial energy policies, that I would consult with them ahead of time. It obviously might be necessary to do some compromising; otherwise, the conference committee report could not function. But my position is still completely compatible with what we proposed to the Congress back in April.

I outlined in my opening statement the three basic principles. One is to protect the interest of American consumers and not to permit windfall profits for the oil companies; secondly, to meet the conservation and conversion goals, and also production goals; and, thirdly, not to seriously unbalance the Federal Government. Within that framework, which is quite constrictive, we will work with the House and Senate leaders.

Q. What about a bill that included any amount of plowback to the oil industry? Could you accept that sort of bill?

THE PRESIDENT. I am not in favor of any plowback to the oil industry. There were proposals made in the Ways and Means Committee starting out at about 80 percent plowback, going all the way down to 20 percent. We opposed all those, and eventually the House rejected this proposal. That's still my position.

STRATEGIC ARMS LIMITATION

Q. Mr. President, the other night in Los Angeles you said that for the first time the Soviet Union has agreed to cut back on or decrease the number of nuclear weapons. And you suggested that a new strategic arms agreement may be in sight, perhaps even in the next few weeks.

Can you tell us anything more about that? Can you tell us what kind of decreases may be in the works and any other specifics about the kind of thing that is shaping up?

THE PRESIDENT. Well, the negotiations between us and the Soviet Union have been characterized in recent weeks by, I would say, constructive cooperation from both sides. My own comments have been mirrored by the comments made by Foreign Secretary Gromyko and also by President Brezhnev.

I would guess that we have a fairly good prospect within the next few weeks of a description of the general terms for a settlement. The details, the exact procedures by which we might verify and so forth, would take a long and tedious negotiation.

As you know, the SALT I agreement, the so-called interim agreement, provides for a heavy disparity between us and the Soviets, with the Soviets having a right to have about one-third more launchers than we have and about one-third more submarines than we have, about one-third more submarine missiles than we have.

The Vladivostok agreement, which, as you know, has never been ratified, set a 2,400 limit on launchers, 1,320 limit on MIRV'd missiles. We hope to reduce those levels, and there's general agreement now that those levels will be reduced.

Also for the first time we have discussed in very strong terms and are close to an agreement on how many land-based ICBM MIRV'd missiles will be permitted. This is a new development. But we've not yet reached final agreement between ourselves and the Soviet Union.

But I think, as I said in both Iowa and Los Angeles, that within a few weeks we'll have a demonstration of real progress. The detailed signing of a treaty will take longer than that.

RICHARD HELMS

Q. Mr. President, Attorney General Griffin Bell said recently he had reached some decision in his own mind as to whether or not it is proper and practical to seek an indictment against former CIA Director Richard Helms. He also discussed some of the ways that he thought might be used to keep sensitive material of national security value from being revealed at any trial that might ensue.

Have you reached any conclusion in your own mind on this matter? And is the issue of revealing national security material sufficiently resolved now so that the judgment can be made on the merits of a possible indictment itself?

THE PRESIDENT. I don't know. The Attorney General has not informed me about what his decision is. In fact, I had not known he had made a decision until I saw it in the press. I would presume, though, that before that discussion is put into final form, that he would discuss it with me. He has not yet done so.

ASSESSMENT OF ADMINISTRATION
POLICIES

Q. Mr. President, Mr. Rhodes, the Republican leader of the House, says that your administration is inept. And as you know, a lot of people have been suggesting that you have not been able to cope with all of these problems and with all of these initiatives.

Assuming you don't think there's a word of truth in any of that, would you tell us why you think the perception is abroad to that extent, and whether you believe that there's anything to the idea that people still think, as a Georgian, that you don't belong here?

THE PRESIDENT. I remember in this room last May someone asked me if my administration was all image and no substance, or all style and no substance. Lately the criticisms have been that there's too much substance and not enough style.

My own attitude toward leadership and politics, when I was Governor of Georgia and since I've been President and during the campaign itself, was to try to analyze the most difficult questions that face our Nation and not to be timid or reticent about seeking solutions for them, recognizing that some of them are historic in nature, some of them have very difficult aspects that almost defy solution, but that they're all important to our country.

The Mideast question is maybe a thousand years old or more, but we're working hard to try to solve it under the most difficult of circumstances.

To put a limit on the spread of atomic weapons is something that has defied solution for the last 35 years. And to work harmoniously with the Soviet Union in reducing strategic weapons with which we could destroy each other is one that has been addressed by all of my predecessors, not yet successfully by any of us.

The energy policy of our country has escaped political decision for years because, perhaps, it is so difficult. The welfare problem is predictably controversial.

The social security system was going into bankruptcy, had not something been done about it. Our Nation is now taking a leadership role in Africa.

And I believe that any one of these questions could be assumed difficult and controversial and not easy of solution, but I could not bring myself as President, responsible for our people's security and for the welfare of our citizens, for the redressing of some longstanding problems, to delay them simply to avoid controversy.

It might take us 3 or 4 more years to reach a final conclusion on welfare reform or tax reform, but I think it's better to get it on the table, have an open debate, let the people be involved in it, let the Congress start learning about it, let me learn more about it, let the private sector of our country become involved in the debate, the universities, the economists, the business leaders, the labor leaders. And I don't see anything wrong with it or anything that I would have done differently.

The fact that the easy solutions have not come forward immediately don't concern me, because they are not questions that can be resolved easily.

But I think that in the long run, certainly in retrospect after this year goes by, there will be a general realization that none of these questions should have been delayed.

I was thinking the other day about what new major innovative proposals might be forthcoming next year and the year after. I can't think of any. I think we've addressed all of the major problems already. There may be some new ones that evolve in an unpredictable way that we'll have to address. But I think most of the major debates now have already been initiated, some will be concluded this year, some have already been concluded by Congress this year, and I think we'll have additional success next year. So, I feel good about it.

Q. Do you think the people will hold that against you?

THE PRESIDENT. The Georgians don't hold it against me. [*Laughter*] No, I don't think being from Georgia is something that is of genuine concern to people. That might be a contrived additional reason not to want me to be in office.

SOUTH AFRICA

Q. Sir, in addition to the mandatory arms embargo which you mentioned, what other unilateral steps do you think the United States will be taking outside the boundaries of a resolution, such as the Ex-Import Bank, commercial sales guarantees, things of this kind? And are you ruling out for now any trade embargo of a general nature or investment embargo?

THE PRESIDENT. We are not deciding at this point on any sort of general trade embargo or investment embargo.

The additional steps that might be taken beyond an arms embargo that would be mandatory have not yet been decided.

G. GORDON LIDDY

Q. Mr. President, when he got out of jail recently, Gordon Liddy expressed gratitude for his early release, and he said that he felt himself bound to carry out any orders from the Commander in Chief. Given that situation, and in order to put the record straight at long last, do you think it would be proper for you to instruct him to say what he was doing in the Watergate, what he was looking for, who authorized the burglary, and any other information he might have?

THE PRESIDENT. Well, I've not had any contact with Mr. Liddy at all, either before or after he was released from prison. And my remote assessment of Mr. Liddy is that he will not voluntarily release the information that he has about the Watergate situation.

ASSESSMENT OF ADMINISTRATION POLICIES

Q. Mr. President, if I could follow up on Sam Donaldson's [ABC News] question, Pat Caddell and Jerry Rafshoon were in to see you a couple of weeks ago— they're supposed to have spent about 2 hours with you. There's speculation that they may have asked to see you to express some sort of reservations they had about the way things were going in general around the Carter administration and perhaps even to make some recommendations about changes.

Could you tell us a little bit more about that meeting and whether, as a result of that or anything else, there are any organizational or personal changes in the wind here at the White House?

THE PRESIDENT. Well, the meeting resulted from my own initiative. I invited them to have lunch with me, along with my wife, and we did discuss some of the poll results which, the way I look at them, are fairly good. They varied greatly from one pollster to another. I think the Roper poll shows that I was below 50 percent, the Gallup poll about 60 percent. Of course, I would like to have higher than either one of those. But I think that the controversial nature of some of the things that we've put forward inherently cause concern about me and reduce my standing in the polls.

Although I didn't want the prediction to come true, when I announced that I would put forth an energy package, I predicted that my poll rating would drop 15 percent. There is a general feeling in this country of optimism about the future, as revealed by Pat Caddell's poll and others. The economy has some very good attributes in it that ought to be recognized more vividly. The inflation rate is coming down fairly rapidly. We have an underlying inflation rate, though, of about 6 percent.

The unemployment rate is coming down slowly but, I think, surely. The balance of trade is better than it was. We have a high rate of business investments.

I think we have a lot to be proud of in this country. I don't believe there's any other nation that has a stronger underlying economic base and more to be thankful for than our Nation does. But most of what I hear as President, in delegations that come to see me and large group meetings that I have, is complaining and expressions of despair, quite often in hopes that as the Government makes decisions, that the squeaking wheel will get more grease and that they'll get more benefits from Federal Government policies.

But I think the general sense of the polls that we discussed at that luncheon meeting was that there's an inherent optimism in our country, there's a concern about the multiplicity of programs that we are addressing at this point, and the fact that the American people can't understand all that many proposals at one time.

And one of the things we discussed is what I said earlier, that I would think that after this year, as far as I can see in my own plans, most of those modern problems would be addressed. But it was a friendly meeting and there was nothing to be concerned about.

HUMAN RIGHTS

Q. Mr. President, at a press conference earlier this year, you mentioned the Palestinians have a right to a homeland and to compensation for losses they have suffered. From your perspective, do the Palestinians have any other legitimate rights?

THE PRESIDENT. Well, the Palestinians have rights, as I described in my United Nations speech, as do all human beings. The Palestinians are one major group of refugees that have been created in the Mideast. Obviously, there are Jewish refugees also. But I think all human beings have the same basic yearning for freedom, for human self-respect, for a home in which they can live, for a right to raise a family, to have education, health care, food. So, I would say in that respect they have the same rights as others do.

Q. Mr. President, could I raise another policy issue for a second?

THE PRESIDENT. Let me get Ms. Compton [Ann Compton, ABC News]. I promised her.

SOUTH AFRICA

Q. Mr. President, is there any grounds for critcism of your approach to the South African problem that you are meddling in internal affairs? Do you worry about getting to a point, responding to what's going on internally in South Africa, the United States is trying to dictate its internal policies?

THE PRESIDENT. No. I don't believe—there are certainly grounds for criticism, but I don't think that this is a legitimate criticism of us. We have not tried to tell South Africa what to do about their internal affairs. We've never laid out any specific action they should take nor any time schedule that they should follow.

We have worked harmoniously with South Africa in some ways in trying to evolve a solution to the Namibian question, formerly Southwest Africa, over which South Africa still has control, and to try to get them to work with the Rhodesian Government in changing

Zimbabwe to a majority rule government with predemocratic elections.

I do feel that it's proper for us to deplore, not only in South Africa but in other nations as well, blatant deprivation of basic human rights.

In my speech in Los Angeles, I pointed out for instance in Czechoslovakia that recently there have been four people tried there as dissidents. Their only crime was that they dissented from what government action has been taken.

But I think it's proper for us to either enhance or reduce our trade with a country depending upon its own policies that are important to us and to the world. I think it's important for us to decide when we should and should not sell weapons to other countries, when we should and should not invest in another country, when we should and should not encourage government programs, loans, and grants to apply to another nation. I don't look upon that as an interference in the internal affairs of another country.

MR. CORMIER. Thank you, Mr. President.

THE PRESIDENT. Thank you, sir.

NOTE: President Carter's eighteenth news conference began at 2:30 p.m. in Room 450 of the Old Executive Office Building. It was broadcast live on radio and television.

Domestic Airline Industry

Statement on Action by the Senate Committee on Commerce, Science, and Transportation To Reduce Regulation of the Industry. October 27, 1977

I would like to commend Senators Cannon and Magnuson and the members of the Senate Commerce Committee for voting today to report, by an 11–2 margin, the Cannon-Kennedy bill to reduce regulation of the domestic airline industry.

This is a breakthrough in our effort to remove outdated regulatory burdens and to make sure that Federal regulatory programs are responsive to the public interest. This bill will eliminate bureaucratic obstacles which have discouraged airlines from charging lower fares where they are possible and kept new, innovative carriers from offering their services to the public. In addition, it modernizes the Federal assistance program to small communities, so that air service to small communities can be improved.

I recently approved an order permitting Laker Airways to fly between London and New York at drastically reduced prices. And I have overruled the CAB to permit carriers to lower their fares on many North Atlantic markets. These decisions have made international travel more affordable for Americans and have otherwise brought substantial benefits to people traveling in international markets.

I do believe that the Government should stop denying similar opportunities to American consumers who need to travel within the United States. That is why this legislation is important, and why we are pleased by today's favorable action by the Senate Commerce Committee.

Similar legislation is pending in the House Aviation Subcommittee of the House Public Works and Transportation Committee. Transportation Secretary Brock Adams joins me in urging the House Committee to move quickly to resolve this important issue.

Susquehanna River Basin Commission

Appointment of Patrick J. Delaney as Alternate Federal Member.   October 27, 1977

The President today announced the appointment of Patrick J. Delaney, of

Long Island City, N.Y., to be alternate Federal member of the Susquehanna River Basin Commission. He would replace Thomas C. H. Webster, resigned.

Delaney was born December 15, 1940, in New York City. He received a B.S. from Providence College in 1963.

From 1965 to 1973, Delaney was a stockbroker in New York. From 1973 to 1975, he was special assistant to the chairman of the New York State Racing and Wagering Board. He served as Assistant Director of the White House Domestic Council from 1975 to 1976, and as Associate Director for Intergovernmental Relations from 1976 to 1977.

Upper Mississippi River Basin Commission

Appointment of Neil S. Haugerud as Chairman. October 27, 1977

The President today announced the appointment of Neil S. Haugerud, of Preston, Minn., to be Chairman of the Upper Mississippi River Basin Commission. He replaces George W. Griebenow, resigned.

Haugerud was born July 3, 1930, in Canton Township, Minn. He served in the U.S. Marine Corps from 1948 to 1952.

Haugerud was sheriff of Fillmore County, Minn., from 1961 to 1969. Since 1969 he has been a member of the Minnesota House of Representatives. He has served as chairman of the State Department's Division of the Appropriations Committee, and as a member of the Legislative Commission on Minnesota Resources, a joint House-Senate committee. He was chairman of the Joint Senate-House Commission for the Review of Administrative Rules.

In addition to his legislative duties, Haugerud is owner and operator of a family farm. Previously, he owned and managed a real estate and insurance agency.

Social Security Financing Bill

White House Statement on House Action on the Bill. October 27, 1977

We commend the action of the House of Representatives today in passing the social security financing bill [H.R. 9346]. The President requested such legislation on May 9, 1977, and it now appears possible that a bill can be enacted this year.

The House bill contains many provisions requested by the administration, including the correction of the inflation adjustment mechanism, maintenance of benefit levels in the future, and the use of general revenues as an insurance policy to protect the trust funds against a future economic downturn. We would like to see more moderate increases in the tax rate for workers. In particular, we are concerned that the removal of the earnings limitation passed by the House will require too great a tax increase. We expect that the tax levels will be moderated in the final measure passed by Congress.

The American people deserve a social security system which is financially sound. The response of the House to the President's initiative is an important first step toward that goal. We are confident that the Senate will soon take action on the bill to be reported from the Finance Committee.

We look forward to working with the Members of the House and Senate in the coming weeks in a joint effort to ensure the financial integrity of the social security system into the middle of the next century.

Bills Concerning Indochina Refugees and Prisoner Transfers With Mexico and Canada

Remarks on Signing H.R. 7769 and S. 1682 Into Law.   October 28, 1977

THE PRESIDENT. *Good morning, everybody.*

This is one of those days and one of those occasions when our Nation puts its best foot forward. One of the most difficult things for a strong and proud country to do is to acknowledge its own commitment to a difficult political principle like the one of human rights.

It's easy for us to preach to other countries, to criticize South Africa, to criticize Czechoslovakia, to be concerned about Eastern Europe and the Soviet Union, and to talk about prisoners in Chile. But when it comes down to our own Nation, we are so proud of our past achievements that quite often it's hard for us to acknowledge our own needs for compassion.

I doubt if any other group of refugees in my lifetime have been so devastated by war than those from Vietnam and Laos, Cambodia. And it's been a very controversial thing domestically to have people come into our country who don't know the language, who are not, at the time they come, self-sufficient, and who, when they receive language training and vocational training and education and job placement, compete for scarce jobs.

But the Congress again has shown that we are a great nation, not just militarily and economically but in our commitment to principles.

This bill from the House, number 7769, acknowledges our gratitude and also our debt, also our commitment to a better life for the refugees who have been here for a number of months, even years, from Southeast Asia and those who have come just this year. It permits the granting to them of additional opportunity for language training, for vocational training, for basic education principles, for counseling, for job placement.

It also gives them legal resident alien status which they can obtain after they have been here 2 years. Most of them have already been here that long and became eligible for citizenship.

I think this is a great step forward. Although the citizenship procedures take 5 years, it puts them on an equal basis with others who come to our country with renewed hope for their lives.

I'm very glad, also, that this provides us with a means, at some significant expense to the Federal Treasury, to help State and local governments, who have been bearing an inordinate financial responsibility for these refugees. And now it puts it on a firm financial basis so that there can be an assurance, leading up to an ultimate conclusion of this program as these people are assimilated into our society, that they will be cared for properly.

So, it's with a great deal of pleasure that I sign this bill, House of Representatives bill 7769, that provides human rights to the refugees from Southeast Asia.

I particularly want to thank those in the Congress behind me who worked so hard on this. I won't try to name them all, but I'm very grateful to them. And I believe that this exemplifies, in a fine spirit, what our country stands for.

[*At this point, the President signed H.R. 7769 into law.*]

I think before I ask some of the Congress Members to say a word that I'll cover the other bill as well. It has the same general tone, but kind of a mirror image.

This bill carries out the principles of treaties with our closest neighbors and allies, Canada and Mexico. And we have the Ambassadors here from those countries to take part in this ceremony.

We have about 2,000 American prisoners incarcerated in foreign lands. Historically we've had an arrangement with the Scandanavian countries that when we have their prisoners in our jails or when they have our prisoners in their jails, that we exchange those American citizens and their citizens. And now we are extending this principle to Mexico and also to Canada.

We have 575 Americans in Mexican prisons, and we have 250 Americans in Canadian prisons. And after negotiating these treaties, we now have implemented that process legally by which these prisoners might be exchanged.

If they so desire, Mexican and Canadian prisoners in our jails can go back to their own lands to serve out their terms, and vice versa concerning our own American citizens in Mexican and Canadian prisons.

I think this is a major step forward. It indicates a compatibility between our own country and our neighbors. It shows that we have a respect for their judicial system, the fairness of their courts, and the trial processes. It also, I think, will be contributory toward better rehabilitation.

I think it's always easier for someone who is in prison in their own land to have closer connections with their peer groups and with their neighbors, with those who love them, with their future potential employers, so that they can work harder toward a rehabilitation effort.

Of course, in Mexico, for instance, there is no opportunity for parole for good service in prison. When these young men and women mostly come back to our land, then they'll be given that opportunity if they perform well and demonstrate their own rehabilitation.

So, I'm very grateful that we have passed this Senate bill 1682 which carries out the provisions of the treaties already signed with Canada and Mexico. And we will commence an immediate exchange of prisoners after this legislation is signed today.

Again, I want to congratulate the Members of Congress who have been so effective in getting this legislation passed.

[*At this point, the President signed S. 1682 into law.*]

Well, congratulations, all of you, and thank you.

Pete, would you like to say a word?

REPRESENTATIVE RODINO. *Mr. President, my colleagues, and my friends:*

Let me say that this marks, as the President has stated so eloquently, another expression of America's commitment to human rights and a deep commitment indeed to justice. And more importantly, I think it is an expression of the American people's willingness to carry out the great concepts of this country and to be understanding and to be compassionate, even though sometimes we have got to bear a bigger burden.

I congratulate the President for his leadership, and the members of my committee for the work they did, and all of those who together brought this about.

Thank you very much, Mr. President.

THE PRESIDENT. Mr. Eilberg.

REPRESENTATIVE EILBERG. Mr. President, I want to thank you very much for the opportunity to be here. It's pleasure enough just to be here at the bill signing, but to be called upon to say a few words is something that I will remember all the rest of my life.

I want to say that without the leadership of Peter Rodino, without the subcommittee that we have, without the extreme support of a totally dedicated staff—and it's really there that the credit belongs—that this wonderful legislation, both pieces, would not be before us today.

I hope that the world really takes note of what we're doing here, because I think once again the United States is doing a wonderful thing, showing the world what should be done, what can be done in a humanitarian way. And I hope other nations will respond in similar ways.

Thank you, Mr. President.

THE PRESIDENT. Thank you.

SENATOR SPARKMAN. Well, Mr. President, I can only echo what these others have said. I think it is a great day.

With reference to the treaties involving the same matters, I think I'm correct in saying that every one of them passed through the Senate with a unanimous vote.

The PRESIDENT. I hope all the rest of the treaties that you face will do the same thing. [*Laughter*]

SENATOR SPARKMAN. Well, we'll have to wait a little while on some of those. [*Laughter*]

THE PRESIDENT. Thank you very much. Thank you very much, sir.

SENATOR KENNEDY. I too want to join in congratulating the President in the leadership that he has shown in terms of pointing the way for the American people to meet its responsibilities to the 115,000 people that have come from Southeast Asia and have joined the American people.

This is an extraordinary act of continuing generosity. It's a great tribute to the voluntary agencies, the church agencies, which represent all the great faiths of this country, who have worked so hard with local communities to help to provide a new opportunity for these citizens to join with our fellow citizens.

As the President understands, there still remains a problem—some 15,000 additional boat cases that homes are going to have to be found for. And so, as we're mindful of this continued step forward that will provide for language training, for counseling, for job training, will help and assist local communities, help and assist States, we're mindful of our continuing responsibility.

Mr. President, I think, as you know, the employment rates among the Vietnamese refugees are about a half of what it is for other Americans. These men and women who have come to this country, have shown their commitment to the ideals of this Nation, their willingness to participate in our country, and I think we ought to recognize their contribution as well.

I congratulate you on your leadership and congratulate the Members of the Congress in responding to what is in our great tradition as a humanitarian nation.

THE PRESIDENT. Thank you, Senator.

I won't call on others, but I know that you recognize that Frank Church and Joe Biden and Pete Stark and Hamilton Fish and many others here have done a great deal of work on this legislation.

I'm very proud of all of you. It's a good day for our country. And I believe that this will indicate to the American people, who always have some concern about the impact of refugees, that as a nation we ought to open our arms and open our hearts to these fine men and women, courageous men and women who have lost their homes because they formed a partnership with us and because they formed ties of kinship and brotherhood and sisterhood with us for a common purpose, that is, human freedoms.

Thank you very much.

NOTE: The President spoke at 9:30 a.m. at the signing ceremony in the Rose Garden at the White House.

As enacted, H.R. 7769 is Public Law 95–145, and S. 1682 is Public Law 95–144, approved October 28.

National Newspaper Association

Question-and-Answer Session by Telephone With Members Attending the Association's Annual Convention. October 28, 1977

THE PRESIDENT. Well, I'm very glad to be able to talk to you all, and I want to say first that I've been pleased at the administration's progress so far. We've addressed a lot of very difficult and controversial, long overdue issues.

I think the Senate is now hard at work on energy legislation. The House has taken its stand on it, and also social security. They're beginning to debate over the welfare proposals. We're making some progress on SALT. And I think that, in general, we've repaired the relationship that was fairly weak between ourselves and the developing nations of the world, particularly Africa.

I think we've strengthened our ties of friendship with the Latin American countries, made good progress on the nonproliferation of nuclear weapons, and I'm very pleased so far.

We have a heavy agenda, but I particularly wanted to get most of the controversial and very important items on the table for debate and congressional action this first year.

I would guess that the pace of introduction of major items would drop off substantially next year, and I would like to say that I want to express my appreciation to the National Newspaper Association for letting me have a chance to open with this brief comment. But I would like to spend most of my time answering questions, and I'm prepared to answer those now if you're prepared to ask them.

AGRICULTURAL EXPORTS

GEORGE JOPLIN. Thank you, Mr. President. We also appreciate your taking the time to be with us this morning.

Mr. President, our first question is, it has been suggested the economy of our country could be boosted by resuming promotion of our agricultural products in world trade. Why do you not advocate such a program, or what do you propose to boost our farm produce for export?

THE PRESIDENT. We've just gotten the figures for the last 12 months, and we've had the highest sale of agricultural products in the history of our Nation, a little more than $24 billion. In addition to that, in spite of fairly good crops around the world and, as you know, high reserve supplies of the basic feed grains and food grains on hand, we're mounting a major effort to increase sales this year over what we had anticipated earlier. We've just approved in the last few weeks, for instance, an increase from 8 million tons to 13 million tons of the grain that the Soviet Union can buy, before they have to go and start reporting individual purchases from us.

We've not been very successful in selling wheat to China this past few years. Most of their purchases have been from Argentina, Australia, and Canada, but we hope to improve this in the future. We're increasing the allotment of time of the Secretary of Agriculture who, as you know, made a trip throughout the world during the summer, particularly in the southeastern part of the Pacific area.

So, we are mounting an all-out effort to hold up foreign sales as much as we possibly can, and I think we've had remarkable success so far with the highest sales on record.

STATE OF TEXAS

Q. Mr. President, I'm Harold Hudson, with the Perryton Texas Herald. You said in Denver last week that the United States bought and paid for Texas. Was this a misstatement, or is it indeed a fact that Texas was bought and paid for? [*Laughter*]

THE PRESIDENT. No, sir. Anybody who lives among as many people who have moved out of Georgia, including my own ancestors, to go to Texas and fight for Texas independence, neighbor of Tennessee and North Carolina and South Carolina and Alabama, who provided people who fought for the independence of Texas, know the history of your great and courageous State.

Only a small part of the territory that was originally claimed by Texas was actually bought by the United States. As you know, we paid, I think, about $15 million for areas that had been previously claimed by Texas but that don't lie within the Texas boundaries now. This was territory to the west of Texas. But I know, and I think everybody in this country knows, that Texas was independent, voluntarily became a State of our Nation, and I'm very proud that some of my ancestors participated in that process.

REPUBLIC OF SOUTH AFRICA

Q. Mr. President, I'm Bob Bailey with the Buhl, Idaho, Herald. And my question is, recent events in South Africa contradict this Nation's basic philosophy of equal rights for all humans. Are you going to impose sanctions against the Republic of South Africa, and if so, what sanctions do you plan?

THE PRESIDENT. All right, thank you. We have tried to work as best we could with the South African Government during this last 10 months and have had some cooperation with them on resolving the problems in Namibia, which was formerly Southwest Africa, and also the Rhodesian-Zimbabwe question, where they have a major influence on Ian Smith. At the same time, we've tried to use our influence on the South African Government, not to tell them how to run

their own affairs, but to let them know the condemnation that exists in the rest of the world for the apartheid system, for the requirement that the majority of their citizens carry passes, that they're not given equal opportunities for employment, promotion, educational opportunities, and so forth.

What precipitated the deepest possible concern, however, was an almost complete abolition of any voices of dissent in South Africa last week among groups representing black citizens and the taking away of the privileges of newspapers to publish the facts to the South African people.

As a result of this action they took last week, we are supporting sanctions against South Africa, working with the allies that we have in the Western World, and also working, hopefully, with some of the leaders of the African nations themselves. These sanctions will consist of a mandatory embargo on the shipment of weapons to South Africa. This has been a voluntary imposition in the past.

Our belief is that this will be overwhelmingly passed by the Security Council. We hope that because of its action, the South Africans will take more constructive action in the future.

I might add one other point. There are other matters, of course, that will be considered. We are quite concerned about Prime Minister Vorster's statement this past week that they had not given us assurances against the testing of atomic weapons. In both a public statement that we've made and also in private dispatches through diplomatic channels and a private message directed to me from Vorster, they had unequivocally committed themselves not to design nor produce nor to test any atomic explosions at all, either peaceful or weapons. So, we have some concerns about South Africa.

I think at this time we'll limit our United Nations sanctions to an arms embargo and we hope that will make progress with the South Africans' attitude toward the rest of the world and toward their own people.

UNDOCUMENTED ALIENS AND INDOCHINA
REFUGEES

Q. Mr. President, I'm Jim Gill with the Hemet, California, News. My question is, on the West Coast and the four border States in the Southwest, we are very perturbed over the Government's position in allowing many people from the Asiatic countries, particularly the bringing of thousands of entire families from Vietnam to the United States, plus the thousands of illegal aliens in the United States from Mexico every month.

This migration, we think, has reached a breaking point when the unemployment of our own citizens and their care continues to soar. What are your plans to halt this situation so we can take care of our own citizens first?

THE PRESIDENT. You've covered two very important issues. On the subject of illegal aliens from Mexico, from China, and from many other nations around the world, for the first time, so far as I know, of any administration, we have submitted to the Congress for consideration a very strong, I think, very adequate legislation.

I hope the Congress will pass it next year. It's supported by a wide range of Members of the Congress—Peter Rodino in the House and his committee, working with Congressman Eilberg, and in the Senate, Senator Eastland from Mississippi and Senator Kennedy from Massachusetts are joint sponsors of the legislation.

This would provide an inventory, through registration of those illegal aliens who are already in our country, and tighten up considerably on border control. And I believe for the first time, we'll have a handle on a rapidly increasing problem for our country.

It's controversial legislation. We're trying at the same time to protect the basic civil rights of those who are of Chinese or Mexican descent and who have legal rights to be in this country. We don't want them to feel any sign of discrimination on employment and so forth.

On the Southeastern Asian refugees, as you know, this is a fairly tiny group. And in the past, immediately after the Vietnam war and the war in Laos and Cambodia, our country accepted about 150,-000 of these refugees. We encouraged other nations to do the same. The only expansion of this will be for about 15,000 of those kinds of refugees who have been living on boats for many years. And the Congress has just recently signed or passed a law, which I've signed, authorizing these to come in.

That's a tiny portion of the people who have suffered so severely in that area. We are providing for them language instruction, vocation-technical training, and also job counseling, to make sure that the impact on the labor markets are not excessive.

I think this is a proper thing to do. I do support it. But as far as our national population is concerned, it's a tiny portion of the problem that we have—150,000. The illegal alien problem, though, is one that consists of 7 or 8 million, perhaps, and is a profound problem. But I hope that the Congress next year will take our own advice, and I believe that this legislation we have proposed and which is widely supported will be passed.

FEDERAL TERMS OF OFFICE

Q. Mr. President, I'm Milton Chilcott with the Sheridan, Wyoming, Press. My question is, many Americans suggest that limitation of the Presidential term, as well as terms of Senators and Representatives, would be a positive contribution to better government. Would you care to comment?

THE PRESIDENT. Well, I hope you're not thinking about cutting it down below 4 years. I would certainly hate to see that done, certainly, you know, within the next few months. [*Laughter*]

I believe that the present arrangement is the best one. I've seen proposals made and highly publicized to change the Presidential term from two 4-year terms to one 6-year term.

I think if you look back on the Presidential tenure in office since Eisenhower, for instance, with Kennedy, Johnson, Nixon, and Ford, you see that the American people have, either through tragedy or through votes or voluntary withdrawals by Presidents from running for reelection, had a very tight control over the Presidency itself. Even with President Truman, I think that the pressures of the office and, perhaps, a very low popularity after he discharged General MacArthur caused him to decide not to run for reelection.

So, I believe that the present arrangement is the best one, with accountability every 4 years, and in times of strife or turmoil or lack of confidence, the President either voluntarily deciding not to run for reelection or the voters deciding to change. So, my summary is leave it like it is.

ADMINISTRATION'S POSTAL POLICY

Q. Mr. President, I'm John Andrist from the Crosby, North Dakota, Journal. My question is, do you realize that the postal policy announced by your administration on September 20, if implemented, would literally destroy many small newspapers?

THE PRESIDENT. No, sir. I don't recognize that it would destroy many small newspapers. I recognize, though, that the small newspapers, the large newspapers, the magazines, and also the companies that sell books would like to have a much more liberal postal policy than the one that we advocate.

I believe that the position that we took is reasonable. It does provide direct aid or subsidies for postal costs. We recommend a line-item approval for this subsidy, and I believe that the small newspapers would have a very high priority within the Congress and certainly would with my own administration.

We are faced with a very high budget impact if all those groups that I described got what they wanted. We're talking about 3, 4, perhaps even 5 billion dollars a year which, over the 4-year period that we are talking about, would mean about 15 or 16 billion dollars in drain on the American Government Treasury.

But I believe that if we put it on the basis that we advocated, with the line-item or individual decision by Congress on which subsidies should be supported, that the small newspapers will come out very well.

LABOR LAW REFORM BILL

Q. Mr. President, George Joplin, again. The so-called labor law reform bill, recently passed in the House and now pending in the Senate, would impose severe economic sanctions against employers, deprive employers of their rights in representation elections, and give unrecognized unions access to the premises and time of employers. It says nothing about the rights of the employers. Why do you so strongly support this, what seems to be one-sided and unfair legislation?

THE PRESIDENT. Well, George, I have to say that if I agreed with your description of it, I would not support it. [*Laughter*]

I have gone over every item in this labor reform package. It's much more moderate or conservative or much more inclined toward the employer's position than it was in its original form because I have the same concern that you do.

I am a businessman, I have been an employer, and I want to be sure that both the rights of workers and their employers are protected. I consider the proposal to be very modest in its scope, and the major thrust of it is to expedite whatever decision is made.

I have seen in Georgia, for instance, that when the application of the present law was attempted, that because of subterfuge or delay, a final determination in the labor dispute might be dragged out 2, 3, 4 years. And I don't think it's right to circumvent the law by unnecessary delay. This would expedite it.

Also, I don't think that any worker should be punished through immediate discharge who tries to seek the rights that are applicable in almost all parts of the country for workers.

But I think if you would get the copy of the law as it was proposed by us and passed by the House and go over it paragraph by paragraph, I would like very much to have you communicate with me directly, Mr. Joplin, and let me know what your specific concerns might be.

I was concerned about the legislation originally. The deeper I got into it, the more I could see that it was fair, was moderate, and had a primary thrust of expediting decisions that ultimately had to be dragged out through the courts for several years and quite often hurt employment and hurt the economic stability and strength and prosperity in the small communities, in particular.

So, how about taking a look at the individual component parts and let me have, either by telegram or direct letter from you, how you feel about the individual paragraphs?

Q. All right, sir, I certainly will, and I appreciate the opportunity.

NATURAL GAS DEREGULATION

Q. Mr. President, this is Harold Hudson from Texas. During the campaign, you said you favored the deregulation of natural gas prices, and now you're opposed to this. Why have you changed your position?

THE PRESIDENT. As I said in my campaign and also as I said to the Congress when I made my energy speech in April, we are working toward deregulation of natural gas. I said in my speech that I would work with the Congress toward this ultimate goal. I don't think we ought to do it all at once, Mr. Hudson. It would just be too much of an impact on our national economy.

The present price for natural gas, as you know, is about $1.45. We advocated raising it immediately to $1.75, which is a substantial increase and, I think, about 600 percent higher than it was 5 or 6 years ago; also, that we provide a step-by-step increase in the price of natural gas from one year to another, bringing it up to the equivalent price for international oil and, I thought, with a fairly liberal definition of what is new gas, to have an incentive for the production and exploration, particularly in the new gas areas.

So, my goal is still to deregulate natural gas. I believe that we made a major step in that direction. I just don't want to do it too rapidly, and I don't want to define old gas which has actually already been discovered and is being produced as new gas.

I think that the House of Representatives has gone along with our position. It's been supported both publicly and privately by some Members who represent gas-producing States, and I think it confirms my campaign promise and my speech to the Congress that we are working toward ultimate deregulation. I just don't want to do it too fast.

SOCIAL SECURITY

Q. Mr. President, this is Bob Bailey. My next question is, what is your plan to salvage the social security system? Do you agree with pending legislation that would drastically increase amounts that employees pay in social security taxes and end the equality of tax between employer and employee? Is this not inflationary, and what effect will it have on employment?

THE PRESIDENT. Our position on the social security package has been already promulgated with a message from me to Congress early this year and also by legislation that we drafted and presented.

The House action is fairly compatible with what we proposed. The fact is that one of the major social security funds will be completely bankrupt in about 2 years if we don't take action, and another one of the three major funds will be running out of money within about 5 years.

What we are trying to do is to put the social security funds, all three of them, on a sound financial basis, permanently, and to make sure that we have a minimum adverse impact on the economy and on the working people of our country.

I think that this is, to some degree, inflationary. But I believe that the major impact might be a dampening effect on our economy. I have announced yesterday that we're going to hold off our tax reform proposals until we can see what Congress does on social security. And I would guess that a major factor would be that if the social security tax increase is substantial after the Congress gets through, we'll try to compensate for this in the tax reform package. But there's no alternative that we have. We've got to increase the contributions to the social security system so it won't go broke.

And this one decision which the Congress is making—I hope this year; the House has already passed it—will put the social security system on a sound basis permanently, certainly throughout the rest of this century. And we'll try to compensate for the inflationary impact or the tax increase on working people by other means to make sure that the economy is not severely damaged by this action.

IRRIGATION OF LAND

Q. Mr. President, this is Jim Gill from California. My next question is, why has your Secretary of the Interior, Mr. Andrus, resurrected a bit of legislation enacted in 1902 that irrigation waters should no longer be available to any rancher who is farming more than 160 acres? The reenactment of this ruling is most archaic today.

Farming methods are geared to production of food on a large scale, which is the backbone of our Nation. It is not economically feasible to continue farming parcels of 160 acres. Are you going to stand by and permit our most needed industry—the feeding of millions of people—to be scuttled by a misinformed member of your Cabinet? [*Laughter*]

THE PRESIDENT. Mr. Gill, I appreciate your very fair and objective analysis of the question. [*Laughter*]

Let me respond briefly, because this is a matter that is very widely misinterpreted in some parts of California. I've been down to Brawley and in the Imperial Valley area as a candidate and have been thoroughly familiar at that time, even, with the circumstances. This was more than a year ago.

The action that's being taken even by the Interior Department was not initiated by us, including, of course, the Secretary of Interior. This action is a result of very long, very controversial judicial decisions where nongovernmental persons filed a lawsuit saying that the 1902 law was passed by Congress, signed by the President, and had been violated.

When the State and the Federal courts made a ruling, they said that the law must be enforced and directed the Secretary of Interior to take action to enforce the law, which, as you know, had not been enforced in the past. And that's what we're doing. We did not initiate this action. We're carrying out the court order. Both I and all the Members of Congress have taken an oath to uphold the Constitution of the United States and the laws of our country as interpreted by the courts.

I'm a farmer myself, as you know. I own 2 or 3 thousand acres of land, and I recognize that the scale of farming is quite different from what it was in 1902; in fact, even what it was in 1952, when we were still plowing with mules down home.

As you know, a husband and a wife of a farm family can own 160 acres each, which makes a total of 320 acres. I doubt that this is the final word about the subject. The Congress is monitoring this very carefully. Legislation might be introduced to modify the 1902 law. I think that there ought to be some larger permits for land holdings—I can't say the exact acreage right now. But in the meantime, we'll have to comply with the Federal court rulings.

I might say that at the banquet that was held in Los Angeles this past weekend, we had a very large contingent there of Imperial Valley farmers to support me and also the Democratic Party and what we are trying to do. We are trying to approach it in an objective and fair fashion, but we're constrained to enforce the law and we'll continue to do so.

But we did not take the initiative. We are familiar with the problems there. I think some modification might very well be made in the law in the future, but in the meantime, we'll have to carry out the court directive.

U.S. POSTAL SERVICE

Q. Mr. President, George Joplin again. Labor costs currently account for about 86 percent of postal service expenses. In light of this, it is clear nothing can be done about the rising rates and declining services unless the labor cost problem is dealt with. How do you intend to deal with this?

THE PRESIDENT. As you know, I don't have any authority over the Post Office. This is a matter that was decided by the Congress just a few years ago, to make an independent Postmaster General who is not appointed by the President and who is not accountable to me, and also a rate-making board which is an independent board.

At the time this new legislation was passed, the postal employees were among the lowest paid Federal employees. They've had a very rapid increase in salaries, and now they are among the highest paid Federal employees. They are separate from the others because of the independence of the Post Office, as determined by the Federal law that was passed by Congress.

We've advocated to the Congress that the Postmaster General be a Presidential appointee, that he serve for 6 years, that his appointment be ratified by the Senate, and that he be accountable, not only to the public but also, at least to that degree, to me as President.

I just believe that there has been progress made in making the Post Office more efficient. The rapid rise in wages, the rapid rise in inflationary pressures have created serious problems, but we will continue to subsidize the postal rate structure. And we will also single out for the rate of subsidy those elements of postal users who provide the greatest and most ad-

1927

vantageous services to the American people. And of course, that would include, in my opinion, the local newspapers whom you represent.

But I think it's good to set the record straight that there is absolutely no accountability now from the Post Office department to the President. The only rights that we have are through the Congress when supplementary appropriations are required. And this is established, as you know, by formula.

We'll do the best we can through public expressions of concern, and we're trying to work with the Congress now to have more accountability built in.

I want to say one other thing in closing. My grandfather was a postmaster, and my mother worked in the Post Office. My mother-in-law has just retired at the age of 70 from the Post Office in Plains— my grandfather was the one who proposed to Georgia Congressmen the establishment of rural free delivery of mail system. So, I've seen the problem from both sides, and now, of course, I'm seeing it from the viewpoint of the Presidency.

I know that you have, speaking to your convention, congressional leaders, committee chairmen who will be evolving legislation. I've also consulted with the Senators, particularly Senator John Glenn, who is very interested on the Senate side. But I believe that we'll come out with a proposal that will be not everything that you want, but highly sensitive to the special needs of the newspapers represented by the National Newspaper Association, because our country recognizes the tremendous contribution that you do make in providing a better life for our people.

Let me say that I'm grateful for this chance to exchange ideas with you. The questions asked me were very sharp and pertinent and, in some instances, difficult to answer. I don't know all the answers. I'm learning as best I can.

I think we have put to the Congress and to the people, proposed solutions to some of the most controversial issues. And it's always beneficial to me as President to have a chance to explain with you, George Joplin, and with Mr. Hudson, Bailey, and others, the questions that you proposed to me.

Good luck to all of you. I hope you have a very successful convention, and I look forward to hearing from you often. And particularly, I'm looking forward, Mr. Joplin, to having your analysis of the labor reform legislation. Thank you very much.

MR. JOPLIN. Thank you, Mr. President.

NOTE: The President spoke at 10:45 a.m. from the Oval Office by telephone hookup to members of the association meeting in Houston, Tex. George Joplin was the outgoing president of the association.

The Cyprus Conflict

*Message to the Congress Reporting on Progress Toward a Negotiated Settlement.
October 28, 1977*

To the Congress of the United States:

Pursuant to Public Law 94–104, this report describes the efforts that the United States has made over the past sixty days to promote a settlement on Cyprus.

There have been no further intercommunal talks under U.N. auspices since the submission of my last report to the Congress in August, and none are presently scheduled. This negotiating pause could easily last for several months more, through the forthcoming Greek elections in November and the Cyprus Presidential elections in February. However, we have not allowed ourselves to proceed on this assumption. Instead, we have continued actively to encourage a resumption of the intercommunal talks and, more importantly, have sought to ensure that, once these do reconvene, there will be meaningful discussion of the major unresolved issues.

We directed our attention to this goal during the special U.N. Security Council consideration of the Cyprus issue requested by the Government of Cyprus in late August and early September. A consensus resolution eventually emerged that was both equitable and nonpolemical, which called upon the parties to avoid provocative acts and resume intercommunal negotiations.

At the same time, we consulted with the Greek and Turkish governments to set the stage for a series of meetings in New York in which Secretary Vance and my Special Representative, Clark Clifford, met with President Kyprianou and Foreign Minister Christofides of Cyprus and with Foreign Ministers Bitsios and Caglayangil of Greece and Turkey. These New York meetings have encouraged us to believe that progress on Cyprus may be possible in the months ahead. We noted a growing recognition in the region that a just solution to the Cyprus issue will serve the long-term interests of all the nations in the Eastern Mediterranean.

Secretary Vance also met in New York with U.N. Secretary General Waldheim and with the Foreign Ministers of Great Britain, the Federal Republic of Germany, and other interested Western allies. All view the situation in the Eastern Mediterranean much as we do, and urgently wish to see progress towards a Cyprus settlement.

So too do the Cypriots. While in New York for the U.N. General Assembly, I had a useful discussion with Cyprus President Spyros Kyprianou. I assured him that the United States sincerely wishes to help the people of Cyprus find a just and lasting settlement, and that we stand ready, as in the past, to support the current U.N. negotiating effort in any way we can. President Kyprianou in turn assured me of his people's earnest desire for a settlement and of their hope that the United States can help bring this about.

In sum, therefore, I believe that I can record here—as I have not been able to do in the last two such reports—a cautious anticipation that movement toward meaningful Cyprus negotiations may soon be possible.

JIMMY CARTER

The White House,
   October 28, 1977.

National Science Foundation

Nomination of James A. Krumhansl To Be an Assistant Director.   October 28, 1977

The President today announced that he will nominate James A. Krumhansl, of Trumansburg, N.Y., to be an Assistant Director of the National Science Foundation. He would replace Edward C. Creutz, resigned.

Krumhansl was born August 2, 1919, in Cleveland, Ohio. He received a B.S. in electrical engineering from the University of Dayton in 1939, an M.S. from Case Institute of Technology in 1940, and a Ph. D. in physics from Cornell University in 1943.

Krumhansl was a physicist for the Stromberg-Carlson Co. from 1944 to 1946, and was on the faculty at Brown University from 1946 to 1948. He was on the faculty at Cornell University from 1948 to 1955, serving as an assistant professor, then associate professor.

Krumhansl was at the National Carbon Co. from 1955 to 1958, serving as assistant, then associate, director of research.

Since 1959 he has been a professor of physics at Cornell University.

Krumhansl has been a consultant to industry and has served on advisory committees for the Atomic Energy Commission, the Defense Department, and the National Academy of Sciences. He was director of the Laboratory of Atomic and Solid State Physics from 1960 to 1964. He has been an editor and contributor to a number of professional journals.

Digest of Other White House Announcements

The following listing includes the President's daily schedule and other items of general interest as announced by the White House Press Office during the period covered by this issue. Events and announcements printed elsewhere in the issue are not included.

October 21

Following the Jefferson-Jackson Day dinner in Des Moines, Iowa, the President went to the farm of Mr. and Mrs. Woodrow W. Diehl in Indianola, where he stayed overnight.

October 22

In the morning, the President met with a group of Iowa farmers at the Diehl home.

October 23

The President returned to the White House after his 3-day trip.

October 25

The President met at the White House with:

—David L. Aaron, Deputy Assistant to the President for National Security Affairs;

—the Democratic congressional leaders;

—Vice President Walter F. Mondale;

—Mr. Aaron and Adm. Stansfield Turner, Director of Central Intelligence;

—James T. McIntyre, Jr., Acting Director of the Office of Management and Budget.

October 26

The President met at the White House with:

—Zbigniew Brzezinski, Assistant to the President for National Security Affairs;

—Senator Gaylord Nelson of Wisconsin, Vice President Mondale, Secretary of Energy James R. Schlesinger, and Frank B. Moore, Assistant to the President for Congressional Liaison;

—Secretary of Commerce Juanita M. Kreps, Vice President Mondale, and Jack H. Watson, Jr., Secretary to the Cabinet and Assistant to the President for Intergovernmental Relations;

—Representatives Toby Moffett of Connecticut, Edward J. Markey of Massachusetts, Andrew Maguire of New Jersey, Jim Guy Tucker of Arkansas, Bob Eckhardt of Texas, Abner J. Mikva of Illinois, and Albert A. Gore, Jr., of Tennessee.

October 27

The President met at the White House with:

—Dr. Brzezinski;

—Members of the House and Senate steel caucuses, Ambassador Robert S. Strauss, Special Representative for Trade Negotiations, Sidney L. Harman, Under Secretary of Commerce, Robert Carswell, Deputy Secretary of the Treasury, and Robert J. Brown, Under Secretary of Labor, to discuss the steel industry;

—Representative Dan Rostenkowski of Illinois;

—David D. Newsom, United States Ambassador to the Philippines;

—former Vice President Nelson A. Rockefeller and Dr. Brzezinski.

October 28

The President met at the White House with:

—Vice President Mondale, Secretary of State Cyrus R. Vance, and Dr. Brzezinski;

—Dr. Brzezinski;

—Representative Frank Thompson, Jr., of New Jersey;

—Mrs. Carter, for lunch;

—a group of editors, publishers, and broadcasters (transcript will be printed next week);

—a group of economic and budget advisers for a budget overview meeting.

The President left the White House for a weekend stay at Camp David, Md.

NOMINATIONS SUBMITTED TO THE SENATE

The following list does not include promotions of members of the Uniformed Services, nominations to the Service Academies, or nominations of Foreign Service officers.

Submitted October 25, 1977

HAROLD W. CHASE, of Minnesota, to be Deputy Assistant Secretary of Defense for Reserve Affairs, vice Will Hill Tankersley, resigned.

DAVID T. WOOD, of Guam, to be United States Attorney for the District of Guam for the term of 4 years, vice Duane K. Craske, resigned.

WILLIAM J. PERRY, of Virginia, to be Under Secretary of Defense for Research and Engineering (new position).

ELSIJANE TRIMBLE ROY, of Arkansas, to be United States District Judge for the Eastern

NOMINATIONS—Continued

Submitted October 25—Continued

and Western Districts of Arkansas, vice Oren Harris, retired.

GERALD D. FINES, of Illinois, to be United States Attorney for the Southern District of Illinois for the term of 4 years, vice Donald B. Mackay, resigned.

AUDREY A. KASLOW, of California, to be a Commissioner of the United States Parole Commission for the term of 6 years, vice Paula A. Tennant, term expired.

SAMUEL D. ZAGORIA, of Maryland, to be a member of the Federal Election Commission for a term expiring April 30, 1983, vice William L. Springer, term expired.

Submitted October 26, 1977

B. MAHLON BROWN III, of Nevada, to be United States Attorney for the District of Nevada for the term of 4 years, vice Lawrence J. Semenza.

JOSEPH F. TIMILTY, of Massachusetts, to be Chairman of the National Commission on Neighborhoods (new position).

Submitted October 27, 1977

STELLA B. HACKEL, of Vermont, to be Director of the Mint for a term of 5 years, vice Mary T. Brooks, resigned.

ALEXANDER O. BRYNER, of Alaska, to be United States Attorney for the District of Alaska for the term of 4 years, vice G. Kent Edwards, resigned.

LARRY D. PATTON, of Oklahoma, to be United States Attorney for the Western District of Oklahoma for the term of 4 years, vice David L. Russell, resigned.

HARRY D. MANSFIELD, of Tennessee, to be United States Marshal for the Eastern District of Tennessee for the term of 4 years, vice Bruce R. Montgomery.

JOSEPH N. NOVOTNY, of Indiana, to be United States Marshal for the Northern District of Indiana for the term of 4 years, vice James W. Traeger.

Submitted October 28, 1977

JAMES ARTHUR KRUMHANSL, of New York, to be an Assistant Director of the National Science Foundation, vice Edward C. Creutz, resigned.

1931

CHECKLIST OF WHITE HOUSE PRESS RELEASES

The following releases of the Office of the White House Press Secretary, distributed during the period covered by this issue, are not included in the issue.

Released October 25, 1977

News conference: on the President's meeting with Foreign Minister Prince Saud of Saudi Arabia—by Jerrold L. Schecter, Associate Press Secretary

Announcement: nomination of B. Mahlon Brown III to be United States Attorney for the District of Nevada

Released October 27, 1977

Announcement: nomination of Alexander O. Bryner to be United States Attorney for the District of Alaska; Larry D. Patton to be United States Attorney for the Western District of Oklahoma; Harry D. Mansfield to be United States Marshal for the Eastern District of Tennessee; and Joseph N. Novotny to be United States Marshal for the Northern District of Indiana

Released October 28, 1977

Announcement: signing into law of H.R. 5675, which will enable the Treasury to earn an additional $50 to $100 million per year on the investment of its short-term cash balances

---

ACTS APPROVED BY THE PRESIDENT

Approved October 23, 1977

S. 2169_____ Public Law 95–141
An act to name a certain Federal building in Washington, District of Columbia, the Hubert H. Humphrey Building.

ACTS APPROVED—Continued

Approved October 25, 1977

H.R. 3_____ Public Law 95–142
Medicare-Medicaid Anti-Fraud and Abuse Amendments.

H.R. 1613_____ Private Law 95–10
An act for the relief of certain postmasters charged with postal deficiencies.

Approved October 26, 1977

H.R. 6415_____ Public Law 95–143
An act to extend and amend the Export-Import Bank Act of 1945.

Approved October 28, 1977

H.R. 4836_____ Public Law 95–146
An act to extend for seven months the term of the National Commission on New Technological Uses of Copyrighted Works.

H.R. 5675_____ Public Law 95–147
An act to authorize the Secretary of the Treasury to invest public moneys, and for other purposes.

H.R. 7769_____ Public Law 95–145
An act to authorize the creation of a record of admission for permanent residence in the cases of certain refugees from Vietnam, Laos, or Cambodia, and to amend the Indochina Migration and Refugee Assistance Act of 1975 to extend the period during which refugee assistance may be provided, and for other purposes.

S. 1682_____ Public Law 95–144
An act to provide for the implementation of treaties for the transfer of offenders to or from foreign countries.

PRESIDENTIAL DOCUMENTS

Interview With the President

Remarks and a Question-and-Answer Session With a Group of Regional Columnists. October 28, 1977

THE PRESIDENT. Good afternoon, everybody. I feel a little emotional. I just had a visit from a couple whose son had been in a Mexican prison for 2½ years. He was arrested just as a child. They were supposed to be here this morning for the signing ceremony for the legislation for prisoner exchange. They had to circle over Washington 2 hours before they could land, and then, when they got on the ground, they were in a taxicab and they got caught in a traffic jam. They had to change clothes in the taxi, and they got here too late. So, I just welcomed them. They hope their son will be home before Christmas.

I'm glad to welcome you here. I know that you represent a very special group of people in our country, columnists and editorial writers, who help to shape opinion and help to provide people with a deeper analysis of the significance of what we do than, perhaps, sometimes a spot news might do.

I know some of you—Hank Drane [Florida Times Union] over here is a friend of mine—and I'm glad to have you come to the White House.

ADMINISTRATION POLICIES

I'd just like to make a brief comment and then answer your questions. We have undertaken, I think, a very full agenda for this administration, and I think we're making very good progress.

The keystone to our first year's work is obviously the energy legislation which the Senate is now considering and which will then go to conference in its entirety. We've already passed four bills through the House and Senate out of five, and the other one, of course, is the tax measure which is now being debated and voted on by the Senate itself.

But we've had other matters that the Congress has already addressed. Many of them are quite controversial and, I think, long overdue in being considered by me and by the people of our Nation and, also, by the Congress. Some of them, like the foreign matters—we hope to have an agreement with the Soviets on the SALT measures. We're working hard on a comprehensive test ban to eliminate the testing of all nuclear weapons. We have, I think, drawn the line on the proliferation issue, whereas a year ago there was kind of a hopeless feeling that it was too late to do so. We're making good progress on that.

We will make proposals to the Soviets before long on the constraint of conventional arms sales around the world. We're the worst violator at this time; the Soviets, perhaps, next; and the French, British, Belgians, Germans to some degree participate in this excessive arms sale. We all feel that it should be cut back. How to do it is another matter, of course, that's very difficult to address.

We have gotten deeply involved in African affairs, an area of the world that we had neglected for too long, in my opinion. And we there face the question of Zimbabwe, Namibia, and we are debating, as you know, in the United Nations this week, how to handle the recent retrogression of South Africa in its dealing with freedom of the press and with freedom of expression of opinion. I think we'll have almost unanimity when we finally vote on the resolution to declare a mandatory arms embargo.

In addition, we've tried to strengthen NATO, our commitment there, which had been in doubt among many of our European allies. We're working harmoniously with the OPEC nations, trying to restrain any increase in the price of oil in 1978. It's going to be a difficult achievement if it is accomplished.

We are putting a lot of time on the Mideast settlement, and I won't go into any further details, but I think you recognize them.

In addition, we've addressed some of the more controversial issues that I understand concern some of you—how to handle our nationwide water policy to make sure that the funds that we do have to expand are spent in the most efficacious way for our people. I think we have an adequate supply of water, a greater commitment to conservation.

We've got authority now for 3 years to reorganize the executive branch of Government; we're making good progress on that.

The Congress has begun hearings on a welfare reform bill that I think will put the emphasis on work, which I believe is a good step in the right direction. It's highly likely that the Congress will get the social security funds restored to a position of integrity, whereas one of them was going into bankruptcy within the next 2 years, another one would follow shortly behind that.

After the Congress adjourns and we see what they do on energy taxation, social security, and after we assess the quality of our Nation's economy, we'll make the final judgments on the tax reform package that will be presented to the Congress before they come back into session in 1978.

We've had an opportunity to address other items that, in my opinion, were long overdue. And I would guess that this first year's work has been one that's perhaps overly full, judged by some standards, but I don't think so. There are none of the matters that I've described to you, or perhaps a dozen more that I could list, that could stand to be delayed any further. And the fact that the Congress is now debating these issues, the public is becoming aware of them, I think, is a very good step in the right direction.

I'd be glad to answer any questions that you might have. I'll try to be brief with my answers.

QUESTIONS

INDIAN LAND CLAIMS AND LORING AIR
FORCE BASE IN MAINE

Q. Mr. President, John Day of the Bangor News, Bangor, Maine. I'd like to ask you a two-part question on a couple of issues which are of vital concern to Maine people. First of all, what are your current thoughts on an equitable resolution of the Maine Indian land suit case, and when will you present your recommendations to Congress?

The second part is, will you play any personal role in the Air Force's proposed decision to close down Loring Air Force Base, and will you meet with Members of the Maine congressional delegation prior to any final determination on the Loring case?

THE PRESIDENT. I appointed, as you know, Judge William Gunter to act as a judge and, to some degree, a mediator in the Indian land claims suit. I believe that Judge Gunter's recommendations were fair and equitable. Now, of course, the problem arises on the acceptance of them by the State, by the Indians, and private landowners, and the Congress. I don't intend to play any additional role in that.

As you know, if his own recommendations are rejected, then the matter would fall either into the courts or into the Congress. We are in a unique position here with Maine Indian claims because it's possibly a precursor to later and even greater legal controversies.

Under the Constitution of our country, under the laws that have existed for many years, the executive branch of Government represents the Indians. Both the Department of Interior and the Attorney General have a legal charge to represent the Indians' case, and so we are not at liberty to do anything that would contravene the rights of Indians. But I think that Judge Gunter's recommendations were fair, and I hope that everybody will move to resolve those differences soon. We have a similar case of a more minor nature, perhaps, in Massachusetts, that we're now working with, and potential Indian claims in the West of much more far-reaching significance, including old treaty terms that say the Indians have a right to all the water that flows through a State, and so forth.

Another question that you asked was about the Loring Air Force Base. Your Senators have been on me—[*laughter*]—almost daily ever since I've been in the White House about that matter. And I have discussed it thoroughly with the Department of Defense, including the Secretary of Defense, himself.

My position on that particular matter, as it has been with other military base closures around the country, is to let them make a judgment on the basis of what's best for our country, and if there is any doubt about the economic or military advantages to be derived from a closure or transfer, to leave the status quo prevailing.

I don't intend to change my position specifically for political purposes, and it would be nice if I could accommodate the desires that are so strongly expressed by your Senators. But I think that if the Defense Department continues to feel that the closing or transfer of all or part of Loring's functions are in the best interests of our country, that I would support that position.

U.S.-SOVIET JOINT STATEMENT ON THE MIDDLE EAST

Q. Mr. President, my name is William Frank, and I'm from Wilmington, Delaware.

There's a movement being started in the city where I live to send you a lot of letters. The text seems to be that the joint Soviet-United States statement on the Mideast[1] represented a severe erosion of the United States posture, and they also will tell you that the abandonment by the United States of solemn promises to Israel raises the question of the reliability of the American commitments. Do you have any comment on that?

---

[1] The text of the October 1 statement is printed in the Department of State Bulletin of November 7, 1977, page 639.

THE PRESIDENT. On the fact that the letters will be sent or the accuracy of the letter itself?

Q. This is a ——

THE PRESIDENT. I welcome the letters. That description of the position is completely erroneous in two respects; I think you only raised two respects. One is that the joint U.S.-Soviet statement, I think, is a major move in the right direction to bringing about an ultimate, peaceful resolution of the longstanding Middle Eastern dispute. The Soviets and we, after long weeks of negotiation, agreed on a common approach which did not contravene any public or private commitments that I've ever made to Israel or to the American public and which represented a substantial change in the previous Soviet commitment, almost uniquely, to the PLO and the Syrian positions.

The Soviets, for instance, for the first time spelled out the need for a peace treaty, for full definitions of peace, which we had espoused. We incorporated the basic language of U.N. Resolution 242 on territories. The PLO was not mentioned. There was an abandonment of the previous Soviet position calling for the recognition of Palestinian national rights and an adoption of our own position that we described earlier.

So, I think it was a major step forward. As you know, ever since 1973 we and the Soviets have been cochairmen of the Geneva conference. This was something established, as I said, 4 years ago. And to have a cochairman who might be publicly and privately opposing any peaceful resolution or openly espousing the unilateral positions of the Arab countries would have been a very serious problem for us to overcome.

I think this is a public commitment of the Soviets to take a much more objective and fair and well-balanced position. So,

I think it's a major step in the right direction.

And the other part of your question is that I have never violated any commitments made to the Israelis, either by my administration or by the previous administrations. Both I and Foreign Minister Dayan, within the last month or two, reviewed in a confidential way all of the publicly disclosed and private agreements that had been reached between Mr. Kissinger and the Israeli Government, and between the Presidents who preceded me here and between myself and the Israeli Government. There has not been and will not be any violation of those commitments.

NEW JERSEY GUBERNATORIAL ELECTION

Q. Mr. President, we have an election of a Governor coming up in New Jersey in 2 weeks.

THE PRESIDENT. Yes, I know.

Q. Ex-President Ford was in a week ago and saw the possibility of this being an expression of your popularity or lack of it. Do you see it that way at all?

THE PRESIDENT. No, except to the extent that I have an utmost confidence in Brendan Byrne, in his ability and in his integrity. I think he's done a good job as Governor under very difficult circumstances, and I've let this be known to the New Jersey people without any equivocation.

I've been up there for a half day to work with him on his campaign. My wife has been up there also. And I think on the same day my wife was there, former President Ford was in Newark with Byrne's opponent.

Back in the first part of this year, I think Brendan only had about a 23-percent support, according to some polls I've seen. And I've seen a recent New York Times poll, that I presume is objective and fair, that shows that he and his opponent are almost equal in popularity.

So, I think the growth in his popularity from a hopeless position, politically, up to one of at least equal potential for victory is already an indication of confidence in him. And I think that in the private polls I've seen, my popularity in New Jersey is fairly high. But I think it's primarily a judgment on the two candidates, and I would guess that the impact of a voter's approval or disapproval of me or President Ford would be a very minor, inconsequential factor.

GOVERNOR REUBIN ASKEW OF FLORIDA

Q. Mr. President——

THE PRESIDENT. Mr. Drane.

Q. I'm flattered you remember me, by the way.

THE PRESIDENT. I think I met you when I was in my lonely days and you were one of the few people that paid any attention to me down there—[*laughter*]—so, I thank you for it.

Q. This is sort of a regional question. I hope my colleagues will forgive me for it, but I think it is important. Governor Askew has strongly indicated he wants to join your administration, perhaps in some foreign post. And I wonder if you have talked with him about this, and if not, if he does talk with you about it later, what are his chances of joining your administration if there is a suitable opening?

THE PRESIDENT. I've not heard about that before. When I was putting my Cabinet together, I called Reubin Askew and asked him if he would accept a Cabinet position, because I think he's one of the superb political leaders in our Nation and because I've known him well and respect him so much.

He told me that he wanted to be Governor of Florida and that he would not accept any position other than the one that he held. I've never discussed with him, nor he with me, any appointment after he leaves the office of Governor. But there is no position that I could think of in Government, including the Presidency itself, for which he would not be qualified.

ADMINISTRATION'S RELATIONS WITH THE
BLACK COMMUNITY

Q. Mr. President, I am D'Army Bailey. I'm from Memphis, Tennessee, with the Commercial Appeal.

You have come under increasing criticism from blacks as to what many of us view as a lack of leadership at the executive level with regard to some of the most pressing problems that the black community faces, particularly with regard to employment and housing. I know that Benjamin Hooks, who is from my own hometown, and my good friend Vernon Jordan have criticized the lack of effective leadership from the national level.

And we've got increasing unemployment among youth, black youth in particular, and we've got what appears to be a hiatus in national concern and movement toward resolving the problems of race that are generations old.

We, as blacks who voted for your Presidency and black people giving you everything that a black could give you, a substantial percentage of the black vote—and yet we don't see coming out of the White House the effective leadership.

Some of the Congressmen I know, the black Congressmen, are criticizing the White House for its failure to move effectively. There's been a suggestion that the White House has not followed through on a commitment to meet regularly with the Black Caucus.

THE PRESIDENT. Do you have a question? [*Laughter*]

Q. At what point, Mr. President, can we expect to see some movement from the White House with regard to resolving the problems that the black people face in this country and getting down to problems of unemployment, getting down to the problems of poor housing?

THE PRESIDENT. Apparently you haven't observed what has gone on in the country for the last 10 months. We've passed, with the help of the Black Caucus and other Congress Members who are up here working hard for their constituents, a broad range of job opportunity bills, with a stimulus package that's now providing about 30,000 jobs per week. We've passed a local public works program—4, 4½ billion dollars—with, for the first time in the history of our country, a guarantee that 10 percent of those projects would be carried out by minority-owned contractors. This has never been done before.

The housing program is under the control of Patricia Harris. I think anyone who has observed the Washington scene would say that the Housing and Urban Department had been a dormant department for many years, even an embarrassing department. And I think anyone, including the leaders that you've named, would agree that it has come to life, that programs that build homes have been successful.

We've got the highest homebuilding rate now in years, over 2 million homes being built per year. The programs for low-income families, guaranteed loans for those who already own their homes and want to renovate them, downtown, urban reconstitution and development programs, have been pursued by Patricia Harris, who happens to be a black woman, in case you didn't know. And the Congress has responded to her request. I signed a housing and urban development bill a couple of weeks ago that provides $12 billion for this purpose.

I work very closely with the Black Caucus. As a matter of fact, yesterday I was talking to Parren Mitchell, who happens to be the chairman of the Black Caucus, to Charles Diggs, about the South African question in the United Nations. Earlier this week, Andy Young conversed, consulted with them on our United Nations posture concerning South Africa. I have a good relationship—and I wish you'd call them to doublecheck what I say—with Vernon Jordan and with Benjamin Hooks. I think that what we've done so far on these items that I've described, and many others, have been the limit of what either I or the Congress could do with the budget constraints and also with the time constraints.

As far as top officials are concerned who happen to be black, we've had an unprecedented success in getting them appointed and confirmed by the Senate. As you know, in the Justice Department, the Secretary of the Army and Secretary of Housing and Urban Development and other places, this has been done.

So, I think that the picture that you present in the preliminary to your question is one of substantial distortion and inaccuracy. And I would ask you, while you're in Washington, to call Parren Mitchell, for instance, and find out if my description is accurate on what I and the Congress have been able to do. And I would like for you to call Benjamin Hooks and Vernon Jordan and see if they have as critical an assessment of our administration's accomplishments as you do.

TAX CREDITS FOR COLLEGE TUITION

Q. Sir, a majority of the Senate has sponsored a bill with Senators Moynihan and Packwood that would allow tax credits for tuition. There is some talk, apparently in the Senate, of adding that to a tax reform bill. Would you support such a concept of tax credits for tuition if it were added in the tax reform bill that you send up, or would you entertain any thought of putting it in the bill yourself?

THE PRESIDENT. I don't know. We have a limit to how many additional tax credits and tax benefits can be put in the legislation and still have equity and fairness and a progressive tax structure. It's obvious that each individual item proposed for tax reform is attractive. You know, when the parents who have children in college don't pay those taxes, somebody's got to pay it for them. And the ones that pay it for them are the parents who don't have children in college.

Quite often, the parents who don't have children in college are older people whose children have passed that college age or the very poor families in our Nation or the working families in our Nation who just can't afford to put a child in college. So, I have doubts about it, although I wouldn't say that I'll veto a bill or work against that particular proposal.

We are trying to have three things come out of the tax reform measure: One is greater equity or fairness, with an end to or a reduction, at least, in the loopholes and tax credits and privileges that have been there for a long time. Another one is a more progressive, overall income tax rate. And, of course, the third one, and perhaps the most important for the taxpayers, is simplicity, so that everybody feels when they fill out the tax form that they are being treated fairly. So, I can't answer your specific question any better than I have now.

INTERNATIONAL TERRORISM

Q. Mr. President, may I ask you, in the area of terrorism—incidentally, I'm Claude Lewis from Philadelphia, Pennsylvania. In dealing with terrorists, is the posture of the U.S. Government going to be one of complete noncooperation with the terrorists, such as has been developed in Japan and West Germany and other nations? And, also, I understand you disagree with the U.N. resolution insofar as how far it goes; you feel it should be much stronger. Can you tell us a little bit about that—your position on that?

THE PRESIDENT. Yes. We have taken a position—I would say, among the strongest of any nation—against terrorism, seeking to get the United Nations to agree with us on all nations refusing to accept aircraft that have been hijacked, for instance, and also agreeing to return the hijackers or terrorists to the country from which they committed a terrorist act.

I believe that we'll have some success, particularly because of the high publicity that accrued to the recent Lufthansa hijacking that terminated, as you know, in Somalia. We encouraged the Somalian Government to cooperate with the West Germans. We worked closely with the West Germans in providing information that we had about the terrorist organizations. And we learned from them and from the Israelis, for instance, after they had an actual experience in rescuing kidnaped passengers from planes.

It's a matter that concerns all countries. And recently, we've had some indications, through United Nations statements and otherwise, that the Soviets were moving toward a more responsible position in deploring and working against terrorism.

There are still some countries, like Libya and Algeria, for instance, who feel that they ought to open their borders to terrorists and to let them land there. And their position that they take publicly is that they save lives by doing so, that there has to be some place for the airplane to land once it is hijacked.

We are also cooperating and trying to ensure that the very strict security measures that we take in our own country of examining people as they go into the airport loading facility is mirrored around the world.

So, we are doing everything we can on a unilateral basis, also on a multilateral basis through the United Nations and through the airline arrangements that we have with cooperative countries, to hold down this particular form of terrorism.

We recognize that there are other forms of terrorism, but I was responding just to that particular part because that was part of your question.

GOVERNOR GEORGE WALLACE OF ALABAMA

Q. Mr. President, I'm Bob Ingram from Montgomery, Alabama, Magazine.

In all likelihood, barring a political miracle, Governor Wallace will be joining you in Washington in 1979 as a Member of the United States Senate. My question is, do you look forward to his Senate service, if it develops, with anticipation or trepidation? [*Laughter*]

THE PRESIDENT. Well, let me say that I don't want to get caught in an expression of preference between him and any of his potential Democratic opponents—certainly not including Senator Sparkman, who has worked very closely with us as chairman of the Foreign Relations Committee.

But if it should happen that the Alabama people choose Governor Wallace, he would come to Washington as a friend of mine. I worked with him very well when he was Governor. After the Ohio/New Jersey primary date, he was the first one who called to congratulate me and also to offer his support, which I'll always remember. And he and I have communicated frequently since I've been in the White House about matters of interest to the Alabama people.

So, if that should be the choice of the Alabama voters, then I would certainly welcome Governor Wallace to the Senate. But I don't want that to be interpreted as a preference that he be chosen over Senator Sparkman, for instance. I don't want to get involved in that particular question.

ELIGIBILITY FOR SOCIAL SECURITY PAYMENTS

Q. Mr. President, I'm Doug Parker with the Salt Lake Tribune. I was wondering how you felt about the inclusion in this social security bill of the allowance to let people earn all they want after they retire and still be eligible for social security.

THE PRESIDENT. Yes. During the campaign, I deplored the $3,000 limit and said that it should be raised. And I still feel that way.

The position that I took—I've forgotten the exact figure, but I think we arbitrarily chose a $5,000 earnings limit. I don't object to a higher limit. Whether the House and Senate will go along with a complete elimination of a limit, I don't know. I don't think the cost in the social security system is likely to be very high, and I would certainly sign a bill that had that provision in it.

DEREGULATION OF NATURAL GAS

Q. Mr. President, as you are probably aware, some officials in Texas feel very strongly that you committed yourself to work for a natural gas price deregulation, and they think that you now reversed that position. Governor Briscoe displays a letter in which you seem to indicate that you would work with the Congress for deregulation. How do you explain your change in position?

THE PRESIDENT. I don't believe that I've changed my position. I don't interpret it that way. My position was that I would work with Congress, as had President Ford, for deregulation of natural gas.

And when I made my energy speech to the Congress—it's the only one I've made—last April, I repeated this commitment. The difference is in the rapidity with which natural gas is deregulated.

We have proposed a substantial step toward ultimate deregulation of natural gas by moving from $1.47 to $1.75 in price. We, I think, proposed a reasonable definition of what new gas is and pledged ourselves to increase the price of natural gas step by step, until it reached a price equivalent to the international oil price.

I think that this is a move toward deregulation. But I think it would be quite disruptive and very costly to the American people, and I don't believe it would result in a substantial increase in the quantity of natural gas produced, to completely deregulate it right now. So, it's a matter of time scale and not a matter of commitment that causes a difference between me and Governor Briscoe.

I know that he and Governor Boren and others—Governor Edwards from Louisiana, Boren from Oklahoma—prefer immediate and complete deregulation. But I just think that would be too rapid and too high a price change at this time. And I think it would be too heavy a burden on consumers and it would be highly inflationary.

CHAIRMANSHIP OF SENATE JUDICIARY
COMMITTEE

Q. Mr. President, Bill Minor from Jackson, Mississippi.

It's been said in some quarters in Mississippi that you have persuaded Senator Jim Eastland to abandon his plans to retire and run for reelection, as if he needed to be persuaded. But it was rumored very strongly that he was planning to step out, but that you may have entered into some of the persuasion in order for

him to remain as chairman of the Senate Judiciary Committee because it would have meant the elevation of Senator Kennedy to the chairmanship. Did you have any role in that at all?

THE PRESIDENT. Well, that's a long question that has several facets.

Let me say that when I went down to Mississippi recently to visit Yazoo City, Senator Eastland was with me, as you know, on part of the trip. And after we came back, I had breakfast with Senator Eastland and eight or nine other Democratic Senators as part of a series.

And after the breakfast one morning, I told him that one of the most frequent comments that I received from Mississippians along the side of the road and in the public meetings with whom I spoke was that they hoped that Senator Eastland would run for reelection.

And I relayed the opinion of those Mississippians to him. He didn't tell me what his plan was, and I have had no indication that he might want to step down or might stay on. I doubt that my own relaying of that often expressed opinion to him would affect his ultimate decision. And I have no preference about who should be the chairman of the Judiciary Committee. I think in some of the more controversial issues that Senators Eastland and Kennedy act in concert. As you know, they've jointly worked on a complete revision of the criminal code—one of the most important measures, I think, that will come out of the Congress—and on some highly controversial issues like, for instance—let me think of an example—well, the matter of illegal aliens. Both Senator Eastland and Senator Kennedy have agreed to be joint sponsors of the legislation, so I don't think the incompatibility between the two men is nearly so great as might be thought. But I think Senator Eastland is a good man and a good Senator. He's been very supportive of my own positions, and so has Senator Kennedy.

But I think that describes my complete involvement in the process. It's up to Mississippi people to decide who they want as their U.S. Senator. It's certainly up to Senator Eastland to decide whether he wants to come back or not.

BILLY CARTER

Q. David Mannwiler with the Indianapolis News. Please forgive a facetious question. It was brought up at lunch.

THE PRESIDENT. It's all right.

Q. We were talking about the fact that your brother, Billy, who has been in and out of our State and region quite often, is very able to comment on your performance. We didn't think we'd ever seen your comments on his performance. And why on Earth aren't you considering running this man for treasurer of the Democratic national party? [*Laughter*]

THE PRESIDENT. Well, Billy has been, as you know, making his own decisions. I could probably have more influence on Senator Eastland or Governor Wallace or Sparkman than I do on Billy. [*Laughter*]

He has been concerned about the economic problems of the country. He's pretty well put the beer industry back on its feet, for instance. [*Laughter*] I think he's shown his ability as a bellybust diver in Canada. He's promoted a lot of good projects like automobile racing and so forth.

Billy is a very intelligent, very competent, very likable person, and he's my only brother, as you know. And I admire the way he lives his own life. I've never had any occasion to be embarrassed by Billy, nor have I ever tried to interfere in Billy's lifestyle. I think he's probably at least as well known as I am, and probably his popularity rating would exceed mine right at this time.

I don't get to see him very often, because he does stay busy, but Billy is a good man, and I'm proud that he is my brother.

Maybe one more question. I promised the gentleman on the end.

SENATOR RUSSELL B. LONG OF LOUISIANA

Q. Sam Hanna from Louisiana. We keep hearing in Louisiana how powerful Senator Long is here now, and he keeps saying that he does not want that reputation. How closely will the White House have to work with him and his committee to pass an energy bill?

THE PRESIDENT. Very closely. Senator Long is a powerful man in the Congress, and I don't deplore it. There is no more brilliant person in Washington than he is, and he works hard. He does his homework. He studies legislation. And I think the members of his committee respect him, and so do I. I enjoy being with him when we have a few minutes alone on occasion.

The Finance Committee in the Senate has such a broad range of responsibilities. Many of the things we've talked about today come under his purview—the controversial energy legislation, social security, welfare reform, and so forth. I do work very closely with Senator Long, and I think he goes out of his way to help me on controversial issues.

For instance, on the energy tax measures, with the exception of the user tax that would impact on Louisiana very heavily, which he opposed, he gave his support to the other tax matters even though a majority of his committee did not. And he and I and Senator Byrd and others consult quite closely as the Senate evolves its own will on the energy matters. He and Senator Jackson will be the two lead Senators in the conference on this energy program.

So, I think, in closing, I should say that he is a relatively modest man. It embarrasses him when the authority and influence that he has is publicly described. But I think it is great, and it's because of his own leadership qualities that he has this influence.

I don't think he's ever abused it. I think he's been a very good man. He has a strong interest in Louisiana. And whenever there's a conflict between the national interest and Louisiana, more parochial interest—as I would be in the Senate—he's inclined to go with Louisiana. But that doesn't always happen.

Although I was not here, I think when the question of the oil depletion allowance faced the Senate for the major oil companies, he voted to do away with the oil depletion allowance, which was a very courageous thing to do.

He and his wife were over at the White House not too long ago for supper with just me and Rosalynn. And we reaffirmed our friendship.

But I think if the truth were known, not only with Senator Long but with Senator Sparkman and with Senator Eastland and others, we have a very good relationship. And the controversies and the hot debates and the differences of opinion are the things that attract the news media, which is understandable and predictable, and I don't particularly deplore it. But the good working relationship that I have developed with people like Senator Long—and with whom we disagree on occasion—is one that provides a basis for continuity and a sense of partnership. And I believe that when this Congress goes home, there will be a general inventory of accomplishments that will be a credit to our country.

So, he represents, in my opinion, one of the fine qualities of leadership that the Congress has provided. When I've been asked in the past what's been the biggest surprise that I've found, I have often said it's the quality of the individual Members of Congress and the depth with which they understand complicated issues, because after they've been here a few years, they start concentrating or specializing in a certain aspect of America's life, either domestic or foreign.

And I've found that a quiet conversation with a chairman of a committee or subcommittee about a specific, highly technical issue is one of the best sources of information and advice that I can get.

Let me say in closing that I'm very grateful to have a chance to talk to you. I wish I could have answered more questions, but the breadth of your own questions indicates the breadth of my responsibilities. I've enjoyed being President very much, and I was well prepared for the controversy, having served as Governor for 4 years and having campaigned for 2 years. And I think that many of the controversial issues that have to be faced are a credit to our Government and not a cause for apology.

When I do have a difficult decision to make on the Mideast or on energy or on tax reform, on illegal aliens, I feel much surer that I'll make the right decision, ultimately, if the American public had been involved in the discussion. I think in the past, there's been too much done secretly and privately and at the last minute revealed to the American people. And although it does create confusion and a sense of lack of discipline and control when these matters are opened up for free and open debate and controversy, I think it's healthy because ultimately the American people have sound judgment, and the more they have a role to play with their government decisions, the less chance we have of making a serious error.

As you know, we've made some serious errors in the last few years. And I don't want to see us come up with another Vietnam or another Watergate or another CIA episode that brings embarrassment on our country. And I don't think those things would have materialized had there been an absolute truth and a complete revelation of those questions when they were in the initial stages of decision.

I want to thank you for the constructive role you play in the very process that I've described. I've enjoyed being with you.

Thank you.

NOTE: The interview began at 1:02 p.m. in the Cabinet Room at the White House.

The transcript of the interview was released on October 29.

United States Metric Board

Nomination of Chairman and Members of the Board.   October 29, 1977

The President today announced that he has nominated Louis Polk, of Dayton, Ohio, to be Chairman of the U.S. Metric Board for a term of 6 years. He also announced 14 other persons who have been nominated as members of the Metric Board.

Polk, 73, is an authority on international metrology and has represented the United States at numerous conferences on the subject. He was Chairman of the Advisory Panel of the National Metric Study conducted by the Commerce Department. He has officially visited the national bureau of standards of most leading industrial nations. Polk was a director of the Bendix Corp. from 1956 to 1975. He was chairman of the board of State Fidelity Federal Savings and its predecessors from 1948 to 1977, and is now emeritus, and served from 1947 to 1975 as a

director and executive committee member of Winters National Bank and Trust Co. in Dayton, Ohio.

Those nominated as members of the Metric Board are:

For 6-year terms:

SYDNEY D. ANDREWS, of Florida, director of the division of standards, Florida Department of Agriculture and Consumer Services.

JOYCE D. MILLER, of New York, vice president and director of social services for the Amalgamated Clothing and Textile Workers Union.

GLENN NISHIMURA, of Arkansas, executive director of Arkansas Consumer Research and of ACR: Public Interest Citizen Action.

SATENIG S. ST. MARIE, of Connecticut, divisional vice president and director of consumer affairs for the J. C. Penney Co.

ADRIAN G. WEAVER, of Connecticut, director of standards practices for IBM Corp.

For 4-year terms:

PAUL BLOCK, JR., of Ohio, publisher of the Toledo Blade and a research professor of chemistry at the University of Toledo.

THOMAS A. HANNIGAN, of Maryland, assistant to the international secretary of the International Brotherhood of Electrical Workers.

FRANK H. HARTMAN, of Michigan, Federal liaison for the Michigan Department of Education.

SANDRA R. KENNEY, of Maryland, continuity director at the Maryland Center for Public Broadcasting.

ROGER E. TRAVIS, of Massachusetts, president of Medi, Inc., and an expert on metals joining.

For 2-year terms:

CARL A. BECK, of Pennsylvania, president of the Charles Beck Machine Corp. and chairman of the Government Liaison Committee of the American National Metric Council.

FRANCIS R. DUGAN, of Ohio, president of the Dugan and Meyers Construction Co. in Cincinnati.

EDWARD L. GINZTON, of California, chairman of the board of Varian Associates in Palo Alto.

HENRY KROEZE, of Wisconsin, chairman of the department of engineering and computer science at the University of Wisconsin Center in Waukesha, Wis.

National Energy Plan

Statement on a Resolution Adopted by the National Conference of Black Mayors. October 29, 1977

The President was informed that the National Conference of Black Mayors, meeting in Washington, D.C., adopted a resolution supporting the proposed National Energy Plan. He issued the following statement from Camp David:

"This is an important statement of support from an organization of leaders representing a sizable constituency in America. I appreciate this action by the National Conference of Black Mayors.

"The mayors have shown that they recognize that a failure to face up to our energy problem will most adversely affect poor people and black people. It shows recognition that passage of the energy program is not a contest between the branches of Government--that, instead, it is a test of our national will. It is my hope that this action by the mayors will add momentum to passage of the National Energy Plan."

NOTE: The statement was made available by the White House Press Office. It was not issued in the form of a White House press release.

Consumer Product Safety Commission

Nomination of R. David Pittle To Be a Commissioner.   October 31, 1977

The President today announced that he will nominate R. David Pittle, of Rockville, Md., for reappointment as a Commissioner of the Consumer Product Safety Commission.

Pittle was born October 7, 1938, in Washington, D.C. He received a B.S. in electrical engineering from the University of Maryland and an M.S.E.E. and Ph.D. in electrical engineering from the University of Wisconsin.

From 1963 to 1969, he was an instructor in electrical engineering at the University of Wisconsin. He also taught for 2 years at the Wisconsin School of Electronics. He taught electrical engineering and public affairs at Carnegie-Mellon University from 1969 until his appointment to the Consumer Product Safety Commission in 1973.

Between 1971 and 1973, Pittle served as president of the Alliance for Consumer Protection, a voluntary consumer organization in Pittsburgh.

Prior to his appointment to the Commission, Pittle was a member of the consumer advisory committee of the Pennsylvania Insurance Department, the consumer relations panel of the National Association of Homebuilders, the Consumer Federation of America, the American Council on Consumer Interests, the consumer standards committees of the American Society for Testing and Materials, and the American National Standards Institute.

A frequent lecturer on consumer protection, Pittle was the principal investigator for a 3-year National Science Foundation grant entitled "Research on Improving Consumer Safety Through Innovative Consumer Education." In June 1977, he received the first annual Eastern Consumer Conference Award "for his outstanding work for the Commission on behalf of consumers and their concerns."

National Endowment for the Arts

Nomination of Livingston L. Biddle, Jr., To Be Chairman.   October 31, 1977

The President today announced that he will nominate Livingston L. Biddle, Jr., of Washington, D.C., to be Chairman of the National Endowment for the Arts for a 4-year term. He would replace Nancy Hanks, term expired.

Biddle was born May 26, 1918, in Bryn Mawr, Pa. He received an A.B. from Princeton University in 1940. From 1942 to 1945, he served as a volunteer ambulance driver overseas with American Field Service.

From 1946 to 1962, Biddle was self-employed as an author. He wrote four novels—"Main Line," "Debut," "The Village Beyond," and "Sam Bentley's Island"—and numerous shorter works of fiction and nonfiction.

From 1963 to 1965, Biddle served as special assistant to Senator Claiborne Pell and drafted the legislation which led to the establishment of the National Council on the Arts and the National Endowment for the Arts. In 1966 and 1967, he served as Deputy to the first Chairman of the National Endowment for the Arts, Roger L. Stevens.

From 1968 to 1970, Biddle was a professor and chairman of the division of arts at Fordham University, where he established and directed a new educational program including all major art forms. In 1971 and 1972, he was chairman of the board of directors of the Pennsylvania Ballet Company.

In 1972 Biddle worked on Senator Pell's reelection campaign, and in 1973 and 1974 he again worked in the Senator's office on reauthorizing legislation for the Arts and Humanities Act and on the Museum Services Act. In 1975 he was Congressional Liaison Director for the National Endowment for the Arts. Since 1976 he has been director of the Senate Subcommittee on Education, Arts and Humanities.

Exemption From Mandatory Retirement

Executive Order 12016.   October 31, 1977

EXEMPTION OF G. JOSEPH MINETTI FROM MANDATORY RETIREMENT

G. Joseph Minetti, Member, Civil Aeronautics Board, became subject to mandatory retirement for age on July 31, 1977, under the provisions of Section 8335 of Title 5 of the United States Code unless exempted by Executive Order. Mr. Minetti was exempted from mandatory retirement until September 30, 1977, by Executive Order No. 12006 of July 29, 1977, and until October 31, 1977, by Executive Order No. 12011 of September 30, 1977.

In my judgment, the public interest requires that G. Joseph Minetti continue to be exempted from such mandatory retirement.

Now, THEREFORE, by virtue of the authority vested in me by subsection (c) of Section 8335 of Title 5 of the United States Code, I hereby exempt G. Joseph Minetti from mandatory retirement until January 31, 1978.

JIMMY CARTER

The White House,
    October 31, 1977.

[Filed with the Office of the Federal Register, 12:15 p.m., November 1, 1977]

NOTE: The Executive order was announced by the White House Press Office on October 31. It was not issued in the form of a White House press release.

Fair Labor Standards Amendments of 1977

Remarks on Signing H.R. 3744 Into Law.
November 1, 1977

THE PRESIDENT. I see a lot of happy faces here this morning.

In 1938, which was 39 years ago, President Roosevelt, in the presence of Senator Jennings Randolph and also in the presence of President George Meany, signed the first Fair Labor Standards Act. This was a time of great depression. It was a time when our Nation suffered. It was a time when unemployment was rampant, when the standard of living of most of our people was quite low. And it was a time when discouragement about the future preyed upon the shoulders of almost all American people.

And this bill said that Americans who had to work with their hands, the laborers of our Nation, those from low-income families, should be treated fairly. They should be given a right to an income which would at least buy the necessities of life. It was an innovative, almost a revolutionary idea, and the American people accepted it somewhat reluctantly. There were predictions of economic catastrophe, that inflation would run rampant, that people would lose their jobs, because a 25-cent hourly wage was more than the economy could bear.

I first came into the labor force in 1941 when the minimum wage was 40 cents an hour, and that was my first job. And each time that we've tried to boost the lower level of salary for the most underpaid workers, there have been predictions of catastrophe. But each time, in my opinion, the change has helped our Nation and its economic strength.

Again, the Congress has acted, perhaps belatedly in each instance, but wisely, be-cause the history of the minimum wage laws has been that the administrations in authority then and the Congress would raise the minimum wage up to an equivalent position compared to other wages. And then year by year as other manufacturing wages rose, the minimum wage stayed the same. And after 3, 4, 5, 6, or 7 years, finally there would be another catchup phase, and those workers at the lower levels of the economic scale would be given what they deserve.

The Congress has now passed House of Representatives bill 3744, which sets a new scale of minimum wage to be raised in January of next year to $2.65 an hour, then step by step each year succeeding that up to maintain an appropriate relationship with other manufacturing wages.

It has been a step in the right direction, again. Again, there are predictions that there will be an adverse effect on inflation. There will be some slight increase in inflation, perhaps, and some people, perhaps, might not gain a job that they would have otherwise. But the overall impact of this bill, again, is good.

Annually, there will be added to the low- and middle-income families about $2 billion in increased income, which will increase the wealth of our Nation. It goes to the hands of those who will spend it for the necessities of life. And the stimulative impact on our economy, I think, will be very beneficial.

We are concerned about youth unemployment. And we've tried to make compensatory steps this year effective with the help of the Congress, in a comprehensive youth employment act, increase in the CETA programs, local public works programs, and an overall stimulative package. And we face future opportunities to compensate for any deleterious effects of this bill. But I'm very glad to have a chance to sign it into law.

We will establish with the passage of this bill a Minimum Wage Study Commission to make sure that in the future, when minimum wage legislation is considered, that the overall impact will be beneficial, that the direct effect on the inflation rate, possible unemployment, will be very carefully considered and that we won't play the drop-far-behind/catchup game in the future. This commission will be an independent one. It will be appointed—I think two representatives each, chosen by Labor, Agriculture, Commerce, and HEW. And they'll analyze within the next few months how we can best approach the minimum wage question in the future.

And so, it's with a great deal of pleasure and appreciation to the bold and, I think, well-considered action of Congress that I sign this bill into law.

[*At this point, the President signed H.R. 3744 into law.*]

I would like to call on two or three Members of the Congress to respond. The first one is a man who, perhaps, deserves most of the credit among many fine leaders, and that's Congressman Dent.

REPRESENTATIVE DENT. Thank you, Mr. President.

THE PRESIDENT. I might say that Congressman Perkins, the chairman of the committee, specifically asked that John Dent be called upon to speak because of his leadership in this legislation.

REPRESENTATIVE DENT. Mr. President, I want to thank you on behalf of millions of Americans who have no other source of support except through the Congress of the United States and the President of the United States. While it's difficult for Congress to achieve much, it's even tougher on a President, who has to face the barrage of opposition singly. Whereas we have 435 Members to take a little bit each, you have to take it all. [*Laughter*]

And every President that has signed a minimum wage bill has done so with heavy opposition against it. All of the things they have predicted have never come true. All that has ever come out of minimum wage is a little bit better way of life for a great number of people who have no other place to go except to the Congress and to the President.

I want to thank the Congress as the sponsor for many years and thank you, Mr. President, for helping these people out.

THE PRESIDENT. I might point out that since President Roosevelt signed the first bill, that six other Presidents have also taken the same action. So, I haven't been alone or lonely in that procedure.

REPRESENTATIVE DENT. Mr. President, I'm not going to horn in, but I was here, too. [*Laughter*]

THE PRESIDENT. Was anyone else here in 1938? Mr. Biemiller, were you there?

MR. BIEMILLER. Yes.

THE PRESIDENT. So, four of you were here when the first bill was signed.

Pete Williams, I'd like to ask you to say a few words.

SENATOR WILLIAMS. Thank you, Mr. President. I think most all of the important things on this bill, as far as those of us in Congress are concerned, have been said over the last few months.

This is a great day for people at the lowest rung of our economic ladder. And while you, Mr. President, and the House and the Senate came to minimum wage legislation this year with the same theme, there were variations. I think it is one of the best examples of our processes that we've come together with a measure that we all know is of great importance to this land.

I am delighted, though, that Jennings Randolph is here from the Senate. He was here at the beginning, and we've had a continuity in this great legislation. And I thank you, Mr. President.

THE PRESIDENT. Thank you very much. Senator Javits.

SENATOR JAVITS. Mr. President, this legislation is, as have been many things and as I hope will be many more, a triumph of bipartisanship and executive-congressional cooperation. We did it all together, and it's a magnificent job for the American people.

There are those who would express lack of confidence in our country, Mr. President. If we can afford to go from 25 cents to $2.90, for openers, there's no reason for lack of confidence in America. And the votes of our colleagues demonstrated that they, too, have that confidence.

And finally, Mr. President, those who would seek differentials for youth or others are begging the question. It means about 10 percent of those who will benefit from the minimum wage. We have to do very much more for American youth to get it employed. That would just be confession and avoidance.

And so, Mr. President, I congratulate you, my colleagues in the Congress. And I feel very deeply moved and honored to have played a small part in this great event.

THE PRESIDENT. Thank you very much.

I'm not going to get myself any more deeply involved in deciding who should speak, but anyone else who'd like to say a word—[*laughter*]——

MR. MITCHELL. Mr. President, I'm Clarence Mitchell, the head of a coalition of American citizens of all races and faiths who got together for the purpose of trying to get this legislation passed.

You were gracious enough to receive Mr. Meany, who is here, and others of us in the early stages of this, when we talked about the knotty problems that were ahead of us. I want to say to you, Mr. President, and to your staff people, we had the most wonderful cooperation.

I want to say, too, that this was a bipartisan effort, as these constructive matters usually are in our country. We could not get along without the constructive people in both parties.

One of the footnotes in this legislation is that there are some half million blacks in this Nation who will today, when this law becomes effective, receive a higher and more meaningful wage. They are already working for $2.30 an hour, but they had to get relief in order to come up to the lowest standard of living. This will help to bring them up there. And on their behalf, Mr. President, I want to thank you and Mr. Meany and the Vice President and the members of the committee for this step forward.

THE PRESIDENT. Thank you very much.

President Meany, would you say a word?

MR. MEANY. Thank you. Mr. President, I want to express to you and to the Members of the Congress who are here, who were involved in this legislation, a word of thanks from a group of people that I have no right to officially speak for, because the recipients of the minimum wage are not, by and large, members of our organization. But I'm sure that I can speak for them and express their deep appreciation for your action, for the action of the Congress in raising the minimum wage.

To me it's not only the question of these people individually, which is a humane question in a way, but if our economy is to have any base, it must have a base in the mass purchasing power in the hands of the great mass of the people. In other words, it's not enough for the people in the upper brackets to be prosperous. If we're going to have a viable, progressive economy, it must come from that base. And I think this provides the base.

Thank you very much.

NOTE: The President spoke at 9:30 a.m. at the signing ceremony in the Rose Garden at the White House. George Meany is president and Andrew Biemiller is director of the Legislative Department of the AFL–CIO, and Clarence J. Mitchell is executive director of the National Association for the Advancement of Colored People.

As enacted, H.R. 3744 is Public Law 95–151, approved November 1.

United States Participation in the United Nations

Message to the Congress Transmitting a Report.   November 1, 1977

To the Congress of the United States:

I am pleased to send to the Congress this 31st annual report on the principal activities of the United States in the United Nations and its constituent organizations during calendar year 1976.

This report describes the main UN activities concerning issues affecting the security and well-being of the American people, such as the Middle East, Southern Africa, Cyprus, law of the sea, North-South economic relations, food, the environment, drug control, science and technology, human rights, terrorism, and disarmament. It emphasizes the work of US representatives in these forums and the positions they adopted, and it explains our government's stand on the issues. In sum, the report portrays an active year during which our country worked hard with others in the UN to advance the causes of peace, economic progress, and justice.

In the area of peace and security, the United Nations continued to serve as a valuable forum for the discussion of political disputes even where progress on the underlying issues was not always possible. In the Middle East and Cyprus, UN peacekeeping units performed their vital tasks while the search for a durable peace continued. The Security Council also worked to defuse other problems in such areas as Southern Africa, Djibouti, and the Comoros. In all, the Security Council met 113 times in 1976—more often than in any year since 1948, and twice as often as in 1975.

The 31st General Assembly adopted a number of resolutions in the area of disarmament and arms control. The two most significant of these were a resolution opening the Environmental Modification Convention for signature and one calling for a special session of the General Assembly in 1978 devoted to disarmament issues.

On the recommendation of the Security Council, and with US support, Secretary General Kurt Waldheim was reappointed by the 31st General Assembly to a second five-year term.

In the area of economic cooperation, the developing and developed countries continued efforts begun at the Seventh Special Session of the General Assembly to find common ground on a wide variety of issues. The UN Conference on Trade and Development (UNCTAD) held its fourth ministerial session in Nairobi and reached partial consensus on the critical issues of commodities, technology transfer, debt, and assistance to the poorest countries. The General Assembly also devoted considerable attention to economic questions. The United States co-sponsored a resolution in the General Assembly calling for a UN Conference on Science and Technology for Development, to be held in 1979.

The UN's record with respect to human rights was disappointing. The unwarranted linking of Zionism with racism was an impediment to serious consideration of human rights matters and the US continued to resist it by all possible means. In a number of cases, failure to take effective action belied the commitment to human rights that all UN members have accepted. International concern over human rights issues continues to broaden, however, and the acceptance of an international competence to consider these issues has become more firmly established.

During 1976, the United States participated in the International Labor Organization under the first year of its two-year notice of intent to withdraw from the organization. A favorable development was the increased cohesion of the industrialized free market countries at the June 1976 conference, but I have yet to decide whether sufficient progress has been made to justify continued US membership.

These were some of the most dramatic developments in the United Nations during the last year but there are a great many other UN activities discussed in this report. Much of this work—the "quiet side" of the United Nations—is not well known to the public because it is noncontroversial and seldom reported in the news media. But these economic, social, and technical activities, which account for the use of nearly 90 percent of the total resources of the UN system, are of great importance to our prosperity, security, and well-being. They include such activities as:

—Establishing safety standards for international civil aviation;
—Maintaining a World Weather Watch;
—Improving health conditions and standards worldwide;
—Combatting ocean and air pollution;
—Improving international food standards and preventing the spread of plant and animal disease;
—Providing assistance to the less-developed countries; and
—Working to curb illicit drug production and abuse.

Since assuming the Presidency, I have pledged my Administration to full support for the work of the United Nations and to greater use of its machinery in the conduct of our foreign relations. The wide-ranging activities described above show clearly the importance of the work done by the UN and its associated agencies. It is work that cannot be accomplished by nations acting alone or even through bilateral diplomacy. It is only through multi-lateral forums such as the UN that many of the world's most pressing issues can be effectively approached.

I am proud of America's role in creating the United Nations, in advancing global cooperation through its various agencies, and in providing, over the years, the largest share of its financial support. As the UN begins its 33rd year, I welcome the opportunity to submit this report to the Congress and to reaffirm my Administration's commitment to this increasingly vital institution.

JIMMY CARTER

The White House,
November 1, 1977.

NOTE: The report is entitled "U.S. Participation in the UN—Report by the President to the Congress for the Year 1976" (Government Printing Office, 426 pp.).

International Labor Organization

Statement on the Termination of U.S. Membership. November 1, 1977

Two years ago, the United States gave official notice that we would leave the International Labor Organization unless corrective measures were taken to restore that organization's commitment to its original purposes. Because such measures have not been taken, I direct that United States membership in ILO be terminated. The United States remains ready to return whenever the ILO is again true to its proper principles and procedures.

NOTE: Secretary of Labor F. Ray Marshall read the statement at a news conference at the White House on November 1. It was not issued in the form of a White House press release.

Transatlantic Air Service

Announcement of the Designation of U.S. Carriers To Serve Certain U.S. Gateway Cities. November 1, 1977

The President has approved the Civil Aeronautics Board's decision on one portion of the Transatlantic Route Proceeding, the designation of U.S. carriers to serve existing U.S. gateway cities.

At present, eight U.S. cities receive air service to London from two competing U.S. carriers. The Bermuda II agreement reduced the number of U.S. cities which may receive such competitive service from eight to two. The agreement requires the United States to indicate by November 1 which two cities will continue to receive competitive service to London, and which single carrier will serve each of the other six gateways.

This decision specifies that the cities to receive competitive service will be New York and, on an interim basis, Boston. The Board will consider further evidence on whether Los Angeles should replace Boston as the second city receiving competitive service.

For the other six cities, Pan Am will be the exclusive carrier for Washington, De-troit, and San Francisco, and TWA will serve Philadelphia, Chicago, and, pending the decision on whether it should receive competitive service, Los Angeles.

Department of the Air Force

Nomination of John A. Hewitt, Jr., To Be an Assistant Secretary. November 2, 1977

The President today announced that he will nominate John A. Hewitt, Jr., of Princeton, N.J., to be an Assistant Secretary of the Air Force. He would replace Everett T. Keech, resigned, and his area of responsibility would be financial management.

Hewitt was born July 20, 1943. He received a B.S. in engineering management from the U.S. Air Force Academy in 1965, and an M.B.A. in production management from UCLA in 1966. He served in the Air Force from 1966 to 1971, serving as a captain at Headquarters, Space and Missile Systems Organization, and project officer responsible for program management of large military satellite systems.

Since 1971 Hewitt has worked for the Chase Manhattan Bank. From 1971 to 1974, he was vice president for corporate planning, and since 1974 he has been vice president and staff group executive for trust and fiduciary investment.

World Jewish Congress

Remarks at the Meeting of the General Council. November 2, 1977

Chairman Phil Klutznick and President Nahum Goldmann, members of the World Jewish Congress:

As my friend Phil Klutznick pointed out, sometimes praise is not forthcoming for a Democratic President, and I want to thank you especially for that warm welcome, which I haven't heard in quite a long time. Thank you very, very much for it.

I'm deeply honored to receive this medal. I accept it with a sense of gratitude because of the organization from which it comes and because of the man for whom it is named. For more than half a century, Dr. Nahum Goldmann has been a scholar and a political leader and a fighter for the rights of all people. His career is proof that a man who is outspoken and sometimes controversial can still be a brilliant and an effective statesman. As the head of this organization and many others, he has played a more significant role in world affairs than have many heads of state. He's stepping down now as president of the World Jewish Congress, but his presence will remain, for he is the kind of man whose moral authority transcends any title or any office.

The World Jewish Congress has always sought to promote human rights in a universal way. In this, it is faithful to the ethical traditions from which it springs, for Jewish teaching has helped to shape the consciousness of human rights that is, I believe, now growing throughout the world.

In large measure, the beginnings of the modern concept of human rights go back to the laws and the prophets of the Judeo-Christian traditions. I've been steeped in the Bible since early childhood, and I believe that anyone who reads the ancient words of the Old Testament with both sensitivity and care will find there the idea of government as something based on a voluntary covenant rather than force—the idea of equality before the law and the supremacy of law over the whims of any ruler; the idea of the dignity of the individual human being and also of

the individual conscience; the idea of service to the poor and to the oppressed; the ideas of self-government and tolerance and of nations living together in peace, despite differences of belief. I know, also, the memory of Jewish persecution and especially of the holocaust lends a special quality and a heartrending sensitivity to your own commitments to human rights.

This organization has made a major contribution to ensuring that human rights became part of the Charter of the United Nations as one of its three basic purposes, along with the preservation of peace and social and economic progress. The principal authors of Universal Covenant on Human Rights were Eleanor Roosevelt, an American Protestant, Charles Malik, a Lebanese Catholic, and René Cassin, a French Jew. Because of their work and the work of others, no government can now pretend that its mistreatment of its own citizens is merely an internal affair.

These accomplishments have helped start a process by which governments can be moved forward, exemplifying the ideals which they publicly profess. Our own actions in the field of human rights must vary according to the appropriateness and effectiveness of one kind of action or another, but our judgments must be made according to a single standard, for oppression is reprehensible whether its victims are blacks in South Africa or American Indians in the Western Hemisphere or Jews in the Soviet Union or political dissidents in Chile or Czechoslovakia.

The public demonstration of our own Government's commitment to human rights is one of the major goals that my administration has set for United States foreign policy. The emphasis on human rights has raised the level of consciousness around the world and is already beginning to help overcome the crisis of spirit which recently has afflicted the nations of the West.

We are also trying to build a more cooperative international system. We are consulting more closely with our own allies, and we place special emphasis on better relations with people in South America and in Asia and in Africa. And we are searching for new areas of cooperation with the Soviet Union, especially in the area where we and the Soviets now most intensely compete—in the race for nuclear weapons.

We must halt that race. In the last few months, we've tried to work closely with the Soviets to eliminate the testing of peaceful nuclear explosives. And just in thet last 24 hours, Mr. Brezhnev, President Brezhnev, has announced that the Soviets are finally coming to agree with us. And we have good hopes that we might, without too much delay, realize a comprehensive test ban that would eliminate this threat from the Earth. We hope so.

But at the same time we seek cooperation, we recognize that competition is also part of international life, and we will always remain capable of defending the legitimate interests of our people. We are addressing other global problems which threaten the well-being and the security of people everywhere. They include nuclear proliferation, the excessive sales of conventional arms, food supplies and energy, and the quality of the environment. These things affect all nations of the world. And we are also seeking solutions to regional conflicts that could do incalculable damage, if not resolved.

Our efforts toward a new treaty with Panama are one example. Bringing about peaceful change in southern Africa is another. But none is more important than finding peace in the Middle East.

Sixty years ago today, November 2, 1917, the British Foreign Secretary, Lord Balfour——

[*At this point, the President was interrupted by demonstrators. After making the following comment on the interruption, he continued his remarks.*]

One of the basic human rights that we cherish in our country is the right to speak, and I have no objection to it.

As I was saying, exactly 60 years ago today, November 2, 1917, the British Foreign Secretary, Lord Balfour, informed Lord Rothschild of his government's support for the establishment of a national home for the Jewish people in Palestine. At that time, the idea seemed visionary and few dared to believe that it could actually be translated into reality. But today Israel is a vital force, an independent and democratic Jewish state whose national existence is accepted and whose security is stronger today than ever before.

We are proud to be Israel's firm friend and closest partner, and we shall stand by Israel always.

I doubt that anyone in the history of our country has traveled more than I have in my campaign for President, nor talked to more groups, nor listened to more questions, nor heard more comments. And when I say that we will always stand with Israel, I speak not only for myself as President, not only for our Government, all three of its branches, but I speak not just for American Jews but for all Americans. This is one of our deepest felt commitments, and I have no doubt that I speak accurately for the overwhelming portion of the American people, now and forever.

Despite its great accomplishments, however, Israel has yet to realize the cherished goal of living in peace with its neighbors. Some would say that peace cannot be achieved because of the accumulated mistrust and the deep emotions which divide Israelis from Arabs. Some would say that we must realistically resign ourselves to the prospect of unending struggle and conflict in the Middle East. With such an attitude of resignation, Israel would never have been created. And with such an attitude now, peace will never be achieved. What is needed is both vision and realism so that strong leadership can transform the hostility of the past into a peaceful and constructive future.

This was a vision of the Zionist movement in the first generation after the Balfour declaration, and it can be the achievement of Israel in its second generation as an independent state.

Since becoming President, I've spent much of my time in trying to promote a peace settlement between Israel and her Arab neighbors. All Americans know that peace in the Middle East is of vital concern to our own country. We cannot merely be idle bystanders. Our friendships and our interests require that we continue to devote ourselves to the cause of peace in this most dangerous region of the world.

Earlier this year, I outlined the elements of a comprehensive peace—not in order to impose our views on the parties concerned, but rather as a way of defining some of the elements of an overall settlement which would have to be achieved through detailed negotiations.

I continue to believe that the three key issues are, first, the obligations of real peace, including the full normalization of political, economic, and cultural relations; second, the establishment of effective security measures, coupled to Israeli withdrawal from occupied territories, and agreement on final, recognized, and secure borders; and third, the resolution of the Palestinian question.

These issues are interrelated in complex ways, and for peace to be achieved that's permanent and real, all of them will have to be resolved. Recently, our diplomatic efforts have focused on establishing a framework for negotiations so that the parties themselves will become engaged in the resolution of the many substantive issues that have divided them so long. We can offer our good offices as mediators, we can make suggestions, but we cannot do the negotiating.

For serious peace talks to begin, a reconvening of the Geneva conference has become essential. All the parties have accepted the idea of comprehensive negotiations at Geneva. An agreement has already been reached on several of the important procedural arrangements. Israel has accepted, for Geneva, the idea of a unified Arab delegation, which will include Palestinians, and has agreed to discuss the future of the West Bank and the Gaza Strip with Jordan, with Egypt, and with Palestinian Arabs. This can provide the means for a Palestinian voice to be heard in the shaping of a Middle East peace, and this represents a positive and a very constructive step.

Israel has also repeated its willingness to negotiate without preconditions and has stressed that all issues are negotiable. This is an attitude that others must accept if peace talks are to succeed.

For their part, the Arab states have accepted Israel's status as a nation. They are increasingly willing to work toward peace treaties and to form individual working groups to negotiate settlement of border issues and other disputes. No longer do they refuse to sit down at the negotiating table with Israel, nor do they dispute Israel's right to live within secure and recognized borders.

That must be taken as a measure of how far we have come from the intransigent positions of the past. The procedural arrangements hammered out at the 1973 Geneva Conference can provide a good basis for a reconvened conference. Even a year ago—just think back—the notion of Israelis and Arabs engaging in face-to-face negotiations about real peace, a peace embodied in signed, binding treaties, seemed like an illusion; yet, today, such negotiations are within reach. And I'm proud of the progress that has been achieved by all nations concerned to make this dream at least possible.

But to improve the atmosphere for serious negotiations, mutual suspicions must be further reduced. One source of Arab concern about Israeli intentions has been the establishment of civilian settlements in territories currently under occupation, which we consider to be a violation of the Fourth Geneva Convention. On the Arab side, much still needs to be done to remove the suspicions that exist in Israel about Arab intentions. It was not so long ago, after all, that Arab demands were often expressed in extreme and sometimes violent ways. Israel's existence was constantly called into question. The continuing refusal of the Palestinian Liberation Organization to accept U.N. Resolution 242 and Israel's right to exist, along with the resort to violence and terror by some groups, provides Israelis with tangible evidence that their worst fears may in fact be justified.

Differences naturally exist not only between Arabs and Israelis but among the Arab parties themselves. And we are actively engaged in an effort, a very difficult effort, to narrow these differences so that Geneva can be reconvened. And we've called on the other cochairman of the Geneva conference, the Soviet Union, to use its influence constructively.

We will continue to encourage a solution to the Palestinian question in a framework which does not threaten the interests of any of the concerned parties, yet respects the legitimate rights of the Palestinians. The nations involved must negotiate the settlement, but we ourselves do not prefer an independent Palestinian state on the West Bank.

Negotiations will no doubt be prolonged and often very difficult. But we are in this to stay. I will personally be prepared to use the influence of the United States to help the negotiations succeed. We will not impose our will on any party, but we will constantly encourage and try to assist the process of conciliation.

Our relations with Israel will remain strong. Since the war in 1973, we have provided $10 billion in military and economic aid to Israel, about two-thirds of which was direct grants or concessional loans. The magnitude of this assistance is unprecedented in history. It's greatly enhanced Israel's economic and military strength. Our aid will continue.

As difficult as peace through negotiations will be in the Middle East, the alternative of stalemate and war is infinitely worse. The cost of another war would be staggering in both human and economic terms. Peace, by contrast, offers great hope to the peoples of the Middle East who have already contributed so much to civilization.

Peace, which must include a permanent and secure Jewish state of Israel, has a compelling logic for the Middle East. It would begin to bring Arabs and Israelis together in creative ways to create a prosperous and a stable region. And the prospect of coexistence and cooperation would revive the spirits of those who, for so long, thought only of violence and of struggle for survival itself.

Peace would lift some of the enormous burdens of defense and uplift the people's quality of life. The idea of peace in the Middle East today is no more of a dream than was the idea of a national home for the Jews in 1917. But it will require the same dedication that made Israel a reality and has permitted it to grow and to prosper.

We may be facing now the best opportunity for a permanent Middle East peace settlement in our lifetime. We must not let it slip away. Well-meaning leaders in Israel and in the Arab nations, African, European, South American, North American, all over the world, are making an unprecedented and a concerted effort to resolve the deep-seated differences in the Middle East.

This is not a time for intemperance or partisanship; it's a time for strong and responsible leadership and a willingness to explore carefully, perhaps for the first time, the intentions of others. It's a time to use the mutual strength and the unique friendship and partnership between Israel and the United States and the influence of you and others who have a deep interest and concern to guarantee a strong and permanently free and secure Israel, at peace with her neighbors and able to contribute her tremendous human resources toward the realization of human rights and a better and more peaceful life throughout the world.

The Old Testament offers a vision of what that kind of peace might mean in its deepest sense. I leave you with these lines from the Prophet Micah—who's still one of my favorites—lines and words which no summary or paraphrase could possibly do justice. It's from the Fourth Chapter and the first five verses:

"But in the last days it shall come to pass, that the mountain of the house of the Lord shall be established in the top of the mountains, and it shall be exalted above the hills; and people shall flow into it.

"And many nations shall come, and say, Come, and let us go up to the mountain of the Lord, and to the house of the God of Jacob; and he will teach us of his ways, and we will walk in his paths: and the law shall go forth from Zion, and the word of the Lord from Jerusalem.

"And he shall judge among many people, and rebuke strong nations afar off; and they shall beat their swords into plowshares, and their spears into pruninghooks: nation shall not lift up a sword against nation, neither shall they learn war any more.

"But they shall sit every man under his vine and under his fig tree; and none shall make them afraid: for the mouth of the Lord of hosts hath spoken it.

"For all people will walk every one in the name of his god, but we will walk in the name of the Lord our God for ever and ever."

However we may falter, however difficult the path, it is our duty to walk together toward the fulfillment of this majestic prophesy.

Thank you very much.

NOTE: The President spoke at 8:45 p.m. at the Capital Hilton Hotel. Prior to his remarks, he was presented with the Nahum Goldmann Medal.

World Weather Program

Message to the Congress Transmitting a Report. November 3, 1977

To the Congress of the United States:

The memory of the severe winter of 1976–1977 in the eastern United States and its effects on our people and the national economy is still fresh in our minds. The continuing drought in the western United States is affecting not only agriculture and power generation but even basic community water supplies. Droughts, floods and freezes in the USSR, the African Sahel, the Indian subcontinent and Brazil in recent years have unsettled world markets and inflicted misery and often death upon untold numbers of people.

Senate Concurrent Resolution 67 of the 90th Congress dedicated the United States to participate in the World Weather Program in order to develop improved worldwide weather observations and services and to conduct a comprehensive program of research to extend our understanding and prediction of global weather and climate variations. I am pleased to transmit, in accordance with that Resolution, this annual World Weather Plan that describes significant activities and accomplishments and outlines the planned participation of Federal agencies for the coming fiscal year. The progress already achieved in this vital program demonstrates that we truly can do something to help our people anticipate and cope with the effects of the world's weather.

JIMMY CARTER

The White House,
 November 3, 1977.

NOTE: The report is entitled "World Weather Program—Plan for Fiscal Year 1978" (Government Printing Office, 73 pp.).

tain words of the Code have, on occasion, caused confusion resulting in training divergencies.

Now, THEREFORE, by virtue of the authority vested in me as President of the United States of America, and as Commander-in-Chief of the Armed Forces of the United States, in order to clarify the meaning of certain words, Article V of the Code of Conduct for Members of the Armed Forces of the United States, attached to and made a part of Executive Order No. 10631 of August 17, 1955, is hereby amended to read as follows:

"When questioned, should I become a prisoner of war, I am required to give name, rank, service number and date of birth. I will evade answering further questions to the utmost of my ability. I will make no oral or written statements disloyal to my country and its allies or harmful to their cause.".

JIMMY CARTER

The White House,
 November 3, 1977.

[Filed with the Office of the Federal Register, 3:51 p.m., November 3, 1977]

NOTE: The Executive order was announced by the White House Press Office on November 3. It was not issued in the form of a White House press release.

American Prisoners of War

Executive Order 12017. November 3, 1977

AMENDING THE CODE OF CONDUCT FOR MEMBERS OF THE ARMED FORCES OF THE UNITED STATES

The Code of Conduct has been an established standard of behavior for all members of the Armed Forces of the United States for more than twenty years. It has helped individuals in captivity to sustain their moral and physical strength and to survive extreme torture and abuse. However, experience indicates that cer-

American Prisoners of War

Executive Order 12018.   November 3, 1977

AMENDING THE MANUAL FOR COURTS-MARTIAL, UNITED STATES, 1969 (REVISED EDITION)

Members of the Armed Forces of the United States who are captured and held prisoner by a hostile armed force are effectively outside the direct operational control of United States military authorities. Recent conflicts involving members of the Armed Forces indicate a need for establishing and maintaining a chain of command among prisoners of war or detained personnel. The senior member of all Services must be provided the necessary command authority over all members of the Armed Forces with whom he is imprisoned or detained. The present wording in the Manual for Courts-Martial should be amended to provide such authority.

Now, THEREFORE, by virtue of the authority vested in me by the Uniform Code of Military Justice (Chapter 47 of Title 10 of the United States Code) and as President of the United States of America, the Manual for Courts-Martial, United States, 1969 (Revised Edition), prescribed by Executive Order No. 11476 and amended by Executive Order No. 11835, is hereby further amended as follows:

SECTION 1. The third paragraph within paragraph 168 is amended by striking out the third sentence and inserting the following in place thereof:

"A commissioned officer of one armed force is not *'his* superior commissioned officer' with respect to a member of another armed force merely because of higher rank. However, a commissioned officer of one armed force is, within the meaning of Article 89, *'his* superior commissioned officer' with respect to a member of another armed force if duly placed in the chain of command over that person. In addition, when members of more than one armed force are prisoners of war or otherwise detained by a hostile entity so that circumstances prevent resort to the normal chain of command, a commissioned officer of one armed force who is not a medical officer or chaplain is *'his* superior commissioned officer' with respect to a member of another armed force who is his junior in rank.".

SEC. 2. The first paragraph within paragraph 170*a* is amended by inserting the following after the second sentence:

"A warrant officer, noncommissioned officer, or petty officer of one armed force who is senior in rank to a member of another armed force is senior to that member under the same circumstances that a commissioned officer of one armed force is the superior commissioned officer of a member of another armed force for the purpose of Article 89 and 90. See 168.".

SEC. 3. The first paragraph within paragraph 171*b* is amended by inserting the following after "See 138*b*":

"A member of one armed force who is senior in rank to a member of another armed force is the superior of that member with authority to issue orders which that member has a duty to obey under the same circumstances as a commissioned officer of one armed force is the superior commissioned officer of a member of another armed force for the purposes of Articles 89 and 90. See 168.".

JIMMY CARTER

The White House,
    November 3, 1977.

[Filed with the Office of the Federal Register, 3:52 p.m., November 3, 1977]

NOTE: The Executive order was announced by the White House Press Office on November 3. It was not issued in the form of a White House press release.

Defense Meritorious Service Medal

Executive Order 12019.   November 3, 1977

ESTABLISHING THE DEFENSE MERITORIOUS SERVICE MEDAL

By virtue of the authority vested in me as President of the United States of America, and as Commander in Chief of the Armed Forces, it is hereby ordered as follows:

SECTION 1. There is hereby established a Defense Meritorious Service Medal, with accompanying ribbons and appurtenances, for award by the Secretary of Defense to any member of the Armed Forces of the United States who has rendered outstanding non-combat meritorious achievement or service while assigned to the Office of the Secretary of Defense, the Organization of the Joint Chiefs of Staff, a specified or unified command, a Defense agency, or other such joint activity as may be designated by the Secretary of Defense.

SEC. 2. The Defense Meritorious Service Medal, with accompanying ribbons and appurtenances, shall be of appropriate design approved by the Secretary of Defense and shall be awarded under such regulations as the Secretary of Defense may prescribe. These regulations shall place the Defense Meritorious Service Medal in an order of precedence after the Medal of Honor, the Distinguished Service Cross, the Defense Distinguished Service Medal, the Distinguished Service Medal, the Silver Star Medal, the Defense Superior Service Medal, the Legion of Merit Medal, and the Bronze Star Medal, but before the Meritorious Service Medal.

SEC. 3. No more than one Defense Meritorious Service Medal shall be awarded to any one person, but for each succeeding outstanding meritorious achievement or service justifying such an award a suitable device to be worn with that medal may be awarded under such regulations as the Secretary of Defense may prescribe.

SEC. 4. The Defense Meritorious Service Medal or device may be awarded posthumously and, when so awarded, may be presented to such representative of the deceased as may be deemed appropriate by the Secretary of Defense.

JIMMY CARTER

The White House,
   November 3, 1977.

[Filed with the Office of the Federal Register, 3:53 p.m., November 3, 1977]

NOTE: The Executive order was announced by the White House Press Office on November 3. It was not issued in the form of a White House press release.

Survey of Congressional Constituent Problems

Memorandum for the Heads of Executive Departments and Agencies. October 28, 1977

Memorandum for the Heads of Executive Departments and Agencies

Subject: Survey of Congressional Constituent Problems

Senators and Congressmen devote a good portion of their time and staff resources, as you know, to helping individual constituents deal with government agencies. Richard Pettigrew, my Assistant for Reorganization, recently conducted a survey of Senate and House offices aimed at identifying those areas of government causing constituents the most problems. This survey has yielded a wealth of information on the daily concerns of both the Congress and the average citizen in dealing with their government.

Responses received so far reflect a strong consensus as to the need for improved program effectiveness in particular areas. They provide us a unique opportunity to improve government's competence in serving the average citizen. They suggest problems, moreover, which are historic in nature and predate this Administration. These problems affect the daily lives of millions. The success we have in dealing with them will therefore bear substantial benefits for great numbers of people. For this reason, their correction deserves priority attention.

By its very nature, congressional casework highlights trouble spots and may not present a full picture of agency performance. I am aware too that departments and agencies are already taking action to address problems identified in the survey. Some of these problems may be beyond agencies' immediate control and have a statutory basis. Because these complaints involve the direct, day-to-day dealings of average citizens with their government, however, I would like to report to the public and the Congress as soon as possible on the steps we are taking to address them.

Please report to the Office of Management and Budget the efforts you now have underway, or the specific efforts you plan to take, to address those complaints involving your agency. This information should be included as part of your regular monthly reorganization progress report which is due December 5.

JIMMY CARTER

NOTE: The text of the memorandum, together with a fact sheet on the survey, was released on November 3.

Office of Rail Public Counsel

Nomination of Howard A. Heffron To Be Director. November 3, 1977

The President today announced that he will nominate Howard A. Heffron, of Bethesda, Md., to be Director of the Office of Rail Public Counsel.

Heffron was born October 3, 1927. He received an A.B. from Columbia Univer-

sity in 1948 and an LL.B. from Harvard Law School in 1951.

From 1953 to 1957, he was Assistant U.S. Attorney for the Southern District of New York. From 1959 to 1961, he was first assistant to the Assistant Attorney General, Tax Division, and Special Assistant to the Attorney General of the United States.

From 1965 to 1967, Heffron was a general consultant to the President's Commission on Law Enforcement and the Administration of Justice. From 1967 to 1969, he was Chief Counsel for the Federal Highway Administration, where he directed a staff of 57 lawyers providing a full range of legal services to agencies administering the automobile safety and motor carrier safety regulatory programs.

Since 1969 Heffron has practiced law in Washington and New York. Since 1975 he has also been a consultant on criminal justice for the German Marshal Fund of the United States.

Bills Concerning the Environment

Remarks on Signing H.R. 2817 and H.R. 4297 into Law. November 4, 1977

First of all, I want to welcome all of you here this morning for an occasion that's very important to our country in the symbolism and the actual accomplishment to this legislation.

One of the difficult questions that I had to face as Governor of Georgia was how to preserve our inland wetlands from inevitable and very rapid destruction. And when I sent Congress an environmental message earlier this year, I pointed out that every year we lose 300,000 acres of these extremely valuable component parts of our national ecology.

House of Representatives bill 2817, which has been supported very strongly by Congressman Bob Edgar, authorizes the expansion and the completion of the Tinicum National Environmental Center in Pennsylvania, on the outskirts of Philadelphia. This is the culmination of about 15 years of work by local people, as well as the Members of Congress in both House and Senate.

The pressure is great around any urban center to expand the industrial development into areas of great natural importance. And city dwellers, particularly, need to have near their own homes— particularly those that are not financially able to travel far and wide—a part of the Earth and environment as it was originally granted to us for our stewardship. I think this legislation goes a long way toward achieving that end.

With continued local support that I'm sure will be realized, Tinicum will become an exceptional wildlife preservation. Part of it has already been changed in form. This will be restored. And this will be a good experimental area to learn how to restore other similar regions around our country. It's also a place where Philadelphians can find a moment of solitude and rest, a part of life that I remember with great relish—[*laughter*]—and miss very much.

But I'm thankful that this is an action that Congress has taken, and I'd like now, at this moment, to sign legislation, House of Representatives bill 2817, which will preserve the Tinicum area near Philadelphia.

[*At this point, the President signed H.R. 2817 into law.*]

The other legislation, coincidentally, has been pursued aggressively by Members of the House and Senate from Delaware to New York, but it also encompasses a very serious problem for our whole country. This is House resolution

act 4297, which amends the Marine Protection Research and Sanctuaries Act. One of the most severe threats to the heavily used and very valuable seashore areas, particularly in Delaware, New Jersey, New York, Pennsylvania, has been the problem of ocean dumping, where— historically, when populations were low and the effluent was fairly well small in volume, dumping of city waste in the ocean was an acceptable practice because the ocean currents could disseminate it without destroying the beauty of the coastline.

But recently, Governors such as Governor Byrne in New Jersey and others have recognized, along with Congress, the great threat to the beauty of life and the very valuable tourist resource of the damage to the ocean beaches because of city wastes that were washed up on those beaches. In this bill, Congress has put into law the policy of this administration to end the dumping of sewage sludge into the ocean by December 31, 1981. This will provide large cities with an opportunity to find landfill sites and other alternative measures for eliminating or disposing of their wastes.

We've already made some progress, but we still have a very serious problem. And I particularly want to compliment Chairman John Murphy of the House Merchant Marine Committee, Jennings Randolph in the Senate, Representative Bill Hughes of New Jersey, and Governor Byrne, who's represented here this morning by Jean Byrne, his wife, for their innovative and very aggressive, sometimes discouraging work to control this practice.

I believe this demonstrates the commitment of Congress and the administration, as well, to protect and preserve one of mankind's most precious possessions— our oceans and our seashores. So, congratulations to you Members of Congress for this very fine work. And I now sign House of Representatives bill number

4297, which will control the dumping of municipal and other wastes into the oceans, which destroy our national seashores.

[*At this point, the President signed H.R. 4297 into law.*]

I think the importance of this legislation is indicated by the degree of commitment and the intense interest that's shown in it, particularly along the eastern seaboard, where population explosions have put special pressure on the beauty of our surroundings. And I again want to thank all of you for being here and for making it possible, through this ceremony, to dramatize this tremendous step forward.

Thank you again.

NOTE: The President spoke at 9:32 a.m. at the signing ceremony in the Indian Treaty Room of the Old Executive Office Building.

As enacted, H.R. 2817 is Public Law 95–152, and H.R. 4297 is Public Law 95–153, approved November 4.

JOYCE H. LOWINSON, director of the Drug Abuse Service and associate clinical professor of psychiatry at the Albert Einstein College of Medicine, Bronx, N.Y.;

DAVID F. MUSTO, associate professor of psychiatry and history, Yale University;

CHARLES B. O'KEEFFE, JR., White House adviser on health issues and drug abuse;

DONALD D. POMERLEAU, police commissioner of Baltimore, Md.;

HARVEY I. SLOANE, M.D., mayor of Louisville, Ky.

The President has designated Peter Bourne, his Special Assistant for Health Issues, as Executive Director of the Council. Other members are Secretary of State Cyrus Vance, Secretary of the Treasury Michael Blumenthal, Secretary of Defense Harold Brown, Attorney General Griffin Bell, Secretary of Health, Education, and Welfare Joseph Califano, Acting OMB Director James McIntyre, and Veterans Affairs Administrator Max Cleland.

Strategy Council

Appointment of Seven Members and Designation of Executive Director. November 4, 1977

The President today announced the appointment of seven persons to the Strategy Council. The Strategy Council was created by the Drug Abuse Office and Treatment Act of 1972, but members have not previously been appointed. The Council is charged with the responsibility of developing a comprehensive, coordinated, long-term strategy for all drug abuse prevention and drug traffic prevention functions of the Federal Government.

The seven persons appointed are:

MILTON F. BRYANT, an Atlanta surgeon and medical researcher and associate professor of surgery at Emory University;

VERNON JORDAN, JR., executive director of the National Urban League;

International Communication Agency

Message to the Congress Transmitting Amendments to Reorganization Plan No. 2 of 1977. November 1, 1977

To the Congress of the United States:

I herewith transmit amendments to Reorganization Plan No. 2 of 1977, which I transmitted to you on October 11, 1977. Except as specifically amended hereby, Reorganization Plan No. 2 remains unmodified.

JIMMY CARTER

The White House,
    November 1, 1977.

AMENDMENTS TO
REORGANIZATION PLAN No. 2 of 1977

Prepared by the President and transmitted to the Senate and the House of Representatives in Congress assembled November 1, 1977, pursuant to the provisions of chapter 9 of title 5 of the United States Code.

Reorganization Plan No. 2 of 1977, which was transmitted to the Senate and the House of Representatives in Congress assembled on October 11, 1977, is hereby amended as follows:

A. The title is amended to read: "International Communication Agency."

B. Section 1 is amended to read:

"Section 1. *Establishment of the International Communication Agency.*

"There is hereby established in the executive branch an agency to be known as the International Communication Agency (the "Agency")."

C. Section 4 is amended to read:

Section 4. *Associate Directors*

"The President, by and with the advice and consent of the Senate, may appoint four Associate Directors, who shall perform such duties and exercise such powers as the Director may from time to time prescribe. One Associate Director shall be known as the Associate Director for Educational and Cultural Affairs and one Associate Director shall be known as the Associate Director for Broadcasting. Each Associate Director shall be entitled to receive compensation at the rate now or hereafter prescribed by law for Level IV of the Executive Schedule."

D. Section 7(a)(12) is amended to read:

"(12) Section 9(b) of the National Foundation on the Arts and Humanities Act of 1965 (20 U.S.C. 958(b)), to the extent that such functions are vested in the Secretary of State;"

E. Section 8(a) is amended to read:

"(a) There is hereby established an advisory commission, to be known as the United States Advisory Commission on

International Communication, Cultural and Educational Affairs (the "Commission"). The Commission shall consist of seven members who shall be appointed by the President, by and with the advice and consent of the Senate. The members of the Commission shall represent the public interest and shall be selected from a cross section of educational, communications, cultural, scientific, technical, public service, labor and business and professional backgrounds. Not more than four members shall be from any one political party. The term of each member shall be three years except that of the original seven appointments, two shall be for a term of one year and two shall be for a term of two years. Any member appointed to fill a vacancy occurring prior to the expiration of the term for which a predecessor was appointed shall be appointed for the remainder of such term. Upon the expiration of a member's term of office, such member may continue to serve until a successor is appointed and has qualified. The President shall designate a member to chair the Commission."

NOTE: The message was not issued in the form of a White House press release.

The text of the amendments was released on November 4.

International Communication Agency

Message to the Congress Transmitting Amendments to Reorganization Plan No. 2 of 1977. November 3, 1977

To the Congress of the United States:

I herewith transmit amendments to Reorganization Plan No. 2 of 1977, which I transmitted to you on October 12, 1977, and certain amendments to which I transmitted on November 1, 1977. Except as specifically amended hereby and by the amendments transmitted November 1,

1977, Reorganization Plan No. 2 remains unmodified.

JIMMY CARTER

The White House,
November 3, 1977.

FURTHER AMENDMENTS TO
REORGANIZATION PLAN NO. 2 OF 1977

Prepared by the President and transmitted to the Senate and the House of Representatives in Congress assembled November 3, 1977, pursuant to the provisions of Chapter 9 of Title 5 of the United States Code.

Reorganization Plan No. 2 of 1977, which was transmitted to the Senate and the House of Representatives in Congress assembled on October 12, 1977, and certain amendments to which were transmitted November 1, 1977, is hereby further amended as follows:

A. Section 7 is further amended by adding thereto a new subsection, to read:

"(c) The Director shall insure that the scholarly integrity and nonpolitical character of educational and cultural exchange activities vested in the Director are maintained."

B. Section 8(b) is amended by adding at the end thereof a new sentence, to read:

"The Commission's reports to the Congress shall include assessments of the degree to which the scholarly integrity and nonpolitical character of the educational and cultural exchange activities vested in the Director have been maintained, and assessments of the attitudes of foreign scholars and governments regarding such activities."

NOTE: The message was not issued in the form of a White House press release.

The text of the amendments was released on November 4.

Digest of Other White House Announcements

The following listing includes the President's daily schedule and other items of general interest as announced by the White House Press Office during the period covered by this issue. Events and announcements printed elsewhere in the issue are not included.

October 30

The President returned to the White House after a weekend stay at Camp David, Md.

October 31

The President met at the White House with:

—Zbigniew Brzezinski, Assistant to the President for National Security Affairs;

—senior White House staff members;

—the Cabinet;

—Secretary of Defense Harold Brown and Dr. Brzezinski;

—Gov. Robert W. Straub of Oregon;

—Robert D. Patridge, executive vice president and general manager, and other representatives of the National Rural Electric Cooperative Association;

—Vice President Walter F. Mondale, Landon Butler, Deputy Assistant to the President, George Meany, president, and J. Lane Kirkland, secretary-treasurer, AFL–CIO, to discuss energy and United States membership in the International Labor Organization.

November 1

The President met at the White House with:

—Dr. Brzezinski;

—Senator Alan Cranston of California;

—Secretary of Labor F. Ray Marshall;

—Vice President Mondale, Adm. Stansfield Turner, Director of Central Intelligence and Dr. Brzezinski;

—James T. McIntyre, Jr., Acting Director of the Office of Management and Budget;

—Douglas A. Fraser, president of the International Union of the United Auto Workers;

—the Democratic congressional leadership.

The White House announced that King Hassan II of Morocco has accepted the invitation of the President to pay a state visit to the United States, beginning with meetings in Washington on December 7 and 8.

November 2

The President met at the White House with:

—Dr. Brzezinski;

—Mrs. Carter, for lunch.

November 3

The President met at the White House with:

—Dr. Brzezinski;

—Members of the Georgia congressional delegation;

—Charles L. Schultze, Chairman of the Council of Economic Advisers;

—Secretary Brown.

November 4

The President met at the White House with:

—Vice President Mondale, Secretary of State Cyrus R. Vance, and Dr. Brzezinski;

—Dr. Brzezinski;

—Secretary Vance, Clark M. Clifford, the President's Personal Emissary to Greece, Turkey, and Cyprus, and

Dr. Brzezinski, to discuss the situation in Cyprus;

—Bert Lance, former Director of the Office of Management and Budget;

—a group of representatives of environmental action groups.

NOMINATIONS SUBMITTED TO THE SENATE

The following list does not include promotions of members of the Uniformed Services, nominations to the Service Academies, or nominations of Foreign Service officers.

Submitted October 28, 1977

The following-named persons to the positions indicated:

LOUIS POLK, of Ohio, to be Chairman of the United States Metric Board for a term of 6 years (new position).

To be members of the United States Metric Board for the terms indicated (new positions):

For a term of 2 years

CARL A. BECK, of Pennsylvania
FRANCIS R. DUGAN, of Ohio
EDWARD L. GINZTON, of California
HENRY KROEZE, of Wisconsin

For a term of 4 years

PAUL BLOCK, JR., of Ohio
THOMAS A. HANNIGAN, of Maryland
FRANK HARTMAN, of Michigan
SANDRA R. KENNEY, of Maryland
ROGER ELLIS TRAVIS, of Massachusetts

For a term of 6 years

SYDNEY D. ANDREWS, of Florida
JOYCE D. MILLER, of New York
GLENN NISHIMURA, of Arkansas
SATENIG S. ST. MARIE, of Connecticut
ADRIAN G. WEAVER, of Connecticut

Submitted October 31, 1977

R. DAVID PITTLE, of Maryland, to be a Commissioner of the Consumer Product Safety Commission for the remainder of the term expiring October 26, 1982, vice Thaddeus A. Garrett, Jr.

LIVINGSTON L. BIDDLE, JR., of the District of Columbia, to be Chairman of the National Endowment for the Arts for a term of 4 years, vice Nancy Hanks, term expired.

NOMINATIONS—Continued

Submitted November 1, 1977

MICHAEL H. WALSH, of California, to be United States Attorney for the Southern District of California for the term of 4 years, vice Terry J. Knoepp.

Submitted November 2, 1977

JOHN ARNOT HEWITT, JR., of New Jersey, to be an Assistant Secretary of the Air Force, vice Everett T. Keech, resigned.

MONROE G. McKAY, of Utah, to be United States Circuit Judge for the Tenth Circuit, vice David T. Lewis, retiring.

JOHN L. KANE, JR., of Colorado, to be United States District Judge for the District of Colorado, vice Alfred A. Arraj, retired.

ROBERT F. COLLINS, of Louisiana, to be United States District Judge for the Eastern District of Louisiana, vice Alvin B. Rubin, elevated.

Submitted November 3, 1977

HOWARD A. HEFFRON, of Maryland, to be Director of the Office of Rail Public Counsel for a term of 4 years (new position).

Submitted November 4, 1977

JAMES K. LOGAN, of Kansas, to be United States Circuit Judge for the Tenth Circuit, vice Delmas C. Hill, retired.

ROBERT S. VANCE, of Alabama, to be United States Circuit Judge for the Fifth Circuit, vice Walter P. Gewin, retired.

CHECKLIST OF WHITE HOUSE PRESS RELEASES

The following releases of the Office of the White House Press Secretary, distributed during the period covered by this issue, are not included in the issue.

Released November 1, 1977

Announcement: nomination of Michael H. Walsh to be United States Attorney for the Southern District of California

News conference: on his meeting with the President to discuss national energy legislation—by Douglas A. Fraser, president of the International Union of the United Auto Workers

News conference: on the President's decision to terminate United States membership in the International Labor Organization—by Secretary of Labor F. Ray Marshall

CHECKLIST—Continued

Released November 2, 1977

Announcement: nomination of Monroe G. McKay to be United States Circuit Judge for the Tenth Circuit; Robert F. Collins to be United States District Judge for the Eastern District of Louisiana; and John L. Kane, Jr., to be United States District Judge for the District of Colorado

Advance text: remarks to the general council of the World Jewish Congress

Released November 3, 1977

Announcement: signing of Executive Orders 12017, 12018, and 12019, concerning the Department of Defense

Released November 4, 1977

Announcement: nomination of James K. Logan to be United States Circuit Judge for the Tenth Circuit and Robert S. Vance to be United States Circuit Judge for the Fifth Circuit

ACTS APPROVED BY THE PRESIDENT

Approved October 31, 1977

H.R. 7797_____ Public Law 95–148
Foreign Assistance and Related Programs Appropriations Act, 1978.

Approved November 1, 1977

H.J. Res. 573_____ Public Law 95–149
A joint resolution commemorating General Thaddeus Kosciuszko by presenting a memorial plaque in his memory to the people of Poland on behalf of the American people.

H.R. 3744_____ Public Law 95–151
Fair Labor Standards Amendments of 1977.

S. 393_____ Public Law 95–150
Montana Wilderness Study Act of 1977.

Approved November 4, 1977

H.R. 2817_____ Public Law 95–152
An act to provide for certain additions to the Tinicum National Environmental Center.

H.R. 4297_____ Public Law 95–153
An act to amend the Marine Protection, Research, and Sanctuaries Act of 1972 to authorize appropriations to carry out the provisions of such Act for fiscal year 1978.

Activity of Korean Agents in the United States

Letter to Congressional Leaders Transmitting a Report on the Justice Department Investigation. November 4, 1977

In accordance with Section 28 of the International Security Assistance Act of 1977 (Public Law 95–92), I am transmitting herewith a report concerning the extent to which the Republic of Korea is cooperating with the Department of Justice investigation into allegations of improper activity in the United States by agents of the Republic of Korea.

Sincerely,

JIMMY CARTER

COOPERATION BY THE REPUBLIC OF KOREA WITH JUSTICE DEPARTMENT INVESTIGATIONS

This report is submitted in accordance with Section 28 of the International Security Assistance Act of 1977 (Public Law 95–92), enacted August 4, 1977. Subsection (a)(2) of Section 28 requests that the President report to the Congress within ninety days of the enactment of the Act concerning "the extent to which the Republic of Korea is cooperating with" the Department of Justice investigation into allegations of improper activity in the United States by agents of the Republic of Korea.

The principal cooperation sought from the Government of the Republic of Korea by the Department of Justice has been the important testimony which could be supplied by Korean businessman Tongsun Park (Pak Tong-son). The Department of Justice considers Mr. Park's verifiable and truthful testimony essential to the full investigation and successful prosecution of illegal acts by U.S. officials in the United States. The cooperation needed from Mr. Park involves both his early interrogation in connection with Grand Jury investigations and his eventual appearance before trial juries in resulting prosecutions in the United States.

The United States Government has sought the full cooperation of the Republic of Korea Government in securing the return of Mr. Tongsun Park to the United States. At the time of this report to the Congress, our two governments are in the midst of active and delicate discussions, and proposals are being considered in an effort to reach a mutually satisfactory agreement. The present report is therefore an interim report which will summarize the efforts made by the United States Government to date to obtain cooperation, and the responses of the Government of Korea thereto.

In April, the Department of State, on behalf of and in full coordination with the Department of Justice, initiated discussions with the Government of the Republic of Korea. United States Ambassador to Korea Richard L. Sneider, in a series of meetings with President Chung Hee Park, Foreign Minister Tong-jin Park and other senior officials of the Korean Government, stressed that Mr. Tongsun Park's testimony was critical to the satisfactory conclusion of the Justice Department investigation and urged that efforts be made by the Korean Government to have him fully cooperate. The Korean Government responded that whether Mr. Park cooperated with the Department of Justice investigation was entirely for him to decide as a private person.

In early July, the United States Government delivered an offer by the Department of Justice to grant Mr. Park complete immunity from criminal prosecution if he returned to the United States and testified in a full and truthful manner concerning his knowledge of illegal payments involving U.S. officials. It was explained that the scandal created by Mr. Park's illegal activities in the U.S. could not be resolved without Mr. Park's cooperation.

The Korean Government in July advised the U.S. Government that it was seeking to persuade Mr. Park (who was then in London) to return to the United States to testify under the guarantee of immunity. The U.S. Government was subsequently informed by the Korean Government that Mr. Park would not agree to return to the United States, and that the Korean Government could not force him to return against his will.

On August 18, Mr. Tongsun Park arrived in Korea from Europe. As he was now directly within the jurisdiction of the Republic of Korea, the United States Government intensified its requests to the Korean Government to help it obtain Mr. Park's truthful testimony in order to bring the investigation to a just and early conclusion.

In late August, President Carter sent a letter to President Park expressing grave concern at the effect Tongsun Park's lack of cooperation was having on our mutual interests. The President urged that the Korean Government assist in getting Mr. Park to return immediately to the United States in order that these matters be concluded satisfactorily as soon as possible.

On two occasions the Korean Government provided statements by Mr. Tongsun Park, including a statement to the Seoul District Prosecutor. These statements, however, were not requested by the United States and were totally unhelpful to the Justice Department investigation.

The Korean Government informed Ambassador Sneider in early September that Foreign Minister Tong-jin Park had talked with Mr. Park in an effort to persuade him to return to the United States. According to the Foreign Minister, Mr. Park nevertheless expressed an unwillingness to return to the United States. Furthermore, the Korean Government pointed out that there is no extradition treaty between the United States and the Republic of Korea, and that it had no legal means to force him to return to the United States.

After the indictment of Mr. Park by the Grand Jury in the U.S. District Court of the District of Columbia, Ambassador Sneider informed the Korean Government that Mr. Park was now considered a fugitive from U.S. justice. Therefore, his return was even more urgent.

On September 12, President Park responded to President Carter, expressing hope that an early resolution of the problem could be effected within the principles of national laws and international practice. President Park stated that the Korean

Government could not compel Mr. Park to go to the United States.

On September 21, Secretary of State Vance and Korean Foreign Minister Park met in Washington. The Secretary expressed strong disappointment at the failure of the Korean Government to respond to the U.S. request. In view of the evidence which was available to the United States Government, the Secretary noted that Mr. Park's situation was different from that of purely a private citizen. The Korean Government's failure therefore to persuade Mr. Park to return to the United States to testify was not the response expected of a close ally. His absence was impeding the course of justice in the United States.

Several further high-level meetings occurred in the days following the Foreign Minister's meeting with the Secretary of State, in the course of which the Korean Government proposed that United States Justice Department officials go to Seoul to discuss the problem with Korean Justice Ministry officials. On September 30, following a second meeting in New York between the Secretary of State and Foreign Minister Park, the two governments simultaneously announced agreement that: ". . . representatives of the U.S. Department of Justice will go to Seoul and meet with Korean Ministry of Justice officials to discuss satisfactory terms and conditions for communicating with Mr. Park Tong-son."

Assistant United States Attorney General Benjamin Civiletti and two other officials of the Department of Justice proceeded to Korea under this agreement and met in more than 30 hours of direct discussions with Korean Ministry of Justice officials from October 17 through October 20, 1977. The Korean side in the talks was headed by Vice Minister of Justice Chong Won Lee.

During these discussions, the United States proposed interrogation of Tongsun Park in a third country under conditions which would provide verification of the truthfulness of his testimony. If sufficient evidence were thereby gained of indictable offenses by United States officials, Mr. Park's later appearance would be required in the United States for trial testimony. The United States proposed that, if Mr. Park faithfully completed these steps, the Justice Department would seek dismissal of the indictment against him. The basis of these U.S. proposals was the need to secure truthful and effective testimony for successful prosecutions at trials in the United States.

The United States proposals were rejected by the Korean side, which advised that Mr. Park was determined not to go to a third country or return to the United States.

The Korean representatives proposed that questions be submitted to Mr. Park through a Korean prosecutor or court, with U.S. prosecutors present only as observers. In making this proposal, the Korean representatives cited their understanding of the arrangements which had been made in the United States at the request of the Japanese Government in the case of the Lockheed Aircraft Corporation. The United States representatives stressed that these Korean proposals were inadequate to the requirements of the present case.

In view of the absence of any agreement on either the fundamental issue of direct examination of Mr. Park under circumstances of trustworthiness, or on his eventual availability to testify at trials in the United States, these negotiations were terminated on October 20 and the U.S. representatives returned to Washington.

Following its analysis of the negotiations between Justice officials in Seoul, the Government of the Republic of Korea on October 31 transmitted to the United States Government an important new proposal relating to interrogation of Mr. Tongsun Park. Active discussions between our two governments are underway in connection with this proposal for cooperation. It is therefore inappropriate and premature to characterize in detail our negotiations at this point. The United States position, however, continues to be guided by the necessity to be able successfully to prosecute illegal acts in the United States in court trials.

In accordance with Public Law 95–92, a further report will be transmitted to the Congress on this matter on or before January 31, 1978.

NOTE: The report to the Congress was enclosed with identical letters addressed to the Honorable Walter F. Mondale, President of the Senate, the Honorable Thomas P. O'Neill, Jr., Speaker of the House of Representatives, the Honorable Robert C. Byrd, majority leader of the Senate, the Honorable John Sparkman, chairman of the Senate Committee on Foreign Relations, and the Honorable Clement J. Zablocki, chairman of the House Committee on International Relations.

The texts of the letters and the report to the Congress were released on November 5.

Veto of Department of Energy Authorization Bill

Message to the Senate Returning S. 1811 Without Approval. November 5, 1977

To the Senate of the United States:

I am returning, without my approval, S. 1811, the Department of Energy Authorization Act of 1978—Civilian Applications.

This bill authorizes fiscal year 1978 appropriations for the Department of Energy's nuclear and non-nuclear energy research, development, and demonstration projects; however, funds for most of these programs, except the Clinch River Breeder Reactor Demonstration Plant, already have been appropriated and made available to the Department.

I cannot approve this legislation because:

• It mandates funding for the Clinch River Breeder Reactor Demonstration Plant, that will result in a large and unnecessarily expensive project which, when completed, would be technically obsolete and economically unsound. This decision would channel scarce and much needed effort away from a broad-based breeder reactor development program into a production model which will not be required or economical for many years.

• It seriously inhibits the President from pursuing effectively an international policy to prevent the proliferation of nuclear weapons and nuclear explosive capability.

• It puts burdensome limitations on the President and the new Department of Energy in exercising necessary judgment to provide an effective energy research and development program.

• It puts unwise limitations on our ability to implement the new spent fuels policy which I recently announced, to aid our non-proliferation goals.

• It limits the constitutional authority of the President through three one-House veto provisions. One of these provisions could also limit the Administration's ability to recover a fair price for the uranium enrichment service provided by the Federal government.

S. 1811 severely limits the flexibility of the Executive Branch in expending funds appropriated for the Clinch River project pursuant to this authorization. This is inconsistent with my strong belief that proceeding beyond completion of the systems design phase of the Clinch River facility would imperil the Administration's policy to curb proliferation of nuclear weapons technology. Further, completion of the Clinch River facility would cost American taxpayers an additional $1.4 billion on a facility that is technically and economically unnecessary.

In 1970, when the Clinch River facility was first authorized it was estimated to cost $450 million. Its total cost estimate now exceeds $2.2 billion. The Federal government's share of the cost of the project has risen from $250 million to $2 billion. Yet current projections of the increase in the need for nuclear-generated electric power in the year 2000 are only one-third of estimates made in 1970. The breeder reactor will, therefore, not be needed in the early 1990's, as had been projected when the Clinch River facility was first authorized.

The Administration is committed to a strong research and development program for advanced nuclear technologies, including base program research on the liquid metal fast breeder, research into alternative breeder cycles, and an accelerated research and development program for advanced non-breeder technologies. These programs are vital to ensure that energy is available to make the transition over the decades ahead from oil and natural gas to other energy sources. All of these programs will be maintained in the absence of S. 1811. Construction of the Clinch River facility in no way is necessary to ensure continued development of nuclear technologies, including liquid metal fast breeder technology.

In vetoing S. 1811, I intend to pursue the authority at my disposal to terminate construction of the Clinch River facility. Further expenditure on the Clinch River facility should be ended in an orderly fashion, and I intend to analyze all available options, including those under the Congressional Budget and Impoundment Control Act of 1974, to ensure that no further unnecessary expenditures on this facility are made.

In addition to those features relating to the Clinch River Breeder Reactor, S. 1811 also contains additional provisions which are not consistent with Administration policies and the national interest.

The bill would further impede our nonproliferation goals by imposing limitations on the ability of the United States to provide for the storage of spent fuel from foreign reactors in those instances where such an action would serve those goals.

It permits a one-House veto over the criteria and prices which the Administration can adopt, infringing on the Administration's ability to recover the full cost of those enrichment services.

S. 1811 would impede the ability of the Secretary of Energy to organize effectively the research and development activities of the new Department of Energy, in contravention of legislation passed in August establishing the Department.

Finally, it would impose a variety of specific and unnecessary technical restrictions on energy research and development programs, establish one-House veto provisions relating to geothermal facility loan guarantees, and impose a six-month requirement for a recommendation on the purchase and/or operation of the Barnwell reprocessing facility.

I am committed to a vigorous energy research and development strategy to ensure maximum progress on shifting the energy base of the United States away from oil and natural gas. However, I am also concerned about the risk of introducing the plutonium economy through an unnecessary commercial demonstration facility. I believe that we should continue our research and development program without large, unnecessary expenditures for a technologically obsolete project and without imperiling our shared desire for halting the uncontrolled spread of nuclear weapons capability.

JIMMY CARTER

The White House,
    November 5, 1977.

Emergency Medical Services Week, 1977

Proclamation 4535.   November 5, 1977

By the President of the United States of America

A Proclamation

Each week more than one thousand Americans lose their lives due to accidents and illnesses because emergency medical assistance is either unavailable or inadequate.

In 1968 the Department of Transportation issued a national uniform standard, "Emergency Medical Services," under the Highway Safety Act of 1966. This Federal initiative has provided essential training courses for emergency medical personnel, vital communications for citizen access, quicker responses and physician direction, and important specifications for ambulances, including necessary medical equipment and uniform colors and markings.

We salute the Nation's emergency personnel, upon whose skill and dedication we all depend.

Now, THEREFORE, I, JIMMY CARTER, President of the United States of America, do hereby designate the week beginning November 6, 1977, as Emergency Medical Services Week.

I call upon the Governors and Mayors and all other State and local officials to assist hospital administrators and physicians, fire departments, public safety agencies and ambulance services in improving emergency medical services.

I call upon Federal agencies, especially the Departments of Transportation and Health, Education, and Welfare to continue, with renewed emphasis, their assistance to States and communities in their efforts to help those in need of emergency medical assistance.

I call upon the American people to lend their support to these efforts in order that we may assure that no individual in this country will suffer due to the lack of available or adequate emergency help when in need.

IN WITNESS WHEREOF, I have hereunto set my hand this fifth day of November, in the year of our Lord nineteen hundred seventy-seven, and of the Independence of the United States of America the two hundred and second.

JIMMY CARTER

[Filed with the Office of the Federal Register, 4:28 p.m., November 7, 1977]

NOTE: The text of the proclamation was released on November 7.

Federal Deposit Insurance Corporation

Nomination of William M. Isaac To Be a Member of the Board of Directors. November 7, 1977

The President today announced that he will nominate William M. Isaac, of Louisville, Ky., to be a member of the Board of Directors of the Federal Deposit Insurance Corporation (FDIC). He would replace Robert Barnett, resigned.

Isaac was born December 21, 1943, in Bryan, Ohio. He received a B.S. in business administration from Miami University of Ohio in 1966 and a J.D. from Ohio State University in 1969.

From 1969 to 1974, Isaac was an attorney with the Wisconsin law firm of Foley & Lardner, where he had a general corporate practice specializing in banking law and antitrust law.

Since 1974 Isaac has been vice president, general counsel, and secretary of the First Kentucky National Corp. and its subsidiaries.

Isaac is the author of several articles on banking and is a frequent lecturer on various banking and bank holding company topics.

Environmental Protection Agency

Nomination of Stephen J. Gage To Be an Assistant Administrator. November 7, 1977

The President today announced that he will nominate Stephen J. Gage, of Bethesda, Md., to be an Assistant Administrator of the Environmental Protection Agency (EPA). He would replace Wilson K. Talley, resigned, and his area of responsibility would be research and development.

Gage was born September 27, 1940, in Palisade, Nebr. He received a B.S. in mechanical engineering from the University of Nebraska in 1962 and an M.S. (1964) and Ph.D. (1966) from Purdue University in nuclear engineering.

In 1965 Gage joined the faculty of the mechanical engineering department of the University of Texas at Austin as an assistant professor. In 1966 he became director of the university's nuclear reactor laboratory. He was promoted to the rank of associate professor in 1970.

From 1971 to 1973, Gage served in the National Resources Group of the White House Office of Science and Technology as a White House Fellow. He specialized in energy resources, energy conversion technology, and environmental effects of energy resource extraction, conversion, and use.

Gage then served as senior staff member for energy programs at the Council on Environmental Quality. From 1972 to 1973, he was a member of the Council's Federal Impact Evaluation Staff.

Gage joined EPA in 1974 as the Acting Director of the Office of Energy Research. Since 1975 he has been Deputy Assistant Administrator for Energy, Minerals, and Industry, in the Office of Research and Development at EPA. In this position he has been responsible for the planning and management of a comprehensive research and development program for the assessment of the environmental impacts of energy, minerals, and industrial operations.

Export-Import Bank of the United States

Nomination of Thibaut de Saint Phalle To Be a Member of the Board of Directors. November 7, 1977

The President today announced that he will nominate Thibaut de Saint Phalle, of Princeton, N.J., to be a member of the Board of Directors of the Export-Import Bank of the United States. He would replace R. Alex McCullough, resigned.

De Saint Phalle was born July 23, 1918, in Tuxedo Park, N.Y. He received an A.B. from Columbia College in 1939 and an LL.B. and J.D. from Columbia Law School in 1941. He served in the U.S.

Navy and Office of Strategic Services from 1942 to 1946.

From 1941 to 1950, he was an associate attorney with the New York firm of Chadbourne, Wallace, Parke & Whiteside. From 1950 to 1954, he was a consultant to the State Department and negotiated the Military Aid Treaty with the United States, France, and Indochina in 1950. From 1950 to 1958, he was a partner and head of the corporate law department at the New York firm of Lewis and Mac-Donald.

From 1958 to 1967, de Saint Phalle was director of Becton, Dickinson and Co. in Rutherford, N.J., where he was in charge of all legal matters. From 1962 to 1966, he was also senior partner at Coudert Brothers, an international law firm.

From 1965 to 1970, de Saint Phalle was an investment banker, serving as vice chairman of the board of directors of Stralem, Saint Phalle & Co. from 1968 to 1970, and limited partner and president of Witter Overseas Finance Corp. from 1967 to 1968.

From 1971 to 1976, de Saint Phalle was a professor of international finance and law at the Centre d'Etudes Industrielles in Geneva, Switzerland, and a consultant to multinational companies and banks on legal and financial matters. Since 1976 he has been a visiting professor at the Centre d'Etudes Industrielles, a lecturer at Fairleigh Dickinson University in New Jersey, and a counsel at Coudert Brothers in New York City.

Strategy Council

Remarks to Members of the Council.
November 7, 1977

I'd like to say a few things to start with before I ask you to report on what you have decided.

This Strategy Council, as you know, is responsible under the law for evolving broad policy matters for the drug control program.

Dr. Bourne, who is working in the White House, will coordinate what you decide and work very closely with the agencies involved as well. We've had remarkable success, I think, already in this first 10 months.

The purity of heroin is at the lowest point that it's been in 7 years. We've had, as well as that, an increase of 25 percent in heroin prices on the street, which is another good indication of the scarcity of it. In the first 6 months of this year, we've had about a 7-percent reduction in the National Crime Index, which I think is quite often directly related to heroin use, at least in some types of crimes.

We've also had good, perhaps even unprecedented, communication and cooperation among the agencies involved—between Justice and Treasury, for instance, and between HEW and State, Agriculture, the United Nations—as we try to not only control the sources of heroin but provide alternative crops to be produced and approach the United Nations and other countries, other than ourselves, to join with us in holding down drug traffic.

We've got an opportunity, I think, as we go into the new domestic programs, to provide adequate treatment for those who are addicted to drugs, including alcohol. And I'm particularly interested in pursuing—working with HEW and others—the control of the so-called legal drugs, barbiturates, that have probably caused almost as many deaths as most of the other drugs. And this overprescription of barbiturates by medical doctors is almost a matter of habit in some communities of our country, and we need to make sure that they aren't used in a destructive way to the health of the people who are inclined toward over-reliance on drugs because of some psychological problem.

NOTE: The President spoke at 11:45 a.m. at a meeting of the Council in the Cabinet Room at the White House.

Schneider was Deputy Director of the Office of Space-Environmental Science Affairs at State in 1968 and 1969 and country director for India from 1969 to 1973. Since 1973 he has been Deputy Chief of Mission in New Delhi.

United States Ambassador to Bangladesh

Nomination of David T. Schneider.
November 8, 1977

The President today announced that he will nominate David T. Schneider, of Bethesda, Md., to be Ambassador Extraordinary and Plenipotentiary of the United States to the People's Republic of Bangladesh. He would replace Edward E. Masters, transferred.

Schneider was born November 20, 1922, in Cincinnati, Ohio. He received a B.A. from Yale University in 1947. He served in the U.S. Army Air Force from 1943 to 1945.

From 1947 to 1949, Schneider was a personnel methods analyst for the Federal Security Agency, and in 1949 he was an intelligence specialist for the Air Force. From 1950 to 1953, he was consular, political, and administrative officer in Karachi.

From 1953 to 1955, Schneider was consular officer in Asmara. He took Hindi language and area training in 1955-56 and served as political officer in Bombay from 1956 to 1958. From 1958 to 1962, he was chief of the political section in New Delhi.

From 1962 to 1966, Schneider was officer in charge of India, Ceylon, and Nepal affairs at the State Department. He attended the National War College in 1966-67 and served as Deputy Chief of Mission in Rawalpindi in 1967 and 1968.

United States Ambassador to Burundi

Nomination of Thomas J. Corcoran.
November 8, 1977

The President today announced that he will nominate Thomas J. Corcoran, of Washington, D.C., to be Ambassador Extraordinary and Plenipotentiary of the United States to the Republic of Burundi. He would replace David E. Mark, resigned.

Corcoran was born September 20, 1920, in New York City. He received a B.S.S. from Saint John's University in 1940. He served in the U.S. Navy from 1942 to 1947.

Corcoran joined the Foreign Service in 1948 and served as consular officer in Barcelona from 1948 to 1950 and as political officer in Saigon from 1950 to 1953. He took Thai language and area training in 1953-54.

Corcoran was principal officer in Hanoi in 1954 and 1955 and political officer in Saigon in 1955 and 1956. He was a supervisory international relations officer at the State Department from 1956 to 1959. In 1959-60 he was detailed to the Armed Forces Staff College.

In 1960 and 1961, Corcoran was political officer for POLAD/CINCPAC in Honolulu, and in 1961 and 1962 he was deputy political officer for POLAD/CINCPAC. He was Deputy Chief of Mission in Ouagadougou from 1962 to 1964.

In 1964 and 1965, Corcoran was an international relations officer at the State

Department, and in 1965 and 1966 he was political officer in Saigon. He was principal officer, then consul general, in Hué in 1966 and 1967.

Corcoran attended the National War College in 1967–68. He was country director for Laos-Cambodia at the State Department from 1968 to 1972. In 1972 and 1973, he was a personnel officer at the State Department, and in 1973 and 1974 he was Deputy Chief of Mission in Port-au-Prince.

In 1974 and 1975, Corcoran was principal officer in Quebec. Since 1975 he has been Deputy Chief of Mission in Vientiane.

Alaska Natural Gas Transportation System

Remarks at the Bill Signing Ceremony.   November 8, 1977

THE PRESIDENT. This joint resolution to approve the construction of the major natural gas pipeline from Alaska down through Canada to our country is a very important demonstration of our Nation's commitment to provide adequate energy supplies in the future, to protect the quality of the environment in our two nations, to work harmoniously in one of the most complicated and most expensive engineering projects ever undertaken by human beings.

I'm very proud that the House and Senate have approved the route that was chosen by ourselves and the Canadians for this major project. This will provide, when it's fully in operation, about 3.6 billion cubic feet of natural gas per day. It's the largest single project ever undertaken for the provision of energy and, perhaps, the largest single engineering project ever undertaken of any kind.

Over a period of 25 years, which is the estimated life of this pipeline—it will probably be longer—it would save the American people more than $6 billion, compared to the alternative route assessed.

But this is just the first very minor step in what's going to be a long journey in engineering, planning, financing, designing and construction and operation of this tremendous pipeline project.

Tonight I will talk to the American people about the energy problem and the enormity of it now and in the future. This is roughly a $14 billion project. Natural gas makes up about 25 percent of our energy needs. This project, in spite of its enormous size, will provide about 5 percent of our Nation's natural gas. So, what we are talking about here, to show you the size of the energy problem and the energy industry, is about 1 percent of the energy supplies of just one nation.

I'm particularly glad that the Ambassador for Canada is here. I hope that he will relay directly to Prime Minister Trudeau my deep gratitude at the cooperative attitude that has been taken by the Canadians in working with us on this project.

I particularly want to thank the Alaskan delegation who are here, the Congress Members who have been so instrumental in the passage of this resolution. Many of them are the same Members of Congress who are now working on the energy conference committee—Senator Jackson, Congressman Udall, John Dingell, Congressmen Staggers, Roncalio, and others. I want to thank them again for their timely and very effective approval of this project.

Dr. Schlesinger, the Secretary of Energy, will now begin his detailed work along with Cecil Andrus, the administrator of the Interior Department—the Secretary—and also other agencies of the Federal Government. So, I think, this is a good time for our country, for Canada, and for the future of the American people.

Again, I want to congratulate the Members of Congress for doing such a good job in helping to make this possible.

[*At this point, the President signed H.J. Res. 621 into law.*]

Now, Jim, you can go ahead and start working.

SECRETARY SCHLESINGER. I think what the President has said underscores the close relationships that we should maintain with Canada in regard to what are common problems, that this will help restore an era of good feelings between the two countries, and that this project, large as it is, is a splendid symbol of that cooperation.

THE PRESIDENT. Mike?

SENATOR GRAVEL. I think that it's not only of benefit to the Nation but, I think, it does lay aside the differences that have arisen in the contest of where the line would go—our differences with Canada. I think if there's any nation that we have a proximity to, it's that great country. I think the gas that we've been blessed with in Alaska we've brought to market efficiently and effectively through this pipeline.

We are grateful to the leadership of the Executive, under you, Mr. President, Mr. Schlesinger, and with the alacrity that the Congress acted in seeing that this resolution got to your desk as soon as possible.

THE PRESIDENT. Thank you. I don't think there were any dissenting votes. It was a voice vote. I didn't hear any——

SENATOR GRAVEL. There were none.

THE PRESIDENT. Congressman Staggers?

REPRESENTATIVE STAGGERS. I'd just say that it's a red-letter day for America and our future.

THE PRESIDENT. Ted?

SENATOR STEVENS. Mr. President, I think this is just the first of a series of transportation systems to bring Alaska's resources to what we call the South 48. We have a lot more oil and gas and we'll hopefully get on to those other areas, too, soon. So, I congratulate you. I think this is the first time that the Vice President and I have been on the same side. We both lost. He favored the Arctic route, and I favored the El Paso route. But we're both happy today. [*Laughter*]

OTHER SPEAKER. Mr. President, the Vice President did not lose on this issue. [*Laughter*]

THE PRESIDENT. I think all Americans won. Although we don't look on Canada as coming under the purview of the Foreign Relations Committee, Frank—because they are so much a part of our country—would you like to say just a word?

SENATOR CHURCH. Thank you, Mr. President. I think the route that's been chosen is the correct one. It happens that the first leg of that route will be built into my State, which may have some influence. [*Laughter*] But I commend you for another milestone, and I think this bill will serve the country well.

THE PRESIDENT. John?

MR. McMILLIAN. It's my pleasure. This is my project. I want to thank you for choosing it, the confidence you had in us. We're going to uphold that confidence of both yourself and the Congress and do what we said to bring this energy source to you as quickly and reasonably as we can.

THE PRESIDENT. We worked very closely with Jim in preparing this, and I want to thank you for it.

MR. McMILLIAN. Thank you, sir.

REPRESENTATIVE DINGELL. Mr. President, I just look forward to being back with you when you sign the energy bill very shortly. [*Laughter*]

NOTE: The President spoke at 1:45 p.m. at the signing ceremony in the Cabinet Room at the White House. John G. McMillian is chairman of Northwest Pipeline Corp.

As enacted, H.J. Res. 621 is Public Law 95–158, approved November 8.

Alaska Natural Gas Transportation System

Statement on Signing H.J. Res 621 Into Law. November 8, 1977

The energy crisis presents an unprecedented challenge that calls for creative solutions. That is why I take special pride in signing today the joint resolution of the Senate and House of Representatives approving my choice of the Alcan project to carry Alaskan natural gas through Canada to the lower 48 States.

This pipeline project will span almost 5,000 miles across the North American Continent. It will be the largest privately financed energy project ever undertaken. It will deliver an additional 1 trillion cubic feet of reasonably priced natural gas to American markets every year. It will save American consumers $6 billion over what other routes would cost during a 20-year period.

But despite the scope of this project, it is sobering to realize that it will add only 5 percent to the Nation's supply of natural gas. And natural gas itself will account for only 25 percent of our total energy supply. Even with the Alcan project we will continue to be gravely dependent on imported oil to meet our energy needs. Later this evening I will discuss with the Nation in more detail the enormous challenge which lies ahead, and the consequences of our failure to act on a comprehensive national energy program.

I want to compliment the Congress on their swift response to my recommendation in the midst of their consideration of the National Energy Plan. I also want particularly to thank Senator Jackson, the floor leader in the Senate, and chairmen Morris Udall and Harley Staggers in the House, as well as subcommittee chairmen John Dingell and Teno Roncalio for their efforts in securing early approval of the resolution.

I am asking Ambassador Towe to convey to Prime Minister Trudeau the proud sense of partnership we feel today at embarking upon this new joint venture. As the Prime Minister and I observed when our agreement was announced, the two countries working together can transport more energy more efficiently than either working alone. The United States will gain the use of our Alaskan gas reserves at the lowest possible cost, and Canada will benefit through access to its frontier gas reserves and the economic activity of constructing and operating this project.

Ultimately, it will be our willingness to consider solutions like this that may well determine this Nation's ability to survive the threats posed by the energy crisis. I will talk more about that tonight. Alcan is just one step in a long series of steps—represented in part by the National Energy Plan—that we must take. We should be both proud of the progress we mark today and humbled by the task that lies ahead.

NOTE: As enacted, H.J. Res. 621 is Public Law 95–158, approved November 8.

Educational Benefits for Veterans and Dependents

Executive Order 12020.   November 8, 1977

PAYMENT OF EDUCATIONAL BENEFITS TO
VETERANS AND DEPENDENTS WHEN
SCHOOLS ARE TEMPORARILY CLOSED
TO CONSERVE ENERGY

By virtue of the authority vested in me by clause (A) of Section 1780(a) of Title 38 of the United States Code, and as President of the United States of America, in order to establish a national policy in regard to payment of educational benefits to veterans and their dependents during periods in which schools are closed to conserve energy, it is hereby ordered as follows:

SECTION 1. Whenever an educational institution submits evidence which satisfies the Administrator of Veterans' Affairs that energy consumption will be abnormally high during the winter months or that available energy supplies will be inadequate to meet the needs of the school, and that, in the interest of energy conservation, the institution plans to close between semesters or terms for a period not to exceed 45 days, the Administrator may continue to pay monthly educational assistance benefits to veterans and eligible persons enrolled in such schools. Such authority may be exercised only once during any 12-month period with respect to any educational institution.

SEC. 2. The Administrator shall advise veterans and other eligible persons of the effect of accepting educational assistance benefits under the provisions of Section 1 of this Order on their period of entitlement.

JIMMY CARTER

The White House,
    November 8, 1977.

[Filed with the Office of the Federal Register,
    4:20 p.m., November 8, 1977]

NOTE: The Executive order was not issued in the form of a White House press release.

NATIONAL ENERGY PLAN

Address to the Nation.   November 8, 1977

Good evening.

More than 6 months ago, in April, I spoke to you about a need for a national policy to deal with our present and future energy problems, and the next day I sent my proposals to the Congress.

The Congress has recognized the urgency of this problem and has come to grips with some of the most complex and difficult decisions that a legislative body has ever been asked to make.

Working with Congress, we've now formed a new Department of Energy, headed by Secretary James Schlesinger. We have the ability to administer the new energy legislation, and congressional work on the National Energy Plan has now reached the final stage.

Last week the Senate sent its version of the legislation to the conference committees, where Members of the House and Senate will now resolve differences between the bills that they've passed. There, in the next few weeks, the strength and courage of our political system will be proven.

The choices facing the Members of Congress are not easy. For them to pass an effective and fair plan, they will need your support and your understanding—your support to resist pressures from a few for special favors at the expense of the rest of us and your understanding that there can be no effective plan without some sacrifice from all of us.

Tonight, at this crucial time, I want to emphasize why it is so important that we have an energy plan and what we will risk, as a nation, if we are timid or reluctant to face this challenge. It's crucial that you understand how serious this challenge is.

With every passing month, our energy problems have grown worse. This summer we used more oil and gasoline than ever before in our history. More of our oil is coming from foreign countries. Just since April, our oil imports have cost us $23 billion—about $350 worth of foreign oil for the average American family.

A few weeks ago, in Detroit, an unemployed steelworker told me something that may reflect the feelings of many of you. "Mr. President," he said, "I don't feel much like talking about energy and foreign policy. I'm concerned about how I'm going to live. . . . I can't be too concerned about other things when I have a 10-year-old daughter to raise and I don't have a job and I'm 56 years old."

Well, I understand how he felt, but I must tell you the truth. And the truth is that you cannot talk about economic problems now or in the future without talking about energy.

Let me try to describe the size and the effect of the problem. Our farmers are the greatest agricultural exporters the world has ever known, but it now takes all the food and fiber that we export in 2 years just to pay for 1 year of imported oil—about $45 billion.

This excessive importing of foreign oil is a tremendous and rapidly increasing drain on our national economy. It hurts every American family. It causes unemployment. Every $5 billion increase in oil imports costs us 200,000 American jobs. It costs us business investments. Vast amounts of American wealth no longer stay in the United States to build our factories and to give us a better life.

It makes it harder for us to balance our Federal budget and to finance needed programs for our people. It unbalances our Nation's trade with other countries. This year, primarily because of oil, our imports will be at least $25 billion more than all the American goods the we sell overseas.

It pushes up international energy prices because excessive importing of oil by the United States makes it easier for foreign producers to raise their prices. It feeds serious inflationary pressures in our own economy.

If this trend continues, the excessive reliance on foreign oil could make the very security of our Nation increasingly dependent on uncertain energy supplies. Our national security depends on more than just our Armed Forces; it also rests on the strength of our economy, on our national will, and on the ability of the United States to carry out our foreign policy as a free and independent nation. America overseas is only as strong as America at home.

The Secretary of Defense said recently, "The present deficiency of assured energy sources is the single surest threat . . . to our security and to that of our allies."

Yesterday, after careful consideration, I announced the postponement of a major overseas trip until after Christmas because of the paramount importance of developing an effective energy plan this year. I have no doubt that this is the right decision, because the other nations of the world—allies and adversaries alike—await our energy decisions with a great interest and concern.

As one of the world's largest producers of coal and oil and gas, why do we have this problem with energy, and why is it so difficult to solve?

One problem is that the price of all energy is going up, both because of its increasing scarcity and because the price of oil is not set in a free and competitive market. The world price is set by a foreign cartel—the governments of the so-called OPEC nations. That price is now almost five times as great as it was in 1973.

Our biggest problem, however, is that we simply use too much and waste too much energy. Our imports have more than tripled in the last 10 years. Although all countries could, of course, be more efficient, we are the worst offender. Since the great price rise in 1973, the Japanese have cut their oil imports, the Germans, the French, the British, the Italians have all cut their oil imports. Meanwhile, although we have large petroleum supplies of our own and most of them don't, we in the United States have increased our imports more than 40 percent.

This problem has come upon us suddenly. Ten years ago, when foreign oil was cheap, we imported just 2½ million barrels of oil a day, about 20 percent of what we used. By 1972, we were importing about 30 percent. This year, when foreign oil is very expensive, we are importing nearly 9 million barrels a day—almost one-half of all the oil we use.

Unless we act quickly, imports will continue to go up, and all the problems that I've just described will grow even worse.

There are three things that we must do to avoid this danger: first, cut back on consumption; second, shift away from oil and gas to other sources of energy; and third, encourage production of energy here in the United States. These are the purposes of the new energy legislation.

In order to conserve energy, the Congress is now acting to make our automobiles, our homes, and appliances more efficient and to encourage industry to save both heat and electricity.

The congressional conference committees are now considering changes in how electric power rates are set in order to discourage waste, to reward those who use less energy, and to encourage a change in the use of electricity to hours of the day when demand is low.

Another very important question before Congress is how to let the market price for domestic oil go up to reflect the cost of replacing it while, at the same time, protecting the American consumers and our own economy.

We must face an unpleasant fact about energy prices. They are going up, whether we pass an energy program or not, as fuel becomes more scarce and more expensive to produce. The question is, who should benefit from those rising prices for oil already discovered? Our energy plan captures and returns them to the public, where they can stimulate the economy, save more energy, and create new jobs.

We will use research and development projects, tax incentives and penalties, and regulatory authority to hasten the shift from oil and gas to coal, to wind and solar power, to geothermal, methane, and other energy sources.

We've also proposed, and the Congress is reviewing, incentives to encourage production of oil and gas here in our own country. This is where another major controversy arises.

It's important that we promote new oil and gas discoveries and increased production by giving adequate prices to the producers.

We've recommended that the price, for instance, of new natural gas be raised each year to the average price of domestic oil that would produce the same amount of energy. With this new policy, the gross income of gas producers would average about $2 billion each year more than at the present price level. New oil prices would also rise in 3 years to the present world level and then be increased annually to keep up with inflation. This incentive for new oil production would be the highest in the whole world.

These proposals would provide adequate incentives for exploration and production of domestic oil and gas, but some of the oil companies want much more—tens of billions of dollars more. They want greatly increased prices for "old" oil and gas—energy supplies which have already been discovered and which are being produced now. They want immediate and permanent deregulation of gas prices, which would cost consumers $70 billion or more between now and 1985. They want even higher prices than those we've proposed for "new" gas and oil, and they want the higher prices sooner. They want lower taxes on their profits.

These are all controversial questions, and the congressional debates, as you can well imagine, are intense. The political pressures are great because the stakes are so high, billions and billions of dollars. We should reward individuals and companies who discover and produce new oil and gas, but we must not give them huge windfall profits on their existing wells at the expense of the American people.

Now the energy proposal that I made to Congress last April has three basic elements to ensure that it is well balanced. First, it's fair both to the American consumers and to the energy producers, and it will not disrupt our national economy. Second, as I've said before, it's designed to meet our important goals for energy conservation, to promote a shift to more plentiful and permanent energy supplies and encourage increased production of energy in the United States. And third, it protects our Federal budget from any unreasonable burden. These are the three standards by which the final legislation must be judged. I will sign the energy bills only if they meet these tests.

During the next few weeks, the Congress will make a judgment on these vital questions. I will be working closely with them. And you are also deeply involved in these decisions. This is not a contest of strength between the President and the Congress, nor between the House and the Senate. What is being measured is the strength and will of our Nation—whether we can acknowledge a threat and meet a serious challenge together.

I'm convinced that we can have enough energy to permit the continued growth of our economy, to expand production and jobs, and to protect the security of the United States—if we act wisely.

I believe that this country can meet any challenge, but this is an exceptionally difficult one because the threat is not easy to see and the solution is neither simple nor politically popular.

I said 6 months ago that no one would be completely satisfied with this National Energy Plan. Unfortunately, that prediction has turned out to be right. There is some part of this complex legislation to which every region and every interest group can object. But a common national sacrifice to meet this serious problem should be shared by everyone— some proof that the plan is fair. Many groups have risen to the challenge. But, unfortunately, there are still some who seek personal gain over the national interest.

It's also especially difficult to deal with long-range, future challenges. A President is elected for just 4 years, a Senator for 6, and our Representatives in Congress for only 2 years. It's always been easier to wait until the next year or the next term of office, to avoid political risk. But you did not choose your elected officials simply to fill an office. The Congress is facing very difficult decisions, courageously, and we've formed a good partnership. All of us in Government need your help.

This is an effort which requires vision and cooperation from all Americans. I hope that each of you will take steps to conserve our precious energy and also join with your elected officials at all levels of government to meet this test of our Nation's judgment and will.

These are serious problems, and this has been a serious talk. But our energy plan also reflects the optimism that I feel about our ability to deal with these problems. The story of the human race is one of adapting to changing circumstances. The history of our Nation is one of meeting challenges and overcoming them.

This major legislation is a necessary first step on a long and difficult road. This energy plan is a good insurance policy for the future, in which relatively small premiums that we pay today will protect us in the years ahead. But if we fail to act boldly today, then we will surely face a greater series of crises tomorrow—energy shortages, environmental damage, ever more massive Government bureaucracy and regulations, and ill-considered, last-minute crash programs.

I hope that, perhaps a hundred years from now, the change to inexhaustible energy sources will have been made, and our Nation's concern about energy will be over. But we can make that transition smoothly—for our country and for our children and for our grandchildren—only if we take careful steps now to prepare ourselves for the future.

During the next few weeks, attention will be focused on the Congress, but the proving of our courage and commitment will continue, in different forms and places, in the months and the years, even generations ahead.

It's fitting that I'm speaking to you on an election day, a day which reminds us that you, the people, are the rulers of this Nation, that your

Government will be as courageous and effective and fair as you demand that it be.

This will not be the last time that I, as President, present difficult and controversial choices to you and ask for your help. I believe that the duties of this office permit me to do no less. But I'm confident that we can find the wisdom and the courage to make the right decisions—even when they are unpleasant—so that we might, together, preserve the greatness of our Nation.

Thank you very much.

NOTE: The President spoke at 9 p.m. from the Oval Office at the White House. His remarks were broadcast live on radio and television.

Federal Mine Safety and Health Amendments Act of 1977 and Air Cargo Deregulation Bill

Remarks on Signing S. 717 and H.R. 6010 Into Law.   November 9, 1977

THE PRESIDENT. This morning I'll sign two bills of great importance to our country. I think every American knows that a major contributing factor to our own economy is the courageous and sometimes endangered miners who go deep beneath the earth to bring to the surface, for our use, coal and other minerals.

This morning I will be signing a mine safety bill which goes far forward in protecting not only the miners in the coal fields of our country but also previously uncovered miners in the areas that produce minerals other than coal.

This sometimes is not highly publicized, but last year, 1976, we had 113 miners who were killed and more than 7,000 who were disabled in mines other than coal mines. This bill extends the same safety and health standards to those mines as has been the case with coal. In addition, in the past, the enforcement of the existing coal mining regulations has not been rapidly assured.

We all remember the tragedy in the Scotia mine, where repeated findings of ventilation faults, I think 63 or 64 of them, were uncorrected. And then we had a major tragedy in that mine. This bill permits a more rapid enforcement of the coal mining safety and health standards when defects are found.

The other very important aspect of this bill is that it transfers the enforcement of the mine safety and health acts to the Labor Department. These were formerly in the Interior Department. Ray Marshall is here, the Secretary of Labor, and I believe that there's a general recognition among the miners of our Nation and among the administration officials, including the Secretary of Interior, that this will mean a much closer relationship between the enforcement of this law by the Federal Government agency and those who live with their lives constantly in danger.

It's with a great deal of pleasure that I sign this legislation. I would particularly like to congratulate Carl Perkins, a Congressman who's been instrumental in this field for many, many years; Pete Williams, who can't be here. He's in New Jersey. New Jersey is almost covered with water. He felt that he ought to be with his own people today. And I particularly thank Senator Jennings Randolph for coming here today. His wife had an operation yesterday, and I'm very thankful that he's reported she came through in good condition.

This is a good step forward, and I'm very glad now to sign into law Senate bill 717, a new mine safety bill.

[At this point, the President signed S. 717 into law.]

Now, to change the subject to one that will be of growing importance during the next 3 years and, I hope, without delay. This is a bill which was originated in the House, bill number 6010, which deregulates air cargo. I hope this is just the first of many steps to get the Government out of the regulatory business, which quite often works contrary to the interests of consumers.

This bill will, at the moment it's signed, permit airlines, small and large, who haul exclusively cargo, to operate without constraint and let the workings of the market determine whether or not they enter this competitive field.

If an airline is reliable and properly and safely operated, it can begin to compete. This is a major step forward, and I hope that without delay this same general principle can be applied to the carrying of passengers.

This bill also helps with the first steps toward deregulation of passenger carrying. It permits the interrelationship between intrastate airlines and interstate airlines, where passengers can now, with a single transaction, change from one to another. Intrastate airlines, in carrying passengers, as you know, are not regulated by the Federal Government.

This also permits lower fares, if the airlines desire to use this authority for elderly people and for those who are handicapped, on a seat-available basis. And I'm sure that some airlines will now begin to offer this extra service to those who need special care in air transportation.

We have great work to do in this field. And I'm particularly grateful that Senator Cannon and the Senate committee have already reported out the air passenger deregulation bill. This is going to be a controversial measure, and I hope that the House will soon follow suit and that both Houses of Congress will move to approve this legislation.

I'm particularly grateful to Congressman Glenn Anderson and to Howard Cannon, the Senator, for this good work on air cargo deregulation and hope it is just a preview of what's going to come with the deregulation of other transportation industries.

Thank you very much, gentlemen.

[At this point, the President signed H.R. 6010 into law.]

Well, I'm very proud of all of you. These are two good bills, and you've done very good work. I know part of it is quite controversial, and I think now you've got a big responsibility on your hands.

SENATOR RANDOLPH. And it will speed up the processing of the cases that are backed up.

THE PRESIDENT. I know. I hope you'll all make sure that Ray does a good job now. *[Laughter]*

We're very hopeful that we can have a new stimulation of coal production industries.

Good luck to all of you. Thank you.

SENATOR RANDOLPH. That last bill, Mr. President, the aid to the handicapped in travel, is very important.

THE PRESIDENT. I know. I hope some airlines will immediately do that.

SENATOR RANDOLPH. They will. Thank you.

NOTE: The President spoke at 9:03 a.m. at the signing ceremony in the Roosevelt Room at the White House.

As enacted, S. 717 is Public Law 95–164, and H.R. 6010 is Public Law 95–163, approved November 9.

Federal Mine Safety and Health Amendments Act of 1977

Statement on Signing S. 717 Into Law. November 9, 1977

Mining has long been recognized as an exceptionally hazardous and demanding occupation. To a large degree, this Nation's economy has been built on the labors of its miners. Their health, safety, and welfare are matters of paramount concern, particularly as we expand production of coal and other needed minerals.

I am exceptionally pleased today to sign S. 717, the Federal Mine Safety and Health Amendments Act of 1977. For the first time, all the Nation's miners will be protected under one comprehensive mine safety and health law. Building on experience gained under previous mine safety and health laws, the bill makes needed improvements which strengthen the protections which should rightly be afforded the Nation's miners and provides that the Secretary of Labor is to administer this new law.

I would note with pleasure that this is a bill which represents the close cooperation of the administration with both Houses of Congress. I particularly want to recognize the efforts of Senator Wil-

liams and Congressman Perkins in passing this legislation.

I would note with pleasure that this is a bill which represents the close cooperation of the administration with both Houses of Congress. I particularly want to recognize the efforts of Senator Williams and Congressman Perkins in passing this legislation.

I would also note that the new law, which transfers responsibilities for mine safety and health programs from the Department of the Interior to the Department of Labor, is a significant contribution to our efforts to reorganize the Federal Government to perform more efficiently and effectively.

This administration will be sensitive to the economic impacts of this legislation to ensure that the mining industry stays productive and efficient while, at the same time, the lives and health of the Nation's miners are protected.

I look forward to working together with miners, their representatives, and with the operators of the Nation's mines to implement this vital legislation.

NOTE: As enacted, S. 717 is Public Law 95–164, approved November 9.

Visit of Prime Minister Robert D. Muldoon of New Zealand

Remarks of the President and the Prime Minister at the Welcoming Ceremony. November 9, 1977

THE PRESIDENT. This morning, I want to welcome to our country Prime Minister Muldoon and his wife, Thea, who have come here from New Zealand, a nation which has, for the last 125 years, had strong diplomatic ties to the United States. As we know, many generations before that, American merchant seamen and whaling ships were received with open arms by the people of New Zealand as they visited those ports of call.

Prime Minister Muldoon is a strong and able leader. He comes here to express the common bonds that bind his country with our own. We have a very strong alliance between Australia, New Zealand, and the United States. And this has been the basis for a firm foundation of economic and political and military comradeship, which has sustained us in times of testing and times of trial and times of danger.

New Zealanders have fought shoulder to shoulder with American fighting men in World War I and World War II, in the Korean war, and in Vietnam. And this is a country which is in a strategic part of the world and, in addition to their military alliances, have worked closely with us for the economic development of the southern Pacific region.

It's very important that we understand the trade benefits that come to both our countries by this close and friendly relationship, consultation on economic matters, and planning for the future. We are very pleased that this relationship does exist.

Prime Minister Muldoon is a man who has a particular interest in the economic well-being of his own people. He has, since he has been in office, reduced the adverse balance of trade in New Zealand much more than 50 percent. The unemployment rate in New Zealand is only 1 percent, which shows what a good leader he is and also shows the commitment of the New Zealand people to hard and honest work for the benefit of one another.

We had one of our nuclear cruisers go into New Zealand recently, a port in Wellington. The New Zealand people, on their own initiative, had a program called Dial-A-Sailor. The private families in that

capital city were encouraged to invite American seamen to come to their homes for a visit, and every sailor on that ship received between five and eight invitations to visit homes in Wellington. I'm very proud that this kind of natural friendship exists, not only at the governmental level but also between the people of our countries.

Prime Minister Muldoon has shown a great interest in my own administration since the first weeks, and I look forward to working with him during this day to make sure that we recommit ourselves to the principle that peace and cooperation and security are indivisible.

Mr. Prime Minister, I, on behalf of the 215 million Americans, welcome you as a friend to our country. Thank you, sir.

THE PRIME MINISTER. *Mr. President, Your Excellencies, and ladies and gentlemen:*

Thank you, sir, for the warmth of your welcome and for your very kind words about my country.

The ties that draw together New Zealand and the United States are of long standing. Americans, as you've said, were amongst the earlier visitors to our shores. Indeed, in 1840, when the British Government formally claimed sovereignty over New Zealand by the Treaty of Watangi, there were probably more American whalers in the country than there were British residents.

We, like you, are part of the New World. We, like you, were settled by men and women who came to find a new life in a new land. We were Britain's frontier as you were Europe's. Those who made our two countries, Mr. President, shared similar hopes and aspirations. Their experience developed in them a respect for self-reliance and individual enterprise and a healthy distaste for class privilege, affectation, and pretension. In New Zealand, as in the United States, a man was judged by what he was and did, not by his country of origin, his wealth, or his family background. That remains true today for both of us.

New Zealanders and Americans, then, are very much the same sort of people. The taproots of our relationship are bedded deep in our common experience, and they continue to nourish the growth of its various branches.

In two World Wars New Zealanders and Americans fought side by side and died side by side to preserve the individual freedoms and democratic ideals to which we are committed. From the second of those great conflicts, we both learned that distance offered little defense and that even the vast reaches of the Pacific Ocean were no barrier to a resourceful and determined enemy. That experience led to the establishment of the ANZUS Treaty, the collective defense arrangement that draws us together with Australia in a common commitment to help keep free from threat the region of which all of us are a part and the environment in which our three peoples live and trade and travel.

The preservation of peace, Mr. President, demands more of us than that we should be prepared for war. Legitimate aspirations too long denied can be as real a threat to security and stability as the rattling saber or the sounding bugle.

Together, we are playing our part in the Pacific and elsewhere to help those who want to help themselves attain for their people the chance to live decent, satisfying, and useful lives. Life, liberty, and the pursuit of happiness are words, Mr. President, over the meaning of which philosophers may squabble. But to those of common sense—our ordinary bloke, your honest Joe—their meaning is plain.

Like the United States, New Zealand not only believes in democracy but practices it. There are all too few in the world who do. But that's no reason why we should not be prepared to stand up and be counted, and, indeed, it's the very reason why we should.

New Zealand and the United States, Mr. President, are two countries that have long heard the beat of the same drummer. I have every confidence that over the coming years we shall continue to step out together along the same path.

NOTE: The President spoke at 10:55 a.m. on the South Lawn of the White House.

Visit of Prime Minister Muldoon of New Zealand

Joint Statement Issued Following the Meetings Between the President and the Prime Minister. November 9, 1977

At the invitation of President Carter, the Prime Minister of New Zealand, Rt. Hon. R. D. Muldoon, is paying an official visit to Washington DC, November 9–10, 1977. The President held discussions with the Prime Minister on 9 November, followed by a luncheon at the White House. The talks between the two leaders covered a wide range of political, security, economic and other subjects of common concern.

The President and Prime Minister Muldoon reviewed bilateral relations between the two countries. They agreed that these were exceptionally warm and close, and securely based on a common commitment to human rights, democracy and the rule of law. They agreed that cooperation in traditional fields including foreign policy, trade and defense should be sustained, and welcomed the recent growth of cooperation in energy and other scientific and technical subjects.

In their discussions on international affairs the President and the Prime Minister paid special attention to Asian and South Pacific affairs. President Carter reiterated the intention of the United

States to remain actively involved in Asian and Pacific affairs, and in particular, reaffirmed the strength of the United States' ties to New Zealand and its commitment to the ANZUS treaty.

The Prime Minister outlined recent changes in the South Pacific, including the rapid movement of many island groups to political independence and the progress towards regional cooperation represented by the South Pacific Forum. He emphasized the importance of the imminent declaration of maritime economic zones, and of the optimum development of the fish resoucres contained within them. The President and the Prime Minister confirmed the continuing importance of efforts to promote the well-being of the peoples of the South Pacific.

The President and the Prime Minister agreed that the two countries should sustain their close consultation on all these matters.

The President and the Prime Minister also exchanged views on other international subjects such as Southern Africa, the Middle East situation, the Antarctic, arms control and disarmament, and the Panama Canal treaties. The Prime Minister welcomed the initiatives that the President was taking to achieve solutions of these important issues.

The President and the Prime Minister discussed economic and trade issues in depth. They noted the serious problem raised by the balance of payments deficit of the non-oil producing developing countries and the primary producers. They agreed on the need for the major industrialized countries to continue their efforts to stimulate world economic recovery. The two leaders particularly stressed the need to expand world markets and improve trading opportunities for agricultural products. They agreed to continue their efforts to achieve this aim, especially at the present time in the context of the current multilateral trade negotiations.

The President and the Prime Minister agreed, within the context of the ANZUS treaty, that the economic health of each of the two partners was important to the other, especially as it affected the positive role each desired to play in their common endeavors to contribute to the welfare of the peoples of the Pacific and Asia and to the stability of the area.

Attending the meeting in the Cabinet room were:

American side:

The President

The Vice President

Secretary of State Cyrus Vance

Zbigniew Brzezinski—Assistant to the President for National Security Affairs

Richard Holbrooke—Assistant Secretary of State

Armistead I. Selden Jr.—Ambassador to New Zealand

Michael Armacost—National Security Council

New Zealand side:

The Prime Minister

Mr. F. H. Corner—Secretary of Foreign Affairs

Mr. W. N. Plummer—Head of the Australian and Americas Division, Ministry of Foreign Affairs

Mr. B. V. Galvin—Permanent Head of Prime Minister's Department

Ambassador Lloyd White—Ambassador to the United States

National Family Week, 1977
Proclamation 4536. November 9, 1977

By the President of the United States of America

A Proclamation

Patterns of living and working have changed during our two centuries as a Nation, and the American family has changed with them. Participation in family life is more and more a personal choice, less and less an economic and social necessity.

But even as customs have changed and many of the traditional sanctions have lost their force, the overwhelming majority of Americans have still chosen the rewards of family life. It is within the family that we first learn to communicate with other people, to give and receive love and understanding, to work together for common goals, and to respect the rights, needs and talents of others. The family teaches us responsibility and compassion, it encourages our best efforts, and it forgives our failures. It fills many of the gaps left by other institutions in our society. As a Nation we must strengthen and support the values of family life for they are inseparable from our finest national traits.

In honoring the family it is especially appropriate to acknowledge those Americans who, through adoption, open their homes and hearts to wanted children. They bring a special commitment to the family and share a special reward in nurturing their children and seeing them grow in love.

Now, THEREFORE, I, JIMMY CARTER, President of the United States of America, in accordance with a joint resolution of the Congress, approved August 15, 1977 (91 Stat. 836) do hereby proclaim the week of November 20, 1977, as National Family Week and call upon the American people to observe that week with appropriate ceremonies, programs and activities.

IN WITNESS WHEREOF, I have hereunto set my hand this ninth day of November in the year of our Lord nineteen hundred seventy-seven and of the Independence of the United States of America the two hundred and second.

JIMMY CARTER

[Filed with the Office of the Federal Register, 4:50 p.m., November 9, 1977]

Veto of Bill Providing for Mandatory Inspection of Rabbit Meat

Message to the House of Representatives Returning H.R. 2521 Without Approval. November 9, 1977

To the House of Representatives:

I am returning, without my approval, H.R. 2521, an Act "To provide for the mandatory inspection of domesticated rabbits slaughtered for human food and for other purposes."

This Act would establish a new mandatory federal inspection program for domesticated rabbits and rabbit products processed for human consumption. The program would be similar to that already applicable to poultry products, and would apply to imported rabbit meat as well as rabbit meat processed in the United States.

In my view, the costs to the general taxpayer associated with H.R. 2521 cannot be justified on several grounds:

—A voluntary inspection program operated by the Department of Agriculture, but paid for by the processors of rabbit meat, is already available to processors wishing to enjoy the marketing benefits of federal wholesomeness certification and grading. Moreover, rabbit meat marketed in the United States (including imports) is subject to inspection by the Food and Drug Administration to ensure sanitation and wholesomeness. Neither the Agriculture Department nor the Food and Drug Administration has been able to substantiate a significant health problem with rabbit meat in this country.

—Existing federal inspection programs are intended to apply to meats consumed

1993

by large numbers of Americans. Rabbit is essentially a specialty food purchased by a relatively small number of consumers. I believe that it would be inequitable to require all taxpayers to support extension of federal inspection of specialty meats to include rabbits. While the initial federal cost is small, once in the law, the subsidy may grow increasingly over the years. Moreover, signing this bill would provide an incentive for federal payments for the inspection of other exotic or specialty foods.

—Requirements for on-site inspection of foreign processing facilities by Department of Agriculture employees would strain relations with the People's Republic of China, a major exporter of domesticated rabbit meat to the United States. Extensive Food and Drug Administration inspection of Chinese imports have uncovered no health problems.

The primary beneficiaries of this special interest legislation would be a few large processors of rabbit meat which would no longer be required to reimburse the Federal Government for inspection services required to market their product as USDA inspected and graded. A significant source of competition from the People's Republic of China also would be severely restricted or eliminated with little or no improvement in consumer health protection.

Accordingly, I do not believe that approval of H.R. 2521 would be in the best interest of the American people.

JIMMY CARTER

The White House,
    November 9, 1977.

NOTE: The text of the message was released on November 10.

The House of Representatives reconsidered H.R. 2521 on November 29, and the bill was referred to committee.

THE PRESIDENT'S NEWS CONFERENCE OF NOVEMBER 10, 1977

THE PRESIDENT. Mr. Pippert [Wes Pippert, United Press International].

UNEMPLOYMENT

Q. Mr. President, you said a lot last year about a lot of people out of work, yet unemployment persists at around 7 percent. It's twice as high among blacks, and yesterday, the head of the Black Caucus said that your programs, in his words, "have not even begun to dent the unemployment that wracks our communities." Why has the administration been unable to dent unemployment, and what are you going to do about it?

THE PRESIDENT. There's no easy answer, of course, to the unemployment question. Last December the unemployment rate was, I think, 8.1 percent. It came down in April or May to about 7 percent, and it has leveled off at that figure. We had an economic stimulus package with a heavy emphasis on jobs and tax reductions, amounting to about $21 billion, which is now beginning to be felt, I hope.

Last quarter, about $3 billion of that program was in effect. By the end of this quarter, $18 billion will be in effect and, in the first quarter of next year, the full amount. We believe that this will have a beneficial impact on unemployment rates, but it certainly won't solve the problem. We will by next June, for instance, have 725,000 jobs under the comprehensive education and training program. This is the highest level for jobs of this category supported directly by the Federal Government since the New Deal days under Roosevelt.

But it's a tedious, slow process. I think the general, worldwide economic slowdown is causing this problem to be felt in all nations. We hope, though, that it will come down next year as it began to come down this year.

Q. Could I follow?

THE PRESIDENT. Please.

Q. Will you accept a Humphrey-Hawkins full employment bill that sets a goal of 4 percent unemployment within 5 years?

THE PRESIDENT. We've been working very closely with the congressional leaders, including my personal conversations with Congressman Hawkins and Senator Humphrey. The Humphrey-Hawkins bill is a concept that I endorse and support. This bill has been constantly modified since it was introduced several years ago, as you know.

We expect to have an announcement about the administration's position on Humphrey-Hawkins within the next few days. There are some important aspects of the bill that have been modified recently. One is to inject into the bill's concepts a strong anti-inflation commitment in addition to the anti-unemployment commitment. Also, from the bill have been removed the direct authorizations for programs that might have been very costly. They would have to be considered step by step by the Congress as required.

Another thing that has been added to the recent version of the bill is some flexibility to accommodate changing times in the future. My belief is that these specific modifications by the authors of the bill and their staffs, working with my staff, can be realized. And my expectation is that we will have a successful conclusion of these negotiations and then that the bill will be presented to the Congress with my endorsement.

NATIONAL HEALTH INSURANCE

Q. Mr. President, you had a meeting yesterday on national health insurance.

And I know that you don't have a program to present at this time, but can you give us some clue as to your thinking of where you are going with national health insurance, and have you got any kind of timetable in mind?

THE PRESIDENT. It's too early yet to lay down specifics on a national health insurance program. This was a concept that was endorsed by all the candidates for President last year, and it's a need in our country that this entire health care system be improved. One of them is to cut down the exorbitant increases in national health care, particularly hospital costs.

We've already initiated a major effort on a hospital cost containment bill. These costs have been doubling every 5 years, which makes it almost impossible to give better health care because the costs have gone up so rapidly there.

Also, there are many facets of national health care in addition to just health insurance. Physical fitness is obviously one; air and water pollution problems, prevention of disease, expansion of the medical personnel that can give health care. And we've just signed a bill that provides for so-called physician extenders to let registered nurses and others do more of the work in health care.

I would say, since this was just an exploratory talk, and my first one, yesterday, with my top staff members and Cabinet members, that it's too early to lay down a schedule. But we'll be working on this now with increasing commitment, and I think by early next year, the principles of the national health program will be outlined to the American people.

RICHARD HELMS

Q. Mr. President, Mr. Helms' attorney says that his client will wear his conviction on charges of failing to testify fully before Congress as a badge of honor. Do you think it's a badge of honor, and do you think a public official has a right to lie in public about his business under any circumstances?

THE PRESIDENT. No, it is not a badge of honor, and a public official does not have a right to lie.

The Helms case is one that we inherited. I've never met Mr. Helms. I don't believe the Attorney General has ever met Mr. Helms.

This is a serious problem that evolved in years past. We had three major facets of this question: One is to uphold the law; the second was to uphold the veracity requirement, the truthfulness requirement of those who testify before Congress; and the third one was to make the best judgment we could on how to protect the security of our Nation.

I think the decision that was made by the Attorney General, confirmed by the courts, was the right decision and the best decision. It does fulfill all three of those requirements. It does not condone lying, it does uphold the law, and I think it did protect, as best we could, the security of our country.

THE MIDDLE EAST

Q. Mr. President, it's our understanding that some of your top national security advisers met yesterday in the White House Situation Room to sort of reassess the situation in the Middle East in light of the recent trouble on the Lebanon border. Can you give us some assessment this morning, especially what effect this might have on the Middle East peace conference later this year?

THE PRESIDENT. This new outburst of violence is a great concern to us and, I think, to the nations in the Middle East, to all people of the world. The unwarranted and continuing terrorist attacks have been part of the Middle East picture for years. The retaliatory measures taken by nations who were attacked by terror-

ists has been a part of the picture in the Middle East for years. I think it shows the volatile nature there of the continuing problems.

I think it shows in a much more vivid way than perhaps in the past, recent past, the need for an immediate convening of the Geneva conference as soon as we can get these national leaders to sit down, or their representatives to sit down on a continuing basis and work out face to face these divisions that have existed in the Middle East for generations.

Loss of life is deplorable. But the situation is never going to be improved, in my opinion, until those nations there are willing to step beyond the procedural debates and squabbles about exactly how to go and exactly what representation will be present and start dealing with the real issues. I've been pleased that the Israeli Government has adopted the procedures for the Geneva conference that we've proposed. I was pleased with the statement yesterday by President Sadat that he was willing to go to Geneva or anywhere else and begin to consult directly with Israel and with the other Arab nations without quibbling any more about the detailed wording of the procedures. That's our position.

I hope that Jordan and Syria and Lebanon very quickly will make a similar response to us, and that we can then convene the Geneva conference. But the major all-encompassing question in the Middle East is that the bloodshed, in my opinion, will not be stopped until the nations are willing to negotiate on the basic divisions that have separated them so long.

Q. Well, do you think the Israeli attack was justified—the retaliation?

THE PRESIDENT. Well, I think this is a question that's hard for me to answer—whether Israel can sit dormant and quiescent and accept repeated attacks on their border villages without retaliation, whether the retaliation was excessive. Those are questions that I think both answers would be, perhaps, yes. There ought not to be any attacks. If there are continued attacks, some retaliation is required.

I don't know the details of it, but I think the overriding consideration is not to condemn Israel at this point for retaliation, but just to say that if the provocations were absent that the retaliation would have been unnecessary. And the best way to resolve it is for Lebanon, Syria, and Israel, relating to that region of the Mideast, for Jordan and Egypt and Israel to start direct negotiations. The whole thing is just sitting and teetering on another outbreak of even more major violence. And I think that at this time, a condemnation of people is probably inappropriate, but an urge for all nations now to stop this present, recent outbreak and to move toward major consultations is the only answer that I can give.

DAM SAFETY INSPECTIONS

Q. Mr. President, I'm asking you, sir, about the question of safety of the 50,000 dams in the United States. It's 5 years since Congress authorized an inspection program, but money has never been put up for it. Last weekend, Mrs. Carter went down to Florida [Georgia] to inspect the latest disaster and, presumably, reported back to you, and presumably you have some ideas on what to do next about it. Could you tell us, sir?

THE PRESIDENT. Yes. Again, this has been, as you know, a historic question in that it lasts from one year to another, from one decade to another, even generations.

There are now about 50,000 dams in this country that need to be inspected without delay. We've allocated $15 million to the Corps of Engineers to commence this examination procedure.

The priorities for inspection of dams will be established depending upon the number of people who are endangered by these potentially unsafe dams. Only about 2,000, I believe, out of the 50,000 are Federal dams. The rest of them are privately owned or, in some instances, owned by the State or local governments—water reservoirs and so forth.

This is a project that requires a broad range of participation. State governments and local governments ought to participate as well. And private owners of dams ought to reassess both the need for the reservoir to continue in existence, or filled with water, or the repair or examination of the dam by letting the water down, or by other means.

I think that these tragedies that occur restimulate interest which has, in the past, died down after a few weeks. I don't intend to let this interest die down. The tragedy in Toccoa, Georgia, was one that was very narrowly defined. This was a small, privately owned dam just above a 200-foot waterfall. Below that waterfall was a very small college, and 37 people have been found dead; 2 more are missing.

We acted immediately there. We've got even more extensive flooding with a number of people's lives being lost in North Carolina. But I intend to pursue this dam safety inspection now without surcease. It will not be postponed any further.

ABORTION

Q. Mr. President, with the Senate and House conferees deadlocked over federally funded abortions, a young woman in Texas recently was unable to obtain an abortion, went across the border into Mexico, obtained a cheap, botched-up operation, and died.

My question is, sir, does this prompt you to any second thoughts about your recent comments that life is unfair when you compare the plight of these poor women with people in better economic circumstances who can pay this relatively small cost for a safe, legal abortion?

THE PRESIDENT. My stand on Federal financing of abortions has not changed. But, obviously, I deplore any sickness or loss of life. I deplore unwanted pregnancies, and we are trying to take other means to make sure that abortions are not necessary. But I'm not in favor, as I've said before, of Federal financing for abortions.

RICHARD HELMS

Q. Mr. President, I'd like to go back to the Helms case for just a moment. In light of the July 25 meeting at the White House that involved you and the Attorney General and others in which you fully discussed the Helms case, I wonder, sir, if you could give us the reasons for your statement on September 29 that you had not consulted with the Attorney General about the Helms case? And the second part of my question is, was one consideration to avoid a public trial at all costs to keep the secret secret?

THE PRESIDENT. The September 25 (The President meant July 25)[1] meeting was not, in the first place, a thorough discussion of the Helms case. It was a brief meeting at which the Helms case was outlined with no secret material discussed, no documents examined, no mention made of people or others who might be involved if the trial did go to conclusion.

There was a general discussion there, fairly brief. Our hope at that time, expressed by the Attorney General, by me, the Vice President, I think by the National Security Advisor, was that a negotiated settlement might be reached. Then, we did not think that was a likely prospect.

_____
[1] Printed in the White House Press Office transcript.

The second question that arose was, if we have to go to trial because of an indictment, should it be concluded aggressively or would the question of national security revelations have to be faced? And we postponed that decision with the understanding that if that prospect did present itself to me, that I would then be briefed on the consequences of those prospects. That never did occur.

The question that was raised in September was based on a statement by Admiral Turner, who heads up the CIA, the national intelligence community, that we were faced with a prospect of two alternatives: One was a decision not to prosecute at all, and the other alternative that Admiral Turner mentioned, which was in the reporter's question, that the complete trial would be held with the revelation of national security secrets. I replied that the Attorney General had never presented that information to me, which was true.

The only other contact that I had after September 25 (The President meant July 25)[1] with the Attorney General on this subject at all was that one day in passing, I think after a Cabinet meeting, he pointed out that there was an inclination on the part of Mr. Helms' attorney to act in a proper way, or patriotic way. But I have never been given any briefings about secret documents that might be revealed, nor people to be involved, because fortunately we did not have to face that prospect.

MONEY SUPPLY AND INFLATION

Q. Mr. President, Chairman of the Federal Reserve Board Arthur Burns said he is going to have to continue to restrain the growth in money supply in order to control inflation, which, of course, is your goal also. But this can drive up interest rates. And I wonder what threat you see from this to the business expansion, which is needed to reduce unemployment.

THE PRESIDENT. Well, you always have that inherent conflict, which is one that was pointed out earlier about the unemployment rate in the Humphrey-Hawkins bill. On the one hand, economic stimulation leads to rapid growth, more employment, at least on a temporary basis; and on the other hand, you have the high inflationary pressures develop when you have an excessive supply of money, an excessive stimulation of the economy.

I strongly support the autonomy and independence of the Federal Reserve. We have had a 2-percent increase in interest rates this year because of action taken by the Federal Reserve. But there's a fairly good balance now, in my opinion, between the Federal Reserve on the one hand, controlling the supply of money in the marketplace to some degree; the Congress, which has direct authority to act, which indirectly controls the supply of money by changes in the tax laws, rebates, and so forth; and the President, of course, participates with the Congress in establishing budget levels, the rapidity with which programs are carried out once the money is authorized by Congress, and so forth. I wouldn't want to change that basic structure. I think it's good.

I might say that the press reports of disharmonies or arguments or a lack of friendship or cooperation between me and Chairman Burns are completely erroneous. We have meetings regularly. We discuss the economic issues openly and freely. The Director of the Office of Management and Budget, the Secretary of Treasury, the Vice President attend those meetings.

Coincidentally, today is one of those monthly meetings when I'll be with Mr. Burns. We've never had any disagreements on those subjects. So, I don't think that I have any inclination to criticize the actions that have been taken by Mr. Burns.

NATIONAL ENERGY PLAN

Q. Mr. President, you canceled your trip overseas in order to be here for the last stages of the fight over your energy bill. You gave a speech on television the other night. What else do you personally intend to be doing, during this period when you would have been traveling, to bring about a result that's acceptable to you?

THE PRESIDENT. I don't know of anything that's more important for me to do as President, other than defending our Nation and guaranteeing its security, than to have the Congress conclude their long year's work with a successful result, spelling out legislation and an energy policy for our Nation to help resolve a serious problem.

Energy waste threatens our country's economy, jobs, inflation. Energy waste threatens our Nation's own security, makes us overly dependent on foreign imports, which might be interrupted at any time. And I think that the best thing I can do the rest of this year is to work closely with the Congress, individually with Members of the Congress, with the conferees who are now engaged in very productive work. And I canceled the trip reluctantly, but with the additional realization that our relationship with the countries that I would have visited will be much better in the future if the United States takes this belated action to provide a workable energy policy.

The Congress is making, I think, good progress. There are five major elements of the energy package, five separate bills that will come to my desk eventually. They have almost completed work on two of them; the others are highly controversial. Perhaps the most wide disparity between the House and Senate is on taxation itself. They are dealing with one that's of crucial importance to consumers, and that is electric rate structures, to eliminate the great advantage that has been going, in the past, to those that waste electricity.

So, I think the Congress is making good progress. But I don't think there's any doubt—I know there's no doubt in my mind that I did the right thing to stay here while the Congress is in its crucial weeks of the conferees' work.

Q. Mr. President, do you expect to meet with members of the House-Senate conference committee personally during their deliberations?

THE PRESIDENT. Yes, sir.

Q. Have you done so this week, and will you be doing so in the immediate future?

THE PRESIDENT. Yes. As a matter of fact, tomorrow I have another meeting scheduled with the House chairman, Congressman Staggers. I have met with him previously and with Senator Long. Senator Jackson and I had a long meeting Sunday afternoon, and I've met with Senator Byrd Saturday afternoon for a couple of hours. I meet with the House and Senate leadership weekly at a breakfast.

In the past, I've called in the entire subcommittees that relate to particular aspects of the energy package. I consider this to be my overriding responsibility at this time. And between now and the time that the conferees conclude their work and the House and Senate vote on the conference reports, I'll put this as a top priority for myself.

EMPLOYMENT

Q. Mr. President, do you share the philosophy of those who say that every American has a right to a job? Does that influence you in your decision on Humphrey-Hawkins?

THE PRESIDENT. Yes, it does. We also, I think, have proposed to the Congress a move in that direction in the Program for Better Jobs and Income, the welfare reform proposals.

Included within that proposal is an additional 1.2 million jobs, most of which would be in the private sector. This is above and beyond the programs that we've already initiated this year. We have a heavy emphasis in almost everything we do to cut down unemployment in our country. It's multi-faceted in nature. And I believe that every person in our country that's able to work ought to have an opportunity for a job.

IRBY TURNER, JR.

Q. Are you aware, Mr. President, that one of your nominees, your most recent nominee to the Corporation for Public Broadcasting, was a very active member of the White Citizens Council in Mississippi and worked very hard to keep schools from being integrated down there? If that is true, would that make any difference to you in making that nomination?

THE PRESIDENT. No, I was not aware of it, and I'd have to know more about the circumstances before I would consider withdrawing a nomination.

There have been in the past, in the South and in other places, alignments with white citizens council groups and groups even more radical in nature.

I always think it's good to give people a chance to change if they will. But I have not known about that allegation, but I'll look into it.

TAX REFORM

Q. Mr. President, now that you've given yourself more time on tax reform, are you rethinking or changing your mind on any of the reforms that are most unsettling to business, specifically the capital gains, special treatment, and the three-martini expense account lunch? [*Laughter*]

THE PRESIDENT. We will continue to assess all aspects of tax reform, including the three-martini business lunch, which might be of special interest to this group. [*Laughter*]

I'm not sure about that, but I think that this is a time for us now to assimilate the action that Congress has taken and is taking on social security, which has major tax impact, and on the energy package, which also has a major impact on our tax structure.

Following that decision or those decisions by Congress, we will combine what we know then with what we know about our national economy prospects, give us another month or so to assess the changes, and then I'll make decisions on specific component parts of the tax reform package. But I've not added in, nor excluded yet, any component individual portions.

UNSPENT APPROPRIATIONS

Q. Mr. President, it is now clear, sir, that the executive branch has failed to spend billions of dollars appropriated by Congress over the last few months. Do you know the size of that shortfall and what effect it has had on the economy, specifically jobs?

THE PRESIDENT. I believe that we're up to date in expending money for jobs. Both Secretary Kreps with Commerce and Secretary Marshall, the head of the Labor Department, have reported to me no later than last Friday that in the local public works program and the jobs program under Labor, that they are at least current or ahead of schedule.

There has been, however, this past fiscal year, a so-called shortfall, in that several billions of dollars, approximately 10 billions of dollars that had been appropriated by Congress, were not spent. Some of that, I think a substantial portion of it, was in the Defense Department, and this has been the case in many years in the past.

We are trying now to put a much more accurate means in effect of assessing how much money we spend each month, compared to what the Congress has authorized and what we want to spend, so that we won't have this major shortfall in the past.

It does have two component effects. One is it saves money for the taxpayers, but the other one is it quite often tends to put a dampening effect on the economy by extracting money that would have been added to stimulate. And also, of course, in cases where programs that are needed are delayed, that creates a problem for those who might receive the benefits. But I don't believe there's any evidence that this has been done in the case of jobs. We've been very insistent that the programs designed to stimulate our economy this year and to give our people jobs stay on schedule.

FRANK CORMIER [Associated Press]. Thank you, Mr. President.

THE PRESIDENT. Thank you, sir.

NOTE: President Carter's nineteenth news conference began at 10:30 a.m. in Room 450 of the Old Executive Office Building. It was broadcast live on radio and television.

National Bureau of Standards

Nomination of Ernest Ambler To Be Director. November 10, 1977

The President today announced that he will nominate Ernest Ambler, of Bethesda, Md., to be Director of the National

Bureau of Standards. He would replace Richard W. Roberts, resigned.

Ambler was born November 20, 1923, in Yorkshire, England. He became a U.S. citizen in 1958. He received B.A., M.A., and Ph. D. degrees from Oxford University.

Ambler has worked for the National Bureau of Standards since 1953. In 1961 he became Chief of the Cryogenics Section; in 1965 he was appointed Chief of the Inorganic Materials Division; and in 1968 he became Director of the Institute for Basic Standards, where he was responsible for directing the development and maintenance of standards and measurement techniques for such quantities as length, mass, time and frequency, and temperature, and advancing the state of the art in measurement science. In 1973 he was appointed Deputy Director of the National Bureau of Standards, and he has been serving as Acting Director since 1975.

Ambler is the recipient of numerous awards, honors, and fellowships. He is a fellow of the American Physical Society and a member of the Washington Academy of Sciences.

National Science Foundation

Nomination of Joseph M. Pettit To Be a Member of the National Science Board. November 10, 1977

The President today announced that he will nominate Joseph M. Pettit, of Atlanta, Ga., to be a member of the National Science Board. He would replace Robert H. Dicke, whose term has expired.

Pettit was born July 15, 1916. He received a B.S. from the University of California at Berkeley in 1938 and an E.E. (1940) and Ph. D. (1942) from Stanford University.

Pettit was a professor of electrical engineering at Stanford from 1947 to 1955. He was associate dean of engineering there from 1955 to 1958, and dean of the School of Engineering from 1958 to 1972. Since 1972 he has been president of Georgia Institute of Technology.

Budget Deferrals

Message to the Congress.   November 10, 1977

To the Congress of the United States:

In accordance with the Impoundment Control Act of 1974, I herewith report four new deferrals totalling $908.6 million in budget authority. The deferrals affect the Departments of Defense and Energy, the National Science Foundation, and the Emergency refugee and migration assistance fund.

In addition, I am reporting revisions to five deferrals previously transmitted. Three of these revisions change the agency name and related identifiers of the deferrals from the abolished Energy Research and Development Administration to the new Department of Energy. The amount deferred for the Department of Energy's Plenum Fill experiment has also been increased by $0.8 million. In addition, two supplementary reports for deferrals in the Office of the Secretary of the Treasury report an increase of $26.3 million in the amount deferred.

The details of each deferral are contained in the attached reports.

JIMMY CARTER

The White House,
November 10, 1977.

NOTE: The attachments detailing the deferrals are printed in the FEDERAL REGISTER of November 15, 1977.

The message was announced by the White House Press Office on November 10. It was not issued in the form of a White House press release.

United Negro College Fund

Remarks at a Meeting With Officials of the Fund. November 11, 1977

Well, first of all, let me say how grateful I am to you, the leaders of our Nation who have joined together to promote the $50 million capital fund for the United Negro College Fund.

When I was elected President, I decided that I would not endorse nor participate in any fundraising effort unless I felt that it was uniquely committed to the best interests of our Nation as a whole. And it's been just a rare occasion when I have let my own name as President be used. The International Red Cross and the Boy Scouts would be two examples. But I feel that the United Negro College Fund is another effort that has the same connotation and the same broad-based benefit to influence the future of our country.

Having been Governor of Georgia and, as Tom has said, participated in this very beneficial effort in the past as a private citizen and as a public official, I know the impact of the courageous private colleges who have predominantly black student bodies on the course of our Nation. They have acted in times of great difficulty, and although their financial status is quite weak and quite uncertain, even today, their academic contributions and their social contributions have been superb.

They've never been weak. They've never been uncertain. They've never been doubtful. Their accomplishments have been recognized by all those who have observed them.

One of the most beneficial entities in the Southland in the crucial years of searching for civil rights have been the black colleges there who, with a staunchness and a commitment that was indeed inspirational even to those who opposed

their purposes at that time, ensured success.

This is an effort that you are undertaking which will help them in the uncertain years ahead, because now that some major civil rights accomplishments have been given, we still have the necessity to recognize that society continues to change. And when change comes, that's extraordinarily expensive for those who are on the cutting edge of beneficial change.

Fifty million dollars is an awfully small amount for 41 colleges to share, but it's a very difficult thing to raise this amount of money. And only by the involvement of the President and the Vice President and the Governors of States and very influential corporate, business, and professional leaders like yourselves can the effort be successful.

I have confidence in the future of these negro colleges. They have come through a testing period where their strength and commitment and quality have already been proven. And we should not ever lessen our commitment to them simply because they are becoming more acceptable in the broad-based American societal life as a probing point for quality, for change, for the benefits derived to all our people regardless of race.

One of the obvious purposes is to give a superb education to those students in our Nation who could not otherwise afford it. Another one is to preserve the uniqueness of a curriculum and a student body commitment that mirror quite often the yearnings and the frustrations and the desires and the hopes and the dreams and aspirations of families of those students who, because of racial prejudice and discrimination, did not have a chance for a good education or to broaden their hearts and their minds. And in many ways these modern-day students of minority groups represent not only themselves but they represent their families and their other ancestors who have been so severely deprived.

We have an obligation to them to redress longstanding grievances and to let the progress in the future mirror not just a degree which represents the progress of the rest of our Nation's educational society, but a much more rapid rate of progress to overcome some of the handicaps that have been inflicted upon these people in the past.

I think we have a lot to learn, also, from the predominantly black colleges of our Nation. They have come to represent a unique symbol of human rights in all its broad categories. Because of the well-organized effort, quite often they represent, perhaps even inadvertently, other groups in our American society who are not so well organized, not so well represented as you are represented around this table, and who don't have a well-publicized effort to correct wrongs.

So, for all of these reasons, I, as President, am not only proud of the predominantly black colleges of our Nation represented by the fund, but also am proud of you for being willing to contribute your very valuable time to this effort. I'm available on this occasion and others to help you.

I know that you recognize that the hard work of fundraising has to be in your hands, but I can't think of a better project for you to undertake. It's a tribute to you, and I know it's an inspirational thing for you to be involved in so worthy a cause. So, good luck in your fundraising efforts. I'm a proud partner with you in one of the finest commitments for the benefit of all the American people that I can imagine. Thank you very much.

NOTE: The President spoke at 9:15 a.m. in the Roosevelt Room at the White House, where officials of the fund and corporate executives were meeting with White House staff members on the inauguration of the 2-year Capital Fund Campaign.

Thanksgiving Day, 1977

Proclamation 4537.   November 11, 1977

By the President of the United States of America

A Proclamation

Although the first years of America's struggle for independence were often disheartening, our forebears never lost faith in the Creator, in their cause, or in themselves. Upon learning of the American victory at Saratoga in 1777, Samuel Adams composed the first National Thanksgiving proclamation, and the Continental Congress called upon the governors of every state to designate a day when all Americans could join together and express their gratitude for God's providence "with united hearts." By their actions they extended a revered regional custom into a national tradition.

Precisely two centuries have now passed since that time. We have tamed a continent, established institutions dedicated to protecting our liberties, and secured a place of leadership among nations. But we have never lost sight of the principles upon which our Nation was founded. For that reason we can look to the future with hope and confidence.

Now, THEREFORE, I, JIMMY CARTER, President of the United States of America, in accord with Section 6103 of Title 5 of the United States Code, do hereby proclaim Thursday, November 24, 1977, as Thanksgiving Day. I ask all Americans to gather on that day with their families and neighbors in their homes and in their houses of worship to give thanks for the blessings Almighty God has bestowed upon us.

IN WITNESS WHEREOF, I have hereunto set my hand this eleventh day of November, in the year of our Lord nineteen hundred seventy-seven, and of the Independence of the United States of America the two hundred and second.

JIMMY CARTER

[Filed with the Office of the Federal Register, 4 p.m., November 11, 1977]

Digest of Other White House Announcements

The following listing includes the President's daily schedule and other items of general interest as announced by the White House Press Office during the period covered by this issue. Events and announcements printed elsewhere in the issue are not included.

November 5

The President met at the White House with Zbigniew Brzezinski, Assistant to the President for National Security Affairs.

The President has declared a major disaster for the State of Arizona as a result of severe storms and flooding, beginning about October 6, which caused extensive public and private property damage.

November 7

The President met at the White House with:

—Dr. Brzezinski;
—senior White House staff members;
—the Cabinet;
—Vice President Walter F. Mondale;
—James T. McIntyre, Jr., Acting Director of the Office of Management and Budget;

—Secretary of the Treasury W. Michael Blumenthal.

The President attended a briefing on the Panama Canal treaties, given for State officials and business and political leaders from Alaska, Rhode Island, and Missouri in the State Dining Room.

The President declared a major disaster for the State of Georgia as a result of the collapse of an earthen dam backing up Kelley Barnes Lake and the resultant flooding beginning on November 6, which caused extensive public and private property damage.

November 8

The President met at the White House with:

—Dr. Brzezinski;
—former Prime Minister Golda Meir of Israel;
—Vice President Mondale, Adm. Stansfield Turner, Director of Central Intelligence, and Dr. Brzezinski;
—Mrs. Carter, for lunch.

November 9

The President met at the White House with:

—David L. Aaron, Deputy Assistant to the President for National Security Affairs;
—members of the Congressional Black Caucus, Vice President Mondale, and Dr. Brzezinski;
—Representative James C. Corman of California;
—a group of administration officials to discuss national health insurance.

November 10

The President met at the White House with:

—Dr. Brzezinski;
—Vice President Mondale, Secretary Blumenthal, Mr. McIntyre, Charles

L. Schultze, Chairman of the Council of Economic Advisers, and Arthur F. Burns, Chairman of the Board of Governors of the Federal Reserve System;

—Nikolay Aemenovich Patolichev, Minister of Foreign Trade of the Union of Soviet Socialist Republics;

—Secretary Blumenthal, Secretary of Energy James R. Schlesinger, Mr. Schultze, Ambassador Robert S. Strauss, Special Representative for Trade Negotiations, and a group of business leaders.

The President attended a briefing on the Panama Canal treaties, given for representatives of women's organizations in the State Dining Room.

The President has declared a major disaster for the State of North Carolina as a result of severe storms and flooding, beginning about November 4, which caused extensive public and private property damage.

November 11

The President met at the White House with:

—Vice President Mondale, Secretary of State Cyrus R. Vance, and Dr. Brzezinski;

—Dr. Brzezinski;

—Representative Harley O. Staggers of West Virginia;

—Vice President Mondale and Mr. Schultze;

—Mayor Abraham Beame of New York;

—a group of editors, publishers, and broadcasters (transcript will be printed next week);

—a group of economic and budget advisers for a budget review meeting.

NOMINATIONS SUBMITTED TO THE SENATE

The following list does not include promotions of members of the Uniformed Services, nominations to the Service Academies, or nominations of Foreign Service officers.

Submitted November 7, 1977

STEPHEN JOHN GAGE, of Maryland, to be an Assistant Administrator of the Environmental Protection Agency, vice Wilson K. Talley, resigned.

THIBAUT DE SAINT PHALLE, of New Jersey, to be a member of the Board of Directors of the Export-Import Bank of the United States, vice R. Alex McCullough, resigned.

WILLIAM M. ISAAC, of Kentucky, to be a member of the Board of Directors of the Federal Deposit Insurance Corporation for a term of 6 years, vice Robert E. Barnett, resigned.

Submitted November 8, 1977

THOMAS J. CORCORAN, of the District of Columbia, a Foreign Service officer of Class one, to be Ambassador Extraordinary and Plenipotentiary of the United States of America to the Republic of Burundi.

DAVID T. SCHNEIDER, of Maryland, a Foreign Service officer of Class one, to be Ambassador Extraordinary and Plenipotentiary of the United States of America to the People's Republic of Bangladesh.

Submitted November 12, 1977

LARRY R. McCORD, of Arkansas, to be United States Attorney for the Western District of Arkansas for the term of 4 years, vice Robert E. Johnson.

ERNEST AMBLER, of Maryland, to be Director of the National Bureau of Standards, vice Richard W. Roberts, resigned.

JOSEPH MAYO PETTIT, of Georgia, to be a member of the National Science Board, National Science Foundation, for a term expiring May 10, 1982, vice Robert Henry Dicke, term expired.

CHECKLIST OF WHITE HOUSE PRESS RELEASES

The following releases of the Office of the White House Press Secretary, distributed during the period covered by this issue, are not included in the issue.

CHECKLIST—Continued

Released November 7, 1977

News conference: on the President's telephone calls to Henry Howell, gubernatorial candidate in Virginia, and Gov. Brendan Byrne, candidate for reelection in New Jersey—by Jody Powell, Press Secretary to the President

Released November 8, 1977

Advance text: address to the Nation on the National Energy Plan

Released November 9, 1977

Remarks: announcement of the Home Loan Bank Board's anti-redlining regulations—by Vice President Walter F. Mondale

News conference: on the Home Loan Bank Board's anti-redlining regulations—by Robert H. McKinney, Chairman of the Board

News conference: on the President's meeting with Prime Minister Robert D. Muldoon of New Zealand—by Jerrold L. Schecter, Associate Press Secretary

Released November 10, 1977

Announcement: nomination of Larry R. McCord to be United States Attorney for the Western District of Arkansas

ACTS APPROVED BY THE PRESIDENT

Approved November 7, 1977

H.J. Res. 611_____ Public Law 95–154
A joint resolution to extend the authority of the Federal Reserve banks to buy and sell certain obligations.

S. 455_____ Private Law 95–11
An act for the relief of Ermelinda Rossi.

S. 556_____ Private Law 95–12
An act for the relief of Lee Young Soo.

S. 948_____ Private Law 95–13
An act for the relief of Chin Ah Park and Chin Suk Park.

S. 1003_____ Private Law 95–14
An act for the relief of Me Young Lee.

Approved November 8, 1977

H.J. Res. 621_____ Public Law 95–158
A joint resolution approving the Presidential decision on an Alaska natural gas transportation system, and for other purposes.

H.R. 2850_____ Public Law 95–160
An act to suspend until the close of June 30, 1978, the duty on certain latex sheets, and for other purposes.

ACTS APPROVED—Continued

Approved November 8—Continued

H.R. 2982_____ Public Law 95–161
An act to suspend until the close of June 30, 1980, the duty on synthetic tantalum/columbium concentrate, and for other purposes.

H.R. 3093_____ Public Law 95–162
An act to provide duty-free treatment for certain copying lathes used for making rough or finished shoe lasts and for parts of such lathes, and for other purposes.

H.R. 3259_____ Public Law 95–159
An act to continue to suspend for a temporary period the import duty on certain horses, and for other purposes.

H.R. 3461_____Private Law 95–17
An act for the relief of Chin-Ho An.

H.R. 5101_____ Public Law 95–155
Environmental Research, Development, and Demonstration Authorization Act of 1978.

H.R. 9090_____ Public Law 95–156
An act to exempt disaster payments made in connection with the 1977 crops of wheat, feed grains, upland cotton, and rice from the payment limitations contained in the Agricultural Act of 1970 and the Agricultural Act of 1949.

S. 1005_____ Private Law 95–15
An act for the relief of Young Shin Joo.

S. 1551_____ Private Law 95–16
An act for the relief of In Hea Kim and Myung Sung Kwon.

S. 2149_____ Public Law 95–157
An act to create the District Court for the Northern Mariana Islands, implementing article IV of the Covenant to Establish a Commonwealth of the Northern Mariana Islands in Political Union with the United States of America.

Approved November 9, 1977

H.J. Res. 643_____ Public Law 95–165
A joint resolution making further continuing appropriations for the fiscal year 1978, and for other purposes.

H.R. 6010_____ Public Law 95–163
An act to amend title XIII of the Federal Aviation Act of 1958 to expand the types of risks which the Secretary of Transportation may insure or reinsure, and for other purposes.

S. 717_____ Public Law 95–164
Federal Mine Safety and Health Amendments Act of 1977.

ACTS APPROVED—Continued

Approved November 10, 1977

H.R. 1139_____ Public Law 95–166
National School Lunch Act and Child Nutrition Amendments of 1977.

Approved November 11, 1977

S. 810_____ Public Law 95–168
An act granting an extension of patent to the United Daughters of the Confederacy.

S. 2208_____ Public Law 95–167
An act to amend the Federal charter of the Big Brothers of America to include Big Sisters International, Incorporated, and for other purposes.

Interview With the President

Remarks and a Question-and-Answer Session With a Group of Editors and News Directors.   November 11, 1977

THE PRESIDENT. This is another in a series of meetings with news editors of all kinds from around the country. I always look forward to them, and I really appreciate your giving me this chance to learn about your concerns. And it also gives me a chance to learn about the rest of the Nation outside of Washington.

What I'd like to do is take about 5 minutes to outline some of the things on which I'm working right at this moment, just for illustrative purposes, and then spend the balance of our time answering your questions.

ADMINISTRATION POLICIES

On the domestic scene, of course, the major issue that we face now is the energy package, which the Congress is discussing. This is five major bills. They've just about finished work on two of them and still have three to go, the more controversial ones still to come—automobiles, natural gas, and taxation, with the crude oil equalization tax.

In addition, there are about 19 other conference committees, I believe, that are now functioning. One of the most important is on social security legislation. I'm quite concerned that the very attractive benefits that are awarded to retired people will be excessive, because the working people and employers now have to pay those benefits. And we presented a reform package to the Congress without any increase in the level of benefits for those who receive them, and we are hopeful that the Congress will not come forward with too generous a package which will add substantially to the tax burden of the working people and employers.

In addition, as you know, this year we've tried to address some of the other serious problems. I've already presented to the Congress a welfare reform program, what we call Better Jobs and Income Program. And we've gotten reorganization authority, which was a struggle at first, but the Congress gave me that for 3 years. We've tried to cut back on paperwork, reporting forms, straighten out OSHA so that it wouldn't be so onerous to people. We've passed major legislation in agriculture with a 5-year farm bill; put into effect about a $21 billion stimulus package, economic stimulus package, over half of which will be felt by the end of this quarter and the balance of which will be felt in the first quarter of 1977 [1978].

The unemployment rate has come down about 1 percent, but it's been fairly level since late April at roughly the 7-percent level.

The latest figures on inflation show some progress on the consumer price index. But those monthly figures fluctuate so wildly that they are not really dependable. We think we have an underlying inflation rate of about 6 or 6½ percent.

The growth rate this year will probably reach our predicted level, an average of about 5 percent. The likelihood now is it will go down a little bit next year.

So, on the domestic scene, we've got a broad range of issues that have been and are being addressed.

On the foreign affairs and defense scene, we are working with the Soviets now on a comprehensive test ban. Last week President Brezhnev adopted our position, that we've been pursuing for months, to include the peaceful nuclear explosions in with the military tests to be prohibited. This was a pleasant development, and I think might make it possible, if we can work out the very difficult details on verification, that we can have a comprehensive test ban concluded. Nobody can predict accurately what will happen.

We are working with the Soviets, in addition to that, on a continuation of the SALT talks that have been going on now almost since the Soviets got into the nuclear field. I think we've got a good basic package evolved. There are still some very important differences that remain, but we've achieved most of our own objectives.

This will be SALT II. We will immediately continue with a SALT III effort. We've searched for equity, balanced forces; we've searched for verification so that any conclusions drawn, any agreements reached could be verified on a regular basis and an acceptable basis. And we are looking for reductions on both sides.

We have proposed to the Soviets that we begin discussions on prohibiting antisatellite weapons. They are taking this under advisement, and I would guess that negotiations might commence on this subject before too many weeks go by.

We have, in addition, one of the most difficult and complicated questions, and that is a comprehensive settlement of the Mideast disputes. I doubt that any foreign negotiating effort has ever been attempted that's more complicated, more thankless, and sometimes more frustrating. But I believe that world peace is dependent upon a resolution of those major differences.

We have evolved now a so-called negotiating paper that has been accepted by some of the parties involved, publicly by Israel and by Egypt. We hope that Jordan, Lebanon, and Syria will agree to go to Geneva without too much more delay.

That's just the first step, but in the negotiations on how the Geneva conference might take place, obviously many of the issues have been raised. The three most important ones, of course, are to achieve real peace—this is something the Arabs have never been willing to acknowledge before—is a need for open borders, free trade, the exchange of tourism, student exchange, ultimate diplomatic relations, genuine peace to live in harmony. Another thing that the Arabs have always refused to do is to negotiate directly with Israel. They have now agreed to that. They have also agreed, as you know, to conclude the discussions, if they are successful, with actual signed peace treaties.

The second question is the territorial boundaries and defense lines and the security of the nations involved who, at the present time, obviously don't trust each other very much. And the third thing is the Palestinian question, how it might be resolved. This involves both refugees and also those who live in the West Bank, the

Gaza Strip. And with tedious negotiations, we've made some progress on that. Nobody yet knows whether it will be successful.

The last thing I'd like to mention very quickly, to give you more time for questions, is the southern Africa difficulties in three general categories: One is Rhodesia or, as the black Africans call it, Zimbabwe; the second one in Namibia, which was formerly Southwest Africa; and the third one, of course, is South Africa itself.

We've not had much involvement in African affairs up until a little more than a year ago, when Secretary Kissinger did make a trip through there and evolved proposals which I thought were good ones but which didn't prove to be acceptable, primarily with Rhodesia.

The United Nations plays a major role in Namibia, working under the general auspices of five of us major nations—ourselves, Canada, Great Britain, France, and Germany—negotiating with South Africa on their withdrawal from Namibia.

We've got additional problems, as you know, in the Horn of Africa, also in Angola, which still has about 20,000 troops. The Cubans have, in effect, taken on the colonial aspect that the Portuguese gave up in months gone by. And we hope that there will be some inclination on the part of the Cubans to withdraw their forces from Angola. They are now spreading into other countries in Africa, like Mozambique. Recently, they are building up their so-called advisers in Ethiopia. We consider this to be a threat to the permanent peace in Africa.

So, that outlines in general some of the foreign policies that we are pursuing. I know that you have special questions to ask, and I'd like now to have your questions.

QUESTIONS

CHAIRMAN OF THE FEDERAL RESERVE BOARD

Q. I'm Ed Wishcamper, Abilene, Texas, Reporter-News. In the Washington Star last evening, Charles Walker wrote about the prospect of Arthur Burns perhaps being reappointed as Chairman of the Federal Reserve Board. At this time, that decision is 2 months away. What will be done?

THE PRESIDENT. I haven't decided about a reappointment yet and haven't had a chance to discuss this with my own staff or my economic advisers. As I said in my press conference this week, the highly publicized disagreements and disharmonies between me and Chairman Burns just do not exist. We talk on the telephone quite frequently; either he calls me or I call him. We have a monthly session with the Vice President, the head of the Office of Management and Budget, the Secretary of Treasury, and my economic advisers. We had one, coincidentally, yesterday.

And I don't understand how these kinds of stories evolve. But I think it's accurate, what I said in the press conference, that I've never had an argument with Mr. Burns. And even in our monthly lunch sessions, when we have a very free discussion, it's always been very harmonious and friendly. There are differences of opinion expressed on long-range trends and so forth, but it's been very harmonious. I have not decided what to do about his reappointment.

NUCLEAR ENERGY

Q. I'm Ben Plastino from Idaho Falls. I think I interviewed you about 2 years ago. My question is, what is your feeling now on the development of nuclear energy aside from the breeder reactor, and are you behind the SAREF [1] project?

THE PRESIDENT. I'm glad to see you again. I remember my visit there. I think that was when you were having a gubernatorial election, and I came in to help Cecil Andrus, who's now helping me. By the way, I used to go to your area, to Arco, Idaho, and Pocatello when I was in the nuclear submarine program and we had our experimental units out there.

My veto of the Clinch River breeder reactor is no conclusion at all that I'm against nuclear power nor against the breeder reactor program. The reasons for the veto are multiple in nature. In addition to the Clinch River breeder reactor, there are several facets of that authorization bill which encroached upon the prerogatives of the President in an unprecedented way. I think it's a mistake to spend more than $2 billion on an actual production model of a particular breeder reactor design which, when it is completed, will already be obsolete. We don't need to go into the plutonium society this early. We need to continue our research and development, small pilot project construction, to test the three or four major types of breeder reactors that might ultimately prove to be most feasible when they are needed, maybe 20, 25 years from now.

I think the commitment that we are making to the nuclear power program is adequate at the Federal Government level. There's no inclination to phase it out.

One thing that we are trying to do is to decrease the time required for the approval of projects once they are submitted for licensing. It now takes about 10 years in our country, as contrasted to about 3 years [2] in a nation, for instance, like Japan, to put into operation a major nuclear powerplant once it is conceived and desired.

We have had another major international effort of which I'm proud—and we've made good progress—and that is to cut down on the proliferation of nuclear explosives around the world. A year ago, I think there was a general feeling of despair that it was too late to do anything about the nuclear genie being out of the bottle. But now there's a general sense among the developed nations of the world, those who do have nuclear power capability, that we can stop the spread of nuclear weapons, although in the past it seemed to be hopeless. We recently, this month as a matter of fact, had 36 nations come into Washington to study the long-range nuclear fuel cycle, including the deposits of uranium, enrichment of thorium and uranium into usable degrees of purity, how to distribute those very useful fuel supplies, how to account for the wastes, how to prevent their being transferred into explosives themselves.

And I think this study will be helpful. So, we are making a major effort around the world to do two things simultaneously. One is to give nations who want and need nuclear power access to fuel and access to technology to generate electricity and, on the other hand, to stop or minimize the opportunity that they might have, and sometimes desire, to make nuclear weapons. It's a difficult proposition, very complicated, but we are making good progress.

PRESIDENT'S RELATIONSHIP WITH THE AMERICAN PEOPLE

Q. Al Fitzpatrick, the Beacon Journal, Akron, Ohio. When you were in Akron

---

[1] Safety Reactor Experimental Facility. [Printed in the White House press release.]

[2] According to the Department of Energy, the time frame for Japan is 5–7 years. [Printed in the White House press release.]

last year, sir, you met with a group of men, and you indicated that you wanted to develop a personal relationship with the people in that room that would continue even after you were elected. Do you feel that you've been able to maintain that kind of relationship?

THE PRESIDENT. That was a religious group?

Q. No, it was primarily a group of minority leaders.

THE PRESIDENT. Yes, I remember. I came there for another reason, but I met with them after the banquet.

Yes, I think so. We've had, I think, as much success in keeping me available to the public as any administration has been able to do. At the conclusion of this year, for instance, I will have met personally and answered questions from about 400, perhaps more, editors and radio and TV executives like yourselves.

This morning I had a meeting with a group, for instance, that was involved in the Negro College Fund. Yesterday I met with about 40 small businessmen at the middle-business level—for instance, Van Heusen Shirt Company and Radio Shack, about that level—that have several thousand employees, but are not the biggest ones. I've made 5 or 6 different—well, more than that—I probably made 15 visits to individual communities around the Nation and ordinarily have either a forum that's publicized or call-in shows, or I have a press conference every 2 weeks, twice a month. We've never missed that yet.

In addition, I've had three fireside chats and one session in the Oval Office where people called me on the telephone for a couple of hours. Walter Cronkite helped me with that. We have a stream of visitors who come here during the week—some meet with me, some, the Vice President, some, top members of my staff.

Although it's never adequate, you know, I've done the best I could to devote a lot of time to this contact directly with the people from around the country.

And as far as the black leadership is concerned—I mentioned the United Negro College Fund, but I met earlier this week with the Black Caucus, and I've done the same thing with women's groups.

I met yesterday afternoon with the national leaders of about 75 different women's organizations over in the White House and made a brief talk and answered their questions. So, although you are never completely satisfied, I think we've done the best we could in keeping my contact directly with the people.

AGRICULTURE

Q. Mr. President, recently in Statesboro, there was a tractor motorcade of 3,000 tractors. These men were protesting low farm prices and high production costs. Do you have any good words to give these farmers?

THE PRESIDENT. Tell them I'm one of them—[*laughter*]—say we've got a dirt farmer in the Secretary of Agriculture's office who understands their problems as well.

We've passed this year one of the most far-reaching farm bills, the most far-reaching farm bill that's ever been passed in this country. I would say the total amount of indirect or direct Federal aid this year, this coming year, will be about $11 billion.

Prices now are growing, are going up fairly well—soybeans, corn, wheat. The price of peanuts, which is important down around Swainsboro and Statesboro, as you know, is fixed at a reasonable price. We are trying to get the Government out of the unwarranted interference in the agriculture picture as best we can.

We've got large farm stocks on hand of wheat and corn. We'll have the highest yield this year in history of both corn and soybeans. We'll have the second highest yield in the history of wheat. At the same time, two-thirds of all the counties in the Nation are designated as disaster counties, which shows the accuracy of concentrating financial aid where it deserves to be.

Georgia had a complete zero production of corn—you might be interested in knowing—I'd say not more than 5-percent yield. And that 5 percent is all permeated with aflatoxin mold and can't be sold.

But I think that in general, the agriculture situation next year is a good one. The reason that the prices are low now is because the yield has been high, and so the gross income per acre is maintained fairly well.

What creates a serious problem, obviously, is when you have a good yield in most parts of the country and a very low yield in certain communities because of weather patterns.

There's been a fairly good yield around the world this year on grains, not nearly as high as last year. As you noticed, President Brezhnev announced that they were going to come up about 20 million tons short of what their goal had been and about 10 million tons short of what we had anticipated their yield to be this year. That was primarily because of bad weather during harvest time.

We have now authorized an increase from 8 million tons of grain to be sold in the Soviet Union up to 15 million tons that can be sold to the Soviet Union. This still leaves us adequate stocks for our own domestic use.

We are concentrating on exports. This past fiscal year, which concluded the end of September, we had $24 billion in farm exports from our Nation, which is the highest we've ever seen in history. And with the better yields, we might not export that much this fiscal year, but we are

trying to. So, I would say, in general, the agriculture picture looks good for the future.

ENERGY PRICES

Q. Mr. President, Bob Reed from the Lowell Sun in Massachusetts. We remember interviewing you, too.

THE PRESIDENT. Yes, I remember coming there. I rode over to Lowell on the train.

Q. Up in New England, we are paying double the national average for energy prices. And in view of your comments on your program, that it's designed to be both fair and equal, is there anything you can do to give us some hope that these prices will come down, particularly in view of John O'Leary's comments the other day that in 1985 we'll still be paying one and a half times the national average? Do you have any hope for relief for us?

THE PRESIDENT. I don't think there's any doubt that the energy prices are going to go up for everybody. But we hope that with Alaskan oil coming down to the Gulf Coast and being distributed, with Alaskan gas coming down to the Midwest with the new pipeline, with an increasing supply of coal, particularly from the Appalachian region, that can be moved into New England—this would require an improvement in the quality of railroads, for instance, coming out of West Virginia, Pennsylvania, to the coast, say, into the Norfolk region or Philadelphia region, and then shipped by freight up to Boston and other New England ports—with a more orderly structure of pricing in oil and gas, encouragement of domestic production, increasing use of solar power over a period of years, that we can reduce substantially the present disparity in prices.

I think it's obvious that you have a much higher price to pay in New England than the rest of the country. Just one small item that I mentioned in passing is the railroad quality. The average speed, for instance, of the coal trains coming out of West Virginia to the coast is 12 miles per hour because the roadbeds have been permitted to deteriorate so badly. So, in the future, I think we are going to see a much better distribution of available energy supplies.

You've almost had to quit using coal in New England because of that purpose. I think the new technology that we hope to evolve in the future, the fluidized bed burning of coal, can let it be used in an increasing percentage, at least in our country and also in the total tons consumed, with minimum adverse effect on the environment, environmental quality.

So, I'd say technology, distribution, shift to new sources of supply, and the new pipelines coming down through Canada will all help to alleviate New England's problem.

GOVERNMENT'S ROLE IN BUSINESS COMMUNITY

Q. Jack Beckland from Destin Log in the Florida Panhandle. In our area, we hear a lot of concerns by small businessmen that somehow the Government is stacking the deck against them in the form of high minimum wages and the probable big jump in social security contributions and, generally, redtape. Would you care to comment on this?

THE PRESIDENT. Well, I have a kinship with you. I have a small business, as you know, too, probably much smaller than the ones you are talking about. I don't believe that you could accurately say that the minimum wage and social security single out small business.

I think in the past, when decisions have been made in Washington, the natural place for, say, President Nixon, President Ford to turn to would be the Business Roundtable, or the National Association of Manufacturers, which is heavily inclined toward the perspective of big business.

And I'm trying to make sure that doesn't happen. This coming 3 or 4 months, I will meet with about 400 key leaders from around the Nation who represent just small business, ranging in size from 10 or 15 employees up to 2,000 or 3,000 total employees. I think this gives me a much different perspective.

I'll just give you one example. Among the very large businesses, when I asked them what they prefer in the way of tax relief, they've said what they want is lower corporate tax rates.

This group I had in yesterday—there were about 40—when I asked them, "What would you prefer, lower corporate tax rates, investment tax credit improvement, say, from 8 to 12 percent with a broader coverage, or removing the double taxation of dividends," I would say 80 percent of them said they would like to have the investment tax credits improved. That's a difference in perspective, I think, between the middle and small businessman or businesswoman and the very large corporations.

So, the only thing I can say is that some of those changes are inevitable on energy costs, social security, minimum wage, but I believe giving the small business leader more voice in government before a decision is made is better.

That brings up another point, and that is that the large corporations can quite often handle unwarranted Government intrusion better than the small ones can. OSHA requirements, ERISA reporting, HEW, Labor forms to be filled out—these are a much greater burden on a small businessperson than they are on a very large corporation that have their own legal staff and own accounting firms and so forth, that work just within them.

We are trying to cut back on that. I set a goal for this first fiscal year, up to October 1, to cut back 7 million man-hours on the time required to process reports coming into the Government.

We tried to abbreviate the reports, to eliminate those that we could, to cut out duplication from one department to another where the same information is required by the Federal Government, to two or three different departments from a single businessperson and, also, to lessen the frequency of the reports. Sometimes when they are required quarterly, we are changing it to semiannually or annually; when they're required monthly, we're changing them to quarterly and sometimes semiannually.

So, 7 million was our goal. In one department alone, the Department of HEW, they have already cut back 14 million man-hours. So that's a 33-percent cutback. So, we are trying to do some things for small business there, because I know from experience how onerous and burdensome it is.

I might say that I know that a lot of your readers are concerned about the minimum wage being increased. But historically, we have had the minimum wage stay at a level of about 50 percent or 52 percent of the prevailing manufacturer's wage, and we've always let it get behind 5, 6, 7 years, and then Congress will pass a law to let it catch up to the roughly 50-percent, 52-percent level. That's what we've done this year.

And on social security, we had no alternative. I inherited a lot of problems, and of course, all my predecessors have inherited problems, too. I'm not complaining about it. But we were faced with the fact that the medical fund part of the social security is going to go bankrupt in

1979; the old age portion of the Social Security Fund is going to go bankrupt in 1983, unless we do something. So, we put forward a minimum increase in tax payments to support the Social Security Funds that we could evolve. And as I mentioned when the national news media were in here, what the Congress has done is added a great and very liberal group of benefits to the social security payments.

Well, you can justify all of them, but somebody has got to pay for them. And as the conferees work on this question in the next few weeks, we are trying to hold down those benefits that we didn't recommend in the first place and, also, at the same time, obviously hold down our contributions to them.

I mentioned minimum wage and social security because that was the two examples that you described.

NATIONAL ENERGY PLAN

Q. Mr. President, I was impressed with the moderation of the tone of your energy message Tuesday night. Have you been able to measure its effect on the conferees?

THE PRESIDENT. As you know, the fireside chat format is not a proper one for going into specific details on the technicalities of the law. It's designed—that particular speech was designed to let the American people know about the seriousness of our energy problem and some of the prospects for even worse problems in the future, unless we took action.

Also, when I made the speech in April, I didn't cover the impact of the very high imports on our Nation's economy and as it affects the average American family. I wanted to pursue that as well. What the Congress leaders wanted me to do is exactly what I did. I had met with Senator Byrd, with Tip O'Neill, Senator Long, Dingell, Staggers, and others. What they needed is to have the American people become supportive of an overall energy package, component parts of which were not attractive. And this is what I tried to do, is to let the American people know the importance of it, to let them know the difficulty of it, to let them know some of the consequences if the Congress didn't hear from the public and didn't have public support.

Obviously, the special interest groups, some of whom are quite benevolent, are here, and their voice is heard every hour or every day by every Member of Congress. That would include the UAW, the automobile manufacturers, the oil and gas producers, the electric power companies, large manufacturing entities, and so forth. They all let their voice be heard. But when you don't hear from the general public, the consumers, there's an unbalanced impression made on the Congress, and the Members of Congress need some support.

So, I think the speech has been almost universally praised by the Members of Congress, and we've probably checked with 60 or 70 of them. I don't know of anyone that thought it was a wrong tone.

It also pointed out that this legislation is extremely complicated, extremely difficult, extremely technical, and not popular, and that it's not a test of strength or will between the President and the Congress, between the House and the Senate. It's not even a test of will between the oil and gas producers and the oil and gas consumers. It's really a test of our national will to deal with a complicated question in a forceful and courageous way.

And the other thing I want to point out is just one thing on the imports. It's a direct threat to our security to be increas-

ingly dependent upon imports. We've gotten up now to where roughly 50 percent of our oil that we burn in this country or use in this country comes from overseas. This is creating about a $45 billion cost to our Nation this year.

If we didn't have oil, we'd have about a $15 or $20 [billion] trade surplus. As it is, we are going to wind up with about a $30 billion trade deficit. And that's $30 billion that goes out of our economy that could be used to build new factories, to expand presently existing businesses, and to provide new jobs. And it's getting worse.

It's almost like a hemorrhage, and unless we do take this action, we're going to be in very serious problems in the future economically, militarily, and for the benefit of our country's living standards.

NEWS LEAKS ON SALT NEGOTIATIONS

Q. Don Corbet, the Arkansas Radio Network. I was talking to our Senator Bumpers earlier this week. He seems extremely concerned, sitting on a subcommittee that heard bimonthly reports on the SALT talks, about the news leaks and to the effect that they might have an effect on the SALT talks themselves. Do you have a comment?

THE PRESIDENT. Well, that's one of the most difficult things I've had to face in Washington, how to deal with breaches of secrecy. It's obvious that the American people need to know what's going on, but I'm not in a position, as President, to go to the American people and reveal our negotiating positions when I and President Brezhnev, our negotiators and the Soviet negotiators, have agreed to keep the negotiating points confidential until some agreement is reached.

I think the revelation of the details of our negotiating position has been ill-advised in some instances. I don't know where the blame lies.

Senator Bumpers is one of those—I have not talked to him about this, but he's one of those who has deplored the revelation to the public of secret information given to the committee by the Secretary of State, Secretary of Defense, and others.

I can't answer the question about whether or not it will present an obstacle to a successful SALT negotiation. I don't think it will be that much of an obstacle.

The Soviets have complained to their Ambassador about these revelations of negotiating points. We have found, in recent weeks, the Soviets to be very amenable to changing their positions enough to accommodate our concerns, and we are making good progress.

So, without saying that these news revelations have hurt, they do cause me some concern. And I believe, though, that in spite of that, we will not find our efforts to be frustrated. My prediction is that we will have a SALT agreement.

I think our time is up. Let me say one thing in closing. I wish I could spend all afternoon answering your questions, because the kind of questions that you all ask me from different parts of the country give me a fairly good indication of what matters are of concern to your readers and your listeners and your viewers.

Because I know that you have very little chance directly to present a question to the President, I'm sure you very carefully decide what is the most important question that you could present to me. But you can see from the brief discussion we've had, the broad range of subjects that are presented to me.

I've enjoyed being President. I think we've got a superb Cabinet. We've had a very good relationship with the Congress. And I believe that when the Congress does adjourn, if the Congress does ad-

journ this year—*[laughter]*—that a tabulation or an inventory of what has been done will be pleasing to the American people.

It's an honor for me to have you here. Looking around the room, I know that many of you have been very hospitable to me and to my political opponents during the campaign. And that's one of the best ways that I had to learn about our Nation, was meeting with you individually, or with your editorial board, and being cross-examined when I was a nonentity, when you didn't know who I was. And it gave me a chance to get to know you, and for your folks to know me.

So, I'm very grateful that you would come here and spend this much of your time. And I think this is the kind of interrelationship with the people out in the country that makes it very beneficial to me in making the right decisions.

If I do face difficult problems that in the past have been too secret, like SALT, which I've discussed in my press conferences and which I've discussed publicly, and the controversial portions of the Middle East and the exact proposal that we made, for instance, on Rhodesia—those things do create, perhaps, a disturbance in the country as people begin to debate about them and argue about them and disagree on them. And sometimes even the news media are critical of causing that confusion, that debate, that disturbance, and those differences.

But I feel much more sure of myself when I make a final decision, as President, if the American people have been involved in the process. And so you play a crucial role in that, as you well know.

And I just want to again express my thanks for the constructive attitude that you take. I think I've been well treated by the news media, I think, adequately examined, adequately criticized, but I don't have any complaints about it. I think you've been fair.

Thank you, again.

NOTE: The interview began at 1:03 p.m. in the Cabinet Room at the White House.

The transcript of the interview was released on November 12.

Sugar, Sirups, and Molasses Imports

Proclamation 4538. November 11, 1977

IMPORT FEES ON SUGAR, SIRUPS, AND MOLASSES

By the President of the United States of America

A Proclamation

1. The Secretary of Agriculture has advised me that he has reason to believe that certain sugars, sirups, and molasses, derived from sugar cane or sugar beets, classified under items 155.20 and 155.30, of the Tariff Schedules of the United States (TSUS) (19 U.S.C. 1202), are being, or are practically certain to be, imported into the United States under such conditions and in such quantities as to render or tend to render ineffective, or to materially interfere with, the price support operations now being conducted by the Department of Agriculture for sugar cane and sugar beets, or to reduce substantially the amount of any product being processed in the United States from domestic sugar beets and sugar cane.

2. I agree that there is reason for such belief by the Secretary of Agriculture. Therefore, I am requesting the United States International Trade Commission to make an immediate investigation with respect to this matter pursuant to section 22 of the Agricultural Adjustment Act, as amended (7 U.S.C. 624), and to report its findings and recommendations to me as soon as possible.

3. The Secretary of Agriculture has also determined and reported to me, with regard to such sugars, sirups, and molasses, that a condition exists which requires emergency treatment, and that the import fees hereinafter proclaimed should be imposed without awaiting the report and recommendations of the United States International Trade Commission.

4. I find and declare that the imposition of import fees hereinafter proclaimed, without awaiting the recommendations of the United States International Trade Commission with respect to such action, is necessary in order that the entry, or withdrawal from warehouse, for consumption of certain sugars, sirups, and molasses, described below by value, use and physical description, and classified under TSUS items 155.20 and 155.30, will not render or tend to render ineffective, or materially interfere with, the price support operations now being conducted by the Department of Agriculture for sugar cane or sugar beets, or reduce substantially the amount of any product processed in the United States from domestic sugar beets or sugar cane.

Now, THEREFORE, I, JIMMY CARTER, President of the United States of America, acting under the authority vested in me by the Constitution and Statutes of the United States of America, including section 22 of the Agricultural Adjustment Act, as amended, do hereby proclaim that Part 3 of the Appendix to the TSUS is amended as follows:

(a) A new headnote is added which reads as follows:

4. Sugar, sirups, and molasses
Licenses may be issued by the Secretary of Agriculture or his designee authorizing the entry of articles exempt from the fees provided for in items 956.10, 956.20, 957.10 and 957.20

of this part on the condition that such articles will be used only for the production (other than by distillation) of polyhydric alcohols, except polyhydric alcohols for use as a substitute for sugar in human food consumption. Such licenses shall be issued under regulations of the Secretary of Agriculture which he de-

termines are necessary to insure the use of such articles only for such purposes.

(b) The following new items, in numerical sequence, are added following items 955.06:

Item	Articles	Import Fees
	"Sugars, sirups, and molasses, derived from sugar cane or sugar beets, except those entered pursuant to a license issued by the Secretary of Agriculture in accordance with headnote 4:	
	Principally of crystalline structure or in dry amorphous form, provided for in item 155.20, part 10A, schedule 1:	
956.10	Valued at not more than 6.67 cents per pound____	50% ad. val.
956.20	Valued at more than 6.67 cents per pound but not more than 10.0 cents per pound _____	3.32 cents per lb. less the amount per lb. by which the value exceeds 6.67 cents per lb.
	Not principally of crystalline structure and not in dry amorphous form, containing soluble non-sugar solids (excluding any foreign substance that may have been added or developed in the product) equal to 6% or less by weight of the total soluble solids, provided for in item 155.30, part 10A, schedule 1:	
957.10	Valued at not more than 6.67 cents per pound of total sugars_____	50% ad. val.
957.20	Valued at more than 6.67 cents per pound of total sugars but not more than 10.0 cents per pound of total sugars_____	3.32 cents per lb. of total sugars less the amount per lb. of total sugars by which the value exceeds 6.67 cents per lb. of total sugars."

The fees established by items 956.10, 956.20, 957.10 and 957.20 shall apply to articles entered, or withdrawn from warehouse, for consumption on or after the date of this Proclamation, and shall continue to apply to such articles pending the report and recommendations of the United States International Trade Commission and action that I may take on them. However, such fees shall not apply to articles (a) exported to the United States before 12:01 A.M. (U.S. Eastern Standard Time) on the date of this Proclamation or (b) imported to fulfill forward contracts entered into before 12:01 A.M. (U.S. Eastern Standard Time) on the date of this Proclamation, *Provided,* That articles referred to in (a) and (b) are entered, or withdrawn from warehouse, for consumption on or before January 1, 1978.

In WITNESS WHEREOF, I have hereunto set my hand this eleventh day of November, in the year of our Lord nineteen hundred and seventy-seven, and of the Independence of the United States of America the two hundred and second.

JIMMY CARTER

[Filed with the Office of the Federal Register, 10:49 a.m., November 14, 1977]

NOTE: The text of the Executive order was released on November 12.

Sugar, Sirups, and Molasses Imports

Proclamation 4539.   November 11, 1977

MODIFICATION OF TARIFFS ON CERTAIN SUGARS, SIRUPS, AND MOLASSES

By the President of the United States of America

A Proclamation

1. By Proclamation 4334, of November 16, 1974, the President modified Subpart A, Part 10, Schedule 1 of the Tariff Schedules of the United States (19 U.S.C. 1202, hereinafter referred to as the "TSUS") to establish, effective January 1, 1975, following expiration of the

Sugar Act of 1948, a rate of duty and quota applicable to sugars, sirups and molasses described in items 155.20 and 155.30 of the TSUS. By Proclamation 4463 of September 21, 1976, as amended by Proclamation 4466, of October 4, 1976, the President modified the rate of duty applicable to such sugars, sirups and molasses.

2. The President took these actions pursuant to authority vested in him by the Constitution and statutes of the United States, including section 201(a)(2) of the Trade Expansion Act of 1962 (19 U.S.C. 1821(a)(2)), and in conformity with Headnote 2 of Subpart A of Part 10 of Schedule 1 of the TSUS, hereinafter referred to as the "Headnote". The Headnote was part of a trade agreement that embodied the results of the "Kennedy Round" of international trade negotiations. That agreement is known formally as the 1967 Geneva Protocol to the General Agreement on Tariffs and Trade, and the agreement includes, as an Annex, "Schedule XX", a schedule of United States trade concessions made during those negotiations. This agreement was concluded pursuant to section 201(a) of the Trade Expansion Act of 1962 (19 U.S.C. 1821(a)), and was implemented by Proclamation No. 3822, of December 16, 1967, (82 Stat. 1455) which, *inter alia,* added the Headnote to the TSUS.

3. The Headnote provides, in relevant part, as follows:

"(i) . . . if the President finds that a particular rate not lower than such January 1, 1968, rate, limited by a particular quota, may be established for any articles provided for in item 155.20 or 155.30, which will give due consideration to the interests in the United States sugar market of domestic producers and materially affected contracting parties to the General Agreement on Tariffs and Trade, he shall proclaim such particular rate and such quota limitation, . . .

"(ii) . . . any rate and quota limitation so established shall be modified if the President finds and proclaims that such modification is

2021

required or appropriate to give effect to the above considerations; . . ."

4. Section 201(a)(2) of the Trade Expansion Act authorizes the President to proclaim the modification or continuance of any existing duty or other import restrictions, or such additional import restrictions as he determines to be required or appropriate to carry out any trade agreement entered into under the authority of that Act, except that pursuant to section 201(b)(2) of the Act, the President may not by proclamation increase a rate of duty to a rate more than 50% above the rate existing on July 1, 1934. The currently applicable tariff rates in rate column numbered 2 for sugars, sirups, and molasses, described in items 155.20 and 155.30, are treated as the rates "existing on July 1, 1934", for the purposes of the President's proclaiming authority.

5. General headnote 4(b) of the TSUS provides that a rate of duty proclaimed pursuant to a concession granted in a trade agreement shall be reflected in the column numbered 1 of the TSUS and, if higher than the then existing rate in column numbered 2, shall also be reflected in the latter column.

6. I find that the modifications hereinafter proclaimed of the rates of duty applicable to items 155.20 and 155.30 of the TSUS are appropriate to carry out that portion of the Kennedy Round trade agreement set forth in the Headnote, and as provided for therein, give due consideration to the interests in the United States sugar market of domestic producers and materially affected contracting parties to the General Agreement on Tariffs and Trade.

Now, THEREFORE, I, JIMMY CARTER, President of the United States of America, acting under the authority vested in me by the Constitution and statutes, including section 201 of the Trade Expansion Act of 1962, and pursuant to General Headnote 4(b), and Headnote 2, Subpart A of Part 10 of Schedule 1, of the TSUS, do hereby proclaim until otherwise superseded by law:

A. The rates of duty in rate columns numbered 1 and 2 for items 155.20 and 155.30 of Subpart A, Part 10, Schedule 1 of the TSUS, are modified, and the following rates are established:

155.20_____2.98125¢ per lb. less 0.0421875¢ per lb. for each degree under 100 degrees (and fractions of a degree in proportion) but not less than 1.9265625¢ per lb.

155.30_____dutiable on total sugars at the rate per lb. applicable under Item 155.20 to sugar testing 100 degrees.

B. Those parts of Proclamation 4334 of November 16, 1974, Proclamation 4463 of September 21, 1976, and Proclamation 4466 of October 4, 1976, which are inconsistent with the provisions of paragraph (A) above are hereby terminated.

C. The provisions of this Proclamation shall apply to articles entered, or withdrawn from warehouse, for consumption on and after the date of this Proclamation. However, the provisions of this Proclamation shall not apply to articles (a) exported to the United States before 12:01 A.M. (U.S. Eastern Standard Time), on the date of this Proclamation, or (b) imported to fulfill forward contracts entered into before 12:01 A.M. (U.S. Eastern Standard Time), on the date of this Proclamation, *Provided,* that articles referred to in (a) and (b) above are entered, or withdrawn from warehouse, for consumption on or before January 1, 1978.

IN WITNESS WHEREOF, I have hereunto set my hand this eleventh day of November, in the year of our Lord nineteen hundred and seventy seven and of the Independence of the United States of America, the two hundred and second.

JIMMY CARTER

[Filed with the Office of the Federal Register, 11:01 a.m., November 14, 1977]

NOTE: The text of the Executive order was released on November 12.

Full Employment and Balanced Growth Bill

Statement by the President.
November 14, 1977

In recent months, members of my administration have met on a number of occasions with Senator Humphrey, Congressman Hawkins, and their representatives to discuss the full employment and balanced growth act. I am very pleased that these discussions have reached a fruitful conclusion. The care and time devoted to the discussions were justified by the seriousness of the issues and the need to develop legislation that will command broad support across our Nation and help us achieve our goal of full employment.

The amended full employment and balanced growth act that the administration is now endorsing would accomplish a number of important objectives. It will:

• Establish the commitment of the Federal Government to achieve full employment.

• Establish the commitment of the Federal Government, simultaneously, to achieve reasonable price stability.

• Establish a framework for economic policy decisions. The administration would transmit to the Congress its goals for employment, unemployment, production, and income over a 5-year period. The Congress would have the responsibility to consider these goals and to establish its own goals.

• Establish as the goal for 1983 an overall unemployment rate of 4 percent, with flexibility to modify that goal if necessity requires. This is an ambitious objective and one that may prove very difficult to achieve, but setting our sights high challenges us to do our best.

• Recognize that high unemployment must be fought with a variety of weapons, including special government efforts, but that primary emphasis should be placed on expanding job opportunities in the private sector.

• Recognize that the achievement of full employment and price stability must be sought through the use of monetary and fiscal policies, together with structural measures designed to improve the functioning of the Nation's labor and capital markets—not through government planning or control of private production, wages, and prices.

Title II of the bill sets out considerations to guide the President and the Congress in the event that new programs and appropriations are needed to fight unemployment. This feature of the bill does not authorize such programs, but commends them for use, if necessary, to implement the goals of the legislation.

Title III of the bill sets forth procedures for congressional consideration of the President's goals and policy recommendations. While the specific procedures are for the Congress to determine, it is important, in my judgment, that the Congress in its deliberations on Title III of the bill, establish procedures to integrate

2023

its decisions on economic goals with its decisions on the budget.

I would like to thank Senator Humphrey, Congressman Hawkins, and their representatives who have worked diligently and in a spirit of cooperation with me and representatives of my administration to reach agreement on this important legislation. I look forward to working with the Congress to enact this legislation.

National Council on the Arts

Nomination of Three Members of the Council.
November 14, 1977

The President today announced that he will nominate Theodore Bikel, Maureen Dees, and Jacob Lawrence to be members of the National Council on the Arts.

Bikel, 53, would replace Thomas Schippers, resigned, and serve until September 3, 1980. Bikel is an actor in Broadway theater, motion pictures, and television.

Dees, 40, would replace Rosalind R. Brisson, deceased, and serve until September 3, 1978. She is with the Southern Poverty Law Center in Montgomery, Ala., and has had experience working with community theaters and local development of the arts in medium-sized and small communities. She is one of the founders of the Montgomery Theatre Guild, a program to train actors and directors for regional community theaters.

Lawrence, 60, would replace Judith Jamison, resigned, and serve until September 3, 1978. He is a painter who has had numerous exhibitions and whose work is represented in many public collections. He is a professor of art at the University of Washington in Seattle.

Board for International Broadcasting

Nomination of Rita E. Hauser and
Frank Markoe, Jr., To Be Members.
November 14, 1977

The President today announced that he will nominate Rita E. Hauser and Frank Markoe, Jr., to be members of the Board for International Broadcasting.

Hauser, of New York City, will serve the remainder of the term expiring April 28, 1980, replacing John P. Roche, resigned. Hauser was born December 7, 1934, in New York City. She received an A.B. from Hunter College in 1954, a Ph. D. from the University of Strasbourg, France, in 1955, and an LL.B. from New York University Law School in 1959.

Hauser has practiced law with various firms in New York City since 1960. Since 1972 she has been with the firm of Stroock & Stroock & Lavan. She served on the U.S. Advisory Commission on Educational and Cultural Affairs from 1974 to 1977. She is a member of the Institute on International Education, the Legal Aid Society of New York, and the Council on Foreign Relations.

Markoe, of Far Hills, N.J., will serve the remainder of the term expiring May 20, 1980, replacing Foy D. Kohler, resigned. Markoe was born September 5, 1923, in Baltimore. He received an A.B. from Washington and Lee University in 1947 and an LL.B. from the University of Maryland in 1950. He served in the U.S. Army Air Force from 1942 to 1945.

Markoe practiced law from 1950 to 1955. From 1955 to 1958, he was with Emerson Drug Co. in Baltimore, serving as general counsel and director, then administrative vice president. Since 1958 he has been with Warner-Lambert Co. in Morris Plains, N.J. He has been executive vice president of Warner-Lambert since 1973.

on the District of Columbia and legislative assistant to Senator Thomas Eagleton. Since earlier this year, Manatos has been Counselor to the Secretary of Commerce for Congressional Liaison.

National Commission on the Observance of International Women's Year

Appointment of Rita Elway as a Member. November 14, 1977

The President has appointed Rita Elway, of Seattle, Wash., to be a member of the National Commission on the Observance of International Women's Year. She replaces March Fong Eu, who has resigned from the Commission. Elway, 26, is a partner and co-owner of Communications Design of Seattle, a public opinion research firm. She teaches communications and Asian American studies at the University of Washington, and serves on the board of directors of the Japanese-American Citizens League.

Department of Commerce

Nomination of Andrew E. Manatos To Be an Assistant Secretary. November 14, 1977

The President today announced that he will nominate Andrew E. Manatos, of Bethesda, Md., to be an Assistant Secretary of Commerce. This is a new position which was created by the signing of S. 1019, the authorization bill for marine programs in the Commerce Department.

Manatos was born December 7, 1944. He received a B.A. and an M.A. from American University. From 1969 to 1973, he was on the staff of the Senate Committee on the Post Office and Civil Service. From 1973 to 1976, he was associate staff director of the Senate Committee

Federal Cash Management

Memorandum for the Heads of Executive Departments and Agencies. November 14, 1977

Memorandum for the Heads of Executive Departments and Agencies

Subject: Federal Cash Management

I have directed my reorganization staff, in conjunction with the Treasury Department, to conduct a comprehensive review of cash management policies, practices and organization throughout the Federal government.

The purpose of this effort is to identify further opportunities to apply modern cash management techniques to our massive cash flow. Within the constraints of monetary and economic policy, and building on the continuing work of the Treasury Department, the effort will seek ways to use our cash more efficiently with a view toward reducing Federal debt requirements and interest costs. The study will pay special attention to how effectively the government collects and disburses money, compensates banks and other financial institutions for services, controls cash balances, and provides incentives to make Federal managers more aware of the cash management implications of their decisions.

Representatives of my reorganization staff will contact you. They may ask you for help, advice, staff resources, or to participate in reviewing your own cash management activities. Inasmuch as I consider this to be a major management improvement effort, I trust you will share my enthusiasm and cooperate to the fullest extent possible.

In order to inform all affected parties that this review is underway, I have directed that this memorandum be published in the FEDERAL REGISTER.

JIMMY CARTER

NOTE: The text of the memorandum was released on November 15.

Visit of Mohammad Reza Pahlavi, Shahanshah of Iran

Remarks of the President and the Shah at the Welcoming Ceremony. November 15, 1977

THE PRESIDENT. This morning, our Nation and its people are indeed honored to have visiting us from Iran His Imperial Majesty and Empress Farah, long-time friends of our country, historically bound together. We are very delighted that the Shah could come here with his beautiful wife.

The first American President with whom the Shah met was Franklin Roosevelt, in 1943 at a Tehran conference. He's met with seven Presidents. And this is a great honor for me to have him come this first year that I'm in office, to share with me the historical ties that have bound our nations together and the pledges of friendship and cooperation and mutual purpose, indeed, partnership as we face the coming years.

When the Shah took over the leadership of his nation 36 years ago, Iran was occupied by foreign powers. Since that time, the progress in his country and his

growth into a world leader has indeed been remarkable and has aroused the admiration of the world.

This is a time for a searching analysis of the beneficial influence that can be exerted upon the other people of the world in energy, trade, and with us, a partnership and a mutual defense which binds our countries together and which provides us with an opportunity to preserve the peace in the Middle East.

Iran is strong and it is at peace with its neighbors. We now have working relationships between Iran and our country within 50 different universities. There are about 30,000 Iranian students here and about 40,000 Americans in Iran. This is a wonderful opportunity for us to share experiences and to plan together for the future.

Your Imperial Majesty, we welcome you and the Empress Farah to our country.

THE SHAH. Mr. President, Mrs. Carter, thank you very much for your very warm words of welcome in describing the close relations existing between our two countries.

I remember the days when I first met with President Roosevelt in our own capital city, in what, in those days, we thought the future shape of the world would be decided. Obviously, we had hopes that those shapes would be for peace, happiness, and prosperity.

History is not always as one plans it. But this doesn't mean that those of good will should not try again and again. What we hope in our country is to see this new leadership in the United States provide and nurture the hopes that millions of people have for a better future, and the leadership that the United States of America and the President of the United States of America could give and bring towards that great future, because you can do it.

By mentioning the numbers of Iranians living in America, and also the numbers of Americans living in Iran, I think that you touched on a very important issue, the great numbers of people from both sides getting to know each other every day, better and better, and developing personal friendships and friendship between the two nations. This is a very good guarantee that we shall stay, hopefully, always together, because basically we believe in the same principles, in the same ideals.

We attach utmost importance to our relations with the United States and your friendship for us, because since the beginnings of our relations, America has always shown a very unselfish and, many times, very friendly attitude towards us. We have never had the slightest shadow casting over our relations, and I pray God that this will continue always in the future.

Thank you again, Mr. President, for your very warm welcome.

THE PRESIDENT. Thank you very much.

NOTE: The President spoke at 10:36 a.m. on the South Lawn of the White House.

Anniversary of the Adoption of the Articles of Confederation

Proclamation 4540.   November 15, 1977

By the President of the United States of America

A Proclamation

In the midst of our struggle for independence the Continental Congress, meeting in York, Pennsylvania, recognized that the new Nation would require a permanent central government. Not only was unity necessary if that struggle was to be successfully concluded, but it was essential if the new Nation was to be able to deal effectively with such matters as regulating trade, disposing of western lands, and controlling finance.

Although the colonists shared a common heritage and spoke a common language, their customs, traditions and economic needs varied. Because of this their loyalties were regional in nature. These differences were overcome and, on November 15, 1777, the Continental Congress adopted the Articles of Confederation.

The Articles of Confederation became our first constitution and served the new Nation from 1781, when they were ratified, until 1789. Much of what we learned about government during that period became part of our Constitution and our heritage.

Now, THEREFORE, I, JIMMY CARTER, President of the United States of America, do hereby proclaim Tuesday, November 15, 1977, as a Day of National Observance of the Two Hundredth Anniversary of the Adoption of the Articles of Confederation by the Continental Congress convened in York, Pennsylvania, and I call upon the people of the United States to observe that day with appropriate ceremonies and activities.

IN WITNESS WHEREOF, I have hereunto set my hand this fifteenth day of November, in the year of our Lord nineteen hundred seventy-seven, and of the Independence of the United States of America the two hundred and second.

JIMMY CARTER

[Filed with the Office of the Federal Register, 1:07 p.m., November 15, 1977]

National Highway Safety Advisory Committee

Appointment of 12 Members to the Committee. November 15, 1977

The President has appointed 12 persons as members of the National Highway Safety Advisory Committee for terms expiring March 15, 1980. They are:

OSCAR H. EDMONDS, JR., 53, of Memphis, Tenn., president of Edmonds Material and Equipment Co. and Mid-South Equipment and Supply Co.

HAROLD A. FENNER, JR., M.D., 53, of Hobbs, N. Mex., an orthopedic surgeon and consultant on medical aspects of automotive safety.

CARLTON FISHER, 42, of Decatur, Ga., Georgia Governor's highway safety representative and a former Georgia state trooper.

CHARLES H. HARTMAN, 44, of Delta, Pa., president of the Motorcycle Safety Foundation and a former Deputy Administrator of the National Highway Traffic Safety Administration.

DEBORAH KAPLAN, 27, of Washington, D.C., director of the Disability Rights Center and chairperson of the National Disabled Women's Caucus.

WILLIAM O. MAYS, M.D., 42, of Bloomfield Hills, Mich., a practitioner of internal medicine and former Wayne County (Michigan) medical examiner.

BETSY F. RAHN, 65, of Walnut Creek, Calif., judge of the municipal court of the Walnut Creek-Danville Judicial District.

J. PHILLIP RICHLEY, 51, of Youngstown, Ohio, recently elected mayor of Youngstown and former director of the Ohio Department of Highways.

KALISTE J. SALOOM, JR., 59, judge of the city and juvenile courts of Lafayette, La.

BASIL Y. SCOTT, 52, of East Greenbush, N.Y., administrative director of the New York State Department of Motor Vehicles and Chairman of the National Motor Vehicle Safety Advisory Council.

LYNNE SMITH, 33, of Washington, D.C., an analyst and writer for the Insurance Institute for Highway Safety and former director of the Center for Auto Safety's highway safety project.

REBECCA C. YOUNG, 43, of Madison, Wis., deputy secretary of the Wisconsin Department of Administration and former commissioner of the Wisconsin Highway Commission.

Visit of the Shah of Iran

White House Statement Issued Following the First Meeting Between the President and the Shah. November 15, 1977

President Carter and His Imperial Majesty the Shahanshah of Iran met in the Cabinet Room for 90 minutes. The President was accompanied by Vice President Mondale; Secretary of State Cyrus Vance; Zbigniew Brzezinski, Assistant to the President for National Security Affairs; Alfred L. Atherton, Jr., Assistant Secretary of State for Near Eastern and South Asian Affairs; U.S. Ambassador to Iran William Sullivan; and Gary Sick, National Security Council staff member; and His Majesty, by Foreign Minister, His Excellency A. A. Khalatbary; and Iranian Ambassador to the United States Ardeshir Zahedi.

The President began by expressing his personal pleasure at meeting His Imperial Majesty for the first time, noting that this visit will enable them to establish close personal ties of friendship. The President expressed his appreciation for His Majesty's message of condolence to the families of those who lost their lives in the recent disaster in Georgia.

The President reaffirmed to His Majesty that he fully supports the special relationship which the two countries have developed over the last 30 years and gave his personal commitment to strengthen further our ties. The President emphasized the broad mutuality of our interests in the region and globally, and expressed appreciation for the support which Iran has extended in achieving our shared objectives. The President reiterated the importance that he attaches to a strong, stable, and progressive Iran under the leadership of His Imperial Majesty. To that end, he emphasized that it remains the policy of the United States to cooperate with Iran in its economic and social development programs and in continuing to help meet Iran's security needs.

The President and His Majesty discussed in some detail the current situation in the Middle East. The President reviewed the diplomatic efforts the United States is making to bring about a reconvening of the Middle East Peace Conference in Geneva. The President noted that Iran has a unique position in the area in that it has good ties with all the countries involved and that Iran's economic assistance to several of these countries and its trade with them were valuable contributions to the stability of the area. The President welcomed the support Iran has extended for our diplomatic efforts to achieve peace in the area. They also discussed developments in the Middle East region as a whole, and such matters of mutual interest as developments in Africa and South Asia and our discussions with the Soviet Union on SALT II and the Indian Ocean.

The President expressed his disappointment that it has been necessary to postpone his visit to Iran but reiterated his desire to make the trip as soon as possible. The President emphasized his determination to obtain the comprehensive national energy program, which is currently before Congress. His Majesty expressed his support for the President's effort. They gave special attention to the needs to develop alternative energy sources, including so-

lar, and agreed that both countries would work closely together in this area. They agreed that effective energy conservation programs are essential to help meet future world energy needs as oil supplies dwindle. In this discussion, they exchanged views on how to maintain a healthy world economy. The President emphasized the very great importance to the international community of maintaining world oil price stability, and expressed his strong hope that there would be no oil price increase over the coming year. He expressed his pleasure at His Imperial Majesty's understanding of this issue.

The President also expressed his appreciation for the strong support we have received from Iran on nuclear nonproliferation matters.

His Majesty stated that he looks forward to receiving the President in the near future in Tehran.

The President and Mrs. Carter are giving a State dinner for His Majesty and the Shahbanou this evening, and the President will meet again tomorrow morning with His Majesty to continue their discussions.

Visit of the Shah of Iran

Toasts of the President and the Shah at a Dinner Honoring the Shah. November 15, 1977

THE PRESIDENT. First of all, I want to welcome all of you here this evening to join with me in expressing our own appreciation that the Shah and Empress would come here to represent their wonderful people of Iran.

There's one thing I can say about the Shah—he knows how to draw a crowd. [*Laughter*]

I really thought today, when the tear gas came across the South Lawn, that the Shah showed a tremendous amount of self-assurance and graciousness and also courage in giving his speech to the people of our country without hesitation, and I deeply appreciate that exhibition of your strength.

THE SHAH. Thank you.

THE PRESIDENT. This is one time when the news reporters were accurate about me. I saw on the evening television that they said it was one of the briefest speeches I had made. [*Laughter*] I was glad to turn the microphone over to the Shah. [*Laughter*]

We've had a wonderful chance to visit and get to know one another. Our country was blessed a few weeks ago to have Empress Farah come here and travel around our Nation. She came to visit Rosalynn and me. We are very delighted to have personal friends, as well as leaders of one of the great nations of the world.

There's an old saying in the East that history is a mirror to the past and a lesson for the future. And if there was ever a country which has blossomed forth under enlightened leadership, it would be the ancient empire of Persia, which is now the great country of Iran.

When the Shah assumed a mantle of leadership in his own country 36 years ago, he faced a very dismal future. His country was occupied then by foreign forces. His father had started some social change that was very doubtful about its own success. At that time, there were about 1,000 people in Iran who had advanced college degrees, and there are now 15 colleges and universities in Iran, 175,-000 students in the college, and the Shah just told me that in 10 years, they'll have 500,000 college students in Iran. This is a remarkable demonstration of leadership and growth in the spiritual and also knowledge of the people of that great country.

As you well know, Iran has always been kind of a crossroads. The cultural history of Iran is absolutely remarkable. And Empress Farah has taken on her own shoulders a responsibility for preserving that ancient culture so that they can learn from the past and preserve the beauty for the future.

There's also been a growth in the well-being of the people there. They've expanded the opportunity for good health care as well as education.

Just not much more than 15 years ago, their average per capita income in Iran was not much more than a hundred dollars per year. The Shah just told me it was now $2,220 per year last month, and it's probably more this month. [*Laughter*] That shows what a tremendous job he is doing.

Iran has recognized that their great natural resources need to be husbanded and invested to guarantee a sound and a prosperous future in the years to come.

Iran is a country that is strong militarily, is strong politically, and is strong in the commitment and in the spirit of its people, and also is at peace with its neighbors, is well respected.

Iran is a nation, and its leadership is epitomized by a man who has a trust of other countries. Even those that historically have been enemies now look upon the Shah and the people of Iran with a great deal of confidence and trust, recognizing that they are a stabilizing influence in that region, indeed, throughout the Persian Gulf, the Indian Ocean, and with a growing degree of influence, in the Western World, in Japan, and in Africa.

I had a chance today to listen to the Shah explain to me the perspective of the region and the rest of the world as viewed from the great country of Iran. And I learned a great deal from him as he talked about the history and the present and future possibilities of the people in Pakistan and Afghanistan, of Burma, India, Iraq, other nations in the Middle East, in the Horn of Africa, things that I had not seen from that particular point of view. And it helped me greatly to understand the special challenges that face us as a great nation and the importance of the partnership that we have with the people of Iran.

We are bound together with unbreakable ties of friendship, of past history, a mutual commitment to the present and to the future. Our military alliance is unshakable, and it's an alliance that is beneficent in its impact on the rest of the world. Iran seeks no dominion over other people. They seek no territorial gains. They just want peace, and they have spread their influence, because of the great leadership of the Shah, very rapidly.

We look upon Iran's strength as an extension of our own strength, and Iran looks upon our strength as an extension of theirs. We derive mutual benefit from this close relationship. The Shah has been to our country more than a dozen times. His first meeting with an American President was in 1943, when President Roosevelt was in Tehran at a conference there; and subsequently he's met with every President we've had—with Truman and with Eisenhower, with Kennedy and with Nixon, with Ford and myself, with President Johnson. And this is a continuation of a growing understanding of one another.

The Shah is very gracious in his attitude toward Americans. In addition to the 175,000 students in his own colleges, there are about 30,000 Iranian students in the colleges of the United States. And this guarantees an investment in the future of understanding of one another. We

have about 40,000 Americans in Iran, and in a very gracious demonstration of friendship which was not well publicized at all, the Shah has provided extra allotments of funds and educational opportunities for American young students there—boys and girls who are at the grammar school and high school level. This is something that he didn't have to do, but it was just an extra demonstration of how valuable they consider our friendship with them.

I would like to say, in closing, that we look upon Iran as a very stabilizing force in the world at large. We don't fear the future when we have friends like this great country.

There are some emerging nations who are assuming regional leadership roles which, in the past, has not been recognized. But I think that Iran is undoubtedly one of those great countries. And with the spreading of their own influence, the world is guaranteed a greater degree of assurance for peace.

We're proud that Empress Farah, perhaps one of the most beautiful leaders in the world, has come to see us again. She's admired by all. Her next-door seatmate here, Mr. Wasserman,[1] has been trying to get her to join him in making a film as a movie star. [*Laughter*] I promised that if he made a film, I'd be the first one to buy a ticket to see her. [*Laughter*] But she's a gracious woman who has taken a lot of interest in the personal lives of the people of her country.

And the Shah has a young son, who's now 17 years old, who will come here for his flight training when he reaches the age of 18. And I think this shows a mutual investment in the future by them in our country and by us in their country.

---

[1] Lew R. Wasserman, president of Music Corporation of America, Inc.

Your Majesty, it's a great honor for me to have you here with us at the White House to renew your old friendship for our country and to express our renewed commitment for friendship in the future. And on behalf of the people of our Nation, I would like to propose a toast to the Shah and to the Empress of Iran and to the great people of that country who are our close, present, and future friends.

THE SHAH. *Mr. President, Mrs. Carter, ladies and gentlemen:*

It is not very easy to speak after the warmth and the kind words that the President of the United States of America has pronounced towards my country, our people, and the Shahbanou and myself. But I would like to reemphasize once more that we look to your country, to your people, and today, to the new President that you have elected, as such good and trusted friends, that this gives us even more fortitude and courage to pursue our goals which are understood so well and which have been said so eloquently by your President.

My personal association with your country is a long one, but even before that, the United States has always shown towards our country and our people what could be expected of a great, unselfish, humanitarian nation which is standing by high principles of honor and dignity.

The reassuring words that the President has pronounced tonight will be felt deeply in my country with appreciation and gratitude. This is a world in which those who stand for the same ideals have to get even closer together. You can rest assured that with us you will find such people who, through any circumstances, will cherish their friendship and their ties with the United States of America and with their noble people.

I must say that since you took this high office, Mr. President, I was looking forward to meeting you, knowing you, and hoping to establish personal relationships. I can say with happiness and with pride that what I saw was absolutely equal, if not more than, anything that I could have expected.

I will take back with me to my country this memorable impression that I have had through my talks with you, through your great understanding of problems, through your vision of our present world and the world of tomorrow.

The important thing is that what we do for today could also serve the future. And I can see that you have that vision, and very clearly, too.

Because of your high position and the importance of your country, we only hope that you will continue to offer the leadership of your country, the potentials of your country, for a future world assured of peace and dignity and the certainty that it will be a better world to live in, better chances for all people of every race, of every creed, of every belief, that, together, we can surmount all the difficulties that can face us by the turn of this century.

I would like to reassure you that you will always find in my country and my people wholehearted support in your noble task, which is to serve your country and also human mankind.

I have to express also our deep appreciation for your hospitality and the friendship that you have shown towards us and, through us, towards our people, and ask all the friends gathered tonight here to join with me in a toast to the President of the United States of America and Mrs. Carter.

THE PRESIDENT. Thank you very much.

NOTE: The President spoke at 9:40 p.m. in the State Dining Room at the White House.

In his remarks, the President referred to an incident which occurred outside the White House grounds. Tear gas was used during an attempt by police forces to separate two groups of demonstrators, one supporting and one opposing the Shah and his visit to the United States.

Visit of the Shah of Iran

White House Statement Issued Following the Second Meeting Between the President and the Shah. November 16, 1977

President Carter and His Imperial Majesty The Shahanshah of Iran met November 16 in the Cabinet Room for 90 minutes. The President was accompanied by Vice President Mondale; Secretary of State Cyrus Vance; Zbigniew Brzezinski, Assistant to the President for National Security Affairs; Alfred L. Atherton, Jr., Assistant Secretary of State for Near Eastern and South Asian Affairs; U.S. Ambassador to Iran William Sullivan; and Gary Sick, National Security Council staff member; and His Majesty, by Foreign Minister, His Excellency A. A. Khalatbary and Iranian Ambassador to the United States Ardeshir Zahedi.

The President and His Majesty this morning, as well as in their discussions last evening, concluded their review of broad international developments of key interest to them both. In this discussion the President reviewed his approach to human rights throughout the world.

The meeting this morning centered largely on bilateral issues. They discussed the broad economic ties between our two countries and noted that the economic cooperation will continue to expand. In this part of the conversation, they examined the progress of our negotiations to reach accord on an agreement on the peaceful uses of nuclear energy. The President also offered suggestions for resolving some points that remain pending and expressed confidence that agreement can be achieved within his nonproliferation policy.

The President and His Majesty reviewed a number of military supply issues. The President again reaffirmed our support for a strong Iran, noting that Iran's security is a matter of the highest priority for this country. The President informed His Majesty that he would wish to work closely with Congress in meeting Iran's security needs.

The President concluded by expressing his great pleasure at the personal ties he and His Majesty had established during this visit. They agreed that these personal ties are valuable in maintaining the long-standing and close relations between our two countries. They look forward to resuming their discussions during the visit the President hopes to make soon to Tehran.

Urban Mass Transportation Act of 1964 Amendments

Statement on Signing H.R. 8346 Into Law. November 16, 1977

I am signing H.R. 8346 today even though I have serious reservations about several of its provisions. I decided to sign it primarily to avoid any possibility that certain commuter rail services might be disrupted.

This bill essentially benefits those who now use subsidized commuter trains.

Special legislation providing temporary Federal assistance for these services was enacted in 1976. It was intended to help assist in an orderly transition to locally supported service. I am disappointed that the affected cities have not arranged to live within these original Federal emergency payments.

The administration is looking at more equitable ways to deal with urban transportation, including commuter rail service, on a long-term basis. Early next year, I will submit legislation providing a more flexible program of transit and highway assistance to urban areas. This expanded program would supplant funds made available by this bill for commuter train services and allow resources to be used for various kinds of transit, including commuter trains where local communities decide they are appropriate.

We should move away from the establishment of a new categorical grant program affecting only a few cities to a comprehensive surface transportation program.

NOTE: As enacted, H.R. 8346 is Public Law 95–187, approved November 16.

Federal Employment of Women

Memorandum for Heads of Departments and Agencies. November 17, 1977

Memorandum for Heads of Departments and Agencies

Executive Order 11375, signed by President Johnson on October 13, 1967, prohibited discrimination on the basis of sex in Federal employment. Ten years later, it is an appropriate time to reaffirm the Executive Order, assess the progress we have made, and evaluate our current efforts to be a truly equal opportunity employer.

In recent months we have made substantial progress in appointing women to responsible non-career positions; I would like to carry this commitment and effort into the career service as well.

Special efforts will be required from all of us to achieve our goal. I have already asked each of you to cooperate in eliminating sex discrimination from our laws and policies. Today I ask that you work, aggressively and creatively, to provide maximum employment opportunities for women in the Federal career service. This means developing, within merit principles, innovative programs to recruit and hire qualified women and to be sure they have the opportunity for satisfying career development.

As part of the President's Reorganization Project, the Personnel Management Project will soon propose program and policy changes for the civil service system. These proposals will have an impact on the employment and advancement of women, and that impact will receive thoughtful consideration.

I will also be receiving reports from the Chairman of the Civil Service Commission on the progress that you are making in increasing the numbers of women in the mid- and senior levels of your organizations. I expect to see significant improvements made in your department or agency as a result of your personal initiatives, and I hope you will be especially sensitive to the concerns of older women and women from minority groups.

JIMMY CARTER

Regulatory Reform

Announcement of Proposed Executive Order To Reform the Government's Regulatory Procedures. November 17, 1977

The President today announced that he will seek public comment on a proposed Executive order to reform the Government's regulatory procedures. For the first time, an order will not be final until the public response has been received and analyzed. Executive orders have always been published in final form in the FEDERAL REGISTER with no opportunity for the public to suggest changes in the text. This order will be published in draft form with a notice inviting public suggestions and comments.

The President's regulatory reform program aims to simplify and improve Government regulations which are often unnecessarily complex, confusing, and burdensome. Federal regulation is often cited as a source of frustration by consumers, businessmen, State and local governments, and nonprofit institutions. Difficulty in making private views known to Federal regulatory agencies is another source of frustration.

The proposed Executive order addresses some of these problems by requiring agencies to take the following actions:

—Publish a semiannual agenda of upcoming regulatory actions in order to allow all interested parties an early opportunity to provide their views on the regulation. This includes consumers, business, Congress, State and local governments, and other public groups.

—Develop a plan for all significant regulations which assures that the public's views are considered in the agency's decisions; that the regulation does not conflict with those of other agencies; that the regulation is written clearly; and that there is a specific official accountable for the regulation.

—Increase oversight by policy officials of the regulation development process to assure that regulations are in the best interest of the public.

—Prepare a regulatory analysis for all major regulations to assure that feasible alternatives have been analyzed and that

the most effective and least burdensome approach has been chosen.

—Undertake a review of existing regulations.

Agencies will be allowed some flexibility to adapt these requirements to meet their unique needs.

The draft Executive order has been reviewed by all departments and agencies and many Members of Congress. The FEDERAL REGISTER notice is scheduled to appear on Friday, November 18, 1977, and solicits public comments on several specific questions related to the order. The public has until December 18 to provide comments.

Digest of Other White House Announcements

The following listing includes the President's daily schedule and other items of general interest as announced by the White House Press Office during the period covered by this issue. Events and announcements printed elsewhere in the issue are not included.

November 12

The President met at the White House with Zbigniew Brzezinski, Assistant to the President for National Security Affairs.

The President and Mrs. Carter attended the Navy-Georgia Tech football game in Annapolis, Md.

The President declared a major disaster for the State of Virginia as a result of severe storms and flooding, beginning about October 31, which caused extensive public and private property damage.

The President declared a major disaster for the State of Tennessee as a result of severe storms and flooding, beginning about November 4, which caused extensive public and private property damage.

November 14

The President met at the White House with:

—Dr. Brzezinski;
—senior White House staff members;
—the Cabinet;
—Mr. and Mrs. Hugh A. Carter, Sr., of Georgia, the President's cousins;
—Vice President Walter F. Mondale;
—a group of administration officials to discuss the budget;
—Representatives Al Ullman of Oregon and Harley O. Staggers of West Virginia, to discuss energy.

The President has appointed four officials as members of the Board of Trustees of the American Folklife Center. They are: Assistant Secretary of Health, Education, and Welfare Mary F. Berry, Assistant Secretary of Agriculture Alex P. Mercure, Assistant Secretary of the Interior Forrest J. Gerard, and National Park Service Director William Whalen.

November 15

The President met at the White House with:

—Dr. Brzezinski;
—a group of administration officials to discuss the budget.

November 16

The President met at the White House with:

—David L. Aaron, Deputy Assistant to the President for National Security Affairs;
—Secretary of Transportation Brock Adams;
—James T. McIntyre, Jr., Acting Director of the Office of Management and Budget;
—Charles L. Schultze, Chairman of the Council of Economic Advisers;
—R. Heath Larry, president of the National Association of Manufacturers.

November 17

The President met at the White House with:

—Dr. Brzezinski;
—Kenneth M. Curtis, chairman, and Paul D. Sullivan, secretary-treasurer, Democratic National Committee;
—Vice President Mondale, Adm. Stansfield Turner, Director of Central Intelligence, and Dr. Brzezinski;
—Mrs. Carter, for lunch;
—Vice President Mondale, Secretary of Defense Harold Brown, Gen. George S. Brown, Chairman of the Joint Chiefs of Staff, Charles W. Duncan, Jr., Deputy Secretary of Defense, and Dr. Brezezinski;
—Vice President Mondale, Secretary Brown, General Brown, Mr. Duncan, Dr. Brzezinski, and other officials, to discuss the strategic arms limitation talks.

In a ceremony on the North Lawn at the White House, the President planted a red maple tree from Georgia.

The President attended a reception in the State Dining Room in recognition of the 10th anniversary of the American Film Institute (transcript will be printed next week).

The President has appointed Stuart E. Eizenstat, Assistant to the President for Domestic Affairs and Policy, as a member of the Board of Trustees of the Woodrow Wilson International Center for Scholars.

The President and Mrs. Carter attended the American Film Institute's 10th Anniversary Benefit Gala at the Kennedy Center.

November 18

The President met at the White House with:

—Vice President Mondale, Secretary of State Cyrus R. Vance and Dr. Brzezinski;
—Dr. Brzezinski;

—Dr. Hafdan Mahler, Director General of the World Health Organization, and Peter G. Bourne, Special Assistant to the President for Health Issues;

—Mr. McIntyre;

—Adm. Hyman G. Rickover, Deputy Commander for Nuclear Propulsion, Naval Sea Systems Command, Department of the Navy;

—Ambassador Arthur J. Goldberg, Chairman of the U.S. Delegation to the Belgrade meeting of the Conference on Security and Cooperation in Europe, to discuss the progress of the Belgrade Conference;

—Soviet Ambassador to the United States A. F. Dobrynin, who delivered a message to the President from President L. I. Brezhnev;

—a group of economic and budget advisers for a budget review meeting.

The President attended a reception in the East Room for the National Panama Canal Citizens Committee.

The White House announced that on November 17, Israeli Ambassador to the United States Simcha Dinitz delivered a message to the President from Prime Minister Menahem Begin concerning the upcoming visit of Egyptian President Anwar al-Sadat to Jerusalem. Prime Minister Begin thanked the President for his efforts which contributed to bringing about the meeting.

NOMINATIONS SUBMITTED TO THE SENATE

The following list does not include promotions of members of the Uniformed Services, nominations to the Service Academies, or nominations of Foreign Service officers.

Submitted November 14, 1977

ANDREW E. MANATOS, of Maryland, to be an Assistant Secretary of Commerce (new position).

NOMINATIONS—Continued

Submitted November 14—Continued

JOHN H. CARY, of Tennessee, to be United States Attorney for the Eastern District of Tennessee for the term of 4 years, vice John L. Bowers, Jr.

The following-named persons to be members of the Board for International Broadcasting for the terms indicated:

RITA E. HAUSER, of New York, for a term expiring April 28, 1980, vice John P. Roche, resigned.

FRANK MARKOE, JR., of New Jersey, for a term expiring May 20, 1980, vice Foy D. Kohler, term expired.

The following-named persons to be members of the National Council on the Arts for the terms indicated:

MAUREEN DEES, of Alabama, for the remainder of the term expiring September 3, 1978, vice Rosalind Russell Brisson, deceased.

JACOB LAWRENCE, of Washington, for the remainder of the term expiring September 3, 1978, vice Judith Jamison, resigned.

THEODORE BIKEL, of Connecticut, for the remainder of the term expiring September 3, 1980, vice Thomas Schippers, resigned.

Withdrawn November 14, 1977

ROBERT H. MENDELSOHN, of California, to be an Assistant Secretary of the Interior, vice Ronald G. Coleman, resigned, which was sent to the Senate on May 5, 1977.

Submitted November 17, 1977

THOMAS ARNY RHODEN, of Mississippi, to be United States Marshal for the Southern District of Mississippi for the term of 4 years (reappointment).

CHECKLIST OF WHITE HOUSE PRESS RELEASES

The following releases of the Office of the White House Press Secretary, distributed during the period covered by this issue, are not included in the issue.

Released November 14, 1977

Announcement: nomination of John H. Cary to be United States Attorney for the Eastern District of Tennessee

Fact sheet: proposed full employment and balanced growth bill

CHECKLIST—Continued

Released November 15, 1977

Announcement: nomination of Thomas A. Rhoden for reappointment as United States Marshal for the Southern District of Mississippi

Released November 18, 1977

News conference: following his meeting with the President—by Arthur J. Goldberg, Chairman of the U.S. Delegation to the Belgrade meeting of the Conference on Security and Cooperation in Europe

ACTS APPROVED BY THE PRESIDENT

Approved November 12, 1977

H.R. 1403_____ Private Law 95–18
An act to authorize the Secretary of the Interior to convey the interest of the United States in certain lands in Adams County, Mississippi, notwithstanding a limitation in the Color-of-Title Act (45 Stat. 1069, as amended; 43 U.S.C. 1068).

H.R. 2527_____ Public Law 95–169
An act to authorize the Secretary of Agriculture to convey certain lands in the Sierra National Forest, California, to the Madera Cemetery District.

H.R. 2849_____ Public Law 95–170
An act to suspend until July 1, 1978, the rate of duty on mattress blanks of latex rubber, and for other purposes.

H.R. 3373_____ Public Law 95–172
An act to extend for an additional temporary period the existing suspension of duties on certain classifications of yarns of silk, and for other purposes.

H.R. 3387_____ Public Law 95–171
An act to extend certain Social Security Act provisions, and for other purposes.

S. 1019_____ Public Law 95–173
Maritime Appropriation Authorization Act for Fiscal Year 1978.

S. 2118_____ Public Law 95–174
An act to authorize the Secretary of Agriculture to convey certain homesites within the Chugach and Tongass National Forests, Alaska.

Approved November 14, 1977

H.R. 4458_____ Public Law 95–176
An act to amend certain provisions of the Internal Revenue Code of 1954 relating to distilled spirits, and for other purposes.

ACTS APPROVED—Continued

Approved November 14—Continued

S. 1142_____ Private Law 95–19
An act for the relief of Kam Liu Cheung.

S. 2052_____ Public Law 95–175
An act to extend the supervision of the United States Capitol Police to certain facilities leased by the Office of Technology Assessment.

Approved November 15, 1977

H.R. 2501_____ Private Law 95–21
An act to eliminate a conflict between the official cadastral survey and a private survey of the so-called Wold Tract within the Medicine Bow National Forest, State of Wyoming.

H.R. 7278_____ Public Law 95–177
An act to amend section 10 of the Merchant Marine Act, 1936.

H.R. 8499_____ Public Law 95–178
An act to amend the Alaska Native Claims Settlement Act.

H.R. 8992_____ Public Law 95–179
An act to amend title 3 of the United States Code to change the name of the Executive Protective Service.

H.R. 9512_____ Public Law 95–180
An act to amend the Higher Education Act of 1965 to include the Trust Territory of the Pacific Islands in the definition of the term "State" for the purpose of participation in programs authorized by that Act.

H.R. 9704_____ Public Law 95–181
An act to amend the Federal Crop Insurance Act, and for other purposes.

H.R. 9836_____ Public Law 95–182
An act to authorize the Architect of the Capitol to furnish chilled water to the Folger Shakespeare Library.

S. 854_____ Private Law 95–20
An act to authorize the Secretary of Commerce to sell two obsolete vessels to Mid-Pacific Sea Harvesters, Incorporated, and for other purposes.

S. 1062_____ Public Law 95–185
An act to amend section 441 of the District of Columbia Self-Government and Governmental Reorganization Act.

S. 1339_____ Public Law 95–183
Energy Research and Development Administration Authorization Act of 1977 and 1978—Military Applications.

ACTS APPROVED—Continued

Approved November 15—Continued

S. 1863_____ Public Law 95–184
Department of Defense Supplemental Appropriation Authorization Act, 1978.

Approved November 16, 1977

H.R. 8346_____ Public Law 95–187
An act to amend the Urban Mass Transportation Act of 1964 to revise the program of Federal operating assistance provided under section 17 of such Act.

H.R. 9019_____ Public Law 95–186
An act to rescind certain budget authority contained in the message of the President of July 19, 1977 (H. Doc. 95–188), transmitted pursuant to the Impoundment Control Act of 1974.

ACTS APPROVED—Continued

Approved November 16—Continued

H.R. 9710_____ Public Law 95–188
An act to extend the authority for the flexible regulation of interest rates on deposits and accounts in depository institutions, to promote the accountability of the Federal Reserve System, and for other purposes.

S. 1269_____ Private Law 95–22
An act for the relief of Camilla A. Hester.

S. 1528_____ Public Law 95–190
Safe Drinking Water Amendments of 1977.

S. 2281_____ Public Law 95–189
An act authorizing an increase in the monetary authorization for nine comprehensive river basin plans.

American Film Institute

Remarks at a Reception on the Occasion of the 10th Anniversary of the Institute. November 17, 1977

Rosalynn and I are very deeply grateful and honored to have a chance to welcome to the White House a group of people who have contributed so much to our Nation, what it is, what it stands for, and the image of it around the world.

James Agee said that the most tremendous possibility for a popular art form was the motion pictures, since the time of Shakespeare. That was a number of years ago. He's one of my favorite authors, and I think his predictions are increasingly coming true.

The movies have touched all our lives—mine as a farmboy. It gave me a vision of the outside world. I'm sure the first time I saw the White House was in the back seat of the movie theater. [*Laughter*] And we also have had a chance to tie our highly diverse American society together. Those who were rich could learn what poverty was, and those who were poor could see the vision of a better life. Those of us who were happy could learn about sorrow, and those who were stricken with hunger or sorrow could learn about happiness.

The motion pictures have, in effect, painted the history of our country—I don't think too distorted in their conglomerate form—and one of the things the Institute is trying to do is to take 14,000 films that are in the Library of Congress and restore them and preserve them for the future. I'm sure the motion pictures don't distort history any more than the day-by-day life of our Nation is distorted in the reporting of it. [*Laughter*]

We've seen also evolve over a number of years the fact that for many hundreds of millions of people in the world America is the movies. That's all they know about us. And the image that we've projected to them overseas, in its total form, again, is probably a quite accurate picture of what our Nation has been and is.

Last night was a good example of it. We had the Shah of Iran and Empress Farah with us, one of the most beautiful women in the world. I was sitting between the Shah and Empress Farah. My preference was to talk—[*laughter*]—well, I won't tell you what my preference is; I'll let you guess. [*Laughter*] Unfortunately, Empress Farah was sitting between me and Lew Wasserman.[1] I was wanting to talk about oil prices, and Lew Wasserman was talking about the motion pictures, and I won't tell you what Empress Farah's preference was. [*Laughter*]

---

[1] Lew R. Wasserman, president of Music Corporation of America, Inc.

But in the process, I had to talk to the Shah about oil prices. And perhaps the motion pictures last night, through Lew Wasserman's influence, helped to hold down the price of oil next year, because I talked to the Shah about that. [*Laughter*]

We are proud to meet all the famous people. I had a chance to put my arms around Olivia De Havilland and Lillian Gish and many others whom I've loved from a distance. And the great actors who are here tonight also have been an inspiration to many of us.

I went to a lot of movies when I was young, whenever I could. In the South, we date life either before "Gone With the Wind" and after "Gone With the Wind," as you know. [*Laughter*]

When "Gone With the Wind" first came out, every school in Georgia was closed, and all the students were hauled to the theaters on the schoolbuses. And it made a great impact on our lives. I think, perhaps, we saw a different version from what was seen in the rest of the country. [*Laughter*] One of my favorite scenes was the burning of Schenectady, New York—[*laughter*]—just before Grant surrendered to Robert E. Lee. It was a great movie. It's not quite as good now as it was then.

But I think all of us realize, because I can tell from the expressions on your face, that the motion pictures have had a tremendous beneficial effect on our country. And on behalf of about 220 million Americans, tonight I would like to express my deep thanks to those who have written and produced and directed and performed and written music for this wonderful art form which is unique in being a true people's art form.

I can't express adequately what it has meant to me personally and to our Nation, and I'm truly grateful to those of you who have made these wonderful films brighten the lives of all Americans and,

perhaps, almost all the people around the world.

Thank you from the bottom of my heart.

NOTE: The President spoke at 6:10 p.m. in the East Room at the White House.

Visit of President Anwar al-Sadat to Israel

Statement Following the Arrival of the Egyptian President in Tel Aviv for Talks With Prime Minister Menahem Begin. November 19, 1977

The arrival of President Sadat in Israel is an historic occasion. The hopes and prayers of all Americans are with these two men as they seek progress toward peace for the people of the Middle East and, indeed, for the entire world.

NOTE: The statement was made available by the White House Press Office. It was not issued in the form of a White House press release.

Visit of President Anwar al-Sadat to Israel

Informal Exchange With Reporters on Departure From the First Baptist Church. November 20, 1977

REPORTER. Could you tell us how your prayer for peace in the Middle East went? What was your prayer, Mr. President?

THE PRESIDENT. My prayer was one that recognized this whole world wants peace; that Christ, our Savior, is the Prince of Peace; that the Middle East has been particularly afflicted by war, which no one there wanted, constantly—almost day by day—conflict, and four major wars in the last 30 years; that yesterday Prime Minister Begin, who is a very deeply religious man, worshipped God in a Jewish temple; this morning President Sadat worshipped the same God in a Moslem mosque and later worshipped the same God in a Christian holy place where Christ was buried; and that all over the world today people are praying for peace.

I mentioned the fact that sometimes the leaders of nations have been the ones who have been an obstacle to peace that was yearned for by the people of their countries and that I knew that Prime Minister Begin is a deeply religious man—he and I have pledged privately to pray for one another—and that President Sadat is a deeply religious man also. He and I have pledged privately to pray for one another.

And I just hope that the prayers of people all over the world will be heard, that this momentous day might lead the entire world another major step toward the peace that we all desire.

Q. You see the hand of God moving in all of this, don't you?

THE PRESIDENT. I think the fact that the Arabs, the Moslems, the Jews, the Christians all worship the same God and freely acknowledge it is a binding force that gives an avenue of communication and common purpose.

I know that when Crown Prince Fahd was here, he talked about this to the Members of Congress and to me, and it's mentioned frequently by leaders like Prime Minister Begin and President Sadat when they talk to me privately, that we do have this common religious bond that at least provides a possible avenue for peace if we can remove the obstacles that men create.

So, yes, I do see it as a common bond.

Q. Do you think things are going well so far?

THE PRESIDENT. I think so. The fact that President Sadat would be courageous enough to go to Israel will transform, I think, the Middle Eastern peace prospects, regardless of the outcome of this particular visit. It's a breakdown in 30 years, perhaps even centuries, of hatred.

I was particularly touched yesterday when President Sadat walked down the red welcoming carpet and shook hands with Mr. Dayan, and he and Mrs. Meir exchanged a friendship, and he bent and kissed her on the cheek. I thought that was a great occasion. I think it will be a major step forward.

Q. What do you mean that leaders have been an obstacle to peace in the Middle East?

THE PRESIDENT. Well, I think it's obvious that the people of the world want peace and pray for peace. And I think that this action by President Sadat to break down all the barriers that have been created by leaders in the past and go directly to the heart of Israel in Jerusalem has been feared by many as a possible action that would arouse the animosity of his own people. And also there was doubt about how Israel would receive him. But the overwhelming gratitude and excitement that now exists in Israel and in Egypt shows that the people were ready for it, and it was just the reluctance of leaders to take this momentous step that was an obstacle.

I have talked to all of the leaders in the Middle East, both the presidents, the kings, the prime ministers, and the foreign ministers, and I know from personal experience that they genuinely want peace. Some of them, I think, have underestimated the willingness of their own people to accept strong moves toward a new understanding. And I think that Sadat and Begin will show today that the two nations that have constantly been at war with tremendous suffering, whose leaders have only been separated by a 30-minute plane ride, have responded well.

I think this is proof in itself that had we leaders of the world been more aggressive in taking bold steps that the people would have responded.

Q. How much difference does the opposition of the Syrians make?

Q. We understand that even now President Sadat is entering the Knesset in Jerusalem.

THE PRESIDENT. I want to get home to watch the speeches. I promised both men on the telephone this week that I would be watching and listening to every word.

I think the Syrians have perhaps been the most difficult and because they are in the most difficult position. They are a nation that's relatively small in size and not nearly so great as Israel or Egypt in military strength. But they are the tie between the more moderate Arab world and the Arab world that still is perhaps most radical, and in a strange way they have become the spokesmen for others who don't want to see such immediate steps made to recognize Israel.

President Asad, with whom I met in Geneva this past year—this year, this past spring, I think, genuinely wants peace, but he has become kind of a spokesman in a strange way for some of the more radical Arab leaders who don't yet want to move.

And I think that this might very well break down the barrier to peace that has existed for so long.

Also, I think it's obvious that President Asad doesn't want to see Syria left out of the future negotiations. They fear that Egypt and Israel will negotiate a bilateral peace agreement to the exclusion of other Arabs. And this is something that neither Sadat wants, nor I, nor Prime Minister Begin. And I think that once

this meeting is over, if it is successful—and I pray that it will be—then this threat that the rest of the Arabs see in being abandoned by the strong nation of Egypt will be removed.

Q. And you think it will make Geneva more possible?

THE PRESIDENT. I think so.

REPORTER. Thank you, Mr. President.

NOTE: The exchange began at 8:54 a.m.

The transcript of the exchange was made available by the White House Press Office. It was not issued in the form of a White House press release.

National Medal of Science

Remarks at the Presentation Ceremony. November 22, 1977

THE PRESIDENT. In 1959 the Congress established this program, the Medal of Science Awards, to recognize outstanding achievement in the sciences and in engineering.

The first awards were given in 1962 by President Kennedy—I think just one award—and since that time every President each year has recognized the outstanding scientists in the physical sciences, the social sciences, biological sciences, and in engineering for the previous year.

I'm particularly grateful, having had some engineering background, some scientific background, in business, agriculture, politics, to come here as President this morning to express the appreciation of our Nation for the tremendous present and past and future contribution that you distinguished Americans have earned.

Most of you have performed so superbly because of a dedication to your own profession—probably most without any thought that you might ultimately be honored for it, except in a contribution to a better life for the people of this country and for those around the world.

As I've looked down the list of those who are being honored today, the breadth of the interests that you have shown and the broad scope of the contributions that you've made is quite remarkable.

As President, I now have the responsibility to prepare the national budget presentation to Congress, after consultation with Frank Press. He's my Science and Technology Adviser. We were impressed with some of the problems that we have.

The quality of scientific equipment has been falling off rapidly in recent years. The number of top-ranked research centers has been falling off in recent years. The percentage of faculty members who are scientists and who are also young has been falling off rapidly in recent years.

In 1968, about 45 percent of the faculty members were young men and women. Now that's dropped off to only about 25 percent, which shows that in the future we have a problem on our hands unless we take strong action to correct these trends.

I'm assessing each individual agency's budget these days. This afternoon I will have three major agencies to assess. In many instances the heads of those agencies, the Cabinet members and others, have relegated research and development to a fairly low position of priority. But I directed the Office of Management and Budget to boost those research and development items much higher, and they will be funded accordingly.

Finally, I'd like to say that we want to make sure that the climate for research and development in our country is enhanced, with my own imprimatur of approval and interest, with a broad-scale exhibition of interest on numerous occasions by the Members of Congress and my own administration, with publicity accruing to those who have achieved notably in the scientific and engineering field and also in direct budget allocations.

We are not trying to establish nor to maintain a college aid program. I think to the extent that basic research and development commitments can be oriented toward things that improve the quality of our people's lives, enhance the security of our Nation, contribute to our position in world leadership, to that extent these allocations of funds and interests will be more readily acceptable and supported by the American people.

What we do in science in this country has a tremendous impact on the decisions made in other nations, strong and independent nations, because there is, as you know, a scientific community that is drawn together by mutuality of interest that's able to transcend obstacles that are raised by national boundaries. And the exchange of information, the consultation, mutual progress, the sharing of responsibility, even between nations like ourselves and the Soviet Union, is one that lays a basis for future peace and understanding and a sharing of a common purpose for humankind.

So, as President of the world's greatest nation, I'm very grateful this morning to participate in a small way in a ceremony. You have honored our country. We would like to present to you now these Medals of Science to recognize the tremendous contribution that you've made to our Nation. Thank you very much for letting us have this opportunity to recognize your notable achievement.

Thank you.

MR. PRESS. Mr. President, the first medalist is Roger Charles Lewis Guillemin from the Salk Institute, San Diego, California, for demonstrating the presence of a new class of hormones, made in the brain, that regulate the function of the pituitary gland, thereby making pos-

2045

sible improved diagnosis and treatment of numerous endocrine disorders.

Keith R. Porter, University of Colorado, for his many contributions in the use of the electron microscope, coupled with other approaches, to give us a comprehensive and unified picture of the life of cells.

Efraim Racker, Cornell University, Ithaca, New York, for major contributions to the understanding of the subcellular mechanism whereby oxidative and photosynthetic energy is transformed into the specific form of chemical energy used by cells.

Edward O. Wilson, Harvard University, Cambridge, Massachusetts, for his pioneering work on the organization of insect societies and the evolution of social behavior among insects and other animals.

Morris Cohen, MIT, Cambridge, Massachusetts, for original research in metallurgy, leading principally to a better understanding of the properties of steel. This work is serving as the basis for the development of high strength materials that are harder, more fracture-resistant, and more durable in hostile environments.

Peter C. Goldmark, formerly of CBS, now with Goldmark Communication Corporation, Connecticut, for contributions to the development of the communication sciences for education, entertainment, culture, and human service. His work in electronics and television has had widespread applications in our space program, in medicine, in our enjoyment of music, entertainment, and education in our homes.

THE PRESIDENT. Mr. Goldmark evolved the long-playing record, and I'm particularly grateful to you. [*Laughter*]

MR. PRESS. The next award, Mr. President, is awarded posthumously. Mrs. Richard Schwab will receive the medal for her father, Erwin W. Mueller, for his invention of the field-emission microscope, the field-ion microscope, and the atom-probe microscope, which helped to resolve the atomic structures of solids. Through these inventions, man was first able to see collections of individual atoms and eventually to identify a single atom.

K. O. Friedricks, New York University, for bringing the power of modern mathematics to bear on problems of physical sciences. Professor Friedricks' work has contributed to the theory of flight. His concepts have also been used within the the context of the controlled fusion reactor program.

Hassler Whitney, Institute for Advanced Studies, Princeton, New Jersey, for founding and bringing to maturity the discipline of differential topology. This new branch of geometry, as adopted by other scientists, has taken on great potential significance for describing the development of complicated structures, such as occur in biology.

Samuel A. Goudsmit, emeritus from Brookhaven National Laboratory, now at the University of Nevada, for the major discovery, together with George Uhlenbeck, of the electron spin as the source of a new quantum number.

Herbert S. Gutowsky, University of Illinois, Urbana, Illinois, in recognition of pioneering studies in the field of nuclear magnetic resonance spectroscopy, one of the most important tools developed for chemical studies in the last 25 years. Dr. Gutowsky's work has been applied to research in solids, liquids, gases, solutions, metals, and biological substances.

Frederick D. Rossini, Rice University, Houston, Texas, for contributions to basic reference knowledge in chemical thermodynamics. Professor Rossini has been one of the pioneers in the development of techniques for precision thermochemical measurement. His work has laid the groundwork for the optimal use of fossil fuels.

Verner E. Suomi, University of Wisconsin, Madison, Wisconsin. As a distinguished meteorologist, he has provided a new view of the dynamics of our atmosphere which already has brought substantial benefits to the people of this Nation and the world. Dr. Suomi has been a major driving force in the application of space systems for improved weather service to the public.

Henry Taube, Stanford University, Stanford, California, in recognition of contributions to the understanding of reactivity and reaction mechanisms in inorganic chemistry. His recent work contributes to our understanding of the mechanism of nitrogen fixation and of the chemical processes important to fuel cells and energy storage.

The last award is George E. Uhlenbeck of the Rockefeller University, New York, for the major discovery, together with Samuel Goudsmit, of the electron spin as a source of a new quantum number. His long career as a scientist and superb science teacher has brought him worldwide recognition.

THE PRESIDENT. Frank, you might explain how the recipients were chosen.

MR. PRESS. The recipients were chosen by a committee of Presidential appointees. I was a member of that committee. We deliberated for several months. We solicited nominations from all over the country, from institutions, professional societies. And from a list of several hundred, we selected these 15 outstanding gentlemen from all fields of science, from all parts of the country.

THE PRESIDENT. This is the first experimental pressing of a long-playing record. Although I won't play this one, I will be listening to another one. [*Laughter*]

I know all of you appreciate what these wonderful men have done. And I think they would be worthy of a rising round of applause.

NOTE: The President spoke at 10 a.m. in Room 450 of the Old Executive Office Building.

Energy Information Administration

Nomination of Lincoln E. Moses To Be Administrator. November 23, 1977

The President today announced that he will nominate Lincoln E. Moses, of Stanford, Calif., to be Administrator of the Energy Information Administration.

Moses was born December 21, 1921, in Kansas City, Mo. He received an A.B. in social sciences (1941) and a Ph. D. in statistics (1950) from Stanford University.

Moses was an assistant professor of education at Teachers College, Columbia University, from 1950 to 1952. Since 1952 he has been at Stanford University, serving as assistant professor, then associate professor, and since 1959, professor of statistics in the department of statistics and the department of preventive medicine. He also served as associate dean of humanities and sciences from 1965 to 1968 and as dean of graduate studies from 1969 to 1975.

Moses is a member of EPA's Environmental Health Advisory Committee. He has served on the Environmental Pollution Panel of the President's Science Advisory Committee and on the executive committee of the Graduate Record Examination Board. He is coauthor of "Elementary Decision Theory" (1959) and "Tables of Random Permutations" (1962) and the author of numerous articles in professional journals.

2047

Wright Brothers Day, 1977
Proclamation 4541.   November 23, 1977

By the President of the United States of America

A Proclamation

The era of modern aviation began near Kitty Hawk, North Carolina, on December 17, 1903, when Wilbur and Orville Wright, bicycle makers and inventors, made the first successful flight in a heavier-than-air, powered aircraft.

The achievement of the two brothers, almost unnoticed at the time, has since been recognized as one of history's most significant accomplishments. Trips that once took months now take a few hours and all the peoples of the earth have become neighbors.

It is particularly appropriate to remember this first powered flight during 1977, the 50th anniversary of Charles A. Lindbergh's solo, nonstop trans-Atlantic flight on a plane, the "Spirit of St. Louis", which was powered by a Wright Whirlwind engine.

To commemorate the historic achievements of the Wright brothers, the Congress, by a joint resolution of December 17, 1963 (77 Stat. 402, 36 U.S.C. 169), designated the seventeenth day of December of each year as Wright Brothers Day and requested the President to issue annually a proclamation inviting people of the United States to observe that day with appropriate ceremonies and activities.

Now, THEREFORE, I, JIMMY CARTER, President of the United States of America, do hereby call upon the people of this Nation, and their local and national government officials, to observe Wright Brothers Day, December 17, 1977, with appropriate ceremonies and activities, both to recall the accomplishments of the Wright brothers and to provide a stimulus to aviation in this country and throughout the world.

IN WITNESS WHEREOF, I have hereunto set my hand this twenty-third day of November, in the year of our Lord nineteen hundred seventy-seven, and of the Independence of the United States of America the two hundred and second.

JIMMY CARTER

[Filed with the Office of the Federal Register, 3:24 p.m., November 23, 1977]

GI Bill Improvement Act of 1977
Statement on Signing H.R. 8701 Into Law. November 23, 1977

I am pleased to sign into law today H.R. 8701, the GI Bill Improvement Act of 1977, a measure providing expanded benefits for Vietnam era veterans. This measure includes a 6.6-percent increase in monthly educational assistance benefits retroactive to October 1. It will mean larger checks for the approximately 1,700,000 individuals who will train during this fiscal year under the GI bill and the Survivors' Educational Assistance Act. Monthly benefits for a single veteran will increase to $311; a married veteran will receive $370; a married veteran with a child will receive $422.

The VA work-study allowances are increased under this measure, as are special tutorial assistance provisions for veterans having academic difficulties.

This bill is also designed to help veterans attending high-tuition schools by liberalizing the VA direct low-interest educational loan program and increasing it from $1,500 to $2,500 per school year.

Veterans will also be eligible to have a portion of their loan canceled through matching action by the Federal and State Governments.

This means that a single veteran is now eligible for up to $4,745 in grants for a 9-month school year, plus an additional $2,500 in low-interest loans. The current GI bill now has a 65-percent participation rate, which far exceeds the final participation rate under both the Korean conflict program (43 percent) and the World War II GI bill (50 percent). That rate will rise even farther when nearly 1,700,000 veterans benefit from the GI Bill Improvement Act.

The nearly $25 billion that we have spent under the current GI bill has been an excellent investment in our Nation's future. The measure I sign today should further improve this program.

NOTE: As enacted, H.R. 8701 is Public Law 95–202, approved November 23.

Thanksgiving Holiday

Remarks Upon Departure for Camp David, Maryland, for the Holiday Weekend.
November 23, 1977

Happy Thanksgiving, everybody.

I would like to say to the American people that no nation in the history of humankind has been more deeply blessed than have we. We've got a lot to be thankful for. The original settlers of this country, more than 300 years ago, began to express our thanks to God every year for the blessing that came on them. This year, we have just before Thanksgiving a good omen in the Middle East which might bring to humankind one of the greatest blessings of all, and that's peace. And all of us want to remember in our prayers the hopes that we harbor for a peaceful settlement of those differences there and those around the world.

Thanksgiving is historically a family affair. I've just returned from Stevens School and had Thanksgiving dinner prepared by my daughter and the fifth and sixth graders of the public school. It was a very good affair. But I think it's time now for us to look outward as a nation, recognizing that we are leaders, that we have extraordinary good fortune in the material things of life, and remember others, both our neighbors here at home and around the world who are not so fortunate as we.

As President, though, I would like to wish the American people a happy Thanksgiving and urge them to remember those who haven't been blessed so fortunately as we have in our own lives. Also, to the press, I want to say that I'm thankful that I don't have to answer questions now on matters of great moment, except that Thanksgiving is a matter of great moment.

Thank you very much.

NOTE: The President spoke at 2:35 p.m. to reporters assembled on the South Lawn of the White House.

Digest of Other White House Announcements

The following listing includes the President's daily schedule and other items of general interest as announced by the White House Press Office during the period covered by this issue. Events and announcements printed elsewhere in the issue are not included.

November 19

The President met at the White House with David L. Aaron, Deputy Assistant to the President for National Security Affairs.

November 21

The President met at the White House with:

—Dr. Brzezinski;

—senior White House staff members;

—the Cabinet;

—Annie Duitscher, a 106-year-old woman from Glen Burnie, Md., and several members of Mrs. Duitscher's family;

—Vice President Walter F. Mondale;

—James T. McIntyre, Jr., Acting Director of the Office of Management and Budget;

—representatives of environmental organizations who support the President's position on water resource projects.

The White House announced that Prime Minister Menahem Begin of Israel called the President this afternoon to brief him on the weekend's events relating to the visit to Israel of President Anwar al-Sadat of Egypt. The Prime Minister again expressed his appreciation for the President's efforts in the Middle East, which the Prime Minister said made the historical meeting possible. The President expressed his appreciation for the call and characterized the conversation as warm and encouraging.

November 22

The President met at the White House with:

—Dr. Brzezinski;

—Vice President Mondale, Adm. Stansfield Turner, Director of Central Intelligence, and Dr. Brzezinski;

—Mrs. Carter, for lunch;

—a group of administration officials to discuss the budget.

In a ceremony in the Oval Office, the President received diplomatic credentials from Ambassadors Franklyn Dolland of Grenada, Jaakko Olavi Iloniemi of Finland, Ayalew Mandefro of Ethiopia, and Francois de Laboulaye of France.

November 23

The President met at the White House with:

—Dr. Brzezinski;

—Representative James A. Burke of Massachusetts;

—Vice President Mondale and Secretary of Defense Harold Brown;

—Secretary of the Treasury W. Michael Blumenthal.

NOMINATIONS SUBMITTED TO THE SENATE

The following list does not include promotions of members of the Uniformed Services, nominations to the Service Academies, or nominations of Foreign Service officers.

Submitted November 21, 1977

GEORGE C. CARR, of Florida, to be United States District Judge for the Middle District of Florida, vice Charles R. Scott, retired.

A. DAVID MAZZONE, of Massachusetts, to be United States District Judge for the District of Massachusetts, vice Frank J. Murray, retired.

Submitted November 22, 1977

PAUL A. SIMMONS, of Pennsylvania, to be United States District Judge for the Western District of Pennsylvania, vice Ralph F. Scalera, resigned.

ANDREW E. GARDNER, of North Carolina, to be United States Marshal for the Western District of North Carolina for the term of 4 years, vice Max E. Wilson.

EDWARD P. GRIBBEN, of South Dakota, to be United States Marshal for the District of South Dakota for the term of 4 years, vice George L. Tennyson, resigned.

Submitted November 23, 1977

LINCOLN E. MOSES, of California, to be Administrator of the Energy Information Administration (new position).

CHECKLIST OF WHITE HOUSE PRESS RELEASES

The following releases of the Office of the White House Press Secretary, distributed during the period covered by this issue, are not included in the issue.

Released November 21, 1977

Announcement: nomination of George C. Carr to be United States District Judge for the Middle District of Florida

Announcement: nomination of A. David Mazzone to be United States District Judge for the District of Massachusetts

Released November 22, 1977

Announcement: nomination of Paul A. Simmons to be United States District Judge for the Western District of Pennsylvania; Andrew E. Gardner to be United States Marshal for the Western District of North Carolina; and Edward P. Gribben to be United States Marshal for the District of South Dakota

ACTS APPROVED BY THE PRESIDENT

Approved November 18, 1977

H.R. 6348_____ Public Law 95–191
An act to convey to the Ely Indian Colony the beneficial interest in certain Federal land.

H.R. 8777_____ Public Law 95–193
An act to amend the Appalachian Regional Development Act of 1965 to permit an extension of the period of assistance for child development programs while a study is conducted on methods of phasing out Federal assistance to these programs.

S. 106_____ Public Law 95–192
Soil and Water Resources Conservation Act of 1977.

S. 1184_____ Public Law 95–194
An act to extend the provisions of the Fishermen's Protective Act of 1967, relating to the reimbursement of seized commercial fishermen, until October 1, 1978.

S. 1560_____ Public Law 95–195
Siletz Indian Tribe Restoration Act.

ACTS APPROVED—Continued

Approved November 19, 1977

H.R. 2770_____ Public Law 95–196
An act to amend section 142 of title 28, United States Code, relating to the furnishing of accommodations to judges of the courts of appeals of the United States.

Approved November 21, 1977

S.J. Res. 81_____ Public Law 95–197
A joint resolution to express the sense of the Congress that, in the light of history, the third Thursday in December 1977, would be a most appropriate day for designation as the "National Day of Prayer for the Year of 1977", and respectfully to request that the President, under the provisions of Public Law 82–324, issue a proclamation designating such date as a "National Day of Prayer for the Year 1977".

Approved November 23, 1977

H.R. 2661_____ Private Law 95–23
An act for the relief of Patricia R. Tully.

H.R. 422_____ Public Law 95–198
An act to amend the Tariff Schedules of the United States to provide duty-free treatment of any aircraft engine used as a temporary replacement for an aircraft engine being overhauled within the United States if duty was paid on such replacement engine during a previous importation.

H.R. 4049_____ Public Law 95–199
An act to amend the Regional Rail Reorganization Act of 1973 to authorize additional appropriations for the United States Railway Association, and for other purposes

H.R. 7074_____ Public Law 95–200
An act to provide improved authority for the administration of certain National Forest System lands in Oregon.

H.R. 8175_____ Public Law 95–201
Veterans' Administration Physician and Dentist Pay Comparability Amendments of 1977.

H.R. 8701_____ Public Law 95–202
GI Bill Improvement Act of 1977.

S. 1750_____ Public Law 95–203
Saccharin Study and Labeling Act.

John L. McClellan

Statement on the Death of the Senator From Arkansas. November 28, 1977

The unexpected death of Senator John L. McClellan deprives the Senate of a resolute and gifted lawmaker. During his 39 years of service on Capitol Hill—4 in the House of Representatives and almost 35 in the Senate—he persistently spoke out for a strong national defense and upheld integrity in the operations of Government. The economic development of the Arkansas River is an achievement for which he will be long remembered and in which he took a deep personal pride.

I am especially grateful for his wise and generous counsel during the early months of my administration.

In the distinguished history of the Senate, only eight Members have ever served longer than John McClellan. His passing is a loss to the Congress and to the Nation.

NOTE: At his November 29 news conference at the White House, Press Secretary Jody Powell announced that Vice President Walter F. Mondale and Rosalynn Carter would represent the President at funeral services for Senator McClellan in Little Rock, Ark., on November 30.

THE PRESIDENT'S NEWS CONFERENCE OF NOVEMBER 30, 1977

THE PRESIDENT. Good morning. Thank you. I have two brief statements to make.

SENATOR JOHN L. MCCLELLAN

One concerns Senator John McClellan from Arkansas, whose funeral is being held today. He served in the Congress for 39 years and exemplified a deep commitment to his own major committee assignments. He has recently been the chairman of the Appropriations Committee. He was always a strong fighter for an adequate national defense, and he was a man of supreme integrity.

In a few minutes, the Vice President and my wife, the First Lady, will be going to the funeral along with a large delegation of Members of Congress. And I want publicly to express, on behalf of the American people, my admiration for what he has done, my public condolences, in addition to the private condolences I've already extended to his wife, and my appreciation for his tremendous contribution to our country.

2053

THE MIDDLE EAST

The other comment I'd like to make is concerning the Middle East. In the last few days we have seen, I believe, an historic breakthrough in the search for a permanent, lasting peace in the Middle East because of the true leadership qualities that have been exhibited by the courage of President Sadat and the gracious reception of him in Israel by Prime Minister Begin.

This has been, already, a tremendous accomplishment. I think the importance of it is that there has been an initiation of direct, person-to-person negotiations between Israel and the major power in the Mideast among the Arab nations who are Israel's neighbors. Lebanon, Syria, Jordan have a total population of about 12 million; Egypt has a population of 36 million and has by far the greatest military force. And the fact that this strongest Arab country and the nation of Israel are now conducting direct negotiations is a major accomplishment in itself.

Two of Israel's most cherished desires have already been met. One is this face-to-face negotiation possibility, and the other one is a recognition by a major Arab leader that Israel has a right to exist. In fact, President Sadat said, "We welcome you in our midst."

The United States has been very pleased to see this reduction in distrust and a reduction in fear and a reduction in suspicion between the Arabs and the Israelis. We have played a close consultative role with both of these leaders. We have, on several instances recently, acted as intermediaries at their request. Both Prime Minister Begin and President Sadat have publicly expressed their reconfirmation that these exploratory talks are designed to lead toward a comprehensive settlement including Israel and all her neighbors.

Sunday, President Sadat called for a conference in Cairo. This is likely to be held around the 13th of December, about the middle of December. We will participate in that conference at a high level—Assistant Secretary Atherton [1] will represent our Nation. We look on this as a very constructive step. The road toward peace has already led through Jerusalem, will now go to Cairo and ultimately, we believe, to a comprehensive consultation at Geneva.

It's not an easy thing to bring about a comprehensive peace settlement. Immediate expectations have sometimes been exaggerated. The definition of real peace—I think we've made good progress on that already. The resolution of the Palestinian question still has not been decided. And the solution to the problem concerning borders and national security has also not been decided.

We have played, I think, a proper role. I have tried to convince, in the past, Prime Minister Begin of the good intentions of President Sadat and vice versa. When there has been no progress being made, the United States has taken the initiative. Now that progress is being made, a proper role for the United States is to support that progress and to give the credit to the strong leadership that's already been exhibited by Prime Minister Begin and President Sadat and to let our Nation be used, as called upon, to expedite the peace process.

I believe that this is a move that the whole world looks upon with great appreciation. And again, I want to express my congratulations and my appreciation to these two strong leaders for the tremendous progress already made and for their commitment to future progress.

---

[1] Alfred L. Atherton, Jr., Assistant Secretary of State for Near Eastern and South Asian Affairs.

QUESTIONS

THE MIDDLE EAST

Q. Mr. President, what is your reaction to Secretary General Waldheim's suggestion for a post-Cairo, pre-Geneva Middle East conference at the United Nations or on some neutral ground?

THE PRESIDENT. As you know, Secretary General Waldheim has also agreed to send a high-level representative to the conference to be held in Cairo. I don't know yet what position our country will take toward a potential meeting at the United Nations. We've not received any invitation to it. I noticed in the news this morning that Israel has said that they would not participate. But it's too early for us to decide whether or not we will go to any conference, if one is actually held at the United Nations.

Q. Mr. President, Egypt and Israel can legitimately deal with themselves, but can Egypt really represent all the other parties, when they're not even at the conference, and the Palestinians, who have never had a say in their own political destiny?

THE PRESIDENT. Well, I think that President Sadat, in his private communications with me and even in his public statements, has said that he is trying as best he can to represent the Arab position concerning Israeli withdrawal from occupied territories and also the resolution of the Palestinian question.

Obviously, the leaders in Syria, even Jordan, certainly the PLO, have not recognized that Egypt is speaking for them adequately. I think, though, that in his speech to the Knesset, in his followup speech to the People's Assembly in Egypt, President Sadat has evoked very clearly the basic Arab position that I have understood in my private conversations with President Asad from Syria and with the King of Jordan, Hussein.

So, I believe that this is an exploratory effort that does accurately represent the basic differences between Israel and all their neighbors. And the fact that Jordan and Syria have not been willing to participate, I don't think has dampened President Sadat's commitment or enthusiasm at all. It is constructive, and I think what he discovers in his already completed discussions with Prime Minister Begin and those that might be taking place in Egypt in the middle of next month will certainly be conducive to pursuing the Arab cause.

I think it's constructive, because for the first time, the Arab position on those controversial issues has been spelled out very clearly for worldwide understanding. And I think the differences that have been faced by us and others for long years are now much more clearly understood by the public. The differences are still sharp; the resolution of those differences is going to be very difficult. I think that to the best of his ability, President Sadat is speaking for the Arab world.

Q. Mr. President, if the other Arabs refuse—continue to refuse not to sit down with Israel, would the United States oppose it if Egypt and Israel somehow worked out some sort of separate agreement? Would that be a good thing, and what would our position be on that?

THE PRESIDENT. Well, we and Egypt and Israel have all taken the position, publicly, and the same position privately among ourselves, that a separate peace agreement between Egypt and Israel to the exclusion of the other parties is not desirable. This is predicated upon the very viable hope that a comprehensive settlement can be reached among all the parties involved. If at some later date it becomes obvious that Jordan does not want peace or that Syria does not want peace or that Lebanon does not want peace in a settlement with Israel, then an alternative might have to be pursued. But we've certainly not reached that point yet.

I think that the other Arab leaders do want peace with Israel. And I am certainly not even considering, and neither is Sadat nor Begin, any assumption that the possibilities for peace have narrowed down to just two nations.

Walt [Walter Rodgers, Associated Press Radio].

Q. Mr. President, there has been criticism of your earlier decision to bring the Soviet Union into the Middle East, the peace negotiating process, and the Soviets have indeed refused to go to Cairo. Would you please explain to the American people why you think it's important that the Soviets be involved in these Middle East peace negotiations?

THE PRESIDENT. The Soviets have been involved in the peace negotiations ever since 1973. The entire Geneva conference concept was established through the United Nations with the United States and with the Soviet Union as cochairmen. So, this has been established now for at least 4 years. And this is a concept that has been adopted and approved by all the parties involved, including the United Nations overwhelmingly, perhaps even unanimously.

In the past, I think it's accurate to say that the Soviets have not played a constructive role in many instances because they had espoused almost completely the more adamant Arab position. My own feeling is that in recent months, the Soviets have moved toward a much more balanced position as a prelude to the Geneva conference.

We have tried to spell out very clearly—certainly since I've been in office and, I think, my predecessors as well—the

United States position. We disagree in some of those issues with the Soviet Union. We've not concealed those differences. We disagree in some instances because of the procedural items that are being discussed. But there is no division between us and the Soviet Union now that didn't exist before, and I would say that their positions have been much more compatible recently.

I wish that the Soviets had decided to go to Cairo. They've decided not to. But we'll make as much progress as we can, following the leadership of Sadat and Begin, to make real progress in Cairo with the Soviets not present. And my belief is that the desire of the whole world is so great for peace in the Middle East that the Soviets will follow along and take advantage of any constructive step toward peace.

The fact that we do have differences of opinion is well known and I don't think is an obstacle to eventual peace in the Middle East. But we did not bring the Soviets in. They have been in since the very initiation of a Geneva conference.

Do you have a followup?

Q. Yes, sir. Do you think you can have peace in the Middle East without the Soviets involved?

THE PRESIDENT. Well, I think that we or the Soviets ought to play a constructive role. And I think both of us will. We have been the nation then and, I think, now that is uniquely trusted by all the parties involved to act fairly and consistently concerning the Middle East questions. I don't believe that the Soviets occupy that position. And I don't have any doubt that if the nations surrounding Israel can work out an individual peace settlement with Israel leading to peace treaties, that the Soviets will play a constructive role, certainly at that point. It would be contrary to their own interest to be identified as an obstacle to peace. I don't think they are trying to be an obstacle to peace. Their perspective is just different from ours.

NATIONAL ENERGY PLAN

Q. Mr. President, I would like to go to that other set of negotiations, on Capitol Hill over energy. Does it now appear to you, sir, that in order to get an energy bill, you may have to grant Senator Long's desire and agree to some sort of plowback to the oil industry for incentives in order to get the wellhead tax? And would you now think that, perhaps, you're going to have to go above $1.75, even up to $2 for natural gas?

THE PRESIDENT. I've never had any conversation with Senator Long that would either encourage me or require me to change my position from what it was last April. We still maintain that the proposition we put to the House and Senate in the energy proposal is the best. The House-passed version of the comprehensive energy plan is very close to what we've proposed, and we support the House position in almost every instance when there is a disagreement.

I don't have any inclination to modify that position anytime soon. We will be consulting very closely with the particular conferees who most nearly espouse the administration's position, and I would guess that the negotiations leading to some ultimate resolution of differences would be between the Senate conferees, headed by Senator Long and also, of course, Senator Jackson, on the one hand and the House conferee leaders on the other side.

We will add our assistance when we can, but we will not betray the confidence of people who look to us for leadership. And I will not work out any private agreement with Senator Long that would betray the commitments that we've made previously, publicly, I might say, in all instances. So, I don't see any possibility of doing what you propose, or what you ask about.

Obviously, both sides are very likely to compromise. They've already had compromises on literally dozens of issues. The three major issues remaining, as you know, are the electric rate reform—we have a good chance of having that resolved this week—the pricing structure on natural gas—and that conference committee will go back to work tomorrow; Senator Jackson is returning to Washington, D.C., then—and of course, the tax on crude oil. And these are to some degree interrelated. But I think that we've got a good chance, still, for making progress now, and I'm going to maintain the position that we described last April as long as possible, support in every instance the conferees that support our position.

Q. Mr. President, if I understood you correctly, then you think the conferees may have to compromise, but that you, yourself, would maintain the administration position.

THE PRESIDENT. That's correct.

Q. The question then becomes—if they compromise and send you a bill with those items I mentioned—what are you going to do?

THE PRESIDENT. Well, as I spelled out in my last fireside chat to the American people, there are three basic elements that I would require: One is fairness in dealing with consumers; the second one is meeting the goals of both conservation and production in the energy area; and, third, an energy proposal that won't bankrupt this Nation nor seriously disturb the future budgets of our country.

That's a fairly broad base, and I think it's an adequate parameter within which the conferees can work. But if any of those principles are violated, I would not sign the bill.

PRESIDENT'S CAMPAIGN PROMISES

Q. Mr. President, based on the reflection of 10 months in office, more than 10 months, do you think that perhaps you made too many promises in last year's campaign and in such precise language? And taking that a step further, do you think that perhaps you tried to fulfill too many of those promises this first year?

THE PRESIDENT. I'm trying to fulfill all my promises. And I think I was quite reticent in making those promises, certainly compared to some of my opponents. But we've put forward already to the Congress proposals that carry out the major promises that I made—reorganization, energy, welfare reform, and so forth.

We've also been successful, I think—when an analysis is made of what the Congress achieved this year, I think there's going to be a very pleasant reaction from the American people when they see the progress that we've accomplished. So, I don't think I made too many promises, and I think I'm doing an adequate job in trying to fulfill those promises.

There is a very heavy agenda for the Congress. And it's much easier for the administration to evolve a proposal or to present legislation to the Congress than it is for Congress actually to pass it. And so the Congress will inherently follow behind any administration in dealing with very controversial issues that have no easy solution. So, I think so far our relationship with the Congress has been good. The effort to carry out my promises has been adequate. I don't think I made too many promises to the American people.

ARTHUR BURNS

Q. Have you decided yet whether you will reappoint Arthur Burns?

THE PRESIDENT. No.

Q. Well, won't the business community be further unsettled if you don't reap-

point Dr. Burns? Wouldn't it be a risky thing not to do?

THE PRESIDENT. No, I think not. I don't believe anybody is indispensable, you know, a President or the Chairman of the Federal Reserve Board or anyone else. I think that if I should decide to replace Dr. Burns as Chairman of the Federal Reserve, then it would be incumbent on me to get someone who is competent and who would arouse the confidence of the American people, including the business community.

GEORGIANS IN THE ADMINISTRATION

Q. Mr. President, as you know, there are those who say that the high councils of your administration are overloaded with Georgians. First, do you think such a thing is possible, and secondly, in searching for a replacement for Bert Lance, will you perhaps go beyond the boundaries of Georgia?

THE PRESIDENT. Well, the high councils of my administration are comprised by the Cabinet members and the major heads of the agencies involved. I consult on foreign affairs not with members of the immediate White House staff who might be from Georgia, but with Dr. Brzezinski and with Secretary Vance, on transportation with Brock Adams, on defense with Secretary Brown, and so forth.

The members of the Cabinet, I think, are broadly representative of the American people. My immediate White House staff, who don't run the departments—many of them are from Georgia. But I don't think that there's an excessive dependence on them, no more than has been the case in the past when President Kennedy brought large numbers of people from Massachusetts to work intimately with him who had been with him before, or President Johnson, or others.

The other part of your question about the Office of Management and Budget—Jim McIntyre is the head of the OMB and he's doing a very good job. Whether or not I would replace him in the future still has to be decided.

THE MIDDLE EAST

Q. Mr. President, to come back to the Middle East for a minute, is the United States Government taking any concrete steps with some of the other governments that have been reluctant, such as Syria, the PLO, which is not a government, and the other countries, to bring them into this process that has been initiated by Israel and Egypt? And if so, what steps are we taking?

THE PRESIDENT. Yes, not with the PLO; we have no contact with the PLO. But with Jordan and with Syria, with Lebanon and, in a supportive role, with the Saudi Arabians and others, we have played, I think, an adequate role. At the time we discovered that President Sadat was going to make a proposal to go to Jerusalem, we immediately began to use whatever influence we had available to us to encourage the other nations not to condemn President Sadat. This particularly applied to Saudi Arabia, to Jordan, to the European countries, to the Soviet Union, and to Syria. In some instances, either they decided not to condemn him or our influence was successful.

We would like very much to keep any of the nations involved in the immediate Middle Eastern discussions from rejecting an ultimate peace settlement and withdrawing from the prospect of going to Geneva. This includes, of course, Prime Minister Begin and President Sadat. They have not rejected the concept that there must be a comprehensive settlement.

In the meantime, we don't see anything wrong; in fact, we look with great favor on the bilateral negotiations between Israel and Egypt. In the meantime, we are trying to induce the Syrians, the Lebanese, the Jordanians, and, as I say again, in a supporting role, the Saudis and others, to support both the ongoing negotiations that will continue from Jerusalem into Cairo and also to avoid any condemnation of Sadat that might disrupt his influence and put an obstacle to peace in the future.

That's about all we can do. We have no control over any nation in the Middle East. When we find the progress in the Middle East being stopped, we use all the initiative that we can. When we see progress being made by the parties themselves, we support them to move on their own.

I think it's much more important to have direct negotiations between Egypt and Israel than to have us acting as a constant, dominant intermediary. I think this is a major step in the right direction. We hope later that Jordan and Syria and Lebanon will join in these discussions, either individually or as a comprehensive group, dealing with Israel directly.

Q. Mr. President, you used the word "induce." What inducements is the United States Government offering to Syria and the others?

THE PRESIDENT. Well, we are not offering them any payment of money or anything, but we primarily capitalize on their clear determination, their clear desire to have peace. There is no doubt in my mind at all that President Asad, who has been one of the most highly critical leaders of what Sadat did—there's no doubt in my mind that President Asad wants peace with Israel, and there's no doubt in my mind that King Hussein wants peace with Israel. And sometimes it's very difficult for them to communicate directly with Israel.

We act as an intermediary there. We meet with those leaders on both sides. Obviously, if there should be a breakthrough in the future, similar to what occurred between Egypt and Israel—let's say, for instance, that if King Hussein said he would like to negotiate directly with Prime Minister Begin, we would support that enthusiastically and offer our good offices to encourage such an interchange. But we don't have any inclination nor ability to dominate anyone nor to require them to take action contrary to what they think is in the best interests of their nation.

DAM SAFETY INSPECTION

Q. Mr. President, you told us at your last news conference, sir, that you would see to it that Federal inspections started promptly on private dams. You had a meeting on this subject Monday. Could you tell us what happened?

THE PRESIDENT. Yes. I met Monday with the Secretary of Interior, Secretary of Agriculture, Secretary of Army, and the head of the Corps of Engineers. We have 9,000 high-risk dams in this country which are not Federal dams. These are nonfederal dams. We will commence very shortly an inspection of all those dams.

My present intention is to distribute, within the next few days, certain guidelines to be worked out with individual States so that the Corps of Engineers personnel, perhaps assisted by some from the Department of Interior, would begin to inspect the dams that we consider of most danger, about 2,000 the first year. It costs about $7,500 per dam to inspect them, on the average. We've allotted $15 million for this purpose.

In that process, we will train the State personnel who will continue the inspec-

tion process after this original inspection is made. We would then continue this for 2 or 3 additional years until all the 9,000 dams have been inspected. This program then would be taken over primarily by the States because the Federal Government has no direct responsibility for these nonfederal dams. In the meantime, of course, dams that have been built by and are controlled by the Corps of Engineers and the Department of Interior are being inspected, I think adequately, by the personnel in those departments because they are Federal dams.

TAX REFORM

Q. Mr. President, one of the issues you'll be facing in the new year is that of tax reform. There's some discussion that what is needed now is a tax break, a quick fix, if you will, and that comprehensive reform can come further down the road. What do you think, Mr. President?

THE PRESIDENT. 1977 is a year when we are seeing major legislation, long overdue, passed, hopefully, that cause some increases in taxes. And additional taxes are necessary to restore the integrity of the social security system; some wellhead taxes are necessary to carry out a comprehensive energy policy and to hold down unnecessary consumption. I would hope that all those changes in the law that bring about any tax increase would be concluded in 1977.

In 1978, there will be substantial tax reductions, and combined with that will be an adequate proposal for tax reform. I spent several hours this week going over the details of our tax reform package. We can't conclude that analysis until we know what will be done on energy and social security, because they have such a high impact on the tax structure. But there will be substantial tax reductions in 1978, combined with comprehensive tax reform.

Q. Mr. President, you want them to be together. You don't want to separate the two?

THE PRESIDENT. That's correct. They will be together. Some of the more controversial items on tax reform that have been proposed to me—they would be very time-consuming and have very little monetary significance—might be delayed until later on, because I feel that it's necessary to expedite the effectiveness of substantial tax reduction, and I'm committed and the Democratic congressional leaders, at least, are committed to substantial tax reduction in 1978 as soon as we can put it through.

BALANCE OF TRADE

Q. Mr. President, the foreign trade deficit is running about $27 billion a year. I wondered, sir, since this is putting downward pressure on the dollar in some currencies, what can you do about it?

THE PRESIDENT. The revelations about October's balance-of-trade deficit were quite disturbing. We analyzed this and found that the same monthly rate of deficit that had existed ever since last May or June, about $2.4 billion per month, is exactly the average of September and October.

So, we apparently have a fairly stable pattern per month of a $2.4 billion deficit, primarily caused by two factors: One is our extraordinary importation of foreign oil. We import $3.7 billion worth of oil every month. This means that we have, if we didn't import the oil, about a $15 billion trade surplus per year. And we have got to cut down on the excessive importing of oil from overseas before we can hope to get our trade balanced.

The other reason for an adverse balance is that our own economy has improved in the last few years—few months, much more than has the rest of the world. Because of our improvement in the economy, we are much more able to buy and much more willing to buy goods from overseas than those nations are able to buy from us because their economies have not been restored as much as ours.

We have one major element that can be introduced to cut down on our trade deficits—and that's obvious—and that is to reduce oil imports.

FRANK CORMIER [Associated Press]. Thank you, Mr. President.

THE PRESIDENT. Thank you.

[President Carter's twentieth news conference began at 10:30 a.m. in Room 450 of the Old Executive Office Building and was broadcast live on radio and television. Following the news conference, the President remained in the room to answer questions from reporters on an informal basis, as follows:]

Q. *[Inaudible]*

THE PRESIDENT. I haven't decided.

Q. What changed to cause you to release him from the commitment? I mean, he knew back in January that Shapp would have to be out and a new Governor elected.

THE PRESIDENT. I don't know. Pete [1] never discussed it with me directly.

Q. You talked about depoliticizing Justice during the campaign, and do you think that releasing him from this commitment to allow him to get back into politics is going to cut against that trend that you've instituted?

THE PRESIDENT. I don't know enough to comment about that because I was not involved in the hiring of him, nor in his resignation.

Q. Do you know how cold it is in Normandy in January? [*Laughter*] I mean, seriously, let's get down to brass tacks.

THE PRESIDENT. We'll find out.

---

[1] On November 26, Deputy Attorney General Peter F. Flaherty announced his intention to resign in order to explore the possibilities of running for the office of Governor of Pennsylvania.

Q. Are you still committed to the joint Soviet-American statement and the contents? Are you still committed to the contents of the Soviet-American——

THE PRESIDENT. Yes.

Q. By saying "We'll find out," I take it that the trip is announced.

The PRESIDENT. The trip will be announced tomorrow.

Civil Service Rules

Executive Order 12021.   November 30, 1977

AMENDING THE CIVIL SERVICE RULES TO EXEMPT CERTAIN POSITIONS FROM THE CAREER SERVICE

By virtue of the authority vested in me by the Constitution of the United States of America, and Sections 3301 and 3302 of Title 5 of the United States Code, and as President of the United States of America, it is hereby ordered as follows:

SECTION 1. That portion of Section 6.8 of Civil Service Rule VI following the heading "Specified Exceptions." (5 C.F.R. 6.8) is designated subsection (a) and a new subsection (b) is added as follows:

"(b) Positions in the Community Services Administration and ACTION whose incumbents serve as regional director or regional administrator shall be listed in Schedule C for grades not exceeding GS–15 of the General Schedule and shall be designated Noncareer Executive Assignments for positions graded higher than GS–15. Incumbents of these positions who are, on November 29, 1977, in the competitive service shall not be affected by the foregoing provisions of this subsection.".

SEC. 2. That portion of Section 9.11 of Civil Service Rule IX following the heading "Career Executive Assignments; selection and assignment." (5 C.F.R. 9.11) is designated subsection (a) and a new subsection (b) is added as follows:

"(b) The regional director or regional administrator positions in the Defense Civil Preparedness Agency and the General Services Administration shall be designated as Noncareer Executive Assignments and the Limited Executive Assignments of any incumbents of these positions on November 29, 1977, are converted to Noncareer Executive Assignments. Incumbents of these positions who are, on November 29, 1977, serving in Career Executive Assignments shall not be affected by the foregoing provisions of this subsection.".

JIMMY CARTER

The White House,
   November 30, 1977.

[Filed with the Office of the Federal Register,
   4:58 p.m., November 30, 1977]

Department of Energy

Nomination of George S. McIsaac To Be an Assistant Secretary.   December 1, 1977

The President today announced that he will nominate George S. McIsaac, of Washington, D.C., to be an Assistant Secretary of Energy. His area of responsibility would be resource applications.

McIsaac was born July 25, 1930, in Auburn, N.Y. He received a B.S. in industrial administration from Yale University in 1952 and an M.S. in business administration from the University of Rochester in 1961. He served in the U.S. Marine Corps from 1952 to 1954.

From 1954 to 1962, McIsaac was with Eastman Kodak Co., where he served as a group leader in the Management Systems Development Division. Since 1962 he has been with McKinsey & Co., Inc., a Washington consulting firm, as a principal and director.

At McKinsey, McIsaac has served as a consultant to numerous Government agencies, including the Defense Department, the Department of Health, Education, and Welfare, the Department of Housing and Urban Development, and the National Science Foundation. He directed a study to improve resource management throughout the Army, worldwide, from 1966 to 1969 and directed the creation of Amtrak for the Board of Incorporators in 1970–71.

McIsaac has also served as a consultant to industry and financial institutions in the United States and Germany, and to the governments of the Federal Republic of Germany and Tanzania. He currently leads McKinsey's industrial and labor relations practice.

National Advisory Council on Extension and Continuing Education

Messsage to the Congress Transmitting a Report. December 1, 1977

To the Congress of the United States:

Enclosed is the "Annual Report of the National Advisory Council on Extension and Continuing Education for FY 1977," prepared in accordance with the requirement of Section III(b) of Title III of the Higher Education Act of 1965, covering calendar year 1976, preceding my term of office.

This report addresses the need for continuing education programs and the Council's recommendations for policies,

funding and administrative structures toward this end.

The Report of the Council is being carefully studied and evaluated. I am forwarding the Report so that it is available to the Congress for its deliberations.

JIMMY CARTER

The White House,
December 1, 1977.

NOTE: The report is entitled "Continuing Need, Continuing Response, Continuing Education, Annual Report 1977—National Advisory Council on Extension and Continuing Education" (Government Printing Office, 50 pp.).

The message was announced by the White House Press Office on December 1. It was not issued in the form of a White House press release.

Social Security Financing Legislation

Letter to Congressional Leaders. December 1, 1977

I would like to commend you and your colleagues for the progress which has been made on the social security financing legislation I proposed to Congress. I am confident that an effective and equitable bill can emerge from the conference committee.

I believe that it is very important that a social security financing bill be enacted before the end of this year. The continuing problems of the system have eroded public confidence leading many persons to fear that their benefits will not be available when they need them. It is incumbent on us to restore that confidence.

As you know, I submitted to Congress a set of proposals designed to restore the financial integrity of the social security system and keep it strong into the next century. Those measures sought to increase revenues without burdening the average worker and his employer, and reduce expenditures by correcting a flaw which caused double-indexing for inflation. I am pleased to note that the House and Senate versions of the bill incorporate many of these proposals.

I am nevertheless deeply concerned about provisions in the House and Senate bills which would unwisely add to the tax burden borne by all workers and employers, in order to increase benefits for a relative few. These proposed increases are all well intentioned, but we cannot afford them at the present time. The benefit increases called for in the two bills could cost from $7–$10 billion a year by 1983. As a direct result of these increases in expenditures the new tax rates imposed on today's already burdened workers and employers are higher than they need be.

The bill also contains a new income tax credit and an amendment to the veterans pension law which add an additional $1–$2 billion to the cost of the legislation.

I call upon the members of the House and Senate to join me in developing a final fiscally responsible social security financing bill which will be less burdensome to the workers and employers who must pay the taxes, and adequate to restore public confidence in the financial integrity of the social security system. Secretary Califano and his staff stand ready to work with the members of the conference committee in its deliberations.

Sincerely,

JIMMY CARTER

NOTE: This is the text of identical letters addressed to the Honorable Robert C. Byrd, Senate majority leader, the Honorable Russell B. Long, chairman of the Senate Finance Committee, the Honorable Thomas P. O'Neill, Jr., Speaker of the House of Representatives, and the Honorable Al Ullman, chairman of the House Ways and Means Committee.

The text of the letters was made available by the White House Press Office. It was not issued in the form of a White House press release.

National Commission for the Review of Antitrust Laws and Procedures

Executive Order 12022. December 1, 1977

ESTABLISHING THE NATIONAL COMMISSION FOR THE REVIEW OF ANTITRUST LAWS AND PROCEDURES

By virtue of the authority vested in me by the Constitution and statutes of the United States of America, and as President of the United States of America, in accordance with the provisions of the Federal Advisory Committee Act (5 U.S.C. App. I), it is hereby ordered as follows:

SECTION 1. *Establishment.* (a) There is hereby established the National Commission for the Review of Antitrust Laws and Procedures, hereafter referred to as the Commission.

(b) The Commission shall consist of fifteen members to be appointed by the President and shall include:

(1) The Assistant Attorney General in charge of the Antitrust Division of the Department of Justice.

(2) The Chairman of the Federal Trade Commission.

(3) The Chairman of one other appropriate independent regulatory agency.

(4) Three members of the Senate recommended by the President of the Senate.

(5) Three members of the House of Representatives recommended by the Speaker of the House of Representatives.

(6) One judge of a United States District Court.

(7) Five persons from the private sector.

(c) The President shall designate a Chairman or Cochairmen from among the members of the Commission.

SEC. 2. *Functions of the Commission.* (a) The Commission shall, within the framework of existing antitrust laws (as that term is defined in 15 U.S.C. 12), study and make recommendations on the following subjects:

(1) Revision of procedural and substantive rules of law needed to expedite the resolution of complex antitrust cases and development of proposals for making the remedies available in such cases more effective, including:

(i) creation of a roster of district court judges knowledgeable regarding antitrust law and large-case problems to whom such cases may be assigned;

(ii) revision of pleading requirements in order to narrow as quickly and precisely as possible the scope of contested issues of fact and law;

(iii) revision of discovery practices in order to limit expensive and time-consuming inquiry into areas not germane to contested issues;

(iv) the desirability of a grant of judicial authority to restrict and penalize dilatory practices through control of issue formulation and imposition of sanctions for unnecessary delays or failures to cooperate;

(v) amendment of evidentiary practices to expedite introduction of testimony and exhibits at trial;

(vi) simplification of the standards required to establish attempted monopolization in suits brought by the United States under Section 2 of the Sherman Act;

(vii) consideration of structural relief for antitrust violations, and of nonjudicial alternatives for resolution of complex antitrust issues; and

(2) the desirability of retaining the various exemptions and immunities from the antitrust laws, including exemptions for regulated industries and exemptions created by State laws that inhibit competition.

(b) The Commission shall conclude its work not later than six months from the date the last member is appointed and shall submit a final report to the Presi-

dent and the Attorney General within thirty days thereafter. The Commission shall terminate thirty days after submitting its final report.

SEC. 3. *Administrative Matters.* (a) The Commission may request any Federal agency to furnish it with such information, advice, and services as may be useful for carrying out its functions under this Order.

(b) The Department of Justice shall furnish to the Commission a staff director and any necessary staff, supplies, facilities and other administrative services. Such funds as are necessary for ordinary operations of the Commission, to the extent permitted by law, shall be provided from the appropriations available to the Department of Justice.

(c) The Commission may procure, subject to the availability of funds, the temporary professional services of individuals to assist in its work, in accordance with the provisions of Section 3109 of Title 5 of the United States Code.

(d) Members of the Commission shall receive no compensation from the United States by virtue of their service on the Commission but shall be entitled to receive travel expenses, including per diem in lieu of subsistence, as authorized by law (5 U.S.C. 5702 and 5703).

(e) Notwithstanding the provisions of any other Executive order, the functions of the President under the Federal Advisory Committee Act (5 U.S.C. App. 1), except that of reporting annually to the Congress, which are applicable to the Commission shall be performed by the Attorney General in accordance with guidelines and procedures established by the Office of Management and Budget.

JIMMY CARTER

The White House,
December 1, 1977.

[Filed with the Office of the Federal Register, 4:13 p.m., December 1, 1977]

Central Intelligence Agency Retirement and Disability System

Executive Order 12023. December 1, 1977

CONFORMING THE CENTRAL INTELLI-
GENCE AGENCY AND CIVIL SERVICE
RETIREMENT AND DISABILITY SYSTEMS

By virtue of the authority vested in me by Section 292 of the Central Intelligence Agency Retirement Act of 1964 for Certain Employees (90 Stat. 2472; 50 U.S.C. 403 note), and as President of the United States of America, it is hereby ordered as follows:

SECTION 1. The Director of Central Intelligence, hereafter referred to as the Director, shall maintain the Central Intelligence Agency Retirement and Disability System and the Central Intelligence Agency Retirement and Disability Fund, hereafter referred to as the Fund, in accordance with the following principles:

(a) None of the moneys mentioned in the Central Intelligence Agency Retirement Act of 1964 for Certain Employees, as amended (78 Stat. 1043, as amended; 50 U.S.C. 403 note), shall be assignable, either in law or equity, except under the provisions of subsection (b) of this Section, or subject to execution, levy, attachment, garnishment, or other legal process, except as otherwise may be provided by Federal laws.

(b) An individual entitled to an annuity from the Fund may make allotments or assignments of amounts of such annuity for such purposes as the Director in his sole discretion considers appropriate.

(c) No payment shall be made from the Fund unless an application for bene-fits based on the service of the participant is received by the Director before the one hundred and fifteenth anniversary of the participant's birth.

(d) Notwithstanding the provisions of subsection (c) of this Section, after the death of a participant or annuitant, no benefit based on the service of such person shall be paid from the Fund unless an application therefor is received by the Director within 30 years after the death or other event which gives rise to title to benefit.

(e) Sums deducted from salaries pursuant to Section 273 of the Central Intelligence Agency Retirement Act of 1964 for Certain Employees (78 Stat. 1053; 50 U.S.C. 403 note) shall be deposited in the Treasury of the United States to the credit of the Fund.

SEC. 2. The provisions of this Order are effective as follows:

(a) The provisions of Sections 1(a) and 1(b) are effective as of December 23, 1975.

(b) The provisions of Sections 1(c) and 1(d) are effective as of December 31, 1975.

(c) The provisions of Section 1(e) are effective as of October 1, 1976 and shall apply to annuitants serving in appointed positions on and after that date.

SEC. 3. The Director of Central Intelligence is authorized to prescribe such regulations as are necessary to carry out the provisions of this Order.

JIMMY CARTER

The White House,
    December 1, 1977.

[Filed with the Office of the Federal Register, 10:52 a.m., December 2, 1977]

NOTE: The text of the Executive order was released on December 2.

Advisory Committee Functions

Executive Order 12024.   December 1, 1977

RELATING TO THE TRANSFER OF CERTAIN
ADVISORY COMMITTEE FUNCTIONS

By virtue of the authority vested in me by the Constitution and statutes of the United States of America, including the Federal Advisory Committee Act, as amended (5 U.S.C. App. I), Section 301 of Title 3 of the United States Code, Section 202 of the Budget and Accounting Procedures Act of 1950 (31 U.S.C. 581c), and Section 7 of Reorganization Plan No. 1 of 1977 (42 FR 56101 (October 21, 1977)), and as President of the United States of America, in accord with the transfer of advisory committee functions from the Office of Management and Budget to the General Services Administration provided by Reorganization Plan No. 1 of 1977, it is hereby ordered as follows:

SECTION 1. The transfer, provided by Section 5F of Reorganization Plan No. 1 of 1977 (42 FR 56101), of certain functions under the Federal Advisory Committee Act, as amended (5 U.S.C. App. I), from the Office of Management and Budget and its Director to the Administrator of General Services is hereby effective.

SEC. 2. There is hereby delegated to the Administrator of General Services all the functions vested in the President by the Federal Advisory Committee Act, as amended, except that, the annual report to the Congress required by Section 6(c) of that Act shall be prepared by the Administrator for the President's consideration and transmittal to the Congress.

SEC. 3. The Director of the Office of Management and Budget shall take all actions necessary or appropriate to effectuate the transfer of functions provided in this Order, including the transfer of funds, personnel and positions, assets, liabilities, contracts, property, records, and other items related to the functions transferred.

SEC. 4. Executive Order No. 11769 of February 21, 1974 is hereby revoked.

SEC. 5. Any rules, regulations, orders, directives, circulars, or other actions taken pursuant to the functions transferred or reassigned as provided in this Order from the Office of Management and Budget to the Administrator of General Services, shall remain in effect as if issued by the Administrator until amended, modified, or revoked.

SEC. 6. This Order shall be effective November 20, 1977.

JIMMY CARTER

The White House,
    December 1, 1977.

[Filed with the Office of the Federal Register,
    10:56 a.m., December 2, 1977]

NOTE: The text of the Executive order was released on December 2.

Executive Schedule

Executive Order 12025.   December 1, 1977

RELATING TO CERTAIN POSITIONS IN
LEVEL IV OF THE EXECUTIVE SCHEDULE

By virtue of the authority vested in me by Section 5317 of Title 5 of the United States Code, and as President of the United States of America, Section 1 of Executive Order No. 11861, as amended, placing certain positions in Level IV of the Executive Schedule, is further amended by deleting "Associate Attorney General, Department of Justice." in subsection (12) and inserting in lieu thereof "Adviser to the Secretary and Deputy Secretary of Defense for NATO Affairs, Department of Defense."

JIMMY CARTER

The White House,
   December 1, 1977.

[Filed with the Office of the Federal Register, 10:57 a.m., December 2, 1977]

NOTE: The text of the Executive order was released on December 2.

Shippingport Light Water Breeder Reactor

Remarks at a Ceremony Marking the Pennsylvania Facility's Increase to Full Power Production.   December 2, 1977

THE PRESIDENT. You might tell us what to expect.

ADMIRAL RICKOVER. Mr. President, if I may be so bold as to suggest that you stay on my right-hand side. That is what the script says. [*Laughter*]

The Shippingport reactor is now putting out about 90 percent of its power. And the actual megawatts is about 65 to 6 or 7. We're ready to go up to full power at any time that you direct.

As you know, there's a blackboard here. And when you give the directions, they will carry out your orders.

THE PRESIDENT. Very fine.

ADMIRAL RICKOVER. As we all hope to do. [*Laughter*]

[*At this point, the President wrote the following words on a blackboard: "Increase light water breeder reactor to 100%, Jimmy Carter." The blackboard was connected electronically to a screen at the Shippingport Atomic Power Station's control center.*]

THOMAS D. JONES II [in Shippingport]. Mr. President, we have received your instructions and are proceeding to increase power to 100 percent rated reactor power.

THE PRESIDENT. Very fine.

ADMIRAL RICKOVER. Mr. President, while they're getting up the power, which takes a few minutes, as typical of all central station powerplants, I would like to explain to you how this reactor's scope and what its ultimate purpose is. This reactor contains about 1,100 pounds of U–233, which is made out of thorium. The thorium, when it's bombarded, changes first to U–235 [Th–233] [1] and goes through—234, rather, then by its own nuclear reaction goes to U–233.

In addition to that, it contains 40 tons of natural thorium. There's more thorium in the Earth than there is uranium; therefore, if this system can be made to work, it will tremendously magnify the energy we can get not only out of our uranium sources but also by this additional material, thorium.

The reactor itself is about 8 feet high, 8 feet in diameter, and weighs about 90 tons.

Now, the building blocks of the reactor I will now explain. This card shows the different kind of pellets which generate power. The top one is natural uranium [natural thorium].[1] The others are also natural thorium—the others are natural thorium [with U–233],[1] which have been irradiated to some extent and supply the neutrons which bombard this natural uranium and turn some of it into similar material.

There are 3 million of these pellets in the reactor. Now, these pellets are put into zirconium rods. This rod happens to have the natural thorium in it. This is a cutaway section, of course; it's not in there this way. The other three rods show different concentrations of the U–233, and of course, the reason there are differences is to take care of the physics which required it because neutrons are very valuable. We cannot waste a single neutron.

---

[1] White House Press Office correction.

Now, when the neutrons from the U–233 bombard, come out of this, bombard this, they cause—[*inaudible*].

THE PRESIDENT. Well, I understand now we have with the standard liquid water—I mean, light water reactors, enough energy to last 30 or 40 years. And if this breeder principle does work, it would magnify that energy supply maybe to 600 years, is that correct?

ADMIRAL RICKOVER. Yes, sir, very much more if it works. We do expect it to work, as I will discuss later.

THE PRESIDENT. Very good.

ADMIRAL RICKOVER. I don't like to start things that don't work, including yourself. [*Laughter*] Incidentally, Mr. President, I interviewed 260 first-class midshipmen for the last 3 days from morning until midnight. And they're all potential Presidents, if they carry out my admonitions. [*Laughter*]

THE PRESIDENT. Jim, you might come in on what this means to us as far as energy supplies are concerned.

SECRETARY SCHLESINGER. It does two things, Mr. President. First, it enormously expands the potential supply of fissionable material, which would provide us with a backup for our fission-produced power. Secondly, it may substantially extend the life of existing light water reactors by shifting to a different kind of fuel cycle and preserve our investment in those reactors.

THE PRESIDENT. The thorium supply is fairly plentiful, is it not?

ADMIRAL RICKOVER. Yes. This reactor is designed so that it can be placed into the pressure vessels of existing reactors. In that way, it's different than the liquid metal breeder. Of course, the liquid metal breeder would require brand new plants.

THE PRESIDENT. Is this the first actual power production that's useful from a breeder reactor in our country?

ADMIRAL RICKOVER. Yes, this is.

THE PRESIDENT. And when did this reactor go critical? When did it——

ADMIRAL RICKOVER. It went critical several weeks ago. And we've been testing it that whole time for physics and mechanical tests. And I would like to say that the reactor has come within three-tenths of 1 percent of our calculations.

THE PRESIDENT. Very good. What will happen to this energy? Will it be wasted?

ADMIRAL RICKOVER. No, sir. This energy right now is on the grid of the Duquesne Power Company in Pittsburgh.

THE PRESIDENT. So, it feeds into——

ADMIRAL RICKOVER. This is feeding right now into the energy grid. As a result of your order, it is being brought up to full power.

THE PRESIDENT. I see.

ADMIRAL RICKOVER. It soon will be at that.

Now, to go on with the description. This is a grid. By the way, there are 17,000 of these. They're all 8 feet high. You've only seen a small section.

These rods—this shows only the small ones—are placed in what we call a grid. This grid is made out of a very special type of stainless steel, and it took quite a long time to develop it.

Now, there are 300 of these grids. This is the smallest one; there are larger. Each one of them—see, they separate the rods so they don't touch. That's one of the small ones.

Now, the reactor is 8 feet in diameter; it's 8 feet high and weighs about 90 tons. This is built so all parts of that reactor, that huge thing, 8-by-8, weighing 90 tons, is built to the accuracy of 1/1000 of an inch. We have to have that accuracy because we cannot waste neutrons.

So, this whole, huge, 90-ton thing is built to the accuracy of a Swiss watch. That will give you some concept of how difficult, mechanically difficult, in addition to the physics, it is to build a reactor.

THE PRESIDENT. This reactor is cooled by highly purified water?

ADMIRAL RICKOVER. Yes, sir. It's cooled by ordinary water. And that is the difference between it and the liquid metal breeder, which will be a much better breeder. But ultimately, if you go long enough in years—it makes no difference whether it's light water or liquid metal—you will ultimately get the same result on energy usage, although the liquid metal breeder will do it faster.

THE PRESIDENT. So, you create as much fuel in this breeder as you consume.

ADMIRAL RICKOVER. Ultimately, you do, yes, sir.

THE PRESIDENT. I understand. I see we are up to 100 percent, apparently.

ADMIRAL RICKOVER. Mr. Kirby, the chairman of the board of Westinghouse, and Mr. Arthur, the chairman of the board of the Duquesne Light Company, are ready to carry out your orders.

As you know, the Westinghouse Company operates the Bettis Laboratory near Pittsburgh at which this reactor was designed and built.

And Mr. Arthur, with the Duquesne Company, operates the plant for the Energy Department, of which Dr. Schlesinger is the boss. And I would like to say he has backed us fully, both when he was Chairman of the Atomic Energy Commission and his present capacity. I'd like to thank him very much.

I also would like to thank Mr. David Leighton, who has been the project manager for me. And he may have hazed you because—I don't know whether he did; he was a class ahead of you at the Naval Academy. However, Mr. Wegner, who's my deputy, was in a class lower than yours. You may have hazed him. So, I think that calls it quits. [*Laughter*]

THE PRESIDENT. Do we have any report from Mr. Kirby?

ADMIRAL RICKOVER. Yes, sir. Mr. Kirby will now tell you if it is ready. You can tell him. You tell Mr. Kirby that the plant is ready.

THE PRESIDENT. Mr. Kirby, are we ready?

MR. KIRBY [in Shippingport]. Mr. President, this is Robert Kirby speaking. For the Bettis Laboratory and the many hundreds of Westinghouse employees who have worked on developing the light water breeder reactor over the past 12 years, I am pleased to inform you that the reactor is now at 100 percent rated reactor power.

THE PRESIDENT. Mr. Kirby, I'm very glad to hear that. This is indeed an historic day in the life of our country. As a matter of fact, and not coincidentally, 35 years ago today, the first sustained chain reaction in the nuclear cycle was commenced at Stagg Field in Chicago, in 1942.

And as you know, 20 years ago today, December 2, we had the first central powerplant operation at Shippingport, where you are located. So, I think the December 2 date, again, will be commemorating a major step forward in the technological development of our country. This is the first time we have ever had power produced in our country from a breeder reactor which uses a very plentiful supply of fuel that can multiply the power supply maybe 30 times over in the breeder cycle.

And I'm very proud to congratulate you, all the people at Bettis, all the people at Westinghouse, on this remarkable technological achievement.

MR. KIRBY. Thank you, Mr. President.

MR. ARTHUR [in Shippingport]. Mr. President, this is John Arthur, Duquesne Light Company. Based on our experience in operating this light water breeder reactor during the recent checkout phase, our company anticipates reliable performance from the reactor. Also, Mr. President, the Shippingport reactor will be very important to us, as we provide electricity to a half million homes, buildings, and industrial plants in the Pittsburgh area.

THE PRESIDENT. Well, Mr. Arthur, I know that the Duquesne Light and Power Company is very glad to get this supply of additional electricity from the breeder reactor. Not only is it a very fine step forward in engineering and technology but also it has a practical advantage as well.

And Admiral Rickover stated a few moments ago that this core, which is unique in its design, is the same configuration and size as the presently existing light water reactors in the nonbreeder field and, therefore, can possibly be substituted in the future. So, I think this again shows farsighted design.

And I'm very proud to see, also, the close cooperation between the Government on the one hand, the scientific community on the other, and industry, working so closely together in such a major effort.

Congratulations to you and to the people at Duquesne for cooperating and also benefiting from this notable achievement.

MR. ARTHUR. Thank you, Mr. President.

ADMIRAL RICKOVER. Mr. President, I would like to take this occasion now to present to you a memento of this occasion.

THE PRESIDENT. Well, Admiral, you know—go ahead.

ADMIRAL RICKOVER. This is a small part of a grid, a small part of two of the fuel rods.

THE PRESIDENT. Well, I'm very proud of you, and thank you very much for letting me participate.

ADMIRAL RICKOVER. I'm proud of you, too. [*Laughter*]

THE PRESIDENT. Thank you, sir.

Jim, thanks a lot. I appreciate it.

SECRETARY SCHLESINGER. Thank you, Mr. President.

THE PRESIDENT. I think it's a good day for us all. Thank you very much.

NOTE: The President spoke at 10:46 a.m. in the Oval Office at the White House.

Attending the ceremony in Washington and Shippingport were Adm. Hyman G. Rickover, Deputy Commander for Nuclear Propulsion, Naval Sea Systems Command, Department of the Navy; David Trent Leighton, Associate Director for Surface Ships and the Light Water Breeder Reactor, Division of Naval Reactors, Department of Energy; and Thomas D. Jones II, superintendent of the Shippingport Atomic Power Station for the Duquesne Light and Power Company. William Wegner is Deputy Director, Division of Naval Reactors, Department of Energy.

Dam Safety

Statement on the Initiation of a Federal Inspection Program for Nonfederal Dams. December 2, 1977

In my press conference this week, I announced that a safety inspection program for nonfederal dams would begin immediately to help prevent further tragedies like that at Toccoa Falls.

I have directed the Secretary of the Army to commence at once the inspection of more than 9,000 nonfederal dams that present a high potential for loss of life and property if they fail. The inspection program, to be administered by the Corps of Engineers, will take approximately 4 years. We will make $15 million available for the program during this fiscal year and hope to be able to inspect 1,800 nonfederal dams during that year. It is impossible to predict the total cost of the program precisely, but we tentatively estimate it to be $70 million.

I have directed the Secretaries of Interior and Agriculture to cooperate with the Secretary of the Army in developing technical criteria and guidelines for inspections and assisting the States. This dam inspection program cannot be a substitute for effective dam safety programs at the State level; it is intended to stimulate the States to action. The Federal Government will use this initiative to establish a partnership with the States in developing State programs. The Federal program will be limited to initial inspections only, will involve no assumption of Federal liability, and will be completed within 4 years.

Because the inspection program will not resolve specific dam safety problems and will not relieve the States or owners of these structures of their responsibilities for public safety, we will ask for Governors to agree, prior to these inspections, to take certain steps toward establishing an adequate State program for dam safety. States that agree to take these steps will be given priority for Federal inspections and technical assistance. We recognize that some States already have excellent dam safety programs.

I have also asked the Secretary of the Army, in cooperation with the Secretaries of the Interior and Agriculture and the Science Adviser to the President, to report back to me within 1 year on the status of the inspection effort, the development of State programs, and any needed additional actions to assure national dam safety.

In summary, the Federal Government will:

1. Begin immediately to work with all of the States to implement or improve dam safety programs;

2. Update the National Dam Inventory;

3. Fund and administer the inspection of all the approximately 9,000 nonfed-

eral dams in the high hazard potential category by virtue of their location;

4. Fund and administer the inspection of intermediate hazard category dams on Federal property; and

5. Fund and administer the inspection of a limited number of other nonfederal dams determined, on a case-by-case basis, after consultation with State officials, to be in a condition presenting an immediate threat to public safety.

The States will be asked to cooperate fully, by:

1. Assuring implementation of an effective dam safety program;

2. Assisting in implementing the federally financed dam inspections, including participation in State personnel training, and performing actual dam inspections where criteria are met; and

3. Assuring that they will use available means to take remedial actions when unsafe dams are found.

Institute of Museum Services

Nomination of Leila I. Kimche To Be Director. December 2, 1977

The President today announced that he will nominate Leila I. Kimche, of Bethesda, Md., to be Director of the Institute of Museum Services.

Kimche was born June 21, 1934, in New York City. She received a B.S.S. from George Washington University in 1956.

From 1969 to 1974, Kimche was assistant director for special projects for the American Association of Museums in Washington, where she was responsible for the Association's communications with more than 3,000 museums of art, history, and science. Since 1974 she has been executive director of the Association of Science-Technology Centers, an organization of 68 science museums.

Vice President Mondale's Visit to Mexico

Statement Announcing the Visit. December 2, 1977

At the invitation of President López Portillo and the Government of Mexico, Vice President Mondale will pay an official visit to Mexico on January 20–21, 1978.

President López Portillo was the first Chief of State to visit Washington in my administration. Mrs. Carter and Mrs. López Portillo participated respectively in President López Portillo's inauguration ceremonies and my own. Subsequently, Mrs. López Portillo and Mrs. Carter met in Mexico this November.

The Vice President will be visiting Mexico as my personal representative to continue this important process of consultations on both bilateral and multilateral issues with our good friends and neighbors in Mexico. His visit will again underscore the very great importance and value I attach to our relations with Mexico.

NOTE: The statement was made available by the White House Press Office. It was not issued in the form of a White House press release.

Vice President Mondale's Visit to Canada

Statement Announcing the Visit. December 2, 1977

At the invitation of Prime Minister Trudeau and the Government of Canada, Vice President Mondale will pay an official visit to Canada on January 18–19, 1978.

I have asked the Vice President to serve as my personal representative during this visit, which marks a welcome continuation of high-level U.S.-Canadian consultations begun at the outset of my administration with Prime Minister Trudeau's visit to Washington. Canada is one of our very closest friends, allies, and trading partners. The breadth of our bilateral and multilateral interests is great. The Vice President's visit will ensure that with our friends in Canada we continue to address those interests with the greatest possible cooperation and effectiveness.

NOTE: The statement was made available by the White House Press Office. It was not issued in the form of a White House press release.

Dinner Honoring Senator Hubert H. Humphrey

Remarks at the Dinner. December 2, 1977

Early this week, my good friend Charles Kirbo came to Washington. He said he was getting very worried about me, that he couldn't understand how every time he saw me, I looked older and older and Senator Humphrey looked younger and younger.

He said Senator Humphrey always has a smile on his face. He said, "Jimmy, your smile is gone." [*Laughter*] He said, "Your hair is turning gray; his has gotten curly." I said, "Well, the difference is that Senator Humphrey has been here long enough in Washington to know how to handle the political scene and I haven't learned yet."

Last summer, just as the Senate was beginning its long 2-month filibuster, Senator Humphrey went back to Minnesota for a vacation. And at the end of the vacation, when he got ready to come back, again being very conversant with political ways, he called me up and said, "Mr. President, I'd like to come back to Washington." I said, "Well, Senator

Humphrey, we're glad to have you." He said, "Yes, but I need a ride." [*Laughter*] And I said, "Well, that's fine. Maybe I could send the Vice President out to pick you up." He said, "Well, I've never ridden in Air Force One."

So, I went to the west coast and came back via Minnesota and picked him up. But first I said, "Well, why is it you want to come back?" He said, "I think if I come back, I can get the Congress straightened out." He said, "I guarantee you, if you give me a ride back to Washington, I'll have the energy package passed in a week." [*Laughter*]

He is a man who has touched my life and that of my family, as I'm sure he's touched almost everyone here in a strange and very delightful way. And I'm going to tell you just a few brief instances that occurred, actually, long before I had any dreams of coming to Washington myself.

The first time I heard about Senator Humphrey was when I was in the Navy, and he made a famous speech at the Democratic National Convention. He was quite well known in Georgia. I don't think anyone else has kept more Georgia politicians from seeing the end of a Democratic convention than Senator Humphrey has, because it got so that every time he walked in, they walked out and came back home. [*Laughter*]

So, in 1964, when he became the Vice-Presidential candidate, in Georgia it wasn't a very popular thing to be for the Johnson-Humphrey slate. My mother, Lillian, ran the Sumter County Johnson-Humphrey headquarters. And I could always tell when my mother was coming down the road, because she was in a brand new automobile with the windows broken out, the radio antenna tied in a knot, and the car painted with soap. [*Laughter*]

In that campaign, Hubert and Muriel came down to south Georgia to Moultrie

for a Democratic rally. And because of my mother's loyalty, she was given the honor of picking up Muriel at the airport. And Rosalynn and my mother and Muriel and my sister Gloria went down to Moultrie to attend the rally. Senator Humphrey made a speech, and they had a women's reception for Muriel. And they were riding around that south Georgia town getting ready for the reception. Everybody in town was very excited. And as Muriel approached the site, she said, "Are any black women invited to the reception?"

For a long time no one spoke, and finally my sister said, "I don't know." She knew quite well that they weren't. And Muriel said, "I'm not going in." So, they stopped the car, and my sister Gloria went inside to check and let the hostess know that Muriel was not coming to the reception. But in a few minutes, Gloria came back and said, "Mrs. Humphrey, it's okay." So, she went in and, sure enough, there were several black ladies there at the reception. And Muriel never knew until now that the maids just took off their aprons for the occasion. [*Laughter*] But that was the first integrated reception in south Georgia, Muriel, and you are responsible for it.

Ten or eleven years ago, when I was not in political office at all, Senator Humphrey was Vice President. He had been to Europe on a long, tedious, very successful trip. And he came down to Atlanta, Georgia, to visit in the home of a friend named Marvin Schube. And I was invited there to meet him, which was a great honor for me. I have never yet met a Democratic President, and he was the only Democratic Vice President I had ever met. And I stood there knowing that he was very weary because he had just returned from Europe. But he answered the eager questions of those Georgia friends until quite late in the morning, about 2 o'clock. And he was very well briefed, because when I walked in the room, he said, "Young man, I understand that your mother is in the Peace Corps in India."

And I said, "Yes, sir, that's right." He said, "Well, I've been very interested in the Peace Corps. The idea originally came from me, and I've been proud to see it put into effect." He said, "Where's your mother?" And I said, "She's near Bombay." He said, "How's she getting along?" I said, "Well, she's quite lonely, sir. She's been there about 6 months, and she's not seen anybody, even the Peace Corps officials. She's in a little town called Vikhroli."

About a month later, I got a letter from my mother. She was in her room one evening, and the head of the Peace Corps in India had driven up to the little town of Vikhroli. He came in and asked my mother if she needed anything. She said, no, she was getting along quite well, but she would like to go over to Bombay. He said, "Well, can I take you in shopping, Mrs. Carter?" She said, "Yes, I'd like that." So, they went in, and he bought her a very fine supper and brought her back to Vikhroli. When he got out, he handed her a fifth of very good bourbon. [*Laughter*] And he turned around to get in the car to leave, and he finally turned back to her and said, "By the way, Miss Lillian, who in the hell are you, anyway?" [*Laughter*] And that's a true story. It was not until later that my mother knew who she was. [*Laughter*] She was a friend of Hubert Humphrey.

And, of course, the next time he crossed my path was in 1968 when he was our nominee for President. And all of us in this room went through that year of tragedy together when he was not elected to be the leader of our country. And I think he felt then an urging to be loyal to his President, and unfortunately,

many people were not that loyal to him. And his loss was our Nation's even greater loss in 1968.

The next time I saw him was when I was Governor. He came to our home in 1972. All the candidates just happened to stop by to see me that year, and my daughter, Amy, was about 4 years old. And most of the ones who would come into the mansion—she stayed away from them, having an early aversion to politicians. But when Senator Humphrey came in, she loved him instantly.

And I'll never forget sitting in the front Presidential suite of the Georgia Governor's mansion, a very beautiful room, trying to talk to Senator Humphrey. Amy came in eating a soft brownie, and she climbed up on his lap without any timidity at all. In a very natural way, he put his arm around her as though she was his own grandchild. And I'll always remember Senator Humphrey sitting there talking to me about politics and about the campaign, smiling often, with brownie all over his face. [*Laughter*] And each time he frowned, brownie crumbs fell to the floor. And Amy loved him then and has loved him ever since. But I think she recognized in him the qualities that have aroused the love of so many people.

And then, of course, last year all I could hear everywhere I went when I said, "Would you help me become President?" almost invariably they would say, "Well, my first preference is Hubert Humphrey. If he doesn't run, I'll support you." And there again, I learned on a nationwide basis the relationship between Senator Humphrey and the people of this country.

But I think the most deep impression I have of my good friend Hubert Humphrey is since I've been President. I've seen him in the Oval Office early in the morning. I've seen him in meetings with other congressional leaders. I've called him on the phone when I was in trouble. I've gotten his quiet and private and sound advice. And I've come to recognize that all the attributes that I love about America are resident in him. And I'm proud to be the President of a nation that loves a man like Hubert Humphrey and is loved so deeply by him.

Thank you very much.

NOTE: The President spoke at 9:40 p.m. in the International Ballroom at the Washington Hilton Hotel at the fundraising dinner for the benefit of the Hubert H. Humphrey Institute of Public Affairs at the University of Minnesota.

The White House press release of the President's remarks was not available until December 21.

Digest of Other White House Announcements

The following listing includes the President's daily schedule and other items of general interest as announced by the White House Press Office during the period covered by this issue. Events and announcements printed elsewhere in the issue are not included.

November 27

The President returned to the White House after spending the Thanksgiving weekend at Camp David, Md.

November 28

The President met at the White House with:

—Zbigniew Brzezinski, Assistant to the President for National Security Affairs;
—Vice President Walter F. Mondale, Secretary of State Cyrus R. Vance, and Dr. Brzezinski;
—the Cabinet;
—Secretary of the Interior Cecil D. Andrus, Secretary of Agriculture Bob Bergland, Secretary of the Army Clifford L. Alexander, Jr., and Lt. Gen. John W. Morris, Chief of Engineers, U.S. Army, to discuss dam safety inspection;
—Vice President Mondale;
—Vice President Mondale, Secretary Vance, and Dr. Brzezinski;
—James T. McIntyre, Jr., Acting Director of the Office of Management and Budget;
—Vice President Mondale, Secretary of Health, Education, and Welfare Joseph A. Califano, Jr.

November 29

The President met at the White House with:

—Dr. Brzezinski;
—the Democratic congressional leadership;
—Representative Charles E. Bennett of Florida;
—Dr. Abdul Halim Mahmoud, Grand Sheikh of Al-Azhar, an Islamic university in Egypt;
—Adm. Stansfield Turner, Director of Central Intelligence, and Dr. Brzezinski;
—Secretary of the Treasury W. Michael Blumenthal and Charles L. Schultze, Chairman of the Council of Economic Advisers;
—Secretary of Labor F. Ray Marshall.

November 30

The President met at the White House with:

—Dr. Brzezinski;
—Secretary of Defense Harold Brown and members of the Joint Chiefs of Staff;
—a group of administration officials to discuss the budget.

The White House announced that the President has asked Joan Mondale, wife of the Vice President, to be his personal representative at the commemoration of

Finland's 60th anniversary of independence in Helsinki on December 5–6.

December 1

The President met at the White House with:

—Dr. Brzezinski;

—Representative Ralph H. Metcalfe of Illinois;

—Secretary of Housing and Urban Development Patricia Roberts Harris;

—Secretary Califano, Representative James C. Corman, chairman, and members of the House Subcommittee on Public Assistance and Unemployment Compensation, which is considering welfare legislation;

—Mrs. Carter, for lunch.

The President attended a briefing on the Panama Canal treaties, given for staff members of the Senate in the State Dining Room.

The President transmitted to the Congress the 11th annual report on the Operation of the Automotive Products Trade Act of 1965.

The White House announced that the President's foreign trip, postponed on November 7, will be divided into two parts. The first portion—visits to Poland, Iran, India, Saudi Arabia, France, and Belgium—will take place from December 29, 1977, to January 6, 1978. The second portion—visits to Brazil, Nigeria, and Venezuela—will take place sometime in the spring of 1978.

December 2

The President met at the White House with:

—Vice President Mondale, Secretary Vance, and Dr. Brzezinski;

—Dr. Brzezinski;

—Vice President Mondale, Secretary of Energy James R. Schlesinger, and a group of Members of the House of Representatives;

—Vice President Mondale and Dr. Schultze;

—Attorney General Griffin B. Bell;

—a group of administration officials to discuss the budget.

The White House announced that the United States will make available $2 million of disaster relief assistance for victims of the cyclone and tidal wave that devastated southeastern India last week, and that the President has expressed to the Indian Government his deepest personal concern about the tragic loss of human life there.

The President has appointed Richard A. Frank, Administrator of the National Oceanic and Atmospheric Administration, as U.S. Commissioner on the International Whaling Commission.

NOMINATIONS SUBMITTED TO THE SENATE

The following list does not include promotions of members of the Uniformed Services, nominations to the Service Academies, or nominations of Foreign Service officers.

Submitted November 28, 1977

ROBERT M. THOMPSON, of Wisconsin, to be United States Marshal for the Western District of Wisconsin for the term of 4 years, vice Leonard E. Alderson, resigned.

Submitted December 1, 1977

GEORGE S. McISAAC, of the District of Columbia, to be an Assistant Secretary of Energy (Resource Applications) (new position).

Submitted December 2, 1977

LEILA I. KIMCHE, of Maryland, to be Director of the Institute of Museum Services (new position).

CHECKLIST OF WHITE HOUSE PRESS RELEASES

The following releases of the Office of the White House Press Secretary, distributed dur-

CHECKLIST—Continued

ing the period covered by this issue, are not included in the issue.

Released November 28, 1977

Announcement: nomination of Robert M. Thompson to be United States Marshal for the Western District of Wisconsin

Released December 1, 1977

Outline of schedule: President's foreign trip from December 29, 1977, to January 6, 1978

CHECKLIST—Continued

Released December 2, 1977

Fact sheet: Federal inspection program for nonfederal dams

ACTS APPROVED BY THE PRESIDENT

Approved December 2, 1977

H.R. 7345_____ Public Law 95–204 Veterans and Survivors Pension Adjustment Act of 1977.

PRESIDENTIAL DOCUMENTS

Week Ending Friday, December 9, 1977

Meeting With Prime Minister Ahmed Osman of Morocco

White House Statement Issued Following the Meeting. December 3, 1977

The President met at 9:30 this morning with Prime Minister Osman of Morocco, who came to Washington as the emissary of King Hassan to deliver a personal message from the King to President Carter. The Prime Minister was accompanied by Ambassador Benjelloun. The meeting of approximately 1 hour was attended on the U.S. side by Secretary of State Vance, Dr. Brzezinski, U.S. Ambassador to Morocco Robert Anderson, and William Quandt of the NSC staff.

Because of recent developments in the Middle East in which Morocco is deeply interested, the visit of His Majesty King Hassan II to President Carter has been postponed by mutual agreement. In an exchange of personal messages, His Majesty and the President reaffirmed the traditional bonds of friendship between the two countries.

The visit of the Prime Minister, who is the highest ranking official in the Moroccan Government after the King, underlined the importance which King Hassan attaches to his relations with the United States. The President took advantage of the Prime Minister's presence for a friendly exchange of views on a number of issues of mutual interest to the United States and Morocco.

NOTE: The statement was made available by the White House Press Office. It was not issued in the form of a White House press release.

Railroad Retirement Board

Nomination of William P. Adams To Be a Member. December 5, 1977

The President today announced that he will nominate William P. Adams, of Springfield, Va., to be a member of the Railroad Retirement Board. He would replace James Cowen, whose term has expired, and would be the at-large member.

Adams was born August 2, 1926, in Danville, Ill. He received a B.S. from Michigan State University in 1949 and a J.D. from Georgetown University Law Center in 1953.

From 1955 to 1974, Adams was counsel and a professional staff member on the House Committee on Interstate and Foreign Commerce. From 1955 to 1974, he was also assistant counsel in the Office of the Legislative Counsel of the House of Representatives.

Since earlier this year, Adams has been vice president of the Motion Picture Association of America, where he maintains liaison with Congress and keeps member companies of the association informed of legislative developments affecting the motion picture industry.

Delaware River Basin Commission

Appointment of Sherman W. Tribbitt as Alternate Federal Member. December 5, 1977

The President today announced that he has appointed Sherman W. Tribbitt, of Delaware, to be alternate Federal member of the Delaware River Basin Commission. He replaces Thomas F. Schweigert, resigned.

Tribbitt was born November 9, 1922, in Easton, Md. He is a graduate of Beacom College. He owned and operated the Odessa Supply Co. in Odessa, Del., for 28 years.

Tribbitt served in the Delaware House of Representatives from 1957 to 1965 and was speaker of the house from 1959 to 1965. From 1965 to 1969, he was Lieutenant Governor of Delaware. From 1971 to 1973, he was minority leader, and from 1973 to 1977 he was Governor of Delaware.

Energy Department Employees

Executive Order 12026.   December 5, 1977

REINSTATEMENT RIGHTS OF CERTAIN EMPLOYEES OF THE DEPARTMENT OF ENERGY

By virtue of the authority vested in me by Sections 3301 and 3302 of Title 5 of the United States Code, and as President of the United States of America, the service of an employee of the Atomic Energy Commission or of the Energy Research and Development Administration pursuant to a Regular or Regular (Conditional) appointment, other than such service in an attorney position, who was transferred to the Department of Energy pursuant to the Department of Energy Organization Act (91 Stat. 565; 42 U.S.C. 7101 *et seq.*) shall be considered as Career or Career-Conditional service, respectively, for purposes of eligibility for reinstatement in the competitive Civil Service.

JIMMY CARTER

The White House,
   December 5, 1977.

[Filed with the Office of the Federal Register, 3:58 p.m., December 5, 1977]

Executive Development and Other Personnel Functions

Executive Order 12027.   December 5, 1977

RELATING TO THE TRANSFER OF CERTAIN EXECUTIVE DEVELOPMENT AND OTHER PERSONNEL FUNCTIONS

By virtue of the authority vested in me by the Constitution and statutes of the United States of America, including Reorganization Plan No. 2 of 1970 (5 U.S.C. App. II), Section 202 of the Budget and Accounting Procedures Act of 1950 (31 U.S.C. 581c), and Section 301 of Title 3 of the United States Code, and as President of the United States of America, in order to transfer certain functions from the Director of the Office of Management and Budget to the United States Civil

Service Commission, it is hereby ordered as follows:

SECTION 1. The following functions which heretofore have been performed by the Director of the Office of Management and Budget, either alone or in conjunction with the United States Civil Service Commission, are hereby reassigned and delegated to the United States Civil Service Commission:

(a) Providing overall Executive Branch leadership, regulation, and guidance in executive personnel selection, development, and management including:

(1) Devising and establishing programs and encouraging agencies to devise and establish programs to forecast the need for career executive talent and to select, train, develop, motivate, deploy and evaluate the men and women who make up the top ranks of Federal civil service;

(2) Initiating and leading efforts to ensure that potential executive talent is identified, developed and well utilized throughout the Executive Branch and;

(3) Ensuring that executive training and motivation meet current and future needs.

(b) Studying and reporting on issues relating to position classification and the compensation of Federal civilian employees, including linkages among pay systems, and providing reports on average grade levels, work-years and personnel costs of Federal civilian employees.

(c) Providing primary Executive Branch leadership in (1) developing and reviewing a program of policy guidance to departments and agencies for the organization of management's responsibility under the Federal Labor Relations program; and (2) monitoring issues and trends in labor management relations for referral to appropriate Executive Branch

officials including the Federal Labor Relations Council.

SEC. 2. Section 1 of Executive Order No. 11541, as amended, is further amended by adding thereto the following new subsection:

"(d) The delegation to the Director of the Office of Management and Budget of the following executive development and personnel functions (which have been transferred to the Civil Service Commission) is terminated on December 4, 1977:

(1) Providing overall Executive Branch leadership, regulation, and guidance in executive personnel selection, development and management.

(2) Studying and reporting on issues relating to position classification and the compensation of Federal civilian employees, including linkages among pay systems, and providing reports on average grade levels, work-years and personnel costs of Federal civilian employees.

(3) Providing primary Executive Branch leadership in (i) developing and reviewing a program of policy guidance to departments and agencies for the organization of management responsibility under the Federal Labor Relations program; and (ii) monitoring issues and trends in labor management relations for referral to appropriate Executive Branch officials including the Federal Labor Relations Council.".

SEC. 3. Executive Order No. 11491, as amended, is further amended by amending Section 25(a) to read as follows:

"The Civil Service Commission, in conjunction with the Director of the Office of Management and Budget, shall establish and maintain a program for the policy guidance of agencies on labor-management relations in the Federal service and shall periodically review the implementation of these policies. The Civil Service Commission shall be responsible for the day-to-day policy guidance under that program. The Civil Service Commission also shall continuously review the operation of the Federal labor-management relations program to assist in assuring adherence to its provisions and merit system requirements; implement technical advice and information programs for the agencies; assist in the development of programs for training agency personnel and management officials in labor-management relations; and, from time to time, report to the Council on the state of the program with any recommendations ·for its improvement.".

SEC. 4. Section 5(a) of Executive Order No. 11636 of December 17, 1971, establishing an Employee-Management Relations Commission as a committee of the Board of the Foreign Service, is amended by deleting: "The representative of the Office of Management and Budget shall be the Chairman of the Commission" and substituting therefor "The representative of the Civil Service Commission shall be the Chairman of the Commission".

SEC. 5. The records, property, personnel, and unexpended balances of appropriations, available or to be made available, which relate to the functions transferred or reassigned by this Order from the Office of Management and Budget to the United States Civil Service Commission, are hereby transferred to the United States Civil Service Commission.

SEC. 6. The Director of the Office of Management and Budget shall make such determinations, issue such orders, and take all actions necessary or appropriate to effectuate the transfers or reassignments provided by this Order, including the transfer of funds, records, property, and personnel.

SEC. 7. This Order shall be effective December 4, 1977.

JIMMY CARTER

The White House,
December 5, 1977.

[Filed with the Office of the Federal Register, 3:59 p.m., December 5, 1977]

Commissioner on Aging

Nomination of Robert C. Benedict. December 5, 1977

The President today announced that he will nominate Robert C. Benedict, of Mechanicsburg, Pa., to be Commissioner on Aging. He would replace Arthur S. Flemming.

Benedict was born November 29, 1940. He received a B.S. in history and political science from Eastern Michigan University in 1965 and an M.P.A. from the University of Michigan in 1969. He also attended the University of Michigan Institute of Gerontology and was certified as a specialist in aging.

From 1965 to 1967, Benedict was a staff associate for human services with the State Human Resources Council of the Executive Office of the Governor of Michigan. From 1969 to 1972, he was on the faculty of the University of Michigan's Institute of Gerontology and also served as director of short-term training and director of the Residential Institute on Aging program.

Since 1972 Benedict has been director of the Bureau for the Aging and commissioner of the Office for the Aging at the Pennsylvania Department of Public Welfare. He has served as a consultant on aging and is the author of several articles on aging in professional journals.

Department of Justice

Nomination of Benjamin R. Civiletti To Be Deputy Attorney General.   December 6, 1977

The President today announced that he will nominate Benjamin R. Civiletti, of Baltimore, Md., to be Deputy Attorney General. He would replace Peter F. Flaherty, who has resigned.

Civiletti was born July 17, 1935, in Peekskill, N.Y. He received an A.B. from Johns Hopkins in 1957 and an LL.B. from the University of Maryland in 1961. He was admitted to the Maryland bar in 1961. He served as law clerk to U.S. District Judge W. Calvin Chestnut in 1961 and 1962.

From 1962 to 1964, Civiletti was assistant U.S. Attorney for the District of Maryland. He practiced law with the Baltimore firm of Venable, Baetjer, Howard from 1964 until March 1977, when he was appointed Assistant Attorney General for the Criminal Division.

U.S. Steel Industry

Announcement of a Report to the President by an Interagency Task Force.   December 6, 1977

The President has received and approved the recommendations of the Interagency Task Force report on steel prepared by the Under Secretary of the Treasury, Anthony Solomon.

The President indicated that the recommendations in the Task Force report will help revitalize the health of the domestic steel industry, will encourage its modernization, and will assist workers, firms, and communities that have been disadvantaged by its current problems.

The President stressed that these purposes would be achieved:

—with maintenance of existing environmental goals;

—within the framework of existing antitrust laws;

—with a minimum of inflationary impact;

—with modest Federal budget expenditures;

—in a way which encourages greater productivity and modernization in the steel industry;

—consistent with competitive market forces.

The President noted the rapidity with which the administration had responded to the problems of the steel industry and applauded the expeditious work by the Task Force and particularly by Under Secretary Solomon.

NOTE: The 35-page report is entitled "Report to the President—A Comprehensive Program for the Steel Industry."

David K. E. Bruce

Statement on the Death of the Former Ambassador.   December 6, 1977

David K. E. Bruce was not only a diplomat of uncommon character and influence, he was also a man whose breadth of friendships, intellect, and empathy for the feelings of others made him an ideal representative of this Nation abroad. His service as Ambassador to France, Germany, and the United Kingdom fittingly symbolized his personal commitment to help reduce the age-old antagonisms of Europe and forge a bond of Western unity. As our country's first envoy to the People's Republic of China, he carried forward the process of normalizing relations set forth in the Shanghai Communique. In his life, as in his diplomacy, he showed how much could be achieved by "the application of intelligence and tact."

Laurence N. Woodworth

Statement on the Death of the Assistant Secretary of the Treasury. December 7, 1977

The death of Laurence Woodworth is a personal loss to me and a loss to our Nation of one of its most dedicated public servants.

For more than three decades, he served with the Joint Committee on Taxation of the Congress, where his understanding of our tax system was matched only by his determination to improve that system and by his patience in dealing with those who knew far less than he. For the last 11 months, as Assistant Secretary of the Treasury for Tax Policy, he directed this administration's efforts to develop a better, fairer tax system.

Larry Woodworth was the first Assistant Secretary I appointed, and in the last year I worked with him personally more than with any other Assistant Secretary in the Government. In that time I developed a profound respect for his abilities and an admiration for his modest, self-effacing manner.

I extend my deepest sympathy to his wife, Margaret, and their children.

Federal Civilian Employment

Announcement of Employment Levels. December 7, 1977

The President today announced that the administration's efforts to hold Federal civilian employment levels to the minimum necessary for the efficient operation of the Government have been successful.

On September 30, 1977, Federal civilian employment in the executive branch was below the ceiling established for that date. The ceilings were announced on June 17, 1977.

	Full-time permanent	Total *
Ceilings established for Sept. 30, 1977..	1,934,200	2,116,000
Actual employment, Sept. 30, 1977.....	1,908,900	2,107,000
Difference......	25,300	8,900
Percent below estimate......	1.3	0.4

* "Total" employment includes full-time permanent as well as temporary, part-time, and intermittent employees. These figures do not include the Postal Service, which controls its own employment.

Chanukah Torch Relay, 1977

Remarks on Receiving the Maccabean Torch at a Ceremony in the Oval Office. December 7, 1977

I want to thank you very much for letting me participate in this ceremony.

As all of you know, 2,000 years ago— or 2,100 years ago, the Maccabees fought for and achieved a tremendous victory for freedom. This was the first occurrence in the history of humankind when the basic struggle was for religious freedom. And that was a precursor of the constant struggle for the Jewish people to have their own land, free of outside domination, a chance to live in peace, to worship God as they choose.

And I believe that it's a very wonderful thing for the world that the Masada, young people of the Zionist Organization of America, have begun—I think, 11 years ago—this ceremony of going to the Shrine to the Maccabees in Israel, acquiring there a light for the torch, of bringing it to our country so that we could share, as Americans, in a sense of brotherhood and common purpose and a recognition of our historical background, together, the courage of the Maccabees and the recent courage, of course, of the new Israeli state.

For the last more than 30 years, this struggle has been going on. And as Rabbi Sternstein said, in the recent weeks there's been a tremendous breakthrough in the search for peace that we hope and pray will be successful. And I hope that this ceremony will remind all the world that Israel and the United States, we stand together in a spirit of deep commitment, with a common religious background and with a common commitment to peace and a recognition of the great courage that was required more than two centuries ago and which is still required to achieve and to maintain that difficult goal of peace and also freedom, together.

Thank you very much.

NOTE: The President spoke at 2:02 p.m. at the ceremony in the Oval Office. The President received the torch from representatives of Masada, the Youth Movement of the Zionist Organization of America, and handed it to Rabbi Joseph P. Sternstein, president of the organization. Rabbi Sternstein used the flame to light four candles of a menorah in celebration of the fourth day of Chanukah.

Department of Justice

Exchange of Letters on the Resignation of Peter F. Flaherty. December 8, 1977

December 8, 1977

To Peter F. Flaherty

This will acknowledge receipt of your letter of December 2, 1977, submitting your resignation as Deputy Attorney General.

With sincere regret, I accept your resignation. Our Administration will miss the benefit of your talent and energy.

Whatever direction your personal career shall take you in your home state of Pennsylvania, please be assured that you have my personal friendship and best wishes for success and personal gratification.

Sincerely,

JIMMY CARTER

[Honorable Peter F. Flaherty, Deputy Attorney General, U.S. Department of Justice, Washington, D.C. 20530]

December 2, 1977

Dear Mr. President:

With grateful appreciation to you for the honor of serving in your Administration, I hereby submit this letter as my resignation, effective December 9, 1977, from the position of Deputy Attorney General.

As Deputy Attorney General, I have been involved mainly in reorganization and administrative changes at Justice, including LEAA, Freedom of Information, minimum prison standards, the Marshals' Witness Security Program and the elimination of a large number of regional offices in the LEAA, Marshals Service and the Drug Enforcement Administration. Most of these changes are completed or nearing completion.

In my home state of Pennsylvania, there has been much speculation as to my entering the 1978 gubernatorial race. The response has been most encouraging, and a recent poll indicated that I would be the leading Democratic contender. Much exploratory work remains to be done, however, before I make a final decision to enter the race. Obviously, I should not seriously explore the matter from my position as Deputy Attorney General.

Although there were a number of things which I had hoped to accomplish over the next few years at the Department, I feel it best to continue my public service career in my home state of Pennsylvania.

Thank you for permitting me to participate in your Administration.

Sincerely,

PETER F. FLAHERTY

[The President, The White House, Washington, D.C. 20500]

NOTE: The texts of the letters were made available by the White House Press Office on December 9. They were not issued in the form of a White House press release.

Bill of Rights Day, Human Rights Day and Week, 1977

Proclamation 4542. December 9, 1977

By the President of the United States of America

A Proclamation

This month marks the anniversaries of two great events in the long struggle for the rights of human beings: the ratification of the American Bill of Rights on December 15, 1791, and the adoption of the Universal Declaration of Human Rights by the United Nations General Assembly on December 10, 1948.

The Bill of Rights culminated the Founders' efforts to create for their new country a national life grounded in liberty and respect for individual rights. The Declaration of Independence proclaimed the inalienable rights of life, liberty, and the pursuit of happiness. The Constitution formed a "more perfect Union" in which those rights could be fulfilled. And the first ten amendments to the new Constitution placed the keystone on this new

edifice of human rights. The immediate application of those rights extended only to one country, and only to some of the people in it. But because those rights were proclaimed as the natural birthright of all human beings, the documents that embodied them were rightly seen to have a profound and universal significance.

It is a lesson of history that no enumeration of rights, however eloquent, can alone ensure their protection in practice. We Americans struggled, sometimes bloodily, to make the rights promised in our founding documents a reality for all our people. That experience of successful struggle for human rights in our own country was both painful and ennobling, and it propelled us into a leading role in the adoption of the Universal Declaration of Human Rights by the United Nations. As a people, we believe what that Declaration says: that the promotion of respect for human rights is the shared responsibility of the world community. We call on the governments of other nations to join us in discharging this responsibility.

Everywhere on earth, men and women have made great personal sacrifices, even to the laying down of their lives, in the long struggle for justice and human dignity. By their sacrifices, they have already hallowed the human rights anniversaries I proclaim today.

NOW, THEREFORE, I, JIMMY CARTER, President of the United States of America, do hereby proclaim December 10, 1977, as Human Rights Day and December 15, 1977, as Bill of Rights Day, and call on all Americans to observe Human Rights Week beginning December 10, 1977. Let us reflect on the significance of the Bill of Rights, which has given purpose to our national life, and of the Universal Declaration of Human Rights, which holds the promise of greater liberty in the lives of all the inhabitants of our planet. Let us recommit ourselves, as individuals and as a Nation, to the realization of these rights, the guarantee of which we hold to be the essential purpose of the civil order.

IN WITNESS WHEREOF, I have hereunto set my hand this ninth day of December, in the year of our Lord nineteen hundred seventy-seven, and of the Independence of the United States of America the two hundred and second.

JIMMY CARTER

[Filed with the Office of the Federal Register, 3:09 p.m., December 9, 1977]

Director of the Federal Bureau of Investigation

Exchange of Letters on the Withdrawal of Judge Frank M. Johnson, Jr.'s Nomination. December 9, 1977

December 9, 1977

To Judge Frank Johnson

I have your letter of November 29 in which you request that your nomination to be Director of the Federal Bureau of Investigation be withdrawn and it is with sincere regret that I do so.

On behalf of the Nation, I am pleased to express my appreciation for your dedication, energy, and tireless efforts throughout your career with the judicial branch of the government. I want you to know that the people of this country and myself are truly happy that we will continue to have the benefit of your advice, contributions, and services on the Bench.

You have my warmest wishes for a speedy recovery and every happiness in the years ahead.

Sincerely,

JIMMY CARTER

[The Honorable Frank M. Johnson, Jr., Chief Judge, United States District Court, Middle District of Alabama, Montgomery, Alabama 36101]

November 29, 1977

Dear Mr. President:

I write to request that you withdraw my nomination to be the Director of the Federal Bureau of Investigation.

As you are aware, since I agreed in the middle of August, 1977, to accept the Directorship of the Bureau, it was necessary that I undergo major surgery to correct an abdominal aortic aneurysm. While the surgery appears to be completely successful and I am recovering, my rate of recovery is very slow. It is evident to me that it will be several more months before I will regain my strength and stamina. It will not be fair to the Federal Bureau of Investigation or to me to keep this matter pending any longer.

I want you to know that I appreciate the confidence that you have expressed through my nomination and I regret that conditions over which I have no control necessitate this letter requesting withdrawal of the nomination.

Respectfully yours,

FRANK M. JOHNSON, JR.

cc: Attorney General Griffin B. Bell

[The President, The White House, Washington, D.C.]

NOTE: The texts of the letters were made available by the White House Press Office on December 9. They were not issued in the form of a White House press release.

Labor-HEW Continuing Appropriations Bill

Statement on Signing H.J. Res. 662 Into Law. December 9, 1977

I am pleased to sign into law H.J. Res. 662, which incorporates the FY 1978 appropriations for the Department of Labor, the Department of Health, Education, and Welfare, the Community Services Administration, and other agencies.

These departments and agencies perform services which directly or indirectly benefit the lives of every American, particularly the least fortunate among us. Public health, the education of the young, jobs and income security all depend heavily upon the programs supported by this legislation.

H.J. Res. 662 reflects some of the efforts which this administration undertook last February in its FY 1978 budget revisions, for it incorporates provisions which:

—expand the Job Corps by 14,000 positions;

—increase by 400,000 the number of college students receiving Basic Educational Opportunity Grants and raise the maximum award to $1,600 a year;

—provide funds to begin to ensure that every child in America is immunized against dangerous communicable diseases;

—provide additional funds to help residents of rural and inner-city areas get high-quality medical care through the National Health Service Corps.

In signing this resolution, I do want to express my concern about Section 208 of H.R. 7555, which the resolution incorporates. Section 208 places limits, with respect to student transportation, on the enforcement of Title VI of the Civil Rights Act of 1964. I have been advised by the Department of Justice that this section, in its application, may raise new and vexing constitutional questions, adding further complexities to an already complex area of law. Moreover, this section may cause additional expense and delay in resolving issues important to parents, students, and school administrators in numerous school systems throughout the country.

NOTE: As enacted, H.J. Res. 662 is Public Law 95–205, approved December 9.

Digest of Other White House Announcements

The following listing includes the President's daily schedule and other items of general interest as announced by the White House Press Office during the period covered by this issue. Events and announcements printed elsewhere in the issue are not included.

December 3

The President met at the White House with Zbigniew Brzezinski, Assistant to the President for National Security Affairs.

December 5

The President met at the White House with:
—Dr. Brzezinski;
—senior White House staff members;
—the Cabinet;
—Vice President Walter F. Mondale;
—a group of administration officials to discuss the budget.

December 6

The President met at the White House with:
—Dr. Brzezinski;
—Secretary of Health, Education, and Welfare Joseph A. Califano, Jr., and other administration officials to discuss elementary and secondary education reauthorization legislation;
—Vice President Mondale, Adm. Stansfield Turner, Director of Central Intelligence, and Dr. Brzezinski;
—James T. McIntyre, Jr., Acting Director of the Office of Management and Budget;
—a group of administration officials to discuss the budget.

December 7

The President met at the White House with:
—Dr. Brzezinski;

—Senator Walter Huddleston of Kentucky.

The White House announced that, at the invitation of the President, Vice President Mondale will visit Strategic Air Command Headquarters at Offutt Air Force Base in Omaha, Nebr., aboard the U.S. Air Force National Emergency Airborne Command Post, on December 8. He will receive a briefing and a tour of SAC Headquarters similar to the one the President received during his visit in October. He will be accompanied by Charles W. Duncan, Jr., Deputy Secretary of Defense, and Gen. George S. Brown, Chairman of the Joint Chiefs of Staff.

December 8

The President met at the White House with:

—Dr. Brzezinski;
—Secretary Califano, Secretary of the Treasury W. Michael Blumenthal, Charles L. Schultze, Chairman of the Council of Economic Advisers, Stuart E. Eizenstat, Assistant to the President for Domestic Affairs and Policy, and Frank B. Moore, Assistant to the President for Congressional Liaison, to discuss social security legislation;
—Mrs. Carter, for lunch;
—a group of administration officials to discuss the budget.

The President transmitted to the Congress the annual report of the Commodity Credit Corporation for the fiscal year ended June 30, 1976, and the transition quarter ended September 30, 1976.

December 9

The President met at the White House with:

—Secretary Blumenthal, Secretary of Commerce Juanita M. Kreps, Secretary of Labor F. Ray Marshall, Richard N. Cooper, Under Secretary of State for Economic Affairs, Dr. Schultze, Mr. McIntyre, and Mr. Eizenstat;
—Dr. Brzezinski;
—Henry Howell, 1977 Democratic candidate for Governor of Virginia;
—a group of editors, publishers, and broadcasters (transcript will be printed next week);
—a group of administration officials to discuss the budget;
—Mark Chona, Presidential Adviser to President Kenneth Kaunda of Zambia.

The President attended a briefing on the Panama Canal treaties, given for leaders of senior citizens organizations in the Roosevelt Room.

The President left the White House for a weekend stay at Camp David, Md. He was accompanied by Senator Hubert H. Humphrey of Minnesota.

NOMINATIONS SUBMITTED TO THE SENATE

The following list does not include promotions of members of the Uniformed Services, nominations to the Service Academies, or nominations of Foreign Service officers.

Submitted December 5, 1977

ROBERT CLYDE BENEDICT, of Pennsylvania, to be Commissioner on Aging, vice Arthur S. Flemming.

WILLIAM P. ADAMS, of Virginia, to be a member of the Railroad Retirement Board for the term of 5 years from August 29, 1977, vice James L. Cowen, resigned.

Submitted December 6, 1977

CARLON M. O'MALLEY, JR., of Pennsylvania, to be United States Attorney for the Middle District of Pennsylvania for the term of 4 years, vice S. John Cottone.

MACK BURTON, of Arkansas, to be United States Marshal for the Western District of Arkansas for the term of 4 years, vice Lee R. Owen.

COY W. ROGERS, of Oklahoma, to be United States Marshal for the Western District of Oklahoma for the term of 4 years, vice Floyd E. Carrier, term expired.

2089

NOMINATIONS—Continued

Submitted December 8, 1977

LOUIS G. VILLAESCUSA, JR., of California, to be United States Marshal for the Central District of California for the term of 4 years, vice Gaylord L. Campbell, term expired.

Submitted December 9, 1977

BENJAMIN R. CIVILETTI, of Maryland, to be Deputy Attorney General, vice Peter F. Flaherty, resigned.

Withdrawn December 9, 1977

FRANK M. JOHNSON, JR., of Alabama, to be Director of the Federal Bureau of Investigation for the term of 10 years, vice Clarence Marion Kelley, resigning, which was sent to the Senate on September 30, 1977.

CHECKLIST OF WHITE HOUSE PRESS RELEASES

The following releases of the Office of the White House Press Secretary, distributed during the period covered by this issue, are not included in the issue.

Released December 3, 1977

Interview: with a group of editors and news directors—by Vice President Walter F. Mondale (held on December 2)

CHECKLIST—Continued

Released December 6, 1977

Announcement: nomination of Carlon M. O'Malley, Jr., to be United States Attorney for the Middle District of Pennsylvania; Mack Burton to be United States Marshal for the Western District of Arkansas; and Coy W. Rogers to be United States Marshal for the Western District of Oklahoma

News conference: on the recommendations of the Interagency Task Force report on steel— by Anthony M. Solomon, Under Secretary of the Treasury for Monetary Affairs

Released December 8, 1977

Announcement: nomination of Louis G. Villaescusa, Jr., to be United States Marshal for the Central District of California

---

ACTS APPROVED BY THE PRESIDENT

Approved December 9, 1977

H. J. Res. 662_____ Public Law 95–205
A joint resolution making further continuing appropriations for the fiscal year 1978, and for other purposes.

Interview With the President

Remarks and a Question-and-Answer Session With a Group of Editors and News Directors. December 9, 1977

THE PRESIDENT. Good afternoon, everybody. Have a seat, please. I apologize for interrupting your meeting. [*Laughter*]

First of all, I want to thank you for coming to the White House to interview our people and to let me see some old friends. Jody [1] began this program at the beginning of this year over some opposition of mine, because I thought it would be too time-consuming, and I was afraid we couldn't get enough benefit from it and understanding of what we are doing in the White House. This is the 16th meeting we've had so far, more than 450 editors and others from around the country.

Jody tells me every State except three—we haven't had anybody yet from Hawaii or Alaska or, just because of scheduling, Vermont—but 20 percent of the newspapers in the United States have had editors here at the White House this year to talk to me personally and to ask questions in an unrestricted way. It's been a very helpful thing for us in telling the American people accurately what we are doing,

---

[1] Jody Powell, Press Secretary to the President.

what our problems are, what our achievements have been, what our plans are for the future.

As has been my custom, I'd like to take about 5 minutes to outline present circumstances, what's going on right now, and then spend the other 25 minutes answering your questions.

ADMINISTRATION POLICIES

The two major items that the Congress is dealing with, of course, are social security and energy. We've had a very productive year so far, and I think when a tabulation is made of what the Congress has done, it will be well received. We've had a major agenda. The Congress committees have been heavily overloaded, and they've responded very well in my opinion. They certainly have my appreciation and admiration.

In the energy package we've got five major programs. I'd say three of them have been successfully resolved. We have made a good bit of progress lately on the crude oil equalization tax; we still have natural gas pricing to go. But the committees are working in a very difficult, complicated, and politically unattractive field or subject.

I think the American public is in favor of a comprehensive energy package being passed. But they are not in favor of some of the specifics that need to go in the package to make it effective.

And I think the Congress has shown a great deal of both hard work, dedication, and courage in bringing us as far as they are.

I hope that we'll have the complete work by the committees and a chance to vote on the energy package before Christmas. It all depends on unpredictable kinds of agreements between the House and Senate conferees.

The other thing is social security. We faced when I came into office, as was the case in energy, a longstanding problem that nobody had been willing to address. It's not an attractive thing to do to provide adequate taxes to bring the social security reserve funds back into a sound position.

The integrity of the social security system is of intense importance to most Americans. One of the reserve funds would have gone bankrupt in 2 years, another one probably 2 years, another one 5 years. And the Congress has moved on that. We now are down to the point of negotiating on particular subjects, the most controversial of which have absolutely nothing to do with social security. But they've been added on to the social security package, just as a legislative maneuver, so that they could be considered not on their own merits but as part of a package that, because it is attractive, might not be vetoed by me.

We are trying to cut down on the very liberal add-on provisions in social security because somebody has got to pay for it. And the ones that have to pay for it, of course, are the families that still have workers. We are very concerned about this aspect of social security.

In international affairs, Cy Vance arrived this morning in Cairo. He's just attended a NATO conference with all the European foreign ministers. He'll be going from Cairo to Jerusalem, and then he'll be going from there to visit the other Middle Eastern leaders.

We're trying to hold together as best we can a commitment that presently exists in Lebanon, Syria, Jordan, Egypt, and Israel to have a comprehensive peace settlement. I personally believe that the Sadat visit to Jerusalem has broken through what seemed to be insurmountable obstacles and has greatly clarified the issues that have to be still addressed.

I believe that Sadat showed a great deal of courage. And my hope and my expectation is that the Israelis will respond accordingly.

We are trying to keep the door open so that the Syrians can come into the negotiations later on, the Jordanians the same, and also the Lebanese. And we hope that the Saudis, who are not part of the negotiations, will continue their constructive support of Egypt and give their tacit support, at least, to the initiatives that President Sadat has taken.

We have good and substantive talks going on with the Soviet Union on a comprehensive approach to prohibiting the testing of nuclear explosives, a comprehensive test ban, for the first time. We had fairly good progress on that recently. The SALT negotiations—we are proceeding on three levels. One is a 3-year protocol which would temporarily take action. At the end of 3 years, we'd assess that action to see if we want to renew it or to modify it in some degree. A longer agreement, it would go for about 8 years, and then we would initiate an outline of what SALT III would comprise.

My own ultimate goal is to eliminate the use or threat of nuclear weapons altogether. And I personally have been pleased in the last few months, at least since the summer, at the constructive attitude of the Soviet Union. We have to be very careful on technicalities and on major strategic elements of the negotiations to protect our own interests. We've got to be sure that we do have an equal or dominant position on all aspects of strategic deterrent. And I believe that we have that posture now, and I want to be sure to maintain it.

We've tried to open up a new relationship with Africa. We've been successful, I think, so far. We've got a very good relationship with Latin America. I think that could possibly be wiped out overnight if the Senate fails to ratify the Panama Canal treaties, but I hope and believe that the Senate will ratify these treaties.

We've got a good relationship, perhaps better than at any time in recent history, with Canada; strong, constant negotiations on a variety of items with Mexico. And we've, I think, restrengthened our position in Europe. We consult almost constantly with European Community nations and also with our NATO allies on military affairs. Harold Brown has just come back from there—well, I think he's on the way back now.

The other aspect of our foreign policy, of course, extends to the Western Pacific. We are now in hard negotiations with the Japanese on trade matters, and I hope that we can resolve those differences. Japan has a very high positive trade balance. We have a very high negative trade balance. The obstacles to selling our goods in Japan are quite difficult to overcome. But Prime Minister Fukuda, I think, is negotiating in good faith. Perhaps we can have some success there.

I'll be leaving Washington on the 21st, going down to Plains until the day after Christmas, and then I'll come back and leave almost immediately for a trip, beginning in Poland, that would encompass a visit to Brussels, to France, to Iran, Saudi Arabia, and India. And then I'll come back home after about a 10-day trip.

Perhaps you have some questions. I just briefly sketched a few points to arouse your interest.

QUESTIONS

COAL SLURRY PIPELINE

Q. Mr. President, I'm from Cheyenne where water is very scarce, and this is an energy-related question.

THE PRESIDENT. Yes.

Q. I understand you favor the coal slurry pipeline concept. Do you also favor a program under which the water would be recycled or replaced if used in such a pipeline?

THE PRESIDENT. I never endorsed and I would be very cautious about endorsing the use of the coal slurry concept of transportation when water at the origin was scarce. That would not be my highest priority for use of water. Obviously, the use of water for drinking purposes, human use, and for agricultural purposes would come first.

This is a matter that hasn't yet been proposed, so far as I know, in any tangible fashion for the more arid regions of our country. I did support the right of eminent domain in the future if the local courts should decide that it was necessary.

In my opinion, that is important because some of the other competing forms of transportation—say, for instance, the railroad—could permanently block a necessary coal slurry line just to prohibit competition. But I don't favor the escalation of water for coal slurry use above those purposes that I've described to you.

PETER F. FLAHERTY

Q. Mr. President, I'm from Pittsburgh. I'm interested to know whether or not you were surprised by the resignation of Pete

Flaherty, and do you believe it was tied to a reported dispute with Attorney General Bell over the appointment of U.S. attorneys; and just one other part, whether or not Mr. Flaherty has asked you to campaign in any way for him in his anticipated run for the Governor's chair in Pennsylvania?

THE PRESIDENT. Well, let me answer briefly. I was very proud that Pete Flaherty came to work as a Deputy Attorney General. That was an an arrangement that was made really without my prior knowledge between the Attorney General and Pete Flaherty.

Secondly, I did not know ahead of time that Pete was going to resign and go back to Pennsylvania. It was not a result of a dispute or an argument or an incompatibility between him and the Attorney General. It was an action taken by Pete on his own initiative. He did a very good job during the time that he was here. He was basically in charge of reorganization of the Department, doing some long-range studies for management reasons. I think he and the Attorney General were completely compatible. And the only comments that the Attorney General has made to me were in praise of Flaherty.

I have not talked to Pete. I got a written letter saying that he intended to resign, and I've written a letter back to him accepting his resignation and expressing my regret that he was leaving and my good wishes for the future. But he's not discussed with me any involvement in the campaign. My policy has been and will be not to involve myself in any sort of Democratic primary campaign. But I have habitually supported Democratic nominees, after they were chosen, in a general election.

HENRY HOWELL

Q. I notice you met with Henry Howell this morning.

THE PRESIDENT. Yes.

Q. I was wondering if you had offered him a position in the administration and, in view of your campaigning for him, if you felt his defeat was a personal political defeat?

THE PRESIDENT. No. I was disappointed when Henry lost. I know him very well and like him and, as a matter of fact, came into Virginia twice 4 years ago to campaign for him at my own initiative just because I have an admiration for him. But of course that's a judgment that the Virginia people made, and I wouldn't question the soundness of their judgment.

I did not offer him a position in the Government.

VISIT TO NORTH CAROLINA

Q. Mr. President, I'm from North Carolina, Senator Morgan's home county.

THE PRESIDENT. Yes, I know.

Q. We're delighted that you're going to visit the State next week. Will you be able to tell us any more about the plans for your visit there?

THE PRESIDENT. Well, I'm going down Friday afternoon. My youngest sister, Ruth Carter Stapleton—her oldest son is getting married. It's going to be a chance to be with my family. We don't get our whole family together very often.

Q. Will you be there overnight, sir?

THE PRESIDENT. Yes, I'll be there overnight Friday, and I'll be there for a breakfast for the family on Saturday morning, and I'll stay for the wedding Saturday afternoon.

Q. We're neighbors. Would there be any chance of coming down to Dunn, North Carolina? [*Laughter*]

THE PRESIDENT. Well, I doubt if I can. We have to come back immediately. We had to cancel a reception here at the White House for the Secret Service and the ones who serve here and their families. We have rescheduled it for Saturday afternoon, so we'll be having to come back right after the wedding. We don't have often a chance for me and both my sisters and my brother, Billy, and my mother and me all to be in the same place. I hope that Fayetteville, North Carolina, survives our visit. [*Laughter*]

Hi. Good to see you.

ADMINISTRATION'S ACCOMPLISHMENTS

Q. Mr. President, a very general question, nonpolitical. As you look back at the end of this first year, what has been the most personally gratifying accomplishment of your year in the Presidency?

THE PRESIDENT. Well, I think it's hard to pick out the accomplishments. We were very pleased to get the economy moving in the right direction. We had an economic stimulus package that the Congress passed with dispatch. The unemployment rate has dropped about 1 percent. Employment has increased more this year, I think, than ever before in history—4 million people net gain in employment this year; 900,000 last month alone.

Since June, the inflation rate has leveled off at 4 percent. I wish I could predict that it was going to stay that low; I don't think it will. But this shows a good response.

We formed a new Department of Energy, which brings order out of chaos in one of the most serious challenges that might affect our Nation in the future. Formerly, we had 50 different agencies in the Federal Government that were dealing with energy. It was almost impossible to get the answer to a question or to register a complaint or to make a beneficial suggestion.

The Congress, I think, has dealt fairly with my programs. We've got a long-range, very well-considered farm bill that will be in effect now for about 5 years. We've met all the challenges, so far as I know, that I've put to the Congress.

We've made good progress in getting back on the track the negotiations with the Soviet Union. We've protected our own interest; we've shown them that we are firm and can't be pushed around.

We've begun some major reorganization effort, projects. It will take us about 3 years to finish them all; some require a great deal of time. But the Congress has given me almost unlimited authority, subject to subsequent congressional veto, to take over the executive branch now and to bring it into a manageable state. We've cut back tremendously on Government regulations, paperwork, reports to be required.

This past week, OSHA, for instance, eliminated 1,100 regulations that they had evolved over the last number of years. I'm trying to approach the Government as a business manager and also as a small businessman who knows the defects in the Government.

Our family has been brought very close together.

We've had substantial success in the developing nations of the world in being reaccepted as a part of the world community who had some concern about them and who treated them with equality and mutual respect.

I believe we've had a blessing in that we've not had a serious military threat. This, obviously, is something that I hope to maintain throughout my term in office.

I hope that we've taken at least a small step forward in restoring the confidence of the American people in the integrity of the Government and the competence of Government. This is going to be a slow process. It's something that can't come in a year, or even 2 years, because with the horrible shocks of Vietnam and Watergate and the

CIA revelations, the American people had lost confidence that there was something here in Washington that they could trust and admire.

I think the most pleasant surprise to me has been the worldwide impact of our re-emphasis on human rights. I really felt when I came into office that something needed to be done just to raise a banner for the American people to admire and of which they could be proud again. I think that the emphasis on human personal freedom and democratic principles is very important for us to espouse.

And although a year ago, I think, very few national leaders anywhere in the world paid much attention to human rights, I don't believe there's a single one out of the roughly 150 that now doesn't consider, "Before we take action, what is the world going to think about me, the way I'm dealing with political prisoners or out-migration or the reunification of families or the persecution of human beings?" I think the human rights issue has been a great escalation.

We've also made a major move toward nonproliferation of nuclear explosives. And again, I think a year ago there was great despair in the world about whether anybody could ever put the nuclear genie back in the bottle. I think there's a reconfirmation now of effort on the part of even countries that have sold reprocessing plants, like Germany and France, all the rest of us, to try to stop the spread of nuclear explosives and not let it go into nations that haven't had them in the past.

Those are a few things that come to mind.

AGRICULTURE

Q. Mr. President, I'm a publisher from South Dakota, and agriculture is my topic. I'm wondering, what is being considered in the way of alternate markets for agricultural products? I notice the farm strike is focusing on Plains, Georgia, I presume, to get your attention——

THE PRESIDENT. ——and also because we didn't make any crops down there. [*Laughter*]

Q. Biomass fuels could offer some partial solution to energy problems as well as the farm problem.

THE PRESIDENT. That's true.

Q. Could you address that a minute?

THE PRESIDENT. Well, in the first place, as I mentioned briefly in passing, I think we've got a very good farm bill that was passed this year, that will be in effect for the next 5 years. We've had some increase in farm prices since I came into office. Corn prices are up about 38 cents—the last time I checked the market. Wheat prices are up about 60 cents a bushel compared to when I came into office. I certainly don't attribute that to the fact that I'm here. But we have got a Secretary of Agriculture who's a dirt farmer who understands the special problems of farmers.

And with the exception of the time I've served in the Federal (and State) [2] Government, all of my income all my life has come from the farm. And I have a sense, too, of what agriculture does need. I think we've had a very good step forward in having grow, in the Department of Agriculture, a special concern about consumers. We don't have enough farm-supported Members of Congress to prevail in a showdown vote. But the more we can let the average American consumer who comes from, perhaps, the urban areas know how valuable a resource we have in our land and in our food and fiber production, the better off we'll be in prevailing and treating the farmers fairly.

We've got a very good price support, target prices, that approach the cost of production, at least in the areas where the efficiency is high. I think we've got this

---

[2] Printed in the White House press release.

past year, up to the 1st of October, the highest farm export level we've ever had in history—$24 billion worth of American farm products were sold overseas. We've never done that before. We are even emphasizing that effort much more in the future.

We'd like to open up permanent sales possibilities in countries that don't presently buy food from us. My first stop on my trip will be Poland. We want to maintain our sales of agricultural products grown in this country to the so-called Eastern European countries, to the Soviet Union, to the People's Republic of China, as well as to our natural allies and friends in this hemisphere and others.

In the energy package—we've tried to put it together in such a way that it would not only protect the farmers and the agricultural communities but also open the way for increased use of, as you refer to it, biomass, and also forestry products. I spent about 4½ hours this morning—I got up at about 5 o'clock and came over here early to work on it—and I will be spending 2½ hours immediately after this meeting, in this room, working on the budget for the Department of Energy next year.

And I'll be analyzing and making final decisions, pending congressional approval next year, on how much research and development money to put into things like the use of biomass, wood products, forestry products, shale, and other energy supplies. But I think the fact that I do know agriculture, do know farm families' needs, and have an Agriculture Secretary the same way, gives me a sense of judgment that maybe I wouldn't have if I had a different background.

So we've got, I think, a good thrust now to resolve some of the longstanding problems. I disagreed very strongly with some of the policies that Secretary Butz had when he was in office. There are not any

easy answers. I would say that Bob Bergland has one of the most difficult jobs in Washington. It's a tough proposition.

PRESIDENT'S SCHEDULE

Q. Mr. President, this question is on behalf of my 12-year-old son who is a newspaper publisher down in Plains, Virginia.

THE PRESIDENT. Very good.

Q. He looks at fathers as sort of an example. And he had read that during your first year in office, you had been getting up at the hour you mentioned a while ago, 5 o'clock in the morning, and working until midnight. And he said that since the end of the softball season and tennis, that he's afraid you're not getting enough exercise, either. [*Laughter*]

Would you share with us, after 10 or 11 months in office, the kind of a schedule you keep now, and I can assure him that you are getting enough rest and exercise?

THE PRESIDENT. Okay, I'd be glad to. I have a permanent call-in to the Secret Service at 6 o'clock. If I don't call them the night before, they always wake me up at 6:00. On Monday mornings, I have to get up at 5:00, because in addition to my regular work, I have a 2-hour Cabinet meeting and I need to prepare myself for the Cabinet meeting. I also have my weekly senior staff meeting Monday morning immediately before the Cabinet meeting. I would say about three mornings a week I get up at 5:00 or 5:30. I've always done that. It's not a handicap for me; it's not a sacrifice or an extraordinary thing for me to do. I prefer to work early in the morning rather than staying up late.

Most nights I go to bed by 11 o'clock, and so does my wife. And I always set aside some time to go home in the afternoon, 5:30 or 6 o'clock, to be with my daughter and to listen to her play the violin and to brag on her and to go over some of her school studies.

Q. He was worried about that, that you weren't seeing Amy.

THE PRESIDENT. I see her enough. Amy and I planned the treehouse, and we built it together. We go to Camp David whenever we can. We find that that's the most pleasant place for us to go. In fact I'll be leaving for Camp David this afternoon. Amy and Rosalynn can't come until tomorrow morning. This is the first time I've gone without them. But I've invited, as my guest, Senator Humphrey. When I brought him back from Milwaukee [Minneapolis] a few weeks ago, he commented to me that he had never seen Camp David. His wife is temporarily in the hospital, so he and I are going to go up together this afternoon and have a chance to sit in front of the fire and talk about both history and the future.

And in the warm season of the year, I play tennis about three times a week. Amy and I and Rosalynn have bowled twice this week. We have a little—one bowling alley in the White House that was put there by Harry Truman. We go swimming at Camp David and do a lot of hiking, bike riding. I get a good bit of exercise. I keep my weight exactly the same as it was 10, 15 years ago. I weigh about 155.

And although some people say I've aged—the people that say I've aged, I've noticed they've aged, too. [*Laughter*] But to summarize, I enjoy it. I'm in good shape, physically, and I get a thorough examination quite often. I have a full-time doctor that stays with me all the time and have a dentist that comes in about every 6 weeks to check my teeth and make sure I'm in good shape. But I've enjoyed it and get a lot of exercise and don't overwork.

This is a new editor, by the way. Saul [Saul Kohler, Newhouse News Service] is going to Harrisburg, Pennsylvania, to be an editor there. He has been on the White House professional reporting staff.

THE MIDDLE EAST

Q. Thank you, sir. Mr. President, is your commitment to a negotiated settlement in the Middle East deep enough that, if necessary, you would go there yourself to confer with the heads of state of Israel and the Arab countries, notwithstanding the fact that they have all been here?

THE PRESIDENT. Well, Asad has not been here; I met him in Geneva. But I have met with all of them. I don't anticipate any need for me to go to Geneva or to go to the Mideast to bring about a negotiated settlement. My commitment to that is very strong and permanent. If it takes the full time I'm in office to bring about a complete, comprehensive, permanent peace in the Middle East, I'll devote my fullest resources to it, both in convincing the public of this country and the public of the world that it's necessary and in assuaging hurt feelings, trying to bring together leaders who may have been separated by one circumstance or another.

One of the reasons that I wanted Cy Vance to go over is because Asad and Sadat are not presently on very good terms, and I wanted Cy Vance to meet both of them and see what bounds could be reestablished to pull them back together.

But obviously, if I felt sometime in the future—and I don't anticipate this, Saul—but if I felt sometime in the future that my personal presence was the difference between success or failure, obviously I would go, because I consider this to be a very important thing not only for the Middle East but for the world.

If you analyze the quantity of oil that we have to get from the Middle East, it's enormous. But if you look at our allies and friends, Japan, Germany, Italy, and others, they are almost completely dependent on the Middle Eastern oil. And so I don't know of any area that concerns me more. There's nothing in foreign affairs that has equaled the time and effort I've spent both studying long-past history of the Middle Eastern problem and also analyzing possible solutions in the future. So, I would do almost anything within reason if I thought it was necessary to bring permanent peace to the Middle East.

RELATIONSHIP WITH CONGRESS

Q. Mr. President, looking back over your first year in office, is there anything that you would do differently if you could attack that problem again?

THE PRESIDENT. Well, Scotty Reston [James B. Reston, New York Times] asked me that the other day. Always, I think, in your life—and mine as a farmer and mine as a naval officer and mine as a candidate, if I knew everything then that I know now, I would have done some things differently.

I made some mistakes in judgment that weren't fatal. I underestimated, first of all, the quality of the Congress, the intense concentration that individual Members of Congress put on a specific issue, sometimes for 25 or 30 or 40 years. They become experts in that issue. And the quality of their staff work is equivalent completely to the quality of my own staff work here in the White House.

This was something that I had not experienced in the Georgia State Legislature, when they only meet for 40 days and then go home. There's no continuity of the legislative process in my State. And I was pleasantly surprised and underestimated the competence of Congress. I think it's a very good thing that no longer

do you have a dominant White House as sometimes existed—I don't say the country suffered when, say, Franklin Roosevelt was here and he could send up bills to the Congress and almost immediately they would be voted on without thorough analysis.

I overestimated the Congress in its ability to deal with complicated subjects expeditiously. This is particularly the case with the Senate, where every Member of the Senate is autonomous and prides himself on being independent, has the ability if he chooses to delay action on any bill no matter how important it is to the country; a constant threat sometimes realized, some not exercised, of a filibuster. Even when you have enough votes to override a filibuster, it takes 5 or 6 days to go through the legislative procedures to do that.

And I think you've noticed that the burden of work we've put on the Congress has just been more than they could handle in the time allotted, so I've had to delay the implementation of some of the programs that I wanted to put forward much earlier. I had anticipated having a comprehensive tax proposal to the Congress by September. And now, of course, we are ready to go with it as far as the executive branch is concerned, but I don't want to send up a comprehensive tax proposal until I see what the impact on the tax structure might be from social security and, say, energy. And as soon as I get those answers, we'll have the package ready to go.

But I don't know of any serious mistakes we've made; probably expecting a little too much from the Congress on expeditious passage, underestimating their competence on the other hand.

At first, we had a shaky start in just knowing how to deal with the Congress. We were eager to do the best we could.

I've consulted with Congress, perhaps more than any President who has ever served in this office. And I've consulted with the Joint Chiefs more than they've ever seen the President.

I had lunch with the Joint Chiefs last week, and I said, "How do I compare in negotiating with you and getting help and advice from you, compared to previous Presidents? I met with you at the Blair House before I was President. I met with you about 6 or 8 or 10 times since I've been President." We had long discussions about Korea and about China and about Taiwan, and about the Middle East and about SALT and everything else. And they said, "Mr. President, we saw you more than we had ever seen any President that first meeting at Blair House before you ever came into office." [*Laughter*] So, I've learned and I've benefited from it.

I want to thank you again. I got to go, but I want to thank you again for letting me have this chance to meet with you.

This is an enormous job. It's one that taxes any individual human being to encompass the challenges and solutions to problems. The ones that arrive at my desk are obviously the ones that can't be solved in a home or in a city hall or at a State Governor's office, and they come to me. But I've really enjoyed it.

It's been a reassuring thing to have a superb Cabinet. There's not a single weak person on it. I've really been pleasantly surprised with them. And the Congress has given me strong and good support. The differences that have arisen between me and the Congress have been that the much more easy job of my preparing a proposal and drafting legislation, than the Congress debating it and passing it.

There's an inherent delay in the congressional process which I think is very good and very healthy. And as you know, I've never served in Washington before at all. I've got a good, sound White House staff. I use my Cabinet more than previous Presidents have.

We have a full-scale, at least 2-hour session here every Monday morning, with the full Cabinet sitting around this table. Most of the time, we have a 100-percent attendance. And it's a lively discussion, and the Secretary of Agriculture, the Secretary of Health, Education, and Welfare, the Secretary of HUD have a chance to listen to an explanation of what Cy Vance is doing, what Bob Strauss is doing, what the Secretary of Treasury is doing. So, there's a good interchange and good team spirit.

I don't have the same need for a chief of staff or a strong, powerful, autocratic White House staff that President Nixon felt. There will never be an Ehrlichman or a Haldeman in my White House staff that gives orders and commands to the Cabinet members who are trying to run the major agencies of Government.

This is not the way I ran the Governor's office in Georgia. It's not the way I am going to run it here. And some of the local press have deplored the fact that I don't have a similar set-up as was the case when President Nixon was in office. It's just not my way of running things. As you know, President Eisenhower also had a chief of staff, Sherman Adams, who ran things almost like a secondary President.

But I've substituted for that an unprecedented use of the Vice President. He and I are close, personal friends. We have a harmonious partnership. I've grown to respect and like him more every day I've known him. And he has authority and responsibility in foreign and domestic affairs and also in helping to manage the White House staff that no Vice President has ever dreamed of having. And it takes a great deal of the burden off my shoulders.

Formerly, Vice Presidents were over in the Executive Office Building across the street. I asked Fritz specifically to move over and occupy an office right down the hall from me. And so, in effect, he is the one who coordinates the staff work in the White House. He's thoroughly familiar with the Congress. He's been there for 12 years himself. He was on the Finance Committee and also the Budget Committee. So he's familiar with that.

When I have budget hearings 2½, 3 hours here in the afternoon—3½ hours yesterday on defense—Fritz is there at my side. And I've incorporated him in this strategic military chain of command. No other Vice President has ever occupied those positions. And if something should happen to me, he would be thoroughly familiar with all the controversies, all of the foreign affairs considerations, all of the defense considerations, and be ready to act in a proper way.

So, there are some different ways of management that I have brought into the White House that quite often have not been understood, but which I've very carefully evolved and of which I'm quite proud.

I have a note that I haven't read yet. Thank you, Gene [Eugene Johnson, White Bear Press, White Bear Lake, Minn.], very much.

Thank you very much.

NOTE: The interview began at 1 p.m. in the Cabinet Room at the White House.

The transcript of the interview was released on December 10.

Legal Services Corporation

Nomination of Five Members of the Board of Directors.   December 12, 1977

The President today announced five persons whom he will nominate to be members of the Board of Directors of the Legal Services Corporation for terms expiring in 1980. They are:

CECILIA D. ESQUER, 35, of Tempe, Ariz. Esquer is assistant attorney general of Arizona. She is a 1976 graduate of Arizona State University College of Law, where she was on the Committee on Legal Education Opportunity and the Chicano Law Students Association. Her special areas of interest are school law, poverty law, and civil rights.

STEVEN L. ENGELBERG, 35, of Chevy Chase, Md. Engelberg is a partner in the Washington law firm of Price, Grove, Engelberg & Fried. From 1969 to 1973, he was legislative counsel to then-Senator Walter Mondale.

HILLARY RODHAM, 30, of Little Rock, Ark. Rodham practices law in Little Rock and Fayetteville, Ark. She was an assistant professor of law at the University of Arkansas Law School from 1974 to 1977. Her special area of interest is children under the law.

RICHARD A. TRUDELL, 34, of Oakland, Calif. Trudell is the executive director of the American Indian Lawyer Training Program. In 1972 and 1973, he was director of the Robert F. Kennedy Memorial's Fellowship Program. He is a member of the American Indian Bar Association.

JOSEPHINE WORTHY, 43, of Holyoke, Mass. Worthy is youth director of Bethlehem Baptist Church and president of the TOETFERT Housing Project Tenants Association. She is on the advisory board of the Office of Children's Services of the State Department of Social Services. From 1974 to 1976, she was a family life counselor at Holyoke Street School.

Harry S Truman Scholarship Foundation

Nomination of John W. Snyder To Be a Member of the Board of Trustees. December 12, 1977

The President today announced that he will nominate John W. Snyder, of Washington, D.C., for reappointment as a member of the Board of Trustees of the Harry S Truman Scholarship Foundation for a term expiring December 10, 1983.

Snyder was born June 21, 1895, in Jonesboro, Ark. He is a retired colonel, United States Army.

From 1946 to 1953, he was Secretary of the Treasury. He was chairman of the finance committee and president of Overland Corp., Toledo, Ohio, from 1953 to 1965. From 1955 to 1969, he was United States Treasury Advisor to the World Bank Fund.

Nonfuel Minerals Policy

Announcement of a Cabinet-level, Interagency Study. December 12, 1977

The White House today announced a Cabinet-level, interagency study of nonfuel minerals policy. The study, to be chaired by Interior Secretary Cecil D. Andrus, will consider international and domestic minerals supply and demand and the economic health of the minerals industry. It will focus on the most critical minerals.

The Cabinet-level coordinating committee will submit policy options and recommendations to the President within 15 months. The study was initiated by the President in response to congressional and public concerns.

Members of the coordinating committee will be the Secretaries of the Interior, State, the Treasury, Commerce, and Energy; the Administrators of EPA and GSA; the Director of the National Science Foundation; the Assistant to the President for National Security Affairs; the Chairman of the Council of Economic Advisers; the Special Representative for Trade Negotiations; the Chairman of the Council on Environmental Quality; the Director of OMB; and the Director of the Office of Science and Technology Policy.

Some of the concerns to be addressed by the study are whether the trends toward international interdependence and the politicization of certain minerals markets are increasing U.S. vulnerability to foreign supply curtailments and price manipulations; whether U.S. reserves, production capacities, and inventories are adequate to deal with possible supply/price interruptions, or with the economic and social consequences of such disruptions; whether the economic health of the domestic minerals industry is adequate; and whether land use decisions are based on adequate minerals information and analysis.

The study will be the first to use the Domestic Policy Review system, a process designed to ensure high-level, interagency consideration of important issues.

Executive Office of the President

Executive Order 12028. December 12, 1977

OFFICE OF ADMINISTRATION IN THE EXECUTIVE OFFICE OF THE PRESIDENT

By virtue of the authority vested in me by the Constitution and statutes of the United States of America, including the National Security Act of 1947, as amended, Reorganization Plan No. 2 of 1970 (5 U.S.C. App. II), Section 202 of the Budget and Accounting Procedures Act of 1950 (31 U.S.C. 581c), and Reorganization Plan No. 1 of 1977 (42 FR 56101 (October 21, 1977)), and as President of the United States of America, in order to effectuate the establishment of the Office of Administration in the Executive Office of the President, it is hereby ordered as follows:

SECTION 1. The establishment, provided by Section 2 of Reorganization Plan No. 1 of 1977 (42 FR 56101), of the Office of Administration in the Executive Office of the President shall be effective, as authorized by Section 7 of that Plan, on December 4, 1977.

SEC. 2. The Director of the Office of Administration, hereinafter referred to as the Director, shall report to the President. As the chief administrative officer of the Office of Administration, the Director shall be responsible for ensuring that the Office of Administration provides units within the Executive Office of the President common administrative support and services.

SEC. 3. (a) The Office of Administration shall provide common administrative support and services to all units within the Executive Office of the President, except for such services provided primarily in direct support of the President. The Office of Administration shall, upon request, assist the White House Office in performing its role of providing those administrative services which are primarily in direct support of the President.

(b) The common administrative support and services provided by the Office of Administration shall encompass all types of administrative support and services that may be used by, or useful to, units within the Executive Office of the President. Such services and support shall include, but not be limited to, providing support services in the following administrative areas:

(1) personnel management services, including equal employment opportunity programs;

(2) financial management services;

(3) data processing, including support and services;

(4) library, records, and information services;

(5) office services and operations, including: mail, messenger, printing and duplication, graphics, word processing, procurement, and supply services; and

(6) any other administrative support or service which will achieve financial savings and increase efficiency through centralization of the supporting service.

(c) Administrative support and services shall be provided to all units within the Executive Office of the President in a manner consistent with available funds and other resources, or in accord with Section 7 of the Act of May 21, 1920 (41 Stat. 613), as amended (31 U.S.C. 686, referred to as the Economy Act).

SEC. 4. (a) Subject to such direction or approval that the President may provide or require, the Director shall:

(1) organize the Office of Administration;

(2) employ personnel;

(3) contract for supplies or services; and

(4) do all other things that the President, as head of the Office of Administration, might do.

(b) The Director shall not be accountable for the program and management responsibilities of units within the Executive Office of the President; the head of each unit shall remain responsible for those functions.

SEC. 5. The primary responsibility for performing all administrative support and service functions of units within the Executive Office of the President shall be transferred and reassigned to the Office of Administration; except to the extent those functions are vested by law in the head of such a unit, other than the President; and except to the extent those functions are performed by the White House Office primarily in direct support of the President.

SEC. 6. The records, property, personnel, and unexpended balances of appropriations, available or to be made available, which relate to the functions transferred or reassigned by this Order from units within the Executive Office of the

President to the Office of Administration, shall be transferred to the Office of Administration.

SEC. 7. (a) The Director of the Office of Management and Budget shall make such determinations, issue such orders, and take all actions necessary or appropriate to effectuate the transfers or reassignments provided by this Order, including the transfer of funds, records, property, and personnel.

(b) Such transfers shall become effective on April 1, 1978, or at such earlier time or times as the Director of the Office of Management and Budget determines, after consultation with the Director of the Office of Administration and other appropriate units within the Executive Office of the President.

JIMMY CARTER

The White House,
December 12, 1977.

[Filed with the Office of the Federal Register, 3:37 p.m., December 12, 1977]

Career Education Incentive Act

*Statement on Signing H.R. 7 Into Law.
December 13, 1977*

I am pleased to sign into law H.R. 7, which authorizes $325 million in Federal grants over the next 5 years to State and local education agencies. The purpose of these grants is to help the agencies improve career education programs in elementary and secondary schools.

Until now, the Federal Government has had a very limited role in sponsoring career education. While expanding that role, H.R. 7 is designed to ensure that the State and local education agencies take the lead in developing and coordinating

better career education programs. During the first 2 years, the programs will be fully funded by the Federal Government. After FY '80, there will be a system of matching grants; in FY '81, the Federal Government will pay 75 percent of the cost by this bill; in FY '82, 50 percent; and in FY '83, 25 percent. After FY '83, the entire cost will be borne by the State and local education agencies. By that time, the programs authorized under this bill should be well enough established, and clearly enough under the direction of the State and local education agencies, to enable them to continue without Federal financial support.

NOTE: As enacted, H.R. 7 is Public Law 95–207, approved December 13.

Rural Health Clinic Services Bill

*Statement on Signing H.R. 8422 Into Law.
December 13, 1977*

At its best, the American health care system is unsurpassed, but its uneven distribution leaves millions of our people without access to adequate care. This problem affects both urban and rural areas but is more widespread in the latter; two-thirds of the people in areas without adequate health care live in rural America.

One of the most sensible and efficient ways to cope with this problem is to enable physician assistants and nurse practitioners to provide regular, high-quality care in small, convenient outpatient clinics. Through such programs as the National Health Service Corps and the Appalachian Regional Commission, the Federal Government has helped start and support these clinics and train the highly skilled professionals who operate them.

But there has been a major obstacle to the healthy growth of these clinics in the areas that need them: That is the failure of public and private health insurance programs to support them. The legislation I am signing today will correct this defect in our public health insurance programs, by requiring that the Medicare and Medicaid programs pay for the services of physician assistants and nurse practitioners in clinics in rural areas without adequate care. This reform will guarantee greater financial stability for clinics already in existence and help establish new clinics where they are needed most.

This legislation also establishes demonstration projects for reimbursing clinics in urban areas. We must keep in mind that many of our inner city residents also lack access to adequate health care.

This bill has come to my desk after exceptionally close and fruitful cooperation between several committees of Congress. In the Senate, Chairman Herman Talmadge and his colleagues on the Finance Health Subcommittee did a fine job in expediting this legislation. In addition, I'd like to commend Senators Jennings Randolph, Bill Hathaway, Dick Clark, and Patrick Leahy for their early and consistent work on this measure. In the House, Chairman Dan Rostenkowski of the Ways and Means Health Subcommittee and Chairman Paul Rogers of the Interstate and Foreign Commerce Health Subcommittee and their colleagues worked closely to produce this measure. In addition, I would like to express my appreciation to the chairmen of the two full House committees, Al Ullman and Harley Staggers. Congressman Bill Brod-

head was also very helpful in securing the passage of this legislation.

NOTE: As enacted, H.R. 8422 is Public Law 95–210, approved December 13.

Postal Rate Commission

Nomination of Alvin H. Gandal To Be a Commissioner.   December 14, 1977

The President today announced that he will nominate Alvin H. Gandal, of Chevy Chase, Md., to be Commissioner of the Postal Rate Commission for the term expiring October 14, 1982. Upon confirmation Gandal will be designated Chairman.

Gandal was born February 8, 1932, in Cleveland, Ohio. He received an A.B. (1953) and an LL.B. (1956) from Case-Western Reserve University. He was admitted to the Ohio bar in 1956 and the District of Columbia bar in 1961. He was an attorney in the office of the Regional Attorney, U.S. Department of Labor, in Cleveland from 1956 to 1957.

From 1957 to 1960, Gandal was first lieutenant in the Judge Advocate General's Corps at the Pentagon, in the Office of the Labor Advisor to the Secretary of the Army. Gandal was a member of the NLRB from 1960 to 1961. From 1961 to 1969, he practiced law in Washington, D.C.

Gandal was attorney-advisor in the Opinions Division of the Postal Service's General Counsel's office from 1969 to 1973. Gandal was special assistant to the Senior Assistant Postmaster General for Employee and Labor Relations, 1973, and Director of the Office of Arbitration Procedures, U.S. Postal Service, 1973 to 1976. Since 1976 he has been Director of the Office of Contract Analysis.

Business Council

Remarks at a Meeting of the Council.
December 14, 1977

THE PRESIDENT. I understood this is where I was supposed to come to restore business confidence. [*Laughter*]

I'm glad to be with you. John deButts and many of you have been very close friends of mine since I've been in the White House as President, and I've relied upon many of you already to give me advice, to give me your counsel and sometimes, of course, your criticisms, and I've learned from it.

This is a time in our Nation when it's very important for us to realize the strength that we have and to seek as much as we possibly can a common purpose and to probe for a partnership between the leaders in our free enterprise system and the leaders in our freely elected government offices.

One of the things that I thought I might do to restore confidence is to point out to you how hard I work and how much I do each day. [*Laughter*] Tomorrow I hope to meet with three world leaders. I already have appointments with two of them. I'll be meeting with Prime Minister Begin tomorrow morning for an early breakfast and to negotiate with him on questions involving Middle Eastern peace.

I'll be having lunch tomorrow with Prime Minister Manley of Jamaica, and I'm seeking an appointment with Senator Russell Long for tomorrow afternoon. [*Laughter*]

I was looking over the history of the Business Council this afternoon, and I noticed that President Lyndon Johnson said about you that he knew of no other organization that offered to do more for our Nation and asked for so little in re-turn. And that's a tremendous—and I'm sure it was a heartfelt feeling on his part.

I've never asked any of you to come to the White House or to join in an unselfish undertaking involving handicapped people or veterans or the evolution of programs that you didn't respond with enthusiasm and with effectiveness.

My own responsibilities are quite diverse, as you know. I think we are making good progress. We've been negotiating very intimately and productively with the Soviet Union on some of the historically intransigent problems. We've made remarkable progress so far in evolving the terms of a comprehensive test ban.

We have tried for the first time, really, to put an absolute lid and to roll back the level of nuclear weaponry. We're negotiating with the Soviet Union on how to prevent an arms buildup and a military race in the Indian Ocean. They've begun, as a matter of habit, to inform us before they fire their own test missiles so that there will be no misunderstanding between us. And I have high hopes that next year we'll be successful in bringing to a conclusion a SALT II agreement. We will have part of it on a 3-year basis, part of it will be more permanent, several years, and we will lay out the groundwork for a SALT III agreement with much more drastic reductions.

We've been involved, I think for the first time, in seeking a comprehensive settlement of the Middle Eastern question. And there have been some very notable results. I've met with all the leaders in the Middle East. As a matter of fact, I've met this year already with 68 heads of nations to negotiate with them and to seek a common purpose between themselves and us. And I can see very clearly that those who could not bring themselves to negotiate with each other, deep within their own hearts and representing their own people, wanted to have peace and to shift the tremendous financial burden from the always escalating arms race to the economic well-being of their own people.

I tried to convince Prime Minister Begin that President Sadat's interests were the same as his, and vice versa. And I'm very grateful for the courage of these two men and hope that we can extend their own negotiations to find a comprehensive and a permanent peace that will ensure the well-being of the people in the Middle East.

We have sought out common interests with our European allies. And we've tried to escalate, particularly within the State Department, a high degree of attention to economic problems on an international basis. There's remarkable harmony now among the different departments of our government that deal with the economic problems, between Treasury and Commerce, Labor, and State Department, and others, including Agriculture and Labor.

We have a weekly Cabinet meeting where we spend several hours discussing the major problems that confront our country. And when Bob Strauss goes to Japan to negotiate better trade terms with that nation, he speaks with a sure sense that the other members of the Cabinet and myself, the Vice President, understand his position and support it, and this gives us, I believe, a much more firm and secure base for representing our Nation.

We have very little disharmony among our heads of departments in other controversial areas. The Joint Chiefs of Staff meet with me frequently, along with the national security adviser and the Secretary of Defense, to talk about SALT questions, and the Secretary of State is present.

We try to iron out our differences, as you try to iron out your differences in a meeting of your boards of directors, so that everybody has a chance to speak and so that your company's position or your firm's position can be clear, not only in the minds of those who listen but also within your own leaders' minds.

We've had, I believe, a good year so far. Twelve months ago, the rate of increase in our gross national product was only 1 percent, the inflation rate was 10 percent, the unemployment rate was 8 percent.

We have had some degree of success this year, not because of who was in the Office of President, but because of the sense of purpose in our Nation. And we are getting past the despair that was engendered by the Vietnam war and by the Watergate revelations and by the CIA problems, and there's a resurgence, I believe, of commitment to the basic principles on which our Nation has stood. We've got a long way to go. We have had, though, progress in the most tenacious and difficult problem areas.

The unemployment rate is still too high. And there are pockets of unemployment among particular constituency groups that are embarrassing to our country—35- or 40-percent unemployment among young black men, and very high areas in our Nation where the unemployment rate for all citizens is entirely too high. That's in spite of the fact that we've had 4 million net increase in employment this year in our country. We haven't had that high an increase in total employment since the Second World War. But there's a balance between slow, steady progress on the one hand, and very difficult, very tenacious problems that still wait to be resolved.

I realize that among those jobs in our country, five-sixths of them are in the private sector. We've had a net reduction, almost a steady reduction in the last 20 or 25 years, in employment within the Federal Government. The increase has been, in government, in the local and State levels. But most of the increase, of course, comes within the private industrial and employment sector.

Housing starts now are at a very good level, about 2.2 million. This is something that gives us encouragement, but also reminds us that we have a long way to go.

We have had a fairly steady progress for the last 2½ years in our economy. I meet every week with not only my Cabinet members in joint session but also privately with Charlie Schultze to give me economic advice. And today, in preparation for my visit with you, we have analyzed some of the long-range trends.

There are no serious or major imbalances or distortions in our economy that quite often have prevailed in a period of recovery from the depths of a recession or depression. We've got a fairly well balanced economy between business debt and cash availability, between inventory and sales. Most of our major lending institutions don't have a complete dearth or shortage of funds to lend for sound loans. We have also experienced, I believe, some increase in involvement of other nations in redressing the international imbalances.

As you know, our country still imports too much oil. This year $45 billion worth of oil will be imported by the United States, in spite of the fact that we are one of the world's largest oil producers. We have facing us this year an adverse balance of trade of about $30 billion. If it weren't for the oil imports, we'd have a very substantial positive trade balance.

In the last 12 months our agricultural exports have been the highest on record, about $24 billion. We are the world's greatest food producer. But in spite of the tremendous exportation of agricultural products, our oil imports are twice as much as total farm exports.

I've tried to address some of the more longstanding and difficult financial questions that have been avoided in the past. And I'm beginning to see much more clearly now why they were avoided by my predecessors. [*Laughter*]

We've made a lot of progress on evolving a comprehensive energy policy. I doubt that the Congress of the United States has ever addressed a more complicated, more difficult, more politically challenging, more divisive issue in the history of our Nation.

Many friends that have come over here to talk to me from Germany or Italy or France can't understand why we can't very rapidly pass an energy legislation. Well, we're not just a consuming nation, we're not just a producing nation. And that dichotomy in our own constituencies almost guarantees a sharp division.

I met late this afternoon with some of the House and Senate energy conferees, not to negotiate with them, but to encourage them to stick with these difficult problems, since they've made so much progress already, before they adjourn.

The Senate conferees—there are 18 of them—they've been divided 9 to 9 ever since the conference committee started. They've never gotten one Senator to change a position, even when repeated efforts to put forth a compromise have been made.

I think you all know that the Congress has put a great deal of time and effort on this question. I presented to the Congress and to the people, April 2d, an energy package that I thought was adequate, well-balanced, protected the consumers, encouraged production, did not create a heavy strain on our budget in the future. And the House passed a bill very similar to what I introduced the first part of August, and we still don't have that legislation through.

Three of the five major items have already been resolved in principle, and I think they are fairly safe to prevail. We still have the questions, though, of natural gas and how to control the consumption of oil. But we are making some progress.

The other question that we've tried to address is to bring some integrity back to the social security system. This is a matter that's very disturbing to us all, and it's also been highly controversial.

But we have made good progress this year. And I think, when you assess what the Congress has done, you will also be pleased.

We've tried to commit ourselves and retain our commitment to the principles of free trade. One of the unanticipated pressures on me as President has been for evolving various methods of protectionism to erect tariffs or quota barriers against foreign imports. Our country lives on international trade, and this is an easy political question to be demagoged. But I hope that you all will help me to convince the public that this is not in the best interests of our Nation.

There are a lot of things, obviously, that the Government can do. I think that we need a substantial permanent tax reduction next year for business and for individuals. I see the major redressing of our problem with unemployment being in your hands, in the private business sector.

The major means of redressing the permanent underlying inflation rate lies in your hands and in those of people who work for you to increase productivity and, therefore, reduce the basic underlying cause for sustained inflation.

I believe that we have in your hands the possibility of helping to redress our balance of trade by producing highly competitive and quality goods for us to export. We can do a lot in partnership with you. The unnecessary paperwork and regulations and intrusion into the business lives by Government needs to be reduced.

We have here tonight with us the administrator of the Occupational Safety and Health Act. I think it's accurate to say that 12 months ago this was one of the most despised and condemned programs in Government. But Dr. Bingham has brought forward revisions in those administrative procedures that have helped to remove this burden on your shoulders.

This past week, she and Ray Marshall announced the elimination of 1,100 of the OSHA regulations. And we are trying to reduce our total paperwork burden on the business and professional community. Health, Education, and Welfare have already reduced their paperwork requirements 27 percent, and we've set a goal for the whole Nation and for the whole Government to do the same. And we are making some progress. We are trying to make weekly reports changed into monthly reports, monthly into quarterly, quarterly into annually, and some of the reports we are trying to eliminate all together. But we are probing to do a better job with your Government.

I just want to say a couple of other things, and then I'd like to answer a question or two, if you'd let me.

I'm a businessman like yourselves. When I was beginning my Carters Warehouse and producing certified seed and buying and storing and ginning cotton and shelling peanuts, you were the leaders in our Nation that I looked to and admired. I recognized then and now the present achievements that you've already realized and the tremendous beneficial impact that you have had and can have on our country. I've tried to bring into the White House some of those business principles that I learned, as many of you did, the hard way.

I try to evolve with my Cabinet members and other advisers long-range goals and describe them as clearly as I can to the public—what we hope to achieve under conditions that we spell out clearly as a target for maximum unemployment and the maximum inflation rate, a sustained growth in our national product, the percentage of personal income that's collected by the Federal Government in taxes, the percent of our Nation's productivity that's collected and spent by the Federal Government, to provide some stability—so that we can all work toward those same goals. And every decision that I make in my budget hearings, in my evolving and proposing legislation to the Congress, in the signing or modification or vetoing of bills, is determined to a major degree by my commitment to meet those goals.

This is not always possible, of course. I intend to devote most of my State of the Union speech in January to the major purpose of my administration in 1978. It will be concerning our economy and how to restore confidence and how to redress many of the problems that I've described tonight as a national commitment next year.

I think the Nation is ready for this, and I believe the lowest unemployed American, up to those who are proud to receive the minimum wage on a part-time basis, to the leaders of our top businesses and industries—we can harness our own efforts in the private sector with those of us in the public sector to try as best we can to realize the benefits of the finest economic system on Earth.

There's one thing that has concerned me a great deal since I've been in office,

and that is the tendency on the part of us all to emphasize the negative aspects in our Nation's economic system. We've got the greatest country on Earth. We've got the best economic system on Earth. It's been stable and part of our lives for 200 years. God has blessed us with unequaled natural resources. We have access to two oceans without constraint on our international commerce through the sea or through the air.

We have got a diversity of population that brings to us the best from every nation on Earth. And we have an underlying commitment of entrepreneurs and a sense of basic human freedom and a sense of self-respect and personal responsibility that sustains us in times of trial, in times of tension, in times of despair. But we all have too much of an inclination to deplore and to emphasize temporary aberrations that can always be described as catastrophies or insurmountable obstacles. And this creates a sense of discouragement and a lack of commitment to aggressive redressing of those transient problems that is discouraging to me as President.

I just hope that all of you will join me when there is good news to acknowledge it, and when you have a chance to speak to those who look to you for leadership, to point out the things of which we can be proud and for which we can be thankful.

The Presidency, as has often been said, is kind of a lonely job. There are times when a decision has to be made just by me. I use my advisers as much as possible; I have to consult constantly with the Congress; I work closely with my Cabinet, with my White House staff. But eventually the time comes when a decision on international affairs or defense or the well-being of our people or economics has to be made by the President.

I have a sense of confidence about it. I never lacked confidence when I ran my campaign. I learned a lot about this Nation which strengthened my confidence in it. I don't have a lack of confidence now. And the primary reason for that is that I know that I have a partnership with you. We have the same goals in mind. We have the same interests at heart. I can only be successful if you are. You can only be successful if I do a good job as President.

I thank you very much for what you've contributed to our country. I hope that I can perform my job in such a way that will make you proud.

Thank you very much.

QUESTIONS

MR. DEBUTTS. Ladies and gentlemen, the President has graciously agreed to answer two or three questions if you have them.

THE PRESIDENT. I might be taking my political life in my hands. [*Laughter*]

If anybody does have a question, I'll be glad to try to answer it. If not, that's a very gracious way to treat a guest. [*Laughter*]

Yes, sir?

Q. [*Inaudible*]—I would like to ask you one question.

THE PRESIDENT. I cannot answer the question you asked me in the receiving line. That was a decision my daughter made. [*Laughter*]

Q. No, this is different.

THE PRESIDENT. Okay, good. [*Laughter*]

Q. I'm a great believer in the free market system. I think that the Government is trusted to stay out of the free market system, but some of the policies of this administration, and some that you appear to support, I must say bother me, and that's in the agricultural field.

THE PRESIDENT. Yes.

Q. Peanuts, for example, which you're very familiar with, which has been under Government control. In fact, we just bought most of the peanut oil surplus. We're not allowed to buy it on the free market. We got rid of most of the agricultural subsidies, and now they're starting to come back. Sugar is back. Wheat is back. And I suspect that we're going to have others.

I get very concerned when I see the subsidy structure coming back again after we got rid of it in the last administration.

THE PRESIDENT. I don't know of any new subsidy programs that we've commenced. I was not involved because of a conflict of interest in the decisions made about peanuts. But it's a much looser structure than it was a year ago. The new legislation opens up additional production and has a much less constraint on peanuts themselves. We did not change the basic format of legislation on the production of other crops either. We did raise—I think the Congress raised perhaps more than I asked for—the target and support prices on grain. But I agree with you that we ought to have as little Government interference as possible. We do have high surpluses on hand, not brought about by legislation, by new legislation, because the bill, as you know, was not in effect this year.

The high surpluses on hand of agricultural products in most instances is because of fairly good weather on a worldwide basis. And we do have reasonable reserve supplies of soybeans, of wheat and corn. But we're trying to keep as much of that reserve in the hands of farmers themselves as possible.

We're trying to compensate for it by reducing the acreage planted next year in those two or three crops, and we're trying to escalate our effort on foreign sales. But I don't disagree with the philosophy that you've expressed. There have been no new and innovative programs in the agricultural subsidy program. And we have maintained those, however, that were there before.

Q. Mr. President, we've all been told why you reconsidered the timing on your tax proposal. Could you give this group tonight any estimate of when you might come forward with a tax proposal?

THE PRESIDENT. Yes. We evolved the tax proposal in a way that I think you would have done had you been in office. We began this year, after we put together the energy package and the welfare reform proposal and the social security proposals, to put down in a tabular form all the tax reform proposals and changes that were advocated from all sources.

We consulted with many of you, through Bert Lance, through Mike Blumenthal, Juanita Kreps, and others, to get your advice and your counsel, along with those of labor leaders.

Those educators who are involved in economics and my own staff—and we put this program on the schedule to be revealed to the public and presented to the Congress in September or October. We anticipated at that time that the Congress would adjourn the 23d of October, after the Congress had finished work on social security and energy—that was my plan. When it became obvious that the Congress would not finish as scheduled, we put the tax reform proposal in abeyance, until I can see what impact on the economy will be felt by the increases in social security payments and also by the final results of energy.

We've also been trying to estimate the inherent increased income tax rates brought about by the effects of inflation as individual taxpayers are put in a higher and a higher income tax bracket. With no additional purchasing power, of course, their rate of taxation goes up.

And so there will be combined, I think, a moderate but an adequate program for tax reform to make it more equitable.

We intend to have it a little more progressive in nature, and the overall effect on it will be permanent, not temporary, tax reductions, both for business and for individuals.

My plan now is to complete the income tax reform proposals, tax reduction proposals and present them in January.

Maybe one more question and then I probably need to go.

Q. Mr. President, for many years my gravest concern has been inflation.

THE PRESIDENT. Yes; mine, too.

Q. I come from the natural resources part of the Nation where we are engaged in coal mining, copper mining, oil production, and oil refining, and all of the things that go with this and with protection of the natural land and the environment.

THE PRESIDENT. Yes.

Q. Now I have to say this, that the requirements that are imposed upon us by the Government in connection with all of those things are the maximum, most expensive requirements that could possibly be imposed and that the inflationary situation would be improved if instead of that, more consideration was given to the cost of doing many things which have to be done but which could be done less expensively if we were allowed to experiment in smaller ways.

I wonder if you share at all this kind of thinking.

THE PRESIDENT. Yes, I do. One of the initiatives that I've taken is to direct the Council on Wage and Price Stability to analyze the inflationary impact of the major decisions made on regulation of industry and business. This includes, obviously, the pollution decisions, the occupational, safety, and health provisions, and also the matter of strip mining laws. We tabulate those, and that's part of the discussions that we give to the Congress when we have new proposals to put forward and, obviously, part of the considerations within our own decision-making process.

At the present time about, I believe, six percent of all industrial investment is in pollution control devices. I would not advocate to the Congress that we lower the standards on air and water pollution. And I supported and was glad to sign the strip mining law this year.

We can, however, encourage business in its attempt to overcome that drain on capital investment funds by modifications in the income tax laws and rates, by more rapid depreciation for those investments, and also by some modification in investment tax credits—maybe concentrated on those items that don't contribute to business profits, but do contribute to a better life for the people who live in those communities.

I think that's the only way I can explain our attempt to at least partially compensate for that drain on capital that is needed for business investment in the future. I think, though, that there is a growing realization in the Environmental Protection Agency, EPA, that predictability has been lacking in the past. And if a business executive who does have to spend substantial amounts of money for new equipment for meeting air and water pollution standards, if they have some long-range realization of what will be required and the regulations won't be changed every year or two, that that in itself would be of help.

I particularly would be eager for you, through Secretary Kreps or through any member of my staff, to point out now or in the future particularly onerous requirements on you that you think are unfair. And that applies to almost any aspect of Government regulation or decision that affects your lives.

I called in, for instance, all the State school superintendents and some of the leading presidents of our university systems, and they gave me lists of reports and regulations that they thought were both onerous and unnecessary. And we were very glad to get those.

Bert Lance and Jim McIntyre took those recommendations, assessed them; a few of them were found to be required by law. We have presented those to the appropriate congressional committees and asked them to remove those requirements.

Others could be changed by Executive decision. This constant admonition from leaders like yourselves, or complaints about the way government programs are administered is exactly what we need.

I would like to say one thing in closing, and then I have to leave. My own administration has a heavy commitment to the autonomy and responsibility of the members of the Cabinet. In the past there have been Presidents, both Democratic and Republican, who operated the Government in an administrative way out of the Oval Office. I have no inclination to do that.

I do work very closely with the members of the Cabinet in evolving basic policy, and I demand from them that they keep me informed about what's going on. But there has never been and never will be an occasion when any of my staff members in the White House try to run the affairs in administering the major departments of Government.

So, I would urge you to get personally acquainted, if you're not already, with the

Cabinet officers who have a direct responsibility, from the government point of view, in your own professional lives and deal directly with them. They have, I think, an unprecedented degree of independence and autonomy. And I think only in that fashion can you hope to have a constant dialog with them that permits you to tell us when we can take action to improve Government administration.

In most instances the Congress and my predecessors in the White House, when they passed laws, obviously had the best interest of our Nation at heart. But quite often the intent of Congress is lost over a period of years, as it sometimes is in your own firm, by subordinates who get preoccupied with their own responsibilities and forget if they ever knew the purpose of the legislation they are administering.

If you find something to be irrational or improper or unnecessary, that unnecessarily encroaches on your own effectiveness, I hope you'll let either my Cabinet officers or me know, and I'll do the best I can to correct it. I feel like this is a responsibility that you have, and if you will let me have those recommendations, I'll do the best I can to comply with your request.

I want to say again, in closing, that I am honored to be invited to come. Every President has come to speak to you, including Franklin Roosevelt, and since his time. I've got a lot to learn, and I'm learning rapidly. I've had some good teachers.

As I said, I feel at ease with the job. I learned a lot about our country during the long, tedious 2-year campaign. And I had a chance to meet many of the top business leaders. The first year I stood outside the factory gates and shook hands with the workers coming to and from their shops; the last half of the year, quite often,

I would get invited inside the factories and get a chance to meet their employers. [*Laughter*] And I'm glad to meet the top tonight, to meet the top business executives of our Nation.

Thank you very much.

NOTE: The President spoke at 7:49 p.m. in the Grand Ballroom at the Mayflower Hotel. He was introduced by John D. deButts, chairman of the council.

Quetico-Superior Committee
Executive Order 12029.   December 14, 1977

TERMINATION OF A PRESIDENTIAL ADVISORY COMMITTEE

By virtue of the authority vested in me by the Constitution and statutes of the United States of America, and as President of the United States of America, in order to terminate an advisory committee in accordance with the provisions of the Federal Advisory Committee Act (5 U.S.C. App. I), it is hereby ordered as follows:

SECTION 1. (a) The Quetico-Superior Committee is terminated.

(b) Executive Order No. 11342, as amended, is revoked.

SEC. 2. Subsection (e) of Section 1 of Executive Order No. 11948 of December 20, 1976, which extended the above advisory committee until December 31, 1978, is superseded.

JIMMY CARTER

The White House,
    December 14, 1977.

[Filed with the Office of the Federal Register,
    4:37 p.m., December 15, 1977]

NOTE: The text of the Executive order was released on December 15.

THE PRESIDENT'S NEWS CONFERENCE OF DECEMBER 15, 1977

HUMAN RIGHTS

THE PRESIDENT. Good morning, everybody. I have a statement to make first about a subject of great importance to us. This is Human Rights Week around the world. I've worked day and night to make sure that a concern for human rights is woven through everything our Government does, both at home and abroad.

This policy has produced some controversy, but it's very much in keeping with the character and the history of our own country. We became an independent nation in a struggle for human rights. And there have been many such struggles since then, for the abolition of slavery, for universal suffrage, for racial equality, for the rights of workers, for women's rights.

Not all of these struggles have yet been won. But the freedom and the vigor of our own national public life is evidence of the rights and the liberties that we have achieved. I believe that public life everywhere, in all nations, should have that same freedom and vigor.

We have no wish to tell other nations what political or social systems they should have, but we want our own worldwide influence to reduce human suffering and not to increase it. This is equally true whether the cause of suffering be hunger on the one hand or tyranny on the other.

We are therefore working to advance a full range of human rights, economic and social, as well as civil and political.

The universal declaration and other international human rights covenants mean that one nation may criticize another's treatment of its citizens without regarding each other as enemies. We will continue to do this, just as we welcome scrutiny and criticism of ourselves as part of the normal dealings between nations. We have strengthened our foreign policy on human rights, and we are letting it be known clearly that the United States stands for the victims of repression. We stand with the tortured and the unjustly imprisoned and with those who have been silenced.

Other governments and the dissidents in Eastern Europe and the political prisoners in Latin America and Asia know where we stand. We've spoken out against gross violations of human rights in countries like Cambodia and South Africa and Uganda. We've received exiles from many other countries, exiles who represent those who are unable to speak freely in their own lands.

We've encouraged several countries to permit inspection of human rights situations by the International Committee of the Red Cross. We've reduced military relationships which in some countries in the past have seemed to support repressive regimes.

Our foreign assistance programs will now reflect more clearly our concern about human rights. We will continue to lead the fight in the United Nations, sponsored by Costa Rica, to establish an Office of the High Commissioner on Human Rights. We support the private and the independent human rights organizations which gather information and support activities in the human rights field.

In the past year, human rights has become an issue that no government on Earth can now afford to ignore. There have been numerous instances of improvement. Some represent genuine change, some are only cosmetic in nature. But we welcome them all, because they reflect a relief of suffering people and persecuted people.

The results of our human rights policy will seldom be dramatic. There will be tensions along the way, and we will often be perceived as either being too rash or too timid. But this is a small risk, compared to the risk assumed by brave men and women who live where repression has not yet yielded to liberty.

My personal commitment to human rights is very strong. The American people feel as I do. Our Government will continue to express that commitment and not ever hide it. And we will always encourage other nations to join us.

Thank you very much.

I'll be glad to answer questions now.

QUESTIONS

THE MIDDLE EAST

Q. Mr. President, there are reports that Prime Minister Begin is bringing along some of his peace proposals to discuss with you. My question is, if the United States underwrites peace, will we have a say in terms of what real peace is, if it gives economic aid, psychological aid, security, and so forth? And I have a followup.

THE PRESIDENT. Well, our hope and our goal has been that the nations directly involved in the Middle Eastern crisis, the Middle Eastern disputes, would meet directly with one another and reach agreements that would encompass three basic questions. One is the definition of real peace, genuine peace, predictable peace, relationship among human beings that might transcend the incumbency of any particular leader. I think President Sadat has made a major stride already in the achievement of what is real peace. The second one is the withdrawal of the Israelis from territory and, at the same time, the assurance that they would have

secure borders. And the third one, of course, is to resolve the Palestinian question.

As I've said before, the direct negotiations between Egypt and Israel is a major step forward. We are attending the Cairo conference and will offer our good services when it's needed. But the basic responsibility will be on the shoulders of the two nations directly involved. As you know, United Nations observers are also there. Other countries were invited by President Sadat to attend—Lebanon, Syria, Jordan, and the Soviet Union. They have not yet accepted that invitation.

We are not trying to define the terms of peace. Anything that is acceptable to Israel and her neighbors will certainly be acceptable to us. But we are always available, I hope, as a trusted intermediary on occasion to break a deadlock or add a supportive word or in a way to introduce one of those leaders to another and convince the opposite party that each leader is acting in good faith.

I have no idea what proposals, if any, Prime Minister Begin will bring to me tomorrow morning. But he and I will meet privately, just the two of us for a while at his request, and I will listen to what his report might be, and we will be constructive as we have been in the past.

Q. Well, do you have any idea of what the outcome of the Cairo conference will be in terms of goals?

THE PRESIDENT. I have hopes, but obviously I can't predict what will occur. We've always hoped that even when some of the nations choose not to participate, that the nations who do negotiate could move a major step forward toward an ultimate, comprehensive peace settlement.

Both Prime Minister Begin and President Sadat have stated publicly and repeatedly that they are not seeking strictly a bilateral or a two-nation agreement.

They recognize that an agreement in the Sinai without involving the West Bank, the Gaza Strip, the Golan Heights, could not be a permanent resolution of territorial differences, and if they ignore the Palestinian question, this would still not result in permanent peace, and if the Palestinian question is not addressed, again, it would not be an adequate step toward permanent peace.

So, I think, obviously, this is a good first step. I would hope that in Cairo itself, even if the other nations don't choose to attend, that Egypt and Israel can make a major stride toward a comprehensive peace that would at least address in definitive terms the questions that also involve Palestinians, Jordanians, Syrians, and Lebanese.

LEGISLATIVE ACCOMPLISHMENTS

Q. Mr. President, this year you've been working with a very heavily Democratic Congress, yet your legislative record, I think, can fairly be described as mixed. You've had some successes, some failures, other things in limbo. Do you think you can improve on your legislative record next year, particularly in view of the fact that a lot of those people are going to be running for an election and may not be devoting as much attention to legislation as they were this year?

THE PRESIDENT. Well, almost all of the major proposals that we put forward to the Congress have either been adopted or are still under active consideration. The two remaining doubts among our major proposals are social security, which has a good possibility to be decided this week, and, of course, the most important of all is energy.

There are three of the five major considerations on energy that have been resolved successfully by the conference committees. The remaining ones are the crude oil equalization tax and how to deal with natural gas. The natural gas question is the one that has been in dispute more than 20 years, and it is the one that's the most difficult. It's also the one that's the most expensive, potentially, to the consumers and most rewarding to the oil and natural gas companies.

I think it's unlikely that the Congress will conclude action on the energy question this year, as I had hoped. But I believe that they have made and will continue to make enough progress so that very early next year they'll complete this year's agenda by taking action on the energy question.

We will have a much more carefully considered agenda for 1978, broadly encompassing the commitments that I've made to the American people and the issues that I've identified since I have been in office as being important.

I'd say it's a more effective presentation, because we now know better when the Congress can move rapidly and when they can't. I think the Congress has made substantial progress even on energy, which has been the only major failure this year, and I believe the basis that they've laid will lead to a rapid conclusion next year.

I'm not discouraged about it. I'm very pleased at what has been accomplished so far, although we didn't conclude 100 percent of what we proposed.

Q. Mr. President, the Vice President is saying that you've had a great year in getting important legislation through Congress. Yet the public perception seems to be to the contrary. How do you account for this?

THE PRESIDENT. Well, my own perception is in harmony with that of the Vice President.

We have created a new Department of Energy. We have instigated a $21 billion economic stimulus program with substantial tax reductions, substantial jobs programs, public works projects, and I believe that this is beginning to pay rich dividends. We've had good progress on many other major items that we've proposed—a comprehensive farm bill, which is a great step forward.

We've had some problems that still exist. I terminated the construction of the B–1 bomber, for instance. We've already completed three of those very expensive airplanes. We have a fourth one now in production that will give us an adequate number to complete a comprehensive research and development program on the advanced, very costly, very fast-moving bomber. The Congress is still insisting, some of the Members of Congress, on building a fifth and sixth airplane at an absolute total waste of about $500 million, a half a billion dollars.

This is the kind of question that's very tenacious and very difficult to address. But I think the sum total of this year, the agenda that we have completed, is a very good one.

Q. Yes, but what about public perception? It doesn't seem to be precisely along these lines.

THE PRESIDENT. Well, I think the public perception, of course, is always affected by reports in the news media, and it's inevitable that most of the attention given during the progress of a congressional session—or legislative session while I was Governor—dwells upon the hot debates and the disputes and the disagreements, and there's not nearly so much attention given when there's a harmonious resolution of a difficult question. But I believe that there will be a turning of attention when the Congress does adjourn for 1977 to an inventory of what has actually been done. And I believe that when that attention is given and that

assessment is made, that the public impression will be good.

THE MIDDLE EAST

Q. Mr. President, I take it from your description of the U.S. role in the Mideast that it is not your intention to endorse specific proposals; that is to say, if Mr. Begin or anyone else presents to you what they hope to do, that they would not be able to go back to a peace conference and say, "Jimmy Carter says that this is what he likes."

THE PRESIDENT. Well, that's a fairly good assessment. I stay in close touch with most of the Middle Eastern leaders, certainly President Sadat. We exchange communications several times a week. Cy Vance is returning from the Middle East tonight, and he will give me a very definitive analysis of the attitude of all the Middle Eastern leaders involved, plus Saudi Arabia, one step removed geographically.

I think I know at least in general terms what would be acceptable to President Sadat, maybe not as a final conclusive agreement, but as an interim step, or major step, toward a final agreement. And if Prime Minister Begin's proposal, in my own personal judgment, is conducive to a step in the right direction and would be acceptable to President Sadat, then I would certainly privately tell him, "This is a very good step." If it should be far short of what I think President Sadat could accept without very serious political consequences and serious disappointment in Egypt and the rest of the world, I would have no reticence about telling Prime Minister Begin privately, "I just don't think this goes far enough." But I would not be the ultimate judge of whether or not it's acceptable or not to the Egyptians. That would be up to President Sadat.

SOCIAL SECURITY LEGISLATION

Q. Mr. President, to what extent are you satisfied or dissatisfied with the results of the social security legislation?

THE PRESIDENT. I think the overwhelming consideration that I had early this year when we proposed legislation to the Congress was to restore the integrity of the social security system itself, to make sure that income to the social security system was adequate to meet committed expenditures.

The Congress conference committee report fulfills that completely. This puts the social security system on a sound financial basis, at least for the next 25 years, throughout the rest of this century.

It's a little more costly than I had hoped it would be. But we were able to stop some of the very costly proposals that either the House or Senate had proposed. I think it's a good resolution of a very serious problem that did exist when I took office, that is, that the social security system was on the road toward bankruptcy. Now it's sound. The American people will pay more taxes into the social security system, but in return they'll know that it will be there permanently and in a sound condition.

THE SOVIET UNION

Q. Mr. President, may I ask you about the role of the Soviet Union in the Middle East? Do you feel that the Soviet Union in recent months has been in any way helpful in trying to bring peace to the Middle East, and how do you regard U.S.-Soviet relations, as we come to the end of this year?

THE PRESIDENT. I think our relations with them are much better than they were shortly after I became President. I think they've gotten to know me and my attitudes; I think I've gotten to know

them and their attitudes much better than before. On SALT, a comprehensive test ban, the Indian Ocean, and many other items, we've had a very constructive relationship with the Soviet Union which I think is constantly improving.

I think the Soviets have been much more constructive in the Middle East than they formerly had. Obviously, they've not been as constructive as I would like to have seen.

The Soviets, for instance, were invited to attend the Cairo conference, along with other nations. They were invited by President Sadat. They chose to decline the invitation. I wished that they had accepted. The Syrians have chosen to decline. I have no evidence that the Soviets have had to use their influence on the Syrians to prevent their attendance. I think this was a decision made by President Asad in Syria.

So, I would say the Soviets have not been very constructive yet. They have not been nearly as much of an obstacle as they apparently were in the past.

Our general relationships with the Soviets are very good, and my hope is that they will continue to cooperate in the future when we go past Cairo toward an ultimate Geneva conference. I was well pleased with the joint Soviet and American statement. Although it's not a definitive solution, obviously, it has no obstacles in it which would prevent an ultimate resolution of the Middle East differences.

So, I'd say it's a mixed assessment. In general, though, they could have been much worse.

THE MIDDLE EAST

Q. Mr. President, your preference for a general or comprehensive settlement in the Middle East is quite understandable, one that could be endorsed by all the interested parties. But I wonder if you think, in light of what has happened since President Sadat's visit, since many people feel that Israel has no real worries about a one-front war, that if an agreement, formal or informal, even a real warming takes place between Israel and Egypt, that you could have de facto peace in the Middle East, perhaps not as neat and wrapped up as a treaty, that would be a major accomplishment in itself? And do you think that it may have to come to that as a result of President Asad's opposition to the talks and the PLO?

THE PRESIDENT. Well, our immediate hope and goal is that any peace move made by Israel and Egypt would be acceptable to the moderate Arab leaders in the Middle East, certainly King Hussein in Jordan, certainly the Saudi Arabians. We have had good indications in my personal visits with President Asad that he wants to resolve the differences. Lebanon is heavily influenced, as you know, by Syrian presence there. The PLO have been completely negative. They have not been cooperative at all.

In spite of my own indirect invitation to them and the direct invitations by Sadat and by Asad, by King Hussein, by King Khalid in Saudi Arabia, the PLO have refused to make any move toward a peaceful attitude. They have completely rejected United Nations Resolutions 242 and 338. They have refused to make a public acknowledgement that Israel has a right to exist, to exist in peace. So, I think they have, themselves, removed the PLO from any immediate prospect of participation in a peace discussion.

But I certainly would not ascribe that short of intransigence or negative attitude toward any of the other parties who have been mentioned as possible participants. We want to be sure that at least moderate Palestinians are included in the discussions. And this is an attitude that's mirrored not only by myself but also by Prime Minister Begin, President Sadat, and others. So, I think they are all major steps, already having been taken, to delineate those who are immediately eager to conclude a step toward peace—those like President Asad, who will wait a while and see what does occur, to see if the Golan Heights question can be resolved and so forth, and those who have in effect removed themselves from serious consideration like the PLO.

AGRICULTURAL POLICIES

Q. Mr. President, I'd like to ask you about the farm strike. Some of the Nation's farmers are on strike today. As you know, there was a meeting at the White House last weekend, and some of the farmers present noted your absence and said if you really cared about their problems as a farmer yourself you would have been there. How do you respond to that, Mr. President? And do you plan any actions because of the farm strike?

THE PRESIDENT. Well, I have deep sympathy for the farmers. I'm one of them. I understand their particular concerns at this time. They have enormous investments, capital investments. In my own county, for instance, the average farm family has a much greater investment than does the average businessman or industrialist. Their income on their investment is exceedingly low.

We've made some major strides in 1977 to help ease those problems. The last time I checked, the price of wheat was up about 60 cents. The price of corn was up about 38 cents from a year ago. So, the trends are in the right direction. The target prices, the support prices, passed by Congress in the new farm bill, are much more favorable to the farmers than was the case with the previous legislation under which farmers had to live.

Most of the farm strike impetus has been from those areas of our Nation who have been affected by adverse weather conditions, something over which the Government has no control. Georgia had a devastating drought. We had less than a 5-percent corn yield compared to the average year, and the corn that was harvested was heavily affected, damaged by aflatoxin mold, and the farmers in Georgia have suffered because of it.

I think we've made a strong move to increase agricultural exports. This past 12 months, we exported $24 billion worth of farm goods, more than we've ever exported in the past. We are creating a reserve supply of key feed and food grain stocks not held by the Government but primarily held on farms by farmers, and we're trying to form international arrangements to eliminate as much as possible the wild fluctuations up and down in farm prices.

So, we've already made great strides toward alleviating the problems of the farmers. The ones who are primarily suffering, as I said earlier, are not suffering from farm legislation or the absence of it, but from weather conditions over which no one has any control.

Q. So you don't think the strike is quite really representative, then, of the rest of the farmers in the country?

THE PRESIDENT. No—although I have to say that I think all farmers would like to get more money for their crops. We have passed a bill this year that will provide about $6½ billion in Government payments to farmers. I've never been in favor of guaranteeing a farmer a profit. We have tried, though, to create an orderly marketing system, where wild fluctuations will not devastate individual farm families, some stable price system and some adequate reserve system and an adequate way to sell our farm products

overseas that we don't need on the domestic scene.

We've made good progress in that respect. In addition to having a farmer in the White House, we've got a working dirt farmer who's thoroughly familiar with the life and problems of farm families in the Secretary of Agriculture.

I think when Bob Bergland goes to meet with these farm groups and talks to them, they understand that. But they are hurt very seriously financially. And a stable, healthy farm economy is very important to me.

Q. Mr. President, if you were still in Plains, would you join the strike, if you were on your farm in Georgia?

THE PRESIDENT. Well, my cousin Hugh, who's not a farmer, participates in the strike. My sister, who is a farmer, drove a tractor to Atlanta as part of the farm strike. My brother, Billy, supports the farm strike. And I think if I were in Sumter County, I would also participate, at least in the demonstration of need and the demonstration of the plight of the farmers actively. Now, where the strike will go from here, I don't know. I doubt that many of the farmers involved will actually stop producing crops. It would be a very hard blow on themselves, it would be a self-sacrificial effort and perhaps would hurt their families more than they can bear.

But the actual prohibition against producing food and fiber is something in which I would not participate. The demonstration of the tangible and demonstrable need of farmers is something in which I would participate.

PRESIDENT'S FOREIGN TRAVEL

Q. Mr. President, your foreign trip is taking you to a disparate range of countries, and the schedule offers fairly limited time for exchanges with other heads of state. Can you tell us what overall objective you have in mind for this trip and if there is any foreign policy theme that you want to accomplish? And I'd like to add to that, do you intend to press this issue of human rights, that you mentioned earlier, in your stops in Poland and Iran?

The PRESIDENT. Yes, I do intend to press the subject of human rights. My time set aside for negotiation with foreign leaders where I'll visit is equivalent to the time that I set aside for discussions with foreign leaders who come here and visit me. There are literally weeks of preparation that go into the visit to any country, days of preparation on my own part. I'll spend a lot of my time over the Christmas holidays reading thick notebooks on the nations to be visited. Each nation is different.

I'll start off my trip with Poland. I think it's very important that an American President indicate our interest in Eastern European countries. Poland is one that has very close ties to us. We have strong trade relationships with Poland, and my presence there is just as important as is the presence of President Brezhnev when he visits a nation like France or Germany. And we will be discussing a broad range of questions with Poland.

We are just making a brief stop in Saudi Arabia and Iran, to and from India. But we'll have time for several hours of intensive discussions with the leaders in those two Middle Eastern countries. They are major suppliers of oil to ourselves and to the rest of the country (world).[1] They have a major political and military influence in the Middle East. And it is very important that I let their people and those leaders know that I care about our friendship with them and vice versa.

---

[1] Printed in the White House Press Office transcript.

India, as you know, is the world's largest democracy, with hundreds of millions of people. In the past under Mrs. Gandhi, their primary orientation shifted toward friendship with the Soviet Union. I would like very much for the people of India, for Prime Minister Desai, with whom I have a continuing correspondence, to know how much we value a restoration of those strong ties of friendship, trade, commerce with India. And I think this is a very important consideration for me.

I have already visited England. Early next summer or late spring, I'll be visiting West Germany, and I particularly wanted to visit France as well. When I was in London last May, President Giscard particularly asked me if I could come to France later this year, late this year. I replied that I would if I could schedule it. And so, I am very eager to negotiate major problems with France. They have a much greater historical presence, for instance, in Africa than we do. I think many of the African nations, particularly those that speak French, look toward France as a source of advice and counsel, economic aid to them. And it will help me to have a better avenue or understanding of Africa to meet with Giscard.

France is not a member of NATO. But they are very supportive of the European defense effort. They retain very rigidly their autonomy and independence from the influence of other countries, which is good. But I want to discuss with Giscard our negotiations with the Soviet Union, our influence in the Middle East, our growing influence in Africa.

Of course, to visit NATO headquarters is important as well, because we are trying to increase our contribution and our influence in NATO.

Those trips are not tied harmoniously or homogeneously together, because each country is unique, each visit will be unique, and I'll prepare each one to get maximum benefit from it.

TAX REDUCTION

Q. Mr. President, how large a tax cut are you going to ask to offset the social security tax increases, especially the very large increases for those now making $20,000 a year and more?

THE PRESIDENT. I don't know yet. We had hoped that I could have the final version of the energy bill and the social security bill and understand the tax consequences of each before we put together the final version of an income tax reduction. The reductions will be substantial, and we will have a clearer picture of the social security tax impact before I put the final version of the income tax reductions together.

That's by far greater, by the way, than will any possible combination of taxes resulting from the energy bills. I just don't know yet. We will have simplicity; we'll have a major tax reduction for both business and individuals. We'll have a greater progressivity, giving the tax breaks where they are most needed, and we will have substantial tax reform. But the exact dollar amount that will be recommended to the Congress is something that I won't decide until early in January.

FRANK CORMIER [Associated Press]. Thank you, Mr. President.

THE PRESIDENT. Thank you very much. Have a Merry Christmas, everybody.

[*President Carter's twenty-first news conference began at 11 a.m. in Room 450 of the Old Executive Office Building and was broadcast live on radio and television. Following the news conference, the President remained in the room to answer questions from reporters on an informal basis, as follows:*]

Q. Are you still going to Fayetteville?

THE PRESIDENT. Yes, tomorrow night.

Q. Mr. President, you said we stand with the unjustly imprisoned. Where do we stand on the Wilmington 10, who have been in jail for over a year on the testimony of witnesses who have recanted?

THE PRESIDENT. Well, as you undoubtedly know, Mary [Mary McGrory, Washington Star], the Wilmington 10 are not tried in Federal court. It's a State case. And until that case should some day get to the Federal courts, I would have no jurisdiction.

Q. But do you have any feelings about it? Amnesty International, which defines violations of human rights in the world, says that the Wilmington 10 are unjustly imprisoned. I wondered what your own view was, since you're an advocate——

THE PRESIDENT. Well, I'm against unjust imprisonment. And the Attorney General is obviously monitoring the case. I think a group of Congressmen have been to North Carolina to look into it.

But I just don't feel like it's proper for me to comment on a particular case that's in the courts until its appeal procedures have been concluded. I don't know the testimony. I've never studied the transcripts of the case. Obviously, I want justice to be carried out, but I don't have any knowledge of that.

Q. I mean, it is kind of an international situation now because Brezhnev called in, as I understand, our Ambassador Malcolm Toon at the Soviet Embassy and said, "What about this? How can you talk about our cases when you have this one?"

THE PRESIDENT. Well, you know, I've seen many cases go through the judicial system of our Nation, and in almost every instance that I remember, the ultimate decision was the right one.

Q. But you have no inclination to call up Governor Hunt, your fellow southern Governor?

THE PRESIDENT. No.

Q. Are you going to meet Mr. Begin more than once, or are those 3 hours tomorrow morning about it?

THE PRESIDENT. I'll be meeting with Cy Vance this afternoon at 6:15, when he returns, to get a report from him on all the visits that he concluded in the Middle East. But I only have one meeting scheduled with Prime Minister Begin so far tomorrow. If he and I can't conclude our discussions inside the time allotted, then I would cancel some of my other appointments to meet further with him.

Q. You know, one of the interesting things is that Mr. Vance is not a low-level official of this Government. He was in Jerusalem last week.

THE PRESIDENT. Yes, I know.

Q. Why does the Prime Minister have to come all the way here just to look you in the eye for about 3 hours?

THE PRESIDENT. You'd have to ask him about that. He sent word to me that he would like to come over here and meet with me. He has not told me what the subject of his conversation would be. But quite often I have an inclination to talk directly to heads of state and not just to the foreign minister, and I think that the work of Secretaries of State and foreign ministers are a good precursor to the more final discussions between heads of state.

I don't think Prime Minister Begin would have made this long and arduous trip had he not had something important to discuss with me. I look forward to it with a great deal of anticipation.

Q. Mr. President, when do you think you will get an energy bill?

THE PRESIDENT. At the latest, early next year. I think if the conference committees can lay down the principles of natural gas regulation and oil taxation, I think the conferees' staff members can be working on that between now and January. I think everybody wants to conclude this as rapidly as possible. It's probably the most difficult and complicated and politically divisive issue that the Congress has ever addressed. You have to remember that we are not a nation of consumers alone. We are a nation of major producers, one of the largest oil-producing nations in the world, and also the greatest consumer of all in the world. And there are inherent conflicts.

The Senate conferees, as you know, have been rigidly divided nine to nine. They've never been able to break that deadlock so far. But I can see progress being made, because many Members of the Congress come and discuss with me or with Frank Moore or with Jim Schlesinger their own private feelings about what they could accept. And there's much more flexibility among the members of the conference committee individually than there has been so far in the public statements or the actual votes. I think we'll have a general agreement, and I think the action on the energy measures will be concluded quite early in the next year's session.

Federal Property Council

Executive Order 12030. December 15, 1977

TERMINATION OF THE FEDERAL PROPERTY COUNCIL

By virtue of the authority vested in me by the Constitution and statutes of the United States of America, including Section 205(a) of the Federal Property and Administrative Services Act of 1949, as amended (40 U.S.C. 486(a)), and as President of the United States of America, it is hereby ordered as follows:

SECTION 1. (a) The Federal Property Council is terminated.

(b) Section 1 of Executive Order No. 11954 of January 7, 1977, which reconstituted the Federal Property Council, is revoked.

(c) Sections 2, 3, 4, 5, and 6 of Executive Order No. 11954 are redesignated as Sections 1, 2, 3, 4, and 5, respectively.

SEC. 2. In order to permit the Director of the Office of Management and Budget to resolve disputes concerning underutilized real property, the provisions of Executive Order No. 11954 which were redesignated as Section 4 by Section 1(c) of this Order are amended to read as follows:

"Sec. 4. The Director of the Office of Management and Budget shall review Federal real property policies and the objectives of the Executive branch of the Government; and, shall review the reports made by the Administrator of General Services pursuant to Section 3 of this Order, as well as other reports relating to resolving conflicting claims on, and alternate uses for, any property described in those reports, consistent with laws governing Federal real property. The Director shall submit such recommendations and cause reports to be submitted to the President as may be appropriate.".

JIMMY CARTER

The White House,
December 15, 1977.

[Filed with the Office of the Federal Register, 4:38 p.m., December 15, 1977]

Budget Deferrals

Message to the Congress. December 15, 1977

To the Congress of the United States:

In accordance with the Impoundment Control Act of 1974, I herewith report three new International security assistance deferrals totalling $806.4 million in budget authority and one new deferral of $3.4 million in outlays for the Antirecession financial assistance fund in the Department of the Treasury.

In addition, I am reporting routine revisions to four deferrals previously transmitted. A deferral for the Emergency refugee and migration assistance fund is increased by $5.8 million in budget authority. Three deferrals of funds provided to the Department of the Treasury are increased by a total of $13.3 million of which $11.9 million is deferred budget authority and $1.3 million is an increase to a deferral which only affects outlays.

The details of each deferral are contained in the attached reports.

JIMMY CARTER

The White House,
December 15, 1977.

NOTE: The attachments detailing the deferrals are printed in the FEDERAL REGISTER of December 21, 1977.

The message was announced by the White House Press Office on December 15. It was not issued in the form of a White House press release.

Christmas Pageant of Peace

Remarks on Lighting the National Community Christmas Tree. December 15, 1977

Thank you. Merry Christmas, everybody.

This is a time of year when we try to forget our worries and our tribulations, our arguments and our differences, our doubts and fears about the future, and look on the positive side of life.

We try to search for confidence and for security. We try to reach out our hands to our friends, those whom we see every day and those whom we tend to forget during the rest of the year.

Christmas is also a time of tradition. This is a time to look back, to see the fine things of life that, because they are so good and decent, have been preserved.

This evening, we have a ceremony that will commemorate one of those commitments. For more than 50 years, since Calvin Coolidge lived in the White House, every single President has been over to join in the lighting of the National Christmas Tree. This also commemorates a continuity of beliefs—belief in one another, belief in our Nation, belief in principles like honesty and justice and freedom, and our religious beliefs, above all.

Ours is a nation of peace, and I thank God that our Nation is at peace. We not only preserve a peaceful life for those who live in the United States, but one of the major commitments of our leaders before me and now is to try to institute an opportunity for peaceful existence for others. In regions that might be torn with war, we try to bring friendship, and in regions of the world that are torn by disputes, we try to bring understanding.

We've seen two great leaders in recent weeks, the President of Egypt, the Prime Minister of Israel, lead in a dramatic way and, indeed, inspire the world with courage. And it is strange, isn't it, that it requires courage just to search for peace under some circumstances. Well, our Nation has been a bulwark where those who want peace can turn, and the staunchness of our commitment has been and can be an inspiration to others.

A few months ago, I designated December 15, today, as a day of prayer. And I hope that all of you in this great audience and all who watch and listen on television, radio, will make a special promise to yourselves during this holiday season to pray for guidance in our lives, purposes, guidance for the wisdom and commitment and honesty of public officials and other leaders, guidance that we can see our Nation realize its great potential and the vision that formed it 200 years ago, and guidance that we will fulfill our deepest moral and religious commitments.

We look back on our own personal lives. Cecil Andrus remembered his family. I remember my own when I was a child and when Christmas was a day that we thought about 365 days a year—looking forward with anticipation, trying to measure up with standards, looking around our shoulders to see who was watching our performance. And sometimes I know that when we look back, we tend to put a rosy attitude or picture of what actually occurred. My favorite poet is Dylan Thomas, and he wrote "A Child's Christmas in Wales," and he tried to point out the confusion that sometimes exists in the mind of an adult about childhood, when he said he couldn't remember whether it snowed 6 days and 6 nights when he was 12 or snowed 12 days and 12 nights when he was 6. But it didn't really matter, because the memory was precious even though it was slightly confused.

We've never seen it snow in Plains on Christmas, but we're going back to Plains next week to be with our friends, to be with our families, to be with those who have loved us throughout a lifetime and those whom we still love, for Christmas is also a time of celebration, of festivity, of enjoyment, of pleasure, of self-gratification, even. And there is no incompatibility between memories, religious beliefs, tradition, peace, and going back home and being happy. They all kind of tie together.

Our Nation is not one of solemn faces and sad demeanors, but our Nation is one of hope and vision and even happiness. And Christmas is a time to remind us that even when we do suffer and are disappointed in the United States and live even a dismal life, compared to our own immediate neighbors, compared to most of the rest of the world, we indeed have a joyous life and a wonderful life. God has blessed us in this country.

Well, in closing, let me say that Christmas has a special meaning for those of us who are Christians, those of us who believe in Christ, those of us who know that almost 2,000 years ago, the Son of Peace was born to give us a vision of perfection, a vision of humility, a vision of unselfishness, a vision of compassion, a vision of love.

Those are exactly the same words that describe our theme this year. The theme is "The American Family." And I hope that we'll make every effort during this Christmas season not only to bring our immediate family together but to look at the family of all humankind, so that we not any longer cherish a commitment toward animosity or the retention of enemies but that we forgive one another and, indeed, form a worldwide family where every human being on Earth is our brother or our sister.

Thank you for letting me come and meet with you and to remind each of you that Christmas is a time for recommitment of each life to the finest ideals that we can possibly envision.

Thank you very much.

NOTE: The President spoke at 5:45 p.m. on the Ellipse. Following his remarks, he lit the National Community Christmas Tree with the help of his daughter, Amy.

Secretary of the Interior Cecil D. Andrus also spoke at the ceremonies.

Meeting With Prime Minister Menahem Begin of Israel

White House Statement Issued Following the First Meeting.   December 16, 1977

The President was happy to have the opportunity to welcome Prime Minister Begin again to the United States.

The Prime Minister and the President met privately for an hour, and subsequently others joined. The entire discussions lasted 2 hours. The President was able to hear firsthand from Prime Minister Begin his impressions and evaluations of the momentous events in the Middle East set in train by President Sadat's historic visit to Jerusalem and his reception by the people, parliament, and government of Israel.

All aspects of the current Middle East situation were discussed in the context of the search for a comprehensive peace.

Obviously, a particular focus was on the direct talks which have commenced between Egypt and Israel. The Prime Minister and the President discussed the most effective ways to continue the momentum and to turn to the broader goal of negotiating a comprehensive peace.

In this respect, the Prime Minister and the President discussed underlying principles which could guide future negotiations. The Prime Minister outlined proposals concerning the future relations between Egypt and Israel and a process for resolving the issue of Palestinian Arabs.

The President thanked the Prime Minister for his thoughts in both of these areas and promised to give them serious consideration.

The President told Prime Minister Begin that the United States is convinced that the course of direct negotiations on which Prime Minister Begin and President Sadat have embarked offers a unique opportunity for peace. We, of course, recognize that in these new circumstances the test of acceptability of the provisions of a negotiated settlement will lie in the judgments of those who will ultimately sign the peace treaties. The United States will continue to remain in the closest possible consultation with both sides in the effort to help them find common ground.

The President and the Prime Minister will meet again tomorrow evening at 7 p.m.

Export-Import Bank of the United States

Nomination of H. K. Allen To Be First Vice President.   December 16, 1977

The President today announced his intention to nominate H. K. Allen, of Temple, Tex., to be First Vice President of the Export-Import Bank of the United States. He will succeed Delio E. Gianturco, resigned.

Allen was born July 24, 1926, in Dallas, Tex. He is a graduate of the University of Texas and holds B.S., B.B.A., and LL.B. degrees. From 1944 to 1946, Allen was in the Navy Flight Officers Training program. In 1951 he was recalled to active duty and served 19 months sea duty.

After an honorable discharge, he returned to Temple where he entered the banking business. Since 1953 he has been chairman of Temple National Bank. Allen is chairman of the Farmers & Merchants State Bank, Ballinger, Tex., and also the chairman of the First State Bank, Rogers, Tex. He is a member of the board of directors of the American Founders Life Insurance Co., Austin, Tex.

Meeting With Prime Minister Michael Manley of Jamaica

White House Statement Issued Following the Meeting.   December 16, 1977

Prime Minister Manley of Jamaica and President Carter met today for an hour and 15 minutes in the Cabinet Room and then proceeded to a working luncheon for an hour and a half. They discussed a wide range of subjects of mutual interest. Mr. Manley was invited to have lunch at the White House by Mrs. Carter during her visit to Kingston in May of this year, and the December 16 date was selected as the time most convenient to both the President and Prime Minister Manley.

The Prime Minister and President Carter discussed multilateral and bilateral issues during their meeting and luncheon. Jamaica, as Chairman of the Group of 77, plays an important role as spokesman for many developing countries. The Prime Minister and the President reviewed the general state of the North-South dialog, as well as several individual issues of importance including the assistance needs of developing countries and the negotiations on a common fund.

The two leaders also discussed certain bilateral issues, including our efforts to assist Jamaica resolve its economic difficulties and Jamaica's contribution to a broader hemispheric commitment to human rights. Several important regional issues were discussed, including the question of Belize. Prime Minister Manley recently hosted a conference of seven Latin American and Caribbean leaders to discuss the future status of Belize, and the Prime Minister related some of the conclusions of that conference to the President, and they explored in general terms ways to ensure a peaceful and durable settlement to that problem. The two leaders also discussed the Panama Canal treaties and regional cooperation in the Caribbean.

The meeting was extremely cordial.

Attending on the Jamaican side were Prime Minister Manley, Mrs. Manley, P. J. Patterson, Minister of Foreign Affairs, Trade and Tourism; Alfred Rattray, Jamaican Ambassador; Richard Fletcher, Minister of State, Ministry of

Finance; Keith Rodd, Member of Parliament; Owen Jefferson, Director, Program Division, Ministry of Finance and Planning; Gordon Wells, Permanent Secretary, Office of the Prime Minister; E. Frank Francis, Permanent Secretary, Ministry of Foreign Affairs, Foreign Trade and Tourism; and Herbert Walker, Permanent Representative to the Jamaican Mission to the Specialized Agencies of the United Nations at Geneva.

Attending on the United States side were President Carter; Vice President Mondale; Secretary of State Cyrus Vance; Zbigniew Brzezinski, Assistant to the President for National Security Affairs; David Aaron, Deputy Assistant to the President for National Security Affairs; Terence A. Todman, Assistant Secretary of State for Inter-American Affairs; Frederick Irving, American Ambassador to Jamaica; and Robert Pastor, National Security Council staff member. The following United States officials also attended the luncheon: Anthony M. Solomon, Under Secretary of the Treasury for Monetary Affairs, and Guy Erb, National Security Council staff member.

NOTE: The statement was made available by the White House Press Office. It was not issued in the form of a White House press release.

Digest of Other White House Announcements

The following listing includes the President's daily schedule and other items of general interest as announced by the White House Press Office during the period covered by this issue. Events and announcements printed elsewhere in the issue are not included.

December 10

The President declared a major disaster for the State of Washington as a result of severe storms, mudslides, and flooding, beginning about December 1, which caused extensive public and private property damage.

December 11

The President returned to the White House after a weekend stay at Camp David, Md.

December 12

The President met at the White House with:

—Zbigniew Brzezinski, Assistant to the President for National Security Affairs;

—senior White House staff members;

—the Cabinet;

—Vice President Walter F. Mondale;

—a group of administration officials to discuss the budget;

—Senator Kaneaster Hodges, Jr., who is filling the term of the late Senator John L. McClellan of Arkansas, members of the Hodges family, and Mrs. John L. McClellan.

December 13

The President met at the White House with:

—Dr. Brzezinski;

—James T. McIntyre, Jr., Acting Director of the Office of Management and Budget;

—a group of administration officials to discuss the budget.

The President and Mrs. Carter hosted a Christmas reception at the White House for Members of Congress and their families.

December 14

The President met at the White House with:

—Vice President Mondale, Secretary of Defense Harold Brown, Deputy Secretary of Defense Charles W. Duncan, Jr., and members of the Joint Chiefs of Staff;

—Dr. Brzezinski;

—a group of black leaders;

—Mrs. Carter, for lunch;

—Charles L. Schultze, Chairman of the Council of Economic Advisers;

—a group of women members of the administration who attended the International Women's Year Conference in Houston, Tex.

The President and Mrs. Carter hosted a Christmas reception for the children of members of the diplomatic corps.

December 15

The President met at the White House with:

—Dr. Brzezinski;

—Senators Henry M. Jackson of Washington and Sam Nunn of Georgia;

—a group of leaders of the Arab American community;

—Attorney General Griffin B. Bell;

—a group of administration officials to discuss the budget;

—Nobuhiko Ushiba. Minister for External Economic Affairs of Japan;

—Vice President Mondale, Secretary of State Cyrus R. Vance, Deputy Secretary of State Warren M. Christopher, Dr. Brzezinski, and David L. Aaron, Deputy Assistant to the President for National Security Affairs.

December 16

The President met at the White House with:

—a group of leaders of church-related educational organizations;

—a group of administration officials to discuss the budget.

The President left the White House for a trip to Fayetteville, N.C., to attend the wedding of his nephew, Sydney Scott Stapleton.

NOMINATIONS SUBMITTED TO THE SENATE

The following list does not include promotions of members of the Uniformed Services, nominations to the Service Academies, or nominations of Foreign Service officers.

Submitted December 12, 1977

DONALD J. KINDT, of Ohio, to be United States Marshal for the Northern District of Ohio for the term of 4 years, vice Robert G. Wagner, term expired.

JOHN W. SNYDER, of the District of Columbia, to be a member of the Board of Trustees of the Harry S Truman Scholarship Foundation for a term expiring December 10, 1983 (reappointment).

The following-named persons to be members of the Board of Directors of the Legal Services Corporation for terms expiring July 13, 1980:

CECILIA DENOGEAN ESQUER, of Arizona, vice Rodolfo Montejano, term expired.

STEVEN L. ENGELBERG, of Maryland, vice Samuel D. Thurman, term expired.

HILLARY DIANE RODHAM, of Arkansas, vice William J. Janklow, resigned.

RICHARD ALLAN TRUDELL, of California, vice Marshall Jordan Breger, term expired.

JOSEPHINE MARIE WORTHY, of Massachusetts, vice Marlow W. Cook, term expired.

Submitted December 15, 1977

ALVIN HARRY GANDAL, of Maryland, to be a Commissioner of the Postal Rate Commission for the term expiring October 14, 1982, vice Frank P. Saponaro, term expired.

CHECKLIST OF WHITE HOUSE PRESS RELEASES

The following releases of the Office of the White House Press Secretary, distributed during the period covered by this issue, are not included in this issue.

Released December 10, 1977

News conference: on social security legislation—by Secretary of Health, Education, and Welfare Joseph A. Califano, Jr.

CHECKLIST—Continued
Released December 12, 1977

Announcement: nomination of Donald J. Kindt to be United States Marshal for the Northern District of Ohio

Released December 13, 1977

Announcement: the President's acceptance of a request from Prime Minister Menahem Begin of Israel for a meeting in Washington on December 16

ACTS APPROVED BY THE PRESIDENT

Approved December 12, 1977

H.R. 1904_____ Public Law 95–206
An act to suspend until July 1, 1980, the duty on intravenous fat emulsion, and for other purposes.

ACTS APPROVED—Continued
Approved December 13, 1977

H.R. 7_____ Public Law 95–207
Career Education Incentive Act.

H.R. 3313_____ Private Law 95–24
An act for the relief of Mark Charles Mieir and Liane Maria Mieir.

H.R. 5555_____ Private Law 95–25
An act for the relief of Adelaida Rea Berry.

H.R. 8159_____ Public Law 95–208
International Safe Container Act.

H.R. 8422_____ Public Law 95–210
An act to amend titles XVIII and XIX of the Social Security Act to provide payment for rural health clinic services, and for other purposes.

S. 1131_____ Public Law 95–209
An act to authorize appropriations for Nuclear Regulatory Commission for the fiscal year 1978, and for other purposes.

Fayetteville, North Carolina

*Remarks in a Telephone Interview With
Jeff Thompson of WFNC Radio.
December 17, 1977*

MR. THOMPSON. Good morning, Mr.
President.

THE PRESIDENT. Good morning, Jeff.
Can you hear me all right?

MR. THOMPSON. Yes, fine, thank you.
We're very honored and privileged that
you took the time to call. Thank you, sir.

THE PRESIDENT. Well, during the campaign I told you I would when I came
back to Fayetteville, and I wanted to
honor my promise.

MR. THOMPSON. Have you got time
for a few questions?

THE PRESIDENT. Yes, I have. About 5
minutes is what they said you wanted.

THE MIDDLE EAST

MR. THOMPSON. Your meeting with
Prime Minister Begin yesterday, to be followed upon your return to Washington by
another, suggests some imminent urgency
in progressing developments in the Middle East. Can you tell us your administration's current role in that conciliation
effort?

THE PRESIDENT. Well, our role is the
same as it always has been, to encourage
direct negotiations between the nations
involved in the Middle East dispute and
to give support whenever they call on us.

We also are very insistent that they do
as much as possible on their own, and we
want to be sure they trust us to relay messages accurately and to describe accurately the positions of the leaders who,
quite often, have not communicated at all
in the past.

Prime Minister Begin will be meeting
with President Sadat within another week
or so, and both he and Sadat communicate with me quite frequently to give me
their positions. We think this is a good
step toward a comprehensive peace. Although it will involve primarily the two
leaders from Egypt and Israel, we hope
that Jordan, Syria, Lebanon will come in
later on if progress can be made.

But we're just offering our good services. And to the extent that we are trustworthy, they use our services very eagerly.

TOBACCO PRICE SUPPORTS

MR. THOMPSON. Mr. President, on a
matter of considerable statewide interest
here in North Carolina, there is growing
intensity in the Congress to significantly
reduce or even abolish the price support
program for tobacco. Although you have
supported the support program consistently, can you say uncategorically that
you would veto any legislation that would
reduce or abolish the tobacco support
program?

THE PRESIDENT. Well, as you know, tobacco is just as important for Georgia as
it is North Carolina, and the tobacco sup-

port program will not be abolished while I'm President.

THE NATION'S DEFENSE

MR. THOMPSON. In view of your decision to stop production of the B–1 bomber, I'm sure a lot of our listeners in the Fort Bragg area would like an assessment from you on our Nation's defense stature. It seems to have been slipping a bit at a time when the Russians are still in a position to capitalize on expansion of their own defense posture. How, in a few words, do you assess our country's military readiness in terms of present and immediate needs?

THE PRESIDENT. As a matter of fact, during the years immediately following the Vietnam war, our defense effort did decrease. But under President Ford and continuing under me, the contribution for our defense effort has gone up in real dollars. In other words, we've compensated for the inflation rate and then added on top of that an additional amount to increase our defense spending—quite a reversal of what had been done in the past.

This is a nationwide commitment. We are trying to focus our attention on the elements of our defense posture which I think were in most serious need, immediate strike forces on hand in this country, as is the case with Fort Bragg. We are strengthening our forces in NATO. We're trying to encourage our NATO partners to do the same, whereas in previous years, I think their commitment to NATO had been decreasing somewhat both in financial contribution and also in attitude.

So, our defense posture will be kept strong. We have a very fine research and development and testing and evaluation program going on with new weapons. And in technology, in competence, I think that our military forces are unexcelled in the world.

The Soviets do have a superiority in some respects—the number of tanks, for instance, in Europe. But as you know, we're trying to make sure that those tanks are vulnerable, and also, we're developing new weapons of our own. So, I don't think anyone needs to worry about the United States being second in total military strength to anybody.

ACCESS TO THE PRESIDENT

MR. THOMPSON. In contrast to recent past administrations, you have continued your campaign image of being very approachable. Has it paid off for you? Do folks feel there is an open door at the White House?

THE PRESIDENT. Well, I hope so. It pays off not just in that respect that you've described, but also it gives me a sense that when I make a final decision on a very controversial issue, that the American people have been included in the debate, that they have been aware of the developing decision. And whether it's the Middle East issues or defense or agriculture programs or whatever, we've tried to get a maximum amount of contribution and advice and counsel, support and, sometimes, criticism from people all around the Nation.

For instance, just to give you an example, I've met with editors and radio and television executives from 47 States this year and—I think a total of about 450 of them at different sessions—every 2 weeks I meet with 35 or 40 of the top news leaders of the country to answer any question they ask me. Quite often, these are questions that are important just on a local area. And in that process not only do they learn about their President and their Government's attitude, but I also learn about their attitude, which makes it much more likely that when I make a final decision it's compatible with what the American people want.

So, the accessibility thing is a two-way street. The people benefit from knowing what I plan and what I am doing. I learn on a daily basis in the White House what the American people want done.

VIEWS ON THE PRESIDENCY

MR. THOMPSON. Mr. President, very briefly, one final question. It's been almost a year now for you as President. A lot of those campaign promises have probably been more difficult than perhaps you imagined. How does the responsibility of holding the single most powerful position in the world differ from what you expected before taking the oath?

THE PRESIDENT. Well, I think the difference between what I expected and what was sometimes covered by the news media has been different. When someone running for a 4-year term of office makes promises to do certain things—in the Middle East, in defense, in agriculture, in education, social security, energy—that doesn't mean that you think you can do it the first year and that nothing will be left to be done the other 3 years.

Another point to be made is that I can evolve a comprehensive program in energy, in welfare, social security, and present it to the Congress much more rapidly than the Congress can actually pass it into law. So there's always a delay, inherently in our system, for Congress to take action on a proposal made by the President.

I believe that we've made excellent progress. And when an inventory is conducted of what this Congress did achieve, I believe the American people will be very pleased and very thankful.

We took major strides forward. The only major disappointment that I have experienced is not getting the comprehensive energy package passed. But I think this will be done early next year. The conference committees are still at work. And this is probably the most complicated, complex, confusing, and politically divisive issue that the Congress has ever attacked in the last 200 years. It is so confusing to simultaneously try to resolve, I think, 113 different proposals that we've presented to the Congress just on the energy question alone. And since our Nation is both a producing country—one of the largest on Earth—and also the biggest consumer nation on Earth, there's an inherent conflict.

But the Congress has performed superbly, in my opinion. We've had a good relationship between the White House and Capitol Hill. And I believe that those important issues to the American people will be realized and handled very well.

MR. THOMPSON. Mr. President, again thank you so very much for calling. We're deeply grateful. Do come back to Fayetteville.

THE PRESIDENT. Thank you, Jeff. I've been pleased, so has my whole family, at the friendship and hospitality that was extended to us yesterday on our arrival here. It gave us a chance to get our family together, which is a rare occasion for us now.

I'll always remember the confidence that North Carolina people had in me both in the primary and the general election. I've tried to act in the White House in such a way to make the North Carolina people proud of me.

Thank you very much, Jeff.

MR. THOMPSON. Thank you again so much.

NOTE: The interview began at 9:16 a.m. and was recorded for later use by WFNC Radio. The President placed the call from the home of his sister, Ruth Carter Stapleton, where he was staying during his visit to Fayetteville.

Administration's First-Year Accomplishments

Summary of Domestic and National Security and Foreign Policy Accomplishments. December 17, 1977

SUMMARY AND OUTLINE OF FIRST-YEAR DOMESTIC ACCOMPLISHMENTS

SUMMARY

The President's domestic policy achievements during the first year of his administration can be summarized as follows:

I. The President *tackled directly and comprehensively major domestic problems that had been almost completely ignored in previous years.* If actions had not been taken early in this administration, these problems would have worsened, making any future efforts at resolution far more difficult and costly. Among the *major* problems confronted were:

1. *Energy.* The country had no comprehensive energy plan. There was no coherent way to reduce foreign imports (costing the United States $45 billion annually), shift to more abundant energy sources, conserve energy use, or provide fair incentives to encourage domestic energy production. The President proposed a National Energy Plan designed to achieve these goals by:

- reducing the growth rate in energy consumption to 2 percent per year;
- reducing gasoline consumption by 10 percent;
- cutting imports of foreign oil to less than 6 million barrels a day, about half the amount that would otherwise be imported;
- establishing a strategic petroleum reserve supply of at least 1 billion barrels, which could meet all domestic needs for 10 months;
- increasing coal production by more than two-thirds, to over 1 billion tons a year;
- insulating 90 percent of American homes and all new buildings;
- using solar energy in more than 2½ million homes.

The National Energy Plan was the President's most important domestic priority during the year. A House-Senate conference committee is now considering the plan, with final congressional passage expected early next year.

2. *Welfare Reform.* For years, the country has suffered from a welfare system that treats people with similar needs differently, provides incentives for family breakup, discourages work, fails to assist with employment efforts, and leads to waste, fraud, and redtape.

The President proposed a comprehensive overhaul of the Nation's welfare system, the Program for Better Jobs and Income, that will provide cash benefits to 32 million people out of 36 million eligible (current programs—30 million receive benefits out of 40 million eligible). The major elements of the program include:

- creation of 1.4 million public service jobs for low-income families, which provide a job opportunity for every poor family with children;
- tax reduction of $4.9 billion for the working poor, through an increase in the Earned Income Tax Credit;
- improved recipient benefits—establishing a basic benefit of $4,200 for single parent families (higher than the AFDC benefit in 14 States);
- fiscal relief to the States and local governments of $2.1 billion;
- work incentives to ensure that those who work will have higher incomes than those who do not;

• ensuring that every family with a working adult would have a total income above the poverty line.

The Congress is beginning its consideration of the President's welfare package. The Special Welfare Reform Subcommittee established in the House moved quickly on major elements of the proposal and has endorsed several key provisions of the administration plan.

3. *Social Security.* The social security system was in serious danger of having its major trust funds depleted in 1979 (disability fund) and in 1983 (old age and survivors fund). The system was projected to have an estimated deficit of 8.2 percent of taxable payroll over the next 75 years. Since 1975, expenditures by social security have exceeded income, and unless changes were made in the way the system is financed, that trend would continue and worsen.

The President proposed a refinancing of the social security system that would:

• prevent the default of the trust funds;

• bring income and expenses into balance in 1978 and maintain that balance through the end of the century;

• create sufficient reserves to protect the system against sudden declines in revenue caused by unemployment or other economic uncertainties;

• protect the system's financial integrity through the end of the century;

• avoid tax rate increases to workers beyond those already scheduled in law and spread burdens more equitably through the wage base.

The Congress passed a social security bill which incorporates many of the major elements of the administration's proposals, which will ensure the financial stability of the system throughout the rest of the century.

II. *Economic Recovery.* When the President was elected, unemployment was at 8 percent, and the country was still struggling to recover from a severe recession. There were 7.5 million Americans out of work, and 1.4 million full-time workers had been forced to take part-time jobs. It was estimated that the economy operated at approximately $132 billion below its high employment potential. The country lost nearly $35 billion in Federal tax revenues and $10 billion in State and local revenues because of the economy's poor performance.

To alleviate those problems, the President proposed and signed into law a comprehensive package of economic stimulus legislation, totaling $21 billion in Federal expenditures. The main elements of the stimulus package, many of whose effects have already been felt throughout the economy, are:

• $4 billion in public works programs (creating about 200,000 jobs);

• $5 billion in tax reductions, primarily through an increase in the standard deduction, largely benefiting moderate- and low-income workers;

• $1 billion increase in countercyclical revenue sharing;

• expansion by 425,000 job slots (to 725,000 slots) in public service employment and training programs;

• $1.5 billion youth employment program which will create over 200,000 jobs for young people and will double the size of the Job Corps.

As a result, in part, of the stimulus package, the economy *has* improved—unemployment has declined to 6.9 percent; employment has increased to 92 million workers (the largest number in the country's history); per capita, after-tax income (adjusted for inflation) has increased 4 percent over the past 12 months; gross average weekly salary has increased since January from $179 to $195; housing starts have increased 27 percent over the past 12 months; corporate dividends have risen 18 percent over the past 12 months; and consumer savings have increased 14 percent over the past 12 months.

III. The President initiated a number of efforts to make the *Federal Government more efficient and effective.* Among the more significant of those steps are the following:

1. *Reorganization Authority*—proposed and signed into law legislation authorizing the President to reorganize executive agencies and departments, subject to congressional veto.

2. *Reorganizations*—completed three individual reorganizations requiring congressional assent:

  • Department of Energy (legislation combining and streamlining 11 Government entities into one new major department);
  • Executive Office of the President (reorganization plan reducing size of Executive Office of the President by seven entities and reducing the White House staff by 28 percent, compared to the size of the staff inherited from the previous administration);
  • International Communication Agency (reorganization plan combining and streamlining United States Information Agency and cultural functions of the State Department);
  • also completed numerous major intradepartmental and other reorganizations not requiring congressional assent, especially regarding HEW, USDA, DOT, and the intelligence functions of CIA and DOD.

3. *Advisory Committees*—eliminated or proposed to Congress the elimination of over 40 percent of the 1,200 advisory committees extant at the beginning of the administration.

4. *Paperwork Reduction*—initiated a Government-wide paperwork reduction program which, by September 30, reduced the gross paperwork burden imposed by the Federal Government on the private sector by 10 percent and resulted in numerous individual paperwork reforms.

IV. The President initiated several efforts toward *making the Government more open and honest:*

1. *Accessibility by the President.* The President made himself more accessible to the American people than any President in modern history and set a tone for the rest of his administration by the following:

  • holding a regular news conference every 2 weeks;
  • meeting regularly for interviews with non-Washington editors;
  • holding town hall meetings in Clinton, Mass., and Yazoo City, Miss.
  • visiting each Cabinet department and answering questions from its employees;
  • holding a radio call-in show at the White House and a television call-in show in Los Angeles;
  • providing complete financial disclosure of his income and assets;
  • making three trips to different parts of the country, stayed in the homes of citizens and met with a broad range of citizens and officials;
  • holding public policy conferences on energy, water policy, and the problems of the poor.

2. *Financial Disclosure.* The President required, for the first time, that all Cabinet, sub-Cabinet, and White House staff members agree to disclose publicly their income and assets. This has been fully implemented.

3. *Ethics Legislation.* The President proposed ethics legislation requiring public financial disclosure by all public offi-

cials, strengthening restrictions on post-Government service activities of Federal officials, and establishing an Office of Ethics in the Civil Service Commission. It has passed the Senate and is making good progress in the House.

4. *Revolving-Door.* The President required, for the first time, that all Cabinet, sub-Cabinet, regulatory agency, and White House staff members pledge, when they leave Government service, not to conduct business before their former employer for 2 years.

5. *Security Classification*—initiated a comprehensive review of the security classification system; provided for public comment a draft Executive order that would, if issued, greatly reduce unnecessary classifications.

V. The President has reversed years of neglect and treated the problems of poor and middle-class citizens with *compassion and understanding.* Among the major steps taken in that effort are the following:

1. *Food Stamp Reform.* The President proposed and signed into law reforms of the food stamp program which make food stamps available to 2.2 million additional Americans. Among the reforms was the elimination of the purchase requirement.

2. *Minimum Wage.* The President proposed and signed into law an increase in the minimum wage to enable the lowest paid workers to recover from and keep pace with inflation. The minimum wage would increase to $2.65-an-hour by January 1, 1978, increasing the earnings of 4.5 million workers by $2.2 billion. Successive increases would raise the hourly rate to $2.90 in 1979, $3.10 in 1980, and $3.35 in 1981.

3. *Farm Bill.* The President proposed and signed into law a comprehensive agriculture and food bill, giving security to farmers over the next 4 years in the form of price supports, loans, and other programs designed to assure them an adequate income from their products.

4. *Welfare Reform.* The President proposed a comprehensive reform of the welfare system, a Program for Better Jobs and Income. It includes creation of 1.4 million public service jobs by 1981 and the establishment of the uniform cash assistance program to low-income citizens.

5. *Hospital Cost Containment.* The President attempted to control the spiraling costs of hospitalization which often make needed health care too expensive by imposing limits on the annual increase in hospital revenues.

6. *Energy Fuel Assistance.* $200 million was provided to grant emergency fuel assistance to poor people adversely affected by last winter's high energy costs.

7. *Handicapped.* HEW issued regulations prohibiting discrimination against the handicapped in any program receiving Federal financial assistance from HEW, effectively extending civil rights protection to the handicapped.

OUTLINE BY TOPIC OF FIRST-YEAR
DOMESTIC ACCOMPLISHMENTS

Agriculture

1. *Food and Agriculture Act*—proposed and signed into law a comprehensive food and agriculture bill which removes inequities in community programs; establishes the principle that price support loans should be kept at levels enabling American food and fiber to remain competitive in world markets; uses a cost-of-production concept to set income support levels; improves administration of the P.L. 480 (Food for Peace) program; improves the food stamp program by eliminating the purchase requirement, standardizing deductions, lowering net income eligibility limits, and (because of the elimination of the purchase require-

ment) making as many as 2 million persons eligible for food stamps for the first time.

2. *Grain Reserve*—initiated plan to place 30–35 million metric tons of food and feed grains in reserve during the next year.

3. *International Grain Agreement*—initiated negotiations with major grain exporting and importing nations to reach an international agreement stabilizing world grain prices.

4. *Sugar*—negotiated an international sugar agreement which will protect domestic sugar producers while stabilizing world sugar prices (congressional ratification pending).

5. *Emergency Drought Assistance*—proposed and signed into law legislation designed to help farmers hit by the severe droughts of the past spring and summer; provided over $800 million in emergency drought assistance.

Civil Rights and Equal Opportunity

1. *Bakke*—Filed an *amicus* brief in the *Bakke* case supporting affirmative action in college admissions programs, provided they use flexible targets or goals instead of inflexible quotas.

2. *Sex Discrimination*—reaffirmed the validity of and importance of compliance with Executive Order 11375, which prohibits discrimination on the basis of sex in Federal employment.

3. *Title VII*—placed the White House Office under Title VII of the Civil Rights Act, which prohibits discrimination in employment on the basis of sex, race, national origin, or religion.

4. *Equal Employment*—filed the first statewide Federal suit to force employment of women and blacks by police and fire departments (affecting 54 cities and parishes in Louisiana).

5. *Handicapped*—issued Section 504 regulations to guarantee equal access to programs receiving Federal financial assistance.

6. *Minority Business*—took several actions to aid businesses owned by members of minority groups:

—placed $100 million in Federal deposits into minority-owned banks;

—supported and signed a public works act requiring that 10 percent of the $4 billion in public works contracts let during 1977–78 be "set aside" for minority-owned programs;

—approved 15 percent "set-aside" for minority businesses in construction on the Northeast Corridor railroad;

—directed Federal agencies to double their purchases of services and goods from minority-owned firms during the next 2 years, reaching a total of $2 billion.

7. *High-Level Appointments*—appointed more blacks, women, and members of ethnic minorities to executive-level positions than any other administration in history.

Civil Service

1. *Pay Raise*—approved a 7.05 percent cost-of-living pay raise for Federal employees.

2. *Hatch Act Reform*—supported reform of the Hatch Act to permit most civil service employees to participate more fully in the political process, without politicizing the civil service. This has passed the House.

3. *Civil Service Reorganization and Reform*—initiated, under the Federal Personnel Management Project, a review of the Civil Service Commission and the civil service employment and promotion laws and regulations. Announcement of proposed reforms will come next year.

4. *Part-time Employment*—directed Cabinet members and agency heads to increase the number of part-time jobs, so that the elderly, the handicapped, and

those with children can more easily obtain Federal employment.

5. *Presidential Interns*—created a Presidential Management Intern Program to bring 250 public administration students annually to Washington for one year of service in the Federal Government.

6. *Protection*—directed that Federal employees not lose their Federal employment solely because of reorganization.

Consumer Protection

1. *Consumer Agency*—proposed the creation of a consumer protection office to represent consumer interests throughout the Federal Government; passed House committee.

2. *Fair Debt Collection Practices*—supported and signed into law the Fair Debt Collection Practices Act, which will prohibit abusive and unfair techniques of debt collection.

3. *Citizen Participation*—supported legislation to reimburse citizens for participation in court and agency proceedings, to expand class action authority, and to expand citizens' standing to sue the Government.

4. *Appointments*—appointed consumer advocates to major regulatory positions.

5. *Passive Restraints*—required automobile occupant crash protection through passive restraints, which will save 9,000 lives and prevent tens of thousands of injuries each year.

Economy

1. *Unemployment*. Unemployment decreased from 8 percent last November to 6.9 percent this November.

2. *Employment*. Employment has increased during the past 12 months by almost 4 million—from 88 million to 92 million. This is the largest number of people with jobs in the Nation's history. In addition, the proportion of the population holding civilian jobs has increased to 57.8 percent, a record high.

3. *Inflation.* The rise in the Consumer Price Index declined from an annual rate of approximately 9 percent early this year to an annual rate of 4 percent in October.

4. *Duration of Unemployment.* The average duration of unemployment has decreased during the past 12 months from 15.5 weeks to 13.8 weeks. The number of persons out of work for 15 weeks or longer has decreased during this period by 25 percent.

5. *After-Tax Income.* After-tax income per person, adjusted for inflation, has increased 4 percent during the past 12 months.

6. *Salaries.* Gross average weekly salary has increased since January from $179 to $195.

7. *Housing Starts.* Housing starts have increased 27 percent during the past 12 months; residential building permits have increased 25 percent during the same period. Housing starts are at a yearly rate of over 2 million units.

8. *Industrial Production.* Industrial production has increased 7 percent during the past 12 months. Since late 1976, the use of industrial capacity has increased about 3 percent.

9. *Economic Profits.* Economic profits of corporations (before taxes) have increased 11 percent during the past year.

10. *Corporate Dividends.* Corporate dividend payments have risen 18 percent during the past 12 months.

11. *Business Capital Outlays* (adjusted for inflation). Business capital outlays are 7 percent more than they were this time last year.

12. *Consumer Savings.* Consumer savings in the form of time and savings deposits have increased 14 percent during the past 12 months.

Elderly

1. *Mandatory Retirement*—supported raising from 65 to 70 years of age the coverage of the Age Discrimination in Employment Act, thereby prohibiting employers from requiring retirement prior to age 70; supported removal of a mandatory retirement age from the civil service laws. Bills have passed both Houses of Congress and are now in conference.

2. *Social Security*—proposed a comprehensive refinancing of the social security system in order to ensure the financial stability of the system for the rest of this century. Social security legislation incorporating many of the administration's proposals was enacted on December 15.

3. *Medicare*—proposed and signed into law the Medicare and Medicaid Anti-Fraud and Abuse Act, which will substantially reduce fraud and help to lower patient costs; cancelled, as part of the revised FY '78 budget, the proposed increase in Medicare patient payments.

4. *Trans-Bus*—required public transportation authorities receiving Federal funds to purchase Trans-Bus, a vehicle accessible to the elderly and physically handicapped, after 1979.

5. *Hospital Cost Containment*—proposed legislation to control the rapidly increasing costs of hospitalization by limiting total hospital revenues.

6. *Housing Assistance*—provided $850 million in FY '78 for assistance to the elderly for 25,000 to 30,000 homes.

7. *Emergency Fuel Assistance*—provided $200 million to help the poor, many of whom were elderly, pay their fuel bills during the past winter; provided additional money for weatherization and winterization programs for the elderly poor.

Employment

1. *Unemployment*—unemployment rate was 8 percent at the time of the 1976 election; latest figures (November) show that it has dropped to 6.9 percent.

2. *Public Service Jobs*—proposed and signed into law an expansion of the public service jobs program (CETA) from 300,000 jobs to 725,000 jobs by March 1978. This is the largest public service jobs program since the 1930's.

3. *Youth Jobs*—proposed and signed into law three new youth jobs programs—the National Youth Conservation Corps, the Youth Community Conservation and Improvement Projects, and the Comprehensive Employment and Training Programs—creating 200,000 new jobs; also, doubled the size of the Job Corps.

4. *Public Works Job*—proposed and signed into law a $4-billion public works program, which will create nearly 200,000 jobs.

5. *Minimum Wage*—proposed increasing the minimum wage to enable the lowest paid workers to recover from and keep pace with inflation; signed a bill increasing the minimum wage to $2.65 an hour by January 1, 1978, directly increasing the earnings of 4.5 million workers by $2.2 billion. Successive increases will raise the hourly rate to $2.90 in 1979, $3.10 in 1980, and $3.35 in 1981.

6. *Mine Safety and Health*—supported and signed into law a bill to improve the safety and health of the Nation's 400,000 miners, by placing all mines under a single safety and health program administered in the Labor Department.

7. *Labor Law Reform*—proposed the first set of comprehensive labor law reforms in 30 years. The reforms would eliminate delays in NLRB procedures and strengthen NLRB sanctions against labor law violators; passed the House.

8. *Undocumented Aliens*—proposed a comprehensive program to control the presence of millions of undocumented aliens in the country. The program in-

cludes a prohibition against employers' hiring undocumented aliens.

9. *Welfare Reform*—proposed comprehensive reform of the Nation's welfare system, including the creation of 1.4 million public service jobs by 1981.

10. *Supplemental Unemployment Benefits*—supported and signed into law a bill to extend Federal supplemental unemployment benefits for 26 additional weeks.

11. *Humphrey-Hawkins*—endorsed the Humphrey-Hawkins full employment bill, establishing a 4-percent unemployment rate and reasonable price stability as national goals for 1983.

Energy

1. *National Energy Plan*—proposed the Nation's first comprehensive energy policy. Bills have passed both Houses of Congress and are now in conference.

2. *Emergency Natural Gas*—proposed and signed into law a bill that permitted the President to make emergency allocations of natural gas during last winter's shortage and permitted emergency purchase of unregulated gas.

3. *Department of Energy*—proposed and signed into law a bill to combine 11 Government entities into one Cabinet-level Department of Energy.

4. *Alaska Natural Gas*—negotiated an agreement with Canada concerning a joint transportation route (the ALCAN Project) for Alaskan natural gas; secured congressional approval of the route decision.

5. *Strategic Petroleum Reserve*—undertook to expand the National Strategic Petroleum Reserve from 500 million barrels to 1 billion barrels of oil, giving the country a 10-month stockpile.

6. *Nuclear Nonproliferation*—proposed legislation to control the worldwide spread of nuclear fuels by applying uniform standards for licensing of nuclear exports, establishing criteria for the negotiation of new nuclear technology exchange agreements, and authorizing regulations for more expeditious review of nuclear export licenses; passed the House.

Environment

1. *Clean Air*—supported and signed into law amendments to the Clean Air Act, including strict auto emission and stationary air standards.

2. *Strip Mining*—supported and signed into law a strip mining bill (twice vetoed by Ford), which will set the first Federal environmental standards for strip mining.

3. *Water Resource Projects*—initiated a major review of Federal water resource development projects to ensure that those recommended for funding in FY '78 and future years are economically and environmentally sound as well as safe; signed legislation halting nine previously authorized projects.

4. *Redwoods*—proposed a moratorium on logging in Redwood National Park; submitted legislation to expand the park and protect it from further commercial use.

5. *Water Pollution*—proposed amendments to the Federal Water Pollution Control Act, involving reform of the sewage treatment construction grant program and strict protection for Federal wetlands; amendments have passed a House-Senate conference.

6. *Environmental Message*—submitted to Congress a comprehensive environmental message which included support for four new wilderness areas, eight new wild and scenic parks, and water resource policy reforms.

7. *Whaling*—ordered protection of whales within 200 miles of U.S. coast; cooperated with the International Whaling Commission on bowhead whales; and

supported a 10-year, worldwide moratorium on commercial whaling.

8. *Alaska Lands*—proposed to Congress the protection of 93 million acres of Alaska Federal lands (d–2 lands), permitting the creation or expansion of 19 national parks and reserves, 14 national wildlife refuges, and 42 wild and scenic rivers.

9. *Water Policy*—began work on a comprehensive Federal water policy.

10. *Oil Spills*—proposed legislation establishing liability for oil tanker spills and leading to the development of regulations to prevent future spills.

Government Efficiency, Reorganization, and Regulatory Reform

1. *Reorganization Authority*—proposed and signed into law legislation authorizing the President to reorganize executive agencies and departments, subject to congressional veto.

2. *Reorganizations*—completed three individual reorganizations requiring congressional assent:

—Department of Energy (legislation combining and streamlining 11 Government entities into one new major department);

—Executive Office of the President (reorganization plan reducing size of Executive Office of the President by seven entities and reducing the White House staff by 28 percent, compared to the size of the staff inherited from the previous administration);

—International Communication Agency (reorganization plan combining and streamlining United States Information Agency and cultural functions of the State Department);

—also completed other reorganizations not requiring congressional as-

sent, including HEW, USDA, DOT, and the intelligence functions of CIA and DOD.

3. *Advisory Committees*—eliminated or proposed to Congress the elimination of over 40 percent of the 1,200 advisory committees extant at the beginning of the administration.

4. *Paperwork Reduction*—initiated a Government-wide paperwork reduction program which, by September 30, had reduced the gross paperwork burden imposed on the public by 12 percent and which had achieved such particular reforms as these:

—10 items were cut from the standard 1040A income tax form, which will reduce the time required to fill out 1977 returns by an estimated 19 million hours;

—OSHA is reducing its paperwork burdens (particularly on small businesses) by 50 percent;

—HEW has reduced its required paperwork by over 10 million hours, a 23-percent reduction, including a cut of 5½ million hours in the Office of Education's reporting requirements on students.

5. *Reduction in Regulatory Burden*—initiated a program to reduce the burden of Federal regulation, including:

—promulgation of an Executive order requiring all agencies to disclose in advance their agendas for regulatory action; assuring that agency heads will subject regulation writers to managerial control; establishing procedures for public comment on proposed regulations before they take effect; and establishing procedures to review and discard outmoded regulations;

—establishment of reform programs in HEW, where "Operation Common Sense" will rewrite all regulations within 5 years, and in OSHA, which has eliminated 1,100 unnecessary regulations and other practices that annoy small businesses to no good purpose;

—development of programs to find and eliminate overlapping and duplicative regulations, especially those affecting equal employment opportunity enforcement and toxic substances;

—establishment of policies to replace regulation with competition, especially in the airline, motor carrier, and communications industries.

6. *Zero-Based Budgeting*—ordered the use of zero-based budgeting by OMB and the executive departments in assessing the merits of all Federal programs.

7. *Written Regulations*—took steps to make Federal regulations shorter and more nearly comprehensible.

Health

1. *Hospital Cost Containment*—proposed legislation limiting increases in hospital revenues; passed Senate Health Subcommittee.

2. *Mental Health Commission*—established a Mental Health Commission, with Rosalynn Carter as honorary Chairman, to review national efforts in mental health services; final report due in April 1978.

3. *Medicare and Medicaid Fraud*—supported and signed into law a bill designed to halt Medicare and Medicaid fraud.

4. *Immunization Program*—began an immunization program for more than 20 million children unprotected against communicable childhood diseases.

5. *CHAP*—proposed legislation increasing from 55 percent to 75 percent the average Federal payment to the States for health care for poor children.

CHAP is the proposed new Child Health Assessment Program.

6. *Physician Assistants*—supported and signed into law a bill making Medicare and Medicaid reimbursement available to physician assistants in rural clinics.

7. *Medical Uses of Illegal Drugs*—directed the scientific reexamination of marijuana and heroin for possible medical uses, particularly in the treatment of cancer.

8. *Public Health Service Hospitals*—restored money in FY '78 budget to keep open eight public health service hospitals; signed into law.

9. *Health Professionals*—proposed $101-million increase for FY '78 budget for health professionals training; signed into law.

10. *National Health Insurance*—established National Health Insurance Advisory Group to help develop a comprehensive national health insurance plan; conducted hearings in all 50 States.

Housing and Community Development

1. *Increased Funding*—proposed and signed into law the Housing and Community Development Act, which ensures housing for an additional 344,000 low- and moderate-income families; increases FHA mortgage insurance limits for a single family home from $45,000 to $60,000 and lowers downpayment requirements; increases community development levels by total of $12.5 billion over 3 years, giving a disproportionate share of the money to the most distressed urban areas; and creates the Urban Development Action Grant program to provide an additional $1.2 billion over 3 years to the most distressed urban areas.

2. *Supplemental Housing Authorization*—proposed and signed into law a bill increasing subsidies for housing construc-

tion, public housing operations, and houses for Indians.

3. *Increased Assisted Housing Starts*—doubled to 114,000 the total starts for assisted housing programs between FY '76 and FY '77. This represents the highest level in HUD's history.

4. *Eviction Moratorium*—imposed moratorium on evictions from HUD-owned properties pending the development of a policy to assist tenants in foreclosed FHA-insured properties.

5. *Housing Counseling*—inaugurated counseling programs for people contemplating the purchase of their first home and for homeowners in danger of defaulting on their mortgages.

6. *Office of Neighborhoods*—created special office at HUD to help communities and neighborhoods with programs of local revitalization.

7. *Urban and Regional Policy Group/ National Urban Policy*—reactivated the interagency Urban and Regional Policy Group and made it responsible for drafting a comprehensive national urban policy.

8. *Anti-Redlining Regulations*—promulgated regulations prohibiting discriminatory mortgage credit practices.

9. *South Bronx*—created an interagency task force to prepare plans for completely rehabilitating the South Bronx.

10. *Urban Homesteading*—extended the Urban Homesteading program to 15 more cities, helping to restore neighborhoods while increasing home ownership opportunities for families of modest means.

Integrity and Openness

1. *Financial Disclosure*—required all Cabinet, sub-Cabinet, and White House staff appointees to disclose publicly their income and assets.

2. *Revolving Door*—required all Cabinet, sub-Cabinet, regulatory agency, and White House staff appointees to pledge not to conduct business with their agency until at least 2 years after leaving it.

3. *Ethics Legislation*—proposed ethics legislation requiring public financial disclosure by all Federal officials; increasing the restrictions on their service after leaving Federal employment; establishing an Office of Ethics in the Civil Service Commission; and authorizing appointment of a temporary special prosecutor to handle cases involving certain executive branch officials; passed the Senate.

4. *Lobbying Reform*—supported strong registration and disclosure legislation.

5. *Security Classification System*—initiated a comprehensive study of the Government's security classification system; proposed reforming the system and reducing unnecessary classification in a draft Executive order which is now being circulated for public comment.

Justice

1. *Pardon*—issued pardon for all selective service law violators from the Vietnam war period.

2. *Merit Selection*—established merit selection panels for the U.S. Circuit Courts of Appeals.

3. *Prisoner Exchange*—supported and signed into law legislation to implement treaties permitting the exchange of prisoners with Mexico and Canada; these transfers are now taking place.

4. *LEAA*—initiated a thorough review of the operations of the LEAA, which will soon lead to an announcement of its comprehensive reform.

5. *Juvenile Justice*—supported and signed into law a bill extending the Juvenile Justice and Delinquency Prevention Act through 1980 and strengthening Federal efforts against juvenile delinquency.

6. *Foreign Intelligence Wiretapping*—developed legislation that would, for the first time, require court warrants for foreign intelligence wiretapping done by the U.S. Government; passed Senate Judiciary Committee.

7. *Marijuana*—supported the elimination of all Federal criminal penalties for the possession of up to one ounce of marijuana.

8. *Court Reform*—developed legislation to reduce court delays by expanding the jurisdiction of Federal magistrates; passed the Senate.

9. *Criminal Code*—helped revise a bill consolidating and simplifying the criminal code.

10. *Fraud*—began using advanced computer technology at HEW to uncover Medicaid fraud by physicians and pharmacists, as a result of which more than 2,000 cases of suspected fraud are now in the hands of Federal and State prosecutors; also began a nationwide effort to identify Federal employees who are illegally receiving welfare benefits.

Social Services

1. *Food Stamps*—proposed and signed into law as part of the farm bill, major reforms in the food stamps program simplifying it, increasing participation by the poor, and eliminating the purchase requirement. As a result, 2.2 million more people will become eligible for food stamps.

2. *Summer Food Service Program*—proposed and signed into law stricter requirements for Summer Food Service program sponsors, more assistance to poor children, and harsher penalties for fraud.

3. *Title XX*—proposed a permanent increase of $200 million for day care services.

4. *Child Care*—proposed improvements in the foster care program, procedural protection for children, subsidized adoptions for hard-to-place children, and more money for child welfare children services; passed by the Senate Finance Committee.

5. *Indochina Refugees*—proposed and signed into law an extension of the Indochina Refugee Assistance Act, which helps the States resettle Indochinese refugees.

6. *Handicapped*—issued regulations prohibiting discrimination against the handicapped in any program receiving money from HEW—similar requirements will be issued by other departments; sponsored the White House Conference on Handicapped Individuals.

7. *Emergency Fuel Assistance*—provided $200 million to help the poor pay their fuel bills last winter; program administered through CSA.

8. *Welfare Reform*—proposed a comprehensive reform of the welfare system, substituting in place of existing programs a Program for Better Jobs and Income, which includes a consolidating cash assistance proposal, 1.4 million public service jobs, and $3.3 billion in tax relief for the working poor.

9. *Public Broadcasting*—proposed legislation to increase Federal support for public radio and television, insulate them better from political influences, and increase the amount of public participation in decisions affecting them.

Trade

1. *Color TV's*—negotiated an orderly marketing agreement to reduce imports of color television sets from Japan from 2.7 million in 1976 to 1.75 million annually for the next 3 years, a 35-percent reduction.

2. *Shoes*—negotiated orderly marketing agreements to reduce imports of shoes from Taiwan and South Korea from 200

million pairs in 1976 to an average of 162 million pairs during the next 4 years.

3. *Anti-Boycott*—helped to develop and signed into law a bill prohibiting American participation in secondary economic boycotts by foreign countries such as the Arab boycott of Israel.

4. *Steel*—announced a comprehensive program to help the domestic steel industry by establishing a "reference price system," which will curb the dumping of under-priced, imported steel.

Transportation

1. *U.S.–U.K. Air Agreement*—negotiated a new air services agreement with the United Kingdom.

2. *Passive Restraint*—ordered airbags or automatic belts to be placed on all new cars by 1984. Such a program is expected to save 9,000 lives and prevent tens of thousands of injuries per year.

3. *Auto Efficiency Standards*—raised fuel efficiency standards for new cars to 22 mpg in 1981, 24 mpg in 1982, 26 mpg in 1983, and 27 mpg in 1984. These will save approximately 1 million barrels of oil per day by 1990.

4. *Concorde Noise Rules*—proposed the first noise rules to govern domestic flights of the Concorde SST and any future SST's. The proposed rules would permit Concordes to use domestic airports only if they meet reasonable, nondiscriminatory noise rules set by local airport operators. New SST's would be required to meet the 1969 subsonic noise standards.

5. *Trans-Bus*—required public transportation authorities receiving Federal funds to purchase Trans-Bus, a vehicle accessible to the handicapped, after 1979.

6. *Airline Deregulation*—supported congressional efforts to deregulate the airline industry; passed Senate Commerce Committee.

7. *International Airfares*—approved Laker Airways' application for low-cost, transatlantic service and subsequent applications from other airlines offering reduced transatlantic and advance-purchase fares.

8. *Northeast Corridor Construction*—began work on the $1.7 billion Northeast Corridor railbed improvement program which will facilitate high-speed rail travel between Boston and Washington, D.C.

9. *Waterway Use Fees*—urged congressional passage of waterway user fees; different versions have passed the Senate and House.

10. *Vehicle Safety*—improved the vehicle safety defect program, causing the recall of 8 million vehicles for safety-related defects.

11. *Cargo Airline Deregulation*—supported and signed into law a bill to deregulate the cargo airline industry.

Veterans

1. *Discharge Review*—established a discharge review program to permit upgrading of less-than-honorable discharges for Vietnam era veterans; signed a bill expanding this principle to cover all veterans.

2. *Disability Compensation*—proposed and signed into law a bill giving a 6.6 percent cost-of-living increase to recipients of veterans disability compensation, benefiting 2.5 million people.

3. *GI Bill Benefits*—proposed and signed into law a bill raising by 6.6 percent the GI bill educational assistance benefits for 1.7 million Vietnam-era veterans.

4. *Pensions*—proposed and signed into law a 6.5-percent increase in pensions for 2.3 million veterans.

5. *Project HIRE*—established, in association with the National Alliance of

Businessmen, Project HIRE to provide jobs in private enterprise for Vietnam veterans.

6. *CETA Jobs*—proposed that 35 percent of the jobs under the new CETA Title VI program be reserved for Vietnam veterans; signed legislation giving priority to Vietnam veterans in the CETA Jobs program.

Education

1. *Comprehensive Education Policy.* The Federal Interagency Committee on Education is drafting the Government's first comprehensive education policy. Their proposal examines the rationale for Federal aid and sets forth priorities for educational support.

2. *Increased Funding.* The administration proposed the first major increase in Federal aid to elementary and secondary education in 8 years, adding about $1 billion to the Ford FY '78 budget. The money bolstered basic grants student aid, programs for disadvantaged and handicapped children, school desegregation, and Project Head Start.

Miscellaneous

To date (12/15/77), the President has:

—sent 49 treaties and legislative messages to Congress

—signed 235 bills and allowed no bills to become law without his signature

—vetoed two bills (the ERDA authorization bill and the rabbit meat inspection bill)

—held 27 bill signing ceremonies

—held 21 national press conferences

—given 16 interviews to groups of non-Washington reporters

—given 28 individual interviews

—held 60 meetings with foreign heads of state or government

—hosted 17 state and working dinners at the White House

—received 2.3 million letters and cards.

SUMMARY OF FIRST-YEAR ACCOMPLISHMENTS IN NATIONAL SECURITY AND FOREIGN POLICY

In his commencement address at the University of Notre Dame on May 22, the President outlined the objectives of his foreign policy and described "the strands that connect our actions overseas with our essential character as a nation."

He declared his belief that "we can have a foreign policy that is democratic, that is based on fundamental values, and that uses power and influence . . . for humane purposes. We can also have a foreign policy that the American people both support . . . and understand . . .

"Our policy must be open; it must be candid; it must be one of constructive global involvement, resting on five cardinal principles . . .

"First, we have reaffirmed America's commitment to human rights as a fundamental tenet of our foreign policy . . .

"Second, we have moved deliberately to reinforce the bonds among . . . democracies . . .

"Third, we have moved to engage the Soviet Union in a joint effort to halt the strategic arms race . . .

"Fourth, we are taking deliberate steps to improve the chances of lasting peace in the Middle East . . .

"And fifth, we are attempting . . . to reduce the danger of nuclear proliferation and the worldwide spread of conventional weapons . . ."

The administration, by its work in international affairs this year, has sought to carry out the objectives which the President set forth at Notre Dame. Among the principal accomplishments in the realm of foreign policy and national security are these:

HUMAN RIGHTS

The President has strengthened our human rights policy, and we are letting it be known clearly that the United States stands with the victims of repression. We are also working to advance the full range of human rights, economic and social as well as civil and political. He has signed the American Convention on Human Rights, the International Covenant on Economic, Social, and Cultural Rights. Our foreign assistance programs will reflect more clearly our human rights concerns. We have encouraged several countries to permit inspection visits from the International Committee of the Red Cross. We are strongly supporting international organizations concerned with human rights, particularly the Inter-American Commission on Human Rights, whose budget was tripled this year.

NUCLEAR PROLIFERATION

The administration has developed a comprehensive policy covering domestic and export activities and has initiated an international, technical evaluation of the entire nuclear fuel cycle. The President signed Protocol I of the Treaty of Tlatelolco, which creates a nuclear weapons-free zone in Latin America.

ARMS TRANSFERS

For the first time, the United States has adopted a policy of restraining both the number and the kinds of American arms sold abroad. We have also begun to discuss restraint with other major arms suppliers.

STRATEGIC ARMS LIMITATION TALKS

At the end of the last administration, the SALT negotiations were at a stalemate. The efforts of this administration, beginning with the March proposal set forth by Secretary Vance in Moscow, have resulted in major progress in the SALT negotiations. We are now working on a comprehensive settlement consisting of a treaty to last through 1985, a 3-year protocol, and a Statement of Principles to guide the SALT III negotiations. Almost all the major issues are now resolved, and we anticipate completion of a SALT II treaty in the early part of next year.

PANAMA CANAL TREATIES

After 14 years of negotiations under four U.S. Presidents, the United States and Panama adjusted their relationship as it applies to the Panama Canal. President Carter and General Omar Torrijos signed two canal treaties on September 7, 1977, which would gradually transfer responsibility for the operation and defense of a neutral canal to Panama. The treaties give the United States the permanent right to defend the canal's neutrality.

COMPREHENSIVE TEST BAN

Negotiations are underway on a treaty banning all nuclear explosions.

NORTH-SOUTH RELATIONS

The United States image in the less-developed world and the United Nations has changed dramatically from that of an adversary to that of a potential partner. In the Security Council debate on Africa, we played a mediating role. Our arms control policies have made a favorable impression on the United Nations' annual review of disarmament issues. We played a constructive role in the Maputo and Lagos conference. And we participated, for the first time, in an ASEAN (Association of Southeast Asian Nations) ministerial meeting. The appointment of Ambassador Andrew Young highlighted our concern for the Third World.

WESTERN EUROPE

The administration has: participated in a successful Belgrade CSCE conference (Conference on Security and Cooperation in Europe), including a review of human rights; prepared another MBFR (mutual and balanced force reductions) proposal to advance talks; inaugurated four NATO efforts (the long-term defense program; the short-term improvements; the "two-way street" in defense purchases; the East-West study); agreed to provide a $300-million loan and forged a multination consortium to help democracy in Portugal; and secured a major IMF loan for Italy.

SOVIET UNION-EASTERN EUROPE

The administration has put the U.S.-Soviet relationship on a more reciprocal, realistic, and what we hope will be an ultimately more productive basis for both nations. The administration has improved relations with various Eastern European countries, including Yugoslavia, as a result of the Vice President's visit, and Poland, as a result of Secretary Kreps' visit and the President's scheduled state visit.

ARAB-ISRAELI CONFLICT

The administration stressed the need for a comprehensive settlement which has three core elements: definition of the nature of the peace, establishment of recognized borders and security, and resolution of the Palestinian question. We have urged, with considerable success, the Arabs and the Israelis to be forthcoming on peace commitments, direct negotiations, and peace treaties. We have supported the Sadat-Begin dialog.

PEOPLE'S REPUBLIC OF CHINA

The administration has followed the Shanghai Communique in efforts toward normalization of relations, while emphasizing the mutuality of efforts necessary to complete the process. Recognizing their strategic importance, we have also continued to develop a consultative relationship with the Chinese on global affairs.

KOREA

The details of the Korean ground troop withdrawal plan have been designed to alleviate major Asian apprehensions that the United States is in the process of disengaging from the region.

VIETNAM

The administration has started the process of normalizing relations through talks in Paris and has established a mechanism to continue to try to account for our servicemen still missing in action.

AFRICA

Vice President Mondale informed Prime Minister Vorster in Vienna that U.S.-South Africa relations depended upon South Africa moving away from apartheid. With the British, we offered a plan for Rhodesian independence. We initiated a Five Power Group to negotiate toward an independent Namibia. We have restored good relations, based on mutual respect, with black African states of all political leanings.

LATIN AMERICA

The administration has developed a new global approach to Latin America and the Caribbean, one which recognizes the diversity of the region rather than one which pretends a single policy identified by a simple slogan. (This approach has been well received in the region.) The President signed the Panama Canal treaties. Through direct negotiations with Cuba, we have concluded a fisheries agreement and established an interest section in each country. We have ratified an exchange of prisoners treaty with Mexico and negotiated one with Bolivia. We have adopted a comprehensive policy for the Caribbean and have been joined by 28 nations and 16 international institutions to establish a Caribbean Group for Cooperation in Economic Development. We have dramatically improved our relations with a number of countries, including Venezuela, Jamaica, Peru, and Mexico.

LONDON SUMMIT

With the leaders of major industrial democracies, the President reached agreement at the London Summit on a common program for international economic cooperation.

MULTILATERAL TRADE NEGOTIATIONS

The administration has reached agreement with the European Economic Community on a timetable for negotiations, breaking a long stalemate.

DEFENSE AND SECURITY

The administration has formulated a comprehensive, national defense strategy which includes an overall American posture toward the Soviet Union. The President reached a decision not to produce the B-1 bomber but to proceed with cruise missiles.

INTELLIGENCE

The administration has reorganized the intelligence agencies and has taken comprehensive steps to protect telecommunications.

INTERNATIONAL COMMUNICATIONS

The administration has established a new International Communication Agency to replace the United States Information Agency and the Bureau of Educational and Cultural Affairs in the Department of State.

DEFENSE BUDGET REDUCTION

The President met his campaign pledge to cut military spending by $5 to $7 billion. The Ford budget for fiscal year 1978 was $123 billion. The Carter budget is $117 billion, as approved by Congress.

Meeting With Prime Minister Menahem Begin of Israel

White House Statement Issued Following the Second Meeting.   December 17, 1977

The President and Prime Minister Begin and their advisers tonight continued the round of discussions begun yesterday morning. They explored further Prime Minister Begin's latest proposals for progress toward comprehensive peace in the Middle East and the next steps to be taken to advance the peace negotiations. The President expressed his appreciation for the Prime Minister's constructive approach and his conviction that Prime Minister Begin and President Sadat, together, are taking important steps down the road to a just and comprehensive peace.

President Carter welcomed the direct talks which will soon be held between Prime Minister Begin and President Sadat. President Carter told the Prime Minister that he believes the current discussions between Israel and Egypt, based on the good will and dedication to peace both have manifested, now more than ever hold out promise of real progress. The United States considers that the understanding and statesmanship which the Prime Minister is demonstrating make a notable contribution.

The President pledged the continuing cooperation of the United States in whatever ways the parties find useful. The President undertook to remain in close touch with Prime Minister Begin and President Sadat and will look forward to learning of their further progress in the mutual search for a comprehensive peace. The President shares with them their dedication to fulfilling this historic opportunity to bring peace to a region too long burdened with misunderstanding and war.

NOTE: Secretary of State Cyrus R. Vance read the statement to reporters in the Briefing Room at the White House following the meeting between the President and the Prime Minister.

National Commission on Neighborhoods

Appointment of 15 Members to the Commission. December 19, 1977

The President today announced the appointment of the following persons to be members of the National Commission on Neighborhoods. They are:

DR. ETHEL D. ALLEN, 48, of Philadelphia, Pa., surgeon and a member of the city council in Philadelphia;

ANNE BARTLEY, 33, of Little Rock, Ark., commissioner of the Little Rock Planning Commission;

NICHOLAS R. CARBONE, 41, of Hartford, Conn., majority leader of the city council in Hartford;

GALE CINCOTTA, 45, of Chicago, Ill., executive director of the National Training and Information Center;

HAROLD W. GREENWOOD, 46, of Minneapolis, Minn., chairman of the board and president of Midwest Federal Savings & Loan Association;

MAYNARD JACKSON, 39, of Atlanta, Ga., mayor of Atlanta;

NORMAN KRUMHOLZ, 50, of Cleveland, Ohio, director of the Cleveland City Planning Commission;

DAVID C. LIZARRAGA, 36, of Los Angeles, Calif., executive director of the East Los Angeles Community Union;

JOHN MCCLAUGHRY, 40, of Concord, Vt., president of the Institute for Liberty and Community;

VICTORIA M. MONGIARDO, 38, of Hyattsville, Md., with the National Center for Urban Ethnic Affairs;

ARTHUR J. NAPARSTEK, 39, of Washington, D.C., director of the Washington Public Affairs Center;

ROBERT B. O'BRIEN, JR., of Newark, N.J., president, director, and chief executive officer of Carteret Savings and Loan Association;

MACLER C. SHEPARD, 59, of St. Louis, Mo., president of Jeff-Vander-Lou, Inc.;

PETER SANDOR UJVAGI, 28, of Toledo, Ohio, vice president for sales at E & C Manufacturing Co., Inc.;

BATHRUS B. WILLIAMS, 62, of Washington, D.C., with the National Institute of Health Project.

Social Security Amendments of 1977

Remarks at the Bill Signing Ceremony. December 20, 1977

THE PRESIDENT. Since the social security system was evolved under the administration of Franklin Roosevelt, it's been a sacred pact between the employees and the employers with the framework established and guaranteed by the Government to be sure that the working people of this Nation had some guarantee of security after they reached the age of retirement or after they were disabled and unable to earn their own livelihood.

In recent years, because of the highest unemployment rate since the Great Depression and the greatest inflation rate since the Civil War, the integrity of the social security system has been in doubt. This was an unanticipated drain on the resources of the reserve funds.

When I campaigned throughout the country for 2 years, one of the most frequent questions asked me by working family members and also by those who had already retired was what can be done to assure us that the integrity of the social security system will be maintained. It's a very difficult issue.

It is never easy for a politically elected person to raise taxes. But the Congress has shown sound judgment and political courage in restoring the social security system to a sound basis.

This legislation is wise. It's been evolved after very careful and long preparation. It focuses the increased tax burdens, which were absolutely mandatory, in a way that is of least burden to the families of this Nation who are most in need of a sound income.

The level of payments were raised for those who are wealthier in our country where they can most easily afford increased payments. In the past they've avoided the rate being applied to their much higher income than the average working family.

At the same time, the Congress has removed the unnecessarily stringent limits on how much a retired person can earn and still draw [from] the social security system for which that person has paid during his or her working years. The limit will now be increased to $6,000-per-year income over 2 or 3 years without losing social security benefits.

This legislation also moves to eliminate discrimination because of sex. It removes references to the sex of the recipient.

The most important thing, of course, is that without this legislation, the social security reserve funds would have begun to be bankrupt in just a year or two, by 1979. Now this legislation will guarantee that from 1980 to the year 2030, the social security funds will be sound.

I want to congratulate the congressional leaders assembled behind me here—the chairmen of the appropriate committees, Senator Long, Ullman, Tip O'Neill, our Speaker, Bob Byrd, Senator Nelson, and many other Members who have worked so long and hard to guarantee that this legislation might be passed. It was not an easy task, but I believe that everyone in this Nation who values the concept of social security has been well served. And I want to thank these courageous and farsighted congressional leaders for their bold and appropriate action.

[*At this point, the President signed H.R. 9346 into law.*]

Well, Mr. Chairmen, you all did a good job.

REPRESENTATIVE TUCKER. Mr. President, I am flattered. I guess as one of the younger members of this crowd and of the Congress——

THE PRESIDENT. You'll pay more into the system. [*Laughter*]

REPRESENTATIVE TUCKER. That's right. Frankly, I hope the time is not too far distant when I can pay more on my own salary, as younger people all over the country have to pay on their salary.

My father was manager of the social security system in Arkansas all of my life before his death. I grew up with a respect and understanding of social security and its importance for the working people of this country.

And I am very proud that it was a Democratic President, Democratic committee chairmen, Democratic congressional leaders, and a Democratic administration that could give us this painful but absolutely necessary help to the social security system of this country. It's why I supported you and voted for you. I knew you had the guts to do it. And I'm proud to be here today.

THE PRESIDENT. Thank you, Jim Guy, very much.

SENATOR LONG. Mr. President, nobody really enjoys voting for taxes if he has to run for office. I know you know that as well as all the rest of us do. But in view of the fact that we are going to be paying anyway, I think that most people would prefer to pay a little more if need be, as they will, and have a sound program rather than be worried about whether or not the program will be financed.

Nelson Cruikshank and some others who were advocating the original social security bill are here, and Wilbur Cohen was here, who was part of it back at that time. And they advocated and visualized a system where people would be free of fear in old age. And that's what we're doing with this bill. We are proud to participate with you.

THE PRESIDENT. Thank you very much.

REPRESENTATIVE ULLMAN. Mr. President, I am sorry that our subcommittee chairman, Jim Burke, isn't here.

THE PRESIDENT. Yes, I was hopeful he would be.

REPRESENTATIVE ULLMAN. He is back in Massachusetts, but he was chairman of the subcommittee. This has been a long, onerous, difficult task, as you know. It's never easy to set a program straight by adding taxes, but this does it in a very responsible way. And I wanted to mention Jim Burke; he's been very important in this operation.

THE PRESIDENT. I understand. Well, with the help of these same leaders of Congress in 1978 we'll have tax reductions—[*laughter*]—which for every taxpayer will result in a lesser tax burden, even in spite of the fact that this does increase taxes to some degree. But I know that all of these leaders will be working with me to give us a tax reform package in 1978 which will be more progressive in nature, that is, put the burden of taxation where it can best be borne, will be greatly simplified, and will also be substantially reduced. So, we are looking forward to good tax reductions in 1978.

REPRESENTATIVE ULLMAN. That will be easy to pass. [*Laughter*]

THE PRESIDENT. Thank you very much, everybody.

NOTE: The President spoke at 8:30 a.m. in the Indian Treaty Room at the Old Executive Office Building.

As enacted, H.R. 9346 is Public Law 95–216, approved December 20.

Social Security Amendments of 1977

Statement on Signing S. 305 Into Law. December 20, 1977

Before I became President, the concern expressed to me most often was the fear that the social security system was in danger of bankruptcy. This fear was backed up by facts:

—A flaw had been introduced into the benefit formula which overcompensated for inflation and threw the system out of actuarial balance.

—Declines in birth rates meant that there would be fewer workers to support the system in the future—down from over 100 to 1 when the system started, to 14 to 1 in 1950, to 3 to 1 today, and to 2 to 1 in the next century.

—The worst recession since the Great Depression and the worst inflation since the Civil War had depleted the reserves in the trust funds to the point that the Disability Trust Fund would be depleted by 1979 and the

Old Age and Survivors Trust Fund would run out by 1983.

—A majority of Americans did not believe that their social security benefits would be there when they needed them.

I am happy to be here today to sign legislation which will reassure the 33 million people who are receiving benefits and the 104 million workers now making contributions that the social security system will be financially sound well into the next century.

I congratulate the Members of Congress for the courage and leadership they have shown in enacting this bill this year. The public overwhelmingly supports the purposes of the social security system, and a clear majority feel that the Congress is showing real courage in raising additional taxes to save the system, according to a recent poll.

Although the final bill differs in some respects from the proposals I submitted last May, it does fulfill all of the campaign promises I made on social security:

—Eliminates the yearly deficits of the social security system and restores the trust funds reserves to healthy levels.

—The delayed retirement credit is increased to reward those who choose to work beyond age 65 before claiming benefits.

—Corrects the flaw in the benefit formula and protects the purchasing power of present and future beneficiaries.

—Raises additional money primarily through increases in the taxable wage base making the system more progressive and minimizing the added burden for low- and moderate-income workers.

—Eases the earnings test, permitting recipients to earn as much as $6,000 without losing any benefits and those over 70 to continue with full benefits no matter how much they might earn.

—Several provisions are of great importance to women: It removes from the Social Security Act references to the sex of applicants, permits older persons to remarry without the fear of losing some of their social security benefits, and it makes homemakers who are divorced after 10 years of marriage eligible for benefits.

—Most importantly, it ensures our senior citizens today that their social security benefits will be protected during their retirement and further assures today's workers that the hard-earned taxes they are paying into the system today will be available upon their retirement.

Taken together, these are tremendous achievements and represent the most important social security legislation since the program was established.

The social security program is a pact between workers and their employers that they will contribute to a common fund to ensure that those who are no longer a part of the work force will have a basic income on which to live. It represents our commitment as a society to the belief that workers should not live in dread that a disability, death, or old age could leave them or their families destitute.

This bill was enacted this year in a spirit of compromise. The taxes are higher than those I proposed, but I believe that much of the increase can be offset by my income tax reduction proposals next month and additional reform in the social security system. I am happy that the Congress accepted my advice and avoided costly benefit increases at this time.

It should be clear to everyone that although we may have differed on some of the means to be used, we have been in full agreement on the goals of this legislation. I am particularly grateful to Senator Long, Congressman Ullman, Senator Nelson, Congressman Burke, and the House and Senate leadership for the efforts they put into making this bill a reality. I am pleased at how quickly we were able to move this massive piece of legislation through the Congress so that it could be signed today.

It is with great pleasure that I sign H.R. 9346.

NOTE: As enacted, H.R. 9346 is Public Law 95–216, approved December 20.

Foreign Corrupt Practices and Investment Disclosure Bill

Statement on Signing S. 305 Into Law. December 20, 1977

I am pleased to sign into law S. 305, the Foreign Corrupt Practices Act of 1977 and the Domestic and Foreign Investment Improved Disclosure Act of 1977.

During my campaign for the Presidency, I repeatedly stressed the need for tough legislation to prohibit corporate bribery. S. 305 provides that necessary sanction.

I share Congress belief that bribery is ethically repugnant and competitively unnecessary. Corrupt practices between corporations and public officials overseas undermine the integrity and stability of governments and harm our relations with other countries. Recent revelations of widespread overseas bribery have eroded public confidence in our basic institutions.

This law makes corrupt payments to foreign officials illegal under United States law. It requires publicly held corporations to keep accurate books and rec-

ords and establish accounting controls to prevent the use of "off-the-books" devices, which have been used to disguise corporate bribes in the past. The law also requires more extensive disclosure of ownership of stocks registered with the Securities and Exchange Commission.

These efforts, however, can only be fully successful in combating bribery and extortion if other countries and business itself take comparable action. Therefore, I hope progress will continue in the United Nations toward the negotiation of a treaty on illicit payments. I am also encouraged by the International Chamber of Commerce's new Code of Ethical Business Practices.

NOTE: As enacted, S. 305 is Public Law 95–213, approved December 19.

Exemption From Mandatory Retirement

Executive Order 12031.   December 21, 1977

EXEMPTION OF JEROME K. KUYKENDALL FROM MANDATORY RETIREMENT

Jerome K. Kuykendall, Chairman, Indian Claims Commission, will become subject to mandatory retirement for age on December 31, 1977, under the provisions of Section 8335 of Title 5 of the United States Code unless exempted by Executive order.

In my judgment, the public interest requires that Jerome K. Kuykendall be exempted from such mandatory retirement.

Now, THEREFORE, by virtue of the authority vested in me by subsection (c) of Section 8335 of Title 5 of the United States Code, I hereby exempt Jerome K.

Kuykendall from mandatory retirement until September 30, 1978.

JIMMY CARTER

The White House,
    December 21, 1977.

[Filed with the Office of the Federal Register, 11:59 a.m., December 21, 1977]

NOTE: The Executive order was announced by the White House Press Office on December 21.

Transatlantic Air Service

Announcement of Approval of Expanded Air Service Between the United States and Europe. December 21, 1977

The President today announced that he has approved major portions of a Civil Aeronautics Board decision significantly expanding air service between the United States and Europe. The President's decision approves 11 new cities for direct service to Europe. These cities are: Atlanta, Cleveland, Dallas, Denver, Houston, Kansas City, Minneapolis/St. Paul, New Orleans, Pittsburgh, St. Louis, and Tampa. It will also permit three new carriers to provide United States-to-Europe service, and it expands the route system of carriers currently providing such service. By increasing competition on the North Atlantic routes, the decision will result in better service opportunities for the public.

Today's decision approves the following portions of the Civil Aeronautics Board's recommendations:

—Northwest Airlines will replace Pan American on various routes between U.S. cities (Seattle, Portland, Los Angeles, Minneapolis/St. Paul, Chicago, Detroit, Washington/Baltimore, New York/Newark, and Boston) and Glasgow and points in Denmark, Norway, Sweden, Finland, and Iceland.

—Trans World Airlines' existing authority is renewed, and TWA is authorized to serve additional U.S. cities (Pittsburgh, Denver, St. Louis, Cleveland, Minneapolis/St. Paul, and Kansas City) as co-terminals on direct or nonstop transatlantic routes.

—Delta is granted authority to serve the Atlanta-London route.

—Pan American World Airways' certificate is amended to renew most of its existing authority, to authorize Miami-Madrid nonstop service, and to add Houston-London authority.

—National Airlines is awarded routes between Miami, New Orleans, and Tampa to Paris.

The President disapproved two portions of the decision. First, the President directed the Board to submit an order adding Amsterdam and Frankfurt to National Airlines' route system.

Second, the President directed the Board to submit an order designating Braniff Airways to serve the Dallas/Fort Worth-London route.

The decision to certificate Braniff Airways to serve the Dallas/Fort Worth-London route and National Airlines to serve Amsterdam and Frankfurt is based on the President's judgment that the certification of strong regional domestic carriers to serve international markets is important to his foreign policy of relying to the maximum extent possible on competitive forces in international aviation. To achieve this goal, the administration, in close cooperation with the Civil Aeronautics Board, is seeking more competitive bilateral air agreements with foreign countries. The President has also recently approved reduced fares on the North Atlantic and has permitted carriers such as Laker Airways to enter the market and provide service at substantially reduced rates. The decision to permit competitive pricing, however, depends on authorizing additional new carriers to serve international markets, as new competitors are an important source of price innovation. The President's decision to certificate Braniff, Delta, National, and Northwest—all of which are strong regional carriers—to serve new European markets is an important step in the pursuit of this overall foreign policy objective.

The Board was correct in relying upon regional carriers to provide competitive service in the North Atlantic. As the dissent points out, however, the refusal of the Civil Aeronautics Board to certificate Braniff Airways to serve Dallas/Fort Worth and the Southwest region is inconsistent with the remainder of the Board's decision, which permit strong regional carriers to serve their regions; for example, Delta and National to serve the Southeast and Northwest to serve the upper Midwest. The President believes that Texas and the Southwest region should have the same opportunity for innovative, competitive service as other regions.

United States Balance of Trade and Payments

Statement Announcing Measures To Improve the U.S. Trade Position.   December 21, 1977

The United States balance of trade and payments has shifted this year to a large deficit position. The two main causes appear to be large oil imports by the United States and relatively slow economic growth in Japan, Germany, and other nations.

These deficits have contributed to some disorder in the exchange markets and rapid movements in exchange rates. Heightened uncertainty and increased exchange market pressure in recent weeks have coincided with the delay in congressional action on our energy legislation. A mistaken belief that the United States is not prepared to adopt an effective energy program has been partly responsible for recent, unsettled conditions in the exchange markets. We have a responsibility to protect the integrity of the dollar. Prompt action is needed in energy and other fields to reduce our deficits.

Last April, I submitted to the Congress a comprehensive conservation and conversion program to reduce our dependence on foreign oil. I am confident that the Congress will not allow this situation to continue to deteriorate through inaction. I am equally confident that the American people will fully support this critically important program. When enacted, the measures now under consideration will have increasingly beneficial effect in coming years and exert their main impact by 1985.

The United States is currently importing petroleum at a cost of about 45 billion a year. In 1978, taking account of planned production of Alaskan oil, our oil imports will be stable, despite substantial purchases for our Strategic Petroleum Reserve. Nevertheless, it is essential that we take further steps to curtail these imports in order to reduce both our excessive dependence on imported oil and the burden on our balance of payments. The energy measures I am now proposing are designed to serve these ends.

I have instructed the Department of Energy to pursue efforts to:

—expand production of oil at the Elk Hills Naval Petroleum Reserve;

—encourage an expansion of production at Prudhoe Bay above the 1.2 million barrels a day planned for early 1978;

—maintain production of California crude at a high level;

—work with appropriate governmental and private interests in expediting provision of adequate pipeline capacity for transport of Alaskan and Californian oil east of the Rocky Mountains.

Combined with conservation measures, these efforts offer good promise.

The new measures will take effect in the period immediately ahead and serve as a bridge until the implementation of the more comprehensive legislative program begins to exert fundamental changes in our energy balance in the years ahead.

I have also instituted measures to expand U.S. exports:

—We have doubled Commodity Credit Corporation credits to support agricultural exports.

—In 1978, we will increase sharply lending activity by the Export-Import Bank to support exports generally.

We will not engage in unfair competition for export markets; we will fully respect our understandings with other Governments regarding export credit terms. But within these understandings, there is room for a more active effort to expand our exports. Through such an effort, I believe we can achieve substantial increases in exports in 1978, as well as in subsequent years.

With these measures, the prospects for an improvement in our trade position will be good. Some of these measures will begin to take effect in 1978. When fully implemented, these measures, energy and non-energy, should produce an annual improvement in our trade position of several billion dollars and will improve the U.S. balance of payments.

There has been a great deal of public discussion in recent weeks about the large U.S. trade and payments deficits and the movement of rates in the exchange markets, mainly between the dollar and the German mark and Japanese yen. The American economy and the dollar are fundamentally sound; U.S. products on the whole are competitive. While some exchange rate adjustment has been understandable in light of economic developments in Germany, Japan, and the United States, recent exchange market disorders are not justified.

The new energy measures strike directly at a key part of the balance of trade problem. The export measures will enable us to respond effectively to expanding export opportunities. Together, the energy and export measures represent action to strengthen our balance of payments and deal with our trade deficit in a substantive way, by improving the underlying conditions upon which the value of the dollar fundamentally depends.

Furthermore, next month I shall be presenting to the Congress a comprehensive economic program designed to ensure a healthy and growing economy, to increase business capital investment, to expand industrial capacity and productivity, and to maintain prudent budgetary policies while counteracting inflationary pressures. These and related measures will promote economic progress and underscore our commitment to a strong and sound U.S. economy.

In the discharge of our responsibilities, we will, in close consultation with our friends abroad, intervene to the extent necessary to counter disorderly conditions in the exchange markets. The measures I have enumerated will deal with the root causes of these market disturbances in a more direct and fundamental way.

Central Intelligence Agency

Nomination of Frank C. Carlucci To Be Deputy Director.   December 22, 1977

The President today announced his intention to nominate Frank C. Carlucci, currently the United States Ambassador to Portugal, to be the Deputy Director of Central Intelligence.

Mr. Carlucci, 47, a native of Scranton, Pa., graduated from Princeton University in 1952 and served 2 years in the United States Navy. He joined the Foreign Service in 1956 and served in several African countries. He served as Counselor for Political Affairs in Rio de Janeiro, 1965–69; as Assistant Director for Operations and, later, as Director of the Office of Economic Opportunity, 1969–71; as Associate Director and Deputy Director, Office of Management and Budget, 1971–72; as Under Secretary of the Department of Health, Education, and Welfare, 1972–74; and as United States Ambassador to Portugal from December 1974 to the present.

United States Ambassador to Portugal

Nomination of Richard J. Bloomfield. December 22, 1977

The President today announced his intention to nominate Richard J. Bloomfield, of Derby, Conn., as Ambassador to Portugal. He would succeed Frank C. Carlucci.

Bloomfield, 50, received a B.S.F.S. in 1950 from Georgetown University and an M.P.A. in 1960 from Harvard University. He served from 1945–46 in the United States Coast Guard and from 1950–51 in the United States Air Force.

He entered the Foreign Service in 1952 and has served in La Paz, Salzburg, Monterrey, and Montevideo. He was Deputy Director, Office of Regional Economic Policy, Bureau of Inter-American Affairs from 1965–67; he was Country Director for Ecuador-Peru in 1967–68; and he was economic counselor and Associate Director, AID, in Rio de Janeiro from 1968–71. He was a fellow at Harvard University Center for International Affairs in 1971–72, and from 1973–76, he was Director, Office of Policy Planning and Coordination, Bureau of Inter-American Affairs. Since 1976 he has been Ambassador to Ecuador.

National Energy Plan

White House Statement on Congressional Action.   December 22, 1977

The President appreciates the hard work and good faith effort by many Members of the Congress and the conference committees to produce a fair and effective National Energy Plan.

However, today's decision to adjourn until January 23 is in his opinion "regrettable." He would like to emphasize that our energy problems "will not go away between now and January 23. They will simply continue to get worse."

Indochina Refugees

Announcement Concerning the Admission of Additional Refugees to the United States. December 22, 1977

The President has authorized the Secretary of State to request the Attorney General to exercise his parole authority to admit up to 7,000 additional Indochinese refugees. In doing so, the President approved the Secretary's request as submitted. Parole authority is vested in the Attorney General under section 212 (d) (5) of the Immigration and Nationality Act.

Digest of Other White House Announcements

The following listing includes the President's daily schedule and other items of general interest as announced by the White House Press Office during the period covered by this issue. Events and announcements printed elsewhere in the issue are not included.

December 17

The President returned to the White House from Fayetteville, N.C.

The President met at the White House with:

—Zbigniew Brzezinski, Assistant to the President for National Security Affairs;

—Vice President Walter F. Mondale, Secretary of State Cyrus R. Vance, and Dr. Brzezinski.

The President and Mrs. Carter hosted a Christmas reception for members of the Secret Service and their families.

December 19

The President met at the White House with:

—Dr. Brzezinski;

—Vice President Mondale, Secretary of the Treasury W. Michael Blumenthal, Secretary of Commerce Juanita M. Kreps, Secretary of Labor F. Ray Marshall, Richard N. Cooper, Under Secretary of State for Economic Affairs, Charles L. Schultze, Chairman of the Council of Economic Advisers, James T. McIntyre, Jr., Acting Director, Office of Management and Budget, Frank B. Moore, Assistant to the President for Congressional Liaison, Stuart E. Eizenstat, Assistant to the President for Domestic Affairs and Policy, and Jack H. Watson, Jr., Assistant to the President for Intergovernmental Affairs, to discuss economic policy;

—Senator Edmund S. Muskie of Maine;

—a group of administration officials and Members of Congress, to discuss economic policy;

—members of the executive committee and chairmen of the standing committees of the National Governors' Conference;

—a group of administration officials to discuss the budget.

The President and Mrs. Carter hosted a Christmas reception for members of the White House staff.

December 20

The President met at the White House with:

—Dr. Brzezinski;

—a group of administration officials to discuss the budget;

—Vice President Mondale, Adm. Stansfield Turner, Director of Central Intelligence, and Dr. Brzezinski;

—Secretary of the Interior Cecil D. Andrus;

—former President Gerald R. Ford;

—Senator Edward M. Kennedy of Massachusetts.

The President and Mrs. Carter hosted separate Christmas receptions for Residence staff members and their families and members of the White House press corps.

December 21

The President met at the White House with Dr. Brzezinski.

The President left the White House to spend the Christmas holidays in Plains, Ga.

NOMINATIONS SUBMITTED
TO THE SENATE

NOTE: The Congress having adjourned *sine die* on Thursday, December 15, no nominations were submitted during the period covered by this issue.

CHECKLIST OF WHITE HOUSE
PRESS RELEASES

The following releases of the Office of the White House Press Secretary, distributed during the period covered by this issue, are not included in the issue.

Released December 17, 1977

White House statement: on the President's meeting with Prime Minister Menahem Begin of Israel (as read by Secretary of State Cyrus R. Vance to reporters in the Briefing Room at the White House)

Released December 22, 1977

Announcement: the President's participation in a nationally broadcast interview with correspondents from the four American television networks to be held on December 28, from 8 to 9 p.m.

ACTS APPROVED BY
THE PRESIDENT

Approved December 19, 1977

H.R. 3722_____ Public Law 95–211
An act to amend the Securities Exchange

ACTS APPROVED—Continued

Act of 1934 to authorize appropriations for the Securities and Exchange Commission for fiscal year 1978.

H.R. 9378_____ Public Law 95–214
An act to amend title IV of the Employee Retirement Income Security Act of 1974 to postpone, for two years, the date on which the corporation first begins paying benefits under terminated multiemployer plans.

H.R. 9418_____ Public Law 95–215
An act to amend the conditions for schools receiving capitation grants under section 770 of such Act, and for other purposes.

S. 305_____ Public Law 95–213
An act to amend the Securities Exchange Act of 1934 to make it unlawful for an issuer of securities registered pursuant to section 12 of such Act or an issuer required to file reports pursuant to section 15(d) of such Act to make certain payments to foreign officials and other foreign persons, to require such issuers to maintain accurate records, and for other purposes.

S. 1316_____ Public Law 95–212
An act to authorize appropriations for fiscal years 1978, 1979, and 1980 to carry out State cooperative programs under the Endangered Species Act of 1973.

S. 2328_____ Private Law 95–26
An act to amend Private Law 95–21 to make a technical correction therein.

Approved December 20, 1977

H.R. 9346_____ Public Law 95–216
Social Security Amendments of 1977.

Editor's Note

Note Concerning the Closing Time of This Issue

The President was in Plains, Ga., at the closing time of this issue. Releases issued there but not received in time for inclusion in this issue will be printed next week.

Interstate 75 Dedication

Remarks by Telephone to Participants in the Dedication Ceremonies in Marietta, Georgia. December 21, 1977

GOVERNOR GEORGE BUSBEE. Hello, Mr. President.

THE PRESIDENT. Hi. How is it going?

GOVERNOR BUSBEE. Everything is going wonderfully well.

THE PRESIDENT. Well, we have had two great transportation achievements in Georgia in one day.

GOVERNOR BUSBEE. Well, let me say, Mr. President, that we have with us on the platform your Secretary of Transportation on this, the most historic day in the history of transportation for our State.

And the audience is aware of the fact that today we are opening the first highway corridor from Canada to the Gulf of Mexico, through Georgia. But what they are unaware of is the fact that you have just made possible on the same day the direct flight from Atlanta to London. So, I would like to announce that at this time.

Bert Lance is standing here, too, and he said also he sold his stock today. So, this is a real great day here in Georgia now. [*Laughter*]

THE PRESIDENT. Well, it's been a wonderful occasion for all of us to see such a fine completion of the most important interstate route in the Nation. And this is an achievement, I think also, George and those who are listening, for a proper interrelationship between those who are concerned about the beauty and the quality of life in Georgia, who also want a good transportation system.

Dr. Eugene Odum,[1] working with Bert Lance and me several years ago, resolved some very difficult environmental questions. And you and the Department of Transportation in Georgia have brought it to a very rapid conclusion. And I think the whole Nation is going to benefit from this superb route through the most beautiful regions of the country.

Brock Adams has done a good job in forming a close working partnership with the Governors throughout the country, and I know it's a time of celebration for the whole State.

I am very glad that we finally got another joint project on which you and I were able to work, and that is direct international airline flights from Atlanta into Europe. And I believe that Georgia and Atlanta, under your superb leadership, is really making great progress.

GOVERNOR BUSBEE. Mr. President, let me say that Senator Nunn had asked me—he is on the platform with us—to express his appreciation. Senator Talmadge

---

[1] Dr. Eugene P. Odum, director of the Institute of Ecology at the University of Georgia.

could not be with us, but I know that he and the Congressmen on the platform today join with me in thanking you for making this day possible in Georgia.

And we are also delighted to have you back in Georgia for what I hope will be a very merry Christmas today.

THE PRESIDENT. Thank you very much, George.

One of the things that is extraordinary about the completion of I–75 is that under the good work of seven different contractors, the highway has been completed in 3 years, which is one year ahead of the original work schedule. And it's going to mean a lot to people trying to go to and from Atlanta in the holiday season to have I–75 open.

And I am very proud of what you have done, what the Department of Transportation has done in Georgia, and we look forward to concluding the other interstate highway systems as rapidly as we can.

But Tom Moreland [2] and Bert Lance made good partners for you and me. And, of course, the Congress has worked also as a part of that close partnership.

I am very glad to be back in Georgia, and I hope that you will extend to everyone there my thanks for a wonderful welcome back home, for the good support I've had in the first year as President. And I'm very proud to have a home where friendship and harmony exist in the State government. And we have benefited greatly in the White House from this strong support from back in Georgia.

So, good luck to you, George, and my congratulations to all those who were involved in this rapid completion of a superb connector link now up and down our

---

[2] Thomas D. Moreland, commissioner of the Georgia Department of Transportation and State highway engineer.

entire Nation. I know that it will help the people in Florida, in the Midwest, and all those in between.

So, congratulations again. Merry Christmas to everybody. I'm very proud of the work you've done.

GOVERNOR BUSBEE. Good day, Mr. President, and Merry Christmas.

THE PRESIDENT. Thank you, George; same to you.

NOTE: The President spoke at 1:34 p.m. from his home in Plains, Ga., to participants in the dedication at the Cobb County Civic Center in Marietta, Ga.

Farm Program

Exchange of Letters With Mrs. Eston Luke of Baxley, Georgia. December 21, 1977

December 21, 1977

Dear Mrs. Luke:

Thank you for writing about the problems farmers are facing.

Well publicized demonstrations in Georgia and around the country have brought home forcefully to the American people the fact that the welfare of American consumers and American farm families cannot be separated. This ability of farmers to act together and focus public attention upon the problems of American agriculture is a new and healthy development.

You and others who have written and called are asking what this administration is doing to help farmers and how, as a farmer, I view the whole situation.

This has been an even more difficult year than usual for many farmers. Drought has done terrible damage to some sections of our country.

Our own home state has been one of the hardest hit. Last year Georgia produced 134 million bushels of corn. This year only 24 million bushels.

There is a word for that situation and others like it across the country—"disaster"—and the disaster programs we inherited were sadly inadequate to deal with so widespread a problem.

Farmers have had to pay higher and higher prices for machinery, fuel, fertilizer, land and everything else needed to produce crops. When production expenses are going up and prices are going down, I know firsthand how impossible that situation can seem.

In the 11 months since I took office, I've tried to face up to those problems with the best interests of both farmers and consumers in mind. I'd like to tell you about some of the steps we have taken since January, both through administrative action and by working with the Congress, that will ease the problems that now affect farmers.

We passed a new farm bill this year—in record time—because both I and the Congress were aware that existing policies and programs were inadequate. That bill went into effect this October and will be of great help to farmers next year.

The new farm bill has several important features. It raises both loan levels and target prices. Target prices were increased 17 percent and will continue to increase each year as production costs go up. As I promised during the campaign, the bill links income support levels to cost of production. Also, the bill authorized formation of a farmer-held grain reserve to help stabilize farm markets in a way that will avoid a repeat of the mistakes of the early 1970's.

The new Food and Agriculture Act of 1977 also authorized $1.2 billion in wheat deficiency payments, more than $800 million above the amount authorized under the old act. By December 1, checks were on their way to about 1.8 million farmers under this program.

In April, even before the farm bill was passed, we reduced the interest rates on commodity and storage loans, boosted feed grain loan prices, and established a farmer-owned wheat and rice reserve. We later expanded this program, and announced a feed grain reserve. To keep excess grain from being turned over to the government, we liberalized the farm storage loan program.

In May, the administration provided $479 million in emergency loans to help producers who had been hurt by the drought. Three months later I authorized another $50 million in loans. Later I signed legislation authorizing disaster payments based upon acreage planted instead of upon outdated allotments.

On August 31, we increased the loan rates for feed grains again.

During these last 11 months, we have also made progress in international negotiations that affect our farmers. The results here were good: An international sugar agreement has been formulated, an international wheat reserve is under discussion, and the multilateral trade negotiations are again underway.

Farm exports this year will be the highest in the history of our country, and we will be making an even greater effort to sell American farm products abroad next year.

We have not solved our farm problems, but these efforts—along with record loan activity and stronger demand for our farm products—have pulled farm prices up. By the end of this year agricultural exports will be at their highest level in our Nation's history. The price of wheat climbed from a season low of $2.03 a bushel in June to $2.48 in November.

The price of corn rose from $1.60 a bushel in September to $1.91 in November.

A hundred pounds of sorghum sold for $2.52 in September, and $3.15 in November. The average price received by farmers for soybeans moved from a season low of $5.27 to a November average of $5.68 a bushel.

Farm prices and income are still too low, but they have improved. Farm production costs are rising but not as fast as they did before. The prices of supplies, interest, taxes and wage rates have been essentially unchanged for the last three months.

I hope farmers will continue to use the farm programs. They are now redesigned to help through periods, like the present one, when supplies are abundant and prices too low.

One other chronic problem is that even when prices are high in the supermarket, they're still too low on the farm. Farmers know—but most consumers don't—how little of the food dollar actually goes to those who take the risks and produce the food. I promised as a candidate to try to hold down the "middleman" portion of food costs. We have taken steps to deal with this problem, too.

My Agriculture Secretary, Bob Bergland, a family farmer himself, has ordered the Agricultural Marketing Service to conduct a full-scale investigation into the pricing of meat between the farmer and the consumer. The investigation is focused on pricing at the wholesale level, to see whether the current system blocks competition.

We are spending $1.5 million this fiscal year to set up direct farmer-to-consumer marketing, a system which would eliminate the substantial costs associated with middleman mark-up.

The Agriculture and Transportation Departments are jointly studying the food transportation system, looking mainly at inequities in the system that prevent more efficient and less costly means for the movement of food.

We have given our support to the idea of a food marketing commission. That commission would look into the whole food marketing system, including pricing at the middleman level. In commenting publicly on this issue, officials of this administration have focused particularly on the costs associated with transportation, advertising and packaging of food.

I hope this letter answers some of your questions; I wish it were possible for government action to solve all the problems that farmers face. But you know that the combination of nature's chance and the farmer's determination makes that impossible; that very challenge is what has drawn so many of us to farming. I respect that spirit, and I am glad for a chance to explain my views to you.

I cannot promise that I will solve every problem. I know that is not what you want, and you know that no President and no government can do that.

I cannot promise a guaranteed profit, but I have never met a farmer who asked for that.

What farmers want is a fair chance, and I do believe we can and have begun to change the policies of this government so that the farm family gets a decent break. If the changes we've made this year don't have the results we expect, they will themselves be changed.

Sincerely,

JIMMY CARTER

[Mrs. Eston Luke, Route 6, Box 201, Baxley, Georgia 31513]

December 14, 1977

Dear Sir:

Please help farmers in their efforts to get better prices for their crops. We deserve a decent living for our hard work as U.S. farmers produce such a fine fare for all Americans and many others.

Thank you,

Mrs. Eston Luke
Route 6, Box 201
Baxley, Georgia 31513

NOTE: The texts of the letters were released at Plains, Ga.

Plains, Georgia

*Informal Exchange With Hugh Carter, Sr., at Mr. Carter's Antique Shop.
December 22, 1977*

MR. CARTER. On this farm thing, you know, they came over here; couldn't get anybody to give them a welcome. I went over there.

THE PRESIDENT. I am glad you did. I mentioned you in my press conference.

MR. CARTER. I know you did. I heard it. That's great. But, you know, I knew you were for them, but it was hard for me to—they were a little angry, you know. They wanted you down here. They started shouting, you know, "We want Jimmy. We want Jimmy. Where's Jimmy?"

THE PRESIDENT. [*Inaudible*]—going to hear about the letter to the farmer. I know they have got the headlines in the Columbus paper. I just wonder if they got it in the Atlanta paper. Have you looked at it?

MR. CARTER. I haven't gone through this yet. I just got it. You want to look at it?

THE PRESIDENT. No, I don't—there it is. I just wanted to be sure it was covered.

I got a letter from a woman in Baxley, a widow, and she and her young son run the farm. So, I just sent her—the paper says a seven-page telegram explaining the way I felt about the farm program.

The new bill that we passed didn't go into effect until October, and it will take care of a lot of our problems. Of course, we have still got a serious problem when we don't make a crop. And land prices, as you know, have leveled off. They were going up 10 to 15 percent a year, which kept prices going up. They have kind of leveled off. And there's also, you know, farmers have got a tremendous capital investment, much more than the average businessman.

MR. CARTER. Well, that's true. Another thing, you know, Jimmy, some of them need to keep their cool. You know, a lot of them are getting mad, and I think this is wrong.

THE PRESIDENT. I think they had some violence in Texas.

MR. CARTER. I know. I saw it on TV last night.

THE PRESIDENT. As long as the farmers let consumers know they have got a problem, that's good. But if they ever turn the consumers against them, they will be worse off than they were before. What's best for the consumers is to have the family farmers strong and have a sound financial base to keep prices from fluctuating so wildly.

NOTE: The exchange began at approximately 8:45 a.m.

Plains, Georgia

Informal Exchange With Reporters During a Walking Tour of Plains.   December 22, 1977

REPORTER. Mr. President, what is the story about the OPEC decision this morning?

THE PRESIDENT. I'm just glad that they decided to freeze the price, and I hope it will be for the whole year of 1978.

Q. How much was a hunting license the last time you bought it? Do you remember?

THE PRESIDENT. The same thing, I believe.

Q. $4.25?

THE PRESIDENT. But I buy one every year.

Q. What are you going to be doing while you are down here?

THE PRESIDENT. I might do a little reading.

Q. On your trip coming up?

Q. What about the budget and taxes?

THE PRESIDENT. Well, I've got all the notebooks on the different countries we are going to go to after Christmas. Then I am going to put the final touches on the Executive order on the intelligence community. I'll do that while I am here.

Q. Have you pretty much finished with the budget, your final decisions now?

THE PRESIDENT. Yes. I signed off on all the decisions yesterday morning. I'll have a brief session when I get back after Christmas just to look at the summary. And they are what they call "scrubbing" the budget now to make sure that the estimates are the best we can——

Q. What's the price?

THE PRESIDENT. I'll tell you later.

Q. A balanced budget is still a goal and not a dream now?

THE PRESIDENT. Absolutely.

Q. How about this Executive order on the intelligence community. Is that to set up the whole intelligence——

THE PRESIDENT. Yes. I've already been over it once. It's in the final form now. But I've got to read it before I sign it.

I'll see you all later.

NOTE: The exchange began at approximately 9 a.m.

Plains, Georgia

Exchange With Reporters Following a Meeting With a Group of Farmers. December 24, 1977

REPORTER. Mr. President, could you tell us about the meeting, sir?

THE PRESIDENT. It was a good meeting. I sympathize with them and understand a lot of things that they say. Many items that farmers buy have gone up 300, 400, 500 percent. Farmers are heavily dependent on energy, for instance, not just oil and natural gas for drying crops but that's where fertilizer comes from. And the same fertilizer that I used to sell down at Carters Warehouse when I was here 4 or 5 years ago cost $40 and now costs $95 or $100. 5–10–15 is a—[*inaudible*]—that's a standard around here. The same way with nitrogen; it's gone up probably——

Q. We are having a little difficulty hearing you, Mr. President; I'm sorry.

THE PRESIDENT. Ann [Ann Compton, ABC News], I didn't want to have a press conference.

I sympathized with them. They are good folks and they are trying to do things peacefully and let the consumers of the country know that farmers have a problem.

Q. Did they outline their five points to you, sir?

THE PRESIDENT. Yes, I was familiar with them already.

Q. Your stand earlier on the farm bill and the fact that it was recently signed and the effect won't be felt for some time—did you express that point of view with them?

THE PRESIDENT. Yes. I had talked to some of the leaders here on the phone yesterday; we went to that particular point. The new farm bill didn't go into effect until October 1, and it will have a beneficial impact next year. Of course, we have got the emergency farm loans, too, to tide the ones over that had failure this year. But that's primarily restricted to areas of the country where the weather caused a crop loss. But they've got a really serious problem, and we are working hard on it.

Q. Do you think you can do anything more for them?

THE PRESIDENT. Well, Bob Bergland is going to meet with the State leaders from all 50 States, I think, the 4th and 5th of January. So, I'll be talking to Bob between now and then.

Q. Do you feel that they were satisfied with the meeting today?

THE PRESIDENT. I think so.

Q. What's wrong with their demand for 100 percent parity?

THE PRESIDENT. Well, it would be difficult for us to compete with international prices on many of our export items if the price were substantially higher than it is now. But I believe that compared to other products that farm prices almost inevitably will have to go up in the years ahead.

As land becomes actually less available, with the encroachment on acreage that's presently devoted to agriculture, and as the population of the world expands, obviously agricultural products from the farmer will be more valuable compared to other products. But in the last few years it's—[inaudible]—very rapidly.

Q. Did you ask them to keep on planting?

THE PRESIDENT. Yes. I think most of these will keep on planting. Also, I told them that any sort of violence or interference in other people's lives by the strikers would have an adverse effect on them.

I think that the reactions so far to the farm demonstrations have been basically favorable from consumers, and they understand that there is always a threat of a few more radical farmers or nonfarmers who joined the parade that might do something that would bring discredit on them. They are very concerned about that, and they want the demonstrations to be peaceful and not interfere illegitimately with other people's lives.

Q. Have you heard from Mr. Sadat or Mr. Begin?

THE PRESIDENT. No, but I probably will before they meet.

Q. Are you going to do anything today?

THE PRESIDENT. Not much.

Q. Quail hunt?

THE PRESIDENT. I doubt it.

REPORTER. Merry Christmas.

THE PRESIDENT. Merry Christmas. I will probably see you later on today.

NOTE: The exchange began at 8:30 a.m. at the President's home in Plains, Ga.

Christmas 1977

Message of the President.   December 24, 1977

At this joyous season, Rosalynn and I extend our warmest wishes to all of our fellow citizens who celebrate Christmas. This is a very special Christmas for us and our family. We are deeply grateful for all the help and affection the American people have given us during this challenging and rewarding year.

Our country has been especially blessed throughout our history. In this season of hope we seek, as individuals and as a nation, to serve as instruments to bring the ancient promises of peace and good will closer to fulfillment for all the peoples of the earth.

May you have a merry Christmas and very satisfying and happy New Year.

JIMMY CARTER

NOTE: The text of the message was released at Plains, Ga.

Plains, Georgia

Informal Exchange With Reporters Prior to Visiting Allie Smith.   December 25, 1977

REPORTER. Merry Christmas.

THE PRESIDENT. Same to you. It's a shame to get you up so early so far away from home.

REPORTER. Well, on Christmas, you get up early anyway when you have family.

THE PRESIDENT. Yes, I know. We always get up about 5:00.

Q. Tell us how Christmas has gone so far.

THE PRESIDENT. Well, it's fine. I just placed a phone call to President Sadat and Prime Minister Begin. And they're in Ismailia, and I was at the Pond House. So, the connection was pretty bad. I could just barely hear them. So, I relayed a message through to them that they have my best wishes and support and that the whole world awaits the peace that they can bring us on this Christmas Day. They are together in Ismailia, and we hope that they will be successful.

We've had a good Christmas ourselves so far. We will be visiting Rosalynn's mother now, already been out to my mother's house, already had Santa Claus at our house. And then we will go to Sunday school and church.

Q. Are you going to talk to them again after they've talked together?

THE PRESIDENT. After they finish this day's work, yes.

Q. Will we get a report from you, perhaps, later?

THE PRESIDENT. Perhaps.

Q. Mr. President, what did you get for Christmas?

THE PRESIDENT. Well, I got some binoculars, and I got a coat that Mother gave me that came from Ireland, a handwoven tweed coat. And I got several books, and I got two shirts from Chip and Jeffrey. I got a pretty good haul so far—got several albums—got Mahler's Eighth Symphony.

Q. Can you say how Mr. Sadat and Mr. Begin's talks are—have they been conferring some already?

THE PRESIDENT. They just are getting started, and we didn't go into any detail about it. We've had very close and thorough discussions with Prime Minister Begin in Jerusalem, with our Ambassador there, and also with our Ambassador and President Sadat in Cairo precedent to this meeting. But we haven't had a chance to meet or talk to them since they've been conversing.

Q. Do you think that in that you are going to meet with Jordan's King Hussein, it might also be possible to meet with President Asad on your trip?

THE PRESIDENT. I don't know. It would suit me fine if it could be worked out. I think the only time that I would have available to talk to him was if we could perhaps meet in Riyadh, but I don't know if it's possible.

Q. Is there any possibility you might go to Cairo?

THE PRESIDENT. I don't think so. If I did, it would—it's not something we've thought about or plan now.

Q. Have you suggested to the Syrians or President Asad the possibility of such a meeting?

THE PRESIDENT. No, I haven't. When Secretary Vance was over there, he talked to the different leaders about the possibility of my meeting with some of them while I was over in the Middle East area. But the only time I would have available is either Tehran or Riyadh. And nothing has been worked out with President Asad, but Secretary Vance had long discussions with all of them, which is probably adequate.

Q. Do you think it's possible to have a meaningful peace solution in the Middle East if the Palestinians don't have an independent state, an independent entity?

THE PRESIDENT. Well, I've never favored a separate nation or an independent state for the Palestinians. I think that they ought to be tied in, in some way at least, with Jordan. That's my preference. But anything that Prime Minister Begin would work out with the Jordanians or the Palestinians or the Egyptians would suit us.

We have no prohibition against any arrangement, including a tie with Jordan or otherwise. This is going to be a dual discussion between President Sadat and Prime Minister Begin—one on a bilateral basis concerning the Sinai region and the relationship directly between Israel and Egypt. The other one, of course, would relate to a much broader range of questions concerning the West Bank, the Gaza Strip, and how the Palestinian Arabs would be treated in a final settlement.

One of the things that is being discussed is an interim arrangement for several years so that they might feel their way toward more sense of security. I think Israel feels very deeply that leaders come and go. Myself, Begin, and Sadat, you know, won't be in office after a number of years. And there has to be a firm foundation of peace between the peoples involved so that any yielding of territory or any lessening of security would be at least more carefully considered and

weighed in the balance of historical times.

But I think that if I've ever seen two people who were determined to be successful under the most difficult negotiating positions, it is Begin and Sadat. I've talked to both of them at length. We've had long and voluminous messages through diplomatic channels as well. And, of course, Cy Vance has been over there to visit with both of them recently. And I know that they are determined to be successful.

There's a difference, as you know, between the governments in Israel and Egypt. Prime Minister Begin is constrained by the parliamentary system. He has a cabinet and a parliament, the Knesset, and he has to negotiate with them and deal with them. I think, so far, he's been successful in selling his proposal that he is making to Sadat today to his own leadership. And I've read news reports and have had private reports that there had been a good bit of disagreement originally. But they gave him their vote of confidence in the cabinet. So, he is negotiating from a strong position among his own people.

Sadat, of course, being a President, being a very strong and powerful constitutional officer in the system of government Egypt has, can speak much more quickly, make decisions much more rapidly. He has to do much less consultation with other Egyptian officials than does Begin. But I think the recent attitudes among the general public in both those countries is conducive to peace.

I think Sadat has the overwhelming support of his own people. I think Begin has the overwhelming support of the people of Israel. So, I have good hopes about it. But I've seen enough of the detailed subjects for negotiation already to know how difficult it is. Past positions taken, past statements made, you know, have to be undone. And if it weren't for the strength of these two men and their deep dedication to peace, there would be very little likelihood of a rapid settlement. But I think their strength and their determination might very well prevail.

Q. Mr. President, do you think that when you meet with King Hussein in Iran that you'll be able to talk him into joining this effort? Do you have hopes in that direction?

THE PRESIDENT. Well, he's never rejected coming into the discussions at some later date. Obviously, any permanent arrangement made concerning the Palestinian question and the West Bank would have to involve King Hussein. And he's being kept thoroughly advised about the negotiations.

He's, I think, taken a very positive attitude toward the Cairo-Ismailia meetings. And he's, I think, willing to participate whenever the time comes. But his absence is not an obstacle to progress at this point.

Q. Is it the Syrians that are the real problem then at the moment?

THE PRESIDENT. Well, as you know, the only territorial matter that involves the Syrians is the Golan Heights area. Of course, the Syrians are also deeply interested in the question of the Palestinian Arabs and the West Bank as well.

But there's no reason for them to be directly involved in those negotiations. There could be a complete settlement of the Gaza Strip, West Bank, Palestinian Arab question without the Syrians' participation.

We are hopeful, though, that they will come into the discussions. And Secretary Vance was encouraged by Asad's attitude toward Sadat when he was there.

I think the private expressions of his opinion were much less abusive or nega-

tive than the public reports had been. So, I think although there might be individual discussions required before we can get ready for the comprehensive peace settlement, there's no doubt in my mind that if progress can be made, that later the Lebanese, Syrians, and Jordanians will come into the discussions.

Q. Is a comprehensive settlement foreseeable within the next year?

THE PRESIDENT. I think it's foreseeable. And the major responsibility now is on the Egyptians and the Israelis, with the Jordanians being thoroughly informed, because the Arab position is being represented by President Sadat as it relates not only to the Sinai but also to the West Bank and the Gaza Strip.

So, I think it's foreseeable. But I can't predict it because I don't know what will happen. I think after today, after these series of meetings, there will be likely followup by technicians on the political aspects of questions and defense matters, both bilateral and on a multinational basis. But I think today is a crucial day for it.

Thank you. I'll see you all later.

REPORTER. Thank you. Merry Christmas.

NOTE: The exchange began at 8 a.m. at the home of Allie Smith, Mrs. Carter's mother.

Plains, Georgia

Informal Exchange With Reporters After Visiting Alton Carter. December 25, 1977

REPORTER. How is Uncle Buddy doing?

THE PRESIDENT. He is much better.

Q. Is he?

THE PRESIDENT. We are really proud of that.

Q. Is that a new jacket? Is that a Christmas present?

THE PRESIDENT. No, this is an old one. I've had this 10 years.

Q. Can you tell us, have you heard anything from the Middle East, or have you heard back from President Sadat or Mr. Begin?

THE PRESIDENT. I've gotten some dispatches about it, but I don't know enough about it to comment.

Q. When do you think you will talk to them today?

THE PRESIDENT. I don't know. I get a report from them a couple of times a a day, but sometimes they want to make announcements themselves, and I would rather defer to them.

Q. Mr. President, what did Amy get for Christmas?

THE PRESIDENT. Well, she got a roomful of stuff.

Q. Did she?

THE PRESIDENT. Yes.

Q. What was her big present?

THE PRESIDENT. I can't remember all she got. She got books and electric trains.

Q. She enjoy running around a little in her bare feet today, did she?

THE PRESIDENT. Yes, it's pretty warm. If you all fall, it's not my fault. [*Laughter*]

Q. No, we won't sue.

Q. Have you been doing homework for the foreign trip?

THE PRESIDENT. Yes, I've already studied Poland and Iran and India. And now I am working on Saudi Arabia and France and Belgium. By the time midnight comes, I'll be through.

Q. The influenza epidemic, are you looking to get the report from Atlanta this week, from the Center for Disease Control?

THE PRESIDENT. Yes, I know. No, I haven't got any report yet. I'm sure I will when I get back. I get those on a routine basis.

Q. Will you be coming back to Plains more often now? It seems a little quieter to us. We don't seem quieter, but——

THE PRESIDENT. Well, all over the Nation, November and December are the slowest months. I think there will probably be a few more people in town after Christmas.

Q. But it looks a little more normal, doesn't it?

THE PRESIDENT. It's much better, yes. It's more like it always was.

Well, I am sorry you all had to be down here for Christmas and not at home.

Q. Well, we miss our families, but——

THE PRESIDENT. I know. Are you going to go to Europe with me?

Q. Yes.

THE PRESIDENT. Very good.

Q. Spend New Year's with the Shah of Iran.

THE PRESIDENT. That's right. I will meet with King Hussein there. I don't know exactly where we'll meet yet. They haven't worked out the details.

Q. And does it look likely that President Asad would be willing to see you while you are over there?

THE PRESIDENT. I don't believe so. I don't know anything about that.

Q. Well, have the rest of a merry Christmas, and we'll see you tomorrow.

THE PRESIDENT. All right. 'Bye.

Q. Is that it for tonight? Can we go off to our Christmas party now?

THE PRESIDENT. I don't know. I have to check with my wife.

NOTE: The exchange began at approximately 5:30 p.m. at the home of Alton "Buddy" Carter, the President's uncle.

Warner Robins Air Force Base, Georgia

Informal Exchange With Reporters on Boarding Air Force One.   December 26, 1977

THE PRESIDENT. I talked to Prime Minister Begin just before I left my home, about 10 minutes of 11.

Let me wait for Helen [Helen Thomas, United Press International]. Helen, I wanted to wait for you. [*Laughter*]

I just told them that I talked to Prime Minister Begin just before I left home. He called me to give me a report. He says their visit to Ismailia was very successful, that he was pleased. They set up military and political committees to continue their work. And they'll meet for the first time January 15, one in Egypt and one in Jerusalem.

Q. Is Secretary Vance going to be joining the talks at all?

THE PRESIDENT. I don't know yet.

Q. Have there been any discussions of that?

THE PRESIDENT. Prime Minister Begin said that they would like for Secretary Vance to join them, but I don't know if he will or not.

Q. There are some reports now that perhaps the meetings did not come out as well as was anticipated. Are you going to try to do anything to keep the momentum going?

THE PRESIDENT. We'll do all we can.

Q. Are you still optimistic?

THE PRESIDENT. Well, Prime Minister Begin was very pleased.

NOTE: The exchange began at 11:55 a.m.

Office of Management and Budget

Remarks Announcing the Nomination of James T. McIntyre, Jr. To Be Director. December 27, 1977

THE PRESIDENT. I hope all of you had a merry Christmas.

It's a great pleasure for me to announce that I've asked Jim McIntyre, James McIntyre, to serve as permanent Director of the Office of Management and Budget. I have known Jim McIntyre for 7 years.

He's a professional in every sense of the word, a dedicated career public servant. He's had long experience in establishing policy, in long-range planning, in preparation of budgets, in the management of government, in reorganization, in zero-base budgeting, and, as you know, he has served here as the Deputy Director of OMB for a while and now in the last few months as the Acting Director of the Office of Management and Budget.

He has been successful in putting together the fiscal year 1979 budget, leading a very able and professional staff, I think, in a superlative way. He's worked harmoniously with me and he's worked well with the Members of Congress and with the Cabinet members as well.

I am very proud of Jim McIntyre. This is a thankless job, but it's one that he has undertaken in a very dedicated fashion, and I have complete confidence in him.

Jim, I want to congratulate you on the 1979 budget. We will be printing it up after our last meeting tomorrow. Our goal is to have the Federal budget be adequate, but to reduce the percentage of the gross national product of our country that goes into the Federal Government from the taxpayers and which is dispensed by the Government itself. And we have made a good start in that direction.

I think when the fiscal year '79 budget is analyzed, there will be many well-deserved accolades coming to Jim McIntyre.

Jim, I thank you and congratulate you on this appointment.

MR. McINTYRE. Thank you, Mr. President.

Mr. President, I want to thank you for the confidence and the trust that you have shown in me.

In recent weeks, we at OMB have pulled together the President's budget. As we've worked on his and other proposed programs and initiatives, my respect and admiration for President Carter's leadership, his intellect, and his diligence to duty and country has been reinforced.

As I look forward to continuing to serve the President and the country at OMB, I am both cautious and confident. Having worked at the agency for almost a year, I realize the size and scope, the responsibilities and the challenges. I also realize that at times we at OMB wouldn't win any popularity prizes, especially at the budget time. But I am confident that I can carry out the President's initiatives and directives.

A major reason for my confidence stems from the highly capable and effective staff at OMB. Our Executive Associate Directors, Bo Cutter and Harrison Wellford, their staffs, our congressional support through Herky Harris, Bob Dietsch and our Public Information Office, and all of the people at the agency have been of invaluable help to me and to the President. I take comfort that they will be there ready to help again.

I also feel confident that I can work with the Congress. While serving as Acting OMB Director, I have made a special effort to meet with a long list of Senators and Representatives, and I look forward to continuing our cooperation.

Next month we will send Congress the Federal budget for fiscal year 1979, the year which begins next October 1. It is President Carter's first full budget, and it will reflect his priorities. It will show the country the President's determination to be fiscally responsible, but it will also show that he will not neglect the country's domestic needs and problems. Thus, while the budget can be described as tight, it also can be described as responsive—responsive to the problems of our environment, our youth, the disadvantaged, and the unemployed. It will reflect the President's determination to make our Government work more effectively. All of us at OMB look forward to working with the Congress in implementing the President's budget.

Mr. President, I will always do my best to carry out OMB's assignments and responsibilities and your own directives. I appreciate your confidence in me. Thank you.

THE PRESIDENT. Thank you very much. Thank you, everybody. You have got a good boss.

NOTE: The President spoke at 2:15 p.m. to reporters assembled in the Briefing Room at the White House. The White House press release also includes the transcript of Mr. McIntyre's remarks in a question-and-answer session with reporters.

National Commission for the Review of Antitrust Laws and Procedures

Letter to the Speaker of the House and the President of the Senate. December 27, 1977

Dear Mr. Speaker: (Dear Mr. President:)

On November 30, 1977, I signed an Executive Order establishing a National Commission for the Review of Antitrust Laws and Procedures. A copy of the Order is enclosed.

The Commission will study and make recommendations on legislative or other proposals for expediting complex antitrust cases and making the remedies in such cases more effective, and on the desirability of retaining the various exemptions and immunities from the antitrust laws. The Commission shall conclude its work within six months and submit its final report to the Attorney General and me within thirty days after completing its work.

By the terms of the Executive Order, I must appoint three of the Commission's fifteen members upon your recommendation. I would appreciate your providing me with your recommendations at an early date, by submitting the names to the Attorney General.

I believe it is essential that our antitrust enforcement efforts not be allowed to become outdated or inefficient. This Commission will have the important responsibility of helping to ensure that this does not occur.

I wish to thank you in advance for your kind cooperation.

Sincerely,

JIMMY CARTER

NOTE: This is the text of identical letters addressed to the Honorable Thomas P. O'Neill, Jr., Speaker of the House of Representatives, and the Honorable Walter F. Mondale, President of the Senate.

The letter was not issued in the form of a White House press release.

For the text of Executive Order 12022, establishing the Commission, see page 2064 of this volume.

Imports of Petroleum and Petroleum Products

Proclamation 4543. December 27, 1977

MODIFYING PROCLAMATION No. 3279, AS AMENDED, RELATING TO IMPORTS OF PETROLEUM AND PETROLEUM PRODUCTS, AND PROVIDING FOR THE LONG-TERM CONTROL OF IMPORTS OF PETROLEUM AND PETROLEUM PRODUCTS THROUGH A SYSTEM OF LICENSE FEES

By the President of the United States of America

A Proclamation

It is necessary that the United States complete the establishment of a Strategic Petroleum Reserve as quickly as possible.

The imposition of license fees on imports of crude oil and products for such

Reserve would not carry out the purposes of Proclamation No. 3279, as amended, and could create administrative and other problems with respect to the expeditious completion of the Reserve.

Now, THEREFORE, I, JIMMY CARTER, President of the United States of America, by virtue of the authority vested in me by the Constitution and the laws of the United States of America, including Section 232 of the Trade Expansion Act of 1962, as amended (19 U.S.C. 1862), do hereby proclaim that, effective as of October 1, 1977, Proclamation No. 3279, as amended, is further amended as follows:

Clauses (i) and (ii) of subparagraph (1) of paragraph (a) of Section 3 are revised to read as follows:

"(i) with respect to imports of crude oil (other than that imported by the Department of Energy, or by another person or agency of the Federal Government acting on behalf of the Department, for the Strategic Petroleum Reserve Program) and natural gas products over and above the levels of imports established in Section 2 of this Proclamation, such fees shall be $0.21 per barrel;

(ii) with respect to imports of motor gasoline, unfinished oils, and all other finished products (except ethane, propane, butanes, asphalt and finished products imported by the Department of Energy, or another person or agency of the Federal Government acting on behalf of the Department of Energy, for the Strategic Petroleum Reserve Program), over and above the levels of imports established in Section 2 of this Proclamation, such fees shall be $0.63 per barrel;".

IN WITNESS WHEREOF, I have hereunto set my hand this twenty-seventh day of December, in the year of our Lord nineteen hundred seventy-seven, and of the Independence of the United States of America the two hundred and second.

JIMMY CARTER

[Filed with the Office of the Federal Register, 3:55 p.m., December 27, 1977]

Best wishes for a healthy and happy and successful 1978.

JIMMY CARTER

NOTE: The text of the telegram was released on December 28.

On the same day, the President met at the White House with Chairman Curtis and Deputy Secretary White.

Democratic National Committee

Telegram to Members on Recommendation of John C. White To Be Chairman. December 27, 1977

I want to inform you, prior to official release to the press, of my recommendation of John White of Texas, to you as Chairman of the DNC. White, currently the Deputy Secretary of Agriculture has a long and outstanding public and party record, serving as Commissioner of Agriculture of Texas for 26 years, and serving in a leadership capacity in every Democratic Presidential campaign in Texas from 1952 to 1976. He served for two years as a member of the National Democratic Charter Commission. Through thick and thin, John White has been a loyal and dedicated Democrat—a talented organizer, an articulate spokesman, a tough and fair leader. He has the attributes that will make him an outstanding Chairman of our Party. He has my fullest support, and I hope he will have yours as well.

I am sending you a follow up letter to this telegram, to detail more specifically the reasons I am recommending John White to you. Chairman Curtis will notify you shortly about the time, date and place of the special meeting of the DNC that will handle the election.

I would like to thank Ken Curtis for all he has done for our party during his term as Chairman.

Clean Water Act of 1977

Statement on Signing H.R. 3199 Into Law. December 28, 1977

I am pleased to sign the Clean Water Act of 1977, which amends the Federal Water Pollution Control Act of 1972. This act reaffirms our national commitment to protect the quality of our waters and the health of our people.

I particularly want to thank Senators Randolph and Muskie and Congressmen Johnson and Roberts for their outstanding leadership in resolving the many difficult issues embodied in this act. I am also grateful for the consistent cooperation of Senator Stafford and Congressman Harsha and the other conferees and for the dedication of the staff and EPA Administrator Costle in this effort.

This act culminates 3 years of hard work by the Congress to make the necessary midcourse corrections in our national water pollution control program. This is a fine example of how close cooperation between the administration and the Congress can produce major legislation of national significance.

The Clean Water Act of 1977 embraces many of the principles and proposals put forward by my administration. The Congress has agreed to long-term funding for the municipal sewage treatment construction grant program which I urged in my environmental message earlier this year. This will help States and communities plan and implement effectively programs to clean up backlogs of municipal pollution.

The bill also emphasizes the importance of controlling toxic pollutants which endanger the public health—a focus which my administration has urged.

The Nation's wetlands will continue to be protected under a framework which is workable and which shares responsibilities with the States. Certain farming and forestry activities that were never intended to be covered under the original act are specifically exempted from requirements to obtain permits. I am concerned that congressionally approved Federal projects are also exempted from this permit program. Accordingly, I have directed EPA and other Federal agencies to take administrative steps to ensure that Federal projects meet standards comparable to those which nonfederal projects must meet.

The bill also:

- helps small communities meet the requirements of the 1972 act;
- encourages industry to experiment with the treatment of waste water and sludge;
- allows the Federal and State Governments to recover their costs in mitigating damages from spills of oil and other hazardous substances.

Amendments to the oil and hazardous spill provisions of the 1972 act will extend domestic jurisdiction to the ocean beyond the contiguous zone, where the fisheries and other natural resources of the United States may be adversely affected. Oil pollution is a global problem, and accidents on the oceans prove the need for effective international solutions.

We have been working through international forums to achieve broader acceptance for higher worldwide pollution standards. I believe that the legislation I am signing may raise issues of consistency with international law, and I know that many Members of the Congress share this concern. Our clear objective is to achieve maximum consistency with applicable principles of international law regarding the protection of the marine environment and to encourage ongoing and future international efforts to combat pollution of the ocean. If that objective should require amendments to the act that I am signing into law, I am confident that the Congress and the administration will work together next year to make any necessary adjustments.

This act also requires Federal agencies to comply with all Federal, State, and local substantive and procedural requirements concerning the control and abatement of water pollution. I strongly support this requirement because it demonstrates the Federal Government's own commitment to cleaning up the water while also recognizing that certain exemptions may be needed in the national interest. For example, during this period of energy crisis, it may be necessary to exempt certain activities such as the Strategic Petroleum Reserve program from the strict application of this requirement. The amendments which I am signing do not limit my authority to grant exemptions which may be needed to avoid unnecessary delays in implementing the important energy program.

NOTE: As enacted, H.R. 3199 is Public Law 95–217, approved December 27.

Congressional Visit to the People's Republic of China

Announcement of Plans for the Visit to China by a Bipartisan Congressional Delegation. December 28, 1977

The Chinese People's Institute of Foreign Affairs of the People's Republic of

China has invited a bipartisan congressional delegation to visit China during January.

The delegation will depart January 2 and return January 17. The group will be led by Senator Alan Cranston, Democrat of California, with Representative Charles Whalen, Republican of Ohio, as the deputy leader.

Other members of the group include:

Senators

CHARLES MATHIAS (R-Md.)
JAMES ABOUREZK (D-S. Dak.)
GARY HART (D-Colo.)
RICHARD LUGAR (R-Ind.)

Representatives

JAMES WEAVER (D-Oreg.)
STEPHEN NEAL (D-N.C.)
FREDERICK RICHMOND (D-N.Y.)
STEPHEN SOLARZ (D-N.Y.)

The Congressmen will be accompanied by Allyn Kreps, legislative assistant to Senator Cranston; Douglas Bennet, Assistant Secretary of State for Congressional Relations; Dan Tate, Deputy Director of the White House congressional liaison office; and Herbert Horowitz of the Department of State.

Since the first congressional delegation went to the People's Republic of China in 1972, there have been over 70 Members of Congress who have visited China.

The present delegation was scheduled to visit China last November, but the continuation of the congressional session forced postponement of the original timing.

The exchange relationship fulfills that part of the Shanghai Communique in which both sides pledged to foster broader understanding and engage in cultural and scientific exchanges.

Generalized System of Preferences for Developing Countries

Executive Order 12032.   December 27, 1977

AMENDING THE GENERALIZED SYSTEM OF PREFERENCES

By virtue of the authority vested in me by the Constitution and statutes of the United States of America, including Title V and Section 604 of the Trade Act of 1974 (88 Stat. 2066, 19 U.S.C. 2461 *et seq.;* 88 Stat. 2073, 19 U.S.C. 2483), and as President of the United States of America, in order to modify, as provided by Section 504(c) of the Trade Act of 1974 (88 Stat. 2070, 19 U.S.C. 2464(c)), the limitations on preferential treatment for eligible articles from countries designated as beneficiary developing countries, and to adjust the original designation of eligible articles taking into account information and advice received in fulfillment of Sections 503(a) and 131–134 of the Trade Act of 1974, it is hereby ordered as follows:

SECTION 1. In order to subdivide existing items for purposes of the Generalized System of Preferences (GSP), the Tariff Schedules of the United States (TSUS) are modified as provided in Annex I, attached hereto and made a part hereof.

SEC. 2. Annex II of Executive Order No. 11888 of November 24, 1975, as amended, listing articles that are eligible for benefits of the GSP when imported from any designated beneficiary developing country, is further amended as provided in Annex II, attached hereto and made a part hereof.

SEC. 3. Annex III of Executive Order No. 11888, as amended, listing articles that are eligible for benefits of the GSP when imported from all designated beneficiary countries except those specified in General Headnote 3(c)(iii) of the

TSUS, is amended as provided in Annex III, attached hereto and made a part hereof.

SEC. 4. General Headnote 3(c)(iii) of the TSUS, listing articles that are eligible for benefits of the GSP except when imported from the beneficiary countries listed opposite those articles, is amended as provided in Annex IV, attached hereto and made a part hereof.

SEC. 5. (a) The amendment made by Annex IV, paragraph (a) of this Order with respect to item 613.18, TSUS, made part hereof by Section 4 above, shall be effective with respect to articles that are both: (1) imported on or after January 1, 1976, and (2) entered for consumption, or withdrawn from warehouse for consumption, on or after March 1, 1977.

(b) The other amendments made by this Order shall be effective with respect to articles that are both: (1) imported on or after January 1, 1976, and (2) entered or withdrawn from warehouse for consumption, on or after January 1, 1978.

JIMMY CARTER

The White House,
    December 27, 1977.

[Filed with the Office of the Federal Register, 12:11 p.m., December 28, 1977]

NOTE: Annexes I, II, III, and IV are printed in the FEDERAL REGISTER of December 29, 1977.

The text of the Executive order was released on December 28.

Executive Office of the President

Appointment of Richard Harden as Director of the Office of Administration. December 28, 1977

The President has appointed Richard Harden, his Special Assistant for Information Management, as Director of the Office of Administration. This new position was created by Reorganization Plan No. 1.

Harden, 33, will continue to serve as Special Assistant to the President. He was commissioner of administrative services, then commissioner of the Department of Human Resources, during then-Governor Carter's administration in Georgia. Harden worked on the Carter Presidential campaign as budget and finance director.

Committee for the Preservation of the White House

Appointment of 16 Members to the Committee. December 28, 1977

The President today announced the appointment of the following persons as members of the Committee for the Preservation of the White House:

VICKI L. BAGLEY, a member of the board of the North Carolina School of Arts and active in the Corcoran Art Gallery and the Kennedy Center;

NORMAN B. CHAMP, JR., president of Champ Spring Co. in St. Louis;

MRS. ATHALIE IRVINE CLARKE, currently on the Committee and a contributor to the White House;

MRS. LAMMOT DUPONT COPELAND, currently a member of the Committee and on the board of trustees of the Henry Francis duPont Winterthur Museum;

MRS. CHARLES W. ENGELHARD, chairman of the board of Engelhard Hanovia in New Jersey and currently a member of the Committee;

HENRY FORD II, president of Ford Motor Company;

MRS. JAMES STEWART HOOKER, of Palm Beach, Fla., a member of the Metropolitan Opera Guild and benefactor of the Metropolitan Museum of Art;

DONELSON F. HOOPES, visiting curator of the M. H. De Young Memorial Museum in San Francisco and associate editor of American Art Review in Los Angeles;

EDWARD VASON JONES, currently a member of the Committee and an architectural and design adviser to the Committee;

Mrs. WILLIAM GERALD McMURTRIE, of Maryland, a member of the board of Mount Vernon College and member of the Children's Hearing and Speech Committee of Children's Hospital;

ROBERT L. McNEIL, JR., currently on the Committee and retired chairman of McNeil Laboratories;

BILL O. MEAD, chairman of the board and chief executive officer of Campbell Taggart, Inc., in Dallas, Tex.;

WALTER H. SHORENSTEIN, chairman of the board of the San Francisco Chamber of Commerce and a real estate executive;

SHIRLEY VERRETT, opera star;

PHILIP M. WALDEN, owner of Capricorn Records in Macon, Ga.;

Mrs. LEW WASSERMAN, of Beverly Hills, who is active in civic affairs there.

Securities Investor Protection Corporation

Nomination of Hugh F. Owens To Be a Director. December 28, 1977

The President today announced that he will nominate Hugh F. Owens, of Washington, D.C., for reappointment as a Director of the Securities Investor Protection Corporation for a term expiring December 31, 1979. The President also indicated that on confirmation by the Senate, Owens would be redesignated Chairman of the Corporation.

Owens was born October 15, 1909, in Muskogee, Okla. He received an A.B. from the University of Illinois in 1931 and an LL.B. from the University of Oklahoma in 1934.

Between 1934 and 1959, Owens practiced law in Illinois, Texas, and Oklahoma. He served in the U.S. Navy as lieutenant commander from 1942 to 1945. From 1959 to 1964, he was administrator of the Oklahoma Securities Commission.

Owens was appointed a member of the Securities and Exchange Commission by President Johnson in 1964. He served on the SEC until 1973, when he resigned to accept appointment as Chairman of the Securities Investor Protection Corporation.

Federal Reserve System

Remarks Announcing the Nomination of G. William Miller To Be Chairman of the Board of Governors. December 28, 1977

THE PRESIDENT. Good afternoon, everybody.

I'm very proud to announce that G. William Miller will be my nominee as Chairman of the Board of Governors of the Federal Reserve System.

For the last 8 years, through two terms as Chairman, Dr. Arthur Burns has done an outstanding job of directing the Federal Reserve System. He has symbolized the integrity of our monetary system and the independence of the Federal Reserve. He has defended the strength of the dollar at home and abroad. In this and in every other public position which he has held, he has served the people of our country well and has earned our respect and our gratitude. And I am very thankful that he has also become my close, personal friend.

There are few positions more demanding than the chairmanship of the Federal Reserve, and few appointments that any President makes that have a greater influence on our country. Apart from the President himself, no one else plays a larger part in determining our Nation's economic policy.

I believe that an independent Federal Reserve must be led by a person of strong character, broad experience, and firsthand knowledge of how to cope effectively with our Nation's economic problems. That is why Dr. Burns has served his two terms so well and that is also why I have now chosen Bill Miller to be the new Chairman.

Extensive consultations with a wide range of business and financial leaders have convinced me that Bill Miller enjoys the highest respect and the confidence of everyone who knows him. His record as a businessman has won him a position of leadership in the American business community. In 1960, at the age of 35, he became president of Textron, Inc., and later became chief executive officer and chairman of the board. He is also chairman of the Conference Board, which represents top American business leadership as a business and an economic research group. Bill Miller has extensive experience and knowledge in international business and finance. He's familiar with the workings of the Federal Reserve System, having served under Dr. Burns as a Director of the Federal Reserve Bank of Boston for 7 years.

I'm particularly impressed that his success as a businessman has not kept him from consistent public service. As chairman of the National Alliance of Businessmen, he has helped to find new ways to harness the resources of the business community to meet some of our most pressing public problems, especially the need to create new jobs. It was because I recognized the importance of this appointment that I consulted widely before making it and because I value the continuity of Federal monetary and economic policy.

I have been very gratified to hear Dr. Arthur Burns express his confidence in Bill Miller.

Bill, thank you very much for being willing to serve. I'd now like to introduce to you and to the Nation G. William Miller, who will be the next Chairman of the Federal Reserve.

Bill?

MR. MILLER. *Mr. President, Mr. Vice President, Chairman Burns:*

It is an important time in our economic situation in the United States, and it came, I suppose, as somewhat of a surprise to me that the President asked me to take on this new role. I recognize that Dr. Burns has served long and wisely, is universally admired and respected, and that he has made an indelible contribution to the monetary system and to the defense of the dollar, to the fight against inflation, and to the stability of our economic system. Yet, we continue to face the problems, the twin problems, of inflation and high unemployment. We need to continue the policies of Dr. Burns and those of the President, to assure that we have full employment with price stability and that we do again have a sound dollar that is the cornerstone of the world monetary system.

I cannot profess to have the qualifications to step into Dr. Burns' shoes, but I do, Mr. President, assure you that all of the energy, drive, capacity that I have will be devoted to continuing the work that has been done and continuing the programs so that over time we can overcome both inflation and unemployment and return this Nation to a period of economic growth and stability.

Thank you very much.

THE PRESIDENT. Dr. Burns?

CHAIRMAN BURNS. *Mr. President, Mr. and Mrs. Miller, Mr. Vice President:*

I think this is a good day. The President informed me of his decision today, and I didn't have to think. I've known Mr. Miller for many years, and I responded at once, "Mr. President, you have chosen wisely and well." And I meant every word literally. I spoke from the bottom of my heart.

Now, Mr. Miller will bring to his Federal Reserve responsibilities not only great energy, not only exceptional knowledge of the business world; he also brings to it the knowledge of the Federal Reserve System. And what is most important of all, he brings to his tasks moral integrity, a fine character, and these are the most important attributes for that high position.

I think, Mr. President, you are to be congratulated on your choice, and I am confident that Mr. Miller will serve this country and will serve it well. You have my very best wishes and my respect.

MR. MILLER. Thank you very much, Dr. Burns.

THE PRESIDENT. We would have time for two or three questions if anyone has any.

REPORTER. Will Dr. Burns stay on the Federal Reserve as a member?

THE PRESIDENT. I would be very pleased if he would, but that's a decision that he would have to make.

Dr. Burns, I don't know if you want to respond or not.

CHAIRMAN BURNS. The good Doctor is in the habit of thinking now and then. He'll think this one over carefully. [*Laughter*]

Q. May I ask Mr. Miller a question?

THE PRESIDENT. Certainly.

Q. Mr. Miller, you've kind of a balance between unemployment and inflation—how to fine-tune it, if you can. Is it your view that perhaps we need to work more on unemployment than we have been, that perhaps the Fed needs to sort of tilt a little bit more?

MR. MILLER. I think we need to work on both at once. It's very interesting that in the Public Agenda Foundation research done in 1976, there was a widespread opinion that one or the other had to be given priority, but the public at large felt that both could be worked on simultaneously, and I happen to share

that view. And I think that working in harmony with the fiscal policies of the President, the monetary policies of the Federal Reserve, I think we can tackle both at once and achieve what we really need—full employment with price stability.

Q. If I may follow that up, can you tighten every discount rate? For instance, you are acting on the money supply, and it has an impact which isn't balanced, isn't six of one and half a dozen of the other.

MR. MILLER. I think we will move from here in the context of the economy as it develops over the next year, and I'm sure that we can find ways in which we can tackle both issues simultaneously, and we certainly shall try.

Q. [*Inaudible*]

MR. MILLER. Well, I think we'll have to let Dr. Burns, who's Chairman now, decide that. And when I'm Chairman, perhaps, I'll have a say.

Q. Sir, how will your policies differ from Dr. Burns'?

MR. MILLER. My policies will be one of seven Board of Governors, and I hope that I will play a leadership role in continuing the policies that Dr. Burns has stood for so well and so long, and that as the economy goes through its natural evolution and develops in its natural ways, that we can continue to be creative and innovative and responsive to the needs in the way in which they exist during the coming years.

I think the past is prologue. We must learn from the past and we must extrapolate from that and always seek to improve and to be creative.

Q. Mr. Miller, now one more question. Do you feel that the American Government should do more to bolster the dollar on the foreign market?

MR. MILLER. I think we should bring about conditions where the dollar is stronger, and that, of course, depends upon fundamental economics and it depends upon our balance of payments and it depends upon the strength of our domestic economy.

If we bring about the normal progress that we were speaking about a moment ago, I think we will again see a strong and favorable dollar and this would, I think, be favorable to our Nation.

Q. Can we ask the President one more question? Dr. Burns has the confidence of the business community to such a great extent that there is a lot of speculation about if he wasn't reappointed there'd be a loss of business confidence. Do you think Mr. Miller has the same reputation, widely, in the business community, or do you think there's a problem there?

THE PRESIDENT. No, I don't think there is a problem. I have consulted either directly or indirectly with dozens of leaders in the business and financial community, and there's been a unanimous and an overwhelming expression of confidence and approbation for Bill Miller to be Chairman. Many of those leaders have also, of course, expressed their hope that the basic principles espoused by Chairman Burns would be continued.

I think the transition period will be a time for Bill Miller to learn and for Dr. Burns and others to teach, but I don't think there's any doubt that the leaders in the business community of our country will respond very well to the appointment of Bill Miller.

Thank you very much, everybody.

REPORTER. Thank you.

NOTE: The President spoke at 5:07 p.m. to reporters assembled in the Briefing Room at the White House.

The White House Press Office also released the following biographical information on Mr. Miller:

Mr. G. William Miller is chairman of Textron, Inc., a diversified company headquartered in Providence, R.I., with 180 plants and facilities in the United States and in several foreign countries. Textron employs 65,000 persons and had sales in 1976 of $2.6 billion.

Mr. Miller is a Director of the Federal Reserve Bank of Boston and chairman of the Conference Board and chairman of the National Alliance of Businessmen.

Mr. Miller is a native of Oklahoma, born in Sapulpa in 1925, and was raised in the Southwest. He graduated from the U.S. Coast Guard Academy in 1945, serving as an officer in the Far Pacific and China.

In 1952 Mr. Miller received his J.D. degree from the University of California and practiced law in New York with the firm of Cravath, Swaine and Moore before joining Textron in 1956 as assistant secretary.

In June of 1960, at age 35, Mr. Miller was elected president of Textron, and in 1968 he assumed the additional post of chief executive officer. In 1974 he was elected chairman of the board.

Mr. Miller is a director of the Allied Chemical Corp., Con Rail, and Federated Department Stores. He is a member of the Business Council and the Business Roundtable. He is also Chairman of the President's Committee for HIRE (veterans employment).

He is cochairman of both the U.S.–U.S.S.R. Trade and Economic Council and the Polish-U.S. Economic Council. In 1977 Mr. Miller was Chairman of the U.S. Industrial Payroll Savings Bond Committee and has served as the first Chairman of the Industry Advisory Committee of the President's Committee on Equal Employment Opportunity and as a member of the National Council on the Humanities.

Mr. Miller is married to the former Ariadna Rogajarski.

Presidential War Powers Bill

**Statement on Signing H.R. 7738 Into Law.
December 28, 1977**

I am today signing H.R. 7738, an act "with respect to the powers of the President in time of war or national emergency."

H.R. 7738 is the result of a cooperative effort by the Congress and this administration. Its broad purpose is to differentiate between those economic powers available to the President in time of war and those available in time of declared national emergency. The bill is largely procedural. It places additional constraints on use of the President's emergency economic powers in future national emergencies and ensures that the Congress and the public will be kept informed of activities carried out under these powers. Enactment of the bill will not affect embargoes now being exercised against certain countries, nor does it affect the blockage of assets of nationals of those and other countries.

In approving the bill, I must note my serious concern over the provision contained in Section 207(b), which would allow Congress to terminate a national emergency declared by the President by concurrent resolution.

Provisions such as these raise profound constitutional questions, since Article I, Section 7, of the Constitution requires that congressional action having the force of law be presented to the President for his signature or veto. In addition, such provisions have the potential of involving Congress in the execution of the laws—a responsibility reserved exclusively to the President under the Constitution. This feature of the bill may be unconstitutional. I will therefore treat the provision as requiring only that I "notify and wait" with respect to national emergencies covered by Section 207(b) of this act.

NOTE: As enacted, H.R. 7738 is Public Law 95–223, approved December 28.

Conversation With the President

Remarks in an Interview With Tom Brokaw of NBC News, Bob Schieffer of CBS News, Robert MacNeil of the Public Broadcasting Service, and Barbara Walters of ABC News. December 28, 1977

THE PRESIDENT. This year we have had fireside chats and television programs and telephone call-in shows and press conferences twice a month and meetings with editors from almost every State in the Nation. And I've been very pleased to stay in touch with the American people.

Tonight we have four distinguished news reporters from the four major networks in our country. And I want to welcome you here as another opportunity for me to speak to the American people with tough interrogations from those who understand our country very well.

I understand Mr. Brokaw has the first question.

THE PRESIDENT'S OVERSEAS TRIP

MR. BROKAW. Mr. President, there are a number of subjects that we want to cover tonight, including some news developments that are going on even as we speak. I want to begin, however, with a question about the trip that you leave on tomorrow. It was originally postponed because you did not yet have the energy bill passed. It still has not been passed.

My question is this: Aren't you playing into the twin themes of your critics who complain that your energy bill has not been passed, that you have failed on the major domestic priority of your administration, and that your foreign policy has no real definition, because this trip seems to have no urgent theme to it?

THE PRESIDENT. Well, the only major legislation that did not pass the Congress this year and which I was expecting to pass, was energy. Speaker of the House Tip O'Neill said that it was the most productive session since the first term of Franklin Roosevelt. I'll let him be the judge of that.

The energy legislation, I think, will be the first item on the agenda when the Congress reconvenes in January. And there's no doubt that wherever I go on this trip—to Eastern Europe, to Western Europe, to the Mideast, to India—what our Nation does about energy will be a prime question.

We are the leader of the world. We are one of the major oil producers. We are the greatest consumer. And until Congress does take action on the energy proposal that I put forward last April, and which the House of Representatives passed in August, that cloud will hang over the determination and leadership qualities of our country.

So, I am disappointed about that. As far as the trip is concerned, it's carefully planned. We began working on this trip last March, and the nations that we will visit are important to us both domestically and in our foreign relations.

Poland—in Eastern Europe, a Communist government with close ties to the Soviet Union but also friendships with us, heavy trade with the Western nations, relatively willing to give people their religious freedom and other freedoms. We will have a good meeting, I think, in Poland.

We go from there to Iran, very close military ally of ours, a strong trade partner of ours with whom we share many political responsibilities.

And then we go to India, the biggest democracy in the world, one that in recent years has turned perhaps excessively toward the Soviet Union, but under the new leadership of Prime Minister Desai is moving back toward us and assuming a good role of, I would say, neutrality. And we have a strong friendship with

India. It's a strong country. They are almost self-sufficient now. They have food surpluses.

We come back from there to Saudi Arabia, our major supplier of imported oil, a nation that's worked closely with us in foreign affairs in many parts of the world.

From there back to France, our historic ally, keystone in Europe. I'll have long discussions with President Giscard there and then go back to Brussels to strengthen our relationships with the European Community and with NATO.

So, every stop will be productive for us. I'll be taking the word and the good will and the sense of importance of the American people toward them in learning about those countries in the process.

But energy will be the tie that will bind us together on this trip, and I hope that this will demonstrate to the American people and to the Congress the necessity for rapid action on one of the most controversial and divisive issues that the Congress has ever faced, and that is to give our country for the first time a comprehensive energy policy.

THE MIDDLE EAST

MR. SCHIEFFER. Mr. President, I know we'll all want to get back to just how you plan to go about getting that energy policy. But while we are on foreign policy, I'd like to ask you about the Middle East. President Sadat, I think everyone agrees, made a spectacular gesture that opened up a whole new era here. Do you feel that the Israelis have as yet made a comparable gesture? Have they been flexible enough in your view?

THE PRESIDENT. Both President Sadat and Prime Minister Begin have been bold and courageous. We've been dealing with the Mideast question as a nation for decades, in a leadership role at least within the last two administrations. And we see the complexities of the questions and the obstacles to progress. When I first became President, we spelled out the basic issues: withdrawal from occupied territories, secure borders, the establishment of real peace, the recognition of Israel's right to be there, and dealing with the Palestinian question.

We are now in a role of supporter. We encourage them to continue with their fruitful negotiations. We try to resolve difficulties, to give advice and counsel when we are requested to do it. This is a better role for us. In the past, we've been in the unenviable position and sometimes unpleasant position, sometimes nonproductive position as mediator among parties who wouldn't even speak to each other. So, I think that the progress that has been made in the last month and a half has been remarkable and has been much greater than I had anticipated.

And I know Sadat and Begin well and personally and favorably. If any two leaders on Earth have the strength and the determination and the courage to make progress toward peace in the most difficult region that I've ever known, it is Prime Minister Begin and President Sadat. There is no reason for us to be discouraged about it. We will help in every way we can to let their progress be fruitful. I think that President Sadat and Prime Minister Begin could have reached a fairly quick solution of just the Egyptian-Israeli problem in the Sinai region. But this is not what they want.

They both want to try to resolve the other questions: What is real peace? Will Israel be recognized as a permanent neighbor to the countries that surround them? Can the Palestinian question, the West Bank, the Gaza Strip be addressed successfully? And knowing how difficult these questions are, I have nothing but admiration for them, nothing but con-

gratulations for them on what they have achieved so far.

Mr. MacNeil. Mr. President, you are going to see King Hussein of Jordan in Tehran. President Sadat said in an interview that was broadcast on public television last night that King Hussein had told him that he was fully behind his efforts. In public until now, King Hussein's opinion has been relatively mysterious. Do you have any information that would make you agree with Mr. Sadat, and are you going to discuss that with King Hussein and urge him to support the Sadat initiative when you see him?

The President. I don't intend to put any pressure on King Hussein—I couldn't if I wanted to—to immediately begin to negotiate with Israel and Egypt as a partner. If he wants to do it, we would certainly welcome that. What I will try to learn, however, is what role Jordan is willing to play in the resolution of the Palestinian-West Bank problem, at what point he thinks it would be advisable for him to enter the negotiations personally as a government leader, and what we can do to get him to give his open support and encouragement to both Begin and Sadat as they struggle to resolve the differences between them.

I think King Hussein has indeed, in his private discussions with Secretary Vance and his personal communications to me, shown a very positive attitude. And in his travels around the Middle East to visit with other leaders, some who don't encourage the talks, like President Asad, those who are very hopeful for progress, like those in Saudi Arabia, I think he's shown a constructive attitude already. But it helps me to understand on a current basis the remaining problems and in what way they can be brought in to achieve a comprehensive peace.

I think they all trust our country. Our motives are good. We've never misled them. We've been honest and as a person, as a country that carried messages from one to another. And I think that this puts us in a position to exert legitimate influence. But what we've always hoped for is direct negotiations or discussions, communications among the leaders involved with our offering good offices when we are requested to do it.

Ms. WALTERS. Mr. President, the chief stumbling block right now does seem to be what we might call the right of return of the Palestinians to the West Bank and the Gaza. You have in the past come out against an independent nation per se on the West Bank, but you have also talked of the legitimate rights of the Palestinians, and you have been in favor of some kind of an entity—although people are still a little obscure about what that means—an entity perhaps linked to Jordan.

Would you, in the light of the developments now, clarify your views for us today, tell us if they have changed, and if they have not, is it because the United States has decided to be neutral on this subject?

THE PRESIDENT. Well, you've described my position very well. We do favor a homeland or an entity wherein the Palestinians can live in peace. I think Prime Minister Begin has taken a long step forward in offering to President Sadat, and indirectly to the Palestinians, self-rule.

President Sadat so far is insisting that the so-called Palestinian entity be an independent nation. My own preference is that they not be an independent nation but be tied in some way with the surrounding countries, making a choice, for instance, between Israel and Jordan.

President Sadat has not yet agreed to that position of ours. Prime Minister Begin has offered that the citizens who live in the West Bank area or the Gaza Strip be given an option to be either Israeli citizens or Jordanian citizens, to

actually run for the Knesset as candidates and to vote in elections, both national, Israeli and Jordan, or local elections in the occupied territories once they are released.

But we don't have any real choice. I've expressed an opinion. But if Israel should negotiate with the surrounding countries a different solution, we would certainly support it.

But my own personal opinion is that permanent peace can best be maintained if there's not a fairly radical, new independent nation in the heart of the Middle Eastern area.

Ms. WALTERS. In view of the deadlock now, however, have you tried to convince either side of your opinion? You've had conversations with both.

THE PRESIDENT. I've expressed this opinion to President Asad, to King Hussein, to President Sadat, to Crown Prince Fahd, and also to Prime Minister Begin, privately. And, of course, they have heard my statements publicly. Our preference is not to have an independent nation there, but we are perfectly willing to accept any reasonable solution that the parties themselves might evolve.

MR. SCHIEFFER. If I could just get back to the question I asked you, do I take it that you would not pass judgment in public, at least at this point, on whether the Israelis have been flexible enough in the negotiating so far? Do you think that the position that they put forward—Mr. Begin said today that there would always be Israeli troops on the West Bank and that all who wanted peace would have to know that—is that a realistic negotiating position?

THE PRESIDENT. Yes. It's certainly a realistic negotiating position.

MR. SCHIEFFER. But would Mr. Sadat ever accept that?

THE PRESIDENT. I don't know. There is a great deal of flexibility there—the number of military outposts, the length of time when this interim solution might be in effect—I think Prime Minister Begin said it would be reassessed at the end of 5 years—the degree of participation of the governments of Israel and Jordan in a possible administrative arrangement—all these questions could add a tone of progress or a possibility for resolution of what seems to be insurmountable obstacles.

So, I think that Prime Minister Begin already has shown a great deal of flexibility. Obviously, President Sadat and King Hussein and others would have to accept whatever proposal is put forward.

But the length of time when the interim agreement would be in effect would be negotiable and the exact relationship between the new self-rule government as far as its autonomy is concerned, its dependence upon or subservience to the Jordanians or the Israelis—all these things are still to be negotiated. So, I think there is enough flexibility at this point.

MR. MacNEIL. Could I just ask one followup on that?

THE PRESIDENT. Please.

MR. MacNEIL. Has either Egypt or Israel, or both, asked the United States formally yet to provide guarantees for any agreement that is made?

THE PRESIDENT. Well, in my private conversations with some of them, they have expressed to me that if a guarantee arrangement between ourselves and Israel should be worked out, that it would be acceptable to the Arab leaders. But we've never discussed this between ourselves and Israel in any definitive form.

My preference would be that our involvement would be minimized after an agreement has been reached. But if it became a matter of having the negotiations break down completely, our hav-

ing some limited role as mutually accepted among those parties involved, then we would consider it very, very favorably.

STRATEGIC ARMS LIMITATION TALKS

MR. BROKAW. Mr. President, if we may move along in another area of foreign policy for just a moment, there now seems to be some signals coming out of Geneva, and even from friends of this administration, that we will not have a SALT agreement in 1978, or at least one will not get before the Senate. That's the word from Senator Alan Cranston, who is known as a very good vote counter in the Senate. Is that your thinking as well, that we are not going to have a SALT agreement with the Russians during this next year?

THE PRESIDENT. I would be disappointed if we don't have a SALT agreement this year. We've made good progress on SALT. We started out with SALT I, the Soviets having a very heavy advantage, about a 3-to-2 ratio in their favor. President Ford and Secretary Kissinger made great progress, I think, at Vladivostok and in their subsequent negotiations, to provide the first indication of equality. And we will maintain that posture of mutual advantage between ourselves and the Soviets.

We have added a new dimension, to have tight constraints on future deployment of weapons, both quantitatively and also the quality of the weapons, and to reduce actually the number of destructive weapons permitted.

We still have some negotiating to do. But we have made good progress on SALT. We have also been pleased with the results of negotiations with the Soviet Union on the comprehensive test ban to prohibit any testing of nuclear weapons at all.

And we have made progress, also, in trying to stop a military buildup in the Indian Ocean. My guess is that President Brezhnev would be likely to want to come here to visit after those three negotiations have made some substantial progress and when there is a prospect of immediate resolution of the remaining differences.

I would never approve a SALT agreement nor present one to the Congress that didn't have an adequate degree of verification of compliance and which didn't protect the right of our own country to defend itself and to carry out our domestic and foreign policy. Whatever I put forward to the Congress will be good for our Nation.

We've had a maximum degree of involvement by the Congress. We've even had Senators in Europe at the negotiating table. And we've kept them informed as the progress is made.

So, my guess is that 1978 will see us successful, and my guess is that when we present it to the Congress, the SALT agreement will be approved.

ARTHUR F. BURNS

Ms. WALTERS. Mr. President, there are so many questions I think we all have on foreign policy, but we are aware of the time. So, perhaps we might slide into the domestic issues.

Shortly before we went on the air you made news yourself about Arthur Burns and his replacement. Mr. Burns still has 2 years to go before he would retire from being on the Board itself of the Federal Reserve. Are you—or have you specifically asked him to stay? Obviously, some words from you might make the difference. Or do you have any other plans for him in government?

THE PRESIDENT. When I met with Chairman Burns, I told him that I understood he wanted to stay on the Board and

that that would please me very much. He said that he had not yet made a decision. I then responded that if he decided not to stay on the Board, after a new Chairman is sworn in, that I would like very much to have him serve in some capacity. He is so wise, he has so much experience, his record is so superb, his integrity is perfect, almost, that I think he would still have good service to offer to our country. He said that he would not want to make any decisions within the next period just ahead, but that he would like to hear from me in the future. And I think the first decision that he would make is whether or not he would stay on the Board. My hope is that he will.

Ms. WALTERS. But did you give him any possibilities so that he would have some choices perhaps to make of what some of these governmental positions might be?

THE PRESIDENT. Not yet. I think either in economic affairs or foreign affairs, the field of human rights, the enhanced involvement of American citizens in taking initiative outside of government in the private sector—these are four areas where he and I have had discussions during this preceding year. He's shown an intense interest in them. He's been very excited about our progress in human rights. He's never seen me a single time this year that he didn't initiate a discussion about human rights, how profound he thought it was and how it exemplified what our Nation stands for. But what he would choose to do would have to be up to him. I would cooperate in every way to encourage him to continue to serve in some capacity.

MR. SCHIEFFER. Mr. President, you sound like a man describing someone you've just reappointed. Why did you replace him? [*Laughter*]

THE PRESIDENT. Well, Chairman Burns—I think he served longer than anyone ever has before. He served two full terms. And I thought it was time for us to have new leadership there. I particularly wanted to bring someone in, Bob, from the business community.

I think there ought to be some change in emphasis from time to time. I also wanted to get someone that would have the confidence of business and financial leaders here and around the world. As a matter of fact, when I informed Chairman Burns of my choice, he said that is a wise and worthy choice. He has known Bill Miller for years, and he said that he had been making a list of those that he hoped I might consider, and he had made a list of some he hoped I didn't consider.

Fritz Mondale said, "Well, why don't we share lists sometimes?" And he said, "Well, I can tell you a few of those that I was hoping you might consider." And the first two or three names he mentioned were leaders in the business community.

So, these are the reasons that I thought it was time for a change. It's certainly no reflection on him.

Mr. MacNeil. But surely Dr. Burns was the very symbol of what business wanted in that job.

The President. I can't deny that.

Mr. MacNeil. And if Mr. Miller's philosophy is not very different from Dr. Burns', it's difficult to see why it was necessary to replace Dr. Burns.

The President. Well, that was not an easy decision to make.

Mr. MacNeil. Or was it for personal reasons?

The President. No, not at all.

Mr. MacNeil. Personal antipathy?

The President. Not at all. I think it's accurate to say—and Dr. Burns would confirm this—that he and I have a close personal friendship. We have never had any sort of disagreements when we were together. I have never criticized Chairman Burns either publicly or privately. But I've already explained the reasons why I thought it was time to make a change. I think two full terms there is adequate. That's as long as a President can serve, and I think bringing in some new leadership into the Federal Reserve System will be beneficial.

THE NATION'S ECONOMY

Mr. Brokaw. Mr. President, I want to sketch a scenario for you if I can. If, as the reports have it, you are considering recommending a tax cut of about $25 billion to Congress when it reconvenes, there are many who say that that will just about offset the increased taxes that we will have as a result of higher taxes on energy and social security. So, it won't stimulate the economy in the manner that you might like it to, and then in 1979 or 1980 you'll have to come back and ask for another tax cut, and if you do that, you will surely have defeated your goal of balancing the budget by 1981. Do you have trouble with that scenario?

The President. Well, I think the benefits to be derived from tax cuts in 1978 and 1979 will exceed any tax burdens that have been added onto the American people's shoulders by the Congress.

We have had fairly good economic success this year. The unemployment rate has dropped from about 8 percent a year ago to a little bit less than 7 percent now. Still, pockets of high unemployment concern me very much. We've added eight million net new jobs this year, the most we've ever added since the Second World War. We have about 92 million people employed now. In the last half of this year, the inflation rate has dropped to less than 5 percent, although the underlying inflation rate is still 6 or 6½ percent. It's obvious that we need some economic stimulus next year, and also I don't want the Federal budget to continue to grow in its proportion of the gross national product of our Nation. It's now—it had gotten up to about 23 percent. We are cutting it down now to a little above 22 percent. And by the time my term is over in 1980, I would like to get this down to about 21 percent through careful management and wise spending of our funds.

I have to judge, though, between how much money I retain in the Federal budget, in the Federal Treasury in order to balance the budget quickly, compared to how much we give back to the taxpayers in the form of tax cuts, to let them have the money to spend and to let the private enterprise system produce more jobs and a better life for us.

So, I think that we have done well so far, and I think we'll make a much wiser decision on the tax reform package and tax reduction package for next year having gotten a good, firm realization of the social security tax changes and a fairly good hope of what the energy package will be as well.

MR. BROKAW. I guess the question still is, do you think that a balanced budget by 1981, which was a campaign promise, is a realistic goal for a man who is now in office, given all of the claims on the Federal budget?

THE PRESIDENT. Well, obviously, I can't guarantee that. We've always known that balancing the budget would be difficult. It depends upon how fast business invests, how many people are at work, which cuts down obviously on expenditure for unemployment compensation and welfare payments, and there has to be some tradeoff.

If there was an absolutely rigid fixation on a balanced budget, then there would be no chance for tax cuts. But I think when you take into consideration that we have $25 billion tax reductions for the people next year with about $6 billion tax reductions this year—that's $31 billion—that's a major benefit to the people. I just can't give a firm commitment on how we will balance tax cuts versus a balanced budget by 1981.

MR. SCHIEFFER. But aren't you going to have just super growth, faster growth rate than anyone really predicts, to be able to balance the budget by 1981? Isn't that what it boils down to?

THE PRESIDENT. It would take about a 10-percent annual increase in real terms in business investment with the present projections of economic need. We want to cut the unemployment rate down considerably, and of course, we want to deal with the problems of the cities. We want to meet the legitimate needs of our people and at the same time not let inflation get out of hand.

So, balancing all these factors is something that you have to do almost daily in making decisions from the White House.

ADMINISTRATION PRIORITIES; PANAMA
CANAL TREATY

Ms. WALTERS. Mr. President, it is reported that Vice President Mondale, with you, of course, is working on a list of your top priorities for next year with the feeling perhaps that you had too many top priorities this year to give to Congress. Can you tell us what the top two or three priorities would be, and can you tell us if it would include a national health insurance program, which organized labor feels you promised to introduce this year?

THE PRESIDENT. Yes, I intend to introduce a national health program to the Congress this year, late in this session. They can't pass it this year, but it will be introduced.

Dealing with the economy, which we've just discussed, would be a top priority. Completing work on the energy package would be the first specific thing that we'll do. One of the most important is to resolve the Panama Canal Treaty question.

About 75 years ago in the middle of the night the American Secretary of State signed the Panama Canal Treaty that presently is in existence. No Panamanian has ever signed it; no Panamanian ever saw it before it was signed. It was signed by a Frenchman who benefited financially from the terms of the treaty on behalf of the Panamanians.

That treaty gave us a chance to do a tremendous job in building the Panama Canal, keeping it open for international shipping. It's helped our country a lot. It's something of which we can be proud.

Presidents Eisenhower and Kennedy recognized that the present treaty was inadequate. President Johnson started negotiations to change it. Presidents Nixon and Ford continued. And we concluded it this year.

It's one of the most difficult political questions that we'll have to deal with. It's going to take a lot of time in the Congress to pass it.

What we wanted was one that treated us and Panama fairly, and we got it. We wanted a treaty that did not put a financial burden on the American taxpayer, and we got it. We wanted treaties that would guarantee proper operation of the Panama Canal itself, for us and for foreign shipping, and we got it. We wanted treaties that would also guarantee us permanently the right to take what action we think necessary to keep the canal safe, to defend it, and to keep it open for us to use, and we got it.

We wanted treaties—two treaties there are—that would give us the right for expeditious passage in time of need or emergency, for our ships to go to the head of the line and go through the canal without delay, and we got it. We wanted treaties also that would be acceptable in the eyes of the international community, particularly in Latin America, and we got them.

So, this is what we have tried to do under four Presidents, and we have finally succeeded. And I would say that would be one of the most difficult challenges that we have politically this year. It is absolutely crucial that the Senate ratify these treaties, and I think the terms are very favorable to us and to Panama.

MR. BROKAW. You've got all that in the treaty, Mr. President. Do you have the votes in the Senate?

THE PRESIDENT. I think we will get the votes in the Senate.

MR. BROKAW. Do you not now have them?

THE PRESIDENT. I can't say for sure that we do because many Senators still haven't expressed their commitment to me or their opinion. But I was talking to President Ford this past week, who's strongly supportive of the treaties, along with Secretary Kissinger and others, and he said that in his speeches to college groups and others around the Nation, that he is getting an increasingly favorable response from the audience. I think public opinion is building up for the treaties as they know the terms of them.

MR. MacNEIL. Could we interpret this as the beginning of a new campaign on your part to get out and sell the treaty? You've been criticized for having left the ground to the opposition somewhat. Are you going to make a major effort personally to try and sell it?

THE PRESIDENT. Yes. I consider it one of my most important responsibilities.

MR. MacNEIL. And can you meet the deadline that President Torrijos has set of April, which he says is urgent, and that Panama's patience could be exhausted.

THE PRESIDENT. Well, no, I don't feel any constraint to operate under a deadline. But both Senator Byrd and I and the leaders of the Senate all hope that we can resolve that issue early in the year, certainly I think by April.

MS. WALTERS. On that—since, by the way, just to get back to my original questions—it seems that your priorities next year are very similar to your priorities this year, energy and the economy. But in October, you and President Torrijos issued a statement—a joint statement to remove the doubts about the rights of the United States to defend the neutrality of the canal and also the right of ships to pass promptly through it. A number of Senators have felt that they might be more comfortable with this if it were actually written into the treaty.

Would you be willing to see the treaty amended so that it would reflect this understanding, this statement between you and General Torrijos?

THE PRESIDENT. No. I think it would be good to have a signed agreement between me and President Torrijos, and he has indicated he would be glad to sign that statement that was made, and of course, I would too. I think the Senate could express an understanding that the treaty was being approved by them with the understanding that this was a proper interpretation. But to actually amend the treaty would require Panama to have another referendum on the subject, and they've already had one.

Many people in Panama think that the treaties are too favorable to the United States. And I don't think it would be fair to them after they negotiated in good faith to cause them to have a completely new referendum. I would certainly hate to have two ratification votes in the Senate, separated by several months. So, I

think that the Senate can very well express its understanding of what the treaties mean. We can exchange documents with the Panamanian leader. To amend the treaties, though, I think would be inadvisable.

ENERGY LEGISLATION

MR. SCHIEFFER. Mr. President, since we are talking about the Congress, what are you going to do about the energy bill now? It's been going on for 6 months now. There seems to be a deadlock there in the conference committee. I saw a poll taken by your pollster the other day that said 44 percent of the people in this country still are undecided about whether it's a good bill or not. What do you do now? Do you start over?

THE PRESIDENT. No.

MR. SCHIEFFER. Do you stay with the conference committee? What happens?

THE PRESIDENT. Well, there's not a problem with the Congress. There's not a problem with the House. The problem is with the Senate conference committee that is dealing with the crucial issue of natural gas. There are 18 members on the Senate conference committee. They've been divided nine and nine ever since the conference began. And I would hope that a compromise could be worked out that could be acceptable to me, to the House Members, and to the Senate conferees and to the Senate quite early in the next session.

MR. SCHIEFFER. There isn't any sign of that yet.

THE PRESIDENT. Well, there are private signs, Bob. [*Laughter*]

MR. SCHIEFFER. Tell us about them.

MS. WALTERS. Could I ask one part of that?

THE PRESIDENT. Please do.

MS. WALTERS. Would you be willing to sign legislation that permitted natural gas prices to go above the figure of $1.75

per thousand cubic feet if that would mean that it would get passed?

THE PRESIDENT. Well, I haven't excluded any reasonable compromise solution from a bill that I would sign. My only requirements are that the bill in my judgment be fair to the consumers of this country, that the bill in my judgment give an adequate shift away from excessive consumption of oil and natural gas to other alternative supplies and also have conservation of energy on top of that and also that the bill not bankrupt the Nation, not be too great a burden on the budget itself.

If those requirements are met, then I will sign the bill. I still favor the proposal that I made to the Congress last April 20, and very close to that is what the House passed back in August. I can see good indications of compromise solutions that would meet my requirements that have already been divulged to me by conferees. When I come back from my overseas trip in 10 days from now, we will play an active role in trying to encourage the Senate leadership and the conferees to negotiate with a great deal of enthusiasm. And I think there will be a growing realization in our country of the importance of this bill.

It hurts our domestic economy, it hurts our foreign economy, it weakens the price, the value of the dollar. We imported this year about $45 billion worth of oil in addition to what we consumed of our own oil. It's a very heavy drain on our economy, on international oil supplies, and the Nation needs it very badly.

And I think as the conferees and the Members of Congress see this need in a more and more dramatic way expressed here in our own country and by leaders overseas, then I think they will act. We've also had encouraging word from the OPEC nations this past week when they

froze the price of oil for another year. I think they did that at least partially on the basis that the Congress would act to cut down on the excessive consumption of oil in this country.

And I think there will be a great pressure internationally for increased prices of oil and, therefore, higher inflation if the Congress doesn't act. It is a very important issue. I think most of the Congress Members still now feel the importance of what they are about to do. I don't think there's any doubt that they will pass this legislation early in the session.

DOMESTIC ISSUES

MR. MACNEIL. Mr. President, looking back a little retrospectively over your first year in domestic issues, is there any domestic issue which just baffles you?

THE PRESIDENT. There are a lot of them that I don't completely comprehend. I've been criticized for introducing too much legislation. I've been criticized for not introducing enough legislation. I've been criticized for dealing too much in specifics and trying to learn too much about the Government and how it works, how the economy functions and what the Congress does, the attitudes and organization of the Congress and the Federal Government agencies.

But this is my nature. I think having come into Washington for the first time to serve in the Federal Government, I had an obligation to learn. I enjoy it. And I obviously realize that there are many things that I don't completely comprehend.

UNEMPLOYMENT

MR. MACNEIL. I had an example in mind of a particularly intractable thing about which in the plethora of proposals that have come out there is no sort of very innovative solution yet, and that is the question of unemployment among black youth in this country, very very high percentages. Is that one of those issues that at the moment just looks baffling and intractable—how to deal with it, given the other priorities?

THE PRESIDENT. The unemployment rate in general is intractable and difficult. The inflation rate seems to be frozen at about 6 or 6½ percent, and there are pockets of unemployment among black youth, in particular, that have been a great challenge to me, that we have not yet successfully resolved, either me or my predecessors. We did add 425,000 new jobs, and most of them were specifically oriented toward people who have been chronically unemployed.

In addition, we had about a $4 billion public works program. Ten percent of that money had to be spent with minority contractors to help emphasize black young employment.

We also contemplate in the 1979 fiscal year budget emphasizing anew our interest in solving high unemployment rate among black young people. But this is one of those problems that is difficult to solve.

When I went to London in May for the International Economic Summit, this was the issue that every foreign leader said was becoming their most difficult and crucial issue. In England, in Germany, in France, in Japan, in Canada, in Italy, there was unanimous agreement among us that this was one of the most intractable and difficult issues of all.

Just recently, in Rome, Secretary Marshall from our Department of Labor went on an international meeting concerning youth unemployment.

We are making some progress in our country. We had during the summer and fall, as a result of a $21 billion economic stimulus package, more people put to work every week even than during the

New Deal days with the WPA and the CCC. But it's a hard thing to solve.

We've added 4 million new jobs this year and still have a high unemployment rate. But I think we are making progress. The basic thing is that government can't provide all those jobs. They have to be initiated through business investment brought about by proper tax decisions and proper economic decisions made by Congress and by business themselves. But I think the progress that we will make in '78 will be even greater than this year.

MR. BROKAW. Mr. President, I wonder about unemployment generally, whether we don't have to, as a society, as a system of government, redefine what is an acceptable level of unemployment.

It's now been running at about 7 percent, and people talk about an unemployment rate of 4, 4½ percent as being acceptable. That's a long drop, to get to 4½ percent. Do you think that we have to redefine what is acceptable at around 6 percent——

THE PRESIDENT. No, I'd hate to do that.

MR. BROKAW. ——realistically?

THE PRESIDENT. No, I would hate to do that.

MR. BROKAW. Well, politically, it's not very attractive, but economically and practically it's very hard to see how it can be dropped that far that fast.

THE PRESIDENT. I believe we can get it below that. We have, as you know, a different system economically than most, even democratic democracies. We provide welfare systems and unemployment compensation for people who are out of work. And habitually in our Nation when demand drops off for a product, the companies lay off even temporarily some of their workers. In a nation like Japan, they keep those workers on the job, they pay them a lower salary, and the production is held down by partial unemployment.

But I have seen good progress made. I think it was either October or November we added 900,000 new jobs, but there were just about that many new people who came into the labor market that month. Nobody anticipated that.

One reason for that is that as people see their neighbors getting jobs, who had been unemployed for a long time, then housewives or students who are still in high school and others apply for jobs and they become part of the labor market, which makes the unemployment rate stay high even though employment goes up to the highest level in the history of our Nation.

MR. MACNEIL. Go ahead, Barbara.

CRITICISM OF THE PRESIDENT

MS. WALTERS. Mr. President, it's almost the end of your first year in office, and it's almost New Year's Eve, and that's the time for people to take stock. And maybe when they take stock, they are a little more critical than they should be. However, I would like to give you a list of people who currently say that they are unhappy about you.

Labor is unhappy, because they say that you are dragging your feet on the medical insurance bill and on full employment. Business has said it's unhappy; they just don't have confidence in you. The blacks are unhappy, again because of full employment and the lack of it and what Robin just brought out. And I talked with Vernon Jordan, who had expressed his unhappiness with you last July and still feels the same way, he says. Many women are unhappy because of your stand on Federal aid to abortion, and there aren't enough women appointed to administration posts. Striking farmers are rolling up their tractors in Plains. [*Laughter*] Who is your constituency, or to put it another way, who's happy?

THE PRESIDENT. Well, Barbara, I think this is inherent and almost inevitable in a free nation like ours. The news media legitimately reports the disharmony and the arguments and the debates because they are more exciting than the achievements.

It's good for us to remember at the end of this year that we live in the strongest nation on Earth—militarily the strongest, economically the strongest, politically the strongest—a nation that is a leader worldwide, that's trusted, that's making progress, dealing with the developing nations, the Western European nations, Latin America, making progress toward controlling atomic weapons.

Domestically, God has blessed us with tremendous natural resources, a free enterprise system that lets people benefit from their own contributions, their own initiative.

We have so much in common. We are a nation of highly diverse people, different people, but we are one people, and we've come from almost nothing 200 years ago to this position of sustained leadership and prosperity. The standard of living in our country for even the poorest person far exceeds the average living standard in many nations of the world. We are unselfish. And I think the threat to our country is that we might, in grasping for advantage or in emphasizing differences, lose that sense of common commitment and common purpose and a common future that binds us together and makes us great.

I don't have any fear about the future. I think that when I make mistakes or when the Congress makes mistakes or when we delay in solving apparently insoluble questions, our country is so strong and so vital and the people are bound together so closely that we can prevail in any case.

And I think the expressions of dissatisfaction, although they are legitimate in many instances, are overemphasized. I think our country is much greater than that.

MR. MACNEIL. Excuse me, Bob.

MR. SCHIEFFER. Go ahead.

STYLE OF THE PRESIDENCY

MR. MACNEIL. Again, looking back on this first year of the Presidency, Senator Hart wrote—Senator Gary Hart—wrote a piece recently in which he said that you had demythologized the imperial Presidency, but he wondered whether you also had not sacrificed some of the psychological weight and power that the Presidency had accumulated since Roosevelt's time to your detriment.

And I was wondering, for instance, you spoke out very strongly against the oil companies, accusing them of trying to rip off the American people, very, very strong words, and yet the oil companies seem relatively unperturbed. Are you at all concerned that in making yours the Presidency of the common man and ridding yourself of some of the imperial trappings you may have thrown away some of the clout?

THE PRESIDENT. Many people think so. The pomp and ceremony of office does not appeal to me, and I don't believe it's a necessary part of the Presidency in a democratic nation like our own. I'm no better than anyone else. And the people that I admire most who have lived in this house have taken the same attitude. Jefferson, Jackson, Lincoln, Truman have minimized the pomp and ceremony and the pride, personal pride, that accrues sometimes to Presidents.

I don't think we need to put on the trappings of a monarchy in a nation like our own. I feel uncomfortable with it. But I doubt if I feel quite as uncomfortable as the average citizen.

REFLECTIONS ON FIRST YEAR IN OFFICE

MR. SCHIEFFER. Mr. President, speaking of Abraham Lincoln, Abraham Lincoln said just toward the end of his Presidency, he said, "I must confess that events have controlled me rather than the other way around." I wonder, looking back over your first year, how do you feel about this first year?

THE PRESIDENT. I feel good about it. It's been an exciting and stimulating and challenging and sometimes frustrating experience for me.

MR. SCHIEFFER. Were you controlled by events?

THE PRESIDENT. I think—yes, I think so. I've tried to represent what the American people want me to be and what they are. I noticed one of the news commentators the other night said that when I said during the campaign that I wanted a government as good as the American people are, that it was demagoguery.

I don't think that's accurate. You know, the American people are good and decent and idealistic. And I think they want their Government to be good and decent and idealistic.

One of the most popular things that I've tried to do is to express to the world our own people's commitment to basic human rights, to freedom and independence and autonomy, the worth of a human being, whether they live here or in Russia or in South America or in Uganda or China. And I doubt that there's a national leader in the world now who doesn't think about human rights every day and how his or her actions are measured against a standard that the world is beginning to demand.

So, I think what I've tried to do is to see what is good in our Nation, in our people, in our past, and try to preserve it and to deal with changing events to the best of my ability. I've got a good

Cabinet. I've had good cooperation and support from the Congress, who recognized my newness in Washington. And overall, although I see great problems ahead of us, I feel confident.

I got my staff—the National Security Council—today to give me an analysis of the world situation as it was a year ago, and the comparison doesn't look bad. I think we are trusted now where we weren't before, say in Africa, primarily because of the influence of Andrew Young. I believe that our intentions are recognized as being good. So, in all I think it's been a good year for us.

MR. BROKAW. Mr. President, do you ever come back from the Oval Office, which is not that many feet away, and come back to the Residence and sit down and reflect on the day's events and what's going on in the world and think, "My God, this is a bigger job than I expected it to be. I'm not sure that I'm up to this"? Do you ever have those moments of self-doubt?

THE PRESIDENT. Well, I have sober moments when I'm not sure that I can deal with problems satisfactorily. But I have a lot of confidence in myself. Sometimes I go in a back room and pray a while. And a few times I've walked through this Mansion where every President has lived except George Washington, since 1801, and I've thought about the difficulties and the tragedy that existed in the lives of many of them and feel myself to be fortunate. But I don't feel inadequate because I feel that even political opponents want me to succeed. And I couldn't have asked for better cooperation and support than I've gotten from those who help me in this job.

MS. WALTERS. Mr. President, can you tell us what you think has been your greatest single achievement this past year and also, even though we hear that you don't have sleepless nights—everyone makes mistakes—what you think your biggest mistake has been?

THE PRESIDENT. I think my biggest mistake has been in inadvertently building up expectations too high. I underestimated the difficulty and the time required for Congress to take action on controversial measures. It's much easier for me to study and evolve and present legislation to the Congress than it is for them to pass it in its final form. And I've dashed some hopes and disappointed people that thought we might act quicker.

I think that the achievements are not measured in how many bills were passed and how many bills I've signed or even my harmony with the Congress. If I have achieved anything, it's been to restore a tone to our Nation's life and attitude that most accurately exemplifies what we stand for. I use the human rights issue as one example. It gratifies me to know that the nations in Africa now look to us with friendship and with trust, whereas, just a short time ago, they wouldn't permit our Secretary of State to come in their country.

It gratifies me to see a burgeoning friendship with Latin American nations and to see our NATO allies now recommitting themselves to strong military commitments. And it gratifies me to see some progress being made in relieving tensions between ourselves and the Soviet Union. We are making slow, steady progress. We are attempting many things simultaneously. Sometimes they get confusing because they are so voluminous and there are so many of them.

But I think having our Nation and its Government represent more accurately the hopes and dreams of the American people is a general accomplishment of which I am most proud.

MR. MACNEIL. Mr. President, when you were still running for office, you told me in an interview—when I asked you, perhaps embarrassingly, what your weakness was, you said perhaps a difficulty to compromise. It had been difficult with the Georgia Legislature, and it might be a difficulty with the Congress. Has this year in Washington been an education in compromise?

THE PRESIDENT. Well, yes. I'm not sure if I had an adequate education yet, because I still find it difficult to compromise. But I'm learning. One way that I have learned since I've been here to avoid having to compromise so much is by involving the congressional leaders in the decision in the initial stages. When we evolved the reorganization bill and when we put together the Energy Department, when we evolved the social security bill and other measures that were controversial, we consulted very closely with congressional leaders ahead of time. So I'm trying to avoid having to yield to my weakness, which is a difficulty in compromising. I'm learning every day, I think.

MR. BROKAW. Mr. President, maybe we can all come back next year at this same time.

THE PRESIDENT. Well, I hope so.

MR. BROKAW. On behalf of all my colleagues, thank you very much for having us here this evening, however.

THE PRESIDENT. Thank you, Tom. I've enjoyed it very much.

MR. BROKAW. Thank you, Mr. President.

NOTE: The interview began at 8 p.m. in the Red Room at the White House. It was broadcast live on radio and television.

The President's Overseas Trip

Remarks on Departure From the White House. December 29, 1977

THE PRESIDENT. Good morning, everybody.

I depart today on a journey that reflects both the diversity of the world we live in and also our own Nation's ability and desire to deal creatively and constructively with that diversity.

It's a rapidly changing world, a world in which the old ideological labels have less meaning than ever, in which the universal desire for freedom and for a better life is being expressed more strongly and in more ways than ever before, a world in which political awakening, economic independence, and technological progress have created new demands on the foreign policy of our people.

The variety of places that we will visit over the next 9 days is symbolic of the breadth and the variety of American interest in this new world.

In France and in Western Europe, we will reaffirm the historic bonds and our common values, and we will explore ways to meet the common problems of the industrial democracies.

In Poland, the ancestral home of millions of Americans, we will nourish the improving relationships between the United States and the peoples of Eastern Europe.

In Iran and in Saudi Arabia, we will discuss key economic relationships and press for a continuation of the dramatic progress that is being made in bringing peace to the Middle East.

In India, which is the largest democracy on Earth, we will seek new paths of cooperation and communication between the developing nations of the world and the industrial north.

And in all these places, we will be reaffirming our dedication to peace and our support of justice and of human rights.

It is a changing world, a different world, and I believe that it's also a different America whose message we will carry, an America more confident and more united, at peace with other nations and also at peace with itself, an America which is ready and able to cooperate wherever possible and to compete when necessary.

After a long period of doubt and turmoil here, we are finding our way back to the values that made us a great nation. And in this new spirit we are eager to work with all countries and all peoples in building the kind of world and the kind of world community that serves the individual and common needs of all.

We undertake this trip to express our own views clearly and proudly, but also to learn and to understand the opinions and the desires of others. We will try to represent our Nation and our people well, and I'll take the good will of America everywhere we go. Thank you very much.

THE VICE PRESIDENT. Mr. President, we wish you and Mrs. Carter well as you undertake this most important mission on behalf of our Nation. I know that I speak for everyone here and for the American people when I say you take with you not only our best wishes but our love as well. We know it'll be a successful journey, and we eagerly await your return.

NOTE: The President spoke at 7:35 a.m. on the South Lawn of the White House. Following the remarks, the Presidential party proceeded to Andrews Air Force Base, Md., where they departed for Poland.

Warsaw, Poland

Remarks of the President and First Secretary Edward Gierek at the Welcoming Ceremony. December 29, 1977

THE FIRST SECRETARY. *Mr. President, Madam Carter, ladies and gentlemen:*

On behalf of the highest authorities of the Polish People's Republic, in the name of our people, I greet you cordially, Mr. President, on the Polish soil.

We are happy to be able to play host to you and Mrs. Carter, as well as to per-

sons accompanying you. We are welcoming and greeting you, Mr. President, as the highest representative of the great American people for which we entertain our sentiments of friendship.

History has linked our two nations by manifold ties. They were molded by the great sons of the Polish people through their participation in the struggle for American independence. They were shaped by the scores of Polish emigrants who have contributed their significant and valuable share to the development and might of the United States. They have been further strengthened in our joint strife for the freedom of all peoples within the great anti-Nazi coalition.

Our desire is to cultivate those traditions in the present-day peaceful and friendly Polish-American cooperation.

We trust your visit will contribute to its further expansion, beneficial to our peoples and promoting the dearest cause to all nations, the cause of peace.

You are arriving in Poland, Mr. President, at a time when the process of international détente—so important as it is to all mankind and the world at large—has been again rejuvenated by the constructive dialog of states and the expectations of nations.

You no doubt understand, Mr. President, that to the people of Poland, which has so dreadfully experienced the atrocities of war, security is the supreme value, while life and peace is the fundamental right.

We view your present visit, Mr. President, as a reaffirmation of the friendly feelings of the American people towards Poland and an expression of the interest in our active peaceful policies. We see in it, too, a manifestation of your personal involvement in the further expansion of Polish-American cooperation in cultivating the traditional friendship between our nations.

We are glad, indeed, that we shall be able to acquaint you with the record of accomplishment of Socialist Poland, with its plans and aspirations with all that at a price of a relentless effort, painstaking and self-sacrificing labors our nation has built on the ruins and ashes.

Ours is the desire that your visit to Poland serve actions which link our peoples together and that it may engrave well in the good memories of yourself, Mr. President, Mrs. Carter, and the members of your party.

Welcome on the Polish soil, Mr. President, in the spirit of the Polish hospitality.

THE PRESIDENT. *First Secretary Gierek, distinguished officials from Poland and from other nations, the people of Poland:*

We are delighted to be in your great country. When I left the United States this morning, I told the people of my Nation that this journey reflects the diversity of a rapidly changing world. It is a world in which old ideological labels have lost their meaning and in which the basic goals of friendship, world peace, justice, human rights, and individual freedom loom more important than ever.

I am proud to begin this journey in Poland—friend of the United States since the time our Nation was founded. Poland is the ancestral home of more than six million Americans, partner in a common effort against war and deprivation.

Relations are changing between North and South, between East and West. But the ties between Poland and the United States are ancient and strong.

Not far from our home in the State of Georgia, a great patriot of both our nations, Casimir Pulaski, was mortally wounded while leading a cavalry legion in the fight for American independence. The home of my son's wife is Pulaski County, Georgia, named for this hero from Poland.

Also, for his military skill and bravery, Thaddeus Kosciuszko won the respect of our first President, George Washington, during wartime. And for his commitment to freedom and justice, he won the admiration of our third President, Thomas Jefferson, in time of peace.

These brave men fought alongside Americans in the era which produced three of the great documents in the struggle for human rights. One was the Declaration of Independence from America. The second was the Declaration of the Rights of Man from France. And the third was the Polish Constitution of May 3, 1791.

Our shared experience in battle has also taught us the paramount importance of preventing war, which has brought devastation to Poland twice in this century. At the end of World War I, a great American, Herbert Hoover, came to Poland to help you ease the suffering of war and to observe the reestablishment of an independent Poland. Circumstances were different and the struggle was long, but Hoover said, and I quote, "If history teaches us anything, it is that from the unquenchable vitality of the Polish race, Poland will rise again from these ashes." And his prediction came true.

I have come not only to express our own views to the people of Poland but also to learn your opinions and to understand your desires for the future. Building on the historical ties between us, recognizing the new and changing realities of life, I look forward to strengthening Polish-American friendship on my visit here in Warsaw.

We deeply appreciate the warm welcome extended to us tonight by First Secretary Gierek and by the Polish people.

Thank you very much.

NOTE: The exchange began at 10:40 p.m. at the Civilian Terminal, Okecie International Airport. First Secretary Gierek spoke in Polish, and his remarks were translated by an interpreter.

THE PRESIDENT'S NEWS CONFERENCE OF DECEMBER 30, 1977

Held in Warsaw, Poland

THE PRESIDENT'S VISIT TO POLAND

THE PRESIDENT. Good afternoon. *Dzien dobry.*

It's a great honor for me to be here in Poland to reaffirm and to strengthen the historic and strong ties of friendship and mutual purpose which exist between our two countries. I have had very fruitful discussions with First Secretary Gierek and the other officials of Poland on bilateral questions, on questions involving NATO and the Warsaw Pact countries, matters relating to SALT, mutual and balanced force reductions, and general commitments to peace in the future.

This morning I had a chance to visit memorials to the brave people of Poland, and particularly of Warsaw. I doubt that there is any nation on Earth which has suffered more from the ravages of war. In the Second World War the Nazis killed 800,000 people in Warsaw alone and 6 million Poles. And I was able to pay homage to their courage and bravery.

I also visited the Ghetto Monument, a memorial to Polish Jews who stood alone to face the Nazis but who will forever live in the conscience of the world.

This afternoon I would like to answer questions from the reporters assembled here. There were a few who wanted to attend who were not permitted to come. Their questions will be answered by me in writing. And now I would be glad to respond to questions, beginning with Mr. Wojna [Riczrd Wojna, Tribuna Ludu].

QUESTIONS

U.S.-SOVIET RELATIONS

Q [in Polish]. Mr. President, Poland and the entire world has attached great importance to the relations between the United States and the Soviet Union. Could you answer what is your assessment of the chance for a prompt conclusion on SALT talks and in other discussions on strategic matters, and how in this respect do you assess the latest pronouncement by Leonid Brezhnev in an interview for the Pravda Daily?

THE PRESIDENT. In the last few months, the United States and the Soviet Union have made great progress in dealing with a long list of important issues, the most important of which is to control the deployment of strategic nuclear weapons. We hope to conclude the SALT II talks this year, hopefully in the spring. We have resolved many of the major issues. A few still remain. We have made good progress in recent months.

At the same time, we have made progress for the first time in establishing principles on which there can be a total prohibition against all tests of nuclear explosives in the future. We've made progress on prohibiting additional military buildup in the Indian Ocean, recently commenced talks to reduce the sale of conventional weapons to other nations in the world. And I will pursue this same subject with President Giscard next week.

In addition, the Soviets and we are making progress in how we can prevent the use in the future of chemical and biological warfare, and we hope that we can reinstigate progress in the mutual and balanced force reductions which have been stalemated in Vienna for a number of years. So, I would say that in summary I am very encouraged at the new progress that I have witnessed personally among our negotiators.

When Foreign Minister Gromyko was in Washington recently, in a few hours we resolved many of the difficult issues. Our negotiators are at work on all those subjects at this present time. There has been no cessation of effort. And I believe that 1978 will see a resolution of many of these issues.

Mr. Cormier [Frank Cormier, Associated Press].

THE MIDDLE EAST

Q. Mr. President, are you likely to go to Egypt next Wednesday, and if you do, will it be primarily because President Sadat has urged you to go, or for some other purpose, or why?

THE PRESIDENT. Well, I have a standing invitation from President Sadat to visit Egypt that he extended to me on his trip to Washington. And he's reemphasized it several times since that date. We have had no discussions with President Sadat on that particular visit to Egypt while I'm on this trip. We will try to keep our schedule flexible. If it's mutually convenient and desirable, we would certainly consider it. But we have no plans at this time to stop in Egypt next Wednesday or any other time on this trip.

I might say that our own relations with the Arab nations, including, certainly, Egypt, are very good and harmonious. There has been no change in our own position relating to the Middle Eastern talks. And we communicate almost daily with the Egyptian and Israeli leaders. And as you know, I will be meeting King Hussein in Tehran on our next stop on this trip.

Helen [Helen Thomas, United Press International].

Q. You said you often don't intend and don't desire to dictate the terms of a Middle East settlement.

THE PRESIDENT. Yes. This is true.

Q. And yet President Sadat seems to think that you have pulled the rug out from under him and that you are in fact dictating terms when you are backing an Israeli military presence on the West Bank at Gaza after there would be a settlement.

THE PRESIDENT. We don't back any Israeli military settlement in the Gaza Strip or on the West Bank. We favor, as you know, a Palestinian homeland or entity there. Our own preference is that this entity be tied in to Jordan and not be a separate and independent nation. That is merely an expression of preference which we have relayed on numerous occasions to the Arab leaders, including President Sadat when he was with me in Washington. I've expressed the same opinion to the Israelis, to King Hussein, and to President Asad, and also to the Saudi Arabians. We have no intention of attempting to impose a settlement. Any agreement which can be reached between Israel and her Arab neighbors would be acceptable to us. We are in a posture of expressing opinions, trying to promote intimate and direct negotiations and communications, expediting the process when it seems to be slow, and adding our good offices whenever requested. But we have no intention or desire to impose a settlement.

Let me go back to the Polish side. Yes, sir.

RELIGION

Q [in Polish]. I will speak Polish. Let me welcome you not only as the President of the United States but as an eminent American Baptist. I am a Baptist myself. I am preoccupied with editing a Baptist magazine in Poland, and I would like to express my gladness that you have been elected to the post of the President of the United States, as a man, as a believer who is not ashamed of it and of his evangelical convictions. This prompts me to wish you and your family the best of the very best in 1978 and also in your activity in strengthening peace the world over.

And now over to our question. We all know that you are a practicing Christian, as every Baptist should be—as every good Baptist should be. And I would like to ask whether your religious convictions help you in executing the job of a President of such a big country. Can you quote an example in how the evangelical principles helped you in solving any complicated problem?

And the second question, we the Polish Baptists live in an extra-Catholic country, and on occasions we are discriminated against. As a believer, as a Baptist, can you influence the change of a situation?

THE PRESIDENT. Well, as you know, the United States believes in religious freedom. And I'm very grateful for the degree of religious freedom that also exists in Poland.

Dr. Brzezinski, my national security adviser, and my wife, Rosalynn, had a visit with Cardinal Wyszynski this morning and did this as an expression of our appreciation for the degree of freedom to worship in this country.

This is a matter of conscience, as a Baptist and as an American leader. We believe in separation of church and state, that there should be no unwarranted influence on the church or religion by the state, and vice versa. My own religious convictions are deep and personal. I seek divine guidance when I make a difficult decision as President and also am sup-

ported, of course, by a common purpose which binds Christians together in a belief in the human dignity of mankind and in the search for worldwide peace—recognizing, of course, that those who don't share my faith quite often have the same desires and hopes.

My own constant hope is that all nations would give maximum freedom of religion and freedom of expression to their people, and I will do all I can, within the bounds of propriety, to bring that hope into realization.

POLISH AUTONOMY

Q. Mr. President, during those Presidential debates, in a celebrated exchange, President Ford claimed that Eastern Europe was not under Soviet domination. And you replied, "Tell it to the Poles." Well, now that you're here, is it your view that this domination will continue almost into perpetuity, or do you see a day when Poland may be actually free? And if so, how would that come about?

THE PRESIDENT. Well, this is obviously a decision for the Polish leaders and the Polish people to make. Our nation is committed to the proposition that all countries would be autonomous, they would all be independent, and they would all be free of unwanted interference and entanglements with other nations.

The Polish people have been bound very closely to the Soviet Union since the Second World War, and they belong to a Warsaw Pact military alliance, which is, of course, different from the NATO relationship to which we belong.

My own assessment within the European theater, Eastern European theater, is that here, compared to some other nations, there is a great religious freedom and otherwise, and I think this is a hope that we all share and cherish. I think this has been the origin of the Polish nation more than a thousand years ago, and it's a deep commitment of the vast majority of the Polish people, a desire and a commitment not to be dominated.

Q. You don't deny that they are dominated here, Mr. President?

THE PRESIDENT. I think I've commented all I wish on that subject.

CONFERENCE ON SECURITY AND COOPERATION IN EUROPE

Q [in Polish]. Mr. President, what is the potential for realization of the Helsinki Final Act as an integral entity, especially in the view of the Belgrade meeting? And what is your opinion about Chancellor Schmidt's [1] proposal to repeat in one or another form the meeting on the top level?

THE PRESIDENT. I think the Helsinki agreement, which calls for cooperation and security in Europe and which has, as a so-called Third Basket component, an insistence upon maximum enhancement and preservation of human rights, is an agreement that is important to the Poles and also to our country and other signatories of that treaty.

We believe that the Belgrade conference has been productive. This is a question that must be approached on a multinational basis. The treaty terms provide for open and frank criticism of other signatories when standards are not met. There has been a free exchange of opinion between ourselves and the Soviet Union and indeed all the nations involved.

We hope that this session will come to a rapid and successful conclusion and that there will be repeated scheduled meetings based upon the Belgrade conference that would be held in the future so that all nations who participated in the Helsinki agreement and all those who didn't become signatories would have a constant reminder before them of the importance of cooperation, mutual security, the sharing of information, the recombination of families, free emigration, and the preservation of basic human rights.

So, I hope that this will be a continuing process scheduled repeatedly and that this issue of human rights will never be forgotten.

Yes, Judy [Judy Woodruff, NBC News].

HUMAN RIGHTS

Q. Mr. President, then how satisfied are you that your concept of the preservation of human rights is currently being honored here in Poland?

THE PRESIDENT. I think that our concept of human rights is preserved in Poland, as I've said, much better than (some) [2] other European nations with which I'm familiar. There is a substantial degree of freedom of the press exhibited by this conference this afternoon; a substantial degree of freedom of religion, demonstrated by the fact that approximately 90 percent of the Polish people profess faith in Christ; and an open relationship between Poland and our country and Poland and Western European countries in trade, technology, cultural exchange, student exchange, tourism.

So, I don't think there's any doubt that the will of the Polish people for complete preservation and enhancement of human rights is the same as our own.

Q. What steps, then, do you believe should be taken here in Poland to come closer to reaching your concept?

THE PRESIDENT. Well, I think Poland shares with us a commitment, which is sometimes embarrassing for us and them, to have our own faults publicized evocatively at conferences like the one in Belgrade, where there's a free and open discussion and criticism and a singular point-

---

[1] Chancellor Helmut Schmidt of the Federal Republic of Germany.

[2] Printed in the White House Press Office transcript.

ing out of violations of high standards of human rights preservation. We have been criticized at Belgrade, sometimes legitimately; sometimes, I think, mistakenly. The same applies to nations in Eastern Europe and to the Soviet Union.

And I think this is the best thing that we can do at this point, is to continue to insist upon a rigid enforcement and interpretation of the human rights section of the Helsinki agreement.

ENERGY

Q [in Polish]. Mr. President, the Polish Radio.

The United States is facing an energy crisis which is also an international problem. How can you see the possibilities of solving that crisis, like a multilateral conference, a European conference or bilateral agreements, and are you of the opinion that the cooperation between the United States and Poland in this respect is possible?

THE PRESIDENT. One of the worst domestic problems that we have is the overconsumption and waste of energy. I have no doubt that every country I visit on this tour will be pressing us on the question of what will the United States do to save energy and not to import too much of very scarce oil, in particular, which is available on the world markets. We are addressing this as a top priority among domestic issues.

Poland is, as you know, self-sufficient in both hard coal and also brown coal, which is increasing in production in Poland itself. We call it lignite in our own country. One of the things that we can do is on a worldwide basis to try to hold down unnecessary demand for oil and natural gas, therefore providing stable prices.

Another is to consume those energy sources which we have most available in our country and in yours, coal; shift to permanent sources of energy, primarily those derived from solar power; and share research and development information and commitments, a subject which I was discussing early today with First Secretary Gierek.

How to burn lignite coal so that it will have minimum effect on the environment and also have maximum heat derivation is a question of importance to you and to us. We are now shifting to the production and consumption of lignite coal in our own country, for instance, and so are you.

So, I think sharing, on an international basis, of data and technological advantages and progress in the energy field and conservation of scarce energy sources for all nations would be the two basic things which we could do jointly.

Q. Mr. President?

THE PRESIDENT. Yes, sir?

Q [in Polish]. I have got one question.

THE PRESIDENT. Go right ahead.

Q. Can I?

THE PRESIDENT. Go ahead.

Q. May I?

THE PRESIDENT. Yes.

U.S.-POLISH RELATIONS

Q. What is involved in the entity of Polish-American cooperation, so far, and what is your opinion as far as this cooperation, between Poland and the United States is concerned, and how in the light of today's talks can you see the prospects for the development of such cooperation as well as what the United States wants to do to contribute to this development?

THE PRESIDENT. We already have a good relationship with Poland in cultural exchange, in technological and scientific cooperation, and in rapidly growing level of trade.

About 4 years ago we had a total trade with Poland of only about $500 million. In 1978, the level of trade will probably exceed $1 billion.

I have just informed First Secretary Gierek that in addition to the $300 million in commodity credit grain sales that has been authorized by our own country, that we will increase that by $200 million more worth of food and feed grains.

Poland has had a devastating and unprecedented 4 years of crop failure because of adverse weather conditions; 3 years of drought, the last year, of excessive floods. We, on the other hand, have had very good and bountiful harvests. And we want to share our grain with Poland on legal credit terms which have already been established by our government.

I think another thing that Poland can help with is to improve even further the better relationships that we are working out with the Soviet Union. Poland is a nation that has good communications and cooperation with the nations in Western Europe—with Germany, Belgium, Holland, France and others—and also are an integral part of the Warsaw Pact nations. And I think this ease of communication and this natural and historical friendship is a basis on which Poland can provide additional cooperation and communication between ourselves and the Soviet Union.

I don't say this to insinuate that we have a lack of communication now. But Poland's good offices can be of great benefit to us.

Yes, sir.

Q. Mr. President, in your discussions earlier today with First Secretary Gierek and other Polish leaders, did they in your mind express any viewpoints on international questions that diverged in tone or substance from the viewpoints generally expressed by the Soviet Union?

THE PRESIDENT. We discussed a wide range of subjects. I didn't detect any significant differences of opinion between ourselves and the Polish leaders, and we did not go into detail on matters that now are not resolved between ourselves and the Soviets.

For instance, the details of the SALT negotiations and the comprehensive test ban were not discussed by me and Mr. Gierek. So, I would say that we found no disharmonies of any significance between ourselves and the Poles, or between the Poles and the Soviet Union.

Mr. Gierek did express a concern that there might be a bilateral agreement between Israel and Egypt in the Middle East, to the exclusion of the other Arab countries. This is an opinion also held by the Soviet Union. It's an opinion also held by us and by Israel and Egypt.

I pointed out to Mr. Gierek that had the Egyptians and Israelis wanted to seek a solution only for the Sinai region and the Egyptian-Israeli relationship, they could probably already have consummated such an agreement. But President Sadat and Prime Minister Begin do not want such an agreement. I pointed out this to Mr. Gierek and he was relieved to hear this.

He also was quite concerned about the lack of progress on the mutual and balanced force reductions, which have been stalemated in Vienna for years. He pointed out that the primary responsibility lay on the shoulders of the United States and the Soviet Union.

This is not exactly the case, because we consult very closely with our NATO allies before any common opinion or proposition is put forward. I hope to relieve this stalemate shortly. And we are consulting closely with the Germans and others in the Western European theater and also with the Soviets on this matter.

He was very pleased that we want to reduce international sales of conventional weapons. This is a subject on which we have just begun to talk with the Soviet Union, and perhaps Poland is ahead of the Soviet Union in this particular subject. But I hope that they will be amenable to that same suggestion.

So, the answer is, I don't know of any disagreements between the Poles and the Soviets that came out this morning, nor do I know any significant disagreements that came out between ourselves and the Poles.

Yes, sir.

TACTICAL NUCLEAR WEAPONS

Q [in Polish]. Mr. President, the Soviet leader, Leonid Brezhnev, has put forward a suggestion recently that the Eastern and Western countries renounce the neutron bomb together. Would you be ready to accept such a proposal?

THE PRESIDENT. One of the disturbing failures up until this point in nuclear weaponry has been a complete absence of discussions concerning tactical or theater nuclear weapons. The only discussions that have ever been held between ourselves and the Soviets related only to strategic weapons, those that can be fired from one continent to another or from the sea into a continent.

I would hope that as a result of the SALT II talks we might agree with the Soviets to start addressing the question of the so-called tactical nuclear weapons, of which the enhanced radiation or neutron bomb would be one.

This weapon is much less destabilizing in its effect, if it should be deployed, than, for instance, some of the advanced new Soviet weapons like the SS–20 missile, which is much more destructive than any weapon held by the NATO allies and has a much greater range.

So, my hope is that in general we can reduce the threat of nuclear destruction in the European area. There are now several thousand tactical nuclear weapons already deployed on both sides in the European theater. And the whole matter must be addressed in its entirety, rather than one weapon at the time.

We would not deploy the neutron bomb or neutron shells unless it was an agreement by our NATO allies. That's where the decision will be made. But there are other new weapons, including the SS–20, much more threatening to the balance that presently exists.

Yes, sir.

POLISH EMIGRATION

Q. Mr. President, you said that you have agreed to expand the agricultural credits to Poland.

THE PRESIDENT. Yes.

Q. In talking with us the other day, your advisers have linked that with a human rights concern, namely, that the reunification of families between the Eastern and Western blocs be improved in Poland. Have the Poles agreed to do that? Have they given you any satisfaction that this, too, would be done?

THE PRESIDENT. One of the first subjects which I discussed with First Secretary Gierek in our private talks today was the reunification of families between Poland and the United States. In the last 4 years there have been about 15,000 Poles who have been permitted to emigrate to our country. We still have about 250 families—we call them nuclear families, that is, a father, mother, and children—who desire to be unified, and permission has not yet been obtained.

First Secretary Gierek said that he would give his own personal attention to alleviating this problem. And he directed his Foreign Minister and I directed our Secretary of State to proceed with this discussion during this afternoon. Their assurance was that our concern would be alleviated.

MR. CORMIER. Thank you, Mr. President.

THE PRESIDENT. Thank you very much.

NOTE: President Carter's twenty-second news conference began at 5:30 p.m. in the Grand Ballroom at the Victoria Hotel in Warsaw, Poland. It was broadcast live via satellite on radio and television in the United States and was taped for broadcast later that evening in Poland.

Several of the reporters spoke in Polish, and their questions were translated by an interpreter.

Earlier in the day, the President attended a working luncheon with First Secretary Gierek at the Parliament Building.

Warsaw, Poland

Toasts of the President and First Secretary Gierek at a State Dinner. December 30, 1977

THE FIRST SECRETARY. *Dear Mr. President, dear Mrs. Carter, ladies and gentlemen:*

I wish to express, Mr. President, our satisfaction of your visit to Poland. I rest assured that together with the highest authorities of the Polish People's Republic, it is indeed shared by the entire people of Poland.

We take great pleasure in seeing Mrs. Carter in our midst. We also welcome prominent members of the party accompanying you on this visit.

In your visit, Mr. President, we see a reaffirmation of the friendly feelings of the American people for the people of Poland and a reflection of the intentions to further expand cooperation between our two countries. Indeed, these feelings and intentions enjoy our full reciprocity as the expansion of Polish-American cooperation remains in keeping with the tradition of friendship between our two peoples.

It is in the interest of our two countries. It helps deepen détente and shape up constructive international relations. Rich and noble are the traditions we jointly refer to. Poles were among the first settlers on the American soil. In the American struggle for independence, a splendid chapter has been written by Kosciuszko, Pulaski, and other great Polish patriots, for whom the cause of freedom of their own land was inseparably linked with that of all peoples.

It can be assumed with all certainty that from the outset of and all through the Bicentennial of the United States, which, along with the American people, we marked here with friendly observances, a significant share to the expansion of the American economy, civilization, and culture has been contributed by Poles.

We are glad that today the overwhelming majority of the multimillion masses of Americans of Polish extraction as good United States citizens keep maintaining their sentimental and cultural ties with the land of their ancestors, that they wish favorable development of cooperation with the Polish People's Republic. The people of Poland are also cognizant of our common struggle in the great anti-Nazi coalition.

Mr. President, I trust that the paramount cause guiding us mutually is the consolidation of peace. The Polish people in particular only too well know both its price and value, for wasn't it so that the city of Warsaw—which we have risen from the ashes—had been doomed to total extinction? For its heroic resistance, for its contribution for the victory of nations over the fascists, our nation paid the price of more than 6 million human lives, of the loss of over 40 percent of the national wealth.

It paid the price of most cities turned to ruins and thousands of villages reduced to ashes. The memory of those tragic experiences impressed forever in the Polish minds and hearts imposes the loftiest of obligations upon us to do all in our power to ensure security and peaceful development.

It is with lasting peace, the joy of which we want to share with all other countries of Europe and the world, that we are linking our aspirations, our plans and expectations, for today and for tomorrow. Hence, it is only natural and understandable, Mr. President, that we view with due attention and support warmly actions which serve that great and supreme cause to all nations.

The key factor of the process of détente we perceive in relations between your country, Mr. President, and the Soviet Union. The dialog between the two big powers determines the climate, the overall climate, of international relations in saving mankind from a nuclear holocaust.

This is why theirs is a special responsibility for world peace. Hence, our profound satisfaction over the incipient progress in the talks on offensive strategic arms limitation. Hence our hopes, in fact shared by the broadest public opinion, for a prompt new agreement, as well as for positive results of discussions between the two powers on other important questions.

Together with its Socialist allies and friends, Poland spares no effort to consolidate the process of détente and make it irreversible, for détente is the only alternative. It indeed represents a great chance of our times. Its proper utilization depends in particular on containing the arms race, which weighs heavily upon international relations, wastes economic resources, and poses great threats.

I am sure you are aware, Mr. President, that Poland has always attached special significance to preventing proliferation of nuclear armaments. We have been advancing our own initiatives to this effect, which have enjoyed general recognition.

Today, when the danger of proliferation of those armaments and the introduction of new kinds of weapons of mass destruction is greater than ever before, we are bound to appeal for moderation for the containment of the dangerous phenomenon, for the strengthening and extension of the system of treaties to protect against it.

Remembering, as we do, what you, yourself, Mr. President, have been saying on that matter, we trust it will be given the maximum of attention. By the same token, we lend our full support to the initiative made by Leonid Brezhnev to conclude an agreement to mutually renounce the production of neutron weapons.

Poland proceeds from the principle of full and integrated implementation of the decisions and recommendations of the Final Act of the Helsinki conference, which we treat as the magna carta of peace in Europe. Guided by its principles, we are favorably shaping up our bilateral relations with all states, signatories of the Final Act to take efforts to achieve positive results of the Belgrade meeting.

Progress in the Vienna talks on the reduction of armed forces and armaments in Central Europe would, too, no doubt, serve to strengthen the general sense of security.

There is much to be said, Mr. President, of the climate of international relations. There is need for mutual understanding and trust; only in such circumstances there can be progress in constructive and friendly international cooperation.

Dear Mr. President, we are glad that you share our desire of continuation of the positive processes in Polish-American relations. Our constructive discussions today have confirmed this.

In recent years, important joint statements, agreements, and contracts were signed between our two countries. They do provide a good basis for further mutually beneficial cooperation. Our economic relations have dynamically expanded. As you know, we attach special significance to them and wish to continue expanding them. Our scientific and technical exchanges have grown, constantly enriching is our cultural cooperation, as is the growing tourist traffic, more frequent, our contact serving to get our respective nations to know better and bring them closer together.

It gives me satisfaction to expect that your visit will effect in a further growth of Polish-American cooperation.

Mr. President, we are sorry you are visiting us for such a short time. We would certainly wish that you could get to know our country better, a country of great progress and, at the same time, still overcoming century-old underdevelopment.

Following the gravest tragedy in its own history, our nation has made a choice which offers it lasting safeguards of independence, sovereignty, and security, which provides for the best premises for development. These premises comprise its own ever more growing potential of present-day Poland, its alliances with the Soviet Union and other friends.

Today Poland belongs to the group of countries of the world which are having the greatest development scale as far as production in industry is concerned. And for the last 7 years, we are maintaining very high indices of further growth.

There has been a tremendous revival, biological revival, of our people. In the current decade, the age of maturity is being reached by 7 million of young Polish girls and boys. We ensure to all of them education and work. We have created just, democratic, socio-political conditions. We are implementing the fullest possible code of socio-economic and political rights.

In maintaining and cultivating all what has been most precious in our national tradition, we are enriching contemporary life of Poles by new, profoundly humanistic contents.

Our greatest achievement is the moral and political unity of our people, in which we perceive the paramount safeguard for successful implementation of all noble aspirations of Poles and also a dignified place of our country among other states of Europe and the world.

Mr. President, tomorrow you will be leaving Poland, departing for other countries. May I be permitted to express my conviction that the impressions you will be taking with you from the first leg of your trip and, first of all, the friendly feelings of the Polish people to the American people and our strivings to peace and cooperation will stay in your good memory for long.

I wish to propose a toast and ask all those present to join me to drink to you, Mr. President, and Mrs. Carter, to the successes of the great American people, to the further expansion of friendly Polish-American relations.

THE PRESIDENT. *First Secretary and Mrs. Gierek, distinguished leaders in politics, the military, music, drama, art, poetry, education, science, engineering:*

We are very proud to be here in Poland and to have had a chance to meet with and to learn from First Secretary Gierek. We have already become close personal friends. He has taught me things that I can use in my own Nation. He has this afternoon discussed with me—and tonight—how he proposes to have a balance of trade in Poland. He sells hare or rabbits to adjacent countries for a lease in hunting preserves, and the rabbits are trained to return to Poland. [*Laughter*]

When I was running for President of the United States for 2 years, I met hundreds of thousands of Americans of Polish ancestry. I saw very quickly that they had a deep love for the United States and, simultaneously, for Poland. They recognize the historical ties which have bound our nations together since the very origins of our country. They have a natural hospitality inherited from their ancestors, and this made us look forward to this trip with great anticipation.

Our country has observed closely the distinguished Poles who have affected world history and our own Nation—ancient and modern scientists like Copernicus and Madam Curie, favorite authors like Joseph Conrad, musicians, Artur Rubinstein, who still loves Poland very deeply, and one of the greatest engineers of all time, Admiral Hyman Rickover, who developed the peaceful use of atomic power.

We have much to learn from Poland—how to use coal, and particularly brown coal, efficiently in this day of short energy supplies. We share cultural and scientific and engineering knowledge.

A hundred and twenty thousand Americans each year come back to visit their homeland here. And today I have seen at firsthand at your memorials a demonstration of affection for those who suffered so bravely in recent wars.

Georgia's capital city of Atlanta was completely destroyed in war, as was the city of Warsaw. But although we have suffered greatly, no other nation has borne such suffering as Poland. In the World War, six million Poles died—800,-000 in Warsaw alone. Poles were the first people to fight the horrors of Nazism and

earn the admiration and appreciation of the world. You were the ones who demonstrated a deep commitment to human rights, a belief in the value of human freedom and human life.

You have seen the horrible consequences of racial hatred when the Polish Jews were exterminated by Nazi terrorists. From these terrible experiences, valuable lessons have been learned. There is a tendency for those in the West to distrust those nations in the East. Sometimes, perhaps, you distrust our motives and our judgment. Sometimes we feel that you might be a danger to us as the NATO allies face the Warsaw Pact nations. But I know in more vivid terms than before that nations like your own and like the Soviet Union, which have suffered so deeply, will never commence a war unless there is the most profound provocation or misunderstanding brought about by lack of communication.

We also want peace and would never start a war except by mistake, when we didn't understand the motives and attitudes and desire for peace on the part of our potential adversaries.

I am pleased to know that there is increasing communication, consultation, and cooperation between the Socialist nations and the nations of the West. Although we belong to different military alliances, our hunger for peace is the same. We are working closely with the Soviet leaders to eliminate the constant and horrible threat of atomic destruction. This is an extremely complicated and technical discussion, but good motivations and common purposes can resolve those differences.

I have every expectation that this next year will bring success. We will do our utmost to realize this dream. We want to prevent the development of new and more powerful weapons and also to prevent any tests of atomic explosions. We want to prevent nations which do not presently have atomic explosions from desiring those capabilities. We want to reduce the sale of conventional weapons to nations around the world. And we want to seek in every possible way closer communications, better trade, closer friendship between our countries.

Poland and your leaders have an ability and experience to look knowledgeably both to the East and to the West, and you can contribute greatly to the mutual efforts of ourselves and the Soviet Union to reach those agreements which we both desire.

The ancient alliance between the United States and Poland in peace and war has given our people good lives. We have helped to establish and to maintain the independence of one another. This sharing of culture, blood kinship, and close cooperation in the past can give us a basis for even better future together.

I hope that at the earliest convenient time we might be permitted to repay the hospitality to your leaders, First Secretary Gierek and others, that you have extended to us on this visit. It is very valuable to have Polish and American friendship combined together to give us what all men and women want—peace throughout the world.

On behalf of the people of the United States, I would like to propose a toast to the indomitable spirit and to the freedom of the Polish people, to your enlightened leaders—particularly First Secretary Gierek and his wife—and to peace throughout the world.

NOTE: The exchange began at 9:27 p.m. at the Palace of the Council of Ministers. First Secretary Gierek spoke in Polish, and his remarks were translated by an interpreter.

Following the dinner, the President met with First Secretary Gierek at the Palace.

Warsaw, Poland

Joint United States-Poland Communique Issued at the Conclusion of the President's Visit. December 31, 1977

The President of the United States of America and Mrs. Carter paid an official visit to Poland December 29–31, 1977, at the invitation of the highest authorities of the Polish People's Republic. The President was accompanied by Secretary of State Cyrus R. Vance and by Assistant to the President for National Security Affairs Zbigniew Brzezinski.

The President laid a wreath at the Tomb of the Unknown Soldier and placed flowers at the Nike Monument to the Heroes of Warsaw and at the Monument to the Heroes of the Ghetto. He also saw some districts of Warsaw, acquainting himself with its reconstruction and development.

During the visit, the President held talks with the First Secretary of the Central Committee of the Polish United Workers' Party, Edward Gierek.

In the plenary talks, which were chaired by the President and the First Secretary, there took part:

From the American side:
Secretary of State Cyrus R. Vance,
Assistant to the President Zbigniew Brzezinski,
and other officials.

From the Polish side:
The Chairman of the Council of State, Henryk Jabloński;
Chairman of the Council of Ministers Piotr Jaroszewicz,
and other officials.

Secretary of State Cyrus R. Vance also held talks with Minister of Foreign Affairs Emil Wojtaszek.

The President and the First Secretary expressed their satisfaction with the conversations they had held as well as their conviction that continued visits at the highest levels, as well as visits by other leading personalities of both countries, serve the interests of both countries and the development of détente and international cooperation.

President Carter expressed his gratitude to the First Secretary and to Mrs. Gierek for the splendid hospitality accorded in Poland to him, Mrs. Carter, and the entire delegation.

President Carter invited First Secretary Gierek to visit the United States. The invitation was accepted with pleasure. The dates for this visit will be agreed upon through diplomatic channels.

NOTE: The text of the joint communique was released at Warsaw, Poland.

Tehran, Iran

Remarks of the President and Mohammad Reza Palavi, Shahanshah of Iran at the Welcoming Ceremony. December 31, 1977

THE SHAH. Mr. President, on behalf of the Shahbanou, myself, and the Iranian people, I welcome you, Mrs. Carter, and your delegation on Iranian soil.

We cherish your arrival as the head of state of a country with which Iran always had unshakable bonds and the best of relations and at the same time as an exalted friend and a most esteemed guest.

We sincerely hope that you will take back with you happy memories of your short visit to our country, and in the meantime we sincerely hope that all the stages of your present trip will be marked by the best of successes.

For the Shahbanou and I, it is great pleasure to be your host only a few weeks after our trip to your country. Your distinguished personality, sincerity, good will, moral virtues, and also the hospitality

and kindness of Mrs. Carter have remained close to our hearts.

On behalf of all the people of Iran, welcome to our country.

THE PRESIDENT. *Your Imperial Majesties, distinguished officials, and citizens of Iran:*

My own Nation has been blessed this year by an official visit of His Imperial Majesty, the Shah, and by the Shahbanou, Empress Farah. This was a fine gesture of friendship. And we also benefited from extensive discussions between the Shah and myself of important issues for Iran and for the United States. I am proud and pleased to be able to come to Iran at the end of this year, my first year in office and, I believe, your 27th year (37th year)[1] as a leader of this great nation, and to begin another new year with our close friends and allies.

In these times of endings and beginnings, I look forward to consulting with the Shah about two of the issues that have most dominated our thoughts in the year just past and will require our best actions in the years ahead.

One is finding solutions to the economic problems of the world's rich and the world's poor. None of these problems is more important than that of energy. Neither producer nor consumer nations can survive and prosper if we recklessly exhaust the world's limited supplies of oil, and neither group of nations can solve the problem without the cooperation of the other. It is because my Nation takes this problem seriously that we are determined soon to have a comprehensive energy plan designed to eliminate waste and to develop alternate sources of energy supplies. We are cooperating closely with Iran, and it is because I respect the leadership of the Shah in this area that

---

[1] Printed in the White House press release.

I have come to him for consultation and for advice.

The other great issue is bringing peace to the troubled areas of the world and turning back the rising tide of armaments and dissension. The Shah and I share a hope that peace will come soon to the Middle East and that as our military alliance remains unshakable, we may help to reduce the level of tension and armaments throughout the world.

The interests of our nations are built on the interests of individuals. And in all of our discussions, both public and private, we emphasize guaranteeing our citizens the fullest economic and political human rights.

I come with warm, personal feelings for the leaders of Iran, and I bring best New Year greetings from the United States for the people of this great country.

Thank you very much, Your Majesties, for this warm and hospitable welcome.

NOTE: The exchange began at 4:45 p.m. at the Imperial Pavilion at Mehrabad International Airport.

Following the arrival ceremony, the President met with the Shah at Saadabad Palace.

Tehran, Iran

Toasts of the President and the Shah at a State Dinner.   December 31, 1977

THE SHAH. *Mr. President, Mrs. Carter, Excellencies, ladies and gentlemen:*

It gives the Shabanou and myself great pleasure to welcome you to our country. This reception is particularly auspicious since it takes place on the eve of 1978, and your presence here represents a New Year's gift for your Iranian friends.

In our country, according to ancient tradition, the visit of the first guest in the new year is an omen for that year. And although the annual new year is cele-brated with the advent of spring, nevertheless, since the distinguished guest tonight is such a person of good will and achievement, naturally we consider it as a most excellent omen.

Mr. President, you now have come to a country which has always had unshakable links with your country and your great nation. We are united together by a special relationship made all the closer by a wide community of mutual interests, which we share in our firm determination to contribute to the maintenance of world peace and security in assuring human progress and betterment.

History has been witness to the growth and development of an outstanding relationship between two nations motivated by common trust, good will, and respect which has repeatedly withstood the test of time.

Humanitarianism, liberty, good will, constructiveness, and creativeness, which are the distinctive qualities of the great American nation, have always been highly regarded by us. Fortunately, our American friends have also perceived this friendship and regard of our people from the very beginning.

The Reverend Mr. Smith, the first American that set foot on the land of Iran in the year 1832, wrote in his assignment report that living among good people like Iranians and serving them was more pleasant for him than anything else, and that he considered the best days of his life those spent in this country.

It gives me pleasure to state that the fruitful cooperation, the social and cultural fields between our two nations have commenced even prior to the establishment of diplomatic relations.

The first modern school was established in Iran in the year 1836 by American missionaries. The American College in Tehran, which was established 100 years ago, was an outstanding center for the education and training of Iranian youth during the whole course of its activities. Our people carry such good memories of its beloved principal, Dr. Samuel Jordan, that one of the highways of Tehran has been named after him.

Now that we are reminiscing on our meritorious American friends, it is perhaps suitable to cherish the memory of Howard Baskerville, a young American who, upon completion of his studies at Princeton, was assigned as a teacher in the Memorial School at Tabriz and, during the constitutional revolution of Iran, heroically and bravely lost his life in the fight for freedom.

This feeling towards Iran has always been evidenced in the literary works of your nation. For instance, the poetry of Ralph Waldo Emerson, in glorifying Iran, is one of the most beautiful examples of its kind in the world of literature. The basic and comprehensive work of Arthur Upham Pope regarding the art of Iran is the best research work that has ever been prepared in this field. Likewise, the extensive studies of William Jackson regarding the culture and civilization of Iran are among the most valuable researches in the history of Iranology.

Numerous universities in the United States have expanded activities in the fields of Iranian studies and its language. Also valuable treasures of the culture and art of Iran are preserved in various libraries and museums of your country. Moreover, American archeologists have played an eminent role in archeological discoveries in Iran.

In the political field, our nation carries unforgettable memories of the role of America in our crisis and times of stress, from the beginning of the present century. For instance, we will never forget that in the great political and economic adversity of our country, in the second decade of this century, William Morgan Shuster, upon the invitation of the government of Iran, sincerely endeavored to bring order into the finances of Iran. Moreover, when, following the 1919 agreement, Iran was in danger of losing its independence, America raised its voice to the world in support of the sovereignty of Iran, as also in the years after the Second World War, America provided us with vital economic and political assistance.

During World War II, I personally had the pleasure of meeting President Franklin Roosevelt in our capital city. Since then I had the opportunity of welcoming in Iran several Presidents of the United States. And I personally have also traveled repeatedly to your great country. I am glad to state that all these visits have been accompanied with the spirit of friendship and cooperation, which is the distinct quality of our relationship.

An example of this cooperation is the long-term economic exchange agreement between Iran and the United States, which was recently signed and, in its scope, is the largest agreement ever signed between us and any other country.

Almost 100 years ago the first American Ambassador, Samuel G. W. Benjamin, who had been assigned by President Chester Alan Arthur, came to Iran. In his book, "Persia and the Persians," he wrote, "Iran today is a weak and unknown country, but certainly this country will step into the path of progress and in the not too distant future will again play an important role in the world."

Now with this prediction coming true, our country has started its role within its potentialities and possibilities. Perhaps it need not be mentioned, but this is a positive and constructive role and in conformity with the principles that your great country has always supported independent and of which you, Mr. President, are the most notable advocate.

From the early days of your election campaign you indicated how much you will attach to high ideals of right and

2219

justice, moral beliefs in human values. These are all qualities that have elevated the American society in such a short period of time to its present high prestige in the world, and a nation like ours with its ancient culture can very well feel to what extent such concepts in moral principles are vital, especially in the world of today, which is suffering from some sort of a civilization crisis.

I entertain excellent memories of the fruitful discussions which I had with you in Washington a few weeks ago. The cordial hospitality extended by Mrs. Carter and yourself and the warmth of your attitude and the understanding which you showed in our discussions have deeply touched me. I am glad that our discussions were so meaningful, particularly in the case of energy, which is one of the most important and vital problems of our era.

We, who are among the greatest producers, share the same view that the present unrestricted use of oil—which is an expendable and finite resource—is not logical and that this valuable commodity, instead of the present, normal daily use, should be utilized mainly in the petrochemical industry. In the meantime, efforts should be exerted to find a substitute in new resources of energy.

Fortunately, we enjoy close cooperation with your country in the field of energy, which will no doubt be consolidated in the future. We also share the same opinions regarding the establishment of an honorable and durable peace, and we sincerely hope that 1978, which begins tomorrow, will be a year of such a peace of which you are the harbinger.

I wish every success to you, Mr. President, and Mrs. Carter, who has proved to be such a successful ambassador of good will, motivated, as she is, by high humanitarian ideals in your present tour, and hope that this will prove to be fruitful

trips in the interest of the whole world and that of peace, security, and welfare for human society.

With this hope I propose a toast, Mr. President, for your and Mrs. Carter's health and happiness, for the further progress and prosperity of the great and noble American people, for the ever-increasing friendship and cooperation between our two countries, and for international peace and understanding.

THE PRESIDENT. *Your Majesties and distinguished leaders of Iran from all walks of life:*

I would like to say just a few words tonight in appreciation for your hospitality and the delightful evening that we've already experienced with you. Some have asked why we came to Iran so close behind the delightful visit that we received from the Shah and Empress Farah just a month or so ago. After they left our country, I asked my wife, "With whom would you like to spend New Year's Eve?" And she said, "Above all others, I think, with the Shah and Empress Farah." So we arranged the trip accordingly and came to be with you.

These visits and the close cooperation that we share, the intense personal and group negotiations and consultations are very beneficial to both our countries. They are particularly beneficial to me as a new leader of the United States. I might pause parenthetically and say I apologize for taking 10 years off your service this afternoon when I said 27 years. It should have been 37 years. And Empress Farah, thank you very much for correcting me on that. The Shah said he felt 10 years younger when I did that. [*Laughter*]

But we do have a close friendship that's very meaningful to all the people in our country. I think it is a good harbinger of things to come—that we could close out this year and begin a new year with those in whom we have such great confidence and with whom we share such great responsibilities for the present and for the future.

As we drove in from the airport this afternoon to the beautiful white palace where we will spend the night, and saw the monument in the distance, I asked the Shah what was the purpose of the beautiful monument. And he told me that it was built several years ago, erected to commemorate the 2500th anniversary of this great nation. This was a sobering thought to me. We have been very proud in our Nation to celebrate our 200th birthday, a couple of years ago. But it illustrates the deep and penetrating consciousness that comes from an ancient heritage and a culture that preceded any that we've ever known in our own lives.

Recently, Empress Farah gave us a beautiful book called "The Bridge of Turquoise"—and we get many gifts of that kind from visitors—and for a few days I have to admit that we didn't pay enough attention to it. And one night I started to thumb through the pages, and I called my wife, Rosalynn, and I called my daughter, Amy, who climbed into my lap, and we spent several hours studying very carefully the beautiful history that this book portrays of Persia, of Iran, of its people, of its lands, of its heritage and its history, and also of its future. It caused me to be reminded again of the value of ancient friendships and the importance of close ties that bind us as we face difficult problems.

Iran, because of the great leadership of the Shah, is an island of stability in one of the more troubled areas of the world. This is a great tribute to you, Your Majesty, and to your leadership and to the respect and the admiration and love which your people give to you.

The transformation that has taken place in this nation is indeed remarkable under your leadership. And as we sat together this afternoon, discussing privately for a few moments what might be done to bring peace to the Middle East, I was profoundly impressed again not only with your wisdom and your judgment and your sensitivity and insight but also with the close compatibility that we found in addressing this difficult question.

As we visit with leaders who have in their hands the responsibility for making decisions that can bring peace to the Middle East and ensure a peaceful existence for all of us who live in the world, no matter where our nations might be, it's important that we continue to benefit from your sound judgment and from your good advice.

We also had a chance to discuss another potential troubled area, the Horn of Africa. And here again we live at a great distance from it. But this region, which already sees the initiation of hostility and combat, needs to be brought under the good influence of you and others who live in this region. And we will be glad to cooperate in any way that we can. We want peace to return. We want Somalia and Ethiopia to be friends again, border disputes to be eased and those of us who do have any influence at all to use that influence for these purposes.

We have also known about the great benefits that we derive in our own nation from the close business relationships that we have with Iran.

As I drove through the beautiful streets of Tehran today with the Shah, we saw literally thousands of Iranian citizens standing beside the street with a friendly attitude, expressing their welcome to me.

And I also saw hundreds, perhaps even thousands of American citizens who stand there welcoming their President in a nation which has taken them to heart and made them feel at home. There are about 30,000 Americans here who work in close harmony with the people of Iran to carve out a better future for you, which also helps to ensure, Your Majesty, a better future for ourselves.

We share industrial growth, we share scientific achievements, we share research and development knowledge, and this gives us the stability for the present which is indeed valuable to both our countries.

We are also blessed with the largest number of foreign students in our country from your own nation. And I think this ensures, too, that we share the knowledge that is engendered by our great universities, but also that when these young leaders come back to your country for many years in the future, for many generations in the future, our friendship is ensured. We are very grateful for this and value it very much.

I have tried to become better acquainted with the culture of Iran in the preparation for my visit here. I was particularly impressed with a brief passage from one of Iran's great poets, Saadi. And I would like to read a few words from him. Empress Farah tells me that he lived about 600 years ago.

"Human beings are like parts of a body, created from the same essence. When one part is hurt and in pain, others cannot remain in peace and quiet. If the misery of others leaves you indifferent and with no feeling of sorrow, then you cannot be called a human being."

I asked Empress Farah why this poet was so famous here in Iran, because he had impressed me so greatly, too. And she said that because he had the greatest facility for professing profound thoughts in the simplest possible words that the average citizen could understand.

Well, this brief passage shows that there is within the consciousness of human beings a close tie with one's neighbors, one's family, and one's friends, but it also ties us with human beings throughout the world. When one is hurt or suffers, all of us, if we are human beings, are hurt and we suffer.

The cause of human rights is one that also is shared deeply by our people and by the leaders of our two nations.

Our talks have been priceless, our friendship is irreplaceable, and my own gratitude is to the Shah, who in his wisdom and with his experience has been so helpful to me, a new leader.

We have no other nation on Earth who is closer to us in planning for our mutual military security. We have no other nation with whom we have closer consultation on regional problems that concern us both. And there is no leader with whom I have a deeper sense of personal gratitude and personal friendship.

On behalf of the people of the United States, I would like to offer a toast at this time to the great leaders of Iran, the Shah and the Shahbanou and to the people of Iran and to the world peace that we hope together we can help to bring.

NOTE: The exchange began at 10:18 p.m. in the Niavaran Palace.

Later in the evening, the President met with the Shah and King Hussein of Jordan at the Niavaran Palace.

Digest of Other White House Announcements

The following listing includes the President's daily schedule and other items of general interest as announced by the White House Press Office during the period covered by this issue. Events and announcements printed elsewhere in the issue are not included.

December 26

The President returned to the White House from Plains, Ga.

December 27

The President met at the White House with Zbigniew Brzezinski, Assistant to the President for National Security Affairs.

December 28

The President met at the White House with:

—Dr. Brzezinski;
—Secretary of Energy James R. Schlesinger;
—a group of administration officials to discuss the budget;
—Vice President Walter F. Mondale and Arthur F. Burns, Chairman of the Board of Governors of the Federal Reserve System.

The President has reappointed Alfred E. Kahn as Chairman of the Civil Aeronautics Board for a term expiring December 31, 1978.

NOMINATIONS SUBMITTED TO THE SENATE

NOTE: The Congress having adjourned *sine die* on Thursday, December 15, 1977, no nominations were submitted during the period covered by this issue.

CHECKLIST OF WHITE HOUSE PRESS RELEASES

The following releases of the Office of the White House Press Secretary, distributed during the period covered by this issue, are not included in the issue.

CHECKLIST—Continued

Released December 26, 1977

Tentative summary schedule: the President's foreign trip

Released December 27, 1977

Biographical information: James T. McIntyre, Jr., Director-designate, Office of Management and Budget

Released December 28, 1977

News conference: on the recommendation of John C. White to be chairman of the Democratic National Committee—by Kenneth M. Curtis, chairman, Democratic National Committee, and John C. White, Deputy Secretary of Agriculture

ACTS APPROVED BY THE PRESIDENT

Approved December 27, 1977

H.R. 3199_____ Public Law 95–217
Clean Water Act of 1977.

Approved December 28, 1977

H.J. Res. 674_____ Public Law 95–221
A joint resolution relative to the convening of the second session of the Ninety-fifth Congress, and for other purposes.

H.R. 6666_____ Public Law 95–222
Legal Services Corporation Act Amendments of 1977.

H.R. 7738_____ Public Law 95–223
An act with respect to the powers of the President in time of war or national emergency.

H.R. 8212_____ Private Law 95–27
An act for the relief of Charles P. Bailey.

H.R. 9794_____ Public Law 95–219
An act to bring the governing international fishery agreement with Mexico within the purview of the Fishery Conservation Zone Transition Act.

S. 904_____ Public Law 95–220
Federal Program Information Act.

S. 1063_____ Public Law 95–218
An act to amend the District of Columbia Self-Government and Governmental Reorganization Act with respect to the payment of certain revenue bonds issued by the Council of the District of Columbia.

Index

Bill Signings

U. S. GOVERNMENT PRINTING OFFICE : 1978 O - 20-300